CASES AND MATERIALS

HIGHER EDUCATION AND THE LAW

by

JUDITH AREEN
Paul Regis Dean Professor of Law and Dean Emeritus
Georgetown University Law Center

FOUNDATION PRESS

2009

Mat #40570921

© 2009 By THOMSON REUTERS/FOUNDATION PRESS

     195 Broadway, 9th Floor
     New York, NY 10007
     Phone Toll Free 1–877–888–1330
     Fax (212) 367–6799
     foundation–press.com

Printed in the United States of America

ISBN 978–1–59941–283–2

 TEXT IS PRINTED ON 10% POST CONSUMER RECYCLED PAPER

*For my teachers who exemplified the best of higher education:
Thomas Emerson, Anna Freud, Andrew Hacker, Jay Katz,
Margaret Mead, Louis Pollak, and John Simon*

*

PREFACE

Higher education is a subject of considerable interest in the United States. On the one hand, it is widely acknowledged to be one of the most successful parts of our economy. A recent ranking of the best universities in the world, for example, placed ten American universities among the top fifteen.[a] On the other hand, the rising costs of higher education threaten to put it out of reach for more and more students. Recent scandals involving financial aid officers and profligate spending by some university presidents have further strained the public's generally positive view. It is striking, therefore, how little attention has been paid to how and why American institutions of higher education developed as they did or to their internal governance structures.

For the most part, the colonial colleges were humble imitations of European universities. Not until the Revolution did the idea of developing distinctive American institutions of higher education take hold. George Washington complained:

> It has always been a source of serious regret with me to see the youth of these United States sent to foreign countries for the purpose of education, often before their minds were formed, or they had imbibed any adequate ideas of happiness of their own, contracting, too frequently, not only habits of dissipation and extravagance, but *principles unfriendly to republican government.*[b]

Over time, a new kind of American university did emerge. The first agent of change was direct investment by the government. Beginning with the set-aside of land by the Continental Congress, the nation consistently has made major investments in higher education, including the Morrill Acts of 1862 and 1890 and, after World War II, the GI Bill and major funding for scientific and medical research conducted at both private and public colleges and universities. This pattern of public investment helped to build a higher education sector that is admired around the world. It also ensured that throughout most of its history, the United States has educated a larger segment of its population to a higher level than almost any other country in the world.[c]

Beginning with John Harvard's bequest in 1638, there has been investment by the private sector as well. With the emergence of huge

---

a. Times Higher Education Supplement, The World's Top 200 Universities (2007), *available at* www.timeshighereducation.co.uk/hybrid.asp?typeCode=144.

b. GEORGE WASHINGTON, XI, THE WRITINGS OF GEORGE WASHINGTON 3 (Jared Sparks ed., Am. Stationers' Co. 1834–1837).

c. The United States leads all other nations except Canada in the proportion of 35–64 year old adults with college degrees. NATIONAL CENTER FOR PUBLIC POLICY AND HIGHER EDUCATION, MEASURING UP 2006: THE NATIONAL REPORT CARD ON HIGHER EDUCATION 7 (2006).

private fortunes in the late nineteenth century, private philanthropists established entire universities that were dedicated to research as well as teaching.

A second major force for change was the establishment of a new form of academic governance, a change that resulted more from necessity than choice. Unlike the universities of Paris, Oxford, and Cambridge, which were founded and governed by scholars, the earliest colonial colleges were founded by various religious denominations. Because there were not enough experienced scholars available, the colonial colleges established lay governing boards ("lay" in the sense of nonfaculty), a structure that endures to this day.

Faculty at first had almost no voice in college or university governance. Over time, their role increased at least with respect to academic matters. The corporate structure that worked well when faculty were hired to transmit knowledge and religious doctrine did not function as effectively by the late nineteenth century when faculties became communities of scholars dedicated to producing new knowledge. Some faculty members even criticized the views and livelihoods of members of the governing boards, a development that led to major confrontations at a number of universities. Scholars sought respect for their expertise and right to speak out by banding together in national organizations established to support academic freedom and tenure.

The third agent of change was democracy itself. Just as the right to vote was expanded after the Civil War to citizens of every race and, in the twentieth century, to women, so, too, admission to colleges and universities was democratized over time, although it has lagged the expansion of the franchise. The Supreme Court did not announce a constitutional basis for prohibiting discrimination on the basis of race in university admissions until 1950[d] and on the basis of gender until 1996.[e] Spurred by the extension of Title VII to educational institutions in 1972,[f] the composition of faculties also became more diverse.

The presence of more diverse student bodies in turn further democratized governance. Beginning in the 1960s, students fresh from involvement in the Civil Rights movement successfully pressured universities for speech rights and for participation in university governance.

By 1956, David Riesman could report that America no longer looked abroad for inspiration for educational advances; rather "Europeans and Japanese, West Africans and Burmese, now come here to look for models or invite American professors to visit and bring with them the 'American Way' in higher education. . . . [O]ur universities . . . are in their energy and accomplishments as good as any the planet offers."[g]

d. Sweatt v. Painter, 339 U.S. 629 (1950).

e. United States v. Virginia, 518 U.S. 515 (1996).

f. 86 Stat. 102.

g. DAVID RIESMAN, CONSTRAINT AND VARIETY IN AMERICAN EDUCATION 33 (1956).

But much remains to be done. Overt barriers to admissions based on race and gender may have been lowered, but other barriers persist. It remains very difficult for students who are the first in their family to attend college or those from low income families to enter college, much less to graduate. Today, seventy-five percent of students whose families are in the top income quartile receive a bachelor's degree by age twenty-four; only nine percent of students whose family income is in the bottom quartile do.[h]

If you consider the college age population rather than the population as a whole, fourteen other nations, including Japan, the United Kingdom, and Poland, now educate more of their young people beyond high school than does the United States. In Australia, Iceland, and New Zealand, more than half of young people earn college degrees, while in the United States, only one-third do.[i]

This casebook examines the complex relationship between higher education and the law in the United States as it has evolved over more than three centuries. The goal is to enable readers to understand better the nature of American institutions of higher education and the legal rights and responsibilities of the institutions and their primary constituencies: faculties, presidents, governing boards, students, alumni, and staff.

The cases and materials chosen cut across the traditional legal categories of contract, torts, antitrust, employment, and constitutional law, among others. This organizational approach is intended to reflect the way the institutions experience legal problems, opportunities and constraints. It also enables readers to use legal standards developed in one area of the law to resolve problems in another.

Chapter One examines historic milestones in the development of American colleges and universities. Chapters Two through Five explore the differences between public and private institutions of higher education, the special issues raised by religion, state and local regulation of higher education, and the financing of higher education.

The chapters in Part II are devoted to faculty matters, particularly academic freedom, tenure, and shared governance. The Part ends with a look at the challenge of reconciling modern workplace antidiscrimination standards with tenure.

Part III examines student access to higher education both in the admissions process and as it is influenced by financial aid.

Part IV takes up student rights and responsibilities, including the different constitutional standards that apply to academic and to nonacademic student misconduct. It also covers students' rights to speech, press, association and religion. The section concludes with an examination of the obligations of colleges and universities to students.

h. Kati Haycock, Educ.Trust, Promise Abandoned: How Policy Choices and Institutional Practices Restrict College Opportunities 5 (2006).

i. Organisation for Economic Co-operation and Development, Education at a Glance: OECD Indicators tbl.A3.1 (2007).

Part V is devoted to university governance, and the roles of governing boards, presidents, and administrators.

Part VI examines the promise and peril of regulation by licensing and accrediting bodies, and by the Federal government.

I want to thank Norman Birnbaum, J. Peter Byrne, Stephen Dunham, Matthew Finkin, Jane Genster, Michael Gottesman, Marcia Greenberger, Vicki Jackson, Jonathan Knight, Ada Meloy, Patricia McGuire, Martin Michaelson, James Mingle, David Rabban, Kathleen Santora, Kent Syverud, John Thelin, Mark Tushnet, and Harold Wechsler for their invaluable guidance and suggestions. My special thanks go to President John DeGioia and Dean Alexander Aleinikoff for their encouragement and support of this project. I am also grateful to the students who helped to research and to edit this draft: Matthew Berns, Sarah Dilks, Matthew Edgar, Marissa Hornsby, Melissa Joy Jackson, Pamela Millard, Julie Shapiro, and Jacob Siler and to Jennifer Locke Davitt for handling copyright permissions and Anna Selden for reviewing the manuscript.

JUDITH AREEN

Washington D.C.
August, 2008

Note on Editing

Deletions from materials are indicated by ellipses except when the omitted material consists only of citations or footnotes. Footnotes in the excerpted sections are numbered according to the original source. New footnotes are indicated by ascending lower case letters.

ACKNOWLEDGMENTS

Excerpts from the following books and articles appear with the kind permission of the copyright holders:

American Association of University Professors. 1940 Statement of Principles on Academic Freedom and Tenure with 1940 and 1970 Interpretive Comments. Reprinted with permission.

American Association of University Professors. 1966 Statement on Government. Reprinted with permission.

Becker, Carl. Cornell University: Founders and The Founding (1943). Copyright © 1943 by Cornell University. Copyright © renewed by Frederick D. Becker. Reprinted with permission of Cornell University Press.

The Berkeley Student Revolt (Seymour Lipset and Sheldon Wolin, eds., 1965). Copyright © 1965 by Seymour Martin Lipset and Sheldon S. Wolin. Reprinted with permission of Doubleday, a division of Random House, Inc.

Bok, Derek. Beyond the Ivory Tower: Social Responsibilities of the Modern University (1982). Reprinted with permission of the publisher: Harvard University Press. Copyright © 1982 by the President and Fellows of Harvard College.

———. Universities in the Marketplace: The Commercialization of Higher Education (2003). Reprinted with permission of Princeton University Press.

———. 2006–07 Annual Report, Harvard Magazine, August 18, 2007. Copyright © 2007 Derek Bok. Reprinted with permission of Harvard Magazine. All rights reserved.

Bowen, William G., Martin A. Kurzweil, and Eugene M. Tobin. In collaboration with Susanne C. Pichler. Equity and Excellence in American Higher Education (2005). Copyright © 2005. University of Virginia Press. Reprinted with permission of the publisher.

Byse, Clark and Louis Joughin. Tenure in American Higher Education, Plans, Practices, and the Law (1959). Reprinted with permission.

Caputo, Philip. 13 Seconds: A Look Back at the Kent State Shootings (2005). Reprinted with permission of Philip Caputo.

Carnesale, Albert. The Public–Private Gap in Higher Education, Chronicle of Higher Education (January 15, 2006). Reprinted with permission of Albert Carnesale, Chancellor Emeritus and Professor, University of California, Los Angeles.

Creighton, Joanne. Why We Need Women's Colleges, The Boston Globe, May 21, 2007, at A9. Reprinted with permission of Joanne Creighton, President, Mt. Holyoke College.

The Economist. Special Report: Meritocracy in America (2005). Reprinted with permission.

Fish, Stanley. Conspiracy Theories 101, New York Times, July 23, 2006, at 13. Copyright © 2006 the New York Times. All rights reserved. Used by permission and protected by the copyright laws of the United States.

Fritschler, A. Lee. Government Should Stay Out of Accreditation, Chronicle of Higher Education, May 18, 2007, at B20. Reprinted with permission of A. Lee Fritschler.

Giamatti, A. Bartlett. A Free and Ordered Space: The Real World of the University (1988). Copyright © 1988. Reprinted with permission of the Estate of A. Bartlett Giamatti.

Jaffe, Harry. Let Them Eat Truffles, Washingtonian, April 2006, at 76. Reprinted with permission.

Karable, Jerome. The Chosen: The Hidden History of Admission and Exclusion at Harvard, Yale and Princeton (2005). Copyright © 2005 by Jerome Karabel. Reprinted by permission of Houghton Mifflin Company. All rights reserved.

Katz, Stanley. What Has Happened to the Professoriate, Chronicle of Higher Education (October 6, 2006). Reprinted with permission of Stanley Katz, Professor, Woodrow Wilson School, Princeton University.

Keohane, Nannerl O. Higher Ground: Ethics and Leadership in the Modern University (2006). Copyright © 2006, Duke University Press. All rights reserved. Reprinted by permission of the publisher.

Kerr, Clark. Fall of 1964 at Berkeley: Confrontation Yields in Reconciliation, in The Free Speech Movement: Reflections on Berkeley in the 1960s (Robert Cohn & Reginald E. Zelnick eds., 2002). Copyright © 2002 by University of California Press–Books. Reprinted by permission of the University of California Press via Copyright Clearance Center.

_____. The Uses of the University (5th ed. 2001). Reprinted by permission of the publisher: Harvard University Press, Copyright © 1963, 1972, 1995, 2001 by the President and Follows of Harvard College.

Lawrence, Charles R. Two Views of the River: A Critique of the Liberal Defense of Affirmative Action, 101 Columbia Law Review 928 (2001). Copyright © 2001 by Columbia Law Review Association, Inc. Reprinted with permission of Columbia Law Review Association via Copyright Clearance Center.

Lively, Kit. A Close Look at How Duke U. Sets Tuition and Spends Money, Chronicle of Higher Education (May 30, 1997). Copyright 2008, The Chronicle of Higher Education. Reprinted with permission.

Lowell, A Lawrence. The Relation between Faculties and Governing Boards, in At War With Academic Traditions in America 283–85 (1934). Reprinted by permission of the publisher: Harvard University Press, Copyright © 1934 by the President and Fellows of Harvard College.

McConnell, Michael M. Academic Freedom in Religious Colleges and Universities, 53 Law and Contemporary Problems 202 (Summer 1990). Reprinted with permission of the Honorable Michael McConnell.

Metzger, Walter P. The 1940 Statement of Principles of Academic Freedom and Tenture. 53 Law and Contemporary Problems 3, 12, 15–16, 20, 23–25, 47, 50, 62–63 (Summer 1990). Reprinted with permission of Walter Metzger.

Morison, Samuel Eliot. The Founding of Harvard College (1935). Reprinted by permission of the publisher: Harvard University Press, Copyright © 1935 by the President and Fellows of Harvard College. Copyright renewed 1963 by Samuel Eliot Morison.

_____. Harvard College in the Seventeenth Century (1936). Reprinted by permission of the publisher: Harvard University Press. Copyright © 1936 by the President and Fellows of Harvard College. Copyright renewed 1964 by Samuel Eliot Morison.

_____. Three Centuries of Harvard, 1636–1935. Reprinted by permission of the publisher: Harvard University Press, Copyright © 1936 by the President and Fellows of Harvard College. Copyright © renewed 1964 by Samuel Eliot Morison.

Note, 114 Harvard Law Review 1414 (2001). Copyright © 2001 by Harvard Law Review Association. Reprinted with permission of Harvard Law Review Association via Copyright Clearance Center.

Oakshott, Michael. The Character of a University Education in What is History? And Other Essays 373 (Luke O'Sullivan ed., 1970). Copyright © Imprint Academic 2004. Reprinted with permission.

Rabban, David M. Functional Analysis of "Individual" and "Institutional" Academic Freedom Under the First Amendment. 53 Law and Contemporary Problems 227, 242 (Summer 1990). Reprinted with permission of David Rabban, Dahr Jamail, Randall Hage Jamail, and Robert Lee Jamail Regents Professor of Law, University of Texas.

Rhodes, Frank H.T. The Creation of the Future: The Role of the American University (2001). Reprinted with permission.

Rosovsky, Henry. The University, An Owner's Manual (1990). Reprinted with permission of Henry Rosovsky, Geyser University Professor Emeritus, Harvard University.

Thomson, Judith Jarvis and Matthew Finkin. Academic Freedom and Church-Related Higher Education: A Reply to Professor McConnell. 53 Law and Contemporary Problems 419 (Summer 1990). Reprinted with permission of the authors.

*

SUMMARY OF CONTENTS

*

TABLE OF CONTENTS

PART II. FACULTY MATTERS

*

TABLE OF CASES

Principal cases are in bold type. Non-principal cases are in roman type. References are to Pages.

*

CASES AND MATERIALS

HIGHER EDUCATION AND THE LAW

*

PART I

Higher Education in the United States

Higher education has been considered an essential part of the United States from the nation's earliest days. In 1788, Benjamin Rush answered skeptics who thought the new nation "too extensive for a republic" by saying that the United States would endure because we would educate our citizens.[a] In 1796, President George Washington used his farewell address to proclaim the importance of higher education: "[p]romote then as an object of primary importance, institutes for the general diffusion of knowledge. In proportion as the structure of government gives force to public opinion, it is essential that public opinion should be enlightened."[b] By the 1830s, with new colleges opening throughout the nation, Alexis de Tocqueville wrote to a friend in Paris that "[t]he effort made in this country to spread instruction is truly prodigious. The universal and sincere faith that they profess here in the efficaciousness of education seems to me one of the most remarkable features of America...."[c]

The remarkable faith in education fostered the growth over time of higher education institutions of great diversity and quality. Today, American colleges and universities attract students from around the world and higher education is considered one of the most successful sectors in the national economy. Yet surprisingly little attention has been paid to how and why America's institutions of higher education developed as they did.

The book begins by asking what is higher education. It then introduces the complex issue of university governance by asking who speaks for a university. The first chapter concludes by examining key milestones in the history of American higher education. As you read the materials in the first chapter, consider the following questions:

1. Is education necessary for a democracy to flourish? Is higher education?

2. Has democracy in turn influenced American colleges and universities? How?

3. Why were colleges founded so early in the colonization of America? How much did the early colleges influence the structure of today's colleges and universities?

4. What are the strengths of the lay governing board model adopted by most American institutions of higher education? What are its greatest weaknesses?

5. Colonial colleges were modeled on English colleges and universities. The first American universities, by contrast, which developed in the late nineteenth century, drew inspiration from German universities. How do modern American colleges and universities differ from their European counterparts?

6. What is the role of faculty in colleges and universities today? Are they employees or something more?

a. Benjamin Rush, *Plan of a Federal University*, American Museum, Nov. 1788, at 442.

b. George Washington, Farewell Address, Sept. 19, 1796, 1 American State Papers: Speeches and Messages of the Presidents of the United States to Both Houses of Congress 34, 36 (1833).

c. George Wilson Pierson, Tocqueville and Beaumont in America 194 (1938).

7. Why did students have so little voice in higher education until the 1960s? Has their increased participation improved American colleges and universities?

8. Would the higher education sector be as robust as it is if there were only public colleges and universities in the United States? Only private colleges and universities?

9. Most institutions of higher education receive both public and private funding. What impact do these diverse funding sources have on university governance?

A.   WHAT IS HIGHER EDUCATION?

Michael Oakeshott, *The Character of a University Education*

in WHAT IS HISTORY? AND OTHER ESSAYS 373, 374–75, 378–80, 382–84 (Luke O'Sullivan ed., 2004).

The world is usually full of doubts and confusion, and among them is a very considerable confusion about the nature of a university and the character of a university education. Perhaps, this confusion is greatest in those parts of the world where, because universities are an old-established feature of the landscape, they have, until recently, been accepted without very much reflection. Moreover, universities have always been manifold and somewhat ambiguous institutions which naturally resist attempts to define their character.

. . .

I will make my beginning with a university as a place of learning and teaching.

. . .

What distinguishes human beings is not their unusually long period of helplessness and dependence, nor is it (as Aristotle thought) their ability to speak to one another and to engage in rational discourse: these are merely symptoms of human character. What distinguishes them is that each is born heir to an inheritance to which he can succeed only in a process of learning.... [E]very man is born heir to an inheritance of human achievements; an inheritance of feelings, emotions, images, visions, thoughts, beliefs, ideas, understandings, intellectual and practical enterprises, languages, relationships, organizations, religions, canons, and maxims of conduct, procedures, rituals, skills, works of art, books, musical compositions, tools, artifacts and utensils.

The components of this inheritance are beliefs, not physical objects; facts not "things"; "expressions" which have meanings or uses which require to be understood because they are the "expressions" of human minds. The starry heavens above and the moral law within, not less than Dante's "Divina comedia" and the city of London, are human achievements.

Now this world of human achievement can be entered, possessed and enjoyed only in a process of learning....

. . .

It is difficult to think of any circumstances where learning may be said to be impossible.... Thus, the random utterances of anyone, however foolish or ignorant, may serve to enlighten a learner, who receives from them as much or as little as he happens to be ready to receive, and receives often what the speaker did not know he was conveying.

But such casual utterances are not teaching; and he who scatters them is not, properly speaking, a teacher. Teaching is the deliberate and intentional initiation of a pupil into the world of human achievement, or into some part of it. The teacher is one whose utterances (or silences) are designed to promote this initiation in respect of a pupil—that is, in respect of a learner whom he recognizes to be ready to receive what he has resolved to communicate. In short, a pupil is a learner known to a teacher, a learner for whom he has taken specific responsibility; and teaching, properly speaking, is impossible in his absence.

The part of a teacher ... is to hold up the mirror of human achievement before a pupil; and to hold it in such a manner that it reflects not merely what has caught the fancy of a current generation, but so that it reflects something which approximates more closely to the whole of that inheritance. His business (indeed, this may be said to be his peculiar quality as an agent of civilization) is to release his pupils from servitude to the current dominant feelings, emotions, images, ideas, beliefs, and even skills, and to bring to their notice what the current world may have neglected or forgotten.

. . .

... A university, as a place where a number of young people are gathered together for a few of the most impressionable years of their career on earth, will inevitably be the place where many will find themselves acquiring interests which will be with them for life, making decisions which, for themselves, may be momentous, entering into relationships which may be the most durable they will ever enjoy, all of which may be thought of as "learning." ... And from this point of view, all that need be said is that those who make and manage universities should recognize that this is what a university will unavoidably be for its students.... On the other hand, a university is not merely a scene of happenings....

. . .

Now, to regard our inheritance of human achievements as a collection of skills to be learned, and of inventions, devices, and enterprises in which we have learned to impress ourselves upon the world, exploit its natural resources, and make it the sort of place we want to live in, is one way of looking at it; but it is not the only way. Those who hand these skills from generation to generation, each adding its own improvements, are certainly agents of civilization; but this is not all there is to be handed on. And, in my view, a university, and learning in a university, represents a complementary way of regarding this inheritance. For this inheritance of human achievement, which we can succeed to only in a process of learning, and in relation to which we become and are human beings, contains something else; namely, the various enterprises of understanding and explaining ourselves and the world we find ourselves in. And these are what I think a university is concerned with.

[T]here is an important difference between learning which is concerned with the degree of understanding necessary to practice a skill, and learning which is expressly focused upon an enterprise of understanding and explaining. . . .

A "science," for example, for the learner of a practical skill, is a collection of information capable of being used; but a "science" in a university is an intellectual pursuit, an explanatory manner of thinking and speaking, being explored. From time to time, no doubt, it may throw off these useless pieces of information; but to do so is not its business. Doctrines, ideas, facts and theories which are invested elsewhere to yield practical profits (like the Mendelian theory of biological inheritance or the molecular structure of matter), in a university are recognized as temporary achievements, valued solely for their explanatory value, in an enterprise of understanding which is, in principle, both endless and autonomous. . . .

Thus, when a student, entering a university, chooses for himself a field of study—chemistry, biology, economics, sociology—which in some cases may look all too like the opportunity of acquiring the knowledge necessary to practice a skill, what he is really doing is choosing to be initiated into one of the great explanatory enterprises which belong to his human inheritance.

Moreover, there are many enterprises of understanding pursued in universities, like history or philosophy, which cannot be expected to throw off any such by-products of readily useable conclusions and which, consequently, may scarcely be mistaken for anything but autonomous enterprises of understanding.

In short, our inheritance of human achievements includes, not only the skills we need for transforming the world, but also (and independently) these great, autonomous, enterprises of understanding ourselves and the world. And, whatever the adventitious appearances to the contrary, it is with these that learning at a university is concerned. It is participation in this which is the common character of all the faculties of a university; it is this common character which makes nonsense of the modish notion of "two cultures"; and it is this common engagement in understanding which gives to the activity of teaching in a university its distinctive character. For teaching, here, is not imparting information; it is holding up the mirror of a civilization in such a manner that what is to be seen in it is men thinking, men engaged in the supremely intellectual activity of understanding the world and themselves.

Moreover, it is the manner in which teaching is carried on in a university which stands in the way of our mistaking these enterprises of understanding ... for other skills. . . .

In a university, a "science" is taught by one who is actually engaged in exploring it, history is taught by historians, philosophy by philosophers. But students who come to study a "science," or history, or philosophy are not regarded as apprentices to a particular explanatory skill. It is possible that some of them will become "scientists," or historians, but the vast majority will not. And what a teacher in a university is doing, is not educating successors to himself ..., it is imparting to his pupils some familiarity with one of the enterprises of understanding as autonomous intellectual pursuits. What he is doing is showing them what it is like to think as a "scientist" or as an historian.

. . .

[T]he most important gift of a university to the society in which it has a place is not the provision of the useful by-products thrown off by some enterprises of understanding, but the opportunity it offers, to many or few, of not going through life without having had a glimpse, though perhaps not more than a glimpse, of that part of their human inheritance to which these enterprises belong: the opportunity to possess, more completely than falls to the lot of everybody, the whole of this inheritance of human endeavour and achievement.

. . .

Not being comparable to a light-industry (having no product, in the strict sense), nor to a store (having no sales-list of items for disposal) a university is apt to confound the accountants. Profit and loss, cost and return on capital are not easily calculable; indeed, there is something inappropriate in making the calculations.

Edward W. Said, *Identity, Authority, and Freedom: The Potentate and the Traveler*

in THE FUTURE OF ACADEMIC FREEDOM 214, 224–28 (Louis Menand ed., 1996).

None of us can deny the sense of luxury carried inside the academic sanctum, as it were, the real sense that as most people go to their jobs and suffer their daily anxiety, we read books and talk and write of great ideas, experiences, epochs. In my opinion there is no higher privilege. But in actuality no university or school can really be a shelter from the difficulties of human life and more specifically from the political intercourse of a given society and culture.

This is by no means to deny that, as Newman said so beautifully and so memorably,

> [A university] has this object and this mission; it contemplates neither moral impression nor mechanical production; it professes to exercise the mind neither in art nor in duty; its function is intellectual culture; here it may leave its scholars, and it has done its work when it has done as much as this. It educates the intellect to reason well in all matters, to reach out towards truth, and to grasp it.[1]

... Newman says in another place,

> Knowledge ... [is] something intellectual, something which grasps what it perceives through the senses; something which takes a view of things, which sees more than the senses convey; which reasons upon what it sees; and while it sees; which invests it with an idea.

. . .

These are incomparably eloquent statements, and they can only be a little deflated when we remind ourselves that Newman was speaking about English men, not women, and then also about the education of young Catholics. Nonetheless, the profound truth in what Newman says is ... designed to undercut any partial or somehow narrow view of education.... Perhaps like many of his Victorian contemporaries ... Newman was arguing

---

1. John Cardinal Newman, THE IDEA OF A UNIVERSITY (1853, 1858: New York: Doubleday and Co., 1962), p. 149.

earnestly for a type of education that placed the highest premium on English, European, or Christian values in knowledge. But sometimes, even though we may mean to say something, another thought at odds with what we say insinuates itself into our rhetoric.... Suddenly we realize that although he is obviously extolling what is an overridingly Western conception of the world, with little allowance made for what was African or Latin American or Indian (or even Irish, since he was speaking in Dublin) his words let slip the notion that even an English or Western identity wasn't enough, wasn't at bottom or at best what education and freedom were all about.

[W]hat happens when we take Newman's prescriptions about viewing many things as one whole, or, we transpose these notions to today's world of embattled national identities, cultural conflicts, and power relations? Is there any possibility for bridging the gap between the ivory tower of contemplative rationality ostensibly advocated by Newman and our own urgent need for self-realization and self-assertion with its background in a history of repression and denial?

I think there is. I will go further and say that it is precisely the role of the contemporary academy to bridge this gap, since society itself is too directly inflected by politics to serve so general and so finally intellectual and moral a role.... For those of us just emerging from marginality and persecution, nationalism is a necessary thing: a long-deferred and long-denied identity needs to come out into the open and take its place among other human identities. But that is only the first step. To make all or even most of education subservient to this goal is to limit human horizons without either intellectual or ... political warrant....

A single overmastering identity at the core of the academic enterprise, whether that identity be Western, African, or Asian, is a confinement, a deprivation. The world we live in is made up of numerous identities interacting, sometimes harmoniously, sometimes antithetically. Not to deal with that whole—which is in fact a contemporary version of the whole referred to by Newman as a true enlargement of the mind—is not to have academic freedom. We cannot make our claim as seekers after justice that we advocate knowledge only of and about ourselves. Our model for academic freedom should therefore be the migrant or traveler; for if, in the real world outside the academy we must needs be ourselves and only ourselves, inside the academy we should be able to discover and travel among other selves, other identities, other varieties of the human adventure.... We must always view the academy as a place to voyage in, owning none of it but at home everywhere in it.

It comes, finally, to two images for inhabiting the academic and cultural space provided by school and university. On the one hand, we can be there in order to reign and hold sway. Here, in such a conception of academic space, the academic professional is king and potentate. In that form you sit surveying all before you with detachment and mastery. Your legitimacy is that this is your domain, which you can describe with *authority* as principally Western, or African, or Islamic, or American, or on and on. The other model is considerably more mobile, more playful, although no less serious. The image of a traveler depends not on power, but on motion, on a willingness to go into different worlds, use difference idioms, and understand a variety of disguises, masks, and rhetorics. Travelers must suspend the claim of customary routine in order to live in new rhythms and rituals. Most of all, and most unlike the potentate who must guard only one place and defend its frontiers, the traveler *crosses over*, traverses territory, and abandons fixed positions, all the time.... To join the academic world is therefore to enter a ceaseless quest for knowledge and freedom.

Questions and Comments on Oakeshott and Said

What does Oakeshott believe constitutes a university education? Do you agree? What does it mean to teach? To learn? Consider the best teachers you have had. What made them particularly effective? President James A. Garfield famously asserted that the ideal college consisted of Mark Hopkins (the highly respected president of Williams) at one end of a log and a student on the other. Could that be right? Did most of what you learned in college come from the faculty? From books? How much did other students contribute to your education? Were you encouraged or required to study other cultures?

What is the role of research in teaching? Consider the approach of philosopher Friedrich Schleiermacher: "The teacher must produce everything he says before his listeners: he must not narrate what he knows, but rather reproduce his way to knowledge, the action itself. The listeners should not only collect knowledge. They should directly observe the activity of intelligence producing knowledge and, by observing it, learn how to do it themselves." A History of the University in Europe 21 (Walter Ruegg ed., 2004).

What do Oakeshott and Said consider to be the purpose or purposes of a college or university education? Is it to train graduates to earn a living? To lead a fuller life? To improve the competitive position of the nation in the world economy? All of the above?

B.   Who Speaks for The University?

Henry Rosovsky, The University, An Owner's Manual 12–15 (1990).

Whenever approaching an unfamiliar object—for example, a new refrigerator or a personal computer—I have found manuals useful and comforting. Sometimes lacking style and clarity, they have nevertheless become a major literary genre of our civilization. Perhaps because of my love for automobiles ... I am especially familiar with texts pertaining to cars. Invariably they strike an optimistic and practical tone. Let me quote briefly from Datsun 1978. No doubt it would make more of an impression to cite Mercedes–Benz 1986 or Jaguar 1988, but these authors are not generally found in professorial glove compartments. "Thank you for choosing a Datsun. We're sure you will be happy you did." Two sentences that are spoken each fall—with suitable name changes—by some president, provost, or dean on nearly every campus in America. Next, consider a few headings from a representative table of contents: Economy Hints, Instruments and Controls, Comfort and Convenience Features, In Case of Emergency....

Is there a resemblance between refrigerators, personal computers, automobiles, and universities? Only in the sense that we may be confronting the unfamiliar. Many students are the first in their families to try higher education. A larger proportion of faculty members are the first in their families to pursue academic careers.[1] Social mobility is a sure sign of American vigor, but as a result our system of higher education has to accomplish very special tasks. We can take little for granted by way of preparation or common background. In many older, developed countries the transition from secondary school to university is a relatively small step for a select few—smooth, well rehearsed, and comfortable. For Americans, it is likely to be a more jarring experience. A didactic manual showing which knob to pull or when to schedule preventive maintenance might be useful.

But why a manual for *owners?* After all, one cannot buy a university and acquire it as a personal possession. Given current levels of tuition fees in some private institutions, parents may feel that they are buying significant portions of universities on the installment plan, but that is not what I have in mind. I am thinking of ownership in a broader, more sophisticated sense. People say: this is *my country.* That is the notion of ownership I wish to suggest to my readers.

Many claimants can be identified from this enlarged perspective. Faculty members often assert that they are the university. Teaching and research, acknowledged to be the key missions of higher learning, are in their hands. Without professors, it is hard to conceive of a university. Academic administrators have been known to behave as if the university belonged to them. In the United States there are large numbers of chairmen, deans, provosts, chancellors, vice presidents, presidents, and so on in control of private fiefdoms. I am personally certain that the quality of a school is negatively correlated with the unrestrained power of administrators, but that is a matter for later discussion.

Students are another important group claiming proprietary rights. They frequently claim to be the *raison d'etre* of a university. A university is a school, and without students scholarship would eventually wither away. Every social organism needs the young to replace the old in order to survive. When students graduate, they assume other "ownership" roles by becoming teachers, alumni, donors, and trustees. Furthermore, undergraduate students spend an average of four precious years pursuing a degree, and many believe that this entitles them to some control over curriculum, faculty selection, university investment policies, parietal regulations, quality and kind of food served in dining halls, who can and cannot speak on campus, and the selection of presidents and deans. The list is endless, and some of these claims are more valid than others.

Faculty, administrators, and students are the primary focus of this manual. There are, however, other categories that appear indirectly and only make occasional appearances. I have already mentioned three over-

---

1. In 1900, only 238,000 students—a little over 2 percent of the 18 to 24 year-old population—went to college. At the end of World War II, the figure had climbed to 2,078,000, and by 1975, 9.7 million—over one-third of the 18 to 24 year-olds enrolled in accredited institutions of higher education. Obviously many young people are the first in their families to go to college.

As to the parents of academics, surveys taken in 1969 and 1975 indicate that only 4 percent of the fathers of professors were college or university teachers and administrators.

On both points, see Seymour Martin Lipset & Everett C. Ladd, Jr., *The Changing Social Origins of American Academics*, in QUALITATIVE AND QUANTITATIVE SOCIAL RESEARCH 319, 321 (Robert K. Merton, James S. Coleman, & Peter H. Rossi eds., 1979).

lapping groups: trustees, alumni, and donors. These are the bodies that formally ratify major policies, give money, and care deeply about the reputation of *their* schools. The range of concerns tends to be broad, and typically includes quality of teaching, prowess of the football team, politics of students and faculty, admission policies, the sexual preferences of the community, and much else.

There are still other part-owners. One such is the government (federal, state, and local): financier of research, banker to students and universities, regulator, judge and jury of many academic activities. In the case of public institutions, the influence of legislatures and taxpayers is, of course, overwhelmingly strong. But the point is that virtually no university in this country can function without federal support and in many cases without state support. That means being owned in some fashion by government.

A last group to consider is the general public and in particular the self-appointed voice of that constituency: the press. The right to know is deeply engrained in our national tradition, most particularly with respect to public figures and public entities. What happens in America's major universities is national news; events at smaller centers of learning matter locally. New scientific discoveries make headlines. Curriculum debates—especially if they can be described in simple slogans such as "Back to Basics"—receive extensive newspaper and magazine coverage. So do all manner of university opinion surveys, particularly those featuring anything related to alcohol and sex. Editorial writers regularly offer advice to universities. I regret to note that currently one finds more criticism than praise. However, that is not the issue. All we need to understand is that universities are viewed as public property and many of their inhabitants are treated as public figures. That is a limitation on freedom—a requirement of accountability to yet another proprietor.

Questions and Comments on *THE UNIVERSITY: AN OWNER'S MANUAL*

Dean Rosovsky introduces the reader to the complexities of governance of colleges and universities. For the most part, institutions of higher education are hybrids that combine a corporate structure that reports on the business of the institution to a governing board on the one hand, with more horizontal governance by faculty over academic matters, on the other. As you examine the material in the casebook, consider the strengths and weakness of this hybrid model. Is it possible for governance to be shared? What constraints may be imposed by donors and founders? By students? Alumni? Accreditors? Government?

CHAPTER 1

FORMATION

A. THE COLONIAL COLLEGES, 1636–1776

1. GOVERNANCE AND FUNDING

Higher education arrived in America more than a century before the American Revolution. Nine colleges were granting degrees by the time the Declaration of Independence was signed. Harvard, the oldest, founded in 1636, was also the first corporation established in North America.[a] The colonists consciously tried to replicate the curriculum and student life of Oxford and Cambridge. But they adopted a new governance structure—one that gave authority to governing boards made up of political and religious leaders rather than to the faculty. The establishment of "lay" (in the sense of nonfaculty) governing boards was more a matter of necessity than choice; there simply were not enough scholars available. Harvard did not appoint its first faculty member until 1722. Until then, students were taught by the president with the assistance of tutors, who were generally unmarried men in their twenties who were studying for master's degrees or waiting for a desirable pulpit to open. The leaders of the colony were not willing to turn control of their new college over to such "youthful amateurs."[b]

The same form of lay governance was adopted at William and Mary toward the end of the seventeenth century, and it remains the dominate form of college and university governance in the United States today.

Although they largely abandoned faculty governance, colonial colleges followed the same approach to funding in place at Oxford and Cambridge. Thus, from the beginning, colonial colleges accepted both public and private funds. This pattern also remains in place today; private colleges and universities receive public funds (in the form of student financial aid and grants for research) as well as private funds, while public ones receive private funds (in the form of tuition payments and corporate research grants) as well as public funds. As you read the founding documents, consider whether it is possible to classify seventeenth-and eighteenth-century Harvard or William and Mary as public or private institutions.

a. The other eight colonial colleges were William and Mary (1693), The Collegiate School at New Haven (Yale) (1701), The College of Philadelphia (University of Pennsylvania) (1740), The College of New Jersey (Princeton) (1746), King's College (Columbia) (1754), The College of Rhode Island (Brown) (1764), Queen's College (Rutgers) (1766), and Dartmouth (1769).

b. RICHARD HOFSTADTER & WALTER P. METZGER, THE DEVELOPMENT OF ACADEMIC FREEDOM IN THE UNITED STATES 124–28 (1955); SAMUEL ELIOT MORISON, 1 HARVARD COLLEGE IN THE SEVENTEENTH CENTURY 13–21 (1936).

The Act Establishing the Overseers of Harvard College

At a General Court held in Boston in the year 1642 *in* CONSTITUTIONAL ARTICLES AND LEGISLATIVE ENACTMENTS RELATIVE TO THE BOARD OF OVERSEERS AND THE CORPORATION OF HARVARD UNIVERSITY 3–4 (Cambridge, Folsom 1835), *available at* http://hul.harvard.edu/huarc/refshelf/Founding Documents.htm.

Whereas, through the good hand of God upon us, there is a College founded in Cambridge, in the county of Middlesex, called HARVARD COLLEGE, for the encouragement whereof this Court has given the sum of four hundred pounds, and also the revenue of the ferry twixt Charlestown and Boston, and that the well ordering and managing of the said College is of great concernment:

It is therefore ordered by this Court, and the authority thereof, that the Governor and Deputy Governor for the time being, and all the Magistrates of this jurisdiction, together with the teaching Elders of the six next adjoining towns, viz. Cambridge, Watertown, Charlestown, Boston, Roxbury, and Dorchester, and the President of the said College for the time being, shall, from time to time, have full power and authority to make and establish all such orders, statutes, and constitutions, as they shall see necessary for the instituting, guiding, and furthering of the said College, and the several members thereof, from time to time, in piety, morality, and learning: As also to dispose, order, and manage to the use and behoof of the said College, and the members thereof, all gifts, legacies, bequeaths, revenues, lands, and donations, as either have been, are, or shall be conferred, bestowed, or any ways shall fall, or come to the said College.

Questions and Comments on the Founding of Harvard College

1. In 1636, only six years after Governor John Winthrop arrived from England with some four hundred men, women, and children to establish the Massachusetts Bay Colony, their governing body, the Great and General Court of Massachusetts, voted to establish a college and allocated £400 for that purpose. 1 RECORDS OF THE GENERAL COURT 183, *reprinted in* JOSIAH QUINCY, THE HISTORY OF HARVARD 586 (photo. reprint 2006) (1860). Historian Samuel Eliot Morison noted how unusual it was that "a colony of a few thousand people, poor even by the modest standards of the day, had the audacity to plan and the energy to achieve a university college of equal status with the ancient foundations of England and Scotland." SAMUEL ELIOT MORISON, THE FOUNDING OF HARVARD COLLEGE 4 (1935).

It was Winthrop who famously cautioned the colony that they would be "a city upon a hill" in the sense that: "The eyes of all people are upon us; so that if we shall deal falsely with our God in this work we have undertaken ... we shall shame the faces of many of God's worthy servants, and cause their prayers to be turned into curses upon us till we be consumed out of the good land whither we are going." John Winthrop, *Christian Charity, A Model Hereof, in* PURITANS IN THE NEW WORLD: A CRITICAL ANTHOLOGY 164, 169 (David D. Hall ed., 2004).

The colonists' own words reveal how important they considered higher education to be for their future: "After God had carried us safe to *New England*, and wee had builded our houses, provided necessaries for our liveli-hood, rear'd convenient places for Gods worship, the next things we longed for, and looked after was to advance *Learning* and perpetuate it to Posterity. . . ." *New Englands First Fruits* (1643), *reprinted in* SAMUEL ELIOT MORISON, THE FOUNDING OF HARVARD COLLEGE 432 (1935).

Their respect for education was undoubtedly strengthened by the presence of a relatively large number of college graduates in the colony. By 1640, there were more than seventy graduates of Oxford or Cambridge in Massachusetts Bay, or about one for every forty families. This was a much larger percentage of educated men than could be found anywhere in England at the time. SAMUEL ELIOT MORISON, BUILDERS OF THE BAY COLONY 184 (1930).

2. The college faced major problems in the early years. The first head of the school, Nathaniel Eaton, was dismissed for neglecting and misusing his students and severely beating his assistant. The college did not even have a name until the death in 1638 of John Harvard, a young minister who had only recently emigrated to the Colony. He bequeathed his library and half of his estate to the new college.

The value of the estate Harvard received from John Harvard remains uncertain. Although the estate is estimated to have been worth £800, Morison was able to confirm only £375 was ever received by the College. SAMUEL ELIOT MORISON, THE FOUNDING OF HARVARD COLLEGE 223 (1935).

The £400 contributed by the General Court may have been smaller than John Harvard's bequest but it was still a formidable amount for the community to contribute, representing as it did more than half the entire colony tax levy for 1635 and almost one-quarter of that for 1636. *Id.* at 168–69. Given the significant public support provided, and the governing structure adopted in 1642, is it possible to classify Harvard College in the seventeenth century as either a public or a private institution?

The Charter of the President and Fellows of Harvard College, May 31, 1650

reprinted in SAMUEL ELIOT MORISON, 1 HARVARD COLLEGE IN THE SEVENTEENTH CENTURY 5–8 (1936).

Whereas, through the good hand of God, many well devoted persons have been, and daily are moved, and stirred up, to give and bestow, sundry gifts, legacies, lands, and revenues for the advancement of all good literature, arts, and sciences in Harvard College, in Cambridge in the County of Middlesex, and to the maintenance of the President and Fellows, and for all accommodations of buildings, and all other necessary provisions, that may conduce to the education of the English and Indian youth of this country, in knowledge and godliness:

It is therefore ordered and enacted by this Court, and the authority thereof, that for the furthering of so good a work and for the purposes aforesaid, from henceforth that the said College . . . shall be a Corporation, consisting of seven persons, to wit, a President, five Fellows, and a Treasurer or Bursar: . . . and that the said seven persons, or the greater number of them, procuring the presence of the Overseers of the College, and by their counsel and consent, shall have the power, are hereby authorized at any time or times, to elect a new President, Fellows or Treasurer, so oft, and from time to time, as any of the said person or persons shall die, or be removed, which said President and Fellows, for the time being, shall for ever hereafter, in name and fact, be one body politic and corporate in law, to all intents and purposes; and shall have perpetual succession; and shall be called by the name of President and Fellows of Harvard College. . . .

And that the said President . . . and Fellows, or the major part of them, from time to time, may meet and choose such officers and servants for the College, and make such allowance to them, and them also to remove, and after death, or removal, to choose such others, and to work of the College as they shall think fit: Provided, the said order be allowed by the Overseers.

... And further be it ordered by this Court, and the authority thereof, that all the lands, tenements, or hereditaments, houses or revenues, within this jurisdiction, to the aforesaid President or College appertaining, not exceeding the value of five hundred pounds per annum, shall, from henceforth, be freed from all civil impositions, taxes, and rates. . . .

Notes on Harvard Governance

1. The Corporation was established because the leaders of the college found that the Board of Overseers was both too large and too difficult to assemble to govern the ordinary business of the college. SAMUEL ELIOT MORISON, HARVARD COLLEGE IN THE SEVENTEENTH CENTURY 3–4 (1936). The request of Henry Dunster, the second head but first president of Harvard, for a corporate charter was facilitated by the execution of King Charles I in 1649, although Morison still found remarkable the "serene assumption" by the General Court that it had authority to grant such a charter. *Id.* at 5.

2. The Harvard Corporation continues to consist of five fellows along with the president and treasurer and is the oldest corporation in continuous existence in North America. MORISON at 8–9.

3. Notice that the Charter does not mention the education of ministers. Instead, Harvard is described as for "the education of the English and Indian youth of this country." This language was apparently adopted to assist the college in raising money from a fund that had been set up by Parliament for the education and conversion of Indian children. Although money was provided to Harvard from the fund, few Indians were ever admitted. The first did not enroll until 1660, and by 1675 only one was enrolled. Bobby Wright, *"For the Children of the Infidels"?: American Indian Education in the Colonial Colleges, in* THE HISTORY OF HIGHER EDUCATION 74–75 (Lester Goodchild & Harold Wechsler eds., 1997).

4. The Massachusetts Bay colonists understood the importance of a charter. In the early seventeenth century, other joint-stock companies had been granted Royal charters by the Crown to oversee foreign colonies, including the East India Company in 1600. Those charters typically provided that the company would hold its stockholder meetings in London. But the Massachusetts Bay charter was different. "Whether by accident or by greasing the palm of some government clerk who drafted the document, this important proviso was left out of [the Massachusetts Bay charter]." SAMUEL ELIOT MORISON, BUILDERS OF THE BAY COLONY 66 (1930). The Virginia charter had been easily confiscated by the Crown in 1624 because it was physically in London. Perhaps emboldened by the absence of language requiring meetings in London, the Bay colonists decided to take their charter with them, thereby becoming a self-governing commonwealth. They elected John Winthrop, a lawyer, as their governor after their first governor decided not to emigrate. The "General Court" that founded Harvard was the equivalent of a modern corporate board of directors. *Id.* at 71–76; SAMUEL ELIOT MORISON, THE FOUNDING OF HARVARD COLLEGE 150–55 (1935).

5. The last governance links between Harvard and the State of Massachusetts were not severed until 1865. At that time, all *ex officio* members of the Board of Overseers were abolished except the President and Treasurer of the University, and the power to elect the thirty Overseers was taken from the State and given to the alumni of the University. An Act in Relation to the Board of Overseers of Harvard College, 1865 Mass. Acts 565–67. For more discussion of the increasing separation of college and state in the late nineteenth century see JOHN S. WHITEHEAD, THE SEPARATION OF COLLEGE AND STATE: COLUMBIA, DARTMOUTH, HARVARD, AND YALE, 1776–1876, at 65 (1973).

6. Although the Board of Overseers provided lay control at Harvard, over time the faculty lost their places on the Corporation as well. A. Lawrence Lowell, *The Relation*

Between Faculties and Governing Boards, in AT WAR WITH ACADEMIC TRADITIONS IN AMERICA 281, 283–85 (1934):

[I]n 1721 there had been for some time only one Fellow in the Corporation who was a teacher at the College. In that year two of the Tutors presented to the Overseers a memorial claiming places in the Corporation, apparently on the ground that they were resident fellows giving instruction in the College and as such were the Fellows intended by the Charter of 1650. The Overseers sustained their claim; as did the House of Representatives, and the controversy dragged on for several years until it was finally brought to naught by the opposition of the Governor, backed eventually by his Council. The question was interwoven with an acute religious quarrel and a desire to remove the ministers in the Corporation whose ecclesiastical views were unpopular. Although the Corporation was not overborne, and the obnoxious Fellows were not removed, it yielded so far as to elect Tutors in the next vacancies that occurred, so that by 1725 three of them were members of the body.

There continued to be two or three Tutors or Professors in the Corporation until 1779, when a notable change began. [The Corporation, under pressure from the Revolution and university growth, began replacing clerical non-resident Fellows with] men of experience in business and practically acquainted with public affairs.

.   .   .

... The change, however, did not take place without subsequent protest. In 1824, a memorial signed by eleven members of the instructing staff, claiming that according to the intent of the charter the Fellows ought to be resident, paid teachers, was presented first to the Corporation and then to the Overseers.... On January 25, 1825, the Overseers voted unanimously: ... "That it does not appear to this board that the resident instructors of Harvard University have any exclusive right to be chosen members of the Corporation...." The Overseers seem, however, to have thought that the instructing staff should be represented among the Fellows, for they refused to confirm the election to the next vacancy of Judge Jackson, one of their own number, until the Corporation stated its desire and purpose to elect a resident instructor a Fellow as soon as a proper occasion should offer. Within ten years Joseph Story and James Walker were appointed professors while Fellows, and retained their places on the Corporation; so that in a certain way the instructing staff was represented there; but the proper occasion for electing a resident instructor did not come until 1884, and the professor so chosen continued a Fellow for only two years. In short, the question of giving to the instructing staff a representation upon the Corporation was virtually settled in 1825, has never been seriously revived, and there appears to be no desire to revive it today.

Note on Governance at Oxford University

The governance structure of Oxford has changed little over more than seven centuries. There is a twenty-six member Council that makes policy for the University on some matters, but final responsibility rests with Congregation, a body that includes some 4,000 members of the academic, senior research, library, museum and administrative staff. News: Next steps for Oxford governance, http://www.admin.ox.ac.uk/po/ 051212.shtml (last visited Jan. 4, 2008). A White Paper published in May 2006, proposed significant changes that would have resulted in a governing structure similar to that of an American university. The proposals were strongly supported by the Vice–Chancellor. According to the White Paper, the Council was to be reduced in size from twenty-six to fifteen members. It would have seven internal and seven lay [meaning nonfaculty] members and a lay chair. All members would be approved by Congregation. A new Academic Board would also be created and chaired by the

Vice–Chancellor. It would have responsibility for overseeing the academic affairs of the university. A majority of its members would be from Congregation and the colleges.

On November 28, 2006, after a debate that lasted nearly three hours, members of Congregation voted against the proposal 730 to 456. The Vice–Chancellor elected to take the matter to all of Congregation in December by postal ballot. This time, more than 2,500 members of Congregation voted, and again the proposal was rejected, with more than 60 percent of those who voted opposing the change.

Representative of the opposition was the statement of Professor D. G. Fraser (Worcester College):

> The issue of governance is quite simple. It was summed up for me by a quietly-spoken colleague. He said there are two issues: (1) it is dangerous to concentrate too much power in the hands of too few individuals; (2) why should we give up something good, merely to conform to some sector norm?
>
> . . .
>
> The success of the present governance of Oxford and Cambridge is that both allow plurality, so that an anomalously high concentration of very able, very ambitious, very creative academics can cohabit with goodwill and trust. It is governance that has successfully evolved and is responsible to all. . . .
>
> Evolutionary biologists will tell you that diverse communities tend to be healthy and long-lived. One of the key reasons why Oxford academics are so committed to the University is that they have real independence and a genuine personal stake in the system. Oxford is a democratic partnership, not a top-down, managerial structure.
>
> . . .
>
> How ironic that today's leading businesses are moving in the opposite direction from the failed 1970s policies of the White paper. Dynamic knowledge-based businesses are moving away from large, centrally administered monoliths, towards small, self-organizing entrepreneurial cells, flexibly connected and practically self determining—just look at the campus models of companies like 3M, Google and Apple. In fact, just like Oxford colleges. You want an example? Look at Gerry Rubin, Head of the Howard Hughes Medical Institute. They have just set up a Hughes campus to look at Neuroscience—it is called the Janelia Farm Research Campus; and the management structure? Small groups, collegiality, minimal management, trust in the past excellence of the people they employ.

Compare the remarks of Professor P.J. Donnelly (St Anne's College):

> . . . Earlier in my academic career I worked at five different institutions, for my sins, before this one. . . . Two of those were major universities in the U.S., three in the UK, and all of them had systems of governance with substantial external representation. I know many colleagues have been in similar situations. What is it like on a day-to-day basis? Very much like it is here. The university infrastructure tries hard to support one's teaching and one's research with varying degrees of success and muddle-headedness. What of the loftier values of the academy, values of scholarship, of learning, of teaching, and research? They are valued every bit as keenly in other institutions with external representatives, not least by the externals, and certainly they are enjoyed with as least as much freedom as we have here. . . .
>
> We have heard arguments in favour of the external representation, in terms of transparency, of rigour, of links with the outside world and while I think they all have weight they are not for me the most compelling. The most compelling arguments are the ones to do with avoiding vested interests and bringing additional expertise. I may not be the only one here who has

had difficulty sitting on committees either in college or University in working out how to go forward with major capital projects and feeling massively at sea.... That is one example where external expertise would be helpful....

Oxford University Gazette: Report of Congregation Discussion on Governance, Dec. 7, 2006, *available at* www.ox.ac.uk/gazette/2006–7/supps/1_4791.htm.

How would you have voted on the proposal if you had been a member of Congregation? Why? What are the major benefits and drawbacks of Oxford's governing structure compared to that of Harvard?

Note on Early Philanthropy for Higher Education

In 1641, three members of the Bay Colony were sent to London to raise funds for the struggling college. England had a tradition of making private contributions to higher education, having given almost forty thousand pounds between 1621 and 1630. Although the fundraisers met with some success, they felt the need for promotional literature. The resulting pamphlet, published under the title *New England's First Fruits,* contained a section devoted to Harvard College which mentioned the gift from John Harvard and observed that God had been pleased "to stir up [his] heart." MORISON, THE FOUNDING OF HARVARD COLLEGE at 432.

In 1719, Thomas Hollis, a London merchant, gave the first of several large gifts to Harvard College. Harvard's president, John Leverett, informed Hollis that the school lacked a divinity professor and asked if he would endow a position for one. Hollis agreed, stipulating that an annual salary of forty pounds be paid to the professor from the income of the money he had already given. He did not impose a religious requirement on the holder of the chair, but in a section of the "Orders" he drafted pertaining to student scholarships, Hollis, a Baptist, specified that "none be refused on account of his belief and practice of adult baptism, if he be sober and religiously inclined." I JOSIAH QUINCY, THE HISTORY OF HARVARD UNIVERSITY 531 (photo. reprint 2006) (1860). His restrictions were acceptable to the Corporation, but not to the more orthodox Board of Overseers. Hollis was more successful in fostering change at the College with a later gift, the establishment in 1727 of the Hollis Professorship of Mathematics and Natural and Experimental Philosophy, which created the first toehold for science in the otherwise classical curriculum at Harvard. MERLE CURTI & RODERICK NASH, PHILANTHROPY IN THE SHAPING OF AMERICAN HIGHER EDUCATION 14–18 (1965) *available at* Harvard Hauser Center for Nonprofit Organizations website, http://www.ksg.harvard.edu/hauser/ (last visited Aug. 18, 2007).

Hollis was following a well-established tradition of using philanthropy to shape a university. As early as 1546, Regius professorships were established by King Henry VIII at Oxford and Cambridge as a way to control appointments in sensitive academic areas. HUGH KEARNEY, SCHOLARS AND GENTLEMEN: UNIVERSITIES AND SOCIETY IN PRE-INDUSTRIAL BRITAIN 1500–1700, at 21 (1970). As Lawrence Stone has noted, when the universities enrolled a significant number of gentry during the sixteenth century, they found themselves for the first time in charge of the secular power elite in some of their most impressionable years. It became important, therefore, for the state to ensure the religious and political conformity of the faculty. In addition to philanthropy, "the English government increasingly interfered in the election of Headships of Houses, Fellowships, and Scholarships by letters of recommendation, lobbying and even threats." Lawrence Stone, *The Ninnyversity?,* THE N.Y. REV. OF BOOKS, Jan. 28, 1971.

Bracken v. Visitors of William & Mary College

Supreme Court of Virginia, 1790.
7 Va. (3 Call) 573.

William & Mary, in the fourth year of their reign [1693], granted a charter of incorporation to Francis Nicholson and others, for the foundation of a College in Virginia, to bear their name.

The introductory part of the charter is in these words: "For as much as our well beloved and faithful subjects constituting the General Assembly of our colony of Virginia, have had it in their minds, and have proposed to themselves, to the end that the church of Virginia may be furnished with a seminary of Ministers of the Gospel, and that the youth may be piously educated in good letters and manners, and that the christian faith may be propagated among the Western Indians to the glory of Almighty God, to make, found and establish, a certain place of universal study or perpetual College of divinity, philosophy, languages, and other good arts and sciences, consisting of one president, six masters or professors, and an hundred scholars, more or less, according to the ability of the said College and the statutes of the same, to be made, increased, diminished or changed there by certain trustees, nominated and elected by the General Assembly aforesaid, to wit: our faithful and well beloved Francis Nicholson, & c., gentlemen, or the major part of them, or of the longer livers of them on the south side of a certain river, &c."

The first section of the charter "grants that the said Francis Nicholson and others, or a major part of them, or of the longer livers of them, for promoting the studies of true philosophy, languages, and other good arts and sciences, and for propagating the pure Gospel of christianity, only mediator to the praise and honor of Almighty God, may have power to erect, found and establish, a certain place of universal study or perpetual College, for divinity, philosophy, languages and other good arts and sciences, consisting of one president, six masters or professors, and a hundred scholars, more or less, graduates and non-graduates as above-said, according to the statutes and orders of the said College, to be made, appointed and established upon the place by the said Francis Nicholson, & c., or the major part of them, to continue for all times coming."

The second section enables the trustees to take property, real and personal, and to transfer it to the president and masters, or professors of the College [when the said college shall ... be erected and founded....]

The fourth section gives to Francis Nicholson and others, and their successors, or the major part of them, power to elect and nominate other fit persons into the places of the masters or professors of the said College; and, that after the death, resignation, or deprivation of the said president or professors, or any of them, the said Francis Nicholson, & c., and their successors, or a major part of them, shall have power to put in and substitute a fit person or persons, from time to time, into his or their places, according to the orders and statutes of the said College, to be made, enacted and established for the good and wholesome government of the said College, and of all that bear office or reside therein by the said Francis Nicholson, & c., or their successors, or the major part of them.

The fifth and sixth makes the president and masters, or professors and their successors, a body politic and corporate, with power to sue and be sued, and to take property of every sort.

The ninth section constitutes the said Francis Nicholson, & c., and their successors, true, sole, and undoubted Visitors and Governors of the said College, forever, with full and absolute liberty, power and authority of making, enacting, framing and establishing such and so many rules, laws, statutes, orders and injunctions, for the good and wholesome government of the said College, as by the said Francis Nicholson, & c., and their successors shall, from time to time, according to their various occasions and circumstances, seem most fit and expedient. All which rules, laws, statutes and injunctions so to be made as aforesaid, we will have to be observed under the penalty therein contained: Provided, notwithstanding, that the said rules, &c., be no way contrary to our prerogative royal, nor to the laws and statutes of our kingdom of England, or our colony of Virginia aforesaid, or to the canons and constitution of the Church of England, by law established.

The twelfth section enables the Visitors to convocate and hold a certain Court on convocation, where they may treat, confer, consult, advise and decree, concerning statutes, orders and injunctions for the said College.

. . .

The eighteenth section gives the president and masters, and their successors, a right to elect a member to represent them in the Assembly of Virginia.

[In 1727, the surviving trustees passed several statutes, one of which provided for:]

The Grammar School. To this school, belongs a school master, and if the number of scholars requires it, an usher. The school master is one of the six masters of whom, with the President and scholars, the college consists.

In this Grammar School, let the latin and greek tongues be well taught.

[In 1779, in a bid to shift the curriculum from classics to law, science, and modern languages, the Board passed a statute discontinuing the Grammar School.]

At a meeting of the Visitors on the 1st of April, 1777, Mr. Bracken was appointed grammar master and professor of humanity. He was removed by the statute of the 4th of December, 1779, and, in October, 1787, a rule was made in the General Court, on the Governors or Visitors of the College, to show cause on the third Saturday of the following term, why a writ of mandamus should not be awarded, to cause them to restore Mr. Bracken to his place and office of grammar master, and professor of humanity.

Counsel having been heard, the case was adjourned, on account of difficulty, to this Court.

[John] Marshall, for the College. Contended:

1st. That a mandamus was not grantable in such a case as this: And,

2dly. If the Court could take jurisdiction, still a mandamus ought not to be granted, because the Visitors or Governors had not exceeded the powers given them by the charter.

The Court have no jurisdiction of the subject in the form the case now wears, because this is a mere Eleemosynary institution, with Visitors appointed for its government and direction. (Mr. Marshall was here stopped, and the position that a mandamus will not lie in the case of a private Eleemosynary institution, where Visitors were appointed, was admitted to be law.)

This is an Eleemosynary institution. It comes completely within the description of Chief Justice Holt, in the case of *Philips v. Bury*, 1 Ld. Raym. 8. It is founded on charity. That the donations proceeded from the King and from the government, is perfectly immaterial, as Visitors are appointed. Colleges are considered as mere Eleemosynary institutions, as entirely as hospitals.

But, if the Court have jurisdiction, it ought not to issue a mandamus, because the Visitors have not exceeded the powers given them in the charter.

The charter establishes one president and six masters or professors for divinity, philosophy, languages and other good arts. It is not necessary, under the charter, that a grammar master should form a part of the system. The professor of modern languages satisfies its requisitions. The Visitors or Governors have power to make such laws for the government of the College, from time to time, according to their various occasions and circumstances, as to them should seem most fit and expedient. The restraining clause annexed, serves to shew the extent of the grant: "Provided that the said laws, & c. be no way contrary to our prerogative royal, & c." Their power of legislation, then, extended to the modification of the schools, in any manner they should deem proper, provided they did not depart from the great outlines marked in the charter; which are divinity, philosophy, and the languages. It was proper, that this discretion should be given to the Visitors, because a particular branch of science, which at one period of time would be deemed all important, might at another, be thought not worth acquiring. In institutions, therefore, which are to be durable, only great leading and general principles, ought to be immutable.

If, then, the Visitors have only legislated on a subject upon which they had a right to legislate, it is not for this Court to enquire, whether they have legislated wisely, or not, and if the change should even be considered as not being for the better, still it is a change; still the grammar school is lawfully put down; and there can be no mandamus to restore a man to an office, which no longer exists. One of the statutes, enacted by the trustees themselves, authorizes the Visitors to change even those very statutes, one of which creates the grammar school.

John Taylor, contra.

The ... question is, whether the visitorial act of 1779, exceeds their powers as limited by the charter?

. . .

This new instrument does, either expressly or virtually, repeal the old charter, or constitution of the College, in a variety of instances.

1. The old charter has the support of religion for an object. The modern one deserts it.

2. The old constitution appoints a professor of religion. The modern one exchanges it for the "rarer parts of science as more immediately subordinate to the leading objects of society."

3. The old charter established a grammar school to teach the ancient languages. The modern one barters these for the modern languages and the fine arts.

4. Under the old charter, the masters held large estates, a right of representation in the Legislature, fixed salaries, and were a body corporate: nor could any individual lose these rights, except by "death, resignation, or

deprivation." By the new, he holds them at the will and pleasure of the Visitors, and may be dismissed without any reason whatsoever.

5.   By the old charter, the College, as then established or erected, was to subsist forever. By the new one, its existence is determined; and if, in the revolution of things, the Visitors should incline to erect it into a Turkish mosque, here is a precedent for it.

6.   By the old constitution, the trustees only had power to erect schools, or appoint professorships. Under the new one, the Visitors assume this power, and exercise it.

The trustees, under the old charter, convey to professors of theology and the master of the grammar school, who then, under the charter, are to hold to them and their successors. The new regulation breaks this succession.

.   .   .

The Visitors seem wholly to have mistaken their office. They seem to have considered themselves as the incorporated society; and the president and masters as an appendage depending upon them: Whereas, the president and masters form the body politic, for the government of which, not for its annihilation, the Visitors are to form rules.

If it were otherwise, the body politic, consisting of the president and masters, were under a government as completely tyrannical, as human cunning could have formed; in which, not even a sham trial, not even a detestable *quo warranto*, was necessary to rob the whole body of its rights and privileges. The fiat of the Visitors—"Let the grammar school be discontinued: Let all the schools be discontinued: Let the grammar master be dismissed; Let all the masters be dismissed: Let there be light and there was light:" The fiat of the Visitors, in a moment, in the twinkling of an eye, was to deprive the whole body politic, not only of their political existence, but, perhaps, of their natural existence, by reducing them to a state of beggary.

But, the president and masters were a lay corporation, having rights, privileges and emoluments, of which they could not be deprived; at least, without some form of trial.

■ OPINION: By the Court.

Let it be certified that, on the merits of the case, the General Court ought not to award a writ of mandamus to restore the plaintiff to the office of grammar master and professor of humanity in the said College.

Questions and Comments on *Bracken*

1.   The charter provided that William and Mary, like Harvard, would have two governing bodies. It granted greater powers to the Board of Visitors, however, than were granted to the Board of Overseers at Harvard. What powers were given to the President and faculty (masters)? Does the division of governance authority reflect the relevant skills of each group?

In its third section, the charter made the Reverend James Blair, head of the Anglican Church in Virginia, president of the college for life and a Visitor. It was Blair who had secured the royal charter. Francis Nicholson, the Lieutenant Governor of Virginia, was also made a Visitor. I AMERICAN HIGHER EDUCATION: A DOCUMENTARY HISTORY 33–39 (Richard Hofstadter & Wilson Smith eds., 1961). In this way, as at Harvard, church and state were given authority over the new college.

2. It is understandable that William and Mary retained the young John Marshall to represent the College in the litigation. From 1790 until 1800, when he was elected to Congress, Marshall was involved in most of the major issues that went to the highest court of Virginia, arguing 113 cases during those years. II ALBERT J. BEVERIDGE, THE LIFE OF JOHN MARSHALL 177 (1916).

Marshall's first argument in *Bracken* was that a writ of mandamus is a common law procedure to compel a government official to act. If the college was private, as Marshall contended, then it was not an appropriate remedy to grant. Did he persuade the court on this point?

3. Marshall's arguments in *Bracken* prefigured positions he would take later when he served as Chief Justice of the United States. See especially his opinion in the *Dartmouth College Case*, set forth at pp. 42–47 *infra*. In *Bracken*, Marshall argued that the college's charter should be interpreted broadly because "[i]n institutions . . . which are to be durable, only great and general principles, ought to be immutable." Later he would make the same argument for interpreting the Constitution broadly. In *Bracken*, Marshall also argued for judicial restraint. Although he greatly expanded the power of the Supreme Court, most famously by the establishment of judicial review in *Marbury v. Madison*, 5 U.S. (1 Cranch) 137 (1803), as Chief Justice of the United States, Marshall generally exercised judicial restraint. After *Marbury*, for example, he never again held a statute of Congress unconstitutional.

4. In 1906, William and Mary became a public institution. All college property was transferred to the Commonwealth by act of the General Assembly and with the approval of the faculty and Board of Visitors. The College of William and Mary Historical Facts, 1900–1925, http://www.wm.edu/vitalfacts/ twentieth1.php (last visited Nov. 9, 2007).

2. ADMISSIONS, CURRICULUM, AND STUDENT LIFE

The governance structure of higher education and its dependence on both private and public funding have changed little since colonial times. By contrast, the standards for admission, the curriculum, and the daily life of students have changed significantly.

Harvard's Laws, Liberties and Orders makes clear that the first curriculum was designed for religious ends. But students are not always amenable to indoctrination. Carl Becker found that by the middle of the eighteenth century, students were reading the classics not simply for grammatical or oratorical training, but as sources of political wisdom that guided them as they remade their world.

The Laws, Liberties, and Orders of Harvard College, circa 1646

Reprinted in SAMUEL ELIOT MORISON, THE FOUNDING OF HARVARD COLLEGE 333–37 (1935).

1. When any Scholar is able to read Tully or such like classical Latin Author *ex tempore*, and make and speak true Latin in verse and prose . . . and decline perfectly the paradigms of Nouns and verbs in the Greek tongue, then may he be admitted into the College, nor shall any claim admission before such qualifications.

2.   Everyone shall consider the main End of his life and studies, to know God and Jesus Christ which is Eternal life. *John* 17:3

. . .

7.   They shall honor as their parents, Magistrates, Elders, tutors and aged persons, by being silent in their presence (except they be called on to answer) not gainsaying showing all those laudable expressions of honor and reverence in their presence, that are in use as bowing before them standing uncovered or the like.

8.   They shall be slow to speak, and eschew not only oaths, lies, and uncertain rumors, but likewise all idle, foolish, bitter scoffing, frothy wanton words and offensive gestures.

9.   None shall pragmatically intrude or intermeddle in other men's affairs.

10.   During their residence, they shall studiously redeem their time, observe the general hours appointed for all the Scholars, and the special hour for their own Lecture, and then diligently attend the Lectures without any disturbance by word or gesture: And if of any thing they doubt they shall inquire as of their fellows so in case of non-resolution modestly of their tutors.

11.   None shall under any pretense whatsoever frequent the company and society of such men as lead an ungirt and dissolute life.

Neither shall any without the license of the Overseers of the College be of the Artillery traine-band.

Nor shall any without the license of the Overseers of the College, his tutor's leave, or in his absence the call of parents or guardians go out to another town.

12.   No Scholar shall buy sell or exchange any thing to the value of six-pence without the allowance of his parents, guardians, or tutors. . . .

13.   The Scholars shall never use their Mother-tongue except that in public exercises of oratory or such like, they be called to make them in English.

14.   If any Scholar being in health shall be absent from prayer or Lectures, except in case of urgent necessity or by the leave of his tutor, he shall be liable to admonition (or such punishment as the President shall think meet) if he offend above once a week.

15.   Every Scholar shall be called by his surname only till he be invested with his first degree; except he be fellow-commoner or a Knight's eldest son or of superior nobility.

16.   No Scholars shall under any pretense or recreation or other cause whatever (unless foreshowed and allowed by the President or his tutor) be absent from his studies or appointed exercises above an hour at morning-bever, half an hour at afternoon-bever; an hour and an half at dinner and so long at supper.

17.   If any Scholar shall transgress any of the Laws of God or the House out of perverseness or apparent negligence, after twice admonition he shall be liable if not adultus to correction, if adultus his name shall be given up to the Overseers of the College that he may be publicly dealt with after the

desert of his fault but in grosser offenses such gradual proceeding shall not be expected.

18.   Every Scholar that on proof is found able to read the original of the Old and New Testament into the Latin tongue, and to resolve them logically withal being of honest life and conversation and at any public act hath the approbation of the Overseers, and Master of the College may be invested with his first degree.

19.   Every Scholar that gives up in writing a Synopsis or summa of Logic, Natural and Moral Philosophy, Arithmetic, Geometry, and Astronomy, and is ready to defend his theses or positions, withal skilled in the originals as aforesaid and still continues honest and studious, at any public act after trial he shall be capable of the second degree of Master of Arts.

Questions and Comments on the *Laws of Harvard College*

1.   Harvard's first statutes were modeled on the statutes of Cambridge University. SAMUEL ELIOT MORISON, THE FOUNDING OF HARVARD COLLEGE 337 (1935).

2.   The word "college" originally meant simply a place were poor scholars could secure room and board. One was established as early as 1180 at the University of Paris. It was at Oxford and Cambridge that colleges came to be the most characteristic feature of university life. Over time, the English colleges took over most of the teaching as well as social life, leaving only examining and degree-conferring to the university.

3.   The position of "fellow-commoner" referred to in the statutes was applied to sons of the nobility who dined with the fellows, but were understood to have no serious scholastic intentions. They were charged double tuition.

4.   According to Morison, a key principle that shaped the early Harvard curriculum was that no student should study more than one subject on a given day. A major constraint was that the President had to provide most of the instruction, which was possible only because there were not many students. Following the pedagogy established at the University of Paris in the sixteenth century, a lecture was followed by individual study and then time to discuss and dispute (debate) so students could practice and apply what they had learned. SAMUEL ELIOT MORISON, HARVARD COLLEGE IN THE SEVENTEENTH CENTURY 140 (1936).

On Mondays and Tuesdays at Harvard, President Dunster would first lecture freshmen on Logic (Physics in the fourth quarter of the term), then the second years on Ethics or Politics, and finally the third years on Arithmetic and Geometry (Astronomy in the fourth quarter). (For the first ten years of the college, the course for a bachelor's degree was only three years long). In the afternoon he would moderate disputations by the classes in three successive hours. On Wednesdays it was Greek etymology and syntax for freshmen, Greek prosody and dialects for second years, and Greek Theory (principles of composition) for third years. Thursday was for Hebrew and Oriental languages (Aramaic and Syriac). Fridays were for Rhetoric and Saturday was Divinity Day. Freshman had an afternoon history class in winter and botany in summer. *Id.* at 142–43.

The College's curriculum was based on the seven Liberal Arts that had dominated European education for a thousand years: the *Trivium* (Grammar, Rhetoric, and Logic) and the *Quadrivium* (Music, Arithmetic, Geometry, and Astronomy). Grammar meant Latin grammar, and most of the textbooks, even the Greek and Hebrew grammars, were in Latin. Rhetoric, the art of persuasion, was studied using ancient Latin authors, particularly Virgil, Ovid, and Cicero. *Id.* at 8–9.

5.   A student also had to meet the demands of upperclassmen:

Once entered, the freshman found that besides his studies he was expected to play errand-boy and unpaid servant to the sophisters (upperclassmen). These "abuses" in sending freshman upon "private Errands" were complained of by the Overseers as early as 1667.... One of his first duties was to procure bread and beer for his seniors at the buttery hatch, for "morning bever," as breakfast was called, consisted of nothing else and was consumed in the students' chambers or in the Yard if the weather was warm and pleasant.

Morning bever was preceded by college prayers at five o'clock, and followed by a study hour before the eight o'clock lecture. Lectures were generally of the medieval sort: the class tutor read aloud from some prescribed textbook in Latin, and the students took notes, or followed the reading in a text of their own. Dinner came at eleven, or noon. It was a formal feast in the college hall.... Resident fellow and fellow-commoners sat at a head or high table adorned with silver ...; the undergraduates eating from wooden trenchers, drinking beer from pewter "cue-cups" and providing their own knives and spoons....

After dinner came the recreation hour; then recitations in your tutor's chamber, where you were quizzed on the morning lecture, or disputations in hall for the sophisters, moderated by the President. Around half-past four or five the college bell tolled for "afternoon bever," ... as the butler stood ready to serve out more ... bread and beer. Evening prayers came at five; then a study hour and supper at half-past seven. A recreation hour extended after supper until nine; and except in summer it was probably spent around the hall fire, talking and smoking....

SAMUEL ELIOT MORISON, THREE CENTURIES OF HARVARD 27–28 (1936).

6. By the eighteenth century, student misbehavior had become a problem at Harvard:

Students spent large amount of time and money in drinking, eating, and entertaining with others, male and female, both at college and off the premises. Drunkenness was rampant and other crimes fed upon it including fighting, lying, swearing, and card playing. In the class of 1728, for example, twenty-two students were variously punished for "nocturnal expeditions" and "entertainments" beginning with stealing and roasting geese and ending up with drunken routes. Gambling was the primary vice of the classes from 1731–1740.

. . .

With an increase in enrollment came an increase in the number of students participating in illegal group activities, referred to at the time as routs or riots.... A famous one, the Bad Butter Rebellion of 1766, began as a complaint against bad food in the commons but escalated to a highly charged debate between the students, headed by the governor's son, and the board of overseers, headed by the governor, over the obligation to obey an unjust sovereign. The whole episode was shot through with obvious and ironic parallels with the rising political debates in the colony. In Harvard's case, the rebellion ended with a negotiated settlement in which the rebels signed a mass confession but received no other punishments.

Kathryn M. Moore, *Freedom and Constraint in Eighteenth Century Harvard, in* THE HISTORY OF HIGHER EDUCATION 108, 109–10 (Lester Goodchild & Harold Wechsler eds., 1997).

CARL BECKER, CORNELL UNIVERSITY: FOUNDERS & THE FOUNDING
3–10 (1943).

Among the ideas ... brought [by the first settlers] to America were the ideas then prevailing in England about schools and universities.... At almost no other time . . . could the first settlers have brought to these shores a set of ideas more restricted or less promising for the promotion of learning in the new world.

In seventeenth-century England, as in Europe generally, the prevailing idea was that schools and universities should teach nothing that would discredit the established religion or the authority of kings and magistrates. There were, it is true, some voices raised in protest. Francis Bacon protested, and with good effect, against an arid scholasticism and a slavish worship of ancient writers. Milton complained that professors "take from young men the use of reason by charms compounded of metaphysics, miracles and absurd scriptures"; the result of which was that at Cambridge he had misspent his own youth trying to digest "an asinine feast of sow-thistles and brambles." . . . But such voices were for the most part unheeded. . . . Even Leibnitz opposed academic freedom, and Hobbes thought the chief use of universities was to teach subjects their duty to the king. . . .

This totalitarian conception of schools and universities was brought to the new world by the first settlers. The unexamined assumption that made it acceptable to them was that learning is essentially dangerous; and they were aware that, so far as schools and universities were concerned, the danger could be met in one of two ways, either by not having any schools or by preventing them from teaching any but familiar and accepted ideas. William Berkeley, Governor of Virginia, preferred the first way. "Thank God there are no free schools nor printing, and I hope we shall not have these hundred years; for learning has brought disobedience and heresy . . . into the world, and printing has divulged them. . . . God keep us from both." . . .

Schools . . . were perhaps more necessary in New England than elsewhere, because there the first settlers came with the deliberate intention of establishing, as Winthrop said, "a due form of government both civil and ecclesiastical." What this due form of government was, the leaders knew with great certainty, and they took care accordingly that their followers should be like-minded men. . . . Yet in spite of every precaution unlike-minded men were found among them. "Many untoward servants," says William Bradford, "were brought over"; parents in England were glad to be rid of children that "would necessarily follow their dissolute courses"; ship masters, making a business of transporting settlers, "to advance their profit cared not who the persons were, so they had money to pay them" and so, the kindly governor ends on a plaintive note, "the country became pestered with many unworthy persons, who, being come-over, crept into one place or another."[3] Besides, even like-minded men were apt to turn perverse. There was Roger Williams, who believed in soul-liberty, and even went so far as to say that the land belonged to the Indians. There was . . . Mistress Anne Hutchinson, who "speaking from the mere motion of the spirit," criticized the ministers for preaching a covenant of good works. Obviously, having no schools or printing would not meet the danger inherent in learning, since the Devil was always around to mislead the people anyway.

Of this profound truth the founders of Massachusetts Bay were well aware. Accordingly, the General Court enacted a law to the effect that, "it being one of the chief projects of that old deluder Satan to keep men from a

---

3. WILLIAM BRADFORD, HISTORY OF PLYM-OUTH PLANTATION 476–77 (Boston, 1898) (1620–1647).

knowledge of the Scriptures, as in former times by keeping them in an unknown tongue, so in these later times by persuading from the use of tongues, there should be established a free school in each town in the province." This was in 1642. In the same year Harvard College held its first Commencement, graduating nine men. If we may go by the printed rules of [Harvard] College, these nine men had been instructed, intermittently and superficially, in Logic, Mathematics, Physics, Politics, Rhetoric, Moral Philosophy, Divinity, History, and the nature of plants; and more constantly and thoroughly, in those tongues (Greek and Latin) in which the old deluder Satan wished to keep the Scriptures hidden. But the chief aim . . . was that every student should be "plainly instructed and earnestly pressed to consider well the main end of his life and studies, . . . to know God and Jesus Christ, which is eternal life." To this end every student was required to "exercise himself in reading the Scriptures twice daily"; and "if in anything they are in doubt, they shall enquire as of their fellow, so (in case of nonsatisfaction) modestly of their Tutors." What the tutors should do if in anything they doubted, the rules do not say; but it is recorded that in 1654 President Dunster, having doubted the doctrine of infant baptism, was admonished on Lecture Day, and forced to resign his office.

Harvard College was founded to promote learning, but not quite in the sense understood by Abelard, one of the founders of the University of Paris in the twelfth century. "By doubting," said Abelard, "we are led to questioning, and by questioning we arrive at truth." At Harvard College, in the seventeenth century, doubt was evidently regarded as the chief obstacle to learning. There the rule was: by doubting we run into error, we arrive at truth by enquiring, modestly, of the tutors.

. . . [I]n the eighteenth century no less than in the seventeenth century, the colleges were supported by the ruling classes (a flexible, mixed aristocracy, composed of the educated and wealthy families who thought of themselves as "the better sort") in order to provide the leaders of the community with a liberal education; and it was taken for granted that a liberal education would safeguard them against subversive political ideas, and fortify their faith, if not the tenets of any particular sect, at least in what the Prospectus of King's College [today Columbia] called "the Great Principles of Christianity and Morality in which all true Christians in each of the denominations are generally agreed." Certainly nothing was further from the intention of the founders of these institutions than that their most distinguished alumni should become the leaders of a revolution dedicated to the principle that all men are endowed by their Creator with an inalienable right to abolish any form of government, civil or ecclesiastical, which did not in their opinion derive its authority from the consent of the governed. Yet this is what came to pass; and if we ask where Jefferson, the brace of Adamses, and their confreres got those subversive ideas, the answer is that they got them in part in college, by reading works in those tongues in which, according to the founders of Massachusetts Bay, the old deluder Satan had hidden the Scriptures.

To establish centers of learning on the assumption that, properly supervised, no subversive ideas will be generated in them is to take a great risk. . . .

[I]t is a fact that Jefferson . . . and many other leaders of the American Revolution attended one or other of the colleges and there learned to read and prize the classical authors. They read the Scriptures too, no doubt, but they seem to have liked the pagans better . . . preferring Demosthenes to Deuteronomy, Cicero to Solomon and St. Augustine; Plutarch and Livy to Eusebius or Orosius. Reading the pagan authors, they found the content more interesting than the grammar, no doubt because the content confirmed them in the notion, already current in the eighteenth century, that history and politics were both more interesting and more relevant than theology. . . . [T]he young John Adams . . . while studying in Harvard College . . . failed to find in the Scriptures any precept "requiring . . . creeds, confessions, oaths, subscriptions, and whole cart-loads of trumpery that we find religion encumbered with these days." Concluding . . . that "the design of Christianity was not to make . . . good mystery mongers, but good men, good magistrates, and good subjects" he was drawn to "that science by which mankind have raised themselves from the . . . state in which nature leaves them, to the full enjoyment of the social union."

In classical literature Adams and his fellows found an engaging if not entirely true account of what the social union was in ancient Greece and Rome, and took it as in some sense a model of what the social union should be in modern times. . . . Admiring the ancient republican heroes, it seemed to them that the golden age of freedom and enlightenment had ended when Caesar crossed the Rubicon, to be followed by a thousand years of despotism and superstition. But from this long Dark Age the world was in their own time emerging, the eternal struggle against tyranny was again the central issue, and in resisting the unwarranted measures of the British government were they not themselves standing at Armageddon? What better then could honest men do than to cultivate the civic virtues of the ancient republican heroes . . . ?

Questions and Comments on CARL BECKER, CORNELL UNIVERSITY: FOUNDERS & THE FOUNDING

Becker reports that Jefferson, Adams, and others drew from their college studies lessons that undermined the social foundations their professors and college benefactors sought to protect. Does that mean that their professors succeeded or failed? Does that result comport with Said's theory of education? With Oakeshott's?

B.   HIGHER EDUCATION IN THE NEW DEMOCRACY, 1787–1862

At the beginning of the American Revolution, only Oxford and Cambridge were authorized to grant degrees in England, in contrast to the nine degree-granting colleges in America. Although the colonial colleges were quite small, with typically at most one hundred students in a class, their graduates were very influential in both the Revolution and the new government. Five of the six first presidents of the United States were college graduates.[a] Washington, the only one of the six who did not attend college, valued education and was passionately devoted to the idea of establishing a national university.

a. John Adams (Harvard); Jefferson (William & Mary); Madison (Princeton); Monroe (William & Mary); John Quincy Adams (Harvard).

None of the nine colonial colleges was permanently closed as a result of the Revolution, but two were expropriated for a time by their states, as the materials in this section reveal.

1.   THE FOUNDING FATHERS AND HIGHER EDUCATION

BENJAMIN FRANKLIN, PROPOSALS RELATING TO THE EDUCATION OF YOUTH IN PENNSYLVANIA (1749)

available at http://www.archives.upenn.edu/primdocs/1749proposals.html.

It has long been regretted as a Misfortune to the Youth of this Province, that we have no Academy, in which they might receive the Accomplishments of a regular Education.

The following Paper of Hints towards forming a Plan for the Purpose . . . .[a]

The good Education of Youth has been esteemed by wise Men in all Ages, as the surest Foundation of the Happiness both of private Families and of Commonwealths. Almost all Governments have therefore made it a principal Object of their Attention, to establish and endow with proper Revenues, such Seminaries of Learning, as might supply the succeeding Age with Men qualified to serve the Public with Honor to themselves, and to their country.

. . . It is proposed that some persons of leisure and public Spirit, apply for a Charter . . . to erect an Academy for the Education of Youth. . . .

That the Rector be a Man of good Understanding, good Morals, diligent and patient; learned in the Languages and sciences, and a correct pure Speaker and Writer of the English Tongue; to have such Tutors under him as shall be necessary.

That the boarding Scholars diet together, plainly, temperately, and frugally.

That to keep them in Health, and to strengthen and render active their Bodies, they be frequently exercised in Running, Leaping, Wrestling, and Swimming.

. . .

As to their Studies, it would be well if they could be taught every Thing that is useful, and every Thing that is ornamental: But Art is long, and their Time is short. It is therefore proposed that they learn those Things that are likely to be most useful and most ornamental. . . .

All should be taught to write a fair Hand, and swift, as that is useful to All. And with it may be learnt something of Drawing . . . and some of the first principles of Perspective.

Arithmetic, Accounts, and some of the first Principles of Geometry and Astronomy.

a. Franklin quotes five prominent authors in his Proposals: John Milton; John Locke, particularly his *Treatise on Education*; Frances Hutcheson, a professor at Glasgow; Obadiah Walker, author of *A Treatise on the Education of a Young Gentleman*; Charles Rollin, French author of *The Method of Teaching and Studying the Belles Lettres*; and George Turnbull, Chaplain to the Prince of Wales and author of *Observations on Liberal Education*.

The English Language might be taught by Grammar; in which some of our best writers, as Tillotson, Addison, Pope, Algernoon Sidney, Cato's Letters, etc., should be Classics.... Reading should also be taught, and pronouncing, properly, distinctly, emphatically; not with an even Tone, which under-does, nor a theatrical, which over-does Nature.

. . .

But if History be made a constant Part of their Reading, such as the Translations of the Greek and Roman historians, and the modern Histories of ancient Greece and Rome may not almost all Kinds of useful Knowledge be that way introduced to Advantage, and with Pleasure to the Student.

. . .

Morality, by decanting and making observations on the Cause of the Rise or Fall of any Man's Character, Fortune, Power, mentioned in History; the Advantages of Temperance, Order, Frugality, Industry, Perseverance.... Indeed the general natural Tendency of Reading good History must be to fix in the Minds of Youth deep Impressions of the Beauty and Usefulness of Virtue of all Kinds, Public Spirit, Fortitude, etc.

. . .

When Youth are told, that the Great Men whose Lives and Actions they read in History, spoke two of the best Languages that ever were, the most expressive, copius, beautiful; and that the finest Writings, the most correct Compositions, the most perfect Productions of human Wit and Wisdom, are in those Languages; ... that no Translation can do them Justice, or give the Pleasure found in Reading the Originals; ... they may be thereby made desirous of learning those Languages ... All intended for Divinity should be taught the Latin and Greek, for Physick, the Latin, Greek and French, for Law, the Latin and French....

With the History of Men, Times and Nations, should be read ... some of the best Histories of Nature.... Natural History will also afford Opportunities of introducing many Observations, relating to the Preservation of Health....

The History of Commerce, of the Invention of Arts, Rise of Manufactures ... will be useful to all.... Accounts ... of the prodigious Force and Effect of Engines and Machines used in War will naturally introduce a Desire to be instructed in Mechanics....

The Idea of what is true Merit, should also be often presented to Youth, explained and impressed on their Minds, as consisting in an Inclination joined with an Ability to serve Mankind, one's Country, Friends, and Family; which Ability is (with the Blessing of God) to be acquired or greatly increased by true Learning; and should indeed be the great Aim and End of all Learning.

Questions and Comments on Franklin and Jefferson

1. Benjamin Franklin had little formal education. When he was eight, his father sent him to Boston Latin School with the goal of having him attend Harvard and become a minister. Franklin was at the top of his class at Boston Latin, but his father nonetheless decided to send him to a local school the following year. Although his

formal education was cut short after two years, Franklin throughout his life wanted to know more. As a young man in Philadelphia he organized the Junto, a club of ambitious young men who wanted to help other Pennsylvanians. For a time the members brought books to their meeting place to give each other access to more books. In 1751, he arranged for fifty people to put up forty shillings each to begin a library open to all subscribers. The Library Company of Philadelphia still flourishes today. *See generally* EDMUND S. MORGAN, BENJAMIN FRANKLIN 55–60 (2002); WALTER ISAACSON, BENJAMIN FRANKLIN: AN AMERICAN LIFE 18–19 (2003); GORDON S. WOOD, THE AMERICANIZATION OF BENJAMIN FRANKLIN 18–49 (2004).

Franklin never thought much of the education provided by colleges like Harvard; as Silence Dogood, Franklin wrote that most Harvard students " 'were little better than Dunces and Blockheads.' This was not surprising, since the main qualification for entry . . . was having money. Once admitted, the students 'learn little more than how to carry themselves handsomely, and enter a Room genteely, (which might as well be acquire'd at a Dancing School,) and from whence they return, after Abundance of Trouble and Charge, as great Blockheads as ever, only more proud and self-conceited.' " GORDON S. WOOD, THE AMERICANIZATION OF BENJAMIN FRANKLIN 21 (2004) (quoting Benjamin Franklin, *Silence Dogood, No. 4, in* 1 THE PAPERS OF BENJAMIN FRANKLIN 14 (Leonard W. Labaree at al. eds., 1959)).

Franklin did more than write about education; he arranged to distribute his Proposals Relating to the Education of Youth free to prominent Philadelphians, explaining later that he presented it "not as an Act of mine, but of some *publick-spirited gentlemen*; avoiding as much as I could, according to my usual Rule, the presenting myself to the publick as the Author of any Scheme for their Benefit." He organized a group to buy an available building which enabled the Academy of Philadelphia to open in 1751. It later became the University of Pennsylvania. JURGEN HERBST, FROM CRISIS TO CRISIS: AMERICAN COLLEGE GOVERNMENT 1636–1819, at 88–89 (1982).

2. In 1779, Joseph Reed, president of the Pennsylvania State Assembly, said of the College of Philadelphia that "an institution framed with such manifest attachment to the British government and conducted with a general inattention to the authority of the state" did not deserve the protection of the government. JURGEN HERBST, FROM CRISIS TO CRISIS: AMERICAN COLLEGE GOVERNMENT, 1636–1819, at 177 (1982). The assembly proceeded to dissolve the College's Board of Trustees and amended the college's charter to rename it the University of the State of Pennsylvania. The board of the new institutions included six public officials, six ministers of different denominations, and thirteen other individuals, including Benjamin Franklin. The College resisted until, in 1789, the legislature voted to restore the rights of the college and its trustees. In 1791, the college and university merged to form the University of Pennsylvania, a private corporation with its own board of self-perpetuating trustees. *Id.* at 177–82.

3. Thomas Jefferson, a graduate of William and Mary, became the governor of Virginia in 1779, which meant he also became the ex officio head of the Board of Visitors of William and Mary. It was under his leadership of the Board that the grammar and divinity schools were discontinued in 1784, triggering the *Bracken* law suit discussed in the last section. ROY J. HONEYWELL, THE EDUCATIONAL WORK OF THOMAS JEFFERSON 56 (1964).

The *Bracken* dispute was about curriculum as much as governance. The faculty wanted to continue the classical curriculum, while Jefferson and a majority of the Board wanted to introduce the study of law, science, and modern languages.

Classical learning continued to form the core of most college education in America until the late nineteenth century. Indeed, nearly half the faculty at colleges during the nineteenth century were classical scholars. CAROLINE WINTERER, THE CULTURE OF CLASSICISM: ANCIENT GREECE AND ROME IN AMERICAN INTELLECTUAL LIFE, 1780–1910, at 1–2 (2002).

Benjamin Rush, *Address to the People of the United States*

THE AMERICAN MUSEUM, Jan. 1787, at 8.

To conform the principles, morals, and manners of our citizens to our republican form of government, it is absolutely necessary that knowledge of every kind, should be disseminated through every part of the united states.

For this purpose, let congress, instead of laying out half a million of dollars in building a federal town, appropriate only a fourth of that sum in founding a federal university. In this university, let every thing connected with government, such as history—the law of nature and nations—the civil law—the municipal laws of our country—and the principles of commerce—be taught by competent professors. Let masters be employed, likewise, to teach gunnery—fortification—and every thing connected with defensive and offensive war. Above all, let a professor, of, what is called in the European universities, economy, be established in this federal seminary. His business should be to unfold the principles and practice of agriculture and manufactures of all kinds: and to enable him to make his lectures more extensively useful, congress should support a traveling correspondent for him, who should visit all the nations of Europe, and transmit to him, from time to time, all the discoveries and improvements that are made in agriculture and manufactures. To this seminary, young men should be encouraged to repair, after completing their academical studies in the colleges of their respective state. The honours and offices of the united states should, after a while, be confined to persons who had imbibed federal and republican ideas in this university.

. . .

Our own citizens act [an] absurd part, when they cry out, after the experience of three or four years, that we are not proper materials for republican government. Remember, we assumed these forms of government in a hurry, before we were prepared for them. Let every man exert himself in promoting virtue and knowledge in our country, and we shall become good republicans. . . .

Note on Benjamin Rush

Benjamin Rush graduated from Princeton and studied medicine at the University of Edinburgh. He returned to American to become a professor of chemistry in the new College of Philadelphia. He inoculated Patrick Henry against smallpox and provided Tom Paine with the title for his pamphlet *Common Sense*. He was a signer of the Declaration of Independence, Surgeon General for the Middle Department during the Revolution, and a member of the Continental Congress. HENRY STEELE COMMAGER, THE EMPIRE OF REASON: HOW EUROPE IMAGINED AND AMERICA REALIZED THE ENLIGHTENMENT 23–24 (1977). When this article appeared, there were more than 500 subscribers to THE AMERICAN MUSEUM including George Washington, Benjamin Franklin, Alexander Hamilton, Thomas Jefferson, and James Madison. DAVID MADSEN, THE NATIONAL UNIVERSITY: ENDURING DREAM OF THE USA 16–18 (1966).

Education and the Constitution

Given the importance attached to education by founders of the new nation, it is striking that there is nothing on the subject in the Constitution. The absence of any mention of elementary or secondary education reflected the widespread belief that the lower levels of education were for states to oversee. The subject of higher education, by contrast, was at least discussed at several points during the Constitutional Convention. On August 18, 1787, James Madison proposed that nine specific powers should be granted to the Congress including the power "to establish an University" and "to encourage by premiums and provisions, the advancement of useful knowledge and discoveries...."[a]

His proposals were referred to the Committee of detail. On the same day, Charles Pinckney, delegate from South Carolina, proposed additional powers for Congress including the powers:

"To establish seminaries for the promotion of literature and the arts & sciences"

"To grant charters of incorporation"

"To grant patents for useful inventions"

"To secure to Authors exclusive rights for a certain time...."[b]

Pinckney's proposal was also unanimously referred to the Committee of detail.

Toward the end of the convention, Madison and Pinckney again took up the issue. On September 14, 1787, they moved to insert into the list of powers of Congress the power "to establish an University, in which no preferences or distinctions should be allowed on account of religion."[c] Gouverneur Morris, a delegate from Pennsylvania, argued that it was not necessary to list this power, saying, "The exclusive power at the Seat of Government, will reach the object."[d] When the delegates voted on the question, the proposal lost,[e] leaving to posterity the question of why it was rejected.

George Washington, Message to Congress, January 8, 1790

1 AMERICAN STATE PAPERS: SPEECHES AND MESSAGES OF THE PRESIDENTS OF THE UNITED STATES TO BOTH HOUSES OF CONGRESS 11 (1833).

Fellow-citizens of the Senate and House of Representatives.

I embrace with great satisfaction, the opportunity which now presents itself of congratulating you on the present favorable prospects of our public affairs....

. . .

The advancement of agriculture, commerce, and manufactures, by all proper means, will not, I trust, need recommendation; but I cannot forbear intimating to you the expediency of giving effectual encouragement as well to the introduction of new and useful inventions from abroad, as to the exertions of skill and genius in producing them at home.

Nor am I less persuaded that you will agree with me in opinion, that there is nothing which can better deserve your patronage, than the promotion of Science and Literature. Knowledge is, in every country, the surest basis of public happiness. In one in which the measures of government

---

a. 2 THE RECORDS OF THE FEDERAL CONVENTION OF 1787 321 (Max Farrand ed., Yale Univ. Press 1937).

b. *Id*. at 325.

c. *Id*. at 616.

d. *Id*.

e. *Id*.

receive their impression so immediately from the sense of the community as in ours, it is proportionably essential. To the security of a free constitution it contributes in various ways; by convincing those who are intrusted with the public administration, that every valuable end of government is best answered by the enlightened confidence of the people; and by teaching the people themselves to know and to value their own rights; to discern and provide against invasions of them; to distinguish between oppression and the necessary exercise of lawful authority; between burthens proceeding from a disregard to their convenience and those resulting from the inevitable exigencies of society; to discriminate the spirit of liberty from that of licentiousness—cherishing the first, avoiding the last, and uniting a speedy, but temperate vigilance against encroachments, with an inviolable respect to the laws.

Whether this desirable object will be best promoted by affording aids to seminaries of learning already established, by the institution of a national university, or by any other expedients, will be well worthy of a place in the deliberations of the legislature. . . .

George Washington, Message to Congress, December 7, 1796

1 AMERICAN STATE PAPERS: SPEECHES AND MESSAGES OF THE PRESIDENTS OF THE UNITED STATES TO BOTH HOUSES OF CONGRESS 31 (1833).

The Assembly to which I address myself, is too enlightened not to be fully sensible how much a flourishing state of the arts and sciences contributes to national prosperity and reputation. True it is, that our country, much to its honor, contains many seminaries of learning highly respectable and useful; but the funds upon which they rest, are too narrow, to command the ablest professors, in the different departments of liberal knowledge, for the Institution contemplated, though, they would be excellent auxiliaries.

Amongst the motives to such an Institution, the assimilation of the principles, opinions, and manners of our countrymen, but the common education of a portion of our youth from every quarter, well deserves attention. The more homogeneous our citizens can be made in these particulars; the greater will be our prospect of permanent union; and a primary object of such a National Institution should be, the education of our youth in the science of government. In a republic, what species of knowledge can be equally important and what duty, more pressing on its legislature, than to patronize a plan for communicating it to those, who are to be the future guardians of the liberties of the country?

The institution of a military academy is also recommended by cogent reasons. However pacific the general policy of a nation may be, it ought never to be without an adequate stock of military knowledge for emergencies. The first would impair the energy of its character, and both would hazard its safety, or expose it to greater evils when war could not be avoided. Besides that war might often not depend upon its own choice. In proportion as the observance of pacific maxims might exempt a nation from the necessity of practising the rules of the military art, ought to be its care in preserving and transmitting, by proper establishments, the knowledge of that art. Whatever argument may be drawn from particular examples, superficially viewed, a thorough examination of the subject will evince, that the art of war is at once comprehensive and complicated; that it demands much previous study; and that the possession of it, in its most improved and perfect state, is always of great moment to the security of a nation. This, therefore, ought to be a serious care of every government; and for this purpose an academy, where a regular course of instruction is given, is an obvious expedient, which different nations have successfully employed.

Questions and Comments on Washington's Support for a National University

1. Washington's speech to both Houses of Congress on January 8, 1790, was the first of his presidency. Although a national university never was established, his proposal for a military academy was more successful. Congress established the United States Military Academy at West Point in 1802, and the United States Naval Academy at Annapolis, Maryland in 1845.

Washington continued to look for ways to establish a national university:

> Washington used his executive authority to set aside land in the capital city as a site for the national university in the evident hope that Congress would act or that private contributions would be raised to fund the institution. Yet Congress refused to act even on the limited basis of establishing a corporation to receive private donations in support of the president's plan.... Washington's hope for a national university could not be dissipated, however, and he left his country a gift in his will to be used as endowment for the university when established.

GEORGE RAINSFORD, CONGRESS AND HIGHER EDUCATION IN THE NINETEENTH CENTURY 21 (1972).

In his will, Washington further explained why he considered a national university to be so important:

> It has always been a source of serious regret with me to see the youth of these United States sent to foreign countries for the purpose of education, often before their minds were formed, or they had imbibed any adequate ideas of the happiness of their own; contracting, too frequently, not only habits of dissipation and extravagance, but *principles unfriendly to republican government,* ... which thereafter are rarely overcome; for these reasons it has been my ardent wish to see a plan devised, on a liberal scale, which would have a tendency to spread systematic ideas through all parts of this rising empire, thereby to do away with local attachments and State prejudices, as far as the nature of things would, or indeed ought to admit, from our national councils. Looking anxiously forward to the accomplishment of so desirable an object as this is, (in my estimation), my mind has not been able to contemplate any plan more likely to effect the measure, than the establishment of a university in the central part of the United States, to which the youths of fortune and talents from all parts thereof may be sent for the completion of their education in all branches of polite literature, in the arts and sciences, in acquiring knowledge in the principles of politics and good government.

XI GEORGE WASHINGTON, THE WRITINGS OF GEORGE WASHINGTON 3 (Jared Sparks ed., American Stationers' Company 1834–1837).

2. Thomas Jefferson expressed equally strong objections to sending American youth to Europe for an education:

> Let us view the disadvantages.... To enumerate them all would require a volume. I will select a few. If he goes to England he learns drinking, horse-racing, and boxing. These are the peculiarities of English education.

> The following circumstances are common to education in that and other countries of Europe. He acquires a fondness for European luxury and

dissipation and contempt for the simplicity of his own country; he is fascinated with the privileges of the European aristocrats, and sees with abhorrence the lovely equality which the poor enjoys with the rich in his own country. He contracts a partiality for aristocracy or monarchy, he forms foreign friendships which will never be useful to him, and loses the season of life for forming in his own country those friendships which of all others are the most faithful and permanent.... He returns to his own country a foreigner, unacquainted with the practices of domestic economy necessary to preserve him from ruin.... It appears to me ... that an American coming to Europe for education loses in his knowledge, in his morals, in his habits, and in his happiness.

Letter from Thomas Jefferson to John Banister, Jr., 1785, reprinted in HENRY STEELE COMMAGER, THE COMMONWEALTH OF LEARNING 63–64 (1968).

3. The first six presidents of the United States all favored a national university. Jefferson and John Quincy Adams joined Washington and Madison in asking Congress to establish one, but Congress did not act. Would a national university have benefited the United States? Would it have led to more federal control over education?

In 2007, Senators Hillary Rodham Clinton and Arlen Specter and Representatives James P. Moran, Jr., and Christopher Shays reintroduced legislation to create a Public Service Academy in the United States. The school would offer a free college education to some 5,000 undergraduates in exchange for their commitment to work for at least five years in public-service jobs at the local, state, or federal level. Senator Clinton suggested there was a need to have an institution comparable to the military academies that would prepare leaders on the civilian side. The proposed school would be administered by the Department of Homeland Security. Stephen Barr, *Federal Diary: A Push to Create a Fresh Class of Public Servants*, WASH. POST, Mar. 23, 2007, at D4. Would the proposed academy amount to a national university?

Letter from Thomas Jefferson to Joseph Priestly (January 18, 1800)

in VII THE WRITINGS OF THOMAS JEFFERSON 407–09 (Paul Leicester Ford ed., 1892–99).

We have in that state a college (Wm. & Mary) just well enough endowed to draw out the miserable existence to which a miserable constitution has doomed it. It is moreover eccentric in it's position, exposed to bilious diseases as all the lower country is, & therefore abandoned by the public care, as that part of the country itself is in a considerable degree by it's inhabitants. We wish to establish in the upper & healthier country, & more centrally for the state, an University on a plan so broad & liberal & *modern,* as to be worth patronizing with the public support, and be a temptation to the youth of other states to come and drink of the cup of knowledge & fraternize with us. The first step is to obtain a good plan; that is, a judicious selection of the sciences, & a practicable grouping of some of them together, & ramifying of others, so as to adapt the professorships to our uses & our means. In an institution meant chiefly for use, some branches of science formerly esteemed, may be now omitted; so may others now valued in Europe, but useless to us for ages to come.... I will venture even to sketch the sciences which seem useful & practicable for us, as they occur to me while holding my pen. Botany, Chemistry, Zoology, Anatomy, Surgery, Medicine, Nat. Philosophy, Agriculture, Mathematics, Astronomy, Geology, Geography, Politics, Commerce, History, Ethics, Law, Arts, Fine Arts.... We should propose that the professors follow no other calling, so that their whole time may be given to their academical functions; and we should propose to draw from Europe the first characters in science, by considerable temptations, which would not need to be repeated after the first set should have prepared fit successors & given reputation to the institution. From some splendid characters I have received offers most perfectly reasonable & practicable.

Note on Efforts to Hire European Faculty for the University of Virginia

Francis Walker Gilmer was born in Virginia in 1790. He graduated from William and Mary and read law with William Wirt who later served as Attorney General for both President Monroe and President John Quincy Adams. Although he declined an appointment as professor of law at the University of Virginia, Gilmer agreed to go to Great Britain to recruit professors for the new university, and managed to bring back five. He wrote several letters to Jefferson during his trip explaining why it was so difficult to recruit faculty:

> Education at the universities has become so expensive, that it is almost exclusively confined to the nobility and the opulent gentry, no one of whom we could expect to engage. Of the few persons at oxford, or cambridge who have any extraordinary talent, I believe 99 out of 100, are designed for the profession of law, the gown, or aspire to political distinction; and it would be difficult to persuade one of these, even if poor, to repress so far the impulse of youthful ambition as to accept a professorship in a college, in an unknown country. They who are less aspiring, who have learning, are caught up at an early period in their several colleges; soon become fellows, & hope to be masters, which with the apartments, garden, and 4, 5, or 600 £ sterling a year, comprises all they can imagine of comfort or happiness. Just at this time too, there are building at Cambridge, two very large colleges attached to Trinity, and King's which will be the most splendid of all. This creates a new demand for professors, and raises new hopes in the graduates.

Letter from Francis Walker Gilmer to Thomas Jefferson, July 20, 1824, *in* CORRESPONDENCE OF THOMAS JEFFERSON AND FRANCIS WALKER GILMER, 1814–1836, at 92–94 (Richard Beale Davis ed., 1946).

Letter from Thomas Jefferson to John Adams, January 8, 1825

II THE *ADAMS-JEFFERSON* LETTERS 605–06 (Lester J. Capon ed., 1959).

It is long since I have written to you. This proceeds from the difficulty of writing with my crippled wrists, and from an unwillingness to add to your inconveniences of either reading by the eyes, or writing by the hands of others.... I am comforted and protected from other solicitudes by the cares of our University. In some departments of science we believed Europe to be in advance of us, and thought it would advance ourselves were we to draw thence instructors in these branches, and thus to improve our science, as we have done our manufactures, by borrowed skill. I have been much squibbed for this; perhaps by disappointed applicants for professorships to which they were deemed incompetent. We wait only the arrival of three of the professors engaged in England to open our university.

Letter from John Adams to Thomas Jefferson, January 22, 1825

II THE *ADAMS-JEFFERSON* LETTERS 606–07 (Lester J. Capon ed., 1959).

Your university is a noble employment in your old age, and your ardor for its success does you honor; but I do not approve of your sending to Europe for Tutors, and Professors. I do believe there are sufficient scholars in America, to fill your Professorships and Tutorships with more active ingenuity and independent minds, than you can bring from Europe. The

Europeans are all deeply tainted with prejudices, both Ecclesiastical, and Temporal, which they can never get rid of. They are all infected with Episcopal and Presbyterian creeds, and confessions of faith.... And until this awful blasphemy is got rid of, there never will be any liberal science in the world.

2.   THE FIRST PUBLIC UNIVERSITIES

The Northwest Ordinance, 1787

32 JOURNALS OF THE CONTINENTAL CONGRESS 334–43 (Worthington Chauncey Ford et al. eds., 1904–37).

It is hereby ordained and declared ... That the following articles shall be considered as articles of compact between the original States and the people and States in the said territory and forever remain unalterable, unless by common consent, to wit:

. . .

Art. 3. Religion, morality, and knowledge being necessary to good government and the happiness of mankind, schools and the means of education shall forever be encouraged....

Notes on Early National Support for Higher Education

1.   The first expression of interest in education at the national level appeared in the Land Ordinance of 1785. 28 JOURNALS OF THE CONTINENTAL CONGRESS 375–78 (Worthington Chauncey Ford et al. eds., 1904–37). In it the Continental Congress authorized the sale of public lands in the Northwest, which later became the states of Ohio, Indiana, Illinois, Michigan, Wisconsin, and the part of Minnesota east of the Mississippi. The Ordinance provided that before being sold, the land was to be surveyed and divided into townships of thirty-six sections each. (A section is 640 acres.) The Ordinance further provided that one section of every township (about 2.78 percent of each township) should be reserved for maintaining public schools. SIDNEY W. TIEDT, THE ROLE OF THE FEDERAL GOVERNMENT IN EDUCATION 16 (1966).

On July 23, 1787, following passage that year of the Northwest Ordinance and after much bargaining, the Continental Congress authorized the sale of nearly five million acres of the land to the Ohio Company at a price that amounted to about nine cents an acre. They further provided for "Not more than two complete townships to be given perpetually for the purposes of an university, to be laid off by the purchaser or purchasers, as near the centre as may be, so that the same shall be of good land, to be applied to the intended objects by the legislature of the state." GEORGE N. RAINSFORD, CONGRESS AND HIGHER EDUCATION IN THE NINETEENTH CENTURY 38 (1972).

By 1799, the townships reserved for higher education under the Ohio contract had been located, surveyed, and settled. On January 2, 1802, the territorial legislature of Ohio chartered American Western University, which in 1804 became Ohio University, using the educational land grant in the 1787 contract as the principal source of income. When Ohio became a state in 1802, the land set aside for the university was given to the state, establishing a precedent that the federal government would not supervise the management of the land granted for education. RAINSFORD at 39–43.

2.   All but five states that entered the Union after the Constitution was adopted received educational land grants or their equivalent. Four of those five (Maine, Kentucky, Vermont, and West Virginia) were carved out of states that had been among the thirteen original colonies. Texas, the fifth, retained title to all the public land within its boundaries when it was admitted to the union. RAINSFORD at 44. Overall, more than 98 million acres were granted by the federal government for the benefit of public education. TIEDT at 17.

3.   Unfortunately, much of the reserved land was sold rather than leased, and often for less than its fair market value. In Michigan, the legislature favored the squatters already on the land, and required the University to sell to them at below market rates. ALICE RIVLIN, THE ROLE OF THE FEDERAL GOVERNMENT IN FINANCING HIGHER EDUCATION 12 (1961). Ohio passed legislation designed to avoid this problem by authorizing the land to be leased "for a term of ninety years, renewable forever" but with the stipulation that the value of the land would be reevaluated after thirty-five, sixty and ninety years and the rent adjusted accordingly. 2 Ohio L. 193 (1804). When the statute was challenged in 1841, the Supreme Court of Ohio upheld its terms in *McVey v. Ohio University*, 11 Ohio 134 (1841), only to have their decision overturned by the state legislature. An Act to Regulate the Sale of Ministerial and School Lands, and the Surrender of Permanent Leases Thereto, 1843 Ohio Laws 20–23.

Charter of the University of Georgia, January 27, 1785

A Digest of the Laws of the State of Georgia . . . to 1798, 299–302 (Robert Watkins & Georgia Watkins eds., 1800), *reprinted in* III A DOCUMENTARY HISTORY OF EDUCATION IN THE SOUTH BEFORE 1860, at 5–9 (Edgar Knight ed., 1953).

As it is the distinguishing happiness of free governments, that civil order should be the result of choice, and not necessity, and the common wishes of the people become the laws of the land, their public prosperity, and even existence, very much depends upon suitably forming the minds and morals of their citizens. Where the minds of the people in general are viciously disposed and unprincipled, and their conduct disorderly, a free government will be attended with great confusions, and with evils more horrid than the wild uncultivated state of nature: It can only be happy where the public principles and opinions are properly directed, and their manners regulated. This is an influence beyond the sketch of laws and punishments, and can be claimed only by religion and education. It should therefore be among the first objects of those who wish well to the national prosperity, to encourage and support the principles of religion and morality, and early to place the youth under the forming hand of society, that by instruction they may be moulded to the love of virtue and good order. Sending them abroad to other countries for their education will not answer these purposes, is too humiliating an acknowledgment of the ignorance or inferiority of our own, and will always be the cause of so great foreign attachment, that upon principles of policy it is not admissible.

. . . THEREFORE the representatives of the freemen of the State of Georgia . . . enacted, ordained, and declared.

1st.   The general superintendance and regulation of the literature of this State, and in particular of the public seat of learning, shall be committed and entrusted to the governor and council, the speaker of the house of assembly, and the chief justice of the State, for the time being, who shall, ex official, compose one board, denominated the Board of Visitors, hereby vested with all the powers of visitation, to see the intent of this institution is carried into effect, and John Houston, James Nation Brownson, etc., who shall compose another board, denominated the Board of Trustees. These two boards united, or a majority of each of them, shall compose the Senatus Academicus of the University of Georgia.

. . .

7th.   The trustees shall have the power of filling up all vacancies of their own board, and appointing professors, tutors, secretary, treasurers, and any other officers which they may think necessary, and the same to discontinue or remove, as they may think fit; but not without seven of their number, at least, concurring in such acts.

8th.   The trustees shall prescribe the course of public studies. . . .

9th.   All officers appointed to the instruction and government of the university, shall be of the Christian religion. . . .

10th.   The president, professors, tutors, students, and all officers and servants of the university whose office require their constant attendance, shall be, and they are hereby excused from military duty, and from all other such like duties and services; and all lands and other property of the university is hereby exempted from taxation.

11th.   The trustees shall not exclude any person of any religious denomination whatsoever, from free and equal liberty and advantages of education, or from any of the liberties, privileges, and immunities of the university in his education, on account of his, her, or their speculative sentiments in religion, or being of a different religious profession.

.   .   .

14th.   All public schools, instituted or to be supported by funds or public monies in this State, shall be considered as parts or members of the university, and shall be under the foregoing directions and regulation.

Note on State Support for Higher Education

1.   The charter of the University of Georgia put politicians in charge of the proposed university, and indeed, of all public schools in the state. (John Houston and James Nathan were former governors of the state.) Is there anything in the proposed structure that would encourage academic quality? One noteworthy provision contained in section 11 is that the university would be open to women.

2.   Georgia was the first state to charter a state university, but funds for its support were not appropriated by the state legislature until 1881. North Carolina in 1795 was the first state to open a public university. JOHN BRUBACHER & WILLIS RUDY, HIGHER EDUCATION IN TRANSITION 146 (4th ed. 2007).

3.   The first governmental endorsement of higher education in the new nation came at the state level. The Pennsylvania Constitution of 1776, for example, provided:

> A school or schools shall be established in each county by the legislature for the convenient instruction of youth, with such salaries to the masters paid by the public as may enable them to instruct youth at low prices: And all useful learning shall be duly encouraged and promoted in one or more universities.

PA. CONST. of 1776, ch. II, § 44.

> The North Carolina Constitution of 1776 had a similar provision:

> That a school or schools shall be established by the Legislature, for the convenient instruction of youth, with such salaries to the masters, paid by the public, as may enable them to instruct at low prices; and all useful learning shall be duly encouraged and promoted, in one or more universities.

N.C. CONST. of 1776, § 41.

The 1777 Vermont Constitution provided:

One grammar school in each county and one university in this State, ought to be established by direction of the General Assembly.

VT. CONST. of 1777, ch. 2, § 40.

4. It is difficult to categorize the early colleges as public or private. Between 1814 and 1823, for example, Harvard was given $100,000 by Massachusetts in ten annual installments. Bowdoin and Williams each received $30,000 as part of the same legislative act. An Act for the Encouragement of Literature, Piety and Morality, and the Useful Arts and Sciences, 1814 Mass. Gen. Laws 407–08. In Connecticut, Yale persuaded the legislature to award it the funds provided by the Morrill Act. In exchange, Yale's Sheffield Scientific School offered forty free scholarships to Connecticut students. In 1893, however, the Connecticut legislature decided to move future Morrill funds to the Storrs Agricultural College, later the University of Connecticut. Yale sued alleging breach of contract, *Yale College v. Sanger*, 62 F. 177 (C.C.D. Conn. 1894), and received a cash settlement of more than $154,000—the largest amount the state had ever given to Yale. JOHN S. WHITEHEAD, THE SEPARATION OF COLLEGE AND STATE: COLUMBIA, DARTMOUTH, HARVARD, AND YALE, 1776–1876, at 181–82 (1973).

3. CONSTITUTIONAL PROTECTION FOR PRIVATE COLLEGES AND UNIVERSITIES

Higher education soon became the nation's "cottage industry." By 1800 there were twenty-five colleges; by 1820 there were fifty-two, with the post-colonial schools roughly equally divided between public and private.[a] There was even greater growth during the next three decades; by 1860 there were 241 colleges and universities (not including 40 schools that opened and closed during the period).[b]

Christopher Jencks and David Riesman found little to praise in the early colleges:

[W]hile the pre-Jacksonian college was almost always a pillar of the establishment, it was by no means a very important pillar. An American "college" was in some respects more like today's secondary schools than today's universities. It did not employ a faculty of scholars. Indeed, only one or two pre-Jacksonian college teachers exercised any significant influence on the intellectual currents of their time. An always upright and usually erudite clergyman served as the president. He then hired a few other men (usually young bachelors and often themselves aspiring clergymen) to assist in the teaching. There were only a few professorships in specialized subjects. In most cases everyone taught almost everything, usually at a fairly elementary level.

Nor did these colleges have much of an impact on the character of the rising generation. Only a minority of those who controlled the established institutions of pre-Jacksonian America sent their children to college, and an even smaller minority had itself been to a college. Even those who attended seldom seem to have regarded the experience as decisive for their later development, at least

---

a. JURGEN HERBST, FROM CRISIS TO CRISIS: AMERICAN COLLEGE GOVERNMENT, 1616–1819, at 241 (1982).

b. JOHN R. THELIN, A HISTORY OF AMERICAN HIGHER EDUCATION 41–42 (2004).

judging by the relative scarcity of references to colleges in the literature of the time. . . .

With the wisdom of hindsight it is tempting to conclude that these colleges influenced neither the intellectual nor the social history of their era. Indeed, it could be argued that America overinvested in higher education during the pre-Jacksonian years. Perhaps the resources devoted to colleges might have been better allocated to libraries, scientific societies, or primary schooling. But . . . Americans during these years were eager to have the outward trappings of equality with the mother country, even if these trappings were neither relevant to the American setting nor productive in the mother country itself.

JENCKS & RIESMAN, THE ACADEMIC REVOLUTION 1–2 (1968).

Can you reconcile the critique of Jencks and Riesman with Carl Becker's statement that some of the founders favored independence from England in part because of the education they received in college?[c]

Trustees of Dartmouth College v. Woodward

Supreme Court of the United States, 1819.
17 U.S. (4 Wheat.) 518, 4 L.Ed. 629.

■ CHIEF JUSTICE MARSHALL.

This is an action of trover, brought by the Trustees of Dartmouth College against William H. Woodward . . . for the book of records, corporate seal, and other corporate property, to which the plaintiffs allege themselves to be entitled.

.   .   .

The Superior Court of Judicature of New–Hampshire rendered a judgment . . . for the defendant, which judgment has been brought before this Court by writ of error. . . .

.   .   .

["The Trustees of Dartmouth College" were incorporated by charter in 1769. In addition to "the usual corporate privileges and powers," the original twelve-member body and its successors had authorization to fill all trustee vacancies.

In June 1816, the New Hampshire legislature, in "an act to amend the charter, and enlarge and improve the corporation of Dartmouth College," increased the number of trustees to twenty-one, gave appointment power to the governor, and created a twenty-five-member board of overseers, which would be appointed by the governor and council and have "power to inspect and control" the trustees. Dartmouth College was also renamed Dartmouth University.]

---

c. *See* THE AMERICAN COLLEGE IN THE NINE-TEENTH CENTURY (Roger L. Geiger ed., 2000) for a good introduction to more recent scholarship on the period. Geiger demonstrates the weakness of selecting arbitrary dates in history to capture the developments in higher education whether Jackson's presidency or the Civil War.

The majority of the trustees of the college have refused to accept this amended charter, and have brought this suit for the corporate property....

It can require no argument to prove, that the circumstances of this case constitute a contract. An application is made to the crown for a charter to incorporate a religious and literary institution. In the application, it is stated that large contributions have been made for the object, which will be conferred on the corporation, as soon as it shall be created. The charter is granted, and on its faith the property is conveyed. Surely in this transaction every ingredient of a complete and legitimate contract is to be found.

The points for consideration are,

1. Is this contract protected by the constitution of the United States?

2. Is it impaired by the acts under which the defendant holds?

1. On the first point it has been argued, that the word "contract," in its broadest sense, would comprehend the political relations between the government and its citizens, would extend to offices held within a State for State purposes, and to many of those laws concerning civil institutions, which must change with circumstances, and be modified by ordinary legislation; which deeply concern the public, and which, to preserve good government, the public judgment must control. That even marriage is a contract, and its obligations are effected by the laws respecting divorces. That the clause in the constitution,[d] if construed in its greatest latitude, would prohibit these laws. Taken in its broad unlimited sense, the clause would be an unprofitable and vexatious interference with the internal concerns of a State, would unnecessarily and unwisely embarrass its legislation, and render immutable those civil institutions, which are established for purposes of internal government, and which, to subserve those purposes, ought to vary with varying circumstances. That as the framers of the constitution could never have intended to insert in that instrument a provision so unnecessary, so mischievous, and so repugnant to its general spirit, the term "contract" must be understood as intended to guard against a power of at least doubtful utility, the abuse of which had been extensively felt; and to restrain the legislature in future from violating the right to property. That anterior to the formation of the constitution, a course of legislation had prevailed in many, if not in all, of the States, which weakened the confidence of man in man, and embarrassed all transactions between individuals, by dispensing with a faithful performance of engagements. To correct this mischief, by restraining the power which produced it, the State legislatures were forbidden "to pass any law impairing the obligation of contracts," that is, of contracts respecting property, under which some individual could claim a right to something beneficial to himself; and that since the clause in the constitution must in construction receive some limitation, it may be confined, and ought to be confined, to cases of this description; to cases within the mischief it was intended to remedy.

... The provision of the constitution never has been understood to embrace other contracts, than those which respect property, or some object of value, and confer rights which may be asserted in a court of justice. It

---

d. "No State shall ... pass any ... Law impairing the Obligation of Contracts...."
U.S. Const. ART. I, § 10.

never has been understood to restrict the general right of the legislature to legislate on the subject of divorces. . . .

The parties in this case differ less on general principles, less on the true construction of the constitution in the abstract, than on the application of those principles to this case, and on the true construction of the charter of 1769. . . . If the act of incorporation be a grant of political power, if it creates a civil institution to be employed in the administration of the government, or if the funds of the college be public property, or if the State of New–Hampshire, as a government, be alone interested in its transactions, the subject is one in which the legislature of the State may act according to its own judgment, unrestrained by any limitation of its power imposed by the constitution of the United States.

But if this be a private eleemosynary institution, endowed with a capacity to take property for objects unconnected with government, whose funds are bestowed by individuals on the faith of the charter; if the donors have stipulated for the future disposition and management of those funds in the manner prescribed by themselves; there may be more difficulty in the case, although neither the persons who have made these stipulations, nor those for whose benefit they were made, should be parties to the cause. . . .

[Justice Marshall reviewed the fundraising activities in England of Dartmouth founder Rev. Eleazer Wheelock, the charter granted by the British monarchy, and the incorporation of the trustees. He concluded that "the funds of the college consisted entirely of private donations."]

Whence, then, can be derived the idea, that Dartmouth College has become a public institution, and its trustees public officers, exercising powers conferred by the public for public objects? Not from the source whence its funds were drawn; for its foundation is purely private and eleemosynary—not from the application of those funds; for money may be given for education, and the persons receiving it do not, by being employed in the education of youth, become members of the civil government. Is it from the act of incorporation? Let this subject be considered.

A corporation is an artificial being, invisible, intangible, and existing only in contemplation of law. Being the mere creature of law, it possesses only those properties which the charter of its creation confers upon it, either expressly, or as incidental to its very existence. These are such as are supposed best calculated to effect the object for which it was created. Among the most important are immortality, and, if the expression may be allowed, individuality; properties, by which a perpetual succession of many persons are considered as the same, and may act as a single individual. They enable a corporation to manage its own affairs, and to hold property without the perplexing intricacies, the hazardous and endless necessity, of perpetual conveyances for the purpose of transmitting it from hand to hand. It is chiefly for the purpose of clothing bodies of men, in succession, with these qualities and capacities, that corporations were invented, and are in use. By these means, a perpetual succession of individuals are capable of acting for the promotion of the particular object, like one immortal being. But this being does not share in the civil government of the country, unless that be the purpose for which it was created. Its immortality no more confers on it political power, or a political character, than immortality would confer such power or character on a natural person. It is no more a State instrument, than a natural person exercising the same powers would be....

. . .

Yet a question remains to be considered, of more real difficulty.... Neither the founders of the college, nor the youth for whose benefit it was founded, complain of the alteration made in its charter, or think themselves injured by it. The trustees alone complain, and the trustees have no beneficial interest to be protected. Can this be such a contract, as the constitution intended to withdraw from the power of State legislation? ...

... Dr. Wheelock, acting for himself, and for those who, at his solicitation, had made contributions to his school, applied for this charter, as the instrument which should enable him, and them, to perpetuate their beneficent intention. It was granted. An artificial, immortal being, was created by the crown, capable of receiving and distributing forever, according to the will of the donors, the donations which should be made to it. On this being, the contributions which had been collected were immediately bestowed. These gifts were made, not indeed to make a profit for the donors, or their posterity, but for something in their opinion of inestimable value; for something which they deemed a full equivalent for the money with which it was purchased. The consideration for which they stipulated, is the perpetual application of the found to its object, in the mode prescribed by themselves. Their descendants may take no interest in the preservation of this consideration. But in this respect their descendants are not their representatives. They are represented by the corporation. The corporation is the assignee of their rights, stands in their place, and distributes their bounty, as they would themselves have distributed it, had they been immortal. So with respect to the students who are to derive learning from this source. The corporation is a trustee for them also....

. . .

It is more than possible, that the preservation of rights of this description was not particularly in the view of the framers of the constitution, when the clause under consideration was introduced into that instrument.... But although a particular and a rare case may not, in itself, be of sufficient magnitude to induce a rule, yet it must be governed by the rule, when established, unless some plain and strong reason for excluding it can be given. It is not enough to say, that this particular case was not in the mind of the Convention, when the article was framed, nor of the American people, when it was adopted. It is necessary to go farther, and to say that, had this particular case been suggested, the language would have been so varied, as to exclude it, or it would have been made a special exception. The case being within the words of the rule, must be within its operation likewise, unless there be something in the literal construction so obviously absurd, or mischievous, or repugnant to the general spirit of the instrument, as to justify those who expound the constitution in making it an exception.

On what safe and intelligible ground can this exception stand. There is no expression in the constitution, no sentiment delivered by its contemporaneous expounders, which would justify us in making it....

... Religion, Charity, and Education, are, in the law of England, legatees or donees, capable of receiving bequests or donations in this form.

They appear in Court, and claim or defend by the corporation. Are they of so little estimation in the United States, that contracts for their benefit must be excluded from the protection of words, which in their natural import include them? Or do such contracts so necessarily require new modeling by the authority of the legislature, that the ordinary rules of construction must be disregarded in order to leave them exposed to legislative alteration?

All feel, that these objects are not deemed unimportant in the United States. The interest which this case has excited, proves that they are not. The framers of the constitution did not deem them unworthy of its care and protection. They have, though in a different mode, manifested their respect for science, by reserving to the government of the Union the power "to promote the progress of science and useful arts, by securing for limited times, to authors and inventors, the exclusive right to their respective writings and discoveries." They have so far withdrawn science, and the useful arts, from the action of the State governments. Why then should they be supposed so regardless of contracts made for the advancement of literature, as to intend to exclude them from provisions, made for the security of ordinary contracts between man and man? No reason for making this supposition is perceived.

If the insignificance of the object does not require that we should exclude contracts respecting it from the protection of the constitution; neither, as we conceive, is the policy of leaving them subject to legislative alteration so apparent, as to require a forced construction of that instrument in order to effect it. These eleemosynary institutions do not fill the place, which would otherwise be occupied by government, but that which would otherwise remain vacant. They are complete acquisitions to literature. They are donations to education; donations, which any government must be disposed rather to encourage than to discountenance. It requires no very critical examination of the human mind to enable us to determine, that one great inducement to these gifts is the conviction felt by the giver, that the disposition he makes of them is immutable. It is probable, that no man ever was, and that no man ever will be, the founder of a college, believing at the time, that an act of incorporation constitutes no security for the institution; believing, that it is immediately to be deemed a public institution, whose funds are to be governed and applied, not by the will of the donor, but by the will of the legislature. All such gifts are made in the pleasing, perhaps delusive hope, that the charity will flow forever in the channel which the givers have marked out for it. If every man finds in his own bosom strong evidence of the universality of this sentiment, there can be but little reason to imagine, that the framers of our constitution were strangers to it, and that, feeling the necessity and policy of giving permanence and security to contracts, of withdrawing them from the influence of legislative bodies, whose fluctuating policy, and repeated interferences, produced the most perplexing and injurious embarrassments, they still deemed it necessary to leave these contracts subject to those interferences. The motives for such an exception must be very powerful, to justify the construction which makes it.

. . .

The opinion of the Court, after mature deliberation, is, that this is a contract, the obligation of which cannot be impaired, without violating the constitution of the United States. . . .

2. We next proceed to the inquiry, whether its obligation has been impaired by those acts of the legislature of New–Hampshire, to which the special verdict refers.

. . .

By the revolution, the duties, as well as the powers, of government devolved on the people of New–Hampshire. It is admitted, that among the latter was comprehended the transcendent power of parliament, as well as that of the executive department. It is too clear to require the support of argument, that all contracts, and rights respecting property, remained unchanged by the revolution. The obligations then, which were created by the charter to Dartmouth College, were the same in the new, that they had been in the old government. The power of the government was also the same. A repeal of this charter at any time prior to the adoption of the present constitution of the United States, would have been an extraordinary and unprecedented act of power, but one which could have been contested only by the restrictions upon the legislature, to be found in the constitution of the State. But the constitution of the United States has imposed this additional limitation, that the legislature of a State shall pass no act "impairing the obligation of contracts."

. . .

On the effect of this law, two opinions cannot be entertained. Between acting directly, and acting through the agency of trustees and overseers, no essential difference is perceived. The whole power of governing the college is transferred from trustees appointed according to the will of the founder, expressed in the charter, to the executive of New–Hampshire. The management and application of the funds of this eleemosynary institution, which are placed by the donors in the hands of trustees named in the charter, and empowered to perpetuate themselves, are placed by this act under the control of the government of the State. The will of the State is substituted for the will of the donors, in every essential operation of the college. This is not an immaterial change. The founders of the college contracted, not merely for the perpetual application of the funds which they gave, to the objects for which those funds were given; they contracted also, to secure that application by the constitution of the corporation. They contracted for a system, which should, as far as human foresight can provide, retain forever the government of the literary institution they had formed, in the hands of persons approved by themselves. This system is totally changed. The charter of 1769 exists no longer. It is reorganized; and reorganized in such a manner, as to convert a literary institution, moulded according to the will of its founders, and placed under the control of private literary men, into a machine entirely subservient to the will of government. This may be for the advantage of this college in particular, and may be for the advantage of literature in general; but it is not according to the will of the donors, and is subversive of that contract, on the faith of which their property was given.

. . .

It results from this opinion, that the acts of the legislature of New–Hampshire . . . are repugnant to the constitution of the United States. . . . The judgment of the State Court must, therefore, be reversed.

Questions and Comments on *Trustees of Dartmouth College v. Woodward*

1. Eleazar Wheelock, the founder of Dartmouth, was authorized by the charter to name his successor. He chose his son, John, who became president when his father died in 1779. By 1809, the governing board, whose membership had changed significantly over the years, began to challenge John's authority. The breaking point came when the board decided that Wheelock could no longer teach the senior class. Wheelock in 1815 published a pamphlet giving his side of the struggle, and asked the state legislature to investigate the actions of the trustees. The college board found that Wheelock's actions constituted "gross and unprovoked libel on the institution" and dismissed him as president, trustee, and professor. JOHN WHITEHEAD, THE SEPARATION OF COLLEGE AND STATE: COLUMBIA, DARTMOUTH, HARVARD, AND YALE, 1776–1876, at 54– 58 (1973). The Jeffersonian Republicans in the state took up Wheelock's cause. In 1816, Republican William Plumer was elected governor of New Hampshire. In his inaugural address he attacked the Dartmouth charter for having "emanated from royalty." *Id.* at 61. He also escalated the dispute to the national level by sending a copy of his address to Thomas Jefferson who, in reply, criticized those who believe that "the earth belongs to the dead, and not to the living." JURGEN HERBST, FROM CRISIS TO CRISIS: AMERICAN COLLEGE GOVERNMENT, 1636–1819, at 236 (1982). The state legislature soon passed statutes intended to supersede the royal charter by transform- ing Dartmouth into a public university and imposing a board of twenty-five Overseers with power over the trustees. By 1817 there were two Dartmouths in New Hamp- shire: Dartmouth University, a public institution operated on Jeffersonian Republican principles, and Dartmouth College, a private institution whose trustees regarded themselves as defenders of true religion and private property. The board of the college sued its former treasurer, William Woodward, who had defected to the university, to recover the original charter and other corporate property. *Id.* at 236– 37.

2. The *Dartmouth College* decision played a major role in the preservation and development of private colleges and universities in the United States when it placed clear limits on public intervention:

> For a corporation charter to be altered, the corporation had to agree to the changes or else be convicted of wrongdoing by due process in a duly constituted court of law. No longer could a legislature unilaterally interfere in college affairs in disregard of the rights and privileges guaranteed by the charter. There might still be disputes over the meaning and implications of charter provisions, and a legislature might reserve to itself in the charter powers of interference or charter alternation. But no longer could legislators on their own determination and without recourse to reserve powers alter, ignore, or abolish a charter.

HERBST at 241.

3. In a recent essay exploring why America's system of higher education is so successful, the ECONOMIST singled out three characteristics or principles:

> The first principle is that the federal government plays a limited part. America does not have a central plan for its universities. It does not treat its academics as civil servants, as do France and Germany. Instead, universities have a wide range of patrons, from state governments to religious bodies, from fee-paying students to generous philanthropists. The academic land- scape has been shaped by rich benefactors such as Ezra Cornell, Cornelius Vanderbilt, and John D. Rockefeller. And the tradition of philanthropy survives to this day: in fiscal 2004, private donors gave $24.4 billion to universities.
>
>   . . .
>
> The second principle is competition. Universities compete for every- thing, from students to professors to basketball stars. Professors compete for

federal research grants. Students complete for college bursaries or research fellowships. This means that successful institutions cannot rest on their laurels.

The third principle is the right to be useful. Bertrand Russell once expressed astonishment at the worldly concerns he encountered at the University of Wisconsin: "When any farmer's turnips go wrong, they send a professor to investigate the failure scientifically." America has always regarded universities as more than ivory towers. Henry Steele Commager ... noted of the average 19th century American that "education was his religion"—provided that it "be practical and pay dividends."

Secrets of Success, ECONOMIST, Sept. 10, 2005, at 6. Do you agree that these three principles explain why higher education has flourished in America? Would the first two principles characterize our system of higher education today if the decision in the *Dartmouth College Case* had gone the other way? Is education still America's religion?

4. EARLY EFFORTS TO DEMOCRATIZE ACCESS TO HIGHER EDUCATION

At first little attention was paid in the new nation to the question of who should have access to higher education. Gradually, however, more citizens embraced Jefferson's idea of developing a natural aristocracy of talent to replace what he termed the "artificial" one based on wealth or birth. Jefferson oversaw the founding of the University of Virginia, but he was not able to persuade Virginia to develop a system of public education that would have included not only free public schools but also a free university education for the best students:

At the first session of our legislature after the Declaration of Independence, we passed a law abolishing entails. And this was followed by one abolishing the privilege of Primogeniture, and dividing the lands of intestates equally among their children, or other representatives. These laws, drawn by myself, laid the axe to the root of Pseudo-aristocracy. And had another which I prepared been adopted by the legislature, our work would have been compleat. It was a Bill for the general diffusion of learning. This proposed to divide every county into wards of 5 of 6 miles square, like your townships; to establish in each ward a free school for reading, writing and common arithmetic; to provide for the annual selection of the best subjects from these schools who might receive at the public expence a higher degree of education at a district school; and from these district schools to select a certain number of the most promising subjects to be completed at an University, where all the useful sciences should be taught. Worth and genius would thus have been sought out from every condition of life, and completely prepared by education for defeating the competition of wealth and birth for public trusts.

... The law for religious freedom, which made a part of this system, having put down the aristocracy of the clergy, and restored to the citizen the freedom of the mind, and those of entails and descents nurturing an equality of condition among them, this on Education would have raised the mass of the people to the high ground of moral respectability necessary to their own safety, and to orderly government; and would have completed the great object of qualifying them to select the veritable aristoi, for the trusts of government, to the exclusion of the Pseudalists. . . .

With respect to Aristocracy, we should further consider that, before the establishment of the American states, nothing was known to History but the Man of the old world, crowded within limits either small or overcharged, and steeped in the vices which that situation generates. . . . Here everyone may have land to labor for himself if he choses; or, preferring the exercise of any other industry, may exact for it such compensation as not only to afford a comfortable subsistence, but wherewith to provide for a cessation from labor in old age. Everyone, by his property, or by his satisfactory situation is interested in the support of law and order. And such men may safely and advantageously reserve to themselves a wholesome control over their public affairs. . . .

[E]ven in Europe a change has sensibly taken place in the mind of Man. Science had liberated the ideas of those who read and reflect. . . . An insurrection has consequently begun, of science, talents and courage against rank and birth, which have fallen into contempt.[a]

Emma Willard, A Plan for Improving Female Education (1819).

The object of this Address, is to convince the public, that a reform with respect to female education is necessary; that it cannot be effected by individual exertion, but that it requires the aid of the legislature; and further, by shewing the justice, the policy, and the magnanimity of such an undertaking, to persuade that body to endow a seminary for females, as the commencement of such reformation.

. . .

. . . Male education flourishes, because, from the guardian care of legislature, the presidencies and professorships of our colleges are some of the highest object to which the eye of ambition is directed. Not so with female institutions.

. . .

Not only has there been a want of system concerning female education, but much of what has been done, has proceeded upon mistaken principles.

One of these is, that, without a regard to the different periods of life, proportionate to their importance, the education of females has been too exclusively directed, to fit them for displaying to advantage the charms of youth and beauty. Though it may be proper to adorn this period of life, yet, it is incomparably more important, to prepare for the serious duties of maturer years. . . .

a. Letter from Thomas Jefferson to John Adams (October 18, 1813), *in* THE *ADAMS-JEF-* *FERSON* LETTERS 387, 390–91 (Lester J. Cappon ed., 1959).

Another error is, that it has been made the first object in educating our sex, to prepare them to please the other. But reason and religion teach, that we too are primary existences; that it is for us to move, in the orbit of our duty, around the Holy Centre of perfection, the companions, not the satellites of men; else, instead of shedding around us an influence, that may help to keep them in their proper course, we must accompany them in their wildest deviations.

. . .

It is the duty of government, to do all in its power to promote the present and future prosperity of the nation, over which it is placed. This prosperity will depend on the character of its citizens. The characters of these will be formed by their mothers; and it is through their mothers, that the government can control the characters of its future citizens, to form them such as will ensure the country's prosperity. If this is the case, then it is the duty of our present legislators to begin now, to form the characters of the next generation, by controlling that of the females, who are to be their mothers, while it is yet with them a season of improvement.

[Willard next considers the appropriate curriculum. In addition to instruction in religion and domestic arts, she turns to "literary instruction."]

To make an exact numeration of the branches of literature, which might be taught, would be impossible. . . .

It is highly important, that females should [also] be conversant with those studies, which will lead them to understand the operations of the human mind. . . . The ductile mind of the child is intrusted to the mother: and she ought to have every possible assistance, in acquiring a knowledge of this noble material, on which it is her business to operate, that she may best understand how to mould it to its most excellent form.

Natural philosophy has not often been taught to our sex. Yet why should we be kept in ignorance of the great machinery of nature, and left to the vulgar notion, that nothing is curious but what deviates from her common course? If mothers were acquainted with this science, they would communicate very many of its principles to their children in early years. From the bursting of an egg buried in the fire, I have heard an intelligent mother, lead her prattling inquirer, to understand the cause of the earth-quake. But how often does the mother, from ignorance on this subject, give her child the most erroneous and contracted views of the cause of natural phenomena; views, which, though he may afterwards learn to be false, are yet, from the laws of association, ever ready to return, unless the active powers of the mind are continually upon the alert to keep them out. A knowledge of natural philosophy is calculated to heighten the moral taste, by bringing to view the majesty and beauty of order and design; and to enliven piety, by enabling the mind more clearly to perceive, throughout the manifold works of God, that wisdom, in which he hath made them all.

. . .

An opinion too generally prevails that our present form of government, though good, cannot be permanent. Other republics have failed, and the historian and philosopher have told us, that nations are like individuals; that, at their birth, they receive the seed of their decline and dissolution.

. . .

In those great republics, which have fallen of themselves, the loss of republican manners and virtues, has been the invariable precursor, of their loss of the republican form of government. But is it not in the power of our sex, to give society its tone, both as to manners and morals? And if such is the extent of female influence, is it wonderful, that republics have failed, when they have calmly suffered that influence, to become enlisted in favour of luxuries and follies, wholly incompatible with the existence of freedom.

Questions and Comments on Higher Education for Women

1. Willard's full title for her work was "An Address to the Public; Particularly to the Members of the Legislature of New York, Proposing a Plan for Improving Female Education." Given her intended audience, what do you think of the quality of her advocacy?

2. Willard was raised in Connecticut and educated first at a district school, then at an academy in Berlin, Connecticut. I THOMAS WOODY, A HISTORY OF WOMEN'S EDUCATION IN THE UNITED STATES 305 (1929). She began teaching when she was seventeen, and at the age of twenty was put in charge of a female academy or boarding school in Middlebury, Vermont. In 1809 she married Dr. John Willard, a physician. He encouraged her to read his books on everything from medicine to philosophy, an experience that led her realize the inadequacies of the education offered at most female academies. *See generally* EZRA BRAINERD, MRS. EMMA WILLARD'S LIFE AND WORK IN MIDDLEBURY (1900).

3. Then-governor of New York, DeWitt Clinton, perhaps moved in part by Emma Willard who sent him a copy of her plan, I WOODY at 305–07, complained that "beyond initiatory instruction, the education of the female sex is utterly excluded from the contemplation of our laws." DeWitt Clinton, Speech to Legislature (Jan. 19, 1819), *in* II STATE OF NEW YORK MESSAGES FROM THE GOVERNORS 972 (Charles Z. Lincoln ed., 1909). In 1820, he recommended state subsidies for female education. DeWitt Clinton, Speech to Legislature (Jan. 4, 1820), *in* II STATE OF NEW YORK MESSAGES FROM THE GOVERNORS 1018 (Charles Z. Lincoln ed., 1909). Although many schools for women were chartered between 1819 and 1828, there was little legislative activity or support.

4. The first institution to offer women a college level curriculum was Oberlin. Founded in 1833 by Presbyterians who were fervent abolitionists, Oberlin was designed to admit students without regard to race, color, or sex. Although at first women were limited to enrolling in the secondary or preparatory department, by 1837 four qualified for admission to the college course and were accepted. Women made up at least ten percent (and never more than twenty-five percent) of the student body; by 1866 eighty-four women had graduated from Oberlin. II WOODY at 232–33.

Mount Holyoke, which opened in 1837, first as a seminary for women and later as a college, is generally considered the first college for women. It was also the first established by appeals for contributions. Mary Lyon, the founder, not only planned the school, she personally raised the funds. I WOODY at 358–62. Although other women's colleges opened in the second half of the nineteenth century and a few of the new private schools, including Cornell and Stanford, admitted women as well as men, most of the elite colleges remained closed to women for another century. Charles Eliot, Harvard's president for four decades beginning in 1869, was a particularly firm opponent of coeducation:

> [He] established his position in his inaugural address, declaring that the policing of hundreds of young men and women of marriageable age would be impossible. He had doubts, moreover, about what he called the "natural mental capacities" of the female sex.

... In 1872 a group of Cambridge and Boston ladies formed the Women's Education Association and invited President Eliot to a meeting to consider women's admission to Harvard.

Eliot's opposition to coeducation was unyielding, and he cited reasons that ranged from the already overcrowded state of the College to the violation of moral and religious tenets. The discussion about coeducation at Harvard during these years extended well beyond the president, as students and faculty articulated the principles of manliness that they regarded as the essence of the College's identity. Barrett Wendell, professor of English, proclaimed that there must be no deviation from the tenet that had ruled since the founding of the College in 1636: "that the influences amid which education should be obtained here must remain purely virile." Even more than an "institution of learning," Harvard was, he affirmed, "a traditional school of manly character." The [student newspaper] described coeducation as "a dangerous tendency in American society," best left to the likes of Oberlin, Cornell, and Boston University, and resisted by elite schools like Yale and Harvard. The *Harvard Graduates Magazine* was gratified that the university was not being "incautious" by precipitously embracing women's education.

Drew Gilpin Faust, *Mingling Promiscuously: A History of Women and Men at Harvard, in* YARDS AND GATES: GENDER IN HARVARD AND RADCLIFFE HISTORY 317, 318 (Laurel Thatcher Ulrich ed., 2004).

Note on Race and Education

1. Oberlin led the way on breaking down barriers of race as well as gender in higher education, but not without struggle. In 1834, Oberlin faced unpaid debts and inadequate funding. Several able faculty at a nearby college were willing to be recruited to Oberlin, but they had two conditions: first, that faculty and students would have freedom of speech on all reform issues, and second, that blacks would be admitted to the school. Although Oberlin was strongly anti-slavery, the proposal to integrate the student body was at first resisted by the Board of Trustees. In the end, however, they gave the faculty the authority to control admissions, and that meant race would no longer be a bar. ROBERT SAMUEL FLETCHER, A HISTORY OF OBERLIN COLLEGE: FROM ITS FOUNDATION THROUGH THE CIVIL WAR 167–78 (1943).

2. In 1853, Mrs. Margaret Douglass, a white woman who lived in Norfolk, Virginia, was fined and sentenced to a month in jail because she taught "free colored" children to read and write in her home, in violation of Virginia law. At her sentencing, the judge observed:

> There are persons, I believe, in our community, opposed to the policy of the law in question. They profess to believe that universal intellectual culture is necessary to religious instruction and education, and that such culture is suitable to a state of slavery; and there can be no misapprehension as to your opinions on this subject, judging from the indiscreet freedom with which you spoke of your regard for the colored race in general. Such opinions in the present state of our society I regard as manifestly mischievous. It is not true that our slaves cannot be taught religious and moral duty, without being able to read the Bible and use the pen....

>   . . .

> The law under which you have been tried and found guilty is not to be found among the original enactments of our legislature. The first legislative provision upon this subject was introduced in the year 1831, immediately succeeding the bloody schemes of the memorable Southhampton insurrection....

> There might have been no occasion for such enactments in Virginia, or elsewhere, on the subject of negro education, but as a matter of self-defense

against the schemes of Northern incendiaries, and the outcry against holding our slaves in bondage. Many now living well remember how, and when, and why the anti-slavery fury began, and by what means its manifestations were made public. Our mails were clogged with abolition pamphlets and inflammatory documents, to be distributed among our Southern negroes to induce them to cut our throats.

Trial of Mrs. Douglas for Teaching Colored Children to Read, in III AMERICAN STATE TRIALS 56–59 (J. D. Lawson ed., 1914–1916).

C. THE FIRST RESEARCH UNIVERSITIES, 1852–1940

The turn to research and science that took place in the last half of the nineteenth century has been termed a "revolution in American higher education."[a] Ideas that had been only discussed before the Civil War—the elective system, graduate instruction, scientific courses—became realities.

Three primary factors produced the change. First, a number of influential educators, including Daniel Coit Gilman of Johns Hopkins, Henry Philip Tappan of the University of Michigan, and Andrew Dickson White of Cornell, admired the emphasis on research and on post-graduate study that characterized German universities and determined to follow their lead. Second, for the first time there were American donors with the capacity to fund entire universities. Large gifts from Ezra Cornell, Johns Hopkins, and John Rockefeller, among others, provided enough resources to build not just new universities, but universities committed to research and to graduate study. At the same time public opinion increasingly turned against the classical curriculum still in place in most institutions of higher education:

> Ever since the Jacksonian period, college enrollments had remained static amid a growing national population. In the years after 1865, these discouraging figures drew more and more notice within academic circles. During the 1870s attendance at twenty of the "oldest leading colleges" rose only 3.5 per cent, while the nation's population soared 23 percent. In 1885 less than a quarter of all American congressmen were college graduates, as compared with 38 per cent ten years earlier. "In all parts of the country," Charles Kendall Adams of Michigan declared, "the sad fact stares us in the face that the training which has long been considered essential to finished scholarship has been losing ground from year to year in the favor of the people."[b]

A fourth major force in the development of the new American universities was the increased professionalization of faculty. It began with an increase in doctoral degrees:

> As late as 1884[,] on a faculty of 189, Harvard had but 19 professors with the degree of Ph.D.; Michigan, with a faculty of 88, had but 6.... By the 1890s Johns Hopkins and the newer graduate schools were moving into high gear, and by then the men with the Ph.D. degrees were beginning to overtake their less fully trained col-

a. RICHARD HOFSTADTER & WALTER METZGER, THE DEVELOPMENT OF ACADEMIC FREEDOM IN THE UNITED STATES 277 (1955).

b. LAWRENCE R. VEYSEY, THE EMERGENCE OF THE AMERICAN UNIVERSITY 4 (1965).

leagues. Between 1888 and 1895 men with the doctorate moved into the majority at a place like Brown.... The University of Illinois in 1905 looked to its reputation and declared that future appointments to the rank of professor would be drawn exclusively from men who had known the rigors of training for the Ph.D.[c]

With specialization, faculties began to organize themselves into departments ("physics," "history," "philosophy," etc.) and to publish scholarly journals. Johns Hopkins led the way in 1877 with *The American Journal of Mathematics*. But the increased stature and independence of faculty also led to clashes with the lay governing boards.

1. THE ACADEMIC LEADERS

Henry Philip Tappan, University Education
42–45, 50–51, 54–55, 65–67 (1851).

That the English Universities are improvable, and improving, we fully believe. But never, while paralyzed by high-church influence, can they fully develop their great capacities, and collect within their precincts, and under their government, schools of philosophy and science formed of the great wits and profound thinkers of England....

We have spoken of the German universities as model institutions. Their excellence consists in two things: first, they are purely Universities, without any admixture of collegial tuition. Secondly, they are complete as Universities, providing libraries and all other materials of learning, and having professors of eminence to lecture on theology, law, and medicine, the philosophical, mathematical, natural, philological, and political Sciences, on history and geography, on the history and principles of Art, in fine, upon every branch of human knowledge. The professors are so numerous that a proper division of labor takes place, and every subject is discussed. At the University, every student selects the courses he is to attend. He is thrown upon his own responsibilities and diligence.... Collegial tuition in the German Universities does not exist, because wholly unnecessary, the student being fully prepared at the Gymnasium before he is permitted to enter the University. Without the Gymnasium, the University would be little worth. The course at the Gymnasium embraces a very thorough study of the Latin and Greek languages, a knowledge of the mathematics below the Differential and Integral Calculus, general history, and one or two modern languages besides the German, and Hebrew if the student design to study theology. The examinations are full and severe, the gradations of merit are accurately marked, and no one below the second grade is permitted to enter the University.

The Educational System of Germany, and particularly in Prussia, is certainly a very noble one. We cannot well be extravagant in its praise. Thorough in all its parts, consistent with itself, and vigorously sustained, it furnishes every department of life with educated men, and keeps up at the Universities themselves, in every branch of knowledge, a supply of erudite and elegant scholars and authors, for the benefit and glory of their country, and the good of mankind.

 .   .   .

c. FREDERICK RUDOLPH, THE AMERICAN COLlege & University 395–96 (1962).

In our country we have no Universities. Whatever may be the names by which we choose to call our institutions of learning, still they are not Universities. They have neither the libraries and material of learning, generally, nor the number of professors and courses of lectures, not the large and free organization which go to make up Universities. Nor does the connection of Divinity, Law and Medical Schools with them give them this character. For law and medicine a thorough preparatory classical discipline is not required. In this respect the last is the most deficient of the two, and great numbers receive the academical degree of Doctor of Medicine who have never received an academical education. . . .

. . . Instead of erecting Universities, we have only pressed into our four years' course a greater number of studies. The effect has been disastrous. We have destroyed the charm of study by hurry and unnatural pressure, and we have rendered our scholarship vague and superficial. We have not fed thought by natural supplies of knowledge. We have not disciplined mind by guiding it to a calm and profound activity; but, we have stimulated acquisition to preternatural exertions, and have learned, as it were, from an encyclopedia the great names of sciences, without gaining the sciences themselves.

. . .

We have increased the number of our colleges to one hundred and twenty, that is, about four for every State. We have enlarged greatly the number of college studies. We have cheapened education—we have reduced it to costs. . . . [I]t would appear from the Report of the Corporation of Brown University, we have lowered rather than elevated the character of our scholarship. "All of them (the colleges) teach Greek and Latin, but where are our classical scholars? All teach mathematics, but where are our mathematicians? We might ask the same questions concerning the other sciences taught among us. . . ."

"The effect of this system on the mind of the teacher is equally obvious. He must teach, generally, from textbooks composed by others. His mind can act but imperfectly on the mind of the pupil. The time of the recitation is commonly quite occupied in ascertaining whether the pupil has learned his daily task. He cannot mark out such a course as he would wish to teach, but must teach as much as he can in the fragment of the time allotted to him. The books which he teaches soon become familiar to him. He has no motive to increase his knowledge, derived from the business to which he has consecrated his life. He already knows more than he has opportunity to communicate. There is no stimulus to call for exertion. There is no opportunity to progress. . . ."

. . .

. . . [I]f we educate men as men, we prepare them for all the responsibilities and duties of men. And educating men on this principle, we should in due time have great examples of the true form; and charm, and power, and dignity of learning would become apparent to all. And then education would stand out, as in truth it is, not as a mere preparation for the facile doing of the business of the world, but as the highest end of the human being. . . . In this way we should raise up a powerful counter influence against the excessive commercial spirit, and against the chicanery and selfishness of demagogueism which now prevail. Men thus worthily built up would get into all the relations of society, and throw a new aspect over the arts, commerce, and politics, and a high-minded patriotism and philanthropy would everywhere appear.... Then the host of penny-a-liners, stump orators, discoursers upon socialism, bigots, and partisans would give way before sound writers, true poets, lofty and truthful orators, and profound philosophers, theologians and statesmen. We should have a pure national literature and a proud national character.

Questions and Comments on Henry Tappan

In 1852, Tappan became the first president of the University of Michigan after the position was first offered and turned down by two other educators of the time. Tappan accepted because he thought the university was one of the few American institutions that might adopt the ideas he had put forth in his book the previous year. He eliminated Latin and Greek in the science curriculum and awarded the first bachelor of science degrees in 1855. Enrollments grew and the calendar altered to provide faculty with three months in the summer for research and travel. Tappan invited prominent speakers to the campus, including Ralph Waldo Emerson in 1856 and Edward Everett in 1857. Tensions developed with the Board of Regents over Tappan's indifference as to whether students drank beer and his selection of faculty members for their scholarship and not their church affiliations. In 1863 he was removed as president. HOWARD H. PECKHAM, THE MAKING OF THE UNIVERSITY OF MICHIGAN, 1817–1992, at 37, 42–44, 54 (Margaret L. Steneck & Nicholas H. Steneck eds., 1994).

Andrew Dickson White, Autobiography
256–57, 278–79, 287–88, 294, 297–99, 336–37, 340–42, 346–48, 397–401 (1905).

[A]t the [Yale] commencement of 1856, while lounging with my classmates in the college yard, I heard some one say that President Wayland of Brown University was addressing the graduates in the Hall of the Alumni. Going to the door, I looked in, and saw at the high table an old man, strong-featured, heavy-browed, with spectacles resting on the top of his head, and just at that moment he spoke very impressively as follows: "The best field of work for graduates is now in the *West*; our country is shortly to arrive at a switching-off place for good or evil; our Western States are to hold the balance of power in the Union, and to determine whether the country shall become a blessing or a curse in human history."

I had never seen him before; I never saw him afterward. His speech lasted less than ten minutes, but it settled a great question for me. I went home and wrote to sundry friends that I was a candidate for the professorship of history in any Western colleges....

. . .

On arriving at the University of Michigan in October, 1857, ... I took charge of the sophomore class....

. . .

Every winter Dr. Tappan went before the legislature to plead the cause of the university, and to ask for appropriations. He was always heard with pleasure, since he was an excellent speaker; but certain things militated against him. First of all, he had much to say of the excellent models furnished by the great German universities, and especially those of Prussia. This gave demagogues in the legislature, anxious to make a reputation ... a great chance. They orated to the effect that we wanted an American and not a Prussian system.

The worse difficulty by far which he had to meet was the steady opposition of the small sectarian colleges scattered throughout the State. Each, in its own petty interest, dreaded the growth of any institution better than itself; each stirred the members of the legislature from its locality to oppose all aid to the State university; each, in its religious assemblage, its synods, conferences, and the like, sought to stir prejudice against the State institution as "godless." . . .

. . .

To Trinity Hall at Hobardt College may be assigned whatever honor that shadowy personage, the future historian, shall think due the place where was conceived and quickened the germ idea of Cornell University. In that little stone barrack on the shore of Seneca Lake, rude in its architecture but lovely in its surroundings, a room was assigned me during my first year at college and in a neighboring apartment, with charming views over the lake and distant hills, was the library of the Hermean Society. . . . One day I discovered in it Huber and Newman's book on the English universities. . . .

As I . . . poured over the engraved views of quadrangles, halls, libraries, chapels . . . my heart sank with me. Every feature of the little American college seemed all the more sordid. But gradually I began consoling myself by building air-castles. This took the form of structure suited to a great university:—with distinguished professors in every field, with libraries as rich as the Bodleian, halls as lordly as that of Christ Church or of Trinity . . . quadrangles as beautiful as those of Jesus and St. John's. . . . This dream became a sort of obsession. . . . But this university, though beautiful and dignified, like those at Oxford and Cambridge, was in two important respects very unlike them. First, I made provision for other studies besides classics and mathematics. There should be professors in the great modern literatures—above all, in our own; there should also be a professor of modern history and a lecturer on architecture. And next, my university should be under control of no religious organization; it should be free from all sectarian or party trammels; in electing its trustees and professors no questions should be asked as to their belief or their attachment to this or that sect or party. So far, at least, I went in those days along the road toward the founding of Cornell.

. . .

On the very first day of the year 1864, taking my seat for the first time in the State Senate in Albany, I found among my associates a tall, spare man, apparently very reserved and austere, and soon learned his name—Ezra Cornell.

. . .

. . . I was one day going down from the State Capitol, when Mr. Cornell joined me and began conversation. . . .

On this occasion, after some little general talk, he quietly said, "I have about half a million dollars more than my family will need: what is the best thing I can do with it for the State?" I answered: "Mr. Cornell, the two things most worthy of aid in any country are charity and education; but, in our country, the charities appeal to everybody ... but the institutions of the highest grade ... can be appreciated by only a few."

... [N]ot long afterward he came to me and said: "I agree with you ... that there should be a new institution fitted to the present needs of the State and the country. I am ready to pledge to such an institution a site and five hundred thousand dollars as an addition to the land grant endowment."

    . . .

We now held frequent conferences as to the leading features of the institution to be created. In these I was more and more impressed by his sagacity and largeness of view; and, when the sketch of the bill was fully developed,—its financial features by him, and its educational features by me,—it was put into shape by Charles J. Folger of Geneva, then chairman of the judiciary committee of the Senate, afterward chief judge of the Court of Appeals, and finally Secretary of the Treasury of the United States. The provision forbidding any sectarian or partisan predominance in the board of trustees or faculty was proposed by me, heartily acquiesced in by Mr. Cornell, and put into shape by Judge Folger. The State-scholarship feature and the system of alumni representation on the board of trustees were also accepted by Mr. Cornell at my suggestion.

I refer to these things especially because they show one striking characteristic of the man—namely, his readiness to be advised largely by others in matters which he felt to be outside his own province. . . .

    . . .

Just previously to my election to the university presidency [in 1865] I had presented a "plan or organization," which having been accepted and printed by the trustees, formed the mold for the main features of the new institution; and early among my duties came the selection and nomination of professors. In these days one is able to choose from a large body of young men holding fellowships in the various larger universities of the United States; but then, with the possible exception of two or three at Harvard, there was not a fellowship, so far as I can remember, in the whole country. . . . Therefore it was that I broached, as a practical measure ... to take into our confidence the leading professors in the more important institutions of learning, and to secure from them, not the ordinary, conventional paper testimonials, but confidential information as to their young men likely to do the best work in various fields, to call these young men to our resident professorships, and then to call the most eminent men we could obtain for non-resident professorships or lectureships. . . . [T]hus it was that I was enabled to secure a number of bright, active, energetic young men as our resident professors, mingling with them two or three older men, whose experience and developed judgment seemed necessary in the ordinary conduct of our affairs.

    . . .

On the 7th of October, 1868, came the formal opening of the university. . . . [My ideas] were grouped in four divisions. The first of these related to "Foundation Ideas," which were announced as follows: First, the close union of liberal and practical instruction; second, unsectarian control; third, a living union between the university and the whole school system of the State; fourth, concentration of revenues for advanced education. The second division was that of "Formative Ideas"; and under these—First, equality between different courses of study. In this I especially developed ideas which had occurred to me as far back as my observations after graduation at Yale, where the classical students belonging to the "college proper" were given a sort of supremacy, and scientific students relegated to a separate institution at considerable distance, and therefore deprived of much general, and even special, culture which would have greatly benefited them. Indeed, they seemed not considered as having any souls to be saved, since no provision was made for them at the college chapel. Second, increased development of scientific studies. The third main division was that of "Government Ideas"; and under these—First, "the regular and frequent infusion of new life into the governing board." Here a system at the time entirely new in the United States was proposed. Instead of the usual life tenure of trustees, their term was made five years and they were to be chosen by ballot. Secondly, it was required that as soon as the graduates of the university numbered fifty they should select one trustee each year, thus giving the alumni one third of the whole number elected. Third, there was to be a system of self-government administered by the students themselves. As to this third point, I must frankly confess that my ideas were vague, unformed, and finally changed by the logic of events. As the fourth and final main division, I presented "Permeating Ideas"; and of these—First, the development of the individual man in all his nature, in all his powers, as a being intellectual, moral, and religious. Secondly, bringing the powers of the man thus developed to bear usefully upon society.

. . .

As regards student discipline in the university, I had dwelt in my "plan of organization" upon the advisability of a departure from the system inherited from the English colleges, which was still widely prevailing.... I had ... taken the ground that, so far as possible, students should be treated as responsible citizens; that, as citizens, they should be left to be dealt with by the constituted authorities; and that members of the faculty should no longer be considered as policemen....

. . .

For some years before the organization of Cornell, I had thought much upon the education of women, and had gradually arrived at the conclusion that they might well be admitted to some of the universities established for young men.... [P]erhaps the strongest influence in this matter was exercised upon me by my mother. She was one of the most conservative of women ... and generally averse to modern reforms; but on my talking over with her some of my plans for Cornell University, she said: "I am not sure about your other ideas, but as to the admission of women you are right. My main education was derived partly from a boarding-school ... and partly from Cortland Academy. In the boarding-school we had only young women, but in the academy we had both young men and young women; and I am sure that the results of the academy were much better than those of the boarding school. The young men and young women learned to respect each other, not merely for physical, but for intellectual and moral qualities."

. . .

... In conversations between Mr. Cornell and myself on this subject, I found that we agreed; and in our addresses at the opening of the university we both alluded to it. ...

... The following year came the first application of a young woman for admission. Her case was strong, for she presented a certificate showing that she had passed the best examination of the State scholarship in Cortland County; and on this I admitted her. ... The only room for students in those days on the University Hill were in the barracks filled with young men; and therefore the young woman took rooms in town, coming up to lectures two or three times a day. It was a hard struggle. ... She bore the fatigue patiently until winter set in; then she came to me, expressing regret at her inability to toil up the icy steep, and left us. On my reporting this to the trustees, Mr. Sage made his proposal. I had expected from him a professorship or a fellowship; but to my amazement he offered to erect and endow a separate college of young women in the university. ...

. . .

My report ... favored the admission of women, and was adopted by the trustees unanimously. ... None of the prophecies of evil so freely made by the opponents of the measure have ever been fulfilled. Every arrangement was made in Mr. Sage's building to guard the health of the young women; and no one will say that the manliness of men or the womanliness of women has ever suffered in consequence of the meeting of the two sexes in classrooms, laboratories, chapel or elsewhere. ...

Questions and Comments on Cornell and Johns Hopkins

1. Cornell brought a new approach to governance when it established places for alumni on the governing board. Interestingly, 1865 is the same year that the power to elect the thirty Overseers at Harvard was taken from the state and given to the alumni of the university. What are the strengths of having alumni on a university governing board? Weaknesses?

2. After Andrew White graduated from Yale in 1853, he sailed for Europe with his friend Daniel Coit Gilman, Yale '52. MORRIS BISHOP, A HISTORY OF CORNELL 33 (1962). In 1876, Gilman became the founding president of Johns Hopkins. Like White, Gilman was deeply influenced by what he saw of German universities, *see* FABIAN FRANKLIN, THE LIFE OF DANIEL COIT GILMAN 23–32 (1910), as well as by universities in other nations. In order to plan for the new university, Gilman was encouraged by the board to travel freely. He first visited Cambridge, Glasgow and Dublin, then Paris, Berlin, Heidelberg, Strasburg, Freiburg, Leipsig, Munich and Vienna. DANIEL COIT GILMAN, THE LAUNCHING OF A UNIVERSITY 13 (1906). The faculty who helped him to plan the new university reflected a similarly broad range of backgrounds: "Two ... had been professors in the University of Virginia, two had received degrees in German universities and others had studied abroad, two had been connected with New England colleges, two had been teachers in scientific schools, and one had been at the head of a State university." *Id.* at 48.

One of Gilman's greatest contributions to American higher education was the establishment in 1876 of graduate "fellowships" for "young men from any place." Hopkins soon attracted an extraordinary group of graduate fellows including Josiah Royce, Thorstein Veblen, Woodrow Wilson, and John Dewey. RICHARD HOFSTADTER & WALTER P. METZGER, THE DEVELOPMENT OF ACADEMIC FREEDOM IN THE UNITED STATES 377 (1955). Between 1878 and 1889, Hopkins awarded 151 Ph.D.s. By contrast, Harvard awarded only 43 and Yale 101. HUGH HAWKINS, PIONEER: A HISTORY OF JOHNS HOPKINS

UNIVERSITY, 1874–1889, at 23, 66, 80, 122. The use of graduate fellows not only spurred other universities to adopt similar programs, it transformed the education of faculty. In 1926, only fifty years after its founding, 1,000 of Hopkins's 1,400 graduates were on college and university faculties. FREDERICK RUDOLPH, THE AMERICAN COLLEGE & UNIVERSITY 336 (1990).

Charles Eliot, who was president of Harvard from 1869–1909, would later acknowledge Gilman's important contributions to higher education. "I want to testify that the graduate school of Harvard University, started feebly in 1870 and 1871, did not thrive, until the example of Johns Hopkins forced our Faculty to put their strength into the development of our instruction for graduates." HAWKINS at 77. Edward Shils considered the founding of Hopkins to be "perhaps the most decisive single event in the history of learning in the Western hemisphere." EDWARD SHILS, THE ORDER OF LEARNING 14 (Philip G. Altbach ed., 1997).

3. Toward the end of the century, competition eroded Hopkins's near-monopoly position in graduate education. Competition came primarily from Harvard, Yale and, after 1892, the new University of Chicago which had an endowment provided by John D. Rockefeller that dwarfed the size of the Hopkins bequest. Hopkins's position was further compromised beginning in the late 1880s when the major holding in its endowment, stock in the B & O railroad that had been donated by Johns Hopkins with directions not to sell the stock, paid no dividends. HAWKINS, *supra* note 2, at 319, 325.

2.   FUNDING BY POLITICIANS AND PHILANTHROPISTS

The Morrill Act of 1862

Act of July 2, 1862, ch.130, 12 Stat. 503, later codified as amended at 7 U.S.C. § 301 et seq.

Be it enacted by the Senate and House of Representatives of the United States of America in Congress assembled, That there be granted to the several States, for the purposes hereinafter mentioned, an amount of public land, to be apportioned to each State a quantity equal to thirty thousand acres for each senator and representative in Congress to which the States are respectively entitled by the apportionment under the census of eighteen hundred and sixty: Provided, That no mineral lands shall be selected or purchased under the provisions of this Act.

Sec. 2. *And be it further enacted*, That the land aforesaid, after being surveyed, shall be apportioned to the several States in sections or subdivisions of sections, not less than one quarter of a section; and whenever there are public lands in a State subject to sale at private entry at one dollar and twenty-five cents per acre, the quantity to which said State shall be entitled shall be selected from such lands within the limits of such State, and the Secretary of the Interior is hereby directed to issue to each of the States in which there is not the quantity of public lands subject to sale at private entry at one dollar and twenty-five cents per acre, to which said State may be entitled under the provisions of this act, land scrip to the amount in acres for the deficiency of its distributive share: said scrip to be sold by said States and the proceeds thereof applied to the uses and purposes prescribed in this Act, and for no other purpose whatsoever: *Provided,* That in no case shall any State to which land scrip may thus be issued be allowed to locate the same within the limits of any other State, or of any Territory of the United States, but their assignees may thus locate said land scrip upon any of the unappropriated lands of the United States subject to the sale at private entry at one dollar and twenty-five cents, or less, per acre: *And provided, further,* That not more than one million acres shall be located by such assignees in any one of the States. . . .

Sec. 3. *And be it further enacted,* That all the expenses of management, superintendence, and taxes from date of selection of said lands, previous to their sales, and all expenses incurred in the management and disbursement of the moneys which may be received therefrom, shall be paid by the States to which they may belong, out of the treasury of said States, so that the entire proceeds of the sale of said lands shall be applied without any diminution whatever to the purposes hereinafter mentioned.

Sec. 4. *And be it further enacted,* That all moneys derived from the sales of lands aforesaid by the States . . . shall be invested in bonds of the United States or of the States or some other safe bonds. . . . Provided, That the moneys so invested . . . shall constitute a perpetual fund, the capital of which shall remain forever undiminished (except so far as may be provided in section 5 of this Act), and the interest of which shall be inviolably appropriated, by each State . . . to the endowment, support, and maintenance of at least one college where the leading object shall be, without excluding other scientific and classical studies and including military tactics, to teach such branches of learning as are related to agriculture and the mechanic arts, in such manner as the legislatures of the States may respectively prescribe, in order to promote the liberal and practical education of the industrial classes on the several pursuits and professions in life.

Sec. 5. *And be it further enacted,* That the grant of land and land scrip hereby authorized shall be made on the following conditions. . . .

First. If any portion of the fund invested, as provided by the foregoing section, or any portion of the interest thereon, shall, by any action or contingency, be diminished or lost, it shall be replaced by the State to which it belongs. . . . so that the capital of the fund shall remain forever undiminished. . . .

Second. No portion of said fund, nor the interest thereon, shall be applied, directly or indirectly, under any pretence whatever, to the purchase, erection, preservation, or repair of any building or buildings.

Third. Any State which may take and claim the benefit of the provisions of this act shall provide, within five years from the time of its acceptance as provided in subdivision seven of this section, at least not less than one college, as described in the fourth section of this act, or the grant to such State shall cease. . . .

    . . .

Sixth. No State while in a condition of rebellion or insurrection against the government of the United States shall be entitled to the benefit of this act.

Questions and Comments on the Morrill Acts of 1862 and 1890

1. The Morrill Act was sponsored by Justin Smith Morrill, then a representative (1854–66) and later a senator (1866–98) from Vermont. The bill was passed by Congress in 1859, but vetoed by President James Buchanan. In 1861, Morrill resubmitted the bill with one small change: the proposed institutions would teach military tactics as well as engineering and agriculture. *See* Section 4 of the Act. Aided by the secession of many states that did not support the plan, the bill was again passed by Congress in 1862 and this time signed into law by President Lincoln on

July 2, 1862. GEORGE RAINSFORD, CONGRESS AND HIGHER EDUCATION IN THE NINETEENTH CENTURY 91–92 (1972).

Morrill's stated objectives changed over time. During the debate on the bill, he stressed the need to do something for farmers. CONG. GLOBE, 37th Cong., 2nd Sess. 257 (1862). In 1864, during a floor debate of an amendment, he said "as I understand it, the object of the original donation was to enable the industrial classes of the country to obtain a cheap, solid, and substantial education." CONG. GLOBE, 38th Cong., 1st Sess. 1284 (1864). By the 1870s, Morrill talked not about colleges for agriculture and mechanical arts, but of "national colleges for the advancement of general science and industrial education." RAINSFORD at 101.

2. There was little public enthusiasm for the Act when it was passed. Lincoln signed it without comment. Horace Greeley, who was one of the main supporters of the legislation, declared he would be satisfied if only five schools were founded as a result. It appears that the bill passed primarily because it appealed to the Republicans in landless eastern states, rather than because of support for higher education. GEORGE N. RAINSFORD, CONGRESS AND HIGHER EDUCATION IN THE NINETEENTH CENTURY 93 (1972).

3. The Act forced states to put most of the land scrip on the market at once, depressing prices. Rhode Island, for example, assigned its 120,000 acres of scrip to Brown University, which, in turn, sold it to a private speculator for 42 cents an acre. The spectacular exception to this pattern was in New York where Ezra Cornell purchased almost all of the 989,920 acres of scrip assigned to the state at the market price of 60 cents per acre. He then located 499,126 acres of land to claim with the scrip in Wisconsin which, when sold, brought an average price of $8.82 per acre, providing Cornell University with an endowment of over $5 million. RAINSFORD at 103–04.

4. In 1890, a second Morrill Act was passed that required each state either to show that race was not an admissions criterion or to designate a separate land-grant institution for persons of color. The 1890 Act also authorized annual cash appropriations, rather than land, but provided that the recipient schools would still be considered land-grant colleges. With the increase in funding came additional students. Although the land-grant colleges grew slowly initially and experienced high student attrition, by 1900 more than 19,000 students were enrolled in sixty-five land-grant colleges. ROGER L. WILLIAMS, THE ORIGINS OF FEDERAL SUPPORT FOR HIGHER EDUCATION: GEORGE W. ATHERTON AND THE LAND-GRANT COLLEGE MOVEMENT 3 (1991).

Today there are more than 100 land-grant institutions which enroll more than 1.3 million students. Most are public, including the University of California system, but some are private (MIT) and others are a mix of both (Cornell). Most belong to the National Association of State Universities and Land Grant Colleges. A list of the original and current land grant institutions may be found at http://www.nasulgc.org.

5. Clark Kerr drew an interesting parallel between the establishment of Johns Hopkins and the land grant movement:

> Along with the Hopkins experiment came the land grant movement— and these two influences turned out to be more compatible than might at first appear. The one was Prussian, the other American; one elitist, the other democratic; one academically pure, the other sullied by contact with the soil and the machine. The one looked to Kant and Hegel, the other to Franklin, Jefferson, and Lincoln. But they both served an industrializing nation and they both did it through research and the training of technical competence. Two strands of history were woven together in the modern American university.

CLARK KERR, THE USES OF THE UNIVERSITY 11–12 (1963).

ANDREW CARNEGIE, THE GOSPEL OF WEALTH (1889).

The contrast between the palace of the millionaire and the cottage of the laborer with us today measures the change which has come with civilization. This change, however, is not to be deplored, but welcomed as highly beneficial.... The "good old times" were not good old times. Neither master nor servant was as well situated then as today. A relapse to old conditions would be disastrous to both—not the least so to him who serves— and would sweep away civilization with it....

. . .

The question then arises ... what is the proper mode of administering wealth after the laws upon which civilization is founded have thrown it into the hands of the few? ... It will be understood that fortunes are here spoken of, not moderate sums saved by many years of effort, the returns from which are required for the comfortable maintenance and education of families. This is not wealth, but only competence, which it should be the aim of all to acquire, and which it is for the best interest of society should be acquired.

There are but three modes in which surplus wealth can be disposed of. It can be left to the families of the decedents; or it can be bequeathed for public purposes; or, finally, it can be administered by its possessors during their lives.... The first is the most injudicious.... Why should men leave great fortunes to their children? If this is done from affection, is it not misguided affection? ... Beyond providing for the wife and daughters moderate sources of income, and very moderate allowances indeed, if any, for the sons, men may well hesitate; for it is no longer questionable that great sums bequeathed often work more for the injury than for the good of recipients....

. . .

As to the second ... [i]n many cases the bequests ... so used ... become only monuments of his folly. It is well to remember that it requires the exercise of not less ability than that which acquires it, to use wealth so as to be really beneficial to the community....

The growing disposition to tax more and more heavily large estates left at death is a cheering indication of the growth of a salutary change in public opinion....

. . .

There remains, then, only one mode of using great fortunes; but in this we have the true antidote for the temporary unequal distribution of wealth, the reconciliation of the rich and the poor—a reign of harmony, another ideal, differing, indeed, from that of the Communist in requiring only the further evolution of existing conditions, not the total overthrow of our civilization....

If we consider the results which flow from the Cooper Institute, for instance, to the best portion of the race in New York not possessed of means, and compare these with those which would have ensued for the good of the masses from an equal sum distributed by Mr. Cooper in his lifetime in the form of wages ... we can form some estimate of the possibilities for the improvement of the race which lie embedded in the present law of the accumulation of wealth. . . .

Poor and restricted are our opportunities in this life, narrow our horizon, our best work most imperfect; but rich men should be thankful for one inestimable boon. They have it in their power during their lives to busy themselves in organizing benefaction from which the masses of their fellows will derive lasting advantage and thus dignify their own life. . . .

This, then, is held to be the duty of the man of wealth: To set an example of modest, unostentatious living, shunning display or extravagance; to provide moderately for the legitimate wants of those dependent upon him; and, after doing so, to consider all surplus revenues which come to him simply as trust funds, which he is called upon to administer, and strictly bound as a matter of duty to administer in the manner which, in his judgment, is best calculated to produce the most beneficial results for the community—the man of wealth thus becoming the mere trustee and agent for his poorer brethren, bringing to their service his superior wisdom, experience, and ability to administer, doing for them better than they would or could do for themselves.

. . .

Thus is the problem of rich and poor to be solved. The laws of accumulation will be left free, the laws of distribution free. Individualism will continue, but the millionaire will be but a trustee for the poor. . . . [T]he day is not far distant when the man who dies leaving behind him millions of available wealth, which was free to him to administer during life, will pass away "unwept, unhonored, and unsung," no matter to what uses he leaves the dross which he cannot take with him. Of such as these the public verdict will then be: "the man who dies thus rich dies disgraced."

Questions and Comments on *The Gospel of Wealth*

1. This essay first appeared in CXLVIII NORTH AMERICAN REVIEW 653–64 (1889). Do you agree with Carnegie? Consider Robert H. Bremner's analysis of the essay:

> His view resembled that of John Winthrop and William Penn, except in one important respect. Carnegie did not say, as those men had, that the great ones owed their distinction to peculiar arrangements ordained of God. He attributed the eminence of the millionaire class to fitness to survive and triumph in the competitive struggle. The trusteeship Carnegie proposed thus differed from the traditional doctrines of stewardship. The millionaire, a product of natural selection, was an agent of the public, of the forces of civilization, rather than a servant of God. Trusteeship devolved on the man of wealth because he was fittest to exercise it. In the exercise of his trust he was responsible only to his own conscience and judgment of what was best for the community.

AMERICAN PHILANTHROPY 106 (1960).

2. Peter Cooper, inspired by a friend's description of the Ecole Polytechnique in Paris, founded Cooper Union in 1859. He later explained "[H]ow glad I would have been, if I could have found such an institution in my youth in [New York City], with its doors open to give instruction at night, the only time that I could command for study. And I then reflected at the fact that there must be a great many young men in this country, situated as I was, who thirsted for the knowledge they could not reach, and would gladly avail themselves of opportunities which they had no money to procure." FIFTEENTH ANNUAL REPORT OF THE TRUSTEES OF THE COOPER UNION FOR THE ADVANCEMENT OF SCIENCE AND ART 18–19 (1874), *quoted in* MERLE CURTI & RODERICK NASH, PHILANTHROPY IN THE SHAPING OF AMERICAN HIGHER EDUCATION (1965), *available at* http://www.ksg.harvard.edu/hauser/philanthropyclassics/pdf_files/Curti_and_Nash.pdf.

3. In 1889, Carnegie announced that he intended to devote less time to business. After publishing his *Gospel of Wealth*, he did live largely according to the principles set forth in his essay. A large portion of his philanthropy was directed to higher education. In 1900, for example, he made a gift of two million dollars to Pittsburgh for a technical school that later became the Carnegie Institute of Technology. CURTI & NASH at 82. In 1904, Carnegie received a proposal from Henry Pritchett, the President of M.I.T., asking him to provide retirement pensions for the M.I.T. faculty. Carnegie instead asked Pritchett to look into the possibility of providing such pensions to a broader group of schools. Pritchett's report said that pensions could be provided for the faculty at 92 colleges and universities at a total cost of $10 million. In 1903 Carnegie donated that amount to what became the Carnegie Foundation for the Advancement of Teaching. Pritchett resigned from M.I.T. to become the first president of the new foundation. He soon realized that he could do more than merely provide income for retired professors; he reasoned that he could use the money to raise standards at participating schools. The Carnegie Foundation required participating schools to limit admissions to students who had completed four years of secondary education. They also required them to have a least six full professors and an endowment of $200,000. Some faculty criticized the program as a mere sop given in the place of salary increases. The Foundation initially barred state universities from participating, but Carnegie himself overruled that part of the policy.

By 1916, Pritchett admitted the failure of his efforts to construct a system of higher education composed of only a few, favored institutions. In 1918, the pension program was reorganized as the Teachers Insurance and Annuity Association (today TIAA–CREF) and required participating professors to contribute 5 percent of their salary toward retirement benefits. CURTI & NASH at 220–22.

In 1901 Carnegie sold his company to J.P. Morgan for $480 million. Two years later he retired from business to devote himself to full time philanthropy. He gave more than $60 million to build more than 3,000 public libraries in the United States, United Kingdom, and other English speaking countries from Canada to Fiji. By 1911, when he established the Carnegie Corporation (a grant-making foundation) Carnegie was seventy-six and tired of philanthropy. Although he had given away nearly $180 million, he still had almost that much remaining. Encouraged by his wife and Elihu Root, his lawyer, Carnegie decided to transfer the remaining assets to the Corporation so that he could continue personally to supervise the distribution of assets as long as he was able and die assured that he had indeed given away his fortune. ELLEN CONDLIFFE LAGEMANN, THE POLITICS OF KNOWLEDGE: THE CARNEGIE CORPORATION, PHILANTHROPY, AND PUBLIC POLICY 12 (1989); ROBERT M. LESTER, FORTY YEARS OF CARNEGIE GIVING 7 (1941).

The Carnegie Corporation in the years since his death has provided substantial funds to a range of institutions and programs including the National Research Council of the National Academy of Sciences, the American Law Institute, and Sesame Street. *See generally* LAGEMANN, *supra*.

3. EARLY CHALLENGES TO ACADEMIC FREEDOM

As the number and expertise of faculty grew in the late nineteenth century, it was perhaps inevitable that there would be clashes with governing boards. One of the most publicized conflicts involved Edward A. Ross, a prominent economist at Stanford, whose advocacy of free silver and opposition to the importation of foreign labor offended Mrs. Leland Stanford, the sole trustee of the university that she and her late husband had founded in memory of their only child, Leland, Jr., who died of typhoid at age 15.[a] She asked David Starr Jordan, the president of Stanford, to fire Professor Ross. Although Mrs. Stanford was the leading benefactor of the university, Jordan delayed acting for several years and tried to change her mind. Ultimately, however, he capitulated and in November, 1900, forced out Ross. Although most senior faculty at Stanford supported Jordan, a number of professors in the social sciences resigned in protest, including philosopher Arthur Lovejoy.[b] Ross sought the assistance of the American Economic Association, which had been founded in 1885. They agreed to organize a committee to look into the matter. The report of the committee presented evidence that Ross had been fired for his opinions. It was sent to leading social scientists, and fifteen signed in support of its findings.[c]

In 1914, in response to the Ross incident as well as challenges to academic freedom at other universities, eighteen full professors at Johns Hopkins issued a call to faculty at nine other universities to form a national association for the support of academic freedom.[d] Delegates from seven attended the organizational meeting: Clark, Columbia, Cornell, Harvard, Princeton, Wisconsin, and Yale. After initial arrangements were completed, invitations were extended to other distinguished full professors to join. Ultimately 867 professors from 60 institutions of higher education became charter members of the American Association of University Professors.[e]

American Association of University Professors, 1915 Declaration of Principles on Academic Freedom and Academic Tenure[f]

1 AAUP Bulletin 17–39 (December 1915).

General Declaration of Principles

The term "academic freedom" has traditionally had two applications—to the freedom of the teacher and to that of the student, *Lehrfreiheit* and

a. ORRIN LESLIE ELLIOTT, STANFORD UNIVERSITY: THE FIRST TWENTY-FIVE YEARS 11 (1937).

b. MARY O. FURNER, ADVOCACY AND OBJECTIVITY: A CRISIS IN THE PROFESSIONALIZATION OF AMERICAN SOCIAL SCIENCE, 1865–1905, at 241–42 (1975). Mrs. Leland Stanford had two years earlier forced the firing of sociologist Harry Huntington Powers but no one took notice. The difference was that Ross was an established scholar who had "earned respect in the profession." *Id.* at 227. He was not uncontroversial, however, given his strong support for Aryan supremacy.

c. Nebraska appointed Ross to its faculty. Harvard invited Ross to deliver a series of lectures in 1902. Five years later, after publishing a number of important works, Ross was appointed to a chair of sociology at Wisconsin which he held for thirty years. FURNER at 252–53.

d. *A National Association of University Professors*, 39 SCIENCE 458, 458–59 (1914).

e. WALTER METZGER, *The Age of the University, in* RICHARD HOFSTADTER & WALTER METZGER, THE DEVELOPMENT OF ACADEMIC FREEDOM IN THE UNITED STATES 476–77 (1955).

f. The Principles were drafted by a committee of fifteen appointed by John Dewey, president of the association. The committee included:

Edwin R.A. Seligman (Economics), Columbia University, Chairman

Charles E. Bennett (Latin), Cornell University

James Q. Dealey (Political Science), Brown University

Richard T. Ely (Economics), University of Wisconsin

Henry W. Farnam (Political Science), Yale University

Frank A. Fetter (Economics), Princeton University

Guy Stanton Ford (History), University of Minnesota

Lernfreiheit. It need scarcely be pointed out that the freedom which is the subject of this report is that of the teacher. Academic freedom in this sense comprises three elements: freedom of inquiry and research; freedom of teaching within the university or college; and freedom of extramural utterance and action. The first of these is almost everywhere so safeguarded that the dangers of its infringement are slight. It may therefore be disregarded in this report. The second and third phases of academic freedom are closely related, and are often not distinguished. The third, however, has an importance of its own, since of late it has perhaps more frequently been the occasion of difficulties and controversies than has the question of freedom of intra-academic teaching. All five of the cases which have recently been investigated by committees of this Association have involved, at least as one factor, the right of university teachers to express their opinions freely outside the university or to engage in political activities in their capacity as citizens. The general principles which have to do with freedom of teaching in both these senses seem to the committee to be in great part, though not wholly, the same. In this report, therefore, we shall consider the matter primarily with reference to freedom of teaching within the university, and shall assume that what is said thereon is also applicable to the freedom of speech of university teachers outside their institutions, subject to certain qualifications and supplementary considerations which will be pointed out in the course of the report.

. . .

1. *Basis of Academic Authority*. American institutions of learning are usually controlled by boards of trustees as the ultimate repositories of power. Upon them finally it devolves to determine the measure of academic freedom which is to be realized in the several institutions. It therefore becomes necessary to inquire into the nature of the trust reposed in these boards, and to ascertain to whom the trustees are to be considered accountable.

The simplest case is that of the proprietary school or college designed for the propagation of specific doctrines prescribed by those who have furnished its endowment. It is evident that in such cases the trustees are bound by the deed of gift, and, whatever be their own views, are obligated to carry out the terms of the trust. . . . [Proprietary institutions] do not, at least as regards one particular subject, accept the principles of freedom of inquiry, of opinion, and of teaching; and their purpose is not to advance knowledge by the unrestricted research and unfettered discussion of impartial investigators, but rather to subsidize the promotion of the opinions held by the persons, usually not of the scholar's calling, who provide the funds for their maintenance. Concerning the desirability of the existence of such institutions, the committee does not desire to express any opinion. But it is manifestly important that they should not be permitted to sail under false colors. Genuine boldness and thoroughness of inquiry, and freedom of

Franklin H. Giddings (Sociology), Columbia University

Edward C. Elliott (Education), University of Wisconsin

Charles A. Kofoid (Zoology), University of California

Arthur O. Lovejoy (Philosophy), The Johns Hopkins University

Frederick W. Padelford (English), University of Washington

Roscoe Pound (Law), Harvard University

Howard C. Warren (Psychology), Princeton University

Ulysses G. Weatherly (Sociology), Indiana University

speech, are scarcely reconcilable with the prescribed inculcation of a particular opinion upon a controverted question.

.   .   .

Leaving aside, then, the small number of institutions of the proprietary type, what is the nature of the trust reposed in the governing boards of the ordinary institutions of learning? Can colleges and universities that are not strictly bound by their founders to a propagandist duty ever be included in the class of institutions that we have just described as being in a moral sense proprietary? The answer is clear. If the former class of institutions constitute a private or proprietary trust, the latter constitute a public trust. The trustees are trustees for the public. In the case of our state universities this is self-evident. In the case of most of our privately endowed institutions, the situation is really not different. They cannot be permitted to assume the proprietary attitude and privilege, if they are appealing to the general public for support. Trustees of such universities or colleges have no moral right to bind the reason or the conscience of any professor. All claim to such right is waived by the appeal to the general public for contributions and for moral support in the maintenance, not of a propaganda, but of a nonpartisan institution of learning. It follows that any university which lays restrictions upon the intellectual freedom of its professors proclaims itself a proprietary institution, and should be so described whenever it makes a general appeal for funds; and the public should be advised that the institution has no claim whatever to general support or regard.

This elementary distinction between a private and a public trust is not yet so universally accepted as it should be in our American institutions. While in many universities and colleges the situation has come to be entirely satisfactory, there are others in which the relation of trustees to professors is apparently still conceived to be analogous to that of a private employer to his employees; in which, therefore, trustees are not regarded as debarred by any moral restrictions, beyond their own sense of expediency, from imposing their personal opinions upon the teaching of the institutions, or even from employing the power of dismissal to gratify their private antipathies or resentments. An eminent university president thus described the situation not many years since:

> In the institutions of higher education the board of trustees is the body on whose discretion, good feeling, and experience the securing of academic freedom now depends. There are boards which leave nothing to be desired in these respects; but there are also numerous bodies that have everything to learn with regard to academic freedom. These barbarous boards exercise an arbitrary power of dismissal. They exclude from the teachings of the university unpopular or dangerous subjects. In some states they even treat professors' positions as common political spoils; and all too frequently, both in state and endowed institutions, they fail to treat the members of the teaching staff with that high consideration to which their functions entitle them.[2]

2. From "Academic Freedom," an address delivered before the New York Chapter of the Phi Beta Kappa Society at Cornell University, May 29, 1907, by Charles William Eliot, President of Harvard University.

It is, then, a prerequisite to a realization of the proper measure of academic freedom in American institutions of learning, that all boards of trustees should understand—as many already do—the full implications of the distinction between private proprietorship and a public trust.

2. *The Nature of the Academic Calling.* The above-mentioned conception of a university as an ordinary business venture, and of academic teaching as a purely private employment, manifests also a radical failure to apprehend the nature of the social function discharged by the professional scholar. While we should be reluctant to believe that any large number of educated persons suffer from such a misapprehension, it seems desirable at this time to restate clearly the chief reasons . . . why it is to the public interest that the professional office should be one both of dignity and of independence.

If education is the cornerstone of the structure of society and if progress in scientific knowledge is essential to civilization, few things can be more important than to enhance the dignity of the scholar's profession, with a view of attracting into its ranks men of the highest ability, of sound learning, and of strong and independent character. This is the more essential because the pecuniary emoluments of the profession are not, and doubtless never will be, equal to those open to the more successful members of other professions. It is not, in our opinion, desirable that men should be drawn into this profession by the magnitude of the economic rewards which it offers; but it is for this reason the more needful that men of high gifts and character should be drawn into it by the assurance of an honorable and secure position, and of freedom to perform honestly and according to their own consciences the distinctive and important function which the nature of the profession lays upon them.

That function is to deal at first hand, after prolonged and specialized technical training, with the sources of knowledge; and to impart the results of their own and of their fellow specialists' investigation and reflection, both to students and to the general public, without fear or favor. The proper discharge of this function requires (among other things) that the university teacher shall be exempt from any pecuniary motive or inducement to hold, or to express, any conclusion which is not the genuine and uncolored product of his own study or that of fellow-specialists. Indeed, the proper fulfillment of the work of the professoriate requires that our universities shall be so free that no fair-minded person shall find any excuse for even a suspicion that the utterances of university teachers are shaped or restricted by the judgment, not of professional scholars, but of inexpert and possibly not wholly disinterested persons outside of their ranks. The lay public is under no compulsion to accept or to act upon the opinions of the scientific experts whom, through the universities, it employs. But it is highly needful, in the interest of society at large, that what purport to be the conclusions of men trained for, and dedicated to, the quest for truth, shall in fact be the conclusions of such men, and not echoes of the opinions of the lay public, or of the individuals who endow or manage universities. To the degree that professional scholars, in the formation and promulgation of their opinions, are, or by the character of their tenure appear to be, subject to any motive other than their own scientific conscience and a desire for the respect of their fellow-experts, to that degree the university teaching profession is corrupted; its proper influence upon public opinion is diminished and vitiated; and society at large fails to get from its scholars, in an unadulterated form, the peculiar and necessary service which it is the office of the professional scholar to furnish.

These considerations make still more clear the nature of the relationship between university trustees and members of university faculties. The latter are the appointees, but not in any proper sense the employees, of the former. For, once appointed, the scholar has professional functions to perform in which appointing authorities have neither competency nor moral right to intervene. The responsibility of the university teacher is primarily to the public itself, and to the judgment of his own profession; and while, with respect to certain external conditions of his vocation, he accepts a responsibility to the authorities of the institution in which he serves, in the essentials of his professional activity his duty is to the wider public to which the institution itself is morally amenable. So far as the university teacher's independence of thought and utterance is concerned—though not in other regards—the relationship of professor to trustees may be compared to that between judges of the Federal courts and the Executive who appoints them. University teachers should be understood to be, with respect to the conclusions reached and expressed by them, no more subject to the control of the trustees than are judges subjects to the control of the President with respect to their decisions; while of course, for the same reason, trustees are no more to be held responsible for, or to be presumed to agree with, the opinions or utterances of professors than the President can be assumed to approve of all the legal reasonings of the courts. . . .

3. *The Function of the Academic Institution.* The importance of academic freedom is most clearly perceived in the light of the purpose for which universities exist. These are three in number.

   a. To promote inquiry and advance the sum of human knowledge.

   b. To provide general instruction to the students.

   c. To develop experts for various branches of the public service.

   . . . In the earlier stages of a nation's intellectual development, the chief concern of educational institutions is to train the growing generation and to diffuse the already accepted knowledge. It is only slowly that there comes to be provided in the highest institutions of learning the opportunity for the gradual wresting from nature of her intimate secrets. The modern university is becoming more and more the home of scientific research. There are three fields of human inquiry in which the race is only at the beginning: natural science, social science, and philosophy and religion, dealing with the relations of man to our nature, to his fellow men, and to ultimate realities and values. . . . In all of these domains of knowledge, the first condition of progress is complete and unlimited freedom to pursue inquiry and publish its results. Such freedom is the breath in the nostrils of all scientific activity.

The second function—which for a long time was the only function—of the American college or university is to provide instruction for students. It is scarcely open to question that freedom of utterance is as important to the teacher as it is to the investigator. No man can be a successful teacher unless he enjoys the respect of his students, and their confidence in his intellectual integrity. It is clear, however, that this confidence will be impaired if there is suspicion on the part of the student that the teacher is not expressing himself fully or frankly, or that college and university teachers in general are a repressed and intimidated class who dare not speak with that candor and courage which youth always demands in those whom it is to esteem. . . .

The third function of the modern university is to develop experts for the use of the community. If there is one thing that distinguishes the more recent developments of democracy, it is the recognition by legislators of the inherent complexities of economic, social and political life, and the difficulty of solving problems or technical adjustment without technical knowledge. The recognition of this fact has led to a continually greater demand for the aid of experts in these subjects, to advise both legislators and administrators. . . . It is obvious that here again the scholar must be absolutely free not only to pursue his investigations but to declare the results of his researches, no matter where they may lead him or to what extent they may come into conflict with accepted opinion. To be of use to the legislator or the administrator, he must enjoy their complete confidence in the disinterestedness of his conclusions.

It is clear, then, that the university cannot perform its threefold function without accepting and enforcing to the fullest extent the principle of academic freedom. . . .

. . .

The attempted infringements of academic freedom at present are probably not only of less frequency than, but of a different character from, those to be found in former times. In the early period of university development in America the chief menace to academic freedom was ecclesiastical, and the disciplines chiefly affected were philosophy and the natural sciences. In more recent times the danger zone has been shifted to the political and social sciences—in some of our smaller institutions. But it is precisely in these provinces of knowledge in which academic freedom is now most likely to be threatened, that the need for it is at the same time most evident. No person of intelligence believes that all of our political problems have been solved, or that the final stage of social evolution has been reached. Grave issues in the adjustment of men's social and economic relations are certain to call for settlement in the years that are to come; and for the right settlement of them mankind will need all wisdom, all the good will, all the soberness of mind, and all the knowledge drawn from experience, that it can command. Toward this settlement the university has potentially its own very great contribution to make; for if the adjustment reached is to be a wise one, it must take due account of economic science, and be guided by that breadth of historic vision which it should be one of the functions of a university to cultivate. But if the universities are to render any such service toward the right solution of the social problems of the future, it is the first essential that the scholars who carry on the work of the universities shall not be in a position of dependence upon the favor of any social class or group, that the disinterestedness and impartiality of their inquiries and their conclusions shall be, so far as is humanly possible, beyond the reach of suspicion.

The special dangers to freedom of teaching in the domain of the social sciences are evidently two. The one which is the more likely to affect the privately endowed colleges and universities is the danger of restrictions upon the expression of opinions which point toward extensive social innovations, or call in question the moral legitimacy or social expediency of economic conditions or commercial practices in which large vested interests are involved. In the political, social, and economic field almost every question, no matter how large and general it at first appears, is more or less affected with private or class interests; and, as the governing body of a university is naturally made up of men who through their standing and ability are personally interested in great private enterprises, the points of possible conflict are numberless. When to this is added the consideration that benefactors, as well as most of the parents who send their children to privately endowed institutions, themselves belong to the more prosperous and therefore usually to the more conservative classes, it is apparent that, so long as effectual safeguards for academic freedom are not established, there is a real danger that pressure from vested interests may, sometimes deliberately and sometimes unconsciously, sometimes openly and sometimes subtly and in obscure ways, be brought to bear upon academic authorities.

On the other hand, in our state universities the danger may be the reverse. Where the university is dependent for funds upon legislative favor, it has sometimes happened that the conduct of institution has been affected by political considerations; and where there is a definite governmental policy or a strong public feeling on economic, social, or political questions, the menace to academic freedom may consist in the repression of opinions that in the particular political situation are deemed ultra-conservative rather than ultra-radical. The essential point, however, is not so much that the opinion is of one or another shade, as that differs from the views entertained by authorities. The question resolves itself into one of departure from accepted standards; whether the departure is in the one direction of the other is immaterial.

This brings us to the most serious difficulty of this problem; namely, the dangers connected with the existence in a democracy of an overwhelming and concentrated public opinion. The tendency of modern democracy is for men to think alike, to feel alike, and to speak alike. Any departure from the conventional standards is apt to be regarded with suspicion. Public opinion is at once the chief safeguard of a democracy, and the chief menace to the real liberty of an individual. It almost seems as if the danger of despotism cannot be wholly averted under any form of government. In a political autocracy there is no effective public opinion, and all are subject to tyranny of the ruler; in a democracy there is political freedom, but there is likely to be a tyranny of public opinion.

An inviolable refuge from such tyranny should be found in the university. It should be an intellectual experiment station, where new ideas may germinate and where their fruit, though still distasteful to the community as a whole, may be allowed to ripen until finally, perchance, it may become part of the accepted intellectual food of the nation or of the world. Not less is it a distinctive duty of the university to be the conservator of all genuine elements of value in the past thought and life of mankind which are not in the fashion of the moment. Though it need not be the "home of beaten causes," the university is, indeed, likely always to exercise a certain form of conservative influence. For by its nature it is committed to the principle that knowledge should precede action, to the caution (by no means synonymous with intellectual timidity) which is an essential part of the scientific method, to a sense of the complexity of social problems, to the practice of taking long views into the future, and to a reasonable regard for the teachings of experience. One of its most characteristic functions in a democratic society is to help make public opinion more self-critical and more circumspect, to check the more hasty and unconsidered impulses of popular feeling, to train the democracy to the habit of looking before and after. It is precisely this function of the university which is most injured by any restriction upon academic freedom; and it is precisely those who most value this aspect of the university's work who should most earnestly protest against any such restriction. For the public may respect, and be influenced by, the counsels of prudence and of moderation which are given by men of science, if it believes those counsels to be the disinterested expression of the scientific temper and of unbiased inquiry. It is little likely to respect or heed them if it has reason to believe that they are the expression of the interests, or the timidities, of the limited portion of the community which is in a position to endow institutions of learning, or is most likely to be represented upon their boards of trustees. And a plausible reason for this belief is given the public so long as our universities are not organized in such a way as to make impossible any exercise of pressure upon professorial opinions and utterances by governing boards of laymen.

Since there are no rights without corresponding duties, the considerations heretofore set down with respect to the freedom of the academic teacher entail certain correlative obligations. The claim to freedom of teaching is made in the interest of integrity and of the progress of scientific inquiry; it is, therefore, only those who carry on their work in the temper of the scientific inquirer who may justly assert this claim. The liberty of the scholar within the university to set forth his conclusions, be they what they may, is conditioned by their being conclusions gained by a scholar's method and held in a scholar's spirit; that is to say, they must be the fruits of competent and patient and sincere inquiry, and they should be set forth with dignity, courtesy, and temperateness of language. The university teacher, in giving instruction upon controversial matters, while he is under no obligation to hide his own opinion under a mountain of equivocal verbiage, should, if he is fit in dealing with such subjects, set forth justly, without suppression or innuendo, the divergent opinions of other investigators; he should cause his students to become familiar with the best published expressions of the great historic types of doctrine upon the questions at issue; and he should, above all, remember that his business is not to provide his students with ready-made conclusions, but to train them to think for themselves, and to provide them access to those materials which they need if they are to think intelligently.

It is, however, for reasons which have already been made evident, inadmissible that the power of determining when departures from the requirements of the scientific spirit and method have occurred, should be vested in bodies not composed of members of the academic profession. Such bodies necessarily lack full competency to judge of those requirements; their intervention can never be exempt from the suspicion that it is dictated by other motives than zeal for the integrity of science; and it is, in any case, unsuitable to the dignity of a great profession that the initial responsibility for the maintenance of its professional standards should not be in the hands of its own members. It follows that university teachers must be prepared to assume this responsibility for themselves. They have hitherto seldom had the opportunity, or perhaps the disposition, to do so. The obligation will doubtless, therefore, seem to many an unwelcome and burdensome one; and for its proper discharge members of the profession will perhaps need to acquire, in a greater measure than they at present possess it, the capacity for impersonal judgment in such cases, and for judicial severity when the occasion requires it. But the responsibility cannot, in this committee's opinion, be rightfully evaded. If this profession should prove itself unwilling to purge its ranks of the incompetent and the unworthy, or to prevent the freedom which it claims in the name of science from being used as a shelter for inefficiency, for superficiality, or for uncritical and intemperate partisanship, it is certain that the task will be performed by others—by others who lack certain essential qualifications for performing it, and whose action is sure to breed suspicions and recurrent controversies deeply injurious to the internal order and the public standing of universities. Your committee has, therefore, in the appended "Practical Proposals" attempted to suggest means by which judicial action by representatives of the profession, with respect to the matters here referred to, may be secured.

There is one case in which the academic teacher is under an obligation to observe certain special restraints—namely, the instruction of immature students. In many of our American colleges, and especially in the first two years of the course, the student's character is not yet fully formed, his mind is still relatively immature. In these circumstances it may reasonably be expected that the instructor will present scientific truth with discretion, that he will introduce the student to new conceptions gradually, with some consideration for the student's preconceptions and traditions, and with due regard to character-building. The teacher ought also to be especially on his guard against taking unfair advantage of the students' immaturity by indoctrinating him with the teacher's own opinions before the student has had an opportunity fairly to examine other opinions upon the matters of question, and before he has sufficient knowledge and ripeness in judgment to be entitled to form any definitive opinion of his own. It is not the least service which a college or university may render to those under its instruction, to habituate them to looking not only patiently but methodically on both sides, before adopting any conclusion upon controverted issues. By these suggestions, however, it need scarcely be said that the committee does not intend to imply that it is not the duty of an academic instructor to give to any students old enough to be in college a genuine intellectual awakening and to arouse in them a keen desire to reach personally verified conclusions upon all questions of general concernment to mankind, or of special significance for their own time. There is much truth in some remarks recently made in this connection by a college president:

> Certain professors have been refused re-election lately, apparently because they set their students to thinking in ways objectionable to the trustees. It would be well if more teachers were dismissed because they fail to stimulate thinking of any kind. We can afford to forgive a college professor what we regard as the occasional error of his doctrine, especially as we may be wrong, provided he is a contagious center of intellectual enthusiasm. It is better for students to think about heresies than not to think at all; better for them to climb new trails, and stumble over error if need be, than to ride forever in upholstered ease in the overcrowded highway. It is a primary duty of a teacher to make a student take an honest account of his stock of ideas, throw out the dead matter, place revised price

marks on what is left, and try to fill his empty shelves with new goods.[3]

It is, however, possible and necessary that such intellectual awakening be brought about with patience, considerateness, and pedagogical wisdom.

There is one further consideration with regard to the classroom utterances of college and university teachers to which the committee thinks it is important to call the attention of members of the profession, and of administrative authorities. Such utterances ought always to be considered privileged communications. Discussions in the classroom ought not to be supposed to be utterances for the public at large. They are often designed to provoke opposition or arouse debate. It has, unfortunately, sometimes happened in this country that sensational newspapers have quoted and garbled such remarks. As a matter of common law, it is clear that the utterances of an academic instructor are privileged, and may not be published, in whole or part, without his authorization. But our practice, unfortunately, still differs from that of foreign countries, and no effective check in this country has been put upon such unauthorized and often misleading publication. It is much to be desired that test cases should be made of any infractions of the rule.[4]

In their extramural utterances, it is obvious that academic teachers are under a peculiar obligation to avoid hasty or unverified or exaggerated statements, and to refrain from intemperate or sensational modes of expression. But subject to these restraints, it is not, in this committee's opinion, desirable that scholars should be debarred from giving expression to their judgments upon controversial questions, or that their freedom of speech, outside the university, should be limited to questions falling within their own specialties. It is clearly not proper that they should be prohibited from lending their active support to organized movements which they believe to be in the public interest. And, speaking broadly, it may be said in the words of a nonacademic body already once quoted in a publication of the Association, that "it is neither possible nor desirable to deprive a college professor of the political rights vouchsafed to every citizen."[5]

It is, however, a question deserving of consideration by members of the Association, and by university officials, how far academic teachers, at least those dealing with political, economic, and social subjects, should be prominent in the management of our great party organizations, or should be candidates for state or national offices of a distinctly political character. It is manifestly desirable that such teachers have minds untrammeled by party loyalties, unexcited by party enthusiasms, and unbiased by personal political ambitions; and that universities should remain uninvolved in party antagonisms. On the other hand, it is equally manifest that the material available for the service of the State would be restricted in a highly undesirable way, if it were understood that no member of the academic profession should ever be called upon to assume the responsibilities of public office. This question

---

3. William T. Foster, President of Reed College, in THE NATION, November 11, 1915.

4. The leading case is *Abernathy vs. Hutchinson*, 3 L.J., Ch. 209. In this case, where damages were awarded, the court held as follows: "That persons who are admitted as pupils or otherwise to hear these lectures, although they are orally delivered and the

parties might go to the extent, if they were able to do so, of putting down the whole by means of shorthand, yet they can do that only for the purpose of their own information and could not publish, for profit, that which they had not obtained the right of selling."

5. REPORT OF THE WISCONSIN STATE BOARD OF PUBLIC AFFAIRS, December 1914.

may, in the committee's opinion, suitably be made a topic for special discussion at some future meeting of this Association, in order that a practical policy, which shall do justice to the two partially conflicting considerations that bear upon the matter, may be agreed upon.

It is, it will be seen, in no sense the contention of this committee that academic freedom implies that individual teachers should be exempt from all restraints as to the matter or manner of their utterances, either within or without the university. Such restraints as are necessary should in the main, our committee holds, be self-imposed, or enforced by the public opinion of the profession. But there may, undoubtedly, arise occasional cases in which the aberrations of individuals may require to be checked by definite disciplinary action. What this report chiefly maintains is that such action cannot with safety be taken by bodies not composed of members of the academic profession. Lay governing boards are competent to judge concerning charges of habitual neglect of assigned duties, on the part of individual teachers, and concerning charges of grave moral delinquency. But in matters of opinion, and of the utterance of opinion, such boards cannot intervene without destroying, to the extent of their intervention, the essential nature of a university—without converting it from a place dedicated to openness of mind, in which the conclusions expressed are the tested conclusions of trained scholars, into a place barred against the access of new light, and pre-committed to the opinions or prejudices of men who have not been set apart or expressly trained for the scholar's duties. It is, in short, not the absolute freedom of utterance of the individual scholar, but the absolute freedom of thought, of inquiry, of discussion, and of teaching, of the academic profession, that is asserted by this declaration of principles. . . .

Practical Proposals

As the foregoing declaration implies, the ends to be accomplished are chiefly three:

First: To safeguard freedom of inquiry and of teaching against both covert and overt attacks, by providing suitable judicial bodies, composed of members of the academic profession, which may be called into action before university teachers are dismissed or disciplined, and may determine in what cases the question of academic freedom is actually involved.

Second: By the same means, to protect college executives and governing boards against unjust charges of infringement of academic freedom, or of arbitrary and dictatorial conduct—charges which, when they gain wide currency and belief, are highly detrimental to the good repute and the influence of universities.

Third: To render the profession more attractive to men of high ability and strong personality by insuring the dignity, the independence, and the reasonable security of tenure, of the professorial office.

The measures which it is believed to be necessary for our universities to adopt to realize these ends—measures which have already been adopted in part by some institutions—are four:

A.   Action by Faculty Committees on Reappointments. Official action relating to reappointments and refusals of reappointment should be taken only with the advice and consent of some board or committee representative of the faculty. Your committee does not desire to make at this time any suggestion as to the manner of selection of such boards.

B.   *Definition of Tenure of Office.* In every institution there should be an unequivocal understanding as to the term of each appointment; and the tenure of professorships and associate professorships, and of all positions above the grade of instructor after ten years of service, should be permanent (subject to the provisions hereinafter given for removal upon charges). In those state universities which are legally incapable of making contracts for more than a limited period, the governing boards should announce their policy with respect to the presumption of reappointment in the several classes of positions, and such announcements, though not legally enforceable, should be regarded as morally binding. No university teacher of any rank should, except in cases of grave moral delinquency, receive notice of dismissal or of refusal of reappointment, later than three months before the close of any academic year, and in the case of teachers above the grade of instructor, one year's notice should be given.

C.   *Formulation of Grounds for Dismissal.* In every institution the grounds which will be regarded as justifying the dismissal of members of the faculty should be formulated with reasonable definiteness; and in the case of institutions which impose upon their faculties doctrinal standards of a sectarian or partisan character, these standards should be clearly defined and the body or individual having authority to interpret them, in case of controversy, should be designated. Your committee does not think it best at this time to attempt to enumerate the legitimate grounds for dismissal, believing it to be preferable that individual institutions should take the initiative in this.

D.   *Judicial Hearings Before Dismissal.* Every university or college teacher should be entitled, before dismissal[6] or demotion, to have the charges against him stated in writing in specific terms and to have a fair trial on those charges before a special or permanent judicial committee chosen by the faculty senate or council, or by the faculty at large. At such a trial the teacher accused should have full opportunity to present evidence, and, if the charge is one of professional incompetency, a formal report upon his work should be first made in writing by the teachers of his own department and of cognate departments in the university, and, if the teacher concerned so desire, by a committee of his fellow specialists from other institutions, appointed by some competent authority.

Questions and Comments on the AAUP 1915 Declaration of Principles

1. The 1915 AAUP Declaration was also known as the Seligman Report after its chair, Columbia economist E.R.A. Seligman. It was immediately acclaimed by scholars as a work of seminal significance, but that did not mean it was accepted by the governing boards of any colleges or universities. Only one year after it was issued, the Wharton School at the University of Pennsylvania dismissed Professor Scott Nearing, described by Walter Metzger as a "nonrevolutionary Marxist." His dismissal did not bode well for the effort to strengthen academic freedom, although that same year A. Lawrence Lowell, who had succeeded Charles Eliot as president of Harvard, made

---

6. This does not refer to refusals of reappointment at the expiration of the terms of office of teachers below the rank of associ- ate professor. All such questions of reappointment should, as above provided, be acted upon by a faculty committee.

headlines by refusing to discipline a professor for his pro-German utterances, a refusal that put at risk a large bequest from an irate alumnus. Walter P. Metzger, *The 1940 Statement of Principles on Academic Freedom and Tenure, in* FREEDOM AND TENURE IN THE ACADEMY 12, 18–19 (William W. Van Alstyne ed., 1993).

2. Does the Declaration make a persuasive case that university governing boards should recognize academic freedom? Consider the view set forth in a contemporary New York Times editorial entitled "The Professors' Union:"

> "Academic freedom," that is, the inalienable right of every college instructor to make a fool of himself and his college by ... intemperate, sensational prattle about every subject under heaven, to his classes and to the public, and still keep on the payroll or be rift therefrom only by elaborate process, is cried to all the winds by the organized dons....
>
> It may be worthwhile to make the perhaps too obvious remark that the "science" about which the uplift professors are apt to be most cocksure are pseudo-sciences, mere opinions. A sociologist, for example, cannot speak with the certainty of a mathematician or chemist....

N.Y. TIMES, Jan. 21, 1916, at 8.

Would the AAUP have had more success in building support for its views if the members had worked with representative presidents or governing board members in preparing their statement? This is the approach they took in preparing the 1940 Statement on Principles on Academic Freedom and Tenure which is set forth in Appendix 1, *infra*. The Statement, which was drafted jointly with the Association of American Colleges (now the Association of American Colleges and Universities), has been endorsed by more than 200 higher education associations.

3. Another famous confrontation over academic freedom involved Richard Ely, one of the drafters of the 1915 AAUP Statement and, like Ross, a professor of economics, who was tried in 1894 by a committee of the Regents of the University of Wisconsin. His main accuser, Oliver E. Wells, was the state superintendent of public instruction and an ex officio member of the board. In a letter to the editors of THE NATION, Wells asserted that Ely supported strikes and practiced boycotts. He quoted Ely as saying that it was better to employ "a dirty, dissipated, unmarried, unreliable and unskilled" union man than "an industrious, skillful, trustworthy, non-union man who is head of a family." Oliver E. Wells, Letter to the Editor, 59 NATION 27 (1894). Ely denied the charges and sought the aid of the president of the university, Charles Kendall Adams. Theron F. Schlabach, *An Aristocrat on Trial: The Case of Richard T. Ely, in* ACADEMIC FREEDOM ON TRIAL: 100 YEARS OF SIFTING AND WINNOWING AT THE UNIVERSITY OF WISCONSIN-MADISON 46 (W. Lee Hansen ed., 1998). In the end, the Regents unanimously exonerated Ely and affirmed the board's devotion to academic freedom in what has become known as the sifting and winnowing statement:

> As Regents of a university with over a hundred instructors supported by nearly two millions of people who hold a vast diversity of views regarding the great questions which at present agitate the human mind, we could not for a moment think of recommending the dismissal or even the criticism of a teacher even if some of his opinions should, in some quarters, be regarded as visionary. Such a course would be equivalent to saying that no professor should teach anything which is not accepted by everybody as true. This could cut our curriculum down to very small proportions. We cannot for a moment believe that knowledge has reached its final goal, or that the present condition of society is perfect. We must therefore welcome from our teachers such discussions as shall suggest the means and prepare the way to which knowledge may be extended, present evils removed and others prevented. We feel that we would be unworthy of the position we hold if we did not believe in progress in all departments of knowledge. In all lines of academic investigation it is of the utmost importance that the investigator should be absolutely free to follow the indications of truth wherever they

may lead. Whatever may be the limitations which trammel inquiry elsewhere we believe the great state University of Wisconsin should ever encourage that continual and fearless sifting and winnowing by which alone the truth can be found.

Id. at 66–67.

Acceptance of the statement, however, was not without controversy. A later Board of Regents was reluctant to accept a bronze plaque containing the sifting and winnowing statement presented by the class of 1910. The plaque was accepted in 1912 but stored in the basement of a university building and not displayed until 1915. Nonetheless, during World War I, the Regents withheld the degrees of several students who refused military service as conscientious objectors, most of the faculty signed a manifesto denouncing the state's senior senator, Robert M. La Follette, for his antiwar views, and a distinguished professor of German was dismissed for suggesting that an obnoxious colleague, who was, like himself, German born, should demonstrate his sudden American patriotism by wearing his Liberty Loan button on the seat of his pants. E. David Ronon, *Sifting and Winnowing Issues at the University of Wisconsin–Madison, in* ACADEMIC FREEDOM ON TRIAL 244–45 (W. Lee Hansen ed., 1998).

4. Is it appropriate to compare the relationship between trustees and faculty to the relationship between the Executive Branch and federal judges? Did your college experience benefit from the goals set forth in the AAUP Statement? Were your professors free to profess unpopular opinions? Did they? Did they live up to the obligation to teach opinions that diverged from their own?

D. HIGHER EDUCATION AFTER WORLD WAR II

1. INCREASED PUBLIC SUPPORT FOR SCIENCE

Vannevar Bush, *Science—The Endless Frontier* (1945).

It has been a basic United States policy that Government should foster the opening of new frontiers. It opened the sea to clipper ships and furnished land for pioneers. Although these frontiers have more or less disappeared, the frontier of science remains. It is in keeping with the American tradition—one which has made the United States great—that new frontiers shall be made accessible for development by all American citizens.

. . .

From early days the Government has taken an active interest in scientific matters. During the nineteenth century the Coast and Geodetic Survey, the Naval Observatory, the Department of Agriculture, and the Geological Survey were established. Through the Land Grant College Acts the Government has supported research in state institutions for more than 80 years on a gradually increasing scale. Since 1900 a large number of scientific agencies have been established within the Federal Government, until in 1939 they numbered more than 40.

. . . Generally speaking, the scientific agencies of Government are not so concerned with immediate practical objectives as are the laboratories of industry nor, on the other hand, are they as free to explore any natural phenomena without regard to possible economic applications as are the educational and private research institutions. Government scientific agencies have splendid records of achievement, but they are limited in function.

... There is no body within the Government charged with formulating or executing a national science policy. There are no standing committees of the Congress devoted to this important subject. Science has been left in the wings. It should be brought to the center of the stage—for in it lies much of our hope for the future.

There are areas of science in which the public interest is acute but which are likely to be cultivated inadequately if left without more support than will come from private sources. These areas—such as research on military problems, agriculture, housing, public health, certain medical research, and research involving expensive capital facilities beyond the capacity of private institutions—should be advanced by active Government support. To date, with the exception of the intensive war research conducted by the Office of Scientific Research and Development, such support has been meager and intermittent.

[W]e are entering a period when science needs and deserves increased support from public funds.

The publicly and privately supported college, universities, and research institutes are the centers of basic research. They are the wellsprings of knowledge and understanding. As long as they are vigorous and healthy and their scientists are free to pursue the truth wherever it may lead, there will be a flow of new scientific knowledge to those who can apply it to practical problems in Government, in industry, or elsewhere.

Many of the lessons learned in the war-time application of science under Government can be profitably applied in peace. The Government is peculiarly fitted to perform certain functions, such as the coordination and support of broad programs on problems of great national importance. But we must proceed with caution in carrying over the methods which work in wartime to the very different conditions of peace. We must remove the rigid controls which we have had to impose, and recover freedom of inquiry and that healthy competitive scientific spirit so necessary for expansion of the frontiers of scientific knowledge.

Scientific progress on a broad front results from the free play of free intellects, working on subjects of their own choice, in the manner dictated by their curiosity for exploration of the unknown. Freedom of inquiry must be preserved under any plan for Government support of science in accordance with the Five Fundamentals.[a]

a. (1) Whatever the extent of support may be, there must be stability of funds over a period of years to that long-range programs may be undertaken.

(2) The agency to administer such funds should be composed of citizens selected only on the basis of their interest in and capacity to promote the work of the agency. They should be persons of broad interests in and understanding of the peculiarities of scientific research and education.

(3) The agency should promote research through contracts or grants to organizations outside the Federal Government. It should not operate any laboratories of its own.

(4) Support of basic research in the public and private colleges, universities, and research institutions must leave the internal control of policy, personnel, and the method and scope of research to the institutions themselves. This is of the utmost importance.

(5) While assuring complete independence and freedom for the nature, scope, and methodology of research carried on in the institutions receiving public funds, and while retaining discretion in the allocation of

Note on Science and Higher Education

1. The Vannevar Bush report was produced in response to a letter from President Roosevelt asking Bush to report on "What can the Government do now and in the future to aid research activities by public and private organizations." Bush at the time was head of the Office of Scientific Research and Development, the wartime agency that had responsibility for mobilizing civilian science. He had spent most of his prewar career on the electrical engineering faculty of M.I.T. It is believed that he had a hand in drafting Roosevelt's letter. Daniel J. Kevles, *Preface* to VANNEVAR BUSH, SCIENCE: THE ENDLESS FRONTIER ix, xiii (Nat'l Sci. Found. 1990).

The report was intended in part to present an alternative to the postwar science policy that had been proposed by Senator Harley M. Kilgore of West Virginia. Kilgore's proposal was intended to recognize the stake nonscientists had in the direction of scientific research. His bill would have distributed at least some of the research money on a geographical basis rather than according to the evaluation of scientists. Kilgore also wanted to free science and its economic benefits from domination by big business; his bill would have required government ownership of patents arising from federally sponsored research. In the end, neither bill passed, and the National Science Foundation that was established in 1950 was both smaller and less significant than either sponsor had hoped. JESSICA WANG, AMERICAN SCIENCE IN AN AGE OF ANXIETY: SCIENTISTS, ANTICOMMUNISM, AND THE COLD WAR 26–27, 37 (1999).

Today, the federal government funds roughly sixty-four percent of the research and development conducted at colleges and universities. The bulk of the remaining funds come from the schools themselves; only five percent is from industry. Over the past forty years, federal funding for university research has increased five-fold, as measured in constant dollars. The amount of research done by universities has also increased. They now provide more than fifty percent of the nation's basic research up from thirty-six percent in 1960. Most federal research funding (sixty-three percent) is for medical research and it comes primarily in the form of grants from the National Institutes of Health. *See* American Association for the Advancement of Science, Research and Development at Colleges and Universities, http://www.aaas.org/spp/rd/guiuniv.htm (last visited Aug. 18, 2007).

2. Because the Constitution does not list support for scientific and medical research as an enumerated power of Congress, some questioned whether Congress had sufficient power to provide such support under the general welfare clause. From the beginning, however, the government of the United States was structured to embrace scientific development. The Constitution, in Article 1, Section 8, grants Congress the power "to promote the Progress of Science and Useful Arts, by securing for limited Times to Authors and Inventors the exclusive Right to their respective Writings and Discoveries." The first patent law was passed by Congress in 1790 at the request of President Washington. Between 1837 and 1860, the number of patents annually granted increased from 436 to 4,778. GEORGE N. RAINSFORD, CONGRESS AND HIGHER EDUCATION IN THE NINETEENTH CENTURY 72–73 (1972). In 1836, the Franklin Institute of Philadelphia, under the first federal research contract, provided the Treasury Department with a report on the causes of steam boiler explosions. *See generally* BRUCE SINCLAIR, EARLY RESEARCH AT THE FRANKLIN INSTITUTE: THE INVESTIGATION INTO THE CAUSES OF STEAM BOILER EXPLOSIONS, 1830–1837 (1966). The constitutional qualms were overcome in 1862—a breakthrough year. Congress not only passed the first Morrill Act but also, pursuant to its power to spend for the general welfare, created the Department of Agriculture and directed it to employ "chemists, botanists, entomologist and other persons skilled in the natural sciences pertaining to agriculture." 12 Stat. 388 (1862) (current version codified at 7 U.S.C. § 2210 (1976)). In *United States v. Butler*, 297 U.S. 1 (1936), the Supreme Court held that federal

funds among such institutions, the Foundation proposed herein must be responsible to the President and Congress. Only through such responsibility can we maintain the proper relationship between science and other aspects of a democratic system.

spending could be used to support the general welfare, finally putting the constitutional controversy to rest. *See* LAWRENCE GOSTIN, JUDITH AREEN, PATRICIA KING, STEVEN GOLDBERG & PETER JACOBSON, LAW SCIENCE AND MEDICINE 346 (3d ed. 2005). *See generally* Steven Goldberg, *The Constitutional Status of American Research*, 1979 U. ILL. L. REV. 1.

3. Despite the efforts of some of the founders, science was slow to make inroads in higher education. Chairs of chemistry were established in 1802 at Columbia and 1803 at Yale, but the curriculum remained primarily classical. The first school to emphasize a more practical curriculum was West Point, founded in 1802, which was the nation's principal source of engineers for the first half of the nineteenth century. RAINSFORD at 75.

An important early scientist was Benjamin Peirce, father of Charles Peirce, who was appointed professor of mathematics and natural philosophy at Harvard in 1833 at the age of twenty-four. Peirce championed the career of Alexander Dallas Bache, a great-grandson of Benjamin Franklin, and helped to get him appointed superintendent of the United States Coast Survey (today known as the Coast and Geodetic Survey) the oldest government scientific agency in America. LOUIS MENAND, THE METAPHYSICAL CLUB 152, 157 (2001).

In the 1840s Bache, Peirce, and Louis Agassiz (a Swiss-born scientist who in 1845 was appointed to a Lawrence Scientific School at Harvard and who was a fierce critic of Darwinism) were in a position to control much of the institutional development of science:

> They were a clique, and were careful to keep it that way. At first they called themselves the Florentine Academy (in honor of an oyster bar favored by Bache), but they eventually became known as the Lazzaroni—"the beggars"—for their success in soliciting government funds for science and then directing the money to work they approved. In 1848 they took over the Association of American Geologists and Naturalists, making membership more selective and changed the name to the American Association for the Advancement of Science, an organization they proceeded to dominate for the next decade.... Still, despite their reforms, the Lazzaroni came to find the Association too democratic. They envisioned a national scientific organization modeled on the French Academy—a body that would be frankly elitist, with limited membership and whose pronouncements would carry incontrovertible authority—and in 1863 they persuaded a wartime Congress to establish the National Academy of Sciences as the official scientific advisory body of the federal government. Bache became its first president....

MENAND at 157–58.

President Lincoln signed the law establishing the National Academy of Sciences. The Act provided that:

> the Academy shall, whenever called upon by any department of the Government, investigate, examine, experiment, and report upon any subject of science or art, the actual expense of such investigations, examinations, experiments, and report to be paid from appropriations which may be made for the purpose, but the Academy shall receive no compensation whatever for its services to the Government of the United States.

An Act to Incorporate the National Academy of Sciences, 37 CONG. REC. 806–07 (3d Sess. 1863) (enacted).

4. The first federal agency devoted to education was also established during the middle of the nineteenth century. In 1865, Congressman Ignatius Donnelly of Minnesota introduced a motion calling for a national Bureau of Education "whose duty shall be to enforce education, without regard to race or color, upon the population of all such states as shall fall below a standard to be established by the Congress." CONG. GLOBE, 39th Cong., 1st Sess. 60 (1865). The bill ultimately passed, and a Department of Education was established March 2, 1867. Within a year, however, it was reduced to a Bureau of Education and placed under the Secretary of the Interior. RAINSFORD at 102.

2. DEMOCRATIZING STUDENT ACCESS

The GI Bill

The Serviceman's Readjustment Act[a] was signed into law on June 22, 1944, by President Roosevelt. Better known as the GI Bill of Rights, it had been proposed by the American Legion and included grants for education, employment services, and a home loan program for returning veterans. After passing both houses, the legislation deadlocked in a conference committee chaired by Representative John Rankin of Mississippi who objected to the portion of the bill that would provide benefits to blacks as well as whites. A flight to Washington had to be arranged for Representative John Gibson of Georgia to break the tie, just four days after the D–Day landings at Normandy Beach.[b]

The legislation did more than reward those who fought World War II. As President Clinton observed on the fiftieth anniversary of the GI Bill, it "opened the door to the American dream of opportunity for advancement to an entire generation of young Americans … and paved the way for an unparalleled period of U.S. economic growth and development."[c] It also transformed higher education. Most had predicted that enrollments would increase by about 150,000 per year. In fact, by 1947 there were 1,164,000 veterans registered for college on the GI Bill, some 49 percent of all students enrolled. Over time the Act helped more than 2.2 million World War II veterans attend college, about half of them the first in their families to do so. Another 3.5 million attended other schools, including business schools, trade schools, and high schools.[d]

The benefits were generous. Veterans who served for ninety days were entitled to one year of full time education plus a period equal to their time in service up to a maximum of forty-eight months. The Act authorized payment for tuition, fees and books, and a monthly stipend.

It has been estimated that for every dollar spent on GI Bill education benefits, the nation received as much as eight dollars in income taxes. Although James Conant, president of Harvard, at first feared that unqualified people would flood the campuses, by 1947 he praised the veterans as "the most mature and promising students Harvard has ever had." At least ten Nobel Prize winners were GIs. About 50 percent of the engineers who later worked for NASA took their degrees with the assistance of the GI Bill.[e] The veterans also improved the culture of higher education.[f]

a. 58 Stat. 284, codified as amended at 10 U.S.C. § 16131.

b. SUZANNE METTLER, SOLDIERS TO CITIZENS: THE GI BILL AND THE MAKING OF THE GREATEST GENERATION 20–22 (2005).

c. Proclamation No. 6703, 59 Fed. Reg. 32,643 (June 21, 1994).

d. MILTON GREENBERG, THE GI BILL: THE LAW THAT CHANGED AMERICA 36 (1997).

e. GREENBERG at 39–47.

f. HAROLD M. HYMAN, AMERICAN SINGULARITY: THE 1787 NORTHWEST ORDINANCE, THE 1862 HOMESTEAD AND MORRILL ACTS, AND THE 1944 G.I.BILL 70–71 (1986) ("the competition veterans offered to nonveteran students swiftened the pace of classrooms. Campus dialogue grew more intense.").

Funding for the program did not keep up with the actual costs of attending college. By 2006, the maximum GI Bill amount available to a veteran was $38,700. The average cost of only one year's tuition, room, and board at public institutions, however, was $12,796.[g] In response to criticism from veterans' groups, Congress drafted a new GI Bill that significantly increases education benefits available to veterans.[h] The Post–911 Veteran's Education Assistance Act of 2008 covers the cost of tuition up to the amount charged by the most expensive public university in the veteran's home state. It also provides a housing allowance and up to $1000 for textbooks, and benefits may be transferred to a service member's spouse or dependent. Veterans are eligible for up to 36 months of benefits.[i]

THE PRESIDENT'S COMMISSION ON HIGHER EDUCATION, I HIGHER EDUCATION FOR AMERICAN DEMOCRACY

5–6, 8, 25, 28, 32, 34–35, 67–68, 103 (1947).

. . .

THE ROLE OF EDUCATION

It is a commonplace of the democratic faith that education is indispensable to the maintenance and growth of freedom of thought, faith, enterprise, and association. Thus the social role of education in a democratic society is at once to insure equal liberty and equal opportunity to differing individuals and groups, and to enable the citizens to understand, appraise, and redirect forces, men, and events as these tend to strengthen or to weaken their liberties.

In performing this role, education will necessarily vary its means and methods to fit the diversity of its constituency, but it will achieve its ends more successfully if its programs and policies grow out of and are relevant to the characteristics and needs of contemporary society. Effective democratic education will deal directly with current problems.

This is not to say that education should neglect the past—only that it should not get lost in the past. . . .

At the same time education is the making of the future. Its role in a democratic society is that of critic and leader as well as servant; its task is not merely to meet the demands of the present but to alter those demands if necessary, so as to keep them always suited to democratic ideals. Perhaps its most important role is to serve as an instrument of social transition, and its responsibilities are defined in terms of the kind of civilization society hopes to build.

. . .

A TIME OF CRISIS

The schools and colleges are not solely or even mainly to blame for the situation in which we find ourselves. . . . But the scientific knowledge and technical skills that have made atomic and bacteriological warfare possible

---

g. Steven Manning, *GI Bill's Buying Power Shrinks*, SEATTLE POST-INTELLIGENCER, May 9, 2007.

h. Kim Clark, *The Surprising History of Military College Benefits*, US NEWS & WORLD REPORT, June 17, 2008.

i. United States Department of Veteran Affairs GI Bill Website, http://www.gibill.va.gov/S22/Post_911_Factsheet.pdf (last visited July 30, 2008).

are the products of education and research, and higher education must share proportionately in the task of forging social and political defenses against obliteration. . . .

In light of this situation, the [Commission] has attempted to select, from among the principal goals for higher education, those which should come first in our time. They are to bring to all the people of the Nation:

Education for a fuller realization of democracy in every phase of living.

Education directly and explicitly for international understanding and cooperation.

Education for the application of creative imagination and trained intelligence to the solution of social problems and to the administration of public affairs.

.   .   .

EDUCATION FOR ALL

Education is by far the biggest and most hopeful of the Nation's enterprises. Long ago our people recognized that education for all is not only democracy's obligation but its necessity. Education is the foundation of democratic liberties. Without an educated citizenry alert to preserve and extend freedom, it would not long endure.

.   .   .

[S]pectacular has been the increase in college attendance. In 1900 fewer than 250,000 students, only 4 percent of the population 18 through 21 years of age, were enrolled in institutions of higher education. By 1940 the enrollment had risen to 1,500,000 students, equal to a little less than 16 percent of the 18–21–year-olds. In 1947, enrollments jumped to the theretofore unprecedented peak of 2,354,000 although approximately 1,000,000 of the students were veterans, older than the usual college age because World War II had deferred their education. . . .

This record of growth is encouraging, but we are forced to admit nonetheless that the educational attainments of the American people are still substantially below what is necessary, either for effective individual living or for the welfare of our society.

.   .   .

BARRIERS TO EQUAL OPPORTUNITY

The old, comfortable idea that "any boy can get a college education who has it in him" simply is not true. Low family income, together with the rising costs of education, constitutes an almost impassable barrier to college education for many young people. For some, in fact, the barrier is raised so early in life that it prevents them from attending high school even when free public high schools exist near their homes.

.   .   .

Under the pressure of rising costs and of a relative lessening of public support, the colleges and universities are having to depend more and more on tuition fees to meet their budgets. As a result, on the average, tuition rates rose about 30 percent from 1939 to 1947.

Nor are tuition costs the whole of it. There are not enough colleges and universities in the country, and they are not distributed evenly enough to bring them within reach of all young people. Relatively few students can attend college in their home communities. So to the expense of a college education for most youth must be added transportation and living costs—by no means a small item.

This economic factor explains in large part why the father's occupation has been found in many studies to rank so high as a determining factor in a young person's college expectancy. . . .

. . .

By allowing the opportunity for higher education to depend so largely on the individual's economic status, we are not only denying to millions of young people the chance in life to which they are entitled; we are also depriving the Nation of a vast amount of potential leadership and potential social competence which it sorely needs.

. . .

RACIAL AND RELIGIOUS BARRIERS

The outstanding example of . . . barriers to equal opportunity, of course, is the disadvantages suffered by our Negro citizens. . . . At the college level, the difference is marked; 11 percent of the white population 20 years of age and over had completed at least 1 year of college and almost 5 percent had finished 4 years; whereas for the nonwhites (over 95 percent of whom are Negroes) only a little more than 3 percent had completed at least a year of college and less than 1 ½ percent had completed a full course.

. . .

At the college level, a different form of discrimination is commonly practiced. Many colleges and universities, especially in their professional schools, maintain a selective quota system for admissions, under which the chance to learn, and thereby to become more useful citizens, is denied to certain minorities, particularly to Negroes and Jews.

This practice is a violation of a major American principle and is contributing to the growing tension in one of the crucial areas of our democracy.

The quota . . . is certainly un-American. It is European in origin and application, and we have lately witnessed on that continent the horrors to which, in its logical extension, it can lead. To insist that specialists in any field shall be limited by ethnic quotas is to assume that the Nation is composed of separate and self-sufficient ethnic groups and this assumption American has never made except in the case of its Negro population, where the result is one of the plainest inconsistencies with our national ideal.

The quota system denies the basic American belief that intelligence and ability are present in all ethnic groups, that men of all religious and racial origins should have equal opportunity to fit themselves for contributing to the common life.

Moreover, since the quota system is never applied to all groups in the Nation's population, but only to certain ones, we are forced to conclude that the arguments advanced to justify it are nothing more than rationalizations to cover either convenience or the disposition to discriminate. The quota system cannot be justified on any grounds compatible with democratic principles.

. . .

NUMBERS WHO SHOULD RECEIVE HIGHER EDUCATION

. . .

The Commission believes that in 1960 a minimum of 4,600,000 young people should be enrolled in nonprofit institutions for education beyond the traditional twelfth grade. Of this total number, 2,500,000 should be in the thirteenth and fourteenth grades (junior college level); 1,500,000 in the fifteenth and sixteenth grades; and 600,000 in graduate and professional schools beyond the first degree.

. . .

In arriving at the enrollment recommended for 1960, this Commission gave consideration to the results of the Army General Classification Test: the one test of mental ability that had been given to a large and representative group. During World War II almost 10,000,000 men entering the enlisted Army through induction centers took this test.

. . .

The test data gave the distribution of AGCT [Army General Classification Test] scores for military personnel by the highest year of schooling each individual had completed by the time of induction. . . . It was thus possible to determine the lowest typical AGCT score of those who had completed a given grade of schooling. There were many individuals with less formal schooling who scored as high or higher than the lowest typical score for a given grade. It follows that those individuals have a reasonable expectation of completing that grade. This consequence is the basis for the Commission's estimate of the proportion of the total population with reasonable expectancies of completing an education at specific levels beyond the high school.

. . .

At least 49 percent of our population has the mental ability to complete 14 years of schooling with a curriculum of general and vocational studies that should lead either to gainful employment or to further study at a more advanced level.

At least 32 percent of our population has the mental ability to complete an advanced liberal or specialized professional education.

EDUCATION ADJUSTED TO NEEDS

To make sure of its own health and strength a democratic society must provide free and equal access to education for its youth, and at the same time it must recognize their differences in capacity and purpose. Higher education in America should include a variety of institutional forms and educational programs, so that at whatever point any student leaves school, he will be fitted, within the limits of his mental capacity and educational level, for an abundant and productive life as a person, as a worker, and as a citizen.

THE COMMUNITY COLLEGE

As one means of achieving the expansion of educational opportunity and the diversification of educational offerings it considers necessary, this Commission recommends that the number of community colleges be increased and that their activities be multiplied.

. . .

Whatever form the community college takes, its purpose is educational service to the entire community, and this purpose requires of it a variety of functions and programs. It will provide college education for the youth of the community certainly, so as to remove geographic and economic barriers to educational opportunity and discover and develop individual talents at low cost and easy access. But in addition, the community college will serve as an active center of adult education. . . .

In the past the junior college has most commonly sought to provide within the local community the freshman and sophomore course of the traditional college curriculum. With notable exceptions, it has concentrated on preparing students for further study in the junior and senior years of liberal arts colleges or professional schools.

But preparatory programs looking to the more advanced course of the senior college are not complete and rounded in themselves, and they usually do not serve well the purpose of those who must terminate their schooling at the end of the fourteenth grade. Half of the young people who go to college find themselves unable to complete the full 4–year course, and for a long time to come more students will end their formal education in the junior college years than will prolong it into the senior college. These 2–year graduates would gain more from a terminal program planned specifically to meet their needs than from the first half of a 4–year curriculum.

For this reason, the Commission recommends that the community college emphasize programs of terminal education.

These terminal programs should include both general education and vocational training. They should be designed both for young people who want to secure as good a general education as possible by the end of the fourteenth grade and for those who wish to fit themselves for semiprofessional occupations.

. . .

Education on the technician level—that is the training of medical technicians, dental hygienists, nurses' aides, laboratory technicians—offers one practical solution for the acute shortage of professional personnel in medicine, dentistry, and nursing.

. . .

If the semiprofessional curriculum is to accomplish its purpose, however, it must not be crowded with vocational and technical courses to the exclusion of general education. It must aim at developing a combination of social understanding and technical competence. Semiprofessional education should mix a goodly amount of general education for personal and social development with technical education that is intensive, accurate, and comprehensive enough to give the student command of marketable abilities.

. . .

FEDERAL AID

The radical character of the adjustments required in higher education, their magnitude, and the pressure of time, all mean that neither individual institutions nor national educational organizations have the resources to effect the necessary changes without outside stimulation and financial assistance. These, the Commission believes, will have to come from the Federal Government.

. . .

The Federal Government assumes responsibility for supplementing State and local efforts in military defense against the Nation's enemies without; surely it may as justifiably assume responsibility for supplementing State and local efforts against educational deficiencies and inequalities that are democracy's enemies within.

Questions and Comments on the Truman Commission Report on Higher Education

1. None of the Commission's recommendations was followed:

> President Truman was a Democrat and yet also a financial conservative. He was reluctant to pursue massive higher-education programs funded by the federal government. The report also suffered from bad timing. Truman was already facing a hostile Congress and an unsupportive press, especially with respect to his international programs and national defense policies. This situation, on top of his existing fiscal caution, made him unwilling to expend political capital pushing for an expanded federal role in higher education. . . . In short, the Truman Commission Report was an intriguing policy program that was all dressed up but with no place to go. It had neither the precedent nor the presidential clout to work its way into congressional subcommittees.

JOHN R. THELIN, A HISTORY OF AMERICAN HIGHER EDUCATION 269–70 (2004).

2. Robert Hutchins, then president of the University of Chicago, was as fierce a critic of the Truman Commission Report as he had been of the GI Bill:

> . . . The Report of the President's Commission on Higher Education reflects the educational system with which it deals. It is big and booming. It is confused, confusing, and contradictory. It has something for everybody. It is generous, ignoble, bold, timid, naive, and optimistic. It is filled with the spirit of universal brotherhood and the sense of American superiority. It has great faith in money. It has great faith in courses. It is anti-humanistic and anti-intellectual. It is confident that vices can be turned into virtues by making them larger. Its heart is in the right place; its head does not work very well.

Hutchins, *Report of the President's Commission on Higher Education*, 29 EDUC. REC. 107 (1948).

3. What do you think of the methodology used by the Commission to estimate how many students have the ability to benefit from higher education? What should be made of that fact that fourteen nations are educating more of the relevant age group to the level of a bachelor's degree or its equivalent than the one-third who reach that level in the United States. A number of those nations are educating more than 50 percent of the relevant age group. See chart page 140, *infra*.

Note on Community Colleges

1. Two year colleges have been called "the most successful institutional innovation in twentieth-century American higher education." STEVEN BRINT & JEROME KARABLE, THE DIVERTED DREAM: COMMUNITY COLLEGES AND THE PROMISE OF EDUCATIONAL OPPORTUNITY IN AMERICA, 1900–1985, at 6 (1989). The first community colleges were established not to increase educational opportunity but at the urging of university presidents who wanted to make their institutions more like German research universities. They decided that the first two years of college should be taught at the secondary level. In California, President David Starr Jordan of Stanford, and Alexis Lange, Dean of the School of Education at Berkeley led the effort to encourage what were known as junction colleges. The first opened in 1910. By 1968, California enrolled one-third of all community college students in the nation. Although many consider community colleges to be a way to qualify to transfer to four year colleges, at no point in time did more than half the students enrolled in fact transfer. National Center for Education Statistics, *Community College Students: Goals, Academic Preparation, and Outcomes*, 2003 U.S. DEPT. OF EDUC. 30. Only seventeen percent of community college students earn an associates' degree; another twenty percent eventually earn a bachelor's degree. *Id.* at 34.

2. The Truman Commission took a strong stand in support of vocational and other terminal degree programs at community colleges. Do you agree with their recommendation?

3. Consider Brint and Karabel on community colleges in the postwar period:

> The rapid rise of the junior college in the postwar years made the American system of higher education, which already enrolled a far higher proportion of young people than did the system of any other country, more accessible than it had ever been. From a comparative perspective, what was new about the community college was not that it did not charge tuition or that it enabled people to attend college while living at home: after all, many European universities had long been free of charge.... The community college's innovative character instead resided in three of its other features: it offered two rather than four (or more) years of education; it provided both academic and vocational programs within the same institution; and it was open to the entire population, including adults.... In a sense, the public 2–year college brought to higher education the comprehensive model that Americans had introduced to secondary education: universal access, relatively weak boundaries between curricular offerings, and an orientation of service to the community. By 1980, over 90 percent of the population was within commuting distance of one of the nation's more than nine hundred community colleges.

BRINT & KARABEL at 221–22.

By 2007, 6.6 million students, or nearly half of all undergraduates in the United States, were enrolled in community colleges. Yet these schools receive less than 30 percent of the state and local financing for higher education. John Merrow, *Dream Catchers*, N.Y.TIMES, April 22, 2007, at Education Life 18.

Sweatt v. Painter

Supreme Court of the United States, 1950.
339 U.S. 629, 70 S.Ct. 848, 94 L.Ed. 1114.

■ VINSON, C.J. delivered the opinion of the Court.

This case and *McLaurin v. Oklahoma State Regents*, 339 U.S. 637 [1950], present different aspects of this general question: To what extent does the

Equal Protection Clause of the Fourteenth Amendment limit the power of a state to distinguish between students of different races in professional and graduate education in a state university.... Because of th[e] traditional reluctance to extend constitutional interpretations to situations or facts which are not before the Court, much of the excellent research and detailed argument presented in these cases is unnecessary to their disposition.

In the instant case, petitioner filed an application for admission to the University of Texas Law School for the February, 1946 term. His application was rejected solely because he is a Negro.[1] Petitioner thereupon brought this suit for mandamus against the appropriate school officials, respondents here, to compel his admission. At that time, there was no law school in Texas which admitted Negroes.

The State trial court recognized that the action of the State in denying petitioner the opportunity to gain a legal education while granting it to others deprived him of the equal protection of the laws guaranteed by the Fourteenth Amendment. The court did not grant the relief requested, however, but continued the case for six months to allow the State to supply substantially equal facilities. [S]uch a school was made available, but petitioner refused to register therein....

[The trial court denied mandamus after finding the new law school offered 'privileges, advantages, and opportunities for the study of law substantially equivalent to those offered by the State to white students at the University of Texas.']

The University of Texas Law School, from which petitioner was excluded, was staffed by a faculty of sixteen full-time and three part-time professors, some of whom are nationally recognized authorities in their field. Its student body numbered 850. The library contained over 65,000 volumes. Among the other facilities available to the students were a law review, moot court facilities, scholarship funds, and Order of the Coif affiliation. The school's alumni occupy the most distinguished positions in the private practice of the law and in the public life of the State. It may properly be considered one of the nation's ranking law schools.

The law school for Negroes which was to have opened in February, 1947, would have had no independent faculty or library. The teaching was to be carried on by four members of the University of Texas Law School faculty, who were to maintain their offices at the University of Texas while teaching at both institutions. Few of the 10,000 volumes ordered for the library had arrived,[2] nor was there any full-time librarian. The school lacked accreditation.

Since the trial of this case, respondents report the opening of a law school at the Texas State University for Negroes. It is apparently on the road

1. It appears that the University has been restricted to white students, in accordance with the State law. See TEX. CONST. ART. VII, §§ 7, 14; Tex. Rev. Civ. Stat. Arts. 2643b, 2719, 2900 (Vernon, 1925 and Supp.).

2. "Students of the interim School of Law of the Texas State University for Negroes (located in Austin, whereas the permanent School was to be located at Houston) shall have use of the State Law Library in the Capitol Building...." Tex. Laws 1947, c. 29, § 11, Tex. Rev. Civ. Stat. (Vernon, Supp.), note to Art. 2643b. It is not clear that this privilege was anything more than was extended to all citizens of the State.

to full accreditation. It has a faculty of five full-time professors; a student body of 23; a library of some 16,500 volumes serviced by a full-time staff; a practice court and legal aid association; and one alumnus who has become a member of the Texas Bar.

Whether the University of Texas Law School is compared with the original or the new law school for Negroes, we cannot find substantial equality in the educational opportunities offered white and Negro law students by the State. In terms of number of the faculty, variety of courses and opportunity for specialization, size of the student body, scope of the library, availability of law review and similar activities, the University of Texas Law School is superior. What is more important, the University of Texas Law School possesses to a far greater degree those qualities which are incapable of objective measurement but which make for greatness in a law school. Such qualities, to name but a few, include reputation of the faculty, experience of the administration, position and influence of the alumni, standing in the community, traditions and prestige. It is difficult to believe that one who had a free choice between these law schools would consider the question close.

Moreover, although the law is a highly learned profession, we are well aware that it is an intensely practical one. The law school, the proving ground for legal learning and practice, cannot be effective in isolation from the individuals and institutions with which the law interacts. Few students and no one who has practiced law would choose to study in an academic vacuum, removed from the interplay of ideas and the exchange of views with which the law is concerned. The law school to which Texas is willing to admit petitioner excludes from its student body members of the racial groups which number 85% of the population of the State and include most of the lawyers, witnesses, jurors, judges and other officials with whom petitioner will inevitably be dealing when he becomes a member of the Texas Bar. With such a substantial and significant segment of society excluded, we cannot conclude that the education offered petitioner is substantially equal to that which he would receive if admitted to the University of Texas Law School.

It may be argued that excluding petitioner from that school is no different from excluding white students from the new law school. This contention overlooks realities. It is unlikely that a member of a group so decisively in the majority, attending a school with rich traditions and prestige which only a history of consistently maintained excellence could command, would claim that the opportunities afforded him for legal education were unequal to those held open to petitioner. That such a claim, if made, would be dishonored by the State, is no answer. "Equal protection of the laws is not achieved through indiscriminate imposition of inequalities." *Shelley v. Kraemer*, 334 U.S. 1, 22 (1948).

It is fundamental that these cases concern rights which are personal and present. This Court has stated unanimously that "The State must provide [legal education] for [petitioner] in conformity with the equal protection clause of the Fourteenth Amendment and provide it as soon as it does for applicants of any other group." *Sipuel v. Board of Regents*, 332 U.S. 631, 633 (1948). That case "did not present the issue whether a state might not satisfy the equal protection clause of the Fourteenth Amendment by establishing a separate law school for Negroes." *Fisher v. Hurst*, 333 U.S. 147, 150 (1948). In *State of Missouri ex rel. Gaines v. Canada*, 305 U.S. 337, 351 (1938), the

Court, speaking through Chief Justice Hughes, declared that "petitioner's right was a personal one. It was as an individual that he was entitled to the equal protection of the laws, and the State was bound to furnish him within its borders facilities for legal education substantially equal to those which the State there afforded for persons of the white race, whether or not other Negroes sought the same opportunity." These are the only cases in this Court which present the issue of the constitutional validity of race distinctions in state-supported graduate and professional education.

In accordance with these cases, petitioner may claim his full constitutional right: legal education equivalent to that offered by the State to students of other races. Such education is not available to him in a separate law school as offered by the State. We cannot, therefore, agree with respondents that the doctrine of *Plessy v. Ferguson*, 163 U.S. 537 (1896), requires affirmance of the judgment below. Nor need we reach petitioner's contention that *Plessy v. Ferguson* should be reexamined in the light of contemporary knowledge respecting the purposes of the Fourteenth Amendment and the effects of racial segregation.

We hold that the Equal Protection Clause of the Fourteenth Amendment requires that petitioner be admitted to the University of Texas Law School. The judgment is reversed and the cause is remanded for proceedings not inconsistent with this opinion.

Questions and Comments on *Sweatt v. Painter*

1. In 1947, Herman Sweatt, a letter carrier, chose to go to court rather than to the new law school that had just been established for minority law students in three small basement rooms in Austin, Texas. Thurgood Marshall, head of the NAACP Legal Defense and Education Fund, was his lawyer. Price Daniel, the Attorney General of Texas represented the state. During the five day trial, Marshall called a number of experts who branded the basement law school a subterfuge. Earl Harrison, the dean of the law school at the University of Pennsylvania, testified that classmates are a very important part of legal education. Robert Redfield, the chairman of the department of anthropology at the University of Chicago, testified that segregation "intensifies suspicion and distrust between Negroes and whites, and suspicion and distrust are not favorable conditions either for the acquisition and conduct of an education, or for the discharge of the duties of a citizen." RICHARD KLUGER, SIMPLE JUSTICE: THE HISTORY OF *BROWN V. BOARD OF EDUCATION* AND BLACK AMERICA'S STRUGGLE FOR EQUALITY 263–64 (1975). The trial court ruled against Sweatt. On appeal, the Legal Defense Fund for the first time urged the Supreme Court to overrule *Plessy v. Ferguson*, 163 U.S. 537 (1896), the decision that had established the doctrine that separate but equal public accommodations were acceptable. Sweatt's position was greatly strengthened when the Justice Department filed a brief in *Sweatt* arguing that *Plessy* should be overturned. KLUGER at 277–78. In the end *Plessy* was not overturned until four years later in *Brown v. Board of Education*, 347 U.S. 483 (1954) set forth in Part 3, *infra*.

2. The Supreme Court did not hold discrimination on the basis of gender in admissions in higher education to be unconstitutional until 1996 in *United States v. Virginia*, 518 U.S. 515, set forth at pages 603–13, *infra*. Why would the constitutionality of discrimination on the basis of race be decided before gender discrimination?

Clark Kerr, The Uses of the University

1–3, 6, 31–32, 95 (5th ed. 2001).

The university started as a single community—a community of masters and students. It may even be said to have had a soul in the sense of a central animating principle. Today, the large American university is, rather, a whole series of communities held together by a common name, a common governing board, and related purposes....

... The modern American university ... is not Oxford nor is it Berlin; it is a new type of institution in the world. As a new type of institution, it is not really private and it is not really public; it is neither entirely of the world nor entirely apart from it. It is unique.

"The Idea of a University" was, perhaps, never so well expressed as by Cardinal Newman when engaged in founding the University of Dublin a little over a century ago. His views reflected the Oxford of his day whence he had come. A University, wrote Cardinal Newman, is "the high protecting power of all knowledge and science, of fact and principle, of inquiry and discovery, of experiment and speculation; it maps out the territory of the intellect, and sees that ... there is neither encroachment nor surrender on any side." He favored "liberal knowledge," and said that "useful knowledge" was a "deal of trash."

Newman was particularly fighting the ghost of Bacon who some 250 years before had condemned "a kind of adoration of the mind ... by means whereof men have withdrawn themselves too much from the contemplation of nature, and the observations of experience, and have tumbled up and down in their own reason and conceits." Bacon believed that knowledge should be for the benefit and use of men....

To this Newman replied that "Knowledge is capable of being its own end. Such is the constitution of the human mind, that any kind of knowledge, if it really be such, is its own reward." ... Newman felt that other institutions should carry on research, for "If its object were scientific and philosophical discovery, I do not see why a University should have any students"—an observation sardonically echoed by today's students who often think their professors are not interested in them at all but only in research. A University training, said Newman, "aims at raising the intellectual tone of society, at cultivating the public mind, at purifying the national taste, at supplying true principles to popular enthusiasm and fixed aims to popular aspirations, at giving enlargement and sobriety to the ideas of the age, at facilitating the exercise of political powers, and refining the intercourse of private life." It prepares a man "to fill any post with credit, and to master any subject with facility."

This beautiful world was being shattered forever even as it was being so beautifully portrayed. By 1852, when Newman wrote, the German universities were becoming the new model.... The gentleman "at home in any society" was soon to be at home in none. Science was beginning to take the place of moral philosophy, research the place of teaching.

   . . .

... The University of California [in 1962] had operating expenditures from all sources of nearly half of billion dollars, with almost another 100 million for construction; a total employment of over 40,000 people, more than IBM and in a far greater variety of endeavors; operations in over a hundred locations, counting campuses, experiment stations, agricultural and urban extension center, and projects abroad involving more than fifty countries; nearly 10,000 courses in its catalogues; some form of contact with nearly every industry, nearly every level of government, nearly every person in its region. Vast amounts of expensive equipment were services and maintained. Over 4,000 babies were born in its hospitals. It is the world's largest purveyor of white mice. It will soon have the world's largest primate colony. It will soon also have 100,000 students—30,000 of them at the graduate level; yet much less than one third of its expenditures are directly related to teaching. It already has nearly 200,000 students in extension courses—including one out of every three lawyers and one out of every six doctors in the state. . . .

. . .

The "Idea of a University" was a village with its priests. . . . "The idea of a Multiversity" is a city of infinite variety. Some get lost in the city; some rise to the top within it; most fashion their lives within one of its many subcultures. There is less sense of community than in the village but also less sense of confinement. . . . There are also more refuges of anonymity—both for the creative person and the drifter. As against the village . . . the "city" is more like the totality of civilization as it has evolved and more an integral part of it; and movement to and from the surrounding society has been greatly accelerated. As in a city, there are many separate endeavors under a single rule of law.

The students in the "city" are older, more likely to be married, more vocationally oriented, more drawn from all classes and races than the students in the village; and they find themselves in a most intensely competitive atmosphere. . . .

The multiversity is a confusing place for the student. He has problems of establishing his identity and sense of security within it. But if offers him a vast range of choices, enough literally to stagger the mind. In this range of choices he encounters the opportunities and the dilemmas of freedom. The casualty rate is high. The walking wounded are many. . . .

. . .

At the outset I quoted Cardinal Newman on his "Idea of a University," reflecting the beautiful ivory tower of Oxford as it once was. It seems appropriate to conclude with Alfred North Whitehead's prophetic words in 1916 on the place of intellect: "In the conditions of modern life the rule is absolute: The race which does not value trained intelligence is doomed. Not all your heroism, not all your social charm, not all your wit, not all your victories on land or sea, can move back the finger of fate. Today we maintain ourselves. Tomorrow science will have moved forward yet one more step, and there will be no appeal from the judgment which will be pronounced on the uneducated."

These are the uses of the university.

CALIFORNIA 1960 MASTER PLAN FOR HIGHER EDUCATION (The Donahoe Act)

Amendment to the CAL. EDUC. CODE §§ 22500–22705.

Chapter 1.   General Provisions

22500. Public higher education consists of (1) all public junior colleges heretofore and hereafter established pursuant to law, (2) all state colleges heretofore and hereafter established pursuant to law, and (3) each campus, branch and function of the University of California heretofore and hereafter established by The Regents of the University of California.

. . .

Chapter 2. University of California

22550. The Legislature hereby finds and declares that the University of California is the primary state-supported academic agency for research.

22551. The university may provide instruction in the liberal arts and sciences and in the professions, including the teaching profession. The university has exclusive jurisdiction in public higher education over instruction in the profession of law, and over graduate instruction in the professions of medicine, dentistry, veterinary medicine and architecture.

22552. The university has the sole authority in public higher education to award the doctoral degree in all fields of learning, except that it may agree with the state colleges to award joint doctoral degrees in selected fields.

22553. The university may make reasonable provision for the use of its library and research facilities by qualified members of the faculties of other institutions of public higher education in this State.

Chapter 3. The State College System

22600. The State College System shall be administered by a board designated as the Trustees of the State College System of California, which is hereby created.

. . .

22604. The Trustees of the State College System shall succeed to the powers, duties and functions with respect to the management, administration and control of the state colleges heretofore vested in the State Board of Education or in the Director of Education, including all powers, duties, obligations, and functions specified in Article 2 (commencing at Section 24501) of Chapter 11 of Division 18 of this code, and all obligations assumed by the State Board of Education pursuant to that article prior to July 1, 1961.

. . .

22605. The State College System shall be entirely independent of all political and sectarian influence and kept free therefrom in the appointment of its trustees and in the administration of its affairs, and no person shall be debarred admission to any department of the state colleges on account of sex.

. . .

Chapter 4. Junior Colleges

22650. The public junior colleges shall continue to be a part of the public school system of this State. The State Board of Education shall prescribe minimum standards for the formation and operation of public junior colleges and exercise general supervision over public junior colleges.

22651. Public junior colleges shall offer instruction through but not beyond the fourteenth grade level, which instruction may include, but shall not be limited to, programs in one or more of the following categories: (1) standard collegiate courses for transfer to higher institutions; (2) vocational and technical fields leading to employment; and (3) general or liberal arts courses. Studies in these fields may lead to the associate in arts or associate in science degree.

Note on the California Master Plan for Higher Education

The Plan was developed by Clark Kerr during the administration of Governor Pat Brown. The state needed a plan that would increase both quality and access. The original plan provided that the top 12.5 percent of graduating high school seniors would be guaranteed a place at one of the University of California campuses; the top third would be eligible to attend one of the schools in the California State University system; all applicants would be accepted by community colleges (then called junior colleges), which would prepare students to transfer to one of the other two systems. *See generally* JOHN A. DOUGLAS, THE CALIFORNIA IDEA AND AMERICAN HIGHER EDUCATION, 1850 TO THE 1960 MASTER PLAN (2000).

Nicholas Lemann has looked into the source of these numbers:

> ... Kerr, the labor economist, calculated that one-third of California's workforce needed to be made up of people with administrative or technical training, and one-eighth of people with graduate or professional training; hence, the state colleges should begin admitting only the top one-third of high school graduates and the university only the top eighth. In truth Kerr would have preferred to limit the university to the top tenth, but he thought there would be too much of an outcry.

NICHOLAS LEMANN, THE BIG TEST: THE SECRET HISTORY OF THE AMERICAN MERITOCRACY 131–32 (1999).

Later the plan was modified to guarantee the top 12.5 percent a spot either at a UC campus or in the CSU system. The plan led to a surge in development in California higher education and is credited with helping to develop the state's economy.

In recent years, the commitment to an affordable place in public higher education for all state residents has eroded. A 2004 report estimated that the rising fees (the term "tuition" in not used in the California system) caused as many as 175,000 students or prospective students to drop out or not enroll. Because of the severe budget shortfall, Governor Schwarzenegger required the UC and Cal State systems to cut freshman enrollment by 10 percent. It was the first time the two systems turned away academically eligible students. Rebecca Trounson, *UC System Accepts Record 55,242 Calif. Applicants for Fall Term*, L.A. TIMES, Apr. 20, 2006, at B4.

UC Berkeley and UC Los Angeles are more economically diverse than most selective universities. Currently, 37 percent of the students enrolled at UC Los Angeles and 34 percent of those enrolled at UC Berkeley receive Pell Grants, which provide up to $4,050 annually in need-based tuition assistance from the federal government. The next most economically diverse selective university is Columbia with 16 percent of its students receiving Pell Grants. *Economic Diversity Among Top Ranked Schools*, U.S. NEWS AND WORLD REPORT, Aug. 28, 2006, at 111.

3. THE FIRST AMENDMENT ON CAMPUS

More than half a century elapsed after the AAUP issued its Declaration of Principles on Academic Freedom before the Supreme Court declared that academic freedom was "a special concern of the First Amendment."[1] Beginning in the 1950s, individual justices discussed the importance of academic freedom in a series of

---

1. Keyishian v. Board of Regents of the University of the State of New York, 385 U.S. 589, 603 (1967).

decisions that arose out of the cold war atmosphere that gripped the nation after the end of World War II. In *Sweezy v. New Hampshire*, for the first time a majority of the Court praised academic freedom, but they could not agree on a constitutional basis for deciding the case.

Sweezy v. New Hampshire

Supreme Court of the United States, 1957.
354 U.S. 234, 77 S.Ct. 1203, 1 L.Ed.2d 1311.

■ MR. CHIEF JUSTICE WARREN announced the judgment of the Court and delivered an opinion, in which MR. JUSTICE BLACK, MR. JUSTICE DOUGLAS, AND MR. JUSTICE BRENNAN join.

This case ... brings before us a question concerning the constitutional limits of legislative inquiry. The investigation here was conducted under the aegis of a state legislature, rather than a House of Congress.... The ultimate question here is whether the investigation deprived Sweezy of due process of law under the Fourteenth Amendment. For the reasons to be set out in this opinion, we conclude that the record in this case does not sustain the power of the State to compel the disclosures that the witness refused to make.

. . .

The investigation in which petitioner was summoned to testify had its origins in a statute passed by the New Hampshire legislature in 1951. It was a comprehensive scheme of regulation of subversive activities. There was a section defining criminal conduct in the nature of sedition. "Subversive organizations" were declared unlawful and ordered dissolved. "Subversive persons" were made ineligible for employment by the state government. Included in the disability were those employed as teachers or in other capacities by any public educational institution. A loyalty program was instituted to eliminate "subversive persons" among government personnel. All present employees, as well as candidates for elective office in the future, were required to make sworn statements that they were not "subversive persons."

In 1953, the legislature adopted a "Joint Resolution Relating to the Investigation of Subversive Activities." It was resolved:

> That the attorney general is hereby authorized and directed to make full and complete investigation with respect to violations of the subversive activities act of 1951 and to determine whether subversive persons as defined in said act are presently located within this state. The attorney general is authorized to act upon his own motion and upon such information as in his judgment may be reasonable or reliable....

. . .

Under state law, this was construed to constitute the Attorney General as a one-man legislative committee. He was given the authority to delegate any part of the investigation to any member of his staff. The legislature conferred upon the Attorney General the further authority to subpoena witnesses or documents. He did not have power to hold witnesses in contempt, however. In the event that coercive or punitive sanctions were needed, the Attorney

General could invoke the aid of a State Superior Court which could find recalcitrant witnesses in contempt of court.

. . .

[The Attorney General summoned petitioner, who answered questions regarding his past conduct, associations, and World War II service with the Office of Strategic Services. Petitioner denied ever belonging to the Communist Party or participating in a "program to overthrow the government by force or violence."]

During the course of the inquiry, petitioner declined to answer several questions [regarding his knowledge of the Progressive Party of New Hampshire, his wife's associations with that party, or his own opinions and beliefs on the grounds that the questions were not pertinent to the state's inquiry or violated the First Amendment]. His reasons for doing so were given in a statement he read to the Committee at the outset of the hearing.[6]

. . .

The Attorney General also turned to a subject which had not yet occurred at the time of the first hearing. On March 22, 1954, petitioner had delivered a lecture to a class of 100 students in the humanities course at the University of New Hampshire. This talk was given at the invitation of the faculty teaching that course. Petitioner had addressed the class upon such

---

6. "Those called to testify before this and other similar investigations can be classified in three categories.

"First there are Communists and those who have reason to believe that even if they are not Communists they have been accused of being and are in danger of harassment and prosecution.

"Second, there are those who approve of the purposes and methods of these investigations.

"Third, there are those who are not Communists and do not believe they are in danger of being prosecuted, but who yet deeply disapprove of the purposes and methods of these investigations.

"The first group will naturally, and I think wholly justifiably, plead the constitutional privilege of not being witnesses against themselves.

"The second group will equally naturally be cooperative witnesses.

"The third group is faced with an extremely difficult dilemma. I know because I belong to this third group, and I have been struggling with its problems for many weeks now. I would like to explain what the nature of that dilemma is. I think it is important that both those conducting these inquiries and the public should understand.

"It is often said: If a person is not a Communist and has nothing to fear, why should he not answer whatever questions are put to him and be done with it? The answer, of course, is that some of us believe these investigations are evil and dangerous, and we do not want to give our approval to them, either tacitly or otherwise. On the contrary, we want to oppose them to the best of our ability and persuade others to do likewise, with the hope of eventually abolishing them altogether. . . .

. . . .

. . . We do not know the whole story, but enough has come out to show that the Attorney General has issued a considerable number of subpoenas and has held hearings in various parts of the state. And so far as the available information allows us to judge, most of those subpoenaed have fallen into one or both of two groups: first professors at Dartmouth and the University of New Hampshire who have gained a reputation for liberal or otherwise unorthodox views, and, second, people who have been active in the Progressive Party. It should be specially noted that whatever may be thought of the Progressive Party in any other respect, it was certainly not devoted to violent overthrow of constitutional forms of government but on the contrary to effecting reforms through the very democratic procedures which are the essence of constitutional forms of government."

invitations in the two preceding years as well. He declined to answer the following questions:

"What was the subject of your lecture?"

"Didn't you tell the class at the University of New Hampshire on Monday, March 22, 1954, that Socialism was inevitable in this country?"

"Did you advocate Marxism at that time?"

"Did you express the opinion, or did you make the statement at that time that Socialism was inevitable in America?"

"Did you in this last lecture on March 22 or in any of the former lectures espouse the theory of dialectical materialism?"

. . .

Following the hearings, the Attorney General petitioned the Superior Court of Merrimack County, New Hampshire, setting forth the circumstances of petitioner's appearance before the Committee and his refusal to answer certain questions. The petition prayed that the court propound the questions to the witness. After hearing argument, the court ruled that the questions set out above were pertinent. Petitioner was called as a witness by the court and persisted in his refusal to answer for constitutional reasons. The court adjudged him in contempt and ordered him committed to the county jail until purged of the contempt.

. . .

There is no doubt that legislative investigations, whether on a federal or state level, are capable of encroaching upon the constitutional liberties of individuals. . . .

In this case, the investigation is governed by provisions in the New Hampshire Subversive Activities Act of 1951. . . .

"Subversive persons" are defined in many gradations of conduct. Our interest is in the minimal requirements of that definition since they will outline its reach. According to the statute, a person is a "subversive person" if he, by any means, aids in the commission of any act intended to assist in the alteration of the constitutional form of government by force or violence. The possible remoteness from armed insurrection of conduct that could satisfy these criteria is obvious from the language. The statute goes well beyond those who are engaged in efforts designed to alter the form of government by force or violence. The statute declares, in effect, that the assistant of an assistant is caught up in the definition. This chain of conduct attains increased significance in light of the lack of a necessary element of guilty knowledge in either stage of assistants. The State Supreme Court has held that the definition encompasses persons engaged in the specified conduct " . . . whether or not done 'knowingly and willfully. . . .' " *Nelson v. Wyman*, 99 N.H. 33, 39, 105 A. 2d 756, 763. The potential sweep of this definition extends to conduct which is only remotely related to actual subversion and which is done completely free of any conscious intent to be a part of such activity.

The statute's definition of "subversive organizations" is also broad. An association is said to be any group of persons, whether temporarily or permanently associated together, for joint action or advancement of views on any subject. An organization is deemed subversive if it has a purpose to abet, advise or teach activities intended to assist in the alteration of the constitutional form of government by force or violence.

The situation before us is in many respects analogous to that in *Wieman v. Updegraff*, 344 U.S. 183. The Court held there that a loyalty oath prescribed by the State of Oklahoma for all its officers and employees violated the requirements of the Due Process Clause because it entailed sanctions for membership in subversive organizations without scienter. A State cannot, in attempting to bar disloyal individuals from its employ, exclude persons solely on the basis of organizational membership, regardless of their knowledge concerning the organizations to which they belonged. . . .

The sanction emanating from legislative investigations is of a different kind than loss of employment. But the stain of the stamp of disloyalty is just as deep. The inhibiting effect in the flow of democratic expression and controversy upon those directly affected and those touched more subtly is equally grave. Yet here, as in *Wieman*, the program for the rooting out of subversion is drawn without regard to the presence or absence of guilty knowledge in those affected.

The nature of the investigation which the Attorney General was authorized to conduct is revealed by this case. He delved minutely into the past conduct of petitioner, thereby making his private life a matter of public record. The questioning indicates that the investigators had thoroughly prepared for the interview and were not acquiring new information as much as corroborating data already in their possession. On the great majority of questions, the witness was cooperative, even though he made clear his opinion that the interrogation was unjustified and unconstitutional. Two subjects arose upon which petitioner refused to answer: his lectures at the University of New Hampshire, and his knowledge of the Progressive Party and its adherents.

The state courts upheld the attempt to investigate the academic subject on the ground that it might indicate whether petitioner was a "subversive person." What he taught the class at a state university was found relevant to the character of the teacher. The State Supreme Court carefully excluded the possibility that the inquiry was sustainable because of the state interest in the state university. There was no warrant in the authorizing resolution for that. The sole basis for the inquiry was to scrutinize the teacher as a person, and the inquiry must stand or fall on that basis.

. . .

The State Supreme Court . . . conceded without extended discussion that petitioner's right to lecture and his right to associate with others were constitutionally protected freedoms which had been abridged through this investigation. These conclusions could not be seriously debated. Merely to summon a witness and compel him, against his will, to disclose the nature of his past expressions and associations is a measure of governmental interference in these matters. These are rights which are safeguarded by the Bill of Rights and the Fourteenth Amendment. We believe that there unquestionably was an invasion of petitioner's liberties in the areas of academic freedom and political expression—areas in which government should be extremely reticent to tread.

The essentiality of freedom in the community of American universities is almost self-evident. No one should underestimate the vital role in a democracy that is played by those who guide and train our youth. To impose any strait jacket upon the intellectual leaders in our colleges and universities would imperil the future of our Nation. No field of education is so thoroughly comprehended by man that new discoveries cannot yet be made. Particularly is that true in the social sciences, where few, if any, principles are accepted as absolutes. Scholarship cannot flourish in an atmosphere of suspicion and distrust. Teachers and students must always remain free to inquire, to study and to evaluate, to gain new maturity and understanding; otherwise our civilization will stagnate and die.

. . .

We do not now conceive of any circumstance wherein a state interest would justify infringement of rights in these fields. But we do not need to reach such fundamental questions of state power to decide this case. The State Supreme Court itself recognized that there was a weakness in its conclusion that the menace of forcible overthrow of the government justified sacrificing constitutional rights. There was a missing link in the chain of reasoning. The syllogism was not complete. There was nothing to connect the questioning of petitioner with this fundamental interest of the State. Petitioner had been interrogated by a one-man legislative committee, not by the legislature itself. . . .

In light of this, the state court emphasized a factor in the authorizing resolution which confined the inquiries which the Attorney General might undertake to the object of the investigation. . . . The New Hampshire legislature specified that the Attorney General should act only when he had information which " . . . in his judgment may be reasonable or reliable." The state court construed this to mean that the Attorney General must have something like probable cause for conducting a particular investigation. It is not likely that this device would prove an adequate safeguard against unwarranted inquiries. . . .

. . .

As a result, neither we nor the state courts have any assurance that the questions petitioner refused to answer fall into a category of matters upon which the legislature wanted to be informed when it initiated this inquiry. The judiciary are thus placed in an untenable position. Lacking even the elementary fact that the legislature wants certain questions answered and recognizing that petitioner's constitutional rights are in jeopardy, we are asked to approve or disapprove his incarceration for contempt.

In our view, the answer is clear. No one would deny that the infringement of constitutional rights of individuals would violate the guarantee of due process where no state interest underlies the state action. Thus, if the Attorney General's interrogation of petitioner were in fact wholly unrelated to the object of the legislature in authorizing the inquiry, the Due Process Clause would preclude the endangering of constitutional liberties. We believe that an equivalent situation is presented in this case. The lack of any indications that the legislature wanted the information the Attorney General attempted to elicit from petitioner must be treated as the absence of authority. It follows that the use of the contempt power, notwithstanding the interference with constitutional rights, was not in accordance with the due process requirements of the Fourteenth Amendment.

. . .

The judgment of the Supreme Court of New Hampshire is [reversed].

■ MR. JUSTICE FRANKFURTER, whom MR. JUSTICE HARLAN JOINS, concurring in the result.

In assessing the claim of the State of New Hampshire to the information denied it by petitioner, we cannot concern ourselves with the fact that New Hampshire chose to make its Attorney General in effect a standing committee of its legislature for the purpose of investigating the extent of "subversive" activities within its bounds. The case must be judged as though the whole body of the legislature had demanded the information of petitioner. It would make the deepest inroads upon our federal system for this Court now to hold that it can determine the appropriate distribution of powers and their delegation within the forty-eight States....

. . .

The New Hampshire Supreme Court, although recognizing that such inquiries "undoubtedly interfered with the defendant's free exercise" of his constitutionally guaranteed right to lecture, justified the interference on the ground that it would occur "in the limited area in which the legislative committee may reasonably believe that the overthrow of existing government by force and violence is being or has been taught, advocated or planned, an area in which the interest of the State justifies this intrusion upon civil liberties." According to the court, the facts that made reasonable the Committee's belief that petitioner had taught violent overthrow in his lecture were that he was a Socialist with a record of affiliation with groups cited by the Attorney General of the United States or the House Un–American Activities Committee and that he was co-editor of an article stating that, although the authors hated violence, it was less to be deplored when used by the Soviet Union than by capitalist countries.

When weighed against the grave harm resulting from governmental intrusion into the intellectual life of a university, such justification for compelling a witness to discuss the contents of his lecture appears grossly inadequate. Particularly is this so where the witness has sworn that neither in the lecture nor at any other time did he ever advocate overthrowing the Government by force and violence.

Progress in the natural sciences is not remotely confined to findings made in the laboratory. Insights into the mysteries of nature are born of hypothesis and speculation. The more so is this true in the pursuit of understanding in the groping endeavors of what are called the social sciences, the concern of which is man and society. The problems that are the respective preoccupations of anthropology, economics, law, psychology, sociology and related areas of scholarship are merely departmentalized dealing, by way of manageable division of analysis, with interpenetrating aspects of holistic perplexities. For society's good—if understanding be an essential need of society—inquiries into these problems, speculations about them, stimulation in others of reflection upon them, must be left as unfettered as possible. Political power must abstain from intrusion into this activity of freedom, pursued in the interest of wise government and the people's well-being, except for reasons that are exigent and obviously compelling.

These pages need not be burdened with proof, based on the testimony of a cloud of impressive witnesses, of the dependence of a free society on free universities. This means the exclusion of governmental intervention in the intellectual life of a university. It matters little whether such intervention occurs avowedly or through action that inevitably tends to check the ardor and fearlessness of scholars, qualities at once so fragile and so indispensable for fruitful academic labor.... Suffice it to quote the latest expression on this subject. It is also perhaps the most poignant because its plea on behalf of continuing the free spirit of the open universities of South Africa has gone unheeded.

> In a university knowledge is its own end, not merely a means to an end. A university ceases to be true to its own nature if it becomes the tool of Church or State or any sectional interest. A university is characterized by the spirit of free inquiry, its ideal being the ideal of Socrates—'to follow the argument where it leads.' This implies the right to examine, question, modify or reject traditional ideas and beliefs. Dogma and hypothesis are incompatible, and the concept of an immutable doctrine is repugnant to the spirit of a university. The concern of its scholars is not merely to add and revise facts in relation to an accepted framework, but to be ever examining and modifying the framework itself.
>
> . . .
>
> ... It is the business of a university to provide that atmosphere which is most conducive to speculation, experiment and creation. It is an atmosphere in which there prevail "the four essential freedoms" of a university—to determine for itself on academic grounds who may teach, what may be taught, how it shall be taught, and who may be admitted to study.

The Open Universities in South Africa 10–12. (A statement of a conference of senior scholars from the University of Cape Town and the University of the Witwatersrand, including A. v. d. S. Centlivres and Richard Feetham, as Chancellors of the respective universities.[1])

I do not suggest that what New Hampshire has here sanctioned bears any resemblance to the policy against which this South African remonstrance was directed. I do say that in these matters of the spirit inroads on legitimacy must be resisted at their incipiency. This kind of evil grows by what it is allowed to feed on. The admonition of this Court in another context is applicable here. "It may be that it is the obnoxious thing in its mildest and least repulsive form; but illegitimate and unconstitutional practices get their first footing in that way, namely, by silent approaches and slight deviations from legal modes of procedure." *Boyd v. United States*, 116 U.S. 616, 635.

. . .

To be sure, this is a conclusion based on a judicial judgment in balancing two contending principles—the right of a citizen to political privacy, as protected by the Fourteenth Amendment, and the right of the

---

1. The Hon. A. v. d. S. Centlivres only recently retired as Chief Justice of South Africa, and the Hon. Richard Feetham is also an eminent, retired South African judge.

State to self-protection. And striking the balance implies the exercise of judgment. This is the inescapable judicial task in giving substantive content, legally enforced, to the Due Process Clause, and it is a task ultimately committed to this Court. It must not be an exercise of whim or will. It must be an overriding judgment founded on something much deeper and more justifiable than personal preference. As far as it lies within human limitations, it must be an impersonal judgment. It must rest on fundamental presuppositions rooted in history to which widespread acceptance may fairly be attributed. Such a judgment must be arrived at in a spirit of humility when it counters the judgment of the State's highest court. But, in the end, judgment cannot be escaped—the judgment of this Court.

And so I am compelled to conclude that the judgment of the New Hampshire court must be reversed.

■ MR. JUSTICE CLARK, with whom MR. JUSTICE BURTON joins, dissenting.

The Court today has denied the State of New Hampshire the right to investigate the extent of "subversive activities" within its boundaries in the manner chosen by its legislature. Unfortunately there is no opinion for the Court, for those who reverse are divided and they do so on entirely different grounds. Four of my Brothers join in what I shall call the principal opinion. They hold that the appointment of the Attorney General to act as a committee for the legislature results in a separation of its power to investigate from its "responsibility to direct the use of that power" and thereby "causes a deprivation of the constitutional rights of individuals and a denial of due process...." This theory was not raised by the parties and is, indeed, a novel one.

. . .

My Brothers FRANKFURTER and HARLAN do not agree with this opinion because they conclude, as do I, that the internal affairs of the New Hampshire State Government are of no concern to us. They do join in the reversal, however, on the ground that Sweezy's rights under the First Amendment have been violated. I agree with neither opinion.

. . .

Since the conclusion of a majority of those reversing is not predicated on the First Amendment questions presented, I see no necessity for discussing them. But since the principal opinion devotes itself largely to these issues I believe it fair to ask why they have been given such an elaborate treatment when the case is decided on an entirely different ground. It is of no avail to quarrel with a straw man.... Since a majority of the Court has not passed on these problems here, and since I am not convinced that the State's interest in investigating subversive activities for the protection of its citizens is outweighed by any necessity for the protection of Sweezy. I would affirm the judgment of the New Hampshire Supreme Court.

Questions and Comments on *Sweezy*

1. The *Sweezy* opinion was released only weeks after the death of Senator Joseph McCarthy. In 1950, McCarthy had made headlines by announcing he had a list of 205 employees of the State Department who were card-carrying Communists. When asked to back up his claim, he bluffed, offering to show the list to a reporter but then

"discovered" he had left it in another suit. McCarthy's attacks escalated until he took on the Army itself in June, 1954. Televised hearings of his attack enabled the American people to judge his actions for themselves; in the ensuing weeks his unfavorable poll ratings rose from 29 to 51 percent. Shortly thereafter the Senate censured him by a vote of 67 to 22. GEOFFREY R. STONE, PERILOUS TIMES: FREE SPEECH IN WARTIME 375–91 (2004).

2. Writing for the plurality in *Sweezy*, Chief Justice Warren stated "there unquestionably was an invasion of *petitioner's* liberties in the areas of academic freedom and political expression." By contrast, Justice Frankfurter in his concurrence quotes the four essential freedoms *of a university*. Why would Frankfurter suggest that academic freedom is a university right rather than an individual right? Is it, or do both individuals and institutions of higher education have rights to academic freedom? Was Frankfurter's concurrence shaped by the fact that Sweezy was not a faculty member? The report Frankfurter quotes says the four freedoms are to be determined "on academic grounds." Does this mean the board of directors or the administration is to decide them on academic grounds or does it mean that faculty must be involved in the determination? How could a board made up of nonfaculty make decisions "on academic grounds?"

3. Do all faculty members, including adjunct faculty and instructors, have as much academic freedom as tenured faculty?

The Free Speech Movement

Although teaching always has been central to the mission of colleges and universities, for centuries students had little say in their education. When German universities developed the concept of *Lehrfreiheit*, or academic freedom for faculty, they also espoused *Lernfreiheit*, or freedom to learn for students. According to Walter Metzger, *Lernfreiheit* amounted to a disclaimer by the university of any control over what a student must study except for courses needed to prepare for state examinations. It also freed the university of any responsibility for the private conduct of students as long as they kept the peace and paid their bills.[a] American colleges and universities, by contrast, followed Cambridge and Oxford in taking a more paternalistic attitude toward their students until the late nineteenth century and the emergence of the first research universities.

The beginning of a major change in the role of students in higher education can be traced quite precisely to the fall of 1964. Ironically, it was the very multiversity celebrated by Clark Kerr that gave birth to what became known as the Free Speech Movement.[b]

During the summer of 1964, students from around the United States traveled to Mississippi to register impoverished African Americans to vote. Todd Gitlin has chronicled the link between Freedom Summer and the Free Speech Movement:

> The boldness of unlettered heroes was part of the spirit that summer volunteers like [Mario] Savio and Jack Weinberg brought back to the Berkeley campus that fall—along with a respect for the

a. Walter P. Metzger, *Profession and Constitution: Two Definitions of Academic Freedom in America*, 66 TEX. L. REV. 1265, 1269 (1988).

b. For more on the Free Speech Movement, *see generally* THE BERKELEY STUDENT REVOLT: FACTS AND INTERPRETATIONS (Seymour Martin Lipset & Sheldon S. Wolin eds., 1965); THE FREE SPEECH MOVEMENT: REFLECTIONS ON BERKELEY IN THE 1960s (Robert Cohen & Reginald E. Zelnik eds., 2002); CLARK KERR, 2 THE GOLD AND THE BLUE: A PERSONAL MEMOIR OF THE UNIVERSITY OF CALIFORNIA 1949–1967 (2003); VERNE A. STADTMAN, THE UNIVERSITY OF CALIFORNIA 1868–1968 (1970).

power of civil disobedience, a fierce moralism, a lived love for racial equality, a distaste for bureaucratic highhandedness and euphemism, a taste for relentless talk at intense mass meetings on the way toward consensus. There were already five years of student protest to build on at Berkeley, but the usual organizers did not expect much to flare up that fall.... Mississippi was the ignition. When University of California administrators knuckled under to local right-wing politicians and refused to permit the recruitment of civil rights demonstrators or the raising of [civil rights] movement money on campus, Savio, Weinberg, and others recognized a paternalism familiar from Mississippi.... On October 1, 1964, Jack Weinberg sat down at his "unauthorized" recruitment table in Sproul Plaza, violating campus rules, and was arrested; the police put him in the back of their car; other students sat down and blocked it for thirty-two hours; Savio among others spoke from its roof; and the Free Speech Movement ... was born.[c]

For a time, students were persuaded by Savio and other student leaders to accept a compromise worked out with Clark Kerr and representatives of the University that expanded their speech rights. But in late November, several FSM leaders, including Savio, received letters that formally charged them for acts that allegedly took place during the police car sit-in including encouragement of the demonstrators and intimidation of police. Believing that the decision to act against the leaders of FSM violated the spirit of the compromise that had been worked out, FSM students scheduled a sit-in for December 2.

At the rally on Sproul Hall steps on December 2, Savio spoke to the crowd:

We have an autocracy which runs this university. It's managed. We asked the following: if President Kerr actually tried to get something more liberal out of the Regents in his telephone conversation, why didn't he make some public statement to that effect? And the answer we received—from a well-meaning liberal—was the following: He said, "Would you ever imagine the manager of a firm making a statement publicly in opposition to his board of directors?" That's the answer! Now, I ask you to consider: if this is a firm, and if the Board of Regents are the board of directors, and if President Kerr in fact is the manager, then I'll tell you something: the faculty are a bunch of employees, and we're the raw material! But we're a bunch of raw material[s] that don't mean to have any process upon us, don't mean to be made into any product, don't mean to end up being bought by some clients of the University, be they the government, be they industry, be they organized labor, be they anyone! We're human beings!

[Applause]

There is a time when the operation of the machine becomes so odious, makes you so sick at heart, that you can't take part; you can't even passively take part, and you've got to put your bodies upon the gears and upon the wheels, upon the levers, upon all the apparatus, and you've got to make it stop. And you've got to

c. TODD GITLIN, THE SIXTIES: YEARS OF
Hope, Days of Rage 163–64 (1993).

indicate to the people who run it, to the people who own it, that unless you're free, the machine will be prevented from working at all![d]

As Joan Baez sang the civil-rights anthem "We Shall Overcome," some one thousand people entered Sproul Hall for a sit-in.

Mario Savio, *An End to History, in* THE BERKELEY STUDENT REVOLT

216–19 (Seymour Martin Lipset & Sheldon S. Wolin eds., 1965).[e]

Last summer I went to Mississippi to join the struggle there for civil rights. This fall I am engaged in another phase of the same struggle, this time in Berkeley. The two battlefields may seem quite different to some observers, but this is not the case. The same rights are at stake in both places—the right to participate as citizens in democratic society and the right to due process of law. Further, it is a struggle against the same enemy. In Mississippi an autocratic and powerful minority rules, through organized violence. In California, the privileged minority manipulates the university bureaucracy to suppress the students' political expressions. That "respectable" bureaucracy masks the financial plutocrats; that impersonal bureaucracy is the efficient enemy in a "Brave New World."

In our free-speech fight at the University of California, we have come up against what may emerge as the greatest problem of our nation—depersonalized, unresponsive bureaucracy. . . . [W]e find it impossible usually to meet with anyone but secretaries. Beyond that, we find functionaries who cannot make policy but can only hide behind the rules. . . .

As a bureaucrat, an administrator believes that nothing new happens. He occupies an a-historical point of view. In September, to get the attention of this bureaucracy which had issued arbitrary edicts suppressing student political expression and refused to discuss its actions, we held a sit-in on campus. We sat around a police car and kept it immobilized for over thirty-two hours. At last, the administrative bureaucracy agreed to negotiate. But instead, on the following Monday, we discovered that a committee had been appointed, in accordance with usual regulations, to resolve the disputes. Our attempt to convince any of the administrators that an event had occurred, that something new had happened, failed. They saw this simply as something to be handled by normal university procedures.

The same is true of all bureaucracies. They begin as tools, means to certain legitimate goals, and they end up feeding their own existence. . . .

. . .

Here is the real contradiction: the bureaucrats hold history as ended. As a result significant parts of the population both on campus and off are dispossessed. . . . It is out of this that the conflict has occurred with the

---

d. Mario Savio, Dec. 2, 1964, http:// www.lib.berkeley.edu/MRC/saviotranscript.html. For online video of the speech, see American Rhetoric: Mario Savio–Sproul Hall Sit–In Address, http://www.americanrhetoric.com/speeches/mariosaviosproulhallsitin.htm.

e. This article was taken from a tape of a speech Savio gave in Sproul Hall during the December sit-in.

university bureaucracy and will continue to occur until that bureaucracy becomes responsive or until it is clear the university cannot function.

The things we are asking for in our ... protests have a deceptively quaint ring. We are asking for ... due process of law. We are asking for our actions to be judged by committees of our peers. We are asking that regulations ought to be considered as arrived at legitimately only from the consensus of the governed. These phrases are all pretty old, but they ... are not being taken seriously on the Berkeley campus.

. . .

The university is a place where people begin seriously to question the conditions of their existence and raise the issue of whether they can be committed to the society they have been born into. After a long period of apathy during the fifties, students have begun not only to question but, having arrived at answers, to act on those answers. This is part of a growing understanding among many people in America that history has not ended, that a better society is possible, and that it is worth dying for.

This free-speech fight points up a fascinating aspect of contemporary campus life. Students are permitted to talk all they want so long as their speech has no consequences.

One conception of the university, suggested by a classical Christian formulation, is that it be in the world but not of the world. The conception of Clark Kerr by contrast is that the university is part and parcel of this particular stage in the history of American society; it stands to serve the need of America industry; it is a factory that turns out a certain product needed by industry or government. Because speech does often have consequences which might alter this perversion of higher education, the university must put itself in a position of censorship. It can permit ... speech which encourages continuation of the status quo. . . . But if someone advocates sit-ins to bring about changes in discriminatory hiring practices, this cannot be permitted. . . .

The administration of Berkeley campus has admitted that external, extra-legal groups have pressured the university not to permit students on campus to organize picket lines. . . . And the bureaucracy went along. Speech with consequences, speech in the area of civil rights, speech which some might regard as illegal, must stop.

Many people here at the university ... are wandering aimlessly about. Strangers in their own lives, there is no place for them here. They are people who have not learned to compromise, who for example have come to the university to learn to question, to grow, to learn—all the standard things that sound like clichés because no one takes them seriously. And they find out at one point or other that for them to become part of society, to become lawyers, ministers, businessmen, people in government, that very often they have to compromise those principles which were most dear to them. They must suppress the most creative impulses that they have; this is a prior condition for being part of the system. The university is well equipped to produce that sort of person. . . .

. . . American society in the standard conception it has of itself is simply no longer exciting. The most exciting things going on in America today are movements to change America. America is becoming ever more the utopia of sterilized, automated contentment. The "futures" and "careers" for which American students now prepare are for the most part intellectual and moral wastelands. This chrome-plated consumers' paradise would have us grow up to be well-behaved children. But an important minority of men and women coming to the front today have shown that they will die rather than be standardized, replaceable and irrelevant.

Note on the Aftermath

1. On December 3, 1964, Governor Brown ordered the arrest of some eight hundred protesting students.

The arrested students were charged with trespass and failure to disperse from a place of unlawful assembly. Those who went limp instead of walking once they had been arrested were also charged with resisting arrest. One of their lawyers later reported that "simply learning who had been arrested and finding a way to facilitate communication were very difficult. This was, after all, decades before everyone was on email." Malcolm Burnstein, *The FSM: A Movement Lawyer's Perspective, in* The Free Speech Movement: Reflections on Berkeley in the 1960s, at 433, 438 (Robert Cohen & Reginald E. Zelnick eds., 2002). Defense counsel moved for a mass jury trial of all defendants on those issues common to everyone. The judge denied the motion. The prosecution wanted to separate those arrested into groups of ten to be tried ten at a time. The compromise agreed to was a single trial before the judge rather than a jury. A representative group of 155 defendants were selected to take part in the actual trial, which took eleven weeks. The judge acquitted the defendants for failing to disperse, but convicted them of trespass and, for those who went limp after arrest, of resisting arrest. For sentencing, the judge asked each defendant to write a letter explaining why he or she had joined in the sit-in. Instead of expressions of contrition or regret, most wrote they felt they had no choice if they were to secure their constitutional rights. (The letters are on file at the Bancroft Library at the University of California). The ten who were considered leaders of the sit-in were sentenced to from 30 to 120 days in jail. The other defendants were sentenced to probation during which they were enjoined from committing civil disobedience. Those who refused that condition were given fines or jail time. Appeals were filed but denied. Burnstein adds that "For years following the trial we received calls from numbers of defendants seeking assistance in obtaining states' licenses where the FSM conviction was being used to deny the license by overzealous or timid state bureaucrats." *Id.* at 444.

2. On December 8, 1964, the Berkeley faculty adopted a resolution by a vote of 824 to 115 that generally supported the position of the FSM. In December, the Regents accepted recommendations from the Berkeley faculty Senate that the University should give student speech the protections provided by the First Amendment. Reasonable time, place, and manner restrictions would be acceptable, but content would not be regulated unless it presented a "clear and present danger" or involved defamation, conspiracy or obscenity. Thus FSM, with the support of the faculty, had won free speech rights for students. On January 5, 1965, FSM was disbanded. Verne A. Stadtman, The University of California 1868–1968, at 462–64 (1970).

The administration's action may have calmed the campus, but not the larger political reaction. In 1966, Ronald Reagan ran for Governor of California in part on a promise of cracking down on radical students. After he was elected, Reagan asked the Regents to fire Kerr and they did at their next meeting on January 20, 1967. Nicholas Lemann, The Big Test: The Secret History of the American Meritocracy 168–71 (1999).

Note on Kent State and Jackson State

1. One of the most tragic events of the period took place on May 4, 1970, at Kent State University in Kent, Ohio, when Ohio National Guardsmen shot and killed four students and wounded nine others. Ohio Governor James Rhodes was in a tough primary campaign. On Saturday, May 2, during the last of four campaign debates, he accused his opponent, Congressman Robert Taft, Jr., of "coddling" students. Donald Janson, *Rhodes Urges Law and Order: Says Taft is Soft on Violence*, N.Y. TIMES, May 5, 1970, at 21. On Sunday, Rhodes called a press conference and compared the student protestors to Nazi brown shirts, describing them as "the worst sort of people we harbor in America" and promised "to use every weapon possible to eradicate the problem." PHILIP CAPUTO, 13 SECONDS: A LOOK BACK AT THE KENT STATE SHOOTINGS 22 (2005).

The events surrounding the shootings are recounted in *United States v. Shaffer*, 384 F.Supp. 496, 498–99 (E.D. Ohio 1974):

> In May, 1970, Kent State University had a student enrollment of approximately twenty thousand. On Friday, May 1st, at 12:00 noon a rally was held on the campus commons to protest former President Nixon's announcement [on April 30] of the incursion of American Troops into Cambodia. Approximately 500 students and faculty attended this rally which was peaceful in nature and without incident. A similar rally was subsequently scheduled for noon on Monday, May 4th.

> Friday night there were several disruptive incidents off-campus in the town of Kent itself. There was some vandalism but no serious personal injury. The Mayor of Kent requested the assistance of the National Guard. Elements of the 145th Infantry and 107th Armored Cavalry were alerted. Both of these units had been in an active duty status since April 29, 1970, because of an unrelated Teamster strike. Troops began entering the city of Kent in the evening of May 2, 1970.

> At approximately 8:30 p.m. on May 2nd, the campus R.O.T.C. building was set afire and firemen were forcefully prevented from putting out the fire. The building was subsequently destroyed and the next few hours were marked by sporadic confrontations between students and law enforcement officers. National Guardsmen proceeded to the scene and their arrival was met by students hurling stones at the troop convoy. The next 36 hours, until the morning of May 4th, followed the established pattern of activity; the campus was quiet by day and restless at night.

> On the morning of May 4th approximately 2,000 students gathered in the vicinity of the victory bell on the commons. An order to disperse went unheeded and tear gas proved ineffective in dispersing the students. The National Guardsmen then advanced on the students with fixed bayonets and loaded weapons. The students were driven up "blanket hill," past Taylor Hall, and on to the Prentice Hall parking lot and the practice football field. Elements of the Guard continued to advance and subsequently took a position on the practice football field. While there the troops were subjected to a barrage of rocks and a stream of verbal abuse. At one point, several guardsmen assumed a "kneeling" position, pointed their rifles, but did not discharge them. This tends to negate any inference that the guardsmen planned or intended to "punish" the students in the crowd, particularly since the rock throwing and verbal abuse reached a crescendo at this point in time.

> Shortly thereafter the Guardsmen on the practice football field retraced their steps and began to return up the hill towards Taylor Hall. This movement was begun in a tactical formation, but, possibly, because of individual fatigue and the severity of the terrain the formation, in part, degenerated into a ragged line. Students began to fill in behind the Guard and follow them up the hill. Some rock throwing continued during this period. As the Guardsmen reached the top of the hill, some, including defendants, turned about and fired their weapons in the direction of the

students who were initially at their rear, but who now were facing them. No order to fire was given nor was there any verbal warning given to the students prior to the fusillade.

From the evidence it would appear that at least 54 shots were fired by approximately 29 Guardsmen. Probably, as indicated by the government's evidence, a single shot immediately preceded the main volley, and may have led to the later shots. The total elapsed time of the actual firing was approximately thirteen seconds. Some of the Guardsmen fired at specific students while others merely fired into or over the crowd. There appears to have been no communication among the guardsmen immediately prior to the shooting. . . .

Eight guardsmen were later indicted by a federal grand jury under 18 U.S.C. § 242 for willfully denying the students their constitutional rights. In 1974, the eight were acquitted. *Id.* at 499, 503–04. The court held that:

In the instant case, the government has not offered sufficient evidence from which reasonable jurors may infer "beyond a reasonable doubt" that the defendants were possessed of any specific intent to deprive any of the students of their constitutional rights.

At best, the evidence presented by the government would support a finding that the amount of force used by defendants was excessive and unjustified; that they intended to harm or frighten at least some of the demonstrators; and that they fired without being ordered to do so.

Id. at 502.

A local Special Grand Jury later brought indictments against a number of students for rioting, and against one professor for inciting the riot. Those indicted, together with other students and a number of faculty, filed suit in federal district court to enjoin the state criminal case and expunge a report written by the grand jury. The court refused to enjoin the criminal case, but agreed to expunge the report. Hammond v. Brown, 323 F.Supp. 326, 342–43 (N.D. Ohio), *aff'd per curiam*, 450 F.2d 480 (6th Cir. 1971). The opinion provides a window into some of the debate of the time:

Part VIII of the [Special Grand Jury] Report begins by saying:

Among other persons sharing responsibility for the tragic consequences of May 4, 1970, then must be included the "23 concerned faculty of Kent State University" who composed and made available for distribution on May 3, 1970, the following document:

The appearance of armed troops on the campus of Kent State University is an appalling sight. Occupation of the town and campus by National Guardsmen is testimony to the domination of irrationality in the policies of our government.

The President of the United States commits an illegal act of war and refers to his opposition as 'bums.' That students and faculty and, indeed, all thinking people reject his position is not only rational but patriotic. True, burning a building at Kent State University is no joke; we reject such tactics. Yet the burning of an ROTC Building is no accident. We deplore this violence but we feel it must be viewed in the larger context of the daily burning of buildings and people by our government in Vietnam, Laos, and now Cambodia.

Leadership must set the example if it is to persuade. There is only one course to follow if the people of this country—young and old—are to be convinced of the good faith of their leaders: The war must stop. The vendetta against the Black Panthers must stop. The Constitutional rights of all must be defended against any challenge, even from the

Department of Justice itself. If Mr. Nixon instead continues his bankrupt, illegal course, the Congress must be called upon to impeach him.

Here and now we repudiate the inflammatory inaccuracies expressed by Governor Rhodes in his press conference today. We urge him to remove the troops from our campus. No problem can be solved so long as the campus is under martial law.

We call upon our public authorities to use their high offices to bring about greater understanding of the issues involved in and contributing to the burning of the ROTC building at Kent State University on Saturday, rather than to exploit this incident in a manner that can only inflame the public and increase the confusion among the members of the University community.

Signed by 23 concerned faculty, Kent State University, Sunday Afternoon, May 3, 1970.

[T]he Report continues:

If the purpose of the authors was simply to express their resentment of the presence of the National Guard on campus, their timing could not have been worse. If their purpose was to further inflame an already tense situation, then it surely must have enjoyed some measure of success. In either case, their action [was] clearly not in the best interests of Kent State University.

. . .

[I]t is determined and declared that these charges, bordering on criminal accusations, against the 23 identifiable faculty members, made by the Special Grand Jury, a formal accusing body of Portage County, irreparably impair and injure the right of these 23 faculty members to their protected right of free expression, protected by the First Amendment made applicable to the states by the Fourteenth Amendment.

. . .

. . . Part IX of the Report of the Special Grand Jury . . . begins by saying:

We find that the major responsibility for the incidents occurring on the Kent State University campus on May 2nd, 3rd, and 4th rests clearly with those persons who are charged with the administration of the university. To attempt to fix the sole blame for what happened during this period on the National Guard, the students or other participants would be inconceivable. The evidence presented to us has established that Kent State University was in such a state of disrepair, that it was totally incapable of re-acting to the situation in any effective manner. We believe that it resulted from policies formulated and carried out by the University over a period of several years, the most obvious of which will be commented on here.

Part IX continues:

The administration at Kent State University has fostered an attitude of laxity, over-indulgence, and permissiveness with its students and faculty to the extent that it can no longer regulate the activities of either and is particularly vulnerable to any pressure applied from radical elements within the student body or faculty.

The first example the Grand Jury gives is the "delegation of a disciplinary authority under a student conduct code which has proven totally ineffective." After devoting several paragraphs to this first example, the Report then states:

A second example of where the University has obviously contributed to the crisis it now faces is the overemphasis which it has placed and allowed to be placed on the right to dissent. Although we fully recognize that the right of dissent is a basic freedom to be cherished and protected, we cannot agree that the role of the University should be to continually foster a climate in which dissent becomes the order of the day to the exclusion of all normal behavior and expression.

. . .

A further example of what we consider an over-emphasis on dissent can be found in the classrooms of some members of the University faculty. The faculty members to whom we refer teach nothing but the negative side of our institutions of government and refuse to acknowledge that any positive good has resulted during the growth of our nation. They devote their entire class periods to urging their students to openly oppose our institutions of government even to the point of where one student who dared to defend the American flag was ridiculed by his professor before his classmates.

We do not mean to suggest that these faculty members represent a majority of the faculty at Kent State University. To the contrary, we suspect that they form a small minority of the total faculty, but this does not mean that their presence should be ignored.

The Report does not identify this assumed "small minority of the total faculty." Since no faculty members are specifically identified and since the Report's reference to the faculty as a class does not either generally or specifically charge violation of any criminal offense, the claim of the . . . plaintiffs based on the Fifth and Sixth Amendments is untenable.

The claimed violation of First Amendment rights violative of Due Process presents a different matter. Let us assume a member of the Kent State faculty reads the Grand Jury's criticism of "over-emphasis on dissent . . . in the classrooms of some members of the University faculty" and the Report's comment that this dissent "becomes the order of the day to the exclusion of all normal behavior and expression." He may reasonably believe that people in the Kent community (university and city) who have read Parts VIII and IX of the Report, may well think the Report may refer to him. People in the community may well believe that a particular faculty member is one of the "small minority of the total faculty" who depart from "all normal behavior and expression."

. . .

. . . Because of the Report instructors have altered or dropped course materials for fear of classroom controversy. For example, an assistant professor of English, after reading the Report, "scratched three poems" from her outline in her Introduction to Poetry course. The poems are "Politics" by William Butler Yeats, "Prometheus" by Lord Byron, and "Dover Beach" by Matthew Arnold.

In "Politics," Yeats writes "And maybe what they say is true/of war and war's alarms."

A university professor may add or subtract course content for different reasons. But when a university professor is fearful that "war's alarm," a poet's concern, may produce "inflammatory discussion" in a poetry class, it is evident that the Report's riptide is washing away protected expression on the Kent campus.

Other evidence cumulatively shows that this teacher's reaction was not isolated. The Report is dulling classroom discussion and is upsetting the teaching atmosphere. This effect was described by other faculty witnesses.

When thought is controlled, or appears to be controlled, when pedagogues and pupils shrink from free inquiry at a state university because of a report of a resident Grand Jury, then academic freedom of expression is impermissibly impaired. This will curb conditions essential to fulfillment of the university's learning purposes.

. . .

Part IX of the Report, exemplified by the quoted excerpts, abridges the exercise of protected expression by the plaintiffs who are members of the Kent State University faculty and other persons of the same class on whose behalf the . . . plaintiffs bring their action. Imposed under the color of state law, Part IX of the Report is determined and declared to deprive these parties of rights guaranteed under the Constitution in violation of 42 U.S.C. § 1983 (1964).

323 F.Supp. at 51–64.

Five cases concerning the burning of the ROTC building went to trial. One non-student defendant was convicted and two others pleaded guilty. One other defendant was acquitted and charges were dismissed against the fifth. In December 1971, all charges against the remaining twenty were dismissed for lack of evidence.

2. The families of the students who were killed sued Governor Rhodes, the Adjutant General of the Ohio National Guard, various other Guard officers and enlisted members, and the university president, charging that they, acting under color of state law, "intentionally, recklessly, willfully and wantonly" caused an unnecessary Guard deployment on the campus and ordered the Guard members to perform allegedly illegal acts resulting in the students' deaths. The litigation reached the Supreme Court in *Scheuer v. Rhodes*, 416 U.S. 232 (1974), where the Court held that the District Court was wrong to summarily dismiss the complaint because officers of the executive branch are entitled not to absolute but only qualified immunity depending upon the scope of discretion and responsibilities of their office and the circumstances existing at the time the challenged action was taken. On remand, the jury returned a verdict for defendants. On appeal, the decision was reversed for a new trial. Krause v. Rhodes, 570 F.2d 563 (6th Cir. 1977), *cert. denied*, 435 U.S. 924 (1978).

In 1979, Ohio's State Controlling Boards approved an out-of-court settlement that paid a total of $675,000 to the victims and families of victims of the Kent State shootings rather than continue to defend against pending litigation. *Ohio Approves $675,000 to Settle Suits in 1970 Kent State Shootings*, N.Y. TIMES, Jan. 4, 1979, at A12.

3. Neil Young famously memorialized the Kent State shootings in the anthemic song "Ohio." Young called the shootings "[p]robably the most important lesson ever learned at an American place of learning." NEIL YOUNG, DECADE (Reprise Records 1977) (liner notes).

4. The Kent State shootings triggered protests on campuses across the country and led to the first nationwide student strike in history. More than 4 million students protested and over 900 American colleges and universities were closed down. On May 9, more than 100,000 people demonstrated in Washington D.C. against the war and the murder of student protestors. On June 13, 1970, President Nixon established a national Commission on Campus Unrest, known as the Scranton Commission. On September 27, the Commission issued and widely publicized the report. It began with a Call to the American People:

The crisis on American campuses has no parallel in the history of the nation.

. . .

On the nation's campuses, and in their neighboring communities, the level of violence has been steadily rising. Students have been killed and injured; civil authorities have been killed and injured; bystanders have been killed and injured. Valuable public and private property, and scholarly products have been burned.

. . .

The shortcomings of the American university are [one] target of student protest. The goals, values, administration and curriculum have been sharply criticized by many students. Students complain that their studies are irrelevant to the social problems that concern them. They want to shape their own personal and common lives, but find the university restrictive. They seek a community of companions and scholars but find an impersonal multiversity. And they denounce the university's relationship to the war and to discriminatory racial practices.

. . .

. . . They see their elders as entrapped by materialism and competition and prisoners of outdated social forms. They believe their own country has lost its sense of human purpose. They see the Indochina War as an onslaught by a technological giant upon the peasant people of a small, harmless and backward nation. The war is seen as draining resources from the urgent needs of social and racial justice. They argue that we are the first nation with sufficient resources to create not only decent lives for some, but a decent society for all and that we are failing to do so. They feel they must remake America in its own image.

But among the members of this new student culture, there is a growing lack of tolerance, a growing insistence that their own views must govern, an impatience with the slow procedures of liberal democracy. . . .

. . .

We urgently call for reconciliation. . . .

. . .

. . . The whole object of a free government is to allow the nation to redefine its purposes in the light of new needs without sacrificing the accumulated wisdom of its living traditions. We cannot do this without each other.

. . .

One of the most valid criticisms of many universities is that their faculties have become so involved in outside research that their commitment to teaching seems compromised. . . .

Large universities should take steps to decentralize or reorganize to make possible a more human scale.

University governance systems should be reformed to increase participation of students and faculty in the formulation of university policies that affect them. But universities cannot be run on a one-man, one-vote basis with participation of all members on all issues.

Universities must become true communities whose members share a sense of respect, tolerance, and responsibility for one another.

THE REPORT OF THE PRESIDENT'S COMMISSION ON CAMPUS UNREST 1, 4–5, 6, 14 (1970).

5. Although events at Jackson State received less national press coverage, ten days after the shootings at Kent State, two African–American students were fatally wounded by police at Jackson State College. There were clear parallels between the two events:

Two nights of campus demonstrations at Jackson State College in May 1970 ended in violent confrontation and tragedy. After 28 seconds of gunfire by

Mississippi Highway Safety Patrolmen and Jackson city policemen, two black youths lay dying and 12 others wounded.

PRESIDENT'S COMMISSION ON CAMPUS UNREST, REPORT 411 (1970).

In 1972, a special committee of the AAUP issued a report on the students deaths at Kent State and Jackson State, NO HEROES, NO VILLAINS 36–37, 83 (1972):

> Although it is impossible for a campus to prevent intrusions by civil authorities, it is both feasible and essential to guard against such intervention.... [T]here are many precautions the president or chancellor can take to safeguard as much campus autonomy as remains.... The authority, the command, and the objectives of such external forces should be ascertained at once. The information should be widely disseminated to the entire campus community. All proper precautions should be taken to avoid confrontations between members of the campus community and outside forces. Close liaison should be maintained between the civil authorities and the campus police or security office. In short, the president should retain control and direction of his own campus as long as possible, no matter how far his autonomy and authority appear to have been wounded.

Healy v. James

Supreme Court of the United States, 1972.
408 U.S. 169, 92 S.Ct. 2338, 33 L.Ed.2d 266.

■ MR. JUSTICE POWELL delivered the opinion of the Court.

This case, arising out of a denial by a state college of official recognition to a group of students who desired to form a local chapter of Students for a Democratic Society (SDS), presents this Court with questions requiring the application of well-established First Amendment principles....

. . .

We mention briefly at the outset the setting in 1969–1970. A climate of unrest prevailed on many college campuses in this country. There had been widespread civil disobedience on some campuses, accompanied by the seizure of buildings, vandalism, and arson. Some colleges had been shut down altogether, while at others files were looted and manuscripts destroyed. SDS chapters on some of those campuses had been a catalytic force during this period. Although the causes of campus disruption were many and complex, one of the prime consequences of such activities was the denial of the lawful exercise of First Amendment rights to the majority of students by the few. Indeed, many of the most cherished characteristics long associated with institutions of higher learning appeared to be endangered. Fortunately, with the passage of time, a calmer atmosphere and greater maturity now pervade our campuses. Yet, it was in this climate of earlier unrest that this case arose.

Petitioners are students attending Central Connecticut State College (CCSC), a state-supported institution of higher learning. In September 1969 they undertook to organize what they then referred to as a "local chapter" of SDS. Pursuant to procedures established by the College, petitioners filed a request for official recognition as a campus organization with the Student Affairs Committee, a committee composed of four students, three faculty members, and the Dean of Student Affairs. The request specified three purposes for the proposed organization's existence. It would provide "a forum of discussion and self-education for students developing an analysis of American society"; it would serve as "an agency for integrating thought with action so as to bring about constructive changes"; and it would endeavor to provide "a coordinating body for relating the problems of leftist students" with other interested groups on campus and in the community. The Committee, while satisfied that the statement of purposes was clear and unobjectionable on its face, exhibited concern over the relationship between the proposed local group and the National SDS organization. In response to inquiries, representatives of the proposed organization stated that they would not affiliate with any national organization and that their group would remain "completely independent."

. . .

With this information before it, the Committee requested an additional filing by the applicants, including a formal statement regarding affiliations. The amended application filed in response stated flatly that "CCSC Students for a Democratic Society are not under the dictates of any National organization." At a second hearing before the Student Affairs Committee, the question of relationship with the National organization was raised again. One of the organizers explained that the National SDS was divided into several "factional groups," that the national-local relationship was a loose one, and that the local organization accepted only "certain ideas" but not all of the National organization's aims and philosophies.

By a vote of six to two the Committee ultimately approved the application and recommended to the President of the College, Dr. James, that the organization be accorded official recognition. . . .

Several days later, the President rejected the Committee's recommendation, and issued a statement indicating that petitioners' organization was not to be accorded the benefits of official campus recognition. . . . He found that the organization's philosophy was antithetical to the school's policies, and that the group's independence was doubtful. He concluded that approval should not be granted to any group that "openly repudiates" the College's dedication to academic freedom.

Denial of official recognition posed serious problems for the organization's existence and growth. Its members were deprived of the opportunity to place announcements regarding meetings, rallies, or other activities in the student newspaper; they were precluded from using various campus bulletin boards; and—most importantly—nonrecognition barred them from using campus facilities for holding meetings. This latter disability was brought home to petitioners shortly after the President's announcement. Petitioners circulated a notice calling a meeting to discuss what further action should be taken in light of the group's official rejection. The members met at the coffee shop in the Student Center ("Devils' Den") but were disbanded on the President's order since nonrecognized groups were not entitled to use such facilities.

[Petitioners sued the State Board of Trustees, the President of the College, and other administrators in U.S. District Court, primarily alleging violations of their First Amendment rights of expression and association. The District Court ruled that the President had denied the students procedural due process by basing his decision on the chapter's affiliation with the national SDS organization, a fact not on the record before him. The court ordered the President to hold a hearing at which the students could introduce evidence regarding their affiliation. After a two-hour hearing, the

President reaffirmed his earlier decision and reasoning, and the District Court dismissed the case.]

Petitioners appealed to the Court of Appeals for the Second Circuit where, by a two-to-one vote, the District Court's judgment was affirmed....

At the outset we note that state colleges and universities are not enclaves immune from the sweep of the First Amendment. "It can hardly be argued that either students or teachers shed their constitutional rights to freedom of speech or expression at the schoolhouse gate." *Tinker v. Des Moines Independent School District*, 393 U.S. 503, 506 (1969). Of course, as Mr. Justice Fortas made clear in *Tinker*, First Amendment rights must always be applied "in light of the special characteristics of the ... environment" in the particular case. And, where state-operated educational institutions are involved, this Court has long recognized "the need for affirming the comprehensive authority of the States and of school officials, consistent with fundamental constitutional safeguards, to prescribe and control conduct in the schools." Yet, the precedents of this Court leave no room for the view that, because of the acknowledged need for order, First Amendment protections should apply with less force on college campuses than in the community at large. Quite to the contrary, "the vigilant protection of constitutional freedoms is nowhere more vital than in the community of American schools." *Shelton v. Tucker*, 364 U.S. 479, 487 (1960). The college classroom with its surrounding environs is peculiarly the " 'marketplace of ideas,' " and we break no new constitutional ground in reaffirming this Nation's dedication to safeguarding academic freedom. *Keyishian v. Board of Regents*, 385 U.S. 589, 603 (1967); *Sweezy v. New Hampshire*, 354 U.S. 234, 249–250 (1957).

Among the rights protected by the First Amendment is the right of individuals to associate to further their personal beliefs. While the freedom of association is not explicitly set out in the Amendment, it has long been held to be implicit in the freedoms of speech, assembly, and petition. There can be no doubt that denial of official recognition, without justification, to college organizations burdens or abridges that associational right. The primary impediment to free association flowing from nonrecognition is the denial of use of campus facilities for meetings and other appropriate purposes....

Petitioners' associational interests also were circumscribed by the denial of the use of campus bulletin boards and the school newspaper. If an organization is to remain a viable entity in a campus community in which new students enter on a regular basis, it must possess the means of communicating with these students. Moreover, the organization's ability to participate in the intellectual give and take of campus debate, and to pursue its stated purposes, is limited by denial of access to the customary media for communicating with the administration, faculty members, and other students. Such impediments cannot be viewed as insubstantial.

Respondents and the courts below appear to have taken the view that denial of official recognition in this case abridged no constitutional rights....

We do not agree with the characterization by the courts below of the consequences of nonrecognition. We may concede, as did Mr. Justice Harlan in his opinion for a unanimous Court in *NAACP v. Alabama ex rel. Patterson*, 357 U.S. at 461, that the administration "has taken no direct action ... to restrict the rights of [petitioners] to associate freely...." But the Constitution's protection is not limited to direct interference with fundamental rights. The requirement in *Patterson* that the NAACP disclose its membership lists was found to be an impermissible, though indirect, infringement of the members' associational rights. Likewise, in this case, the group's possible ability to exist outside the campus community does not ameliorate significantly the disabilities imposed by the President's action....

The opinions below also assumed that petitioners had the burden of showing entitlement to recognition by the College. While petitioners have not challenged the procedural requirement that they file an application in conformity with the rules of the College, they do question the view of the courts below that final rejection could rest on their failure to convince the administration that their organization was unaffiliated with the National SDS. For reasons to be stated later in this opinion, we do not consider the issue of affiliation to be a controlling one. But, apart from any particular issue, once petitioners had filed an application in conformity with the requirements, the burden was upon the College administration to justify its decision of rejection. It is to be remembered that the effect of the College's denial of recognition was a form of prior restraint, denying to petitioners' organization the range of associational activities described above. While a college has a legitimate interest in preventing disruption on the campus, which under circumstances requiring the safeguarding of that interest may justify such restraint, a "heavy burden" rests on the college to demonstrate the appropriateness of that action.

These fundamental errors—discounting the existence of a cognizable First Amendment interest and misplacing the burden of proof—require that the judgments below be reversed. But we are unable to conclude that no basis exists upon which nonrecognition might be appropriate. Indeed, based on a reasonable reading of the ambiguous facts of this case, there appears to be at least one potentially acceptable ground for a denial of recognition. Because of this ambiguous state of the record we conclude that the case should be remanded, and, in an effort to provide guidance to the lower courts upon reconsideration, it is appropriate to discuss the several bases of President James' decision. Four possible justifications for nonrecognition, all closely related, might be derived from the record and his statements. Three of those grounds are inadequate to substantiate his decision: a fourth, however, has merit.

From the outset the controversy in this case has centered in large measure around the relationship, if any, between petitioners' group and the National SDS....

Although this precise issue has not come before the Court heretofore, the Court has consistently disapproved governmental action imposing criminal sanctions or denying rights and privileges solely because of a citizen's association with an unpopular organization. *See, e.g., United States v. Robel,* 389 U.S. 258 (1967); *Keyishian v. Board of Regents,* 385 U.S., at 605–610; *Elfbrandt v. Russell,* 384 U.S. 11 (1966); *Scales v. United States,* 367 U.S. 203 (1961)....

Students for a Democratic Society, as conceded by the College and the lower courts, is loosely organized, having various factions and promoting a number of diverse social and political views, only some of which call for unlawful action.[14] Not only did petitioners proclaim their complete independence from this organization, but they also indicated that they shared only some of the beliefs its leaders have expressed. On this record it is clear that the relationship was not an adequate ground for the denial of recognition.

Having concluded that petitioners were affiliated with, or at least retained an affinity for, National SDS, President James attributed what he believed to be the philosophy of that organization to the local group. He characterized the petitioning group as adhering to "some of the major tenets of the national organization," including a philosophy of violence and disruption. Understandably, he found that philosophy abhorrent. . . .

> The mere disagreement of the President with the group's philosophy affords no reason to deny it recognition. As repugnant as these views may have been, especially to one with President James' responsibility, the mere expression of them would not justify the denial of First Amendment rights. Whether petitioners did in fact advocate a philosophy of "destruction" thus becomes immaterial. The College, acting here as the instrumentality of the State, may not restrict speech or association simply because it finds the views expressed by any group to be abhorrent. . . .

As the litigation progressed in the District Court, a third rationale for President James' decision—beyond the questions of affiliation and philosophy—began to emerge. His second statement, issued after the court-ordered hearing, indicates that he based rejection on a conclusion that this particular group would be a "disruptive influence at CCSC." . . .

If this reason, directed at the organization's activities rather than its philosophy, were factually supported by the record, this Court's prior decisions would provide a basis for considering the propriety of nonrecognition. The critical line heretofore drawn for determining the permissibility of regulation is the line between mere advocacy and advocacy "directed to inciting or producing imminent lawless action and . . . likely to incite or produce such action." *Brandenburg v. Ohio*, 395 U.S. 444, 447 (1969) (unanimous per curiam opinion). In the context of the "special characteristics of the school environment," the power of the government to prohibit "lawless action" is not limited to acts of a criminal nature. Also prohibitable are actions which "materially and substantially disrupt the work and discipline of the school." *Tinker v. Des Moines Independent School District*, 393 U.S. at 513. Associational activities need not be tolerated where they infringe reasonable campus rules, interrupt classes, or substantially interfere with the opportunity of other students to obtain an education.

The "Student Bill of Rights" at CCSC, upon which great emphasis was placed by the President, draws precisely this distinction between advocacy and action. It purports to impose no limitations on the right of college student organizations "to examine and discuss *all* questions of interest to them." (Emphasis supplied.) But it also states that students have no right (1) "to deprive others of the opportunity to speak or be heard," (2) "to invade the privacy of others," (3) "to damage the property of others," (4) "to disrupt

14. *See Hearings before a Subcommittee of the House Committee on Appropriations*, 92d Cong., 2d Sess., pt. 1, p. 916 (1972), in which the former Director of the Federal Bureau of Investigation, J. Edgar Hoover, stated that while violent factions have spun off from SDS, its present leadership is "critical of bombing and violence."

the regular and essential operation of the college," or (5) "to interfere with the rights of others." The line between permissible speech and impermissible conduct tracks the constitutional requirement, and if there were an evidential basis to support the conclusion that CCSC–SDS posed a substantial threat of material disruption in violation of that command the President's decision should be affirmed.

The record, however, offers no substantial basis for that conclusion.... [T]here was no substantial evidence that these particular individuals acting together would constitute a disruptive force on campus. Therefore, insofar as nonrecognition flowed from such fears, it constituted little more than the sort of "undifferentiated fear or apprehension of disturbance [which] is not enough to overcome the right to freedom of expression." *Tinker v. Des Moines Independent School District*, 393 U.S. at 508.

[The] references in the record to the group's equivocation regarding how it might respond to "issues of violence" and whether it could ever "envision ... interrupting a class," suggest a fourth possible reason why recognition might have been denied to these petitioners. These remarks might well have been read as announcing petitioners' unwillingness to be bound by reasonable school rules governing conduct. The College's Statement of Rights, Freedoms, and Responsibilities of Students contains, as we have seen, an explicit statement with respect to campus disruption. The regulation, carefully differentiating between advocacy and action, is a reasonable one, and petitioners have not questioned it directly. Yet their statements raise considerable question whether they intend to abide by the prohibitions contained therein.[22]

> As we have already stated ..., the critical line for First Amendment purposes must be drawn between advocacy, which is entitled to full protection, and action, which is not. Petitioners may, if they so choose, preach the propriety of amending or even doing away with any or all campus regulations. They may not, however, undertake to flout these rules....

Just as in the community at large, reasonable regulations with respect to the time, the place, and the manner in which student groups conduct their speech-related activities must be respected. A college administration may impose a requirement, such as may have been imposed in this case, that a group seeking official recognition affirm in advance its willingness to adhere to reasonable campus law. Such a requirement does not impose an impermissible condition on the students' associational rights. Their freedom to speak out, to assemble, or to petition for changes in school rules is in no sense infringed. It merely constitutes an agreement to conform with reasonable standards respecting conduct. This is a minimal requirement, in the interest of the entire academic community, of any group seeking the privilege of official recognition.

---

22. The Court of Appeals found that petitioners "failed candidly to respond to inquiries whether they would resort to violence and disruption on the CCSC campus, including interruption of classes." 445 F.2d, at 1131. While petitioners' statements may be read as intimating a rejection of reasonable regulations in advance, there is in fact substantial ambiguity on this point.... Indeed, the District Court's failure to identify the question of willingness to abide by the College's rules and regulations as a significant subject of inquiry, coupled with the equivocation on the part of the group's representatives, lends support to our view that a remand is necessary.

Petitioners have not challenged in this litigation the procedural or substantive aspects of the College's requirements governing applications for official recognition. Although the record is unclear on this point, CCSC may have, among its requirements for recognition, a rule that prospective groups affirm that they intend to comply with reasonable campus regulations. Upon remand it should first be determined whether the College recognition procedures contemplate any such requirement. If so, it should then be ascertained whether petitioners intend to comply. Since we do not have the terms of a specific prior affirmation rule before us, we are not called on to decide whether any particular formulation would or would not prove constitutionally acceptable. Assuming the existence of a valid rule, however, we do conclude that the benefits of participation in the internal life of the college community may be denied to any group that reserves the right to violate any valid campus rules with which it disagrees.[24]

. . .

Reversed and remanded.

Questions and Comments on *Healy v. James*

1. The Supreme Court laid out two questions to be answered on remand. First, did CCSC "have, among its requirements for [student group] recognition, a rule that prospective groups affirm that they intend to comply with reasonable campus regulations"? Second, if CCSC had such a rule, were the members of the CCSC SDS "willing to abide by reasonable campus rules and regulations"?

CCSC did have in place regulations regarding student group recognition. CCSC had modeled its policies on the AAUP's 1967 Joint Statement on Rights and Freedoms of Students. Telephone Interview by Matthew Berns with Richard Judd, Former President, Cent. Conn. St. Univ. (Nov. 23, 2007). The Joint Statement provides in part that "[s]tudents and student organizations . . . should always be free to support causes by orderly means that do not disrupt the regular and essential operations of the institution." AAUP, Joint Statement on Rights and Freedoms of Students, http://www.aaup.org/AAUP/pubsVres/policydocs/contents/stud-rights.htm (last visited Jan. 6, 2008).

Richard Judd, then CCSC's Dean of Student Affairs and later President, sought an answer from the SDS students to the court's second question: were they willing to obey the rules? By the time the Supreme Court remanded the case, however, Catherine Healy and many of the other students who had tried to form the SDS chapter had already graduated; the few members still attending CCSC were no longer interested in starting an SDS group. Judd never received a response to his inquiries, and no officially recognized SDS chapter ever formed at CCSC. Telephone Interview by Matthew Berns with Richard Judd, Nov. 23, 2007.

2. A more detailed account of SDS is provided by Philip Caputo in 13 Seconds: A Look Back at the Kent State Shootings 15–19 (2005):

. . . Formed in 1960 at the University of Michigan as the student arm of an old-Left organization, the League for Industrial Democracy, the SDS has been involved in civil rights causes and in inner city community organizing projects during the early sixties. Tom Hayden, a leader of the [1968]

---

24. In addition to the College administration's broad rulemaking power to assure that the traditional academic atmosphere is safeguarded, it may also impose sanctions on those who violate the rules. We find, for instance, that the Student Affairs Committee's admonition to petitioners in this case suggests one permissible practice—recognition, once accorded, may be withdrawn or suspended if petitioners fail to respect campus law.

Democratic convention protests, later a California state assemblyman and one of Jane Fonda's husbands, had been among the SDS's founders. It might have remained a small, obscure band of quasi-socialist idealists had it not been for the galvanizing effect of the Vietnam War. By 1969 it had grown to one hundred thousand members in three hundred chapters across the country.

At its national conference—another Chicago event—a factional fight erupted among the SDS mainstream, a Marxist group called Progressive Labor, and the Revolutionary Youth Movement, putative revolutionaries from middle and upper-middle class backgrounds and with long histories of student activism.... [T]hese disaffected undergraduates issued a manifesto called "You don't need a weatherman to tell you which way the wind blows," a title borrowed from a line in Bob Dylan's countercultural anthem, *The Subterranean Homesick Blues.*

The manifesto expressed disdain for the SDS's policies of peaceful protest ...; rejected Progressive Labor's call for an alliance with the white working class, which the authors considered too conservative and pro-war; and called for a campaign of "exemplary violence" by planting bombs in symbolic targets like the Pentagon, ROTC buildings, military bases, and other "imperialist" bastions.

. . .

The group changed its name to "Weathermen," and, led by charismatic and photogenic figures like Bernadine Dohrn, William Ayres, Kathy Boudin, David Gilbert, and Bill Flanagan, staged its first exemplary violence in Chicago in October 1969. It was called the "Days of Rage."

. . .

In March 1970, the Weathermen—now rechristened the Weather Underground—resurfaced in spectacular, if self-destructive fashion. One of the cells ... had hatched a plot to plant a nail bomb at a dance in the Officer's Mess at Fort Dix, New Jersey.... Fortunately for the intended victims, the device blew up in the Manhattan town house in which it was being constructed, killing Ayer's girlfriend, Diana Oughten, and two other weathermen. Ayers, Rudd, Dohrn, et al., ended up on the FBI's Ten Most Wanted Fugitive list and went on the lam.

3. The student anti-war movement was broader than SDS. Consider Robert Cohen, *The Many Meanings of the FSM, in* THE FREE SPEECH MOVEMENT: REFLECTIONS ON BERKELEY IN THE 1960s 1, 39 (Robert Cohen & Reginald E. Zelnick eds., 2002):

... [T]here is something inherently unfair about using figures like Rudd or Rubin to represent the full array of students who mobilized to protest the Vietnam War and other injustices. As Terry Anderson has shown in his informative chronicle, *The Movement and the Sixties* (1995), at the very time in the late 1960s when the revolutionary posturing was paralyzing New Left organizations, most notably SDS, the antiwar movement grew at an unprecedented rate, and millions of student demonstrated in the same mostly nonviolent way that the FSM had done back in 1964. It may be that as historians follow up on Anderson's pioneering work, they will find that for most student activists who came along later in the decade, the nonviolent approach that the FSM popularized in the early sixties never went out of style, a conclusion reinforced by the finding of the President's Commission on Campus Unrest.

4.   DEMOCRATIZING THE FACULTY

Beginning with the passage of the Civil Rights Act in 1964, Congress enacted a series of federal statutes that prohibit discrimination of various types in the workplace. Title VII of the Civil Rights Act prohibits discrimination on the basis of race, color, religion, sex, or national origin whether by public or private employers. In 1967, the Age Discrimination in Employment Act became law. It was followed by two statutes prohibiting discrimination against individuals with disabilities: the Rehabilitation Act of 1974, which applies to recipients of federal funds, and, in 1990, the Americans with Disabilities Act.

Some colleges and universities sought exemptions from the new laws on the grounds that academic freedom and tenure distinguished them from most workplaces. They were exempted at first from Title VII, but Congress repealed the exemption in 1972, setting the stage for a clash between equality and academic freedom that eventually was heard by the Supreme Court.

University of Pennsylvania v. Equal Employment Opportunity Commission

Supreme Court of the United States, 1990.
493 U.S. 182, 110 S.Ct. 577, 107 L.Ed.2d 571.

■ BLACKMUN, J., delivered the opinion of the Court.

In this case we are asked to decide whether a university enjoys a special privilege, grounded in either the common law or the First Amendment, against disclosure of peer review materials that are relevant to charges of racial or sexual discrimination in tenure decisions.

The University of Pennsylvania, petitioner here, is a private institution. It currently operates 12 schools, including the Wharton School of Business, which collectively enroll approximately 18,000 full-time students.

In 1985, the University denied tenure to Rosalie Tung, an associate professor on the Wharton faculty. Tung then filed a sworn charge of discrimination with respondent Equal Employment Opportunity Commission (EEOC or Commission). As subsequently amended, the charge alleged that Tung was the victim of discrimination on the basis of race, sex, and national origin, in violation of § 703(a) of Title VII of the Civil Rights Act of 1964, 78 Stat. 255, as amended, 42 U.S.C. § 2000e–2(a) (1982 ed.), which makes it unlawful "to discriminate against any individual with respect to his compensation, terms, conditions, or privileges of employment, because of such individual's race, color, religion, sex, or national origin."

In her charge, Tung stated that the department chairman had sexually harassed her and that, in her belief, after she insisted that their relationship remain professional, he had submitted a negative letter to the University's Personnel Committee which possessed ultimate responsibility for tenure decisions. She also alleged that her qualifications were "equal to or better than" those of five named male faculty members who had received more favorable treatment. Tung noted that the majority of the members of her department had recommended her for tenure, and stated that she had been given no reason for the decision against her, but had discovered of her own efforts that the Personnel Committee had attempted to justify its decision "on the ground that the Wharton School is not interested in China-related research." This explanation, Tung's charge alleged, was a pretext for discrimination: "simply their way of saying they do not want a Chinese–American, Oriental, woman in their school."

The Commission undertook an investigation into Tung's charge and requested a variety of relevant information from petitioner. When the University refused to provide certain of that information, the Commission's Acting District Director issued a subpoena seeking, among other things, Tung's tenure-review file and the tenure files of the five male faculty members identified in the charge. Petitioner refused to produce a number of the tenure-file documents. It applied to the Commission for modification of the subpoena to exclude what it termed "confidential peer review information," specifically, (1) confidential letters written by Tung's evaluators; (2) the department chairman's letter of evaluation; (3) documents reflecting the internal deliberations of faculty committees considering applications for tenure, including the Department Evaluation Report summarizing the deliberations relating to Tung's application for tenure; and (4) comparable portions of the tenure-review files of the five males. The University urged the Commission to "adopt a balancing approach reflecting the constitutional and societal interest inherent in the peer review process" and to resort to "all feasible methods to minimize the intrusive effects of its investigations."

The Commission denied the University's application. . . . "The Commission would fall short of its obligation" to investigate charges of discrimination, the EEOC's order stated, "if it stopped its investigation once [the employer] has . . . provided the reasons for its employment decisions, without verifying whether that reason is a pretext for discrimination." The Commission also rejected petitioner's proposed balancing test, explaining that "such an approach in the instant case . . . would impair the Commission's ability to fully investigate this charge of discrimination."

[The U.S. District Court for the Eastern District of Pennsylvania issued an order enforcing the EEOC's subpoena. The Court of Appeals for the Third Circuit affirmed, and the Supreme Court granted certiorari "limited to the compelled-disclosure question."]

As it had done before the Commission, the District Court, and the Court of Appeals, the University raises here essentially two claims. First, it urges us to recognize a qualified common-law privilege against disclosure of confidential peer review materials. Second, it asserts a First Amendment right of "academic freedom" against wholesale disclosure of the contested documents. With respect to each of the two claims, the remedy petitioner seeks is the same: a requirement of a judicial finding of particularized necessity of access, beyond a showing of mere relevance, before peer review materials are disclosed to the Commission.

[W]e cannot accept the University's invitation to create a new [common law] privilege against the disclosure of peer review materials. We begin by noting that Congress, in extending Title VII to educational institutional and in providing for broad EEOC subpoena powers, did not see fit to create a privilege for peer review documents.

When Title VII was enacted originally in 1964, it exempted an "educational institution with respect to the employment of individuals to perform work connected with the educational activities of such institution." Eight years later, Congress eliminated that specific exemption by enacting § 3 of the Equal Employment Opportunity Act of 1972, 86 Stat. 103. This extension of Title VII was Congress' considered response to the widespread and compelling problem of invidious discrimination in educational institutions. The House Report focused specifically on discrimination in higher education, including the lack of access for women and minorities to higher ranking (i.e., tenured) academic positions. Significantly, opponents of the extension claimed that enforcement of Title VII would weaken institutions of higher education by interfering with decisions to hire and promote faculty members. Petitioner therefore cannot seriously contend that Congress was oblivious to concerns of academic autonomy when it abandoned the exemption for educational institutions.

The effect of the elimination of this exemption was to expose tenure determinations to the same enforcement procedures applicable to other employment decisions. This Court previously has observed that Title VII "sets forth 'an integrated, multistep enforcement procedure that enables the Commission to detect and remedy instances of discrimination.'" *EEOC v. Shell Oil Co.*, 466 U.S. 54, 62 (1984), quoting *Occidental Life Ins. Co. v. EEOC*, 432 U.S. 355, 359 (1977).... To enable the Commission to make informed decisions at each stage of the enforcement process, § 2000e–8(a) confers a broad right of access to relevant evidence:

> "The Commission or its designated representative shall at all reasonable times have access to, for the purposes of examination, and the right to copy any evidence of any person being investigated ... that relates to unlawful employment practices covered by [the Act] and is relevant to the charge under investigation."

If an employer refuses to provide this information voluntarily, the Act authorizes the Commission to issue a subpoena and to seek an order enforcing it. § 2000e–9 (incorporating 29 U.S.C. § 161).

On their face, §§ 2000e–8(a) and 2000e–9 do not carve out any special privilege relating to peer review materials, despite the fact that Congress undoubtedly was aware, when it extended Title VII's coverage, of the potential burden that access to such material might create. Moreover, we have noted previously that when a court is asked to enforce a Commission subpoena, its responsibility is to "satisfy itself that the charge is valid and that the material requested is 'relevant' to the charge ... and more generally to assess any contentions by the employer that the demand for information is too indefinite or has been made for an illegitimate purpose." It is not then to determine "whether the charge of discrimination is 'well founded' or 'verifiable.'"

The University concedes that the information sought by the Commission in this case passes the relevance test set forth in *Shell Oil*. Petitioner argues, nevertheless, that Title VII affirmatively grants courts the discretion to require more than relevance in order to protect tenure-review documents. Although petitioner recognizes that Title VII gives the Commission broad "power to *seek* access to all evidence that may be 'relevant to the charge under investigation,'" it contends that Title VII's subpoena enforcement provisions do not give the Commission an unqualified right to *acquire* such evidence. This interpretation simply cannot be reconciled with the plain language of the text of § 2000e–8(a), which states that the Commission "*shall ... have* access" to "relevant" evidence (emphasis added). The provision can be read only as giving the Commission a right to obtain that evidence, not a mere license to seek it.

Although the text of the access provisions thus provides no privilege, Congress did address situations in which an employer may have an interest in the confidentiality of its records. The same § 2000e–8 which gives the Commission access to any evidence relevant to its investigation also makes it "unlawful for any officer or employee of the Commission to make public in any manner whatever any information obtained by the Commission pursuant to its authority under this section prior to the institution of any proceeding" under the Act. A violation of this provision subjects the employee to criminal penalties. To be sure, the protection of confidentiality that § 2000e–8(e) provides is less than complete. But this, if anything, weakens petitioner's argument. Congress apparently considered the issue of confidentiality, and it provided a modicum of protection. Petitioner urges us to go further than Congress thought necessary to safeguard that value, that is, to strike the balance differently from the one Congress adopted. Petitioner, however, does not offer any persuasive justification for that suggestion.

We readily agree with petitioner that universities and colleges play significant roles in American society. Nor need we question, at this point, petitioner's assertion that confidentiality is important to the proper functioning of the peer review process under which many academic institutions operate. The costs that ensue from disclosure, however, constitute only one side of the balance. As Congress has recognized, the costs associated with racial and sexual discrimination in institutions of higher learning are very substantial. Few would deny that ferreting out this kind of invidious discrimination is a great, if not compelling, governmental interest. Often, as even petitioner seems to admit, disclosure of peer review materials will be necessary in order for the Commission to determine whether illegal discrimination has taken place. Indeed, if there is a "smoking gun" to be found that demonstrates discrimination in tenure decisions, it is likely to be tucked away in peer review files. . . .

. . .

Acceptance of petitioner's claim would also lead to a wave of similar privilege claims by other employers who play significant roles in furthering speech and learning in society. What of writers, publishers, musicians, lawyers? It surely is not unreasonable to believe, for example, that confidential peer reviews play an important part in partnership determinations at some law firms. We perceive no limiting principle in petitioner's argument. Accordingly, we stand behind the breakwater Congress has established: unless specifically provided otherwise in the statute, the EEOC may obtain "relevant" evidence. Congress has made the choice. If it dislikes the result, it of course may revise the statute.

. . .

As noted above, petitioner characterizes its First Amendment claim as one of "academic freedom." Petitioner begins its argument by focusing our attention upon language in prior cases acknowledging the crucial role universities play in the dissemination of ideas in our society and recognizing "academic freedom" as a "special concern of the First Amendment." *Keyishian v. Board of Regents of University of New York*, 385 U.S. 589, 603 (1967). In that case the Court said:

"Our Nation is deeply committed to safeguarding academic freedom, which is of transcendent value to all of us and not merely to the teachers concerned." Petitioner places special reliance on Justice Frankfurter's opinion, concurring in the result, in *Sweezy v. New Hampshire*, 354 U.S. 234, 263 (1957), where the Justice recognized that one of 'four essential freedoms' that a university possesses under the First Amendment is the right to "determine for itself on academic grounds *who may teach*" (emphasis added).

Petitioner contends that it exercises this right of determining "on academic grounds who may teach" through the process of awarding tenure. A tenure system, asserts petitioner, determines what the university will look like over time. "In making tenure decisions, therefore, a university is doing nothing less than shaping its own identity."

Petitioner next maintains that the peer review process is the most important element in the effective operation of a tenure system. A properly functioning tenure system requires the faculty to obtain candid and detailed written evaluations of the candidate's scholarship, both from the candidate's peers at the university and from scholars at other institutions. These evaluations, says petitioner, traditionally have been provided with express or implied assurances of confidentiality. It is confidentiality that ensures candor and enables an institution to make its tenure decisions on the basis of valid academic criteria.

Building from these premises, petitioner claims that requiring the disclosure of peer review evaluations on a finding of mere relevance will undermine the existing process of awarding tenure, and therefore will result in a significant infringement of petitioner's First Amendment right of academic freedom. As more and more peer evaluations are disclosed to the EEOC and become public, a "chilling effect" on candid evaluations and discussions of candidates will result. And as the quality of peer review evaluations declines, tenure committees will no longer be able to rely on them. "This will work to the detriment of universities, as less qualified persons achieve tenure causing the quality of instruction and scholarship to decline." Compelling disclosure of materials "also will result in divisiveness and tension, placing strain on faculty relations and impairing the free interchange of ideas that is a hallmark of academic freedom." The prospect of these deleterious effects on American colleges and universities, concludes petitioner, compels recognition of a First Amendment privilege.

In our view, petitioner's reliance on the so-called academic-freedom cases is somewhat misplaced. In those cases government was attempting to control or direct the *content* of the speech engaged in by the university or those affiliated with it. In *Sweezy*, for example, the Court invalidated the conviction of a person found in contempt for refusing to answer questions about the content of a lecture he had delivered at a state university. Similarly, in *Keyishian*, the Court invalidated a network of state laws that required public employees, including teachers at state universities, to make certifications with respect to their membership in the Communist Party. When, in those cases, the Court spoke of "academic freedom" and the right to determine on "academic grounds who may teach" the Court was speaking in reaction to content-based regulation.

Fortunately, we need not define today the precise contours of any academic-freedom right against governmental attempts to influence the content of academic speech through the selection of faculty or by other means,[6] because petitioner does not allege that the Commission's subpoenas are intended to or will in fact direct the content of university discourse toward or away from particular subjects or points of view....

Also, the cases upon which petitioner places emphasis involved *direct* infringements on the asserted right to "determine for itself on academic grounds who may teach." In *Keyishian,* for example, government was attempting to *substitute* its teaching employment criteria for those already in place at the academic institutions, directly and completely usurping the discretion of each institution. In contrast, the EEOC subpoena at issue here effects no such usurpation. The Commission is not providing criteria that petitioner *must* use in selecting teachers. Nor is it preventing the University from using any criteria it may wish to use, except those—including race, sex, and national origin—that are proscribed under Title VII. In keeping with Title VII's preservation of employers' remaining freedom of choice, courts have stressed the importance of avoiding second-guessing of legitimate academic judgments. This Court itself has cautioned that "judges ... asked to review the substance of a genuinely academic decision ... should show great respect for the faculty's professional judgment." *Regents of University of Michigan v. Ewing*, 474 U.S. 214, 225 (1985). Nothing we say today should be understood as a retreat from this principle of respect for *legitimate* academic decisionmaking.

That the burden of which the University complains is neither content based nor direct does not necessarily mean that petitioner has no valid First Amendment claim. Rather, it means only that petitioner's claim does not fit neatly within any right of academic freedom that could be derived from the cases on which petitioner relies. In essence, petitioner asks us to recognize an *expanded* right of academic freedom to protect confidential peer review materials from disclosure. Although we are sensitive to the effects that content-neutral government action may have on speech, and believe that burdens that are less than direct may sometimes pose First Amendment concerns, we think the First Amendment cannot be extended to embrace petitioner's claim.

First, by comparison with the cases in which we have found a cognizable First Amendment claim, the infringement the University complains of is extremely attenuated. To repeat, it argues that the First Amendment is infringed by disclosure of peer review materials because disclosure undermines the confidentiality which is central to the peer review process, and this in turn is central to the tenure process, which in turn is the means by which petitioner seeks to exercise its asserted academic-freedom right of choosing who will teach. To verbalize the claim is to recognize how distant the burden is from the asserted right.

---

6. Obvious First Amendment problems would arise where government attempts to direct the content of speech at private universities. Such content-based regulation of private speech traditionally has carried with it a heavy burden of justification. *See, e.g., Police Dept. of Chicago v. Mosley*, 408 U.S. 92, 95, 98–99 (1972). Where, as was the situation in the academic-freedom cases, government attempts to direct the content of speech at public educational institutions, complicated First Amendment issues are presented because government is simultaneously both speaker and regulator. *Cf. Meese v. Keene*, 481 U.S. 465, 484, n. 18 (1987) (citing *Block v. Meese*, 253 U.S. App. D. C. 317, 327–328, 793 F.2d 1303, 1313–1314 (1986)). *See generally*, M. Yudof, When Government Speaks (1983).

Indeed, if the University's attenuated claim were accepted, many other generally applicable laws might also be said to infringe the First Amendment. In effect, petitioner says no more than that disclosure of peer review materials makes it more difficult to acquire information regarding the "academic grounds" on which petitioner wishes to base its tenure decisions. But many laws make the exercise of First Amendment rights more difficult. For example, a university cannot claim a First Amendment violation simply because it may be subject to taxation or other government regulation, even though such regulation might deprive the university of revenue it needs to bid for professors who are contemplating working for other academic institutions or in industry. We doubt that the peer review process is any more essential in effectuating the right to determine "who may teach" than is the availability of money.

In addition to being remote and attenuated, the injury to academic freedom claimed by petitioner is also speculative. As the EEOC points out, confidentiality is not the norm in all peer review systems. *See, e.g.,* G. Bednash, The Relationship Between Access and Selectivity in Tenure Review Outcomes (1989) (unpublished Ph.D. dissertation, University of Maryland). Moreover, some disclosure of peer evaluations would take place even if petitioner's "special necessity" test were adopted. Thus, the "chilling effect" petitioner fears is at most only incrementally worsened by the absence of a privilege. Finally, we are not so ready as petitioner seems to be to assume the worst about those in the academic community. Although it is possible that some evaluators may become less candid as the possibility of disclosure increases, others may simply ground their evaluations in specific examples and illustrations in order to deflect potential claims of bias or unfairness. Not all academics will hesitate to stand up and be counted when they evaluate their peers.

. . .

Because we conclude that the EEOC subpoena process does not infringe any First Amendment right enjoyed by petitioner, the EEOC need not demonstrate any special justification to sustain the constitutionality of Title VII as applied to tenure peer review materials in general or to the subpoena involved in this case. . . .

The judgment of the Court of Appeals is affirmed.

Questions and Comments on *Univ. of Penn. v. EEOC*

1. Should colleges and universities be treated differently by courts than other workplaces? How necessary is secrecy to tenure decisions? Might some degree of openness actually benefit the decision-making process?

2. Do you think race and gender are ever factors in the peer review process? Has the university's argument about the chilling effect of subpoenas on the peer review proven accurate?

3. In *Sweezy*, the university's interest in maintaining an open intellectual forum coincided with Sweezy's interest in free speech in an academic setting. *University of Pennsylvania v. EEOC* suggests that institutional academic freedom may conflict with a faculty member's assertion of her own academic freedom. Did the Court resolve that conflict appropriately?

E.   STRUCTURE AND MISSION

Degree Granting Institutions in the United States by Type, 2006–2007

Type of Institution	4 years and above	2 year	TOTAL
Public	643	1,045	1,688
Private Nonprofit	1,533	107	1,640
For profit	453	533	986
TOTAL	2,629	1,685	4,314

Source: U.S. Department of Education, National Center for Education Statistics, Integrated Postsecondary Education Data System (IPEDS) Tbl. 255 (2006–2007).

Degrees Awarded by Type of Institution, 2005–2006

	Associate		Bachelor's		Master's		Doctorate		Professional	
Type of Institution	Number	Share of Total	Number	Share of Total	Number	Share of Total	Number	Share of Total	Number	Share of Total
Public	557,134	78%	955,369	64%	293,517	49%	33,767	60%	36,269	41%
Private Nonprofit	46,442	7	467,836	32	255,424	43	20,830	37	50,902	58
For Profit	109,490	15	62,037	4	45,124	8	1,470	3	484	1
TOTAL	713,066	100	1,485,242	100	594,065	100	56,067	100	87,655	100

Source: 55 CHRON. OF HIGHER EDUC., Aug. 29, 2008, at 20.

Campuses with the Largest Enrollments, Fall 2006

University of Phoenix online	165,373	City College of San Francisco	44,392
Ohio State U. main campus	51,818	University of South Florida	43,646
Miami Dade College	51,329	Penn. State U. at University Park	42,914
Arizona State U at Tempe	51,234	U. of Ill. at Urbana–Champaign	42,738
University of Florida	50,912	Houston Comm. College	42,526
University of Minn.–Twin Cities	50,402	U. of Wisconsin at Madison	41,028
University of Texas at Austin	49,697	New York University	40,870
U. of Central Florida.	46,646	North Harris–Montgomery CC	40,846
Michigan State University	45,520	Perdue University main campus	40,609
Texas A & M U. at College Station	45,380	U. of Michigan at Ann Arbor	40,025

Source: 55 CHRON. OF HIGHER EDUC., Aug. 29, 2008, at 17.

**Percentage of U.S. Population Age 25 and
Over by Years of School Completed**

Year	Less than 5 years of elementary school	High school or higher	Bachelor's degree or higher
1910	23.8	13.5	2.7
1920	22.0	16.4	3.3
1930	17.5	19.1	3.9
1940	13.7	24.5	4.6
1950	11.1	34.3	6.2
1960	8.3	41.1	7.7
1970	5.3	55.2	11.0
1980	3.4	68.6	17.0
1990	2.4	77.6	21.3
2000	1.6	84.1	25.6
2007	1.5	85.7	28.7

Source: National Center for Education Statistics, Digest of Education Statistics, Tbl. 8 (2007).

Special Report: *Meritocracy in America*

ECONOMIST, Jan.1, 2005, at 22.

The United States likes to think of itself as the very embodiment of meritocracy: a country where people are judged on their individual abilities rather than their family connections. The original colonies were settled by refugees from a Europe in which the restrictions on social mobility were woven into the fabric of the state, and the American revolution was partly a revolt against feudalism. From the outset, Americans believed that equality of opportunity gave them an edge over the Old World, freeing them from debilitating snobberies and at the same time enabling everyone to benefit from the abilities of the entire population. They still do.

To be sure, America has often betrayed its fine ideals. The Founding Fathers did not admit women or blacks to their meritocratic republic. The country's elites have repeatedly flirted with the aristocratic principle, whether among the Brahmins of Boston or, more flagrantly, the rural ruling class in the South. Yet America has repeatedly succeeded in living up to its best self, and today most Americans believe that their country still does a reasonable job of providing opportunities for everybody, including blacks and women. In Europe, majorities of people in every country except Britain, the Czech Republic and Slovakia believe that forces beyond their personal control determine their success. In America only 32% take such a fatalistic view.

But are they right? A growing body of evidence suggests that the meritocratic ideal is in trouble in America. Income inequality is growing to levels not seen since the Gilded Age, around the 1880s. But social mobility is not increasing at anything like the same pace: would-be Horatio Algers are finding it no easier to climb from rags to riches, while the children of the privileged have a greater chance of staying at the top of the social heap. The United States risks calcifying into a European-style class-based society.

The past couple of decades have seen a huge increase in inequality in America. The Economic Policy Institute, a Washington think-tank, argues that between 1979 and 2000 the real income of households in the lowest fifth (the bottom 20% of earners) grew by 6.4%, while that of households in the top fifth grew by 70%. The family income of the top 1% grew by 184%—and that of the top 0.1% or 0.01% grew even faster. Back in 1979 the average income of the top 1% was 133 times that of the bottom 20%; by 2000 the income of the top 1% had risen to 189 times that of the bottom fifth.

Thirty years ago the average real annual compensation of the top 100 chief executives was $1.3m: 39 times the pay of the average worker. Today it is $37.5m: over 1,000 times the pay of the average worker. In 2001 the top 1% of households earned 20% of all income and held 33.4% of all net worth. Not since pre-Depression days has the top 1% taken such a big whack.

Most Americans see nothing wrong with inequality of income so long as it comes with plenty of social mobility: it is simply the price paid for a dynamic economy. But the new rise in inequality does not seem to have come with a commensurate rise in mobility. There may even have been a fall.

. . .

[M]ore and more evidence from social scientists suggests that American society is much "stickier" than most Americans assume. Some researchers claim that social mobility is actually declining. A classic social survey in 1978 found that 23% of adult men who had been born in the bottom fifth of the population (as ranked by social and economic status) had made it into the top fifth. Earl Wysong of Indiana University and two colleagues recently decided to update the study. They compared the incomes of 2,749 father-and-son pairs from 1979 to 1998 and found that few sons had moved up the class ladder. Nearly 70% of the sons in 1998 had remained either at the same level or were doing worse than their fathers in 1979. The biggest increase in mobility had been at the top of society, with affluent sons moving upwards more often than their fathers had. They found that only 10% of the adult men born in the bottom quarter had made it to the top quarter.

The Economic Policy Institute also argues that social mobility has declined since the 1970s. In the 1990s 36% of those who started in the second-poorest 20% stayed put, compared with 28% in the 1970s and 32% in the 1980s. In the 1970s 12% of the population moved from the bottom fifth to either the fourth or the top fifth. In the 1980s and 1990s the figures shrank to below 11% for both decades. The figure for those who stayed in the top fifth increased slightly but steadily over the three decades, reinforcing the sense of diminished social mobility.

. . .

Not all social scientists accept the conclusion that mobility is declining. Gary Solon, of the University of Michigan, argues that there is no evidence of any change in social-mobility rates, down or up. But, at the least, most people agree that the dramatic increase in income inequality over the past two decades has not been accompanied by an equally dramatic increase in social mobility.

Take the study carried out by Thomas Hertz, an economist at American University in Washington, DC, who studied a representative sample of 6,273 American families (both black and white) over 32 years or two generations. He found that 42% of those born into the poorest fifth ended up where they started—at the bottom. Another 24% moved up slightly to the next-to-bottom group. Only 6% made it to the top fifth. Upward mobility was particularly low for black families. On the other hand, 37% of those born into the top fifth remained there, whereas barely 7% of those born into the top 20% ended up in the bottom fifth. A person born into the top fifth is over five times as likely to end up at the top as a person born into the bottom fifth.

. . .

There is also growing evidence that America is less socially mobile than many other rich countries. Mr. Solon finds that the correlation between the incomes of fathers and sons is higher in the United States than in Germany, Sweden, Finland or Canada. Such cross-national comparisons are rife with problems: different studies use different methods and different definitions of social status. But Americans are clearly mistaken if they believe they live in the world's most mobile society.

This is not the first time that America has looked as if it was about to succumb to what might be termed the British temptation. America witnessed a similar widening of the income gap in the Gilded Age. It also witnessed the formation of a British-style ruling class. The robber barons of the late 19th century sent their children to private boarding schools and made sure that they married the daughters of the old elite, preferably from across the Atlantic. Politics fell into the hands of the members of a limited circle—so much so that the Senate was known as the millionaires' club.

Yet the late 19th and early 20th centuries saw a concerted attempt to prevent America from degenerating into a class-based society. Progressive politicians improved state education. Philanthropists—many of them the robber barons reborn in new guise—tried to provide ladders to help the lads-o'-parts (Andrew Carnegie poured millions into free libraries). Such reforms were motivated partly out of a desire to do good works and partly out of a real fear of the implications of class-based society. Teddy Roosevelt advocated an inheritance tax because he thought that huge inherited fortunes would ruin the character of the republic. James Conant, the president of Harvard in 1933–53, advocated radical educational reform—particularly the transformation of his own university into a meritocracy—in order to prevent America from producing an aristocracy.

The evils that Roosevelt and Conant worried about are clearly beginning to reappear. But so far there are few signs of a reform movement. Why not?

The main reason may be a paradoxical one: because the meritocratic revolution of the first half of the 20th century has been at least half successful. Members of the American elite live in an intensely competitive universe. As children, they are ferried from piano lessons to ballet lessons to early-reading classes. As adolescents, they cram in as much after-school coaching as possible. As students, they compete to get into the best graduate schools. As young professionals, they burn the midnight oil for their employers. And, as parents, they agonise about getting their children into the best universities. It is hard for such people to imagine that America is anything but a meritocracy: their lives are a perpetual competition. Yet it is a competition among people very much like themselves—the offspring of a tiny slither of society—rather than among the full range of talents that the country has to offer.

The second reason is that America's engines of upward mobility are no longer working as effectively as they once were. The most obvious example lies in the education system. Upward mobility is increasingly determined by education. The income of people with just a high-school diploma was flat in 1975–99, whereas that of people with a bachelor's degree rose substantially, and that of people with advanced degrees rocketed.

The educational system is increasingly stratified by social class, and poor children have a double disadvantage. They attend schools with fewer resources than those of their richer contemporaries (school finances are largely determined by local property taxes). And they have to deal with the legacy of what Michael Barone, a conservative commentator, has labeled "soft America". Soft America is allergic to introducing accountability and measurement in education, particularly if it takes the form of merit pay for successful teachers or rewards for outstanding pupils. Dumbed-down schools are particularly harmful to poor children, who are unlikely to be able to compensate for them at home.

America's great universities are increasingly reinforcing rather than reducing these educational inequalities. Poorer students are at a huge disadvantage, both when they try to get in and, if they are successful, in their ability to make the most of what is on offer. This disadvantage is most marked in the elite colleges that hold the keys to the best jobs. Three-quarters of the students at the country's top 146 colleges come from the richest socio-economic fourth, compared with just 3% who come from the poorest fourth (the median family income at Harvard, for example, is $150,000). This means that, at an elite university, you are 25 times as likely to run into a rich student as a poor one.

One reason for this is government money. The main federal programme supporting poorer students is the Pell grant: 90% of such grants go to families with incomes below $41,000. But the federal government has been shifting resources from Pell grants to other forms of aid to higher education. Student loans are unrelated to family resources. Federal tax breaks for higher education benefit the rich. State subsidies for higher education benefit rich and poor alike. At the same time, colleges are increasingly using financial aid to attract talented students away from competitors rather than to help the poor.

Another reason may be "affirmative action"—programmes designed to help members of racial minorities. These are increasingly used by elite universities, in the belief that race is a reasonable proxy for social disadvantage, which it may not be . Flawed as it may be, however, this kind of affirmative action is much less pernicious than another practised by many universities: "legacy preferences", a programme for the children of alumni—as if privileged children were not already doing well enough out of the education system.

In most Ivy League institutions, the eight supposedly most select universities of the north-east, "legacies" make up between 10% and 15% of every class. At Harvard they are over three times more likely to be admitted than others. The students in America's places of higher education are increasingly becoming an oligarchy tempered by racial preferences. This is sad in itself, but even sadder when you consider the extraordinary role that the same universities—particularly Conant's Harvard—played in promoting merito-cracy in the first half of the 20th century.

. . .

In his classic "The Promise of American Life", Herbert Croly noted that "a democracy, not less than a monarchy or an aristocracy, must recognise political, economic, and social distinctions, but it must also withdraw its consent whenever these discriminations show any tendency to excessive endurance." So far Americans have been fairly tolerant of economic distinc-tions. But that tolerance may not last for ever, if the current trend towards "excessive endurance" is not reversed.

Note on Income and the Distribution of Education

Workers eighteen and over with a bachelor's degree earn an average of $51,206 a year in the United States, while those with only a high school diploma earn on average $27,915. Press Release, U.S. Census Bureau, College Degree Nearly Doubles Annual Earnings (March 28, 2005), *available at* http://www.census.gov/Press–Release/ www/releases/archives/education/004214.html. The United States leads all other na-tions except Canada in the proportion of 35–64 year-old adults with college degrees. NATIONAL CENTER FOR PUBLIC POLICY AND HIGHER EDUCATION, MEASURING UP 2006: THE NATIONAL REPORT CARD ON HIGHER EDUCATION 7 (2006), *available at* http://measuring up.highereducation.org/_docs/2006/NationalReport_2006.pdf.

Gary Becker and Kevin Murphy note that:

In 1980, an American with a college degree earned about 30 percent more than an American who stopped at high school. But in recent years, a person with a college education earned roughly 70 percent more. Meanwhile, the premium for having a graduate degree increased from roughly 50 percent in 1980 to well over 100 percent today. The labor market is placing a greater emphasis on education, dispensing rapidly raising rewards to those who stay in school the longest.

The Upside of Income Inequality, AMERICAN.COM, May/June 2007, http://www.american. com/archive/2007/may-june-magazine-contents/the-upside-of-income-inequality/.

They add that education premiums for women and African–Americans have increased as much as, or more than, the premiums for all workers. They conclude that "instead of lamenting the increased earnings gap caused by education, policy-makers and the public should focus attention on how to raise the fraction of American youth who complete high school and then go on for a college education," adding "it will be a disaster if the focus remains so much on the earnings inequality itself that Congress tries to interfere directly with this inequality rather than trying to raise the educational levels of those who are now being left behind." *Id.*

In the early 1990s, the progress that had been made in increasing access to college slowed dramatically. By 2005, the United States ranked only fifteenth in the world in the educational attainment of young adults.

Graduates Awarded Bachelor's Degree or Equivalent, 2005

OECD Country	Ratio of graduates to the population at the typical age of graduation
Australia	59
Iceland	56
New Zealand	51
Finland (2004)	47
Denmark	46
Poland	45
Netherlands	42
Italy	41
Norway	41
United Kingdom	39
Ireland	38
Sweden	38
Hungary	36
Japan	36
United States	**34**
Spain	33
Portugal	32
Slovak Republic	30
Switzerland	27
Czech Republic	25
Greece	25
Austria	20
Germany	20
Turkey	11
OECD Average	**36**

Source: ORG. FOR ECON. COOP. AND DEV., EDUCATION AT A GLANCE 2007, at 67 tbl.A3.1 (2007), *available at* http://www.oecd.org/dataoecd/4/55/39313286. pdf.

The problem can be traced to degree completion. The United States is one of the top five nations in the world in the proportion of young people who enroll in college; but it ranks only sixteenth in degree completion. TRAVIS REINDL, MAKING OPPORTUNITY AFFORDABLE, HITTING HOME: QUALITY, COST, AND ACCESS CHALLENGES CONFRONTING HIGHER EDUCATION TODAY 4 (2007).

CHAPTER 2

DISTINGUISHING PUBLIC FROM PRIVATE COLLEGES AND UNIVERSITIES

Chapter 1 revealed how difficult it can be to classify a college as public or private. As you read the material in this chapter, consider not only the question of how courts should classify particular colleges or universities, but the consequences. When and why does it matter whether a college or university is public or private?

A. FROM PRIVATE TO PUBLIC

Trustees of Dartmouth College v. Woodward

Supreme Court of the United States, 1819.
17 U.S. (4 Wheat.) 518, 4 L.Ed. 629.

[The opinion is set forth at pages 42 to 47, *supra*.]

Rutgers v. Richman

Superior Court of New Jersey, Chancery Division, 1956.
41 N.J.Super. 259, 125 A.2d 10.

■ SCHETTINO, J.S.C.

[In 1956, New Jersey enacted a statute designed to increase the state's control over Rutgers University. The statute would not take effect, however, unless the university's Board of Trustees "accept[ed] and adopt[ed] its provisions" within three months of enactment. Decided within that three-month period, this case addresses the statute's constitutionality and whether the Trustees' fiduciary duties prevented them from accepting the statute. The court also provides a history of Rutgers University, which tells the story of nearly two centuries of increasing public control over a once fully private college.]

Rutgers University has its origin in Queen's College, chartered by George III of Great Britain in 1766 in response to a petition of Dutch settlers of New York and New Jersey. . . .

The original charter provided:

a.   The right and power to establish and conduct a college:

For the education of youth in the learned languages, liberal and useful arts and sciences, and especially in divinity; preparing them for the ministry and other good offices;

b.   The provision that the President shall be a member of the Dutch Reformed Church;

c.   The incorporation of the Trustees in perpetuity, under the name "Trustees of Queen's-College in New Jersey," with appropriate corporate powers;

d.   Full power in the Trustees over the government of the college, to make "ordinances, orders and laws" for the government of the college, and to execute the same;

e.   Election by the Trustees of a President, a Professor of Divinity, professors and tutors, treasurer, the clerk, the steward, and other inferior officers and ministers to serve during the pleasure of the Trustees;

f.   The membership of the Trustees, originally consisting of the Governor or Commander-in-Chief, the President of the Council, the Chief Justice and the Attorney–General of the colony for the time being, and 37 named Trustees of the Colony of New Jersey and the Provinces of New York and Pennsylvania....

After the American Revolution the charter was amended and confirmed by the State of New Jersey in 1781 upon petition of the Board of Trustees, an interesting change being the removal of the one-third restriction upon ordained ministers as trustees. In 1825 the name was changed to "The Trustees of Rutgers College in New Jersey" in recognition of Colonel Henry Rutgers, a generous donor, and the charter was amended in minor respects.

.   .   .

The formal excision from the charter of all religious and sectarian qualifications both generally and with specific reference to the President's membership in the Reformed Church in America and to the maintenance of a professorship of divinity, was made by Board resolution of 1920.

.   .   .

[I]n 1945 Rutgers was recognized by the State and the Board of Trustees as a university, the State University, an instrumentality of the State; and all its parts became subject to a public trust for higher education under the general superintendence of the State Board of Education.

.   .   .

Rutgers is today a university, "an instrumentality of the state for providing public higher education," and its property and educational facilities are impressed with a "public trust for higher education of the people of the State."

It is centered in New Brunswick, with branches in more than a score of other municipalities in New Jersey, consisting of 21 colleges and divisions at graduate and undergraduate levels....

.   .   .

Management of the University is in the Board of 54 Trustees.... Thirty-two of the number are classified as charter trustees, of whom 30 hold indefinite terms and two (women) hold a five-year term; and seven persons are elected by the Board of Trustees for five-year terms on the nomination of the alumni and alumnae of the University. Five trustees are classified as public trustees appointed to five-year terms by the Governor of the State with the advice and consent of the Senate. The balance of the membership comprises nine trustees *ex officio* (officials of the State Government), and the president of the New Jersey Federation of Women's Clubs (*ex officio* by election by the Board)....

Internal control of the University by the Board of Trustees is subject to certain public supervision by the State Board of Education "to examine into its manner of conducting its affairs and to enforce an observance of its laws and regulations and the laws of the State." In addition, the property of the State which the Board of Trustees holds at the University is subject to the visitorial power, and

> The State Board of Education shall investigate and jointly with the State University of New Jersey make recommendations to the Governor and the Legislature respecting the needs for the facilities and services of the State University of New Jersey as an instrumentality of the State for providing public higher education and thereby to increase the efficiency of the public school system of the State.

The State Board of Education has express responsibility and authority with respect to the University's budget ... to "advise with the State University of New Jersey regarding its annual budget ... and jointly with the State University make recommendations to the Governor and to the Legislature in support of such budget...." [T]he State Board of Education annually makes contracts with the University which deal not only with the disposition of the budget but also with matters of admissions, tuitions and state scholarships.

. . .

Chapter 61 of the Laws of 1956 was approved by the Governor.... This act known as "Rutgers, The State University Act of 1956," embodies the proposed reorganization of the University. It will become void unless the Board of Trustees in its discretion accepts and adopts its provisions prior to September 1, 1956.

... The act provides for a Board of Governors for the University which will supersede the Board of Trustees in the general supervision and conduct of the University.

The Board of Governors shall consist of two *ex officio* members without vote, i.e., the Commissioner of Education of New Jersey and the President of Rutgers, and 11 voting members. Of the 11, a majority of six shall be appointed by the Governor of New Jersey with the advice and consent of the Senate, and the minority of five shall be appointed by the Board of Trustees from among the charter, alumni and alumnae trustees, each for a six-year term; they may succeed themselves for one additional six-year term and are appointed to staggered terms.... The Board of Governors shall have general supervision over and be vested with the conduct of the University; specifically, power to determine policy and study the educational and financial needs of the University; preparation of the budget and presentation of it (jointly with the State Board of Education) to the Governor and Legislature;

disbursement of all monies received from any source, including endowment income received through the Board of Trustees; the borrowing of money with the advice and consent of the Board of Trustees; planning, provision and construction of buildings, lands, materials, equipment and supplies; appointment, removal and compensation of all officers, faculty and employees of the University (in the case of the President, with the advice and consent of the Board of Trustees), and establishment with the approval of the State Board of Education of new educational departments or schools. The use and income of hitherto privately-donated properties, funds and trusts, the control of which is retained by the Board of Trustees, are made available to the Board of Governors and continued to be held impressed with a public trust for higher education. Title to properties continues in the corporate body excepting those which are in the name of the State.

> The Board of Trustees is to retain important functions and powers of three distinct types. First, it shall act in an overall advisory capacity. Second, it shall have control of properties, funds and trusts vested in the corporate body as of August 31, 1956 (other than those, broadly speaking, owned by the State or derived from public sources) and of property, funds and trusts thereafter received by the corporate body which, again broadly speaking, the donor may be deemed to intend to entrust to the control of the Board of Trustees as such. Third, the Board of Trustees shall have the right to withhold or withdraw both of those two categories of property from the use and employment of the Board of Governors if such property is not properly applied to the purpose of public higher education, if the State fails to make sufficient provision to permit the fulfillment of the Trustee's public trust through the conduct of a state university with high educational standards, or if certain other terms are not met. . . .

The Board of Trustees consists of the following: (a) two *ex officio* trustees without vote, namely the Commissioner of Education and the President of the Corporation; (b) the public trustees are increased from five to 11, being the five trustees provided for in Laws 1945, chapter 49, section 4; N.J. Stat. Ann. § 18:22–15.4 plus the six appointees of the Governor to the Board of Governors, who automatically serve also as Trustees; (c) the alumni and alumnae trustees will remain at seven in number; and (d) lastly, the present 30 charter trustees with indefinite term will continue to serve until the incidence of vacancies reduces their number to 12, whereafter the number may be maintained at 12 by election of the Board, subject to the election by the Board of three women as charter trustees. All trustees hereafter elected except the *ex officio* trustees and the public trustees serving under the 1945 act shall serve for a six-year term, on a staggered basis, and may succeed themselves for one additional six-year term. . . .

> Each board is given incidental powers appropriate to its respective functions. . . .

The executive management and conduct of the institution under the act remains lodged in the President, who shall be elected by the Board of Governors with the advice and consent of the Board of Trustees and shall hold office at the pleasure of the Board of Governors. Departure from the specified manner of electing the President is made one of the occasions permitting the Board of Trustees' withdrawal of its properties.

The act changes the name of the University from "The Trustees of Rutgers College in New Jersey" to "Rutgers, The State University."

. . . Whereas since 1945 the facilities of the University have remained in the hands of the Board of Trustees impressed with a public trust and subject to the general superintendence of the State Board of Education, under the act the facilities and their use and income will be actually made available to and directly managed by a publicly controlled Board of Governors. The State will receive effective control of an existing and established educational institution valued at many millions of dollars, plus the prospect of future donations. On the other hand, the Board of Trustees will have the State's solemn declaration of its policy that

> (i) the University shall be and continue to be given a high degree of self-government and that the government and conduct of the Corporation and the University shall be free of partisanship, and

> (ii) that resources be and continue to be provided and funds be and continue to be appropriated by the State adequate for the conduct of a State University with high educational standards and to meet the cost of increasing enrollment and the need for proper facilities.

and that

> . . . provision shall . . . be made by the State sufficient to enable the Board of Trustees to discharge its trust to apply the trust assets . . . for public higher education through the conduct of a university with high educational standards.

and further that the assets controlled by the Trustee shall be properly applied and that the name of the University shall not be changed, nor provisions of the act for the essential self-government of the University be substantially altered, without the Board's consent.

We summarize the problems. . . . Plaintiffs are trustees of a very considerable body of assets, for the most part derived from private donations in the cause of higher education over more than a century and a half and including also assets of substantial value derived from grants of the State of New Jersey and the Federal Government. . . .

The two most basic questions presented are, first, whether chapter 61 is a constitutionally valid enactment upon which the plaintiffs may safely rely if they choose to accept its terms, and, second, whether the nature of their fiduciary duties permits them to exercise their choice in favor of accepting it.

Defendants, Grover C. Richman, Jr., Attorney–General, Robert L. Finley, Acting and Deputy State Treasurer, and the State Board of Education acting in their public and official capacities, support the plaintiffs' motion for summary judgment.

. . .

At the outset, it should be emphasized that this court is not called upon to determine the wisdom of the plan of reorganization . . . nor is it required to determine whether the trustees should or should not accept this plan or other alternate plans for the solution of the potential problems of the

University in future years.... Our power is limited and is to pass upon the legal validity of the plan and the legislation....

. . .

A principle of trust law is that trustees, having been chosen as such because of the confidence reposed in them and because of their special competence to effectuate the purposes of a trust, may not delegate important discretionary powers. Here the Governor and Legislature have provided for a shift in the major trust responsibility from the privately controlled Board of Trustees to the publicly controlled Board of Governors....

The first inquiry is directed to determining the nature of the "charitable trust" held and administered by the Trustees of Rutgers College in New Jersey....

By chapter 49 of the Laws of 1945, and the resolution of acceptance, the Trustees of Rutgers College in New Jersey agreed to impress all property, assets and funds held and administered by the corporation as trustee with a public trust for higher education of the people of the State. That public trust must be maintained pursuant to chapter 61, which discloses a strongly enunciated continuation of Rutgers' dedication to the purposes of higher education for the people of New Jersey. Necessarily, the accomplishment of the trust purpose is all important. A trust will not fail because of a change in the identity of the trustee or the method of administration. It is not likely that persons making gifts to the University do so in special reliance upon the fact that no change will be made in the management of the corporation, in view of numerous Rutgers' changes stated above.

Other factors strongly support the conclusion that the Trustees of Rutgers College in New Jersey would not breach their trust duties by adoption of L. 1956, c. 61. The Board of Trustees retains power to withdraw and withhold the use and income of the trust property, assets and funds, presently of the value of $89,000,000, from the Board of Governors in the event that its trust duties for the accomplishment of the trust purposes are not adequately discharged.

. . .

The fundamental change brought about by the use of the additional governing body to be known as a Board of Governors is the granting of a greater voice in management to the State as a *quid pro quo* for greater financial support. Since the majority of voting members of the Board of Governors are appointed by the Governor of the State of New Jersey with the advice and consent of the Senate, the public is granted major control over the policies and administration of the university. Nevertheless, we note the strong statement of "public policy" that the University shall continue to be given a high degree of self-government, free of the partisanship which may be present in State Government. Thus we find here created a hybrid institution—at one and the same time private and public, with the State being granted a major voice in management, and the designation "State University"; and the institution being granted private autonomy and control of physical properties and assets.

Under general legislation dealing with charitable and educational corporations, in the absence of a membership in such a corporation, the trustees are empowered to act in the case of an amendment to the charter or certificate of incorporation. The Board of Trustees, by appropriate resolution, has assented to the plan of reorganization and has accepted the amendments to the charter contained therein, so that the constitutional hurdles evoked by the *Dartmouth College* case are not applicable....

. . .

It is clear that the purposes of the charter, namely, to establish a college "for the education of youth in the learned languages, liberal and useful arts, and sciences," is [sic.] advanced and nurtured by the plan which seeks to effect greater financial support in order to bring the facilities of the University in line with the demands of modern society. The basic functions, purpose and role of the University as an educational institution remain unchanged. The mode or technique of internal management is changed. I find that the modifications are fair and reasonable and consistent with the purposes set forth in the charter and its subsequent amendments.

The more troublesome question is whether the consent of the Trustees is sufficient to validate the changes in the absence of the practical inability to secure the consent of the donors or beneficiaries. Some courts have taken the literal approach to the nature of the trust and have denied the right of the State and the trustees to produce changes without the consent of the founder.

Other states have taken the view that the consent of the trustees is adequate if the amendments are not inconsistent with the basic purposes of the trustees, especially where the donors and beneficiaries are so numerous and unascertainable as to make it wholly impractical to seek their consent.

. . .

The divergent decisions are reviewed and analyzed in an interesting article by Professor Austin W. Scott, entitled *Education and the Dead Hand*, 34 HARV. L. REV. 1 (November, 1920). Professor Scott takes the position that progress demands changes and that as long as the changes are reasonable under the existing circumstances and consistent with the basic purposes of the charitable corporation, the concurrent action of the Legislature and the trustees is adequate to sustain the legal validity. As he points out, "The trustees are peculiarly fit to determine such questions. They hold and administer the properties; they and they alone represent both the donors and the beneficiaries." With this view, I agree.

. . .

I conclude that this court has jurisdiction to grant a final judgment and to give instructions and declaratory judgment with respect to the matters alleged in the amended and supplemental complaint; that fiscal support of Rutgers, The State University, pursuant to chapter 61 of the Laws of 1956 and under enactments of the New Jersey Legislature from time to time granting appropriations to Rutgers, The State University, will not constitute a violation of Article VIII, Section III, paragraph 3 of the Constitution of New Jersey as a donation of land or appropriation of money to or for the use of any society, association or corporation whatever; that chapter 61 of the Laws of 1956 does not constitute an appropriation of money in violation of Article VIII, Section II, paragraph 2 of the Constitution of New Jersey; that chapter 61 of the Laws of 1956 deals with a matter of substantial public concern and is not unconstitutional as an impairment of the obligation of a contract or deprivation of due process of law forbidden by the Constitution of the State of New Jersey or of the United States; that The Board of Trustees of Rutgers College in New Jersey individually, collectively and on behalf of the corporate plaintiff, has power and authority to adopt Chapter 61 of the Laws of 1956 as a valid and constitutional enactment, to amend the Charter of the corporate plaintiff in conformity therewith, and to effectuate the plan of reorganization which is implemented thereby; and the same is a valid and proper exercise of their fiduciary duties which will not of itself subject it or them to liability or penalty for any violation or dereliction of its or their fiduciary duties; that the effectuation of the plan of reorganization of the Trustees of Rutgers College in New Jersey which is implemented by chapter 61 of the Laws of 1956, and the adoption of said act and amendment of said Charter thereby, will not of themselves as a matter of law adversely affect, forfeit or cause a reverter of the corporate plaintiff's interest in the properties and funds held or administered by it or which may in the future inure to its benefit, subject, however, in every case to special conditions subsequent or reversionary or other provisions affecting, and to the proper construction of, any particular gift, bequest, trust, transfer or other applicable instrument, including but not limited to the funds known as the "Beneficiary Funds" and so designated in the annual financial statements of the corporate plaintiff, and to the provisions of chapter 61 of the Laws of 1956 and other applicable laws, and without prejudice whatsoever to the rights and interests of any person or persons therein as may be determined in accordance with law.

Questions and Comments on *Rutgers v. Richmond*

1. Did the statute reviewed in *Rutgers v. Richmond* transform Rutgers into a public institution? Courts have provided conflicting answers. *Compare* Kovats v. Rutgers, 822 F.2d 1303 (3d Cir. 1987) (Rutgers is not entitled to Eleventh Amendment immunity from suit in federal court), *and* Frank Briscoe Co. v. Rutgers, 130 N.J.Super. 493, 327 A.2d 687 (Law Div. 1974) (Rutgers is not a state agency subject to the New Jersey Contractual Liability Act), *with* Keddie v. Rutgers, 148 N.J. 36, 689 A.2d 702 (1997) (Rutgers' spending records for outside counsel are publicly available). The most recent pronouncement from the New Jersey Supreme Court is that "unless public status would frustrate the purposes of the Rutgers charter or the primary purpose of the underlying law or rule, Rutgers should be considered an instrumentality of the state." Fine v. Rutgers, 163 N.J. 464, 750 A.2d 68, 72 (2000).

2. Why did the legislature of New Jersey succeed in taking over a private institution of higher education when the legislature of New Hampshire failed in *The Dartmouth College* case?

B. STATE ACTION DOCTRINE

Hack v. President and Fellows of Yale College

United States Court of Appeals for the Second Circuit, 2000.
237 F.3d 81, *cert. denied*, 534 U.S. 888 (2001).

■ MORAN, SENIOR DISTRICT JUDGE.

Yale College requires all unmarried freshmen and sophomores under the age of 21 to reside in college dormitories, all of which are co-educational.

The plaintiffs were Yale freshmen and sophomores when they brought this suit. They represent that as devout Orthodox Jews they cannot reside in those dormitories because to do so would conflict with their religious convictions and duties. Plaintiffs contend that Yale is a state actor or instrumentality and, therefore, the First, Fourth, and Fourteenth Amendments invalidate the parietal rule pursuant to 42 U.S.C. § 1983; that in any event they are entitled to discovery to explore the interrelationship between Yale and the governments of Connecticut and New Haven; that Yale's mandatory on-campus housing requirement is both an attempt to monopolize a New Haven housing market in violation of § 2 of the Sherman Antitrust Act and a tying arrangement in violation of § 1 of that statute; and that Yale's refusal to exempt religious observers from co-educational housing violates the Fair Housing Act, 41 U.S.C. § 3601 *et seq.*

The district court . . . granted defendants' motion to dismiss for failure to state a claim upon which relief can be granted . . . and plaintiffs appealed. . . .

The threshold inquiry for plaintiffs' constitutional claims is whether Yale can be considered a state actor or instrumentality acting under color of state law. The district court concluded that it could not. . . .

What constitutes state action has been variously described by courts as "an extremely difficult question," "murky waters," "obdurate," and a "protean concept," *see Krynicky v. University of Pittsburgh*, 742 F.2d 94, 97 (3d Cir. 1984). . . . The Court acknowledged in *Lebron v. National RR Passenger Corp.*, 513 U.S. 374 (1995), that "it is fair to say that 'our cases deciding when private action might be deemed that of the state have not been a model of consistency.'" *Id.* at 378 (quoting *Edmonson v. Leesville Concrete Co.*, 500 U.S. 614, 632 (1991) (O'Connor, J., dissenting)). As in *Lebron*, however, we need not "traverse that difficult terrain," because plaintiffs rely almost entirely upon *Lebron* in contending that Yale is not, in reality, a private entity but is, rather, an agency or instrumentality of the State of Connecticut for the purpose of individual constitutional rights.

Plaintiffs begin by describing the significant interrelationships between Yale and the state from colonial days well into the latter nineteenth century. To that end they note that Yale is chartered by special legislation and, indeed, that charter is confirmed in the Connecticut Constitution. They contend that Yale was created to further public, governmental objectives, objectives that are equally valid today. Yale, they point out, must submit its budget and financial report to the Connecticut legislature. Finally, they argue that the presence of the Governor and Lieutenant Governor, as *ex officio* members of the nineteen-member "Fellows of Yale College" governing board, provides further support for the conclusion that Yale is a governmental entity.

In *Lebron*, the Supreme Court determined that Amtrak was a governmental entity:

> We hold that where, as here, the Government creates a corporation by special law, for the furtherance of governmental objectives, and retains for itself permanent authority to appoint a majority of the directors of that corporation, the corporation is part of the Government for purposes of the First Amendment.

In the wake of *Lebron*, other courts have concluded that the Court set forth a three-prong standard: only if (1) the government created the corporate entity by special law, (2) the government created the entity to further governmental objectives, and (3) the government retains "permanent authority to appoint a majority of the directors of the corporation" will the corporation be deemed a government entity for the purpose of the state action requirement. Here, the first two factors are easily satisfied: the State of Connecticut created the corporate entity by special law, and higher education is a governmental objective (although not the exclusive province of government). Two of nineteen board members is, however, a long way from control.

Plaintiffs contend that a three-prong test, with one prong requiring "majority" governmental control, is an overly simplistic reading of *Lebron*. They argue that the two highest executive officers of the state are likely to be far more influential than other members, that they carry with them the aura of official action, and that their participation is at least as significant as the Presidential power to appoint a majority of Amtrak board members from specific lists of recommended private sector nominees. We disagree.

We think *Lebron* means what it says. Indeed, the Court there contrasted Comsat with Amtrak, noting that the President appointed only three of fifteen Comsat directors, and describing it as a private corporation not government-controlled. Moreover, the Court has indicated its reluctance to have the federal courts indulge in evaluations of the effectiveness of governmental persuasion, absent government control. Plaintiffs do not suggest that Connecticut had any involvement in establishing Yale's parietal rules. It is equally clear that the state could not control Yale's policies and operations even if it chose to become involved. Yale, as a private university, did not act under color of law.

. . .

Plaintiffs further allege that Yale's requirement that freshmen and sophomores reside in the dormitories is an attempt to monopolize the New Haven student housing market and that it is an illegal arrangement tying the provision of a Yale education to the purchase of unrelated housing services, all in violation of the Sherman Antitrust Act, 15 U.S.C. §§ 1 and 2.

We begin with the observation that if a parietal rule requiring some students to reside in college or university housing runs afoul of the antitrust laws, it has largely escaped the notice of the many colleges and universities across the country that have had and continue to have those rules and the notice of the millions of students who have attended those institutions in the more than a century since the Sherman Act was enacted. In *Hamilton Chapter of Alpha Delta Phi, Inc. v. Hamilton College*, 128 F.3d 59, 64–65 (2d Cir. 1997), we noted that only one reported case involved an antitrust challenge to university housing policies. And there, *American Nat'l Bank & Trust Co. of Chicago v. Board of Regents for Regency Universities*, 607 F. Supp. 845 (N.D. Ill. 1984), parietal rules similar to those here were not even questioned....

... Plaintiffs insist that there is no substitute for a Yale education, that it is unique, and in a collegiate sense that is undoubtedly so. *See Lee v. Life Ins. Co. of North America*, 23 F.3d 14, 17 (1st Cir. 1994) (considering "uniqueness" of the University of Rhode Island). The annual rankings of colleges and universities in *U.S. News and World Report*, however, illustrates the obvious:

there are many institutions of higher learning providing superb educational opportunities. Those opportunities are not inherently local. Plaintiffs themselves allege that 92.5 percent of the 1997–1998 freshman class came from outside Connecticut. If some of them, including the plaintiffs, were dissatisfied with the Yale parietal rules, they could matriculate elsewhere. The antitrust implications of university housing rules do not depend upon a trier of fact deciding that some universities, or certain departments in some universities, are "unique" and others are not.

     . . .

Plaintiffs further contend that Yale's refusal to exempt religious observers from co-educational housing violates Title VIII of the Civil Rights Act of 1968, known as the Fair Housing Act, 42 U.S.C. § 3601 *et seq.* ("FHA"). The Fair Housing Act provides that "it shall be unlawful to refuse to sell or rent . . . or otherwise make unavailable or deny, a dwelling to any person because of . . . religion." 42 U.S.C. § 3604(a). The FHA also prohibits discrimination "in the terms, conditions, or privileges of sale or rental of a dwelling, or in the provision of services or facilities in connection therewith, because of . . . religion." 42 U.S.C. § 3604(b).

The district court did not reach the merits of plaintiffs' Fair Housing Act claims because it concluded that the plaintiffs lacked standing. We disagree. The Act provides that "an aggrieved person may commence a civil action in an appropriate United States district court. . . ." A party is an "aggrieved person," according to the definition in 42 U.S.C. § 3602(i)(1), if he or she "claims to have been injured by a discriminatory housing practice." The Act requires only that the party "allege 'injury in fact' within the meaning of Article III of the [United States] Constitution, that is, that he allege 'distinct and palpable injuries that are fairly traceable to [defendants'] actions.' " *Leblanc–Sternberg v. Fletcher*, 67 F.3d 412, 424 (2d Cir. 1995). The Supreme Court has repeatedly directed the courts to give a "generous construction" to the Fair Housing Act. *See, e.g., Trafficante v. Metropolitan Life Ins. Co.*, 409 U.S. 205, 211–212 (1972). "Congress intended standing under § 812 to extend to the full limits of Art. III" and thus courts lack authority to create prudential barriers to standing under the Act.

The student plaintiffs claim a tangible, economic injury. Indeed, they do not seek to compel Yale to provide single-sex housing; they ask to be relieved of the burden of paying for rooms they contend are effectively "made unavailable" to them. We conclude that they have amply alleged injury in fact and, accordingly, have standing to pursue Fair Housing Act claims.

Because we disagree with the district court's conclusion that the students lack standing, we must consider Yale's contention that the students failed to state an FHA claim. We begin with the observation that plaintiffs allege no discriminatory intent on Yale's part, no facially discriminatory policy, and no facts sufficient to constitute disparate impact discrimination.

     . . .

     . . . Because the complaint alleges neither intent to discriminate, nor a facially discriminatory policy, nor facts necessary to constitute disparate impact discrimination, nor even that the plaintiffs were excluded from housing, we believe sections 3604(a) and (b) cannot be stretched to cover plaintiffs' claim that the FHA gives them a right to be excluded from Yale housing. Thus, based on our reading of the complaint, we would affirm the district court's dismissal of plaintiffs' FHA claims.

. . .

Plaintiffs' second theory of liability is that Yale impermissibly discriminated against them on the basis of religion because it has a "policy of granting *ad hoc* and other exemptions and accommodations for secular reasons, but not for religious reasons." Nowhere in their complaint do plaintiffs allege that Yale has a system of "*ad hoc*" exemptions. Although they refer loosely to the granting of exemptions "for reasons other than religious conviction and belief," the only other reasons identified are age (over 21) and marital status. These exemptions apply to Orthodox Jews just as they apply to other students. However, even assuming that plaintiffs alleged the widespread grant of "*ad hoc*" exemptions, they would not have stated a claim under the FHA. As we previously discussed, one relevant section of the FHA contemplates a challenge to a denial or refusal of housing and the other relevant section contemplates a challenge to discriminatory terms or conditions offered with respect to housing that is provided or offered. Plaintiffs' allegation that defendants refused to grant them exemptions does not come within either of these sections because they do not allege that Yale's refusal was based on intent to discriminate, was a facially discriminatory policy, constituted disparate impact discrimination by resulting in an under-representation of Orthodox Jews in Yale housing, or even caused them to be denied housing. Therefore, we affirm the district court's dismissal of the students' FHA claim. Having affirmed the dismissal of all of plaintiffs' federal claims, we also affirm the dismissal of plaintiffs' state law claims for lack of supplemental jurisdiction.

Note on State Action

The state action doctrine purports to distinguish between state actors or instrumentalities, which are subject to the limitations of the Fourteenth Amendment, and private conduct or entities, which are not. Four decades ago, Charles Black characterized the doctrine as "a conceptual disaster area," Charles L. Black, Jr., *Foreword: "State Action," Equal Protection, and California's Proposition 14*, 81 Harv. L. Rev. 69, 95 (1967), and little has changed since.

> In its most recent application of the doctrine, the Supreme Court explained:

> Our cases try to plot a line between state action subject to Fourteenth Amendment scrutiny and private conduct (however exceptionable) that is not. The judicial obligation is not only to preserve an area of individual freedom by limiting the reach of federal law and avoid the imposition of responsibility on a State for conduct it could not control, but also to assure that constitutional standards are invoked when it can be said that the State is *responsible* for the specific conduct of which the plaintiff complains.

Brentwood Acad. v. Tennessee Secondary Sch. Athletic Ass'n, 531 U.S. 288, 295 (2001). Almost apologetically, the Court noted that "[w]hat is fairly attributable [to state action] is a matter of normative judgment, and the criteria lack rigid simplicity." *Id.*

Against that background, the Supreme Court held in *Brentwood* that an athletic association, although a private corporation, was pervasively entwined with the state and therefore subject to the Fourteenth Amendment. The association consisted of a number of schools, eighty-four percent of them public, with each having a vote in the choice (from a list of eligible school officials) of the members of the corporation's governing council and board of control. Additionally, members of the state board of education sat as ex officio members of those bodies, and the association's "ministerial employees [were] treated as state employees ... eligible for membership in the state retirement system.... Entwinement will support a conclusion that an ostensibly private organization ought to be charged with a public character and judged by constitutional standards; entwinement to [this degree] requires it." *Id.* at 298–302.

The *Brentwood* Court thus added "pervasive entwinement" to its list of available state action tests, while explicitly noting that the association did not meet the three-prong *Lebron* test applied in *Hack. Id.* at 310. Was the Second Circuit too quick to dismiss the plaintiffs' claim that Yale was a state actor based on *Lebron*? Would Yale pass the pervasive entwinement test?

C. Public Forums

State v. Schmid

Supreme Court of New Jersey, 1980.
84 N.J. 535, 423 A.2d 615, *appeal dismissed,* 455 U.S. 100 (1982).

■ Handler, J.

[Chris Schmid was arrested and convicted of trespass for distributing materials relating to the United States Labor Party on the campus of Princeton, a private university. Schmid was not a Princeton student and the Labor Party was not a recognized student organization. Schmid did not have permission to be on the campus. Schmid earlier had been told that he would be arrested if he returned to the campus, and he knew that Princeton had a policy against allowing "persons not connected with the University to enter campus uninvited and without sponsorship for the purpose of soliciting support or contributions." While Schmid's appeal of his criminal conviction was pending, the Supreme Court of New Jersey certified the case and invited Princeton University to intervene in the appeal.]

Defendant asserts initially that his conviction in this case violated his rights under the First Amendment to the United States Constitution.... The Amendment imposes no limitations upon "the owner of private property used nondiscriminatorily for private purposes only," even though such use may trench upon the speech and assembly activities of other persons. *Lloyd Corp. v. Tanner*, 407 U.S. 551 (1972).

It is clear that public colleges and universities, as instrumentalities of state government, are not beyond the reach of the First Amendment. A public college or university, created or controlled by the state itself, is an arm of state government and, thus, by definition, implicates state action.

A private college or university, however, stands upon a different footing in relationship to the state. Such an institution is not the creature or instrument of state government. Even though such an institution may conduct itself identically to its state-operated counterparts and, in terms of educational purposes and activities, may be virtually indistinguishable from a public institution, a private college or university does not thereby either operate under or exercise the authority of state government. Hence, the state nexus requirement that triggers the application of the First Amendment is not readily met in the case of a private educational institution.

Notwithstanding the primary thrust of the First Amendment against state governmental interference with expressional freedoms, the guarantees of this Amendment may under appropriate conditions be invoked against nongovernmental bodies. In particular settings, private entities, including educational institutions, may so impact upon the public or share enough of the essential features of governmental bodies as to be engaged functionally in "state action" for First Amendment purposes. The more focused inquiry therefore must be turned to those circumstances that can subject an entity of essentially nongovernmental or private character to the requirements imposed by the First Amendment.

One test of such state action involves the presence of an interdependent or symbiotic relationship between the private entity and the state government. This standard was utilized in *Burton v. Wilmington Parking Auth.*, 365 U.S. 715 (1961), in which the Supreme Court held that a privately-owned restaurant which leased premises in a government-owned and government-maintained parking garage was subject to the Equal Protection Clause of the Fourteenth Amendment; the restaurant thus could not refuse to serve blacks. . . .

Another basis for determining the existence of state action is the extent of direct governmental regulation of the private entity. This standard was applied in *Public Utilities Comm'n v. Pollak*, 343 U.S. 451, 463 (1952), wherein the Supreme Court held that the First and Fifth Amendments to the federal Constitution were applicable to a policy decision made by a private transit company operating in the heavily-regulated field of public transportation because that decision was subject to approval by a governmental agency. . . .

. . .

The record reveals that Princeton University, though privately owned and controlled, is involved in a continuous relationship with the State. The University is a state accredited educational institution; it participates in and receives, as do other public and private educational institutions, the advantages of certain State programs, *e.g.*, The New Jersey Educational Facilities Authority Law, N.J. Stat. Ann. 18A:72A–1 *et seq.* (authority created to issue bonds for capital improvements and new construction on the campuses both of public and private post secondary educational institutions); The Higher Education Assistance Authority N.J. Stat. Ann. 18A:72–1 *et seq.* (creating fund to provide loans to New Jersey students attending public or private post secondary educational institutions). Its property and buildings on the central campus, with the exception of its ice skating and hockey facility and its campus parking lots, are tax exempt. The University also receives state budgeted funds through The Independent College and University Assistance Act, N.J. Stat. Ann. 18A:72B–15 *et seq.* In addition, according to the stipulations of the parties, the University Security Department, some of whose employees are deputized to make arrests under the laws of New Jersey, is primarily responsible for providing security services for the entire University community.

Nonetheless, this congeries of facts does not equate with state action on the part of Princeton University. Princeton University is, indisputably, predominantly private, unregulated and autonomous in its character and functioning as an institution of higher education. The interface between the University and the State is not so extensive as to demonstrate a joint and mutual participation in higher education or to establish an interdependent or symbiotic relationship between the two in the field of education.

Moreover, the degree of State regulation does not evince a "close nexus" between the State and Princeton University's policies, particularly with regard to the public's access to the University campus and facilities and even more particularly, with regard to either the distribution of political literature or other expressional activities on University property. Furthermore, the resort by Princeton University to the State's trespass laws to protect its own rights of property does not . . . constitute state action for First Amendment purposes. In the absence of a protectable First Amendment right in the individual, the property owner's recourse to appropriate and otherwise neutral penal sanctions to protect its legitimate interests does not constitute action by the State nor clothe the property owner with a state identity for First Amendment purposes.

. . . [T]here remains to be considered still another standard for determining First Amendment applicability, viz., the "public function doctrine." Even though a private entity is not engaged in "state action," it may nevertheless be required to honor First Amendment rights if its property is sufficiently devoted to public uses. *See Marsh v. Alabama*, 326 U.S. 501, 506 (1946). . . .

A company-owned town which possessed all of the characteristics of a municipality, providing full access to the public to all of its facilities including its shopping district, was held to be subject to the strictures of the First Amendment. *Id.* at 503, 508–509. In *Amalgamated Food Employees Union Local 590 v. Logan Valley Plaza, Inc.*, 391 U.S. 308, 317 (1968), the Supreme Court found "striking" similarities between a company town, as described in *Marsh v. Alabama, supra*, and a privately-owned shopping mall. Specifically noting the common sidewalks and parking areas and the invitation to the public to use the property, the Court held that it was a violation of the First Amendment to apply a trespass statute to union members picketing a non-unionized supermarket located in the privately-owned shopping mall.

A different result was reached in *Lloyd Corp. v. Tanner, supra*. The majority of the Supreme Court in *Lloyd* held that a privately-owned shopping mall could bar the distribution of anti-war handbills on mall property. It distinguished *Logan Valley* on the ground that the subject matter of the handbills in *Lloyd* was unrelated to the shopping center's business. With respect to the public use of the property, the Court noted that the invitation for public use of the shopping mall was not "open ended" or for "any and all purposes." It also found significance in the fact that there were adequate alternative means of communication, *i.e.*, that there were public areas directly outside the mall that were available for the distribution of the anti-war handbills. The Court reinforced the *Lloyd* holding in *Hudgens v. National Labor Relations Board*, 424 U.S. 507 (1976), wherein it ruled that striking warehouse employees who sought to picket their employer's retail store located in a privately owned shopping center were not protected under the First Amendment. A majority of the *Hudgens* Court supported the view that *Lloyd* effectively overruled and substantially constricted the reach of *Logan Valley*. Very recently, in *PruneYard Shopping Center v. Robins*, 447 U.S. 74, 78–88 (1980) the Supreme Court recapitulated this judicial history and observed that the rationale of *Logan Valley* had been "substantially repudiated" by *Lloyd* and had been actually overruled by *Hudgens*.

. . .

We are thus confronted with strong crosscurrents of policy that must be navigated with extreme care in reaching any satisfactory resolution of the competing constitutional values under the First Amendment in this case. These concerns persuade us to stay our hand in attempting to decide the question of whether the First Amendment applies to Princeton University in the context of the present appeal. Defendant, moreover, has presented compelling alternative grounds for relief founded upon the State Constitution, which we now reach.

. . .

Most recently, this Court recognized ... that freedom of the press, intimately associated with individual expressional and associational rights, is strongly protected under the State Constitution (N.J. Const. (1947), Art. I, par. 6), state statutory enactments (e.g., N.J. Stat. Ann. 2A:84A 21 *et seq.* ("shield law")), and state decisional law. The United States Supreme Court itself has acknowledged that the First Amendment, which implicates this important freedom, does not accord to it the degree of protection that may be available through state law. *Branzburg v. Hayes*, 408 U.S. 665, 706 (1972).

A basis for finding exceptional vitality in the New Jersey Constitution with respect to individual rights of speech and assembly is found in part in the language employed. Our Constitution affirmatively recognizes these freedoms, viz.:

> Every person may freely speak, write and publish his sentiments on all subjects, being responsible for the abuse of that right. No law shall be passed to restrain or abridge the liberty of speech or of the press. . . . [N.J. Const. (1947), Art. I, par. 6.]

> The people have the right freely to assemble together, to consult for the common good, to make known their opinions to their representatives, and to petition for redress of grievances. [N.J. Const. (1947), Art. I, par. 18.]

. . .

Against this constitutional backdrop must be addressed the question of whether the State Constitution's guarantees of speech and assembly under Article I, paragraphs 6 and 18 apply to the distribution of political materials by defendant Schmid upon the Princeton University campus on April 5, 1978. . . .

. . .

We are ... constrained to achieve the optimal balance between the protections to be accorded private property and those to be given to expressional freedoms exercised upon such property. In seeking this optimum, we can derive some guidance from certain of the Supreme Court cases, such as *Marsh v. Alabama, supra*; *Lloyd Corp. v. Tanner supra*, and *PruneYard Shopping Center v. Robins, supra*, which recognize generally that the more private property is devoted to public use, the more it must accommodate the rights which inhere in individual members of the general public who use that property. Since it is our State Constitution which we are here expounding, it is also fitting that we look to our own strong traditions which prize the exercise of individual rights and stress the societal obligations that are concomitant to a public enjoyment of private property.

Accordingly, we now hold that under the State Constitution, the test to be applied to ascertain the parameters of the rights of speech and assembly upon privately owned property and the extent to which such property reasonably can be restricted to accommodate these rights involves several elements. This standard must take into account (1) the nature, purposes, and primary use of such private property, generally, its "normal" use, (2) the extent and nature of the public's invitation to use that property, and (3) the purpose of the expressional activity undertaken upon such property in relation to both the private and public use of the property . . .

. . . Application of the appropriate standard in this case must commence with an examination of the primary use of the private property, namely, the campus and facilities of Princeton University. Princeton University itself has furnished the answer to this inquiry in expansively expressing its overriding educational goals, viz.:

> The central purposes of a University are the pursuit of truth, the discovery of new knowledge through scholarship and research, the teaching and general development of students, and the transmission of knowledge and learning to society at large. Free inquiry and free expression within the academic community are indispensable to the achievement of these goals. The freedom to teach and to learn depends upon the creation of appropriate conditions and opportunities on the campus as a whole as well as in classrooms and lecture halls. All members of the academic community share the responsibility for securing and sustaining the general conditions conducive to this freedom.

> . . .

> Free Speech and peaceable assembly are basic requirements of the University as a center for free inquiry and the search for knowledge and insight. . . .

[University Regulations, *supra* (1975 as amended 1976).]

. . .

In examining next the extent and nature of a public invitation to use its property, we note that a public presence within Princeton University is entirely consonant with the University's expressed educational mission. Princeton University, as a private institution of higher education, clearly seeks to encourage both a wide and continuous exchange of opinions and ideas and to foster a policy of openness and freedom with respect to the use of its facilities. The commitment of its property, facilities, and resources to educational purposes contemplates substantial public involvement and participation in the academic life of the University. The University itself has endorsed the educational value of an open campus and the full exposure of the college community to the "outside world," i.e., the public at large. Princeton University has indeed invited such public uses of its resources in fulfillment of its broader educational ideals and objectives.

The further question is whether the expressional activities undertaken by the defendant in this case are discordant in any sense with both the private and public uses of the campus and facilities of the University. There is nothing in the record to suggest that Schmid was evicted because the purpose of his activities, distributing political literature, offended the University's educational policies. The reasonable and normal inference thus to be extracted from the record in the instant case is that defendant's attempt to disseminate political material was not incompatible with either Princeton University's professed educational goals or the University's overall use of its property for educational purposes.[11] Further, there is no indication that even under the terms of the University's own regulations, Schmid's activities in any way, directly or demonstrably "disrupted the regular and essential operations of the University" or that in either the time, the place, or the manner of Schmid's distribution of the political materials, he "significantly infringed on the rights of others" or caused any interference or inconvenience with respect to the normal use of University property and the normal routine and activities of the college community.

. . . [T]he University nevertheless contends that its solicitation regulation was properly invoked against Schmid in this case because it requires that there be a specific invitation from on campus organizations or students and a specific official authorization before an individual may enter upon University premises even for the purpose of exercising constitutional rights of speech and assembly. It points out that Schmid failed to obtain such permission. The University stresses the necessity for and reasonableness of such a regulation.

In addressing this argument, we must give substantial deference to the importance of institutional integrity and independence. Private educational institutions perform an essential social function and have a fundamental responsibility to assure the academic and general well being of their communities of students, teachers and related personnel. At a minimum, these needs, implicating academic freedom and development, justify an educational institution in controlling those who seek to enter its domain. The singular need to achieve essential educational goals and regulate activities that impact upon these efforts has been acknowledged even with respect to public educational institutions. Hence, private colleges and universities must be

---

11. Supportive of this conclusion is the following excerpt from Princeton University President William G. Bowen in "The Role of the University as an Institution in Confronting External Issues" (January 6, 1978):

> Central to the philosophy of education is the proposition that the University has a responsibility to expose students and faculty members to a wide variety of views on controversial questions. . . . Put simply, the University's ability to carry out its basic educational mission requires an environment conducive to the maximum possible freedom of thought and expression for each individual student and faculty member. We are not talking here about something that is merely desirable; we are talking about something that is essential.

In this crucial respect, the University has a special role in the society—a special responsibility for creating a milieu in which every individual, whether the steadiest proponent of the majority viewpoint or the loneliest dissenter, is encouraged to think independently. As noted by Professor Emerson, "freedom of expression is [both] an essential process for advancing knowledge and discovering truth" and "a method of achieving a more adaptable and hence a more stable community, of maintaining the precarious balance between healthy cleavage and necessary consensus." T. EMERSON, THE SYSTEM OF FREEDOM OF EXPRESSION 6, 7 (1970).

accorded a generous measure of autonomy and self governance if they are to fulfill their paramount role as vehicles of education and enlightenment.

In this case, however, the University regulations that were applied to Schmid contained no standards, aside from the requirement for invitation and permission, for governing the actual exercise of expressional freedom. Indeed, there were no standards extant regulating the granting or withholding of such authorization, nor did the regulations deal adequately with the time, place, or manner for individuals to exercise their rights of speech and assembly. Regulations thus devoid of reasonable standards designed to protect both the legitimate interests if the University as an institution of higher education and the individual exercise of expressional freedom cannot constitutionally be invoked to prohibit the otherwise noninjurious and reasonable exercise of such freedoms. . . . It follows that in the absence of a reasonable regulatory scheme, Princeton University did in fact violate defendant's State constitutional rights of expression in evicting him and securing his arrest for distributing political literature upon its campus.

We are mindful that Princeton University's regulatory policies governing the time, place, and manner for the exercise of constitutionally-protected speech and associational rights have been modified substantially since the events surrounding Schmid's arrest and now more fully and adequately define the nature of these restrictions. As we have indicated, the content of such regulations, recognizing and controlling the right to engage in expressional activities, may be molded by the availability of alternative means of communication. These current amended regulations exemplify the approaches open to private educational entities seeking to protect their institutional integrity while at the same time recognizing individual rights of speech and assembly and accommodating the public whose presence nurtures academic inquiry and growth. As noted, however, these regulations were not in place when the University interfered with Schmid's reasonable efforts to communicate his political views to those present on its campus in April 1978. Hence, Schmid suffered a constitutional impairment of his State constitutional rights of speech and assembly and his conviction for trespass must therefore be undone.

Questions and Comments on *Schmid*

1. After losing in state court, Princeton sought review in the United States Supreme Court. Princeton conceded that it could not use academic freedom as a shield against state rules concerning health, safety, and like matters, but it asserted that "the state cannot use its police powers to control in any way the intellectual activities of the university," which are protected by "the ancient right of a university community to determine how its educational philosophy may best be implemented." Jurisdictional Statement of Princeton University at 6, *Princeton Univ. v. Schmid*, 455 U.S. 100 (1982) (No. 80–1576) at 6.

Princeton's defense of the rights of its "university community" did not sit well with some Princeton faculty who took exception to Princeton's argument. The AAUP opposed the petition for certiorari, arguing that "[Princeton's] argument mistakes institutional pluralism for academic freedom. Academic freedom is a scholar's right to be free of institutional (or governmental) control in professional utterance. The dissemination only of established truths is the antithesis of academic freedom. Princeton's "academic freedom" claim cannot be accepted without doing violence to the meaning of the term." Brief for Am. Assoc. of Univ. Professors as Amicus Curiae at 5, *Princeton Univ. v. Schmid*, 455 U.S. 100 (1982) (No. 80–1576). The professors worried that the broad immunity from judicial scrutiny claimed by Princeton would leave private universities with too much discretion to restrict the academic freedom of their own faculty. David M. Rabban, *A Functional Analysis of "Individual" and "Institutional" Academic Freedom Under the First Amendment*, 53 Law & Contemp. Probs. 227, 259 (1990). In the end, the appeal was dismissed. 455 U.S. 100 (1982).

2. What justifies the court's deference to decisions made by private colleges and universities?

3. Other private universities have faced litigation when demonstrators claimed a public forum on campus. In *Commonwealth v. Tate*, 495 Pa. 158, 432 A.2d 1382 (1981), protesters were distributing leaflets on the campus of Muhlenberg College outside a building in which a public official was delivering a speech. Muhlenberg, a private college in Pennsylvania, had previously denied the protesters' request for a permit to distribute leaflets. After refusing the appeal of the Chief of Police to leave campus, the protesters were arrested and convicted of defiant trespass. The Pennsylvania statute for defiant trespass provides a defense if "the premises were at the time open to members of the public and the actor complied with all lawful conditions imposed on access to or remaining on the premises." *See id.* at 1386 (quoting 18 Pa. Cons. Stat. § 3503(c)(2)).

On appeal, the Supreme Court of Pennsylvania held:

> On the day in question the campus was indeed "open to members of the public" within the meaning of § 3503(c)(2). Although privately supported, Muhlenberg College serves in many respect as a community center for Allentown, maintaining upon its campus a United States Post Office station, a public cafeteria, an information and sales booth for tickets to public events, and a federal book depository library, which is required "to be maintained so as to be accessible to the public." All of these facilities are located within a few hundred yards of the site of appellants' arrest. It was established at trial that other members of the public who, like appellants, did not choose to attend the symposium, were present without incident on the Muhlenberg campus on March 26, 1976. Moreover, according to the testimony of the college president, Muhlenberg had "no policy about off-campus visitors," and "a lot of people walk(ed) the campus."

> The college did have a requirement that any person from off campus wishing to distribute materials or offer materials for sale secure the permission of the college beforehand. The only difference between appellants and the other members of the public on the college grounds on the day of the symposium was that appellants attempted to distribute leaflets relating to the symposium without having received permission to do so from the college. As stated earlier, appellants had sought a permit on the previous day but had been refused. The record does not reveal what standards, if any, were applicable to the granting or denial of such permission. It appears, however, from the testimony of the college president, that the college believed itself entitled to exercise its discretion arbitrarily.

> Thus at issue is whether the college's standardless permit requirement constitutes a lawful condition with which appellants were obligated to comply or otherwise face prosecution and conviction as defiant trespassers. Here we are faced with an educational institution which holds itself out to the public as a community resource and cultural center, allows members of the public to walk its campus, permits a community organization to use its facilities as a forum for a public official of national importance, and at the same time arbitrarily denies a few members of the public the right to distribute leaflets peacefully to the relevant audience present at that forum. In these circumstances, we are of the view that the Constitution of this Commonwealth protects appellants' invaluable right to freedom of expression against the

enforcement, by state criminal statute, of the college's standardless permit requirement.

Id. at 1386–87, 1391.

Compare State v. Guice, 262 N.J.Super. 607, 621 A.2d 553 (Law Div. 1993), in which a New Jersey court faced with similar facts ruled in favor of the private university. In *Guice*, the defendants were convicted of criminal trespass for attempting to distribute political literature on the campus of Stevens Institute of Technology. The court applied the *Schmid* three-prong test, but found that while the defendants' actions paralleled those in *Schmid*, Stevens did not open its campus as Princeton did:

> There is no evidence in the record that Stevens encourages a policy of openness and freedom with regard to the use of its facilities. Stevens does not open its campus to the public to the degree that Princeton does. On the contrary, the record below reflects a deliberate policy to maintain the property as private. The gates are shut once a year to protect its private status. The property is enclosed, not geographically integrated with the town as are parts of Princeton University. Stevens does not allow outsiders on campus without sponsorship or other permission (except for local "Sunday strollers"). The public is invited on campus only for certain events (*e.g.* basketball games); limited commercial activities are permitted under the aegis of the college bookstore.
>
> . . .
>
> This court finds that Stevens Institute issues only limited invitations to the public for specific purposes, and thus cannot be deemed an "open" campus. The facts in this case do not support the granting of constitutional rights to the defendants, unless one is prepared to say that the *Schmid* test as applied to private educational institutions in New Jersey will always find First Amendment obligations.

Id. at 555–56 (affirming defendants' convictions).

4. Why might the *Guice* court have been "[un]prepared to say that the *Schmid* test as applied to private educational institutions in New Jersey will always find First Amendment obligations"? The *Guice* court gave the most weight to the second prong of the *Schmid* test, effectively holding that the limitations on the Stevens Institute's invitations to the public trumped the first and third prongs. Is that approach to the balancing test appropriate? Should a university with "central purposes of . . . the pursuit of truth . . . and the transmission of knowledge and learning to society at large" not be subject to First Amendment obligations if it on occasion closes its doors to the public?

Is it in the legal interests of a university to limit public access? Would the outcome in *Schmid* have been different if Princeton had shut its campus to the public once a year?

5. Does applying the First Amendment to private universities simply shift the decision of what speech to privilege from the university to the state? As a student, which would you prefer as the decision-maker?

Gilles v. Blanchard

United States Court of Appeals for the Seventh Circuit, 2007.
477 F.3d 466, *cert. denied*, 128 S.Ct. 127.

■ Posner, Circuit Judge.

Vincennes University, the oldest institution of higher education in Indiana (founded in 1806 by future President William Henry Harrison before Indiana was admitted to statehood)—and a public institution since its inception—has its main, and only residential, campus in the town of Vincennes (population 18,000) in southwestern Indiana. About 5,000 students, all undergraduate, are enrolled full time at the Vincennes campus. James Gilles ("Brother Jim") is a traveling evangelist—the latest in a line of Christian itinerant preachers stretching back to Saint Paul and prominent in Methodism in nineteenth-century America. Born near Vincennes, Gilles gives the following account of his salvation. As a result of Satan's machinations, he devoted himself as a youth to drugs, sex, booze, and rock and roll. At a rock and roll concert at which the well-known Van Halen band performed, singer David Lee Roth shouted to the crowd: "Not even God can save your soul at a Van Halen concert!" Gilles saw the light, called on God to save him and thus refute Roth, and was saved. The message he preaches, as summarized in his own words, is "Sinner friend, I have good news for you, you also can experience righteousness, peace and joy in the Holy Ghost if you would only forsake your sinful, selfish ways and turn to the Lord and Savior Jesus Christ." Neither the record nor Brother Jim's home page indicates that he is affiliated with any religious organization, although in another case in which he was turned away by a university he is identified as a member of the Free Pentecostal Holiness Churches, *Gilles v. Torgersen*, 71 F.3d 497, 499 (4th Cir. 1995) (dismissed without a decision on the merits), presumably a reference to the Pentecostal Holiness Church, a Protestant denomination with Methodist antecedents. None of this, of course, is important. There is no reason to doubt either his bona fides or that the content of his religious advocacy is protected by the First Amendment. The question is whether the protection extends to a particular site on the university campus.

Vincennes University and Brother Jim first intersected in 2001, when he entered the campus uninvited and walked to a lawn in the middle of the campus, next to the university library. He preached from the lawn and a disturbance ensued, the nature of which is not revealed by the record, although the university's dean of students stated in his deposition that "when I went there, he [Brother Jim] was in the grassy area in front of the library. He had had—he was speaking to a number of students there. There was some—a disturbance, and at one point the campus police felt like he was in danger. And they asked him to leave, and he did." From another case we learn that "when preaching, [Brother Jim] uses a confrontational style that includes calling people in the crowd names, such as whoremonger and drunkard, once the individuals have answered certain questions that he poses to them. He has been arrested on numerous occasions in the past." Brother Jim denied that his preaching at Vincennes in 2001 had caused a disturbance, and in the procedural posture of the case we must credit his denial.

In reaction to the incident—whatever exactly it was—the university for the first time adopted a formal policy governing access to the campus by outsiders to the university community. Entitled "Sales and/or Solicitation Policy," the policy requires prior approval by the dean of students of all sales on campus. In addition, and more to the point of this case, the policy also requires the dean's prior approval of all "solicitations" on campus. Solicitation is defined as "the act of seeking to obtain by persuasion; to entice a person to action; or the recruiting of possible sales." Solicitors, if approved, are limited to soliciting in the brick walkway directly in front of the student union.

. . .

Brother Jim returned to the campus the following year, proceeded to the lawn, was turned back and told he could preach only on the brick walkway. He tried to preach there, but the fact that the walkway is adjacent to a street makes it a noisy locale for a speech. Unable to attract an audience, he broke off and left, and filed this suit against the responsible university officials, contending that the solicitation policy infringes his right of free speech. The district court granted summary judgment for the defendants.

Brother Jim argues that since the lawn is public property and is suitable for speechifying, he can no more be forbidden to preach there than he could be forbidden to preach in a public park. That is incorrect. The Justice Department in Washington has a large auditorium, with a stage, and so would be a suitable venue for a theatrical production. But the First Amendment does not require the department to make the auditorium available for that purpose even when it is not being used for departmental business. Public property is property, and the law of trespass protects public property, as it protects private property, from uninvited guests. "[T]he Government, 'no less than a private owner of property, has power to preserve the property under its control for the use to which it is lawfully dedicated,' *Greer v. Spock*, 424 U.S. 828, 836 (1976)." *Cornelius v. NAACP Legal Defense & Educational Fund, Inc.*, 473 U.S. 788, 800 (1985). Since public and private universities compete with each other, courts hesitate to impose in the name of the Constitution extravagant burdens on public universities that private universities do not bear.

It is not as if requiring a public university to throw open its grounds to itinerant speakers would merely redress the advantage that a public university has over a private one because it has taxpayer support; the requirement would deny the university control over its facilities. The courts reject the proposition "that a campus must make all of its facilities equally available to students and nonstudents alike, or that a university must grant free access to all of its grounds or buildings." *Widmar v. Vincent*, 454 U.S. 263, 268 n. 5 (1981). "The State, no less than a private owner of property, has power to preserve the property under its control for the use to which it is lawfully dedicated." *Adderley v. Florida*, 385 U.S. 39 (1966).

No matter how wonderfully suited the library lawn is to religious and other advocacy, Vincennes University could if it wanted bar access to the lawn to any outsider who wanted to use it for any purpose, just as it could bar outsiders from its classrooms, libraries, dining halls, and dormitories. It wouldn't have to prove that allowing them in would disrupt its educational mission. "[G]overnment may draw permissible status-based distinctions among different classes of speakers in order to preserve the purpose of the forum, even when the proposed uses by those inside the permitted class of speakers and those outside the permitted class of speakers are quite similar." *Goulart v. Meadows*, 345 F.3d 239, 254 (4th Cir. 2003).

What is true is that a university that decided to permit its open spaces to be used by some outsiders could not exclude others just because it disapproved of their message. *E.g.*, *Rosenberger v. Rector & Visitors of University of Virginia*, 515 U.S. 819, 828–30, (1995). But it could use neutral criteria for access, such as that an outsider must be invited to speak on campus by a faculty member or a student group. The difference between invited and uninvited visitors is fundamental to a system of property rights. "The fact that other civilian speakers and entertainers had sometimes been invited to appear at Fort Dix did not of itself serve to convert Fort Dix into a public forum or to confer upon political candidates a First or Fifth Amendment right to conduct their campaigns there. The decision of the military authorities that a civilian lecture on drug abuse, a religious service by a visiting preacher at the base chapel, or a rock musical concert would be supportive of the military mission of Fort Dix surely did not leave the authorities powerless thereafter to prevent any civilian from entering Fort Dix to speak on any subject whatever." *Greer v. Spock*, 424 U.S. 828, 838 n. 10 (1976)....

Brother Jim places great weight on *Bowman v. White*, 444 F.3d 967 (8th Cir. 2006), which held that a public university that allowed anyone to use its outdoor spaces for public speaking could not limit that use by outsiders to five days (per outsider) per semester. The limit did not discriminate against particular viewpoints. It merely gave preference to insiders, which strikes us as eminently reasonable and leads us to doubt the soundness of the decision, for in *Cornelius v. NAACP Legal Defense & Educational Fund, Inc., supra*, 473 U.S. at 806, the Supreme Court said that "control over access to a nonpublic forum can be based on subject matter and speaker identity so long as the distinctions drawn are reasonable in light of the purpose served by the forum and are viewpoint neutral." Our case is in any event distinguishable from *Bowman* because Vincennes University has placed the lawn completely off limits to uninvited outsiders, and if it can't do that without violating the Constitution, public universities cannot control their property. Confining solicitations to the walkway in front of the student union is entirely appropriate because most of the solicitations are of students, and where better to encounter a steady stream of them than outside the student union? Letting solicitors into the middle of the campus would disrupt the campus atmosphere.

But here is the rub. In responding to Brother Jim's lawn preaching in 2001 by promulgating a policy limited to sales and solicitations, the university could be thought to have thrown open the lawn to all outsiders who were *not* selling or soliciting. Brother Jim argues forcefully that he does neither, and he asks us to infer (or allow a jury to infer) that the application of the policy to him was therefore pretextual and discriminatory. Not that the university necessarily disapproves of his message. It may just fear a disturbance. But yielding to a "heckler's veto" infringes a speaker's free speech. *Church of American Knights of Ku Klux Klan v. City of Gary*, 334 F.3d 676, 680–81 (7th Cir. 2003), and cases cited there.

Brother Jim certainly is not selling anything. And he does not solicit or receive contributions or seek to "entice" members of his audiences to "action." He tries merely to save their souls and make them happy. Of course, as he explains, salvation requires them to give up, as he gave up, drugs, sex (Brother Jim means fornication and adultery—he is not a Shaker), booze, and rock and roll. But that is enticement to inaction rather than to action. It is remote from what is ordinarily understood by "solicitation." To solicit, in law as in ordinary language, is to ask someone to do something, usually of a commercial or quasi-commercial character, for the solicitor—so one solicits a prostitute for sex (or the prostitute solicits one), or solicits donations to a charity, or solicits a competitor to join in a price-fixing conspiracy. A priest who urged conversion to the Catholic Church might be thought to be engaged in solicitation, and likewise Jehovah's Witnesses when they go door to door seeking converts. But the Pope is not soliciting when he gives a speech from the balcony of St. Peter's, even though it is implicit or explicit in his message that the listeners should conform their behavior to the teachings of the Church. That is the character of Brother Jim's preaching. If the Pope and Brother Jim are solicitors, almost anyone who opens his mouth to say anything is a solicitor.

The application of the university's solicitation policy to Brother Jim brings him to the verge of victory. The policy as interpreted by the defendants to cover preaching the Gospel is hopelessly vague and thus a supple weapon for excluding from the university lawn those outsiders whose message the university disapproves of. But Brother Jim falls just short of prevailing because he has failed to show that *any* uninvited outsider has ever been permitted to use the lawn for any purpose. No doubt outsiders wander in from time to time. The campus is not fenced, and outsiders are not forbidden to visit. They are classic licensees. But we are given no instance of an outsider's being permitted to do more than stroll on the lawn—no instance of an outsider's being permitted to give a speech, to play the bongo drums, to pitch a tent, to beg, to sunbathe, to play frisbee, or to engage in solicitation—without an invitation, whether from the university or from a faculty member or a student group.

This has long been a norm, and not just a practice: strangers to the university community are not to use the library lawn for purposes other than those unobtrusive, implicitly authorized uses of land (generally as a shortcut or other pathway) that distinguish a licensee from a trespasser. So unlikely is it that a university or any other landowner would, as Brother Jim contends Vincennes University does, give strangers a right to roam the campus speechifying, begging, buttonholing, skateboarding, drag racing, etc., that he had to produce *some* evidence of that unlikely authorization in order to create a genuine issue of material fact—some evidence that would allow a reasonable jury to find that the university has such a permissive policy and merely denies Brother Jim the benefit of it lest his incendiary preaching ignite another disturbance.

Brother Jim does point to numerous expressive activities that have taken place on the library lawn, including religious activities—preaching by a couple named Duncan and the annual distribution of free Bibles by the Gideon Society. But of all the expressive activities that have taken place on the lawn, the record discloses only one that was not by invitation. The Duncans had not been invited. They had preached on the lawn in 1998, three years before Brother Jim's first visit, and the circumstances of their visit are hazy. One unauthorized use of the lawn would not come close to establishing the absence of a policy against use of the lawn by uninvited speakers. Maybe no one complained, and as a result the violation did not come to the attention of the university authorities—indeed, the dean of students attested that he had never learned of the matter. Perfect past compliance with a rule is not a precondition to being allowed to continue enforcing the rule. Otherwise few rules could be enforced, and universities would have to fence their open areas in order to limit access.

Brother Jim lists the following speakers or events that have taken place on the library lawn, in addition to the Duncans' preaching and the Gideons' handing out Bibles: Women of Essence; Black Male Initiative; Indiana National Guard; Kernan and Davis for Indiana campaign; Rebekka Armstrong (an HIV-positive former Playboy Playmate); Mark Sterner (speaker on drunk driving); Mentalist Craig Karges; TB Re–Screening; Student Part

Time Job Fair; The Man Without a Face (an oral cancer survivor who lost half his jaw and part of his tongue); Health Screening; Ariana Huffington; Dr. Peter DeBenedittis (speaker on how the media manipulate consumers); Manufacturing Job Fair; Amanda Persinger (pharmaceutical representative); Prentis Hall Sales Representative; Tupperware Multihost Bingo/Party; Kevin Riggins (speaker against athletic doping); Kelly Craig (speaker against drunk driving); and the Red Cross Blood Drive. This bewildering miscellany refutes an inference of discrimination against disfavored points of view, or of a university administration fearful of controversy and of the disturbances that might ensue. As far as appears, any student group can invite any speaker to speak on the library lawn. The diversity of speakers mirrors the diversity of the university community.

Of course there would be even greater diversity of viewpoints if *anyone*, invited or uninvited, could use the lawn for expressive activity; for apparently no one in the Vincennes University community wants to invite Brother Jim to speak. He wants to turn the lawn into an American version of Speakers' Corner in London's Hyde Park, where anyone can speak on any subject other than the Royal family or the overthrow of the British government. The limits that Vincennes University has placed on the use of the library lawn are consistent with limiting university facilities to activities that further the interests of the university community. The limits are constitutional.

We should note that the defendants wanted us to pitch our analysis on the distinction that the Supreme Court has drawn between "traditional public forums," "designated public forums," and "nonpublic forums." E.g., *Good News Club v. Milford Central School*, 533 U.S. 98, 106–07 (2001); *International Society for Krishna Consciousness, Inc. v. Lee*, 505 U.S. 672, 678–79 (1992). The first consist of streets and parks and other public property that are traditional, and, the Supreme Court has ruled, irrevocable venues for expressive activity (marches, demonstrations, harangues, and so forth). The second consist of public facilities for expression that are nontraditional, such as public theaters, and used for only some types of expressive activity even though they could be used for others as well—a public theater could be used for political rallies. The Court does not require that they be used for expressive activities for which they were not intended to be used, provided that there is no discrimination based on the message of the excluded speaker, or that their use for expressive activity be irrevocable. The third category consists of public facilities like the Justice Department's auditorium that could be used for private expressive activities but are not—and they do not have to be.

The difficulty with using the "forum" template to resolve this case—a difficulty that is common enough where rules are concerned—is that the present case falls into a crack between the rules. The library lawn is not open to all outsiders, or closed to all outsiders, or reserved for some uses but not others. To fill the crack, cases such as *Bowman v. White, supra*, 444 F.3d at 975–76; *Justice for All v. Faulkner*, 410 F.3d 760, 765–69 (5th Cir. 2005), and *Travis v. Owego–Apalachin School District*, 927 F.2d 688, 692 (2d Cir. 1991), have carved out a fourth category—a variant of the second, the "designated public forum." This fourth category is variously (and confusingly) termed the "limited designated public forum" (versus the "true forum"), the "limited public forum," or the "limited forum." The terms denote a public facility reserved for some speakers but not others, here members of the university community and their guests but not uninvited outsiders.

We doubt the utility of multiplying categories in this fashion, thus adding epicycles to an already complex scheme and turning the search for sensible results into a classification game. The issue more simply posed is whether a university should be able to bar uninvited speakers under a policy that by decentralizing the invitation process assures nondiscrimination, and a reasonable diversity of viewpoints consistent with the university's autonomy and right of self-governance. We have tried to explain why the Constitution does not commit a university that allows a faculty member or student group to invite a professor of theology to give a talk on campus also to invite Brother Jim and anyone else who would like to use, however worthily, the university's facilities as his soapbox. To call the library lawn therefore a "limited designated public forum" is an unnecessary flourish.

Affirmed.

Note on Public Forums

Both the *Schmid* and *Gilles* courts expressed dissatisfaction with public forum jurisprudence, noting that the doctrine did little to clarify the conditions in which a university may control expressive activities on their campuses. Legal scholars have been equally critical of the doctrine. *See, e.g.*, Calvin Massey, *Public Fora, Neutral Governments, and the Prism of Property*, 50 Hastings L.J. 309 (1999) (arguing that the Supreme Court's public forum decisions have vacillated between inconsistent conceptions of the free speech guarantee and that this confusion has been compounded by a "Byzantine" categorization of public property); Robert C. Post, *Between Governance and Management: The History and Theory of the Public Forum*, 34 UCLA L. Rev. 1713, 1716–17 (1987) (arguing that "almost none of the special rules characteristic of [public forum] doctrine can withstand analytic scrutiny" and suggesting that courts should focus on the nature of government authority at issue in a given case, not the nature of the government property); Daniel A. Farber & John E. Nowak, *The Misleading Nature of Public Forum Analysis: Content and Context in First Amendment Adjudication*, 70 Va. L. Rev. 1219, 1224 (1984) (arguing that public forum analysis "distracts attention from the first amendment values at stake in a given case").

Many universities have established "free speech" zones as designated public forums. Timothy Zick, *Speech and Spatial Tactics*, 84 Tex. L. Rev. 581, 601–04 (2006). By creating "free speech" zones, university officials implicitly designate all other areas of the campus as "speech-free" zones; this practice is especially troubling when the "free speech" zones are small relative to the size of the campus or inconveniently located. *Id.* West Virginia University, for example, designated two areas the size of classroom as "free speech" zones. After students and faculty complained, the university increased the size of the zone to roughly five percent of the campus. In response to criticism of the new plan, the university then abandoned the zoning approach to free speech. *Id.* at 602. Do safety concerns and the educational mission of the university justify the creation of "free speech" zones, or does the creation of such zones frustrate the free exchange of ideas?

D.   Public and Private

In the Matter of Stoll v. New York State College of Veterinary Medicine at Cornell University

Court of Appeals of New York, 1999.
94 N.Y.2d 162, 723 N.E.2d 65, 701 N.Y.S.2d 316.

■ Chief Judge Kaye.

Petitioner, David Stoll, is the attorney for James Maas, a Cornell University professor disciplined for having sexually harassed several female

undergraduate students (*see Maas v. Cornell Univ.*, 94 N.Y.2d 87 [721 N.E.2d 966] [decided today]). Stoll filed a request under the Freedom of Informa-
tion Law (FOIL) seeking from Cornell any complaints brought under the University's Campus Code of Conduct, "including any complaints made to a supervisor, department head or the Judicial Administrator . . . by or against any administrator, professor or student of any statutory college operated by Cornell pursuant to the New York Education Law," and "any documents, including any written findings, relating to those complaints." The "statutory colleges" referred to in petitioner's request are respondents: the New York State College of Veterinary Medicine, the New York State College of Agriculture and Life Sciences, the New York State College of Human Ecology, and the New York State School of Industrial and Labor Relations.

After respondents denied the request, petitioner brought the instant . . . proceeding to compel production. Supreme Court rejected petitioner's request, ruling that respondents are not State agencies subject to FOIL. The Appellate Division reversed, reasoning that Cornell operated the statutory colleges on behalf of the State University of New York (SUNY), which is a State agency under FOIL; the statutory colleges were State agencies under the State Finance Law; they were subject to the Open Meetings Law; and the State supervises the statutory colleges, approves the appointment of Deans, must be consulted with respect to tuition rates and holds title to their buildings. The court therefore concluded that Cornell performed a governmental function and was subject to FOIL, and it remitted the matter to Supreme Court for consideration of respondents' affirmative defenses.

After respondents' motion for leave to appeal to this Court was dismissed as nonfinal, [the] Supreme Court on remittal . . . ruled that respondents could redact "deliberative materials" and "identifying personal information" but that the records otherwise had to be produced. We granted respondents leave to appeal and now reverse.

The Freedom of Information Law requires that, with certain statutory exceptions, each "*agency* shall . . . make available for public inspection and copying all records." FOIL defines an "agency" as:

> "any state or municipal department, board, bureau, division, commission, committee, public authority, public corporation, council, office or other governmental entity performing a governmental or proprietary function for the state or any one or more municipalities thereof, except the judiciary or the state legislature."

SUNY is an agency under FOIL. Whether Cornell's statutory colleges also qualify as agencies of the State for FOIL purposes is an open question.

Cornell is a private university incorporated under article 115 of the New York Education Law. The University has 18 academic units, including the four "statutory" or "contract" colleges. The Education Law defines "statutory or contract colleges" as colleges "furnishing higher education, operated by independent institutions on behalf of the state pursuant to statute or contractual agreements." The colleges are unique, *sui generis* institutions created by statute—public in some respects, private in others. As statutory creatures, plainly their classification depends on the statutes that define them.

Several aspects of the administration of the colleges have been committed by the Legislature to Cornell's private discretion. Cornell, for example, is specifically charged with creating the academic curriculum, hiring faculty, maintaining discipline and formulating educational policies for the statutory colleges. The SUNY Board of Trustees does not have direct operational authority over the statutory colleges, as it does of SUNY generally. Also unlike SUNY, employees of the statutory colleges are not classified as members of the State civil service.

While the narrow question before us is an open one, the law is settled that, for a number of other purposes, the statutory colleges are *not* State agencies, including: tort law; the regulation of the business activities of public officers; and article 18 of the General Municipal Law, which regulates conflicts of interest.

The statutory colleges are, however, subject to certain oversight by the SUNY Board of Trustees. They are funded with State money, which must be kept separate from Cornell's private funds. Cornell must submit an annual statement detailing the colleges' finances and must consult with the SUNY Board about financial matters, including tuition rates. Cornell selects the Deans of the statutory colleges, but the SUNY Board must approve the appointments. And although Cornell maintains custody and control of the buildings and property used by the statutory colleges, title belongs to the State. In addition, the statutory colleges are technically part of the SUNY system; they are State agencies under section 53–a (5) (b) of the State Finance Law; their employees are eligible for the State University retirement system; and the Third Department has held that they are "public bodies" under the Open Meetings Law.

Given the hybrid statutory character of the colleges, we cannot agree with the dissent that they should be categorically deemed agencies of the State for the purposes at issue because of a compilation of factors on the State side of the column. Of equal significance is the list of statutory indicia that denote a private entity and function, not subject to any State direction or oversight. Nor does the general policy of liberal disclosure under FOIL answer the question before us. At issue is the threshold question whether the statutory colleges are subject to FOIL in the first place. This question cannot be answered by reference to broad classifications, but rather turns on the particular statutory character of these *sui generis* institutions.

The principle that resolves the particular quandary here is that the Legislature has chosen to vest Cornell—the private institution—with discretion over the "maintenance of discipline" at the four statutory colleges. In this respect, there is no statutory provision for oversight by the SUNY Trustees, or for any appeal to the SUNY Board. Consistent with that statutory mandate, Cornell has implemented a single system for administering discipline in the statutory colleges and in its private colleges. Indeed, as is manifest from petitioner's own FOIL request, there is a University-wide Campus Code of Conduct and a Judicial Administrator to whom all such complaints are directed. Thus, the disciplinary records of the statutory colleges and the private colleges are all held by the same private office of the University.

To be sure, whether a governmental agency must turn over a document under FOIL does not depend on "the purpose for which the document was produced or the function to which it relates." (*Matter of Citizens for Alternatives* to *Animal Labs v. Board of Trustees,* [92 N.Y.2d 357, 361], quoting *Matter of Capital Newspapers v. Whalen,* 69 N.Y.2d 246, 253). In *Animal Labs,* for example, we reasoned that a SUNY research facility did not lose its status as an "agency" merely because it was keeping Federally mandated records: the facility itself was fulfilling a State governmental function (*see* 92 N.Y.2d at 360). Here, by contrast, the statutory colleges are a blend of specified private and governmental activities. Thus, unlike *Animal Labs,* the activity in issue becomes significant in defining whether the entity itself is, or is not, a State agency. Finally, in identifying Cornell's disciplinary system as private, the Legislature may well have had in mind the confidentiality of such proceedings and the potential for misuse of disciplinary records.

Finally, we underscore that, by this decision and analysis, we do not "rule that the entire administration of the statutory colleges is not subject to FOIL." We hold only that, given the unique statutory scheme applicable here, Cornell's disciplinary records are not subject to FOIL disclosure. Other, more public aspects of the statutory colleges may well be subject to FOIL, but we need not and do not reach such issues today.

Questions and Comments on Cornell

1. From its beginning, Cornell included both private and public colleges as described in *Stoll*. Historian Carl Becker summarized the influence of Cornell on the reforms of higher education of the late nineteenth century:

> In this education renaissance Cornell University played its part, and that not an insignificant one. Better than any other institution it may be said to have represented, in its organization and in its aims, all of the dominant trends of the time. Located neither in the old East nor in the newer West, it was shaped by the interests and currents of opinion that prevailed in both regions. It was not altogether a state university, like those of Michigan and Illinois, or altogether a privately endowed university, like Harvard and Yale, but a curious combination of both. It managed, with great ingenuity, to obtain munificent gifts from private individuals while holding lands granted by the federal government for a rise in price, and then to induce the state legislature to make additional and substantial appropriates for its support. It was founded by a shrewd, hard-headed farmer and business man with a practical outlook and a Quaker conscience [Ezra Cornell], and organized by a Michigan professor of history who had graduated from Yale and was familiar at first hand with European universities [Andrew Dickson White]; and as a result of their united efforts it was deliberately designed to meet the three cardinal demands of the time—the demand for a liberalization of the college of arts, for the promotion of scientific research, and for advanced professional training in agriculture and the mechanic arts.

CARL L. BECKER, CORNELL UNIVERSITY: FOUNDERS & THE FOUNDING 22 (1943).

2. What do you think of New York State's decision to grant administrative control over public colleges to a private institution? Does a "public college" administered by a private university have First Amendment obligations? *See* Powe v. Miles, 407 F.2d 73 (2d Cir. 1968).

CHAPTER 3

RELIGION AND HIGHER EDUCATION

Beginning with Harvard in 1636, most American colleges and universities were established for religious ends. By the late nineteenth century, however, a trend toward secularization took hold with the result that today, the few remaining institutions of higher education governed by or affiliated with religious denominations sometimes feel out of step. Consider the critique of George Marsden:

> In many of the American colonies all the citizens were taxed for the support of the established religious group, regardless of the citizen's religious affiliation. In the nineteenth century the Protestant establishment became informal and declared itself nonsectarian. Today nonsectarianism has come to mean the exclusion of all religious concerns. In effect, only purely naturalistic viewpoints are allowed a serious academic hearing. As in earlier establishments, groups who do not match the current national ideological norms are forced to fend for themselves outside of the major spheres of cultural influence. Today, almost all religious groups, no matter what their academic credentials, are on the outside of this educational establishment, or soon will be, if present trends continue. American who are concerned for justice ought to be open to considering alternatives.[a]

As you read the material in this chapter, consider whether Marsden is right.

A. RELIGIOUS COLLEGES AND UNIVERSITIES

Tilton v. Richardson

Supreme Court of the United States, 1971.
403 U.S. 672, 91 S.Ct. 2091, 29 L.Ed.2d 790.

■ MR. CHIEF JUSTICE BURGER announced the judgment of the Court and an opinion in which MR. JUSTICE HARLAN, MR. JUSTICE STEWART, and MR. JUSTICE BLACKMUN join.

[Title I of the Higher Education Facilities Act of 1963, 77 Stat. 364, 20 U.S.C. § 711–21, authorized grants to institutions of higher education for the construction of academic facilities. The Act disqualified facilities used or to be used (i) "for sectarian instruction," (ii) "as a place for religious worship," or (iii) "primarily in connection with any part of the program of a

a. GEORGE M. MARSDEN, THE SOUL OF THE AMERICAN UNIVERSITY: FROM PROTESTANT ESTABLISHMENT TO ESTABLISHED NONBELIEF 440 (1994). *See also* JULIE A. REUBEN, THE MAKING OF THE MODERN UNIVERSITY: INTELLECTUAL TRANSFORMATION AND THE MARGINALIZATION OF MORALITY (1996).

school or department of divinity." In administering the Act, the U.S. Commissioner of Education required assurances that applicant institutions would use "no part of the [grant-funded] project" for these disqualified purposes. The Office of Education planned to enforce these restrictions through site inspections for 20 years. Violations would entitle the U.S. to recover the present-day value of the initial grant. After 20 years, the U.S. would no longer retain an interest in the funded buildings.]

. . .

Appellants are citizens and taxpayers of the United States and residents of Connecticut. They brought this suit for injunctive relief against the officials who administer the Act [alleging violations of the First Amendment's Establishment and Free Exercise Clauses]. Four church-related colleges and universities in Connecticut receiving federal construction grants under Title I were also named as defendants. Federal funds were used for five projects at these four institutions: (1) a library building at Sacred Heart University; (2) a music, drama, and arts building at Annhurst College; (3) a science building at Fairfield University; (4) a library building at Fairfield; and (5) a language laboratory at Albertus Magnus College. A three-judge federal court . . . sustained the constitutionality of the Act, finding that it had neither the purpose nor the effect of promoting religion. We noted probable jurisdiction.

We are satisfied that Congress intended the Act to include all colleges and universities regardless of any affiliation with or sponsorship by a religious body. Congress defined "institutions of higher education," which are eligible to receive aid under the Act, in broad and inclusive terms. Certain institutions, for example, institutions that are neither public nor nonprofit, are expressly excluded, and the Act expressly prohibits use of the facilities for religious purposes. But the Act makes no reference to religious affiliation or nonaffiliation. Under these circumstances "institutions of higher education" must be taken to include church-related colleges and universities.

This interpretation is fully supported by the legislative history. Although there was extensive debate on the wisdom and constitutionality of aid to institutions affiliated with religious organizations, Congress clearly included them in the program. The sponsors of the Act so stated . . . and amendments aimed at the exclusion of church-related institutions were defeated.

. . .

[In evaluating the Establishment Clause challenge, the Court considers three questions]: First, does the Act reflect a secular legislative purpose? Second, is the primary effect of the Act to advance or inhibit religion? Third, does the administration of the Act foster an excessive government entanglement with religion? . . .

[1]

The stated legislative purpose appears in the preamble where Congress found and declared that

> "the security and welfare of the United States require that this and future generations of American youth be assured ample opportunity for the fullest development of their intellectual capacities, and that this opportunity will be jeopardized unless the Nation's colleges and universities are encouraged and assisted in their efforts to accom-

modate rapidly growing numbers of youth who aspire to a higher education." 20 U. S. C. § 701.

This expresses a legitimate secular objective entirely appropriate for governmental action.

. . .

The Act itself was carefully drafted to ensure that the federally subsidized facilities would be devoted to the secular and not the religious function of the recipient institutions. It authorizes grants and loans only for academic facilities that will be used for defined secular purposes and expressly prohibits their use for religious instruction, training, or worship. These restrictions have been enforced in the Act's actual administration, and the record shows that some church-related institutions have been required to disgorge benefits for failure to obey them.

Finally, this record fully supports the findings of the District Court that none of the four church-related institutions in this case has violated the statutory restrictions. The institutions presented evidence that there had been no religious services or worship in the federally financed facilities, that there are no religious symbols or plaques in or on them, and that they had been used solely for nonreligious purposes. On this record, therefore, these buildings are indistinguishable from a typical state university facility. Appellants presented no evidence to the contrary.

Appellants instead rely on the argument that government may not subsidize any activities of an institution of higher learning that in some of its programs teaches religious doctrines. . . .

. . .

. . . Two of the five federally financed buildings involved in this case are libraries. The District Court found that no classes had been conducted in either of these facilities and that no restrictions were imposed by the institutions on the books that they acquired. There is no evidence to the contrary. The third building was a language laboratory at Albertus Magnus College. The evidence showed that this facility was used solely to assist students with their pronunciation in modern foreign languages—a use which would seem peculiarly unrelated and unadaptable to religious indoctrination. Federal grants were also used to build a science building at Fairfield University and a music, drama, and arts building at Annhurst College.

There is no evidence that religion seeps into the use of any of these facilities. Indeed, the parties stipulated in the District Court that courses at these institutions are taught according to the academic requirements intrinsic to the subject matter and the individual teacher's concept of professional standards. Although appellants introduced several institutional documents that stated certain religious restrictions on what could be taught, other evidence showed that these restrictions were not in fact enforced and that the schools were characterized by an atmosphere of academic freedom rather than religious indoctrination. All four institutions, for example, subscribe to the 1940 Statement of Principles on Academic Freedom and Tenure endorsed by the American Association of University Professors and the Association of American Colleges.

. . .

[2]

Although we reject appellants' broad constitutional arguments we do perceive an aspect in which the statute's enforcement provisions are inadequate to ensure that the impact of the federal aid will not advance religion. If a recipient institution violates any of the statutory restrictions on the use of a federally financed facility, § 754 (b)(2) permits the Government to recover an amount equal to the proportion of the facility's present value that the federal grant bore to its original cost.

This remedy, however, is available to the Government only if the statutory conditions are violated "within twenty years after completion of construction." ...

. . .

To this extent the Act therefore trespasses on the Religion Clauses. The restrictive obligations of a recipient institution under § 751 (a)(2) cannot, compatibly with the Religion Clauses, expire while the building has substantial value. This circumstance does not require us to invalidate the entire Act, however. "The cardinal principle of statutory construction is to save and not to destroy." ... Nor does the absence of an express severability provision in the Act dictate the demise of the entire statute.

. . .

[3]

We next turn to the question of whether excessive entanglements characterize the relationship between government and church under the Act. Our decision today in *Lemon v. Kurtzman* [403 U.S. 602 (1971)] and *Robinson v. DiCenso* has discussed and applied this independent measure of constitutionality under the Religion Clauses. [The *Lemon* Court considered three factors under the entanglement prong: "the character and purposes of the institutions that are benefited, the nature of the aid that the State provides, and the resulting relationship between the government and the religious authority."] There we concluded that excessive entanglements between government and religion were fostered by Pennsylvania and Rhode Island statutory programs under which state aid was provided to parochial elementary and secondary schools. Here, however, three factors substantially diminish the extent and the potential danger of the entanglement.

In *DiCenso* the District Court found that the parochial schools in Rhode Island were "an integral part of the religious mission of the Catholic Church." There, the record fully supported the conclusion that the inculcation of religious values was a substantial if not the dominant purpose of the institutions....

Appellants' complaint here contains similar allegations. But they were denied by the answers, and there was extensive evidence introduced on the subject. Although the District Court made no findings with respect to the religious character of the four institutions of higher learning, we are not required to accept the allegations as true under these circumstances, particularly where, as here, appellants themselves do not contend that these four institutions are "sectarian."

There are generally significant differences between the religious aspects of church-related institutions of higher learning and parochial elementary and secondary schools. The "affirmative if not dominant policy" of the instruction in pre-college church schools is "to assure future adherents to a particular faith by having control of their total education at an early age." *Walz v. Tax Comm'n*, [397 U.S. 664, 671 (1970)].[3] There is substance to the contention that college students are less impressionable and less susceptible to religious indoctrination.[4] Common observation would seem to support that view, and Congress may well have entertained it. The skepticism of the college student is not an inconsiderable barrier to any attempt or tendency to subvert the congressional objectives and limitations. Furthermore, by their very nature, college and postgraduate courses tend to limit the opportunities for sectarian influence by virtue of their own internal disciplines. Many church-related colleges and universities are characterized by a high degree of academic freedom[5] and seek to evoke free and critical responses from their students.

The record here would not support a conclusion that any of these four institutions departed from this general pattern. All four schools are governed by Catholic religious organizations, and the faculties and student bodies at each are predominantly Catholic. Nevertheless, the evidence shows that non-Catholics were admitted as students and given faculty appointments. Not one of these four institutions requires its students to attend religious services. Although all four schools require their students to take theology courses, the parties stipulated that these courses are taught according to the academic requirements of the subject matter and the teacher's concept of professional standards. The parties also stipulated that the courses covered a range of human religious experiences and are not limited to courses about the Roman Catholic religion. The schools introduced evidence that they made no attempt to indoctrinate students or to proselytize. Indeed, some of the required theology courses at Albertus Magnus and Sacred Heart are taught by rabbis. Finally, as we have noted, these four schools subscribe to a well-established set of principles of academic freedom, and nothing in this record shows that these principles are not in fact followed. In short, the evidence shows institutions with admittedly religious functions but whose predominant higher education mission is to provide their students with a secular education.

Since religious indoctrination is not a substantial purpose or activity of these church-related colleges and universities, there is less likelihood than in primary and secondary schools that religion will permeate the area of secular education. This reduces the risk that government aid will in fact serve to support religious activities. Correspondingly, the necessity for intensive government surveillance is diminished and the resulting entanglements between government and religion lessened. Such inspection as may be necessary to ascertain that the facilities are devoted to secular education is minimal and indeed hardly more than the inspections that States impose over all private schools within the reach of compulsory education laws.

The entanglement between church and state is also lessened here by the nonideological character of the aid that the Government provides. Our cases

---

3. *E.g.*, J. FICHTER, PAROCHIAL SCHOOL: A SOCIOLOGICAL STUDY 77–108 (1958); Giannella, *Religious Liberty, Nonestablishment, and Doctrinal Development, pt. II, The Nonestablishment Principle*, 81 HARV. L. REV. 513, 574 (1968).

4. Giannella, *supra*, n. 3, at 583.

5. M. PATTILLO & D. MACKENZIE, CHURCH-SPONSORED HIGHER EDUCATION IN THE UNITED STATES 96, 167, 204 (1966).

... have permitted church-related schools to receive government aid in the form of secular, neutral, or nonideological services, facilities, or materials that are supplied to all students regardless of the affiliation of the school that they attend. In *Lemon* and *DiCenso*, however, the state programs subsidized teachers, either directly or indirectly. Since teachers are not necessarily religiously neutral, greater governmental surveillance would be required to guarantee that state salary aid would not in fact subsidize religious instruction. There we found the resulting entanglement excessive. Here, on the other hand, the Government provides facilities that are themselves religiously neutral. The risks of Government aid to religion and the corresponding need for surveillance are therefore reduced.

Finally, government entanglements with religion are reduced by the circumstance that, unlike the direct and continuing payments under the Pennsylvania program, and all the incidents of regulation and surveillance, the Government aid here is a one-time, single-purpose construction grant. There are no continuing financial relationships or dependencies, no annual audits, and no government analysis of an institution's expenditures on secular as distinguished from religious activities. Inspection as to use is a minimal contact.

No one of these three factors standing alone is necessarily controlling; cumulatively all of them shape a narrow and limited relationship with government which involves fewer and less significant contacts than the two state schemes before us in *Lemon* and *DiCenso*. The relationship therefore has less potential for realizing the substantive evils against which the Religion Clauses were intended to protect.

We think that cumulatively these three factors also substantially lessen the potential for divisive religious fragmentation in the political arena. This conclusion is admittedly difficult to document, but neither have appellants pointed to any continuing religious aggravation on this matter in the political processes. Possibly this can be explained by the character and diversity of the recipient colleges and universities and the absence of any intimate continuing relationship or dependency between government and religiously affiliated institutions. The potential for divisiveness inherent in the essentially local problems of primary and secondary schools is significantly less with respect to a college or university whose student constituency is not local but diverse and widely dispersed.

[The Court also holds that the Act did not violate the appellant-taxpayers' free exercise rights.]

We conclude that the Act does not violate the Religion Clauses of the First Amendment except that part of § 754 (b)(2) providing a 20–year limitation on the religious use restrictions contained in § 751 (a)(2)....

Note on *Hunt* and *Roemer*

In *Hunt v. McNair*, 413 U.S. 734 (1973), the Supreme Court refined the primary effect portion of the three-prong *Lemon* test by introducing a pervasively sectarian standard:

Aid normally may be thought to have a primary effect of advancing religion when it flows to an institution in which religion is so pervasive that a substantial portion of its functions are subsumed in the religious mission or when it funds a specifically religious activity in an otherwise substantially secular setting.

Id. at 743.

In *Roemer v. Board of Public Works of Maryland*, 426 U.S. 736 (1976), the Court "was asked once again to police the boundary between church and state." *Id.* at 739. Less than a year after *Tilton*, the Maryland legislature enacted a statute providing annual grants to private universities. As long as the institution was fully accredited, awarded more than just theological degrees, and did not use the money for "sectarian purposes," the institution would receive funds on a per student basis. After passing an initial screening process to ensure that the institution awarded more than just theological degrees, the only other review process consisted of an annual report submitted by the institution on the use of the funds. "Any question of sectarian use" of the funds was resolved by a government council "on the basis of information submitted to it by the institution and without actual examination of its books. Failing that, a 'verification or audit' may be undertaken ... taking less than one day." Four Maryland citizens sued to enjoin funds being dispersed to four institutions affiliated with the Catholic Church.

The Supreme Court, applying the *Lemon* test, held that the statute was constitutional. Because the secular purpose of the statute was not contested, the Court focused its analysis on the primary effect and entanglement prongs of the test.

To meet the primary effect test, the grants could neither (1) be awarded to pervasively sectarian institutions nor (2) fund secular activities. The Court noted the District Court findings that:

a) The institutions were formally affiliated with the Catholic Church, but highly autonomous.

b) Catholic services were held on campus, but religious development was only "one secondary objective" of the institutions.

c) Mandatory religious classes were part of the curriculum, but the rest of the curriculum was "taught in an 'atmosphere of intellectual freedom' and without 'religious pressures.' "

d) Some classes began with prayer, were taught by "instructors in clerical garb," and were held in rooms adorned with religious symbols, but these were minor issues.

e) Although two of the colleges inquired into the religious views of applicants, "faculty hiring decisions [were] not made on a religious basis."

f) Students were accepted without regard to their religion.

The Court held that the "general picture" painted by the District Court's findings "of the appellee institutions is similar in almost all respects to that of ... *Tilton* and *Hunt*" and held that the institutions were not pervasively sectarian. The Court further found that the "statutory prohibition against sectarian use" satisfied the second part of the primary effect test. *Id.* at 758–59.

The statute also passed *Lemon*'s three-factor excessive-entanglement test. Because the institutions were primarily secular, there was little need "for close surveillance" of whether "an ostensibly secular [educational] activity [is actually] infused with religious content or significance." *Id.* at 762. The Court did not consider the *form* of aid prong because the appellants questioned only the fund-distribution *process*. On that issue, the Court held that the statute's annual submission and review process was not excessively entangling, although perhaps more so than the one-time grant in *Tilton*, because the State could easily separate "the secular and sectarian activities of the colleges." *Id.* at 764.

Consider the *Tilton* and *Roemer* courts' inquiries into the operations of church-related institutions. Is the judicial review process more "entangling" than the challenged programs themselves?

Columbia Union College v. Clarke

Supreme Court of the United States, 1999.
527 U.S. 1013, 119 S.Ct. 2357, 144 L.Ed.2d 252.

■ JUSTICE THOMAS, dissenting from the denial of certiorari.

Through the program at issue in this case—a program named, ironically, for Father Joseph Sellinger, a Roman Catholic priest—the State of Maryland provides financial aid, on a per student basis, to a wide range of private colleges. Although many of the colleges participating in the Sellinger Program are affiliated with religious institutions, Maryland deemed Columbia Union College, a private liberal arts college affiliated with the Seventh-day Adventist Church, "too religious" to participate. Throughout this litigation, Columbia Union College has maintained that Maryland violated its free speech, free exercise, and equal protection rights by excluding it from the Sellinger Program. The District Court and Court of Appeals for the Fourth Circuit agreed that the State's action infringed one or more of these rights. But, relying on our decision in *Roemer v. Board of Public Works of Md.*, 426 U.S. 736 (1976) (plurality opinion), both courts nonetheless concluded that Columbia Union's exclusion could be justified by Maryland's compelling interest in enforcing the Establishment Clause by ensuring that a "pervasively sectarian" institution did not benefit from public funds.

We invented the "pervasively sectarian" test as a way to distinguish between schools that carefully segregate religious and secular activities and schools that consider their religious and educational missions indivisible and therefore require religion to permeate all activities. In my view, the "pervasively sectarian" test rests upon two assumptions that cannot be squared with our more recent jurisprudence. The first of these assumptions is that the Establishment Clause prohibits government funds from ever benefiting, either directly or indirectly, "religious" activities. The other is that any institution that takes religion seriously cannot be trusted to observe this prohibition.[1]

We no longer require institutions and organizations to renounce their religious missions as a condition of participating in public programs. Instead, we have held that they may benefit from public assistance that is made available based upon neutral, secular criteria. *See Agostini v. Felton*, 521 U.S. 203 (1997) (students attending religious schools eligible for federal remedial assistance); *Rosenberger v. Rector and Visitors of Univ. of Va.*, 515 U.S. 819 (1995) (Christian student organization eligible for student activity funds); *Zobrest v. Catalina Foothills School Dist.*, 509 U.S. 1 (1993) (publicly funded sign language interpreter could assist student in a Catholic school); *Witters v. Washington Dept. of Servs. for Blind*, 474 U.S. 481 (1986) (blind student free to use public vocational assistance to attend bible college). Furthermore, the application of the "pervasively sectarian" test in this and similar cases directly collides with our decisions that have prohibited governments from discriminating in the distribution of public benefits based upon religious status or sincerity. *See Rosenberger, supra* (invalidating university policy denying student activity funds to Christian student newspaper); *Lamb's Chapel v. Center Morich-*

---

1. Typical of this assumption is the plurality's statement in *Tilton v. Richardson*, 403 U.S. 672, 681 (1971), that "there is no evidence that religion seeps into the use of any of these facilities ... the schools were characterized by an atmosphere of academic freedom rather than religious indoctrination."

es Union Free School Dist., 508 U.S. 384 (1993) (invalidating "religious use" restriction on public access to school district property); *Widmar v. Vincent*, 454 U.S. 263 (1981) (invalidating policy prohibiting student religious organizations from using public university's facilities).

We should take this opportunity to scrap the "pervasively sectarian" test and reaffirm that the Constitution requires, at a minimum, neutrality not hostility toward religion. By so doing, we would vindicate Columbia Union's right to be free from invidious religious discrimination.[2] Columbia Union's exclusion from the Sellinger Program "raises the inevitable inference that the disadvantage imposed is born of animosity to the class of [institutions] affected," namely, those schools that insist upon integrating their religious and secular functions. We also would provide the lower courts—which are struggling to reconcile our conflicting First Amendment pronouncements—with much needed guidance.

Although the Court declines to grant certiorari today—perhaps because this case comes to us in an interlocutory posture—the growing confusion among the lower courts illustrates that we cannot long avoid addressing the important issues that it presents.

Questions and Comments on *Columbia Union*

1. Is it possible to reconcile the pervasively sectarian test and the neutrality test?

2. One year after his dissent in *Columbia Union College*, Justice Thomas wrote the plurality opinion in *Mitchell v. Helms*, 530 U.S. 793 (2000), which held that government funding of educational materials used in private religious schools did not violate the Establishment Clause in the First Amendment. The plurality and concurring opinions applied the modified *Lemon* test set forth the in *Agostini v. Felton*, 521 U.S. 203 (1997), which incorporated the entanglement prong into the analysis of whether the primary effect of the statute was to advance religion. *Mitchell*, 530 U.S. at 808. Noting that the secular purpose of the Act was not at issue, the plurality focused on whether the statute had the primary effect of advancing religion. In upholding the law, the plurality dismissed distinctions between direct and indirect aid and emphasized the neutral application of the statute and the role of private choices in directing the aid towards private religious schools. The plurality further noted that "nothing in the Establishment Clause requires the exclusion of pervasively sectarian schools from otherwise permissible aid programs, and other doctrines of this Court bar it. This doctrine, born of bigotry, should be buried now." *Id.* at 829.

Justice O'Connor concurring in *Mitchell* and, joined by Justice Breyer, agreed that neutrality was important but stated that it had never been the sole criteria the Court relied upon in determining a statute's primary effect. *Id.* at 839 (O'Connor, J., concurring).

Because the concurrence did not address the plurality's discussion of the purported demise of the pervasively sectarian factor, should lower courts still consider it to be a factor?

---

2. Indeed, Maryland is not the only State that practices religious discrimination in the distribution of financial aid. *See, e.g.,* Colo. Rev. Stat. § 23–3.5–101–106 (1998) (students attending pervasively sectarian colleges ineligible for Colorado Student Incentive Grant Program); Wash. Rev. Code § 28B.10.814 (1994) (students pursuing a theology degree ineligible for state financial aid programs); Wis. Stat. Ann. § 39.30(2)(d) (Supp. 1998–1999) (state tuition grants shall not be awarded to "members of religious orders who are pursuing a course of study leading to a degree in theology, divinity or religious education").

3.   On remand in *Columbia Union College* from the Fourth Circuit after the denial of certiorari by the Supreme Court, the primary issue was whether Columbia Union College was pervasively sectarian. The district court found that it was not. On appeal, the Fourth Circuit upheld the participation of Columbia Union in the Sellinger program citing the decision of the Supreme Court in *Mitchell*. 254 F.3d 496, 505–08 (2001):

> The neutral features of the Sellinger Program are six in number, and Columbia Union meets each one. First, the institution is a "nonprofit private college or university that was established in Maryland before July 1, 1970." Md. Code Ann. Educ. § 17–103. Second, Columbia Union is "approved by the Maryland Higher Education Commission." *Id*. Third, the college is "accredited by the Commission on Higher Education of the Middle States Association of Colleges and Schools." *Id*. Fourth, Columbia Union has "awarded the associate of arts or baccalaureate degrees to at least one graduating class." *Id*. Fifth, the college "maintain[s] one or more earned degree programs, other than seminarian or theological programs, leading to an associate of arts or baccalaureate degree." *Id*. And sixth, the institution has submitted "each new program and each major modification of an existing program to the Maryland Higher Education Commission for its review and recommendation as to the initiation of the new or modified program." *Id*. The fact that Columbia Union meets every requirement of the statute, and the fact that fifteen other institutions have also satisfied these same requirements, show beyond cavil that the Sellinger Program assigns funds in a neutral and even-handed manner, "without regard to religion." *Mitchell*, 530 U.S. at 810 (plurality opinion).

> Under the plurality opinion [in *Mitchell*] the Sellinger Program's secular purpose and its neutral criteria would practically dispose of this case. And under the analysis of Justice O'Connor and Justice Breyer, the neutrality of the Sellinger Program remains a critical factor in considering its constitutionality. . . . Additional considerations, however, underscore the constitutionality of Sellinger assistance to the college.

> [One] consideration is one precisely identified by Justice O'Connor—the lack of any evidence of *actual* diversion of government aid to religious purposes. It is not of consequence that a sectarian school offers secular courses like computer science because the "presumptions of religious indoctrination are normally inappropriate when evaluating neutral school-aid programs under the Establishment Clause." Instead, plaintiffs must show "*evidence* that the government aid in question *has resulted* in religious indoctrination." *Id*. (emphasis added).

> Here, the State cannot make a showing of actual diversion. . . .

> In addition to the absence of evidence of actual diversion, there are safeguards against future diversion of Sellinger Program funds for sectarian purposes. The statute requires that a qualifying institution "may not use" Sellinger Program funds "for sectarian purposes." Md. Code Ann. Educ. § 17–104. Columbia Union satisfies this prerequisite as well. The President of Columbia Union signed a sworn affidavit stating that the funds would not be used for sectarian purposes. Moreover, the program assigns the amount of aid based on the "number of full-time equivalent students enrolled at the institution," excluding "students enrolled in seminarian or theological programs." *Id*. § 17–104. Indeed, the requirements that funds *not* be used for sectarian purposes and that students enrolled in sectarian programs be excluded from the total number of students signify that, if anything, sectarian colleges are actually at a disadvantage in receiving aid under the Sellinger Program.

>   . . .

A final reason for sustaining the constitutionality of Columbia Union's use of Sellinger Program funds is the fact that Columbia Union is an institution of higher learning. . . .

The Supreme Court has consistently stated that it would scrutinize aid to religiously-affiliated colleges and universities more leniently than aid to primary and secondary schools. Students attending college are more likely to do so by free will and more likely to encounter a variety of influences and opinions while on campus. As the Supreme Court noted in *Tilton*, "there are generally significant differences between the religious aspects of church-related institutions of higher learning and parochial elementary and secondary schools." *Tilton*, 403 U.S. at 685 (plurality opinion). College students are simply "less susceptible to religious indoctrination." *Id*. at 686. "The skepticism of the college student is not an inconsiderable barrier to any attempt or tendency" to try to use secular courses to teach religion at the university level. *Id*.

. . . [T]he fact remains that the Court has never struck down a government aid program to a religiously-affiliated college or university. Thus, even if direct funding of classes raises special constitutional concerns at the primary and secondary level, *see Mitchell*, 530 U.S. at 859–60 (O'Connor, J., concurring in the judgment), direct funding of secular classes at the collegiate level might still survive scrutiny. For at the college level, "there is no danger, or at least only a substantially reduced danger, that an ostensibly secular activity [like] the study of biology [or] the learning of a foreign language . . . will actually be infused with religious content or significance." *Roemer*, 426 U.S. at 762 (plurality opinion). The features of the college environment thus mean that aid is much less likely to have a constitutionally impermissible effect.

. . .

We cannot . . . find any reason even under a pervasively sectarian analysis why Columbia Union should be denied Sellinger Program assistance. The district court found as a matter of fact, after examining the thousands of pages of evidence and conducting a bench trial, that Columbia Union is not pervasively sectarian. Even assuming that *Roemer* is still good law, and that the pervasively sectarian analysis remains relevant for determining violations of the Establishment Clause, Columbia Union is entitled to Sellinger Program funds because the district court was not clearly erroneous in its findings. . . .

Compare Virginia College Building Authority v. Lynn, 260 Va. 608, 538 S.E.2d 682, 693 (2000) (stating that "without a fifth vote the plurality's obituary for analysis of pervasive sectarianism may be premature"). In *Zelman v. Simmons–Harris*, 536 U.S. 639 (2002), the Court upheld a state program providing elementary and secondary students with vouchers to a private school of their choice, explaining that it was a program based on private choice and was neutrally applied. *Id*. at 655. Neither the majority nor the dissent focused on whether the schools were pervasively sectarian. If lower courts can still weigh the pervasively sectarian nature of a school as a factor, how much weight should it be given? See *Lynn*, 538 S.E.2d at 698–99 (holding that, although Regent University is pervasively sectarian, a law issuing government bonds on its behalf is constitutional because of its neutral application and the role of private choices).

4.   Thirty-six state constitutions contain provisions that explicitly prohibit the use of public funds for religious purposes. Martha McCarthy, *Room for "Play in the Joints"—Locke v. Davey*, 33 J.L. & EDUC. 457, 465 (2004). After *Mitchell* and *Zelman*, these state constitutions pose one last barrier for states that want to fund students attending religious universities and colleges.

5. Would the *Columbia Union College* case be decided the same way today? For a lower court's analysis of whether a state can refuse to fund pervasively sectarian colleges *see Colorado Christian University v. Baker*, 2007 WL 1489801 (D. Colo. 2007).

Bob Jones University v. United States

Supreme Court of the United States, 1983.
461 U.S. 574, 103 S.Ct. 2017, 76 L.Ed.2d 157.

■ CHIEF JUSTICE BURGER delivered the opinion of the Court.

. . .

Until 1970, the Internal Revenue Service granted tax-exempt status to private schools, without regard to their racial admissions policies, under § 501(c)(3) of the Internal Revenue Code, 26 U.S.C. § 501(c)(3) and granted charitable deductions for contributions to such schools under § 170 of the Code, 26 U.S.C. § 170.

[That year, the District Court for the District of Columbia issued a preliminary injunction that barred the IRS from continuing to grant tax-exempt status to private schools with racially discriminatory admissions policies and treat as charitable deductions contributions to those schools. The IRS altered its construction of the Code accordingly and made its new policy "applicable to all private schools ... at all levels of education." The District Court then held that discriminatory schools and their donors were not entitled, respectively, to tax-exempt status and charitable deductions, and the IRS formally revised its policy in Revenue Ruling 71–447, 1971–2 Cum. Bull. 230.]

Bob Jones University is a nonprofit corporation located in Greenville, S.C.[4] Its purpose is 'to conduct an institution of learning ... giving special emphasis to the Christian religion and the ethics revealed in the Holy Scriptures.' Certificate of Incorporation, Bob Jones University, Inc., of Greenville, S.C. The corporation operates a school with an enrollment of approximately 5,000 students, from kindergarten through college and graduate school. Bob Jones University is not affiliated with any religious denomination, but is dedicated to the teaching and propagation of its fundamentalist Christian religious beliefs. It is both a religious and educational institution. Its teachers are required to be devout Christians, and all courses at the University are taught according to the Bible. Entering students are screened as to their religious beliefs, and their public and private conduct is strictly regulated by standards promulgated by University authorities.

The sponsors of the University genuinely believe that the Bible forbids interracial dating and marriage. To effectuate these views, Negroes were completely excluded until 1971. From 1971 to May 1975, the University accepted no applications from unmarried Negroes,[5] but did accept applications from Negroes married within their race.

---

4. Bob Jones University was founded in Florida in 1927. It moved to Greenville, S. C., in 1940, and has been incorporated as an eleemosynary institution in South Carolina since 1952.

5. Beginning in 1973, Bob Jones University instituted an exception to this rule, allowing applications from unmarried Negroes who had been members of the University staff for four years or more.

Following the decision of the United States Court of Appeals for the Fourth Circuit in *McCrary v. Runyon*, 515 F.2d 1082 (1975), *aff'd*, 427 U.S. 160 (1976), prohibiting racial exclusion from private schools, the University revised its policy. Since May 29, 1975, the University has permitted unmarried Negroes to enroll; but a disciplinary rule prohibits interracial dating and marriage [or encouraging interracial dating and marriage. The punishment is expulsion.]

The University continues to deny admission to applicants engaged in an interracial marriage or known to advocate interracial marriage or dating.

Until 1970, the IRS extended tax-exempt status to Bob Jones University under § 501(c)(3). By the letter of November 30, 1970 ... the IRS formally notified the University of the change in IRS policy, and announced its intention to challenge the tax-exempt status of private schools practicing racial discrimination in their admissions policies.

. . .

[O]n April 16, 1975, the IRS notified the University of the proposed revocation of its tax-exempt status. On January 19, 1976, the IRS officially revoked the University's tax-exempt status, effective as of December 1, 1970, the day after the University was formally notified of the change in IRS policy. The University subsequently filed returns under the Federal Unemployment Tax Act for the period from December 1, 1970, to December 31, 1975, and paid a tax totaling $21 on one employee for the calendar year of 1975. After its request for a refund was denied, the University instituted the present action, seeking to recover the $21 it had paid to the IRS. The Government counterclaimed for unpaid federal unemployment taxes for the taxable years 1971 through 1975, in the amount of $489,675.59, plus interest.

The United States District Court for the District of South Carolina held that revocation of the University's tax-exempt status exceeded the delegated powers of the IRS, was improper under the IRS rulings and procedures, and violated the University's rights under the Religion Clauses of the First Amendment. The court accordingly ordered the IRS to pay the University the $21 refund it claimed and rejected the IRS's counterclaim.

The Court of Appeals for the Fourth Circuit, in a divided opinion, reversed.

. . .

In Revenue Ruling 71–447, the IRS formalized the policy, first announced in 1970, that § 170 and § 501(c)(3) embrace the common-law "charity" concept. Under that view, to qualify for a tax exemption pursuant to § 501(c)(3), an institution must show, first, that it falls within one of the eight categories expressly set forth in that section, and second, that its activity is not contrary to settled public policy.

Section 501(c)(3) provides that "[corporations] ... organized and operated exclusively for religious, charitable ... or educational purposes" are entitled to tax exemption. Petitioners argue that the plain language of the statute guarantees them tax-exempt status. They emphasize the absence of any language in the statute expressly requiring all exempt organizations to be "charitable" in the common-law sense, and they contend that the disjunctive "or" separating the categories in § 501(c)(3) precludes such a reading.

Instead, they argue that if an institution falls within one or more of the specified categories it is automatically entitled to exemption, without regard to whether it also qualifies as "charitable."

It is a well-established canon of statutory construction that a court should go beyond the literal language of a statute if reliance on that language would defeat the plain purpose of the statute. . . .

Section 501(c)(3) therefore must be analyzed and construed within the framework of the Internal Revenue Code and against the background of the congressional purposes. Such an examination reveals unmistakable evidence that, underlying all relevant parts of the Code, is the intent that entitlement to tax exemption depends on meeting certain common-law standards of charity—namely, that an institution seeking tax-exempt status must serve a public purpose and not be contrary to established public policy.

This "charitable" concept appears explicitly in § 170 of the Code. That section contains a list of organizations virtually identical to that contained in § 501(c)(3). It is apparent that Congress intended that list to have the same meaning in both sections.[10] In § 170, Congress used the list of organizations in defining the term "charitable contributions." On its face, therefore, § 170 reveals that Congress' intention was to provide tax benefits to organizations serving charitable purposes. The form of § 170 simply makes plain what common sense and history tell us: in enacting both § 170 and § 501(c)(3), Congress sought to provide tax benefits to charitable organizations, to encourage the development of private institutions that serve a useful public purpose or supplement or take the place of public institutions of the same kind.

More than a century ago, this Court announced the caveat that is critical in this case:

> "[It] has now become an established principle of American law, that courts of chancery will sustain and protect . . . a gift . . . to public charitable uses, *provided the same is consistent with local laws and public policy* . . . ." *Perin v. Carey*, 65 U.S. (24 How.) 465, 501 (1861) (emphasis added).

. . .

[This and other] statements clearly reveal the legal background against which Congress enacted the first charitable exemption statute in 1894:[14] charities were to be given preferential treatment because they provide a benefit to society.

. . .

10. . . . The language of the two sections is in most respects identical, and the Commissioner and the courts consistently have applied many of the same standards in interpreting those sections. To the extent that § 170 "aids in ascertaining the meaning" of § 501(c)(3), therefore, it is "entitled to great weight," *United States v. Stewart*, 311 U.S. 60, 64–65 (1940).

14. Act of Aug. 27, 1894, ch. 349, § 32, 28 Stat. 556–557. The income tax system contained in the 1894 Act was declared unconstitutional, *Pollock v. Farmers' Loan & Trust Co.*, 158 U.S. 601 (1895), for reasons unrelated to the charitable exemption provision. The terms of that exemption were in substance included in the corporate income tax contained in the Payne–Aldrich Tariff Act of 1909, ch. 6, § 38, 36 Stat. 112. A similar exemption has been included in every income tax Act since the adoption of the Sixteenth Amendment, beginning with the Revenue Act of 1913, ch. 16, § II(G), 38 Stat. 172. *See generally* Reiling, *Federal Taxation: What Is a Charitable Organization?*, 44 A. B. A. J. 525 (1958); Liles & Blum.

A corollary to the public benefit principle is the requirement, long recognized in the law of trusts, that the purpose of a charitable trust may not be illegal or violate established public policy. . . .

When the Government grants exemptions or allows deductions all taxpayers are affected; the very fact of the exemption or deduction for the donor means that other taxpayers can be said to be indirect and vicarious "donors." Charitable exemptions are justified on the basis that the exempt entity confers a public benefit—a benefit which the society or the community may not itself choose or be able to provide, or which supplements and advances the work of public institutions already supported by tax revenues. History buttresses logic to make clear that, to warrant exemption under § 501(c)(3), an institution must fall within a category specified in that section and must demonstrably serve and be in harmony with the public interest. The institution's purpose must not be so at odds with the common community conscience as to undermine any public benefit that might otherwise be conferred.

We are bound to approach these questions with full awareness that determinations of public benefit and public policy are sensitive matters with serious implications for the institutions affected; a declaration that a given institution is not "charitable" should be made only where there can be no doubt that the activity involved is contrary to a fundamental public policy. But there can no longer be any doubt that racial discrimination in education violates deeply and widely accepted views of elementary justice. Prior to 1954, public education in many places still was conducted under the pall of *Plessy v. Ferguson*, 163 U.S. 537 (1896); racial segregation in primary and secondary education prevailed in many parts of the country. This Court's decision in *Brown v. Board* of Education, 347 U.S. 483 (1954), signaled an end to that era. Over the past quarter of a century, every pronouncement of this Court and myriad Acts of Congress and Executive Orders attest a firm national policy to prohibit racial segregation and discrimination in public education.

.   .   .

Few social or political issues in our history have been more vigorously debated and more extensively ventilated than the issue of racial discrimination, particularly in education. Given the stress and anguish of the history of efforts to escape from the shackles of the "separate but equal" doctrine of *Plessy v. Ferguson*, 163 U.S. 537 (1896), it cannot be said that educational institutions that, for whatever reasons, practice racial discrimination, are institutions exercising "beneficial and stabilizing influences in community life," *Walz v. Tax Comm'n*, 397 U.S. 664, 673 (1970), or should be encouraged by having all taxpayers share in their support by way of special tax status.

There can thus be no question that the interpretation of § 170 and § 501(c)(3) announced by the IRS in 1970 was correct. That it may be seen as belated does not undermine its soundness. It would be wholly incompatible with the concepts underlying tax exemption to grant the benefit of tax-exempt status to racially discriminatory educational entities, which "[exert] a pervasive influence on the entire educational process." *Norwood v. Harrison*, [413 U.S. 455, 469 (1973)]. Whatever may be the rationale for such private schools' policies, and however sincere the rationale may be, racial discrimination in education is contrary to public policy. Racially discriminatory educational institutions cannot be viewed as conferring a public benefit within the "charitable" concept discussed earlier, or within the congressional intent underlying § 170 and § 501(c)(3).

[The Court next rejects Petitioners' argument that the IRS exceeded its congressionally delegated authority by issuing the rulings in question.]

Petitioners contend that, even if the Commissioner's policy is valid as to nonreligious private schools, that policy cannot constitutionally be applied to schools that engage in racial discrimination on the basis of sincerely held religious beliefs. As to such schools, it is argued that the IRS construction of § 170 and § 501(c)(3) violates their free exercise rights under the Religion Clauses of the First Amendment. . . .

This Court has long held the Free Exercise Clause of the First Amendment to be an absolute prohibition against governmental regulation of religious beliefs, *Wisconsin v. Yoder*, 406 U.S. 205, 219 (1972); *Sherbert v. Verner*, 374 U.S. 398, 402 (1963); *Cantwell v. Connecticut*, 310 U.S. 296, 303 (1940). As interpreted by this Court, moreover, the Free Exercise Clause provides substantial protection for lawful conduct grounded in religious belief, *see Wisconsin v. Yoder*, supra, at 220; *Thomas v. Review Board of Indiana Employment Security Div.*, 450 U.S. 707 (1981); *Sherbert v. Verner*, *supra*, at 402–403. . . .

On occasion this Court has found certain governmental interests so compelling as to allow even regulations prohibiting religiously based conduct. In *Prince v. Massachusetts*, 321 U.S. 158 (1944), for example, the Court held that neutrally cast child labor laws prohibiting sale of printed materials on public streets could be applied to prohibit children from dispensing religious literature. The Court found no constitutional infirmity in "excluding [Jehovah's Witness children] from doing there what no other children may do." Denial of tax benefits will inevitably have a substantial impact on the operation of private religious schools, but will not prevent those schools from observing their religious tenets.

The governmental interest at stake here is compelling. . . . [T]he Government has a fundamental, overriding interest in eradicating racial discrimination in education discrimination that prevailed, with official approval, for the first 165 years of this Nation's constitutional history. That governmental interest substantially outweighs whatever burden denial of tax benefits places on petitioners' exercise of their religious beliefs. The interests asserted by petitioners cannot be accommodated with that compelling governmental interest, and no "less restrictive means," are available to achieve the governmental interest.

The remaining issue is whether the IRS properly applied its policy. . . .

Petitioner Bob Jones University . . . contends that it is not racially discriminatory. It emphasizes that it now allows all races to enroll, subject only to its restrictions on the conduct of all students, including its prohibitions of association between men and women of different races, and of interracial marriage. Although a ban on intermarriage or interracial dating applies to all races, decisions of this Court firmly establish that discrimination on the basis of racial affiliation and association is a form of racial discrimination, *see, e. g., Loving v. Virginia*, 388 U.S. 1 (1967). . . . We therefore find that the IRS properly applied Revenue Ruling 71–447 to Bob Jones University.

Questions and Comments on *Bob Jones University*

1. After the decision by the Supreme Court, Bob Jones University became a taxable nonprofit educational organization. The University already owned and operated a museum and art gallery on the campus. In 1992 they were separately incorporated as the nonprofit Bob Jones University Museum and Gallery, Inc. Offering free admission to the public, the Museum receives over 2,000 visitors annually, 80 percent of whom have no connection to the University. In 1995, the Museum petitioned the United States Tax Court for a declaratory judgment that it met the requirement of § 501(c)(3) and thus was exempt from federal income tax. The Internal Revenue Service opposed the request, arguing that the University was using the Museum as an alternative way to achieve the tax-exempt status that had been denied by the Supreme Court. The court sided with the Museum. Bob Jones Univ. Museum and Gallery, Inc. v. Commissioner, 71 T.C.M. (CCH) 3120 (1996).

2. In addition to the Museum, the University has established other separately incorporated organizations including a Minority Scholarship Fund, Hispanic Assistance Fund, Demonstrative Need Fund, Science and Engineering Endowment Fund, and Gospel Fellowship Association and holds them out as tax deductible. *See* Bob Jones University: Planned Giving, http:/www.bju.edu/giving/pg/ (last visited Aug. 18, 2007). Do they meet the standards set forth in the *Bob Jones* decision?

B. RELIGION AND PUBLIC COLLEGES AND UNIVERSITIES

Yacovelli v. Moeser

United States District Court for the Middle District of North Carolina, 2004.
324 F.Supp.2d 760.

■ TILLEY, United States District Judge.

The parties in this matter continue to dispute the constitutionality of a freshman orientation program, instituted by the University of North Carolina at Chapel Hill, involving the study of a book about the Qur'an. . . .

. . . The University of North Carolina at Chapel Hill ("UNC") conducts an orientation program for all incoming freshmen prior to the beginning of classes. The stated goals of the orientation program are to: (1) stimulate discussion and critical thinking around a current topic, (2) introduce the student to academic life at UNC, (3) enhance a sense of community between students, faculty and staff, and (4) provide a common experience for incoming students. For the 2002 orientation program, UNC selected portions of MICHAEL SELLS' APPROACHING THE QUR'AN: THE EARLY REVELATIONS (White Cloud Press 1999), stating that a book exploring Islam was highly relevant in light of the terrorist attacks of September 11, 2001.

Two parts of the book were designated: the introduction and an analysis of passages from the Qur'an. Sells states that "the purpose of the introduction is to clarify the cultural and historical matrix in which the Qur'an came to exist, the central themes and qualities of hymnic Suras,[3] and the manner in which the Qur'an is experienced and taken to heart within Islamic societies." The second designation includes a translation of several Suras and accompanying commentary.[4] This portion of the book is dedicated to "issues

---

3. Suras are "hymnic chapters."

4. Sound recordings of the Suras being recited are included in a compact disk at-of interpretation, historical context, and key themes" of Islam as expressed in the early Suras.

UNC originally required all incoming students to read the book and write a paper in response to the book, guided by a series of questions prepared by UNC. UNC later stated that students with religious objections did not have to read the book, and that they could instead write a paper addressing why they chose not to read the book. The student papers, while not graded, were collected. Despite representations by UNC officials that attendance would not be taken at the discussion groups, Plaintiff Jane Roe alleges that her discussion facilitator took attendance.

Plaintiffs filed the instant lawsuit contending that UNC violated the federal Constitution by assigning a book with a positive portrayal of both Muhammad and Islam and by forcing students to read and discuss the book. Further, Plaintiffs allege that forcing students to write about and share their personal religious beliefs subjected them to harassment and ridicule.

. . .

The Free Exercise Clause, made applicable to the states through the Fourteenth Amendment, provides that "Congress shall make no law . . . prohibiting the free exercise" of religion. According to the Supreme Court, "the free exercise of religion means, first and foremost, the right to believe and profess whatever religious doctrine one desires." *Employment Div., Dept. of Human Res. of Or. v. Smith*, 494 U.S. 872, 877 (1990). The government may not "compel affirmation of religious belief, punish the expression of religious doctrines it believes to be false, impose special disabilities on the basis of religious views or religious status, or lend its power to one or the other side in controversies over religious authority or dogma."

Laws designed to suppress religious beliefs or practices may not be adopted "unless justified by a compelling governmental interest and narrowly tailored to meet that interest." However, where the contested government action is a neutral, generally applicable law, the government need not establish a compelling governmental interest "even if the law has the incidental effect of burdening a particular religious practice." Put simply, a law that is neutral and of general applicability "does not offend the Free Exercise Clause, despite any incidental religious burdens it may create."

. . . Accepting all of the Plaintiffs' allegations as true, UNC required students who did not want to read the assigned book to write a paper explaining why they chose not to read the book, and to attend a related discussion group with other students who may or may not have read the book. At the discussion group, students were asked to turn in their papers and to answer any questions, either about the book or about their decision not to read the book, that the facilitator may direct at them.

This Court has already found that the book in question was not a religious reading, but part of an academic exercise. *See Yacovelli v. Moeser*, 2004 WL 1144183 (M.D.N.C.2004). Nonetheless, UNC allowed anyone who objected to reading the book to refrain from doing so. Therefore, the Plaintiffs' only remaining factual allegations are that writing about their

tached to the book because the rhythmic patterns of the Arabic language are "central to the Qur'an."

reasons for not reading the book and/or attending a two-hour discussion group interfered with the exercise of their religious beliefs.

The facts as set out in the Second Amended Complaint are insufficient to state a claim for a Free Exercise Clause violation. The Complaint does not allege a factual basis for the conclusion that UNC either (1) compelled affirmation of any particular religious belief, (2) lent its power to a particular side in a controversy over religious dogma, (3) imposed special disabilities on the basis of religious views or religious status, or (4) punished the expression of any particular religious doctrines.

. . .

. . . Plaintiffs have not provided any factual allegations which would support a finding that they have been burdened in their religious beliefs or practices by any of UNC's actions.

. . . To the contrary, UNC implemented a program asking students to discuss a religion thrust into recent controversy, and to do so from an academic perspective. Part of the purpose of this program was to introduce students to the type of higher-level thinking that is required in a university setting. Students who were not members of the Islamic faith, probably the great majority of students, were neither asked nor forced to give up their own beliefs or to compromise their own beliefs in order to discuss the patterns, language, history, and cultural significance of the Qu'ran.

. . .

Because the Plaintiffs have not alleged a violation of the Free Exercise Clause, Defendants' Motion to Dismiss the Free Exercise Claim will be Granted. . . .

Note on *Scopes*, *Epperson*, and *Kitzmiller*

Religious conflicts over curricula are hardly new, although most have involved elementary or high schools. Perhaps the best known is the Scopes Trial case, which reached the Tennessee Supreme Court in *Scopes v. State*, 154 Tenn. 105, 289 S.W. 363 (1927). At issue was a Tennessee law forbidding the teaching of evolution in any Tennessee public school, including universities. John Scopes, a public high school teacher, was charged with violating the law. When William Jennings Bryan, a three-time Democratic presidential candidate agreed to serve as a special prosecutor at the trial, Clarence Darrow, an eminent advocate for the ACLU, agreed to defend Scopes. At the trial, the judge excluded the jury from hearing most of the defense case; the jury promptly brought in a guilty verdict. The conviction was overturned on appeal to the Tennessee Supreme Court for a technical sentencing error. Because Scopes agreed to leave the state, he was never reprosecuted. *See* EDWARD J. LARSON, SUMMER FOR THE GODS: THE SCOPES TRIAL AND AMERICA'S CONTINUING DEBATE OVER SCIENCE AND RELIGION (1997); William W. Van Alstyne, *Academic Freedom and the First Amendment in the Supreme Court of the United States: An Unhurried Historical Review, in* FREEDOM AND TENURE IN THE ACADEMY 79, 84–85 (William W. Van Alstyne ed., 1993).

In its opinion, the Tennessee Supreme Court made clear that it considered the statute constitutional:

> [Scopes] was under contract with the State to work in an institution of the State. He had no right or privilege to serve the State except upon such terms as the State prescribed. His liberty, his privilege, his immunity to teach and proclaim the theory of evolution, elsewhere than in the service of the State, was in no wise touched by this law.

The statute before us is not an exercise of the police power of the State undertaking to regulate the conduct and contracts of individuals in their dealings with each other. On the other hand, it is an Act of the State as a corporation, a proprietor, an employer. It is a declaration of a master as to the character of work the master's servant shall, or rather shall not, perform. In dealing with its own employees engaged upon its own work, the state is *not hampered* by the limitations of . . . the Fourteenth Amendment to the Constitution of the United States.

Scopes, 289 S.W. at 364–65.

After the decision in *Scopes*, Arkansas adopted a similar law forbidding the teaching of evolution that reached the United States Supreme Court in *Epperson v. Arkansas*, 393 U.S. 97 (1968). In 1968, Susan Epperson, a public school biology teacher, sought a declaration that the statute was void. Although the law had not been enforced for some time, she wanted to ensure there would be no penalty for teaching the evolution chapter in a new biology textbook. The Supreme Court noted that courts should exercise restraint when getting involved in the daily operation of schools, but struck down the law. *Epperson*, 393 U.S. at 104. The Court explained, "[t]here is and can be no doubt that the First Amendment does not permit the State to require that teaching and learning must be tailored to the principles or prohibitions of any religious sect or dogma." *Id.* at 106. Arkansas may not have adopted explicitly religious language as Tennessee had, "but there is no doubt that the motivation for the law was the same: to suppress the teaching of a theory which, it was thought, 'denied' the divine creation of man." *Id.* at 109. Teaching of a scientific theory cannot be restricted solely because of its conflict with a religious belief. *Id.*

Disputes over evolution continue to be brought to court. *See, e.g.*, Edwards v. Aguillard, 482 U.S. 578 (1987) (Louisiana law requiring equal time for teaching creationism if evolution was taught violates the Establishment Clause); Webster v. New Lenox Sch. Dist. No. 122, 917 F.2d 1004 (7th Cir.1990) (teacher's first amendment rights not violated by a prohibition against teaching creationism).

The most recent evolution case is *Kitzmiller v. Dover Area School District*, 400 F.Supp.2d 707 (D.Pa.2005). In *Kitzmiller*, teachers were required to read a disclaimer before teaching evolution that stated:

> The Pennsylvania Academic Standards require students to learn about Darwin's Theory of Evolution and eventually to take a standardized test of which evolution is a part.
>
> Because Darwin's Theory is a theory, it continues to be tested as new evidence is discovered. The Theory is not a fact. Gaps in the Theory exist for which there is no evidence. A theory is defined as a well-tested explanation that unifies a broad range of observations.
>
> Intelligent Design is an explanation of the origin of life that differs from Darwin's view. The reference book, Of Pandas and People, is available for students who might be interested in gaining an understanding of what Intelligent Design actually involves.
>
> With respect to any theory, students are encouraged to keep an open mind. The school leaves the discussion of the Origins of Life to individual students and their families. As a Standards-driven district, class instruction focuses upon preparing students to achieve proficiency on Standards-based assessments.

Kitzmiller, 400 F.Supp.2d at 708–09.

After an extensive analysis, the district court held that the disclaimer violated the Establishment Clause in two ways. First, it was an unconstitutional endorsement of a religious belief. Second, the disclaimer failed the *Lemon* test because its purpose was to promote religion and the effect was "to impose a religious view of biological origins into the biology course." The court continued:

[A]fter a searching review of the record and applicable case law, we find that while ID [intelligent design] arguments may be true, a proposition on which the Court takes no position, ID is not science. We find that ID fails on three different levels, any one of which is sufficient to preclude a determination that ID is science. hey are: (1) ID violates the centuries-old ground rules of science by invoking and permitting supernatural causation; (2) the argument of irreducible complexity, central to ID, employs the same flawed and illogical contrived dualism that doomed creation science in the 1980's; and (3) ID's negative attacks on evolution have been refuted by the scientific community.... ID has failed to gain acceptance in the scientific community, it has not generated peer-reviewed publications, nor has it been the subject of testing and research.

Id. at 735.

For further discussion of evolution and the First Amendment see Asma T. Uddin, *Evolution Toward Neutrality: Evolution Disclaimers, Establishment Jurisprudence Confusions, and a Proposal of Untainted Fruits of a Poisonous Tree*, 8 RUTGERS J.L. & RELIGION 12 (2007). *See also* Selman v. Cobb County Sch. Dist., 390 F. Supp. 2d 1286 (N.D.Ga. 2005) (holding that stickers on biology textbooks saying evolution is a "theory, not a fact" violated the Establishment Clause), *vacated and remanded*, 449 F.3d 1320 (11th Cir. 2006).

Widmar v. Vincent

Supreme Court of the United States, 1981.
454 U.S. 263, 102 S.Ct. 269, 70 L.Ed.2d 440.

■ JUSTICE POWELL delivered the opinion of the court.

This case presents the question whether a state university, which makes its facilities generally available for the activities of registered student groups, may close its facilities to a registered student group desiring to use the facilities for religious worship and religious discussion.

It is the stated policy of the University of Missouri at Kansas City to encourage the activities of student organizations. The University officially recognizes over 100 student groups. It routinely provides University facilities for the meetings of registered organizations. Students pay an activity fee of $41 per semester (1978–1979) to help defray the costs to the University.

From 1973 until 1977 a registered religious group named Cornerstone regularly sought and received permission to conduct its meetings in University facilities.[2] In 1977, however, the University informed the group that it could no longer meet in University buildings. The exclusion was based on a regulation, adopted by the Board of Curators in 1972, that prohibits the use of University buildings or grounds "for purposes of religious worship or religious teaching."[3]

2. Cornerstone is an organization of evangelical Christian students from various denominational backgrounds. According to an affidavit filed in 1977, "perhaps twenty students ... participate actively in Cornerstone and form the backbone of the campus organization." Cornerstone held its on-campus meetings in classrooms and in the student center. These meetings were open to the public and attracted up to 125 students. A typical Cornerstone meeting included prayer, hymns, Bible commentary, and discussion of religious views and experiences.

3. There is no chapel on the campus of UMKC. The nearest University chapel is at the Columbia campus, approximately 125 miles east of UMKC.

Although the University had routinely approved Cornerstone meetings before 1977,

Eleven University students, all members of Cornerstone, brought suit to challenge the regulation in the Federal District Court for the Western District of Missouri.[4] They alleged that the University's discrimination against religious activity and discussion violated their rights to free exercise of religion, equal protection, and freedom of speech under the First and Fourteenth Amendments to the Constitution of the United States.

Upon cross-motions for summary judgment, the District Court upheld the challenged regulation. . . .

The Court of Appeals for the Eighth Circuit reversed. . . .

Through its policy of accommodating their meetings, the University has created a forum generally open for use by student groups. Having done so, the University has assumed an obligation to justify its discriminations and exclusions under applicable constitutional norms.[5] The Constitution forbids a State to enforce certain exclusions from a forum generally open to the public, even if it was not required to create the forum in the first place.

At the same time, however, our cases have recognized that First Amendment rights must be analyzed "in light of the special characteristics of the school environment." *Tinker v. Des Moines Independent School District*, 393 U.S. 503, 506 (1969). We continue to adhere to that view. A university differs in significant respects from public forums such as streets or parks or even municipal theaters. A university's mission is education, and decisions of this Court have never denied a university's authority to impose reasonable regulations compatible with that mission upon the use of its campus and facilities. We have not held, for example, that a campus must make all of its facilities equally available to students and nonstudents alike, or that a university must grant free access to all of its grounds or buildings.

The University's institutional mission, which it describes as providing a "*secular* education" to its students, does not exempt its actions from constitutional scrutiny. With respect to persons entitled to be there, our cases leave no doubt that the First Amendment rights of speech and association extend to the campuses of state universities.

Here UMKC has discriminated against student groups and speakers based on their desire to use a generally open forum to engage in religious worship and discussion. These are forms of speech and association protected

the District Court found that University officials had never "authorized a student organization to utilize a University facility for a meeting where they had full knowledge that the purposes of the meeting [included] religious worship or religious teaching."

4. Respondent Clark Vincent and Florian Chess, a named plaintiff in the action in the District Court, were among the students who initiated the action on October 13, 1977. Named as defendants were the petitioner Gary Widmar, the Dean of Students at UMKC, and the University's Board of Curators.

5. This Court has recognized that the campus of a public university, at least for its students, possesses many of the characteristics of a public forum. "The college classroom with its surrounding environs is peculiarly 'the marketplace of ideas.' " *Healy v. James*, 408 U.S. 169, 180 (1972). Moreover, the capacity of a group or individual "to participate in the intellectual give and take of campus debate . . . [would be] limited by denial of access to the customary media for communicating with the administration, faculty members, and other students." *Id.* at 181–182. We therefore have held that students enjoy First Amendment rights of speech and association on the campus, and that the "denial [to particular groups] of use of campus facilities for meetings and other appropriate purposes" must be subjected to the level of scrutiny appropriate to any form of prior restraint. *Id.* at 181, 184.

by the First Amendment.[6] In order to justify discriminatory exclusion from a public forum based on the religious content of a group's intended speech, the University must therefore satisfy the standard of review appropriate to content-based exclusions. It must show that its regulation is necessary to serve a compelling state interest and that it is narrowly drawn to achieve that end.

In this case the University claims a compelling interest in maintaining strict separation of church and State. It derives this interest from the "Establishment Clauses" of both the Federal and Missouri Constitutions.

The University first argues that it cannot offer its facilities to religious groups and speakers on the terms available to other groups without violating the Establishment Clause of the Constitution of the United States. We agree that the interest of the University in complying with its constitutional obligations may be characterized as compelling. It does not follow, however, that an "equal access" policy would be incompatible with this Court's Establishment Clause cases. Those cases hold that a policy will not offend the Establishment Clause if it can pass a three-pronged test: "First, the [governmental policy] must have a secular legislative purpose; second, its principal or primary effect must be one that neither advances nor inhibits religion . . .; finally, the [policy] must not foster 'an excessive government entanglement with religion.'" *Lemon v. Kurtzman*, 403 U.S. 602, 612–613 (1971).

In this case two prongs of the test are clearly met. Both the District Court and the Court of Appeals held that an open-forum policy, including nondiscrimination against religious speech, would have a secular purpose[10]

6. The dissent argues that "religious worship" is not speech generally protected by the "free speech" guarantee of the First Amendment and the "equal protection" guarantee of the Fourteenth Amendment. If "religious worship" were protected "speech," the dissent reasons, "the Religion Clauses would be emptied of any independent meaning in circumstances in which religious practice took the form of speech." This is a novel argument. The dissent does not deny that speech *about* religion is speech entitled to the general protections of the First Amendment. It does not argue that descriptions of religious experiences fail to qualify as "speech." Nor does it repudiate last Term's decision in *Heffron v. International Society for Krishna Consciousness, Inc.*, which assumed that religious appeals to nonbelievers constituted protected "speech." Rather, the dissent seems to attempt a distinction between the kinds of religious speech explicitly protected by our cases and a new class of religious "speech [acts]" constituting "worship." There are at least three difficulties with this distinction.

First, the dissent fails to establish that the distinction has intelligible content. There is no indication when "singing hymns, reading scripture, and teaching biblical principles," cease to be "singing, teaching, and reading"— all apparently forms of "speech," despite their religious subject matter—and become unprotected "worship."

Second, even if the distinction drew an arguably principled line, it is highly doubtful that it would lie within the judicial competence to administer. Merely to draw the distinction would require the university—and ultimately the courts—to inquire into the significance of words and practices to different religious faiths, and in varying circumstances by the same faith. Such inquiries would tend inevitably to entangle the State with religion in a manner forbidden by our cases.

Finally, the dissent fails to establish the *relevance* of the distinction on which it seeks to rely. The dissent apparently wishes to preserve the vitality of the Establishment Clause. But it gives no reason why the Establishment Clause, or any other provision of the Constitution, would require different treatment for religious speech designed to win religious converts than for religious worship by persons already converted. It is far from clear that the State gives greater support in the latter case than in the former.

10. . . . Because this case involves a forum already made generally available to student groups, it differs from those cases in which this Court has invalidated statutes permitting school facilities to be used for instruc-

and would avoid entanglement with religion.[11] But the District Court concluded, and the University argues here, that allowing religious groups to share the limited public forum would have the "primary effect" of advancing religion.[12]

The University's argument misconceives the nature of this case. The question is not whether the creation of a religious forum would violate the Establishment Clause. The University has opened its facilities for use by student groups, and the question is whether it can now exclude groups because of the content of their speech. *See Healy v. James*, 408 U.S. 169 (1972). In this context we are unpersuaded that the primary effect of the public forum, open to all forms of discourse, would be to advance religion.

We are not oblivious to the range of an open forum's likely effects. It is possible—perhaps even foreseeable—that religious groups will benefit from access to University facilities. But this Court has explained that a religious organization's enjoyment of merely "incidental" benefits does not violate the prohibition against the "primary advancement" of religion....

We are satisfied that any religious benefits of an open forum at UMKC would be "incidental" within the meaning of our cases. Two factors are especially relevant.

First, an open forum in a public university does not confer any imprimatur of state approval on religious sects or practices....[14]

Second, the forum is available to a broad class of nonreligious as well as religious speakers; there are over 100 recognized student groups at UMKC.... At least in the absence of empirical evidence that religious groups will dominate UMKC's open forum, we agree with the Court of

tion by religious groups, but *not* by others. *See, e.g., McCollum v. Board of Education*, 333 U.S. 203 (1948). In those cases the school may appear to sponsor the views of the speaker.

11. We agree with the Court of Appeals that the University would risk greater "entanglement" by attempting to enforce its exclusion of "religious worship" and "religious speech." Initially, the University would need to determine which words and activities fall within "religious worship and religious teaching." This alone could prove "an impossible task in an age where many and various beliefs meet the constitutional definition of religion." *O'Hair v. Andrus*, 198 U. S. App. D. C. 198, 203, 613 F.2d 931, 936 (1979); *see* L. TRIBE, AMERICAN CONSTITUTIONAL LAW § 14–6 (1978). There would also be a continuing need to monitor group meetings to ensure compliance with the rule.

12. In finding that an "equal access" policy would have the primary effect of advancing religion, the District Court in this case relied primarily on *Tilton v. Richardson*, 403 U.S. 672 (1971). , , ,

We do not believe that *Tilton* can be read so broadly. In *Tilton* the Court was concerned

that a sectarian institution might convert federally funded buildings to religious uses or otherwise stamp them with the imprimatur of religion. But nothing in *Tilton* suggested a limitation on the State's capacity to maintain forums equally open to religious and other discussions. Cases before and after *Tilton* have acknowledged the right of religious speakers to use public forums on equal terms with others. See, *e.g., Heffron v. International Society for Krishna Consciousness, Inc.*, 452 U.S. 640 (1981); *Saia v. New York*, 334 U.S. 558 (1948).

14. University students are, of course, young adults. They are less impressionable than younger students and should be able to appreciate that the University's policy is one of neutrality toward religion. See *Tilton* v. *Richardson, supra*, at 685–686. The University argues that the Cornerstone students themselves admitted in affidavits that "[students] know that if something is on campus, then it is a student organization, and they are more likely to feel comfortable attending a meeting." In light of the large number of groups meeting on campus, however, we doubt students could draw any reasonable inference of University support from the mere fact of a campus meeting place....

Appeals that the advancement of religion would not be the forum's "primary effect."

. . .

Our holding in this case in no way undermines the capacity of the University to establish reasonable time, place, and manner regulations. Nor do we question the right of the University to make academic judgments as to how best to allocate scarce resources or "to determine for itself on academic grounds who may teach, what may be taught, how it shall be taught, and who may be admitted to study." *Sweezy v. New Hampshire*, 354 U.S. 234, 263 (1957) (Frankfurter, J., concurring in result); *see University of California Regents v. Bakke*, 438 U.S. 265, 312–313 (1978) (opinion of Powell, J., announcing the judgment of the Court).[20] Finally, we affirm the continuing validity of cases that recognize a university's right to exclude even First Amendment activities that violate reasonable campus rules or substantially interfere with the opportunity of other students to obtain an education.

The basis for our decision is narrow. Having created a forum generally open to student groups, the University seeks to enforce a content-based exclusion of religious speech. Its exclusionary policy violates the fundamental principle that a state regulation of speech should be content-neutral, and the University is unable to justify this violation under applicable constitutional standards.

For this reason, the decision of the Court of Appeals is affirmed.

■ JUSTICE STEVENS concurring in the judgment.

As the Court recognizes, every university must "make academic judgments as to how best to allocate scarce resources." The Court appears to hold, however, that those judgments must "serve a compelling state interest" whenever they are based, even in part, on the content of speech. This conclusion apparently flows from the Court's suggestion that a student activities program—from which the public may be excluded—must be managed as though it were a "public forum." In my opinion, the use of the terms "compelling state interest" and "public forum" to analyze the question presented in this case may needlessly undermine the academic freedom of public universities.

Today most major colleges and universities are operated by public authority. Nevertheless, their facilities are not open to the public in the same way that streets and parks are. University facilities—private or public—are maintained primarily for the benefit of the student body and the faculty. In performing their learning and teaching missions, the managers of a university routinely make countless decisions based on the content of communicative materials. They select books for inclusion in the library, they hire professors on the basis of their academic philosophies, they select courses for inclusion in the curriculum, and they reward scholars for what they have written. In addition, in encouraging students to participate in extracurricular activities, they necessarily make decisions concerning the content of those activities.

---

20. In his opinion concurring in the judgment, Justice Stevens expresses concern that use of the terms "compelling state interest" and "public forum" may "undermine the academic freedom of public universities." As the text above makes clear, this concern is unjustified.... Our holding is limited to the context of a public forum created by the University itself.

Because every university's resources are limited, an educational institution must routinely make decisions concerning the use of the time and space that is available for extracurricular activities. In my judgment, it is both necessary and appropriate for those decisions to evaluate the content of a proposed student activity. I should think it obvious, for example, that if two groups of 25 students requested the use of a room at a particular time—one to view Mickey Mouse cartoons and the other to rehearse an amateur performance of Hamlet—the First Amendment would not require that the room be reserved for the group that submitted its application first. Nor do I see why a university should have to establish a "compelling state interest" to defend its decision to permit one group to use the facility and not the other. In my opinion, a university should be allowed to decide for itself whether a program that illuminates the genius of Walt Disney should be given precedence over one that may duplicate material adequately covered in the classroom. Judgments of this kind should be made by academicians, not by federal judges, and their standards for decision should not be encumbered with ambiguous phrases like "compelling state interest."

Thus, I do not subscribe to the view that a public university has no greater interest in the content of student activities than the police chief has in the content of a soapbox oration on Capitol Hill. A university legitimately may regard some subjects as more relevant to its educational mission than others. But the university, like the police officer, may not allow its agreement or disagreement with the viewpoint of a particular speaker to determine whether access to a forum will be granted. If a state university is to deny recognition to a student organization—or is to give it a lesser right to use school facilities than other student groups—it must have a valid reason for doing so.

In this case I agree with the Court that the University has not established a sufficient justification for its refusal to allow the Cornerstone group to engage in religious worship on the campus. The primary reason advanced for the discriminatory treatment is the University's fear of violating the Establishment Clause. But since the record discloses no danger that the University will appear to sponsor any particular religion, and since student participation in the Cornerstone meetings is entirely voluntary, the Court properly concludes that the University's fear is groundless. With that justification put to one side, the University has not met the burden that is imposed on it. . . .

Nor does the University's reliance on the Establishment Clause of the Missouri State Constitution provide a sufficient justification for the discriminatory treatment in this case. As I have said, I believe that the University may exercise a measure of control over the agenda for student use of school facilities, preferring some subjects over others, without needing to identify so-called "compelling state interests." Quite obviously, however, the University could not allow a group of Republicans or Presbyterians to meet while denying Democrats or Mormons the same privilege. It seems apparent that the policy under attack would allow groups of young philosophers to meet to discuss their skepticism that a Supreme Being exists, or a group of political scientists to meet to debate the accuracy of the view that religion is the "opium of the people." If school facilities may be used to discuss anticlerical doctrine, it seems to me that comparable use by a group desiring to express a belief in God must also be permitted. The fact that their expression of faith includes ceremonial conduct is not, in my opinion, a sufficient reason for suppressing their discussion entirely.

Note on Maturity

For discussion of the doctrinal importance of the difference in maturity between college students and elementary or secondary students, see Deanna N. Pihos, Note, *Assuming Maturity Matters: The Limited Reach of the Establishment Clause at Public Universities*, 90 Cornell L. Rev. 1349 (2005). Pihos argues that the Supreme Court has failed to articulate why the difference between high school and college students should be a decisive factor in Establishment Clause cases and suggests courts should revisit that assumption. First, "To conclude . . . that a student can distinguish an endorsement or advancement of religion in August, though they could not do so at their high school graduation in June, is a questionable distinction on which to create two different standards of Establishment Clause protection." Second, many college students are for the first time in their lives "free from extensive parental supervision or the influence of the communities and institutions that previously shaped their lives" and therefore potentially more, rather than less, "malleable" in the face of state-sponsored religion. *Id.* at 1373.

In *Tilton v. Richardson*, 403 U.S. 672 (1971), the Supreme Court relied on "[c]ommon observation" and a Harvard Law Review article to support its conclusion that college students are less impressionable and less susceptible to religious indoctrination. The cited article noted, without citation, that attempting to impose religious values on "the college student is highly inappropriate, and would probably prove self-defeating, since either his basic religious personality has already been formed or it can be influenced successfully only by stimulating the student to acquire understandings and insight which persuade him to accept certain religious teachings." *See* Donald A. Giannella, *Religious Liberty, Nonestablishment, and Doctrinal Development*, 81 Harv. L. Rev. 513, 583 (1968).

The latest medical research shows that the brain does not fully develop until people reach their early 20s. Jay N. Giedd, *Adolescent Brain Development: Vulnerabilities and Opportunities*, 1021 Ann. N.Y. Acad. Sci. 77, 77 (2004). Would this new research have made a difference to the Court? Based on your own experience, could religious indoctrination occur through college courses? In other college settings?

Note on Prayer at Public Universities

In *Lee v. Weisman*, 505 U.S. 577 (1992), the Supreme Court held that offering nonsectarian prayers at public middle school or high school graduations violated the Establishment Clause. Declining the Solicitor General's "invitation" to abandon the *Lemon* test, the Court held that the prayers violated the constitutional principle that "government may not coerce anyone to support or participate in religion or its exercise." *Id.* at 587. While leaving open the question of whether the rule of *Lee* would apply to colleges and universities, the opinion emphasized the adolescent students' immaturity and susceptibility to pressure to conform. *Id.* at 593–94.

The several Courts of Appeals that have considered prayer in public institutions of higher education have disagreed on the issue, as well as whether *Lee* introduced a new "coercion" rule that must be considered in addition to *Lemon*'s three-prong test. The Sixth and Seventh Circuits applied both tests independently and found no constitutional violation, *see* Chaudhuri v. Tennessee, 130 F.3d 232 (6th Cir. 1997), *cert. denied* 523 U.S. 1024 (1998); Tanford v. Brand, 104 F.3d 982 (7th Cir.), *cert. denied* 522 U.S. 814 (1997); under somewhat different circumstances, the Fourth Circuit applied *Lee* both independently and as a "refinement of *Lemon*'s second prong," and found an Establishment Clause violation. *See* Mellen v. Bunting, 327 F.3d 355, 371 (4th Cir. 2003), *cert. denied* 541 U.S. 1019 (2004).

In *Chaudhuri*, a Hindu professor challenged the use of prayer at "graduation exercises, faculty meetings, dedication ceremonies, and guest lectures" at Tennessee State University in Nashville. In response to Chaudhuri's initial complaints, the university replaced the nonsectarian prayers planned for two graduation ceremonies in 1993. On both occasions, "[t]he moment . . . was less than silent. Someone, or a group of people, began to recite the Lord's Prayer aloud. Many audience members joined in . . . and loud applause followed." Applying the *Lemon* test, the court held first that both nonsectarian prayers and moments of silence served the legitimate secular purpose of solemnizing and dignifying a public occasion. Second, the prayers and moments of silence did not have a principal effect of advancing or inhibiting religion and could not seem to do so to any "reasonable observer." Third, neither prayers nor moments of silence created "any church-state entanglement at all," despite the fact that the university invited a local clergyman to give a benediction and invocation and requested that his prayers not reference Jesus Christ.

Tanford, which addressed a nonsectarian invocation and benediction at Indiana University's graduation ceremony, included several plaintiffs: a professor who disapproved of prayer at graduations, a law student who "would be bothered if her daughter saw a religious figure on the stage . . . giving a prayer," another law student "offended by the giving of a nonsectarian invocation and benediction because it was a form of proselytizing," and an undergraduate, made uncomfortable by prayer, who "believe[d] there should be a separation between church and state in a public institution." The Seventh Circuit held that the university's ceremony did not violate the *Lemon* test because it served the legitimate public purpose of "solemnizing public occasions," did not have a primary effect of endorsing or disapproving religion, and did not create excessive entanglement between the university and the clerics selected—here, a different (but monotheistic) religious group was represented almost every year and the speaker was asked only to give an uplifting and unifying speech.

By contrast, in *Mellen*, the Fourth Circuit held unconstitutional the Virginia Military Institute's "supper roll call," during which cadets were required to stand and be silent as the Cadet Chaplain read a prayer. Under *Lemon*'s first prong, while expressing its inclination to hold that official school prayer is "plainly religious in nature," the court accepted the commanding general's explanation that the prayer served secular functions in developing cadets as leaders, allowing them to develop their own spiritual dimensions, and accommodating their individual free exercise rights. The roll call prayer, however, violated *Lemon*'s second and third prongs: it had "the primary effect of promoting religion, in that it sends the unequivocal message that VMI, as an institution, endorses the religious expressions embodied in the prayer," and was excessively entangling because VMI "composed, mandated, and monitored [the] daily prayer for its cadets." Although the court discussed at length VMI's "rigorous and punishing system of indoctrination" and emphasized this aspect of the case in applying *Lee*'s coercion test, VMI's particularly coercive environment played little, if any, role in the court's *Lemon* analysis.

Despite the apparent circuit-split created by *Mellen*, the Supreme Court denied certiorari. Bunting v. Mellen, 541 U.S. 1019 (2004). Justice Stevens, joined by Justices Ginsburg and Breyer, wrote in support of the denial:

> [One] reason justifying a denial of certiorari is the absence of a direct conflict among the Circuits. . . . Given the unique features of VMI, we do not know how the Fourth Circuit would resolve a case involving prayer at a state university, or, indeed, how the Sixth or Seventh Circuits would analyze the supper prayer at issue in this case.

Id. at 1021. In his dissent from the denial of certiorari, Justice Scalia wrote, "In fact, it might be said that [prayer at VMI] is *more*, rather than *less*, likely to be constitutional, since group prayer before military mess is more traditional than group prayer at ordinary state colleges." *Id.* at 1026.

Imagine you are General Counsel to a large state school. The new university president asks your advice about whether the school should abandon its long-standing practice of having the university chaplain read a nonsectarian, but mono-theistic, prayer over the loudspeaker before every football home game. The president thinks that many students and other audience members would be upset if this tradition were replaced by a moment of silence, so she is disinclined to change the current practice if that too would be legally problematic. What advice would you give her?

Locke v. Davey

Supreme Court of the United States, 2004.
540 U.S. 712, 124 S.Ct. 1307, 158 L.Ed.2d 1.

■ CHIEF JUSTICE REHNQUIST delivered the opinion of the Court.

The State of Washington established the Promise Scholarship Program to assist academically gifted students with postsecondary education expenses. In accordance with the State Constitution, students may not use the scholar-ship at an institution where they are pursuing a degree in devotional theology. We hold that such an exclusion from an otherwise inclusive aid program does not violate the Free Exercise Clause of the First Amendment.

. . . . [T]he Promise Scholarship Program, which provides a scholarship, renewable for one year, to eligible students for postsecondary education expenses. Students may spend their funds on any education-related expense, including room and board. The scholarships are funded through the State's general fund, and their amount varies each year depending on the annual appropriation, which is evenly prorated among the eligible students. The scholarship was worth $1,125 for academic year 1999–2000 and $1,542 for 2000–2001.

To be eligible for the scholarship, a student must meet academic, income, and enrollment requirements. A student must graduate from a Washington public or private high school and either graduate in the top 15% of his graduating class, or attain on the first attempt a cumulative score of 1,200 or better on the Scholastic Assessment Test I or a score of 27 or better on the American College Test. The student's family income must be less than 135% of the State's median. Finally, the student must enroll "at least half time in an eligible postsecondary institution in the state of Washington," and may not pursue a degree in theology at that institution while receiving the scholarship. §§ 250–80–020(12)(f)–(g); *see also* Wash. Rev. Code § 28B.10.814 (1997) ("No aid shall be awarded to any student who is pursuing a degree in theology"). Private institutions, including those reli-giously affiliated, qualify as "eligible postsecondary institution[s]" if they are accredited by a nationally recognized accrediting body. *See* Wash. Admin. Code § 250–80–020(13). A "degree in theology" is not defined in the statute, but, as both parties concede, the statute simply codifies the State's constitu-tional prohibition on providing funds to students to pursue degrees that are "devotional in nature or designed to induce religious faith."

. . .

Respondent, Joshua Davey, was awarded a Promise Scholarship, and chose to attend Northwest College. Northwest is a private, Christian college affiliated with the Assemblies of God denomination, and is an eligible institution under the Promise Scholarship Program. Davey ... decided to pursue a double major in pastoral ministries and business management/administration. There is no dispute that the pastoral ministries degree is devotional and therefore excluded under the Promise Scholarship Program.

Davey brought an action under 42 U.S.C. § 1983 against various state officials (hereinafter State) in the District Court for the Western District of Washington to enjoin the State from refusing to award the scholarship solely because a student is pursuing a devotional theology degree, and for damages. He argued the denial of his scholarship based on his decision to pursue a theology degree violated, *inter alia*, the Free Exercise [Clause of the First Amendment].... The District Court rejected Davey's constitutional claims and granted summary judgment in favor of the State.

A divided panel of the United States Court of Appeals for the Ninth Circuit reversed. 299 F.3d 748 (2002).... We granted certiorari....

The Religion Clauses of the First Amendment ... are frequently in tension. Yet we have long said that "there is room for play in the joints" between them. *Walz v. Tax Comm'n of City of New York*, 397 U.S. 664, 669 (1970). In other words, there are some state actions permitted by the Establishment Clause but not required by the Free Exercise Clause.

This case involves that "play in the joints." ... Under our Establishment Clause precedent, the link between government funds and religious training is broken by the independent and private choice of recipients. As such, there is no doubt that the State could, consistent with the Federal Constitution, permit Promise Scholars to pursue a degree in devotional theology and the State does not contend otherwise. The question before us, however, is whether Washington, pursuant to its own constitution,[2] which has been authoritatively interpreted as prohibiting even indirectly funding religious instruction that will prepare students for the ministry ... can deny them such funding without violating the Free Exercise Clause.

Davey urges us to answer that question in the negative. He contends that under the rule we enunciated in *Church of Lukumi Babalu Aye, Inc. v. Hialeah*, [508 U.S. 520 (1993)], the program is presumptively unconstitutional because it is not facially neutral with respect to religion. We reject his claim of presumptive unconstitutionality, however; to do otherwise would extend the *Lukumi* line of cases well beyond not only their facts but their reasoning. In *Lukumi*, the city of Hialeah made it a crime to engage in certain kinds of animal slaughter. We found that the law sought to suppress ritualistic animal sacrifices of the Santeria religion. In the present case, the State's disfavor of religion (if it can be called that) is of a far milder kind. It imposes neither criminal nor civil sanctions on any type of religious service or rite. It does not deny to ministers the right to participate in the political affairs of the community. And it does not require students to choose between their religious beliefs and receiving a government benefit. The State has merely chosen not to fund a distinct category of instruction.

Justice Scalia argues, however, that generally available benefits are part of the "baseline against which burdens on religion are measured." Because

---

2. The relevant provision of the Washington Constitution, Art. I, § 11, states:

... "No public money or property shall be appropriated for or applied to any religious worship, exercise or instruction, or the support of any religious establishment."

the Promise Scholarship Program funds training for all secular professions, Justice Scalia contends the State must also fund training for religious professions. But training for religious professions and training for secular professions are not fungible. Training someone to lead a congregation is an essentially religious endeavor. Indeed, majoring in devotional theology is akin to a religious calling as well as an academic pursuit. And the subject of religion is one in which both the United States and state constitutions embody distinct views—in favor of free exercise, but opposed to establishment—that find no counterpart with respect to other callings or professions. That a State would deal differently with religious education for the ministry than with education for other callings is a product of these views, not evidence of hostility toward religion.

. . . In fact, we can think of few areas in which a State's antiestablishment interests come more into play. Since the founding of our country, there have been popular uprisings against procuring taxpayer funds to support church leaders, which was one of the hallmarks of an "established" religion.[6] Most States that sought to avoid an establishment of religion around the time of the founding placed in their constitutions formal prohibitions against using tax funds to support the ministry. The plain text of these constitutional provisions prohibited *any* tax dollars from supporting the clergy.... That early state constitutions saw no problem in explicitly excluding *only* the ministry from receiving state dollars reinforces our conclusion that religious instruction is of a different ilk.

Far from evincing the hostility toward religion which was manifest in *Lukumi*, we believe that the entirety of the Promise Scholarship Program goes a long way toward including religion in its benefits. The program permits students to attend pervasively religious schools, so long as they are accredited. As Northwest advertises, its "concept of education is distinctly Christian in the evangelical sense." It prepares *all* of its students, "through instruction, through modeling, [and] through [its] classes, to use . . . the Bible as their guide, as the truth," no matter their chosen profession. And under the Promise Scholarship Program's current guidelines, students are still eligible to take devotional theology courses....

In short, we find neither in the history or text of Article I, § 11 of the Washington Constitution, nor in the operation of the Promise Scholarship Program, anything that suggests animus towards religion. Given the historic and substantial state interest at issue, we therefore cannot conclude that the denial of funding for vocational religious instruction alone is inherently constitutionally suspect.

Without a presumption of unconstitutionality, Davey's claim must fail. The State's interest in not funding the pursuit of devotional degrees is

---

6. Perhaps the most famous example of public backlash is the defeat of "A Bill Establishing a Provision for Teachers of the Christian Religion" in the Virginia Legislature. The bill sought to assess a tax for "Christian teachers," reprinted in *Everson v. Board of Ed. of Ewing*, 330 U.S. 1, 74 (1947) (supplemental appendix to dissent of Rutledge, J.); *see also Rosenberger, supra*, at 853 (Thomas, J., concurring) (purpose of the bill was to support "clergy in the performance of their function of teaching religion"), and was rejected after a public outcry. In its stead, the "Virginia Bill for Religious Liberty," which was originally written by Thomas Jefferson, was enacted. This bill guaranteed "that no man shall be compelled to frequent or support any religious worship, place, or ministry whatsoever." A Bill for Establishing Religious Freedom, reprinted in 2 Papers of Thomas Jefferson 546 (J. Boyd ed. 1950).

substantial and the exclusion of such funding places a relatively minor burden on Promise Scholars. If any room exists between the two Religion Clauses, it must be here. We need not venture further into this difficult area in order to uphold the Promise Scholarship Program as currently operated by the State of Washington.

Axson–Flynn v. Johnson

United States Court of Appeals for the Tenth Circuit, 2004.
356 F.3d 1277.

■ EBEL, CIRCUIT JUDGE.

In 1998, Plaintiff–Appellant Christina Axson–Flynn ("Axson–Flynn"), a member of the Church of Jesus Christ of Latter-day Saints ("Mormon church"), applied to the University of Utah's Actor Training Program (ATP). As part of the application process, she attended an audition conducted by ATP instructors Barbara Smith, Sandy Shotwell, Jerry Gardner, and Sarah Shippobotham (hereinafter "Defendants"). During her audition, Sandy Shotwell asked Axson–Flynn if there was anything she would feel uncomfortable doing or saying as an actor. Axson–Flynn replied that she would not remove her clothing, "take the name of God in vain," "take the name of Christ in vain" or "say the four-letter expletive beginning with the letter F." Although the record is unclear as to whether Axson–Flynn explained at the time why she had those objections, the district court summarized her reasons as follows:

> Her refusal to use the words "God" or "Christ" as profanity is based on one of the Ten Commandments, which prohibits believers from taking "the name of the Lord thy God in vain...." Exodus 20:8. Plaintiff has also explained that her refusal to say the word "fuck" is due to the fact that it is religiously offensive to her because she finds that it vulgarizes what Plaintiff, as a Mormon, believes is a sacred act, appropriate only within the bounds of marriage.

Axson–Flynn v. Johnson, 151 F.Supp.2d 1326, 1328 (D. Utah 2001).

At the audition, after challenging Axson–Flynn's refusal to say "fuck" by giving several examples of when it might be appropriate to do so, Defendant Shotwell asked Axson–Flynn, "Well, see, it isn't black and white, is it?" Axson–Flynn responded, "Well I guess not, and I guess it comes down to the individual actor. But as for myself, I will not say the F word, take the Lord's name in vain, or take off my clothes." Defendants then said "Thank you," and the audition ended. At one point during the exchange (the record is unclear as to exactly when), Axson–Flynn said, "I would rather not be admitted to your program than use these words" and "I will not use these words." Axson–Flynn later explained in her deposition that she did not ask Defendants if they understood her position, because "they're intelligent people. And I would assume that if you say: I will not do this, that they comprehend that. They're teachers."

Axson–Flynn was admitted to the ATP, and she matriculated in the fall of 1998. As part of a class exercise that fall, she was asked to perform a monologue called "Friday" that included two instances of the word "goddamn" and one instance of the word "shit."[2] Without informing her instructor (Defendant Barbara Smith), Axson–Flynn substituted other words for the two "goddamn's" but otherwise performed the monologue as written. Smith did not notice, and Axson–Flynn received an "A" grade for her performance.

[A few weeks later, Smith asked Axson–Flynn to perform a scene from "The Quadrangle." She was to play an unmarried girl who recently had an abortion, and she would be required to say "goddamn" and "fucking." Axson–Flynn refused, but offered to read a different scene from the same play without the offensive language. Smith told Axson–Flynn that she would have to "get over" her language concerns and that she could "still be a good Mormon and say these words." Smith told Axson–Flynn that she would receive a grade of zero if she refused to read the scene. When Axson–Flynn stated that she would accept the zero, Smith relented, stating that she "admired [Axon–Flynn's] character," and allowed her to perform the part without the offensive language. For the rest of the semester Axson–Flynn was allowed to omit any language she found offensive.

At the semester review at the end of the fall semester, Defendants told Axson–Flynn that her refusal to read offensive language was "unreasonable behavior" and suggested that she "talk to some other Mormon girls who are good Mormons, who don't have a problem with this." Finally, the Defendants told her "You can choose to continue in the program if you modify your values. If you don't, you can leave. That's your choice." The next semester, the Defendants continued to pressure Axson–Flynn to use language she found offensive. Axson–Flynn appealed to the ATP's coordinator and its director without success. She then left the ATP and the University of Utah because she felt she would ultimately be asked to leave.]

On February 16, 2000, Axson–Flynn filed suit against Defendants ... for violating her free speech and free exercise rights under the First Amendment. She sought both monetary damages and declaratory relief in the form of a statement that Defendants had violated her constitutional rights.... The district court granted Defendants' motion for summary judgment.... Axson–Flynn timely filed this appeal.

. . .

I. FREEDOM OF SPEECH

. . .

The Supreme Court has long held that the government may not compel the speech of private actors. *See United States v. United Foods, Inc.*, 533 U.S. 405, 413–15 (2001); *Wooley v. Maynard*, 430 U.S. 705, 714–15 (1977); *W. Va. State Bd. of Educ. v. Barnette*, 319 U.S. 624, 642 (1943). Moreover, it is apodictic that public school students do not "shed their constitutional rights to freedom of speech or expression at the schoolhouse gate." *Tinker v. Des Moines Indep. Cmty. Sch. Dist.*, 393 U.S. 503, 506 (1969). At the same time, however, the Court has emphasized that "the First Amendment rights of students in the public schools are not automatically coextensive with the rights of adults in other settings, and must be applied in light of the special characteristics of the school environment." *Hazelwood Sch. Dist. v. Kuhlmeier*, 484 U.S. 260, 266 (1988) (internal quotation marks and citations omitted).

---

2. Axson–Flynn had no religious objections to saying the word "shit." Her objections appear to be limited to the word "fuck" and to the words "goddamn" and its variants.

Nowhere is this more true than in the context of a school's right to determine what to teach and how to teach it in its classrooms.

At the outset, we must determine whether the ATP's classroom should be considered a traditional public forum, designated public forum, or nonpublic forum for free speech purposes. As the *Hazelwood* Court stated, "public schools do not possess all of the attributes of streets, parks, and other traditional public forums that 'time out of mind, have been used for purposes of assembly, communicating thoughts between citizens, and discussing public questions.'" Nothing in the record leads us to conclude that under that standard, the ATP's classroom could reasonably be considered a traditional public forum. Neither could the classroom be considered a designated public forum, as there is no indication in the record that "school authorities have 'by policy or by practice' opened [the classroom] 'for indiscriminate use by the general public,' or by some segment of the public, such as student organizations." We thus find that the ATP's classroom constitutes a nonpublic forum, meaning that school officials could regulate the speech that takes place there "in any reasonable manner."

... There are three main types of speech that occur within a school setting. *Fleming v. Jefferson County Sch. Dist. R–1*, 298 F.3d 918, 923 (10th Cir. 2002). First is student speech that "happens to occur on the school premises," such as the black armbands worn by the students in Tinker. This type of speech comprises "pure student expression that a school must tolerate unless it can reasonably forecast that the expression will lead to 'substantial disruption of or material interference with school activities.'" *Id*. (quoting *Tinker*, 393 U.S. at 514). The speech at issue in the instant case clearly is not of this type, as it occurred in the classroom setting in the context of a class exercise and did not simply "happen[ ] to occur on the school premises."

The second type of speech in the school setting is "government speech, such as the principal speaking at a school assembly." Axson–Flynn is a student, not a school official, and recitation of the play is not being advanced as government speech. Therefore, this speech does not fit into this category either.

The third type of speech is "school-sponsored speech," which is "speech that a school 'affirmatively ... promotes,' as opposed to speech that it 'tolerates.'" *Id*. (quoting *Hazelwood*, 484 U.S. at 270–71). "'Expressive activities that students, parents, and members of the public might reasonably perceive to bear the imprimatur of the school' constitute school-sponsored speech, over which the school may exercise editorial control, 'so long as [its] actions are reasonably related to legitimate pedagogical concerns.'" *Id*. (quoting *Hazelwood*, 484 U.S. at 271, 273). We conclude that Axson–Flynn's speech in this case constitutes "school-sponsored speech" and is thus governed by *Hazelwood*.

In *Hazelwood*, the Supreme Court upheld against a free speech challenge a school's decision to excise two pages from the school newspaper because of content it deemed inappropriate for publication. The Court determined that the newspaper, which was published as part of a journalism class, constituted "school-sponsored" speech—speech that a school "affirmatively ... promotes," as opposed to speech that it merely "tolerates." School-sponsored speech comprises "expressive activities" that "may fairly be characterized as part of the school curriculum, whether or not they occur in a traditional classroom setting, so long as they are supervised by faculty members and designed to impart particular knowledge or skills to student participants and audiences." *Id.* at 271. Because the newspaper was "part of the school curriculum," it was school-sponsored speech. The Court held that school officials may place restrictions on school-sponsored speech "so long as their actions are reasonably related to legitimate pedagogical concerns." *Id.* at 273. The Court then proceeded to find that the school's reasons for excising the two newspaper pages met that standard and that its decision to do so should be upheld. *Id.* at 276.

In *Fleming*, we held that a school project which involved the painting of four-inch-by-four-inch tiles that would be permanently affixed to the school's hallways constituted "school-sponsored speech" under *Hazelwood*. *Fleming*, 298 F.3d at 920–21, 924. . . .

Here, there is no doubt that the school sponsored the use of plays with the offending language in them as part of its instructional technique. The particular plays containing such language were specifically chosen by the school and incorporated as part of the school's official curriculum. Furthermore, if a school newspaper and a project to paint and post glazed and fired tiles in a school hallway can be considered school-sponsored speech, then surely student speech that takes place inside the classroom, as part of a class assignment, can also be considered school-sponsored speech.

Our conclusion that speech which is prescribed as part of the official school curriculum in connection with a classroom exercise is school-sponsored speech is bolstered by the conclusions that other circuits have reached in this context. In *Settle v. Dickson County Sch. Bd.*, 53 F.3d 152 (6th Cir. 1995), a ninth grade teacher refused to permit one of her students to write a required research paper on Jesus Christ. The teacher said that she would accept a paper on religion, as long as the paper "did not deal solely with Christianity or the Life of Christ." *Id.* at 154. Among the teacher's reasons for this decision were the student's failure to follow the required procedure to propose a paper topic; the teacher's concern that the proposed paper would be difficult to evaluate because of the student's strong personal beliefs; and the teacher's concern that because the student already knew a great deal about Jesus Christ, allowing her to write a paper about Jesus Christ would defeat the research-oriented purpose of the exercise. *Id.* When the student refused to comply with the teacher's condition, she received a zero on the assignment. She then sued the teacher and the school board for violating her free speech rights under the First Amendment.

The Sixth Circuit applied a *Hazelwood* analysis and rejected the student's free speech challenge by affirming the grant of summary judgment to the defendants. The court reasoned:

> Where learning is the focus, as in the classroom, student speech may be even more circumscribed than in the school newspaper or other open forum. So long as the teacher limits speech or grades speech in the classroom in the name of learning and not as a pretext for punishing the student for her race, gender, economic class, religion or political persuasion, the federal courts should not interfere.

> Like judges, teachers should not punish or reward people on the basis of inadmissible factors—race, religion, gender, political ideology—but teachers, like judges, must daily decide which argu-

ments are relevant, which computations are correct, which analogies are good or bad, and when it is time to stop writing or talking. *Grades must be given by teachers in the classroom, just as cases are decided in the courtroom; and to this end teachers, like judges, must direct the content of speech.* Teachers may frequently make mistakes in grading and otherwise, just as we do sometimes in deciding cases, but *it is the essence of the teacher's responsibility in the classroom to draw lines and make distinctions—in a word to encourage speech germane to the topic at hand and discourage speech unlikely to shed light on the subject.* Teachers therefore must be given broad discretion to give grades and conduct class discussion based on the content of speech. . . . It is not for us to overrule the teacher's view that the student should learn to write research papers by beginning with a topic other than her own theology.

Id. at 155–56 (emphasis added).

Brown v. Li, 308 F.3d 939 (9th Cir. 2002), arose from university student Christopher Brown's decision to attach a "Disacknowledgements" section to the end of his master's degree thesis. The section began, "I would like to offer special *Fuck You's* to the following degenerates for being an ever-present hindrance during my graduate career. . . ." *Id.* at 943. It then named, among others, the dean and staff of the student's graduate school, the managers of the university library, and a former California governor. Due to the inclusion of this section, Brown's thesis committee declined to approve his thesis, and he was eventually placed on academic probation for failing to complete his degree within the allotted time. After four months of probation, the university relented and awarded Brown his degree based on his earlier submission of a copy of his thesis that had not included the "Disacknowledgements" section. *Id.* at 945. However, because Brown had not submitted the approved version of his thesis to the university library, it was never added to the library's archive of theses. *Id.* As a result, Brown filed suit alleging, *inter alia*, that the defendants' initial withholding of his degree violated his free speech rights under the First Amendment. Among other remedies, Brown sought an injunction compelling the defendants to place his thesis in the university's library. The district court granted the defendants' motion for summary judgment on all counts, and the Ninth Circuit affirmed.

The Ninth Circuit framed the First Amendment question as "whether Defendants violated Plaintiff's First Amendment rights when they refused to approve that ["Disacknowledgements"] section." *Id.* at 947. After acknowledging that there was "no precedent precisely on point," the court began its First Amendment analysis by discussing *Hazelwood* and *Settle*. The court reasoned that those two cases

lead to the conclusion that an educator can, consistent with the First Amendment, require that a student comply with the terms of an academic assignment. Those cases also make clear that the First Amendment does not require an educator to change the assignment to suit the student's opinion or to approve the work of a student that, in his or her judgment, fails to meet a legitimate academic standard. Rather, as articulated by *Hazelwood*, "educators do not offend the First Amendment by exercising editorial control over the style and content of student speech in school sponsored expressive activities so long as their actions are reasonably related to legitimate pedagogical concerns."

Id. at 949 (quoting *Hazelwood*, 484 U.S. at 273).

The court acknowledged that *Hazelwood* explicitly "left open the question 'whether the same degree of deference is appropriate with respect to school sponsored expressive activities at the college and university level.' " *Id.* (quoting *Hazelwood*, 484 U.S. at 273 n.7). However, the *Brown* court concluded that, at least as to curriculum issues, as opposed to extracurricular activities, *Hazelwood* provided a good framework for evaluating free speech claims even at the college level. The court concluded that

> under the Supreme Court's precedents, the curriculum of a public educational institution is one means by which the institution itself expresses its policy, a policy with which others do not have a constitutional right to interfere. The Supreme Court's jurisprudence does not hold that an institution's interest in mandating its curriculum and in limiting a student's speech to that which is germane to a particular academic assignment diminishes as students age. Indeed, arguably the need for academic discipline and editorial rigor increases as a student's learning progresses.

Id. at 951 (citation and emphasis omitted).

. . .

We find the reasoning of ... *Settle* [and] *Brown* ... persuasive. Few activities bear a school's "imprimatur" and "involve pedagogical interests" more significantly than speech that occurs within a classroom setting as part of a school's curriculum. Accordingly, we hold that the *Hazelwood* framework is applicable in a university setting for speech that occurs in a classroom as part of a class curriculum. . . .

Axson–Flynn argues that forcing her, as part of an acting-class exercise, to say words she finds offensive constitutes compelled speech in violation of the First Amendment. . . . There is no question that in the instant case, Defendants attempted to compel Axson–Flynn to speak. Although they never suspended her from the ATP or explicitly threatened her with expulsion, Defendants made it abundantly clear that Axson–Flynn would not be able to continue in the program if she refused to say the words with which she was uncomfortable.

As we have noted earlier, because the speech was to take place in the classroom context as part of a mandated school curriculum, it clearly bore the school's "imprimatur" and "involved pedagogical interests." *Fleming*, 298 F.3d at 924. As such, it is school-sponsored speech. Thus, we will uphold the ATP's decision to restrict (or compel) that speech as long as the ATP's decision was "reasonably related to legitimate pedagogical concerns." We give "substantial deference" to "educators' stated pedagogical concerns."

That schools must be empowered at times to restrict the speech of their students for pedagogical purposes is not a controversial proposition. By no means is such power limited to the very basic level of a teacher's ability to penalize a student for disruptive classroom behavior. For example,

> schools routinely deny students the ability to express themselves by adopting the words of others. A student told to submit an essay about the nineteenth century Russian novel could not fulfill the

obligation by assuring his teacher that he agrees with GEORGE STEINER'S TOLSTOY OR DOSTOEVSKY: AN ESSAY IN THE OLD CRITICISM (1959)—could not do so even if he turned in a brand new, store-bought copy, avoiding any charge of plagiarism or violation of the copyright laws.

Hedges v. Wauconda Cmty. Unit Sch. Dist. No. 118, 9 F.3d 1295, 1302 (7th Cir. 1993). By the same token, schools also routinely require students to express a viewpoint that is not their own in order to teach the students to think critically:

> For example, a college history teacher may demand a paper defending Prohibition, and a law-school professor may assign students to write "opinions" showing how Justices Ginsburg and Scalia would analyze a particular Fourth Amendment question.... Such requirements are part of the teachers' curricular mission to encourage critical thinking (in the hypothetical examples) and to conform to professional norms (in this case).

Brown, 308 F.3d at 953 (concluding that a thesis committee at a university is entitled under *Hazelwood* to put limits on what may be included in the acknowledgments section of a master's thesis); see also *Fleming,* 298 F.3d at 926 ("We conclude that *Hazelwood* allows educators to make viewpoint-based decisions about school-sponsored speech.").

In the instant case, Defendants justified their restriction on speech—the requirement that students, including Axson–Flynn, perform the acting exercises as written—as a methodology for preparing students for careers in professional acting. Defendants argue that requiring students to perform offensive scripts advances the school's pedagogical interest in teaching acting in at least three ways: (1) it teaches students how to step outside their own values and character by forcing them to assume a very foreign character and to recite offensive dialogue; (2) it teaches students to preserve the integrity of the author's work;[11] and (3) it measures true acting skills to be able convincingly to portray an offensive part. Requiring an acting student, in the context of a classroom exercise, to speak the words of a script as written is no different than requiring that a law or history student argue a position with which he disagrees.[13] Both types of restriction on student speech, if not

---

11. In Plaintiff's initial interview, Shotwell explained the importance of appreciating a work of art as a whole: "If you like a piece of art, but you don't like one piece of it, do you cut out that piece and hang it on the wall with a hole in it? Or do you enjoy art as a whole and just accept what you don't like about it."

13. The religious nature of Axson–Flynn's refusal to say the offensive words is not determinative of our disposition of her free speech claim. The Supreme Court has never held that religious speech is entitled to more protection than non-religious speech. *See Capitol Square Review & Advisory Bd. v. Pinette,* 515 U.S. 753, 760 (1995) ("Our precedent establishes that private religious speech, far from being a First Amendment orphan, is as fully protected under the Free Speech Clause as secular private expression.") (em-phasis added); *see also id.* at 766 ("Of course, giving sectarian religious speech preferential access to a forum close to the seat of government (or anywhere else for that matter) would violate the Establishment Clause (as well as the Free Speech Clause, since it would involve content discrimination).") (plurality); *Rosenberger,* 515 U.S. at 846 (O'Connor, J., concurring) ("We have time and again held that the government generally may not treat people differently based on the God or gods they worship, or do not worship.") (quotation marks and citation omitted); *Kreisner v. City of San Diego,* 1 F.3d 775, 790 (9th Cir. 1993) (Kozinski, J., concurring) ("Religious speech is speech, entitled to exactly the same protection from government restriction as any other kind of speech—no more and no less.").

pretextual, can meet the *Hazelwood* standard, which "does not require that the [restrictions] be the most reasonable or the only reasonable limitations, only that they be reasonable." *Fleming*, 298 F.3d at 932. The school's methodology may not be necessary to the achievement of its goals and it may not even be the most effective means of teaching, but it can still be "reasonably related" to pedagogical concerns. A more stringent standard would effectively give each student veto power over curricular requirements, subjecting the curricular decisions of teachers to the whims of what a particular student does or does not feel like learning on a given day. This we decline to do.

Although we do not second-guess the pedagogical wisdom or efficacy of an educator's goal, we would be abdicating our judicial duty if we failed to investigate whether the educational goal or pedagogical concern was pretextual. In *Regents of the Univ. of Mich. v. Ewing*, 474 U.S. 214, 225 (1985), the Supreme Court directed courts not to override a faculty member's professional judgment "unless it is such a substantial departure from accepted academic norms as to demonstrate that the person or committee responsible did not actually exercise professional judgment." Thus, we may override an educator's judgment where the proffered goal or methodology was a sham pretext for an impermissible ulterior motive.

In her amended complaint, Axson–Flynn posits that Defendants forced her to adhere strictly to the script not because of their educational goals as described above, but rather because of "anti-Mormon sentiment." During her deposition, she queried, "They respect other kids' freedom of religion that aren't [Mormon]. Why won't they respect mine?" Additionally, the program's insistence that Axson–Flynn speak with other "good Mormon girls" and that she could "still be a good Mormon" and say these words certainly raises concern that hostility to her faith rather than a pedagogical interest in her growth as an actress was at stake in Defendants' behavior in this case. Viewing the evidence in a light most favorable to Axson–Flynn, we find that there is a genuine issue of material fact as to whether Defendants' justification for the script adherence requirement was truly pedagogical or whether it was a pretext for religious discrimination. Therefore, summary judgment was improper.

For the foregoing reasons, we reverse the district court's grant of summary judgment in favor of Defendants on the free speech claim, and remand for further proceedings.

II.   FREE EXERCISE

Axson–Flynn also argues that by attempting to force her to say words whose utterance would violate her religious beliefs, Defendants violated the free exercise clause of the First Amendment. The district court rejected this argument and granted summary judgment to Defendants. We review that decision de novo and reverse the decision of the district court.

"Depending on the nature of the challenged law or government action, a free exercise claim can prompt either strict scrutiny or rational basis review." *Tenafly Eruv Ass'n, Inc. v. Borough of Tenafly*, 309 F.3d 144, 165 (3d Cir. 2002)....

Neutral rules of general applicability ordinarily do not raise free exercise concerns even if they incidentally burden a particular religious practice or belief. *Church of Lukumi Babalu Aye, Inc. v. City of Hialeah*, 508 U.S. 520, 531

(1993); *Employment Div. v. Smith*, 494 U.S. 872, 879 (1990). When it comes to the enforcement of such rules, "the Free Exercise Clause offers no protection." *Tenafly*, 309 F.3d at 165. By contrast, if a law that burdens a religious practice or belief is not neutral or generally applicable, it is subject to strict scrutiny, and "the burden on religious conduct violates the Free Exercise Clause unless it is narrowly tailored to advance a compelling government interest." *Tenafly*, 309 F.3d at 165.

We first address the threshold requirement of *Smith* of determining whether the strict adherence to offensive script requirement was a "neutral rule of general applicability." A rule that is discriminatorily motivated and applied is not a neutral rule of general applicability. As discussed in the free speech section above, we find a genuine issue of fact in the record as to whether Defendants' requirement of script adherence was pretextual. Therefore, we remand for further proceedings on whether the script adherence requirement was discriminatorily applied to religious conduct (and thus was not generally applicable). Unless Defendants succeed in showing that the script requirement was a neutral rule of general applicability, they will face the daunting task of establishing that the requirement was narrowly tailored to advance a compelling governmental interest.

If Defendants succeed on remand in showing their requirement was not pretextual but rather was a neutral and generally applicable requirement, Axson–Flynn argues that the two exceptions to the *Smith* rule apply, and if she were to be successful in establishing an exemption, Defendants' conduct would not be sheltered by the rational basis test of *Smith*. The first exception, following *Wisconsin v. Yoder*, 406 U.S. 205 (1972), has come to be called the "hybrid rights" exception: when a free exercise claim is coupled with some other constitutional claim (such a free speech claim), heightened scrutiny may be appropriate. *Smith*, 494 U.S. at 881–82. The second exception, following *Sherbert v. Verner*, 374 U.S. 398 (1963), is the "individualized exemption" exception: where a state's facially neutral rule contains a system of individualized exemptions, a state "may not refuse to extend that system to cases of 'religious hardship' without compelling reason." *Smith*, 494 U.S. at 884. The district court held that Axson–Flynn's case fit within neither *Smith* exception. . . .

A.   Hybrid rights

In *Swanson v. Guthrie Indep. Sch. Dist. No. I–L*, 135 F.3d 694, 699 (10th Cir. 1998), we recognized the hybrid-rights free exercise theory discussed in *Smith*, but declined to apply that theory to a claim by a home-schooled student that she should be allowed to attend public school on a part-time basis. We acknowledged in *Swanson* that "it is difficult to delineate the exact contours of the hybrid-rights theory discussed in Smith." We stated that the hybrid-rights theory "at least requires a colorable showing" of infringement of a companion constitutional right which left open for later development the definition of "colorable" in this context.

In defining "colorability" for purposes of hybrid-rights claims, the Ninth Circuit has required the companion claim to have a "fair probability or a likelihood, but not a certitude, of success on the merits." We find these analogies helpful, and will only apply the hybrid-rights exception to *Smith* where the plaintiff establishes a "fair probability, or a likelihood," of success on the companion claim.

Our approach strikes a middle ground between the two extremes of painting hybrid-rights claims too generously and construing them too narrowly....

. . .

Therefore, we have chosen the middle ground of requiring the hybrid-rights claimant to show that the companion constitutional claim is "colorable." We define this to mean that the plaintiff must show a fair probability or likelihood, but not a certitude, of success on the merits. This inquiry is very fact-driven and must be used to examine hybrid rights on a case-by-case basis.

Because we are remanding on the free speech issue for fact development, we cannot at this point discern whether Axson–Flynn has a fair probability or likelihood of success on her pretext argument in her free speech claim. However, a remand as to this hybrid-rights issue would be pointless because ... Defendants are entitled to qualified immunity on the hybrid rights theory.

B.   The individualized-exemption exception

We turn now to Axson–Flynn's argument that her case is covered by the second *Smith* exception, which holds that "in circumstances in which individualized exemptions from a general requirement are available, the government may not refuse to extend that system to cases of religious hardship without compelling reason." *Church of Lukumi Babalu Aye,* 508 U.S. at 537 (citing *Smith,* 494 U.S. at 884) (internal quotation marks omitted). The Court has never explained with specificity what constitutes a "system" of individualized exceptions, and as with the hybrid rights exception, courts and commentators are divided on the question.

Our Circuit has held that a system of individualized exemptions is one that "gives rise to the application of a subjective test." *Swanson,* 135 F.3d at 701. Such a system is one in which case-by-case inquiries are routinely made, such that there is an "individualized governmental assessment of the reasons for the relevant conduct" that "invites considerations of the particular circumstances" involved in the particular case. *Smith,* 494 U.S. at 884.

Perhaps the best example of such a system, and indeed the one in which this exception originated, is a system of unemployment benefits which requires claimants to show "good cause" as to why they are unable to find work. In *Sherbert v. Verner,* 374 U.S. 398 (1963), a Seventh Day Adventist was fired by her employer because she refused to work on Saturdays, which her faith did not permit. Sherbert applied for unemployment benefits but was denied for failing to demonstrate "good cause" for her unemployment. The Supreme Court held that the denial of benefits violated the Free Exercise Clause because it "forced [Sherbert] to choose between following the precepts of her religion and forfeiting benefits, on the one hand, and abandoning one of the precepts of her religion in order to accept work, on the other hand." *Id.* at 404.

In *Sherbert,* then, the "good cause" exemption required an official to examine an applicant's specific, personal circumstances. That is, every unemployment compensation decision was made on a case-by-case basis. This being so, the state could not refuse to accept religious reasons for unemployment on equal footing with secular reasons for unemployment. Or, as the

Smith Court explained the holding in *Sherbert* and the Court's other unemployment compensation cases, "where the State has in place a system of individual exemptions, it may not refuse to extend that system to cases of 'religious hardship' without compelling reason." *Smith,* 494 U.S. at 884.

Smith's "individualized exemption" exception is limited, then, to systems that are designed to make case-by-case determinations. The exception does not apply to statutes that, although otherwise generally applicable, contain express exceptions for objectively defined categories of persons. . . . While of course it takes some degree of individualized inquiry to determine whether a person is eligible for even a strictly defined exemption, that kind of limited yes-or-no inquiry is qualitatively different from the kind of case-by-case system envisioned by the *Smith* Court in its discussion of *Sherbert* and related cases.

With this understanding of the "individualized exemption" exception, we now address whether Axson–Flynn's case falls within the exception. . . .

The syllabus for First–Year Acting (the ATP class that Axson–Flynn was taking in the fall of 1998) contained a curricular requirement to do improvisational work. However, a Jewish student named Jeremy Rische asked for and received permission to avoid doing an improvisational exercise on Yom Kippur without suffering adverse consequences. Defendant Barbara Smith, who taught First Year Acting, gave him this exemption despite the fact that, in Rische's words, "she said it would be an exercise that couldn't be made up, because it was one of the exercises by—an improv exercise that involved the whole class, and it would be almost impossible to make up." Rische was never penalized, his grades were never lowered, and he was never asked to make up the assignment in any way. Axson–Flynn argues that Defendants' willingness to grant an exemption to Rische demonstrates that the ATP had a system of individualized exemptions in place. That Defendants did not grant her an exemption, Axson–Flynn argues, constitutes "discrimination among members of different religious faiths" that violates the Free Exercise Clause.

When this evidence is coupled with the fact that Defendants sometimes granted Axson–Flynn herself an exemption from their script adherence requirement, we find that the record raises a material fact issue as to whether Defendants maintained a discretionary system of making individualized case-by-case determinations regarding who should receive exemptions from curricular requirements.

The "system of individualized exemptions" need not be a written policy, but rather the plaintiff may show a pattern of ad hoc discretionary decisions amounting to a "system." If we were to require the plaintiff to show that the "system of individualized exemptions" was contained in a written policy, we would contradict the general principle that greater discretion in the hands of governmental actors makes the action taken pursuant thereto more, not less, constitutionally suspect. *See e.g., Cantwell v. Connecticut,* 310 U.S. 296, 305 (1940).

Because Axson–Flynn has raised a genuine issue of material fact as to whether Defendants maintained a discretionary system of case-by-case exemptions from curricular requirements, we hold that summary judgment on her free exercise "individualized exemption" claim was improper. Accordingly, we reverse and remand.

CHAPTER 4

STATE AND LOCAL GOVERNMENT REGULATION

Traditionally, church or state was in charge of higher education. The last chapter examined the place of religion in contemporary higher education. This chapter turns to state control. The most overt form of state control is power over public colleges and universities, but states have some power over private college and universities as well. As you study the cases in this chapter, consider what limits there are, if any, on the power of states to regulate institutions of higher education.[a] When the legislature and the leaders of a public college or university disagree about matters of policy, does the legislature always trump? Should they?

Why might university governing boards and state legislators disagree about educational policy or institutional governance? Do the different constituencies of the two groups make conflict inevitable?

Finally, what limits, if any, are there on the power of local governments to regulate colleges and universities?

Shelton College v. State Board of Education

Supreme Court of New Jersey, 1967.
48 N.J. 501, 226 A.2d 612.

■ WEINTRAUB, C.J.

Shelton College (herein Shelton) ... challenges the constitutionality of a statute ... which requires all degree-conferring colleges to obtain a license and ... which requires approval of the basis and conditions for conferring a degree....

First Shelton says it is beyond the power of government to regulate in any way the award of the bachelor degree ... because of the right of free speech guaranteed in Art. I, para. VI of the State Constitution and the First Amendment to the United States Constitution.

It should be noted that the resolution in question does not limit in any way what Shelton may teach. Rather the resolution concerns the power to confer the bachelor degree. Hence Shelton's thesis, logically extended, must be that everyone has the absolute power to bestow degrees evidencing higher educational achievement, no matter how remote the course of instruction may be from the values the educational degree is commonly thought to hold. It contends that society may protect itself from the obvious evils of that proposition only by relying upon private evaluations of colleges, such as

---

a. Federal regulations are reviewed in Chapter 18.

214

those made by the regional accreditation associations which now pass upon the standing of colleges on a voluntary basis.

Shelton points to no authority to support its position. The history of the subject runs strongly the other way. The public interest in higher education has been evident since medieval times. SELDEN, ACCREDITATION: A STRUGGLE OVER STANDARDS IN HIGHER EDUCATION 8–9 (1960).[1] Today in most countries ministries of education control educational standards. . . . The story in the United States has been uniquely different, for here, overall, government has played a modest role. The result has been a chaotic scene with which private interests have had to contend on a wholly cooperative basis. There emerged a system of regional associations which continue to set standards and accredit institutions. Whatever the reason for the modest governmental activity in this area, it was not for doubt as to the power of the States to act. In *Trustees of Dartmouth College v. Woodward*, 4 Wheat. 518, 634 (1819), in which the charter of incorporation was held to be a contract the State could not undo, Chief Justice Marshall said, in axiomatic style:

> That education is an object of national concern, and a proper object of legislation, all admit.

And it is the degree, evidential as it is of academic attainment, which especially is an appropriate object of regulation. As stated in ELLIOTT, THE COLLEGES AND THE COURTS 200 (1936), "The power to confer academic degrees is to be regarded as distinct and separate from the privilege of being incorporated as an educational institution. The privilege of granting degrees is very intimately related to the public welfare, and is unquestionably subject to regulation by the State."

. . .

It was an undisputed need for standardization with respect to degrees, both academic and professional, which sparked the development of private accreditation. But useful as private accreditation has been, it cannot deal directly with the non-accredited school. It cannot stop the substandard school or close the out-and-out degree mill. Hence bogus degrees have been

---

1. The interest of the Church and State in medieval seats of learning is there described in these terms:

> At first these centers of study existed without external authority, but in time princes and popes granted charters, officially creating *studia generalia* and extending to masters and students special privileges including exemption from taxation, from military service, and from trial in courts of civil magistrates; in time, many other privileges were granted. Since most students were not native to the location of a particular university and therefore would not have sufficient protection in a local civil court, the exemption from jurisdiction of the civil courts was particularly important as an inducement to attract students. For an institution to obtain important and adequate recognition outside of its own domain, a grant by papal bull or royal order was required—as the *ius*

ubique docendi, the right to teach anywhere, was dependent on such a grant, and was essential to the tutor who wished to be accepted in a guild of masters.

> Not only was it important for the universities to have papal or royal support, but it also was important for both church and lay authorities to seek the allegiance of the universities, since these two groups sparred with each other for political supremacy. Consequently, popes vied with kings in granting privileges to the universities, which thus were able to maintain a degree of relative autonomy throughout the struggle for their control, which continued for several centuries. And, it should be remembered, this was at a time when scholars were taking a leading part in shaping the ideas of the Church and when the Church held undisputed domination over western thought and culture.

vended, and no doubt still are, not only to citizens here but as well to residents of foreign countries, who, familiar with their own controls over academic standards, cannot "understand that an academic or professional degree from some fly-by-night university or college in the United States may be little more than a scrap of paper." REID, AMERICAN DEGREE MILLS 19 (1959). In 1950 the education editor of the New York Times estimated there were more than 1,000 unethical institutions of which at least 100 were outright diploma mills, with an annual take of $75,000,000 from 750,000 students. REID, *supra*, at 7.

The statute of 1912, which sought for the first time in our State to protect the academic degree by requiring the "approval" of the State Board of Education, was a direct response to the widespread concern over the abuse of the public. Educators themselves had called for legislative intervention.... In 1897 the president of Northwestern University said:

> "The cause of professional as well as academic education suffers from the want of adequate State supervision.... This sort of thing, impossible in Europe, should be made impossible in America. Such a condition of affairs is demoralizing beyond question. The tendency of it is all in the direction of low standards. It imposes on the public a class of educational charlatans and works injury to the students whom it falsely pretends to educate." Quoted in SELDEN, ACCREDITATION: A STRUGGLE OVER STANDARDS IN HIGHER EDUCATION 49 (1960).

In 1897 the National Education Association resolved "that the States should exercise supervision over degree-conferring institutions through some properly constituted tribunal having the power to fix a minimum standard of requirements for admission to or graduation from such institutions, and with the right to deprive of the degree-granting power such institutions not conforming to the standards so prescribed." REID, *supra*, at 13. In 1907 Woodrow Wilson, then president of Princeton University, proclaimed that "We are on the eve of a period when we are going to set up standards," SELDEN, *supra*, at 36, and five years later, as Governor of this State, he signed the 1912 enactment to that end.

. . .

The public stake in education has never been more evident, for today higher education is essential for the survival of man himself. The academic degree is the more meaningful on that account. The State may protect it unless the police power is restrained by some constitutional guaranty.... Shelton relies upon the abstract possibility that a power to regulate could be used illicitly to destroy by indirection a value secured from destruction by the Constitution, and from that premise contends that the power to regulate may not be allowed at all.

Of course the power to regulate does not depend upon a power to destroy. If government were denied the power to regulate unless it could also prohibit, there could hardly be law and order. Our statutes abound with needful restrictions upon rights of the person and of property notwithstanding the Constitution would protect those rights from destruction. Rather the Constitution condemns such exercises of the police power as are arbitrary, and leaves it to its constituted officers to say when the boundaries of that power have been breached. *Meyer v. State of Nebraska*, 262 U.S. 390 (1923).

Here there is no proof whatever that the State Board is bearing down upon Shelton because of Shelton's convictions upon any topic . . . The attack rests wholly upon the untenable proposition that the Constitution guarantees to everyone an absolute right to bestow the degree of bachelor of arts upon any basis or upon none at all.

Next, Shelton says the statute fails to set forth a sufficient standard for the exercise of the legislative power delegated to the State Board and therefore violates our State Constitution, Art. IV, § I, para. 1, and Art. III, para. 1.

. . . N.J. Stat. Ann. 18:2–4 empowers the State Board in subsection "l" to "Advance the education of people of all ages," and to that end equips the Board with sundry powers of which the following may be mentioned here from the catalogue in the section just cited:

"b. Prescribe and enforce rules and regulations necessary to carry into effect the school laws of this State;

. . .

m. Establish standards of higher education;

n. License institutions of higher education as authorized by sections 18:20–5, 18:20–6, and 18:20–7 of this Title;

o. Approve the basis or conditions for conferring degrees as authorized by sections 18:20–8, 18:20–9, and 18:20–10 of this Title;

. . .

u. The State Board shall have all other powers requisite to the performance of its duties."

Shelton's complaint is quite like the one rejected in *Douglas v. Noble*, 261 U.S. 165 (1923). That case involved a state statute concerning the practice of dentistry. The attack made under the Fourteenth Amendment was based upon the claim that the discretion given the board of examiners with respect to licensure was so standardless as to furnish no guard against arbitrariness. Specifically the complaint was the legislature did not itself fix the scope or the character of the qualifying examination but rather left it to the board to decide what would demonstrate fitness to practice dentistry. The highest court of the State had held the statute was not intended to authorize arbitrary action, and of course the United States Supreme Court accepted that judicially found restriction. The Supreme Court unanimously upheld the statute, saying that, although the legislature could itself specify (1) what knowledge and skill will fit one to practice dentistry and leave it to the board to decide (2) whether the individual applicant had the specified knowledge and skill, the legislature was free to commit both matters to the agency, adding that "it is not to be presumed that powers conferred upon the administrative boards will be exercised arbitrarily."

And so in the case at hand, the Legislature, to protect the sundry interests in the integrity and value of the bachelor degree, could itself have written the qualifying specifications for the school and then left it to the Board to decide in each case whether the specifications were met. But the Legislature could decide, as it did, that the wiser course was to leave it to the Board to make the specifications, thus to profit from the expertise of the Board and to permit those specifications to develop with a changing educational scene. Whether that approach to the problem will better serve the public interest is itself a matter which the Constitution commits to the judgment of the Legislature. The judiciary of course may not intervene unless the legislative decision is palpably arbitrary. There is nothing before us to suggest the Legislature exceeded its constitutional authority in deciding to delegate the subject in such fullness to the State Board. Nor is there any reason to suppose the Legislature intended that the power thus delegated may be used by the Board capriciously. On the contrary, it is elementary in our State that delegated power must be exercised reasonably in its substantive aspects and that the procedural demands of due process must be honored whenever they apply. . . .

. . .

The resolution under appeal is therefore affirmed.

Comment on *Shelton College*

Shelton College was "a Bible Presbyterian school for educating preachers and teachers—something of a seminary, something of a liberal arts college." Russell Kirk, *Shelton College and State Licensing of Religious Schools: An Educator's View of the Interface Between the Establishment and Free Exercise Clauses*, LAW & CONTEMP. PROBS., Spring 1981 at 169, 169. It has been described as "not very different from the Harvard or Yale of an earlier time[, conforming] to the familiar pattern of the church-related denominational college in America, with its ministerial guidance and its rural setting." *Id.* at 173.

The New Jersey Supreme Court intimated that Shelton College believed it was being targeted because of its teachings. It is possible that Shelton's chancellor, an "ultra-conservative" with a vocal disdain for Roman Catholics, might have drawn the state's attention to the school? See *id.* at 174. Although the court did not fully address that question, it would have the opportunity to do so in the future.

Following the New Jersey Supreme Court's decision in *Shelton*, the State Board of Higher Education revoked Shelton's temporary license, and in 1971 the school moved to Florida. In 1979, Shelton College again applied for a license to operate in New Jersey. Shelton students began attending classes in Cape May, New Jersey in Fall 1979, with the administration intending to confer degrees through its Florida campus until it obtained a license to grant degrees at the new location. The State obtained a preliminary injunction barring Shelton from "engaging in any form of educational instruction" but allowing current students to finish the semester. The District Court for the District of New Jersey then enjoined the state from enforcing the state court injunction against Shelton. *See* New Jersey–Philadelphia Presbytery of the Bible Presbyterian Church v. New Jersey State Bd. of Higher Educ., 482 F.Supp. 968, 972–73, 979–80 (D. N.J. 1980), *aff'd* 654 F.2d 868 (3d Cir. 1981).

When Shelton's First Amendment challenge to the licensing statute again reached the New Jersey Supreme Court, the court held:

> that the State's program for licensing institutions of higher education is applicable to sectarian institutions and that facially it does not unduly interfere with the free exercise of religion nor create an excessive state entanglement with religion. At the same time, we recognize the good faith with which the students of Shelton College have pursued their educational and religious goals. To accommodate the free exercise interests of the individual students without unduly interfering with the state regulatory program, and in consideration of the difficulty involved in transferring to a different college at the end of three years, we modify the judgment below to allow the awarding of earned credits and degrees to all eligible students through the end of the 1982–83 academic year and to the class of 1984

through the end of the 1983–84 academic year. No other credits or degrees shall be awarded without licensure.

New Jersey State Bd. of Higher Educ. v. Board of Dirs. of Shelton Coll., 90 N.J. 470, 490, 448 A.2d 988 (1982).

Note on *Meyer v. Nebraska* and *Pierce v. Society of Sisters*

The New Jersey Supreme Court in *Shelton* cited *Meyer v. Nebraska*, 262 U.S. 390 (1923), for the proposition that the state could not arbitrarily exercise its regulatory power. In *Meyer*, a German language teacher challenged and the Supreme Court held unconstitutional a Nebraska statute making it a crime to teach any language except English to students below the high school level. The legislation was a product of animosity toward foreigners aroused by World War I. In Nebraska, local anger was directed at Germans and the German language in particular:

> The problem for our determination is whether the statute as construed and applied unreasonably infringes the liberty guaranteed to the plaintiff in error by the Fourteenth Amendment. "No State shall ... deprive any person of life, liberty, or property, without due process of law."

> While this Court has not attempted to define with exactness the liberty thus guaranteed, the term has received much consideration and some of the included things have been definitely stated. Without doubt, it denotes not merely freedom from bodily restraint but also the right of the individual to contract, to engage in any of the common occupations of life, to acquire useful knowledge, to marry, establish a home and bring up children, to worship God according to the dictates of his own conscience, and generally to enjoy those privileges long recognized at common law as essential to the orderly pursuit of happiness by free men. The established doctrine is that this liberty may not be interfered with, under the guise of protecting the public interest, by legislative action which is arbitrary or without reasonable relation to some purpose within the competency of the State to effect. Determination by the legislature of what constitutes proper exercise of police power is not final or conclusive but is subject to supervision by the courts.

> ... The Supreme Court of the State has held that "the so-called ancient or dead languages" are not "within the spirit or the purpose of the act." *Nebraska District of Evangelical Lutheran Synod v. McKelvie*, 187 N.W. 927. Latin, Greek, Hebrew are not proscribed; but German, French, Spanish, Italian and every other alien speech are within the ban. Evidently the legislature has attempted materially to interfere with the calling of modern language teachers, with the opportunities of pupils to acquire knowledge, and with the power of parents to control the education of their own.

> It is said the purpose of the legislation was to promote civic development by inhibiting training and education of the immature in foreign tongues and ideals before they could learn English and acquire American ideals; and "that the English language should be and become the mother tongue of all children reared in this State." It is also affirmed that the foreign born population is very large, that certain communities commonly use foreign words, follow foreign leaders, move in a foreign atmosphere, and that the children are thereby hindered from becoming citizens of the most useful type and the public safety is imperiled.

> That the State may do much, go very far, indeed, in order to improve the quality of its citizens, physically, mentally and morally, is clear; but the individual has certain fundamental rights which must be respected. The protection of the Constitution extends to all, to those who speak other languages as well as to those born with English on the tongue. Perhaps it would be highly advantageous if all had ready understanding of our ordi-

nary speech, but this cannot be coerced by methods which conflict with the Constitution—a desirable end cannot be promoted by prohibited means.

For the welfare of his Ideal Commonwealth, Plato suggested a law which should provide: "That the wives of our guardians are to be common, and their children are to be common, and no parent is to know his own child, nor any child his parent.... The proper officers will take the offspring of the goods parents to the pen or fold, and there they will deposit them with certain nurses who dwell in a separate quarter; but the offspring of the inferior, or of the better when they chance to be deformed, will be put away in some mysterious, unknown place, as they should be." In order to submerge the individual and develop ideal citizens, Sparta assembled the males at seven into barracks and intrusted their subsequent education and training to official guardians. Although such measures have been deliberately approved by men of great genius, their ideas touching the relation between individual and State were wholly different from those upon which our institutions rest; and it hardly will be affirmed that any legislature could impose such restrictions upon the people of a State without doing violence to both letter and spirit of the Constitution.

The desire of the legislature to foster a homogeneous people with American ideals prepared readily to understand current discussions of civic matters is easy to appreciate. Unfortunate experiences during the late war and aversion toward every characteristic of truculent adversaries were certainly enough to quicken that aspiration. But the means adopted, we think, exceed the limitations upon the power of the State and conflict with rights assured to plaintiff in error. The interference is plain enough and no adequate reason therefore in time of peace and domestic tranquility has been shown.

The power of the State to compel attendance at some school and to make reasonable regulations for all schools, including a requirement that they shall give instructions in English, is not questioned. Nor has challenge been made of the State's power to prescribe a curriculum for institutions which it supports. Those matters are not within the present controversy. Our concern is with the prohibition approved by the Supreme Court.... No emergency has arisen which renders knowledge by a child of some language other than English so clearly harmful as to justify its inhibition with the consequent infringement of rights long freely enjoyed. We are constrained to conclude that the statute as applied is arbitrary and without reasonable relation to any end within the competency of the State.

As the statute undertakes to interfere only with teaching which involves a modern language, leaving complete freedom as to other matters, there seems no adequate foundation for the suggestion that the purpose was to protect the child's health by limiting his mental activities. It is well known that proficiency in a foreign language seldom comes to one not instructed at an early age, and experience shows that this is not injurious to the health, morals or understanding of the ordinary child.

The judgment of the court below must be reversed....

262 U.S. at 399–403.

Two years later in *Pierce v. Society of Sisters*, 268 U.S. 510 (1925), the Supreme Court struck down an Oregon statute that required all children under the age of sixteen to attend public schools. As in *Meyer*, the Court held that the statute violated the liberty interests of parents to decide whether to send their children to public or private schools. Thus *Pierce* preserved the private sector for elementary and secondary education much as *Dartmouth College* had for higher education.

University of Illinois v. Barrett

Supreme Court of Illinois, 1943.
382 Ill. 321, 46 N.E.2d 951.

■ SMITH, J.

This is an original petition for *mandamus*. The relators are the Board of Trustees of the University of Illinois and Norval D. Hodges and Sveinbjorn Johnson, individually.... The action is brought against the Attorney General and the Auditor of Public Accounts of the State of Illinois. Its purpose is to compel the payment of salaries alleged to be due to the individual relators; to prevent the Attorney General from interfering with Johnson and Hodges acting as counsel and assistant counsel, respectively, for the university and its Board of Trustees, and from interfering with them in the exercise of the asserted right to represent the Board of Trustees in a case now pending in the circuit court of Cook county.

. . .

The decisive question is whether the Attorney General is, by virtue of his office, and in his official capacity, the sole legal advisor, counsel and attorney for the university and its Board of Trustees. The solution of this question involves a determination of the status of the university as a corporate entity and its relation to the State government, as well as the powers vested in the Attorney General by the constitution and laws of this State.

By an act of July 2, 1862, the Congress of the United States made certain land grants to the several States for the endowment, support and maintenance of at least one college in each State, where the leading object should be to teach such branches of learning as are related to agriculture and the mechanic arts....

. . .

In compliance with these conditions the legislature on February 28, 1867, passed an act creating a corporation to be styled "The Board of Trustees of the Illinois Industrial University."

. . .

By an act of June 19, 1885, the name of the corporation was changed to "University of Illinois." By an act of June 15, 1887, it was provided that the trustees shall be elected from the State at large at regular general elections, instead of being appointed by the Governor, as provided in section 1 of the original act.

. . .

Under the decisions of this court, there is little room for speculation or disagreement as to the character of the University of Illinois as a corporate entity. In the case of *Spalding v. People*, 172 Ill. 40, where the question was directly involved, it was definitely held that while the university is not strictly a municipal corporation, it is nevertheless, a public corporation. It was organized for the sole purpose of conducting and operating the university, as a State institution. It is not a private corporation....

. . .

While it is a public corporation, it was organized and exists for one specific purpose. It is unique in that it has and can own no property in its own right. Whatever property or interest in property it acquires belongs to the State, and is held by it as trustee for the use of the State. It has no taxing powers and no means of raising money or acquiring property, except through the operation of the university. Its power to borrow money and to issue bonds is granted and limited by the act of June 4, 1941. True, it may receive donations and gifts, but whatever it may receive as such, like all other property which it acquires, it holds only as trustee for the State, the beneficial owner. It has no power to select its own trustees or managers. This power is reserved to the State. It functions solely as an agency of the State for the purpose of the operation and administration of the university, for the State. In doing this, it functions as a corporation, separate and distinct from the State and as a public corporate entity with all the powers enumerated in the applicable statutes, or necessarily incident thereto. It has and can exercise no sovereign powers. It is no part of the State or State government....

As such a corporation it may formulate and carry out any educational program it may deem proper with complete authority over its faculty, employees and students, as well as all questions of policy. Incident to its corporate existence and the exercise of its corporate powers, it has the undoubted right to employ its own counsel or engage the services of any other employees it may deem necessary or proper, by contract or otherwise. This power is, however, always subject to the restriction that when such faculty members or other employees are to be paid from State funds, they must be within the classifications for which funds have been appropriated and are available.

.   .   .

The power of the legislature is ... unlimited as to who shall constitute the trustees, managing directors, or other officers or governing body of all public corporations, as well as the manner in which they shall be chosen. There is nothing in the constitution, or in the public policy or laws of this State, to prevent the legislature from providing for the selection of these officers, either by the people of the whole State, or of any part of the State, in the same manner and at the same times, that State officers are elected. It can do this as to all public corporations, or as to cities, counties or other municipal or *quasi*-municipal corporations. The plan adopted may be changed at any time. This principle finds practical demonstration in the history of the statute under consideration. For the first twenty years of its existence the university was governed by trustees appointed by the Governor and approved by the Senate. In 1887 the statute was amended so as to provide for the election of three trustees in the general election in November, 1888, and at each general election every two years thereafter, for terms of six years. It further provided that the trustees so elected, together with the Governor, President of the State Board of Agriculture and the Superintendent of Public Instruction, should constitute the board. Under the statute it seems clear that the sole function of the trustees of the University of Illinois is the management of the corporation. They are not State officers in the sense that the Attorney General is their legal advisor or representative, as contended by respondents in this case.

.   .   .

In the sense that it is a department or branch of the State government, the University of Illinois is not an agency or instrumentality of the State. It is a separate corporate entity, which functions as a public corporation. It is not the duty of the Attorney General to represent either the corporation or the trustees, by virtue of his office, as chief law officer of State. He has no right to do so. Both the university as a public corporation and its trustees are entitled to select their own legal counsel and advisor and to be represented in all suits brought by or against them by counsel of their own choice. As the managing or governing body of the university and all its property, clearly it would be the duty of the Attorney General to institute all appropriate proceedings against the corporation, and its officers and trustees, to either prevent or redress any breach of the trust. He would do this as the representative of the State and not as the representative of the corporation or its trustees. . . .

. . . With reference to relator Johnson, it is alleged in the petition that during the academic year 1941–42 the university, in accordance with its established procedure, certified payroll vouchers covering the position held by him under the following description, "Sveinbjorn Johnson, Professor and Counsel." It sets out the creation of the position of "University Counsel" and his appointment and succession to that office, naming his predecessor, in great detail. His duties as University Counsel are set out at length, as well as his professorial duties. In the payroll vouchers, no division was made as to the amount due him for professorial services and the amount due him as University Counsel. As to relator Hodges, the petition alleges that he performed services during the academic year 1941–42 as "Student Loan Assistant" and "Assistant University Counsel;" that as "Assistant University Counsel" he was entitled to a salary of $900 per year, payable from State appropriations to the University.

. . .

An examination of the appropriations for the University of Illinois for the 1941–42 biennium discloses that no appropriation for either "University Counsel" or "Assistant University Counsel," was made. . . . There is nothing in the appropriations which would authorize the Auditor to issue warrants for salaries or compensation for such officers or employees, when certified as such on the university payroll. Nor do we find any appropriation for the employment of attorneys or counsel, or for legal expenses, in any form or amount.

It is argued by relators, and the petition sets forth, that preceding the appropriations for the 1941–42 biennium, and preceding each appropriation for many years prior thereto, the University of Illinois has submitted, in its internal budget to the General Assembly, the funds needed for the current biennium in the operation of the university; that it has included in such budget, as necessary anticipated expense during the period covered by the budget the positions of "University Counsel" and "Assistant University Counsel." Preceding the passage of the appropriations by the General Assembly, it is alleged that copies of this internal budget have been delivered to each of the individual members of the General Assembly. From this premise it is argued, and the petition alleges, that the ensuing biennium appropriations were based upon the internal budgets so submitted, and that appropriations for these positions were necessarily included in the appropriations because they were included in the internal budgets. This is not the averment of a fact.... With the internal budgets before it, in which were included items for the payment for counsel and assistant counsel, the appropriations made show that the legislature has consistently omitted to include any such items in its appropriations. The logical conclusion is that the legislature did not approve of those particular expenditures and, for that reason, refused to make appropriations herefore.

It follows that there being no averment in the petition of funds available for the payment of warrants, which petitioners ask this court to compel the Auditor to issue, it must be assumed that no such funds are available in any applicable appropriation. It appears from the appropriations made that no such items were included. In this situation, obviously, it was not the duty of the Auditor to issue the warrants, even though the salaries of relators had been duly certified in the university payrolls. The Attorney General was correct in advising the Auditor to refuse to issue the warrants. By the eighth subparagraph of section 4 of the statute prescribing the duties of the Attorney General, it is made his duty "To enforce the proper application of funds appropriated to the public institutions of the state...."

The Auditor was equally justified in refusing to issue the warrants. Any prevailing custom to the contrary, however long followed, cannot aid petitioners in this respect....

. . .

The Attorney General was in error in assuming that he was the sole legal representative of the University of Illinois, or its trustees. He was also in error in appearing in the case described in the petition, pending in the circuit court of Cook County, as attorney for the university and the other defendants therein named.

The writ of *mandamus* is awarded directing the Attorney General to move to withdraw his appearance and all pleadings filed by him in the case of *People of the State of Illinois ex rel. etc., v. University of Illinois et al.*, being an action at law on the docket of the circuit court of Cook County. In all other respects the prayer of the petition is denied.

Regents of the University of Michigan v. State of Michigan

Court of Appeals of Michigan, 1988.
166 Mich.App. 314, 419 N.W.2d 773.

■ WALSH, D.F.

Plaintiff, the body corporate known as the Regents of the University of Michigan, appeals from a circuit court order ... granting summary judgment to defendant, the State of Michigan.... At issue on appeal is the constitutionality of 1982 Mich. Pub. Acts 512, which amended the Civil Rights Act (CRA), Mich. Comp. Laws 37.2101 *et seq.*; MSA 3.548(101) *et seq.*...

... Appearing as amici curiae before this Court are the Board of Governors of Wayne State University; State Representatives Perry Bullard and Virgil Smith, Jr., principal sponsors of Act 512; the Black Student Union of the University of Michigan; the Peace Education Center; the Institute for Global Education; the National Conference of Black Lawyers; the International Union of the United Auto Workers; the National Lawyers Guild; and the American Committee on Africa.

The CRA prohibits discriminatory practices, policies and customs in the exercise of rights based on religion, race, color, national origin, age, sex, height, weight and marital status. Article 4 of CRA addresses the issue of discrimination by educational institutions. Act 512 amended § 402 of Article 4 by adding the requirement that educational institutions, which include public universities, shall not

> (f) Encourage or condone legally required discrimination against an individual on the basis of race or color by knowingly making or maintaining after April 1, 1984, an investment in an organization operating in the republic of South Africa. This subdivision shall not apply to a private educational institution.

> (g) Encourage or condone religious discrimination or ethnic discrimination by knowingly making or maintaining after February 1, 1983, an investment in an organization operating in the Union of Soviet Socialist Republics. . . .

. . . The [Michigan] Constitution confers on plaintiff, as it does on the controlling boards of the other institutions of higher education established by Michigan law and authorized to grant baccalaureate degrees, the "general supervision of its institution and the control and direction of all expenditures from the institution's funds." Const 1963, art 8, §§ 5 and 6. Candidates for membership on the eight-member Board of Regents are nominated at the state convention of each political party. The regents, whose eight-year terms are staggered, are elected at the state general election. They are subject to recall and to removal by impeachment.

On July 15, 1983, plaintiff commenced this action seeking a declaratory judgment that Act 512 is unconstitutional. Plaintiff's principal challenge was that Act 512 contravenes Const 1963, art 8, § 5 in attempting to restrict plaintiff's authority to control and direct expenditures of the university's funds. Attached to plaintiff's complaint was a copy of an April 15, 1983, resolution of the regents whereby, subject to limited exceptions, the chief financial officer of the university was directed to divest the university of its interest in investments in shares of corporate stock and other equities of organizations operating in the Republic of South Africa. Also attached to plaintiff's complaint were lists of university investments in companies doing business in the Union of Soviet Socialist Republics and the Republic of South Africa. The market values of such investments as of June 30, 1983, were $17,756,507.90 and $51,636,241.54, respectively. Each of the listed companies doing business in the U.S.S.R. also did business in South Africa. The parties both moved for summary judgment. The circuit court rejected each of plaintiff's challenges to Act 512 and granted summary judgment to defendant. . . .

. . .

In the Constitution of 1850, provision was first made for the election of regents of the University of Michigan. In addition, in language largely echoed in the 1908 and present constitutions, the Constitution of 1850 conferred on the regents "the general supervision of the University, and the direction and control of all expenditures from the university interest fund." Const. 1850, art 13, § 8. The significance of these developments and of the consequent independent nature of the university has been the subject of considerable comment:

> Under the Constitution of 1835, the legislature had the entire control and management of the University and the University fund. They could appoint regents and professors, and establish departments. The University was not a success under this supervision by the legislature, and, as some of the members of the constitutional convention of 1850 said in their debates, "some of the denominational colleges had more students than did the University." Such was the condition of affairs when that convention met. It is apparent to any reader of the debates in this convention in regard to the constitutional provision for the University that they had in mind the idea of permanency of location, to place it beyond mere political influence, and to intrust it to those who should be directly responsible and amenable to the people.

> . . .

> The result has proved their wisdom, for the University, which was before practically a failure, under the guidance of this constitutional body, known as the "Board of Regents," has grown to be one of the most successful, the most complete, and the best-known institutions of learning in the world.

> . . .

> Obviously, it was not the intention of the framers of the Constitution to take away from the people the government of this institution. On the contrary, they designed to, and did, provide for its management and control by a body of eight men elected by the people at large. They recognized the necessity that it should be in the charge of men elected for long terms, and whose sole official duty it should be to look after its interests, and who should have the opportunity to investigate its needs, and carefully deliberate and determine what things would best promote its usefulness for the benefit of the people. Some of the members of the convention of 1850 referred in the debates to two colleges (one in Virginia and the other in Massachusetts) which had been failures under the management by the State. It is obvious to every intelligent and reflecting mind that such an institution would be safer and more certain of permanent success in the control of such a body than in that of the legislature, composed of 132 members, elected every two years, many of whom would, of necessity, know but little of its needs, and would have little or no time to intelligently investigate and determine the policy essential for the success of a great university. [*Sterling v. Regents of the University of Michigan*, 110 Mich. 369, 374, 377, 379–380, 68 N.W. 253 (1896).]

> . . .

The issue of the extent to which legislative action may, if at all, permissibly impinge on the authority granted to the governing boards of Michigan's state universities is not new to the jurisprudence of our state. The Michigan Supreme Court has repeatedly affirmed the constitutional independence and exclusive authority of art 8, § 5 boards in the face of attempted legislative encroachment.... The [appellate] courts have clearly interpreted the Constitution as conferring general fiscal autonomy on the university boards.

In this case, the circuit court found that Act 512 does not contravene art 8, § 5 because it does not impinge on the "expenditure" of university funds but only on the "investment" of those funds. We agree with plaintiff that reliance on selected dictionary definitions offers an insufficient basis for the constitutional adjudication demanded by this case. As plaintiff additionally notes, any investment of funds entails what even the circuit court would be constrained to agree is the incidental expenditure of funds....

. . .

All agree that the clearly established public policy of our state strictly prohibits racial and religious discrimination in the exercise of civil rights. Const. 1963, art 1, § 2, MCL 37.2101 *et seq.*; MSA 3.548(101) *et seq.* It is also beyond dispute that the apartheid system of South Africa is repugnant to our common sense of morality and justice.[6] Neither the people nor the Legislature, however, have clearly declared that Michigan public policy prohibits investment of public funds in organizations operating in South Africa. Act 512 is directed solely at educational institutions. The Legislature has not prohibited all investment of public funds in organizations operating in South Africa. Such investment of public employees' pension funds, for example, has not been prohibited. While Act 512 has not been the Legislature's only statement concerning investments in South Africa, we find that the investment standards contained in Act 512 do not yet reflect "a clearly established public policy" in this state.... The circuit court found that university autonomy is limited to "the educational sphere." We do not read the *Employment Relations Comm.* case as restricting university autonomy to a strictly "educational sphere." In any event, we agree with plaintiff that the distinction, if any, between the "educational" and "noneducational" spheres of a major research university is indistinct and often indiscernible. The Constitution contains no "educational sphere" limitation.

... Because Act 512 impermissibly encroaches on plaintiff's authority to allocate university funds, it violates Const. 1963, art 8, § 5.

Questions and Comments on *Regents of the University of Michigan v. State of Michigan*

Would the same result have been reached if this controversy had arisen in Illinois rather than Michigan? What would happen if the Michigan legislature passed a law requiring the university to hire a professor in a particular discipline? *See* People v. Regents of Univ. of Michigan, 18 Mich. 469 (1860).

University of Utah v. Shurtleff

Supreme Court of Utah, 2006.
2006 UT 51, 144 P.3d 1109.

■ PARRISH, J.

For many years, the University of Utah has enforced a policy prohibiting its students, faculty, and staff from possessing firearms on campus. During its

---

6. Act 512 prohibits investment not only in South Africa but also in the Soviet Union. The parties have focused their attention on South Africa, however, and we therefore do likewise.

2004 General Session, the Utah Legislature passed Utah Code section 63–98–102, a statute prohibiting state and local entities from enacting or enforcing any ordinance, regulation, rule, or policy that in "any way inhibits or restricts the possession or use of firearms on either public or private property." The conflict between the University's policy and section 63–98–102 requires that we assess the relative authority of the University and the legislature to regulate firearms on the University's campus.

. . .

Utah's Enabling Act requires the University to "forever remain under the exclusive control of" the State of Utah.... To that end, the Utah Legislature created the Utah State Board of Regents, which has authority to "enact regulations governing the conduct of university and college students, faculty, and employees." Utah Code Ann. § 53B–3–103(1) (Supp. 2004). The board of regents has, in turn, enacted regulations giving the University's president the responsibility to maintain a safe and orderly campus, as well as the authority to issue policies aimed at ensuring the safety and security of people and property on the University's campus. The legislature also has authorized the University's president to exercise authority delegated by the board of regents, as well as other "necessary and proper ... powers" not denied the University "by the [board of regents] or by law," to run the University efficiently and effectively. The University enforces its regulations pursuant to those grants of power.

One of the regulations enacted by the University is a firearms policy. The policy, which prohibits students, faculty, and staff from carrying guns on campus and "while conducting University business off campus," authorizes disciplinary action for violations. Numerous University administrative bodies endorse the policy, and those responsible for campus safety view it as a success.

The University's firearms policy became the subject of heated debate in 2001, when Utah Attorney General Mark Shurtleff issued Opinion No. 01–002, in which he opined that a Utah Department of Human Resource Management rule forbidding state employees to carry guns in state facilities violated Utah's Uniform Firearms Act....

. . .

The University then sued the Attorney General in Utah state court, seeking a declaration that its firearms policy was contrary to neither the Uniform Firearms Act, *id.* §§ 76–10–500 to–530 (2003), nor the Concealed Weapon Act, Utah Code Ann. §§ 53–5–701 to–711 (2002). In the alternative, the University sought a declaration that article X, section 4 of the Utah Constitution guaranteed it institutional autonomy over firearms regulation, thereby allowing it to continue to enforce its firearms policy in spite of any contrary Utah law. The Attorney General moved to dismiss the University's suit, and the University countered with a motion for summary judgment.

The district court denied the Attorney General's motion to dismiss and granted the University's motion for summary judgment, holding that the University's firearms policy was not contrary to Utah law....

The Attorney General appealed. Shortly after he filed his initial brief, the legislature passed Senate Bill 48, later codified at sections 63–98–101 to–102 of the Utah Code. *See id.* §§ 63–98–101 to–102 (2004). Section 63–98–102 provides, "Unless specifically authorized by the Legislature by statute, a local authority or state entity may not enact, establish, or enforce any ordinance, regulation, rule, or policy pertaining to firearms that in any way inhibits or restricts the possession or use of firearms on either public or private property." *Id.* § 63–98–102(5). The statutory definition of the phrase "[l]ocal authority or state entity" includes "state institutions of higher education," such as the University. *Id.* § 63–98–102(6)(b). The passage of section 63–98–102 dramatically altered the legal landscape, rendering it clear that Utah's firearms statutes are universally applicable, rather than merely criminal in nature as the district court had concluded, and that the University's firearms policy does, in fact, violate Utah law.

Because the enactment of section 63–98–102 conclusively resolved the statutory interpretation issue in a manner contrary to the holding of the district court, both the University and the Attorney General suggested that the district court's decision on that point had been rendered moot, obviating the need for this court to review that issue. The parties further suggested that the University's constitutional claim, which the district court had not reached, was ripe for adjudication and should be addressed by this court. We agreed and directed the parties to proceed with briefing on the constitutional issue.

The University contends that section 63–98–102 is unconstitutional as applied to the University because the University enjoys institutional autonomy under article X, section 4 of the Utah Constitution. . . .

. . .

[A]rticle X, section 4, the constitutional provision governing higher education . . . provides:

> The general control and supervision of the higher education system shall be provided for by statute. All rights, immunities, franchises, and endowments originally established or recognized by the constitution for any public university or college are confirmed.

Nothing in the first sentence of this section could be read to limit the legislature's right of control over the University. To the contrary, the phrase explicitly confirms the legislature's right to "general control and supervision of the higher education system" through its lawmaking power. Absent any restrictive language, the legislature may supervise and generally control all University functions.

The basis for the University's claimed right of institutional autonomy is the second sentence of article X, section 4, which confirms "[a]ll rights, immunities, franchises, and endowments originally established or recognized by the constitution for any public university or college." The University contends that these rights include the institutional autonomy to disregard legislative enactments that interfere with its academic mission. Because this sentence reserves to the University only those rights "originally established" by the constitution, we must examine the scope of those original rights.

. . .

This court exhaustively examined the historical record and outlined the scope of the University's rights at the time of statehood in the case of *University of Utah v. Board of Examiners*, 4 Utah 2d 408, 295 P.2d 348 (Utah 1956). As explained in that opinion, the University was "instituted and incorporated [in 1850] by an ordinance of the State of Deseret." In 1892, just four years prior to statehood, the territorial legislature enacted a new comprehensive statute governing the University and repealed all other laws in conflict with its provisions (the "1892 Act"). The 1892 Act described the University as "a body corporate with perpetual succession" with "all the property, credits, effects and franchises of the existing corporation, subject to all [its] contracts, obligations and liabilities." It vested management of the University in a board of regents. Finally, it provided that the University "shall be deemed a public corporation and be subject to the laws of Utah, from time to time enacted, relating to its purposes and government."

The University reasons that because the 1892 Act vested management of the University in a board of regents and gave it power to employ instructors and employees, the University has authority to supervise and control University activities and is protected "from legislative interference of the University's autonomy in relation to academic matters." We disagree.

The territorial legislature gave the University broad authority to regulate its day-to-day affairs, and it retained the powers typically bestowed on corporations, such as the authority to make contracts, purchase property, and use the proceeds of such property. But the University was never given the power to act in contravention of legislative enactments. Rather, the authority conferred on the University by the 1892 Act, which was later incorporated into the Utah Constitution, was limited by the language rendering the University "subject to the laws of Utah." As we concluded in *Board of Examiners*, although the University retained certain rights, privileges, immunities, and franchises associated with public corporations, it was never exempt from the obligation of all Utah citizens and entities to follow Utah law. Its authority was subject to general legislative oversight, even to legislative enactments relating to its core academic functions.

.   .   .

The University acknowledges that it is "subject to legislative control regarding its budget and finances," but maintains that this court has never held that the legislature may control the University's central academic purpose. While the University is correct that our prior cases did not involve legislative action directed at the University's academic mission, the fact remains that the reasoning of those cases is incompatible with the University's position. Our prior case law construing article X, section 4 has consistently upheld the power of the legislature to exercise "general control and supervision" over higher education, including the University.

.   .   .

In *Board of Examiners*, this court examined the question of whether "Article X, Section 4 of the Utah Constitution establishe[d] the University as a constitutional corporation free from the control of the Legislature, administrative bodies, commissions and agencies and officers of the State." After an extensive analysis of the constitutional language and historical context of article X, section 4, this court answered the question in the negative.

The *Board of Examiners* opinion distinguished Utah's constitutional language from that of other states whose constitutions vest their institutions of higher learning with the institutional autonomy the University seeks. After discussing the differences between those constitutions and Utah's constitution, it reasoned:

> If the framers of the Utah Constitution had intended to create the University of Utah a constitutional corporation, completely autonomous and free from legislative control, it is difficult to understand why language such as was used in the constitutions of Michigan, Minnesota and the other constitutions referred to was not used.
>
> . . .
>
> That the framers of the Utah Constitution did not adopt language similar to the constitutions of Minnesota and Idaho, even though the convention had before it the constitutions of those states is evidence that a different result was intended.

Id. at 360. It concluded:

> There is not in Article X, Section 4, or elsewhere in the Constitution of Utah any express prohibition against action by the legislature respecting the University. Nor do we believe that the Constitution contains any implied restraint against such action.
>
> . . .

In summary, we simply cannot agree with the proposition that the Utah Constitution restricts the legislature's ability to enact firearms laws pertaining to the University. The plain language of article X, section 4 and this court's prior pronouncements on the issue of university governance compel the conclusion that the University is subject to legislative control, and therefore cannot enforce its firearms policy in contravention of state law.

In this case, we conclude that the legislature has not overstepped its constitutional bounds. The plain meaning of article X, section 4 of the Utah Constitution, supported by history, context, and our prior decisions, is that although the University has broad powers, it is not completely autonomous, and it is ultimately subject to legislative oversight. Policy considerations, no matter how persuasive, cannot dictate a contrary interpretation. The Utah Constitution does not grant the University authority to promulgate firearms policies in contravention of legislative enactments, and it is not our place to do so. To the extent their constituents disagree with the legislature's choice, their remedy is to express their dissatisfaction at the ballot box.

We hold that the University lacks the authority to enact firearms policies in contravention of Utah statutory law. . . .

■ DURHAM, C. J., dissenting:

. . .

Although I agree that *Board of Examiners* rejected the University's claim of absolute autonomy, I disagree that the court in that decision conclusively subjected the University to legislative control on all matters. . . . [T]he 1892 Act designated the University a "public corporation." . . . It does not necessarily follow, however, that all incorporated state universities have only nominal independent power, particularly where the university in question is provided for in the state constitution. . . . Although the language in our state's constitution varies from the language in the constitutions of Idaho, Minnesota, and Michigan, our constitution nevertheless recognizes the University's corporate powers. Article X, section 4 explicitly perpetuated these corporate powers in 1896 and thereafter confirmed them in 1987. In my view, this constitutional recognition of corporate powers raises the status of the University above that of most public corporations.

. . . The proceedings of the constitutional convention indicate that the framers of the 1896 constitution were concerned with the United States Supreme Court case of *Trustees of Dartmouth College v. Woodward*, 17 U.S. 518 (1819), which had held that a legislature may not amend a corporate charter, once granted, unless the legislature expressly retains the right to do so in the original grant. The fact that the framers of the Utah Constitution were careful to preserve the legislature's power to amend the charters of all corporations, private or municipal, except for the University's strongly suggests an intent to preserve the University's corporate powers independent of legislative control and supports my plain language interpretation of article X, section 4.

. . .

I . . . conclude that, aside from the selection of general fields of study, the power to control academic affairs on its campus is among those corporate rights and privileges perpetuated by the 1896 constitution and confirmed by its 1987 revision of article X, section 4. . . . The remaining question, therefore, is whether, as the University argues, the provisions of the University's personnel and student conduct policies that prohibit employees and students from carrying firearms on campus fall within the scope of the University's academic autonomy.

. . . Applying, as they do, only to University employees and students, and only while these individuals are on the University campus, these policies merely reflect the University's judgment on an issue that is within the scope of its academic expertise—namely, the appropriate means by which to maintain an educational environment in its classrooms and on its campus.[7]

It is significant that, even outside the context of federal "academic freedom" analysis, a number of courts have explicitly recognized that a university's academic role extends beyond the classroom itself to the maintenance of an educational atmosphere on its campus. . . . This recognition reflects the fact that a university, by its nature, is more than the sum of its classes. Its educational endeavor extends to unorganized activities and dis-

---

7. The University points out that, in the past thirty-two years, only twenty crimes involving firearms have occurred on its campus, six of which were suicides and four of which involved armed robbery of credit unions. I recognize, of course, that those who wish to carry firearms for their personal protection are concerned with defending themselves not only against attackers who wield firearms but also against those who may otherwise be able to succeed in an assault without using a firearm. However, as there is no evidence in the record demonstrating that attacks by strangers (with or without firearms) against employees or students on campus are common, and as the University's policies do allow students and employees to receive authorization to carry a firearm on an individual basis, I remain unable to conclude that the policies implicate legislative concerns regarding the best way to prevent crime. Students and employees may well have their own concerns regarding the burden University policies place on their constitutional right to bear arms. Such concerns are properly raised by individual students and employees in a claim against the University under article I, section 6.

cussion among its students and faculty in its offices, hallways, cafeterias, libraries, and open spaces on its campus. The maintenance of an appropriate atmosphere within which such activity may occur is directly related to a university's academic mission. Thus, if the University's policies are reasonably connected with its academic mission and the campus environment necessary to that mission, those policies are within its autonomous authority over academic affairs. The record in this case contains extensive evidence that practitioners and experts in higher education are convinced that a no weapons on campus policy is necessary to the educational enterprise; that evidence is uncontroverted. I therefore conclude that the University's policies governing students, faculty, and staff are within its authority to govern academic affairs.

Questions and Comments on *Shurtleff*

Who or what should determine how much autonomy a public university has? The state constitution? The Constitution of the United States? The legislature? The courts?

While the parties argued this case in state court, the University filed a federal lawsuit alleging the firearms statute violated its First and Fourteenth Amendment rights to academic freedom. After the decision by the Utah Supreme Court, the university and the state attorney general obtained permission from the federal district court to see if the issue could be resolved legislatively. University President Michael Young, who was not president of the university when the litigation began in 2001, announced that the university would seek the right to bar firearms in dormitories and stadiums on the grounds that dormitory type communal living is not the best place to have weapons—adding that it is hard to see their utility in athletic venues. President Young also stated that it is preferable to resolve differences with legislators through negotiations rather than in court. A former dean of George Washington University Law School, Young stated "I'm a lawyer, and as any sensible lawyer will tell you, court is the last place to go." Scott Jaschik, *Avoiding a Legal Shootout*, INSIDE HIGHER ED, Dec. 4, 2006, http://insidehighered.com/news/2006/12/04/utah. In the end, the legislature passed and the governor signed a revised law that guarantees students and staff the right to carry concealed firearms on campus with a permit, but allows university students to request to not live with concealed weapons holders in the residence halls. On March 12, 2007, the University's Board of Trustees voted to drop the federal lawsuit, even though the new law did not ban weapons in any parts of campus. *U Drops Its Lawsuit Over Gun Ban*, DESERT MORNING NEWS, Mar. 18, 2007, at B2.

President and Directors of Georgetown College v. District of Columbia Board of Zoning Adjustment

District of Columbia Court of Appeals, 2003.
837 A.2d 58.

■ SCHWELB, ASSOCIATE JUDGE.

.   .   .

Founded in 1789, Georgetown is the Nation's oldest Catholic and Jesuit University. Its campus comprises 104 acres within the Georgetown Historic District. Much of the campus is zoned R–3 (low-to-moderate-density residential row dwellings), but parts are zoned C–1 (commercial). To the north of the campus lie the residential neighborhoods of Burleith and Hillandale.

According to the Board [of Zoning Adjustment] as of March 2001, approximately 77% of the University's "traditional undergraduate students" were living on campus. A new 780–bed residence hall, the Southwest Quadrangle, was scheduled to be completed by the fall of 2003. In support of its proposed Campus Plan, the University represented to the BZA that at least 84% of its undergraduates would live on campus by 2010. The University proposed that the previous enrollment cap of 5627, adopted as part of the 1990 Campus Plan, be raised by 389 to 6016 students, but only after the Southwest Quadrangle was ready for occupancy.

At the proceedings before the Board, testimony or written evidence was presented on behalf of the University, the District's Office of Planning (OP), the Department of Public Works (DPW), Advisory Neighborhood Commission (ANC) 2E, and various neighbors and neighborhood groups. Much of the controversy surrounding this case involved the conduct of Georgetown undergraduates who were living off campus, especially in the Burleith and Hillandale communities.

The Board received evidence, both favorable and unfavorable, regarding the activities of Georgetown and its students in the adjoining neighborhoods. Letters supporting the position of the University referred to the contributions made by the University and its students and faculty, for example, in tutoring elementary school children, providing various types of assistance to public and private schools, teaching adult literacy and other classes, providing medical outreach services, and assisting economic and human development efforts of community organizations.

Many residents of the surrounding communities, however, complained of what they characterized as objectionable living conditions caused by students living off-campus, including frequent loud noise; excessive use of alcohol; disorderly behavior; loud late-night parties; parking violations; accumulations of trash and infestations of rats; poor maintenance of properties rented to students by absentee landlords; vandalism and destructive behavior by students, including causing damage to neighbors' houses, yards, and property; the prevalence of group houses occupied by transient students instead of permanent residents; and the overcrowding of large groups of students into single-family residences.

The Board was obviously impressed by the complaints of the neighbors. The Board found that "the number of undergraduate students at the University's campus is having an adverse impact on the surrounding neighborhoods because of the frequent occurrence of serious student misconduct off-campus and the displacement of permanent, non-student housing as a result of the lack of sufficient on-campus housing." The Board concluded that, unless preventive action was taken, "the insufficient supply of on-campus housing and the repeated occurrences of off-campus student misconduct" were "likely to exacerbate objectionable impacts on neighboring property." According to the Board, "pressures associated with the large numbers of undergraduate students threaten [the] livability and residential character" of neighborhoods adjoining Georgetown's campus. The Board noted the anticipated completion of the Southwest Quadrangle project, and welcomed the submission by the University of a new "Off–Campus Student Affairs Program"(OCSAP).[5] Nevertheless, the Board could not find "conclusively"

5. [In the OCSAP, the University promised to take certain actions to improve the relationship between its off-campus students and their neighbors. The plan included im-

that the anticipated new dormitory and implementation of the off-campus program will in fact rectify the adverse impacts described by OP, the affected ANC, and neighborhood parties in opposition.

The Board therefore ordered that "the cap on undergraduate enrollment of 5,627 adopted as part of the 1990 campus plan should be maintained in the approved 2000 campus plan."

The Board's conclusions must be sustained unless they are "arbitrary, capricious, an abuse of discretion, or otherwise not in accordance with law." D.C. Code § 2–510 (a)(3)(A) (2001). . . .

In all appeals and applications to the Board, including applications for a special exception, "the burden of proof shall rest with the appellant or applicant." The Board, as we have noted, imposed certain conditions on the Campus Plan because it could not find "conclusively" that an adverse impact on the surrounding neighborhoods could be avoided without these conditions. The Board cited no authority for a requirement of "conclusiveness," and we know of none.

. . .

> The relationship between universities and their neighbors—between Town and Gown—has been the subject of considerable controversy and litigation, and the law has evolved significantly over the years. New York (as well as other jurisdictions) have long considered religious, educational and other institutions to be "favored uses" in residential areas, allowed where other nonresidential uses are not. This approach is entirely consistent with a sort of romantic view of a traditional neighborhood, with a neighborhood park, neighborhood elementary school and two or three houses of worship all carefully integrated into an otherwise entirely residential setting.

7 PATRICK R. ROHAN, ZONING & LAND USE CONTROLS § 40.02, at 40.57 (2003) (footnotes omitted). . . . More than half a century ago, the New York Court of Appeals declared that "educational uses . . . [are] clearly in furtherance of the health, safety, morals and general welfare of the community." In *Rutgers, State University v. Piluso*, 60 N.J. 142, 286 A.2d 697, 705 (N.J. 1972), the Supreme Court of New Jersey held "that the growth and development of Rutgers, as a public university for the benefit of all the people of the state,[10] was not to be thwarted or restricted by local land use regulations and that it is immune therefrom." But romantic notions of quaintly traditional neighborhoods and the pristine purity of educational institutions have had to give

---

posing stiffer sanctions for Code of Conduct violations, providing a forum for neighbors to share grievances with the University, cooperating with local police, expanding alcohol education programs, and making public statistics regarding off-campus student conduct. Additionally, in] academic year 2004–05 (one full year after the Southwest Quad is projected to be online), the University would update the BZA on the program with identifiable goals and benchmarks to evaluate its success. This ensures that there is an opportunity for short-term review rather than asking the community or the Board to wait until the 10–year

expiration of the campus plan. At that time, the Board can impose further conditions on the University if, in its judgment, the program has not proven successful. This places the burden squarely on the University to ensure that the program it has designed works and that its relationship with the surrounding community is positively impacted as a result.

10. Georgetown, of course, is a private university, but a private institution can cause problems relating to noise, traffic, and student misbehavior just as readily as any of its "public" counterparts can.

way to the realities of the modern era, including, *inter alia*, traffic jams, trash accumulation, noise pollution, and the spirited and sometimes rowdy behavior of college students who may have celebrated with a beer or two or ten!

. . .

Condition 2 of the BZA's order provides that the University "shall not increase undergraduate enrollment above the cap of 5,627 [traditional students]." The University contends that the Board lacked legal authority to impose any cap at all. In the alternative, the University asserts that even if the BZA did possess such authority, the cap in the present case was arbitrary and capricious in light of the evidence of record. We reject the first of these contentions but discern merit in the second.

On or about August 24, 2000, the University, through its counsel, submitted to the Board the University's Proposed Findings of Fact, Conclusions of Law, and Order. The specific order that the University asked the Board to enter stated, in pertinent part, as follows:

It is ORDERED that [Georgetown's] application is GRANTED SUBJECT to the following CONDITIONS:

4. the cap on traditional undergraduate student enrollment remains at 5,627 until the Southwest Quad is brought on-line. At that time, the University may increase undergraduate enrollment to an outside cap of 6,016 (an additional 389 students) provided this increase is phased in over the remaining years of the Plan.

Notwithstanding its own proposal to the Board, the University now contends that the "number of students living in off-campus housing is not a legitimate concern for land-use regulations" and that "enrollment caps are not the province of land-use regulators."

The University relies on *Summit School v. Neugent*, 82 A.D.2d 463, 442 N.Y.S. 2d 73 (N.Y. App. Div. 2d Dep't 1981). In that case, a municipal Board of Zoning Appeals imposed a cap of 125 students on a private school as a condition of granting the school a "special use" permit. The court stated that "municipalities may place reasonable zoning restrictions upon ... uses carried on by private educational institutions," but that conditions "which may intrude upon the educational processes of the [school], as opposed to [its] use of real property, are contrary to public policy." The court went on to hold that "provisions in a special use permit which '[relate] to the total number of students ... are invalid, because they apply to details of the operation of the business and not to the zoning use of the premises.'" The court was further of the opinion that the Board's actions went beyond land use concerns and "impermissibly impinged on the details of the teaching operation of [the] school facility."

[The court held that the University's submission of a proposed order capping its enrollment precluded it from later arguing that the BZA lacked authority to impose such a cap.]

If the University was seeking a ruling that the imposition of student enrollment caps is beyond the BZA's authority, it was obliged to say so, "loudly and clearly," to the Board. Having failed to do that, it cannot, on this record, successfully argue for such a proposition in this court.

The University's 1990 Campus Plan, as approved by the BZA, contained an enrollment cap of 5627 "traditional" students. In its plan for 2000–2010, the University initially proposed an increase of 500 undergraduates to 6127, but subsequently modified its proposal (in its proposed order) to an increase of 389 and a cap of 6016. On December 5, 2000, at a public meeting, the Board voted to approve the proposed cap of 6016, conditioned upon the University's agreement to delay the increase in the cap until after the Southwest Quad was in place.

When the Board issued its written order on March 29, 2001, however, it reversed its previously announced decision to authorize a delayed increase. Instead, the Board decided to retain, presumptively until 2010, the cap of 5627 undergraduates that it had imposed as a condition of the 1990 Campus Plan. In a footnote to its order of March 29, 2001, the Board described this change as a "clarification" of its intent when it took the earlier vote. . . .

The same evidence that, in the Board's initial view, had warranted the approval of a small phased increase—an average of thirty-nine additional undergraduates per year, for ten years, totaling slightly less than one half of the capacity of the new 780–bed Southwest Quadrangle complex—was now suddenly perceived by the BZA as requiring it to proscribe any increase at all.

We find little, if any, support in the record for the finding that the modest enrollment increase initially authorized but subsequently disapproved by the Board would have contributed to or exacerbated objectionable conditions in the adjoining neighborhoods. The BZA's ultimate refusal to permit the proposed increase may have been influenced by the Board's apparent but erroneous theory that the University's showing of no obvious impact on neighboring communities must be "conclusive." . . .

. . . In their briefs, the District [the Office of Corporation Counsel, representing the BZA] and CAG [Citizens Association of Georgetown] appear to assume that because the zoning regulations require the BZA to include the "number of students" in its calculus, the freezing of the University's enrollment at a level imposed twenty years before the expiration of the current Campus Plan must necessarily be proper.

We do not agree. First, without necessarily viewing all of the court's reasoning in the *Summit School* case, 442 N.Y.S.2d at 75–79, as applicable to the District of Columbia, we are of the opinion that the imposition by the BZA of an enrollment cap at least approaches (if, indeed, it does not cross) the line between the exercise of legitimate zoning and land use authority and an *ultra vires* intrusion upon the University's educational mission. We therefore consider it imperative that, in order to justify a freeze on enrollment under the circumstances presented here, the BZA must make reasonably detailed underlying evidentiary findings in which it specifically identifies the need for continuing the 1990 cap and describes in non-conclusory terms the manner in which the retention of the cap would protect the residents of the adjoining communities.

. . .

In the present case, during the discussion of the proposed increase in the enrollment cap among the members of the Board, one member [suggested that the Board was using the enrollment cap as leverage to force the University to make concessions to the neighboring community.] [I]t is significant that the focus of these remarks was not on whether the modest proposed increase, in itself, would adversely affect the neighboring communities. Rather, it was on the use of the cap as a means by which the Board could place financial pressure on the University and could make Georgetown's "shoe pinch" until the University did what, in this Board member's view, "the community" wanted done.

But the manner in which the zoning regulations are to be enforced cannot depend even on scientifically conducted public opinion polls, and certainly not on speculation as to what some undefined "community" may find desirable. We conclude that the record lacks substantial evidence supporting the BZA's freeze of the University's enrollment, potentially until 2010, at the level set in 1990. . . .

Citizens Association of Georgetown v. D.C. Board of Zoning Adjustment

District of Columbia Court of Appeals, 2007.
925 A.2d 585.

■ WASHINGTON, CHIEF JUDGE:

. . . This matter is back before us after the BZA attempted to address the concerns raised in the original proceeding before this court. *See President & Directors of Georgetown Coll. v. District of Columbia Bd. of Zoning Adjustment,* 837 A.2d 58 (D.C.2003) ("*Georgetown I*"). In that case, we vacated the BZA's order and remanded the case for further proceedings . . . On remand, the BZA reconsidered the evidence presented and approved the Campus Plan with a revised cap and certain other conditions. Petitioner filed the instant petition for review seeking reversal of the latest BZA order approving the Campus Plan. . . .

. . .

On June 22, 2004, in light of this court's decision in *Georgetown I,* the Board held a public meeting and requested that the parties submit a list of issues to be addressed on remand. Thereafter, on October 15, 2004, the Board issued an order directing the parties to submit a proposed order either granting or denying the application in whole or in part, that included findings of fact, conclusions of law, and any proposed conditions that would mitigate any potential adverse impacts identified by the court's decision in *Georgetown I.* . . . The University's proposed order included a Revised Condition 2, setting an enrollment cap of 6,016 full-time students. The proposed order made clear that the enrollment cap proposed by the University was arrived at by averaging the fall and spring traditional undergraduate numbers. . . .

. . . [O]n June 7, 2005, the Board issued its final order approving the Revised Campus Plan. That plan included the University's Revised Condition 2, increasing the enrollment Cap to 6,016. In addition, the Revised Campus Plan eliminated certain conditions that were included in the Original Campus Plan and in the proposed orders submitted by both the CAG and the University. . . .

The CAG contends (1) that the BZA erred when it allowed the University to average its fall and spring semester enrollment to determine compliance with the cap on undergraduate enrollment contained in the 2000–2010

Campus Plan ...; and (2) that the BZA erred when it eliminated uncontested provisions from the Original Campus Plan Order.

In light of our remand order in *Georgetown I,* and after consideration of the original record as it existed in 2001, the Board concluded that the increase of the University's enrollment cap to 6,016, which was calculated as an average over the fall and spring semesters of the academic year, would not become objectionable to neighboring property or have an adverse impact on the neighboring property. In reaching its determination, the Board relied on several factors, including evidence that the completion of the Southwest Quadrangle project would create housing for 84 percent of the traditional undergraduate population, and that the University had implemented new measures and enhanced existing programs to prevent and mitigate the impacts of any off-campus student misconduct in the neighborhoods surrounding the campus. The CAG now takes issue with the Board's determination to increase the enrollment cap, but more vehemently challenges the Board's decision to set a student enrollment cap based on an average of the University's full-time undergraduate enrollment for the fall and spring semesters. According to the CAG, the increase in the enrollment cap along with the approval of the University's averaging methodology, allows the University to "almost double" the number of undergraduate students enrolled in the fall semester. In essence, by permitting averaging, the University can increase its undergraduate student enrollment in the fall semester based on a lower enrollment in the spring semester, without exceeding its enrollment cap.

. . .

Given the substantial evidence in the record regarding the revised cap and the use of averaging as a methodology for calculating student enrollment caps, we see no basis to disturb the BZA's decision in this regard.

Alternatively, the CAG contends that the Board's decision to permit the University to average its fall and spring enrollment figures to determine an appropriate enrollment cap is arbitrary and capricious and thus, must be overturned. In essence, the CAG complains that the type of enrollment cap included in the Revised Campus Plan is not a true enrollment cap because it does not set a finite limit on the number of students that the University can enroll at any one time. While that is certainly another way of defining an enrollment cap, we are not persuaded that the enrollment cap imposed here does not flow rationally from the evidence presented or is otherwise unlawful. As we understand it, the main purpose of including an enrollment cap on the number of students a college or university can enroll as part of a campus plan is to limit the adverse impact the student population will have on the surrounding community. While we certainly appreciate why some limitation on enrollment has to be set, we see no reason why those limits have to be accomplished through the use of a hard cap based on a snapshot in time. In this case, the University explained clearly why it favored the setting of a cap based on the fluctuation it experiences in its seasonal enrollment figures. The Board also heard evidence from the CAG and the ANC about the impact that the University's average number of traditional full-time students would have on the community and decided that the impacts were not likely to become objectionable or adversely affect the use of the neighboring property. In other words, the Board concluded that while there may be some difference in the enrollment numbers in the fall and spring, the differences between a hard enrollment cap and the blended enrollment cap advocated by the University would not have an adverse impact on the surrounding community. Because the Board's decision in this regard seems neither arbitrary nor capricious, and "rationally flow[s] from findings of fact supported by substantial evidence in the record as a whole," we see no basis to disturb the Board's ruling.

Finally, the CAG contends that despite its findings to the contrary, the Board failed to consider how the increase in the enrollment cap would affect the surrounding community. The Board's findings of fact, however, indicate otherwise. With respect to the effects of averaging on the community, the Board found that

> [The University's] proposal to increase its enrollment cap on the number of traditional undergraduate students, calculated as an *average* over the Fall and Spring semesters of the academic year, *is not likely to become objectionable to the neighboring property* or to adversely affect the use of neighboring property. After completion of the new Southwest Quadrangle project, the University will have more than 5,000 beds on campus, a number sufficient to house 84 percent of the traditional undergraduate population. The University has implemented new measures and enhanced existing programs that will help to prevent and mitigate the impacts of any student misconduct off-campus in the neighborhood abutting the campus. (Emphasis added).

Thus, the record indicates that the Board considered how the increase in the enrollment cap would affect the neighboring property. Additionally, the Board's findings also reflect that it gave "great weight" to the ANC's requirement that the University maintain 85% of its undergraduate student population on-campus after completion of the Southwest Quadrangle project. Specifically, the ANC "conditioned its approval of the proposed [C]ampus [P]lan" on the University's recognition and BZA's support that "measures be taken to strengthen the off-campus affairs program." The Board's consideration of the ANC's requirements is also reflected in its order on remand noting that it gave "great weight" to the ANC. As a result, we are satisfied that the Board's decision responded to and accorded "great weight" to ANC's concerns. Finally, because there is evidence in the record to support the Board's findings and the Board's conclusions flow rationally from those factual findings, we hold that the Board did not err in approving Revised Condition 2 of the Campus Plan.

The CAG argues that the Board acted in an arbitrary and capricious manner when it omitted certain conditions that were included both in the Original Campus Plan and the proposed orders of the University and the CAG. We agree. . . . This court is troubled by the fact that the Board found the uncontested conditions necessary and supported by substantial evidence in the Original Campus Plan, but decided to eliminate them without explanation on remand. We find that the Board's failure to give any findings or reasons for the omission of the uncontested conditions to be arbitrary and capricious.

. . .

Accordingly, we conclude that there is substantial evidence in the record to support the BZA's decision capping full-time student enrollment based on averaging the number of full-time students enrolled during the fall and spring semesters, and that averaging for purposes of establishing an enrollment cap flows rationally from the BZA's findings. Thus, we affirm the BZA order to the extent the parties have challenged that provision of the order. However, we again remand the case back to the BZA for an explanation as to why several uncontested provisions included in the Original Campus Plan were not included in the Revised Campus Plan.

Questions and Comments on *Georgetown v. Board of Zoning Adjustment* and *Citizens Ass'n of Georgetown v. Board of Zoning Adjustment*

How much say should the local community have in limiting the growth of a private university? How should the views of the community be measured? By scientifically conducted public opinion polls? By the views expressed by those neighbors who attend civic board meetings? What weight, if any, should be given to the views of students?

CHAPTER 5

FINANCING HIGHER EDUCATION

In early 2000, when the board of trustees of Ursinus College, a small, liberal arts institution in the eastern Pennsylvania countryside, raised its tuition and fees 17.6 percent to $23,460, Ursinus received nearly 200 more applications than it had received the year before. Within four years, the size of the freshman class had risen by thirty-five percent to 454 students.[a] The experience of Ursinus demonstrates that, in the unusual economics of higher education, high tuition is often taken as an indicator of quality.

Although high tuition would seem to be a barrier to students from low-income families, that barrier can be reduced, if not eliminated, by a generous financial aid policy. Ursinus, for example, increased its student aid by nearly twenty percent when it raised tuition, so that a majority of its students now pay less than half full tuition.[b]

To complicate matters, the best-endowed schools spend more per student than is covered by the full tuition charged. In effect these institutions "lose" money on every student they admit. What kind of business model is this? How are the budgets of such schools balanced? What implications does this approach to budgeting have for admissions?

When the first public colleges and universities opened, state legislatures saw them as a way to open access to higher education to all qualified applicants without regard to family income. Over the years, however, the portion of the budgets of public universities has declined. Only fifteen percent of the budget of the University of California at Los Angeles comes from the state. Less than ten percent of the University of Colorado does.

Some critics have complained that public institutions of higher education have further undermined their mission of broad access by raising tuition in their quest to emulate the elite, private schools. Others suggest that public colleges and universities should raise their tuition even closer to the level of private schools and use more of that revenue to provide generous financial aid for high need students. Who is right?

A. TUITION AND PUBLIC SUBSIDIES

Kashmiri v. Regents of the University of California

California Court of Appeal, First District, 2007.
156 Cal.App.4th 809, 67 Cal.Rptr.3d 635, *rev. den.* 2008 Cal. LEXIS 891 (Jan. 23, 2008).

■ LAMBDEN, J.

The Regents set and receive the educational fees for all students attending the University of California (UC). On January 21, 1994, the

---

a. Jonathan D. Glater & Alan Finder, *In Tuition Game, Popularity Rises with Price*, N.Y. TIMES, Dec. 12, 2006, at A1.

b. *Id.*

Regents approved a fee policy that included an educational fee for all UC students and a professional degree fee (PDF) for some UC graduate students.

. . .

[In late 2002, faced with a budget crisis, the Regents initiated a series of increases in ... both the educational fee and PDF. Affected students brought suit for breach of contract.

In adopting the PDF, the Regents stated that that fee should "remain the same for each student for the duration of his or her enrollment in the professional degree program, with increases in the fee applicable to new students only, until such time as the fee for each professional program reaches approximately the average of fees charged for that program by comparable high-quality institutions across the nation." Various university publications, including its website, budget documents, and Boalt Hall School of Law catalogues stated that the PDF would remain constant for individual students during their time at the university and any PDF increases would apply only to incoming students. These statements were sometimes accompanied by additional statements that fees generally were subject to change and that the PDF was only a part of the total fees.

The Regents increased the PDF three times between 1994 and the 2002–2003 academic year, each time applying the increase only to incoming (but not continuing) professional students. In late December 2002, the Regents increased the Spring 2003 PDF for all professional students by between $150 and $400, varying by field of study. For the 2003–2004 academic year, the PDF would increase to a flat rate (between $2,925 and $9,473) for each field of study, regardless of when individual students enrolled, and increase again in each of the next two academic years.

All UC students pay the "educational fee." The Regents voted to increase the educational fee by $135 on December 16, 2002. The University's billing statements for the Spring 2003 term (citing the previous rate) had been mailed over the previous month. Although University press releases had warned of impending fee increases and, in January 2003, the University website stated the likelihood of fee increases, "[n]o [S]pring 2003 student received individualized notice of an increase prior to receiving the original bill ..., and some students did not receive any notification about the increase until after they started spring classes." The University did, however, provide notice of the increase by e-mail, and later in written form, between December 18 and February 5.

Similarly, UC Berkeley and UCLA students were billed in February for the Summer 2003 term, and the Regents voted in May to increase their educational fees. All in-state students for the Summer term received individualized notice of the increase before the deadline for withdrawing from summer courses.

On July 24, 2003, eight students [respondents], on behalf of three subclasses of UC students, sued the University for breach of contract. The first subclass consisted of professional students enrolled prior to the December 2002 PDF increase who subsequently paid the increased PDF. The second "spring 2003" subclass consisted of students who were billed for their

Spring 2003 educational fee or PDF prior to receiving individualized notice of and being charged the increased rate. The third "summer 2003" subclass consisted of students billed for their Summer 2003 fees prior to receiving individualized notice of and being charged the increased rate.]

In the summer of 2004, respondents and the Regents filed cross-motions for summary judgment. . . .

The trial court denied both summary judgment motions on January 24, 2005. . . .

    . . .

The parties entered into stipulations preserving the Regents' legal positions, but permitting the superior court to resolve the case without trial. . . .

On March 2, 2006, the trial court issued its statement of decision granting respondents' motion for summary judgment. . . .

    . . .

Accordingly, the court awarded the professional student subclass $23,901,219 ($34,287,787 less $10,386,568 [the amount grant awards increased during the contested period]), plus prejudgment interest. It gave the spring 2003 student subclass the amount of $2,383,587 ($3,972,645 less $1,589,058), plus prejudgment interest. The summer 2003 student subclass received $1,808,454 ($2,712,681 less $904,227), plus prejudgment interest.

The court concluded that about 1,000 members of the professional student subclass had not yet graduated and it permanently enjoined the University from charging members of the professional student subclass any PDF greater than the amount charged when these students first enrolled in their professional degree program.

The Regents filed a timely notice of appeal.

    . . .

The court in *Zumbrun v. University of Southern California* (1972) 25 Cal. App. 3d 1, 10 [101 Cal.Rptr. 499] (*Zumbrun*) held that the basic legal relationship between a student and a private university is contractual in nature. Although *Zumbrun* concerned a private university, other courts have recognized that a contractual relationship applies equally to state universities. . . .

    . . .

Although courts have characterized the relationship between the student and educational institution as contractual, they have recognized that contract law should not be strictly applied. . . . Universities are entitled to some leeway in modifying their programs from time to time to exercise their educational responsibility properly. . . .

The University insists that the lower court failed to apply this rule of "flexibility" when applying contract law to the present situation. We agree with the University that it is well settled that contract law is not always rigidly applied, especially in actions challenging the academic decision of a university or a student's qualifications for a degree. "There is a widely accepted rule of judicial nonintervention into the academic affairs of schools." *Paulsen v.*

Golden Gate University (1979) 25 Cal.3d 803, 808 [159 Cal.Rptr. 858, 602 P.2d 778] (*Paulsen*).

Our Supreme Court in *Paulsen* applied contract law, although it noted that contract was not always the most apt description of the relationship between the student and educational institution. The court denied a student's breach of contract claim based on the law school's refusal to provide him a degree. The court explained: "[A]fter [the student's] academic disqualification [the law school] agreed to allow him to enroll in additional courses only on the express condition that he would *not* be eligible for a degree. Any contract between the parties would therefore have included that condition, and by its terms would have precluded awarding Paulsen a degree under any circumstances."

The University maintains that no case rejects "the rule of flexibility in a fee case, or states that it applies only to academic matters."

The University, however, ignores the types of cases that have applied the rule of flexibility to the relationship of the student and educational institution. Courts have applied contract law flexibly to actions involving academic and disciplinary decisions by educational institutions because of the lack of a satisfactory standard of care by which to evaluate these decisions. . . . Courts have, however, not been hesitant to apply contract law when the educational institution makes a specific promise to provide an educational service, such as a failure to offer any classes or a failure to deliver a promised number of hours of instruction. Courts have uniformly held that a contract between an educational institution and a student "confers duties upon both parties which cannot be arbitrarily disregarded and may be judicially enforced." A breach of contract action regarding a *specific* promise about the fee to be charged is similar to a breach of contract action based on the failure to provide a specifically promised educational service.

The present action does not involve what is essentially an educational malpractice claim or a decision that involves disciplinary discretion. Moreover, it does not involve a general statement or expectation regarding the PDF. "Ruling on this [fee dispute] would not require an inquiry into the nuances of educational processes and theories, but rather an objective assessment" of the University's performance of its promise. Accordingly, we conclude that contract law applies to the students' claims regarding the increased fees.

. . .

. . . We agree that educational institutions retain the right to raise the fees when that is specified in their catalogues or other publications as long as the increase is reasonable and does not violate any duty of good faith and fair dealing.

The question presented here, however, is not whether the University can retain the right to increase the fees. The pivotal question is whether the statements in the catalogues and on the University's Web site not to raise the PDF for continuing students became a term of the implied-in-fact contract between the professional student subclass and the University. . . .

. . .

In the present case, the University's statement promising not to raise the PDF is not qualified by any language suggesting that this was merely an expectation. The promise regarding the PDF is not a general statement or declaration in the catalogue. Rather, it is a specific promise. The promise is that increases to the PDF "apply to new students only. The Fee will remain the same for each student for the duration of his or her enrollment in the professional degree program."

Since the language regarding the PDF in the catalogues and on the Web site is unequivocal, the reasonable expectation of the parties would be that once the student enrolls in the University and the University accepts his or her payment of the PDF, the PDF will remain the same for the duration of the student's enrollment in that program. It is reasonable that an institution of higher education would promise not to increase the PDF for continuing students in exchange for the student's promise to attend that institution.

Accordingly, we conclude that it was reasonable for students to believe that the general statement that fees could be changed did not apply to the PDF, which, according to the statements set forth by the University, would remain the same for the duration of that student's enrollment in the professional program.

. . .

. . . [T]o the extent the University is arguing that the fiscal crisis excused its performance on the promise not to raise the PDF, we reject this contention. The University argues that even *Zumbrun* establishes that courts interpret seemingly absolute promises to be limited by the governmental power that reasonable students would expect a university to reserve. Although the *Zumbrun* court held that the student had alleged a breach of contract claim when the professor's protest resulted in canceling a number of classes, the court noted in a footnote that its decision did not "foreclose the right of university administrators or faculty members to take appropriate action, including the suspension or cancellation of classes, when faced with demonstrations or threats of demonstrations on campus . . . which present actual danger to lives or property."

Even if we were to agree that *Zumbrun* allows for an emergency exception to an absolute promise by the educational institution, the University has failed to establish an emergency exception amounting to impossibility of performance in the present case. Although the University likens its fiscal crisis to an emergency presenting an "actual danger to lives or property," economic crises do not excuse performance on a contract. "Facts which may make performance more difficult or costly than contemplated when the agreement was executed do not constitute impossibility." *Glendale Fed. Sav. & Loan Assn. v. Marina View Heights Dev. Co.* (1977) 66 Cal.App. 3d 101, 154 [135 Cal.Rptr. 802]. Thus, the fiscal problems experienced by the University did not excuse its performance.

The University's Web site and catalogues last contained the promise not to raise the PDF for continuing students for the 2002–2003 academic year. Thereafter, the promise no longer appeared on the Web site or in catalogues. The University maintains that each term in which the student enrolls constitutes a new contract. Therefore, according to the University, the PDF statement did not apply to the subsequent academic years, such as the academic year of 2003–2004. Consequently, the University asserts, even if it did breach the students' contract when it increased the PDF in the spring of 2003, the subsequent increases did not constitute a breach of contract claim.

The University is again attempting to eschew the effect of the clear language of its promise on its Web site and in the catalogues. The University's promise was not limited to the academic year of the catalogue. Rather, the express language of the promise stated that continuing students would not have to pay an increased PDF for the duration of their enrollment in the professional program. As with any contract, the parties' explicit terms and intentions control.

The contractual relationship between students and educational institutions can encompass promises that expire at the end of the term and other promises that extend throughout the student's enrollment in the program. When an institution of higher learning makes a promise that extends for the entire length of a student's enrollment in the institution or program, courts have not limited the agreement to a single term or semester.

. . .

Students at UC presumably made choices about which professional program to attend based on the University's promises about fees. We will not rewrite the promise not to increase the PDF for the duration of the student's enrollment in the program to a promise not to raise it for that academic term.

For all the foregoing reasons, we reject the University's argument that the students did not have a reasonable expectation that the PDF would not be increased for the duration of their enrollment in their professional program.

Questions and Comments on *Kashmiri*

1. The *Kashmiri* court applied contract law to the students' claims. What were the doctrinal alternatives? The court noted that the *Kashmiri* case did not involve educational malpractice, disciplinary discretion, or the parties' general statements and expectations. What law would apply in a case that did touch upon these issues? Does the opinion suggest that some university decisions are—within certain bounds—not reviewable by courts?

2. On January 23, 2008, the Supreme Court of California declined to review the decision of the Court of Appeal in *Kashmiri*. The University will have to pay some $40 million in refunds; it is likely they will have to raise fees for new students to pay the refunds. Bob Egelko, *UC Ordered to Give Students Partial Refunds*, SAN FRANCISCO CHRON., Jan. 24, 2008 at B1.

Notes on Access to Public Universities

1. Albert Carnesale, former Chancellor of the University of California at Los Angeles, has cautioned that the growing disparities between the financial resources of private and public universities are creating inequities that could have "damaging repercussions" not only for social mobility, but for our ability to compete internationally:

> From 2002 to 2005 alone, state governments reduced higher-education appropriations from $63.65 to $60.29 billion—a cut of almost 10 percent after inflation. The result has been to force public institutions to be more dependent on tuition and other sources of funds. For example, only about 15 percent of the University of California at Los Angeles's budget now comes from the state, as does just 9 percent of the University of Colorado System's.

Albert Carnesale, *The Private–Public Gap in Higher Education*, CHRON. HIGHER EDUC., Jan. 6, 2006, at B20. The resource gap has made it harder to recruit and retain top graduate students and faculty members. Carnesale labels it "wishful thinking" to expect states to close the resource gap.

One alternative is to rely more on out-of-state students. The universities of Michigan and Virginia both enroll about forty percent of their undergraduates from out of state, and the out-of-state students pay more than three times as much as state residents. The problem with that model is that is reduces spaces available for in-state students.

Carnesale recommends instead a "higher fee, higher aid" approach, under which public universities would both receive state support and charge higher fees, but still less than the fees charged by private universities. The fee increase would be used to subsidize state students in the form of need-based aid; that is, the largest subsidies would go the poorest students. He projects that a high-income family in California now pays only about $7000 per year to send a son or daughter to UCLA, less than one-fourth of what they would pay at comparable private universities. If UCLA's tuition increased by $7000 they would still be paying less than half the tuition charged by competitive private institutions. Do you agree with his recommendation?

Some public universities are beginning to offer more need-based aid. The Carolina Covenant at the University of North Carolina at Chapel Hill was started in 2004. It guarantees low-income students enough aid to graduate debt-free. In 2006, about eight percent of the freshman class qualified. The University of Virginia, the University of Washington, and the University of Florida have recently begun similar programs. Tamar Lewin, *Public Universities Vie to Join the Top 10 in Academic Rankings*, N.Y. TIMES, Dec. 20, 2006, at A20.

On the other hand, Danette Gerald and Kati Haycock report that in 2003 the nation's fifty leading public universities spent $257 million on financial aid for students from families that earn more than $100,000 per year, but only $171 million on students from families who earn less than $20,000 per year. DANETTE GERALD & KATI HAYCOCK, EDUCATION TRUST, ENGINES OF INEQUALITY: DIMINISHING EQUITY IN THE NATION'S PREMIER PUBLIC UNIVERSITIES 4 (2006). In only eight years, spending on financial aid for students from high income families increased by $207 million compared to an increase of only $75 million in aid to students from families making $40,000 or less. *Id.*

2. James Garland, the president of Miami University of Ohio, contends that state higher education budgets are not efficiently targeted:

> By way of comparison, consider the food stamp program, which in 2004 paid out $27 billion directly to 24 million low income Americans. Imagine if there were, in its place, a food subsidy program by which the government paid that $27 billion directly to supermarkets. Under such a program needy families would benefit little, because most of the savings would be passed on to customers who didn't need help. That would be an inefficient use of public money. But that is precisely what happens in public higher education.

James C. Garland, *How to Put College Back Within Reach*, WASH. POST, Dec. 30, 2005 at A27. He recommends that states phase out their tuition subsidy to public schools and replace them with scholarships for middle and low income students to attend any accredited four year college in the state, public or private. He the thinks the increased competition would force campuses to be more efficient. What do you think of his proposal?

3. The federal government for the first time in history has surpassed state governments as the primary financial supporter of higher education. Current federal policies provide $61 billion in loans, $18 billion in direct student-aid grants, and $8 billion in tax support—for a total of more than $90 billion—to higher education. All the states combined provide about $74 billion, of which about $7 billion is for financial aid. F. King Alexander, *The States Failure to Support Higher Education*, CHRON. HIGHER EDUC., June 30, 2006, at B16.

Kit Lively, A Close Look at How Duke U. Sets Tuition and Spends Money

CHRON. HIGHER EDUC., May 30, 1997, at A12.

John A. Koskinen remembers that tuition stayed at about $650 for each of the four years he attended Duke University. He graduated in 1961.

The Class of 1997 is paying $19,360 for tuition this year.... Their total tab for a bachelor's degree, including room and board, will be just under $100,000.

Mr. Koskinen, chairman of Duke's Board of Trustees, worries that the university's tuition will scare middle-class students. Still, he considers Duke a good buy. Premier colleges provide an education that is worth much more than the tuition students pay, he and other officials here say.

. . .

A lot of families are willing to find the money for expensive colleges.... But as tuition, fees, room, and board approach $30,000 a year at top private colleges, the public is asking some hard questions: Why does tuition keep rising faster than the rate of inflation? How much longer can elite colleges afford to provide financial aid to all students who need it? Would quality suffer if tuition increases slowed to the rate of inflation or below?

. . .

Duke, founded in a log building in 1839, became Trinity College in 1859 and was renamed in 1924 for James B. Duke, who made it the principal beneficiary of his family's endowment. The university's ascent to the top of national rankings has occurred pretty much in the past few decades....

Duke put itself on the map by aggressively and strategically hiring distinguished faculty members in selected fields, and by making a point of having more senior professors teach undergraduates. Tuition increases were used to pay for many of the costs, in part because Duke's endowment is dwarfed by those of the institutions against which it found itself competing.

In 1996, the endowment was $966.7 million, which is big compared to most colleges. But Harvard University's is $8.8 billion and Yale University's is $4.9 billion. Duke's endowment per student—$87,537—was lower than those of all but one of the 17 competitive private research universities to which it compares itself.

These institutions aren't representative of most colleges. They educate only 1.6 per cent of all American students, and their average tuition and fees this year amounted to $20,637. Duke's price, with fees, comes to $21,041. Only about 60 of the country's 3,700 colleges charge more than $20,000 in tuition and fees.

But however unrepresentative these colleges and universities may be, they define for many Americans—including many policy makers—the type of higher education they want their children to receive.

. . .

When higher-education experts try to explain why tuition is five times what it was 20 years ago at universities like Duke, they offer different reasons for the increases dating from different periods. During the late 1970s and early '80s, inflation was the primary culprit, perhaps exacerbated by a poor job by federal economic planners and college budget officers of anticipating the inflation.

Another cause, college officials often say, is that many core expenses, such as libraries, computers, and salaries, especially for faculty members, rise faster than the rate of inflation.

"It is just a fact," says Nannerl O. Keohane, Duke's president. "You cannot have a faculty and a highly skilled professional set of people working here who will be content to have their salaries go up every year by the rate of inflation."

"Universities have a built-in driver that most corporate entities don't have," she adds. "Most of your budget is payroll—a payroll of people who are expecting some degree of professional advancement."

. . .

Research universities get money from several sources, including private gifts, endowment income, grants, contracts, and, of course, tuition. Duke officials stress that they don't automatically raise tuition when other revenues come in lower than expected. For example, they say, when the recovery of indirect costs on federal research grants last year was about $1 million less than expected, the college of arts and sciences absorbed the loss by filling fewer faculty vacancies than planned.

The trustees' guideline for tuition increases is the Consumer Price Index plus 2 percentage points. Mr. Koskinen, the trustees' chairman . . . says the board has discussed using a lower rate, or some years not raising tuition at all.

This would be a powerful signal that Duke was trying to operate efficiently, he says. It would also be expensive. Forgoing a $1,000 tuition increase would cost about $6 million a year, he says. Duke would need about $150 million more in its endowment to generate income of equal value.

Duke officials maintain that the university is already pretty lean from its years of heightening its academic standing despite relatively modest resources. Still, it's in a competitive market. Its faculty salaries for 1995–96 ranked near the top, from the 80th to 95th percentiles among public and private universities that grant doctorates. Also that year, by Duke's own calculations, it spent almost $4,000 per student on shared central support costs, a broad category that includes general administration, personnel, and subsidies for the Duke Gardens and Chapel. . . .

An independent accountant who is familiar with higher-education finance . . . says the university appears to operate as efficiently as its peers do. The accountant, Karl R. Sening, a partner in the Washington office of Coopers & Lybrand whose clients include several private colleges, says Duke might lower its costs if it "radically changed" the curriculum or the way it delivers education. "But then Duke would not be the institution I think strategically they want to become," he adds.

Most schools are trying to cut costs. However, they all must provide state-of-the-art facilities to attract students. "Wiring the campus for the

Internet has been a very common project," Mr. Sening says. "It seems like they all feel like they need to keep up with the Joneses to stay competitive. Buildings and maintenance are another area. I have seen instances where the state-of-the-art buildings and grounds of a college can significantly impact a student's decision to go."

Duke, like most other private institutions in these days of public scrutiny, does have plans to trim costs. Operations in purchasing and personnel are being streamlined to save an eventual $3 million to $4 million a year. And most administrative offices will not be allowed to grow next year. . . .

Duke has had two major tuition increases in the past decade, one in 1988–89 and one in 1994–95. Both times, its tuition had drifted to the middle of the group of institutions to which it compares itself.

In each case, the trustees split tuition into two levels—one for continuing students and one for new freshmen. Each time, the bigger increase—19.5 per cent in 1988–89—set a new base for freshmen and all classes after them. Continuing students were charged a smaller increase—6 per cent in 1988–89. In subsequent years, tuition rose at the same rate for both groups.

The two-level approach for major increases was Mr. Koskinen's idea. He had worried that large annual increases made it hard for families to plan.

. . .

Trustees earmarked both increases for academic goals that the administration considered most important. With the first increase, the administration proposed hiring faculty members who had already earned academic respect elsewhere, and reducing the number of undergraduate classes taught by graduate students. Because the increased revenues would be limited, many of the new hires would be in such areas as the humanities, where Duke already was strong—and where the university could hire more people with less money because they wouldn't require expensive scientific laboratories.

The first increase raised $8.3 million over four years. Half of the money paid for hiring 52 faculty members, with the biggest gains being in English, history, literature, political science, and Romance languages. The new hires also lowered Duke's student-faculty ratio, making it more competitive with comparable institutions.

The rest of the money went for financial aid, equipment, facilities, and reduced teaching loads for graduate students.

When the trustees approved the second major tuition increase, in 1993, administrators again had an eye on the competition. Duke lagged behind some of the pack in its computing capabilities. Administrators also wanted to renovate classrooms, buy basic laboratory equipment for undergraduates, and provide more sophisticated scientific equipment for new faculty members. The increase, which began in 1994–95, is projected to raise a total of $6.7–million by next year, when it is fully phased in.

Last year, 17 classrooms got new lighting, seating, computer wiring, and acoustics. Tuition revenues also are paying to install multimedia classrooms and computer facilities for teaching calculus.

Officials see a direct connection between the investments financed by the tuition increases and the university's rise in academic prominence. Duke had fared respectably in the National Research Council's 1982 national rankings of graduate programs, with programs in 12 disciplines ranked among the top 25 in the country. None, however, were in the top 5. In 1993, when the

N.R.C. repeated the survey, 20 Duke programs were ranked in the top 25, and 8 were in the top 5. The humanities fared particularly well: The Duke programs earning top–5 rankings included English, French, comparative literature, and Spanish.

Duke has also become more popular and more competitive. The number of applicants grew from 10,296 in 1983, the year before it was proclaimed a "hot college" by The New York Times Magazine, to 13,585 in 1996, an increase of 32 per cent. The proportion of Duke freshmen in the top 10 per cent of their high-school classes is expected to be 87 per cent next fall, up from 76 per cent in 1980.

Meanwhile, the proportion of freshmen from minority groups increased from 8.6 per cent in 1984 to 27.7 in 1996. The proportion of black students increased from 3.7 per cent to 7.7 per cent during that period.

.   .   .

Financial aid is hugely expensive. In 1995–96, Duke spent $22.6 million of its own money on need-based aid for undergraduates, up from $3.6 million in 1984–85. In contrast, the amount Duke spent on merit aid from internal sources grew only from $1.06 million to $2.1 million over that period. (Neither category includes athletic scholarships.)

Despite the expense, Duke has never seriously considered dropping need-blind admissions, officials say. Keeping it, as far as Dr. Keohane is concerned, "says something about the moral commitment of a university—if it can afford it."

Need-blind admissions also enable the university to say it admits students based on merit instead of wealth, an important point in asserting its academic reputation.

In fact, Dr. Keohane says, the three kinds of aid contribute to Duke's image as a place that takes academics, athletics, and educational opportunity seriously. "We would be a different place if we stopped doing any of the three," she says.

.   .   .

Jane and Warren Shapiro, of Long Island, are paying for one daughter at Duke and for her sister at Washington University (Mo.). They are happy with both institutions, but they wonder how carefully such wealthy research universities watch spending.

"We think things could be run more efficiently in higher education," Ms. Shapiro says. "The general complaint, if you ask other parents, is that when you're working five days a week, eight hours a day, you can't understand why a professor can't work a few more hours and still do research and teach."

She and her husband add that they are somewhat bothered that some of their tuition dollars pay for financial aid instead of academic programs. "We are subsidizing a lot of other students who couldn't otherwise come to Duke," Ms. Shapiro says.

Duke officials argue that every student there gets a subsidy, because tuition doesn't come close to covering the university's expenditures for undergraduate education. Officials estimate that in 1995–96, the cost per undergraduate in arts and sciences averaged about $30,355, excluding room, board, and university spending on financial aid. Tuition that year averaged $18,950 for new and continuing students.

Duke's Estimate of the Cost to Educate an Undergraduate, 1995–96

Function	Cost per Student
Education expenses, including salaries of faculty and staff members, computing, supplies, telephones, and other operating costs	$10,499
Shared central support costs, including general administration, accounting, personnel, and subsidies for the Duke Chapel and Duke Forest	3,922
Academic support costs, such as financial-aid offices, libraries, central computing, and undergraduate admissions	2,251
Costs for activities like student affairs, housing and career services; operating costs for arts-and-sciences facilities	3,025
Positions and programs financed through gifts and endowment income	2,673
Special projects financed by president and provost	352
Estimated annual value of campus building usage[1]	7,017
Estimated annual value of library collections[2]	616
TOTAL	**$30,355**
Tuition* (Weighted average of tuitions charged to undergraduates)	$18,950
Subsidy per student	11,405
Tuition as a percentage of costs	62.4%

Note: These calculations cover undergraduates in the college of arts and sciences and exclude financial aid, room, board, and the direct and indirect costs of sponsored research. The categories are derived from the university's budget.

1. "Estimated annual value of campus building usage" is equal to 5.5% of the net facilities replacement value (replacement value less deferred maintenance) allocated to the college of arts and sciences based on its enrollment. If the value of the facilities was invested in the endowment instead, it would produce this amount of income per student.

2. "Estimated annual value of library collections" applies the same calculations as for building usage to the insured value of the library collections.

Note on the Economics of Higher Education

The Duke figures indicate that even a student paying full tuition was receiving an implicit scholarship of more than $11,000 every year. Does this mean that students with a choice should enroll in the best endowed college or university to which they are accepted? Does the total size of the endowment matter more or less than endowment per student? Not surprisingly there is a correlation between endowment size and various rankings of quality, although it is not absolute.

Largest Endowment per Student, 2007
Private Institutions

	Endowment	Enrollment	Endowment per student
Rockefeller University	$2,145,203,000	197	$10,889.355
Princeton University	$15,787,200,000	7085	$2,228,257
Yale University	$22,530,200,000	11,358	$1,983,641
Harvard University	$34,634,906,000	19,514	$1,774,875
Princeton Theological Seminary	$1,108,515,000	635	$1,745,693
Franklin W. Olin College of Engineering	$482,662,000	296	$1,630,615
Stanford University	$17,164,836,000	14,890	$1,152,776
Pomona College	$1,760,902,000	1,531	$1,150,165
Grinnell College	$1, 718,313,000	1,570	$1,094,467
Curtis Institute of Music	$182,248,000	167	$1,091,305
Amherst College	$1,662,377,000	1,656	$1,003,851
Bryn Athyn College of the New Church	$364,358,000	363	$1,003,741
Swarthmore College	$1,441,232,000	1,479	$974,464
Massachusetts Institute of Technology	$9,980,410,000	10,250	$973,699
Rice University	$4,669,544,000	4,932	$946,785
Williams College	$1,892,055,000	2,027	$933,426
Baylor College of Medicine	1,278,011,000	1,398	$914,171
California Institute of Technology	$1,860,052,000	2,086	$891,684
Principia Corporation	$776,864,000	1,027	$756,440
Wellesley College	$1,656,565,000	2,237	$740,530

**Largest Endowment per Student 2007
Public Institutions**

	Endowment	Enrollment	Endowment per student
VMI Foundation, Inc.	$394,848,000	1,265	$312,133
Oregon Health Sciences Foundation	$446,634,000	2,144	$208,318
University of Virginia	$4,370,209,000	21,849	$200,019
University of Michigan	$7,089,830,000	48,703	$145,573
University of Texas System	$15,613,672,000	139,689	$111,775
University of California at San Francisco Foundation	$470,568,000	4,326	$108,777
University of Delaware	$1,397,492,000	15,278	$91,471
College of William and Mary and Foundations	$585,904,000	7,336	$79,867
Texas A & M University System and Foundations	$6,590,300,000	84,212	$78,258
University of North Carolina at Chapel Hill and Foundation	$2,164,444,000	27,717	$78,091
Georgia Tech Foundation	$1,281,162,000	17,027	$75,243
University of Pittsburgh	$2,254,379,000	30,301	$74,399
Citadel	$216,214,000	3,015	$71,713

Source: Largest Endowments Per Student, 55 CHRON. HIGHER EDUC. Aug. 29, 2008, at 29.

The budget is balanced each year at schools like Duke by payout from the endowment and annual gifts from alumni and other donors. From Duke's perspective, when they admit a class of students, they are making a prediction that many of them will be financially able to provide future endowment or annual gifts to enable the University to continue to charge less tuition than it costs to educate students who pay "full" tuition. Of course, for this approach to budgeting to work, alumni must be willing, as well as able, to make gifts to their alma mater. One benefit is that the university and students share an interest in preparing them for a successful career.

In 1965, William Baumol and William Bowen published an article that examined the strained economic circumstances of the performing arts. They cautioned there was little opportunity for using technology to increase productivity. "The output per man-hour of the violinist playing a Schubert quartet in a standard concert hall is relatively fixed, and it is fairly difficult to reduce the number of actors necessary for a performance of *Henry IV, Part II.*" W. J. Baumol & W. G. Bowen, *On the Performing Arts: The Anatomy of Their Economic Problems,* 55 AM. ECO. REV. 495, 500 (1965). Much of higher education, whether one-on-one advising, or small group interactions between students and faculty may be subject to the same limits on productivity noted by Baumol and Bowen for the arts. Or is it? Could universities substitute digital recordings for live lectures and computerized instructional materials for textbooks without significantly reducing the quality of education provided?

B.   FOUNDERS AND DONORS

Coffee v. Rice University

Court of Civil Appeals of Texas, First District, 1966.
408 S.W.2d 269.

■ ASSOCIATE JUSTICE COLEMAN.

This is a suit brought by William Marsh Rice University, and the Trustees thereof, for the purpose of securing an interpretation of the organic instruments by which the institution was created that the Trustees, in the exercise of their discretion, are free to accept as students qualified applicants without regard to color and to charge tuition to those able to pay the same. In the alternative, the University requested the court to apply the equitable doctrines of Cy Pres and deviation if such action was found to be necessary in order that students might be admitted without regard to color and that tuition might be charged those able to pay the same.

. . . . By an instrument dated May 13, 1891, and acknowledged on May 16, 1891, William Marsh Rice gave to James A. Baker, Jr., E. Raphael, C. Lombardi, J. E. McAshan, F.A. Rice, and A. S. Richardson, as Trustees, a promissory note in the sum of $200,000.00 payable at his death. This instrument recited the terms of the note verbatim, and provided that the money donated should be an endowment fund, the interest, income, issues and profits of which should forever be donated "to the instruction of the white inhabitants of the City of Houston, and State of Texas, through and by the establishment and maintenance of a Public Library and Institute for the Advancement of Literature, Science and Art, to be incorporated as hereinafter provided, and to be known by such name as the said parties of the second part (Trustees) may in their judgment select."

This instrument then directed the Trustees to incorporate "forthwith for the purpose of carrying out the uses, intents, and purposes of this trust." The next paragraph provided:

"*THIRD*:—That as soon as the said Public Library and Institute for the Advancement of Science and Art shall have been incorporated, as herein contemplated, then the said *Institute*, through and by its Board of Trustees hereinafter named, shall accept from the said parties of the second part, the Endowment Fund of Two Hundred Thousand Dollars."

The instrument proceeded to appoint as Trustees of the Institute William Marsh Rice and the same people who were Trustees under the trust indenture; provided life tenure; reserved to William Marsh Rice the right to fill vacancies arising during his lifetime; providing that all trustees be inhabitants of the City of Houston, Texas; reserving to William Marsh Rice, "during his natural life," the right to make all decisions in the event he disagreed with the other Trustees.

Numbered Paragraph SEVENTH reads:

"The Endowment Fund, herein mentioned, including all future endowments, donations and bequests that may hereafter be made to the said Institute, not otherwise provided, shall be devoted to the following objects, and purposes, to-wit:

"A. To the establishment and Maintenance of a Free Library, Reading Room, and Institute for the Advancement of Science and Art.

"B. To provide, as soon as the fund will warrant such an expenditure, for the establishment and maintenance of a thorough polytechnic school, for males and females, designed to give instructions on the application of Science and Art to the useful occupations of life; the requirements for admission to which shall be left to the discretion of the Board of Trustees.

"C. Said Library, Reading Room, Scientific Departments, and Polytechnic School, and the instruction, benefits and enjoyments to be derived from the Institute to be free and open to all; to be non-sectarian and non-partisan, and subject to such restrictions only, as in the judgment of the Board of Trustees will conduce to the good order and honor of the said Institute."

. . .

The name of the corporation, established by the charter, was the William M. Rice Institute for the Advancement of Literature, Science and Art.

Article Two (2) of the Corporate Charter reads:

The objects, intents, and purposes of this Institution are declared to be the establishment and maintenance, in the City of Houston, Texas, of a Public Library, and the maintenance of an Institute for the Advancement of Literature, Science, Art, Philosophy and Letters; the establishment and maintenance of a Polytechnic school; for procuring and maintaining scientific collections; collections of chemical and philosophical apparatus, mechanical and artistic models, drawings, pictures and statues; and for cultivating other means of instruction for the white inhabitants of the City of Houston, and State of Texas, to, for, and upon the uses, intents, and purposes, and upon the trusts, and subject to the conditions and restrictions contained in a deed which is in form, substance and words as follows. . . .

After quoting the trust instrument the charter provided that the "office" of the Institute shall be established and remain in the City of Houston, Texas. It provided for a board of seven trustees, naming them, and provided that the "corporation powers of this Institute" shall be managed and exercised by them. The charter then in general terms granted the corporation power "to execute the trusts and powers mentioned in and intended to be created by" the trust indenture quoted, and to hold the endowment with the increase and profits thereof, "including all endowments, donations, and bequests at any time to be made to the said Institute, subject to the conditions and restrictions created in said deed, and to, for and upon the uses, intents, and purposes expressed and provided." The corporation, "and the Board of Trustees thereof", were authorized "to do and perform all and every act and thing whatever, and to carry out and accomplish all and every trust, intent and purpose provided to be done, carried out or accomplished, in and by the aforesaid deed ... and ... to receive all and every endowment, donation and bequest made to it, and to appropriate the same to the uses, intents, and purposes contemplated herein and in said deed."

. . .

Our task in this case is not unlike that of the court in *William Buchanan Foundation v. Shepperd*, Tex. Civ. App. 1955, 283 S.W. 2d 325, *reversed and remanded by agreement* 155 Tex. 406, 289 S.W. 2d 553, where the court summarized the general rules of construction by which we must be guided:

"The cardinal principle to be observed in construing a trust instrument is to ascertain the settlor's intent with the view of effectuating it."

. . .

... From a consideration of the instruments as a whole we are impelled to disagree with the contention of appellants that the quoted phrase must be considered the dominant purpose of the trust.

While the trust instrument at one place stated that the income from the endowment fund should be donated "to the instruction of the white inhabitants of the City of Houston, and State of Texas, through and by the establishment and maintenance of a Public Library and Institute for the advancement of Literature, Science and Art," the phrase is not repeated in paragraph seven, previously quoted. There it is stated that the endowment fund shall be devoted to "the following objects and purposes...." Then, after specific methods of gaining and disseminating knowledge are specified, it is provided that the Library, Reading Room, Scientific Departments and Polytechnic School, and "the instruction, benefits and enjoyments to be derived from the Institute to be free and open to all ... and subject to such restrictions only, as ... will conduce to the good order and honor of the said Institute."

.... While the motivating factor leading to the establishment of the trust was the donor's desire to promote the education of the white inhabitants of the City of Houston, and State of Texas, the dominant purpose of the trust was to establish a free library and an educational institution, the primary aim of which was to contribute to the advancement of human knowledge in the fields of literature, science, art, philosophy and letters. Subsidiary purposes were to be the establishment and maintenance of a polytechnic school, scientific collections, and collections of chemical and philosophical apparatus, mechanical and artistic models, drawings, pictures, and statues, as well as such other means of more directly instructing the white inhabitants of Houston and Texas, as the Trustees might devise.

The institute was repeatedly mentioned in the trust instrument and the corporate charter. The name given the corporation is revealing. The Institute was to be incorporated and the endowment fund was to be managed by the Trustees of the corporation. After provision is made for the establishment and maintenance of the Library and Institute, the Polytechnic School is to be established. A sinking fund was provided for "betterments and improvements" of the Institute. The office of the Institute is to remain in Houston. It must also be noted that the word "Institute" is used in the charter to refer to the corporation. Nevertheless, it is our opinion from a consideration of all provisions of the instruments that the dominant purpose of the donor was to create an educational institution primarily devoted to research and original work calculated to expand the boundaries of human knowledge, the benefits of which would accrue only indirectly to the white inhabitants of Houston and Texas. By reason of the subsidiary purposes and the authority to provide "other means of instruction" the Trustees were given great discretion in formulating the vehicle by which the purposes of the donor were to be accomplished. It should also be noted that the polytechnic school, museums, and "other means of instruction," with the exception of the Library, probably were intended to be functioning components of the Institute, since they were to be established, financed, and managed by the corporation, and the sinking fund was to be established for improvements and betterments of the Institute.

Judicial notice may be taken of the fact that in 1891, when the trust instrument was signed, the University of Texas had been in operation only eight years, and that the number of students attending institutions of higher learning in Texas was small. At that time the opportunities for free education at the college level were limited. The amount of research and creative work being carried out in science and the liberal arts could not have been significant. The number of people qualified by education to do such work was undoubtedly small. The need for such an institution in this State was apparent.

. . .

While the word "university" does not appear in the trust instrument or the charter, it seems clear that an "Institute for the Advancement of Literature, Science and Art" might well be a university. Clearly the Trustees of the corporation were empowered by the donor with the authority to make of the Institute a university of the first class so long as the general purposes and intents disclosed in the trust instrument were accomplished. . . .

. . .

We point out for emphasis that there is no provision in the trust instrument or corporate charter that expressly excludes negroes and other non-white peoples from sharing the "instruction, benefits, and enjoyments to be derived from the Institute," nor do those instruments declare that the "instruction" should be confined to the white inhabitants of Houston and Texas *solely*. On the contrary, in paragraph seven it is directed that the "instruction, benefits and enjoyments *derived* from the Institute" were to be free and *open to all*, to be nonsectarian and non-partisan, and *subject to such restrictions only* as in the *judgment of the Board of Trustees* will conduce to the *good order* and *honor* of the Institute.

The Trustees were further given "full authority" to formulate such rules and regulations for the government of the *affairs* of the Institute *as in their judgment* they may deem proper....

While a reasonable construction of the trust instruments requires the conclusion that the donor intended to benefit the white inhabitants of the City of Houston and State of Texas primarily, reason compels the further conclusion that the instruction, benefits, and enjoyments of the Institute were not intended to benefit them solely. Expanded knowledge in the field of science in the nature of things cannot be excluded from a segment of our society. The selection of a university as the most suitable instrument through which the purpose of the donor could be accomplished was the action of the Trustees, not the donor. It was not required by the terms of the trust, which might have been complied with literally by establishing a foundation to assist scholars, scientists, artists and writers financially; by establishing museums, and art galleries; and by establishing a polytechnical school. We cannot say that the donor had a fixed purpose to establish a university to which students would be admitted free, and from which Negroes would be excluded. It is equally clear, however, that the establishment of such an institution was within the discretionary power of the Trustees.

Nevertheless, to consider the instrument in light of the conditions prevailing at the time it was executed, the fact of segregation of the races cannot be ignored. In 1891 in the State of Texas the segregation of races in public educational institutions was required by law, and such segregation was the invariable custom in private institutions. As a practical matter at that time a school was either a school for white children or one for Negro children. Bearing in mind the expressed intent to instruct the white inhabitants of Texas, the Trustees, when they established an educational institution to which students were to be admitted, understood that Negro students were to be excluded without specific instructions to that effect.

It also follows that, while the injunction that the instruction, benefits, and enjoyment derived from the Institute were to be free and open to all was not a specific instruction that no tuition be required of students of Rice University, it was the expression of a general philanthropic intent which the Trustees properly carried into effect by adopting a policy of requiring no tuition. Since these policies were adopted by the Trustees as their interpretation of the intention of the donor, and since these policies have been consistently followed for fifty years without a question being raised as to their propriety, this Court would not be justified in adopting a construction of the instrument different from that of the Trustees designated by the donor to carry out his purposes unless compelled by the clear language of the trust instrument.

While we have concluded as a matter of law from the language of the trust instruments that the primary purpose of the donor was to establish an educational institution of the first class, the careful trial judge submitted the question to the jury....

In answer to special issues submitted to them, the jury found that William Marsh Rice intended that the funds given the Institute be used for the instruction and improvement of white inhabitants only, but that it is impossible or impracticable under present conditions to carry out said intent.

The jury also found that William Marsh Rice intended that the benefits to be derived from the Institute were to be free of tuition, but that it is impossible or impracticable under present conditions to carry out said intent.

There is no contention that the answers made by the jury to these issues are not supported by the evidence produced at the trial....

.   .   .

Testimony was produced at the trial of this case from the Chancellors and Presidents of most of the universities located in the State of Texas. This testimony, with no material inconsistency or contradiction, established that under present conditions no university that discriminates in the selection of teachers or students on the basis of race could attain or retain the status of a university of the first class because it could not recruit the necessary faculty, and would be at a disadvantage in seeking grants for research from foundations and the government. It was established that it would be impossible to carry on significant research in the field of science without such assistance since the cost of necessary facilities and equipment is prohibitive. It was established that Rice University has attained a position of eminence in selected scientific fields, but has not reached this position in the humanities and literature.

.... While it is well known that Rice University is one of the most richly endowed schools in the South, it is a matter of common knowledge that for some years costs have been increasing faster than the rate of return on invested capital. If Rice University is denied all sources of revenue other than gifts and income from the endowment fund, it is entirely reasonable to conclude that it will inevitably, in the course of time, fall behind those schools receiving large percentages of their operating revenue from tuition or tax sources. The remarkable achievements in science, which have occurred since the death of William Marsh Rice and which make necessary the use of extremely expensive atomic and electronic equipment by educational institutions engaged in scientific research necessary in order to maintain a competitive position in the educational world, could not have been foreseen, and were not foreseen by him. There was a question of fact as to whether it is impossible or impractical to carry out the purpose of William Marsh Rice that the benefits to be derived from the Institute be free of tuition. The jury's determination of this issue of fact is conclusive on this Court since it is supported by evidence.

The judgment entered by the trial court is supported by our construction of the trust instruments, the evidence, the facts found by the jury, and the applicable rules of law. It is, therefore, affirmed.

Note on *Coffee v. Rice University*

Rice University reports that:

On May 13, 1891, Massachusetts-born businessman William Marsh Rice chartered the William Marsh Rice Institute for the Advancement of Literature, Science, and Art as a gift to the city of Houston, where he made his fortune. The terms of the charter required that work on the new institute would begin only after Rice's death.

On September 23, 1900, Rice was chloroformed to death by his valet, Charlie Jones, who had conspired with an unscrupulous lawyer, Albert Patrick, to murder the aging millionaire and claim his estate using a forged will. When an autopsy ordered by Rice's attorney, Captain James A. Baker, revealed evidence of poisoning, Jones agreed to provide state's evidence in return for immunity from prosecution. Patrick was convicted of murder and sent to Sing Sing. He was pardoned in 1912, the same year that classes began at the Rice Institute.

Rice University, A Brief Rice History, http://www.explore.rice.edu/explore/A_Brief_Rice_History.asp (last visited Mar. 2, 2008).

Tennessee Division of the United Daughters of the Confederacy v. Vanderbilt University

Court of Appeals of Tennessee, 2005.
174 S.W.3d 98.

■ KOCH, JR., WILLIAM C.

This appeal involves a dispute stemming from a private university's decision to change the name of one of its dormitories....

[In 1913, 1927, and 1933, the George Peabody College for Teachers entered a series of contracts with the Tennessee Division of the United Daughters of the Confederacy ("Tennessee U.D.C."). Under the terms of the contracts, the Tennessee U.D.C. would donate $50,000 for a dormitory, and Peabody College promised that the dormitory would conform to plans approved by the Tennessee U.D.C., that certain female descendants of Confederate soldiers could live in the dormitory rent-free, and that the dormitory would be called "Confederate Memorial."]

... On June 8, 1934, the Peabody College trustees voted to borrow $100,000 from the school's permanent endowment to supplement the funds raised by the Tennessee U.D.C. On July 12, 1934, the contract for the construction of the new dormitory was awarded to V. L. Nicholson Co. for a guaranteed price of $131,294 or less. Construction drawings dated July 12, 1934 show the words "Confederate Memorial Hall" in incised lettering on the pediment on the front of the building. The building was completed in less than a year, and on June 1, 1935, Peabody College held a dedication ceremony for the new dormitory at which members of the Tennessee U.D.C. spoke.

From 1935 until the late 1970's, women descendants of Confederate soldiers nominated by the Tennessee U.D.C. and accepted by Peabody College lived in Confederate Memorial Hall rent-free. However, by the late 1970's, Peabody College found itself in increasingly dire financial straits. In the spring of 1978, the trustees of the college decided to lease two dormitories, including Confederate Memorial Hall, to Vanderbilt as a way to raise revenue. By that time, only a few students nominated by the Tennessee U.D.C. were living in Confederate Memorial Hall, but Confederate Memorial Hall still housed various artifacts placed there by the Tennessee U.D.C., including Confederate portraits, furniture, and scrapbooks.

... Peabody College's financial situation continued to deteriorate, and it soon became evident that the college would either have to merge with another institution or face bankruptcy. In the fall of 1978, the executive committee of the college's board of trust voted to allow President Dunworth to enter into confidential merger discussions with Vanderbilt. . . .

. . . On April 28, 1979, the trustees of Vanderbilt and Peabody College entered into an agreement effectuating the merger. Under the terms of the merger agreement, Vanderbilt succeeded to all of Peabody's legal obligations.

By the time of the merger, only four students nominated by the Tennessee U.D.C. were still living in Confederate Memorial Hall. Vanderbilt allowed these four students to continue living there at a reduced rental rate, but after they graduated, no other students nominated by the Tennessee U.D.C. were allowed to live in Confederate Memorial Hall rent-free or at a reduced rate.[10]

In 1987 and 1988, Vanderbilt spent approximately $2.5 million to renovate and upgrade Confederate Memorial Hall. During the following academic year, there was much discussion on the Vanderbilt campus regarding the propriety of retaining the name "Confederate Memorial Hall."

[Following a resolution passed by the Vanderbilt Student Government Association in 1989, university officials, in consultation with Tennessee U.D.C. and student groups, placed a plaque at the entrance to Confederate Memorial Hall explaining why it was named "Confederate." In the spring of 2000, the Student Government Association passed a resolution calling on the administration to change the building's name. The resolution noted that the demographic population of Vanderbilt had changed significantly since 1935[12] and that Vanderbilt respected all individuals regardless of their racial identity. In 2002, chancellor E. Gordon Gee was given authority to handle the issue by Vanderbilt's board of trustees, and, without consulting Tennessee U.D.C., he decided to change the name to "Memorial Hall." After the decision to change the name was made public, university officials expressed their gratitude to Tennessee U.D.C. and informed the organization that the plaque explaining the history of the building would remain in place.]

. . .

On October 10, 2002, Chancellor Gee drafted a memorandum to the full Vanderbilt board of trust explaining his decision to rename the building. Chancellor Gee stated that former, current, and prospective students, faculty, and staff had identified the presence on the Vanderbilt campus of a building named "Confederate Memorial Hall" as a barrier to achieving an inclusive and welcoming environment that is essential for a world-class university. He also noted that some individuals had refused to live or attend events in the building; that the building was originally named "Confederate Memorial Hall" to commemorate values that do not reflect those of a university dedicated to educating all and meeting the aspirations of the broader society; and that assigning students to live in a dormitory so named implied an endorsement, if not a celebration, of a system that many people find offensive. Finally, Chancellor Gee observed that having a building on

10. Vanderbilt has continued to use the building as a dormitory to the present day.

12. Vanderbilt did not admit African–American students to its graduate programs until 1953, and the first African–American undergraduates were not enrolled until 1964, the same year that Peabody admitted its first African–American undergraduate students. By the 2002–03 academic year, there were 371 African–American students in the Vanderbilt undergraduate student body.

the campus named "Confederate Memorial Hall" strongly reinforced the worst stereotypes held by many people that Vanderbilt is an institution trapped in a long-distant past.

The Vanderbilt board of trust supported Chancellor Gee's decision to rename Confederate Memorial Hall....

On October 17, 2002, the Tennessee U.D.C. filed suit against Vanderbilt for breach of contract in the Chancery Court for Davidson County. The Tennessee U.D.C. alleged that it had fully performed its obligations under the 1913, 1927, and 1933 contracts and that Vanderbilt's renaming of Confederate Memorial Hall constituted a breach of those contracts. The Tennessee U.D.C. sought an injunction to prevent Vanderbilt from removing the inscription on the pediment on the front of the building, a declaratory judgment specifying Vanderbilt's rights and obligations to the Tennessee U.D.C., and compensatory damages in an amount to be shown at trial.

Vanderbilt answered and ... filed a motion for summary judgment[, which the court granted while denying Tennessee U.D.C.'s motion for partial summary judgment]....

. . .

... [T]he central issue on this appeal is whether the trial court erred by determining that Vanderbilt, rather than the Tennessee U.D.C., was entitled to a judgment as a matter of law....

In order to determine whether it is Vanderbilt or the Tennessee U.D.C. that is entitled to a judgment as a matter of law, we must first determine the precise nature of the legal relationship formed between the Tennessee U.D.C. and Peabody College by the 1913, 1927, and 1933 agreements. Although all three agreements use the word "contract," they do not purport to establish a typical commercial arrangement in which one party provides certain goods or services in return for a sum to be paid by the other party. Instead, the agreements indicate that the $50,000 to be raised by the Tennessee U.D.C. was to be transferred to Peabody College as a gift. Peabody College's status as a non-profit charitable organization dedicated to the advancement of education suggests the possibility of a donative intent on the part of the Tennessee U.D.C., and this possibility is confirmed by the plain language of the three agreements. The 1913 agreement repeatedly describes the $50,000 to be raised and turned over to Peabody College as a "gift" from the Tennessee U.D.C., and the 1927 and 1933 agreements do not in any way modify or retract this description.

The 1913, 1927, and 1933 contracts do not, however, describe the proposed transfer to Peabody College as a gift with no strings attached. The three contracts attach specific conditions to the gift, and the 1927 contract expressly reserves to the Tennessee U.D.C. the right to recall the gift if Peabody College fails or ceases to comply with these conditions....

. . .

Taking all three contracts together, the gift from the Tennessee U.D.C. to Peabody College was subject to three specific conditions. First, Peabody College was required to use the gift to construct a dormitory on its campus conforming to plans and specifications approved by the Tennessee U.D.C. Second, Peabody College was required to allow women descendants of Confederate soldiers nominated by the Tennessee U.D.C. and accepted by

Peabody College to live on the first and second floors of the dormitory without paying rent and paying all other dormitory expenses on an estimated cost basis. Third, Peabody College was required to place on the dormitory an inscription naming it "Confederate Memorial." The contracts do not specify the duration of these conditions. In such circumstances, the court must determine whether a duration can be inferred from the nature and circumstances of the transaction. Given the nature of the project and the content of the conditions, we conclude that these conditions were not meant to bind Peabody College forever but instead were to be limited to the life of the building itself. Thus, as long as the building stands, these three conditions apply to the gift.

In its complaint, the Tennessee U.D.C. claimed that Vanderbilt had already violated the condition requiring an inscription on the building naming it "Confederate Memorial" by publicly and privately announcing its intention to rename the building "Memorial Hall" and that Vanderbilt planned to violate the condition further by removing or altering the inscription on the pediment. . . .

Vanderbilt's claim that the placement of a plaque by the entrance to the building describing the contributions of the Tennessee U.D.C. to the original construction constitutes substantial performance with the inscription condition cannot be taken seriously. The determination of whether a party has substantially performed depends on what it was the parties bargained for in their agreement. Here, the 1933 contract expressly and unambiguously required Peabody College to place an inscription on the building naming it "Confederate Memorial," and we have already concluded that the parties intended the inscription to remain until the building was torn down. Peabody College complied with the condition by placing a large inscription in stone on the pediment of the building reading "Confederate Memorial Hall." Peabody College did so in conformity with Peabody College's own 1934 construction drawings which show these words in large incised lettering on the pediment of the building.

Vanderbilt continued to comply fully with this condition from its 1979 merger with Peabody College until 2002 when it announced its plans to remove the word "Confederate" from the building's pediment. It is doubtful that a party such as Vanderbilt that has willfully changed course after over twenty years of compliance with the literal terms of an agreement could ever rely on the doctrine of substantial performance. Even if it could, no reasonable fact-finder could conclude that replacing a name written in stone in large letters on the pediment of a building with a plaque by the entrance constitutes substantial performance of a requirement to do the former.

Vanderbilt's argument that it should be excused from complying with the inscription condition contained in the 1933 contract because the Tennessee U.D.C. has already received enough value for its original contribution to the construction of the building is likewise without merit. The courts must interpret contracts as they are written, and will not make a new contract for parties who have spoken for themselves. The courts do not concern themselves with the wisdom or folly of a contract, and are not at liberty to relieve parties from contractual obligations simply because these obligations later prove to be burdensome or unwise.

The same is true of conditions contained in a gift agreement. By entering into the 1913, 1927, and 1933 contracts, Peabody College necessarily agreed that the value of the gift it was receiving was worth the value of full performance of the conditions of the gift. 8 CORBIN ON CONTRACTS § 36.2, at 338. In short, Vanderbilt's unilateral assessment that Peabody College gave away too much in the 1913, 1927, and 1933 agreements does not constitute a legal defense that would excuse Vanderbilt from complying with the conditions of the original gift.

Vanderbilt's assertion that principles of academic freedom allow it to keep the gift from the Tennessee U.D.C. while ignoring the conditions attached to that gift is equally unavailing. As Vanderbilt correctly notes in its brief on appeal, the United States Supreme Court has long been solicitous of the independence of private colleges from government control. *See, e.g., Trs. of Dartmouth Coll. v. Woodward*, 17 U.S. 518 (1819). However, the source of the obligation at issue in this case is not the government but Vanderbilt itself. The original obligation to place the inscription on Confederate Memorial Hall is contained in a private gift agreement voluntarily entered into between Peabody College and the Tennessee U.D.C. Vanderbilt's legal obligation to comply with the conditions of that gift agreement arises not from any action on the part of the government but from Vanderbilt's own decision to enter into a merger agreement with Peabody College in 1979 in which it agreed to succeed to Peabody College's legal obligations.

Moreover, we fail to see how the adoption of a rule allowing universities to avoid their contractual and other voluntarily assumed legal obligations whenever, in the university's opinion, those obligations have begun to impede their academic mission would advance principles of academic freedom. To the contrary, allowing Vanderbilt and other academic institutions to jettison their contractual and other legal obligations so casually would seriously impair their ability to raise money in the future by entering into gift agreements such as the ones at issue here.

As noted above, where a donee fails or ceases to comply with the conditions of a gift, the donor's remedy is limited to recovery of the gift. However, it would be inequitable to allow Vanderbilt to "return" the gift at issue here simply by paying the Tennessee U.D.C. the same sum of money the Tennessee U.D.C. donated in 1933 because the value of a dollar today is very different from the value of a dollar in 1933. To reflect the change in the buying power of the dollar, the amount Vanderbilt must pay to the Tennessee U.D.C. in order to return the gift should be based on the consumer price index published by the Bureau of Labor Statistics of the United States Department of Labor. As attested by numerous Tennessee statutes, reference to the consumer price index is the most common way to calculate a change in the value of money over time under Tennessee law. In addition, the Tennessee Supreme Court has endorsed the consumer price index as an accurate measure of the change in the purchasing power of a dollar. Thus, on remand, if Vanderbilt continues to elect not to comply with the terms of the gift, it must pay the Tennessee U.D.C. in today's dollars the value of the original gift in 1933.

Questions and Comments on *Tennessee UDC v. Vanderbilt*

Why was Vanderbilt less successful than Rice in changing the terms of the original gift? What are the implications of this decision for gifts to colleges or universities from corporate entities rather than from individuals?

Carl J. Herzog Foundation v. University of Bridgeport

Supreme Court of Connecticut, 1997.
243 Conn. 1, 699 A.2d 995.

■ NORCOTT, J.

The sole issue in this ... appeal is whether the Connecticut Uniform Management of Institutional Funds Act (CUMIFA), Conn. Gen. Stat. §§ 45a–526 through 45a–534, establishes statutory standing for a donor to bring an action to enforce the terms of a completed charitable gift....

[The Carl J. Herzog Foundation, plaintiff-donor, sought injunctive and other relief on the grounds that the University of Bridgeport, defendant, was not using donated funds for the purposes specified by the plaintiff. In 1986, plaintiff agreed to match up to $250,000 raised by the University for need-based merit scholarships for disadvantaged students pursuing medicine-related studies. The University raised $250,000, and the plaintiff matched that amount in two grants in 1987 and 1988. The grants funded scholarships for nursing students until 1991, when the University closed its nursing school.]

. . .

[The Appellate Court stated:]

The plaintiff's alleged injury is that the funds are no longer being used for their specified purpose. Paragraph fourteen of the revised complaint states: "The [plaintiff] has been given to understand and believes that the said institutional funds have been co-mingled with the general funds of the [defendant], that said institutional funds are not being used in accordance with the 'Gift Instrument' under which said institutional funds were transferred to [the defendant], and that said institutional funds have in fact been spent for general purposes of [the defendant]."

The plaintiff requested a temporary and permanent injunction, ordering the defendant "to segregate from its general funds matching grants totaling $250,000," an accounting for the use of the fund from the date of receipt until present, and a reestablishment of the fund in accordance with the purposes outlined in the gift instrument, and, in the event that those purposes could not be fulfilled, to revert the funds and direct them to the Bridgeport Area Foundation, which is prepared to administer the funds in accordance with the original agreement.

The defendant moved to dismiss the action for lack of subject matter jurisdiction on the ground that the plaintiff lacked standing. The trial court held that the act did not provide a donor with the right to enforce restrictions contained in a gift instrument, and, therefore, the plaintiff lacked standing to bring the action. The trial court noted that the attorney general, pursuant to General Statutes § 3–125, could bring an action to enforce the gift, and it dismissed the action.

The Appellate Court reversed the judgment of the trial court, concluding that Conn. Gen. Stat. § 45a–533 provides donors with standing to enforce the terms of a completed gift, even though no such right of enforcement was provided for in the gift instrument. . . .

. . . The sole basis for standing claimed by the plaintiff is CUMIFA, more particularly, § 45a–533 (a). Our task, therefore, devolves into a question of statutory construction. We must determine whether the legislature intended CUMIFA to provide a donor that has made a completed charitable gift to an "institution" as defined by § 45a–527(1), with standing to bring an action to enforce the terms of that gift where, as here, the gift instrument contained no express reservation of control over the disposition of the gift, such as a right of reverter or a right to redirect.

We begin by noting the common law landscape upon which CUMIFA was enacted. We do so based on the applicability to this case of the well recognized principle of statutory construction that no statute "is to be construed as altering the common law, farther than its words import [and . . . a statute] is not to be construed as making any innovation upon the common law which it does not fairly express." *State v. Luzietti*, 230 Conn. 427, 433, 646 A.2d 85 (1994). . . .

At common law, a donor who has made a completed charitable contribution, whether as an absolute gift or in trust, had no standing to bring an action to enforce the terms of his or her gift or trust unless he or she had expressly reserved the right to do so. . . . [I]t was established that "equity will afford protection to a donor to a charitable corporation in that *the attorney general may maintain a suit* to compel the property to be held for the charitable purpose for which it was given to the corporation." (Emphasis added; internal quotation marks omitted.) *Lefkowitz v. Lebensfeld*, 68 A.D.2d 488, 494–95, 417 N.Y.S.2d 715 (1979). "The general rule is that charitable trusts or gifts to charitable corporations for stated purposes are [enforceable] at the instance of the attorney general. . . . It matters not whether the gift is absolute or in trust or whether a technical condition is attached to the gift."[3]

[I]t is clear that the general rule at common law was that a donor had no standing to enforce the terms of a completed charitable gift unless the donor had expressly reserved a property interest in the gift.[5]

Having concluded that the plaintiff would have had no standing at common law, we now turn to its contention that the common law has been altered by the legislature's adoption of CUMIFA, specifically that portion codified at § 45a–533. . . .

---

3. Public officials, such as the attorney general, had common law standing to enforce charitable trusts because, by virtue of their positions, they are closely associated with the public nature of charities. A leading treatise on the subject states that "the public benefits arising from the charitable trust justify the selection of some public official for its enforcement. Since the attorney general is the governmental officer whose duties include the protection of the rights of the people of the state in general, it is natural that he has been chosen as the protector, supervisor, and enforcer of charitable trusts, both in England and in the several states. . . ." G. Bogert & G. Bogert, Trusts and Trustees (2d rev. ed. 1991) § 411, pp. 2–3. Connecticut is among the majority of jurisdictions which have codified this common law rule and has entrusted the attorney general with the responsibility and duty to "represent the public interest in the protection of any gifts, legacies or devises intended for public or charitable purposes. . . ." Conn. Gen. Stat. § 3–125.

5. By expressly reserving a property interest such as a right of reverter, the donor of the gift or the settlor of the trust may bring himself and his heirs within the "special interest" exception to the general rule that beneficiaries of a charitable trust may not bring an action to enforce the trust, but rather are represented exclusively by the attorney general.

The plaintiff bases its statutory standing claim primarily on the language of subsection (a) of § 45a–533, which provides that "with the written consent of the donor, the governing board may release, in whole or in part, a restriction imposed by the applicable gift instrument on the use or investment of an institutional fund." On the basis of this language, the Appellate Court concluded, and the plaintiff maintains, that "it would be anomalous for a statute to provide for written consent by a donor to change a restriction and then deny that donor access to the courts to complain of a change without such consent." We disagree.

The plaintiff concedes, as it must, that nothing in the plain language of § 45a–533 (a) or any other portion of CUMIFA expressly provides statutory standing for donors to charitable institutions who have not somehow reserved a property interest in the gift such as a right of reverter. In order to demonstrate that the legislature intended to abrogate the common law, therefore, the plaintiff is left only with the legislative history of CUMIFA and the circumstances surrounding its enactment. The history and background of CUMIFA, however, not only do not support the plaintiff's claim of statutory standing, they directly refute it.

. . .

First, it is unmistakable that the drafters of UMIFA [the Uniform Management of Institutional Funds Act, which Connecticut courts use for assistance in interpreting the state statute] regarded charitable institutions, particularly colleges and universities, as the principal beneficiaries of their efforts. The drafters set forth the explanation of their purpose in the prefatory note to UMIFA. "Over the past several years the governing boards of eleemosynary institutions, particularly colleges and universities, have sought to make more effective use of endowment and other investment funds. They and their counsel have wrestled with questions as to permissible investments, delegation of investment authority, and use of the total return concept in investing endowment funds. Studies of the legal authority and responsibility for the management of the funds of an institution have pointed up the uncertain state of the law in most jurisdictions. There is virtually no statutory law regarding trustees or governing boards of eleemosynary institutions, and case law is sparse." UMIFA, prefatory note, 7A U.L.A. 706 (1985).

UMIFA, drafted in the early 1970s, was set against the backdrop of a state of flux for colleges and universities. In a time of dramatic social change that cast new light on many older charitable gift restrictions, these institutions saw their operating costs rise significantly without a similar increase in endowment funds. . . . UMIFA attempted to offer as much relief as possible *to charitable institutions*, without any mention of concern regarding a donor's ability to bring legal action to enforce a condition on a gift.

The specific area of relief to institutions focused upon by the Appellate Court and the plaintiff is that embodied in § 7, of UMIFA, entitled "Release of Restrictions on Use or Investment." The prefatory note to that section provides: "It is established law that the donor may place restrictions on his largesse which the donee institution must honor. Too often, the restrictions on use or investment become outmoded or wasteful or unworkable. There is a need for review of obsolete restrictions and a way of modifying or adjusting them. The Act authorizes the governing board to obtain the acquiescence of the donor to a release of restrictions and, in the absence of the donor, to petition the appropriate court for relief in appropriate cases." In the comment to § 7, the drafters of UMIFA expressly provided that the donor of a completed gift would not have standing to enforce the terms of the gift. "*The donor has no right to enforce the restriction*, no interest in the fund and no power to change the eleemosynary beneficiary of the fund. He may only acquiesce in a lessening of a restriction already in effect." (Emphasis added.) UMIFA, § 7, comment, 7A U.L.A. 724 (1985).

These clear comments regarding the power of a donor to enforce restrictions on a charitable gift arose in the context of debate concerning the creation of potential adverse tax consequences for donors, if UMIFA was interpreted to provide donors with control over their gift property after the completion of the gift. Pursuant to § 170 (a) of the Internal Revenue Code and § 1.170A–1 (c) of the Treasury Regulations, an income tax deduction for a charitable contribution is disallowed unless the taxpayer has permanently surrendered "dominion and control" over the property or funds in question. Where there is a possibility not "so remote as to be negligible" that the charitable gift subject to a condition might fail, the tax deduction is disallowed. See also I.R.C. § 2055; Treas. Reg. § 20.2055–2 (b) (similar provisions for estate tax deductions).

The drafters of UMIFA worked closely with an impressive group of professionals, including tax advisers, who were concerned with the federal tax implications of the proposed act. The drafters' principal concern in this regard was that the matter of donor restrictions not affect the donor's charitable contribution deduction for the purposes of federal income taxation. In other words, the concern was that the donor not be so tethered to the charitable gift through the control of restrictions in the gift that the donor would not be entitled to claim a federal charitable contribution exemption for the gift. See I.R.C. § 170 (a); Treas. Reg. § 1.170A–1 (c).

In resolving these concerns, the drafters of UMIFA clearly stated their position in the commentary. "No federal tax problems for the donor are anticipated by permitting release of a restriction. *The donor has no right to enforce the restriction, no interest in the fund and no power to change the eleemosynary beneficiary of the fund.* He may only acquiesce in a lessening of a restriction already in effect." (Emphasis added.) UMIFA, § 7, comment, 7A U.L.A. 724 (1985). The Appellate Court dismissed this language, reasoning that it is limited to "tax implications when a donor does consent in writing to a release of a restriction" and does not answer the question of whether the sole right to speak to the donor's interest in the release of a restriction "lies with the attorney general, to the exclusion of a donor." We disagree. Although the comments and the prefatory note to UMIFA do recognize that a donor has an interest in a restriction, as analyzed herein, we find no support in any source for the proposition that the drafters of either UMIFA or CUMIFA intended that a donor or his heirs would supplant the attorney general as the designated enforcer of the terms of completed and absolute charitable gifts.

Indeed, it would have been anomalous for the drafters of UMIFA to strive to assist charitable institutions by creating smoother procedural avenues for the release of restrictions while simultaneously establishing standing for a new class of litigants, donors, who would defeat this very purpose by virtue of the potential of lengthy and complicated litigation.

There similarly is nothing in the history of our legislature's adoption of CUMIFA that contravenes the clear statement of the drafters of UMIFA that a "donor has no right to enforce [a] restriction...." UMIFA, § 7, comment, 7A U.L.A. 724 (1985). It is clear that our legislature knows how to establish statutory standing and it has done so unambiguously in a plethora of instances.

Finally, the legislative history of CUMIFA indicates that the legislature was aware of the question of donor standing regarding restrictions, but chose not to establish it. During the legislative debate regarding House Bill No. 8268, Representative James T. Healey stated, "if the donor has seen fit to spell out restrictions, then those restrictions govern. This bill steps in only in the event that he has not spelled out the restrictions."16 H.R. Proc., Pt. 11, 1973 Sess., p. 5732. Representative David Neiditz added that "the bill generally leaves it to the donor to make his own provisions for the matters covered in the bill. The bill applies when the donor has not specified another way." *Id.* at 5726.

On the basis of our careful review of the statute itself, its legislative history, the circumstances surrounding its enactment, the policy it was intended to implement, and similar common law principles governing the same subject matter, we conclude that CUMIFA does not establish a new class of litigants, namely donors, who can enforce an unreserved restriction in a completed charitable gift. Nothing in our review supports the conclusion that the legislature, in enacting CUMIFA, implicitly intended to confer standing on donors.

Questions and Comments on *Herzog Foundation*

In *Russell v. Yale University*, 54 Conn.App. 573, 737 A.2d 941 (1999), the court applied *Herzog Foundation*'s analysis of the common law of charitable trusts to hold that the plaintiffs lacked standing to seek an injunction of Yale's reorganization of its divinity school or a declaratory judgment that the reorganization abused Yale's discretion as trustee. First, the heir of the settlor of a charitable trust lacked standing when the settlor imposed some restrictions on Yale's use of the trust but reserved no property rights in the trust for his heirs. Second, divinity school alumni donors lacked standing despite their status as alumni and contributors or unrestricted charitable gifts. Third, the court, citing *Dartmouth College*, held that "absent special injury to a student or his or her fundamental rights, [current divinity school] students do not have standing to challenge the manner in which the administration manages an institution of higher education."

Is a donor's interest in the use of donated funds left legally unprotected when the state attorney general declines to bring an action to enforce the terms of the gift? Not necessarily. Some scholars suggest that courts are more likely to find that donors have standing to sue when the attorney general does not effectively pursue the public interest in proper administration of donated funds. *See, e.g.,* Evelyn Brody, *From the Dead Hand to the Living Dead: The Conundrum of Charitable–Donor Standing*, 41 GA. L. REV. 1183, 1244 (2007). However, "courts that grant standing to private parties often appear to require an unacceptable level of regulatory neglect, if not an outright disabling conflict of interest that impedes attorney general action[, and] private standing will usually be denied when the attorney general affirmatively determines not to act." *Id.* at 1247. What incentives might an attorney general have to bring suit? What forces might discourage such a suit?

Some courts have denied standing to donors even in the face of a clear conflict of interest between the attorney general and the donee university. For example, in

Warren v. Board of Regents of the University System of Georgia, 247 Ga.App. 758, 544 S.E.2d 190 (2001), the attorney general represented the defendants, the university's board of regents. The court held that the donors nevertheless lacked standing and that a district attorney or special assistant attorney general could sufficiently represent the public interest. *Id.* at 194. Such conflicts of interest are most likely to arise when the donee institution is a public university. In such cases, do you think *any* government lawyer can represent the "public interest" without raising conflict of interest problems?

Notes on Private Philanthropy

1. Over $28 billion dollars was donated to universities and colleges in 2006, an increase of nearly ten percent from the previous year. Alumni gifts made up thirty percent of those donations, and although the percentage of alumni donating has decreased, the size of individual donations has increased. *See* Press Release, Council for Aid to Education, Contributions to Colleges and Universities Up By 9.4 Percent to $28 billion (Feb. 21, 2007), *available at* www.cae.org/content/pdf/VSE 2006 Press Release.pdf.

Universities face a delicate choice when major pledges go unpaid. Although the schools could sue to enforce unpaid pledges, *see, e.g.*, Furman University v. Waller, 124 S.C. 68, 117 S.E. 356 (1923), they rarely do. Faced with the possibility of upsetting other donors and ruining a potentially fruitful future relationship with the delinquent donor, universities often choose to simply ignore unpaid pledges. *See* Geraldine Fabrikant & Shelby White, *Promises, Promises, but Where's the Check?*, N.Y. TIMES, Nov. 15, 2004, at 24.

2. In 1961, Charles Robertson (Princeton '26) and his wife Marie, an heiress to the A & P supermarket chain, created the Robertson Foundation with an endowment of 700,000 shares of A & P stock, then worth $35 million. The Robertsons established the Foundation to support Princeton University's Woodrow Wilson School of Public and International Affairs in training of graduate students for careers in the federal government, especially in international relations. *See* Martin Morse Wooster, *The Robertson Foundation Case: Can Princeton Ignore A Donor's Intent?*, FOUNDATION WATCH (Capital Research Ctr., Washington, D.C.), May 2006, at 1, *available at* http://www.capitalresearch.org/pubs/pdf/FW0506.pdf.

The Robertson Foundation consists of a seven-member board, comprised of four members chosen by the University and three chosen by the Robertson family. In the last four decades, the Robertson gift has grown into an over $800 million endowment, which constitutes more than six percent of the University's endowment.

Within the first decade of the Foundation's existence, Charles Robertson expressed dissatisfaction with its progress; he was concerned that too few graduates were pursuing careers in government. In 1972, only ten of the forty-seven students who graduated from the Woodrow Wilson School with masters in public affairs were hired by the federal government. Wooster at 3. In November 1972, Robertson reiterated the objective of his Foundation in a letter to Princeton University President William Bowen: "Federal government service with international relations and affairs. That was our original goal. It continues to be our goal, and it emphatically always will be our goal!" John Hechinger & Daniel Golden, *Poisoned Ivy: Fight at Princeton Escalates Over Use of a Family's Gift*, WALL ST. J., Feb. 7, 2006, at A1.

Arguing that the intent of the donor has been disregarded, the children and a cousin of the Robertsons filed suit on July 17, 2002 in the New Jersey Superior Court, naming as defendants Princeton University, the Robertson Foundation, University President Shirley Tilghman, and three university-appointed trustees of the Foundation. The plaintiffs allege that the University sought to commingle the funds of the Foundation with those of the general University endowment. This allegation stemmed from the University's plan to shift control over the Foundation's investments from the Foundation's own investment committee to an outside management company. The University selected, and the Robertson Foundation's board ultimately approved, vesting this control in Princeton Investment Company (PRINCO), the same body that manages the University's endowment. Wooster, *supra*, at 4.

The plaintiffs also allege that too few graduates of the Wilson School have pursued careers in government and international relations. In its defense, the University argued that, in the five years prior to the filing of this suit, the Wilson School placed between thirty-seven and fifty-five percent of its graduate students in public service jobs. Silla Brush, *Robertsons Allege Misuse of Wilson School Endowment*, DAILY PRINCETONIAN, Sept. 11, 2002, *available at* http://prince-web1.princeton.edu/archives/2002/09/V11/news/5247.shtml.

The plaintiffs requested, among other forms of relief, that the court (1) sever the relationship between the Robertson Foundation and its sole beneficiary, Princeton University, and (2) reverse the Foundation board's decision that PRINCO manage the Foundation's investments. Public Statement, Cass Cliatt, Princeton University, University Seeks Summary Judgment on Three Key Robertson Litigation Issues (June 25, 2007), http://www.princeton.edu/robertson/statements/viewstory.xml?storypath=/main/news/archive/S13/68/42K81/index.xml. The trial judge set the framework for the continuing litigation in a series of rulings on the parties' motions for summary judgment. First, the judge rejected the Robertsons' demand for a jury trial. Robertson v. Princeton Univ., No. C–99–02, slip op. at 20 (N.J. Super. Ct. Ch. Div. Oct. 25, 2007), http://www.princeton.edu/robertson/documents/docs/Plaintiffs_Jury_Demand_Decision.pdf. Second, the court ruled that under the Foundation's Certificate of Incorporation the University could spend realized gains from its investments, not just dividends and interest. Robertson v. Princeton Univ., No. C–99–02, slip op. at 44 (N.J. Super. Ct. Ch. Div. Oct. 25, 2007), http://www.princeton.edu/robertson/documents/docs/ Article_11c_Summary_Judgment_Decision.pdf. Third, the court denied the Robertsons' motion for summary judgment on the issues of whether the University—as opposed to the University-designated trustees—owes a fiduciary duty to the Foundation and whether the entire fairness rule—rather than the more deferential business judgment rule—applied to the court's review of the University's spending of Foundation funds. Robertson v. Princeton Univ., No. C–99–02, slip op. at 61–89 (N.J. Super. Ct. Ch. Div. Oct. 25, 2007), http://www.princeton.edu/robertson/documents/docs/Fiduciary_Duties_Summary _ Judgment_Decision.pdf. Fourth, the court granted summary judgment to the plaintiffs for certain overcharges admitted by the university while denying summary judgment in respect of other overcharges to the Foundation. At the same time, the court barred Princeton from claiming dollar-for-dollar offsets on certain undercharges to the Foundation. Robertson v. Princeton Univ., No. C–99–02, slip op. at 40–41 (N.J. Super. Ct. Ch. Div. Oct. 25, 2007), http://www.princeton.edu/robertson/documents/docs/Overcharges–Offset_Summary_Judgment_ Decision.pdf. Fifth, the court ruled that although the Foundation's Certificate of Incorporation might not bar the selection of PRINCO to manage the Foundation's funds, the plaintiffs had raised sufficient questions as to "whether the University Trustees have acted in the best interests of the Foundation with regard to the PRINCO transaction." Robertson v. Princeton Univ., No. C–99–02, slip op. at 59 (N.J. Super. Ct. Ch. Div. Oct. 25, 2007), http://www.princeton.edu/robertson/documents/docs/Princo_Summary_Judgment_ Decision.pdf. Finally, the court denied the University's motion for summary judgment on the issue of whether Princeton is the sole beneficiary entitled to receive Foundation funds. Robertson v. Princeton Univ., No. C–99–02 (N.J. Super. Ct. Ch. Div. Oct. 25, 2007), http://www.princeton.edu/robertson/documents/ docs/Sole_Beneficiary_Summary_Judgment_Decision.pdf.

The Robertson dispute raises a number of important questions. Who has the right to challenge how university assets are spent and whether their use conforms to the donor's original objectives? Do the children of large donors have standing to sue to ensure the university is honoring the donor's intent? How broadly may those controlling the endowment interpret a donor's objective? *See* E. Daniel Larkin, *Don't Turn a Donor Into a Plaintiff*, CHRON. OF HIGHER EDUC., May 27, 2005, at 18. Should universities avoid structuring endowments in which control is vested in both the university and an outside party?

In re Estate of Wirth

Court of Appeals of New York, 2005.
5 N.Y.3d 875, 842 N.E.2d 480, 808 N.Y.S.2d 582.

■ Memorandum Opinion

The order of the Appellate Division should be affirmed, with costs.

Shortly before his death in 2000, Raymond Wirth executed a pledge agreement that provides, in part: "In consideration of my interest in education, and intending to be legally bound, I, RAYMOND P. WIRTH, irrevocably pledge and promise to pay DREXEL UNIVERSITY the sum of ONE HUNDRED FIFTY THOUSAND and 00/100 Dollars ($150,000.00)." It is undisputed that the pledge is governed by Pennsylvania law. Pennsylvania's Uniform Written Obligations Act (Pa. Stat. Ann., tit. 33, § 6), enacted in 1927, provides: "A written . . . promise, hereafter made and signed by the person . . . promising, shall not be invalid or unenforceable for lack of consideration, if the writing also contains an additional express statement, in any form of language, that the signer intends to be legally bound."

By the plain terms of the statute, Wirth's pledge was not "invalid or unenforceable for lack of consideration," and Wirth's estate has no other defense to Drexel's claim. The estate argues that there was a "failure" rather than a "lack" of consideration, but this argument rests only on confusion. A "failure of consideration" means a failure to render the performance the parties agreed on (2–5 CORBIN, CONTRACTS § 5.20 [2005]). In this case, there is no basis for asserting that Drexel failed to render any required performance.

Comment on *In re Estate of Wirth*

Following the court's decision, Raymond Wirth's estate paid the full sum of $150,000 to the university. Telephone Interview by Matthew Berns with Carl (Tobey) Oxholm III, General Counsel, Drexel Univ. (Jan. 9, 2008).

Note on Lawsuits Against Donors

Wirth is only one of a number of high-profile donors who recently have failed to fulfill their pledges to colleges and universities. Among the more prominent donors are Larry Ellison, CEO of Oracle, who reneged on a $115 million pledge to Harvard following the departure of President Larry Summers, and J. Howard Marshall II, the husband of Anna Nicole Smith, who fulfilled only part of his multimillion dollar pledge to Haverford College. Sally Beatty & Vauhini Vara, *Giving Back: A Prenup for Donors*, WALL ST. J., Nov. 24, 2006, at W1.

C.   TAX BENEFITS

Bob Jones University v. United States

Supreme Court of the United States, 1983.
461 U.S. 574, 103 S.Ct. 2017, 76 L.Ed.2d 157.

[The opinion is set forth at pages 183–87, *supra*].

City of Washington v. Board of Assessment Appeals

Supreme Court of Pennsylvania, 1997.
550 Pa. 175, 704 A.2d 120.

■ Chief Justice Flaherty

This is an appeal by allowance from an order of the Commonwealth Court which reversed an order of the Court of Common Pleas of Washington County. The court of common pleas had reversed determinations of the Board of Assessment Appeals of Washington County that eighty-seven properties owned by Washington & Jefferson College (W&J) were exempt from real estate tax. The City of Washington, appellant, challenges W&J's tax-exempt status.

W&J is a private, coeducational, nonsectarian, four-year liberal arts college in Washington County. It claims exemption from tax pursuant to the General County Assessment Law, 72 P.S. § 5020–204(a)(3), which provides that all universities and colleges, "with the grounds thereto annexed and necessary for the occupancy and enjoyment of the same, founded, endowed, and maintained by public or private charity" shall be exempt from all county, city, borough, town, township, road, poor, and school taxes. The exemption was enacted pursuant to a provision of the Pennsylvania Constitution which gives the legislature power to exempt from taxation "institutions of *purely public charity*, but in the case of any real property tax exemptions only that portion of real property of such institution which is actually and regularly used for the purposes of the institution." Pa. Const. art. VIII, § 2(a)(v) (emphasis added). At issue in this appeal is whether W&J meets the constitutional prerequisite of being a "purely public charity" so that it can claim the statutory exemption.

In *Hospital Utilization Project v. Commonwealth*, 507 Pa. 1, 487 A.2d 1306 (1985), we set forth the test that determines whether an entity constitutes a purely public charity. The test requires that the entity 1) advance a charitable purpose; 2) donate or render gratuitously a substantial portion of its services; 3) benefit a substantial and indefinite class of persons who are legitimate subjects of charity; 4) relieve the government of some of its burden; and 5) operate entirely free from private profit motive. Here, the record demonstrates that W&J fulfills all of these requirements.

With regard to the first prong of the *Hospital Utilization Project* test, an institution advances a charitable purpose if it benefits the public from an educational, religious, moral, physical or social standpoint. Institutions that provide education have long been regarded by this court as serving to advance the public good and as being charitable in nature. W&J provides education for youths in this Commonwealth and thereby serves a charitable purpose.

The next element of the *Hospital Utilization Project* test is satisfied in that W&J donates or renders gratuitously a substantial portion of its services. It does so by absorbing massive tuition charges that would otherwise be charged to the students. This results in an annual disbursement of substantial amounts of essentially free, or partially free, education for the approximately 1,100 students that comprise W&J's student body.

... [Between the academic years 1991–92 and 1993–94, W&J provided, on average, $533,176 in academic-merit scholarships to 130 students annually. Over the same period, W&J annually provided an average of $4,330,487 to 735 students.][4] Approximately 845 students were recipients of scholarships, grants, and related aid from W&J in 1993–94; 850 were recipients in 1992–93; and 762 were recipients in 1991–92. Scholarships, grants, and aid amounted to 30.5% of the college's total operating budget for 1992–93, and to 25.2% thereof for 1991–92.

In addition, W&J contributes large sums from its endowment to sustain its educational programs. In the academic years 1992–93 and 1991–92, at least 23% of W&J's operating budget was paid from endowment funds. By using these funds to finance educational programs rather than raising tuition prices to reflect true operating costs, W&J effectively subsidizes each and every student for a portion of the cost of his or her education. Further, W&J incurred operating losses in 1993–94, 1992–93, and 1991–92, respectively, in the amounts of $1,071,959 (projected), $470,631, and $939,848. These losses were covered by funds from the endowment, rather than by tuition increases. This demonstrates W&J's charitable character.

Due to the extensive use of scholarships, grants, and endowment funds, the typical student at W&J receives approximately 50% of his or her education without charge. In 1992–93, student tuition payments covered only 46.8% of the college's operating budget. In 1991–92, such payments covered only 51.7% of the budget. As we stated in *Pittsburgh Institute of Aeronautics Tax Exemption Case*, 435 Pa. 618, 624, 258 A.2d 850, 853 (1969), "if the tuition only pays for one half the operating expenses, then every student is effectively getting a 50% scholarship irrespective of the number of formal scholarships offered."

Inasmuch as W&J collects only about half of its operating costs from its students, it essentially provides half of its educational services for free.[6] This level of assistance is well above what we have deemed adequate to qualify as a purely public charity. *See St. Margaret Seneca Place v. Board of Property Assessment Appeals and Review*, 536 Pa. 478, 486, 640 A.2d 380, 384 (1994) (nursing home that collected fees for its services and absorbed only one-sixth of its costs qualified for tax exemption as a purely public charity); *Presbyterian Homes Tax Exemption Case*, 428 Pa. 145, 153, 236 A.2d 776, 780 (1968) (rest home that collected fees from its residents and absorbed only one-fifth of its costs was a purely public charity).

The fact that tuition charges are levied by W&J does not negate the college's status as a charity. *See St. Margaret Seneca Place v. Board of Property Assessment, Appeals and Review*, 536 Pa. 478, 486, 640 A.2d 380, 384 (1994) (collection of fees is appropriate since charities need not provide services that are *wholly* gratuitous); *Presbyterian Homes Tax Exemption Case*, 428 Pa. at 154, 236 A.2d at 780–81 (receipt of payment for services does not conflict with status as a purely public charity); *Hill School Tax Exemption Case*, 370 Pa. at 27, 87 A.2d at 263 (educational institution that levies tuition charges does not thereby lose its status as a purely public charity).

4. In addition to scholarships and grants, which are available to the general student population, tuition remission and assistance are provided for students whose parents are employees of W&J and certain other colleges. The latter sums, however, are small in relation to the total of scholarships and grants.

Tuition remission and assistance [averaged $474,047 between 1991–92 and 1993–94].

6. In addition to providing free educational services, W&J makes many of its facilities available free of charge or at nominal cost for use by numerous community organizations and the public at large.

The scholarships, grants, and other aid provided by W&J were sufficiently substantial that, with the supplemental aid provided by state and federal grant and loan programs, nearly all students were able to pay the required fees, i.e., to pay the remaining portion of the $19,360 annual charge for tuition, room, board, and related fees. In fact, in 1993–94, only seven or eight students were excluded from enrollment as a result of inability or refusal to pay the required fees.

The next prong of the *Hospital Utilization Project* test requires that W&J benefit a substantial and indefinite class of persons who are legitimate subjects of charity. Given our earlier conclusion that W&J advances a charitable purpose by providing youths with college education, it follows that youths seeking education can qualify as legitimate subjects of charity.

In this era when the cost of attending college poses a major obstacle for youths seeking to further their education, even students who are financially secure in other phases of life are often "poor" in relation to the financial outlays that college requires. W&J provides substantial aid for students who would not otherwise be able to afford a college education. Through scholarships and grants, as well as the use of endowment funds to subsidize the education of its students, W&J makes education attainable for innumerable youths who would not otherwise be able to afford it. *See generally Hospital Utilization Project*, 507 Pa. at 19 n.9, 487 A.2d at 1315 n.9 (purely public charity must attempt to serve those who would not otherwise be able to pay the full fees).

The cost of education would climb precipitously if colleges did not use endowment funds and other forms of aid to keep their fees within bounds. For many youths, perhaps even most, the price of education would simply be beyond reach. Institutions such as W&J plainly serve those who would not be able to afford the fees that would prevail in the absence of their benevolence.

The vast majority of the aid that W&J provides is directed to the financially needy, i.e., those who cannot afford the usual charges for tuition, room, and board. In fact, approximately 82% of the total aid that the college provides is comprised of need-based grants. Significantly, too, the admissions policies at W&J do not discriminate against applicants who will need such grants. *Compare Pittsburgh Institute of Aeronautics Tax Exemption Case*, 435 Pa. at 624, 258 A.2d at 853, "[a] school in which the admission of students is almost totally limited to those who are able to pay their own way can hardly be considered a charitable institution. . . ."

The fact that scholarships, a smaller category of aid than grants, are awarded on the basis of academic achievement rather than on the basis of financial need is not inconsistent with W&J's charitable status. The process of awarding scholarships will no doubt result in some awards going to the financially needy and others going to those who would have been able to pay part or all of the cost of their education. There is no requirement, however, that all of the benefits bestowed by a purely public charity go *only* to the financially needy.

Likewise, the existence of academic admissions standards is consistent with W&J's charitable status. As we stated in *Hill School Tax Exemption Case*, [370 Pa. 21, 26, 87 A.2d 259, 262 (1952)], an "institution engaged in education of youth is a 'public charity' if its doors are open to the public generally or a well defined class thereof, subject to reasonable entrance requirements." Consistent with this, enrollment at W&J is open to the public for anyone who can meet its academic requirements.[7]

To satisfy the next element of the *Hospital Utilization Project* test, it is necessary that W&J relieve the government of some of its burden. This element is plainly met inasmuch as W&J, like other independent colleges and universities, relieves the load placed on the state-owned system of colleges and universities. So large is the role of private colleges and universities that they account for nearly 40% of Pennsylvania's undergraduate enrollment. Inasmuch as the Commonwealth has taken on the responsibility of providing higher education for its residents, it is clear that were it not for the existence of independent colleges and universities the demands placed on the state's institutions would be vastly expanded. The legislature has expressly recognized the role of private institutions in this regard by providing them with institutional assistance grants that cover a small percentage of their costs. State assistance received by W&J, for example, averages $391 per student on an annual basis. The legislature has declared that independent colleges and universities "make a significant contribution to higher education in the Commonwealth," 24 P.S. § 5182(a), and that if such institutions were inhibited in their ability to provide such education it would *"increase the burden on public institutions,"* 24 P.S. § 5182(b) (emphasis added).

The final prong of the *Hospital Utilization Project* test requires that W&J operate entirely free from private profit motive. The record demonstrates that W&J has, since its very origin, operated without any intention of producing private gain. The college traces its roots to the eighteenth century when ministers of the Presbyterian Church, who sought not personal profit but rather a means of providing education for youths, created two colleges that were later combined to form W&J. W&J has long been incorporated as a non-profit corporation. Its trustees serve without receiving any salary for their services. No dividends or profits are distributed to any individuals. If W&J were to generate an operating surplus, the surplus would be reinvested in the college. However, as heretofore described, W&J has incurred substantial operating losses in recent years. Given the large sums of aid that the college provides through scholarships, need-based grants, and endowment utilization, it is clear that W&J provides education at far less than its cost. Supplying educational services below cost provides evidence of a lack of profit motive. *Hospital Utilization Project*, 507 Pa. at 17, 487 A.2d at 1314 (enterprises operated for profit do not supply all of their services for less than actual cost.).

We conclude, therefore, that the Commonwealth Court properly held that W&J satisfies all five elements of the *Hospital Utilization Project* test. Hence, W&J can claim exemption from tax as a purely public charity.

Rensselaer Polytechnic Institute v. Commissioner

United States Court of Appeals for the Second Circuit, 1984.
732 F.2d 1058.

■ PRATT, CIRCUIT JUDGE:

The issue before us is not only one of first impression; it is also of considerable financial significance to many of our colleges and universities. . . .

---

7. W&J also offers a program for academically underprivileged students, those with a grade point average of 2.1 or less, and ten percent of the first year class enters this program.

... Rensselaer Polytechnic Institute (RPI) is a non-profit educational organization entitled to tax-exempt status under I.R.C. § 501(c)(3). It owns and operates a fieldhouse which it devotes to two broad categories of uses: (1) student uses, which include physical education, college ice hockey, student ice skating, and other activities related to RPI's tax-exempt educational responsibilities; and (2) commercial uses, which include activities and events such as commercial ice shows and public ice skating, that do not fall within its tax-exempt function. For fiscal year 1974, the net income from commercial use of the fieldhouse constituted "unrelated business taxable income" which was subject to taxation under I.R.C. § 511(a)(1).

The dispute is over the amount of unrelated business tax due from RPI for 1974 and, since there is no disagreement over the gross income, $476,613, we must focus on the deductible expenses. The parties "direct expenses," are those that can be specifically identified with particular commercial uses. For the year in question direct expenses amounted to $371,407, and the parties have always agreed to their deductibility.

. . .

This appeal involves ... "fixed expenses".... The amounts of fixed expenses incurred with respect to the fieldhouse were stipulated to be:

Salaries and fringe benefits	$59,415
Depreciation	29,397
Repairs and Replacements	14,031
Operating Expenditures	1,356
	$104,199

Narrowly stated, the issue is how these fixed expenses should be allocated between RPI's dual uses: the exempt student use and the taxable commercial use. RPI contends it is entitled to allocate the fixed expenses on the basis of relative times of actual use. Thus, in computing that portion of its deductible expenses, RPI multiplies the total amount of fixed expenses by a fraction, whose numerator is the total number of hours the fieldhouse was used for commercial events, and whose denominator is the total number of hours the fieldhouse was used for all activities and events—student and commercial combined.

The commissioner argues that the allocation of fixed expenses must be made not on the basis of times of actual use, but on the basis of total time available for use. Thus, he contends the denominator of the fraction should be the total number of hours in the taxable year. In practical terms, the difference between the two methods of allocation amounts to $9,259 in taxes.

Below, the tax court agreed with RPI's method of allocating on the basis of actual use, finding it to be "reasonable" within the meaning of Treas. Reg. § 1.512(a)–1(c). The commissioner appeals....

It has been the consistent policy of this nation to exempt from income taxes a corporation, like RPI, that is "organized and operated exclusively for ... educational purposes...." I.R.C. § 501(c)(3). This preferred treatment to educational, as well as religious, charitable, and scientific institutions, was established simultaneously with the first income tax enacted by congress in 1913, and has been continued in identical language through a series of revenue acts down to and including the current provision contained in I.R.C. § 501. So firm was the policy shielding educational institutions from taxation that, despite repeated challenges by the commissioner, the statute was consistently interpreted to exempt from taxation all income earned by an exempt corporation, even that obtained from activities unrelated to its tax-exempt educational purposes. *See Mueller Co. v. Commissioner*, 190 F.2d 120 (3d Cir. 1951).

Recognizing, however, the unfair competitive advantage that freedom from income taxation could accord tax-exempt institutions that entered the world of commerce, Congress, in 1950, extended the income tax to the "unrelated business income" of certain tax-exempt institutions, including educational corporations. Pub. L. No. 81–814, § 301, 64 Stat. 906, 947 (1950) (codified at I.R.C. §§ 511–513). Its objective in changing the law was to eliminate the competitive advantage educational and charitable corporations enjoyed over private enterprise, without jeopardizing the basic purpose of the tax-exemption. *See* H.R. Rep. No. 2319, 81st Cong., 2d Sess. 36–38; S. Rep. No. 2375, 81st Cong., 2d Sess. 28–30....

... Section 512 of the code defines as "unrelated business taxable income" gross income derived from unrelated business activities less deductions "directly connected with" such activities. Treas. Reg. § 1.512 (a)–1(a) further defines the term "directly connected with," and provides that "to be 'directly connected with' the conduct of unrelated business for purposes of section 512, an item of deduction must have proximate and primary relationship" to that business. Two subsequent subsections of that regulation define "proximate and primary relationship" in the context of (a) items that are attributable solely to the unrelated business, Treas. Reg. § 1.512(a)–1(b); and (b) as in this case, items that are attributable to facilities or personnel used for both exempt and unrelated purposes, Treas. Reg. § 1.512(a)–1(c). The latter regulation provides:

> (c) *Dual use of facilities or personnel.* Where facilities are used both to carry on exempt activities and to conduct unrelated trade or business activities, expenses, depreciation and similar items attributable to such facilities (as, for example, items of overhead), *shall be allocated between the two uses on a reasonable basis.* Similarly, where personnel are used both to carry on exempt activities and to conduct unrelated trade or business activities, expenses and similar items attributable to such personnel (as, for example, items of salary) *shall be allocated between the two uses on a reasonable basis.* The portion of any such items so allocated to the unrelated trade or business activity is *proximately and primarily related to that business activity, and shall be allowable as a deduction in computing unrelated business taxable income* in the manner and to the extent permitted by section 162, section 167 or other relevant provisions of the Code.

Treas. Reg. § 1.512(a)–1(c) (emphasis added).

. . .

Under this regulation, therefore, the critical question is whether the method of allocation adopted by RPI was "reasonable." The tax court found that it was, and, giving due regard to its expertise in this area, we see no error in that conclusion. Apportioning indirect expenses such as depreciation on the basis of the actual hours the facility was used for both exempt and taxable purposes sensibly distributes the cost of the facility among the activities that benefit from its use. In addition, the method is consistent with that followed by the tax court in the most common dual-use situation, home office deduction cases.

Indeed, the commissioner does not claim that RPI's allocation method is factually unreasonable, but instead contends solely that the method is not "reasonable," because by permitting depreciation during "idle time," when the fieldhouse is not being used at all, it contravenes the statutory requirement that deductible expenses be "directly connected with" RPI's unrelated business activities. By advancing this argument, however, the commissioner ignores his own definition of the concept "directly connected with" included in Treas. Reg. § 1.512(a)–1(a) discussed above. In addition, the commissioner would have us adopt a more stringent interpretation of "directly connected with" in § 512 than has been applied for over sixty years to the same concept in the commissioner's regulations governing the deductibility of ordinary and necessary business expenses. *See* Treas. Reg. § 1.162–1(a). Moreover, the logical extension of his position would require the commissioner to deny depreciation deductions to all businesses for those periods when their assets are idle. Such a view, however, would contravene the basic concepts underlying the commissioner's elaborate regulations governing depreciation generally. *See* Treas. Reg. § 1.167(a)–1 *et seq.*

For an expense to be "directly connected with" an activity, the commissioner argues that it must be one that would not have been incurred in the absence of the activity. But whether or not the fieldhouse is actually put to any business use, depreciation of the facility continues. We cannot accept the commissioner's argument, therefore, because it would in effect eliminate entirely all deductions for indirect expenses such as depreciation, a result that is not required by statute and that is directly contrary to the regulation.

. . .

Furthermore, to apply the statute as the commissioner interprets it would not fulfill the congressional purpose of placing private enterprise on an equal level with competing businesses run by tax-exempt institutions, but would place RPI at a competitive disadvantage. Unlike business enterprises, it would be unable to allocate any of its indirect expenses to those periods when the fieldhouse was not being used at all.

Some concern has been expressed that RPI's allocation method would provide an incentive for educational institutions to abuse their tax-exempt status. The argument is a red herring. Use of educational facilities for producing unrelated business income is not tax abuse; on the contrary, as we have pointed out above, such non-exempt activities have been consistently permitted and, since 1950, expressly approved by congress. Moreover, should the trustees of a particular tax-exempt educational institution so pervert its operations that the institution no longer "engages primarily in activities which accomplish [its exempt purposes]," Treas. Reg. § 1.501(c)(3)–

1(c)(1), the commissioner has adequate remedies available to correct any abuse or even terminate the exemption.

The judgment appealed from is affirmed.

Questions and Comments on UBIT

UBIT grew out of the perception that in the nonprofit sector, universities in particular were abusing their tax-exempt status. One notable instance of the alleged abuse was New York University's purchase of a noodle company. In debating the UBIT legislation, one congressman quipped, "I know New York University pretty well and there is nothing that they teach in New York University that is incidental to spaghetti." Ethan G. Stone, *Adhering to the Old Line: Uncovering the History and Political Function of the Unrelated Business Income Tax*, 54 Emory L.J. 1475, 1551 (2005) (quoting *Proposed Revisions of the Internal Revenue Code: Hearings Before the H. Comm. on Ways and Means*, 80th Cong. 3536 (1947) (statement of Rep. Walter Lynch)). Among the other business activities of universities prior to the passage of UBIT were the "production of automobile parts, chinaware, and food products, and the operation of theatres, oil wells, and cotton gins." United States v. American Coll. of Physicians, 475 U.S. 834, 838 (1986). For an argument that the tax-exempt status of nonprofits does not give them an unfair advantage over for-profit firms and that the UBIT actually disadvantages nonprofits, see Michael Knoll, *The UBIT: Leveling an Uneven Playing Field or Tilting a Level One?*, 76 Fordham L. Rev. 857 (2007)

Although income from the operation of oil wells is taxable under UBIT, trade or business "which is carried on . . . by [a college or university] primarily for the convenience of its members, students, patients, officers, or employees" remains exempt. 26 U.S.C. § 513(a)(2). This exemption may extend to income from university bookstores, cafeterias, and laundry services. *See* Deirdre Dessingue Halloran, *UBIT Update*, 36 Cath. Law. 39, 46 (1995); Stone at 1484. Should the income generated by a university book store be subject to UBIT? Should income generated from intercollegiate sports be considered substantially related to education, and thus exempt from the UBIT? *See* Gabriel A. Morgan, Note, *No More Playing Favorites: Reconsidering the Conclusive Congressional Presumption that Intercollegiate Athletics are Substantially Related to Educational Purposes*, 81 S. Cal. Law Rev. 149 (2007). For an analysis of whether income from university endowments should be subject to the UBIT, see Mark J. Cowan, *Taxing and Regulating College and University Endowment Income: The Literature's Perspective*, 34 J.C. & U.L 507 (2008).

D.   For-Profit Colleges and Universities

United States *ex rel.* Hendow v. University of Phoenix

United States Court of Appeals for the Ninth Circuit, 2006.
461 F.3d 1166, cert. denied, ___ U.S. ___, 127 S.Ct. 2099 (2007).

■ HALL, Senior Circuit Judge:

The False Claims Act makes liable anyone who "knowingly makes, uses, or causes to be made or used, a false record or statement to get a false or fraudulent claim paid or approved by the Government." 31 U.S.C. § 3729(a)(2). In this case, relators have raised allegations that the University of Phoenix knowingly made false statements, and caused false statements to be made, that resulted in the payment by the federal Department of Education of hundreds of millions of dollars. Despite this axiomatic fit between the operative statute and the allegations made, respondent claims that relators' legal theory holds no water. The district court agreed, dismissing the suit for failure to state a claim upon which relief can be granted....

When an educational institution wishes to receive federal subsidies under Title IV and the Higher Education Act, it must enter into a Program Participation Agreement with the Department of Education (DOE), in which it agrees to abide by a panoply of statutory, regulatory, and contractual requirements. One of these requirements is a ban on incentive compensation: a ban on the institution's paying recruiters on a per-student basis. The ban prohibits schools from "provid[ing] any commission, bonus, or other incentive payment based directly or indirectly on success in securing enrollments or financial aid to any persons or entities engaged in any student recruiting or admission activities or in making decisions regarding the award of student financial assistance." 20 U.S.C. § 1094(a)(20). This requirement is meant to curb the risk that recruiters will "sign up poorly qualified students who will derive little benefit from the subsidy and may be unable or unwilling to repay federally guaranteed loans." *United States ex rel. Main v. Oakland City Univ.*, 426 F.3d 914, 916 (7th Cir. 2005), *cert. denied*, 126 S. Ct. 1786 (2006). The ban was enacted based on evidence of serious program abuses.

This case involves allegations under the False Claims Act that the University of Phoenix (the University) knowingly made false promises to comply with the incentive compensation ban in order to become eligible to receive Title IV funds. Appellants, Mary Hendow and Julie Albertson (relators), two former enrollment counselors at the University, allege that the University falsely certifies each year that it is in compliance with the incentive compensation ban while intentionally and knowingly violating that requirement. Relators allege that these false representations, coupled with later claims for payment of Title IV funds, constitute false claims under 31 U.S.C. § 3729(a)(1) & (a)(2).

First, relators allege that the University, with full knowledge, flagrantly violates the incentive compensation ban. They claim that the University "compensates enrollment counselors ... based directly upon enrollment activities," ranking counselors according to their number of enrollments and giving the highest-ranking counselors not only higher salaries but also benefits, incentives, and gifts. Relators allege that the University also "urges enrollment counselors to enroll students without reviewing their transcripts to determine their academic qualifications to attend the university," thus encouraging counselors to enroll students based on numbers alone. Relator Albertson, in particular, alleges that she was given a specific target number of students to recruit, and that upon reaching that benchmark her salary increased by more than $50,000. Relator Hendow specifically alleges that she won trips and home electronics as a result of enrolling large numbers of students.

Second, relators allege considerable fraud on the part of the University to mask its violation of the incentive compensation ban. They claim that the University's head of enrollment openly brags that "[i]t's all about the numbers. It will always be about the numbers. But we need to show the Department of Education what they want to see." To deceive the DOE, relators allege, the University creates two separate employment files for its enrollment counselors—one "real" file containing performance reviews based on improper quantitative factors, and one "fake" file containing performance reviews based on legitimate qualitative factors. The fake file is what the DOE allegedly sees. Relators further allege a series of University policy changes deliberately designed to obscure the fact that enrollment counselors are compensated on a per-student basis, such as altering pay scales to make it less obvious that they are adjusted based on the number of students enrolled.

Third and finally, relators allege that the University submits false claims to the government. Claims for payment of Title IV funds can be made in a number of ways, once a school signs its Program Participation Agreement and thus becomes eligible. For instance, in the Pell Grant context, students submit funding requests directly (or with school assistance) to the DOE. In contrast, under the Federal Family Education Loan Program, which includes Stafford Loans, students and schools jointly submit an application to a private lender on behalf of the student, and a guaranty agency makes the eventual claim for payment to the United States only in the event of default. Relators allege that the University submits false claims in both of these ways. . . .

On May 20, 2004, the district court dismissed the relators' complaint with prejudice under Federal Rule of Civil Procedure 12(b)(6) for failure to state a claim. Relators appealed on June 15, 2004. The United States Department of Justice submitted a brief as amicus curiae supporting the reversal of the district court. Because this case comes to us on a motion to dismiss, we assume that the facts as alleged are true, and examine only whether relators' allegations support a cause of action under the False Claims Act under either of two possible theories. We hold that they do, and that either theory is viable.

. . .

In an archetypal *qui tam* False Claims action, such as where a private company overcharges under a government contract, the claim for payment is itself literally false or fraudulent. The False Claims Act, however, is not limited to such facially false or fraudulent claims for payment. Rather, the False Claims Act is "intended to reach all types of fraud, without qualification, that might result in financial loss to the Government." *United States v. Neifert–White Co.*, 390 U.S. 228, 232 (1968). More specifically, in amending the False Claims Act in 1986, Congress emphasized that the scope of false or fraudulent claims should be broadly construed:

> [E]ach and every claim submitted under a contract, loan guarantee, or other agreement which was originally obtained by means of false statements or other corrupt or fraudulent conduct, or in violation of any statute or applicable regulation, constitutes a false claim.

S. Rep. No. 99–345, at 9 (1986), *reprinted in* 1986 U.S.C.C.A.N. 5266, 5274.

The principles embodied in this broad construction of a "false or fraudulent claim" have given rise to two doctrines that attach potential False Claims Act liability to claims for payment that are not explicitly and/or independently false: (1) false certification (either express or implied); and (2) promissory fraud.

. . .

[U]nder either the false certification theory or the promissory fraud theory, the essential elements of False Claims Act liability remain the same:

(1) a false statement or fraudulent course of conduct, (2) made with scienter, (3) that was material, causing (4) the government to pay out money or forfeit moneys due. The question remaining is whether relators in this case have alleged facts satisfying all four of these elements.

A. Falsity

Relators allege a false statement or course of conduct. They allege that the University violates a statutory requirement, the incentive compensation ban, to which it agreed in writing in the Program Participation Agreement. They allege that the University establishes policies of violating that requirement, and encourages its employees to violate that requirement. They allege specific instances of violation, where higher salaries, benefits, and incentives were given in response to increased enrollment. And they allege that the University did so knowingly, and with the specific intent to deceive the government. Thus, relators properly allege a false statement or course of conduct.

B. Scienter

Relators allege a false statement or course of conduct made knowingly and intentionally. They allege that University staff openly bragged about perpetrating a fraud, that the University had an established infrastructure to deceive the government, and that the University repeatedly changed its policies to hide its fraud. In other words, relators allege that the University provided statements to the government that were "intentional, palpable lie[s]," made with "knowledge of the falsity and with intent to deceive."

The University argues that the incentive compensation ban is nothing more than one of hundreds of boilerplate requirements with which it promises compliance. This may be true, but fraud is fraud, regardless of how "small." The University is worried that our holding today opens it up to greater liability for innocent regulatory violations, but that is not the case— . . . innocent or unintentional violations do not lead to False Claims Act liability. But that is no reason to inoculate institutions of higher education from liability when they *knowingly* violate a regulatory condition, with the intent to deceive, as is alleged here. Relators properly allege false statements or courses of conduct made with scienter.

C. Materiality

Most of the argument in this case centers on whether and how much the University's alleged fraud was material to the government's decision to disburse federal funds. The parties argue at length over, for instance, the enforcement power of the DOE, and whether its authority to take "emergency action"—to withhold funds or impose sanctions where it has information that statutory requirements are being violated—means that the statutory requirements are causally related to its decision to pay out moneys due.

These questions of enforcement power are largely academic, because the eligibility of the University under Title IV and the Higher Education Act of 1965—and thus, the funding that is associated with such eligibility—is *explicitly* conditioned, in three different ways, on compliance with the incentive compensation ban. First, a federal statute states that in order to be eligible, an institution must

> enter into a program participation agreement with the Secretary [of Education]. The agreement *shall condition* the initial and continuing eligibility of an institution to participate in a program *upon compliance* with the following requirements . . . [including the incentive compensation ban.]

20 U.S.C. § 1094(a) (emphasis added).

Second, a federal regulation specifies:

> An institution may participate in any Title IV, HEA program . . . *only if* the institution enters into a written program participation agreement with the Secretary. . . . A program participation agreement *conditions* the initial and continued participation of an eligible institution in any Title IV, HEA program *upon compliance* with the provisions of this part [such as the incentive compensation ban.]

34 C.F.R. § 668.14(a)(1) (emphasis added).

Third and finally, the program participation agreement itself states:

> The execution of this Agreement [which contains a reference to the incentive compensation ban] by the Institution and the Secretary is a *prerequisite* to the Institution's initial or continued participation in any Title IV, HEA program.

(emphasis added).

All of the emphasized phrases in the above passages demonstrate that compliance with the incentive compensation ban is a necessary condition of continued eligibility and participation: compliance is a "prerequisite" to funding; funding shall occur "only if" the University complies; funding shall be "condition[ed] . . . upon compliance." These are not ambiguous exhortations of an amorphous duty. The statute, regulation, and agreement here all explicitly condition participation and payment on compliance with, among other things, the precise requirement that relators allege that the University knowingly disregarded.

The University argues that the ban is merely a condition of *participation*, not a condition of *payment*. But in this case, that is a distinction without a difference. In the context of Title IV and the Higher Education Act, if we held that conditions of participation were not conditions of payment, there would be no conditions of payment at all—and thus, an educational institution could flout the law at will.

To see why this is so, one only need look at the University's semantic argument, in which it claims that for a condition of participation, an institution says it "*will* comply" with various statutes and regulations, but for a condition of payment, an institution says that it "*has* complied." This grammatical haggling is unmoored in the law, and it is undercut by the Program Participation Agreement itself. In the section that the University concedes contains conditions of payment—the section entitled "Certifications Required From Institutions"—the University agrees that it "will" or "shall" comply with various regulations no less than six times. Under the University's logic, these future-tense assertions could not be conditions of payment, and yet it concedes that they are. Its concession is correct; these, and all other promises to comply with the Program Participation Agreement, are conditions of payment. These conditions are also "prerequisites," and "the *sine qua non*" of federal funding, for one basic reason: if the University had not agreed to comply with them, it would not have gotten paid.

Furthermore, we take the University's argument to mean that it believes if it had signed an agreement that stated "the University of Phoenix certifies that it has complied with the incentive compensation ban," then it would have signed a condition of payment. But the DOE and the United States Congress, as evidenced by the statutes, regulations, and contracts implementing the Title IV and Higher Education Act requirements for funding, quite plainly care about an institution's ongoing conduct, not only its past compliance. For purposes of federal funding, the University is not permitted to merely have a history of compliance with the applicable regulations; it must also agree to comply in the future. The Program Participation Agreement, constraining its ongoing conduct, is the condition of payment that the federal government requires—a promise that the University shall not break the law, not merely an assertion that it has not broken the law *yet*. If such promises were not conditions of payment, the University would be virtually unfettered in its ability to receive funds from the government while flouting the law. This cannot be what Congress and the DOE intend when they ask institutions to sign Program Participation Agreements.

Nor was such laissez-faire compliance what the Second Circuit had in mind, we think, when it developed the "participation versus payment" distinction in the first place. The case in which that distinction was first mentioned, [*United States ex rel. Mikes v. Straus*, 274 F.3d 687 (2d Cir. 2001)], is completely distinguishable from the case before us. There, in the Medicare context, the defendant was subject to a statutory requirement that stated:

> "[i]t shall be the obligation" of a practitioner who provides a medical service "for which payment may be made . . . to assure" compliance with [42 U.S.C. § 1320c–5(a)].

274 F.3d at 701.

"Compliance," in that instance, meant maintaining an appropriate standard of care, which was ensured by peer review and extensive monitoring. Dereliction of that duty would result in sanctions only where "a violation was especially gross and flagrant." *Id*. at 702. Defendants were accused of not maintaining the appropriate standard of care, but the Second Circuit held that such a violation could not constitute a breach of a condition of payment under the Medicare statute. This makes sense for two interrelated reasons. First, the statutory duty was not to promise *compliance*, but to promise *assurance* of compliance. The fact that defendants did not meet the appropriate standard of care does not necessarily mean that they were ignoring their duty to try their best to comply; rather, it may have indicated merely that they were not doing a very good job. If the allegation had been that the defendants in *Mikes* were not even trying to comply—that they were not only failing to provide the appropriate standard of care, but also affirmatively and knowingly choosing not to—we imagine the *Mikes* case would have come out differently.

And even if it would not have, the *Mikes* court was dealing with the Medicare context, to which the court specifically confined its reasoning. *Id*. at 700. It imposed an additional requirement on Medicare cases: that the underlying statute "expressly" condition payment on compliance. An explicit statement, however, is not necessary to make a statutory requirement a condition of payment, and we have never held as much.

Therefore, because relators have alleged that the University fraudulently violated a regulation upon which payment is expressly conditioned in three different ways, we hold that they have properly alleged the University engaged in statements or courses of conduct that were *material* to the government's decision with regard to funding.

D. *Claim*

Finally, relators allege that the University submitted a [false] claim against the government fisc. Relators allege that the University submits false claims in a number of ways—either by submitting requests for Pell Grant funds directly to DOE, resulting in a direct transfer of the funds into a University account, or by submitting requests to private lenders for government-insured loans. We agree with the Seventh Circuit that "it is irrelevant how the federal bureaucracy has apportioned the statements among layers of paperwork." All that matters is whether the false statement or course of conduct causes the government to "pay out money or to forfeit moneys due." Relators have properly alleged that the University submitted a claim, for purposes of False Claims Act liability.

Accordingly, because relators in this case have properly alleged (1) a false statement or fraudulent course of conduct, (2) made with scienter, (3) that was material, causing (4) the government to pay out money or forfeit moneys due, their cause of action under the False Claims Act survives a motion to dismiss, and the decision of the district court is reversed.

Note on *Qui Tam* Litigation

Although the University of Phoenix allegedly defrauded the government, the action in *United States ex rel. Hendow* was initiated by former employees of the university. Under 31 U.S.C. § 3730, "[a] person [or "relator"] may bring a civil action for a violation of [the False Claims Act] for the person and for the United States Government." Statutory language allowing such an action by a private party is called a *qui tam* provision, short for the Latin phrase meaning "who as well for the king as for himself sues in this matter." Christina Orsini Broderick, Note, Qui Tam *Provisions and the Public Interest*, 107 COLUM. L. REV. 949, 951 (2007).

Under the False Claims Act, "[i]f a relator brings the claim, it is served on the government, not the defendant. The complaint remains under seal for sixty days, during which time the Attorney General must investigate the claim and decide whether or not to intervene and proceed. If the government elects to intervene, it assumes primary responsibility for prosecuting the action; however, the private party retains a right to continue as a party and to receive up to twenty-five percent of the damages, plus reasonable attorney's fees. If, on the other hand, the government chooses not to intervene the relator may continue with the suit and may receive up to thirty percent of the damages, plus reasonable attorney's fees. However, if the government elects not to intervene it retains the right to do so at a later time upon showing 'good cause.' Additionally, the government may dismiss the case entirely, despite an objection from the relator, if the relator is given a chance to be heard before a court." *Id.* at 952–53.

According to Broderick, *qui tam* actions became more frequent after the 1986 amendments to the False Claims Act. The amendments allowed relators to maintain *qui tam* actions even if the government had prior knowledge of the false claim allegations and decided to take primary responsibility for the action, increased the total damages that could be imposed on false claimants and the percentage of that total that could be awarded to relators, and protected whistle-blowing relators from employer retaliation. *See id.* at 954.

Questions and Comments on *Phoenix*

Founded in 1976, the University of Phoenix currently enrolls more students than any other college or university in the nation. It is also a division of the Apollo Group, a publicly traded corporation. "About 95 percent of instructors are part-time, according to federal statistics, compared with an average of 47 percent across all universities." Sam Dillon, *Troubles Grow for a University Built on Profits*, N.Y. TIMES, Feb. 11, 2007, § 1, at 1. Its graduation rate is sixteen percent as measured by the number of first-time undergraduates who graduate in six years (the federal standard), one of the lowest rates in the nation. *Id.*

Most of its campuses are in office buildings near freeways to keep overhead low. To lessen instructors' preparation time, the University prepares course plans at its headquarters. "Students take one course at a time, online or in evening classes, which meet for four hours, once a week, for five or six weeks.... [S]tudents spend twenty to twenty-four hours with an instructor during each course, compared with about forty hours at a traditional university. The university also requires students to teach one another by working on projects for four or five hours per week in what it calls 'learning teams.' " *Id.* The University of Phoenix's president, on the other hand, argues that concerns about the quality of its students' education are "symptomatic of an elitist bias against nontraditional higher education." Moreover, Phoenix suggests that the federal graduation-rate standard is biased against institutions like Phoenix that serve mostly older students who have been "ignored or excluded by traditional colleges and universities." Bill Pepicello, Letter to the Editor, *For–Profit University*, N.Y. TIMES, Feb. 18, 2007, § 4, at 11.

Will Phoenix drive other "more traditional" colleges and universities out of business? Which institutions are most likely to lose potential students to Phoenix? Would that be good or bad?

E. LICENSING REVENUE

By 2006, there were twenty-eight colleges and universities that earned more than $10 million in annual revenue from their licensing of inventions by faculty and staff. New York University earned the most of any single institution that year with more than $157 million in revenues. The ten–campus University of California system earned $193.5 million, a figure that included a $100 million settlement that the university reached with Monsanto in a patent-infringement lawsuit concerning a genetically engineered growth hormone for cows. Goldie Blumenstyk, *3 More Universities Join $10–Million Club in Annual Revenue from Licensing Inventions*, CHRON. HIGHER EDUC., Dec. 14, 2007, at A22.

*

PART II

FACULTY MATTERS

Stanley Katz, *What Has Happened to the Professoriate?*,

CHRON. HIGHER EDUC., Oct. 6, 2006, at B8.

[E]ven though the general public may think of us as a unitary professoriate, a professorial class, we are in reality a highly variegated and not always well-interrelated set of subclasses. . . .

University professors include those who are primarily undergraduate teachers, those who teach graduate and professional students, and those who spend all or nearly all of their time as researchers. They also include the large class of Ph.D.'s working primarily as university administrators, many of whom seldom see a classroom or laboratory. There are huge differences within each of these categories—between professors in market-driven fields (some of the sciences and professional schools, and some of the social sciences, especially economics) and the rest; between those at private and at public institutions; between those at research universities and at primarily teaching institutions. Professors at four-year liberal-arts colleges constitute another distinctive cohort, but their institutions vary greatly from the elite, purely liberal-arts colleges and the much larger group of colleges increasingly turning to pre-professional education.

There are adjunct faculty members who are paid by the course, and who should probably be thought of as a group of professors with their own identity and interests; independent scholars who earn their living outside the academy but nevertheless carry on (sometimes significant) academic careers. Then there is the huge class of professors who teach in two-year colleges, instructing almost half of American undergraduate students. A large proportion of those faculty members have Ph.D.'s, but many do not. They are not ordinarily expected to do research, and they do not always identify with academic disciplines.

And more. We have a growing community of professors who work for proprietary institutions; free-standing professional schools of theology, law, medicine, business, and so forth. And, let us not forget, there is a significant group of professors (I am thinking for the moment only of those holding the Ph.D.) in secondary education, some of whom conduct research and publish—in many countries around the world, such individuals are called "professors."

In each of those groups, some professors work full time and others part time; some are unionized and many are not; some are handsomely paid, while others barely eke out a living. I am sure that I have omitted some important groups, but the point is clear: The professoriate is a mansion of many rooms. It is very hard to say what it means to be "a professor" in the contemporary United States, and it is difficult to know whether there is still such a thing as "the professoriate."

While there never was a golden age, there surely was a distinctive era of the professoriate during the first half of the 20th century. It was an era characterized by a small but fairly coherent group of scholars trained at a few leading universities, committed both to one another and to the institutions in which they taught. I can still remember visiting my Harvard University graduate-school professor, the historian Frederick Merk, in his Widener Library office in the mid–1950s. His walls were covered with large oblong photographs of gentlemen in black-tie attire (and a handful of ladies in long dresses) at the formal dinners that concluded the annual meeting of the

Mississippi Valley Historical Association (now, a sign of expansion, the Organization of American Historians). Just about every professor who taught American history at the postsecondary level belonged to the Mississippi Valley association and turned up for its dinner. There were a couple of hundred of them, and Mr. Merk knew them all. Today there are more than 9,000 members of the OAH, most of whom do not attend the annual meeting, and I know only a couple of hundred of them. But they are a wonderfully heterogeneous group in every respect, from demography to job descriptions—many of them teach in secondary schools and in community colleges, and certainly their faces are not all white. Their diversity enriches higher education and the history profession. The downside, of course, is that we have far less in common. It is not clear that we are a community in any strong sense.

Most of the contemporary academic disciplines emerged between 1870 and 1920, during the period in which the modern forms of classical higher education took shape. The training of Ph.D.'s in the disciplines provided the human resources for the universities that had evolved from the church-related colleges of the 19th century, and for the liberal-arts colleges that appeared alongside the universities. Doctoral students were broadly educated in their disciplines, examined on the full range of material in their areas. When I received my Ph.D., for instance, I was expected to be able to teach all of American and British history.

And there was not a great deal of job mobility—professors tended to remain in the service of their first employers. That made for institutional stability, with networking provided by the expanding group of national disciplinary organizations. Mr. Merk spent his entire teaching career at Harvard, and his professional world was the overlapping communities of Harvard and the Mississippi Valley Historical Association. I doubt that he ever felt any conflict between his double loyalties. Similarly, my philosopher father-in-law taught his entire career at Mount Holyoke College.

. . . The creation of the American Association of University Professors in 1915 marked both the movement toward professionalization and its response to assaults upon professorial academic freedom and (even more important) conflicts between professors and those who managed their universities for the right to control academic decision making.

The great leader of the AAUP movement was John Dewey, who characterized the problem in his first address to the association: "We are in a period of intense and rapid growth of higher education. No minister of public education controls the growth; there is no common educational legislature to discuss and decide its proper course; no single tribunal to which moot questions may be brought. There are not even long-established traditions to guide the expansive growth. Whatever unity is found is due to the pressure of like needs, the influence of institutional imitation and rivalry, and to informal exchange of experience and ideas. These methods have accomplished great things," Dewey wrote. "But have we not come to a time when more can be achieved by taking thought together?" For Dewey, that was a political as well as professional point, for he believed strongly in the role of professions in sustaining democracy.

It is important to remember that the AAUP aspired to create and represent an academic community, and it helped to do so in its first decades. But the situation then was fairly static, and the community not large. The postwar boom in higher education, both in response to the GI Bill and to efforts to be competitive after the Soviet Union launched Sputnik, changed everything, ushering in an era of exciting and much-needed new vitality. New institutions (and classes of institutions) were created, new disciplines and subdisciplines proliferated, research spending skyrocketed, and an entirely new infrastructure of research emerged. The brave new world of research universities burst upon the scene, with all of its tremendous potential for creating knowledge and teaching a larger and larger cohort of the general population. At the same time, what had been a WASP gentleman's profession began to be democratized, diversified, and internationalized. With expansion, however, Ph.D. training was also distributed across the country and became highly specialized. Job mobility became the norm rather than the exception, and commitment to national disciplinary and research organizations began to displace loyalty to employer institutions.

The reorientation of the profession from teachers to researchers and from local communities to national and international ones has had serious practical consequences. Since we have so little loyalty to our particular universities, we are less likely to serve them well, either in the classroom or in the performance of other necessary functions. . . .

Just as important, the current situation of the professoriate renders it difficult for us to develop and maintain either norms of conduct or of intellectual substance. The proliferation of controversies over academic misconduct, especially plagiarism, bears witness to the weakness of commonly accepted professional standards of behavior, as does the inability of professional associations in the humanities and social sciences to specify and adjudicate standards. And the more and more common intradisciplinary disputes over research methodology (witness recent debates about what counts as evidence in political science) demonstrate the centrifugal character of academic units. The center will not hold.

We simply share too little in terms of either background or experience with our colleagues, and frequently we are genuinely unable to understand where they are coming from. I fear that it may be fair to say that the AAUP itself suffers from this historical dilemma, since it seems to be trying to balance two (hugely important) issues—academic freedom and academic working conditions—rather than creating a Deweyesque single community of professors. But how could it now do otherwise?

. . . I certainly acknowledge that it matters deeply what the public thinks of us. Ours is a public profession. We serve society both by training its young (and, increasingly, its old) and by creating socially necessary knowledge. But in so doing we need to have our own standards and professional imperatives.

The public evidently still gives us high marks in meeting our goals. But it is troubling that so much of the public discussion seems to assume a uniform profession. Is it any wonder? I have become convinced that our most profound problems have to do with our unwillingness to inquire into our own situation. We cannot expect the public to understand the complexity of today's professoriate if we, ourselves, do not.

That is, we need to be clearer about how we see ourselves. For many of us, the academy provides such high pay and satisfying working conditions that the professoriate has become hard to distinguish from other highly professionalized work. Our professorial subgroups are islands, sufficient unto themselves. But isn't there some substantive core of academic professionalism that ought still unite us and give greater meaning to the underlying calling that we share? I would like to think that there is.

If I am correct that we are, professionally, "professors," then each of us, in whatever segment of the professoriate, has a duty to teach. At the very least, we need to ask whether teaching should not once again be the core of our mission, accepting that "teaching" is now a much more complex and variegated activity than it was a century ago. Granted, teaching is more central to the function of a liberal-arts, general-university, or community-college faculty member than it is for those at a research university, but in most academic disciplines we are training all faculty members as though they will inevitably become research-university professors—and few will. Those institutions in which teaching is the central faculty function need to be clear about that fact, and their faculties need to embrace it—although we should keep in mind that they could perform best if their institutions could provide adequate working conditions for them. And research-university faculty members must also accept that every one of them needs to teach and relate to students with the same passion that they bring to their labs and the library.

. . .

We also need to inquire whether our university workplaces cannot once again be the centers of our activity, and whether, indeed, professional responsibility does not include responsibility to our institutions. The problem is not just that the continuing trend toward disciplinarity creates the staggering mobility available to the most-adept researchers and an upper-end professoriate of academic grasshoppers who have little familiarity with either the undergraduates or the future paths of graduate students at the particular way stations along their career route. The problem is also that even among faculty members with fewer prospects for upward professional mobility, many find that outside obligations erode their commitment to local institutions.

If we are to create the conditions in which dedicated teachers and institutional innovators can flourish, we must ask whether it is not possible to devise systems of promotion and reward that more fairly and effectively define the breadth of our educational goals. That, too, is a challenge for the professoriate. The reward structure in too many institutions serves the needs of the research community narrowly defined, but it is commonly recognized that it is dysfunctional for the other crucial functions of the professoriate. It prejudices teaching, community service, nontraditional scholarship, and, in general, academic risk taking. In the end, it is probably not nearly as efficient even for the promotion of research as is commonly assumed. This is the toughest challenge for reform in higher education, and we have put it off too long. If professors were more willing to be self-reflective about their roles and responsibilities, they might begin to meet the challenge. Again, this is the business of professors, not deans.

Nor can we address such issues fully and honestly if we don't ask whether we can expect adjunct professors who spend their time putting together a (poorly paid) career at multiple institutions to participate in any professional and institutional life; whether we are aware how the growth of all kinds of non-tenure-track positions affects our wider professional community (whether or not we, ourselves, have tenured jobs). These are questions of professional ethics, and also of institutional integrity. The professoriate should feel responsible for both.

I believe it all comes back to the values that Dewey espoused a century ago, and to the nature of the professions. Too frequently even the most thoughtful academics are fixated on academic freedom as the crucial challenge. Academic freedom—the freedom to teach and to learn—is central. But it must follow from an acceptance of the duties of professionalism. We have such academic "rights" only if we embrace the duties of a public profession—to instruct the untrained and to create knowledge. That includes the obligation to identify the standards by which practice can be assessed and to enforce adherence to them. Seen from that perspective, professionalism is the core of democratic behavior, since it entails the acceptance of the principled provision of public services, without which a modern democracy cannot be expected to succeed.

Addressing the challenge of professionalism is a huge task for the professoriate, and it must be a focus of our postsecondary institutions, disciplinary associations, higher-education associations, and other groups. But I think it can also at least begin in a simple place—with the willingness of senior members of the professoriate, especially in the elite universities on whom so many other institutions model their behavior, to reconceptualize and reconstruct the role of teacher-scholars and university citizens. All effective reform is local, and it begins with individuals.

The diversification of higher education has had innumerable benefits for society and the professoriate. We are now more diverse, more evenly spread around the country, more capable of performing diverse tasks, and in some ways more robust. But for me, what we have gained through the breathtaking expansion of higher education does not make up for what we have lost. I know that what I regret we have abandoned may seem both nostalgic and elitist. But I would like us to consider whether there are not recoverable values and practices in the world that we have lost—and also new ones more appropriate to the 21st-century professoriate. Shouldn't we at least be asking Dewey's question: "But have we not come to a time when more can be achieved by taking thought together?"

Note on Faculty Composition

The end of World War II began a period of unprecedented growth in the number of faculty in the United States. From 1940 to 1960, the number grew from 120,000 to 236,000. Between 1960 and 1970, the number climbed to 450,000. Most of the growth was at public institutions. In 1940, less than half of all faculty were employed in the public sector. By 1969, seven of ten were. Jack H. Schuster & Martin J. Finkelstein, The American Faculty: The Restructuring of Academic Work and Careers 33 (2006).

The composition of the faculty also changed. What had been an almost exclusively Protestant profession, by 1969 included 32.3 percent faculty with non-Protestant origins. *Id.* at 66. The proportion of women and minorities increased significantly in the last part of the century. In 1969, about one in six (17.3 percent) faculty were women; by 1998, they were more than one third (35.9 percent). *Id.* at 51. In 1969 only 3.8 percent of faculty were racial or ethnic minorities; by 1998, 14.5 percent were. *Id.* at 53–54.

But the road to nondiscrimination was not smooth. When Paul Samuelson came to Harvard as a graduate student in 1935, for example, he was not allowed to teach Economics I, the major course for Harvard undergraduates. He was instead shunted off to statistics and accounting that were generally thought of as "Jewish courses." "The failure to appoint Samuelson became legendary as the most destructive consequence of Harvard anti-Semitism and the source of MIT's decades-long preeminence in Economics." MORTON KELLER & PHYLLIS KELLER, MAKING HARVARD MODERN 81–82 (2001).

The most significant recent change in faculty composition has been the decline in the proportion of full-time faculty. Of the 1,314,506 faculty at colleges that awarded federal financial aid in fall 2005, 624,753, or 47.5 percent, were in part-time positions. NAT'L CTR. FOR EDUC. STATISTICS, U.S. DEP'T OF EDUC., EMPLOYEES IN POSTSECONDARY INSTITUTIONS, FALL 2005 AND SALARIES OF FULL-TIME INSTRUCTIONAL FACULTY, 2005–06, at 6 (2007), *available at* http://nces.ed.gov/pubs2007/2007150.pdf. In addition, the majority of new full-time faculty positions in the past decade have been to non-tenure-eligible or fixed-term-contract positions. Thus, in 2001, only about one-quarter of new faculty appointments were to full-time tenure or tenure track positions. Martin Finkelstein, *The Morphing of the American Academic Profession*, LIBERAL EDUC., Fall 2003, at 6, 6. What has caused this change? Finkelstein suggests that it reflects the fact that higher education is increasingly viewed as a business and the concomitant belief that faculty costs must be reduced by hiring fewer tenured or tenure track faculty. Do you agree? What are the implications for academic freedom? For the quality of education provided? For the future of higher education?

Ronal Ehrenberg warns that "we are offering less educational quality to the students who need it most," explaining that the soaring number of adjunct faculty is more pronounced in community colleges and the less selective public universities. Some of them are great teachers, he explained, but they do not have the support that tenure track faculty have including offices and secretarial help, and their teaching loads are higher. Alan Finder, *Decline of the Tenure Track Raises Concerns at Colleges*, N.Y. TIMES, Nov. 20, 2007, at A1.

A recent study by Solon Simmons and Neil Gross found that only 9.2 percent of college instructors are conservatives, 46.6 percent are moderates, and 44.1 percent are liberals. Political orientation varied by discipline with the social sciences and humanities having the highest percentage of liberals (more than 52 percent) and lowest of conservatives (less than 5 percent) while computer science/engineering and health sciences have the smallest percentage of liberals (less than 21 percent) and among the highest of conservatives (more than 11 percent). Significantly, younger instructors are more moderate (60 percent) and less liberal (32.5 percent) than the average for all instructors which means the trend is toward even more moderation. Liberal arts colleges have the highest concentrations of left-of-center teachers. Only 3.9 percent of their instructors are conservatives. Community colleges have the smallest proportion of liberals (37.1 percent) and the highest proportion of conservatives (19 percent). Selective Ph.D.-granting institutions fall in the middle with 10.2 percent of instructors identifying themselves as conservative. This pattern contrasts with studies conducted in 1969 and 1972 by Everett Carll Ladd Jr. and Seymour Martin Lipset, *The Divided Academy* (1976), who found the fewest conservatives in elite, Ph.D granting institutions. Neil Gross & Solon Simmons, *The Social and Political Views of American Professors* (2007), *available at* http://www.wjh.harvard.edu/?ngross/lounsbery_9–25.pdf. Do these results square with your own knowledge of college faculty? Do you think it is appropriate for faculty to express their political views on topics that are discussed in class? What boundaries, if any, are appropriate for how politicized the classroom becomes?

Faculty by Employment Status and Institution Type, Fall 2003

		Doctoral		Master's		Baccalau-reate	2 year
	All Institutions	Public	Private Nonprofit	Public	Private Nonprofit	Private Nonprofit	Public
Full time Total in thousands	619.8	210.7	82.4	90.5	43.4	42.1	114.7
Sex							
Men	61.9%	68.4%	69.0%	59.2%	57.1%	59.3%	51.3%
Women	38.1	31.6	31.1	40.2	42.9	40.7	48.7
Rank							
Full Professor	29.5%	33.4%	34.6%	31.1%	24.9%	28.8%	21.5%
Associate Professor	22.4	25.4	25.5	23.2	27.4	24.6	11.3
Assistant Professor	23.1	24.1	24.7	28.6	32.8	29.9	10.2
Instructor or Lecturer	15.6	10.4	9.3	12.4	8.4	8.1	39.5
Other or not applicable	0.3	6.8	6.0	4.7	6.5	8.7	17.5
Tenure Status							
Tenured	49.3%	53.0%	47.1%	53.8%	41.9%	42.9%	49.1%
On tenure track	21.3	20.4	19.5	28.3	28.1	25.0	15.6
Not on tenure track	20.9	25.9	28.8	17.0	21.5	21.6	9.3
No tenure system	8.5	0.7	4.5	1.0	8.6	10.5	26.0
Work Activity							
Teaching	67.8%	51.6%	48.6%	81.9%	82.6%	83.4%	85.1%
Research	12.4	25.3	25.0	2.0	0.6	0.7	0.1
Administration	10.5	11.0	11.8	10.7	11.1	10.7	7.6
Other	9.3	12.1	14.6	5.4	5.7	5.2	7.3
Part-time total in Thousands	473.2	60.6	38.8	52.5	53.5	24.6	206.3

Source: *Profile of Faculty Members with Teaching Duties by Employment Status and Type of Institution*, 55 CHRON. HIGHER EDUC., Aug. 29, 2008, at 25.

CHAPTER 6

ACADEMIC FREEDOM AND TENURE

A. PROFESSIONAL ACADEMIC FREEDOM

American Association of University Professors 1915 Declaration of Principles

1 AAUP Bulletin 17–39 (December 1915).

[The text is set forth on pages 68–79, *supra*.]

Questions and Comments on the Declaration

1. The Declaration asserts that academic freedom has two traditional applications that developed in the German system of higher education: *Lehrfreiheit* and *Lernfreiheit*. The German ideal of academic freedom was developed in the late eighteenth century by major scholars of the period including Immanuel Kant. *See* IMMANUEL KANT, THE CONFLICT OF THE FACULTIES 23 (Mary J. Gregor, trans., Nebraska 1992) (1798) ("The university would have a certain autonomy (since only scholars can pass judgment on scholars as such.)"). Liberal reformer Wilhelm von Humboldt was guided by these scholars' ideas when he founded the University of Berlin in 1810. In particular, Humboldt embraced the idea of academic freedom for the University. The University of Berlin was also the first to be dedicated to the importance of research as well as teaching. DANIEL FALLON, THE GERMAN UNIVERSITY: A HEROIC IDEAL IN CONFLICT WITH THE MODERN WORLD 28 (1980).

2. German universities were governed by their faculties rather than lay governing boards. FRIEDRICH PAULSEN, THE GERMAN UNIVERSITIES: THEIR CHARACTER AND HISTORICAL DEVELOPMENT 93–97 (Edward D. Perry, trans., Kessinger Legacy Reprint 2007) (1895). Academic Freedom in Germany, therefore, protected faculty only from government interference. The drafters of the Declaration expanded academic freedom to protect faculty from governing boards as well by endorsing a new governing structure. Thus, Part 2 of the Declaration asserts that faculty should have "equal responsibilities" with the trustees on most matters, and "primary responsibility" with respect to scientific and educational questions. How should trustees and faculty fulfill this shared governance mandate? Can academic freedom in research and teaching exist without shared governance?

3. The Declaration outlines two procedural protections necessary for academic freedom: tenure, and the right of all faculty, whether tenured or not, to a hearing before the faculty (or a duly constituted committee of the faculty) before being disciplined or dismissed for their ideas. Can academic freedom exist without these procedural protections?

Kay v. Board of Higher Education of the City of New York

Supreme Court of New York, New York County, 1940.
173 Misc. 943, 18 N.Y.S.2d 821, *aff'd*, 259 A.D. 879, 20 N.Y.S.2d 1016, *appeal dismissed*, 284 N.Y. 578, 29 N.E.2d 657 (1940).

■ McGeehan, J.

... [P]etitioner seeks to review the action of the board of higher education in appointing Bertrand Russell to the chair of philosophy at City College....

   . . .

... The petitioner contends that the appointment of Bertrand Russell has violated the public policy of the State and of the nation because of the notorious immoral and salacious teachings of Bertrand Russell and because the petitioner contends he is a man not of good moral character.

   . . .

... [T]here are certain basic principles upon which this government is founded.... One of the prerequisites of a teacher is good moral character. In fact, this is a prerequisite for appointment in civil service in the city and State, or political subdivisions, or in the United States. It needs no argument here to defend this statement. It need not be found in the Education Law. It is found in the nature of the teaching profession. Teachers are supposed not only to impart instruction in the classroom but by their example to teach the students. The taxpayers of the city of New York spend millions to maintain the colleges of the city of New York. They are not spending that money nor was the money appropriated for the purpose of employing teachers who are not of good moral character. However, there is ample authority in the Education Law to support this contention.

Section 556 ... article 20, entitled "Teachers and Pupils," reads as follows: "A school commissioner shall examine any charge affecting the moral character of any teacher within his district, first giving such teacher reasonable notice of the charge, and an opportunity to defend himself therefrom; and if he find the charge sustained, he shall annul the teacher's certificate, by whomsoever granted, and declare him unfit to teach; and if the teacher holds a certificate of the Commissioner of Education, or of a former Superintendent of Public Instruction or a diploma of a State normal school, he shall notify the Commissioner of Education forthwith of such annulment and declaration."

It has been argued that this section does not apply. Assuming it does not apply to the board of higher education specifically, it is a declaration of the public policy of this State. It is inconceivable that the board of higher education would dare to contend that they had the power to appoint persons of bad moral character as teachers in the colleges of the city of New York....

   . . .

The contention of the petitioner that Mr. Russell has taught in his books immoral and salacious doctrines, is amply sustained by the books conceded to be the writings of Bertrand Russell, which were offered in evidence. It is not necessary to detail here the filth which is contained in the books. It is sufficient to record the following: From "Education and the Modern World," pages 119 and 120: "I am sure that university life would be better, both intellectually and morally, if most university students had temporary childless marriages. This would afford a solution of the sexual urge neither restless nor surreptitious, neither mercenary nor casual, and of such a nature that it need not take up time which ought to be given to work." From "Marriage and Morals," pages 165 and 166: "For my part, while I am quite convinced that companionate marriage would be a step in the right direction, and would do a great deal of good, I do not think that it goes far enough. I think that all sex relations which do not involve children should be regarded as a purely private affair, and that if a man and a woman choose to live together without having children, that should be no one's business but their own. I should not hold it desirable that either a man or a woman should enter upon the serious business of a marriage intended to lead to children without having had previous sexual experience." ("The peculiar importance attached, at the present, to adultery, is quite irrational." From "What I Believe," p. 50.)

The Penal Law of the State of New York is a most important factor in the lives of our people.... Even assuming that the board of higher education possesses the maximum power which the Legislature could possibly confer upon it in the appointment of its teachers, it must act so as not to violate the Penal Law or to encourage the violation of it. Where it so acts as to sponsor or encourage violations of the Penal Law, and its actions adversely affect the public health, safety and morals, its acts are void and of no legal effect. A court of equity, with the powers inherent in that court, has ample jurisdiction to protect the taxpayers of the city of New York from such acts as this of the board of higher education....

. . .

The Penal Law of the State of New York defines the crime of abduction and provides that a person who uses or procures to be taken or used, a female under eighteen years of age, when not her husband, for the purpose of sexual intercourse, or a person who entices an unmarried female of any age of previous chaste character to any place for the purpose of sexual intercourse is guilty of abduction and punishable by imprisonment for not more than ten years (§ 70). Furthermore, the Penal Law provides that even a parent or guardian having legal charge of a female under eighteen years of age and who consents to her being taken by any person for the purpose of sexual intercourse violates the law and is punishable by imprisonment for not more than ten years (§ 70).

As to the crime of rape the Penal Law provides that a person who perpetrates an act of sexual intercourse with a female not his wife under the age of eighteen years, under circumstances not amounting to rape in the first degree, is guilty of rape in the second degree and punishable by imprisonment for not more than ten years (§ 2010).

Section 100 of the Penal Law makes adultery a criminal offense.

Section 2460 of the Penal Law, among other things, provides that any person who shall induce or attempt to induce any female to reside with him for immoral purposes shall be guilty of a felony and on conviction punishable by imprisonment for not less than two years, nor more than twenty years and by a fine not exceeding $5,000.

When we consider the vast amount of money that the taxpayers are assessed each year to enforce these provisions of the law, how repugnant to the common welfare must be any expenditure that seeks to encourage the violation of the provisions of the Penal Law. Conceding arguendo that the board of higher education has sole and exclusive power to select the faculty of City College and that its discretion cannot be reviewed or curtailed by this court or any other agency, nevertheless, such sole and exclusive power may not be used to aid, abet or encourage any course of conduct tending to a violation of the Penal Law. Assuming that Mr. Russell could teach for two years in City College without promulgating the doctrines which he seems to find necessary to spread on the printed pages at frequent intervals, his appointment violates a perfectly obvious canon of pedagogy, namely, that the personality of the teacher has more to do with forming a student's opinion than many syllogisms. A person we despise and who is lacking in ability cannot argue us into imitating him. A person whom we like and who is of outstanding ability, does not have to try. It is contended that Bertrand Russell is extraordinary. That makes him the more dangerous.... When we consider how susceptible the human mind is to the ideas and philosophy of teaching professors, it is apparent that the board of higher education either disregarded the probable consequences of their acts or were more concerned with advocating a cause that appeared to them to present a challenge to so-called "academic freedom" without according suitable consideration of the other aspects of the problem before them. While this court would not interfere with any action of the board in so far as a pure question of "valid" academic freedom is concerned, it will not tolerate academic freedom being used as a cloak to promote the popularization in the minds of adolescents of acts forbidden by the Penal Law.... Academic freedom does not mean academic license. It is the freedom to do good and not to teach evil. Academic freedom cannot authorize a teacher to teach that murder or treason are good. Nor can it permit a teacher to teach directly or indirectly that sexual intercourse between students, where the female is under the age of eighteen years, is proper....

Academic freedom cannot teach that abduction is lawful nor that adultery is attractive and good for the community. There are norms and criteria of truth which have been recognized by the founding fathers. We find a recognition of them in the opening words of the Declaration of Independence, where they refer to the laws of nature and of Nature's God. The doctrines therein set forth, which have been held sacred by all Americans from that day to this, preserved by the Constitution of the United States and of the several States and defended by the blood of its citizens, recognizing the inalienable rights with which men are endowed by their Creator must be preserved, and a man whose life and teachings run counter to these doctrines, who teaches and practices immorality and who encourages and avows violations of the Penal Law of the State of New York, is not fit to teach in any of the schools of this land. The judicial branch of our government under our democratic institutions has not been so emasculated by the opponents of our institutions to an extent to render it impotent to act to protect the rights of the people. Where public health, safety and morals are so directly involved, no board, administrative or otherwise, may act in a dictatorial capacity, shielding their actions behind a claim of complete and absolute immunity from judicial review. The board of higher education of the city of New York has deliberately and completely disregarded the essential principles upon which the selection of any teacher must rest. The contention that Mr. Russell will teach mathematics and not his philosophy does not in any way detract from the fact that his very presence as a teacher will cause the students to look up to him, seek to know more about him, and the more he is able to charm them and impress them with his personal presence, the more potent will grow his influence in all spheres of their lives, causing the students in many instances to strive to emulate him in every respect.

In considering the power of this court to review the determination and appointment of Dr. Russell by the board of higher education this court has divided the exhibits in this proceeding into two classes, namely, those exhibits which dealt with controversial measures not malum in se as far as the law is concerned, even though abhorrently repulsive to many people, and those considered malum in se by the court.... [W]here the matter transcends the field of controversial issues and enters the field of criminal law, then this court has the power and is under a duty to act. While in encouraging adultery in the language used in the book "Education and the Good Life," at page 221, "I shall not teach that faithfulness to our partner through life is in any way desirable, or that a permanent marriage should be regarded as excluding temporary episodes," it might be urged that he is only encouraging the commission of a misdemeanor rather than a felony, yet that mitigating argument must fall when we are confronted with Dr. Russell's utterances as to the damnable felony of homosexualism, which warrants imprisonment for not more than twenty years in New York State, and concerning which degenerate practice Dr. Russell has this to say in his book entitled "Education and the Modern World," at page 119: "It is possible that homosexual relations with other boys would not be very harmful if they were tolerated, but even then there is danger lest they should interfere with the growth of normal sexual life later on."

Considering Dr. Russell's principles with reference to the Penal Law of the State of New York, it appears that not only would the morals of the students be undermined, but his doctrines would tend to bring them, and in some cases their parents and guardians, in conflict with the Penal Law, and, accordingly, this court intervenes.

The appointment of Dr. Russell is an insult to the people of the city of New York and to the thousands of teachers who were obligated upon their appointment to establish good moral character and to maintain it in order to keep their positions. Considering the instances in which immorality alone has been held to be sufficient basis for removal of a teacher, and mindful of the aphorism "As a man thinketh in his heart, so he is," the court holds that the acts of the board of higher education of the city of New York in appointing Dr. Russell to the department of philosophy of the City College of the City of New York, to be paid by public funds, is in effect establishing a chair of indecency and in doing so has acted arbitrarily, capriciously and in direct violation of the public health, safety and morals of the people and of the petitioner's rights herein, and the petitioner is entitled to an order revoking the appointment of the said Bertrand Russell and discharging him from his said position, and denying to him the rights and privileges and the powers appertaining to his appointment.

Questions and Comments on *Kay*

1. Given the holding of the court, it is ironic that *Kay* is the first court opinion in the United States to use the term "academic freedom." There are also unfortunate parallels between this decision and the trial of Socrates for corrupting the morals of the youth of Athens.

2. Do you agree with the court's assertion that academic freedom is the "freedom to do good and not to teach evil?" At a minimum the court's definition is strangely unrelated to such core academic concerns as teaching and research. Is it a viable standard?

3. When the Board of Higher Education for the City of New York voted unanimously in 1940 to appoint Russell to a philosophy professorship for one year at City College of New York, Russell was serving as a lecturer at the University of California, Los Angeles, and had been chosen to give the William James lectures at Harvard in the fall of 1940. Horace M. Kallen, *Behind the Bertrand Russell Case*, *in* THE BERTRAND RUSSELL CASE 15, 15–18 (John Dewey & Horace M. Kallen eds., 1941) [hereinafter THE BERTRAND RUSSELL CASE]. The *New York Times* considered the appointment newsworthy, even running a photo of Russell above its story that described him as a "noted British philosopher." *Russell to Teach at City College*, N.Y. TIMES, Feb. 27, 1940, at 19. Four days later, a long letter by the Right Rev. William T. Manning, head of the Protestant Episcopal Diocese of New York, appeared in the city's major newpapers. Manning denounced the appointment on the ground that Russell is "a recognized propagandist against religion and morality and who specifically defends adultery." THOM WEIDLICH, APPOINTMENT DENIED: THE INQUISITION OF BERTRAND RUSSELL 14 (2000). After two weeks of protests and letters to the editor of the *New York Times*, the City Council passed a resolution calling on the Board of Higher Education to rescind the appointment. *Council Demands Russell Rejection*, N.Y. TIMES, Mar. 16, 1940, at 1. Three days later, the Board of Higher Education voted to uphold the appointment, although seven of the original nineteen supporters of the appointment now voted against it. *Russell Keeps Post by Vote of 11 to 17*, N.Y. TIMES, Mar. 19, 1940, at 1. After the vote, Mrs. Jean Kay, the wife of a dentist and mother of two children in the New York public schools, brought suit against the Board to order the rescission of the appointment. *Charges are Filed in Fight on Russell*, N.Y. TIMES, Mar. 20, 1940, at 27. One week later, arguments were heard by Judge John McGeehan, and three days after the hearing McGeehan handed down his opinion. *Fight on Russell is Argued in Court*, N.Y. TIMES, Mar. 29, 1940, at 21; *Russell is Ousted by Court as Unfit*, N.Y. TIMES, Mar. 31, 1940, at 1.

Russell appealed to Judge McGeehan for permission to intervene in the case on his own behalf, but his motion was denied on the ground that he had no legal interest in the proceeding. THE BERTRAND RUSSELL CASE, *supra*, at 24. One week after McGeehan's opinion was handed down, Mayor LaGuardia eliminated the position to which Russell had been appointed from the City's budget in order to eliminate grounds for a breach of contract suit. *Mayor Gets Brunt of Russell Clash*, N.Y. TIMES, Apr. 7, 1940, at 9. In mid-April, the Board of Higher Education voted to appeal McGeehan's decision, against the advice of the Corporation Counsel which represented the City in all legal matters. *Russell Decision Will be Appealed*, N.Y. TIMES, Apr. 16, 1940, at 23. The Board hired private counsel and proceeded with their appellate case. *Mayor is Flouted in Russell Appeal*, N.Y. TIMES, Apr. 20, 1940, at 12. In late May, the Appellate Division upheld McGeehan's decision to deny Russell permission to intervene on his own behalf, and in mid-June the Appellate Division upheld McGeehan's decision that the Board did not have the authority to retain private counsel and denied their appeal of the lower decision. *Russell Loses a Point*, N.Y. TIMES, May 25,

1940, at 9; *Appeal on Russell Blocked by Court*, N.Y. TIMES, June 20, 1940, at 25. In October, the Appellate Division denied permission to the Board to appeal their decision refusing permission to substitute counsel and proceed with the case. *School Board Loses Appeal for Russell*, N.Y. TIMES, Oct. 5, 1940, at 15. Finally, in January of 1941, the Court of Appeals of New York denied permission to Bertrand Russell to appeal any of the lower court decisions, ending the litigation. *Court Rejects Plea by Bertrand Russell*, N.Y. TIMES, Jan. 17, 1941, at 18.

After Russell's appointment was blocked, art collector Dr. Albert Barnes hired him to work at the Barnes Foundation in Merion, Pennsylvania. Barnes also funded a report on the entire matter, which was published as THE BERTRAND RUSSELL CASE. John Dewey, the book's co-editor wrote of the controversy:

> ... It is probably true that because the war waged by totalitarian powers came at a time when it distracted attention from the Russell case it became easier for the cohorts of darkness to "get away" with their campaign against the democratic method of discussion. But it would be a bitter irony if protest against totalitarianism abroad should be a factor in fostering recourse to totalitarian methods in this country.

Introduction to THE BERTRAND RUSSELL CASE, *supra*, at 8.

Barnes added:

> It is Democracy that needs to be vindicated, not Bertrand Russell. From the time of the initial charges against Russell until the enforcement of the court decision that wantonly injured him, neither Democracy nor Russell was given an opportunity to raise a voice in their defense. This attempt at character-assassination is a black mark on America's escutcheon, in some respects even deeper in tone than was the bodily assassination of Sacco and Vanzetti; deeper because the Italians were accorded the formality of trial in a court of justice and Russell was not.

Albert C. Barnes, *Foreward* to THE BERTRAND RUSSELL CASE, *supra* at 11.

The job at the Barnes Foundation effectively ended the litigation. On October 21, 1940, the Board of Higher Education voted to take no further steps because, by its own regulations, faculty members could not have more than one position. WEIDLICH, *supra*, at 170.

The McGeehan opinion was criticized in a number of law reviews. For example, Professor Walton Hamilton wrote:

> If [Russell's] equity in a chair at City College is to be resolved by legal law, he is entitled to a fair and honest trial. The challenge must come from a party entitled to make it; it must be entertained by a court of competent jurisdiction; judgment must emerge from the application of established norms to the distinctive circumstances of the instant case. Yet here protest has been taken by a person who can scarcely be accorded a legal interest in the matter; the court presents no convincing proof that it has warrant to hear the cause; the principles by which the facts are commuted into an adverse holding reside in no legal authority.... In an opinion of some five thousand words ... the judge rises to every error which opportunity presents. Nasty names confer the human touch and a preconceived answer supplies the target for a wayward logic.

Walton Hamilton, *Trial by Ordeal, New Style*, 50 YALE L. J. 778, 778–89 (1941).

In 1944, Russell returned to England. In 1950 he was awarded the Nobel Prize for literature, in part for the writings that had been so controversial in New York.

American Association of University Professors and Association of American Colleges,[a] 1940 Statement of Principles on Academic Freedom and Tenure with 1940 and 1970 Interpretive Comments

[The text is set forth in Appendix A, *infra*.]

Questions and Comments on the 1940 Statement

1. Compare the 1940 Statement with the 1915 Declaration, *supra* at 65–76. The Statement is shorter in part because it devotes little space to justifying academic freedom. The Declaration also includes a fairly detailed look at the role of governing boards and quotes with approval Charles William Eliot's denunciation of some boards[b]; the Statement has little to say on the subject apart from calling faculty "educational officers" rather than employees. The Declaration endorses a strong role for faculty in reappointing and terminating faculty by requiring "the advice and consent of some board or committee representative of the faculty" in such decisions; the Statement accepts a weaker faculty role in such matters, saying that termination of continuous appointments or dismissal prior to the expiration of a term appointment "should, if possible, be considered by both a faculty committee and the governing board of the institution."

The most significant difference between the two documents is the large number of organizations that have embraced the 1940 Statement.

2. Walter Metzger has written the definitive history of the 1940 Statement:

> It is common knowledge that the 1940 Statement was co-authored by representatives of the AAUP and representatives of the [AAC], an organization composed of undergraduate academic institutions and run by their top administrators. This knowledge, however, has not commonly excited much curiousity—and it should. Why, it is reasonable to ask, did the only organization in America dedicated to the advancement of academic freedom and tenure need administrators to help them tell the world how this might best be done? . . .
>
>   . . .
>
> . . . More than anything else, an unanticipated change in the planned activities of the association convinced its leaders during its natal year that going it alone would not carry them very far. In 1915, much to their surprise, [the leaders of the AAUP] were inundated by calls for help from faculty members at far-flung campuses who alleged that they were or were about to be dismissed because of their spoken or written views. Despite the empty treasury of the neonate association and their own chronic shortage of free time, this dutiful, unhappy few decided to respond to every seemingly meritorious SOS, not by taking the faculty member's complaint at face value, but by visiting the site of the proposed offense, nosing out the facts,

---

a. Now the Association of American Colleges and Universities.

b. "These barbarous boards exercise an arbitrary power of dismissal. They exclude from the teachings of the university unpopular or dangerous subjects. In some states they even treat professors' positions as common political spoils; and all too frequently . . . they fail to treat the members of the teaching staff with the high consideration to which their functions entitle them." Charles William Eliot, *Academic Freedom* (1907), an address delivered before the New York Chapter of the Phi Beta Kappa Society at Cornell University (May 29, 1907).

interviewing all the parties, trying if possible to set things right, and then, if need be, exposing uncorrected wrongs.

No program could have been better designed to reveal to the AAUP the disadvantages of being the sole source of support for the doctrines set forth in its Declaration. Even as they conducted their investigations, negative reviews of that work began to appear in conservative newspapers and administration journals.... And always in these organs someone could be counted on to make the worst accusation of bias—to call the document the manifesto of a professors' trade union.... Still, it was one thing to encounter the ex parte argument when it appeared in the journals of opinion ... and another to confront it during a campus investigation, where it could serve to deny the AAUP access to the administration, defeat AAUP efforts at mediation, and justify refusals to redress abuses cited in AAUP reports.

· · ·

From all accounts, the early AAUP leaders, had they been forced to choose one and only one set of collaborators, would have picked the presidents of the elite research universities with major graduate schools, the institutions that belonged to the then exclusive Association of American Universities ("AAU"), formed around the turn of the century.... As a group, the AAU presidents had been prominently identified with the secularization of American higher education, a major wellspring of academic freedom on these shores....

· · ·

... The AAUP sought out the AAU, but the AAU did not reciprocate. The journal of the AAU took no notice of the 1915 Declaration; an AAUP questionnaire on items in that report sent out to AAU presidents elicited few replies; the staff of the AAU did not warm to [AAUP] approaches....

· · ·

In 1922, [an AAC] committee issued a ... report that ... described the 1915 Declaration as "highly important" (its new chairman called it "monumental"). It urged all colleges and universities to safeguard academic freedom, which included recognition by the institution that a faculty member in speaking and writing upon subjects beyond the scope of his own field of study is entitled to the same freedom and responsibility as attached to all other citizens. It endorsed the principle of tenure to the extent of urging that faculty members who had demonstrated their competence and compatibility to the satisfaction of the institution should receive a long-term or indefinite appointment, and that the termination of such an appointment for cause should be preceded by a hearing on charges....

· · ·

[T]he AAUP let it be known ... that it would be willing to accept the 1922 report, with minor amendments, as a preliminary draft and basis for discussion.... [The result was a 1925 Conference Statement adopted by both the AAC and the AAUP].

· · ·

In marked contrast with the swift and harmonious exchange of views that cemented the 1925 Statement, the deliberations leading to the 1940 statement were prolonged, volatile, and acrimonious. Not counting a series of informal meetings called by the AAC to protest the AAUP's handling of freedom and tenure cases, the two associations met officially four times between 1937 and 1940 to hammer out a revised freedom and tenure statement....

· · ·

On most matters dealt with by the 1940 Statement, the two camps were not at each other's throats. It is simply not the case that the professors fought for freedom while the presidents fought for restrictions, or that one side believed in tenure while the other side did not. Many differences that cropped up in discussion were over nuances in phrasing and were resolved without personal animosity. But two issues could not be readily resolved, and it was these issues that invited testy egos to do their worst. One issue concerned the AAUP's proposal that all probationary periods be of a standard as well as a fixed duration; more than a technical follow-up to 1915 or 1925, this was a transformative idea that went far beyond contemporary personnel practice. The second issue involved the AAC's desire to subject the public utterances of academics to institutional discipline. . . .

[The AAUP position prevailed as to having a fixed probationary period. As to the second, interpretive comment 4 was added making clear that extramural utterances could serve as a basis for removing tenure].

Afterwards, many AAUP members and officials would be uncertain about just what . . . had been agreed to. One extramural freedom case in particular would show that what had been settled in script had not necessarily been settled in many minds. In 1960, the Board of Regents of the University of Illinois dismissed Leo F. Koch, an assistant professor of Biology, for writing a letter to a student newpaper condoning premarital sexual intercourse between consenting students. . . . To convince the AAUP investigators and the academic world that Koch's academic freedom had not been violated by its action, the board came up with findings that tracked the 1940 Statement: Koch, it held, had not adhered to the standards of "accuracy," "restraint," "respect for others," and dissociation from his institution prescribed by that code for extramural utterances, and he could thus be validly discharged after a due process hearing for not living up to his academic responsibilities. The AAUP team of investigators, headed by Professor Thomas I. Emerson of the Yale Law School, plus every member of the Committee A, agreed that the Illinois administration had not accorded to Koch adequate due process; for this reason, the association voted for censure. But a sharp internal division arose over whether any institutional sanction—even the relatively mild one of a reprimand, which had been recommended by a faculty hearing body—could be imposed on Koch under the 1940 Statement. Professor Emerson, taking vigorous exception to the view that only "responsible" extramural utterances were protected under the insigne of academic freedom, considered the passages in the 1940 Statement so marred by backing and filling as to be almost meaningless. Several members of Committee A, calling attention to the postulate that academics should be accorded the freedom of citizens, argued that the 1940 Statement did not sanction occupational punishments for allegedly untoward public speech. But a majority of the committee, after reviewing the history of failed attempts to find alternatives, concluded that the interpretive footnote plainly did say that a failure to adhere to the verbal standards laid down for extramural utterances could be sued by an administration as a ground for dismissal.

From a yet more distant perspective, it seems abundantly clear today that the Committee A majority in the Koch case was correct.

Walter P. Metzger, *The 1940 Statement of Principles of Academic Freedom and Tenure*, LAW & CONTEMP. PROBS., Summer 1990, at 3, 12, 15–16, 20, 23–25, 47, 50, 62–63.

If you had been a member of Committee A when the Koch matter was heard, what position would you have taken? On which provisions of the 1940 Statement would you ground your argument? Why?

3. By 2007, the AAUP faced serious problems. Membership in 1971 had been 90,000, by 2007 it was down to 43,600. There was also a $250,000 budget deficit, and the chief financial officer had been forced out in 2006 after he failed to produce a credible audit report. Five top staff had left in the past sixteen months. Robin Wilson, *The AAUP, 92 and Ailing: Mismanagement, Declining Membership, and a Schizophrenic Mission Threaten the Premier Faculty Association*, CHRON. HIGHER EDUC., June 8, 2007, at A8. "Most of the AAUP's chapters [were] at regional public universities and second-tier public liberal arts colleges." *Id*. at A9. Columbia University and Johns Hopkins University—homes to the AAUP's founding professors—no longer had chapters. *Id*.

Perhaps the biggest challenge facing the AAUP was what role it should play in collective bargaining. The AAUP began participating in collective bargaining in 1972, and by 2007, most of its membership was part of an AAUP collective-bargaining unit. Michael Bérubé, a member of the AAUP Executive Committee, "says the association is now referred to as both 'toothless and dangerous.' Toothless ... because young faculty members believe they can accomplish more through their own scholarly associations, like the Modern Language Association. Dangerous ... because others believe that the AAUP's union activities corrupt its high-minded professional policies." *Id*.

In June of 2008, the AAUP announced that its members had voted to restructure the organization by dividing it into three separate entities: a professional association that will continue to advocate on behalf of academic freedom and faculty interests, a second entity that will be structured as a union to handle collective bargaining work, and a third charitable organization called the AAUP Foundation that will raise money for the AAUP. Robin Wilson, *Can Reorganization Save the AAUP?*, CHRON. HIGHER EDUC., June 27, 2008, at A4. Do you think this reorganization will resolve the tensions between the various roles of the AAUP?

B. CONSTITUTIONAL ACADEMIC FREEDOM

Although there are similarities between the professional academic freedom supported by the AAUP and the academic freedom protected by the Constitution, there are also important differences. William W. Van Alstyne, for example, describes the 1940 AAUP Statement as "soft law":

> Generally speaking, the 1940 Statement is not policed by the courts. Rather it is policed principally by Committee A of the AAUP and by publication of AAUP's ad hoc committee investigation case reports in the AAUP's professional journal. And while this may understate the 1940 Statement's influence in some respects (for example, as when a university has adopted it and made it part of the faculty's contractual guarantee), the 1940 Statement is certainly not hard law in the ultimate sense one differently associates, say, with the first amendment to the Constitution with its general protection of free speech.... [T]he 1940 Statement generally requires affirmative institutional action of some sort to carry its provisions into legal effect (for example, incorporation by reference into college or university bylaws, into letters of faculty appointment, or collective bargaining agreements).... The Bill of Rights, including the first amendment, is quite different.... Compliance ... is not optional; its protections are enforceable in every court in the United States.[a]

a. William W. Van Alstyne, *Academic Freedom and the First Amendment in the Supreme Court of the United States*, LAW & CONTEMP. PROBS., Summer 1990, at 79, 79–80.

Questions and Comments on Constitutional Protection for Academic Freedom

David Rabban has argued that academic freedom "may provide faculty more protection for professional speech and less protection for unprofessional speech than the free speech clause would afford the same statements by nonacademics." Consider his example:

> The owner of a movie theatre could be punished for showing a film declared obscene by a jury in his community though protected by juries elsewhere, but a professor at the adjacent university might have an academic freedom right to show the same film in an advanced course on the regulation of mass media to make the intellectual point that the definition of obscenity involves close questions on which the community standards vary.

> On the other hand, a professor speaking within his field of expertise may be disciplined without violating constitutional academic freedom for speech that otherwise would be protected under the free speech clause of the first amendment.... Grossly inaccurate speech about the Holocaust, for example, could be cause for dismissing a historian for incompetence, but not for taking any adverse action against a professor in the school of engineering or an employee of the municipal utility commission.

David M. Rabban, *A Functional Analysis of "Individual" and "Institutional" Academic Freedom Under the First Amendment*, LAW & CONTEMP. PROBS., Summer 1990, at 227, 242.

As you read the leading cases on constitutional protection for academic freedom, focus on the differences between constitutional academic freedom and the professional norm and consider whether those differences have been understood by the courts.

1. EARLY ACADEMIC FREEDOM DECISIONS

Wieman v. Updegraff

Supreme Court of the United States, 1952.
344 U.S. 183, 73 S.Ct. 215, 97 L.Ed. 216.

■ MR. JUSTICE CLARK delivered the opinion of the Court.

This is an appeal from a decision of the Supreme Court of Oklahoma upholding the validity of a loyalty oath prescribed by Oklahoma statute for all state officers and employees. Appellants, employed by the State as members of the faculty and staff of Oklahoma Agricultural and Mechanical College, failed, within the thirty days permitted, to take the oath required by the Act. Appellee Updegraff, as a citizen and taxpayer, thereupon brought this suit in the District Court of Oklahoma County to enjoin the necessary state officials from paying further compensation to employees who had not subscribed to the oath. The appellants, who were permitted to intervene, attacked the validity of the Act on the grounds, among others, that it was a bill of attainder; an *ex post facto* law; impaired the obligation of their contracts with the State and violated the Due Process Clause of the Fourteenth Amendment. They also sought a mandatory injunction directing the state officers to pay their salaries regardless of their failure to take the oath. Their objections centered largely on the following clauses of the oath:

> "... That I am not affiliated directly or indirectly ... with any foreign political agency, party, organization or Government, or with any agency, party, organization, association, or group whatever which has been officially determined by the United States Attorney

General or other authorized agency of the United States to be a communist front or subversive organization; ... that I will take up arms in the defense of the United States in time of War, or National Emergency, if necessary; that within the five (5) years immediately preceding the taking of this oath (or affirmation) I have not been a member of ... any agency, party, organization, association, or group whatever which has been officially determined by the United States Attorney General or other authorized public agency of the United States to be a communist front or subversive organization...."

. . .

There can be no dispute about the consequences visited upon a person excluded from public employment on disloyalty grounds. In the view of the community, the stain is a deep one; indeed, it has become a badge of infamy. Especially is this so in time of cold war and hot emotions when "each man begins to eye his neighbor as a possible enemy." Yet under the Oklahoma Act, the fact of association alone determines disloyalty and disqualification; it matters not whether association existed innocently or knowingly. To thus inhibit individual freedom of movement is to stifle the flow of democratic expression and controversy at one of its chief sources.... Indiscriminate classification of innocent with knowing activity must fall as an assertion of arbitrary power. The oath offends due process.

■ MR. JUSTICE FRANKFURTER, whom MR. JUSTICE DOUGLAS joins, concurring.

The times being what they are, it is appropriate to add a word by way of emphasis to the Court's opinion, which I join.

The case concerns the power of a State to exact from teachers in one of its colleges an oath that they are not, and for the five years immediately preceding the taking of the oath have not been, members of any organization listed by the Attorney General of the United States, prior to the passage of the statute, as "subversive" or "Communist-front." Since the affiliation which must thus be forsworn may well have been for reasons or for purposes as innocent as membership in a club of one of the established political parties, to require such an oath, on pain of a teacher's loss of his position in case of refusal to take the oath, penalizes a teacher for exercising a right of association peculiarly characteristic of our people. See Arthur M. Schlesinger, Sr., Biography of a Nation of Joiners, 50 Am. Hist. Rev. 1 (1944), reprinted in Schlesinger, Paths To the Present, 23. Such joining is an exercise of the rights of free speech and free inquiry. By limiting the power of the States to interfere with freedom of speech and freedom of inquiry and freedom of association, the Fourteenth Amendment protects all persons, no matter what their calling. But, in view of the nature of the teacher's relation to the effective exercise of the rights which are safeguarded by the Bill of Rights and by the Fourteenth Amendment, inhibition of freedom of thought, and of action upon thought, in the case of teachers brings the safeguards of those amendments vividly into operation. Such unwarranted inhibition upon the free spirit of teachers affects not only those who, like the appellants, are immediately before the Court. It has an unmistakable tendency to chill that free play of the spirit which all teachers ought especially to cultivate and practice; it makes for caution and timidity in their associations by potential teachers.

The Constitution of the United States does not render the United States or the States impotent to guard their governments against destruction by enemies from within. It does not preclude measures of self-protection against anticipated overt acts of violence. Solid threats to our kind of government—manifestations of purposes that reject argument and the free ballot as the means for bringing about changes and promoting progress—may be met by preventive measures before such threats reach fruition. However, in considering the constitutionality of legislation like the statute before us it is necessary to keep steadfastly in mind what it is that is to be secured. Only thus will it be evident why the Court has found that the Oklahoma law violates those fundamental principles of liberty "which lie at the base of all our civil and political institutions" and as such are imbedded in the due process of law which no State may offend.

That our democracy ultimately rests on public opinion is a platitude of speech but not a commonplace in action. Public opinion is the ultimate reliance of our society only if it be disciplined and responsible. It can be disciplined and responsible only if habits of open-mindedness and of critical inquiry are acquired in the formative years of our citizens. The process of education has naturally enough been the basis of hope for the perdurance of our democracy on the part of all our great leaders, from Thomas Jefferson onwards.

To regard teachers—in our entire educational system, from the primary grades to the university—as the priests of our democracy is therefore not to indulge in hyperbole. It is the special task of teachers to foster those habits of open-mindedness and critical inquiry which alone make for responsible citizens, who, in turn, make possible an enlightened and effective public opinion. Teachers must fulfill their function by precept and practice, by the very atmosphere which they generate; they must be exemplars of open-mindedness and free inquiry. They cannot carry out their noble task if the conditions for the practice of a responsible and critical mind are denied to them. They must have the freedom of responsible inquiry, by thought and action, into the meaning of social and economic ideas, into the checkered history of social and economic dogma. They must be free to sift evanescent doctrine, qualified by time and circumstance, from that restless, enduring process of extending the bounds of understanding and wisdom, to assure which the freedoms of thought, of speech, of inquiry, of worship are guaranteed by the Constitution of the United States against infraction by National or State government.

The functions of educational institutions in our national life and the conditions under which alone they can adequately perform them are at the basis of these limitations upon State and National power. These functions and the essential conditions for their effective discharge have been well described by a leading educator:

> "Now, a university is a place that is established and will function for the benefit of society, provided it is a center of independent thought. It is a center of independent thought and criticism that is created in the interest of the progress of society, and the one reason that we know that every totalitarian government must fail is that no totalitarian government is prepared to face the consequences of creating free universities.

"It is important for this purpose to attract into the institution men of the greatest capacity, and to encourage them to exercise their independent judgment.

"Education is a kind of continuing dialogue, and a dialogue assumes, in the nature of the case, different points of view.

"The civilization which I work and which I am sure, every American is working toward, could be called a civilization of the dialogue, where instead of shooting one another when you differ, you reason things out together.

"In this dialogue, then, you cannot assume that you are going to have everybody thinking the same way or feeling the same way. It would be unprogressive if that happened. The hope of eventual development would be gone. More than that, of course, it would be very boring.

"A university, then, is a kind of continuing Socratic conversation on the highest level for the very best people you can think of, you can bring together, about the most important questions, and the thing that you must do to the uttermost possible limits is to guarantee those men the freedom to think and to express themselves.

"Now, the limits on this freedom, cannot be merely prejudice, because although our prejudices might be perfectly satisfactory, the prejudices of our successors or of those who are in a position to bring pressure to bear on the institution, might be subversive in the real sense, subverting the American doctrine of free thought and free speech."

Tax–Exempt Foundations: Hearing on H. Res. 561 Before the H. Select Comm. to Investigate Tax–Exempt Foundations and Comparable Organizations, 82d Cong. 267, 291–92 (1952) (statement of Robert M. Hutchins, Associate Director of the Ford Foundation).

Questions and Comments on *Wieman v. Updegraff*

1. Justice Douglas dissenting in *Adler v. Board of Education*, 342 U.S. 485 (1952), was the first justice to use the phrase "academic freedom" in a Supreme Court opinion. At issue in *Adler* was the Feinberg law, a New York State statute that provided for the removal from public employment of any person who supported using violence to alter the form of government. A majority of the Court upheld the statute from facial attack, although in 1967 *Adler* was substantially overturned in *Keyshian v. Board of Regents*, described below. In his dissent in *Adler*, Douglas declared there could be no real "academic freedom" given the fear created by the Feinberg law. Do you agree?

2. Justice Frankfurter, like Justice Douglas in his concurrence in *Wieman v. Updegraff*, states that freedom of speech and inquiry are protected by the Fourteenth Amendment for all citizens in our democracy. What then, if anything, is being protected for faculty that isn't protected for all citizens? Frankfurter at one point declares that all teachers, from primary grades on, should have academic freedom, yet the quote he includes from Robert Hutchins speaks of universities only. Can Frankfurter and Hutchins's arguments be reconciled? If you accept the argument that teachers of younger pupils should have academic freedom, should academic freedom mean the same thing for them as it does for university professors? If not, how should their academic freedom differ?

Sweezy v. New Hampshire

Supreme Court of the United States, 1957.
354 U.S. 234, 77 S.Ct. 1203, 1 L.Ed.2d 1311.

[The opinion is set forth at pages 100 to 107, *supra*.]

Questions and Comments on *Sweezy* and *Keyishian v. Bd. of Regents of the State of N.Y.*

1. Although Justice Frankfurter's *Sweezy* concurrence stated that academic freedom was constitutionally protected, it was not until *Keyishian v. Board of Regents for the State of N.Y.*, 385 U.S. 589 (1967), that a majority of the Supreme Court agreed that "academic freedom ... is ... a special concern of the First Amendment, which does not tolerate laws that cast a pall of orthodoxy over the classroom." 385 U.S. at 603. *Keyishian*, like *Adler*, involved a challenge to New York's Feinberg law. This time the Court held that the statute was unconstitutionally vague. The opinion also included the strongest statement yet made about the constitutional position of academic freedom:

> Our Nation is deeply committed to safeguarding academic freedom, which is of transcendent value to all of us and not merely to the teachers concerned. That freedom is therefore a special concern of the First Amendment, which does not tolerate laws that cast a pall of orthodoxy over the classroom. "The vigilant protection of constitutional freedoms is nowhere more vital than in the community of American schools." *Shelton v. Tucker*, [364 U.S. 479, 487 (1960)].

385 U.S. at 603.

2. *Keyishian* was a five-four decision. In 1962, Justice Arthur Goldberg had replaced Frankfurter, and Abe Fortas assumed that same seat in 1965 upon Goldberg's retirement. Justice Fortas joined the *Keyishian* majority, while the two other justices new to the court, Stewart and White, joined Justices Clark and Harlan in dissent. Was Justice Frankfurter's departure significant to the outcome in *Keyishian*? Could Justice Brennan have built a majority without the opinion's emphasis on the vagueness of the New York statutes?

3. Why did courts fail to link academic freedom and the Constitution until after World War II? Consider David M. Rabban, *A Functional Analysis of "Individual" and "Institutional" Academic Freedom Under the First Amendment*, LAW & CONTEMP. PROBS., 227, 237–38 (Summer 1990).

> The term "academic freedom," in obvious contrast to "freedom of the press," is nowhere mentioned in the text of the first amendment. It is inconceivable that those who debated and ratified the first amendment thought about academic freedom. Indeed, before the Civil War, when most institutions of higher education were denominational colleges, "the problem of academic freedom as we now understand it was hardly posed" even as a nonlegal matter.... Only with the emergence of the modern research university in the late nineteenth century did a comprehensive theory of academic freedom, expressed most thoroughly in the 1915 Declaration, emerge in the United States. It took an "educational revolution" following the Civil War to produce the commitment to critical inquiry central to the modern rational for academic freedom, and arguably related to general free speech theories contained within the first amendment. "It may put some of our current difficulties into perspective," wrote [Hofstadter and Metzger] just before the Supreme Court gave the term constitutional meaning, "that

the academic freedom which is now under fire is not an ancient prerogative but an acquisition of relatively recent date."

. . .

The AAUP . . . decided not to submit an amicus brief in *Sweezy*, in part because it reasonably concluded that the Court was unlikely to address the constitutional implications of academic freedom for the first time, but also because it worried about judicial appropriation of a concept the AAUP had largely defined and successfully advocated throughout the academic world. Even a favorable definition of academic freedom under the first amendment would be subject to further judicial interpretation. What the Court gave, many within the AAUP worried, it could also take away.

2. PUBLIC EMPLOYEE SPEECH FROM *PICKERING* TO *GARCETTI*

Pickering v. Board of Education of Township High School

Supreme Court of the United States, 1968.
391 U.S. 563, 88 S.Ct. 1731, 20 L.Ed.2d 811.

■ MR. JUSTICE MARSHALL delivered the opinion of the Court.

[Appellant, Marvin L. Pickering, a teacher in Township High School District 205, wrote a letter to the editor of the local paper attacking the School Board for its handling of bond issue proposals and allocation of financial resources between athletic and educational programs, and the superintendent for allegedly attempting to prevent district teachers from criticizing the bond issue.

The Board moved to dismiss Pickering for publishing his letter. At a hearing, required by Illinois law, the Board argued that statements in the letter were false, "unjustifiably impugned the 'motives, honesty, integrity, truthfulness, responsibility and competence'" and damaged the reputations of the Board and administrators, were potentially disrupting of faculty discipline, and "would tend to foment 'controversy, conflict and dissension' among teachers, administrators, the Board of Education, and the residents of the district." "No evidence was introduced at any point in the proceedings as to the effect of the publication of the letter on the community as a whole or on the administration of the school system in particular, and no specific findings along these lines were made."]

The Illinois courts reviewed the proceedings solely to determine whether the Board's findings were supported by substantial evidence and whether, on the facts as found, the Board could reasonably conclude that appellant's publication of the letter was "detrimental to the best interests of the schools." Pickering's claim that his letter was protected by the First Amendment was rejected on the ground that his acceptance of a teaching position in the public schools obliged him to refrain from making statements about the operation of the schools "which in the absence of such position he would have an undoubted right to engage in." It is not altogether clear whether the Illinois Supreme Court held that the First Amendment had no applicability to appellant's dismissal for writing the letter in question or whether it determined that the particular statements made in the letter were not entitled to First Amendment protection. In any event, it clearly rejected Pickering's claim that, on the facts of this case, he could not constitutionally be dismissed from his teaching position.

To the extent that the Illinois Supreme Court's opinion may be read to suggest that teachers may constitutionally be compelled to relinquish the First Amendment rights they would otherwise enjoy as citizens to comment on matters of public interest in connection with the operation of the public schools in which they work, it proceeds on a premise that has been unequivocally rejected in numerous prior decisions of this Court. *E.g., Wieman v. Updegraff*, 344 U.S. 183 (1952); *Shelton v. Tucker*, 364 U.S. 479 (1960); *Keyishian v. Board of Regents*, 385 U.S. 589 (1967). "The theory that public employment which may be denied altogether may be subjected to any conditions, regardless of how unreasonable, has been uniformly rejected." *Keyishian v. Board of Regents, supra*, at 605–606. At the same time it cannot be gainsaid that the State has interests as an employer in regulating the speech of its employees that differ significantly from those it possesses in connection with regulation of the speech of the citizenry in general. The problem in any case is to arrive at a balance between the interests of the teacher, as a citizen, in commenting upon matters of public concern and the interest of the State, as an employer, in promoting the efficiency of the public services it performs through its employees.

. . .

An examination of the statements in appellant's letter objected to by the Board reveals that they, like the letter as a whole, consist essentially of criticism of the Board's allocation of school funds between educational and athletic programs, and of both the Board's and the superintendent's methods of informing, or preventing the informing of, the district's taxpayers of the real reasons why additional tax revenues were being sought for the schools. The statements are in no way directed towards any person with whom appellant would normally be in contact in the course of his daily work as a teacher. Thus no question of maintaining either discipline by immediate superiors or harmony among coworkers is presented here. Appellant's employment relationships with the Board and, to a somewhat lesser extent, with the superintendent are not the kind of close working relationships for which it can persuasively be claimed that personal loyalty and confidence are necessary to their proper functioning. Accordingly, to the extent that the Board's position here can be taken to suggest that even comments on matters of public concern that are substantially correct . . . may furnish grounds for dismissal if they are sufficiently critical in tone, we unequivocally reject it.

We next consider the statements in appellant's letter which we agree to be false. The Board's original charges included allegations that the publication of the letter damaged the professional reputations of the Board and the superintendent and would foment controversy and conflict among the Board, teachers, administrators, and the residents of the district. However, no evidence to support these allegations was introduced at the hearing. So far as the record reveals, Pickering's letter was greeted by everyone but its main target, the Board, with massive apathy and total disbelief. The Board must, therefore, have decided, perhaps by analogy with the law of libel, that the statements were *per se* harmful to the operation of the schools.

However, the only way in which the Board could conclude, absent any evidence of the actual effect of the letter, that the statements contained therein were *per se* detrimental to the interest of the schools was to equate the Board members' own interests with that of the schools. Certainly an accusation that too much money is being spent on athletics by the administrators of the school system (which is precisely the import of that portion of appellant's letter containing the statements that we have found to be false) cannot reasonably be regarded as *per se* detrimental to the district's schools. Such an accusation reflects rather a difference of opinion between Pickering and the Board as to the preferable manner of operating the school system, a difference of opinion that clearly concerns an issue of general public interest.

In addition, the fact that particular illustrations of the Board's claimed undesirable emphasis on athletic programs are false would not normally have any necessary impact on the actual operation of the schools, beyond its tendency to anger the Board. For example, Pickering's letter was written after the defeat at the polls of the second proposed tax increase. It could, therefore, have had no effect on the ability of the school district to raise necessary revenue, since there was no showing that there was any proposal to increase taxes pending when the letter was written.

More importantly, the question whether a school system requires additional funds is a matter of legitimate public concern on which the judgment of the school administration, including the School Board, cannot, in a society that leaves such questions to popular vote, be taken as conclusive. On such a question free and open debate is vital to informed decision-making by the electorate. Teachers are, as a class, the members of a community most likely to have informed and definite opinions as to how funds allotted to the operation of the schools should be spent. Accordingly, it is essential that they be able to speak out freely on such questions without fear of retaliatory dismissal.

In addition, the amounts expended on athletics which Pickering reported erroneously were matters of public record on which his position as a teacher in the district did not qualify him to speak with any greater authority than any other taxpayer. The Board could easily have rebutted appellant's errors by publishing the accurate figures itself, either via a letter to the same newspaper or otherwise. We are thus not presented with a situation in which a teacher has carelessly made false statements about matters so closely related to the day-to-day operations of the schools that any harmful impact on the public would be difficult to counter because of the teacher's presumed greater access to the real facts. Accordingly, we have no occasion to consider at this time whether under such circumstances a school board could reasonably require that a teacher make substantial efforts to verify the accuracy of his charges before publishing them.[4]

What we do have before us is a case in which a teacher has made erroneous public statements upon issues then currently the subject of public attention, which are critical of his ultimate employer but which are neither shown nor can be presumed to have in any way either impeded the teacher's proper performance of his daily duties in the classroom[5] or to have interfered with the regular operation of the schools generally. In these circumstances we conclude that the interest of the school administration in limiting teachers' opportunities to contribute to public debate is not significantly

4. There is likewise no occasion furnished by this case for consideration of the extent to which teachers can be required by narrowly drawn grievance procedures to submit complaints about the operation of the schools to their superiors for action thereon prior to bringing the complaints before the public.

5. We also note that this case does not present a situation in which a teacher's public statements are so without foundation as to call into question his fitness to perform his duties in the classroom. In such a case, of course, the statements would merely be evidence of the teacher's general competence, or lack thereof, and not an independent basis for dismissal.

greater than its interest in limiting a similar contribution by any member of the general public.

The public interest in having free and unhindered debate on matters of public importance—the core value of the Free Speech Clause of the First Amendment—is so great that it has been held that a State cannot authorize the recovery of damages by a public official for defamatory statements directed at him except when such statements are shown to have been made either with knowledge of their falsity or with reckless disregard for their truth or falsity. *New York Times Co. v. Sullivan*, 376 U.S. 254 (1964); *St. Amant v. Thompson*, 390 U.S. 727 (1968). . . .

This Court has also indicated, in more general terms, that statements by public officials on matters of public concern must be accorded First Amendment protection despite the fact that the statements are directed at their nominal superiors. *Garrison v. Louisiana*, 379 U.S. 64 (1964); *Wood v. Georgia*, 370 U.S. 375 (1962). . . .

While criminal sanctions and damage awards have a somewhat different impact on the exercise of the right to freedom of speech from dismissal from employment, it is apparent that the threat of dismissal from public employment is nonetheless a potent means of inhibiting speech. . . . [I]n a case such as the present one, in which the fact of employment is only tangentially and insubstantially involved in the subject matter of the public communication made by a teacher, we conclude that it is necessary to regard the teacher as the member of the general public he seeks to be.

In sum, we hold that, in a case such as this, absent proof of false statements knowingly or recklessly made by him, a teacher's exercise of his right to speak on issues of public importance may not furnish the basis for his dismissal from public employment. Since no such showing has been made in this case regarding appellant's letter, his dismissal for writing it cannot be upheld and the judgment of the Illinois Supreme Court must, accordingly, be reversed. . . .

Questions and Comments on *Pickering*

Although Pickering was a teacher, the Court does not invoke academic freedom in the case. Rather, the holding turns on the first amendment rights of all public employees. Should teachers have rights greater than those of other public employees? Is it significant that Pickering was not a university or college professor?

The Court noted several issues that were not on the table in *Pickering*. In what situations did the Court suggest a teacher's speech might not be protected by the First Amendment? In those cases, is the First Amendment inapplicable or are the teacher's interests simply outweighed by the interests of the government as an employer? Is it appropriate to balance First Amendment rights against the interest of the state in ensuring efficiency in public services? Is there any justification for the idea that public employees should have less right to express themselves than other citizens?

Connick v. Myers

Supreme Court of the United States, 1983.
461 U.S. 138, 103 S.Ct. 1684, 75 L.Ed.2d 708.

■ JUSTICE WHITE delivered the opinion of the Court.

The respondent, Sheila Myers, was employed as an Assistant District Attorney in New Orleans for five and a half years. She served at the pleasure of petitioner Harry Connick, the District Attorney for Orleans Parish. During this period Myers competently performed her responsibilities of trying criminal cases.

In the early part of October 1980, Myers was informed that she would be transferred to prosecute cases in a different section of the criminal court. Myers was strongly opposed to the proposed transfer and expressed her view to several of her supervisors, including Connick. Despite her objections, on October 6 Myers was notified that she was being transferred. Myers again spoke with Dennis Waldron, one of the First Assistant District Attorneys, expressing her reluctance to accept the transfer. A number of other office matters were discussed and Myers later testified that, in response to Waldron's suggestion that her concerns were not shared by others in the office, she informed him that she would do some research on the matter.

That night Myers prepared a questionnaire soliciting the views of her fellow staff members concerning office transfer policy, office morale, the need for a grievance committee, the level of confidence in supervisors, and whether employees felt pressured to work in political campaigns. Early the following morning, Myers typed and copied the questionnaire. She also met with Connick who urged her to accept the transfer. She said she would "consider" it. Connick then left the office. Myers then distributed the questionnaire to 15 Assistant District Attorneys. Shortly after noon, Dennis Waldron learned that Myers was distributing the survey. He immediately phoned Connick and informed him that Myers was creating a "mini-insurrection" within the office. Connick returned to the office and told Myers that she was being terminated because of her refusal to accept the transfer. She was also told that her distribution of the questionnaire was considered an act of insubordination. Connick particularly objected to the question which inquired whether employees "had confidence in and would rely on the word" of various superiors in the office, and to a question concerning pressure to work in political campaigns which he felt would be damaging if discovered by the press.

Myers filed suit under 42 U.S.C. § 1983 (1976 ed., Supp. V), contending that her employment was wrongfully terminated because she had exercised her constitutionally protected right of free speech. The District Court agreed, ordered Myers reinstated, and awarded backpay, damages, and attorney's fees....

Connick appealed to the United States Court of Appeals for the Fifth Circuit, which affirmed on the basis of the District Court's opinion. Connick then sought review in this Court by way of certiorari, which we granted.

For at least 15 years, it has been settled that a State cannot condition public employment on a basis that infringes the employee's constitutionally protected interest in freedom of expression. Our task, as we defined it in *Pickering*, is to seek "a balance between the interests of the [employee], as a citizen, in commenting upon matters of public concern and the interest of the State, as an employer, in promoting the efficiency of the public services it performs through its employees." The District Court, and thus the Court of Appeals as well, misapplied our decision in *Pickering* and consequently, in our view, erred in striking the balance for respondent.

The District Court got off on the wrong foot in this case by initially finding that, "[taken] as a whole, the issues presented in the questionnaire relate to the effective functioning of the District Attorney's Office and are matters of public importance and concern." Connick contends at the outset that no balancing of interests is required in this case because Myers' questionnaire concerned only internal office matters and that such speech is not upon a matter of "public concern," as the term was used in *Pickering*. Although we do not agree that Myers' communication in this case was wholly without First Amendment protection, there is much force to Connick's submission. The repeated emphasis in *Pickering* on the right of a public employee "as a citizen, in commenting upon matters of public concern," was not accidental. This language, reiterated in all of *Pickering*'s progeny, reflects both the historical evolvement of the rights of public employees, and the common-sense realization that government offices could not function if every employment decision became a constitutional matter.

In all of . . . the precedents in which *Pickering* is rooted, the invalidated statutes and actions sought to suppress the rights of public employees to participate in public affairs. The issue was whether government employees could be prevented or "chilled" by the fear of discharge from joining political parties and other associations that certain public officials might find "subversive." The explanation for the Constitution's special concern with threats to the right of citizens to participate in political affairs is no mystery. The First Amendment "was fashioned to assure unfettered interchange of ideas for the bringing about of political and social changes desired by the people." *Roth v. United States*, 354 U.S. 476, 484 (1957); *New York Times Co. v. Sullivan*, 376 U.S. 254, 269 (1964). "[Speech] concerning public affairs is more than self-expression; it is the essence of self-government." *Garrison v. Louisiana*, 379 U.S. 64, 74–75 (1964). Accordingly, the Court has frequently reaffirmed that speech on public issues occupies the "highest rung of the heirarchy of First Amendment values," and is entitled to special protection. *NAACP v. Claiborne Hardware Co.*, 458 U.S. 886, 913 (1982); *Carey v. Brown*, 447 U.S. 455, 467 (1980).

Pickering v. Board of Education, supra, followed from this understanding of the First Amendment. . . .

Pickering, its antecedents, and its progeny lead us to conclude that if Myers' questionnaire cannot be fairly characterized as constituting speech on a matter of public concern, it is unnecessary for us to scrutinize the reasons for her discharge. When employee expression cannot be fairly considered as relating to any matter of political, social, or other concern to the community, government officials should enjoy wide latitude in managing their offices, without intrusive oversight by the judiciary in the name of the First Amendment. Perhaps the government employer's dismissal of the worker may not be fair, but ordinary dismissals from government service which violate no fixed tenure or applicable statute or regulation are not subject to judicial review even if the reasons for the dismissal are alleged to be mistaken or unreasonable. *Board of Regents v. Roth*, 408 U.S. 564 (1972); *Perry v. Sindermann, supra; Bishop v. Wood*, 426 U.S. 341, 349–350 (1976).

We do not suggest, however, that Myers' speech, even if not touching upon a matter of public concern, is totally beyond the protection of the First Amendment. "[The] First Amendment does not protect speech and assembly only to the extent it can be characterized as political[."] . . . We in no sense suggest that speech on private matters falls into one of the narrow and well-defined classes of expression which carries so little social value, such as obscenity, that the State can prohibit and punish such expression by all persons in its jurisdiction. For example, an employee's false criticism of his employer on grounds not of public concern may be cause for his discharge but would be entitled to the same protection in a libel action accorded an identical statement made by a man on the street. We hold only that when a public employee speaks not as a citizen upon matters of public concern, but instead as an employee upon matters only of personal interest, absent the most unusual circumstances, a federal court is not the appropriate forum in which to review the wisdom of a personnel decision taken by a public agency allegedly in reaction to the employee's behavior. *Cf. Bishop v. Wood, supra,* at 349–350. Our responsibility is to ensure that citizens are not deprived of fundamental rights by virtue of working for the government; this does not require a grant of immunity for employee grievances not afforded by the First Amendment to those who do not work for the State.

Whether an employee's speech addresses a matter of public concern must be determined by the content, form, and context of a given statement, as revealed by the whole record. In this case, with but one exception, the questions posed by Myers to her co-workers do not fall under the rubric of matters of "public concern." We view the questions pertaining to the confidence and trust that Myers' co-workers possess in various supervisors, the level of office morale, and the need for a grievance committee as mere extensions of Myers' dispute over her transfer to another section of the criminal court. Unlike the dissent, we do not believe these questions are of public import in evaluating the performance of the District Attorney as an elected official. Myers did not seek to inform the public that the District Attorney's Office was not discharging its governmental responsibilities in the investigation and prosecution of criminal cases. Nor did Myers seek to bring to light actual or potential wrongdoing or breach of public trust on the part of Connick and others. Indeed, the questionnaire, if released to the public, would convey no information at all other than the fact that a single employee is upset with the status quo. While discipline and morale in the workplace are related to an agency's efficient performance of its duties, the focus of Myers' questions is not to evaluate the performance of the office but rather to gather ammunition for another round of controversy with her superiors. These questions reflect one employee's dissatisfaction with a transfer and an attempt to turn that displeasure into a cause celebre.

To presume that all matters which transpire within a government office are of public concern would mean that virtually every remark—and certainly every criticism directed at a public official—would plant the seed of a constitutional case. While as a matter of good judgment, public officials should be receptive to constructive criticism offered by their employees, the First Amendment does not require a public office to be run as a roundtable for employee complaints over internal office affairs.

One question in Myers' questionnaire, however, does touch upon a matter of public concern. Question 11 inquires if assistant district attorneys "ever feel pressured to work in political campaigns on behalf of office supported candidates." We have recently noted that official pressure upon employees to work for political candidates not of the worker's own choice constitutes a coercion of belief in violation of fundamental constitutional rights. *Branti v. Finkel,* 445 U.S., at 515–516; *Elrod v. Burns,* 427 U.S. 347

(1976). In addition, there is a demonstrated interest in this country that government service should depend upon meritorious performance rather than political service. *CSC v. Letter Carriers*, 413 U.S. 548 (1973); *Public Workers v. Mitchell*, 330 U.S. 75 (1947). Given this history, we believe it apparent that the issue of whether assistant district attorneys are pressured to work in political campaigns is a matter of interest to the community upon which it is essential that public employees be able to speak out freely without fear of retaliatory dismissal.

Because one of the questions in Myers' survey touched upon a matter of public concern and contributed to her discharge, we must determine whether Connick was justified in discharging Myers.

. . .

The *Pickering* balance requires full consideration of the government's interest in the effective and efficient fulfillment of its responsibilities to the public. One hundred years ago, the Court noted the government's legitimate purpose in "[promoting] efficiency and integrity in the discharge of official duties, and [in] [maintaining] proper discipline in the public service." *Ex parte Curtis*, 106 U.S., at 373. As JUSTICE POWELL explained in his separate opinion in *Arnett v. Kennedy*, 416 U.S. 134, 168 (1974):

> To this end, the Government, as an employer, must have wide discretion and control over the management of its personnel and internal affairs. This includes the prerogative to remove employees whose conduct hinders efficient operation and to do so with dispatch. Prolonged retention of a disruptive or otherwise unsatisfactory employee can adversely affect discipline and morale in the work place, foster disharmony, and ultimately impair the efficiency of an office or agency.

We agree with the District Court that there is no demonstration here that the questionnaire impeded Myers' ability to perform her responsibilities. The District Court was also correct to recognize that "it is important to the efficient and successful operation of the District Attorney's office for Assistants to maintain close working relationships with their superiors." Connick's judgment, and apparently also that of his first assistant Dennis Waldron, who characterized Myers' actions as causing a "mini-insurrection," was that Myers' questionnaire was an act of insubordination which interfered with working relationships. When close working relationships are essential to fulfilling public responsibilities, a wide degree of deference to the employer's judgment is appropriate. Furthermore, we do not see the necessity for an employer to allow events to unfold to the extent that the disruption of the office and the destruction of working relationships is manifest before taking action. We caution that a stronger showing may be necessary if the employee's speech more substantially involved matters of public concern.

The District Court rejected Connick's position because "[unlike] a statement of fact which might be deemed critical of one's superiors, [Myers'] questionnaire was not a statement of fact but the presentation and solicitation of ideas and opinions," which are entitled to greater constitutional protection because "under the First Amendment there is no such thing as a false idea." This approach, while perhaps relevant in weighing the value of Myers' speech, bears no logical relationship to the issue of whether the questionnaire undermined office relationships. Questions, no less than forcefully stated opinions and facts, carry messages and it requires no unusual insight to conclude that the purpose, if not the likely result, of the questionnaire is to seek to precipitate a vote of no confidence in Connick and his supervisors. Thus, Question 10, which asked whether or not the Assistants had confidence in and relied on the word of five named supervisors, is a statement that carries the clear potential for undermining office relations.

Also relevant is the manner, time, and place in which the questionnaire was distributed. As noted in *Givhan v. Western Line Consolidated School District*, 439 U.S., at 415, n. 4: "Private expression . . . may in some situations bring additional factors to the *Pickering* calculus. When a government employee personally confronts his immediate superior, the employing agency's institutional efficiency may be threatened not only by the content of the employee's message but also by the manner, time, and place in which it is delivered." Here the questionnaire was prepared and distributed at the office; the manner of distribution required not only Myers to leave her work but others to do the same in order that the questionnaire be completed. Although some latitude in when official work is performed is to be allowed when professional employees are involved, and Myers did not violate announced office policy, the fact that Myers, unlike Pickering, exercised her rights to speech at the office supports Connick's fears that the functioning of his office was endangered.

Finally, the context in which the dispute arose is also significant. This is not a case where an employee, out of purely academic interest, circulated a questionnaire so as to obtain useful research. Myers acknowledges that it is no coincidence that the questionnaire followed upon the heels of the transfer notice. When employee speech concerning office policy arises from an employment dispute concerning the very application of that policy to the speaker, additional weight must be given to the supervisor's view that the employee has threatened the authority of the employer to run the office. Although we accept the District Court's factual finding that Myers' reluctance to accede to the transfer order was not a sufficient cause in itself for her dismissal . . . this does not render irrelevant the fact that the questionnaire emerged after a persistent dispute between Myers and Connick and his deputies over office transfer policy.

Myers' questionnaire touched upon matters of public concern in only a most limited sense; her survey, in our view, is most accurately characterized as an employee grievance concerning internal office policy. The limited First Amendment interest involved here does not require that Connick tolerate action which he reasonably believed would disrupt the office, undermine his authority, and destroy close working relationships. Myers' discharge therefore did not offend the First Amendment. . . .

Our holding today is grounded in our longstanding recognition that the First Amendment's primary aim is the full protection of speech upon issues of public concern, as well as the practical realities involved in the administration of a government office. Although today the balance is struck for the government, this is no defeat for the First Amendment. For it would indeed be a Pyrrhic victory for the great principles of free expression if the Amendment's safeguarding of a public employee's right, as a citizen, to participate in discussions concerning public affairs were confused with the attempt to constitutionalize the employee grievance that we see presented here. The judgment of the Court of Appeals is reversed.

Garcetti v. Ceballos

Supreme Court of the United States, 2006.
547 U.S. 410, 126 S.Ct. 1951, 164 L.Ed.2d 689.

■ JUSTICE KENNEDY delivered the opinion of the Court.

[Respondent, Richard Ceballos, a deputy district attorney in Los Angeles County, was serving as a calendar deputy in the office's Pomona branch when he received a call from a defense attorney stating that the affidavit used to obtain a search warrant was inaccurate. Pursuant to local practice, the defense attorney, who had decided to challenge the warrant, asked Ceballos to investigate the case.

Ceballos "determined that the affidavit contained serious misrepresentations" in its description of the premises to be searched. On March 2, 2000, after the warrant affiant, a Los Angeles County deputy sheriff, failed to provide a satisfactory explanation, Ceballos drafted a memorandum explaining his findings and recommending dismissal of the case. Following Ceballos's submission of the memo, he attended a heated meeting with his supervisors, petitioners Carol Najera and Frank Sundstedt, and representatives of the sheriff's department. When Sundstedt proceeded with the prosecution, the defense called Ceballos, but the trial court ultimately rejected the challenge to the warrant.

Ceballos was subsequently reassigned, transferred, and denied a promotion. Following the denial of an employment grievance, Ceballos sued, alleging retaliation for his March 2 memo, in violation of the First and Fourteenth Amendments. The District Court dismissed on the grounds that the First Amendment did not protect the contents of Ceballos's memo because he wrote it pursuant to his employment duties and, alternatively, that petitioners had qualified immunity because the rights Ceballos asserted were not clearly established. The Court of Appeals for the Ninth Circuit reversed, and the Supreme Court granted certiorari.]

It is well settled that "a State cannot condition public employment on a basis that infringes the employee's constitutionally protected interest in freedom of expression." *Connick v. Myers,* 461 U.S. 138, 142 (1983). The question presented by the instant case is whether the First Amendment protects a government employee from discipline based on speech made pursuant to the employee's official duties.

. . .

Pickering and the cases decided in its wake identify two inquiries to guide interpretation of the constitutional protections accorded to public employee speech. The first requires determining whether the employee spoke as a citizen on a matter of public concern. If the answer is no, the employee has no First Amendment cause of action based on his or her employer's reaction to the speech. If the answer is yes, then the possibility of a First Amendment claim arises. The question becomes whether the relevant government entity had an adequate justification for treating the employee differently from any other member of the general public. This consideration reflects the importance of the relationship between the speaker's expressions and employment. A government entity has broader discretion to restrict speech when it acts in its role as employer, but the restrictions it imposes must be directed at speech that has some potential to affect the entity's operations.

. . .

When a citizen enters government service, the citizen by necessity must accept certain limitations on his or her freedom. *See, e.g., Waters v. Churchill,* 511 U.S. 661, 671(1994) (plurality opinion) ("[T]he government as employer indeed has far broader powers than does the government as sovereign"). Government employers, like private employers, need a significant degree of control over their employees' words and actions; without it, there would be little chance for the efficient provision of public services. . . .

. . .

Ceballos wrote his disposition memo because that is part of what he, as a calendar deputy, was employed to do. It is immaterial whether he experienced some personal gratification from writing the memo; his First Amendment rights do not depend on his job satisfaction. The significant point is that the memo was written pursuant to Ceballos' official duties. Restricting speech that owes its existence to a public employee's professional responsibilities does not infringe any liberties the employee might have enjoyed as a private citizen. It simply reflects the exercise of employer control over what the employer itself has commissioned or created. Contrast, for example, the expressions made by the speaker in *Pickering,* whose letter to the newspaper had no official significance and bore similarities to letters submitted by numerous citizens every day.

. . .

Ceballos' proposed contrary rule, adopted by the Court of Appeals, would commit state and federal courts to a new, permanent, and intrusive role, mandating judicial oversight of communications between and among government employees and their superiors in the course of official business. This displacement of managerial discretion by judicial supervision finds no support in our precedents. When an employee speaks as a citizen addressing a matter of public concern, the First Amendment requires a delicate balancing of the competing interests surrounding the speech and its consequences. When, however, the employee is simply performing his or her job duties, there is no warrant for a similar degree of scrutiny. To hold otherwise would be to demand permanent judicial intervention in the conduct of governmental operations to a degree inconsistent with sound principles of federalism and the separation of powers.

. . .

Two final points warrant mentioning. First, as indicated above, the parties in this case do not dispute that Ceballos wrote his disposition memo pursuant to his employment duties. We thus have no occasion to articulate a comprehensive framework for defining the scope of an employee's duties in cases where there is room for serious debate. We reject, however, the suggestion that employers can restrict employees' rights by creating excessively broad job descriptions. The proper inquiry is a practical one. Formal job descriptions often bear little resemblance to the duties an employee actually is expected to perform, and the listing of a given task in an employee's written job description is neither necessary nor sufficient to demonstrate that conducting the task is within the scope of the employee's professional duties for First Amendment purposes.

Second, Justice Souter suggests today's decision may have important ramifications for academic freedom, at least as a constitutional value. There is some argument that expression related to academic scholarship or classroom instruction implicates additional constitutional interests that are not fully accounted for by this Court's customary employee-speech jurisprudence. We need not, and for that reason do not, decide whether the analysis we conduct today would apply in the same manner to a case involving speech related to scholarship or teaching.

Exposing governmental inefficiency and misconduct is a matter of considerable significance. As the Court noted in [*Connick v. Meyers*, 461 U.S. 138 (1983)], public employers should, "as a matter of good judgment," be "receptive to constructive criticism offered by their employees." The dictates of sound judgment are reinforced by the powerful network of legislative enactments—such as whistle-blower protection laws and labor codes—available to those who seek to expose wrongdoing. *See, e.g.*, 5 U.S.C. § 2302(b)(8). Cases involving government attorneys implicate additional safeguards in the form of, for example, rules of conduct and constitutional obligations apart from the First Amendment. *See, e.g.*, Cal. Rule Prof. Conduct 5–110 (2005) ("A member in government service shall not institute or cause to be instituted criminal charges when the member knows or should know that the charges are not supported by probable cause"). These imperatives, as well as obligations arising from any other applicable constitutional provisions and mandates of the criminal and civil laws, protect employees and provide checks on supervisors who would order unlawful or otherwise inappropriate actions.

We reject, however, the notion that the First Amendment shields from discipline the expressions employees make pursuant to their professional duties. Our precedents do not support the existence of a constitutional cause of action behind every statement a public employee makes in the course of doing his or her job.

The judgment of the Court of Appeals is reversed, and the case is remanded for proceedings consistent with this opinion.

■ JUSTICE SOUTER, with whom JUSTICE STEVENS and JUSTICE GINSBURG join, dissenting.

. . .

The key to understanding the difference between this case and [*Rust v. Sullivan*, 500 U.S. 173 (1991) (upholding regulation prohibiting Title X recipients and their staffs from promoting abortion as a family planning method through on-the-job counseling)] lies in the terms of the respective employees' jobs and, in particular, the extent to which those terms require espousal of a substantive position prescribed by the government in advance. Some public employees are hired to "promote a particular policy" by broadcasting a particular message set by the government, but not everyone working for the government, after all, is hired to speak from a government manifesto. *See Legal Services Corporation v. Velazquez*, 531 U.S. 533, 542 (2001). There is no claim or indication that Ceballos was hired to perform such a speaking assignment. He was paid to enforce the law by constitutional action: to exercise the county government's prosecutorial power by acting honestly, competently, and constitutionally. The only sense in which his position apparently required him to hew to a substantive message was at the relatively abstract point of favoring respect for law and its evenhanded enforcement, subjects that are not at the level of controversy in this case and were not in *Rust*. Unlike the doctors in *Rust*, Ceballos was not paid to advance one specific policy among those legitimately available, defined by a specific message or limited by a particular message forbidden. The county government's interest in his speech cannot therefore be equated with the terms of a specific, prescribed, or forbidden substantive position comparable to the Federal Government's interest in *Rust*, and *Rust* is no authority for the notion that government may exercise plenary control over every comment made by a public employee in doing his job.

It is not, of course, that the district attorney lacked interest of a high order in what Ceballos might say. If his speech undercut effective, lawful prosecution, there would have been every reason to rein him in or fire him; a statement that created needless tension among law enforcement agencies would be a fair subject of concern, and the same would be true of inaccurate statements or false ones made in the course of doing his work. But these interests on the government's part are entirely distinct from any claim that Ceballos's speech was government speech with a preset or proscribed content as exemplified in *Rust*. . . .

The fallacy of the majority's reliance on *Rosenberger*'s understanding of *Rust* doctrine, moreover, portends a bloated notion of controllable government speech going well beyond the circumstances of this case. Consider the breadth of the new formulation:

> Restricting speech that owes its existence to a public employee's professional responsibilities does not infringe any liberties the employee might have enjoyed as a private citizen. It simply reflects the exercise of employer control over what the employer itself has commissioned or created.

This ostensible domain beyond the pale of the First Amendment is spacious enough to include even the teaching of a public university professor, and I have to hope that today's majority does not mean to imperil First Amendment protection of academic freedom in public colleges and universities, whose teachers necessarily speak and write "pursuant to official duties." *See Grutter v. Bollinger*, 539 U.S. 306, 329 (2003) ("We have long recognized that, given the important purpose of public education and the expansive freedoms of speech and thought associated with the university environment, universities occupy a special niche in our constitutional tradition"); *Keyishian v. Board of Regents of Univ. of State of N.Y.*, 385 U.S. 589, 603 (1967); *Sweezy v. New Hampshire*, 354 U.S. 234, 250 (1957).

Questions and Comments on *Garcetti*

Is it possible to reconcile *Garcetti's* view of the First Amendment rights of public employees with the positions taken in *Wieman*, *Sweezy*, and *Keyishian* concerning the academic freedom of public institutions of higher education and their faculty? Are the faculty of public institutions of higher education entitled to greater first amendment protection than other public employees? Consider the concurring opinion of Justices Breyer, Souter and Stevens in *Board of Regents of the University of Wisconsin v. Southworth*, 529 U.S. 217 (2000):

[The opinion of the Court is set forth at pp. 745, *infra. Southworth* involved a challenge to a mandatory student activity fee at the University of Wisconsin. The majority upheld the program but added the requirement that funding must be allocated in a way that is viewpoint neutral. Justice Souter, joined by Justice Stevens and Justice Breyer, concurred in the judgment, but not the opinion. Their concurrence discusses in some detail differences they see between academic freedom and traditional First Amendment principles.]

. . . The question before us is . . . properly cast not as whether viewpoint neutrality is required, but whether Southworth has a claim to relief from this specific viewpoint neutral scheme. Two sources of law might be considered in answering this question.

The first comprises First Amendment and related cases grouped under the umbrella of academic freedom.[3] Such law might be implicated by the University's proffered rationale, that the grant scheme funded by the student activity fee is an integral element in the discharge of its educational mission. Our understanding of academic freedom has included not merely liberty from restraints on thought, expression, and association in the academy, but also the idea that universities and schools should have the freedom to make decisions about how and what to teach. In *Regents of Univ. of Mich. v. Ewing*, 474 U.S. 214 (1985), we recognized these related conceptions: "Academic freedom thrives not only on the independent and uninhibited exchange of ideas among teachers and students, but also, and somewhat inconsistently, on autonomous decisionmaking by the academy itself." Some of the opinions in our books emphasize broad conceptions of academic freedom that if accepted by the Court might seem to clothe the University with an immunity to any challenge to regulations made or obligations imposed in the discharge of its educational mission. So, in *Sweezy v. New Hampshire*, 354 U.S. 234 (1957), Justice Frankfurter, concurring in the result and joined by Justice Harlan, explained the importance of a university's ability to define its own mission by quoting from a statement on the open universities in South Africa:

> "It is the business of a university to provide that atmosphere which is most conducive to speculation, experiment and creation. It is an atmosphere in which there prevail 'the four essential freedoms' of a university—to determine for itself on academic grounds who may teach, what may be taught, how it shall be taught, and who may be admitted to study."

These broad statements on academic freedom do not dispose of the case here, however. *Ewing* addressed not the relationship between academic freedom and First Amendment burdens imposed by a university, but a due process challenge to a university's academic decisions, while as to them the case stopped short of recognizing absolute autonomy. And Justice Frankfurter's discussion in *Sweezy*, though not rejected, was not adopted by the full Court. . . . Our other cases on academic freedom thus far have dealt with more limited subjects, and do not compel the conclusion that the objecting university student is without a First Amendment claim here.[4] While we have

---

3. We have long recognized the constitutional importance of academic freedom. *See* Wieman v. Updegraff, 344 U.S. 183 (1952) (Frankfurter, J., concurring); Sweezy v. New Hampshire, 354 U.S. 234, 250 (1957) (plurality opinion); Shelton v. Tucker, 364 U.S. 479, 487 (1960); Keyishian v. Board of Regents of Univ. of State of N. Y., 385 U.S. 589, 603 (1967).

4. Our university cases have dealt with restrictions imposed from outside the academy on individual teachers' speech or associations, Keyishian v. Board of Regents, 385 U.S. at 591–592; Shelton v. Tucker, *supra*, at 487; Sweezy v. New Hampshire, *supra*, at 236; Wieman v. Updegraff, 344 U.S. at 184–185, and cases dealing with the right of teaching institutions to limit expressive freedom of students have been confined to high schools, Hazel-

spoken in terms of a wide protection for the academic freedom and autonomy that bars legislatures (and courts) from imposing conditions on the spectrum of subjects taught and viewpoints expressed in college teaching, we have never held that universities lie entirely beyond the reach of students' First Amendment rights.[5] Thus our prior cases do not go so far as to control the result in this one, and going beyond those cases would be out of order, simply because the University has not litigated on grounds of academic freedom. As to that freedom and university autonomy, then, it is enough to say that protecting a university's discretion to shape its educational mission may prove to be an important consideration in First Amendment analysis of objections to student fees.

The second avenue for addressing Southworth's claim to a pro rata refund or the total abolition of the student activity fee is to see how closely the circumstances here resemble instances of governmental speech mandates found to require relief. As a threshold matter, it is plain that this case falls far afield of those involving compelled or controlled speech, apart from subsidy schemes. Indirectly transmitting a fraction of a student activity fee to an organization with an offensive message is in no sense equivalent to restricting or modifying the message a student wishes to express. Nor does it require an individual to bear an offensive statement personally, as in *Wooley v. Maynard*, 430 U.S. 705, 707 (1977), let alone to affirm a moral or political commitment, as in *West Virginia Bd. of Ed. v. Barnette*, 319 U.S. 624, 626–629 (1943). . . .

. . .

Second, Southworth's objection has less force than it might otherwise carry because the challenged fees support a government program that aims to broaden public discourse.

. . .

Third, our prior compelled speech and compelled funding cases are distinguishable on the basis of the legitimacy of governmental interest. No one disputes the University's assertion that some educational value is derived from the activities supported by the fee, whereas there was no governmental interest in mandating union or bar association support beyond supporting the collective bargaining and professional regulatory functions of those organizations. Nor was there any legitimate governmental interest in requiring the publication or affirmation of propositions with which the bearer or speaker did not agree. Finally, the weakness of Southworth's claim is underscored by its setting within a university, whose students are inevitably required to support the expression of personally offensive viewpoints in ways that cannot be thought constitutionally objectionable unless one is prepared to deny the University its choice over what to teach. No one disputes that some fraction of students' tuition payments may be used for course offerings that are ideologically offensive to some students, and for paying professors who say things in the university forum that are radically at odds with the politics of particular students. Least of all does anyone claim that the University is somehow required to offer a spectrum of courses to satisfy a viewpoint neutrality requirement. The University need not provide junior

wood School Dist. v. Kuhlmeier, 484 U.S. 260, 262 (1988); Bethel School Dist. No. 403 v. Fraser, 478 U.S. 675, 677 (1986); Tinker v. Des Moines Independent Community School Dist., 393 U.S. 503, 504 (1969), whose students and their schools' relation to them are different and at least arguably distinguishable from their counterparts in college education.

5. Indeed, acceptance of the most general statement of academic freedom (as in the South African manifesto quoted by Justice Frankfurter) might be thought even to sanction student speech codes in public universities.

years abroad in North Korea as well as France, instruct in the theory of plutocracy as well as democracy, or teach Nietzsche as well as St. Thomas. Since uses of tuition payments (not optional for anyone who wishes to stay in college) may fund offensive speech far more obviously than the student activity fee does, it is difficult to see how the activity fee could present a stronger argument for a refund.

Scallet v. Rosenblum

United States District Court for the Western District of Virginia, 1996.
911 F.Supp. 999.

■ MICHAEL, United States District Judge.

Plaintiff, a non-tenured instructor at the University of Virginia's Darden Graduate School of Business ("Darden"), brings this action pursuant to 42 U.S.C. § 1983, alleging that the defendants, three senior Darden faculty members, violated rights secured to Plaintiff under the First Amendment by refusing to renew his teaching contract in retaliation for his outspokenness on issues of "diversity" at Darden. Plaintiff seeks injunctive relief and damages for this alleged violation of his constitutional rights. . . . .

. . . Plaintiff Robert J. Scallet became a full-time faculty member at Darden in 1988. At Darden, Scallet taught a section of the Analysis and Communications course ("A & C"), a writing and speech class that all students are required to take in their first year at Darden. Scallet also had administrative responsibilities within the A & C department, serving as Course Head beginning in 1988. Scallet's responsibilities as Course Head included administering the course, managing other A & C faculty, and developing the curriculum for A & C.

Scallet was a strong advocate of "diversity" while at Darden. By that term, it is understood that Scallet championed, among other things, the goal of broadening both the traditional focus of classroom materials so as to make them more accessible to women and minorities, and the traditional under-pinnings of the business community itself so as to make that sphere more hospitable to the same.

In the fall of 1991, Defendant Smith, an Associate Dean at Darden, asked Scallet to take some "pieces of paper" off of the wall outside his office. Those pieces of paper consisted of various articles and cartoons that Scallet had posted.

In late April or early May of 1992, Defendant Harris, another Associate Dean at Darden, met with Scallet and suggested to him that his contract would be renewed for the 1992–1993 academic year. Defendant Harris made the statement to Scallet "because I, I felt that [Scallet] continued to be able to deliver some good instruction to the Darden students." A few days later, however, Defendants Smith and Harris, together with Defendant Rosen-blum, the Dean of Darden, met with the other members of the A & C faculty to discuss, outside of Scallet's presence, reported problems the A & C faculty were having with Scallet. At that meeting, the faculty members expressed concerns about their collective ability to continue working with Scallet. A short time after this meeting, Dean Rosenblum informed Scallet that he would be relieved of his teaching duties for the 1992–1993 academic year and that his contract would not be renewed thereafter.

In response, Scallet filed a grievance petition with the University in October 1992, seeking review of the adverse action. In his petition, Scallet alleged that Dean Rosenblum failed to renew his contract on account of Scallet's outspoken views regarding issues of diversity and "multiculturalism" at Darden. Scallet's request for review prompted an internal investigation that culminated in a report prepared by Defendant Daniel Hallahan, a Professor in the School of Education and a member of the Faculty Relations Committee. That report contained comments from various faculty members at Darden, including Dean Rosenblum, to the effect that Scallet was an ineffective faculty member who possessed character defects. The report, issued in March 1993, concluded that there was no support for Scallet's contention that he was retaliated against for his remarks about diversity. However, the report contained a comment attributed to Defendant Rosenblum that "there were a few faculty who did not like [Scallet's] activist orientation to the course. . . ."

In March 1994, Scallet filed the current lawsuit. . . .

The speech that Scallet alleges caused defendants to take the adverse action against him falls into three categories: (1) classroom discussions; (2) comments made by Scallet in faculty meetings; and (3) articles and cartoons posted by Scallet on the wall outside of his office. . . .

First, Scallet contends that defendants objected to the content of his classroom discussions. Scallet maintains that "senior faculty members were threatened by . . . the issues Scallet was discussing in the classroom." Scallet points to comments by Defendant Harris to Plaintiff that "[Smith] and the others want all the social and political content stripped from your course." Specifically, Defendant Harris allegedly told Scallet that senior faculty members objected to Scallet's discussion of "power relationships" in corporate organization and his teaching the movie "Roger and Me." Indeed, one senior faculty member expressed concerns about Scallet's showing a "commie" movie at Darden. Furthermore, Defendant Harris allegedly told Scallet that members of the faculty did not approve of two cases he used in class. One involved the target-marketing of cigarettes to African–Americans and the other featured an Asian woman as the key decision-maker. Defendant Harris did not indicate whether the senior faculty disagreed with the social and political content of the materials or if they thought it was pedagogically inappropriate. And as noted above, Defendant Rosenblum told Professor Hallahan that "there were a few faculty who did not like [Scallet's] activist orientation to the course. . . ."

Scallet further contends that his 1991 request for summer funding was denied because he intended to use the grant to develop course materials that touched upon social and political issues. He was allegedly told by Defendant Harris that "we don't want you doing that. Cross that off the list." More generally, Scallet claims that he was reprimanded on one occasion by Defendant Smith who stated that he "hated my tone, he hated . . . the minority material I taught. He found me dangerous, he found me evil, I was undermining his objectives for the school. . . ." During this same discussion, Defendant Smith allegedly intimated to Scallet that he had been trying to get Scallet fired for two years and stated "now I am going to do it." When Scallet ultimately confronted Defendant Rosenblum about the non-renewal and asked whether Defendant Smith was the catalyst for it and further whether Rosenblum felt pressure to support Smith because Smith was an extremely influential member of the Darden faculty who could help safeguard Rosenblum's own position at Darden, Rosenblum allegedly stated, "Yes, you've got most of the story. There are some details you don't have."

Second, Scallet contends that defendants objected to Scallet's expression of views in faculty meetings concerning the "importance of developing case material that ... reflected the experiences of women and minorities in the workplace" and "the ways in which issues of social responsibility in business could be incorporated into classroom discussions." Defendant Harris allegedly told Plaintiff that he should mute his expression of views at faculty meetings because his "advocacy of certain views was ticking people off." Scallet claims that "[s]ome senior faculty objected to my public expression of views related to Darden's pedagogy, the institution's position on academic freedom, faculty governance, the institution's mission statement, and the school's difficulty in incorporating diversity into its core curriculum." Scallet does not provide examples of specific comments to which defendants expressed concerns.

Third, Scallet maintains that defendants objected to the materials Scallet posted on his door and on the wall outside his office. Specifically, Scallet alleges that Defendant Smith "complained about articles on the wall outside of Scallet's office dealing with issues of diversity in communications and ordered Scallet to remove them so that students could not see them." The material at issue included a Guide to Nonsexist Language, a Doonesbury cartoon lampooning the prevalence of dual-track education for boys and girls, and an article concerning business and the environment. Defendant Smith allegedly admonished Scallet that, "I want all this stuff gone," and "I don't like the students reading that stuff."

Thus, it is Scallet's contention that the defendants did not renew his contract for the 1993–1994 academic year, and relieved him of his teaching responsibilities for the 1992–1993 term, because they did not approve of the views he expressed regarding issues of diversity in the contexts discussed above. Scallet makes this argument in light of a political schism Scallet alleges existed on campus between advocates of diversity and those wedded to what Scallet terms "the Darden Way." As evidence of this schism, Scallet points to a May 1992 Report of the Ad Hoc Committee on the Status of Women at Darden, wherein the Committee concluded that "there are widely held perceptions by the faculty that ... there is an inability (or an unwillingness) to address the underlying issues that diversity is creating. This has allowed particular problems to escalate to destructive proportion."

Defendants, in contrast, maintain that Scallet's contract was not renewed because he lacked essential collegiality skills that made it impossible for other members of the A & C faculty to coexist with him. Defendants also suggest that Scallet's classroom discussions disrupted the effective delivery of the A & C course and trenched upon course material taught outside the A & C department.

Defendants maintain that there were at least two complaints lodged against Scallet by members of the A & C faculty. Specifically, some members of the A & C faculty complained that Scallet had threatened them with termination if they did not agree to teach more class hours. In addition, one A & C faculty member, Paula Wenger, protested to Defendant Harris that Plaintiff had excluded her from the hiring process of a potential A & C faculty member. This latter dispute, defendants allege, mushroomed into a heated confrontation in a basement classroom between Scallet and Ms.

Wenger, who was eight-months pregnant at the time. Defendants maintain that Scallet accosted Ms. Wenger so thoroughly about her going to Associate Dean Harris behind Scallet's back that she thereafter feared Scallet, refusing to work with Scallet alone, or even to be in the building with him at the same time. ("She was absolutely white and shaking.... She could hardly speak"). As a result of these complaints, Defendant Harris, in the spring of 1991, relieved Scallet of his management responsibilities over A & C, and took over the administration of the A & C course himself.

The record indicates that Scallet had altercations with other female A & C instructors. During the winter of 1988–1989, Elizabeth Denton, who was pregnant, missed a speech class due to illness and was castigated by Scallet. Ms. Denton eventually left Darden in part because of the treatment she received from Scallet during her tenure. Scallet also allegedly subjected Virginia Germino to unwelcome details of his sex life. There is evidence in the record as well that female students "dreaded" Scallet's classes because he made them feel uncomfortable and because his use of profanity interfered with their ability to focus on the material.

In addition to harassing colleagues, defendants maintain that Scallet fostered division within the A & C faculty and actually sabotaged some of his peers' classes. Defendants cite an instance wherein Scallet allegedly told a colleague, who was preparing to lecture Scallet's and Ms. Wenger's class, to present one type of lecture even though the students were expecting a different type of lecture. Scallet allegedly chuckled when the technician confronted him because, Scallet believed, Ms. Wenger would ultimately be held responsible for the gaffe.

Defendants also point out that each and every member of the A & C faculty who served with Scallet testified that Scallet was extremely difficult to work with because he fostered an environment of fear and distrust, especially among the female faculty.

Defendants argue that Scallet created problems within A & C by failing to teach the same material taught by other A & C faculty. This failure, defendants allege, disrupted the A & C agenda because A & C was supposed to be taught in a uniform fashion so that students from different sections could more easily interact outside the classroom. Scallet's deviations from the program, defendants contend, disrupted the classes of other A & C faculty because students protested the divergence. ("students complained to me at the beginning of class that they did not think they should have to perform the assignment because students in Cid Scallet's class were doing something else. It was a significant disruption in my class"); ("we had to teach a separate course from Cid and that created intolerable tension among us"). Most significantly, defendants allege that the Scallet's classroom material trenched upon material taught by other teachers throughout Darden, some of whom expressed concerns about Scallet's course content. The record indicates that two operations professors expressed concern "that we were teaching material that stepped on the toes of the Operations course." In addition, a Marketing professor asked "what the heck we were doing teaching a marketing case in A & C?" All of these concerns, and some others, were voiced at the May 1992 meeting between the defendants and the other members of the A & C faculty.

Thus, defendants argue that they took the adverse action against Scallet because his disruption of the A & C mandate, accomplished both through the material he taught and through the ways in which he abrasively interacted with his colleagues, created an untenable situation that warranted, indeed necessitated, the action taken.

. . .

In *Pickering v. Board Of Education*, 391 U.S. 563 (1968), the Supreme Court articulated a [balancing] test for identifying the scope of first amendment protection afforded teachers' out-of-class speech [which is], obviously, germane to the analysis of Scallet's out-of-class speech—that is, to Scallet's remarks at faculty meetings and to his placement of articles and cartoons outside his office—and it will be employed for that purpose.

However, Scallet also alleges that the defendants retaliated against him for his in-class speech. The Supreme Court, though, has never spoken to the level of first amendment protection afforded teachers' in-class speech.

Lower federal courts have sought to fill this void in several ways. Some courts have simply appropriated *Pickering's* balancing test for use in the context of the university classroom.[10]

Other courts have looked to such Supreme Court cases as *Tinker v. Des Moines Independent School District*, 393 U.S. 503 (1969) and *Hazelwood School District v. Kuhlmeier*, 484 U.S. 260 (1988), where the Court discussed the scope of students' first amendment rights in the classroom. For example, in *Miles v. Denver Public Schools*, 944 F.2d 773 (10th Cir. 1991), the court adopted a two-prong test derived from *Hazelwood School District v. Kuhlmeier*, 484 U.S. 260 (1988), where the Supreme Court held that "educators do not offend the First Amendment by exercising editorial control over the style and content of student speech in school-sponsored expressive activities so long as their actions are reasonably related to legitimate pedagogical concerns." Extending the holding in *Hazelwood* to the in-class expression of a ninth grade teacher, the *Miles* court held that a school may restrict a teacher's in-class expression if (1) it has a legitimate pedagogical interest in abridging the speech; and (2) the school's restriction on the speech is reasonably related to that interest.

The *Miles* court declined to use the *Pickering* balancing test, stating that while "the *Pickering* test accounts for the state's interests as an employer, it

10. The Second Circuit appeared to adopt the *Pickering* test in *Blum v. Schlegel*, 18 F.3d 1005 (2d Cir. 1994). In that case, a state law school professor claimed that he was denied tenure because "*in classes* and in campus publications, Blum advocated the legalization of marijuana and criticized national drug control policy. For example, Blum in his First Amendment class set a number of hypotheticals in the context of the current drug war. Blum also published two pieces in a campus publication and participated in a debate regarding civil disobedience." The Second Circuit did not distinguish between Blum's in-class remarks and pedagogy on the one hand, and his out-of-class expressions, on the other. Instead, the court simply applied the *Pickering* balancing test to Blum's speech as a whole. Specifically, the court held that Blum's speech interest outweighed the efficiency interest proffered by the University as a justification for restricting Blum's speech. The court held that "the efficient provision of services by a State university's law school actually depends, to a degree, on the dissemination in public fora of controversial speech implicating matters of public concern. Blum's speech, therefore, does not impair the interests of the state in efficient provision of services through its law school." *Id.* Since the court did not distinguish between Blum's out-of-class expressions and his classroom expression, it is difficult to tell whether the court actually endorsed the *Pickering* test for use in the context of a law school classroom. It is clear, however, that the court endorsed a broad conception of protected speech in the graduate school setting.

does not address the significant interests of the state as educator." The court articulated those "significant interests" as assuring "that participants learn whatever lessons the activity is designed to teach, that readers or listeners are not exposed to material that may be inappropriate for their level of maturity, and that the views of the individual speaker are not erroneously attributed to the school." The court acknowledged that *Hazelwood* involved students' expression in a secondary school and not teachers' expression in the classroom. However, the court concluded that there is "no reason to distinguish between students and teachers where classroom discussion is concerned."

Finally, at least one court has fashioned its own balancing test. *See Bishop v. Aronov*, 926 F.2d 1066 (11th Cir. 1991), *cert. denied*, 505 U.S. 1218 (1992).[11]

In the absence of clear guidance, this court will apply the *Pickering* balancing test to determine the level of first amendment protection afforded Scallet's in-class speech. The court notes that the cases in which the *Hazelwood* test is employed do not address the in-class speech of teachers at the university or graduate school level. Rather, those cases deal with the in-class speech of secondary school teachers. Thus, the "significant interests" discussed in *Hazelwood* that justify the restriction, in certain instances, of teachers' in-class speech, are not implicated to the same extent, if at all, in the context of higher education. Certainly the interest in assuring "that readers or listeners are not exposed to material that may be inappropriate for their level of maturity" is not implicated in the graduate school context. Furthermore, the interest in assuring that "the views of the individual speaker are not erroneously attributed to the school" is not as strongly implicated in the context of higher education, where students are not so easily cowed by the assertion of the apparent authority the classroom fosters. In addition, while the Supreme Court has recognized that communities have a legitimate interest in attempting to inculcate certain values in students through public education, *see, e.g.*, *Bd. of Educ. v. Pico*, 457 U.S. 853, 863–64 (1982) (plurality opinion) (courts should allow school boards freedom to set school curriculum in manner that transmits community values to students), achieving some sort of uniform value system is not part of the mandate of higher education. Indeed, it is anathema to the intellectually maverick

---

11. In this case, Dr. Bishop, a university professor of exercise physiology, interjected his religious beliefs into classroom discussions, telling students that he modeled his life after Christ because he felt that it was "the wisest thing I can do." He informed students that they need not share his views but that they should understand his "bias." The university required that Dr. Bishop discontinue his "interjection of religious beliefs and/or preferences during instructional time periods." In analyzing Dr. Bishop's claim that the university's restraint of his classroom speech violated the First Amendment, the court created its own multi-factor test, based upon its reading of *Hazelwood*. First, the court noted the classroom context of the speech, stating that such a context forced the court to consider the "coercive effect upon students that a professor's speech inherently possesses and that the University may wish to avoid." Indeed, student complaints regarding Professor Bishop's reli-gious remarks suggested that the students felt coerced by them. Second, the court considered the university's position as a public employer "which may reasonably restrict the speech rights of employees more readily than the those [sic] of other persons." In this vein, the court considered "the University's authority to reasonably control the content of its curriculum, particularly that content imparted during class time." The court also considered the possibility that classroom speech could "give[ ] the appearance of endorsement by the university." Finally, the court considered "the strong predilection for academic freedom as an adjunct of the free speech rights of the First Amendment." *Id.* at 1075. Applying this balance, the court concluded that "the University's interests in the classroom conduct of its professors are sufficient ... to warrant the reasonable restrictions it has imposed on Dr. Bishop."

environments of the university and graduate school. *See Tilton v. Richardson*, 403 U.S. 672, 685–86 (1971). Thus, the pedagogical interest in restricting teacher's in-class speech is not as strongly implicated in the context of higher education.

... The court notes that it has reservations about extending the *Pickering* analysis to the in-class speech of university professors and graduate school instructors since the test does not explicitly account for the robust tradition of academic freedom in those quarters. However, the court concludes that this interest can be accounted for within the parameters of the balancing test by properly defining the extent of the teacher's interest in the speech.[13] ... Accordingly, the court turns below to the *Pickering* analysis.

. . .

1. Classroom Speech

. . .

Defendants contend that Scallet's classroom speech relates simply to issues of curriculum which cannot be characterized as matters of public concern. Rather, defendants maintain, Scallet was simply discharging his duties as an employee of Darden when he made his classroom remarks, thereby stripping them of any public relevance. . . .

. . .

[D]efendants' argument seriously misconceives the relevance of classroom debate in our democratic society. To suggest that the First Amendment, as a matter of law, is never implicated when a professor speaks in class, is fantastic. "For decades it has been clearly established that the First Amendment tolerates neither laws nor other means of coercion, persuasion or intimidation 'that cast a pall of orthodoxy' over the free exchange of ideas in the classroom." *Dube v. State University of New York*, 900 F.2d 587, 598 (2d Cir. 1990) (quoting *Keyishian v. Board of Regents*, 385 U.S. 589, 603 (1967), *cert. denied*, 501 U.S. 1211 (1991)). Indeed, "the vigilant protection of constitutional freedoms is nowhere more vital than in the community of American schools," *Shelton v. Tucker*, 364 U.S. 479, 487 (1960). . . .

In short, defendants' sweeping argument that a university instructor's classroom remarks, as a matter of law, cannot be characterized as addressing

---

13. The court notes that it declines to rely on the *Bishop* case, *see* n. 11, *supra*, because the Establishment Clause concerns that lurked throughout the analysis in that case are wholly absent from the current case. *See* Bishop, 926 F.2d at 1077 ("Because of the potential establishment conflict, even the appearance of proselytizing by a professor should be a real concern to the University"); *id.* at 1074 (noting that classroom speech could "give[] the appearance of endorsement by the University") Thus, the court concludes that the issue addressed in *Bishop* limits the relevance of its analysis. *See* Michael A. Olivas, Reflections on Professorial Academic Freedom: Sec-

ond Thoughts on the Third "Essential Freedom", 45 Stan. L. Rev. 1835, 1847 (1993) ("The holding exceeds by a wide margin the rationale necessary to find for the University. The court could have fashioned a more carefully reasoned argument, based on higher education precedents, that religion is *sui generis*, that supplementary lectures and personal remarks on religious beliefs are highly suggestive, that religious views are not germane to an exercise physiology (or math) class, and that a faculty committee had reviewed the matter and given Bishop the opportunity to explain his pedagogical choices").

matters of public concern warranting first amendment protection, fails to convince.

. . .

Defendants argue that the defendants' interest in controlling the A & C curriculum outweighs Professor Scallet's interest in his classroom speech.[16] Defendants argue that the course Professor Scallet taught was a "uniform writing and speech course, an integral part of Darden's required first-year curriculum. Each student received the same course material and was to receive the same instruction, although the course was taught in different sections by different instructors. There can be no doubt that Darden as an institution had a powerful interest in the content of the A & C curriculum and its coordination with the content of other required courses. . . ."

Defendants maintain that Scallet's forays into issues of diversity caused significant disruption within the A & C department. Indeed, some students protested the divergence between the material taught in class sections. Defendants also suggest that Scallet's classroom speech intruded on the material taught by other teachers in other courses at Darden. And as an institutional matter, defendants maintain that it is the school's prerogative to decide whether business ethics and diversity issues are taught in the first-year Business Ethics class by a professor with an M.B.A, or by an instructor in the first-year writing and speech class who has no business background. In short, defendants maintain that they needed to take control of the A & C curriculum and that the First Amendment does not prohibit them from doing so.

. . .

... The court finds, as a factual matter, that Scallet's in-class speech, that is, his use of certain materials for classroom discussion, did disrupt Darden's pedagogical mission. The record indicates that tight control over the A & C curriculum was necessary to ensure uniformity across class sections. The record further indicates that Scallet's in-class speech, in the form of the materials he used and the discussions those materials fostered, created disruption within the A & C department, hampering the school's ability effectively to deliver the A & C course to its students. Furthermore, there is evidence in the record that Scallet's use of particular material in his classes created divisions within the A & C faculty, a fact this court considers in striking its balance. Moreover, the record indicates that Scallet's in-class pedagogy adversely affected the functioning of Darden as a whole. It is undisputed that several faculty members outside the A & C department expressed concerns to Scallet about his class trenching upon their own.

The court notes that there is evidence in the record that could suggest that Scallet's classroom speech did not disrupt Darden's mission in any significant way. For example, it is undisputed that the A & C department still utilizes the "Hoffman" case even though that case drew complaints from members of the Darden faculty. If Scallet's use of that case did indeed intrude on other courses or created other problems within A & C, then it would be fair to assume that the case would have been dropped from the

---

16. Defendants do not concede that they took the adverse action against Scallet because of his expressions regarding diversity. Rather, for purposes of summary judgment, they ar-gue that even if they had taken the action to stifle Scallet's speech, they had a legitimate, constitutional reason for doing so.

curriculum. However, the court must look at the entire record, and upon doing so, the court is convinced that Scallet's in-class speech was in fact disruptive.

Given the court's factual finding that Scallet's in-class speech was disruptive, the court concludes, as a matter of law, that the speech is not protected by the First Amendment. The State's interest in the effective administration of its duties outweighs Scallet's interest in teaching his own material, where teaching that material hampers the State's ability to fulfill its duties. Scallet could have found, and no doubt did, other, perhaps more appropriate, outlets for expressing his opinions about diversity.[18]

Thus, the court concludes that Scallet's in-class speech is not protected by the First Amendment.

2. Faculty Meetings

. . .

It is manifest that Scallet's speech at faculty meetings related to matters of public concern. Scallet's expressed desire to reconstruct A & C cases to reflect the psychology of women and African–Americans in the workplace, although curricular in nature, cannot be said to relate to matters solely of institutional or personal concern since it also speaks to the general debate on multiculturalism that currently thrives in all quarters of American society. To characterize Scallet's remarks in faculty meetings as "essentially a 'private' matter between employer and employee," mischaracterizes the nature of the expression. Scallet was speaking not as a disgruntled employee, about some issue of only parochial concern to him or in which he had some vested interest. Rather, Scallet was speaking as a concerned citizen, albeit one within the University community, who wished to advance a dialogue at Darden because he thought changes in society demanded that Darden engage in that dialogue.

And as discussed above, the fact that Scallet expressed his concerns about Darden's lack of sensitivity to issues of diversity in private faculty meetings, and not in the public square, does not strip those comments of their inherently public quality.

Thus, the court concludes that the remarks Scallet made at faculty meetings concerning diversity at Darden relate to matters of public concern.

. . .

Defendants deny that they wished to muzzle Scallet at faculty meetings, but state that to the effect that they did wish to do so it was because of Scallet's confrontational and argumentative style, not because of the content of his remarks. This argument addresses whether defendants would have renewed Scallet's contract "but for" his protected speech and does not

---

18. The court also concludes that Darden's interest in controlling the channels through which its students receive the curriculum outweighs Scallet's interest in his classroom speech. It is proper for Darden, as an institution, to cabin the teaching of certain material within certain fora if it believes that any other pedagogical regime would compromise the delivery of the material. Thus, if school administrators believe, as they apparently do, that a required first-year class on business ethics is the most appropriate forum in which to teach issues of diversity, they are entitled to make that judgment and to bring it to fruition. Otherwise, the court may well be engaged in that "intrusive oversight by the judiciary in the name of the First Amendment."

suggest any counterbalance to Scallet's interest in expression under the present analysis.

Thus, the court concludes that Scallet's advocacy of diversity in faculty meetings is protected under the First Amendment because it relates to matters of public concern and because the defendants offer no competing interest served by stifling that speech.

3.   Posted Articles and Cartoons

Defendants do not contest that the various articles and Doonesbury cartoons that Scallet posted on his office door and wall relate to matters of public concern. Rather, defendants argue that Scallet was instructed to remove the items because they were harming the wallpaper and because they created an inaesthetic environment that harmed Darden's recruiting effort since Scallet's office was across the hall from Darden's Admissions' Office.

The court concludes that defendants' aesthetic interest, if legitimate, does not outweigh Scallet's interest in the expression. The court again notes that "when an employee's speech substantially involves matters of public concern . . . the state must make a stronger showing of disruption in order to prevail." Defendants' aesthetic argument is simply not up to the task.

In summary, the court holds that Scallet's remarks at faculty meetings, and his placement of articles and cartoons outside his office, are protected forms of expression under the First Amendment but that his classroom speech is not so protected.

Defendants, however, may still prevail on their motion for summary judgment if they can demonstrate that the record is clear that Scallet's protected speech—that is his comments at faculty meetings and his posting of articles and political cartoons outside his office—was not the "but for" cause of defendants failure to renew the contract.

.   .   .

. . . The only evidence Scallet musters to support his contention that defendants disapproved of his advocacy at faculty meetings is a statement Scallet attributes to Defendant Harris in May of 1991 to that effect. Even if credited, this statement, taken together with the incident with Defendant Smith, could not support a verdict for Scallet in light of the compelling and substantial evidence of Scallet's misconduct and inability to work with his colleagues in the A & C department.

Underlying this controversy—indeed, at the root of it—is the issue of the proper content of, and method of teaching, the A & C curriculum so as to achieve the course's writing and speech goals. Efforts by Scallet to include divergent diversity and multicultural elements in that curriculum appears to have been at the heart of the disaffections of the other instructors of the A & C classes, though coupled with strong complaints about Scallet's personal interrelations with those instructors. Further, having what it considered to be an integrated overall curriculum in the school, other professors saw this expansion of the A & C curriculum as intruding on their separate course-work and curriculum. As a pedagogical matter, the institution included diversity, for instance, in a course on Business Ethics, where it was believed to fit far better than in a course teaching writing and speech.

Failure by Scallet to observe and follow this institutional determination of which courses should embrace which matters within the particular course curriculum is, as observed above, at the very heart of this dispute. Such determinations are clearly legitimately pedagogical, and so clearly related to the institutional judgments appropriate to such discussions, that failure to appreciate and respond to them by Scallet caused the disruption and dissatisfaction so clearly manifested in the record.

As discussed at length above, the record indicates that Scallet's conduct was disruptive and that the entire A & C faculty had severe problems working with him. Indeed, some of his conduct bordered on sexual harassment. Although Scallet maintains that these proffered reasons for his non-renewal are pretextual, he simply has not mustered sufficient evidence to demonstrate to a jury that defendants retaliated against him either for his advocacy in faculty meetings or because he posted articles and cartoons outside his office. In light of the wealth of evidence supporting defendants' non-retaliatory motivation for failing to renew Scallet's contract, the court concludes that defendants have carried their burden for summary judgment.

For the foregoing reasons, the court grants defendants' motion for summary judgment.

Questions and Comments on *Scallet*

The Court reviews the different approaches to in-classroom speech before concluding that the *Pickering* balancing test is the most appropriate. Do you agree with this conclusion? Does it make sense to use the same approach for in-classroom speech and out-of-class speech?

In applying the *Pickering* balancing test, the court notes that Scallet could have found other outlets for expressing his opinions on diversity. To what extent does the court's holding with respect to Scallet's in-class speech depend on the fact that this was a mandatory class?

Note on *Hong v. Grant*

The *Garcetti* dissenters raised, and the majority declined to answer, the question of *Garcetti*'s implications for academic freedom. In light of the Supreme Court's opinion, should lower courts hold that "expression related to academic scholarship or classroom instruction implicates additional constitutional interests that are not fully accounted for by ... customary employee-speech jurisprudence"?

In *Hong v. Grant*, 516 F. Supp. 2d 1158 (C.D. Cal. 2007), the court granted summary judgment to the Regents of the University of California (University) and six University officials in a 42 U.S.C. § 1983 action on the grounds that the plaintiff professor's speech was not protected by the First Amendment. Professor Juan Hong of University of California, Irvine's Department of Chemical Engineering and Materials Science sued after the University denied him a routine merit increase in pay and increased his teaching duties.

Hong alleged that the University's decisions were in retaliation for several disagreements he had with the administration over the preceding years. First, during his mid-career review of another professor, Hong raised questions about the propriety of certain research grants obtained by that professor. Second, Hong suggested that another faculty member had misrepresented himself in a merit-increase application and then accused the administration of manipulating the application review process. Third, Hong complained to the department chair about what he saw as overuse of lecturers in teaching classes that could be covered by tenured faculty. Finally, Hong had disagreed with the department chair's extension of an informal employment offer before the faculty approved the appointment, believing that the decision violated the faculty's right to self-governance.

The court decided the case in the *Garcetti* framework, suggesting that its decision protected institutional academic freedom:

> If a public employee's speech is made in the course of the employee's job duties and responsibilities, the speech is not protected under the First Amendment. Because all of Mr. Hong's criticisms were made in the course of doing his job as a UCI professor, the speech is not protected from discipline by University administrators. Moreover, Mr. Hong's criticisms pertained to the internal hiring, promotion and staffing practices of UCI and are of very little concern to the public. This Court is not qualified to second guess the wisdom of UCI's practices in this regard and it must allow University administrators wide latitude in managing its affairs if UCI is to accomplish its very important educational and research mission.

Id. at 1161.

Because the University gives faculty a role in departmental governance and faculty appointment and promotion, they held that Hong "has a professional responsibility to offer feedback, advice and criticism about his department's administration and operation from his perspective as a tenured, experienced professor." *Id.* at 1167. Noting that Hong felt professional obligation to participate in faculty review and discussions about the manner of instruction and directed his criticisms only to university administrators and faculty, the court found that the University had "commissioned" Hong's speech and that such speech was not constitutionally protected. Moreover, even if Hong's statements exposed governmental waste, "they are more properly characterized as internal administrative disputes which have little or no relevance to the community as a whole." *Id.* at 1169.

Is this a fair reading of *Garcetti*?

3. ACADEMIC FREEDOM DECISIONS AFTER *PICKERING*

Regents of the University of Michigan v. Ewing

Supreme Court of the United States, 1985.
474 U.S. 214, 106 S.Ct. 507, 88 L.Ed.2d 523.

■ STEVENS, J. delivered the opinion for a unanimous Court.

Respondent Scott Ewing was dismissed from the University of Michigan after failing an important written examination. The question presented is whether the University's action deprived Ewing of property without due process of law because its refusal to allow him to retake the examination was an arbitrary departure from the University's past practice....

In the fall of 1975 Ewing enrolled in a special 6–year program of study, known as "Inteflex," offered jointly by the undergraduate college and the Medical School. An undergraduate degree and a medical degree are awarded upon successful completion of the program. In order to qualify for the final two years of the Inteflex program, which consist of clinical training at hospitals affiliated with the University, the student must successfully complete four years of study including both premedical courses and courses in the basic medical sciences. The student must also pass the "NBME Part I"—a 2–day written test administered by the National Board of Medical Examiners.

In the spring of 1981, after overcoming certain academic and personal difficulties, Ewing successfully completed the courses prescribed for the first four years of the Inteflex program and thereby qualified to take the NBME Part I. Ewing failed five of the seven subjects on that examination, receiving a total score of 235 when the passing score was 345. (A score of 380 is required for state licensure and the national mean is 500.) Ewing received the lowest score recorded by an Inteflex student in the brief history of that program.

On July 24, 1981, the Promotion and Review Board individually reviewed the status of several students in the Inteflex program. After considering Ewing's record in some detail, the nine members of the Board in attendance voted unanimously to drop him from registration in the program.

In response to a written request from Ewing, the Board reconvened a week later to reconsider its decision. Ewing appeared personally and explained why he believed that his score on the test did not fairly reflect his academic progress or potential.[2] After reconsidering the matter, the nine voting members present unanimously reaffirmed the prior action to drop Ewing from registration in the program.

In August, Ewing appealed the Board's decision to the Executive Committee of the Medical School. After giving Ewing an opportunity to be heard in person, the Executive Committee unanimously approved a motion to deny his appeal for a leave of absence status that would enable him to retake Part I of the NBME examination. In the following year, Ewing reappeared before the Executive Committee on two separate occasions, each time unsuccessfully seeking readmission to the Medical School. On August 19, 1982, he commenced this litigation in the United States District Court for the Eastern District of Michigan.

Ewing's complaint against the Regents of the University of Michigan asserted a right to retake the NBME Part I test on three separate theories, two predicated on state law and one based on federal law. As a matter of state law, he alleged that the University's action constituted a breach of contract and was barred by the doctrine of promissory estoppel. As a matter of federal law, Ewing alleged that he had a property interest in his continued enrollment in the Inteflex program and that his dismissal was arbitrary and capricious, violating his "substantive due process rights" guaranteed by the Fourteenth Amendment and entitling him to relief under 42 U. S. C. § 1983.

. . .

The District Court concluded that the evidence did not support either Ewing's contract claim or his promissory estoppel claim under governing Michigan law. There was "no sufficient evidence to conclude that the defendants bound themselves either expressly or by a course of conduct to give Ewing a second chance to take Part I of the NBME examination." With reference to the pamphlet "On Becoming A Doctor," the District Court held that "even if [Ewing] had learned of the pamphlet's contents before he took

---

2. At this and later meetings Ewing excused his NBME Part I failure because his mother had suffered a heart attack 18 months before the examination; his girlfriend broke up with him about six months before the examination; his work on an essay for a contest had taken too much time; his makeup examination in pharmacology was administered just before the NBME Part I; and his inadequate preparation caused him to panic during the examination.

the examination, and I find that he did not, I would not conclude that this amounted either to an unqualified promise to him or gave him a contract right to retake the examination."

With regard to Ewing's federal claim, the District Court determined that Ewing had a constitutionally protected property interest in his continued enrollment in the Inteflex program and that a state university's academic decisions concerning the qualifications of a medical student are "subject to substantive due process review" in federal court. The District Court, however, found no violation of Ewing's due process rights. . . .

[T]he Court of Appeals reversed the dismissal of Ewing's federal constitutional claim. . . .

We granted the University's petition for certiorari. . . .

In *Board of Curators, Univ. of Mo. v. Horowitz,* 435 U.S. 78, 91–92 (1978), we assumed, without deciding, that federal courts can review an academic decision of a public educational institution under a substantive due process standard. In this case Ewing contends that such review is appropriate because he had a constitutionally protected property interest in his continued enrollment in the Inteflex program. But remembering Justice Brandeis' admonition not to "'formulate a rule of constitutional law broader than is required by the precise facts to which it is to be applied,'" *Ashwander v. TVA,* 297 U.S. 288, 347 (1936) (concurring opinion), we again conclude, as we did in *Horowitz,* that the precise facts disclosed by the record afford the most appropriate basis for decision. We therefore accept the University's invitation to "assume the existence of a constitutionally protectible property right in [Ewing's] continued enrollment," and hold that even if Ewing's assumed property interest gave rise to a substantive right under the Due Process Clause to continued enrollment free from arbitrary state action, the facts of record disclose no such action.

As a preliminary matter, it must be noted that any substantive constitutional protection against arbitrary dismissal would not necessarily give Ewing a right to retake the NBME Part I. The constitutionally protected interest alleged by Ewing in his complaint, and found by the courts below, derives from Ewing's implied contract right to continued enrollment free from arbitrary dismissal. The District Court did not find that Ewing had any separate right to retake the exam and, what is more, explicitly "[rejected] the contract and promissory estoppel claims, finding no sufficient evidence to conclude that the defendants bound themselves either expressly or by a course of conduct to give Ewing a second chance to take Part I of the NBME examination." The Court of Appeals did not overturn the District Court's determination that Ewing lacked a tenable contract or estoppel claim under Michigan law, and we accept its reasonable rendering of state law, particularly when no party has challenged it.

The University's refusal to allow Ewing to retake the NBME Part I is thus not actionable in itself. It is, however, an important element of Ewing's claim that his dismissal was the product of arbitrary state action, for under proper analysis the refusal may constitute evidence of arbitrariness even if it is not the actual legal wrong alleged. The question, then, is whether the record compels the conclusion that the University acted arbitrarily in dropping Ewing from the Inteflex program without permitting a reexamination.

It is important to remember that this is not a case in which the procedures used by the University were unfair in any respect; quite the contrary is true. Nor can the Regents be accused of concealing nonacademic or constitutionally impermissible reasons for expelling Ewing; the District Court found that the Regents acted in good faith.

Ewing's claim, therefore, must be that the University misjudged his fitness to remain a student in the Inteflex program. The record unmistakably demonstrates, however, that the faculty's decision was made conscientiously and with careful deliberation, based on an evaluation of the entirety of Ewing's academic career. When judges are asked to review the substance of a genuinely academic decision, such as this one, they should show great respect for the faculty's professional judgment. Plainly, they may not override it unless it is such a substantial departure from accepted academic norms as to demonstrate that the person or committee responsible did not actually exercise professional judgment.

Considerations of profound importance counsel restrained judicial review of the substance of academic decisions. As JUSTICE WHITE has explained:

> Although the Court regularly proceeds on the assumption that the Due Process Clause has more than a procedural dimension, we must always bear in mind that the substantive content of the Clause is suggested neither by its language nor by preconstitutional history; that content is nothing more than the accumulated product of judicial interpretation of the Fifth and Fourteenth Amendments. This is ... only to underline Mr. Justice Black's constant reminder to his colleagues that the Court has no license to invalidate legislation which it thinks merely arbitrary or unreasonable.

Moore v. East Cleveland, 431 U.S. 494, 543–544 (1977) (WHITE, J., dissenting). *See id.* at 502 (opinion of POWELL, J.). Added to our concern for lack of standards is a reluctance to trench on the prerogatives of state and local educational institutions and our responsibility to safeguard their academic freedom, "a special concern of the First Amendment." *Keyishian v. Board of Regents,* 385 U.S. 589, 603 (1967).[12] If a "federal court is not the appropriate forum in which to review the multitude of personnel decisions that are made daily by public agencies," *Bishop v. Wood,* 426 U.S. 341, 349 (1976), far less is it suited to evaluate the substance of the multitude of academic decisions that are made daily by faculty members of public educational institutions— decisions that require "an expert evaluation of cumulative information and [are] not readily adapted to the procedural tools of judicial or administrative decisionmaking." *Board of Curators, Univ. of Mo. v. Horowitz,* 435 U.S., at 89– 90.

This narrow avenue for judicial review precludes any conclusion that the decision to dismiss Ewing from the Inteflex program was such a substantial departure from accepted academic norms as to demonstrate that the faculty did not exercise professional judgment. Certainly his expulsion cannot be

---

12. Academic freedom thrives not only on the independent and uninhibited exchange of ideas among teachers and students, *see* Keyishian v. Board of Regents, 385 U.S., at 603; Sweezy v. New Hampshire, 354 U.S. 234, 250 (1957) (opinion of Warren, C. J.), but also, and somewhat inconsistently, on autonomous decisionmaking by the academy itself, *see* University of California Regents v. Bakke, 438 U.S. 265, 312 (1978) (opinion of POWELL, J.); Sweezy v. New Hampshire, 354 U.S., at 263 (Frankfurter, J., concurring in result). Discretion to determine, on academic grounds, who may be admitted to study, has been described as one of "the four essential freedoms" of a university. University of California Regents v. Bakke, 438 U.S., at 312 (opinion of POWELL, J.) (quoting Sweezy v. New Hampshire, *supra,* at 263 (Frankfurter, J., concurring in result)) (internal quotations omitted).

considered aberrant when viewed in isolation. The District Court found as a fact that the Regents "had good reason to dismiss Ewing from the program." Before failing the NBME Part I, Ewing accumulated an unenviable academic record characterized by low grades, seven incompletes, and several terms during which he was on an irregular or reduced course load. Ewing's failure of his medical boards, in the words of one of his professors, "merely [culminated] a series of deficiencies.... In many ways, it's the straw that broke the camel's back."[13] Moreover, the fact that Ewing was "qualified" in the sense that he was eligible to take the examination the first time does not weaken this conclusion, for after Ewing took the NBME Part I it was entirely reasonable for the faculty to reexamine his entire record in the light of the unfortunate results of that examination. Admittedly, it may well have been unwise to deny Ewing a second chance. Permission to retake the test might have saved the University the expense of this litigation and conceivably might have demonstrated that the members of the Promotion and Review Board misjudged Ewing's fitness for the medical profession. But it nevertheless remains true that his dismissal from the Inteflex program rested on an academic judgment that is not beyond the pale of reasoned academic decisionmaking when viewed against the background of his entire career at the University of Michigan, including his singularly low score on the NBME Part I examination.[14]

The judgment of the Court of Appeals is reversed, and the case is remanded for proceedings consistent with this opinion.

Grutter v. Bollinger

Supreme Court of the United States, 2003.
539 U.S. 306, 123 S.Ct. 2325, 156 L.Ed.2d 304.

■ JUSTICE O'CONNOR delivered the opinion of the Court.

This case requires us to decide whether the use of race as a factor in student admissions by the University of Michigan Law School (Law School) is unlawful.

---

13. Even viewing the case from Ewing's perspective, we cannot say that the explanations and extenuating circumstances he offered were so compelling that their rejection can fairly be described as irrational. For example, the University might well have concluded that Ewing's sensitivity to difficulties in his personal life suggested an inability to handle the stress inherent in a career in medicine. The inordinate amount of time Ewing devoted to his extracurricular essay writing may reasonably have revealed to the University a lack of judgment and an inability to set priorities.

14. Nor does the University's termination of Ewing substantially deviate from accepted academic norms when compared with its treatment of other students. To be sure, the University routinely gave others an opportunity to retake the NBME Part I. But despite tables recording that some students with more incompletes or low grades were permitted to retake the examination after failing it the first time, and charts indicating that these students lacked the outside research and honor grade in clinical work that Ewing received, we are

not in a position to say that these students were "similarly situated" with Ewing. The Promotion and Review Board presumably considered not only the raw statistical data but also the nature and seriousness of the individual deficiencies and their concentration in particular disciplines—in Ewing's case, the hard sciences. The Board was able to take into account the numerous incompletes and makeup examinations Ewing required to secure even marginally passing grades, and it could view them in connection with his reduced course loads. Finally, it was uniquely positioned to observe Ewing's judgment, self-discipline, and ability to handle stress, and was thus especially well situated to make the necessarily subjective judgment of Ewing's prospects for success in the medical profession. The insusceptibility of promotion decisions such as this one to rigorous judicial review is borne out by the fact that 19 other Inteflex students, some with records that a judge might find "better" than Ewing's, were dismissed by the faculty without even being allowed to take the NBME Part I a first time.

The Law School ranks among the Nation's top law schools. It receives more than 3,500 applications each year for a class of around 350 students. Seeking to "admit a group of students who individually and collectively are among the most capable," the Law School looks for individuals with "substantial promise for success in law school" and "a strong likelihood of succeeding in the practice of law and contributing in diverse ways to the well-being of others." More broadly, the Law School seeks "a mix of students with varying backgrounds and experiences who will respect and learn from each other." In 1992, the dean of the Law School charged a faculty committee with crafting a written admissions policy to implement these goals. In particular, the Law School sought to ensure that its efforts to achieve student body diversity complied with this Court's most recent ruling on the use of race in university admissions. *See Regents of Univ. of Cal. v. Bakke*, 438 U.S. 265 (1978). Upon the unanimous adoption of the committee's report by the Law School faculty, it became the Law School's official admissions policy.

The hallmark of that policy is its focus on academic ability coupled with a flexible assessment of applicants' talents, experiences, and potential "to contribute to the learning of those around them." The policy requires admissions officials to evaluate each applicant based on all the information available in the file, including a personal statement, letters of recommendation, and an essay describing the ways in which the applicant will contribute to the life and diversity of the Law School. In reviewing an applicant's file, admissions officials must consider the applicant's undergraduate grade point average (GPA) and Law School Admissions Test (LSAT) score because they are important (if imperfect) predictors of academic success in law school. The policy stresses that "no applicant should be admitted unless we expect that applicant to do well enough to graduate with no serious academic problems."

The policy makes clear, however, that even the highest possible score does not guarantee admission to the Law School. Nor does a low score automatically disqualify an applicant. Rather, the policy requires admissions officials to look beyond grades and test scores to other criteria that are important to the Law School's educational objectives. So-called " 'soft' variables" such as "the enthusiasm of recommenders, the quality of the undergraduate institution, the quality of the applicant's essay, and the areas and difficulty of undergraduate course selection" are all brought to bear in assessing an "applicant's likely contributions to the intellectual and social life of the institution."

The policy aspires to "achieve that diversity which has the potential to enrich everyone's education and thus make a law school class stronger than the sum of its parts." The policy does not restrict the types of diversity contributions eligible for "substantial weight" in the admissions process, but instead recognizes "many possible bases for diversity admissions." The policy does, however, reaffirm the Law School's longstanding commitment to "one particular type of diversity," that is, "racial and ethnic diversity with special reference to the inclusion of students from groups which have been historically discriminated against, like African–Americans, Hispanics and Native Americans, who without this commitment might not be represented in our student body in meaningful numbers." By enrolling a " 'critical mass' of [underrepresented] minority students," the Law School seeks to "ensure their ability to make unique contributions to the character of the Law School."

The policy does not define diversity "solely in terms of racial and ethnic status." Nor is the policy "insensitive to the competition among all students for admission to the Law School." Rather, the policy seeks to guide admissions officers in "producing classes both diverse and academically outstanding, classes made up of students who promise to continue the tradition of outstanding contribution by Michigan Graduates to the legal profession."

Petitioner Barbara Grutter is a white Michigan resident who applied to the Law School in 1996 with a 3.8 grade point average and 161 LSAT score. The Law School initially placed petitioner on a waiting list, but subsequently rejected her application. In December 1997, petitioner filed suit in the United States District Court for the Eastern District of Michigan against the Law School ... [alleging] that respondents discriminated against her on the basis of race in violation of the Fourteenth Amendment; Title VI of the Civil Rights Act of 1964, 78 Stat 252, 42 USC § 2000d; and Rev Stat § 1977, as amended, 42 USC § 1981 [42 USCS § 1981].

Petitioner further alleged that her application was rejected because the Law School uses race as a "predominant" factor, giving applicants who belong to certain minority groups "a significantly greater chance of admission than students with similar credentials from disfavored racial groups." ... Petitioner requested compensatory and punitive damages, an order requiring the Law School to offer her admission, and an injunction prohibiting the Law School from continuing to discriminate on the basis of race....

. . .

[The Court reviews the testimony presented by the parties at trial, noting that the law school did not set a numerical representation threshold for what constitutes a "critical mass" of underrepresented minority students. Rather, the goal was to admit a number of underrepresented minorities so that those students would not feel isolated, and other students would learn that there is no " 'minority viewpoint' " but rather a variety of viewpoints among minority students. To implement the policy, the Director of Admissions for the Law School reviewed "daily reports" that kept track of the racial and ethnic composition of the class to ensure that a critical mass would be reached. Expert testimony indicated that a statistically significant relationship existed between race and admission rates, but that a race-blind admissions system would have a "very dramatic" negative effect on underrepresented minority admissions.]

In the end, the District Court concluded that the Law School's use of race as a factor in admissions decisions was unlawful. Applying strict scrutiny, the District Court determined that the Law School's asserted interest in assembling a diverse student body was not compelling because "the attainment of a racially diverse class ... was not recognized as such by *Bakke* and is not a remedy for past discrimination." The District Court went on to hold that even if diversity were compelling, the Law School had not narrowly tailored its use of race to further that interest. The District Court granted petitioner's request for declaratory relief and enjoined the Law School from using race as a factor in its admissions decisions.

Sitting en banc, the Court of Appeals reversed the District Court's judgment and vacated the injunction....

. . .

We granted certiorari, 537 U.S. 1043 (2002), to resolve the disagreement among the Courts of Appeals on a question of national importance: Whether diversity is a compelling interest that can justify the narrowly tailored use of race in selecting applicants for admission to public universities.

. . .

Since this Court's splintered decision in *Bakke*, Justice Powell's opinion announcing the judgment of the Court has served as the touchstone for constitutional analysis of race-conscious admissions policies. Public and private universities across the Nation have modeled their own admissions programs on Justice Powell's views on permissible race-conscious policies. *See, e.g.*, Brief for Judith Areen et al. as *Amici Curiae* 12–13 (law school admissions programs employ "methods designed from and based on Justice Powell's opinion in *Bakke*"); Brief for Amherst College et al. as *Amici Curiae* 27 ("After *Bakke*, each of the *amici* (and undoubtedly other selective colleges and universities as well) reviewed their admissions procedures in light of Justice Powell's opinion ... and set sail accordingly")....

. . .

[F]or the reasons set out below, today we endorse Justice Powell's view that student body diversity is a compelling state interest that can justify the use of race in university admissions.

. . .

... Before this Court, as they have throughout this litigation, respondents assert only one justification for their use of race in the admissions process: obtaining "the educational benefits that flow from a diverse student body." In other words, the Law School asks us to recognize, in the context of higher education, a compelling state interest in student body diversity.

We first wish to dispel the notion that the Law School's argument has been foreclosed, either expressly or implicitly, by our affirmative-action cases decided since *Bakke*. It is true that some language in those opinions might be read to suggest that remedying past discrimination is the only permissible justification for race-based governmental action. *See, e.g., Richmond v. J. A. Croson Co.*, [488 U.S. 469, 493 (1989)] (plurality opinion) (stating that unless classifications based on race are "strictly reserved for remedial settings, they may in fact promote notions of racial inferiority and lead to a politics of racial hostility"). But we have never held that the only governmental use of race that can survive strict scrutiny is remedying past discrimination.... Today, we hold that the Law School has a compelling interest in attaining a diverse student body.

The Law School's educational judgment that such diversity is essential to its educational mission is one to which we defer. The Law School's assessment that diversity will, in fact, yield educational benefits is substantiated by respondents and their *amici*. Our scrutiny of the interest asserted by the Law School is no less strict for taking into account complex educational judgments in an area that lies primarily within the expertise of the university.

Our holding today is in keeping with our tradition of giving a degree of deference to a university's academic decisions, within constitutionally prescribed limits. *See Regents of Univ. of Mich. v. Ewing*, 474 U.S. 214, 225 (1985); *Board of Curators of Univ. of Mo. v. Horowitz*, 435 U.S. 78, 96, n. 6 (1978); *Bakke*, 438 U.S., at 319, n. 53 (opinion of Powell, J.).

We have long recognized that, given the important purpose of public education and the expansive freedoms of speech and thought associated with the university environment, universities occupy a special niche in our constitutional tradition. In announcing the principle of student body diversity as a compelling state interest, Justice Powell invoked our cases recognizing a constitutional dimension, grounded in the First Amendment, of educational autonomy: "The freedom of a university to make its own judgments as to education includes the selection of its student body." From this premise, Justice Powell reasoned that by claiming "the right to select those students who will contribute the most to the 'robust exchange of ideas,' " a university "seeks to achieve a goal that is of paramount importance in the fulfillment of its mission." Our conclusion that the Law School has a compelling interest in a diverse student body is informed by our view that attaining a diverse student body is at the heart of the Law School's proper institutional mission, and that "good faith" on the part of a university is "presumed" absent "a showing to the contrary."

As part of its goal of "assembling a class that is both exceptionally academically qualified and broadly diverse," the Law School seeks to "enroll a 'critical mass' of minority students." The Law School's interest is not simply "to assure within its student body some specified percentage of a particular group merely because of its race or ethnic origin." That would amount to outright racial balancing, which is patently unconstitutional. Rather, the Law School's concept of critical mass is defined by reference to the educational benefits that diversity is designed to produce.

These benefits are substantial. As the District Court emphasized, the Law School's admissions policy promotes "cross-racial understanding," helps to break down racial stereotypes, and "enables [students] to better understand persons of different races." These benefits are "important and laudable," because "classroom discussion is livelier, more spirited, and simply more enlightening and interesting" when the students have "the greatest possible variety of backgrounds."

The Law School's claim of a compelling interest is further bolstered by its *amici*, who point to the educational benefits that flow from student body diversity. In addition to the expert studies and reports entered into evidence at trial, numerous studies show that student body diversity promotes learning outcomes, and "better prepares students for an increasingly diverse workforce and society, and better prepares them as professionals."

These benefits are not theoretical but real, as major American businesses have made clear that the skills needed in today's increasingly global marketplace can only be developed through exposure to widely diverse people, cultures, ideas, and viewpoints. Brief for 3M et al. as *Amici Curiae* 5; Brief for General Motors Corp. as *Amicus Curiae* 3–4. What is more, high-ranking retired officers and civilian leaders of the United States military assert that, "based on [their] decades of experience," a "highly qualified, racially diverse officer corps . . . is essential to the military's ability to fulfill its principle mission to provide national security." Brief for Julius W. Becton, Jr. et al. as

Amici Curiae 27. The primary sources for the Nation's officer corps are the service academies and the Reserve Officers Training Corps (ROTC), the latter comprising students already admitted to participating colleges and universities. At present, "the military cannot achieve an officer corps that is *both* highly qualified *and* racially diverse unless the service academies and the ROTC used limited race-conscious recruiting and admissions policies." To fulfill its mission, the military "must be selective in admissions for training and education for the officer corps, *and* it must train and educate a highly qualified, racially diverse officer corps in a racially diverse setting." We agree that "it requires only a small step from this analysis to conclude that our country's other most selective institutions must remain both diverse and selective."

We have repeatedly acknowledged the overriding importance of preparing students for work and citizenship, describing education as pivotal to "sustaining our political and cultural heritage" with a fundamental role in maintaining the fabric of society. *Plyler v. Doe*, 457 U.S. 202, 221 (1982). This Court has long recognized that "education ... is the very foundation of good citizenship." *Brown v. Board of Education*, 347 U.S. 483, 493 (1954). For this reason, the diffusion of knowledge and opportunity through public institutions of higher education must be accessible to all individuals regardless of race or ethnicity. The United States, as *amicus curiae*, affirms that "ensuring that public institutions are open and available to all segments of American society, including people of all races and ethnicities, represents a paramount government objective." And, "nowhere is the importance of such openness more acute than in the context of higher education." Effective participation by members of all racial and ethnic groups in the civic life of our Nation is essential if the dream of one Nation, indivisible, is to be realized.

Moreover, universities, and in particular, law schools, represent the training ground for a large number of our Nation's leaders. *Sweatt v. Painter*, 339 U.S. 629, 634 (1950). Individuals with law degrees occupy roughly half the state governorships, more than half the seats in the United States Senate, and more than a third of the seats in the United States House of Representatives. *See* Brief for Association of American Law Schools as *Amicus Curiae* 5–6. The pattern is even more striking when it comes to highly selective law schools. A handful of these schools accounts for 25 of the 100 United States Senators, 74 United States Courts of Appeals judges, and nearly 200 of the more than 600 United States District Court judges.

In order to cultivate a set of leaders with legitimacy in the eyes of the citizenry, it is necessary that the path to leadership be visibly open to talented and qualified individuals of every race and ethnicity. All members of our heterogeneous society must have confidence in the openness and integrity of the educational institutions that provide this training. As we have recognized, law schools "cannot be effective in isolation from the individuals and institutions with which the law interacts." *See Sweatt v. Painter*, *supra*, at 634. Access to legal education (and thus the legal profession) must be inclusive of talented and qualified individuals of every race and ethnicity, so that all members of our heterogeneous society may participate in the educational institutions that provide the training and education necessary to succeed in America.

The Law School does not premise its need for critical mass on "any belief that minority students always (or even consistently) express some characteristic minority viewpoint on any issue." To the contrary, diminishing the force of such stereotypes is both a crucial part of the Law School's mission, and one that it cannot accomplish with only token numbers of minority students. Just as growing up in a particular region or having particular professional experiences is likely to affect an individual's views, so too is one's own, unique experience of being a racial minority in a society, like our own, in which race unfortunately still matters. The Law School has determined, based on its experience and expertise, that a "critical mass" of underrepresented minorities is necessary to further its compelling interest in securing the educational benefits of a diverse student body.

. . .

Since *Bakke*, we have had no occasion to define the contours of the narrow-tailoring inquiry with respect to race-conscious university admissions programs. That inquiry must be calibrated to fit the distinct issues raised by the use of race to achieve student body diversity in public higher education. Contrary to Justice Kennedy's assertions, we do not "abandon[] strict scrutiny." Rather, as we have already explained we adhere to *Adarand*'s teaching that the very purpose of strict scrutiny is to take such "relevant differences into account."

To be narrowly tailored, a race-conscious admissions program cannot use a quota system—it cannot "insulate each category of applicants with certain desired qualifications from competition with all other applicants." Instead, a university may consider race or ethnicity only as a " 'plus' in a particular applicant's file," without "insulating the individual from comparison with all other candidates for the available seats." . . .

. . .

We are satisfied that the Law School's admissions program, like the Harvard plan described by Justice Powell, does not operate as a quota. Properly understood, a "quota" is a program in which a certain fixed number or proportion of opportunities are "reserved exclusively for certain minority groups." . . .

Justice Powell's distinction between the medical school's rigid 16–seat quota and Harvard's flexible use of race as a "plus" factor is instructive. Harvard certainly had minimum *goals* for minority enrollment, even if it had no specific number firmly in mind. What is more, Justice Powell flatly rejected the argument that Harvard's program was "the functional equivalent of a quota" merely because it had some " 'plus' " for race, or gave greater "weight" to race than to some other factors, in order to achieve student body diversity.

The Law School's goal of attaining a critical mass of underrepresented minority students does not transform its program into a quota. As the Harvard plan described by Justice Powell recognized, there is of course "some relationship between numbers and achieving the benefits to be derived from a diverse student body, and between numbers and providing a reasonable environment for those students admitted." "Some attention to numbers," without more, does not transform a flexible admissions system into a rigid quota. Nor, as Justice Kennedy posits, does the Law School's consultation of the "daily reports," which keep track of the racial and ethnic composition of the class (as well as of residency and gender), "suggest[] there was no further attempt at individual review save for race itself" during the final stages of the admissions process. To the contrary, the Law School's admissions officers testified without contradiction that they never gave race any more or less weight based on the information contained in these reports. Moreover, as Justice Kennedy concedes, between 1993 and 2000, the number of African–American, Latino, and Native–American students in each class at the Law School varied from 13.5 to 20.1 percent, a range inconsistent with a quota.

The Chief Justice believes that the Law School's policy conceals an attempt to achieve racial balancing, and cites admissions data to contend that the Law School discriminates among different groups within the critical mass. But, as the Chief Justice concedes, the number of underrepresented minority students who ultimately enroll in the Law School differs substantially from their representation in the applicant pool and varies considerably for each group from year to year.

That a race-conscious admissions program does not operate as a quota does not, by itself, satisfy the requirement of individualized consideration. When using race as a "plus" factor in university admissions, a university's admissions program must remain flexible enough to ensure that each applicant is evaluated as an individual and not in a way that makes an applicant's race or ethnicity the defining feature of his or her application. The importance of this individualized consideration in the context of a race-conscious admissions program is paramount.

Here, the Law School engages in a highly individualized, holistic review of each applicant's file, giving serious consideration to all the ways an applicant might contribute to a diverse educational environment. The Law School affords this individualized consideration to applicants of all races. There is no policy, either *de jure* or *de facto*, of automatic acceptance or rejection based on any single "soft" variable. Unlike the program at issue in *Gratz v. Bollinger*, the Law School awards no mechanical, predetermined diversity "bonuses" based on race or ethnicity. Like the Harvard plan, the Law School's admissions policy "is flexible enough to consider all pertinent elements of diversity in light of the particular qualifications of each applicant, and to place them on the same footing for consideration, although not necessarily according them the same weight."

We also find that, like the Harvard plan Justice Powell referenced in *Bakke*, the Law School's race-conscious admissions program adequately ensures that all factors that may contribute to student body diversity are meaningfully considered alongside race in admissions decisions. With respect to the use of race itself, all underrepresented minority students admitted by the Law School have been deemed qualified. By virtue of our Nation's struggle with racial inequality, such students are both likely to have experiences of particular importance to the Law School's mission, and less likely to be admitted in meaningful numbers on criteria that ignore those experiences.

The Law School does not, however, limit in any way the broad range of qualities and experiences that may be considered valuable contributions to student body diversity. To the contrary, the 1992 policy makes clear "there are many possible bases for diversity admissions," and provides examples of admittees who have lived or traveled widely abroad, are fluent in several languages, have overcome personal adversity and family hardship, have exceptional records of extensive community service, and have had successful careers in other fields. The Law School seriously considers each "applicant's promise of making a notable contribution to the class by way of a particular strength, attainment, or characteristic—*e.g.*, an unusual intellectual achievement, employment experience, nonacademic performance, or personal background." All applicants have the opportunity to highlight their own potential diversity contributions through the submission of a personal statement, letters of recommendation, and an essay describing the ways in which the applicant will contribute to the life and diversity of the Law School.

What is more, the Law School actually gives substantial weight to diversity factors besides race. The Law School frequently accepts nonminority applicants with grades and test scores lower than underrepresented minority applicants (and other nonminority applicants) who are rejected. This shows that the Law School seriously weighs many other diversity factors besides race that can make a real and dispositive difference for nonminority applicants as well. By this flexible approach, the Law School sufficiently takes into account, in practice as well as in theory, a wide variety of characteristics besides race and ethnicity that contribute to a diverse student body....

... Petitioner and the United States argue that the Law School's plan is not narrowly tailored because race-neutral means exist to obtain the educational benefits of student body diversity that the Law School seeks. We disagree. Narrow tailoring does not require exhaustion of every conceivable race-neutral alternative. Nor does it require a university to choose between maintaining a reputation for excellence or fulfilling a commitment to provide educational opportunities to members of all racial groups. Narrow tailoring does, however, require serious, good faith consideration of workable race-neutral alternatives that will achieve the diversity the university seeks.

We agree with the Court of Appeals that the Law School sufficiently considered workable race-neutral alternatives. The District Court took the Law School to task for failing to consider race-neutral alternatives such as "using a lottery system" or "decreasing the emphasis for all applicants on undergraduate GPA and LSAT scores." But these alternatives would require a dramatic sacrifice of diversity, the academic quality of all admitted students, or both.

. . .

We acknowledge that "there are serious problems of justice connected with the idea of preference itself." Narrow tailoring, therefore, requires that a race-conscious admissions program not unduly harm members of any racial group. Even remedial race-based governmental action generally "remains subject to continuing oversight to assure that it will work the least harm possible to other innocent persons competing for the benefit." To be narrowly tailored, a race-conscious admissions program must not "unduly burden individuals who are not members of the favored racial and ethnic groups."

We are satisfied that the Law School's admissions program does not. Because the Law School considers "all pertinent elements of diversity," it can (and does) select nonminority applicants who have greater potential to enhance student body diversity over underrepresented minority applicants. . . .

We are mindful, however, that "[a] core purpose of the Fourteenth Amendment was to do away with all governmentally imposed discrimination based on race." *Palmore v. Sidoti*, 466 U.S. 429, 432 (1984). Accordingly, race-conscious admissions policies must be limited in time. This requirement reflects that racial classifications, however compelling their goals, are potentially so dangerous that they may be employed no more broadly than the interest demands. Enshrining a permanent justification for racial preferences would offend this fundamental equal protection principle. We see no reason to exempt race-conscious admissions programs from the requirement that all governmental use of race must have a logical end point. The Law School, too, concedes that all "race-conscious programs must have reasonable durational limits."

In the context of higher education, the durational requirement can be met by sunset provisions in race-conscious admissions policies and periodic reviews to determine whether racial preferences are still necessary to achieve student body diversity. Universities in California, Florida, and Washington State, where racial preferences in admissions are prohibited by state law, are currently engaged in experimenting with a wide variety of alternative approaches. Universities in other States can and should draw on the most promising aspects of these race-neutral alternatives as they develop.

The requirement that all race-conscious admissions programs have a termination point "assures all citizens that the deviation from the norm of equal treatment of all racial and ethnic groups is a temporary matter, a measure taken in the service of the goal of equality itself." *Richmond v. J. A. Croson Co.*, 488 U.S., at 510 (plurality opinion).

We take the Law School at its word that it would "like nothing better than to find a race-neutral admissions formula" and will terminate its race-conscious admissions program as soon as practicable. It has been 25 years since Justice Powell first approved the use of race to further an interest in student body diversity in the context of public higher education. Since that time, the number of minority applicants with high grades and test scores has indeed increased. We expect that 25 years from now, the use of racial preferences will no longer be necessary to further the interest approved today.

. . . The judgment of the Court of Appeals for the Sixth Circuit, accordingly, is affirmed.

■ JUSTICE KENNEDY, dissenting.

. . .

Justice Powell's approval of the use of race in university admissions reflected a tradition, grounded in the First Amendment, of acknowledging a university's conception of its educational mission. Our precedents provide a basis for the Court's acceptance of a university's considered judgment that racial diversity among students can further its educational task, when supported by empirical evidence.

It is unfortunate, however, that the Court takes the first part of Justice Powell's rule but abandons the second. Having approved the use of race as a factor in the admissions process, the majority proceeds to nullify the essential safeguard Justice Powell insisted upon as the precondition of the approval. The safeguard was rigorous judicial review, with strict scrutiny as the controlling standard....

The Court, in a review that is nothing short of perfunctory, accepts the University of Michigan Law School's assurances that its admissions process meets with constitutional requirements. The majority fails to confront the reality of how the Law School's admissions policy is implemented. The dissenting opinion by The Chief Justice, which I join in full, demonstrates beyond question why the concept of critical mass is a delusion used by the Law School to mask its attempt to make race an automatic factor in most instances and to achieve numerical goals indistinguishable from quotas....

■ JUSTICE THOMAS, with whom JUSTICE SCALIA joins as to Parts I–VII, concurring in part and dissenting in part.

... I believe blacks can achieve in every avenue of American life without the meddling of university administrators. Because I wish to see all students succeed whatever their color, I share, in some respect, the sympathies of those who sponsor the type of discrimination advanced by the University of Michigan Law School (Law School). The Constitution does not, however, tolerate institutional devotion to the status quo in admissions policies when such devotion ripens into racial discrimination. Nor does the Constitution countenance the unprecedented deference the Court gives to the Law School, an approach inconsistent with the very concept of "strict scrutiny."

No one would argue that a university could set up a lower general admission standard and then impose heightened requirements only on black applicants. Similarly, a university may not maintain a high admission standard and grant exemptions to favored races. The Law School, of its own choosing, and for its own purposes, maintains an exclusionary admissions system that it knows produces racially disproportionate results. Racial discrimination is not a permissible solution to the self-inflicted wounds of this elitist admissions policy.

... I believe that the Law School's current use of race violates the Equal Protection Clause....

. . .

... The Law School maintains that it wishes to obtain "educational benefits that flow from student body diversity." This statement must be evaluated carefully, because it implies that both "diversity" and "educational benefits" are components of the Law School's compelling state interest. Additionally, the Law School's refusal to entertain certain changes in its admissions process and status indicates that the compelling state interest it seeks to validate is actually broader than might appear at first glance.

Undoubtedly there are other ways to "better" the education of law students aside from ensuring that the student body contains a "critical mass" of underrepresented minority students. Attaining "diversity," whatever it means,[3] is the mechanism by which the Law School obtains educational

3. "Diversity," for all of its devotees, is more a fashionable catchphrase than it is a useful term, especially when something as serious as racial discrimination is at issue. Because the Equal Protection Clause renders the color of one's skin constitutionally irrelevant to the Law School's mission, I refer to the Law School's interest as an "aesthetic." That is, the Law School wants to have a certain appearance, from the shape of the desks and tables

benefits, not an end of itself. The Law School, however, apparently believes that only a racially mixed student body can lead to the educational benefits it seeks. How, then, is the Law School's interest in these allegedly unique educational "benefits" *not* simply the forbidden interest in "racial balancing," that the majority expressly rejects?

A distinction between these two ideas (unique educational benefits based on racial aesthetics and race for its own sake) is purely sophistic—so much so that the majority uses them interchangeably. Compare ("The Law School has a compelling interest in attaining a diverse student body"), with (referring to the "compelling interest in securing the *educational benefits* of a diverse student body" (emphasis added)). The Law School's argument, as facile as it is, can only be understood in one way: Classroom aesthetics yields educational benefits, racially discriminatory admissions policies are required to achieve the right racial mix, and therefore the policies are required to achieve the educational benefits. It is the *educational benefits* that are the end, or allegedly compelling state interest, not "diversity."

.   .   .

A close reading of the Court's opinion reveals that all of its legal work is done through one conclusory statement: The Law School has a "compelling interest in securing the educational benefits of a diverse student body." No serious effort is made to explain how these benefits fit with the state interests the Court has recognized (or rejected) as compelling, or to place any theoretical constraints on an enterprising court's desire to discover still more justifications for racial discrimination. . . .

.   .   .

Under the proper standard, there is no pressing public necessity in maintaining a public law school at all and, it follows, certainly not an elite law school. Likewise, marginal improvements in legal education do not qualify as a compelling state interest.

While legal education at a public university may be good policy or otherwise laudable, it is obviously not a pressing public necessity when the correct legal standard is applied. . . . The fact that some fraction of the States reject a particular enterprise, however, creates a presumption that the enterprise itself is not a compelling state interest. In this sense, the absence of a public, American Bar Association (ABA) accredited, law school in Alaska, Delaware, Massachusetts, New Hampshire, and Rhode Island, provides further evidence that Michigan's maintenance of the Law School does not constitute a compelling state interest.

. . . [E]ven assuming that a State may, under appropriate circumstances, demonstrate a cognizable interest in having an elite law school, Michigan has failed to do so here.

.   .   .

in its classrooms to the color of the students sitting at them.

I also use the term "aesthetic" because I believe it underlines the ineffectiveness of racially discriminatory admissions in actually helping those who are truly underprivileged.

It must be remembered that the Law School's racial discrimination does nothing for those too poor or uneducated to participate in elite higher education and therefore presents only an illusory solution to the challenges facing our Nation.

The interest in remaining elite and exclusive that the majority thinks so obviously critical requires the use of admissions "standards" that, in turn, create the Law School's "need" to discriminate on the basis of race. The Court validates these admissions standards by concluding that alternatives that would require "a dramatic sacrifice of . . . the academic quality of all admitted students," need not be considered before racial discrimination can be employed. . . . The Court never explicitly holds that the Law School's desire to retain the status quo in "academic selectivity" is itself a compelling state interest, and, as I have demonstrated, it is not. Therefore, the Law School should be forced to choose between its classroom aesthetic and its exclusionary admissions system—it cannot have it both ways.

With the adoption of different admissions methods, such as accepting all students who meet minimum qualifications, the Law School could achieve its vision of the racially aesthetic student body without the use of racial discrimination. The Law School concedes this, but the Court holds, implicitly and under the guise of narrow tailoring, that the Law School has a compelling state interest in doing what it wants to do. I cannot agree. . . .

The Court bases its unprecedented deference to the Law School—a deference antithetical to strict scrutiny—on an idea of "educational autonomy" grounded in the First Amendment. In my view, there is no basis for a right of public universities to do what would otherwise violate the Equal Protection Clause.

The constitutionalization of "academic freedom" began with the concurring opinion of Justice Frankfurter in *Sweezy v. New Hampshire*, 354 U.S. 234 (1957). . . .

. . . According to Justice Frankfurter: "It is the business of a university to provide that atmosphere which is most conducive to speculation, experiment and creation. It is an atmosphere in which there prevail 'the four essential freedoms' of a university—to determine for itself on academic grounds who may teach, what may be taught, how it shall be taught, and who may be admitted to study."

In my view, "it is the business" of this Court to explain itself when it cites provisions of the Constitution to invent new doctrines—including the idea that the First Amendment authorizes a public university to do what would otherwise violate the Equal Protection Clause. The majority fails in its summary effort to prove this point. The only source for the Court's conclusion that public universities are entitled to deference even within the confines of strict scrutiny is Justice Powell's opinion in *Bakke*. Justice Powell, for his part, relied only on Justice Frankfurter's opinion in Sweezy and the Court's decision in *Keyishian v. Board of Regents of Univ. of State of N. Y.*, 385 U.S. 589 (1967), to support his view that the First Amendment somehow protected a public university's use of race in admissions. *Regents of Univ. of Cal. v. Bakke*, 438 U.S. 265, at 312. *Keyishian* provides no answer to the question whether the Fourteenth Amendment's restrictions are relaxed when applied to public universities. . . .

I doubt that when Justice Frankfurter spoke of governmental intrusions into the independence of universities, he was thinking of the Constitution's ban on racial discrimination. . . .

The Court's deference to the Law School's conclusion that its racial experimentation leads to educational benefits will, if adhered to, have serious collateral consequences.... The Court never acknowledges, the growing evidence that racial (and other sorts) of heterogeneity actually impairs learning among black students. *See, e.g.*, Flowers & Pascarella, Cognitive Effects of College Racial Composition on African American Students After 3 Years of College, 40 J. of College Student Development 669, 674 (1999) (concluding that black students experience superior cognitive development at Historically Black Colleges (HBCs) and that, even among blacks, "a substantial diversity moderates the cognitive effects of attending an HBC"); Allen, The Color of Success: African–American College Student Outcomes at Predominantly White and Historically Black Public Colleges and Universities, 62 Harv. Educ. Rev. 26, 35 (1992) (finding that black students attending HBCs report higher academic achievement than those attending predominantly white colleges).

. . .

The majority grants deference to the Law School's "assessment that diversity will, in fact, yield educational benefits." It follows, therefore, that an HBC's assessment that racial homogeneity will yield educational benefits would similarly be given deference. An HBC's rejection of white applicants in order to maintain racial homogeneity seems permissible, therefore, under the majority's view of the Equal Protection Clause. Contained within today's majority opinion is the seed of a new constitutional justification for a concept I thought long and rightly rejected—racial segregation.

. . .

... Since its inception, selective admissions has been the vehicle for racial, ethnic, and religious tinkering and experimentation by university administrators. The initial driving force for the relocation of the selective function from the high school to the universities was the same desire to select racial winners and losers that the Law School exhibits today. Columbia, Harvard, and others infamously determined that they had "too many" Jews, just as today the Law School argues it would have "too many" whites if it could not discriminate in its admissions process.

Columbia employed intelligence tests precisely because Jewish applicants, who were predominantly immigrants, scored worse on such tests. Thus, Columbia could claim (falsely) that " 'we have not eliminated boys because they were Jews and do not propose to do so. We have honestly attempted to eliminate the lowest grade of applicant [through the use of intelligence testing] and it turns out that a good many of the low grade men are New York City Jews.' " In other words, the tests were adopted with full knowledge of their disparate impact.

Similarly no modern law school can claim ignorance of the poor performance of blacks, relatively speaking, on the Law School Admissions Test (LSAT). Nevertheless, law schools continue to use the test and then attempt to "correct" for black underperformance by using racial discrimination in admissions so as to obtain their aesthetic student body. The Law School's continued adherence to measures it knows produce racially skewed results is not entitled to deference by this Court....

Having decided to use the LSAT, the Law School must accept the constitutional burdens that come with this decision....

The Court will not even deign to make the Law School try other methods, however, preferring instead to grant a 25–year license to violate the Constitution. And the same Court that had the courage to order the desegregation of all public schools in the South now fears, on the basis of platitudes rather than principle, to force the Law School to abandon a decidedly imperfect admissions regime that provides the basis for racial discrimination.

... I believe what lies beneath the Court's decision today are the benighted notions that one can tell when racial discrimination benefits (rather than hurts) minority groups, and that racial discrimination is necessary to remedy general societal ills....

... I must contest the notion that the Law School's discrimination benefits those admitted as a result of it. The Court spends considerable time discussing the impressive display of *amicus* support for the Law School in this case from all corners of society. But nowhere in any of the filings in this Court is any evidence that the purported "beneficiaries" of this racial discrimination prove themselves by performing at (or even near) the same level as those students who receive no preferences.

The silence in this case is deafening to those of us who view higher education's purpose as imparting knowledge and skills to students, rather than a communal, rubber-stamp, credentialing process. The Law School is not looking for those students who, despite a lower LSAT score or undergraduate grade point average, will succeed in the study of law. The Law School seeks only a facade—it is sufficient that the class looks right, even if it does not perform right.

The Law School tantalizes unprepared students with the promise of a University of Michigan degree and all of the opportunities that it offers. These overmatched students take the bait, only to find that they cannot succeed in the cauldron of competition. And this mismatch crisis is not restricted to elite institutions. *See* T. Sowell, Race and Culture 176–177 (1994) ("Even if most minority students are able to meet the normal standards at the 'average' range of colleges and universities, the systematic mismatching of minority students begun at the top can mean that such students are generally overmatched throughout all levels of higher education"). Indeed, to cover the tracks of the aestheticists, this cruel farce of racial discrimination must continue—in selection for the Michigan Law Review, *see* University of Michigan Law School Student Handbook 2002–2003, pp 39–40 (noting the presence of a "diversity plan" for admission to the review), and in hiring at law firms and for judicial clerkships—until the "beneficiaries" are no longer tolerated. While these students may graduate with law degrees, there is no evidence that they have received a qualitatively better legal education (or become better lawyers) than if they had gone to a less "elite" law school for which they were better prepared. And the aestheticists will never address the real problems facing "underrepresented minorities,"[11] instead continuing their social experiments on other people's children.

---

11. For example, there is no recognition by the Law School in this case that even with their racial discrimination in place, black *men* are "underrepresented" at the Law School.

See ABA–LSAC Guide 426 (reporting that the Law School has 46 black women and 28 black men). Why does the Law School not also discriminate in favor of black men over black

Beyond the harm the Law School's racial discrimination visits upon its test subjects, no social science has disproved the notion that this discrimination "engenders attitudes of superiority or, alternatively, provoke[s] resentment among those who believe that they have been wronged by the government's use of race." *Adarand*, 515 U.S., at 241 (Thomas, J., concurring in part and concurring in judgment). "These programs stamp minorities with a badge of inferiority and may cause them to develop dependencies or to adopt an attitude that they are 'entitled' to preferences."

It is uncontested that each year, the Law School admits a handful of blacks who would be admitted in the absence of racial discrimination. Who can differentiate between those who belong and those who do not? The majority of blacks are admitted to the Law School because of discrimination, and because of this policy all are tarred as undeserving. This problem of stigma does not depend on determinacy as to whether those stigmatized are actually the "beneficiaries" of racial discrimination. When blacks take positions in the highest places of government, industry, or academia, it is an open question today whether their skin color played a part in their advancement. The question itself is the stigma—because either racial discrimination did play a role, in which case the person may be deemed "otherwise unqualified," or it did not, in which case asking the question itself unfairly marks those blacks who would succeed without discrimination. Is this what the Court means by "visibly open"?

Questions and Comments on *Grutter*

How much did the outcome in *Grutter* turn on judicial deference to academic freedom? Was the deference justified?

One of the "four essential freedoms" of the university first cited by Justice Frankfurther in *Sweezy v. New Hampshire* was that the university should be able "to determine for itself on academic grounds . . . who may be admitted to study." Sweezy v. New Hampshire, 354 U.S. 234, 262 (1957) (Frankfurter, J., concurring). Suppose a public university could conclusively determine that a specific racial balance led to an optimal learning environment for students. Should that university be allowed to make admissions decisions on the basis of race in order to achieve that optimal balance? What considerations would cut against allowing colleges and universities complete control over whom they admit to study?

American Academy of Religion v. Chertoff

United States District Court, Southern District of New York, 2007.
2007 WL 4527504.

■ PAUL A. CROTTY, United States District Judge:

["Tariq Ramadan is a well-known and respected Muslim scholar who accepted an offer to become a tenured professor at the University of Notre Dame in January 2004." In May 2004, the State Department approved Ramadan's H–1B visa application, which permits the three-to six-year residency of college-educated professionals with highly specialized knowledge.

women, given this underrepresentation? The answer is, again, that all the Law School cares about is its own image among know-it-all elites, not solving real problems like the crisis of black male underperformance.

Two months later, the U.S. Embassy in Ramadan's home country of Switzerland revoked the visa. Although no reason was provided Ramadan, a Department of Homeland Security (DHS) spokesperson informed the media that the revocation was based on the Patriot Act's provision excluding anyone who used a "position of prominence within any country to endorse or espouse terrorist activity." Upon the suggestion of U.S. officials, Ramadan reapplied in October 2004 but resigned from the offered Notre Dame position in December when it became clear that the application would not soon be processed. DHS then quickly revoked Ramadan's new application. Although Ramadan had previously traveled to and lectured in the U.S. often under Switzerland's participation in a visa waiver program, which allows ninety days of U.S. travel without a visa, the revocation left Ramadan ineligible for the visa waiver program, requiring him to apply for a visa every time he seeks to travel to the U.S.

In September 2005, Ramadan applied for a nonimmigrant B visa to travel to the U.S. for short periods to attend academic events. During two interviews with DHS officials in late 2005, Ramadan disclosed approximately $1336 in donations to the Association de Secours Palestinien (ASP) between 1998 and 2002. Since 2003, the U.S. Department of the Treasury has listed ASP as a "Specially Designated Global Terrorist" and provider of funds to Hamas.

The typical wait time for B-visa processing is two days, and special clearances usually take up to thirty. Four months after his application and thirty days after his last interview, Ramadan had not received a response to his application. Plaintiffs, the American Academy of Religion, the American Association of University Professors, the PEN American Center, and Ramadan, filed this lawsuit. In an earlier order, the court ordered Defendants Michael Chertoff, the Secretary of DHS and Condoleeza Rice, the Secretary of State, to render a final decision on Ramadan's pending non-immigrant visa application.

In September 2006, the Government denied the application on the grounds that Ramadan had provided material support to Hamas, a terrorist group, making him inadmissible under the Immigration and Nationality Act (INA) § 212(a)(3)(B), codified at 8 U.S.C. § 1182(a)(3)(B)(iv)(VI). In response, the Plaintiffs amended their complaint and moved for summary judgment on the grounds that the Government's reason for excluding Ramadan was not "facially legitimate and bona fine" and that 8 U.S.C. § 1182(a)(3)(B)(i)(VII), the Patriot Act's provision for the exclusion of aliens endorsing or espousing terrorist activity or persuading others to do so or to support a terrorist organization, is unconstitutional under the First and Fifth Amendments.]

. . .

The controlling statute is the Immigration and Nationality Act, as modified by the Patriot Act in 2001, Pub. L. No. 107–56, 115 Stat. 272 (Oct. 26, 2001), and the REAL ID Act in 2005, Pub. L. 109–13, 119 Stat. 231 (May 11, 2005). The relevant provision of the statute bars from the United States any alien who has "engaged in terrorist activity." "Engaging in terrorist activity" is further defined as, *inter alia*, "commit[ting] an act that the actor knows, or reasonably should know, affords material support, including . . . funds, transfer of funds or other material financial benefit" to individuals or organizations engaged in terrorist activities, "unless the actor can demonstrate by clear and convincing evidence that the actor did not know, and should not reasonably have known, that the organization was a terrorist organization." 8 U.S.C. § 1182(a)(3)(B)(iv)(VI).

.   .   .

Also in dispute is the "endorse and espouse" provision of the Patriot Act, which Plaintiffs refer to as the "ideological exclusion" provision. The "endorse and espouse" provision is codified at 8 U.S.C. § 1182(a)(3)(B)(i)(VII) and states that "[a]ny alien who . . . endorses or espouses terrorist activity or persuades others to endorse or espouse terrorist activity or support a terrorist organization . . . is inadmissible." The Plaintiffs challenge the constitutionality of this provision even though the provision was not used to deny Ramadan's visa application. It is true that in August 2004 a DHS spokesperson mentioned the provision as the basis for the revocation of the original H–1B visa. Nonetheless, the Government has since disavowed the statement. . . . The "endorse and espouse provision," therefore, no longer operates as the basis for Ramadan's denial and is challenged on other grounds.

A number of points are not disputed. First, Professor Ramadan has no standing—indeed he has no rights whatsoever—to challenge the consular decision denying his visa. . . . Second, while Plaintiffs assert a First Amendment claim, their claim challenging the visa denial gives rise to only limited First Amendment review. Finally, with respect to their constitutional challenge to the endorse and espouse provision, Plaintiffs admit that they cannot name a single alien they have invited to the country who has been excluded under that provision.

It is well-settled that the decision of a consular official to grant or deny a visa is nonreviewable by courts, absent a Constitutional challenge by a United States citizen. This principle, now firmly rooted in our jurisprudence, has come to be known as the "doctrine of consular nonreviewability." . . .

.   .   .

While the doctrine of consular nonreviewability bars a court from hearing an alien's challenge to a consular decision, a court has jurisdiction over a United States citizen's constitutional claim directly related to a consular decision. *Abourezk v. Reagan*, 785 F.2d 1043, 1051 n.6 (D.C. Cir. 1986); [*Saavedra Bruno v. Albright*], 197 F.3d 1153, 1163. The court does not exercise jurisdiction over the consular decision denying the alien entry, which is protected by consular nonreviewability, but rather, over the citizen's constitutional claim, which is an exercise of jurisdiction squarely within the court's Article III powers. . . .

.   .   .

It is conceded here that Ramadan has no rights—First Amendment or otherwise—to challenge the denial of his visa application. The Plaintiffs' First Amendment challenge to the consular decision, however, provides an opportunity, but a very limited one, to examine the consular determination. The First Amendment claim does not eclipse the consular decision. Rather, the Court neither declines to review the consular decision entirely (as it would under the doctrine of consular nonreviewability), nor does the Court conduct a full-blown First Amendment review (as it would in an ordinary First Amendment case). The doctrine of consular nonreviewability still compels judicial deference to consular decisions. But where there is a First Amendment claim, the Supreme Court has applied a separate test. *Kleindienst v. Mandel*, 408 U.S. 753 (1972).

In *Mandel*, the State Department denied Ernest Mandel, a Belgian academic and editor of a Socialist newspaper, a visa to visit the United States. Similar to Professor Ramadan, Mandel, who had previously visited and lectured in the United States on several occasions, had been invited to speak at various academic conferences throughout the country. The State Department denied his visa on the grounds that he had, on previous visits, "engaged in activities beyond the stated purposes" of his trip. Upon the denial of his visa, Mandel applied to the Attorney General for a waiver of the visa requirement. The Attorney General refused to grant the waiver, and Mandel, along with several university professors, sought review of the decision in federal court claiming that he was excluded on the basis of unpopular speech.[19] There, as here, the professors argued that excluding Mandel abridged their right to "hear his views and engage him in a free and open academic exchange" under the First Amendment.

A three-judge District Court granted an injunction (2–1) which prevented the Government from enforcing certain provisions of the INA which excluded aliens on the basis of their political beliefs. *Mandel v. Mitchell*, 325 F. Supp. 620 (E.D.N.Y. 1971). The district court held that the provisions were impermissible under the First Amendment. It applied a balancing test where it weighed the "dangers" of the expression of Mandel's views against the Plaintiffs' First Amendment right to hear those views. Since the viewpoint could not be excluded, it did not make sense to exclude its proponent—especially when the professors' right to listen (the "free spirit" of academia, as the court called it)—would be adversely impacted. *Id.* Further, the District Court stated that "[i]n this case the admission of [the alien] is but a lever by which the constitutional rights of his prospective citizen audience are to be given effect; they, as the articulately concerned portion of the sovereign people, assert a very high title to support Mandel's admission." . . .

The Supreme Court reversed the decision of the three-judge panel below. . . .

. . .

. . . The standard is clear: when a consular official denies a visa which implicates a United States citizen's First Amendment rights, he or she must have a facially legitimate and bona fide reason for doing so.

. . .

The Supreme Court recognized that the three judge District Court's decision would require courts to weigh the First Amendment rights of citizens against the Government's compelling interest to exclude aliens. It specifically rejected that test. The First Amendment does not trump consular

19. In light of the fact that the decision at issue in *Mandel* was the Attorney General's decision not to waive the visa requirement, and not the underlying consular decision to deny the visa, the *Mandel* decision is not regarded as involving a direct application of the consular nonreviewability doctrine. The Supreme Court determined, however, that the reason given by the consular official was "facially legitimate and bona fide." *Mandel*, 408 U.S. at 769–70. The Court never ruled directly on the reasonableness of the Attorney General's denial of the waiver.

nonreviewability based on a speaker's fame or popularity, or the demand for his presence by learned audiences. When it comes to consular decisions, the Supreme Court refused to hold that the value of academic exchanges and conferences had greater weight, for example, than the value of the presence of an average citizen's alien husband, or mother-in-law, or brother, whose sole purpose in seeking admission to the United States would be to reunite a family. In terms of the strength of the individual interest, the desire to keep a nuclear family intact should arguably be on the same footing as the "right to hear." The Court found that the difficulty of the proposed balancing test, and concerns about giving weight to the "right to hear" based on "the size of the audience or the probity of the speaker's ideas," justified leaving the alien's admissibility decision "in the hands of the Executive." Once the Executive has exercised the discretion allotted by Congress, and has provided a facially legitimate and bona fide reason for doing so, the Court's inquiry must end. The Executive's decisions cannot be overturned by courts balancing the consular decision against First Amendment values.

Plaintiffs argue that the denial of Professor Ramadan's visa violates their First Amendment right to meet face to face with Professor Ramadan here in the United States. Plaintiffs do have that right, but only up to the point of insisting that the reason for Professor Ramadan's exclusion be "facially legitimate and bona fide," as required by *Mandel*. Plaintiffs contend that the reason proffered by the Government for Professor Ramadan's exclusion is neither facially legitimate nor bona fide.

In contrast, the Government argues that its consul in Switzerland has provided a written explanation for denying Professor Ramadan's visa application, the consular decision is nonreviewable, and the Court has no authority to inquire further. If the Court does review the decision, however, the Government contends that it has provided a facially legitimate and bona fide reason for excluding Professor Ramadan.

The Court does not believe that the consular decision at issue here is beyond its review. It comes to this conclusion based on several factors. First and foremost is the presence of the Plaintiffs' First Amendment rights. The values and freedoms inherent in the First Amendment are at the very core of our constitutional scheme. "[T]he First Amendment embodies more than a commitment to free expression and communicative interchange for their own sakes; it has a . . . role to play in securing and fostering our republican system of self-government." *Richmond Newspapers, Inc. v. Virginia*, 448 U.S. 555, 587 (1980) (Brennan, J., concurring). The First Amendment includes not only a right to speak, but also a right to receive information and ideas, and a "right to hear." *See Stanley v. Georgia*, 394 U.S. 557, 564 (1969); *see also Mandel*, 408 U.S. at 762–64. Nevertheless, because "the stretch of [First Amendment] protection is theoretically endless, it must be invoked with discrimination and temperance." *Richmond*, 448 U.S. at 588 (Brennan, J., concurring). There are limits, and they are not to be overcome by "ingenious argument." *Zemel v. Rusk*, 381 U.S. 1, 16–17 (1965). The Court does not hold that every denial of an alien's visa application would result in a First Amendment claim reviewable by federal courts. That holding would interject the Court into business long allocated to the political branches of government whenever able counsel could devise an ingenious First Amendment argument. It would be an obvious end-run around the doctrine of consular nonreviewability. But there are additional factors here besides Plaintiffs' well-pleaded First Amendment complaint.

Unlike most other cases that are shielded by consular nonreviewability, it is uncontested that the decision at issue here was not made solely by consular officials. Consular nonreviewability is premised, at least in part, on Congress' decision to commit the visa authority exclusively into consular hands. Where other agencies and other officials become involved in the decision to grant or deny a visa, it is not clear that Congress intended the same result to apply.

This Court has previously recognized that consular officials were not in complete control of Professor Ramadan's case. DHS was clearly involved, as well. DHS officials made statements to the media regarding Ramadan's exclusion in August 2004, statements now disavowed by the Government. DHS monitored Ramadan's employment status, as evidenced by its contact with Notre Dame in December 2004 to report that Ramadan's visa application had been revoked because he had resigned his position. Indeed, DHS officials conducted the December 2005 visa interview in which Ramadan revealed his donations to the ASP. Under these circumstances, where the decision to deny the visa was not made solely by consular officials, it is not apparent that the doctrine of consular nonreviewability should apply with full force.

Finally, given the entire history of this case including the initial grant of the visa, followed by the unexplained (but claimed "prudential") revocation, and then the long, foot-dragging series of inexplicable delays in proceeding, it is appropriate to inquire whether the reason finally offered is satisfactory. Thus, under the unique circumstances of this case, the Court finds that the Government must have a facially legitimate and bona fide reason for excluding Professor Ramadan. The Court now turns to the question of whether the Government's proffered reason is facially legitimate and bona fide.

As this Court has previously noted, while the *Mandel* Court found that the Government had a "facially legitimate and bona fide" reason for excluding the alien, it did not define the term—nor did it explain its source, or instruct lower federal courts how to determine if the standard had been met. Therefore, to conduct the analysis in Ramadan's case, this Court has fashioned a three-part inquiry.

First, the Court inquires whether or not the Government has provided a reason for denial of the visa. The Government has done so: Ramadan's admitted donations to organizations supporting known terrorist organizations. It is noteworthy, in the context of the First Amendment challenge, that this reason is unrelated to Professor Ramadan's speech. Second, the Court asks whether the Government has a statutory basis for its decision. Here, the Government's reason is based on an appropriate statute, 8 U.S.C. § 1182(a)(3)(B), which permits exclusion when an alien provides material support to individuals or organizations supporting terrorists. Finally, the Court must determine whether the cited provision is properly applied to Professor Ramadan.

Plaintiffs urge that the statute is not properly applied to Professor Ramadan. The Court must resolve two issues: (1) whether the material support provision of the REAL ID Act should be applied retroactively; and (2) whether Ramadan satisfies the knowledge requirement of the statute.

Plaintiffs argue that the material support provision of the REAL ID Act, permitting the exclusion of any alien who commits an act which "affords material support . . . to a terrorist organization," cannot be a facially legitimate and bona fide reason for exclusion as applied to Ramadan because it would require retroactive application of the statute without the requisite clear Congressional intent. 8 U.S.C. § 1182(a)(3)(B)(iv)(VI). Plaintiffs urge that the REAL ID Act's provisions do not contain the header "Retroactive Application" (as did the Patriot Act's effective date provision) and accordingly it should not be given retroactive effect. Further, Plaintiffs contend that retroactivity would cause problems for resident aliens. Since Ramadan's donations to the ASP were not grounds for inadmissibility when they were made, Plaintiffs urge that they should not now provide the basis for denial of his visa.[22] Plaintiffs urge the Court not to allow the phrase "before, on, or after," language which is present in the REAL ID Act, to become a statutory "talisman" for retroactivity.

The Supreme Court has held that "it is beyond dispute that, within constitutional limits, Congress has the power to enact laws with retrospective effect." *INS v. St. Cyr*, 533 U.S. 289, 316 (2001). Nevertheless, "[a] statute may not be applied retroactively . . . absent a clear indication from Congress that it intended such a result." *Id.* Courts, in turn, have routinely found that Congress demonstrates clear intent to give a statute's provisions retroactive effect when Congress includes language applying a statute's effects to events occurring "before, on, or after" the effective date of the legislation.

. . . The Court cannot divorce the word "before" from the plain meaning which Congress clearly intended. Congress selected the word and used it in a way which, in the context of the statute, comports with its ordinary usage. Further, Congress gave no indication that the word "before," or the phrase "before, on, or after," was to have any special meaning or significance other than the plain meaning understood by the average reader. Notwithstanding the objections to trying to divine Congress' intent through an examination of the legislative history, comments in the REAL ID Act's legislative history confirm that lawmakers were aware of, and intended, its potential retroactive effects.

The plain meaning of "before" yields an obvious and intended result—the statute applies to events which occurred "before" its effective date. . . . The material support provision will be applied retroactively.

Plaintiffs argue that the Government failed to demonstrate that Ramadan had the requisite statutory knowledge to fall within the material support provision. In support of this argument, Plaintiffs cite to the dual references to "knowledge" in the statute. The material support provision states:

> to commit an act that *the actor knows, or reasonably should know,* affords material support . . . to a terrorist organization . . . *unless the actor can demonstrate by clear and convincing evidence that the actor did*

---

22.   As discussed in the summary of facts, Professor Ramadan made his donations to the ASP between 1998 and 2002, and the ASP was not listed by the U.S. Department of the Treasury as an entity supporting terrorism by providing funding to Hamas until Aug. 21, 2003. Therefore, at the time the donations were made, they did not fall squarely within the provisions of the REAL ID Act. If the REAL ID Act's provisions apply retroactively, however, then the material support provision applies to the donations that were made before the ASP was designated part of Hamas' European funding network.

*not know, and should not reasonably have known, that the organization was
a terrorist organization.*

8 U.S.C. § 1182 (a)(3)(B)(iv)(VI)(dd) (emphasis added).

Plaintiffs rely on the first knowledge requirement ("knows, or reasonably
should know") to argue that Ramadan did not know that ASP was providing
support to Hamas. Defendants, in contrast, rely on the second knowledge
requirement (requiring the actor to "demonstrate by clear and convincing
evidence that [he] did not know, and should not reasonably have known") to
argue that Ramadan cannot demonstrate that he did not know that ASP was
providing funding to Hamas.

Professor Ramadan admits that his 1998–2002 donations benefited ASP.
Plaintiffs argue, however, that because ASP was not deemed a Specially
Designated Global Terrorist until 2003, he could not have known he was
funding terror. The first reference to knowledge in the statute requires that
Ramadan must have known, or reasonably should have known, that he was
giving money to the ASP itself. Professor Ramadan admits this. Indeed, he
himself brought the ASP donations to the Government's attention at his visa
interview in December 2005. This admission satisfies the first knowledge test.
Since he knew, the statute then imposes on him the second part of the
knowledge requirement. Accordingly, he has the burden to demonstrate "by
clear and convincing evidence" that he "did not know, and should not
reasonably have known, that the organization was a terrorist organization."
The consular official determined that he did not satisfy this burden.

Ramadan offers the Court three critical pieces of evidence regarding his
lack of knowledge that ASP was a terrorist organization. First, he offers his
own statement that he did not know the ASP was supporting Hamas.
Ramadan claims that his intent was to provide humanitarian aid to Palestini-
an refugees, not to support Hamas. This may well be true, but it is self-
serving. It simply does not rise to the level of clear and convincing evidence.
Second, he asserts that at the time of the donations, the ASP was a verified
and legitimate charity according to the Swiss Government. Again, this fact
may be true, but the Swiss endorsement does not provide the "clear and
convincing evidence" required by the statute that Ramadan himself was not
aware of the organization's illegitimate activities. Third, Ramadan offers an
expert declaration opining that somebody in Ramadan's situation would not
have known that ASP was providing funding to Hamas. *See* Decl. of Jonathan
Benthall. This evidence, while objectively illuminating, provides little comfort
to the Court that Ramadan, subjectively, lacked the requisite knowledge.

The statute imposes a heavy burden: it requires Professor Ramadan to
prove a negative, and to do so by clear and convincing proof. But this
outcome is the direct result of the language Congress used. . . . Given the
high standard articulated by Congress, the consular official is then charged
with the duty of determining whether the alien has met his or her burden.
Once the consular official has made this decision, it is not the Court's role—
sitting without the benefit of the subject matter expertise or detailed information on the applicant available to the consular official—to second guess
the result.

The Court finds that the Government has satisfied the limited burden
imposed by *Mandel.* It has given a reason for the visa denial unrelated to
Professor Ramadan's speech, linked the reason to a statutory provision

providing the basis for exclusion, and demonstrated that the statute applies to Professor Ramadan. The Plaintiffs' arguments to the contrary are insufficient. . . .

Plaintiffs also challenge the "endorse and espouse" provision—the so-called "ideological exclusion" provision—of the Patriot Act. Ramadan's visa was not denied under this provision, however. As a result, the Plaintiffs recognize that their challenge creates questions of justiciability and standing.

A court should only render judgments on actual cases and controversies before it. . . . In order to satisfy the standing requirements of Article Ill, plaintiffs must demonstrate that they have suffered an injury in fact, that their injury is traceable to the challenged statutory provision, and that their injury has a likelihood of being redressed by a favorable decision of the court. . . .

Even though Professor Ramadan's visa was not denied on the basis of the endorse and espouse provision, plaintiffs argue that they have four grounds on which to challenge the provision: (1) the provision has a chilling effect on their First Amendment rights because it deters them from inviting scholars to speak, and deters scholars from accepting speaking invitations, for fear they will be subject to ideological scrutiny; (2) there is a credible threat that the provision will be used to exclude Plaintiffs' invitees in the future if scholars decide to accept speaking invitations, thereby subjecting themselves to ideological scrutiny and possibly visa revocation; (3) Plaintiffs have suffered concrete injury because they have suffered financial and administrative losses related to Ramadan's exclusion; and (4) the provision operates as an unconstitutional speech licensing scheme. We reject each of Plaintiffs' arguments.

While a chilling effect may provide the basis for standing under certain circumstances, it cannot do so here.[27] . . . Here the case and controversy arises from Ramadan's exclusion, but does not involve the endorse or espouse provision. There can be no case or controversy based on the hypothetical future exclusion of another—as of yet unidentified—alien, who, on another day, might possibly decline an invitation to some—at present unknown—event, organized by Plaintiffs. Plaintiffs have not identified anyone whom they wished to bring to the United States who has been excluded under the endorse and espouse provision. Their harm is not sufficiently concrete or particularized to confer standing. Nor do the losses they assert in relation to Professor Ramadan's exclusion bear any relevance to the endorse and espouse provision, which was not the reason for his exclusion. Finally,

---

27. Plaintiffs cite to, *inter alia, Dombrowski v. Pfister*, 380 U.S. 479, 494, 85 S.Ct. 1116, 14 L.Ed.2d 22 (1965) and *Abourezk*, 785 F.2d at 1052 n.8, but these cases are inapposite. In *Dombrowksi*, appellants made a Civil Rights Act challenge to a threat of future prosecution under state law, and claimed that the threat of prosecution chilled their speech. No such threat of prosecution exists for Plaintiffs here. If the invited aliens are not permitted to enter the country, Plaintiffs can still interact with the aliens via teleconference or video. Neither the alien nor the Plaintiffs would face threat of prosecution of any kind, or any similar loss of freedom sufficient to create the kind of chill-ing effect discussed in *Dombrowksi*. Moreover, the *Dombrowski* case did not occur in the immigration context, with its accompanying deference to Congress and concerns about separation of powers. In *Abourezk*, the court did address a potential chilling effect that might result when an alien is *actually* excluded on the basis of their speech, but that does not apply to this case. 785 F.2d at 1052 n.8. The only alien *actually* excluded here is Professor Ramadan and he was excluded on the basis of donations he made to a terrorist organization under the material support provision, not on the basis of his speech.

Plaintiffs' argument that our national visa system is an unconstitutional speech licensing scheme is far too broad and is without foundation in the law.

. . .

The Court finds that the reason provided by the Government for the exclusion of Professor Ramadan is facially legitimate and bona fide. The Court recognizes the limits on its authority in this case. The question of admissibility of aliens is a political question, a question which is best left to the Legislative and Executive branches. Having articulated a facially legitimate and bona fide reason to exclude Professor Ramadan, *Mandel* makes clear that the Court has no authority to override the Government's consular decision.

Plaintiffs' motion for summary judgment is denied and Defendants' motion for summary judgment is granted.

Questions and Comments on *American Academy of Religion v. Chertoff*

Is it a violation of academic freedom to encumber travel abroad for academic purposes? *See* Emergency Coal. to Defend Educ. Travel v. U.S. Dep't of Treasury, 498 F. Supp. 2d 150 (D.D.C. 2007) (upholding the Trading with the Enemy Act, 50 U.S.C. app. § 5(b), and the Cuban Assets Control Regulation, 31 C.F.R. § 515, which together require most people, including students, to obtain prior approval from the Office of Foreign Assets Control before traveling to Cuba).

C. ACADEMIC FREEDOM AND RELIGIOUS COLLEGES AND UNIVERSITIES

Curran v. Catholic University of America

District of Columbia Superior Court, 1989.
Civ. Action No. 1562–87.

■ WEISBERG, J.

On July 25, 1986, in a letter to Charles E. Curran, a Catholic priest and a tenured professor of Catholic Theology at The Catholic University of America ("CUA" or "the University"), Joseph Cardinal Ratzinger, the Prefect of the Roman Catholic Church's Sacred Congregation For The Doctrine Of The Faith [and later Pope Benedict XVI], advised Professor Curran that he was "not suitable nor eligible to teach Catholic Theology." This declaration was the culmination of a long investigation of Professor Curran's statements and writing over many years, focused primarily on Curran's vocal dissent from Church doctrine in the area of sexual ethics generally and on the subject of artificial contraception in particular. The Ratzinger letter stated that the decision regarding Professor Curran had been presented to, and was specifically approved by, the Pope on July 10, 1986. A separate letter of July 25, 1986 to James Cardinal Hickey, Chancellor of CUA by virtue of his position as Archbishop of Washington, advised the Chancellor that "[t]he Pontifical approbation of this decision ... renders it a definitive judgment in this case," and it directed the Chancellor to take "appropriate action."

Upon receipt of the Ratzinger letter, Chancellor Hickey began proceedings to withdraw Professor Curran's canonical mission, an ecclesiastical license required to teach in certain Departments at CUA, which are authorized by the Church to confer ecclesiastical degrees. The Department of Theology, where Curran taught, is one such Department. In January of 1987, the Chancellor suspended Curran from teaching the courses he was scheduled to teach that term in the Department of Theology. Ultimately, after hearings before an ad hoc faculty committee which made recommendations to the Board of Trustees, the Board voted on April 12, 1988, to withdraw Curran's canonical mission; and, after an unsuccessful attempt to negotiate an alternative teaching assignment for Professor Curran, the Board issued a resolution on June 2, 1988 barring Curran from teaching Catholic Theology anywhere within the University.

At the present time, Professor Curran retains his tenure, but not his right to teach Catholic Theology, which he contends is his only field of professional competence. He maintains this suit for breach of contract, alleging that the University's actions violate his right to academic freedom. He seeks specific performance of what he asserts is his contractual right to teach in the Department of Theology without a canonical mission or, failing that, his right to teach Catholic Theology in another Department within the University.

The University defends on several levels. It contends that while academic freedom exists as an important value at CUA, the Board of Trustees has never adopted a definition of academic freedom for inclusion in the Faculty Handbook, the document that defines the contractual relationship between the faculty member and the University. The University also contends that academic freedom, by any definition, is not absolute. In the context of this case, the University's position is that academic freedom is limited both by the discipline—the teaching of Catholic Theology—and by the nature of the institution in which the discipline is practiced—the Catholic University of America, a pontifical university chartered by Pope Leo XIII in 1889, which has maintained by choice for one hundred years what the University refers to as a "special relationship with the Holy See." To rule otherwise, according to the University, would be to violate its First Amendment right to the free exercise of its religious beliefs. Finally, the University argues that because of its papal charter and its ecclesiastical faculties, it is governed not only by civil law, but also by canon law; and, to the extent that its actions in this case were dictated by authoritative interpretations of canon law, they are unreviewable and are beyond the legitimate exercise of jurisdiction by the civil courts.

Trial of this matter was held without a jury from December 14 to December 23, 1988. . . .

It is . . . apparent after seven days of trial that many of the parties and witnesses know considerably more than the court about both academic freedom—and the authoritative teachings of the Roman Catholic Church, which is not to say that there is unanimity on either subject. But it is the law of contracts which must govern the decision in this case. As in any other contract case, the central issues are: What are the terms of the contract? Did the University breach it? If so, what is the proper remedy? Within those issues, however, are a number of subsidiary questions. Does Curran's contract with CUA include a guarantee of academic freedom? If it does, and if it is not absolute, what are the limits on academic freedom for which the parties bargained? Does Curran's contract with CUA require him to hold a canonical mission in order to teach in the Department of Theology? If it does, and if the canonical mission was properly withdrawn, what further contractual obligation, if any, did CUA owe to Curran? Assuming that the withdrawal of the canonical mission did not, in and of itself, affect Curran's right to teach Catholic Theology in a non-ecclesiastical faculty, did the parties to the contract intend that Curran could continue to teach Catholic Theology in a non ecclesiastical faculty even if the Holy See, in a definitive judgment, declared that he was no longer "eligible to exercise the function of a Professor of Catholic Theology?" To the extent that the University's actions in the wake of the Holy See's declaration were dictated by canon law, are they immune from judicial scrutiny; and is a remedy barred, even if such actions would constitute a breach of contract as a matter of civil law? Finally, if Curran is entitled to a remedy for breach of contract, is he entitled to specific performance?

Professor Curran's contract with CUA consists of his annual appointment letter and the Faculty Handbook.[3] The Bylaws of the University state:

> The Board of Trustees does hereby authorize the preparation and publication of a Faculty Handbook which shall set forth the relationship of the Faculty members to the University's corporation; guarantees with respect to academic freedom; the nature of the tenure of the members of the Faculty; and other pertinent matters, *all of which, when approved by the Board of Trustees, shall constitute the University's representation to the Faculty generally with respect to such matters.* The Handbook, which will include the Canonical Statutes of the Ecclesiastical Faculties of The Catholic University of America, will, when approved by the Board of Trustees, have the same force of law as do these Bylaws. (emphasis added)

The parties do not disagree about what the core documents of the contract are. The principal area of disagreement is over whether the contract includes a specific guarantee of academic freedom and the extent to which the University's customs and practices regarding academic freedom are part of the contractual relationship between the University and its faculty. If academic freedom, in one form or another is an ingredient of the contractual relationship, the parties also disagree over whether there are limits on academic freedom at CUA and, if so, what those limits are.

Under District of Columbia law, "an employee handbook . . . defines the rights and obligations of the employee and the employer, and is a contract enforceable by—the courts." In a university setting, the employment contract can also include the customs and practices of the university.

. . .

. . . A party seeking to prove the meaning of a university employment contract by reference to the university's customs and practices must establish by "clear satisfactory evidence" that the custom and practice is "definite,

---

3. The Faculty Handbook contains a section on the Government of the University, which includes the charter documents, Bylaws and statutes of the University, a section on Faculty Appointments and a "General Infor-

mation" section. The current edition of the Handbook also includes the 1981 Canonical Statutes, with revisions approved by the Board of Trustees in 1984.

uniform and well known." Finally, as with any question of contract interpretation, if the contract is ambiguous, the court must determine what a reasonable person in the position of the parties would have thought the contract meant. . . .

These general principles of contract interpretation provide the analytical framework in which the court must decide the disputed factual issues presented by this case. In doing so, the court must avoid impermissible entanglement of the "State" in the affairs of the Church. Contract issues are for the civil courts, but they must be resolved according to "neutral principles of law," with due regard for the right of the Church—in this case, the Roman Catholic Church—to decide for itself matters of Church polity and doctrine. *Jones v. Wolf*, 443 U.S. 595, 602 (1979).

The adverse action against Professor Curran following the Chancellor's receipt of the Ratzinger letter occurred in stages. In the first phase, the Chancellor suspended Curran from teaching in the Department of Theology, and he asked the University's Academic Senate to form an ad hoc faculty committee to hold hearings and to make a recommendation to the Board of Trustees on the question of whether "the decision of the Holy See ... constitutes a most serious reason for the withdrawal of Father Curran's canonical mission to teach in the name of the Church."[4] The ad hoc committee held hearings in April and May of 1987 and issued its report in October of that year, recommending that the canonical mission be withdrawn if, but only if, a teaching position was found for Curran in his area of competence within the Department of Theology or elsewhere within the University. There ensued a series of remands back to the ad hoc committee in which first the Chancellor and then the Board of Trustees accused the committee of exceeding its jurisdiction. Each time the committee held to its position. Ultimately, the Board voted on April 12, 1988 to withdraw Curran's canonical mission and directed a triumvirate, consisting of the Chairman of the Board, the Chancellor and the President of the University, to negotiate with Curran to find a teaching position for him that would not be inconsistent with either the withdrawal of the canonical mission or the declaration of the Holy See.

In the second phase of the University's adverse action against Professor Curran attempts were made to locate an alternative teaching assignment for him. Those attempts failed, essentially for two reasons. First, Curran took the position that even if he were to teach courses in social ethics, as the University offered, he would be teaching as a Catholic moral theologian. Second, Curran refused to "accept" the declaration in the Ratzinger letter as binding on him or having any effect on his teaching of theology outside of the Department of Theology. The University rejected both of Curran's positions as being inconsistent with the withdrawal of the canonical mission and the declaration of the Holy See. On June 2, 1988, the Board of Trustees adopted its Resolution declaring, *inter alia*, that it would not allow Curran to

---

4. The 1981 Canonical statutes of the University provide that "[t]he Chancellor grants the canonical mission to teach in the name of the Church" and that he "may withdraw the mission ... only for the most serious reasons and after providing information regarding specific charges and proofs." The canonical Statutes also provide that if requested by the member of the Faculty, certain "procedures of due process ... shall be employed"—including, among other things, a hearing before an *ad hoc* committee of faculty members, the right to a decision by the Board of Trustees on withdrawal of the canonical mission, and the right to appear before the Board before such a decision is made.

teach Catholic Theology anywhere within the University, because to do so in the face of the declaration of the Holy See that he is ineligible, which the Board accepted as "binding upon the University as a matter of canon law and religious conviction," would be "inconsistent with the University's special relationship with the Holy See, incompatible with the University's freely chosen Catholic character, and contrary, to the obligations imposed on the University as a matter of canon law." Effectively, then, the Board's action created a stalemate: Curran could teach anything other than Catholic Theology; but, according to Curran, Catholic Theology is the only thing he teaches. The resulting impasse is what gives rise to this lawsuit.

A.   The Withdrawal of the Canonical Mission

On this aspect of his claim, plaintiff makes two central arguments. First, he contends that his tenure contract with the University dates from 1970 or 1971[5] and at that time there was no requirement that he hold a canonical mission to teach in the Department of Theology. Any such requirement that may have been imposed by the 1931 Apostolic Constitution or by the University statutes enacted in 1937 had, he says, long since fallen into "desuetude." Second, he argues that the University's reintroduction of the requirement of a canonical mission in its 1981 Canonical Statutes can not be applied retroactively to him, because to do so would be in derogation of his contract, by which he was granted tenure without a canonical mission.

The requirement of a canonical mission appears clearly in the University's 1937 statutes, which were enacted by the University pursuant to *Deus Scientiarium Dominus*, the Apostolic Constitution of 1931. . . .

The University's position is that the requirement of the canonical mission has never lapsed since its inception at CUA in 1937. It acknowledges that for many years, and perhaps from the beginning, canonical missions were not explicitly conferred by the Chancellor on teachers of the sacred disciplines, but it urges—it says as a matter of canon law—that each professor in the pertinent faculties held a canonical mission "implicitly." Plaintiff counters that the idea of implicit conferral of the canonical mission is something the University came up with after the fact to get around his argument that requirements recognized for the first time in 1981 can not be applied retroactively to him. He points out that throughout the turmoil of the late sixties—including, among other events, a faculty and student strike in 1967 over the University's threatened non-renewal of Curran's contract, and the Board's partial acceptance of the Marlowe Committee report in 1969 following the public dissent by Curran and others from the papal encyclical *Humanae Vitae*—no one said anything about withdrawing Professor Curran's canonical mission, or even the fact that he had one. He concludes, therefore, that any requirement of a canonical mission dating from the 1930's had surely fallen into desuetude at CUA by 1970 or 1971, if it ever existed in the first place.

The University may be correct that the existence or non-existence of the requirement of a canonical mission is a question of canon law, and therefore that the court must accept its authoritative interpretation of canon law on that question. But the question presented here is not what canon law means

---

5. . . . Both sides agree that Curran enjoyed full academic tenure no later than October of 1971.

on this point, but whether the parties to the contract agreed to be bound by it. Even assuming canon law required Curran to hold a canonical mission in 1970 and 1971 in order to teach in the Department of Theology, that requirement was not sufficiently explicit to be considered a bargained for term of his contract. It is one thing to say that a contract, or part of it, can be based on canon law, if the parties agree to it; it is quite another to say that the contract can be based on secret law, the provisions of which are unknown to one of the parties to the contract. If CUA wanted to make it a condition of Curran's contract that he must maintain his canonical mission, it should have told him so. Having not made the requirement explicit, the University can not now rely on an interpretation of arcane provisions of canon law to read into the contract terms that could not have been understood by the parties, or at least one of the parties, at the time the contract was entered. The court's inquiry on this aspect of the case does not end with the conclusion that the parties did not bargain for the canonical mission requirement in 1970 or 1971. Things change, and some contracts are no exception. It is clear that as of the 1981 Canonical Statutes, professors in the Department of Theology were required to hold a canonical mission.[9] The question is whether that requirement can be applied to Professor Curran, who received his contract with tenure in 1970 or 1971.

Ordinarily, of course, the rights and obligations of the parties to a contract are fixed at the time the contract is made, and one party may not thereafter unilaterally change the terms or add new conditions. In the context of a professor's contract with his or her university, however, ... [b]oth parties to the contract understand that from time to time the university may change its bylaws or other governing documents, which may in turn alter the relationship between the university and its faculty, even those with tenure. If this were not so, the relationship between each faculty member and the university would be defined by whatever the rules and policies were when the faculty member received tenure, with each faculty member enjoying different benefits or bearing different burdens depending on when he or she received tenure.[11]

---

9. Under the 1981 Canonical Statutes, canonical missions are required of Catholics who teach subjects relating to faith or morals in the ecclesiastical faculties. Non–Catholics and those who teach subjects other than those relating to faith or morals must simply have the Chancellor's "permission to teach." Professor Curran is a Catholic priest, who taught subjects relating to faith and morals in an ecclesiastical faculty.

11. Plaintiff does not appear to disagree that the relationship between the university and its faculty is subject to change as the rules and policies of the university change. For plaintiff, however, this doctrine of evolution is a one-way process: changes that expand the rights of tenured faculty become part of the contract, but changes that diminish the rights of tenured faculty do not. This theory of non-mutuality fits nicely with plaintiff's approach to this case, but one is unlikely to find it in Corbin or Williston. The reality is that, as a

tenured faculty member and a member of the Academic Senate, Professor Curran had a right to participate in the process by which the University changed its policies and its governing documents, and the record shows that he was an active participant in that process. It hardly makes sense for the Court to bind the University to the changes Professor Curran likes but to excuse him from his obligations under the changes that did not go his way. Even where universities have lowered the mandatory age of retirement, an essential ingredient of tenure, courts have generally upheld the application of the new policy to tenured faculty without a "grandfather clause" to protect those who had received tenure before the retirement age was lowered. *See, e.g.*, Karlen v. New York University, 464 F.Supp. 704 (S.D.N.Y. 1979); Rehor v. Case Western Reserve University, 43 Ohio St.2d 224, 331 N.E.2d 416 (Ohio 1975).

This doctrine of evolution in the contractual relationship between a tenured faculty member and the university is especially true of the relationship between CUA and its professors in the ecclesiastical faculties. Whether or not the parties specifically intended in 1970 or 1971 that there be a requirement of a canonical mission, certain basic facts were clearly understood and accepted by the parties: they knew that the ecclesiastical faculties are different from the rest of the University; that these faculties are authorized by the Holy See to confer special ecclesiastical degrees, that no other Catholic university in the United States has ecclesiastical faculties; that these faculties are governed by an Apostolic Constitution, as implemented by Canonical Statutes, which in turn must be expressly approved by the Holy See; and that the Holy See might change the requirements for these faculties at any time, imposing on the University an obligation to accommodate such changes or risk losing the authority to confer ecclesiastical degrees. Therefore when *Sapientia Christiana*, the Apostolic Constitution of 1979, and the University's Canonical Statutes of 1981, enacted pursuant to *Sapientia Christiana*, introduced or reintroduced the requirement of a canonical mission, it should have come as no surprise to Professor Curran that he was expected to have one.[12]

As of 1981 then, if not before, Professor Curran had, and was required by his contract to maintain, a canonical mission.[13] The letter from Cardinal Ratzinger to Chancellor Hickey directed the Chancellor to take "appropriate action." The Chancellor, following the due process procedures outlined in the Canonical Statutes, initiated the process to withdraw Professor Curran's canonical mission; and on April 12, 1988, the Board of Trustees withdrew it. Professor Curran maintains the position that he was not required to have a canonical mission, but concedes that the decision to withdraw it was both

12. This might be a different case if, after enactment of the 1981 Canonical Statutes, the Chancellor had gone through the ecclesiastical faculties conferring canonical mission on all the professors except Curran, and then removed Curran from the Department of Theology because he did not have a canonical mission. But that is not what happened. Instead, the Chancellor applied the Statutes as if they contained a "grandfather clause," conferring the canonical mission retroactively on all professors in the ecclesiastical faculties who had received tenure before 1981, including Professor Curran. Thus, it was not the "new" requirement of a canonical mission that cost Professor Curran his position in the Department of Theology, it was the declaration of the Holy See which made him no longer eligible to hold the canonical mission. It is true, of course, that the withdrawal of the canonical mission could not have directly affected Professor Curran's right to teach in the Department of Theology if he was not required by his contract to hold the canonical mission in the first place. But whatever he may have understood about the canonical mission requirement, Professor Curran could not have reasonably believed he had a right under his contract to continue to teach in an ecclesi-

astical faculty if the Holy See declared him ineligible.

13. If the court had come to the opposite conclusion on this issue, it would have been squarely presented with a substantial constitutional question. The University has argued, persuasively, that the canonical mission is a papal authorization "to teach in the name of the Church" and, as such, only the Church can decide who may teach in its name. That decision, according to the University, is governed by canon law, and a civil court may not review authoritative interpretations and applications of canon law by the highest authorities in a hierarchical Church like the Roman Catholic Church. The University's argument on this point is supported by more than one hundred years of Supreme Court jurisprudence. *See, e.g.* Jones v. Wolf, 443 U.S. 595, 602–04 (1979); Serbian Eastern Orthodox Diocese v. Milivojevich, 426 U.S. 696, 710–14 (1976); Gonzalez v. Archbishop, 280 U.S. 1, 16 (1929); Watson v. Jones, 80 U.S. (13 Wall.) 679 (1872). In light of the court's conclusion that Professor Curran's contract required him to have a canonical mission as a condition of teaching in the Department of Theology, it is unnecessary to reach the University's "canon law defense."

substantively and procedurally correct—that is, that there were "most serious reasons" for withdrawing the canonical mission and that proper procedures were followed. The withdrawal of the canonical mission was not a breach of Professor Curran's Contract with the University.[14]

B.   The June 2, 1988 Resolution

The immediate effect of the withdrawal of the canonical mission was that Professor Curran could not teach in an ecclesiastical faculty. Two questions remained: could he teach civil degree students in the Department of Theology; and if not, could he teach Catholic Theology in one of the other, non-ecclesiastical, Departments within the University?

There are three ecclesiastical faculties at CUA: the School of Philosophy, the Department of Canon Law and the Department of Theology. Within the Department of Theology, however, there are both civil degree candidates and ecclesiastical degree candidates. Plaintiff's position is that the canonical mission is required to teach the ecclesiastical degree students but not to teach the civil degree students.

On the issue of whether the Department of Theology is a unitary faculty or a binary faculty, the University has much the better of it.... [P]laintiff failed to produce any credible evidence that the University has ever divided the Department of Theology faculty along those lines or made any distinctions between professors based on whether their students were in one program or the other. Indeed, the weight of the evidence is decidedly the other way on this issue. [P]laintiff has failed to prove by a preponderance of the evidence that he can teach civil degree students in the Department of Theology without the canonical mission. Put another way, plaintiff failed to prove that the University breached his contract by removing him from the Department of Theology after his canonical mission was withdrawn.

The issue of Professor Curran's right, *vel non*, to teach Catholic Theology in a non-ecclesiastical faculty within the University is not as easily resolved. The University has not fired Professor Curran or violated his tenure rights, as such. It says he may teach in an appropriate non-ecclesiastical faculty within the University, but he may not teach Catholic Theology. Curran asserts that everything he teaches is Catholic Theology and argues that the University's decision is, in effect, constructive discharge without the judgment of his peers that he is incompetent within his academic discipline. The first question that must be answered on this aspect of the case is whether the University had any contractual duty to Professor Curran once his canonical mission was withdrawn and he was removed from the Department of Theology. Professor Curran's appointment with continuous tenure was to the School of Sacred Theology, which later became the Department of Theology in the School of Religious Studies. Although there appears to be some debate on the point within the academic community, the great weight

---

14. At trial, the evidence relating to the Chancellor's suspension of Professor Curran received less attention than the evidence relating to the actual withdrawal of the canonical mission. Nonetheless, Curran claims that the suspension was itself a breach of his contract. Curran concedes, however, that *if* he was required to have a canonical mission, which he denies, the declaration in the Ratzinger letter constituted an adequate ground for withdrawing it, and the procedures used by the University to reach that decision were proper. Under the circumstances, the court concludes that the Chancellor's suspension of Professor Curran pending the outcome of withdrawal proceeding was authorized by the Canonical Statutes and did not violate his contract.

of authority, supported by the preponderance of credible evidence in this case, is that a professor's tenure is to a department or a school and not to the university at large. The Faculty Handbook, the core document defining the contractual relationship between CUA and its faculty, stipulates that appointments with continuous tenure are initiated by the Chairman of the Department (or by the Dean of the School if the School does not have Departments) and are based on the needs of the programs, departments or schools concerned. The only situation in which the Handbook imposes on the University a duty to seek alternative teaching assignments for a tenured professor in a Department other than the one to which he or she was tenured is when the professor's program or Department is discontinued or the position is eliminated because of financial exigency. If this were an ordinary case, and if Professor Curran had been dismissed for cause from the Department of Theology based on a judgment of his peers that he is not competent, the University would clearly have no duty to place him in any other Department.

But this is not an ordinary case. For one thing, in Professor Curran's most recent annual appointment letter in 1986, the University, for reasons that are not clear in the record, unilaterally changed his appointment from the Department of Theology to the School of Religious Studies. The School of Religious Studies includes the Department of Theology, but it also includes other Departments, which, unlike the Department of Theology, are not ecclesiastical faculties. More importantly, Professor Curran was not dismissed for cause after peer review of his competence. Throughout the proceedings leading up to the withdrawal of Curran's canonical mission, and in court, the University has consistently said that its actions were not based on a judgment of Curran's competence as a professor. They were based on the judgment of the Holy See that he is not "eligible" to exercise the function of a professor of Catholic Theology and the decision of the Board of Trustees to accept that judgment as binding on the University. The university Handbook does not address this situation, and there is no custom or practice at the University that can be looked to as a source for the contractual rights and duties of the parties in these unusual circumstances. The simple fact is that it has never happened before, at this University or anywhere else.

For these reasons, reference to the traditional norms of academic tenure is not dispositive of plaintiff's claims, and the court prefers to base its decision on other grounds. Like the rest of plaintiff's case, the question comes down to what the contract says and what the parties to it intended. It is fair to assume that neither party in 1970 or 1971 could have anticipated a judgment by the Holy See that was both as broad and as definitive as the Ratzinger letter. No one sat down and spelled out what the rights and obligations of the parties would be if the Holy See, in absolute and definitive terms, declared Curran "unsuitable" and "ineligible" to teach Catholic Theology. But certain things were unmistakably known and understood by the parties. For example, the parties knew that the University, in addition to its civil charter, had a pontifical charter from Pope Leo XIII in 1889. They knew that the Archbishop of Washington serves as the Chancellor of the University and that, under the Bylaws, the Chancellor acts as the liaison between the University and the National Council of Catholic Bishops and between the University and the Holy See. They knew that, under the Bylaws, the University's Board of Trustees consists of 40 trustees, 20 of whom must be Roman Catholic clerics, of whom 16 must be Bishops, and that the cleric members of the Board will usually include all of the Cardinals who are residential ordinaries in the American Catholic hierarchy. And they knew that all of the University's self-descriptions, in the Faculty Handbook and elsewhere, emphasized its unique relationship to the Holy See and its concomitant responsibility to the Roman Catholic Church.[15]

No one—least of all a Catholic priest and a professor of Catholic Theology—could have contracted with CUA without understanding the University's special relationship with the Roman Catholic Church, with all of the implications and obligations flowing from that relationship. Indeed, Professor Curran testified that in fact he did understand at all relevant times that this special relationship existed. As much as he may have wished it otherwise, he could not reasonably have expected that the University would defy a definitive judgment of the Holy See that he was "unsuitable" and "ineligible" to teach Catholic Theology. Whether or not the University is correct that it was obligated to accept the declaration of the Holy See as a matter of canon law, it was surely bound to do so as a matter of religious conviction and pursuant to its long-standing, unique and freely chosen special relationship with the Holy See. Given the history and content of its relationship to the Holy See, CUA could not have given up its right to accept and act upon definitive judgments of the Holy See in its dealings with Professor Curran unless it did so explicitly, which it certainly did not do. The University did not breach its contract with Professor Curran by requiring him to teach courses other than Catholic Theology or, for that matter, by requiring him to agree to be bound by the declaration of the Holy See.

IV.   Remedy

Having concluded that the University did not breach its contract with Professor Curran, it is arguably unnecessary to consider the question of what relief would have been appropriate if the court had ruled for the plaintiff on the liability issue. In the interest of resolving all issues, however, and because a reviewing court may see the liability issue differently, it seems advisable that the court should rule also on the remedy issue.

Even if the court were to find that the University had breached its contract with Professor Curran, it is virtually unthinkable that the court should order specific performance in this case. Such a remedy, the legitimacy of which rests solely in the court's equitable power, would force the Catholic University of America to accept a professor of Catholic Moral Theology who the highest offices of the Roman Catholic Church have expressly declared "unsuitable" and "ineligible" to teach that subject. Indeed, if plaintiff had his way, the court's injunction would go even further and would order the University to let him teach that very subject in open defiance of the Holy See.

---

15. These statements appear, among other places, in the Faculty Handbook in the sections called "Goals of the Catholic University of America," "Aims of the University," and the "Historical Preface" to the Bylaws. Plaintiff correctly points out that there is also language in both the "Goals" and the "Aims" sections that emphasizes CUA's status as a "modem American University," which fosters an environment of academic freedom. Far from abrogating the University's relationship with the Holy See, however, the juxtaposition of this language only serves to point up the natural tension created by the University's commitment to two sets of norms—academic norms of American universities on the one hand, and the norms established by the Holy See on the other. Nothing in the Faculty Handbook or any other statement adopted by the University's Board of Trustees makes one set of norms paramount or subordinate to the other.

Problems of enforcement aside, specific performance is a singularly inappropriate remedy in the unique circumstances of this case. To begin with, personal service contracts in general, and employment contracts in particular, are rarely enforced by a judicial decree of specific performance. Restatement (Second) of Contracts § 367 (1981). Forcing an unwilling employee on an employer smacks of involuntary servitude and is virtually unheard of. *Id.* comment a. Although courts are slightly more receptive to prayers for specific performance by unwanted employees, that remedy is generally reserved for cases in which the employee was discharged in violation of his or her statutory or constitutional rights or a collective bargaining agreement and where little or no direct supervision of the employee by the employer is required. *Id.* comment b. This is not such a case.

The practice of not enforcing employment contracts by specific performance is especially well rooted in academia. As Judge Holtzoff once put it:

> A contract to hire a teacher may not be enforced by specific performance. It is not within those few categories of agreements that are enforceable in equity. It would be intolerable for the courts to interject themselves and to require an educational institution to hire or to maintain on its staff a professor or instructor whom it deemed undesirable and did not wish to employ.

Greene v. Howard University, 271 F.Supp. 609, 615 (D.D.C. 1967), remanded on other grounds, 134 U.S. App.D.C. 81, 412 F.2d 1128 (1969).

If ever there were a case in which a court should decline to force an unwanted teacher on an unwilling educational institution, this must surely be it. Professor Curran is, by all accounts, a popular and highly respected teacher and scholar. But none of the University's decisions in this matter have been based on its judgment of his competence. The simple fact is that the Holy See, in a "definitive judgment," has declared that Professor Curran is "ineligible to exercise the function of a Professor of Catholic Theology." Once that judgment was communicated to the University, through its Chancellor, the Archbishop of Washington, the University felt compelled to execute it as a matter of "religious conviction" and pursuant to "the obligations imposed on the University as a matter of canon law." The University argues forcefully that because its decisions were based in part on its interpretation of its obligations under canon law, they are unreviewable by this court without impermissibly entangling the "State" in the affairs of the Church. More specifically, the University contends that a specific performance decree by this court, enforceable by contempt, ordering the University to permit Professor Curran to teach Catholic Theology would violate the University's rights under the Free Exercise Clause of the First Amendment. Without reaching these global constitutional issues,[18] however,

---

18. The University may be, as defendant asserts, a "juridic person" under both civil law and canon law, but it is less clear that it is a person for purposes of the Free Exercise Clause. *Cf.* First Nat'l. Bank v. Bellotti, 435 U.S. 765 (1978) (speech otherwise protected under the First Amendment does not lose that protection merely because the "speaker" is a corporation); United States v. White, 322 U.S. 694, 698–701 (1944) (privilege against self-incrimination is personal and can not be exercised by or on behalf of any organization, such as a corporation); *but see* Gay Rights Coalition v. Georgetown University, 536 A.2d 1, 30–31 (D.C. 1987) [116 WLR 1]. There is also a question whether this court's decree, requiring nothing more than compliance with its own contract, would constitute sufficient gov-

it is clear to the court, at a minimum, that specific performance in a case such as this would be extremely ill-advised and would not be a proper exercise of the court's equitable power.

At the argument on the University's motion for summary judgment before trial, the court asked counsel for the University a question based on the following hypothetical contract between Professor Curran and the University:

1. The parties to this Contract understand that there exists a unique and special relationship between the University and the Roman Catholic Church.

2. Notwithstanding the foregoing, the University expressly guarantees that the Professor shall have academic freedom, which the parties understand to mean, at a minimum, the following:

a) the University will take no adverse action against the Professor based on the moral or religious content of his speech, writing or teaching;

b) if it is determined that the Professor requires a canonical mission to teach in the Department of Theology, and if the Holy See attempts to withdraw, or to direct the Chancellor to withdraw, the Professor's canonical mission based on the moral or religious content of the Professor's speech, writing or teaching, the University will defend the Professor's right to hold the canonical mission;

c) if, notwithstanding the foregoing, the Professor's canonical mission is withdrawn, the University will guarantee the Professor the right to teach Catholic Theology in an appropriate Department or faculty in which a canonical mission is not required, subject to all the rights and privileges customarily associated with the concept of academic freedom in an American university.

It goes without saying that the University would never write such a contract. But plaintiff's case, in essence, is that this is precisely the contract he had with the University. If plaintiff's evidence had established that this hypothetical contract was real, the result in this case might very well have been different, although the court would still have had serious reservations about entering a decree of specific performance. After all the evidence is in, however, the hypothetical contract remains just that—hypothetical. Plaintiff's evidence describes the University he wanted to work for, maybe even the one he thought he was working for, but not the one with which he contracted.

The bulk of plaintiff's proof at trial was historical. His burden, as he saw it, was to show that the events at CUA in the late 1960's had transformed the University into a place where academic freedom reigned supreme, to the exclusion of all else, including the obligations imposed on the University by virtue of its pontifical charter and its relationship with the Holy See. There is

---

ernmental action against the University to present an issue under the First Amendment. *Cf.* Shelley v. Kraemer, 334 U.S. 1 (1948). In any event, for the reasons stated in the text, it is unnecessary and inadvisable to decide these difficult constitutional questions, particularly where the specific performance issue does not even surface unless the court's ruling for defendant on liability were to be set aside.

little doubt that the late 1960's was an extraordinary time at Catholic University. In many respects the events on that campus were a reflection of the turmoil on college campuses all across the country. These were turbulent times, characterized by persistent testing of institutional limits on all forms of expression of individual freedom, including academic freedom. It is hardly surprising that the Catholic University of America, with its close ties to the Roman Catholic Church, found itself in the middle of these struggles. Nor is it surprising that many of the changes at the University—the Marlowe Committee report and its partial acceptance by the Board of Trustees, new statements about academic freedom at the University and changes in the University's Bylaws and statutes, to list just a few—were directed at strengthening the independence and autonomy of the University and its faculty from interference by outside authorities, not the least of which was the Holy See. Internally, the University had to wrestle with its own ambivalence. On the one hand, it wanted to be recognized as a university—a Catholic university, to be sure—but a full-fledged American university nonetheless. On the other hand, it continued to place transcendent value on its unique and special relationship with the Holy See. Perhaps it can fairly be said that the University wanted it both ways; but on most issues it can also be said that the University could have it both ways. On some issues—and this case certainly presents one of them—the conflict between the University's commitment to academic freedom and its unwavering fealty to the Holy See is direct and unavoidable. On such issues, the University may choose for itself on which side of that conflict it wants to come down, and nothing in its contract with Professor Curran or any other faculty member promises that it will always come down on the side of academic freedom.

Professor Curran has his own view of what this case is about, which is best expressed in his own words excerpted from his trial testimony:

Q. You have asked this Court to order Catholic University to take you back and to permit you to teach theology at Catholic University. Why?

A. Because in the last analysis, I think it's not only good for me, but I think it's good for Catholic University. I told my colleagues on the Faculty Inquiry Committee that in the last analysis I wasn't on trial, but they were. And I still believe that very strongly.... What I want to prove, and I think we have to prove, and I think I have but others might disagree, is that ultimately even academic freedom for the Catholic theologian is ultimately for the good of the Church. That in the last analysis, academic freedom, itself, is for the good of the Church.

Maybe Professor Curran is right. But in adjudicating the breach of contract claim he brings to this court, what is good for Catholic University or for the Roman Catholic Church is not a question presented and not one the court has either the right or the competence to decide. The question presented is whether his contract gives him the right to teach Catholic Theology at Catholic University in the face of definitive judgment by the Holy See that he is ineligible to do so. The court holds today that it does not. Whether that is ultimately good for the University or for the Church is something they have a right to decide for themselves.

Questions and Comments on *Curran v. Catholic University of America*

1. After the court decision, Father Curran was approved for a tenured chair in religion at Auburn University by the faculty, dean, academic vice president, and president of the school. CHARLES E. CURRAN, LOYAL DISSENT: MEMOIR OF A CATHOLIC THEOLOGIAN 166–68 (2006). At the last minute, however, Auburn's president single-handedly blocked the appointment and refused to disclose his reasons. A faculty committee, after investigating the matter, voted to censure the president for violations of academic principles and policies. *Id.* at 169–74. Shortly after his denial of tenure at Auburn, Father Curran was granted tenure at Southern Methodist University, where he currently serves as Elizabeth Scurlock University Professor of Human Values. *Id.* at 175–79.

The AAUP investigated Father Curran's case. The AAUP final report reached a different conclusion than did the court:

The Initial Administrative Action

On August 18, 1986, the day that he conveyed Cardinal Ratzinger's final letter to Professor Curran, Chancellor Hickey informed Professor Curran that he was initiating the withdrawal of his canonical mission and reminded him of his right to due process under the university's Canonical Statutes. On the next day President Byron, while expressing confidence that Professor Curran would continue to serve the Church, announced that, "given the Vatican declaration," he would not be able to do so as a member of the University's Department of Theology.

Under the Canonical Statutes, [which govern the faculties of Philosophy, Canon Law, and Theology at Catholic University,] a faculty member whose canonical mission is to be withdrawn is entitled to due process in accordance with the procedures outlined in the faculty handbook (Part II, Section 4, Article 24). Under this article, the hearing body is prescribed as an *ad hoc* committee of the Academic Senate, and "the burden of proof that adequate cause exists [for action against the faculty member] rests with the institution, and shall be satisfied only by clear and convincing evidence in the record considered as a whole." President Byron's announcement was thus quite precipitate, an anticipation of a decision that a hearing body had not reached and was not yet in existence even to consider.

The Suspension

The university's Canonical Statutes provide that, "in more serious or pressing cases, the Chancellor, with the concurrence of a majority of the episcopal members of the Board, may suspend the member of the Faculty from teaching in an Ecclesiastical Faculty during the period of investigation." Under other provisions of the faculty handbook, which applied to any suspension outside the ecclesiastical faculties, "The faculty member will be suspended, or assigned to other duties in lieu of suspension, only if immediate harm to himself or others is threatened by his continuance"—language that is identical with that in the 1958 *Statement on Procedural Standards in Faculty Dismissal Proceedings* of the Association of American Colleges and the AAUP. With respect to suspension outside the ecclesiastical faculties, the faculty handbook provides that, "before suspending a faculty member, pending an ultimate determination of his status through the hearing procedures, the President or his representative will consult with the Committee on Academic Freedom and Tenure of the Academic Senate." The provisions for suspension in the Canonical Statutes do not set an "immediate harm" standard, nor do they call for consultation with the Senate's Committee....

Chancellor Hickey, proceeding under the Canonical Statutes provisions and apparently viewing the other faculty handbook provisions as not required in Professor Curran's case, consulted with the episcopal members of the board of trustees before imposing the suspension ... on January 9, 1987. There was no consultation by the president or his representative with the senate's Committee on Academic Freedom and Tenure, nor was any indication given as to what immediate harm might be caused to Professor Curran or others by his resumption of teaching, outside as well as inside an ecclesiastical faculty, after his return from leave and pending the outcome of the *ad hoc* committee's deliberations.

Chancellor Hickey's conviction that suspension was necessary was forcefully conveyed in his January 9 letter to Professor Curran:

> In my letter of December 19, I expressly solicited your response to this question: How can you be permitted to retain your canonical mission "to teach in the name of the Church," when the Holy See has expressly declared that you are "not suitable nor eligible to teach Catholic Theology"? In your response to this question, you state that your canonical mission may never be withdrawn if you are successful in your defense in the upcoming hearings. But you articulate no conceivable basis on which a decision could be reached to permit you to retain your canonical mission to teach in the name of the Church, when the highest authorities of the Church have expressly and finally declared that you are not suitable to teach Catholic Theology. As I stated in my letter of December 19, it is difficult to conceive of a more "serious reason" to withdraw the canonical mission, or a "more serious pressing case" for suspension.

> . . .

Obviously the judgment of the Sacred Congregation for the Doctrine of the Faith, endorsed by the Congregation for Catholic Education and approved by Pope John Paul II, was entitled to great respect. It was not entitled to veneration. Cardinal Hickey was the chancellor and in important respects a chief administrative officer of a university with procedures that had been painstakingly developed ... , and those procedures were themselves entitled to respect and observance. The senate's Committee on Academic Freedom and Tenure should have been consulted by the president or his representative before action was taken by the chancellor that had the effect of suspending Professor Curran from teaching outside as well as inside the ecclesiastical faculties. And the suspension should not have been invoked unless it could have been shown that, after twenty-one years of teaching at the Catholic University of America without apparent harm to anyone, Professor Curran's return to teaching would suddenly endanger either himself or others.

Due Process and Tenure

The *ad hoc* committee of the Academic Senate proceeded cautiously and deliberately. In a preliminary hearing it examined opposing counsel on what each considered the appropriate purpose of the full hearing. During the hearing each side was permitted to call and examine witnesses and to submit exhibits. A verbatim record of the hearing was kept and made available to both parties. And the committee, following the completion of its deliberations, issued an extensive report....

Counsel for Chancellor Hickey contended in the preliminary hearing that the Sacred Congregation's "deliberation was binding on the Committee as a matter of canon law" and that no further hearing was necessary.... Counsel for Professor Curran argued that the Sacred Congregation's statement was not binding on the university and that the committee should consider countervailing evidence as well as the potential effects of withdrawing Professor Curran's canonical mission.

That the committee adopted this second approach seems to the [AAUP's] investigating committee both proper for a proposed action of such consequence to a tenured faculty member and consistent with the provisions of the faculty handbook. These provide that the burden of proof "shall be satisfied only by clear and convincing evidence in the record considered as a whole." The *ad hoc* committee saw very clearly not only that Professor Curran's canonical mission might be removed but also that his tenure, in fact if not in name, might be taken along with it. . . .

. . .

. . . [W]ith the withdrawal of Professor Curran's canonical mission the "inherent contradiction" that disturbed the Sacred Congregation was resolved, for he no longer possessed the authority to teach in the name of the Church. Had he been permitted . . . to accept a position in the Department of Religion and Religious Education, which was eager to have him and he was quite willing to join, he would no longer have been teaching in an ecclesiastical faculty. Under the circumstances, it was unnecessary and, in the investigating committee's judgment, improper, for the administration and the board of trustees to place any restrictions on Professor Curran's teaching and, particularly, to insist that he not teach Catholic theology at Catholic University.

When Professor Curran was awarded tenure in 1971, he was adjudged competent by his faculty colleagues and the board of trustees and was assured of the right to teach in his area of competence until his retirement, subject to dismissal only for adequate cause established through due process. Even though he remains on leave of absence and thus nominally a member of the faculty, in not being permitted to teach Catholic theology, in a non-ecclesiastical as well as an ecclesiastical department, he has for all practical purposes been deprived of his tenure without due process and without adequate cause. The outcome that the *ad hoc* committee tried to prevent became a reality through the persistent adherence of the administration and the board to positions that this investigating committee finds untenable.

Academic Freedom

Ultimately Professor Curran lost his position in Catholic University's Department of Theology because of opinions expressed in his published works. As far as the investigating committee knows, no one in the university's administration had publicly raised questions about them. . . . Had it not been for the intervention of the Sacred Congregation for the Doctrine of the Faith, Professor Curran would undoubtedly still be active in the university's Department of Theology, a popular teacher, honored theologian, and respected colleague.

Under the 1940 *Statement of Principles on Academic Freedom and Tenure* . . . "[l]imitations of academic freedom because of religious or other aims of the institution should be clearly stated in writing at the time of the appointment." Catholic University has no statement labeled "Limitations," although . . . [a] relevant statement applying explicitly to faculty members in the Ecclesiastical Faculties, is contained in the Canonical Statutes: "These norms and practices concerning appointments to the Faculties are intended to assure fidelity to the revealing Word of God as it is transmitted by tradition and interpreted and safeguarded by the Magisterium of the Church and to safeguard academic freedom."

A faculty member, formerly dean of the School of Religious Studies, who had a main role in preparing this statement, informed the investigating committee that he looked upon it as a statement of limitations on both the faculty and the magisterium. . . . He noted also that the statement was not intended to preclude dissent from noninfallible teaching.

. . .

The president, chancellor, and board of trustees seemed all too ready, nonetheless, to conclude that the Sacred Congregation's declaration was controlling and that withdrawal of Professor Curran's canonical mission had to follow as a matter of course. . . .

. . . In forcing Professor Curran to relinquish all teaching of Catholic theology at Catholic University, the administration and the board of trustees violated his academic freedom; for they were moved to their decision by a declaration of the Sacred Congregation for the Doctrine of the Faith based upon publications that were protected by academic freedom under the 1940 *Statement of Principles* and the policies of Catholic University itself.

The role of the board of trustees in this connection raises some puzzling questions. At least sixteen of the board's twenty clerical members were required to be members of the National Conference of Catholic Bishops. They were members, in short, of the very body that had set the tone for Catholic theological discussion in the United States since 1968. How could they have not spoken out while Professor Curran was subjected to the humiliation of a seven-year inquisition for exercising a right to dissent that the American bishops' own statement had acknowledged? . . .

. . . The university's autonomy and the academic freedom of its faculty may not have been important to the Sacred Congregation, but they should have been of first importance to the board of trustees. And who can say with assurance that this was not a crisis in the university's affairs, if not in those of Catholic higher education generally? Although initially the inquiry of the Sacred Congregation affected only Professor Curran, its repercussions have been felt throughout the university and far beyond its bounds. . . .

The board by its complicity in the actions against Professor Curran thus failed to protect academic freedom and the university's autonomy, two essential conditions of the kind of university that the Catholic University of America considered itself to be. . . .

Academic Freedom and Tenure: The Catholic University of America, ACADEME, Sept.-Oct. 1989, at 27, 35–38.

Consider the differences in approach and result taken by the AAUP and the *Curran* court. What are the strengths and limits of each approach?

2. Pope Benedict XVI (formerly the same Cardinal Ratzinger who sent the letter that caused the Board of Trustees to withdraw Father Curran's canonical mission) visited Catholic University during his first visit to the United States as pope and gave a speech on academic freedom. During the speech, Benedict endorsed a view of academic freedom that called on scholars to "search for the truth wherever careful analyses of evidence leads. . . ." The Pope was careful to note that academic freedom must be bounded within Catholic doctrine, however, noting, "Any appeal to the principle of academic freedom in order to justify positions that contradict the faith and the teaching of the Church would obstruct or even betray the university's identity and mission." Paul Schwartzman, *Nuanced View of Academic Freedom*, WASH. POST, Apr. 18, 2008, at A16. Are Pope Benedict's views on the appropriate relationship between Catholic doctrine and scholarly research consistent with the profession's view of academic freedom?

Michael W. McConnell,[a] *Academic Freedom in Religious Colleges and Universities,*

in LAW & CONTEMP. PROBS., Summer 1990, at 303, 306–07, 311–12.

Through the middle of the 19th century, an essentially religious, or dogmatic, understanding of truth pervaded higher education in America. . . . The modern university was born in a conscious attempt to free scholarly investigation from the strictures of the single, constrained understanding of the advancement of knowledge. Academic freedom became the central operating tenet of the modern secular university. Under this modern view, colleges and universities exist to advance the frontiers of knowledge; the test of knowledge is its ability to withstand the rigors of debate and disputation; the advancement of knowledge requires that the work of teachers and scholars be free from all constraints other than those of the academic discipline.

. . . This understanding assumed its canonical form in the 1940 State of Principles on Academic Freedom and Tenure. . . .

. . .

The 1940 Statement, however, [r]ecognizing that the older tradition of the pursuit of knowledge was still common . . . said that "[l]imitation of academic freedom because of religious or other aims of the institution should be clearly stated in writing at the time of the appointment." This statement . . . did not explicitly authorize or condone limitations on academic freedom, but it assumed they would exist and regulated them through the requirement of open disclosure.

. . .

The small number of exceptional institutions remaining argues for, not against, their accommodation. When the vast majority of academic institutions are committed to the view of knowledge reflected in the principle of secular academic freedom, there is little to be gained and much to be lost from quelling the few dissenting institutional voices. As *religious* institutions, such schools are more valuable as exemplars of an alternative understanding of knowledge than they could ever be as (in many cases, unexceptional) secular colleges.

As an alternative rational for the religious accommodation, the 1988 subcommittee mentioned (without repudiating or endorsing) the argument that "many of these institutions usefully function as 'decompression chambers' that ease the passage into the larger world for the religiously provincial." The condescension—indeed bigotry—of this suggestion seems to have passed unnoticed.

The AAUPs experts on academic freedom have confessed themselves unable to "discern a principled reason" why religious colleges and universities should not be required to conform to the same standards of academic freedom appropriate to secular institutions. I would suggest three reasons: (1) religiously distinctive colleges and universities make important contributions to the intellectual life of their faculty, their students, and the nation,

---

a. Professor McConnell is now a judge on the United States Court of Appeals for the Tenth Circuit.

and secular academic freedom in its unmodified form would lead quickly to the extinction of these institutions; (2) the insistence on a single model of truth-seeking is inconsistent with the antidogmatic principles on which the case for academic freedom rests; and (3) even if the extension of secular academic freedom to religious institutions were desirable on intellectual grounds, it would subvert the ability of religious communities to maintain and transmit their beliefs, and thus undermine religious freedom.

Judith Jarvis Thomson & Matthew W. Finkin, *Academic Freedom and Church–Related Higher Education: A Reply to Professor McConnell,*

in 53 LAW & CONTEMP. PROBS., Summer 1990 at 419, 420–23.

Professor McConnell gives three reasons for exempting religious institutions from the obligation to allow for academic freedom. . . .

. . .

The academic profession is in no position to ignore consequentialist arguments for or against academic freedom. The 1940 Statement itself justifies the entitlement to academic freedom on consequentialist grounds: it says that "[i]nsitutions of higher education are conducted for the common good," that "[t]he common good depends upon the free search for truth and its free exposition," and that "[a]cademic freedom is essential to these purposes." . . .

The document's consequentialist ground for academic freedom is often expressed in a metaphor: truth is most likely to be discovered in a free marketplace for ideas. McConnell's first consequentialist ground for academic freedom can be thought of as the claim that the marketplace for ideas needs regulation if it is to serve the purpose it is valued for—thus truth is most likely to be discovered in a marketplace for ideas which is so regulated that certain options do not disappear. . . .

Now our own view is that religiously distinctive colleges and universities do make important contributions to intellectual life. And we think it possible that those contributions could not be made—or anyway could not be so effectively made—by any other social organizations or agencies than the religiously distinctive colleges and universities. But three things seem to us to be in doubt.

In the first place, we doubt whether their making those contributions requires them to limit the academic freedom of their faculties. Professor McConnell asserts that requiring those institutions to provide their faculties with "secular academic freedom in its unmodified form would lead quickly to [their] extinction." This seems to us false on its face. It is also an insult to the religions which those institutions represent, for it presupposes that the religions themselves are instrinsically so far unattractive or implausible that the faculties at those institutions cannot be expected voluntarily to advance the denomination's educational ends, and that they will do so only if they labor under the threat of discharge for doctrinal infidelity. . . .

A weaker claim would have been more plausible and less insulting, namely, that requiring those institutions to provide their faculties with "secular academic freedom in its unmodified form" would place the institutions at risk of extinction—given a good governance system, in which the faculty has a voice as to the institution's aims. This brings us to our second doubt. What needs showing, after all, is not merely that it conduces to the common good that there be religiously distinctive institutions of higher education, but that their contribution to the common good is sufficiently great to justify them in coercing their faculties in order to place themselves beyond the risk of extinction.

.   .   .

We think it is unquestionable that much serious religious scholarship is engaged in at the religiously distinctive colleges and universities. We think it is also unquestionable that much serious religious scholarship is engaged in at institutions which, whether religiously distinctive or not, do not coerce their faculties. . . . We suspect . . . that policing a faculty for creedal conformity is unlikely to create a climate in which the very best religious scholarship will emerge. To McConnell, this suspicion may seem no more than an expression of faith, based upon a secular measure of scholarly worth. But to us, it seems historically justified.

. . . Might it not be asked whether the religiously distinctive institutions really are special in the respect McConnell points to here? The religiously distinctive institutions do, as we said, make important contributions to intellectual life; could the same not be said of institutions distinguished by their commitment to a particular body of political or social or economic doctrine? . . . In some views, perhaps McConnell's, the religiously distinctive institutions make a *more important* contribution to the intellectual life than do other doctrinally committed institutions. Our third doubt is whether it is open to the American professoriate—through its organized voice, the AAUP—to take a stand on the substantive question whether they do. [T]he 1940 Statement declined to distinguish religious from "other aims," and we greatly doubt that the AAUP is so much as institutionally competent to make such judgments.

Questions on Academic Freedom and Religious Colleges and Universities

Consider the competing visions of how religious colleges and universities should approach the issue of academic freedom. Which view do you agree with? Should these institutions be limited by religious doctrine?

CHAPTER 7

TEACHING, RESEARCH, AND SHARED GOVERNANCE

A. CLASSROOM BOUNDARIES

Furumoto v. Lyman

United States District Court for the Northern District of California, 1973.
362 F.Supp. 1267.

■ RENFREW, DISTRICT JUDGE.

Plaintiffs, former students at Stanford University, brought this action under 42 U.S.C. §§ 1983 and 1985 and the First, Fifth, Eighth, Ninth and Fourteenth Amendments.... Defendants are members of the Board of Trustees, administration and faculty of Stanford University. The claims arose from plaintiffs' participation in a disturbance in a classroom at Stanford, for which they were given indefinite suspensions from the University. Plaintiffs seek an injunction preventing defendants from enforcing the campus regulations which were applied to them and from continuing plaintiffs' suspensions. Each plaintiff also seeks $125,000 in damages plus interest, attorneys' fees, costs, and any other appropriate relief. Defendants have moved for summary judgment.

On January 18, 1972, shortly after 11:00 A.M., approximately fifteen people, including plaintiffs, entered Room 127, McCullough Building, on the Stanford University campus, where a scheduled quiz in a course on electrical engineering was being given under the supervision of Professor William Shockley.[2] The racial or ethnic composition of the group was mostly non-Caucasian. Although plaintiffs were registered Stanford students it is not clear that all members of the group were Stanford students. The group's sole purpose was to condemn Shockley's view of genetics while demanding that he debate one Cedric Clark publicly. The intrusion was a planned event, with the members of the group acting in concert.

Shockley announced in a loud and clear voice to the group immediately after they had entered that they were interrupting a quiz and should leave the room. They refused to leave. Shockley then asked them to identify themselves, which they also refused to do. Most of the group settled in the rear of the room while a tall, black man, unidentified, went to the front and began to read a statement. An unidentified black woman began passing out copies of the statement to class members. The statement declared that Professor Shockley had been "found" by "Third World People" to be "racist" in his writings, speeches and actions. It called his theories "Nazi race

---

2. Professor Shockley, a winner of the Nobel Prize in 1956 for his work in transistor physics, is also well known for his theories on eugenics and dysgenics. However, at no time prior to January 18, 1972, did Professor Shockley ever lecture on or discuss these theories of eugenics and dysgenics in that course in electrical engineering.

theory" and claimed that he was seeking to justify "killing the future generation of black and other poor people...." It concluded that: *"We will not allow this to happen."* (emphasis in statement) "As a first step," it demanded that Professor Shockley meet one Cedric Clark in a public debate by February 28, 1972.

Shockley took Polaroid snapshots of the intruders, although the latter covered their faces. Mr. Troy Barbee, a member of the University staff, having received word of the intrusion, came to the classroom. Shockley gave the Polaroid exposures to him, but the black man, having finished his statement, walked toward Barbee, grabbed the exposures from him, and passed them to other intruders. They were never recovered. In an attempt to recover them, however, Barbee in effect pushed the black man down to the floor. Other intruders then rose and shouted accusations at Barbee. This event caused high tensions and the possibility of further disturbances, although generally tensions were low throughout the incident.

Before the black man had begun reading his statement, Shockley had turned on a cassette recorder. The black man turned it off, but Shockley turned it back on. After the black man had finished reading the statement, he removed the cassette and threw it along the floor to other intruders. The cassette too was not recovered.

The action of the intruders effectively prevented the students in Shockley's electrical engineering class from taking the scheduled quiz.

During the black man's statement, Shockley corrected his pronunciation of "eugenics" and "dysgenics." Shockley entered into a debate or dialogue, mostly with the black woman. He, in the words of the Stanford hearing officer, "actively, engagingly, seductively, and provocatively contributed to the continuation" of this debate. The intruders made "baiting and accusatory type statements" of Shockley's racism, allegations of genocide, and equated Shockley's views with the racial views of Hitler. After the debate, which lasted less than thirty minutes, Shockley agreed to give serious consideration to a request for a debate made in the conventional manner as long as certain conditions were met. Once this understanding was reached, the intruders left the room.

Plaintiffs, and one other student, were charged in writing with having violated a university policy in disrupting the effective carrying out of a university function or approved activity.[3] In accordance with Stanford's

---

3. Stanford's Policy on Campus Disruption reads as follows:

"Because the rights of free speech and peaceable assembly are fundamental to the democratic process, Stanford firmly supports the rights of all members of the University community to express their views or to protest against actions and opinions with which they disagree.

"All members of the University also share a concurrent obligation to maintain on the campus an atmosphere conducive to scholarly pursuits; to preserve the dignity and seriousness of University ceremonies and public exercises; and to respect the rights of all individuals.

"The following regulations are intended to reconcile these objectives:

"It is a violation of University policy for a member of the faculty, staff, or student body to (1) prevent or disrupt the effective carrying out of a University function or approved activity, such as lectures, meetings, interviews, ceremonies, the conduct of University business in a University office, and public events; (2) obstruct the legitimate movement of any person about the campus or in any University building or facility.

"Members of the faculty, staff, and student body have an obligation to leave a University building or facility when asked

rules, this case was heard by a hearing officer, who was a professor of law. The hearing lasted eight days. The hearing officer concluded that additional warnings by Shockley that the intruders were disrupting the class would have been ignored.

[The hearing officer found that plaintiffs Alice Furumoto, Don Lee, and Kwonping Ho each had knowingly intruded on Professor Shockley's electrical engineering class for the purpose of condemning his genetic theories and demanding a public debate. The hearing officer also found that Furumoto had "made provocative and derisive comments to Professor Shockley" and Ho had "asked one of the students in the course if he 'knew what his professor was advocating.'" The university was unable to prove beyond a reasonable doubt that a fourth individual had been present or aided or abetted the plaintiffs.] After a hearing, the Campus Judicial Panel affirmed the hearing officer's findings and recommended the indefinite suspension of plaintiffs.[4] The President of Stanford, defendant Richard W. Lyman, adopted that recommendation, and plaintiffs were indefinitely suspended from Stanford.

... Plaintiffs claim that defendants denied them exercise of their First Amendment rights; that defendants applied to them unconstitutionally vague and overly broad campus regulations on disruption; that the sanction given them, indefinite suspension, constitutes cruel and unusual punishment in that it is disproportionate to the offense charged; and finally that defendants supported racism by giving Professor Shockley a forum and "academic respectability" for his genetic theories and by punishing plaintiffs for their anti-racist actions, causing them grave and irreparable injury.

In their second cause of action, based on 42 U.S.C. § 1985(3), plaintiffs claim that defendants entered into a conspiracy to deprive them of equal protection of the law in that defendants supported racism and punished plaintiffs' efforts to oppose racism, that defendants sanctioned them but not the University band which had disrupted classes, and that defendants prosecuted them but not others who took similar actions on other occasions.

. . .

The complaint claims that Professor Shockley's writings are racist, "highly offensive" to anyone opposing racism, and "antagonize and anger" those in opposition. These claims upon analysis simply amount to vehement disagreement with another person's exercise of his First Amendment rights, not a statement of a claim under § 1983. The hearing officer's finding that Shockley did contribute to the continuation of the debate in his classroom does not suggest any deprivation of plaintiffs' civil rights. The second cause of action simply includes Shockley in the alleged conspiracy and again is

to do so in the furtherance of the above regulations by a member of the University community acting in an official role and identifying himself as such; members of the faculty, staff and student body also have an obligation to identify themselves when requested to do so by such a member of the University community who has reasonable grounds to believe that the person(s) has violated section (1) or (2) of this policy and who has so informed the person(s)."

4. Indefinite suspension is a two-year minimum suspension from the University with the possibility of future enrollment being contingent upon a finding by the appropriate campus judicial body that reinstatement "serves the interest of the University community."

purely conclusory. Thus, plaintiffs have failed to state a claim upon which relief can be granted against Professor Shockley.

To establish their claims under § 1983, plaintiffs must show that they were deprived of civil rights by the remaining defendants,[11] who in their official capacities were acting "under color of state law." [Plaintiffs failed to prove that the defendants' actions were state actions. California's grants to Stanford of corporate powers and privileges, permission to charge tuition to state residents, certain tax exemptions, and "authorization of the use of eminent domain on Stanford's behalf" do not evidence state control of the university, only the policy of advancing private higher education. In setting requirements for awarding degrees, the state was not exercising control of the university, only protecting individuals against private institutions providing substandard education. "The State's concern for student discipline . . . [does not] amount to direct involvement in Stanford's disciplinary process. Finally, plaintiff's argument that Stanford performs a vital public function which, if Stanford did not exist, the State would have to fulfill, could be extended to virtually all private endeavors. Few institutions, if any, would remain in the private realm."]

. . .

Even if state action were present in this case, plaintiffs' claims fail.

Although it is not entirely clear from plaintiffs' complaint, one element of their claim seems to be that defendants punished them for their expression of opposition to racism, thus denying them their rights under the First Amendment.

That the plaintiffs as students retained their First Amendment rights upon entering the University is clear beyond question. *Tinker v. Des Moines School Dist.*, 393 U.S. 503, 506 (1969); *Healy v. James*, 408 U.S. 169, 180 (1972). But those rights do not include an absolute right to determine how, where, and when such protected expression will take place:

> ". . . conduct by the student, in class or out of it, which for any reason—whether it stems from time, place, or type of behavior— materially disrupts classwork or involves substantial disorder or invasion of the rights of others is, of course, not immunized by the constitutional guarantee of freedom of speech." 393 U.S. at 513.

That the Stanford regulations are consistent with these authorities is clear from a consideration of the history of the problem which led to their adoption and the very nature of a university environment. Although American campus life has become quiescent in the past few months, the history of university up-heavals and turmoil is too recent to require any detailed statement. In the words of the Report of the President's Commission on Campus Unrest (1970) [President's Commission], " . . . the last decade clearly shows a gradual movement toward more disruptive, violent, and even terrorist tactics in campus protest, and a steady and significant growth in the number of radical students and tactical extremists." After studying the history of the campus disturbances, the Commission found that:

---

11. The remaining defendants are Richard W. Lyman, the President of Stanford; John Kaplan, Chairman of the Campus Judicial Panel, which adjudicated the charges against plaintiffs; and Henry Ramsey, Jr., the hearing officer who determined the facts in plaintiffs' cases.

"Universities have not adequately prepared themselves to respond to disruption. They have been without suitable plans, rules, or sanctions. Some administrators and faculty members have responded irresolutely. Frequently, announced sanctions have not been applied. Even more frequently, the lack of appropriate organization within the university has rendered its response ineffective. The university's own house must be placed in order." [President's Commission].

It is to this deficiency which Stanford was plainly responding with its Policy on Campus Disruption. That Policy was not an unreasonable response considering the fragility of a university, the inherent inconsistency of authoritarianism with intellectual freedom, and the need for order:

"An institution committed to intellectual freedom, to individuality, and to the toleration of eccentricity, is bound to be loosely organized at best, and its internal processes of governance and law are bound to be somewhat uncertain." [President's Commission].

Stanford's Policy on Campus Disruption is limited to the most egregious interferences with campus order and the rights of others. It does not approach being prior restraint, as in *Hammond v. South Carolina State College*, 272 F. Supp. 947, 949–950 (D.S.C. 1967). Nor does it interfere with the right of free association. There is no evidence that Stanford officials used the regulations to intimidate plaintiffs or any other members of the academic community.

In this case plaintiffs and other members of the disrupting group had other means available for challenging Professor Shockley to a debate. Even if, as plaintiffs have indicated elsewhere, there was need to have black people confront Shockley, there was no reason given why they could not have waited until after class to present, briefly but completely, their challenge. Even here, they did not, of course, have a right to infringe his personal liberty.

... [C]ounsel for plaintiffs put forward the position that in academic life a professor must debate his views publicly if challenged. While this Court would agree that this may be desirable as a part of intellectual responsibility to consider opposing views and respond to them, that responsibility cannot extend to mandate public debating. Such a requirement would in itself be a potential inhibitor of academic freedom, since many individuals simply do not have the personality or talents to perform comfortably and adequately in oral debating. Such a requirement, if widely adopted, could drive otherwise qualified and valuable scholars from academic life. Professor Shockley thus had a First Amendment right to choose the medium for his response to his challengers or indeed even whether to respond at all. Plaintiffs cannot justify their actions by claiming that Professor Shockley would otherwise have been able to avoid a public debate.

Plaintiffs' counsel also advanced the position that each member of the academic community has the right to respond to activities which he finds morally offensive, determined by his personal standards, in ways that he feels are necessary. While this Court admires the forthrightness of counsel and his belief in the integrity of individual judgment, it views such a principle as ultimately destructive of the university and of free social life in general in that it would likely lead either to anarchy or to the rule of the mob.

For these reasons, this Court holds that the defendants did not deny nor interfere with plaintiffs' First Amendment rights.

. . .

Plaintiffs claim that defendants supported racism by affording Professor Shockley a forum and academic respectability while punishing plaintiffs for their actions in opposition to racism.[30] ... [T]he Supreme Court has held that:

> "... absent proof of false statements knowingly or recklessly made by him, a teacher's exercise of his right to speak on issues of public importance may not furnish the basis for his dismissal from public employment." *Pickering v. Board of Education*, 391 U.S. 563, 574 (1968).

That reasoning appears equally applicable here as to Professor Shockley's right to express his particular views with which plaintiffs disagree. Again, it must be remembered that the record is uncontroverted that at no time prior to January 18, 1972, did Professor Shockley ever lecture on or even discuss his theories of eugenics and dysgenics in the course in electrical engineering which plaintiffs disrupted. In this case, then, unless plaintiffs could meet the *Pickering* criteria with respect to Shockley's views, they could not begin to make a case that defendants supported racism by giving him a position. With respect to theoretical work, in contrast to factual description, a showing of falsity would be extremely difficult if not conceptually impossible.

Since Professor Shockley's views have not been shown by plaintiffs to fall outside the First Amendment and the scope of academic freedom, defendants cannot be charged with racism for giving him an academic position.

In contrast to their claims under § 1983, plaintiffs do not base their § 1985(3) cause of action upon the contention that defendants' actions constituted state action. In *Collins v. Hardyman*, 341 U.S. 651 (1951), the Supreme Court in effect read into § 1985 a state-action requirement. The Court created an exception to this requirement, however, in *Griffin v. Breckenridge*, 403 U.S. 88 (1971). The key language describing the parameters of the exception is as follows:

> "The language requiring intent to deprive of *equal* protection, or *equal* privileges and immunities, means that there must be some racial, or perhaps otherwise class-based, invidiously discriminating animus behind the conspirators' action. The conspiracy, in other words, must aim at a deprivation of the equal enjoyment of rights secured by the law to all." 403 U.S. at 102.

Griffin involved allegations of a racially motivated conspiracy made by plaintiffs who were members of a racial minority and who claimed that they were the targets of the conspiracy. The Court expressly left undecided the question of whether an intent other than racial bias would bring an action within § 1985(3). There is no evidence here that defendants had a particular racial intent in taking action against plaintiffs. Plaintiffs assert again that defendants supported racism "by presenting the views of defendant Shockley on campus" and by denying plaintiffs equal protection of the law. They also

---

30. Stanford has, however, twice rejected, once very recently, the offer by Professor Shockley to teach a course dealing with his genetic theories.

assert a violation of equal protection guarantees by defendants' alleged selective prosecution of plaintiffs (persons of Asian ethnic origin).

The Supreme Court in *Griffin* v. *Breckenridge* stressed that the exception to state action in § 1985(3) was a precisely limited one and did not constitute a "general federal tort law." 403 U.S. at 101–102. In extending *Griffin*, thus, precision must be retained. The only relevant classes in which plaintiffs would appear to fall are "non-white opponents of racism" and "disrupters of university operations for social or political reasons." Neither of these is sufficiently limited to pass the *Griffin* test, and plaintiffs have failed to show or allege other facts demonstrating the necessary class-based, discriminatory intent.

Therefore, plaintiffs' claims do not come within the scope of § 1985(3). Even if § 1985(3) were applicable, however, plaintiffs would fail on the merits.

Plaintiffs allege that the "conspiracy was engaged in to foster, promote, encourage, advocate, and support racism by presenting the views of defendant Shockley on campus and to deny plaintiffs equal protection of the law." The Court has already held that defendants did not support racism by giving Professor Shockley an academic position, and plaintiffs have not in the least demonstrated that defendants closed all other means of expressing their opposition to racism and to Professor Shockley. Nor have they shown that they were "prosecuted" for their anti-racism rather than for violations of valid campus regulations on campus disruption.

Plaintiffs' next charge is selective prosecution in that they were prosecuted but not others who performed similar acts. This charge does not have substance. Plaintiffs contend that they were prosecuted, but not the University band which also disrupted classes during the football season. The band's activities were undoubtedly a legitimate activity upon campus which must be accommodated with other legitimate activities. Plaintiffs' actions, in contrast, were clearly proscribed.

Plaintiffs also contend that other students disrupted classes but were not prosecuted. There were, however, two recent previous prosecutions for classroom disruption at Stanford. The Stanford official in charge of bringing actions against students also offered a reasonable explanation why other charges were not brought, stressing in particular the problem of identifying the students involved.[33] Plaintiffs have not demonstrated that this explanation is unacceptable. Moreover, they fail to satisfy the elements which the Supreme Court has required to establish a violation of equal protection in a *criminal* context:

> " . . . the conscious exercise of some selectivity in enforcement is not in itself a federal constitutional violation. Even though the statistics in this case might imply a policy of selective enforcement, it was not stated that the selection was deliberately based upon an unjustifiable

---

33. Other reasons given were that some professors would adjourn their classes when the disturbance began, thus creating difficult problems of proof. Some professors would welcome those disrupting, with some students later complaining. Professors would in some cases take a vote of their students on whether the intruders would be welcomed or not, with the intruders leaving if the vote went against them. Other cases were found simply not to be sufficiently strong cases of disruption warranting disciplinary action.

standard such as race, religion, or other arbitrary classification." *Oyler v. Boles*, 368 U.S. 448, 456 (1962).

Campus officials must have a wide discretion in determining what action should be taken for violations of campus discipline. As long as the reasons behind their selectivity are not invidious or arbitrary, a court should not intervene.

For these reasons, plaintiffs' claims under § 1985(3) are without merit. There being no genuine issue as to any material fact, the remaining defendants are entitled to summary judgment as a matter of law.

Questions and Comments on *Furumoto*

1. What if the students had not disrupted Shockley's class during an exam, but instead silently entered the classroom with protest signs? What limitations, if any, are there on student speech in a university classroom? *See generally* Part IV, *infra*.

Given the status of the classroom as a place where diverse ideas often come into conflict, and the idea of a university as a place to foster diverse thinking, how should colleges and universities respond to potentially disruptive speech and activities like those at issue in *Furumoto*? Can you draft regulations to deal with these types of disruptions?

2. Law professor Charles Ogletree was a student at Stanford at the time and has written of the events surrounding the *Furumoto* case:

> At Stanford, Shockley became interested in the field of genetics, though he had no genetics training, and began to take positions on race, genetics, and intelligence.... Interestingly, Shockley's ideas were rather summarily dismissed by Stanford scientists with some knowledge of genetics, but, undaunted, he presented his views at forums around the country. His views were so racist and shocking that we could not ignore them. He argued that the future of the American population was threatened because African–Americans had lower IQs and were producing low-IQ children faster than Americans with higher IQs.
>
> . . .
>
> On November 9, 1972, as the chairman of the Stanford BSU, I issued a public challenge to Shockley, to debate his genetics theories with the psychology professor Cedric Clark and the genetics professor L.L. Cavali–Sforza, both of Stanford. The debate was scheduled for January 23, 1973. At the same time that Professor Clark was preparing for the debate with Shockley, he also joined the Nation of Islam. As the debate approached, student, faculty, and public interest reached a fevered pitch. The debate was planned for Memorial Auditorium, which held nearly two thousand people.
>
> ... To no one's surprise, Memorial Auditorium was filled beyond capacity, with people in the aisles, the balcony, and jamming all the doors.... The Stanford Fire Department knew that, but chose not to create any animosity among the Fruit of Islam, the young men who provided security for the Nation of Islam, or the black students.
>
> That night, rather than make a serious case for his views, Shockley instead attacked those African–American students who were at Stanford. Not satisfied simply to restate his views, he went on to declare that the IQ of the average African–American increases one percent for every one percent of Caucasian ancestry. He suggested that Americans could learn from Nazi experiments with eugenics.... Although he was booed after making these points, Shockley had, perhaps unwittingly, accomplished his goal. His debate points were weak, but they probably reinforced the views of those who

believed blacks to be inferior to whites. Shockley lost the public debate, but we, the *Brown* babies, had to contend with the powerful impression even racist ideas can have on vulnerable minds.

> Ultimately, our public strategy was successful.... [Shockley] retired from teaching the year we graduated and never generated any serious following in the academic community in general or in the genetics field in particular.

CHARLES J. OGLETREE, JR., ALL DELIBERATE SPEED 49–50 (2004).

The debate Ogletree describes occurred about one year after the protest at issue in *Furumoto*. Alice Furumoto's descriptions of the events leading up to her protest provide further historical context. Racial strife on the Stanford campus was a problem larger than Professor Shockley; mistreatment of minority students by their professors was "rampant." The students sought to use Shockley's overt racism to call attention to the more widespread problem. Asian students were particularly concerned with Shockley's positions on race because he "used Asians as a cover to say that he wasn't racist against blacks" by happily admitting that Asians scored higher than whites. Furumoto points out, however, that Shockley did not advocate sexual relationships between whites and Asians to increase white intelligence or press for increased college admissions for Asians compared to whites—positions analogous to those he took with respect to blacks and whites. Telephone Interview by Matthew Berns with Alice Furumoto–Dawson (Mar. 6, 2008).

3. What happened to the three students involved in the case?

Alice Furumoto had completed her requirements for graduation when the incident giving rise to the case occurred; Stanford nullified the credits from her last term in order to impose a two-year suspension. She deferred enrollment in the University of Hawaii's School of Medicine to challenge the decision. Furumoto twice applied to terminate the suspension. The first time, a panel consisting of one professor, one graduate student, one undergraduate, and one member of the administration (all white males, Furumoto notes) decided against her re-enrollment. The second panel (a visiting professor from France, a Chicano medical student, a female Caucasian undergraduate, and a member of the administration) voted three-to-one for re-enrollment, with the French professor expressing amusement at the suspension "for so minor and civil a protest action." Stanford removed mention of the suspension from her record, and Furumoto graduated with a Bachelor of Sciences in Biology at age twenty-two. She later obtained a Ph.D. in Epidemiologic Science and now works at the University of Chicago's Center for Interdisciplinary Health Disparities Research, "still engaged in addressing the social injustices of American society, in the field of health inequities." E-mail from Alice Furumoto–Dawson to Matthew Berns (Feb. 14, 2008) (on file with author).

Don Lee, who was a senior at the time of his expulsion, was never able to regain admission to Stanford. *Id.*

The third student, Ho Kwon Ping, now appears as number twenty on *Forbes's* list of Singapore's forty richest people, with a net worth of $195 million. His Banyan Tree resort chain is one of the biggest in Asia. *Singapore's 40 Richest: #20 Ho Kwon Ping*, FORBES.COM, Aug. 24, 2006, http://www.forbes.com/lists/2006/79/06singapore_Ho-Kwon–Ping_YY3K.html. After a backpacking trip in Southeast Asia during his youth that left him "distressed by irresponsible tourism," Ho Kwon Ping has focused his businesses on corporate responsibility and ecological conservation. Adeline Chong, *Ho Kwon Ping: Rooted in Romance*, BRANDCHANNEL.COM, Jan. 31, 2005, http://www.brandchannel.com/ careers_profile.asp?cr_id=52. After his suspension from Stanford, he enrolled as a transfer student at Cornell, but felt displaced and returned to Singapore, where he served in the army and then graduated from the University of Singapore. Upon graduation, he worked as a journalist and was placed in two-months solitary confinement for pro-Communist writings in the *Far Eastern Economic*

Review. Nureza Ahmad, *Ho Kwon Ping*, NATIONAL LIBRARY SINGAPORE, June 9, 2004, http://infopedia.nlb.gov.sg/articles/SIP_434_2005–01–14.html.

White v. Davis

Supreme Court of California, 1975.
13 Cal.3d 757, 533 P.2d 222, 120 Cal.Rptr. 94.

■ TOBRINER, J.

. . .

Plaintiff Hayden White, a professor of history at the University of California at Los Angeles and a resident taxpayer of the City of Los Angeles, instituted this taxpayer's suit against defendant Edward M. Davis, Chief of Police of the City of Los Angeles, seeking to enjoin the alleged illegal expenditure of public funds in connection with the police department's conduct of covert intelligence gathering activities at UCLA. The complaint alleges that with the authorization of Chief Davis, members of the Los Angeles Police Department, serving as "secret informers and undercover agents," have registered as students at UCLA, have attended classes held at the university and have submitted reports to the police department of discussions occurring in such classes. The complaint also alleges that the undercover police agents have joined university-recognized organizations, have attended public and private meetings of such organizations and have made reports on discussions at such meetings. The reports of these under-cover agents are allegedly maintained by the police department in files, "commonly designated as 'police dossiers'." Finally, the complaint alleges that the reports and dossiers compiled by the police pursuant to these covert surveillance activities "pertain to no illegal activity or acts."

Asserting that the expenditure of public funds for such operation is illegal because such activity "inhibits the exercise of freedom of speech and assembly, and abridges the right of due process of law and of privacy" in violation of the federal and state Constitutions, the complaint sought to enjoin the police department from expending funds for such activities in the future.

. . .

The most familiar limitations on police investigatory and surveillance activities, of course, find embodiment in the Fourth Amendment of the federal Constitution and article I, section 13 (formerly art. I, § 19) of the California Constitution. On numerous occasions in the past, these provisions have been applied to preclude specific ongoing police investigatory practices [including the conducting of "warrantless surveillance of private residences by means of concealed microphones" and "routine and continual surveillance of public restrooms"]. . . .

Unlike these past cases involving the limits on police surveillance prescribed by the constitutional "search and seizure" provisions, the instant case presents the more unusual question of the limits placed upon police investigatory activities by the guarantees of freedom of speech. . . . As discussed below, this issue is not entirely novel; to our knowledge, however, the present case represents the first instance in which a court has confronted the issue in relation to ongoing police surveillance of a *university community*.

Our analysis of the limits imposed by the First Amendment upon police surveillance activities must begin with the recognition that with respect to First Amendment freedoms "the Constitution's protection is not limited to direct interference with fundamental rights." *Healy v. James* (1972) 408 U.S. 169. Thus, although police surveillance of university classrooms and organization meetings may not constitute a direct prohibition of speech or association, such surveillance may still run afoul of the constitutional guarantee if the effect of such activity is to chill constitutionally protected activity. "In the domain of these indispensable liberties, whether of speech, press, or association, the decisions of this Court recognize that abridgement of such rights, even though unintended, may inevitably follow from varied forms of governmental action." *N.A.A.C.P. v. Alabama* (1958) 357 U.S. 449. As the United States Supreme Court stated recently in *Healy v. James, supra,* 408 U.S. 169, 183: "We are not free to disregard the practical realities. Mr. Justice Stewart has made the salient point: 'Freedoms such as these are protected not only against heavy-handed frontal attack, but also from being stifled by more subtle governmental interference.' "

As a practical matter, the presence in a university classroom of undercover officers taking notes to be preserved in police dossiers must inevitably inhibit the exercise of free speech both by professors and students. . . .

. . .

. . . As the United States Supreme Court has recognized time and again: "The vigilant protection of constitutional freedoms is nowhere more vital than in the community of American schools." *Shelton v. Tucker,* (1960) 364 U.S. 479, 487.

In the past, threats to academic freedom have generally arisen from governmental conduct involving significantly less intrusion into the academic community than posed by the police activities at issue in the instant case. Thus, prior cases have most frequently involved either state statutes inquiring into teacher's organizational associations, *see, e.g., Shelton v. Tucker, supra,* 364 U.S. 479, or provisions requiring teachers to sign overly broad loyalty oaths. *See, e.g., Wieman v. Updegraff* (1952) 344 U.S. 183. . . . Our research reveals only one previous instance, *Sweezy v. New Hampshire,* (1957) 354 U.S. 234, in which governmental inquiry sought to reach inside the classroom itself; the Supreme Court's stinging condemnation of that intrusive investigative effort illuminates the constitutional issues presented by the instant case. . . . The police investigatory conduct at issue unquestionably poses at least as debilitating a threat to academic freedom as that presented by the governmental inquiry in *Sweezy.* According to the allegations of the complaint, which for purposes of this appeal must be accepted as true, the Los Angeles Police Department has established a network of undercover agents which keeps regular check on discussions occurring in various university classes. Because the identity of such police officers is unknown, no professor or student can be confident that whatever opinion he may express in class will not find its way into a police file. If the after-the-fact inquiry conducted in *Sweezy* threatened to cast a pall of orthodoxy over classroom debates, the covert presence of governmental agents within the classroom itself must cast a deeper shadow.

The crucible of new thought is the university classroom; the campus is the sacred ground of free discussion. Once we expose the teacher or the student to possible future prosecution for the ideas he may express, we forfeit the security that nourishes change and advancement. The censorship of totalitarian regimes that so often condemns developments in art, science and politics is but a step removed from the inchoate surveillance of free discussion in the university; such intrusion stifles creativity and to a large degree shackles democracy.

. . .

In the instant case, defendant's burden of justification is very heavy indeed. Not only does the alleged covert intrusion into university classes and meetings pose a grave threat to the freedom of expression necessary for the preservation of the university as we know it today, but the complaint also alleges that the information gathered by the undercover police officers "pertains to no illegal activity or acts." Because this case arises upon the sustaining of a demurrer, defendant has as yet given no explanation or justification for the alleged surveillance; indeed, defendant has yet to file any answer at all in this case. Thus, inasmuch as we have determined that the complaint does demonstrate a prima facie violation of First Amendment rights, the trial court erred in sustaining defendant's demurrer. The judgment must accordingly be reversed and the case remanded for a trial on the merits.

. . .

As far as we are aware, the extensive, routine, covert police surveillance of university classes and organization meetings alleged by the instant complaint are unprecedented in our nation's history. The dangers implicit in such police operations, however, have long been understood.

The English historian, Sir Thomas Erskine May, writing in the middle of the 19th century, observed: "Next in importance to personal freedom is immunity from suspicions and jealous observation. Men may be without restraints upon their liberty; they may pass to and fro at pleasure: but if their steps are tracked by spies and informers, their words noted down for crimination, their associates watched as conspirators,—who shall say that they are free? Nothing is more revolting . . . than the espionage which forms part of the administrative system of continental despotisms. It haunts men like an evil genius, chills their gayety, restrains their wit, casts a shadow over their friendships, and blights their domestic hearth. The freedom of a country may be measured by its immunity from this baleful agency." (2 May, Constitutional History of England (1863) p. 275.)

The motto of one of our great universities—Stanford University—is "The wind of freedom blows," but the air of its classrooms would be befouled indeed by the presence of secret police. In the course of classroom debate some thoughts will be hazarded only as the trial balloons of new theories. Yet such propositions, that are tentative only, will nevertheless be recorded by police officers, filtered through the minds of the listening informers, often incorrectly misstated to their superiors and sometimes maliciously distended. Only a brave soul would dare to express anything other than orthodoxy under such circumstances. But the classroom of the university should be a forum of free expression; its very function would largely be destroyed by the practices described in the complaint before us.

The judgment is reversed.

Questions and Comments on *White v. Davis*

In 2006, an independent alumni group of the University of California at Los Angeles, the Bruin Alumni Association, established a website on which they offered $100 prizes to students who would turn over extensive documentation of cases in which professors showed political bias in the classroom. Piper Fogg, *Independent Alumni Group Offers $100 Bounties to UCLA Students Who Ferret Out Classroom Bias*, CHRON. HIGHER EDUC., Jan. 19, 2006. The group quickly withdrew the offer, which would have required students to collect "full lecture notes, classroom materials, and tape recordings of every class session for one course," after UCLA informed them that the offer violated university policies. Some members of the group's advisory board, which (according to its website) included a number of University of California professors, resigned over the matter. Piper Fogg, *No Bounty for Reports of 'Bias' at UCLA*, CHRON. HIGHER EDUC., Feb. 3, 2006, at A12. Did the offer violate the law?

Note on *Shelton v. Tucker*

Shelton v. Tucker, 364 U.S. 479 (1960), cited by the court in *White v. Davis*, involved a Fourteenth Amendment challenge to an Arkansas statute that "[compelled] every teacher, as a condition of employment in a state-supported school or college, to file annually an affidavit listing without limitation every organization to which he has belonged or regularly contributed within the preceding five years." B.T. Shelton, a teacher in a Little Rock public school, did not file the affidavit, and the school district declined to renew his contract. As the Court explained, Shelton was "not a member of the Communist Party or of any organization advocating the overthrow of the Government by force" but belonged to the NAACP. Other plaintiffs included Max Carr, an associate professor at the University of Arkansas, and Ernest T. Gephardt, another teacher from Little Rock. The plaintiffs alleged violations of their "rights to personal, associational, and academic liberty."

The Court held that the state has legitimate interests in ensuring public school teachers' fitness and competence, but that the statute's "unlimited and indiscriminate sweep" violated the teachers' associational freedom. The statute "requires [teachers] to list, without number, every conceivable kind of associational tie—social, professional, political, avocational, or religious. Many such relationships could have no possible bearing upon the teacher's occupational competence or fitness."

Justice Frankfurter wrote in dissent:

> . . . [I]t is not that I put a low value on academic freedom. *Wieman v. Updegraff*; *Sweezy v. New Hampshire*. It is because that very freedom, in its most creative reaches, is dependent in no small part upon the careful and discriminating selection of teachers. This process of selection is an intricate affair, a matter of fine judgment, and if it is to be informed, it must be based upon a comprehensive range of information. . . . [T]he information which the statute requires—and which may not be otherwise acquired than by asking the question which it asks—is germane to that selection. . . . Of course, if the information gathered by the required affidavits is used to further a scheme of terminating the employment of teachers solely because of their membership in unpopular organizations, that use will run afoul of the Fourteenth Amendment.

Although the majority emphasized the statute's overbreadth, one particular application of the Arkansas law may have been the court's deepest concern. The majority and both dissents took care to distinguish *Shelton* from *NAACP v. Alabama*, 357 U.S. 449, and *Bates v. Little Rock*, 361 U.S. 516, both of which dealt with a state's efforts to obtain the NAACP's membership lists. The Court had reason to suspect that this statute also specifically targeted NAACP members: listed among the statutory purposes was the need " 'to assist in the solution' of problems raised by 'the decisions of the United States Supreme Court in the school desegregation cases.' " The dissenters argued that the Court could not properly examine the possible uneven application of the statute: "It must be emphasized that [the case does not] actually present[] an issue of racial discrimination. The statute on its face applies to *all* Arkansas teachers irrespective of race, and there is no showing that it has been discriminatorily administered." Writing just two years after *Shelton*, Alexander Bickel noted:

> The decisive factor ... may have been the more-than-tenable surmise that Arkansas would dismiss teachers whom it had found to be members of the NAACP, and that dismissals would actually rest on such membership even though other, spurious grounds would be formally assigned. Despite the Court's assumption that the state may inquire into a teacher's commitments and use of his free time and may require him to disclose the totality of his affiliations, including one with the NAACP, a dismissal for NAACP membership would lack rationality, at least in absence of a showing of some particular interference with the teacher's professional effectiveness.... [L]ittle beyond a peaceable dedication to the ideal of equality of the races can be inferred from adherence to the NAACP, and such an inference without more is not relevant to any purpose the state is permitted to pursue. This problem, however, was not present in the case and might never arise....

ALEXANDER BICKEL, THE LEAST DANGEROUS BRANCH 53–54 (1962).

If Bickel is right, the majority framed *Shelton* as a case about the associational rights of teachers in part because the facial challenge to the statute prevented the Court from addressing the more compelling race question. Nevertheless, the case has come to stand for academic freedom.

Could a state draft legislation to ensure the fitness and character of its teachers without being as overly broad as the statute in *Shelton*?

Stanley Fish, *Conspiracy Theories 101*

N.Y.TIMES, July 23, 2006, at 13.

Kevin Barrett, a lecturer at the University of Wisconsin at Madison, has now taken his place alongside Ward Churchill of the University of Colorado as a college teacher whose views on 9/11 have led politicians and ordinary citizens to demand that he be fired.

Mr. Barrett, who has a one-semester contract to teach a course titled "Islam: Religion and Culture," acknowledged on a radio talk show that he has shared with students his strong conviction that the destruction of the World Trade Center was an inside job perpetrated by the American government. The predictable uproar ensued, and the equally predictable battle lines were drawn between those who disagree about what the doctrine of academic freedom does and does not allow.

Mr. Barrett's critics argue that academic freedom has limits and should not be invoked to justify the dissemination of lies and fantasies. Mr. Barrett's supporters (most of whom are not partisans of his conspiracy theory) insist that it is the very point of an academic institution to entertain all points of view, however unpopular. (This was the position taken by the university's provost, Patrick Farrell, when he ruled on July 10 that Mr. Barrett would be retained: "We cannot allow political pressure from critics of unpopular ideas to inhibit the free exchange of ideas.")

Both sides get it wrong. The problem is that each assumes that academic freedom is about protecting the content of a professor's speech; one side thinks that no content should be ruled out in advance; while the other would draw the line at propositions (like the denial of the Holocaust or the flatness of the world) considered by almost everyone to be crazy or dangerous.

But in fact, academic freedom has nothing to do with content. It is not a subset of the general freedom of Americans to say anything they like (so long as it is not an incitement to violence or is treasonous or libelous). Rather, academic freedom is the freedom of academics to study anything they like; the freedom, that is, to subject any body of material, however unpromising it might seem, to academic interrogation and analysis.

Academic freedom means that if I think that there may be an intellectual payoff to be had by turning an academic lens on material others consider trivial—golf tees, gourmet coffee, lingerie ads, convenience stores, street names, whatever—I should get a chance to try. If I manage to demonstrate to my peers and students that studying this material yields insights into matters of general intellectual interest, there is a new topic under the academic sun and a new subject for classroom discussion.

In short, whether something is an appropriate object of academic study is a matter not of its content—a crackpot theory may have had a history of influence that well rewards scholarly scrutiny—but of its availability to serious analysis. This point was missed by the author of a comment posted to the blog of a University of Wisconsin law professor, Ann Althouse: "When is the University of Wisconsin hiring a professor of astrology?" The question is obviously sarcastic; its intention is to equate the 9/11–inside-job theory with believing in the predictive power of astrology, and to imply that since the university wouldn't think of hiring someone to teach the one, it should have known better than to hire someone to teach the other.

But the truth is that it would not be at all outlandish for a university to hire someone to teach astrology—not to profess astrology and recommend it as the basis of decision-making (shades of Nancy Reagan), but to teach the history of its very long career. There is, after all, a good argument for saying that Shakespeare, Chaucer and Dante, among others, cannot be fully understood unless one understands astrology.

The distinction I am making—between studying astrology and proselytizing for it—is crucial and can be generalized; it shows us where the line between the responsible and irresponsible practice of academic freedom should always be drawn. Any idea can be brought into the classroom if the point is to inquire into its structure, history, influence and so forth. But no idea belongs in the classroom if the point of introducing it is to recruit your students for the political agenda it may be thought to imply.

And this is where we come back to Mr. Barrett, who, in addition to being a college lecturer, is a member of a group calling itself Scholars for 9/11 Truth, an organization with the decidedly political agenda of persuading Americans that the Bush administration "not only permitted 9/11 to happen but may even have orchestrated these events."

Is the fact of this group's growing presence on the Internet a reason for studying it in a course on 9/11? Sure. Is the instructor who discusses the group's arguments thereby endorsing them? Not at all. It is perfectly possible to teach a viewpoint without embracing it and urging it. But the moment a professor does embrace and urge it, academic study has ceased and been replaced by partisan advocacy. And that is a moment no college administration should allow to occur.

Provost Farrell doesn't quite see it that way, because he is too hung up on questions of content and balance. He thinks that the important thing is to assure a diversity of views in the classroom, and so he is reassured when Mr. Barrett promises to surround his "unconventional" ideas and "personal opinions" with readings "representing a variety of viewpoints."

But the number of viewpoints Mr. Barrett presents to his students is not the measure of his responsibility. There is, in fact, no academic requirement to include more than one view of an academic issue, although it is usually pedagogically useful to do so. The true requirement is that no matter how many (or few) views are presented to the students, they should be offered as objects of analysis rather than as candidates for allegiance.

There is a world of difference, for example, between surveying the pro and con arguments about the Iraq war, a perfectly appropriate academic assignment, and pressing students to come down on your side. Of course the instructor who presides over such a survey is likely to be a partisan of one position or the other—after all, who doesn't have an opinion on the Iraq war?—but it is part of a teacher's job to set personal conviction aside for the hour or two when a class is in session and allow the techniques and protocols of academic research full sway.

This restraint should not be too difficult to exercise. After all, we require and expect it of judges, referees and reporters. And while its exercise may not always be total, it is both important and possible to make the effort.

Thus the question Provost Farrell should put to Mr. Barrett is not "Do you hold these views?" (he can hold any views he likes) or "Do you proclaim them in public?" (he has that right no less that the rest of us) or even "Do you surround them with the views of others?"

Rather, the question should be: "Do you separate yourself from your partisan identity when you are in the employ of the citizens of Wisconsin and teach subject matter—whatever it is—rather than urge political action?" If the answer is yes, allowing Mr. Barrett to remain in the classroom is warranted. If the answer is no, (or if a yes answer is followed by classroom behavior that contradicts it) he should be shown the door. Not because he would be teaching the "wrong" things, but because he would have abandoned teaching for indoctrination.

The advantage of this way of thinking about the issue is that it outflanks the sloganeering and posturing both sides indulge in: on the one hand, faculty members who shout "academic freedom" and mean by it an instructor's right to say or advocate anything at all with impunity; on the other hand, state legislators who shout "not on our dime" and mean by it that they can tell academics what ideas they can and cannot bring into the classroom.

All you have to do is remember that academic freedom is just that: the freedom to do an academic job without external interference. It is not the freedom to do other jobs, jobs you are neither trained for nor paid to perform. While there should be no restrictions on what can be taught—no list of interdicted ideas or topics—there should be an absolute restriction on appropriating the scene of teaching for partisan political ideals. Teachers who use the classroom to indoctrinate make the enterprise of higher education vulnerable to its critics and shortchange students in the guise of showing them the true way.

Questions on Fish article

Consider Fish's view with respect to the events described in the *Furumoto* case. How should a college or university administration respond if a professor's views on a subject lead to frequent class disruptions and distract from the learning environment?

Axson-Flynn v. Johnson

United States Court of Appeals for the Tenth Circuit, 2004.
356 F.3d 1277.

[The opinion is set forth at pages 203–13, *supra*.]

Lovelace v. Southeastern Massachusetts University

United States Court of Appeals for the First Circuit, 1986.
793 F.2d 419.

■ PER CURIAM [COFFIN, BREYER and TORRUELLA, Circuit Judges].

Plaintiff-appellant, whose contract to teach at defendant Southeastern Massachusetts University was not renewed, brought this civil rights action complaining of the non-renewal and sundry other matters. . . .

[The court first holds that Plaintiff had no property or liberty interest in obtaining tenure, so had no right to a pre-non-renewal hearing.]

Plaintiff claims that the real reason his contract was not renewed and his grievances were rejected or interfered with is because he refused to inflate his grades or lower his expectations and teaching standards. He contends that, in response to student complaints that homework assignments were too time consuming and that plaintiff's courses were too hard, defendants first threatened not to renew plaintiff's contract unless he appeased the students and then carried out their threat when plaintiff refused to lower his standards. This, plaintiff says, interfered with his academic freedom which, plaintiff maintains, is protected by the first amendment.

It is important to note what plaintiff's first amendment claim is and to separate speech from action. Plaintiff has not contended that he was retaliated against simply because he *advocated* that the university elevate its standards. Indeed, plaintiff would be hard pressed to support such a claim in view of the February 11, 1983 memorandum from Dean Ward which plaintiff placed in the record. The memo indicates that as a result of consultations with plaintiff about the student complaints, the Dean concluded upgrading of the lower level computer courses was warranted. Far from manifesting hostility towards voiced concerns about educational matters, the memo suggests a spirit of receptivity to faculty concerns. Plaintiff's complaint instead is that he was retaliated against when he refused to *change* his standards.

We will assume for purposes of this opinion that plaintiff's refusal to lower his standards was a substantial motivating factor . . . in the decision not to renew his contract. We nevertheless conclude that plaintiff has failed to state a constitutional claim.

Whether a school sets itself up to attract and serve only the best and the brightest students or whether it instead gears its standard to a broader, more average population is a policy decision which, we think, universities must be allowed to set. And matters such as course content, homework load, and grading policy are core university concerns, integral to implementation of this policy decision. *See Regents of the University of California v. Bakke*, 438 U.S. 265, 312 (1978) (the "four essential freedoms" of a university are "to determine for itself on academic grounds who may teach, what may be taught, how it shall be taught, and who may be admitted to study") (quoting *Sweezy v. New Hampshire*, 354 U.S. 234, 263 (1957)). To accept plaintiff's contention that an untenured teacher's grading policy is constitutionally protected and insulates him from discharge when his standards conflict with those of the university[2] would be to constrict the university in defining and performing its educational mission. The first amendment does not require that each nontenured professor be made a sovereign unto himself. *See Palmer v. Board of Education*, 603 F.2d 1271 (7th Cir. 1979) (first amendment rights of probationary kindergarten teacher not violated by discharging her for refusing to teach patriotic subjects; a public school teacher is not free to disregard the prescribed curriculum concerning patriotic matter), *cert. denied*, 444 U.S. 1026 (1980); *Clark v. Holmes*, 474 F.2d 928, 931 (7th Cir. 1972) (rejecting contention that university teacher has first amendment right to disregard established curriculum content), *cert. denied*, 411 U.S. 972 (1973); *Hetrick v. Martin*, 480 F.2d 705 (6th Cir.) (first amendment does not prevent university from terminating untenured teacher whose pedagogical style and philosophy did not conform with those of the school's administration), *cert. denied*, 414 U.S. 1075 (1973).

.   .   .

Having found no merit in any of plaintiff's arguments, we affirm the district court judgment.

Questions and Comments on *Lovelace*

The court did not discuss the process by which the grading curve was set. Should it matter whether the curve was adopted by faculty, or was established by administrators—or would pursuing such an inquiry intrude too much into the institutional autonomy of colleges and universities?

Parate v. Isibor

United States Court of Appeals for the Sixth Circuit, 1989.
868 F.2d 821.

■ Keith, Circuit Judge.

Plaintiff Natthu S. Parate ("Parate"), whose contract to teach at Tennessee State University ("TSU") was not renewed, brought this civil rights action

---

2. It is true that plaintiff contends that his grading policy was in fact in accordance with the university's published criteria. We think, however, that it must be university officials—and not either an untenured teacher in his first year at the university or a federal court—which must be the judge of that, at least in the context of the constitutional claim plaintiff asserts.

Plaintiff also contends that the Federation Agreement guaranteed him academic freedom and this guaranty was violated by the university's alleged action in attempting to coerce plaintiff to alter grades. If that were so, plaintiff at most would state a contract claim, not a constitutional one.

against defendants, various officials of TSU and the State University and Community College System of Tennessee. Parate complained that the defendants violated his First and Fourteenth Amendment rights. The district court dismissed Parate's claims ... and granted summary judgment in favor of the defendants....

[Parate assumed an annually renewable, tenure-track position as associate professor in TSU's Civil Engineering Department in 1982. During his first semester, Parate told his Groundwater and Seepage ("GWS") class that he would award "As" to students earning ninety or more percent of the available points and "Bs" to those earning between eighty and ninety percent. Although these grades would be based on homework, class discussion, and examinations, Parate noted that he would also consider students' extenuating circumstances.

After receiving their grades for GWS, two students—"X" and "Y"— requested their grades, 86.1 and 86.4%, respectively, be changed to "As." Parate changed the grade of Student "X," who demonstrated that a "serious legal matter" had prevented him from doing as well on his final exam as he had earlier in the semester. Parate refused to change the grade of Student "Y," however, whom he had caught cheating on the final exam and had previously presented false medical excuses. Michael Samuchin, the Head of the Department of Civil Engineering, concurred in both grading decisions. Upon hearing that his grade would not be altered, Student "Y" stated that he would get his grade changed "through the Dean"—Edward I. Isibor, Dean of the School of Engineering and Technology.

The court suggested that Student "Y" and Isibor's shared Nigerian background was the basis for Isibor's subsequent actions on Student "Y's" behalf. On March 3, 1983, Isibor called a meeting with Parate and Samuchin and] instructed Parate to change Student "Y's" grade to an "A." Isibor also insisted that Parate sign a memorandum changing his official grading distribution for the "GWS" course so that a grade of 86 would be an "A" instead of a "B." When Parate refused, Isibor began to insult and berate him. Isibor said that Parate did not know how to teach, asked him where he got his degree, and stated that it would be very difficult to renew Parate's contract at TSU.

On the following day, Samuchin again met with Parate. Samuchin had prepared memoranda for Parate's signature that referred to the purported change in the grading criteria for the "GWS" course. The memoranda also requested grade changes for both Students "X" and "Y." Although Parate signed the memoranda, he added a notation to each copy: "as per instructions from Dean and Department Head at meeting." Later the same day, Samuchin returned with retyped memoranda and explained to Parate that there was to be no notation referring to Isibor's instructions. Samuchin then warned Parate that if he failed to sign the retyped memoranda, then Isibor would "mess up" his evaluation. Parate signed the second set of memoranda, but to signify his protest, used a signature different from his normal one. Samuchin then returned with a third set of retyped memoranda, which Parate ultimately signed due to his fear of future reprisals from Isibor.

[Over the next two academic years, Isibor and Samuchin "engaged in a variety of retaliatory acts" against Parate, including challenging his grading criteria, giving him low performance evaluations, denying his requests for travel and other reimbursements impairing his ability to participate in professional conferences, and eventually recommending that his contract not be renewed.]

. . .

. . . [O]n October 4, 1985, Parate held his "Statics" class as scheduled. Isibor and Samuchin, however, had preceded him into the classroom unannounced. After Parate began to call the roll, he was immediately interrupted. Isibor shouted from the back of the room: "Stop the roll call, don't waste time; circulate the paper for a roll call." Adhering to Isibor's directive, Parate began to teach his class, but was again interrupted by Isibor's shouts. Isibor next ordered Parate to complete one of the problems from the textbook. After Parate began to work out the problem on the blackboard and explain it to the students, Isibor again interrupted him. Isibor demanded that Parate complete the problem on the blackboard without addressing the students; that the students complete the problem on paper; and that Samuchin copy Parate's work from the board. Isibor soon approached the blackboard himself and began to work on the same problem that Parate and the students were completing. After severely criticizing Parate's teaching skills in front of his students, Isibor collected the students' papers and left the classroom.

. . . [At a later meeting, Isibor] said that some of Parate's students were more intelligent than their teacher, and that Parate's salary could be stopped at any time. Isibor then removed Parate from his post as instructor of the "Statics" course, but directed Parate to attend the class as a student. Parate attended the class for five or six sessions, but was then told that Isibor no longer wanted him to attend. During that semester, Parate was never reinstated as the instructor of the "Statics" class. In the remainder of Parate's final academic year, 1985–86, Isibor and Samuchin continually sent faculty observers to his classroom.

. . .

The administration of the university rests not with the courts, but with the administrators of the institution. A nontenured professor does not escape reasonable supervision in the manner in which she conducts her classes or assigns her grades. University officials remain free to review a professor's classroom activities when determining whether to grant or deny tenure. The university may constitutionally choose not to renew the contract of a nontenured professor whose pedagogical attitude and teaching methods do not conform to institutional standards. *Hetrick v. Martin*, 480 F.2d 705, 708 (6th Cir.), *cert. denied*, 414 U.S. 1075 (1973). The First Amendment concept of academic freedom does not require that a nontenured professor be made a sovereign unto himself. *See Lovelace v. Southeastern Mass. Univ.*, 793 F.2d 419, 426 (1st Cir. 1986).

. . .

Although judicial concern has been expressed for the academic freedom of the university, the courts have also afforded substantial protection to the First Amendment freedoms of individual university professors. . . .

The individual university professor may claim that his assignment of an examination grade or a final grade is communication protected by the First Amendment. As does any communicative act, assigning a letter grade sends a message to the recipient. The message communicated by the letter grade "A" is virtually indistinguishable from the message communicated by a formal written evaluation indicating "excellent work." Both communicative acts represent symbols that transmit a unique message.

Because the assignment of a letter grade is symbolic communication intended to send a specific message to the student, the individual professor's communicative act is entitled to some measure of First Amendment protection.

The freedom of the university professor to assign grades according to his own professional judgment is of substantial importance to that professor. To effectively teach her students, the professor must initially evaluate their relative skills, abilities, and knowledge. The professor must then determine whether students have absorbed the course material; whether a new, more advanced topic should be introduced; or whether a review of the previous material must be undertaken. Thus, the professor's evaluation of her students and assignment of their grades is central to the professor's teaching method.

The professor's authority over grading was addressed by the Supreme Court in *Board of Curators of the Univ. of Mo. v. Horowitz*, 435 U.S. 78 (1978). The Court stated that "like the decision of an individual professor as to the proper grade for a student in his course, the determination of whether to dismiss a student for academic reasons requires an expert evaluation of cumulative information and is not readily adapted to the procedural tools of judicial or administrative decisionmaking." The court concluded that the professor should retain wide discretion in his evaluation of the academic performance of his students. *Id.* at 96, n. 6 (Powell, J., concurring).

Although the individual professor does not escape the reasonable review of university officials in the assignment of grades, she should remain free to decide, according to her own professional judgment, what grades to assign and what grades not to assign. In the context of protected speech, the difference between compelled speech and compelled silence "is without constitutional significance, for the First Amendment guarantees 'freedom of speech,' a term necessarily comprising the decision of both what to say and what not to say." *Riley v. National Fed'n. of the Blind of N.C.*, 487 U.S. 781 (1988). Thus, the individual professor may not be compelled, by university officials, to change a grade that the professor previously assigned to her student. Because the individual professor's assignment of a letter grade is protected speech, the university officials' action to compel the professor to alter that grade would severely burden a protected activity.

. . .

If the speech of a nontenured professor is compelled by a university administrator, then the professor is not without redress for this violation of her constitutional rights. If a nontenured professor claims that she was not rehired in violation of a First Amendment right, she must first establish that her conduct was constitutionally protected, and then that this conduct was the motivating factor in her not being rehired. *Mt. Healthy City School Dist. Bd. of Educ. v. Doyle*, 429 U.S. 274 (1977).

In the present appeal, we consider the claim of the individual professor, Parate. He argues that his First Amendment right to academic freedom was violated during the March 3, 1983, grading incident. The district court explained that Parate "bases his claim to be free in his assignment of grades on the First Amendment guarantee of academic freedom." The district court then concluded "that a refusal to change a grade does not rise to the level of a constitutionally protected First Amendment right." Thus, the district court construed Parate's claim as being based on a First Amendment right to see that Student "Y" ultimately received the "GWS" course grade that Parate originally assigned him, and the alleged constitutional infringement occurred when the grade was changed. However, based on the foregoing analysis, we conclude that the constitutional issue was mischaracterized below. The defendants' act of *ordering Parate* to change the grade, rather than the act of giving Student "Y" a different grade than Parate desired, gives rise to the constitutional violation.

. . . Parate correctly contends that even as a nontenured professor, he retains the right to review each of his students' work and to communicate, according to his own professional judgment, academic evaluations and traditional letter grades. Parate, however, has no constitutional interest in the grades which his students ultimately receive. If the defendants had changed Student "Y's" "GSW" course grade, then Parate's First Amendment rights would not be at issue. Parate's First Amendment right to academic freedom was violated by the defendants because they ordered *Parate* to change Student "Y's" original grade. The actions of the defendants, who failed to administratively change Student "Y's" grade *themselves*, unconstitutionally compelled Parate's speech and precluded him from communicating his personal evaluation to Student "Y." Thus, the district court misconstrued Parate's First Amendment claim.

Relying on *Hillis v. Stephen F. Austin State Univ.*, 665 F.2d 547 (5th Cir.), *cert. denied*, 457 U.S. 1106 (1982), the district court concluded that Parate's First Amendment claims should be dismissed. In *Hillis*, however, the plaintiff's nontenured professor's contract was not renewed, in part, because he refused to give a student a "B" grade as directed by the head of his department. Unlike the present defendants, the *Hillis* university administrators changed the student's grade. Unlike Parate, the *Hillis* professor was not forced, in violation of his own professional judgment, to personally change his student's grade. Because the *Hillis* professor's speech was not compelled in violation of the First Amendment, as was Parate's, the *Hillis* case is inapplicable here.

The district court next cited *Lovelace v. Southeastern Mass. Univ.*, 793 F.2d 419 (1st Cir. 1986). . . . Unlike the *Lovelace* professor, Parate did not implement his own grading criteria. Parate was compelled to change his "GSW" course grade distribution policy to accomplish a grade change for Student "Y," a Nigerian student, favored by defendant Isibor, a Nigerian dean. Thus, this appeal, unlike the *Lovelace* case, is not a dispute over a nontenured professor's adherence to a university's published grading policy. This appeal is grounded in defendant Isibor's effort to compel a change in Parate's grading to favor Student "Y." Thus, *Lovelace* may also be distinguished from the present appeal.

The district court also relied on *Hetrick v. Martin*, 480 F.2d 705 (6th Cir.), *cert. denied*, 414 U.S. 1075 (1973). In *Hetrick*, this Court found that no First Amendment interests were implicated when a state university did not renew the contract of a nontenured professor because her pedagogical style and teaching methods did not conform to the university's standards. In the present appeal, however, defendants did not try to alter Parate's pedagogical style, but compelled his speech by demanding that he change, against his own professional judgment, a grade previously assigned.

We believe that the acts of the defendants deserve *exacting* First Amendment scrutiny. First, we consider Parate's First Amendment right to academic freedom and his interest in eliminating the defendants' arbitrary interference in the assignment of his course grades. Second, we consider Parate's First Amendment right to be free from compelled speech. By insisting that Parate sign the grade change memoranda without including his reservations or the notation "per the instruction of the Dean," the defendants compelled Parate to conform to a belief and a communication to which he did not subscribe. We then balance Parate's interests against defendants' interest in having Parate personally change Student "Y's" grade. Arguing from their First Amendment right to academic freedom, the defendants assert an interest in supervising and reviewing the grading policies of their nontenured professors. If they deemed Parate's grade assignments improper, however, the defendants could have achieved their goals by administratively changing Student "Y's" grade. We conclude that by forcing Parate to change, against his professional judgment, Student "Y's" grade, the defendants unconstitutionally compelled Parate's speech and chose a means to accomplish their supervisory goals that was unduly burdensome and constitutionally infirm.

Parate next claims that the defendants' actions on October 4, 1985, violated his First Amendment right to academic freedom. Parate contends that the defendants not only precluded him from teaching his "Statics" course, but humiliated him before his students. Parate also alleges that because his contract had not been renewed prior to the classroom incident, the defendants did not intend to evaluate his teaching competence and illegitimately exercised their supervisory functions.

The district court found that the requisite test for evaluating the classroom incident is whether the defendants "cast a pall of orthodoxy over the classroom," and thereby violated Parate's First Amendment rights. *Keyishian*, 385 U.S. at 603. We agree with the district court's conclusion that the defendants' actions on October 4, 1985, did not rise to the level of a constitutional violation.

It has long been recognized that the purpose of academic freedom is to preserve the "free marketplace of ideas" and protect the individual professor's classroom method from the arbitrary interference of university officials. University administrators, however, are free to observe, review or evaluate a nontenured professor's competence. Moreover, because public education in America is committed to the control of local and state authorities, the courts cannot intervene to resolve educational conflicts that do not "sharply implicate basic constitutional values." Although defendants' behavior was unprofessional, their actions on October 4, 1985, did not violate Parate's First Amendment right to academic freedom. First, Parate alleges that the defendants interfered with his classroom teaching on only one occasion. Thus, defendants' incidental conduct could not have resulted in a "pall of orthodoxy" being cast over Parate's "Statics" classroom. Second, Parate failed to allege that the defendants consistently denied him a free and open exchange with his students. Third, because Parate is a nontenured professor, he can allege no First Amendment right to teach a particular class or to be free from the supervision of university officials.

As the district court correctly noted, the defendants' actions on October 4, 1985, rise at most to the level of a tort of defamation which is not cognizable under 42 U.S.C. § 1983.

. . .

After careful review of the record, we reverse the judgment of the district court dismissing Parate's First Amendment claims resulting from the March 3, 1983, grading incident. On this issue, we remand to determine damages and whether Parate was discharged due to the exercise of his First Amendment right to academic freedom. . . .

Questions and Comments on *Parate*

After being contacted by Professor Parate, the AAUP appointed an investigating committee of experts in his field from other universities to look into Parate's situation. Following standard procedure, the report of the investigating committee was approved by Committee A and sent to the administration of Tennessee State University for comment before the final report was prepared. In the section of its final report on grading, the AAUP states:

> The joint *Statement on Government of Colleges and Universities* places primary responsibility with the faculty "for such fundamental areas as curriculum, subject matter, and methods of instruction." The assessment of student academic performance, it follows, is a faculty responsibility, and the faculty member responsible for a course should, under normal circumstances, be the judge of the grades the students receive. . . .

> . . . At the same time, of course, situations do arise in which a student believes that a grade he or she has received is wrong. . . . A suitable mechanism for appeal should thus be available for reviewing allegations that inappropriate criteria were used in determining the grade or that the instructor did not adhere to announced procedures or grading standards. The principles set forth by Committee A indicate that the review of a student complaint over a grade should be by members of the faculty, under procedures adopted by the faculty, and that any resulting change in a grade should be by faculty authorization. Under no circumstances should the administration substitute its judgment for that of the faculty concerning the academic quality of a student's work.

> . . .

> In his January 1987 report and recommendation, the federal magistrate handling Professor Parate's case concluded that the assignment of grades "is not a right which rises to a constitutional level," because it does not implicate issues of "classroom content and method" which the First Amendment protects. The investigating committee's main interest in this matter, of course, is not in the legal issue of a potential constitutional violation, but rather in academic freedom and faculty prerogatives as professional concerns. The committee recognizes that administrative officers have a responsibility to listen to student complaints about grades, to seek clarification, and to attempt to assist in obtaining a resolution. They should not be able on their own authority to change a grade assigned by a faculty member, however, and there is a world of difference between asking the faculty member to consider making the change and ordering that the change be made upon threat of punishment. The investigating committee finds that the administration of the School of Engineering and Technology, in repeatedly interfering with Professor Parate's grading and on at least one occasion changing a grade over his objection, exceeded its proper authority and

infringed upon his prerogatives as an instructor to grade the performance of his students. The investigating committee lacks sufficient evidence to reach a finding on Professor Parate's contention that he was issued notice of non-reappointment because of his protests against the administration's interference with his grading.

Academic Freedom and Tenure: Tennessee State University, ACADEME, May–June 1987, at 39, 42–43.

Does the AAUP's disclaiming interest in the constitutional issue explain why it reached a different conclusion than the courts on the question of whether academic freedom demands that a student receive the grade the professor thinks is deserved? What do you think of the court's distinction between the university administration ordering a professor to change a student's grade and administratively changing the student's grade after the fact? Should a college or university administrator ever change a student's grade, or should such decisions rest in the hands of faculty members, as the AAUP argues?

The AAUP final report found the subsequent interference with Parate's teaching and professional activities, particularly his suspension from teaching statics, even more troubling:

> "Freedom in the classroom" is assured the university teacher by the 1940 *Statement of Principles* and the stated policies of Tennessee State University.
>
> . . .
>
> The investigating committee appreciates that there can be circumstances under which an administrative officer, responding to recurrent student complaints, has warrant to visit a faculty member's classroom to observe that teacher's performance.... Yet even if the dean had grounds for concern about Professor Parate's ability to teach that particular class, the investigating committee believes that there can be no justification for his conducting himself as he did....
>
> . . .
>
> The suspension of a faculty member from all or part of his teaching duties is justified, under generally accepted academic standards ... only pending an appropriate hearing on cause and "only if immediate harm to himself or others it threatened by his continuance." In contrast, Dean Isibor summarily removed Professor Parate from teaching his statics course, without subsequent demonstration before a faculty body that there was adequate cause for his action.... From what the investigating committee can determine ... any immediate harm to the students that Dean Isibor may have thought would be avoided by removing Professor Parate from the statics class was harm created more by Dean Isibor's humiliating treatment of Professor Parate in front of his students than by anything Professor Parate did or did not do.
>
> ... The investigating committee is of the opinion ... that so crass an intrusion by an administrator into a faculty member's classroom can have profound adverse effects on that faculty member's subsequent exercise of his academic freedom and indeed on the willingness of all other faculty members under that administrator's jurisdiction to exercise their academic freedom. The actions of Dean Isibor, which the federal magistrate has described as "boorish," "unprofessional," and "offensive," were not so repugnant, in the magistrate's vew, as to "shock the conscience." The investigating committee is confident, however, that the academic community would strongly disagree with the magistrate's assessment of the seriousness of the offense.

The committee finds that Dean Isibor's assault on Professor Parate's classroom constituted grossly unacceptable behavior under the academic community's norms of conduct and that it bespeaks a climate in Tennessee State University's School of Engineering and Technology that is inimical to academic freedom.

Note on the "Academic Bill of Rights"

Stanley Fish has written that, with the introduction of postmodernism, poststructuralism, gender, ethnic, and sexuality studies to the curriculum, "[t]he left may have won the curricular battle, but the right won the public-relations war." Stanley Fish, *'Intellectual Diversity': The Trojan Horse of a Dark Design*, Chron. Higher Educ., Feb. 13, 2004, at B13. Following recent curricular changes in the academy, much of the general public has come to view colleges and universities as "hotbeds . . . of radicalism and pedagogical irresponsibility where dollars are wasted, nonsense is propagated, students are indoctrinated, religion is disrespected, and patriotism is scorned." *Id.*

Conservative commentator David Horowitz has recently proposed an "Academic Bill of Rights," which he characterizes as an attempt "to remove partisan politics from the classroom." David Horowitz, *In Defense of Intellectual Diversity*, Chron. Higher Educ., Feb. 13, 2004, at B12. According to Horowitz's critique, American higher education is suffering because professors who have "lost sight of the vital distinction between education and indoctrination[,] . . . focus merely on their own partisan agendas and . . . abandon their responsibilities as professional educators with obligations to students of all political persuasions." *Id.* Horowitz's proposed remedy is academic diversity, across faculties and within specific courses: "Requiring readings on more than one side of a political controversy would be appropriate educational policy and would strengthen, not weaken, the democracy that supports our educational system." *Id.*

After unsuccessfully pressing Congress to pass legislation implementing the objectives of the Academic Bill of Rights, Horowitz had some success on the state level. The Pennsylvania House of Representatives, for example, created a select committee to study whether:

> (1) faculty are hired, fired, promoted and granted tenure based on their professional competence and subject matter knowledge and, in the humanities, social sciences and arts, with a view of helping students explore and understand various methodologies and perspectives; (2) students have . . . an environment conducive to learning, the development of critical thinking and the exploration of independent thought and that the students are evaluated based on their subject knowledge or ability to defend their perspective in various courses; and (3) academic freedom and the right to explore and express independent thought is available to and practiced freely by faculty and students. . . .

H.R. 177, 2005 Gen. Assem., Reg. Sess. (Pa. 2005).

Following hearings at a number of Pennsylvania's public universities and colleges, the Committee reported "that legislation requiring the adoption of a uniform statewide academic freedom policy . . . was *not* necessary. . . . [A]cademic freedom violations are rare. . . ." The Committee decided to leave it to universities to decide "whether internal efforts are necessary to encourage diverse political views on campus and to ensure that students receive a balanced and effective education." H. Rep. of Pa., Report of the Select Committee on Academic Freedom in Higher Education Pursuant to House Resolution 177, at 11–12 (2006), *available at* http://www.aaup.org/NR/rdonlyres/F07FA225–3E09–45CB–9046–A40D44625D4D/0/HR177reportfinal.pdf.

Think back to Stanley Fish's article regarding the comments made about 9/11 by Kevin Barrett at the University of Wisconsin. Is Horowitz's Academic Bill of Rights consistent with Fish's thinking on these issues?

Note on AAUP Report on Freedom in the Classroom

In 2007, Committee A on Academic Freedom and Tenure of the AAUP, whose 1940 Statement on Academic Freedom Horowitz has invoked as the precursor to the Academic Bill of Rights, released a report on the freedom of professors in the classroom. COMM. A ON ACADEMIC FREEDOM AND TENURE, FREEDOM IN THE CLASSROOM (2007), *available at* www.aaup.org/AAUP/comm/rep/A/class.htm. It provides in pertinent part:

A.   "Education, Not Indoctrination!"

The caption is taken from a statement of the Committee for a Better North Carolina, which in 2003 condemned the assignment of Barbara Ehrenreich's *Nickel and Dimes: On Not Getting By in America* to incoming students at the University of North Carolina at Chapel Hill. We agree, of course, that indoctrination is to be avoided, but the question is how education is to be distinguished from indoctrination.

It is not indoctrination for professors to expect students to comprehend ideas and apply knowledge that is accepted as true within a relevant discipline. . . .

. . .

. . . [I]ndoctrination occurs whenever an instructor insists that students accept *as truth* propositions that are in fact professionally contestable. . . .

Under this test . . . the Committee for a Better North Carolina could not possibly have known whether the assignment of Ehrenreich's *Nickel and Dimed*, which explores the economic difficulties facing low-wage workers in American, was an example of indoctrination or education. It is fundamental error to assume that the assignment of teaching materials constitutes their endorsement. An instructor who assigns a book no more endorses what it has to say than does the university library that acquire it. . . .

. . .

B.   Balance

. . .

To urge that instruction be "balanced" is to urge that an instructor's discretion about what to teach should be restricted. But the nature of this proposed restriction . . . is fatally ambiguous. Stated most abstractly, the charge of lack of balance evokes a seeming ideal of neutrality. The notion appears to be that an instructor should impartially engage all potentially relevant points of view. But . . . [n]o coherent principle of neutrality would require an instructor in a class on constitutional democracy to offer equal time to "competing" vision of communist totalitarianism or Nazi fascism. . . .

The ideal of balance makes sense only in light of an instructor's obligation to present all aspect of a subject matter that professional standards would require to be presented. If a professor of molecular biology has an idiosyncratic theory that AIDS is not caused by a retrovirus, professional standards may require that the dominant contrary perspective be presented.

. . .

C.   Hostile Learning Environment

. . .

... It is a breach of professional ethics for an instructor to hold a student up to obloquy or ridicule in class for advancing an idea grounded in religion, whether it is creationism or the geocentric theory of the solar system. It would be equally improper for an instructor to hold a student up to obloquy or ridicule for an idea grounded in politics, or anything else.

But the current application of the idea of "hostile learning environment" ... assumes that students have a right not to have their most cherished beliefs challenged. This assumption contradicts the central purpose of higher education, which is to challenge students to think hard about their own perspectives, whatever those might be.... Ideas that are germane to a subject under discussion in the classroom cannot be censored because a student with particular religious or political beliefs might be offended.... This would create a classroom environment inimical to the free and vigorous exchange of ideas necessary for teaching and learning in higher education.

Williams v. Weisser

California Court of Appeal, Second Appellate District, 1969.
273 Cal.App.2d 726, 78 Cal.Rptr. 542.

■ KAUS, P.J.

Defendant Weisser, who does business under the fictitious name of Class Notes, appeals from a judgment which enjoins him from copying, publishing and selling notes of lectures delivered by plaintiff in his capacity as an Assistant Professor of Anthropology at the University of California at Los Angeles ("UCLA"). The judgment also awards plaintiff $1,000 in compensatory and $500 in exemplary damages.

... Defendant does business in Westwood, California as Class Notes selling outlines for various courses given at UCLA. In 1965, defendant paid Karen Allen, a UCLA student, to attend plaintiff's class in Anthropology 1 to take notes from the lectures, and to type up the notes. Allen delivered the typed notes to defendant and defendant placed a copyright notice thereon in defendant's name, reproduced the typed notes, and sold and offered them for sale. Plaintiff objected. Defendant did not cease these activities until served with summons, complaint and temporary restraining order....

... Defendant has used plaintiff's name in selling the publications here in question.

The judgment in plaintiff's favor was based on two grounds: 1. defendant infringed plaintiff's common law copyright in his lectures; and 2, defendant invaded plaintiff's privacy by the use of plaintiff's name....

Certain preliminary observations are in order:

1. The product of the mind in which the plaintiff claims a copyright consists of the extensive notes which he had compiled before the beginning of the course, together with the oral expression at the time of delivery of the lectures, based on the notes, which delivery included charts and diagrams placed on the classroom blackboard. This is, therefore, not a case where the concrete expression of the "composition" consists solely of an intangible oral presentation. As far as this litigation is concerned, the chief importance of the oral presentation is that it provided defendant with access to plaintiff's work and with an argument that there had been a divestive publication.

2. Defendant does not dispute on this appeal that the lectures were properly the subject of a common law copyright....

3. Substantial similarity between the lectures and the notes published by defendant is conceded.

Plaintiff became employed by UCLA starting in July 1965. Defendant's relations with the university started in 1948 when he began to publish and sell to students what purported to be notes of various courses. In 1963 defendant and the university authorities agreed on certain ground rules as a condition to advertising in the Daily Bruin, the student newspaper. Friction arose between defendant and the administration. The matter culminated in a memorandum dated November 19, 1964, addressed to all members of the faculty. It is copied in the footnote.[10]

. . .

We are . . . convinced that in the absence of evidence [to the contrary] the teacher, rather than the university, owns the common law copyright to his lectures. . . .

Defendant claims that the opposite is the law. His sole statutory authority is section 2860 of the Labor Code which reads as follows: "Everything which an employee acquires by virtue of his employment, except the compensation which is due to him from his employer, belongs to the employer, whether acquired lawfully or unlawfully, or during or after the expiration of the term of his employment."

It is obvious that a literal application of that section does not cover the present situation. The code speaks of things which the employee "acquires," not matters which he creates. [T]he section has been applied principally, though not exclusively, to unfair competition carried on by former employees with the use of trade secrets and the like. Even so it has been narrowly employed. We do not believe it applies here.

Defendant also claims that plaintiff is in the position of an employee for hire whose employment calls for the creation of a copyrightable work or, perhaps, of an independent contractor who has been so commissioned. In such cases it is usually presumed that, unless a different intention is shown, the employer or commissioner is the owner of the copyright.

This contention calls for some understanding of the purpose for which a university hires a professor and what rights it may reasonably expect to retain after the services have been rendered. A university's obligation to its students is to make the subject matter covered by a course available for study by various methods, including classroom presentation. It is not obligated to present the subject by means of any particular expression. As far as the teacher is concerned, neither the record in this case nor any custom known to us suggests that the university can prescribe his way of expressing the ideas he puts before his students. Yet expression is what this lawsuit is all about. No reason has been suggested why a university would want to retain the ownership in a professor's expression. Such retention would be useless

---

10. . . . [R]egarding the faculty member's right to control distribution of notes taken in classroom lecture, it appears quite clear that under California's recognition of common law copyright, the lecturer retains a property right to his words spoken before a limited audience. Any unauthorized duplication and distribution of these words, either verbatim or in the form of notes may therefore constitute an infringement of this right. It is emphasized that the common law copyright in a lecture is the property of the lecturer rather than of the University, and therefore any legal actions for the infringement of such right must be brought in the name of the aggrieved faculty member.

except possibly for making a little profit from a publication and for making it difficult for the teacher to give the same lectures, should he change jobs.

Indeed the undesirable consequences which would follow from a holding that a university owns the copyright to the lectures of its professors are such as to compel a holding that it does not. Professors are a peripatetic lot, moving from campus to campus. The courses they teach begin to take shape at one institution and are developed and embellished at another. That, as a matter of fact, was the case here. Plaintiff testified that the notes on which his lectures were based were derived from a similar course which he had given at another university. If defendant is correct, there must be some rights of that school which were infringed at UCLA. Further, should plaintiff leave UCLA and give a substantially similar course at his next post, UCLA would be able to enjoin him from using the material which, according to defendant, it owns.

No one but defendant, an outsider as far as the relationship between plaintiff and UCLA is concerned, suggests that such a state of the law is desirable.

Another strange consequence which would follow from equating university lectures with other products of the mind which an employee is hired to create, is, that in order to determine just what it is getting, the university would have to find out the precise extent to which a professor's lectures have taken concrete shape when he first comes to work. Not even defendant suggests that a contract for employment implies an assignment to the university of any common law copyright which the professor already owns.

The many cases cited by defendant for the general rule probably reach desirable results that are in accord with common understanding in their respective areas, but a rule of law developed in one context should not be blindly applied in another where it violates the intention of the parties and creates undesirable consequences. University lectures are *sui generis*. Absent compulsion by statute or precedent, they should not be blindly thrown into the same legal hopper with valve designs, motion picture background music, commercial drawings, mosaics designed for the Congressional Library in Washington, D.C., high school murals, song stylings, radio scripts, commercial jingles, lists of courses taught by a correspondence school, and treatises on the use of ozone or on larceny and homicide.

On the other hand, there is a short but sturdy line of authorities dealing with lectures. . . .

The first and leading case is *Abernethy v. Hutchinson*, 3 L.J. (Ch.) 209 (1825), 1 H. & T. 28 (1825). . . .

[In holding that Dr. Abernethy, a surgeon, held the copyright to lectures he delivered at a hospital, Lord Eldon noted,] "One question had been, whether Mr. Abernethy, from the peculiar situation which he filled in the hospital, was precluded from publishing his own lectures for his profit; *but there was no evidence before the Court, that he had no such right.* Therefore the defendants must be enjoined in future." Earlier in the opinion the court had likened Doctor Abernethy's position to that of a university professor. From our point of view, the significance of the quoted passage is that in the absence of positive evidence to the contrary the Chancellor assumed as a matter of course that the copyright was with the lecturer and not with the hospital. *A fortiori* it would not belong to a university.

The case which is factually closest in point is *Caird v. Sime* [1887] 12 A.C. 326 (H.L.).... [T]he case turned on the question whether Caird had lost his common law copyright because as a professor in a public university it was his obligation "to receive into his class all comers having the requisite qualification." Therefore, it was argued, "his lectures are really addressed to the public." In answer to this point the court noted that it was a "fact that professors and their representatives have been in frequent use to publish lectures which had been annually delivered for years before such publication, and have enjoyed, without objection or challenge, the privilege of copyright."

. . .

Crossing the Atlantic we find *Sherrill v. Grieves*, 57 Wash. L.R. 286, 20 C.O. Bull. 675, decided by the Supreme Court of the District of Columbia in 1929. [Sherrill, an instructor for the United States Army at Fort Leavenworth's postgraduate school, used his leisure time to plan a book on military sketching, map reading, and surveying. In Sherrill's copyright infringement suit, the defendants argued that a pamphlet based on the book's section on sketching was a "publication of the United States" despite Sherrill's statutory copyright because it had been printed by Fort Leavenworth authorities with his consent.] The plaintiff at the time was employed to give instruction just as a professor in an institution of learning is employed. *The court does not know of any authority holding that such a professor is obliged to reduce his lectures to writing or if he does so that they become the property of the institution employing him.* . . .

There is, of course, a possible distinction between *Sherrill v. Grieves* and the case at bar: the report does state that the material was prepared in Sherrill's "leisure time, not as an incident to his work as instructor."

The distinction is illusory. If the employing institution has any rights at all, they stem from the fact that the teacher, when preparing his lectures, is only doing that which he is hired to do. Since it is not customary for a college to prescribe the hours of the day when a teacher is to prepare for class, it follows that the time when he does so automatically ceases to be leisure time.

In any event, it is quite arguable that plaintiff prepared his notes in his "leisure time" if that concept has any validity. . . . Before arriving at UCLA he had accumulated notes over a period of years. He prepared the notes from which he eventually delivered his lectures during the summer.

There is therefore no real difference between Sherrill and plaintiff. Neither was under a duty to make notes, neither was under a duty to prepare for his lectures during any fixed hours, but the notes that each made did directly relate to the subjects taught.

. . .

Little needs to be said on the point of divestive publication. The question of what manner of publication divests a common law copyright to a lecture is extensively discussed in D. E. Harding, *Copyright in Lectures, Sermons, and Speeches* (1966) 14 Ascap, Copyright Law Symposium 270, 291–324. The author there points out that the authorities approach the problem in two ways. Professor Nimmer's view is that no divestive publication occurs unless there is a distribution of tangible copies of the work. In other words the doctrine of *Ferris v. Frohman*, 223 U.S. 424, that performance does not dedicate, applies. Other authorities make the distinction between "limited" and "general" publication. Under either view the oral delivery of the lectures did not divest plaintiff of his common law copyright to his lectures. Nothing tangible was delivered to the students and every case that has considered the problem of divestment from the limited versus general publication point of view has reached the conclusion that the giving of a lecture is not a general publication. As the court said in *Caird v. Sime*, holding that the publication of the plaintiff's lecture was only limited: " . . . The principle which pervades the whole of that reasoning is, that where the persons present at a lecture are not the general public, but a limited class of the public, selected and admitted for the sole and special purpose of receiving individual instruction, they may make any use they can of the lecture, to the extent of taking it down in shorthand, for their own information and improvement, but cannot publish it. . . ."

. . .

An author who owns the common law copyright to his work can determine whether he wants to publish it and, if so, under what circumstances. Plaintiff had prepared his notes for a specific purpose—as an outline to lectures to be delivered to a class of students. Though he apparently considered them adequate for that purpose, he did not desire a commercial distribution with which his name was associated. Right or wrong, he felt that his professional standing could be jeopardized. There is evidence that other teachers at UCLA did not object to representatives of Class Notes being in the classroom, indeed some cooperated with defendant in revising the product of the note takers. Plaintiff considered the Anthropology 1 notes sold by defendant as defective in several respects, chiefly because of certain omissions. Any person aware of the cooperation given by other faculty members could reasonably believe that plaintiff had assisted in the final product. We think that these considerations easily bring the case within the ambit of *Fairfield v. American Photocopy etc. Co.*, 138 Cal.App.2d 82 [291 P.2d 194]. There the defendant used the plaintiff's name in advertising a certain product. He was said to be one of the many satisfied users of the product. He had been a user, but had returned the product to the defendant. The court held that defendant's conduct was "an unauthorized and unwarranted appropriation of plaintiff's personality as a lawyer for pecuniary gain and profit." We think that the *Fairfield* case is indistinguishable from the one at bar.

. . .

Taking the evidence as a whole, the trial court was amply justified in concluding that defendant was not an innocent layman, caught in the complexities of the law, but a businessman who, for personal profit, was determined to pursue a certain course of action even if it meant riding roughshod over the rights of others.

The judgment is affirmed.

Questions and Comments on *Williams*

1. Are lectures copyrightable? *Williams* recognized a professor's common law copyright on his lecture notes. The court noted that the professor's lecture was not "solely an intangible oral presentation." Whether class lectures are copyrightable may depend on whether the lecture has taken on a tangible form. As one scholar has observed:

> Lectures can pose a problem regarding the "fixed" requirement in copyright.... To copyright a lecture, the lecture must be in a tangible, fixed form. If a professor writes her lecture in a word processing program, or creates an outline or notes, those written versions of the lecture are protected by copyright. Audio or video recording could also fix the lecture. If a professor authorizes students to tape-record their lectures, the tape recording fixes the lecture sufficiently to establish copyright on the live version. However, the permission in making the copy does not transfer any kind of ownership rights in the copyright to the student. The rights to reproduce, distribute, and publicly perform that lecture elsewhere remain with the professor.... Issues of ownership in lecture came into focus early in legal history when someone in the audience tried to publish notes from the lecture.

Elizabeth Townsend, *Legal and Policy Responses to the Disappearing "Teacher Exception," or Copyright Ownership in the 21st Century University*, 4 MINN. INTELL. PROP. REV. 209, 222–23 (2003).

Many universities have taken a stand against unauthorized distribution of lecture notes. The approaches vary by institution and include such measures as official policies prohibiting the practice, cease and desist letters, copyright statements attached to syllabi, and litigation. Ashley T. Barnett, Note, *"Profiting at My Expense": An Analysis of the Commercialization of Professors' Lecture Notes*, 9 J. INTELL. PROP. L. 137, 139–43 (2001). At least one university has unsuccessfully sued a commercial note company for copyright violations. In *University of Florida v. KPB, Inc.*, 89 F.3d 773 (11th Cir. 1996), a jury found that a professor's lecture is largely comprised of facts or ideas that do not belong to anyone, thus rejecting the university's copyright claims. Goldie Blumenstyk, *Putting Class Notes on the Web: Are Companies Stealing Lectures?*, CHRON. HIGHER EDUC., Oct. 1, 1999, at A31.

2. If lecture notes are copyrightable, who owns the copyright? The "teacher exception," recognized by the court in *Williams*, is an exception to the work-for-hire doctrine that employers, rather than employees, own the copyright to an employee's work. Although not mentioned in the 1909 Copyright Act, the teacher exception was carved out of the general work-for-hire rule through judicially developed doctrine. Townsend, *supra*, at 224–25; *see also Williams*, 273 Cal.App.2d at 736–40. When Congress recodified the 1909 statute in the 1976 Copyright Act, it did not incorporate the common law teacher exception, *see* 17 U.S.C. § 201(b) (2000), prompting concern that the doctrine was no longer good law.

Despite its absence in the 1976 Copyright Law, however, the teacher exception continues to be recognized in law and practice. Noting that 1976 Copyright Law permitted employers and employees to contract around the statutory work-for-hire rule, the Seventh Circuit in *Weinstein v. University of Illinois*, 811 F.2d 1091 (7th Cir. 1987), interpreted a professor's contract as incorporating the "teacher exception," which the court stated had "been the academic tradition since copyright law began." *Id.* at 1094; see also Townsend, *supra*, at 235–37. Internal university copyright policies like that in *Weinstein* have become common following the 1976 recodification. *Id.* at 251–74.

B. RESEARCH RESTRICTIONS

Levin v. Harleston

United States Court of Appeals, Second Circuit, 1992.
966 F.2d 85.

■ VAN GRAAFEILAND, CIRCUIT JUDGE:

Bernard W. Harleston and Paul Sherwin, the President and Dean of Humanities, respectively, of The City College of The City University of New

York, appeal from a judgment entered after a bench trial in the United States District Court for the Southern District of New York in a 42 U.S.C. § 1983 action brought by Professor Michael Levin....

... This litigation had its inception in three writings of Levin, a tenured professor at the College, which is a public institution funded in part by the State of New York. The first of these was a letter to the New York Times, the second was a book review published in Quadrant, an Australian journal, the third was a letter published in the American Philosophical Association Proceedings. Because these writings contained a number of denigrating comments concerning the intelligence and social characteristics of blacks, they elicited a mixed response, much of it critical in nature. As will hereafter appear, appellants' response went beyond simple vocal condemnation.

Over Dean Sherwin's objection, Professor Charles Evans, Chairman of the College's philosophy department, assigned Professor Levin to teach a section of Philosophy 101 during the 1990 spring semester. After the appearance in January 1990 of Levin's letter in the American Philosophical Association Proceedings, Dean Sherwin created an "alternative" section of Philosophy 101 for those of Levin's students who might want to transfer out of his class. He wrote to the students in Levin's class on February 1, after the semester had commenced and without notice to Levin, informing them of the alternative section to which they could transfer.

Similar action never before had been taken in the history of City College. Moreover, none of Professor Levin's students ever had complained of unfair treatment on the basis of race. Professor Evans objected to the creation of the "shadow class" as immoral, illegal and an unwarranted interference in his discretionary powers as a department chairman. Faculty members of City College, and of other institutions as well, criticized appellants' acts as a violation of academic freedom. The district court found that the shadow classes "were established with the intent and consequence of stigmatizing Professor Levin solely because of his expression of ideas," and enjoined their continuance.

In addressing the issue of the "shadow classes," we emphasize the great reluctance with which this court intrudes upon the decisions of a university administration. Where, however, basic constitutional values have been infringed, this court will not remain silent. "State colleges and universities are not enclaves immune from the sweep of the First Amendment." *Healy v. James*, 408 U.S. 169, 180 (1972)....

An impermissible purpose does not, of course, end our inquiry if a permissible reason for the governmental act also existed. Formation of the alternative sections would not be unlawful if done to further a legitimate educational interest that outweighed the infringement on Professor Levin's First Amendment rights.... Given the complete lack of evidence to support appellants' claim of a legitimate educational interest, we are unable to say that the district court erred.

Appellants contend that "since, by definition, alternative class sections presuppose that Professor Levin will continue to teach a class section, the creation of such sections cannot, as a matter of law, constitute an infringement of Professor Levin's First Amendment rights." We disagree. Appellants' encouragement of the continued erosion in the size of Professor Levin's class if he does not mend his extracurricular ways is the antithesis of freedom of expression.

Because the alternative sections continue to exist, that part of the district court's judgment permanently enjoining appellants "from creating or maintaining 'shadow' or 'parallel' sections of his classes predicated solely upon Professor Levin's protected expression of ideas," was warranted and is affirmed....

Appellants did not content themselves with simply creating a "shadow" class. At a press conference held on March 28, 1990, President Harleston announced the proposed formation of an Ad Hoc Committee on Academic Rights and Responsibilities to determine whether Professor Levin's views affected his teaching ability. President Harleston was reported as saying that "the process of removing a tenured professor is a difficult one." He also was quoted as saying that "[Levin's] views are offensive to the basic values of human equality and decency and simply have no place here at City College."

In a subsequent memorandum to the City College community, Harleston formally announced the appointment of the Ad Hoc Committee. The Committee was "to review the question of when speech both in and outside the classroom may go beyond the protection of academic freedom or become conduct unbecoming a member of the faculty, or some other form of misconduct." The words "conduct unbecoming" a member of the faculty mirror the language in the College's By–Laws and the Professional Staff contract warranting imposition of discipline on a faculty member. Harleston was aware of this and deliberately chose the language.

Professor Levin testified that, after he saw the above memorandum, he feared President Harleston was going to fire him. As a consequence, he turned down at least twenty invitations to speak or write about his controversial views. When Levin instituted this lawsuit on September 24, 1990, the Committee still was deliberating. Despite the commencement of the litigation and admonitory letters from Levin's counsel, Harleston never assured Levin that he was not subject to discipline for his statements outside the classroom. When the Committee finally reported, it recommended that no disciplinary action be taken against a faculty member for speech outside the classroom and that no disciplinary proceedings be brought against Professor Levin.

It is settled that governmental action which falls short of a direct prohibition on speech may violate the First Amendment by chilling the free exercise of speech. *Laird v. Tatum*, 408 U.S. 1, 11 (1972)....

The district court did not err in finding that the threat of discipline implicit in President Harleston's actions was sufficient to create a judicially cognisable chilling effect on Professor Levin's First Amendment rights. It is not fatal that Harleston never explicitly stated that disciplinary charges would be brought if Levin continued to voice his views. It is the chilling effect on free speech that violates the First Amendment, and it is plain that an implicit threat can chill as forcibly as an explicit threat....

Whether this threat was sufficient to warrant the grant of injunctive relief presents a more difficult problem. No disciplinary proceeding or other investigation of Professor Levin is pending, and the Ad Hoc Committee recommended that none be initiated.... The burden ... remains on the moving party to demonstrate the need for injunctive relief. This requires a showing of irreparable harm.... Because Professor Levin has not made this demonstration, he was not entitled to injunctive relief.

However, since Levin requested "such other and further relief as the Court may deem just," we conclude that an award of declaratory relief is appropriate. Declaratory relief does not share injunctive relief's requirement of irreparable harm. A declaration that disciplinary proceedings, or the threat thereof, predicated solely upon Levin's continued expression of his views outside the classroom violates his First Amendment rights will clarify the relations between the parties and eliminate the legal uncertainties that gave rise to this litigation....

Appellants' final disputed response to Professor Levin's writings was one of inaction rather than action, *i.e.*, their alleged failure to take steps to prevent what they themselves describe as "undisputed facts concerning disruptions" of Levin's classes. The district court devoted several pages of its opinion to a detailed description of these disruptions and the College's responses or lack thereof. It condemned with strong language the "appalling behavior of the shouters, the intimidators and the bullies." We join in this condemnation. However, we are concerned that the district court has not adequately explicated a legal basis for holding that appellants' response or lack of response to the student disruptions violated Professor Levin's constitutional rights. The basis for this concern is the undisputed evidence that the College's response to the disruption of Levin's classes was no different than that accorded to other instances of student disruption. Accordingly, although under some circumstances a state may be guilty of an equal protection violation if it denies disfavored individuals protections and benefits that it freely grants to others, that is not what happened in the instant case. Simply stated, there is no evidence that the College treated student demonstrations directed at Professor Levin any differently than other student demonstrations. Whether this failure to discipline is a wise policy is not the issue herein. Whether the practice breaches a tort or contractual obligation that the College owes its teachers also is beyond the scope of our review. We limit our review to whether Professor Levin's constitutional rights were violated, and we are persuaded that they were not....

Questions and Comments on *Levin*

1. In May 1990, fifty protesters attempted to storm an auditorium at Long Island University's Brooklyn campus, where Professor Levin was giving an address entitled "White Fear of Black Crime Is Morally and Epistemically Correct." Police blockaded the auditorium and arrested nine protestors while six police were injured and Levin was safely escorted away. A university spokesperson stated that "[a] panel of students, faculty members and administrators decided that in the interest of free speech and a free flow of ideas," Levin should be permitted to speak at the seventy-percent-black university. *See 9 Are Arrested in Protest Over a Lecture on Race*, N.Y. TIMES, May 3, 1990, at B2.

2. Professor Levin maintained that he had not overstepped his area of scholarly expertise:

> ... [L]et me highlight the points at which philosophy intersects the issue of race and intelligence. The main argument for affirmative action appeals to compensatory justice, a topic central to ethical inquiry since at least Aristotle. Identifying the tacit factual premise of the affirmative-action argument—that

black underachievement is caused by white oppression—is precisely the sort of things philosophers do.

In addition, a central question of the philosophy of science—one of my areas of expertise—concerns the criteria by which scientists accord existence to unobservable, theoretical entities, such as quarks and magnetic fields. The reality of an all-purpose problem-solving ability never more than partly manifest in behavior is such a question; its discussion by a philosopher would raise no eyebrows were his conclusions more fashionable.

Michael Levin, Letter to the Editor, *Affirmative Action Bears Great Moral Costs*, N.Y. TIMES, June 9, 1990, at 22.

Should all of the writings of Professor Levin at issue in the case be considered "scholarship"? Does the difficulty of answering that question suggest why the AAUP Declaration takes the position that all extramural writing and speech by faculty should be protected by academic freedom?

3. In 2006, tenured engineering professor Arthur Butz of Northwestern University told press in the United States and in Iran that he agreed with Iranian President Mahmoud Ahmadinejad that the holocaust is a myth. Henry Bienen, the President of Northwestern, in response issued a statement that was emailed to all students, faculty, and staff at the University. Bienen said in part:

While I hope everyone understands that Butz's opinions are his own and in no way represent the views of the university or me personally, his reprehensible opinions on this issue are an embarrassment to Northwestern.

Jodi S. Cohen, *NU Rips Holocaust Denial*, CHI. TRIB., Feb. 7, 2006, at NS1.

Did the statement by President Bienen infringe the academic freedom of Professor Butz?

Rouse v. Walters & Associates

United States District Court for the Southern District of Iowa, 2007.
513 F. Supp. 2d 1041.

■ JAMES E. GRITZNER, J.

This matter is before the Court on . . . Motion[s] for Partial Summary Judgment. . . .

Plaintiffs Dr. Gene Rouse (Rouse) and Dr. Doyle Wilson (Wilson) were employed by Iowa State University of Science and Technology (ISU). . . .

Third–Party Defendant Dr. Viren Amin is an Associate Scientist with the ISU Department of Animal Science. Biotronics, Inc., is an Iowa corporation that was formed in 1998 by Wilson, Rouse, Amin, and Craig Hayes.

Defendant Walter & Associates, L.L.C., markets and provides agricultural consulting services throughout the United States, Canada, and Latin America. Defendant Marvin J. Walter is President and Chairman of Walter & Associates, L.L.C., and was a member of the board of directors of the Iowa State University Research Foundation (ISURF) prior to the formation of Walter & Associates. ISURF is a not-for-profit corporation that is a separate entity from ISU. ISURF owns and licenses ISU's intellectual property. The Office of Intellectual Property and Technology Transfer (OIPTT) at ISU is charged with serving ISU as the vehicle for marketing and licensing intellectual property owned by ISURF. Dr. Kenneth Kirkland is the Executive Director of ISURF and the Director of OIPTT. Nita Lovejoy is the Associate Director of ISURF and OIPTT.

[Since the 1980s Rouse and Wilson, professors at ISU, had researched the use of ultrasound technology to predict the beef quality of living cattle, drawing $1.6 million in outside grant funding. Rouse and Wilson eventually developed live animal intramuscular fat prediction software (LAIPS) that used algorithms to predict the percentage of intramuscular fat based on the images output by the Aloka and Classic ultrasound devices. In February 1995, "[b]ecause the LAIPS program arose from the sponsored research, Rouse and Wilson assigned the copyright for the software to ISURF ...," which in turn licensed LAIPS to third parties and provided royalties to Rouse, Wilson, and Amin, who had assisted in developing LAIPS.

"LAIPS requires the use of another software program, a 'front-end' interface program, to serve as a user interface and a means to display the images." Finding their current front-end program too slow, Rouse and Wilson asked Amin to develop a new front-end program that could function with the Windows© operating system. As requested, Amin wrote the USOFT program, which incorporated VisionTools software. Amin signed a license agreement for VisionTools with Evergreen Technologies, Inc., pursuant to which ISU obtained a nonexclusive, nontransferable license to copy the software only for incorporation into ISU's programs and to distribute it noncommercially within ISU's departments, but ISU was prohibited from commercially distributing VisionTools or using, reproducing, sub-licensing, distributing, or disposing of it except as allowed by the terms of the licensing agreement. The VisionTools libraries are a "necessary component" for USOFT to "return and display meaningful data on a computer screen."

According to Amin, "USOFT was created to support the research they were doing into intramuscular fat and some of the other traits they were researching. Rouse testified during his deposition that Amin alone ... wrote the software code but that Rouse and Wilson were involved in calculating and preparing certain algorithms used in the USOFT program...."

"Amin programmed the USOFT menu pages with '© Iowa State University' on each screen in the program...." Amin also wrote messages into the software informing users that it was developed at ISU and copyrighted to ISURF. However, "USOFT was never assigned to ISURF in written form, and an express written agreement regarding the ownership of the USOFT copyright does not exist between Plaintiffs and Amin and ISU."

Rouse, Wilson, and Amin executed a "gold sheet" in October 1997 for a "Centralized Processing of Real Time Ultrasound Images Research Project." Gold sheets are used by ISU researchers to inform ISU of their outside funding and state that they will disclose to ISU any intellectual property resulting from their research. The proposed project involved a two-year, $200,000 grant from the American Angus Association (AAA) for the development of a centralized ultrasound processing (CUP) laboratory, which could later be transitioned to the private sector, and $63,000 in University resources. The CUP lab, which ISU ran on its campus from January 1998 to December 1999, used both USOFT and LAIPS. In addition, ISU's "Department of Animal Science developed an intramuscular fat prediction model for the Classic ultrasound scanner," and Amin incrementally updated the USOFT program.

During this time, ISURF repeatedly requested that Rouse and Wilson disclose their newly developed software, particularly the LAIPS updates, which ISU was required to share with third parties to whom it had licensed the program. These requests stemmed from ISURF's belief that USOFT belonged to ISU and had been developed with ISU resources. Despite multiple requests from ISURF, the researchers never disclosed USOFT to ISURF.

In 2000, ISU decided to transfer the CUP lab to the private sector, and ISURF ultimately entered a licensing agreement with Walter & Associates. Wilson included USOFT on a list of the software necessary for Walter & Associates to run the CUP lab, and Amin informed ISURF that USOFT was "free to anyone who wants it." ISU transferred the CUP lab and a software package including USOFT to Walter & Associates, which used both in private-sector ultrasound scanning of cattle. Walter & Associates continued to use USOFT through 2006.

"In 2002, Rouse, Wilson, and Amin, through their company, Biotronics, decided to establish a commercial business and compete in the ultrasound market. Biotronics would thus be directly competing with Walter & Associates. Biotronics does not use USOFT in the course of its ultrasound business." In 2005, Rouse and Wilson wrote to ISURF that they and Amin were the exclusive owners of USOFT. ISURF, through Kenneth Kirkland, declined to concede that the researchers owned USOFT.]

On approximately May 6, 2005, Lovejoy spoke with Amin, who indicated he would speak to Rouse and Wilson about their opinion on placing USOFT in the public domain. Amin was concerned about liability related to the third-party software, VisionTools, and wanted some assurances ISU would protect him from any liability related to any misuse of VisionTools. On May 11, 2005, Rouse, Wilson, and Amin signed an Agreement Between Joint Owners that stated they are the joint owners of all right, title, and interest in the copyright to the USOFT software program. On June 8, 2005, Wilson, Rouse, and Amin filed a Certificate of Registration with the United States Copyright Office for the USOFT program. The copyright was registered on June 9, 2005. At some time during 2005, prior to the filing of the present suit, Rouse and Wilson sent a cease and desist letter to Walter, claiming USOFT was independently owned by them. Walter & Associates refused to discontinue their use of the USOFT program.

On August 1, 2005, Plaintiffs (Rouse and Wilson) filed a Complaint against Walter & Associates alleging a single claim of copyright infringement based on Walter & Associates' use of the USOFT software. On August 31, 2005, Walter & Associates filed an Answer and included counterclaims against Rouse, Wilson, and Biotronics for declaratory judgment, tortious interference with contract, tortious interference with prospective business relationship, and slander per se. . . .

. . .

Defendants argue that Rouse and Wilson's claims for copyright infringement against Walter & Associates and Walter must be dismissed because (1) Rouse and Wilson cannot establish as a matter of law that USOFT is an expression of their creation, rather than merely their idea, which is not subject to copyright protection; (2) USOFT was created by Amin, Rouse, and Wilson within the scope of their employment at ISU and thus is owned by ISU as work made for hire. . . .

. . .

... The testimony of Wilson, Rouse, and Amin indicates the development of USOFT was a collaborative process, with Wilson and Rouse directing Amin, who was doing the actual drafting and typing of the software program. Considering the facts in the light most favorable to Rouse and Wilson, the Court cannot decide as a matter of law that Plaintiffs did not co-author some protectable interest in the USOFT program with Amin. However, under the circumstances of this case, a finding that Rouse and Wilson co-authored the work with Amin does not end the inquiry regarding standing because the analysis continues into the "work for hire" doctrine, as that doctrine ultimately determines the "author" of a work for purposes of the Copyright Act.

"Copyright in a work protected under this title vests initially in the author or authors of the work. The authors of a joint work are [co-owners] of copyright in the work." 17 U.S.C. § 201(a). "In the case of a work made for hire, the employer or other person for whom the work was prepared is considered the author for purposes of this title, and, unless the parties have *expressly* agreed otherwise in a *written instrument signed by them,* owns all of the rights comprised in the copyright." 17 U.S.C. § 201(b) (emphasis added). Defendants assert that ISU owns the copyright to USOFT as work made for hire. Rouse, Wilson, and Amin contend the work-for-hire doctrine does not apply in this case because Rouse, Wilson, and Amin expressly agreed otherwise in a written instrument.

Plaintiffs contend that at the commencement of their employment with ISU, they signed a "letter of intent" with the University that expressly incorporated into the letter of intent the ISU Faculty Handbook, and that this Faculty Handbook contains a policy that vests ownership rights in the authors unless assigned to ISURF. Plaintiffs further contend that even if the work-for-hire doctrine could apply in this case, the required elements are not met, and disputed issues of material fact exist that preclude summary judgment on the issue of work for hire.

. . .

Defendants assert that as ISU tenured faculty, Rouse and Wilson were expected to and did in fact engage in research activities. Rouse and Wilson argue that the creation of USOFT was not the kind of work they were expected to perform.

Rouse testified that he and Wilson devoted approximately fifteen years of their ISU careers working on the research project relating to the prediction of intramuscular fat in live cattle, bringing in over $1.6–million in sponsored research funding to support such work.... Complementary to that research was the development of ultrasound technology to measure compositional traits in beef cattle.

. . .

Amin testified he began working with the Department of Animal Science after he graduated in 1992, working on beef ultrasound, and that he was still working in the Department of Animal Science when he was developing USOFT. Amin testified that he did research, developed algorithms to analyze the images, assisted in developing a procedure to derive information out of the images, assisted in scanning the images and, wrote source codes. Amin also assisted in making improvements to the LAIPS software program, and he developed a program to interpret images from the Classic scanner. Although Amin stated in his May 24, 2007, declaration that his position was "as a scientist, not a programmer," this more recent declaration contradicts not only Amin's own deposition testimony that in performing work for the Department of Animal Science he had programmed software, but also his own curriculum vitae, in which he included, under the header "Primary areas of interest and expertise," "computer based system and software development for bio-medical and agricultural imaging applications," and under the header "Other Professional Activities," "Developed USOFT and related software products for animal ultrasound researchers."

Given these facts, there exists no genuine issue of material fact that the development of USOFT was within the scope of duties Amin was hired to perform. Amin testified USOFT was developed to support the research they were doing into intramuscular fat and some of the other compositional traits, such as how to measure the depth and area of the fat. Amin testified USOFT allowed them to do their research at ISU in a particular way.

Rouse and Wilson argue that although part of Amin's salary was paid by grant funding, this salary was paid for his work as a scientist, not as a computer programmer. Courts have found that although not hired to program software, where the development of software occurred within the scope of the employee's employment it can be deemed work of the kind the employee was hired to perform.

. . . Wilson and Rouse directed Amin to develop a front-end program, USOFT, in order to provide them with a faster interface for the LAIPS software. This faster interface for LAIPS would certainly assist Rouse and Wilson in continuing their ultrasound research project at ISU and allow them to run the ultrasound processing laboratory more efficiently based on the ability to process the images more quickly. Further, ISURF licensed USOFT, along with LAIPS, to a third party, evidence that USOFT was important to the process of ultrasound imaging and clearly integral to the work and an obvious part of the research task. The Court concludes Plaintiffs have failed to generate a genuine issue of material fact regarding whether directing Amin to develop USOFT, and assisting him in that development, was the type of work Rouse and Wilson were employed to perform. Plaintiffs have also failed to generate a genuine issue of material fact on the issue of whether drafting USOFT at the directive of the professors and creating the software with their assistance was of the type of work Amin was expected to perform at ISU.

Rouse, Wilson, and Amin contend the development of USOFT did not occur substantially within authorized space and time limits, asserting Amin used his own personal computer at home for the "vast" majority of programming the USOFT program.

An employee cannot establish copyright ownership rights solely on the basis that the work was done at home on off-hours. *Avtec Sys., Inc.* [*v. Peiffer*, 21 F.3d 568, 571 (4th Cir. 1994).]

. . .

The facts of this case are strikingly similar to those of *Genzmer v. Public Health Trust of Miami–Dade County* [219 F. Supp. 2d 1275 (S.D. Fla. 2002)]. In that case, Genzmer contended he wrote the software at issue at his home, using his home computer, during off-duty hours. In finding Genzmer's work occurred substantially within the authorized time and space limits, the court noted Genzmer was a salaried employee involved in a research project and stated what mattered was that he performed the work on the software during the time period in which he had been employed to complete the research program. The court also found it was important that Genzmer tested the computer program using the employer's resources.

The USOFT program was developed and tested on ISU computers, and because USOFT utilized the VisionTools software, pursuant to the Vision-Tools Noncommercial Run–Time Software Distribution Agreement between Evergreen Technologies and ISU, the VisionTools software could not be distributed to any computer system other than ISU's computer system. Indeed, both Rouse and Wilson testified USOFT was not operational unless it had VisionTools attached to it, and USOFT required the VisionTools libraries to operate. The source code for USOFT is kept at the Department of Animal Science.

In arguing the creation of USOFT did not occur substantially within authorized time and space limits, Plaintiffs argue ISURF has a specific disclosure form for (1) inventions arising in the employees' work, (2) research that has "used significant university resources," or (3) research that has a commercial application, and that no such disclosure form was submitted to ISURF for the USOFT program. It is undisputed that no disclosure form regarding USOFT was ever given to ISURF. Section 3.1(2) of ISU's Personnel Policy states, "Faculty members have the responsibility of disclosing intellectual property in a timely fashion when it arises in their work." The lack of a disclosure form simply means Plaintiffs, the individuals who would have been responsible for completing such a disclosure form, never gave such a form to ISURF. Plaintiffs may not rely on their own failure to complete the requisite disclosure form as evidence that USOFT was not the type of invention subject to a disclosure form under ISU policies, and the lack of the requisite disclosure form does not generate a *genuine* issue of material fact.

Rouse, Wilson, and Amin make the same argument regarding the absence of a "gold sheet" that specifically pertained to USOFT. This argument is without merit because, again, Rouse, Wilson, and Amin would have been the ones responsible for generating a gold sheet; thus, contrary to the assertions of Plaintiffs, the fact that one does not exist that specifically indicates "USOFT" as the funded research project does not generate a fact issue that USOFT was not created substantially within the authorized time and space limits of the job.

.   .   .

. . . Plaintiffs have failed to generate a genuine issue of material fact regarding whether USOFT was work made for hire.

Where work is deemed "work made for hire," under the Copyright Act such work automatically vests with the employer unless an express, written agreement between the employer and employee exists. . . . Rouse and Wilson assert they do have such a written instrument, arguing that at the time they began their employment, they signed a letter of intent with ISU. Rouse and Wilson contend this letter of intent expressly incorporated the ISU Faculty Handbook policy. . . .

The Faculty Handbook states, "The Faculty Handbook is the official statement of Iowa State University policy governing the rights, responsibilities, and performance of faculty." [The "Policies"] section states as follows:

The university recognizes the vested rights of an author under the Iowa Code. However, if the educational materials are to be developed with university sponsorship, the author is expected to assign these rights for the benefit of the university. It is not intended that this policy affect the traditional university relationship to faculty members' ownership of books or other instructional materials whose preparation was not supported or assisted in a substantial way by the university.

Individuals preparing or planning to prepare educational materials are encouraged to clarify whether the materials are covered by this policy through consultation with the appropriate department chair and dean.

In cases in which a prospective author wishes to receive support from the university in a proposed development of educational materials covered by this document, the university will enter into an agreement with the prospective author prior to the development of the university-sponsored educational materials setting forth the extent of support, if any, associated with their development and providing for payment to the author and/or the distribution of earnings, if any should accrue from the use, rental royalties, or sale of the educational materials.

. . .

Plaintiffs argue that USOFT was "educational" in nature, and thus under Section 8.3.6.3 they retained the authorship to USOFT. There is no evidence in the record to demonstrate USOFT was educational in nature or otherwise used for academic instruction. The record demonstrates USOFT was developed not to assist in educating ISU students, but instead to assist in the ultrasound imaging research. In the absence of more specific language in Section 8.3.6.3 of the Handbook, the unsupported assertion that USOFT was a Section 8.3.6.3 educational material is insufficient to generate a genuine issue of material fact.

. . .

... ISU expressly acknowledges the work-for-hire doctrine applies to employees and faculty members. ISURF and OIPTT policies that pertain to copyright state that the ownership of copyright in traditional scholarly works, such as poems, plays, visual arts, textbooks, and musical compositions, remain with the student or faculty authors. This policy then goes on to state as follows:

Other types of copyrighted works such as software, instructional materials, and works of non-faculty employees are owned by the university or for the benefit of the university when:

* Significant university resources are required to develop a copyrighted work. The current policy requires that an agreement be entered into between the developers and the university prior to the development of work. Concerns about determining whether significant resources will be

used or have been used should be taken to the Department head and/or Dean who may consult with OIPTT. Funded research is considered a use of significant university resources.

* Copyrighted works are produced by university employees in performance of the duties of their position at ISU. These works are considered developed under copyright's work-for-hire doctrine, under which the university is considered the author and owner of the copyright.

* The work may also be patented, such as the case with software. (Note that in these cases, the university reserves the right to pursue multiple forms of legal protection.)

* The work uses any of the university trademarks, including the names ISU, Iowa State, or Cyclones.

Rouse and Wilson argue they never used grant money in creating USOFT; however, both testified they raised over $1.6–million in funding for the ultrasound imaging research, and the record shows a small portion of these funds were used to purchase the computers on which USOFT was developed. Further, both Rouse and Wilson testified they spent over fifteen years at ISU conducting this research, and such a significant amount of time cannot be said to be anything but in the performance of their duties in their position at ISU. The work not only uses the name Iowa State University, USOFT actually has the internationally known copyright symbol "©" in front of Iowa State University's name on the USOFT screen displays. While it is unclear if USOFT is the type of software that actually can be patented, it appears that given the record of this case, the development of USOFT falls into practically every category ISURF and OIPTT have described as being works in which ownership in the copyright will vest in the University.

. . .

Plaintiffs have failed to generate a genuine issue of material facts regarding whether an express, written agreement existed between ISU and the Plaintiffs that exempts USOFT from the "work for hire" doctrine.

. . .

... The record demonstrates that there are no genuine issues of material fact regarding whether USOFT was work for hire under the Copyright Act. The Court concludes USOFT was work made for hire, and therefore pursuant to 17 U.S.C. § 201(b), ISU is considered the author for purposes of the Copyright Act. Because ISU is deemed the owner of the copyright, Rouse and Wilson have no standing to bring a copyright infringement claim with respect to USOFT. . . . Defendants' Motion for Summary Judgment therefore must be granted.

Note on Patents and the Bayh–Dole Act

1. In 1980, Congress passed the Universities and Small Business Patent Procedures Act (otherwise known as the Bayh–Dole Act) Pub. L. No. 96–517, 94 Stat. 3015 (1980) (codified at 35 U.S.C. §§ 200–212 (2000)). Although the Act was intended simply to standardize the rules governing ownership of patents on inventions created using federal research funds, it has been credited with bringing huge returns to universities. *See generally* Lorelei Ritchie de Larena, *The Price of Progress: Are Universities Adding to the Cost?*, 43 HOUSTON L. REV. 1373 (2007). *Compare* DAVID C. MOWERY, RICHARD R., NELSON, BHAVEN N. SAMPAT & ARVIDS A. ZIEDONIS, IVORY TOWER AND INDUSTRIAL INNOVATION: UNIVERSITY-INDUSTRY TECHNOLOGY TRANSFER BEFORE AND AFTER THE BAYH–DOLE ACT (2004). Mowery et al., by contrast, report that university patenting had begun to grow long before passage of the Act. Indeed, the "patent propensity," meaning the patents per dollar of academic research and development spending, grew steadily after World War II with no sharp break in the trend after 1980. U.S. patent policy also broadened the range of patentable subject matter in the biomedical sciences during this same period. Growth in patents was particularly large in molecular biology many of which were of high value to the pharmaceutical industry. *Id.* at 181–82.

Although returns to a university can be quite high, the beneficial effects of the Bayh–Dole Act are not without cost to traditions of scholarship. As one scholar has noted:

> By most measures, the numbers are pretty impressive. In fiscal year 2004 alone, approximately 154 U.S. universities reaped over $1 billion in net patent licensing income, executed 3928 new licenses, and were issued over 3800 U.S. patents, largely as a result of university-industry technology transfer initiatives. By comparison, in 1991, ninety-eight universities garnered a mere $123 million in gross licensing income. These funds provide needed revenue to university coffers, stimulate economic growth in surrounding municipalities, and provide beneficial products to consumers here and abroad.

> But these achievements have not come without a cost to academia. Historically, universities have existed for the purpose of promoting inquiry and advancing the sum of human knowledge. To further these goals, university researchers would publish and present their scientific findings as soon as possible in accordance with communal norms promoting the prompt and open sharing of data. But today, academic researchers are being encouraged by technology transfer offices ("TTOs") and industry sponsors to delay publishing and presenting their work until after filing a patent application and sometimes even longer than that. In addition, the growth in patent-related litigation involving universities and the much-hyped "tragedy of the anticommons" in the patenting of basic research tools are both costs attributable, at least in part, to technology transfer initiatives. While not amenable to precise quantification, the stifling of discourse and the erosion in the norms of sharing and colloquy historically associated with the scholarly enterprise are costs that must be balanced against the technology transfer gains.

> Both the impressive numbers and the negative side effects are usually traced to the 1980 Bayh–Dole Act, which allows universities to elect ownership of inventions developed with federal funds, enabling them to offer exclusive licenses to companies interested in commercializing the inventions.

Margo A. Bagley, *Academic Discourse and Proprietary Rights: Putting Patents in their Proper Place*, 47 B.C. L. REV. 217, 217–19 (2006) (internal citations omitted). For a thoughtful critique of university rights to the results of federally funded research, see Rebecca S. Eisenberg, *Public Research and Private Development: Patents and Technology Transfer in Government–Sponsored Research*, 82 VA. L. REV. 1663 (1996).

2.   It is common for multiple researchers, often including graduate students, to work together on new technologies. This often makes the process of determining who is the inventor complicated and, at times, acrimonious. For a good discussion of academic mentor-mentee patent disputes, see Sean B. Seymore, *My Patent, Your Patent, or Our Patent? Inventorship Disputes Within Academic Research Groups*, 16 ALB. L.J. SCI. & TECH. 125 (2005–2006).

Radolf v. University of Connecticut

United States District Court for the District of Connecticut, 2005.
364 F. Supp. 2d 204.

■ MARK R. KRAVITZ, UNITED STATES DISTRICT JUDGE.

This case arises out of a bitter dispute between Plaintiff Justin D. Radolf, M.D., a tenured professor, and his colleagues at the University of Connecticut Health Center ("UCHC") and the University of Connecticut School of Medicine. . . .

. . . Dr. Radolf seeks prospective injunctive relief against the Defendants in their official capacities and monetary damages against the Defendants in their individual capacities. . . .

The basic facts of this case are not in serious dispute. Dr. Radolf joined the faculty of the UCHC as a tenured professor in April 1999 in order to establish the UCHC Center for Microbial Pathogenesis (the "Center") and to serve as its Director. Defendant Peter J. Deckers, M.D., is the Executive Vice President for Health Affairs of the UCHC and Dean of the University of Connecticut School of Medicine. Defendant Richard Berlin, Ph.D., is Associate Dean for Research Planning and Coordination at UCHC. Defendant Stephen Wikel, Ph.D., is a full professor with tenure in the Department of Physiology at UCHC and the Interim Director of the Center for Microbial Pathogenesis.

[In 2001, a UCHC Special Review Board found that "Dr. Radolf had falsified data on two grant proposals submitted to the U.S. Department of Agriculture and Connecticut Innovations, Inc." The University placed a letter of reprimand in Dr. Radolf's file, put him on three-year academic probation, and required a faculty committee to review all his grants, contracts, and philanthropic proposals for regulatory compliance and research integrity. At the same time, the Department of Health and Human Services's Federal Office of Research Integrity (ORI) began investigating Dr. Radolf's academic misconduct. In 2003, Dr. Radolf and ORI signed a Voluntary Exclusion Agreement, in which he admitted scientific misconduct in National Institutes of Health (NIH)-funded research and accepted five years of academic probation for activities connected to the U.S. Public Health Service. Although UCHC and the Defendants were not parties to the Voluntary Exclusion Agreement, UCHC was required to submit a Supervisory Plan, similar to that already in place at the University, for ORI approval.]

Dr. Radolf continues to be employed as a full professor with tenure at UCHC and he may still work at the Center for Microbial Pathogenesis, though the parties were unclear about that latter fact at oral argument on January 31, 2005. t their core, Dr. Radolf's claims in this lawsuit arise from the actions and decisions of the Defendants in their attempt to navigate the difficult terrain of continuing to employ a tenured professor who was on academic probation imposed by the UCHC and under investigation by the federal government for scientific misconduct, an investigation which eventually resulted in an extended term of academic probation. . . .

. . .

. . . Dr. Radolf alleges that his First Amendment right to academic freedom was violated when Drs. Deckers and Berlin prevented him from participating in the formulation of a grant proposal to the Department of

Defense entitled "Anti-vector vaccines to control mosquito and tick transmitted diseases" (the "DOD Grant"), and in subsequent research funded by that grant. . . .

It is important at the outset to emphasize precisely what Dr. Radolf claims was a violation of his First Amendment right to academic freedom. He does not assert that Defendants prevented him from teaching or performing research on any subject matter. Nor does he claim . . . that Defendants retaliated against him for engaging in protected First Amendment activities, by, for example, denying him the opportunity to participate in a grant available to others because of his speech on matters of public concern. Rather, Dr. Radolf asserts that he had a constitutional right, derived from and based on the First Amendment right to academic freedom, to participate in research projects for which he was qualified, and Defendants violated that right when they allegedly denied Dr. Radolf the opportunity to participate in the DOD Grant.

There are plenty of factual disputes on the nature of the research in the DOD Grant, and on whether and/or why Dr. Radolf was denied participation in this research project. For purposes of summary judgment, the Court draws all ambiguities and inferences in favor of Dr. Radolf, and thus accepts his version of the events surrounding the DOD Grant. . . .

. . .

. . . [C]ourts understandably have been hesitant to define the precise contours of the First Amendment right to academic freedom. The right to academic freedom is often formulated as a right of a university or other academic institution to be free from government interference with its curriculum and its decisions on who may or may not teach or be admitted to study.

In some instances, however, courts have acknowledged that an individual professor or student possessed an individual right to academic freedom. *See, e.g.,* Vega v. Miller, 273 F.3d 460, 467 (2d Cir. 2001) ("*Dube* serves as a caution to governmental administrators not to discipline a college teacher for expressing controversial, even offensive, views lest a pall of orthodoxy inhibit the free exchange of ideas in the classroom.") (citing *Dube* [*v. State Univ. of New York*, 900 F.2d 597, 589, 598 (2d Cir. 1990)]); *East Hartford Education Assoc. v. Board of Education*, 562 F.2d 838, 843 (2d Cir. 1977) ("Freedom to teach in the manner of one's choice is a form of academic freedom that is universally recognized, if not invariably protected, at the college level."). And some courts have also suggested that the right of academic freedom may extend to research done in a laboratory. *See, e.g., Dow Chem. Co. v. Allen*, 672 F.2d 1262, 1275 (7th Cir. 1982) (academic freedom "extends as readily to the scholar in the laboratory as to the teacher in the classroom.") (quoted in *McMillan v. Togus Reg'l Office, Dep't of Veterans Affairs*, 294 F. Supp. 2d 305, 317 (E.D.N.Y. 2003)).

Nonetheless, what is clear from the available case law in this admittedly amorphous area of First Amendment jurisprudence is that no court has ever held that a university professor has a First Amendment right of academic freedom to participate in writing any particular grant proposal or performing research under any particular grant. . . . The cases Dr. Radolf cites in support of his argument all concern a public actor (a university or other government entity) either directly forbidding a teacher from teaching a particular subject or preventing a researcher from performing research on a certain subject, or otherwise chilling the teacher's or researcher's expressive rights—factual circumstances that are not even alleged here. *Cf. Dow Chemical*, 672 F.2d at 1275 (addressing the question of the extent to which administrative subpoenas seeking enormous amounts of primary data would "threaten substantial intrusion into the enterprise of university research," stating that "there are several reasons to think they are capable of chilling the exercise of academic freedom").

. . . [E]ven if the Court is wrong and Dr. Radolf did have a First Amendment right to participate in the DOD Grant, Defendants would nonetheless have qualified immunity from his claims in this lawsuit because that supposed constitutional right was not clearly established at the time of the events in question—or, for that matter, even today. "Government officials performing discretionary functions generally are shielded from liability for civil damages insofar as their conduct does not violate clearly established statutory or constitutional rights of which a reasonable person would have known." *Harlow v. Fitzgerald*, 457 U.S. 800, 818 (1982).

Questions and Comments on *Radolf*

1. The *Radolf* court cited *Dow Chemical Co. v. Allen*, 672 F.2d 1262 (7th Cir. 1982), for the proposition that researchers might have an academic freedom interest in their laboratory activities that protects them from state action that might have a chilling effects on their expressive rights. Dow Chemical, faced with EPA cancellation of certain herbicides it produced, obtained a subpoena from an administrative law judge ordering "University of Wisconsin researchers to disclose all of the notes, reports, working papers, and raw data relating to on-going, incomplete animal toxicity studies so that it may evaluate that information with a view toward possible use at the cancellation hearings." *Id.* at 1265–66. Dow believed that the researchers' ongoing study would yield information proving that the herbicides would have no ill effects below certain concentrations. The Seventh Circuit affirmed the District Court's refusal to enforce the subpoena on two grounds: overburdensomeness on the researchers and academic freedom.

In considering whether a subpoena is unduly burdensome, courts balance the party seeking the subpoena's need for the material against the burden imposed on the party holding the subpoenaed information. After accepting the District Court's conclusion that Dow's need for the researchers' information was not great, *id.* at 1272–73, the Court of Appeals outlined the burdens issuing the subpoena would impose on the researchers:

> that public access to the research data would make the studies an unacceptable basis for scientific papers or other research; that peer review and publication of the studies was crucial to the researchers' credibility and careers and would be precluded by whole or partial public disclosure of the information; that loss of the opportunity to publish would severely decrease the researchers' professional opportunities in the future; and that even inadvertent disclosure of the information would risk total destruction of months or years of research.

Id. at 1273.

After concluding that these burdens outweighed Dow's need for the research data, the court went on to address the case's implications for academic freedom (an issue not discussed by the District Court but raised on appeal by the State of Wisconsin as amicus). The Seventh Circuit concluded, "whatever constitutional protection is afforded by the First Amendment extends as readily to the scholar in the laboratory as to the teacher in the classroom." *Id.* at 1275. The subpoena, which would have required the researchers to submit both existing and future data:

> threaten[ed] substantial intrusion into the enterprise of university research, and there are several reasons to think [it] capable of chilling the exercise of academic freedom.... [E]nforcement of the subpoenas would leave the researchers with the knowledge throughout continuation of their studies that the fruits of their labors had been appropriated by and were being scrutinized by a not-unbiased third party whose interests were arguably antithetical to theirs. It is not difficult to imagine that that realization might well be both unnerving and discouraging.... In addition, the researchers could reasonably fear that additional demands for disclosure would be made in the future. If a private corporation can subpoena the entire work product of months of study, what is to say further down the line the company will not seek other subpoenas to determine how the research is coming along? ... Clearly, enforcement of the subpoenas carries the potential for chilling exercise of First Amendment rights.

Id. at 1276.

Concurring, Judge Pell wrote that the court need not have reached the academic freedom issue and called attention to the fact:

> that this was not an independent investigation engaged in by faculty researchers and financed by the University. The research is being conducted pursuant to a grant application to the Department of Health, Education, and Welfare. The fact that it is being financed by government money, I assume, would not mean that the ongoing study was automatically subject to public disclosure at each step and stage thereof. Nonetheless, it is quite reasonable to assume that the undertaking of the study was directly limited to whether or not the product being researched should continue in the public marketplace....

Id. at 1279 (Pell, J., concurring).

Why might Wisconsin, which, as a state, is subject to First Amendment limitations on its actions, have encouraged the Seventh Circuit to adopt an expansive interpretation of academic freedom encompassing the laboratory?

Do you agree with Judge Pell's suggestion that research should have less First Amendment protection when funded by the government? Consider Judge Pell's argument in light of Charles Reich's classic article *The New Property*, 73 YALE L.J. 733, 774 (1964):

> Reduced to simplest terms, "the public interest" has usually meant this: government largess may be denied or taken away if this will serve some legitimate public policy. The policy may be one directly related to the largess itself, or it may be some collateral objective of government. A contract may be denied if this will promote fair labor standards. A television license may be refused if this will promote the policies of the antitrust laws.... Most of these objectives are laudable, and all are within the power of government. The great difficulty is that they are simplistic. Concentration on a single policy or value obscures other values that may be at stake. Some of these competing values are other public policies; for example, the policy of the best possible television service to the public may compete with observance of antitrust laws. The legislature is the natural arbiter of such conflicts. But the conflicts may also be more fundamental. In the regulation of government largess, achievement of specific policy goals may undermine the independence of the individual. Where such conflicts exist, a simplistic notion of the public interest may unwittingly destroy some values.

How significant to the decision in *Dow Chemical* was the fact that the subpoena was sought by a private party that was actually challenging the government's tentative policy decision? Would the outcome have been different had the government itself sought access to the researchers' data before the completion of the study?

2. The issue raised in *Dow Chemical* is not uncommon. A similar case arose out the the Microsoft antitrust litigation. Microsoft sought a subpoena for the research materials for a not-yet-published book, *Competing on Internet Time: Lessons from Netscape and the Battle with Microsoft* by Michael A. Cusumano and David B. Yoffie, tenured professors at MIT's Sloan School of Management and Harvard Business School, respectively. In researching their book, the professors had conducted confidential interviews with employees of Netscape, a Microsoft competitor, and Microsoft sought the notes, recordings, and transcripts of those interviews. Microsoft explained that these materials could show that Microsoft's dominance in the internet browser market resulted from Netscape's business mistakes, not Microsoft's alleged illegal and anti-competitive behavior.

On appeal from the District Court's denial of Microsoft's motion to compel production of the research materials, the First Circuit held that "[a]cademicians engaged in pre-publication research should be accorded protection commensurate to that which the law provides journalists." *In re* Cusumano, 162 F.3d 708, 714 (1st Cir. 1998).

> Journalists are the personification of a free press, and to withhold . . . protection would invite a "chilling effect on speech," and thus destabilize the First Amendment. The same concerns suggest that courts ought to offer similar protection to academicians engaged in scholarly research. After all, scholars too are information gatherers and disseminators. If their research materials were freely subject to subpoena, their sources likely would refuse to confide in them. As with reporters, a drying-up of sources would sharply curtail the information available to academic researchers and thus would restrict their output. Just as a journalist, stripped of sources, would write fewer, less incisive articles, an academician, stripped of sources, would be able to provide fewer, less cogent analyses. Such similarities of concern and function militate in favor of a similar level of protection for journalists and academic researchers.
>
> . . .
>
> . . . [A]llowing Microsoft to obtain the notes, tapes, and transcripts it covets would hamstring not only the [Cusumano and Yoffie's] future research efforts but also those of other similarly situated scholars. This loss of theoretical insight into the business world is of concern in and of itself. Even more important, compelling the disclosure of such research materials would infrigidate the free flow of information to the public, thus denigrating a fundamental First Amendment value.

Id. at 714, 717.

The Seventh Circuit in *Dow Chemical* extended researchers' laboratory rights as far as the teacher's classroom rights. In *Cusumano*, the First Circuit compared researchers' privileges to those of journalists. Which analogy seems to be a better fit? Which provides researchers greater protections? The right kind of protections?

3. Companies have also sought access to researchers' data in lawsuits against the researchers. In 1998, for example, Beverly Enterprises Inc., a nursing-home chain, sued Kate L. Bronfenbrenner, a Cornell labor researcher, for libel and slander. The company sought $225,000 in damages for Bronfenbrenner's allegedly false statements to members of Congress regarding Beverly's dispute with a union. Over 700 scholars protested Beverly's pre-trial request for copies of Bronfenbrenner's research, which included confidential information on union organizing strategies. A district court held that Bronfenbrenner's statements to Congress were legally protected. *Judge Dismisses Company's Defamation Lawsuit Against Cornell U. Researcher*, CHRON. HIGHER EDUC., June 5, 1998, at A9.

For further discussion about compelling professors to share the fruits of their research, see generally *Court-Ordered Disclosure of Academic Research: A Clash of Values of Science and Law*, LAW & CONTEMP. PROBS., Summer 1996, at 1.

Note on Defamation and Research

Professors sometimes sue each other. The most prominent example of such scholarly litigation is the defamation lawsuit by economist John R. Lott, Jr., against Steven D. Levitt, another economist and co-author of *Freakonomics*. The lawsuit stems from a 2005 e-mail from Levitt to a third economist and from passages of *Freakonomics* critical of Lott. David Glenn, *Dueling Economists Reach Settlement in Defamation Lawsuit*, CHRON. HIGHER EDUC., Aug. 10, 2007, at A10.

In 2007, Levitt and Lott reached a tentative settlement agreement regarding the e-mail, in which Levitt stated that a *Journal of Law & Economics* article by Lott had not been peer-refereed. The settlement agreement required Levitt to write a "clarification letter" to the recipient of the e-mail, stating that the article had been peer-refereed and that Levitt had in fact been one of the referees. Still, "Lott appear[ed] to have won little from his 15 months of litigation. No money . . . change[d] hands, and the settlement d[id] not require a formal apology from Mr. Levitt." *Id.*

At the time of the proposed settlement on the claim stemming from the e-mail, Lott was still pursuing the defamation claims resulting from *Freakonomics* itself, although the court had previously dismissed that part of the suit. *See* Lott v. Levitt, 469 F. Supp. 2d 575 (N.D. Ill. 2007). Lott particularly objected to passages of the book that criticized his work *More Guns, Less Crime. Freakonomics* states, "[T]here was the troubling allegation that Lott actually invented some of the survey data that support his more-guns/less-crime theory. Regardless of whether the data were faked, Lott's admittedly intriguing hypothesis [that places allowing law-abiding people to carry weapons have less violent crime] doesn't seem to be true. When other scholars have tried to replicate his results, they found that right-to-carry laws simply don't bring down crime." STEVEN D. LEVITT & STEPHEN J. DUBNER, FREAKONOMICS 133–34 (2005).

Other disputes asserting defamation in research arise in the context of scholarly research that contradicts previous researchers findings and studies. In 1993, Edward Ezrailson co-authored an article suggesting that patients with silicone breast implants have elevated levels of antibodies directed at the silicone. The article hypothesized that an assay researched and developed by Ezrailson as CEO of Emerald Biomedical Sciences could help determine whether breast implants were leaking silicone gel into the body. Emerald sought to market the assay commercially, but the FDA made an assessment that the assay had not been proven effective. In 1996, a group of three medical science researchers employed by the University of Texas Southwestern Medical Center published an article based on a study of whether silicone causes the body to form antibodies. These researches found that the assay used in the 1996 study was "similar" to the one developed by Ezrailson, but there were also important differences. The article concluded that the results of the study "raise questions about the validity and reproducibility of the . . . assay. . . ." Furthermore, the article called into question the ability of the assay to detect implant ruptures.

Ezrailson sued the researchers, claiming that their statements were false and defamatory. On appeal, the court held for the researchers. After noting that "no person of ordinary intelligence would perceive the article as defaming Ezrailson personally," the court discussed the relationship between defamation law and medical research:

> Scientists continuously call into question and test hypotheses and theories; this questioning advances knowledge. In another context, the United States Supreme Court has described scientific conclusions as "subject to

perpetual revision." *See Daubert v. Merrell Dow Pharms., Inc.*, 509 U.S. 579, 597 (1993). The Court noted:

> The scientific project is advanced by broad and wide-ranging consideration of a multitude of hypotheses, for those that are incorrect will eventually be shown to be so, and that in itself is an advance.

Id. Here, appellees' hypothesis was shown to be incorrect; "and that in itself is an advance." *Id.* If advancement in medical scientific knowledge is essential to society, "inquiries into these problems, speculations about them, stimulation in others of reflection upon them, must be left as unfettered as possible." *See Sweezy v. New Hampshire*, 354 U.S. 234, 262 (1957) (Frankfurter, J., concurring).

Note on Scientific Misconduct and Conflicts of Interest

1. Beginning in 1989, in response to several high profile cases involving allegations of scientific misconduct, both the Public Health Service (PHS) and the National Science Foundation (NSF) issued regulations defining and prohibiting misconduct in science they funded. By law, institutions conducting funded research have primary responsibility for making formal findings of misconduct, 42 C.F.R. § 93.307 (2005), and for then reporting their investigation findings to the federal government. 42 C.F.R. § 93.403 (2005). *See generally* Debra Parrish, *Scientific Misconduct and the Plagiarism Cases*, 21 J.C. & U.L. 517 (1995).

In 2002 the NSF revised its regulations to provide:

> Research misconduct means fabrication, falsification, or plagiarism in proposing or performing research funded by NSF, reviewing research proposals submitted to NSF, or in reporting research results funded by NSF.

Research Misconduct, 45 C.F.R. § 689 (2007).

The regulations define plagiarism as "the appropriation of another person's ideas, processes, results or words without giving appropriate credit."

Comparable revisions were adopted by the PHS in 2005. Public Health Service Policies on Research Misconduct, 70 Fed. Reg. 28,370 (May 17, 2005) (to be codified at 42 C.F.R. § 93).

For a summary of federal definitions of misconduct and their application, see generally Debra Parrish, *Research Misconduct and Plagiarism*, 33 J.C. & U.L. 65 (2006). From 1989 to 2004, the Office of Research Integrity of the Public Health Service evaluated 123 allegations of plagiarism and found misconduct in twenty-four of them. *Id.* at 78–79. From 1989 to 2000, the National Science Foundation evaluated 110 cases of alleged plagiarism, and found misconduct in sixteen of them. *Id.* at 80.

2. In 1992, the United States Agency for International Development (USAID) entered into a Cooperative Agreement with an institute of Harvard University to establish a program to assist Russia in developing capital markets. In *United States v. President and Fellows of Harvard College*, 323 F.Supp.2d 151 (D. Mass. 2004), Andrei Shleifer, a Harvard professor of economics who served as director of the program, and Harvard were denied summary judgment in a civil case brought by the government. The government charged that Shleifer and another employee of the project wrongfully invested and conducted business in Russia during the government-sponsored program in violation of the conflict-of-interest provisions of the agreement. In 2005, Harvard agreed to pay the government $26.5 million to settle the litigation, and Shleifer agreed to pay $2 million. Shleifer said he believed that he would have been vindicated had the case gone to trial, but he settled to avoid large legal fees. Marcella Bombardieri, *Harvard Finishes Ethics Investigation in Russian Investment*, BOSTON GLOBE, Oct.13, 2006. A faculty committee investigated Shleifer's actions in the matter and in 2006 reported their findings to the dean of the Faculty of Arts and Sciences. The dean issued a statement that "This case raised important issues which have been thoroughly investigated according to the published procedures of the Faculty, and appropriate action has been taken." He declined to say what action he took, citing a policy of not discussing personnel matters. *Id*. What action would you have recommended?

3.   In 2008, Senator Charles Grassley began a congressional inquiry into apparent conflicts of interest by academic researchers who failed to disclose payments received from pharmaceutical manufacturers. The inquiry revealed that psychiatrist Charles B. Nemeroff of Emory University, author of more than 850 research reports, had signed a letter on June 15, 2004, promising the administration of Emory that he would earn less than $10,000 that year from GlaxoSmithKline, when in fact he earned $170,000 from the company that year. He was at the time the principal investigator of a $3.9 million grant from the National Institute of Mental Health for which GlaxoSmith-Kline provided drugs. Gardiner Harris, *Top Psychiatrist Didn't Report Drug Makers' Pay, Files Show*, N.Y. TIMES, Oct. 4, 2008, at A1. The National Institutes of Health have conflict-of-interest rules that require researchers to inform an institute if they have income of more than $10,000 in a year from a company whose products are being studied. NIH relies on universities to oversee compliance with its rules. If a university does not provide adequate oversight, the agency has the authority to suspend all NIH grants to that university. *Id*.

Senator Grassley has introduced legislation called the Physician Payment Sunshine Act, which would require drug and device manufacturers to disclose publicly any payments to doctors that exceed $500. Several states already require such disclosures. *Id*.

Grimes v. Kennedy Krieger Institute

Court of Appeals of Maryland, 2001.
366 Md. 29, 782 A.2d 807.

■ Opinion by CATHELL, J.

Prologue

We initially note that these are cases of first impression for this Court. For that matter, precious few courts in the United States have addressed the issues presented in the cases at bar. In respect to nontherapeutic research using minors, it has been noted that "consent to research has been virtually unanalyzed by courts and legislatures." Robert J. Katerberg, *Institutional Review Boards, Research on Children, and Informed Consent of Parents: Walking the Tightrope Between Encouraging Vital Experimentation and Protecting Subjects' Rights*, 24 J.C. & U.L. 545, 562, quoting National Commission for the Protection of Human Subjects of Biomedical and Behavioral Research, Report and Recommendations [National Commission]: Research Involving Children 79–80 (1977). Our research reveals this statement remains as accurate now as it was in 1977.

In these present cases, a prestigious research institute, associated with Johns Hopkins University, ... created a nontherapeutic research program[2] whereby it required certain classes of homes to have only partial lead paint

---

[2].   At least to the extent that commercial profit motives are not implicated, therapeutic research's purpose is to directly help or aid a patient who is suffering from a health condition the objectives of the research are designed to address—hopefully by the alleviation, or potential alleviation, of the health condition.

Nontherapeutic research generally utilizes subjects who are not known to have the condition the objectives of the research are designed to address, and/or is not designed to directly benefit the subjects utilized in the research, but, rather, is designed to achieve beneficial results for the public at large (or, under some circumstances, for profit).

abatement modifications performed, and in at least some instances, ... arranged for the landlords to receive public funding by way of grants or loans to aid in the modifications. The research institute then encouraged, and in at least one of the cases at bar, required, the landlords to rent the premises to families with young children. In the event young children already resided in one of the study houses, it was contemplated that a child would remain in the premises, and the child was encouraged to remain, in order for his or her blood to be periodically analyzed. In other words, the continuing presence of the children that were the subjects of the study was required in order for the study to be complete. Apparently, the children and their parents involved in the cases *sub judice* were from a lower economic strata and were, at least in one case, minorities.

The purpose of the research was to determine how effective varying degrees of lead paint abatement procedures were. Success was to be determined by periodically, over a two-year period of time, measuring the extent to which lead dust remained in, or returned to, the premises after the varying levels of abatement modifications, and, as most important to our decision, by measuring the extent to which the theretofore healthy children's blood became contaminated with lead, and comparing that contamination with levels of lead dust in the houses over the same periods of time. In respect to one of the protocols presented to the Environmental Protection Agency and/or the Johns Hopkins Joint Committee on Clinical Investigation, the Johns Hopkins Institutional Review Board (IRB), the researchers stated: "To help insure that study dwellings are occupied by families with young children, City Homes[3] will give priority to families with young children when renting the vacant units following R & M [Repair and Maintenance] interventions."

The same researchers had completed a prior study on abatement and partial abatement methods that indicated that lead dust remained and/or returned to abated houses over a period of time. In an article reporting on that study, the very same researchers said: "Exposure to lead-bearing dust is particularly hazardous for children because hand-to-mouth activity is recognized as a major route of entry of lead into the body and because absorption of lead is inversely related to particle size." Mark R. Farfel & J. Julian Chisolm, *Health and Environmental Outcomes of Traditional and Modified Practices for Abatement of Residential Lead–Based Paint*, 80 American Journal of Public Health 1240, 1243 (1990). After publishing this report, the researchers began the present research project in which children were encouraged to reside in households where the possibility of lead dust was known to the researcher to be likely, so that the lead dust content of their blood could be compared with the level of lead dust in the houses at periodic intervals over a two-year period.

Apparently, it was anticipated that the children, who were the human subjects in the program, would, or at least might, accumulate lead in their blood from the dust, thus helping the researchers to determine the extent to which the various partial abatement methods worked. There was no complete and clear explanation in the consent agreements signed by the parents of the children that the research to be conducted was designed, at least in significant part, to measure the success of the abatement procedures by

3. City Homes apparently was a non-profit entity affiliated with the Enterprise Foundation, that owned and/or managed low income housing in Baltimore City.

measuring the extent to which the children's blood was being contaminated. It can be argued that the researchers intended that the children be the canaries in the mines but never clearly told the parents. (It was a practice in earlier years, and perhaps even now, for subsurface miners to rely on canaries to determine whether dangerous levels of toxic gasses were accumulating in the mines. Canaries were particularly susceptible to such gasses. When the canaries began to die, the miners knew that dangerous levels of gasses were accumulating.)

The researchers and their Institutional Review Board apparently saw nothing wrong with the research protocols that anticipated the possible accumulation of lead in the blood of otherwise healthy children as a result of the experiment, or they believed that the consents of the parents of the children made the research appropriate. Institutional Review Boards (IRB) are oversight entities within the institutional family to which an entity conducting research belongs. In research experiments, an IRB can be required in some instances by either federal or state regulation, or sometimes by the conditions attached to governmental grants that are used to fund research projects.[4] Generally, their primary functions are to assess the protocols of the project to determine whether the project itself is appropriate, whether the consent procedures are adequate, whether the methods to be employed meet proper standards, whether reporting requirements are sufficient, and the assessment of various other aspects of a research project. One of the most important objectives of such review is the review of the potential safety and the health hazard impact of a research project on the human subjects of the experiment, especially on vulnerable subjects such as children. Their function is *not* to help researchers seek funding for research projects.

[T]he IRB involved here, the Johns Hopkins University Joint Committee on Clinical Investigation, in part, abdicated that responsibility, instead suggesting to the researchers a way to miscast the characteristics of the study in order to avoid the responsibility inherent in nontherapeutic research involving children. In a letter dated May 11, 1992, [the University's IRB wrote to Dr. Farfel that, by characterizing the "control group" as a group of children "being studied to determine what exposure outside the home may play in a total lead exposure," he could indicate that those children received the benefit of learning whether safe housing was sufficient to produce acceptable blood-lead levels. Doing so would allow him to skirt the strict federal guidelines for *"using children as controls in projects in which there is no potential benefit"* to the particular children.] . . .

While the suggestion of the IRB would not make this experiment any less nontherapeutic or, thus, less regulated, this statement shows two things: (1) that the IRB had a partial misperception of the difference between therapeutic and nontherapeutic research and the IRB's role in the process and (2) that the IRB was willing to aid researchers in getting around federal

4. In respect to research conducted or supported by any federal agency, Institutional Review Boards, among other requirements, must furnish the agency with: a list of IRB members, their degrees, representative capacity, experience, and employment relationships between the member and the research entity. Each IRB is required to have at least five members of varying backgrounds; there must be racial, gender, and cultural diversity. Each IRB has to contain at least one scientific member and one non-nonscientific member and one member who is not affiliated with the institution in any way. No member of an IRB can have a conflicting interest. 45 C.F.R. Subtitle A, sections 46.103 and 46.107.

regulations designed to protect children used as subjects in nontherapeutic research. An IRB's primary role is to assure the safety of human research subjects—not help researchers avoid safety or health-related requirements. The IRB, in this case, misconceived, at least partially, its own role.

. . .

Otherwise healthy children, in our view, should not be enticed into living in, or remaining in, potentially lead-tainted housing and intentionally subjected to a research program, which contemplates the probability, or even the possibility, of lead poisoning or even the accumulation of lower levels of lead in blood, in order for the extent of the contamination of the children's blood to be used by scientific researchers to assess the success of lead paint or lead dust abatement measures. Moreover, in our view, parents, whether improperly enticed by trinkets, food stamps, money or other items, have no more right to intentionally and unnecessarily place children in potentially hazardous nontherapeutic research surroundings, than do researchers. In such cases, parental consent, no matter how informed, is insufficient.

. . . [T]he very inappropriateness of the research itself cannot be over-looked. It is apparent that the protocols of research are even more important than the method of obtaining parental consent and the extent to which the parents were, or were not, informed. If the research methods, the protocols, are inappropriate then, especially when the IRB is willing to help researchers avoid compliance with applicable safety requirements for using children in nontherapeutic research, the consent of the parents, or of any consent surrogates, in our view, cannot make the research appropriate or the actions of the researchers and the Institutional Review Board proper.

The research relationship proffered to the parents of the children the researchers wanted to use as measuring tools should never have been presented in a nontherapeutic context in the first instance. Nothing about the research was designed for treatment of the subject children. They were presumed to be healthy at the commencement of the project. As to them, the research was clearly nontherapeutic in nature. The experiment was simply a "for the greater good" project.[6] The specific children's health was put at risk, in order to develop low-cost abatement measures that would help all children, the landlords, and the general public as well.

. . .

The research project at issue here, and its apparent protocols, differs in large degree from, but presents similar problems as those in the Tuskegee Syphilis Study conducted from 1932 until 1972 (*The Tuskegee Syphilis Study*, 289 New England Journal of Medicine 730 (1973)), the intentional exposure of soldiers to radiation in the 1940s and 50s (*Jaffee v. United States*, 663 F.2d 1226 (3d Cir. 1981), *cert. denied*, 456 U.S. 972 (1982)), the tests involving the exposure of Navajo miners to radiation (*Begay v. United States*, 591 F. Supp. 991 (1984), *aff'd*, 768 F.2d 1059 (9th Cir. 1985)), and the secret administration of LSD to soldiers by the CIA and the Army in the 1950s and 60s (*United*

6. . . . At least one of the consenting parents in one of these cases was on public assistance, and was described by her counsel as being a minority. The children of middle class or rich parents apparently were not involved. [The court pointed to vulnerable populations, which were particularly at risk of abusive human experimentation: prisoners, children, the elderly, racial and ethnic minorities, women, the poor, and the under-educated.]

States v. Stanley, 483 U.S. 669 (1987); *Central Intelligence Agency v. Sims*, 471 U.S. 159 (1985)). The research experiments that follow were also prior instances of research subjects being intentionally exposed to infectious or poisonous substances in the name of scientific research. They include the Tuskegee Syphilis Study, aforesaid, where patients infected with syphilis were not subsequently informed of the availability of penicillin for treatment of the illness, in order for the scientists and researchers to be able to continue research on the effects of the illness, the Jewish Hospital study,[8] and several other post-war research projects. Then there are the notorious use of "plague bombs" by the Japanese military in World War II where entire villages were infected in order for the results to be "studied"; and perhaps most notorious, the deliberate use of infection in a nontherapeutic project in order to study the degree of infection and the rapidity of the course of the disease in the Rose and Mrugowsky typhus experiments at Buchenwald concentration camp during World War II. These programs were somewhat alike in the vulnerability of the subjects; uneducated African American men, debilitated patients in a charity hospital, prisoners of war, inmates of concentration camps and others falling within the custody and control of the agencies conducting or approving the experiments. In the present case, children, especially young children, living in lower economic circumstances, albeit not as vulnerable as the other examples, are nonetheless, vulnerable as well.

It is clear to this Court that the scientific and medical communities cannot be permitted to assume sole authority to determine ultimately what is right and appropriate in respect to research projects involving young children free of the limitations and consequences of the application of Maryland law.... [The IRBs] are, primarily, in-house organs. In our view, they are not designed, generally, to be sufficiently objective in the sense that they are as sufficiently concerned with the ethicality of the experiments they review as they are with the success of the experiments. This has been the subject of comment in a constitutional context, in dissent, in a case involving the use of psychiatric medication on mental patients without their consent....

In footnote two of his dissent [in *Washington v. Harper*, 494 U.S. 210 (1990)], Justice Stevens noted:

> The Constitution's promise of due process of law guarantees at least compensation for violations of the principle stated by the Nuremberg Military Tribunals "that the 'voluntary consent of the human subject is absolutely essential ... to satisfy moral, ethical and legal concepts[.]' "; The Fourteenth Amendment protects the "freedom to care for one's health and person[.]"

494 U.S. at 238.

... Justice Steven's doubts as to the effectiveness of such in-house review to assess the ethics of research were warranted. Here, the IRB ... encouraged the researchers to misrepresent the purpose of the research in order to bring the study under the label of "therapeutic" and thus under a lower

---

8. Generally known as the Jewish Chronic Disease Hospital study where chronically ill and debilitated patients were injected with cancer cells without their consent. *See Zeleznik v. Jewish Chronic Disease Hosp.*, 47 A.D.2d 199, 366 N.Y.S.2d 163 (1975); *Application of Hyman*, 42 Misc.2d 427, 248 N.Y.S.2d 245, *rev'd*, *Hyman v. Jewish Chronic Disease Hospital*, 21 A.D.2d 495, 251 N.Y.S.2d 818 (1964), *rev'd*, 15 N.Y.2d 317, 206 N.E.2d 338, 258 N.Y.S.2d 397 (1965).

safety standard of regulation. The IRB's purpose was ethically wrong, and its understanding of the experiment's benefit incorrect.

The conflicts are inherent. This would be especially so when science and private industry collaborate in search of material gains. Moreover, the special relationship between research entities and human subjects used in the research will almost always impose duties.

. . .

I. The Cases

Two separate negligence actions involving children who allegedly developed elevated levels of lead dust in their blood while participating in a research study with respondent, Kennedy Krieger Institute, Inc., (KKI) are before this Court. Both cases allege that the children were poisoned, or at least exposed to the risk of being poisoned, by lead dust due to negligence on the part of KKI. Specifically, they allege that KKI discovered lead hazards in their respective homes and, having a duty to notify them, failed to warn in a timely manner or otherwise act to prevent the children's exposure to the known presence of lead. Additionally, plaintiffs alleged that they were not fully informed of the risks of the research.

. . . [W]e granted certiorari to address [this issue:]

Was the trial court incorrect in ruling on a motion for summary judgment that as a matter of law a research entity conducting an ongoing non-therapeutic scientific study does not have a duty to warn a minor volunteer participant and/or his legal guardian regarding dangers present when the researcher has knowledge of the potential for harm to the subject and the subject is unaware of the danger?

We answer in the affirmative. The trial court was incorrect. Such research programs normally create special relationships and/or can be of a contractual nature, that create duties. The breaches of such duties may ultimately result in viable negligence actions. Because, at the very least, there are viable and genuine disputes of material fact concerning whether a special relationship, or other relationships arising out of agreements, giving rise to duties existed between KKI and both sets of appellants, we hold that the Circuit Court erred in granting KKI's motions for summary judgment in both cases before this Court. Accordingly, we vacate the rulings of the Circuit Court for Baltimore City and remand these cases to that court for further proceedings consistent with this opinion.

II. Facts & Procedural Background

[In 1993, the Environmental Protection Agency (EPA) awarded KKI a $200,000 contract to research the effectiveness and costliness of various Repair and Maintenance methods of reducing levels of residential lead dust (and, thereby, the levels of lead in children's blood). The effectiveness of those methods would be measured in part by the increases or decreases in lead levels in children's blood. KKI's clinical investigation consent forms acknowledge the dangers to children's health of lead exposure. The study included 125 houses, divided into five groups. Three groups included houses with high levels of lead dust, with each group receiving assigned amounts of Repair and Maintenance; one group consisted of houses that previously had high levels of lead dust but had since received "a supposedly complete abatement of lead dust"; the fifth group consisted of new houses where lead dust had never been present.

"The ultimate aim of the research was to find a less than complete level of abatement that would be relatively safe, but economical, so that Baltimore landlords with lower socio-economical rental units would not abandon the units.... The cost of full abatement of such housing at times far exceeded the monetary worth of the property.... As a result, some lower rental properties containing lead based paint in Baltimore had been simply abandoned and left vacant. The study was attempting to determine whether a less expensive means of rehabilitation could be available...."]

One way the study was designed to measure the effectiveness of such abatement measures was to measure the lead dust levels in the houses at intervals and to compare them with the levels of lead found, at roughly the same intervals, in the blood of the children living in the respective houses. The project required that small children be present in the houses. To facilitate that purpose, the landlords agreeing to permit their properties to be included in the studies were encouraged, if not required, to rent the properties to tenants who had young children.

In return for permitting the properties to be used and in return for limiting their tenants to families with young children, KKI assisted the landlords in applying for and receiving grants or loans of money to be used to perform the levels of abatement required by KKI for each class, of home.

. . .

[Ericka Grimes's mother signed a consent form for her to participate in KKI's study in March 1993. The consent form did not state that the study might cause Ericka to accumulate lead in her blood or that Ericka would need to remain in their current house so that the fluctuations in her blood lead levels could be monitored. The Consent Form described how children acquire lead poisoning and stated that the Repair and Maintenance work would not remove all lead from the home. According to the Consent Form, KKI would test the home for lead 8 to 9 times and provide children between 6 months and 7 years with free blood lead testing 8 to 9 times over the next 2 years. Parents were also asked to fill out a questionnaire every 6 months.

In a section called "BENEFITS," the Consent Form stated, "To compensate you for your time answering questions and allowing us to sketch your home we will mail you a check in the amount of $5.00. In the future we would mail you a check in the amount of $15 each time the full questionnaire is completed. The dust, soil, water, and blood samples would be tested for lead at [KKI] at no charge to you. We would provide you with specific blood-lead results. We would contact you to discuss a summary of house test results and steps that you could take to reduce any risks of exposure."

KKI collected samples at Ericka's house six times over the next two years. Although the first test revealed "hot spots" with levels of lead higher than those in a completely abated house, KKI did not inform Ericka's mother until nine months later, after Ericka was found to have high levels of blood lead. Although Ericka's blood lead levels were "Normal" on the first testing (less than or equal to 9 micrograms of lead per deciliter of blood (μg/dL), under Centers for Disease Control (CDC) standards), over the next year she twice tested in the "Highly elevated" category (20 to 44 μg/dL).]

In her Complaint filed in the Circuit Court for Baltimore City, Ms. Hughes sought to hold KKI liable for negligence for failing to warn of, or abate, lead-paint hazards that KKI allegedly discovered in the Monroe Street property during the research study. Specifically, she alleged:

As part of the [Research] Study, [appellant's] mother agreed to allow [KKI] to periodically inspect the Monroe Street property for the presence of lead-paint hazards. Upon inspection, [KKI] discovered the existence of lead-paint hazards within [appellant's] home, but failed to inform and/or warn [appellant] and her mother of such hazards and failed to take any action to abate said hazards. As a consequence, [appellant] and her mother continued to reside in the home unaware of the hazards and unaware of the dangers to which [appellant] was being exposed.

KKI filed a Third Party Complaint against JJB, Inc., (JJB) the owners of the [appellant's] property. Appellant filed an Amended Complaint to add JJB as an additional defendant alleging negligence and violations of the Maryland Consumer Protection Act. KKI filed a Motion for Summary Judgment on the grounds that it did not owe any duty to appellant that it had breached. . . .

On appeal, appellant seeks review of the Circuit Court's decision granting KKI summary judgment. She contends that KKI owed a duty of care to appellant based on the nature of its relationship with appellant and her mother arising out of: (1) a contract between the parties; (2) a voluntary assumption by KKI; (3) a "special relationship" between the parties; and (4) a Federal regulation. She argues that KKI's failure to notify her of the lead dust hazards . . . until after more than nine months had passed since the samples had been collected, and until after Ericka Grimes's blood was found to be lead poisoned, constituted negligence on the part of KKI in the performance of its duties to Ericka arising out of the nature of the relationship between the parties.

· · ·

III.   Discussion

· · ·

Initially, we note that we know of no law, nor have we been directed to any applicable in Maryland courts, that provides that the parties to a scientific study, because it is a scientific, health-related study, cannot be held to have entered into special relationships with the subjects of the study that can create duties, including duties, the breach of which may give rise to negligence claims. We also are not aware of any general legal precept that immunizes nongovernmental "institutional volunteers" or scientific researchers from the responsibility for the breaches of duties arising in "special relationships." Moreover, we, at the very least, hold that, under the particular circumstances testified to by the parties, there are genuine disputes of material fact concerning whether a special relationship existed. . . . When a "special relationship" can exist as a matter of law, the issue of whether, given certain facts, a special relationship does exist, when there is a dispute of material fact in that respect, is a decision for the finder of fact, not the trial judge. We shall hold initially that the very nature of nontherapeutic scientific research on human subjects can, and normally will, create special relationships out of which duties arise. Since World War II the specialness or nature of such relationships has been frequently of concern in and outside of the research community.

As a result of the atrocities performed in the name of science during the Holocaust, and other happenings in the World War II era, what is now known as The Nuremberg Code evolved. Of special interest to this Court, the Nuremberg Code, at least in significant part, was the result of legal thought and legal principles, as opposed to medical or scientific principles, and thus should be the preferred standard for assessing the legality of scientific research on human subjects. Under it, duties to research subjects arise.

. . .

> The Nuremberg Code is the "most complete and authoritative statement of the law of informed consent to human experimentation." It is also "part of international common law and may be applied, in both civil and criminal cases, by state, federal and municipal courts in the United States." However, even though courts in the United States may use the Nuremberg Code to set criminal and civil standards of conduct, none have used it in a criminal case and only a handful have even cited it in the civil context. Even where the Nuremberg Code has been cited as authoritative, it has usually been in dissent, and no United States court has ever awarded damages to an injured experimental subject, or punished an experimenter, on the basis of a violation of the Nuremberg Code. There have, however, been very few court decisions involving human experimentation. It is therefore very difficult for a common law: of human experimentation to develop. This absence of judicial precedent makes codes, especially judicially-crafted codes like the Nuremberg Code, all the more important.

George J. Annas, *Mengele's Birthmark: The Nuremberg Code in United States Courts,* 7 Journal of Contemporary Health Law & Policy 17, 19–21 (Spring, 1991).

> Why wasn't the Nuremberg Code immediately adopted by United States courts as setting the minimum standard of care for human experimentation? One reason, perhaps, is that there was little opportunity. As remains true today, almost no experiments resulted in lawsuits in the 1940's, 50's, and 60's. A second reason may be that the Nazi experiments were considered so extreme as to be seen as irrelevant to the United States. This may explain why our own use of prisoners, the institutionalized retarded, and the mentally ill to test malaria treatments during World War II was generally hailed as positive, making the war "everyone's war." Likewise, in the late 1940's and early 1950's, the testing of new polio vaccines on institutionalized mentally retarded children was considered appropriate. Utilitarianism was the ethic of the day.... Noting that the Code applied primarily to the type of outrageous nontherapeutic experiments conducted during the war, physician groups tended to find the Code too "legalistic" and irrelevant to their therapeutic experiments, and set about to develop an alternative code to guide medical researchers. The most successful and influential has been the World Medical Association's (WMA) Declaration of Helsinki....

Mengele's Birthmark, supra, at 24 (footnotes omitted). In his conclusions the author noted:

> However, since American judges promulgated the [Nuremberg] Code under both natural and international law standards, it is disturbing that we have not taken it more seriously in areas where there is no question that it has direct application. . . .
>
> . . . We have yet to succeed in eradicating our birthmark that impels us to trample human rights and welfare when either society's welfare seems in jeopardy, or the promise of "progress" is dangled before us. . . . Neither Alymer nor Mengele will be called to account in a world that puts expediency over ethics, and exalts progress over human rights.

Id. at 43–44.

       . . .

Just recently the research community has been subjected to question as a result of genetic experimentation on a Pennsylvania citizen. Jesse Gelsinger consented to participate in a research project at the University of Pennsylvania's Institute of Human Gene Therapy. After Gelsinger's death, the U.S. Food and Drug Administration ordered a halt to eight human gene therapy experiments at the Institute. Additionally, other similar projects were halted elsewhere. The FDA took the action after a "discovery of a number of serious problems in the Institute's informed consent procedures and, more generally, a lapse in the researchers' ethical responsibilities to experimental subjects." Jeffrey H. Barker, *Human Experimentation and the Double Facelessness of a Merciless Epoch,* 25 New York University Review of Law and Social Change 603, 616 (1999).

Gelsinger had a different type of ornithine transcarbamylase deficiency (OTC) disease, than that addressed by the research. His particular brand of the disease was under control. There was no possibility that the research being conducted would directly benefit him. It was thus, as to him, as it was to the children in the case at bar, nontherapeutic; a way to study the affects on the subjects (in the present case, the children) in order to measure the success of the experiment. In Gelsinger's case, the research was to test the efficiency of disease vectors. In other words, weakened adenovirus (common-cold viruses) were used to deliver trillions of particles of a particular OTC gene into his artery and thus to his liver. Gelsinger experienced a massive and fatal immune system reaction to the introduction of the common-cold virus.

There were problems with the extent of the informed consent there obtained. Barker noted that:

> . . . Informed consent has suffered from pressure to get results—as quickly as possible. . . . Informed consent procedures, properly followed, are troublesome, time-consuming, costly, and may even threaten proprietary information valuable to the biotech companies. The ethical face of the research subject can be obscured by such factors.
>
>   . . .
>
> . . . Researchers, under competitive pressure and also financial pressure from corporate backers, operate under a paternalistic

approach to research subjects, asserting professional expertise and arguing experimental necessity while minimizing the right to self-determination—a key aspect of the exercise of autonomy—of their subjects. The result is a greater or lesser degree of ethical efface-ment.

Id. at 617–20.

Because of the way the cases *sub judice* have arrived, as appeals from the granting of summary judgments, there is no complete record of the specific compensation of the researchers involved.... Neither is there in the record any development of what pressures, if any, were exerted in respect to the researchers obtaining the consents of the parents and conducting the experi-ment. Nor, for the same reason, is there a sufficient indication as to the extent to which the Institute has joined with commercial interests, if it has, for the purposes of profit, that might potentially impact upon the research-er's motivations and potential conflicts of interest—motivations that generally are assumed, in the cases of prestigious entities such as John Hopkins University, to be for the public good rather then a search for profit.

We do note that the institution involved, the respondent here ... is a highly respected entity, considered to be a leader in the development of treatments, and treatment itself, for children infected with lead poisoning. With reasonable assurance, we can note that its reputation alone might normally suggest that there was no realization or understanding on the Institute's part that the protocols of the experiment were questionable, except for the letter from the RB requesting that the researchers mischarac-terize the study.

· · ·

It is important for us to remember that appellants allege that KKI was negligent. Specifically, they allege that KKI, as a medical researcher, owed a duty of care to them, as subjects in the research study, based on the nature of the agreements between them and also based on the nature of the relationship between the parties. They contend specifically that KKI was negligent because KKI breached its duty to: (1) design a study that did not involve placing children at unnecessary risk; (2) inform participants in the study of results in a timely manner; and (3) to completely and accurately inform participants in the research study of all the hazards and risks involved in the study.

In order to establish a claim for negligence under Maryland law, a party must prove four elements: "(1) that the defendant was under a duty to protect the plaintiff from injury, (2) that the defendant breached that duty, (3) *that the plaintiff suffered actual injury or loss*[33] and (4) that the loss or injury proximately resulted from the defendant's breach of the duty." (Emphasis added.) Because this is a review of the granting of the two summary judgments based solely on the grounds that there was no legal duty to protect the children, we are primarily concerned with the first prong—whether KKI was under a duty to protect appellants from injury.

· · ·

33. We note that there was little sugges-tion of actual permanent injury to the chil-dren involved with these two cases. Our opin-ion is not directed to the matter of whether damages can be proven in the present cases.

The relationship that existed between KKI and both sets of appellants in the case at bar was that of medical researcher and research study subject. Though not expressly recognized in the Maryland Code or in our prior cases as a type of relationship which creates a duty of care, evidence in the record suggests that such a relationship involving a duty or duties would ordinarily exist, and certainly could exist, based on the facts and circumstances of each of these individual cases. . . .

IV. The Special Relationships

Both sets of appellants signed a similar Consent Form prepared by KKI. . . .

By having appellants sign this Consent Form, both KKI and appellants expressly made representations, which, in our view, created a bilateral contract between the parties. At the very least, it suggests that appellants were agreeing with KKI to participate in the research study with the expectation that they would be compensated, albeit, more or less, minimally, be informed of all the information necessary for the subject to freely choose whether to participate, and continue to participate, and receive promptly any information that might bear on their willingness to continue to participate in the study. This includes full, detailed, prompt, and continuing warnings as to all the potential risks and hazards inherent in the research or that arise during the research. KKI, in return, was getting the children to move into the houses and/or to remain there over time, and was given the right to test the children's blood for lead. As consideration to KKI, it got access to the houses and to the blood of the children that had been encouraged to live in a "risk" environment. In other words, KKI received a measuring tool—the children's blood. Considerations existed, mainly money, food coupons, trinkets, bilateral promises, blood to be tested in order to measure success. "Informed consent" of the type used here, which imposes obligation and confess consideration on both researcher and subject (in these cases, the parents of the subjects) may differ from the more one-sided "informed consent" normally used in actual medical practice. Researcher/subject consent in nontheraputical research can, and in this case did, create a contract.

The consent form did not directly inform the parents of the fact that it was contemplated that some of the children might ingest lead dust particles, and that one of the reasons the blood of the children was to be tested was to evaluate how effective the various abatement measures were.

A reasonable parent would expect to be clearly informed that it was at least contemplated that her child would ingest lead dust particles, and that the degree to which lead dust contaminated the child's blood would be used as one of the ways in which the success of the experiment would be measured. The fact that if such information was furnished, it might be difficult to obtain human subjects for the research, does not affect the need to supply the information, or alter the ethics of failing to provide such information. A human subject is entitled to *all* material information. The respective parent should also have been clearly informed that in order for the measurements to be most helpful, the child needed to stay in the house until the conclusion of the study. Whether assessed by a subjective or an objective standard, the children, or their surrogates, should have been additionally informed that the researchers anticipated that, as a result of the experiment, it was possible that there might be some accumulation of lead in the blood of the children. The "informed" consent was not valid because full material information was not furnished to the subjects or their parents.

. . .

[T]he trial courts appear to have held that special relationships out of which duties arise cannot be created by the relationship between researchers and the subjects of the research. While in some rare cases that may be correct, it is not correct when researchers recruit people, especially children whose consent is furnished indirectly, to participate in nontherapeutic procedures that are potentially hazardous, dangerous, or deleterious to their health. As opposed to compilation of already extant statistics for purposes of studying human health matters, the creation of study conditions or protocols or participation in the recruitment of otherwise healthy subjects to interact with already existing, or potentially existing, hazardous conditions, or both, for the purpose of creating statistics from which scientific hypotheses can be supported, would normally warrant or create such special relationships as a matter of law.

. . .

A duty may be prescribed by a statute, or a special relationship creating duties may arise from the requirement for compliance with statutory provisions. Although there is no duty of which we are aware prescribed by the Maryland Code in respect to scientific research of the nature here present, federal regulations have been enacted that impose standards of care that attach to federally funded or sponsored research projects that use human subjects. *See* 45 C.F.R. Part 46 (2000). 45 C.F.R. Part 46, Subpart A, is entitled "Basic HHS[37] Policy for Protection of Human Research Subjects" and Subpart D of the regulation is entitled "Additional Protections for Children Involved as Subjects in Research." . . . [T]his study was funded, and co-sponsored, by the EPA and presumably was therefore subject to these federal conditions. These conditions, if appropriate administrative action has been taken, require fully informed consent in any research using human subjects conducted, supported, or otherwise subject to any level of control or funding by any federal department or agency. 45 C.F.R. section 46.116 provides in relevant part:

> Sec. 46.116 General requirements for informed consent.
>
> Except as provided elsewhere in this policy, no investigator may involve a human being as a subject in research covered by this policy unless the investigator has obtained the *legally effective* informed consent of the subject or the subject's legally authorized representative. *An investigator shall seek such consent only under circumstances that provide the prospective subject or the representative sufficient opportunity to consider whether or not to participate and that minimize the possibility of coercion or undue influence.* The information that is given to the subject or the representative shall be in language understandable to the subject or the representative. No informed consent, whether oral or written, may include any exculpatory language through which the subject or the representative is made to waive or appear to waive any of the subject's legal rights, or releases or

---

37. HHS refers to the Department of Health and Human Services.

appears to release the investigator, the sponsor, the institution or its agents from liability for negligence.

(a) Basic elements of informed consent.... [T]he following information shall be provided to each subject: ["(2) A description of any reasonably foreseeable *risks* or discomforts to the subject; ... (4) A disclosure of appropriate alternative procedures or courses of treatment, if any, that might be advantageous to the subject; ... (6) For research involving more than minimal *risk*, an explanation as to whether any compensation and an explanation as to whether any medical treatments are available in injury occurs and, if so, what they consist of, or where further information may be obtained."]

(b) Additional elements of informed consent. When appropriate, one or more of the following elements of information shall also be provided to each subject:

> (1) A statement that the particular treatment or procedure may involve risks to the subject (or to the embryo or fetus, if the subject is or may become pregnant) which are currently unforeseeable;
>
> . . .
>
> (5) *A statement that significant new findings developed during the course of the research which may relate to the subject's willingness to continue participation will be provided to the subject....* [Emphasis added.]

Subpart D of the regulation concerns children involved as subjects in research. 45 C.F.R. section 46.407 therefore additionally provides:

HHS will conduct or fund research that the IRB does not believe meets the requirements of Sec. 46.404, Sec. 46.405, or Sec. 46.406 only if:

(a) The RB finds that the research presents a reasonable opportunity to further the understanding, prevention, or alleviation of a serious problem affecting the health or welfare of children; *and*

(b) *The Secretary,*[8] *after consultation with a panel of experts in pertinent disciplines (for example: science, medicine, education, ethics, law) and following opportunity for public review and comment, has determined either:*

> (1) That the research in fact satisfies the conditions of Sec. 46.404, Sec. 46.405, or Sec. 46.406, as applicable, or
>
> (2) The following:
>
> (i) The research presents a reasonable opportunity to further the understanding, prevention, or alleviation of a serious problem affecting the health or welfare of children;
>
> (ii) *The research will be conducted in accordance with sound ethical principles;*

---

8. We have found no indication in the record that the research protocols were approved by The Secretary. We again emphasize, however, that these cases were determined on summary judgment motions and the record is, accordingly, incomplete. Moreover, perhaps because of the limiting effect of summary judgment procedures early in the case, there is no indication that we can find in the record, or to which we were directed, that indicates that a "National Review" was conducted.

> (iii) Adequate provisions are made for soliciting the assent
> of children and the permission of their parents or guard-
> ians, as set forth in Sec. 46.408. [Emphasis added.]

These federal regulations, especially the requirement for adherence to sound ethical principles, strike right at the heart of KKI's defense of the granting of the Motions for Summary Judgment. *Fully informed* consent is lacking in these cases. The research did not comply with the regulations. There clearly was more than a minimal risk involved. Under the regulations, children should not have been used for the purpose of measuring how much lead they would accumulate in their blood while living in partially abated houses to which they were recruited initially or encouraged to remain, because of the study.

> . . .

Clearly, KKI, as a research institution, is required to obtain a human participant's fully informed consent, using sound ethical principles. It is clear from the wording of the applicable federal regulations that this requirement of informed consent continues during the duration of the research study and applies to new or changing risks. In this case, a special relationship out of which duties might arise might be created by reason of the federally imposed regulations. The question becomes whether this duty of informed consent created by federal regulation, as a matter of state law, translates into a duty of care arising out of the unique relationship that is researcher-subject, as opposed to doctor-patient. We answer that question in the affirmative. In this State, it may, depending on the facts, create such a duty.

. . . The Nuremberg Code specifically requires researchers to make known to human subjects of research "all inconveniences and hazards reasonably to be expected; and the effects upon his health or person which may *possibly* come from his participation in the experiment." (Emphasis added.) The breach of obligations imposed on researchers by the Nuremberg Code, might well support actions sounding in negligence in cases such as those at issue here. . . .

V. The Ethical Appropriateness of the Research

> . . .

The determination of whether a duty exists under Maryland law is the ultimate function of various policy considerations as adopted by either the Legislature, or, if it has not spoken, as it has not in respect to this situation, by Maryland courts. In our view, otherwise healthy children should not be the subjects of nontherapeutic experimentation or research that has the potential to be harmful to the child. It is, first and foremost, the responsibili-ty of the researcher and the research entity to see to the harmlessness of such nontherapeutic research. Consent of parents can never relieve the researcher of this duty. . . .

. . . A researcher's duty is not created by, or extinguished by, the consent of a research subject or by IRB approval. The duty to a vulnerable research subject is independent of consent, although the obtaining of consent is one of the duties a researcher must perform. All of this is especially so when the subjects of research are children. Such legal duties, and legal protections, might additionally be warranted because of the likely conflict of interest between the goal of the research experimenter and the health of the human subject, especially, but not exclusively, when such research is commercialized. There is always a potential substantial conflict of interest on the part of researchers as between them and the human subjects used in their research. If participants in the study withdraw from the research study prior to its completion, then the results of the study could be rendered meaningless. There is thus an inherent reason for not conveying information to subjects as it arises, that might cause the subjects to leave the research project. That conflict dictates a stronger reason for full and continuous disclosure.

. . . A special relationship giving rise to duties, the breach of which might constitute negligence, might also arise because, generally, the investigators are in a better position to anticipate, discover, and understand the potential risks to the health of their subjects. Practical inequalities exist between researchers, who have superior knowledge, and participants "who are often poorly placed to protect themselves from risk." "Given the gap in knowledge between investigators and participants and the inherent conflict of interest faced by investigators, participants cannot and should not be solely responsible for their own protection."

This duty requires the protection of the research subjects from unreasonable harm and requires the researcher to completely and promptly inform the subjects of potential hazards existing from time to time because of the profound trust that participants place in investigators, institutions, and the research enterprise as a whole to protect them from harm. "Faced with seemingly knowledgeable and prestigious investigators engaged in a noble pursuit, participants may simply assume that research is socially important or of benefit to them individually; they may not be aware that participation could be harmful to their interests."

. . .

While we acknowledge that foreseeability does not necessarily create a duty, we recognize that potential harm to the children participants of this study was both foreseeable and potentially extreme. A "special relationship" also exists in circumstances where such experiments are conducted.

VII. Conclusion

We hold that in Maryland a parent, appropriate relative, or other applicable surrogate, cannot consent to the participation of a child or other person under legal disability in nontherapeutic research or studies in which there is any risk of injury or damage to the health of the subject.

We hold that informed consent agreements in nontherapeutic research projects, under certain circumstances can constitute contracts; and that, under certain circumstances, such research agreements can, as a matter of law, constitute "special relationships" giving rise to duties, out of the breach of which negligence actions may arise. We also hold that, normally, such special relationships are created between researchers and the human subjects used by the researchers. Additionally, we hold that governmental regulations can create duties on the part of researchers towards human subjects out of which "special relationships" can arise . . . . .

The determination as to whether a "special relationship" actually exists is to be done on a case by case basis. The determination as to whether a special relationship exists, if properly pled, lies with the trier of fact. We hold that there was ample evidence in the cases at bar to support a fact finder's determination of the existence of duties arising out of contract, or out of a special relationship, or out of regulations and codes, or out of all of them, in each of the cases.

We hold that on the present record, the Circuit Courts erred in their assessment of the law and of the facts as pled in granting KKI's motions for summary judgment in both cases before this Court. Accordingly, we vacate the rulings of the Circuit Court for Baltimore City and remand these cases to that court for further proceedings consistent with this opinion.

ON MOTION FOR RECONSIDERATION PER CURIAM.

The Court has considered the motion for reconsideration and the submissions by the various amici curiae. The motion is denied, with this explanation.

Some of the issues raised in this case, in the briefs and at oral argument, were important ones of first impression in this State, and the Court therefore attempted to address those issues in a full and exhaustive manner. The case reached us in the context of summary judgments entered by the Circuit Court, which entailed rulings that the evidence presented by the plaintiffs, for purposes of the motions, even when taken in a light most favorable to them, was insufficient as a matter of law to establish the prospect of liability. We disagreed with that determination. Although we discussed the various issues and arguments in considerable detail, the only conclusion that we reached as a matter of law was that, on the record currently before us, summary judgment was improperly granted—that sufficient evidence was presented in both cases which, if taken in a light most favorable to the plaintiffs and believed by a jury, would suffice to justify verdicts in favor of the plaintiffs. Thus, the cases were remanded for further proceedings in the Circuit Court. Every issue bearing on liability or damages remains open for further factual development, and any relevant evidence not otherwise precluded under our rules of evidence is admissible.

Much of the argument in support of and in opposition to the motion for reconsideration centered on the question of what limitations should govern a parent's authority to provide informed consent for the participation of his or her minor child in a medical study. In the Opinion, we said at one point that a parent "cannot consent to the participation of a child . . . in nontherapeutic research or studies in which there is any risk of injury or damage to the health of the subject." . . . [B]y "any risk," we meant any articulable risk beyond the minimal kind of risk that is inherent in any endeavor. The context of the statement was a non-therapeutic study that promises no medical benefit to the child whatever, so that any balance between risk and benefit is necessarily negative. As we indicated, the determination of whether the study in question offered some benefit, and therefore could be regarded as therapeutic in nature, or involved more than that minimal risk is open for further factual development on remand.

Questions and Comments on *Grimes*

1. After the Court of Appeals decision, the plaintiffs and the Kennedy Krieger Institute reached a confidential settlement. *Don't Keep Your Distance*, 437 NATURE 451 (2005). Although the court denied the motion for reconsideration, the denial arguably restricted the scope of the original holding. Even if most of the opinion is technically dicta, does it put researchers on notice as to how other courts might react to comparable research protocols? In the wake of *Grimes*, the Institute of Medicine of the National Academies published a two hundred page volume entitled *Ethical Considerations for Research on Housing–Related Health Hazards Involving Children*, which included a recommendation for community oversight of research: "Partners in the community can help researchers . . . by highlighting flaws in study design, recruiting participants, and strengthening the informed-consent process." *Id.*

2.   "Lead levels of 20 [μ/dL] or above have been shown in studies to lead to reduced IQs, while levels of 24 or above have been shown to increase the chances of mental retardation, according to the American Academy of Pediatrics." Manuel Roig–Franzia, *"My Kids Were Used as Guinea Pigs"*, WASH. POST, Aug. 25, 2001, at A1. "Now, [Ericka's mother] wonders whether the lead is responsible for her daughter's learning disabilities, attention problems and troubles at George Washington Elementary School, where Ericka had to repeat the second grade. [She] wonders most on the days when Ericka comes home crying and asks: 'Mommy, I'm stupid?' " *Id.*

3.   On July 21, 2001, the federal Office for Human Research Protections (OHRP) suspended all federally supported research projects at Johns Hopkins and several affiliated institutions following the death of Ellen Roche, a twenty-four year-old technician at the Johns Hopkins Asthma and Allergy Center who was a volunteer in a study that involved inducing asthma symptoms in the subjects. OHRP cited the asthma-inducing drug lacking FDA approval and the internal review board's inadequate oversight as the reasons for suspension. *Family of Fatality in Study Settles With Johns Hopkins*, N.Y. TIMES, Oct. 12, 2001, at A20 [*Family of Fatality*]. The suspension was lifted after Hopkins quickly took corrective action. For a detailed analysis of the entire episode, see Robert Steinbrook, *Protecting Research Subjects—The Crisis at Johns Hopkins*, 347 NEW ENG. J. MED. 716 (2002). Hopkins also reached a settlement for an undisclosed amount with Roche's family. *Family of Fatality, supra*, at A20.

4.   Institutional Review Boards (IRBs), which grew out of condemnation of medical research projects such as the Tuskegee Syphillis Study, have extended their reach to an increasing amount of social science research. J. Michael Oakes, *Risks and Wrongs in Social Science Research: An Evaluator's Guide to the IRB*, 26 EVALUATION REV. 443, 444 (Oct. 2002). There are now more than 5,500 IRBs. Patricia Cohen, *As Ethics Panels Expand Grip, No Field is Off Limits*, N.Y. TIMES, Feb. 28, 2007, at A15. They have not only increased their scrutiny of social science protocols, they "often mistakenly apply standards of clinical and biomedical research to social science research, to the detriment of the latter. . . ." AMERICAN ASSOCIATION OF UNIVERSITY PROFESSORS, RESEARCH ON HUMAN SUBJECTS: ACADEMIC FREEDOM AND THE INSTITUTIONAL REVIEW BOARD (2006), *available at* http://www.aaup.org/AAUP/comm/rep/A/humansubs.htm (last visited Feb. 6, 2008). One incident cited in the AAUP report involved a review board asking a linguist studying a preliterate tribe to "have the subjects read and sign a consent form." *Id.*

The AAUP report acknowledges that some social science research may pose serious harm to subjects, so some IRB review is appropriate. The report mentions the example of the possible long-term effect on the participants in the experiments conducted at Yale University in the 1960s by Stanley Milgrim. Milgrim devised a test in which participants thought they were administering electrical shocks to other "volunteers." But the report recommends exempting low-risk research from IRB review; low-risk is defined as "research whose methodology consists entirely of collecting data by surveys, conducting interview, or observing behavior in public places." Do you agree with that recommendation?

5.   Some scholars have alleged that the prior approval required by IRBs violates the First Amendment. Do you agree? What are the strongest arguments that these scholars could make against IRBs?

6. For thoughtful proposals to improve the functioning of IRBs, including providing basic First Amendment training, see Dale Carpenter, *Institutional Review Boards, Regulatory Incentives, and Some Modest Proposals for Reform*, 101 Nw. U. L. Rev. 687 (2007); *see generally* Symposium, *Censorship and Institutional Review Boards*, 101 Nw. U. L. Rev. (2007).

Board of Trustees of Stanford University v. Sullivan

United States District Court for the District of Columbia, 1991.
773 F.Supp. 472.

■ Greene, United States District Judge.

The principal legal issue in this lawsuit—the extent to which the government may curtail the speech of a recipient of a government grant—is related to that which was recently resolved by the Supreme Court in *Rust v. Sullivan*, [500 U.S. 173] (1991), a case involving abortion counseling in family planning clinics....

In August 1989 the National Heart, Lung, and Blood Institute (Institute) of the National Institutes of Health[2] issued a notice that it planned to award contracts for a five-year research project on an artificial heart device. The research was to be conducted at two separate academic institutions, each of which was to receive a government grant of approximately $1.5 million. The notice indicated that the contract might include a clause known as the Confidentiality of Information Clause (confidentiality clause) which would require researchers to obtain government approval before publishing or otherwise publicly discussing preliminary research results. In October 1989 Dr. Philip Oyer, a professor of cardiovascular surgery at Stanford Medical School, submitted a proposal on behalf of Stanford in response to the notice. Stanford's proposal objected to several provisions of the notice, particularly the confidentiality clause, and ultimately, when Stanford and the government could not agree with respect to the clause, the government withdrew the contract from Stanford and awarded it elsewhere.[3]

Stanford argues that the confidentiality clause constitutes an illegal prior restraint and an unconstitutional condition on a government benefit. The relief requested is a declaratory judgment that this clause is unconstitutional and an injunction requiring the Institute to re-award the contract to Stanford.

The confidentiality clause requires researchers to give the government advance notice of their intent to publish preliminary findings, and it allows the government's contracting officer to block such publication. More specifi-

2. The National Institutes of Health are component parts of the Department of Health and Human Services which is headed by Secretary Louis Sullivan.

3. In June 1990, the Institute sent the research contract—which included the clause—to Stanford for its concurrence. Stanford signed the contract, but it made its agreement to the contract contingent upon the "mutually satisfactory resolution" of several issues, including its objection to the confidentiality clause. During July and August, Stanford negotiated with the Institute about the

clause. At the end of August 1990, when no agreement could be reached, the Institute withdrew the contract from Stanford and a week later awarded it to St. Louis University Medical Center, which apparently did not object to the clause. There have been some delays with respect to the start of this research, and St. Louis University has not yet begun the human trials of the artificial heart device. The government agrees that a resolution of this case in favor of Stanford would not significantly injure St. Louis University or any other third party.

cally, under the clause, a researcher must give forty-five days advance notice that he plans to publish preliminary findings. If the contracting officer objects to the publication, the researcher may file a written claim with him, and the contracting officer then has an additional sixty days in which to decide that claim. The contracting officer's ultimate decision is final and binding (except that the researcher may file suit in court). *See* 48 C.F.R. § 52.233–1.

It is well established that under the law this procedure constitutes a prior restraint on speech in that it allows the government to suppress the dissemination of information in advance of publication.[7] Prior restraints are permitted "only in exceptional cases." *Near v. Minnesota*, 283 U.S. 697, 716 (1931). . . .

These principles apply to the kind of speech involved in this case. The most typical prior restraint cases involve political or artistic speech. It is equally settled, however, though less commonly the subject of litigation, that the First Amendment protects scientific expression and debate just as it protects political and artistic expression.

The defendants now concede[8] that the government could not impose the kind of restraint contemplated by the regulation on scientists whose research is not paid for by a government grant or contract. The question before the Court therefore is whether the grant of public funds takes the present situation out of the category of impermissible suppression of speech.

Prior to the issuance by the Supreme Court of the decision earlier this year, the law regarding speech-type conditions attached to government grants was less than clear. Although there were factual differences among the cases which could be, and were, cited as responsible for the particular results reached in the various cases, it has become increasingly difficult to discern a principled rule applicable to all the various situations.

.   .   .

In *Rust v. Sullivan*, the Supreme Court upheld a regulatory restriction which prohibits health professionals in government-funded family planning clinics from discussing abortion with their patients. . . . There are, however, two bases upon which, under the *Rust* Court's own language, the *Rust* result does not follow here.

First. The Supreme Court made a sharp distinction . . . between the denial of a benefit to an individual on account of his speech or expression (which is constitutionally prohibited) and an insistence that public funds be spent for the program purposes for which they were authorized (which the Constitution allows). Said the Court:

7. It is immaterial that the restraint does not last forever. Even a restraint of speech for a limited period is inconsistent with the First Amendment. *See, e.g.*, New York Times Co. v. United States, 403 U.S. 713 (1971).

8. Further, although at one stage of this litigation defendant appeared to contend to the contrary, this case does not involve commercial speech. Stanford seeks to engage in five years of research, not to "propose a commercial transaction." Defendants later conceded this point. Equally unpersuasive is the defendants' claim that, inasmuch as the government could have hired scientists as employees, a diminution of the free speech rights of scientists affiliated with a university receiving government monies is less offensive to the law than it might otherwise be. Even assuming that the premise is correct, that kind of an argument could be made with respect to almost any activity, and its acceptance would in practice erode First Amendment freedoms on the widest scale.

The Secretary's regulations do not force the Title X grantee to give up abortion-related speech; they merely require that the grantee keep such activities separate and distinct from Title X activities. Title X expressly distinguishes between a Title X grantee and a Title X project.... The Title X grantee can continue to perform abortions, provide abortion-related services, and engage in abortion advocacy; it simply is required to conduct these activities through programs that are separate and independent from the project that receives Title X funds.

In contrast, our "unconstitutional conditions" cases involve situations in which the government has placed a condition on the recipient of the subsidy rather than on a particular program or service, thus effectively prohibiting the recipient from engaging in the protected conduct outside the scope of the federally-funded program.

111 S. Ct. at 1774.

The regulations at issue in the instant case broadly bind the grantee and not merely the artificial heart project. Dr. Oyer and the other individuals working for Stanford on the project are prohibited by defendants' regulations from discussing preliminary findings of that project without permission. Unlike the health professionals in *Rust*, the Stanford researchers lack the option of speaking regarding artificial heart research on their own time, or in circumstances where their speech is paid for by Stanford University or some other private donor, or not paid for by anyone at all. Regardless of the circumstances, during the contract's five-year life they may not speak about the project's results or its progress without ... express prior permission from defendants' contracting officer.

The Supreme Court's discussion in *Rust* which, notwithstanding the result reached there, specifically reaffirmed the unconstitutionality of speech-related restrictions applicable to recipients of government funds as such, compels the conclusion that the defendants' restrictions in the instant case lack constitutional validity. The regulation at issue here is not tailored to reach only the particular program that is in receipt of government funds; it broadly forbids the recipients of the funds from engaging in publishing activity related to artificial heart research at any time, under any auspices, and wholly apart from the particular program that is being aided.[13]

Second. Other language of the Supreme Court has a similar impact on the issues in this case. The Court recalled in *Rust* that it had previously "recognized that the university is a traditional sphere of free expression so fundamental to the functioning of our society that the Government's ability to control speech within that sphere by means of conditions attached to the

---

13. Defendants' ban on preliminary reporting could not validly be defended on the basis that it is tied to the heart research program rather than the researchers, for the latter, as noted, would be precluded from speaking or publishing about artificial heart research even on their own time. Any attempt to examine such speech or publication with a view to determining whether or not the information came to these scientists as a consequence of their work on the federally-financed project or from their general familiarity with the subject would require such intrusive examination into thought processes that it could not conceivably be undertaken. It should be noted in this connection that Dr. Oyer has worked for almost twenty years on the development of a self-contained artificial heart device.

expenditure of Government funds is restricted by the vagueness and over-breadth doctrines of the First Amendment." This explicit exception to the broader ruling in *Rust* is directly on point here. The plaintiff is of course a university. The subject of this lawsuit is the very free expression that the *Rust* Court held to be so important for the functioning of American society that it may be curtailed through conditions attached to grants or contracts only if these conditions are not vague or overbroad. Yet, the conditions imposed by the defendants are plainly in that category.

The regulations permit the contracting officer to prevent Stanford from issuing "preliminary unvalidated findings" that "could" or that might have "adverse effects on ... the Federal agency." 48 C.F.R. § 352.224–70. In the view of this Court, these standards are impermissibly vague. Under what circumstances are preliminary findings regarded as "validated"? Who will decide whether the conclusions drawn by Stanford are erroneous—the non-scientist contracting officer?[15] What is meant by the phrase that a report "could" create erroneous conclusions? How would it be determined that such a conclusion "might threaten public health or safety,"[16] and to what degree of certainty would there have to be a threat to public health and safety? What kind of a threat? What would be regarded as an adverse effect "on the Federal agency?" Would such an effect have to be concrete, financial, reputational, or of some other nature? To pose these questions, and others that could be asked, is to reveal the vagueness of the standards.

There is the related problem of the chilling effect of these vague and overbroad conditions. It is impossible for a grantee such as Stanford and its chief researcher Dr. Oyer to know what might be regarded as a violation of these amorphous standards. Because of the vagueness and subjectivity of the administrative regulation, a responsible grantee could be certain of not being in violation only if it refrained from publishing any preliminary findings not endorsed by the contracting officer. Thus, the qualifying phrases referred to above are not likely to effect any real diminution of the otherwise unfettered authority of the contracting officer, and no prudent grantee is likely to publish that which the contracting officer has not cleared even if the reasons for the refusal to clear appear to be wholly invalid. In sum, this case fits snugly in the "free expression at a university" category that carved out of its general ruling on speech conditions attached to grants.

Defendants' approach to this case is that, since public funds will be expended on the artificial heart research at issue here, the burden is on plaintiff Stanford University to explain why and under what circumstances it

---

15. The contracting officer need not even be, and in this instance he apparently is not, a medical doctor or a scientist.

16. In fact, defendants' claim that the condition is designed to protect public health and safety, is also off the mark. Defendants point to cases in which government agencies tried to protect members of the public from false claims by commercial purveyors of medicine and therapies. But no such public health hazard is posed in this case if only because only twenty of the artificial heart devices will be made available, and their availability will be strictly controlled under the research regime. And of course there is not the slightest reason to believe that the Stanford scientists—who are not in the business of selling patent medicines—will be making fraudulent claims when they publish learned articles on artificial heart research. Defendants' stated goal of protecting prospective patients from unwarranted hope (that might result from the issuance of preliminary findings by Stanford scientists not screened in advance by a government contracting officer), constitutes a strange and attenuated way of protecting health and safety. Neither these defendants nor any other public officials have statutory or other authority to regulate citizens' hopes.

should be relieved of the obligation to submit its publications on this subject to the government for its prior approval. That approach views the issue from the wrong end of the telescope.

Stanford University, a premier academic institution, engaged in significant scientific and medical research for the benefit of the American people, is not ipso facto compelled under the law to surrender its free speech rights and those of its scientific researchers to a "contracting officer" merely because a regulation issued by defendants so directs. There exists, after all, the First Amendment to the Constitution, the supreme law of the land, which protects those very rights.

. . . The *Rust* decision opened the door to government review and suppression of speech and publication in areas which had theretofore been widely thought immune from such intrusion; the government's position in this case, if endorsed by the courts, would take that door off its hinges.

That position must be viewed in the context of the fact that few large-scale endeavors are today not supported, directly or indirectly, by government funds—from the health care of senior citizens, to farm subsidies, to the construction of weaponry, to name but a few of the most obvious. Defendants' proposal would, at least potentially, subordinate the free speech rights of the participants in the programs receiving such federal monies to the government's wishes. To put it another way, if the Supreme Court decision were to be given the scope and breadth defendants advocate in this case, the result would be an invitation to government censorship wherever public funds flow, and acceptance by the courts of defendants' position would thus present an enormous threat to the First Amendment rights of American citizens and to a free society.

This Court, like all lower courts, is of course bound by the *Rust* decision. But for the reasons stated, the Court will not, without explicit appellate direction, further narrow the speech and expression rights of citizens and organizations, or subject to government censorship the publications of institutions of higher learning and others engaged in legitimate research. No such appellate direction has been given; on the contrary, as explained above, *Rust* is consistent with a decision to allow Stanford to use its own judgment on when and what to publish, notwithstanding that its research is supported with federal funds. The Court will accordingly issue an injunction which will have the effect of prohibiting defendants from interfering with the university's freedom to publish.

What remains to be decided is what relief is appropriate. Defendants argue that their Department should be given the opportunity "to resolicit the contract following appropriate procurement procedures." However, it is plain that the contract would have remained with Stanford but for the illegal confidentiality clause. Under these circumstances, a court may order that the contract be awarded to the disappointed party without an additional round of procurement proceedings. The judgment being issued contemporaneously herewith therefore so provides.

Note on Conflicts Between Academic Freedom and Private Funding of Research

1. In his farewell speech to the nation in 1961, President Eisenhower warned of the dangers posed by the military-industrial complex. Less attention has been paid to the fact that he also warned of the risks posed by government funding to universities (he had been president of Columbia before being elected president of the United States):

> [T]he free university, historically the fountainhead of free ideas and scientific discovery, has experienced a revolution in the conduct of research. Partly because of the huge costs involved, a government contract becomes virtually a substitute for intellectual curiosity. . . .

> The prospect of domination of the nation's scholars by Federal employment, project allocations, and the power of money is ever present—and is gravely to be regarded.

President Dwight D. Eisenhower, Farewell Radio and Television (Jan. 17, 1961), *available at* http://www.eisenhower.archives.gov/speeches/Eisenhower_speeches.html,

2. Corporate funding also often comes with limitations on publication. Consider the warning of Derek Bok:

> Although the results of university research may eventually be made public, companies continually press for more and more restrictions while the research they support is underway in an effort to keep any word of new discoveries from leaking prematurely to their competitors. Many firms try to prohibit the researchers they fund from speaking about their work at conferences. Some corporate agreements can be interpreted to require scientists to obtain clearance before merely talking on the telephone with colleagues. A few professors have actually declared their laboratories off-limits to colleagues and students in their own departments. While no one can measure the impact of such restrictions with precision, the likely effect is to inhibit scientific progress to some extent, by limiting the flow of information and the ideas that investigators need in order to advance their work.

> Surprisingly, many universities, their affiliated hospitals, and other biomedical research organizations have not done much to keep secrecy to the minimum necessary to protect legitimate commercial interests. In one comprehensive study, only 12 percent of these institutions had policies specifying clear time limits on keeping discoveries secret. Some had no written policy at all. Others do not rigorously enforce their own rules. As a result, company research directors report that they seldom have difficulty obtaining as much secrecy as they want.

> . . .

> Even more troubling are a handful of cases involving heavy-handed attempts by drug companies to suppress unfavorable findings by university scientists. For example, Betty Dong of the University of California, San Francisco, received a grant from a pharmaceutical firm to determine whether its expensive drug Synthroid was in fact superior to cheaper generic alternatives. Against expectations, including her own, she found no significant difference (which meant that patients were paying several hundred million dollars more per year for Synthroid than they needed to spend). Informed of these embarrassing results, the company accused Dong of numerous methodological errors and unspecified ethical lapses and even hired a private investigator to look for conflicts of interest (which proved to be nonexistent). When Dong went ahead and submitted her findings to a professional journal, the company threatened suit, invoking a clause in the research agreement she had signed prohibiting publication without the firm's consent. Although the university had never reviewed the contract nor warned her not to sign, it declined to assist her, leaving her to fight the company alone. Only after seven years did she finally succeed in publishing her paper.

DEREK BOK, UNIVERSITIES IN THE MARKETPLACE 64–65, 72 (2003).

3. In 1965, more than sixty percent of all research and development in the United States was financed by the federal government. By 2006, sixty-five percent was paid for by private industry. Jennifer Washburn, *Science's Worst Enemy: Corporate Funding*, DISCOVER, Oct. 11, 2007, *available at* http://discovermagazine.com/2007/oct/sciences-worst-enemy-private-funding. Washburn warns that corporate money often comes with questionable strings:

> University policies governing conflicts of interest and research integrity vary widely from campus to campus—and most still have a lot of holes.... One 2005 study examining more than 100 academic medical centers found that half would allow the corporate sponsor to write manuscripts reporting on study results and only allow faculty to "suggest revisions"—a policy basically authorizing commercial ghostwriting of academic research. Thirty-five percent allowed the sponsor to store clinical trial data and release only portions to the investigator; 62 percent allowed the sponsor to alter the study design after the researchers and the sponsor had signed an agreement.

In November 2007, the University of California at Berkeley together with the Lawrence Berkeley National Laboratory and the University of Illinois at Urbana–Champaign signed a contract with BP to establish a new $500 million Energy Biosciences Institute. Nearly one third of the expected $50 million a year that BP will provide for the institute will be designated for confidential research in laboratory space rented from Berkeley or Illinois. The products of that research will be owned by BP. BP also has the right to negotiate for exclusive licenses on the results of other parts of the research venture and pay no more than $100,000 a year in royalties per license. Although the right to negotiate for exclusive rights is common in such agreements, capping the royalties in advance is most unusual and "not necessarily prudent." Goldie Blumenstyk, *BP Gets Good Terms in U. of California Deal*, CHRON. HIGHER EDUC., Nov. 23, 2007, at A21. Although the initial proposal called for a governing board of five members with two from BP and one each from the three academic partners, the final agreement has a governing board of eight, with half from BP. Charles Burress, *BP Research Partnership Contract Is Finally Signed*, SAN FRAN. CHRON., Nov. 15, 2007, at B3.

C.   SHARED GOVERNANCE

Although the court decisions in this section primarily address the collective bargaining rights of faculty, they also grapple with the issue of the role of faculty in university governance. As you read the material, consider whether the decisions shed useful light on faculty governance. The term "shared governance" emerged early in the last century. Does the term capture the essence of what Justice Frankfurter meant in *Sweezy v. New Hampshire*[a] when he quoted the four essential freedoms of a university to be "to determine for itself on academic grounds who may teach, what may be taught, how it shall be taught, and who may be admitted to study?"[b] What is to be shared, and what is to be allocated entirely to the faculty—or, in the alternative, allocated entirely to the president and board. Should some decisions allocated to the board require faculty consent as well? What did Frankfurter mean when he said that the university should "determine for itself on academic grounds." Does the phrase mean that governing boards may decide without faculty involvement so long as the board believes the decision to be academically sound? On what basis can they make such a

a. 354 U.S. 234 (1957).   **b.** 354 U.S. at 263.

determination? May the president of the college or university decide to grant tenure to a particular faculty member without faculty involvement?

1966 Statement on Government of Colleges and Universities
AAUP Policy Documents & Reports 135 (10th ed. 2006).

[The text is set forth in Appendix B, *infra*.]

Questions and Comments on Shared Governance

1. Consider the views of Peter Eckel:

    Much of the current thinking on shared governance is shaped by the 1966 *Statement on Government of Colleges and Universities* jointly formulated by the American Association of University Professors (AAUP), the American Council on Education (ACE), and the Association of Governing Boards of Universities and Colleges (AGB). The *Statement*, although not intended to serve as a blueprint for institutional decision making, outlines roles for faculty, administrators, and trustees in governance decisions. For example, it suggests that issues such as managing the endowment be assigned to the trustees, maintaining and creating the new resources to the president, and developing the curriculum to the faculty. Not all decisions fall neatly into the domain of one of the three groups. It notes that, therefore, much of institutional governance is (or should be) conducted jointly. Decisions about general education policy, the framing and execution of long-range plans, budgeting, and presidential selection should be made jointly.

    The *Statement* may cause as much confusion as clarity. Because of its broad categories of responsibilities, different groups can easily make a case that a specific decision falls in their domain. For example, how can an institution determine if a change like offering a new continuing education program is the responsibility of the president (who, according to the *Statement*, is responsible for maintaining and creating new resources), the faculty (who are responsible for the curriculum), or the trustees (who are the conduit between the public with its needs and the institution)? Or is this new initiative part of long-range planning, which the *Statement* identifies as a joint effort? If so, is participation equal? Answers to questions about who takes the lead on institutional decisions most likely depend on where one sits and the case each party can make for ownership. When high stakes are involved, the probability of conflict over who decides most likely rises.

    Peter D. Eckel, *The Role of Shared Governance in Institutional Hard Decisions: Enabler or Antagonist*, 24 REV. OF HIGHER EDUC. 15, 17 (2000).

2. Compare The University of Chicago Faculty Handbook (1999):

    The University of Chicago is an institution governed by its faculty through representative Ruling Bodies. Past and present members of the faculty have deliberated the policies and procedures that presently govern the conduct of individuals and academic units in the University. Such deliberations are ongoing, in response to faculty initiatives, changes in intellectual and cultural currents, or the law.

    It may not be immediately apparent to many members of the faculty that these Statutes and policies much affect what they do: faculty at the University are engaged primarily with research and teaching. However, teaching and research—as well as the whole range of departmental and professional school decisions—are pursued within an institutional framework of policies that have evolved, through the processes of faculty governance, to foster and support research and teaching. These policies express publicly the University's commitment to integrity not only in scholarship but in all of its activities. Breaches of University policies thus may damage not only the individuals involved but the University as a whole. Members of the University of Chicago faculty, as members of a self-governing community, owe it to themselves and the broader community to be familiar with the University's policies in their professional school and departmental activities. Particularly at the departmental or professional school level, every faculty member has a responsibility to participate with colleagues in self-government and insure that the department and its members follow University policies. Members of the faculty, as members of the Senate and other Ruling bodies, also have the opportunity to propose new policies or modify existing ones.

3. Consider also the University of Michigan Faculty Handbook, *available at* http://www.provost.umich.edu/faculty/handbook/:

> The following statement of general principles for faculty participation in institutional and academic unit level governance ... was developed by the Academic Affairs Advisory Committee (AAAC) of the Senate Assembly. These principles were unanimously endorsed by the Senate Assembly on April 21, 1997, and were subsequently distributed to all members of the faculty....
>
> A. General Principles for Faculty Participation in Institutional Governance
>
> 1. The faculty has primary responsibility for such fundamental areas as curriculum, subject matter and methods of instruction, research, faculty status, standards and procedures for admission of students, and those aspects of student life which relate to the educational process.
>
> 2. The faculty sets the degree requirements, determines when the requirements have been met, and otherwise qualifies students and recommends them to the president and Board of Regents to grant the degrees thus achieved.
>
> 3. Considerations of faculty status and related matters are primarily a faculty responsibility; this area includes matters relating to academic titles, appointments, reappointments, decisions not to reappoint, promotions, the recommending of tenure and dismissal. Policies and procedures shall be developed for the implementation of these faculty responsibilities.
>
> 4. The faculty shall participate in the determination of policies and procedures governing compensation of faculty.
>
> 5. Agencies for faculty participation in the government of the college/school or university shall be established at each level where faculty responsibility is to be met. A faculty-elected campus-wide body shall exist for the presentation of the views of the whole faculty. The agencies may consist of meetings of all faculty members of a department, school, college, division, or university system, or they may take the form of faculty-elected executive committees in departments and colleges/schools, and a faculty-elected body for larger divisions or for the institution as a whole.
>
> 6. Budgetary policies and decisions directly affecting those areas for which the faculty has primary responsibility—such as, but not limited to, curriculum, subject matter and methods of instruction, research, faculty status, admission of students and those aspects of student life which relate to the educational process—shall be made in concert with the faculty.
>
> 7. The preceding faculty responsibilities remain in effect when there is a delegation of faculty governance to agencies or administrative officers. Faculty must exercise diligence and provide oversight to ensure that its agencies act in keeping with its policies and recommendations, and that they are implemented in an appropriate manner.

B.   Academic Unit Level Governance Principles

1.   Although the principles of governance apply to all academic units the forms of faculty governance may vary among units.

2.   Every academic unit at the University of Michigan shall have a set of written rules and procedures for its governance, copies of which are to be available to each faculty member.

3.   The governing faculty of each academic unit shall establish the responsibilities and authority of each academic unit governance entity and each administrative entity within that unit. This applies to the lines of decision-making authority of these entities in relation to: curriculum; admission requirements; graduation requirements; major operating procedures such as departmental organization, committee organization, committee appointments; budget; faculty appointments, reappointments, decisions not to reappoint; faculty promotion and tenure; and policies concerning reviews of faculty for merit salary increases.

4.   The governing faculty of each academic unit shall establish the operating procedures of its academic unit governance entities including, but not limited to: procedures for agenda setting, establishment of a quorum, determination of membership and voting rights, qualification of attendance by persons other than members, appointment of a faculty secretary, distribution of minutes, and the retention/filing of minutes.

5.   For those academic units where the faculty delegates authority to an executive committee the following principles apply:

    a.   Procedures for nomination and election of executive committee members shall be determined by the governing faculty of the unit.

    b.   All recommendations to the Regents concerning a unit executive committee or other unit governance entity shall be based on a vote of the governing faculty of the unit.

    c.   The governing faculty shall establish the membership criteria for the executive committee with consideration for balance among various components of the unit, such as unit programs and departments, to make the executive committee representative of the governing faculty of the unit.

    d.   The governing faculty shall establish criteria for those eligible to serve on the executive committee, e.g., membership in the governing faculty or in the professional faculty, fraction of appointment, and holding of administrative positions.

    e.   The governing faculty shall establish policies and procedures by which a vote by secret ballot among nominees for membership on the executive committee will be conducted, and for the transmission of the names of those elected to the Regents.

    f.   The governing faculty shall establish policies and procedures to be used to fill a vacancy if a member of the executive committee must take a leave of absence or is otherwise unable to complete the original term of office.

    g.   The governing faculty shall establish policies and procedures regarding the term of office of elected members and any other restrictions on terms of office.

Do these regulations make the lines of authority clear? Are there any changes you would recommend?

N.L.R.B. v. Yeshiva University

Supreme Court of the United States, 1980.
444 U.S. 672, 100 S.Ct. 856, 63 L.Ed.2d 115.

■ MR. JUSTICE POWELL delivered the opinion of the Court.

Supervisors and managerial employees are excluded from the categories of employees entitled to the benefits of collective bargaining under the National Labor Relations Act. The question presented is whether the full-time faculty of Yeshiva University fall within those exclusions.

Yeshiva is a private university which conducts a broad range of arts and sciences programs at its five undergraduate and eight graduate schools in New York City. On October 30, 1974, the Yeshiva University Faculty Association (Union) filed a representation petition with the National Labor Relations Board (Board). The Union sought certification as bargaining agent for the full-time faculty members at 10 of the 13 schools.[2] The University opposed the petition on the ground that all of its faculty members are managerial or supervisory personnel and hence not employees within the meaning of the National Labor Relations Act (Act). A Board-appointed hearing officer held hearings over a period of five months, generating a voluminous record.

The evidence at the hearings showed that a central administrative hierarchy serves all of the University's schools. Ultimate authority is vested in a Board of Trustees, whose members (other than the President) hold no administrative positions at the University. The President sits on the Board of Trustees and serves as chief executive officer, assisted by four Vice Presidents who oversee, respectively, medical affairs and science, student affairs, business affairs, and academic affairs. An Executive Council of Deans and administrators makes recommendations to the President on a wide variety of matters.

University-wide policies are formulated by the central administration with the approval of the Board of Trustees, and include general guidelines dealing with teaching loads, salary scales, tenure, sabbaticals, retirement, and fringe benefits. The budget for each school is drafted by its Dean or Director, subject to approval by the President after consultation with a committee of administrators.[3] The faculty participate in University-wide governance through their representatives on an elected student-faculty advisory council. The only University-wide faculty body is the Faculty Review Committee, composed of elected representatives who adjust grievances by informal negotiation and also may make formal recommendations to the Dean of the affected school or to the President. Such recommendations are purely advisory.

---

2. The schools involved are Yeshiva College, Stern College for Women, Teacher's Institute for Women, Erna Michael College, Yeshiva Program, James Striar School of General Jewish Studies, Belfer Graduate School of Sciences, Ferkauf Graduate School of Humanities and Social Sciences, Wurzweiler School of Social Work, and Bernard Revel Graduate School.

3. At Yeshiva College, budget requests prepared by the senior professor in each subject area receive the "perfunctory" approval of the Dean "99 percent" of the time and have never been rejected by the central administration. A council of elected department chairmen at Ferkauf approves the school's budget allocations when discretionary funds are available. All of these professors were included in the bargaining unit approved by the Board.

The individual schools within the University are substantially autonomous. Each is headed by a Dean or Director, and faculty members at each school meet formally and informally to discuss and decide matters of institutional and professional concern. At four schools, formal meetings are convened regularly pursuant to written bylaws. The remaining faculties meet when convened by the Dean or Director. Most of the schools also have faculty committees concerned with special areas of educational policy. Faculty welfare committees negotiate with administrators concerning salary and conditions of employment. Through these meetings and committees, the faculty at each school effectively determine its curriculum, grading system, admission and matriculation standards, academic calendars, and course schedules.[4]

Faculty power at Yeshiva's schools extends beyond strictly academic concerns. The faculty at each school make recommendations to the Dean or Director in every case of faculty hiring, tenure, sabbaticals, termination and promotion. Although the final decision is reached by the central administration on the advice of the Dean or Director, the overwhelming majority of faculty recommendations are implemented.[5] Even when financial problems in the early 1970's restricted Yeshiva's budget, faculty recommendations still largely controlled personnel decisions made within the constraints imposed by the administration. Indeed, the faculty of one school recently drew up new and binding policies expanding their own role in these matters. In addition, some faculties make final decisions regarding the admission, expulsion, and graduation of individual students. Others have decided questions involving teaching loads, student absence policies, tuition and enrollment levels, and in one case the location of a school.

A three-member panel of the Board granted the Union's petition in December 1975, and directed an election in a bargaining unit consisting of all full-time faculty members at the affected schools. The unit included Assistant Deans, senior professors, and department chairmen, as well as associate professors, assistant professors, and instructors.[7] Deans and Di-

---

4. For example, the Deans at Yeshiva and Erna Michael Colleges regard faculty actions as binding. Administrators testified that no academic initiative of either faculty had been vetoed since at least 1968. When the Stern College faculty disagreed with the Dean's decision to delete the education major, the major was reinstituted. The Director of the Teacher's Institute for Women testified that "the faculty is the school," while the Director of the James Striar School described his position as the "executive arm of the faculty," which had overruled him on occasion. All decisions regarding academic matters at the Yeshiva Program and Bernard Revel are made by faculty consensus. The "internal operation of [Wurzweiler] has been heavily governed by faculty decisions," according to its Dean.

5. One Dean estimated that 98% of faculty hiring recommendations were ultimately given effect. Others could not recall an instance when a faculty recommendation had been overruled. At Stern College, the Dean in

six years has never overturned a promotion decision. The President has accepted all decisions of the Yeshiva College faculty as to promotions and sabbaticals, including decisions opposed by the Dean. At Erna Michael, the Dean has never hired a full-time faculty member without the consent of the affected senior professor, and the Director of Teacher's Institute for Women stated baldly that no teacher had ever been hired if "there was the slightest objection, even on one faculty member's part." The faculty at both these schools have overridden recommendations made by the deans. No promotion or grant of tenure has ever been made at Ferkauf over faculty opposition. The Dean of Belfer testified that he had no right to override faculty decisions on tenure and nonrenewal.

7. "Full-time faculty" were defined as those "appointed to the University in the titles of professor, associate professor, assistant professor, instructor, or any adjunct or visiting thereof, department chairmen, division chair-

rectors were excluded. The Board summarily rejected the University's contention that its entire faculty are managerial, viewing the claim as a request for reconsideration of previous Board decisions on the issue. Instead of making findings of fact as to Yeshiva, the Board referred generally to the record and found no "significan[t]" difference between this faculty and others it had considered. The Board concluded that the faculty are professional employees entitled to the protection of the Act because "faculty participation in collegial decision making is on a collective rather than individual basis, it is exercised in the faculty's own interest rather than 'in the interest of the employer,' and final authority rests with the board of trustees." 221 N.L.R.B. 1053, 1054 (1975).

The Union won the election and was certified by the Board. The University refused to bargain, reasserting its view that the faculty are managerial. In the subsequent unfair labor practice proceeding, the Board refused to reconsider its holding in the representation proceeding and ordered the University to bargain with the Union. When the University still refused to sit down at the negotiating table, the Board sought enforcement in the Court of Appeals for the Second Circuit, which denied the petition.

. . .

There is no evidence that Congress has considered whether a university faculty may organize for collective bargaining under the Act. Indeed, when the Wagner and Taft–Hartley Acts were approved, it was thought that congressional power did not extend to university faculties because they were employed by nonprofit institutions which did not "affect commerce." *See NLRB v. Catholic Bishop of Chicago*, 440 U.S. 490, 504–505 (1979). Moreover, the authority structure of a university does not fit neatly within the statutory scheme we are asked to interpret. The Board itself has noted that the concept of collegiality" does not square with the traditional authority structures with which th[e] Act was designed to cope in the typical organizations of the commercial world." *Adelphi University*, 195 N.L.R.B. 639, 648 (1972).

The Act was intended to accommodate the type of management-employee relations that prevail in the pyramidal hierarchies of private industry. In contrast, authority in the typical "mature" private university is divided between a central administration and one or more collegial bodies. This system of "shared authority" evolved from the medieval model of collegial decisionmaking in which guilds of scholars were responsible only to themselves. At early universities, the faculty were the school. Although faculties have been subject to external control in the United States since colonial times, traditions of collegiality continue to play a significant role at many universities, including Yeshiva.[10] For these reasons, the Board has recognized that principles developed for use in the industrial setting cannot be

---

men, senior faculty and assistant deans, but excluding ... part-time faculty; lecturers; principal investigators; deans, acting deans and directors; [and others not relevant to this action]." 221 N.L.R.B., at 1057. The term "faculty" in this opinion refers to the members of this unit as defined by the Board.

   10. See the inaugural address of Williams College President Paul Ansel Chadbourne, quoted in Kahn, The NLRB and Higher Education: The Failure of Policymaking Through Adjudication, 21 UCLA L. Rev. 63, 70, n. 16 (1973) (" 'Professors are sometimes spoken of as working for the college. They *are* the college' ") (emphasis in original); Davis, Unions and Higher Education: Another View, 49 Ed. Record 139, 143 (1968) ("The president ... is not the faculty's master. He is as much the faculty's administrator as he is the board [of trustees']"); n. 4, *supra*.

"imposed blindly on the academic world." *Syracuse University*, 204 N.L.R.B. 641, 643 (1973).

The absence of explicit congressional direction, of course, does not preclude the Board from reaching any particular type of employment. Acting under its responsibility for adapting the broad provisions of the Act to differing workplaces, the Board asserted jurisdiction over a university for the first time in 1970. *Cornell University*, 183 N.L.R.B. 329 (1970). Within a year it had approved the formation of bargaining units composed of faculty members. *C. W. Post Center*, 189 N.L.R.B. 904 (1971).[11] The Board reasoned that faculty members are "professional employees" within the meaning of § 2(12) of the Act and therefore are entitled to the benefits of collective bargaining. 189 N.L.R.B., at 905; 29 U.S.C. § 152(12).[12]

Yeshiva does not contend that its faculty are not professionals under the statute. But professionals, like other employees, may be exempted from coverage under the Act's exclusion for "supervisors" who use independent judgment in overseeing other employees in the interest of the employer,[13] or under the judicially implied exclusion for "managerial employees" who are involved in developing and enforcing employer policy. Both exemptions grow out of the same concern: That an employer is entitled to the undivided loyalty of its representatives. *Beasley v. Food Fair of North Carolina*, 416 U.S. 653, 661–662 (1974); *see NLRB v. Bell Aerospace Co.*, 416 U.S. 267, 281–282 (1974). Because the Court of Appeals found the faculty to be managerial employees, it did not decide the question of their supervisory status. In view of our agreement with that court's application of the managerial exclusion, we also need not resolve that issue of statutory interpretation.

Managerial employees are defined as those who "formulate and effectuate management policies by expressing and making operative the decisions of their employer." *NLRB v. Bell Aerospace Co., supra*, at 288 (quoting *Palace Laundry Dry Cleaning Corp.*, 75 N.L.R.B. 320, 323, n. 4 (1947)). These employees are "much higher in the managerial structure" than those explicitly mentioned by Congress, which "regarded [them] as so clearly outside the Act that no specific exclusionary provision was thought necessary." 416 U.S. at 283. Managerial employees must exercise discretion within, or even independently of, established employer policy and must be aligned with management. Although the Board has established no firm criteria for determining when an employee is so aligned, normally an employee may be excluded as managerial only if he represents management interests by taking

---

11. The Board has suggested that Congress tacitly approved the formation of faculty units in 1974, when the Act was amended to eliminate the exemption accorded to nonprofit hospitals. Although Congress appears to have agreed that nonprofit institutions "affect commerce" under modern economic conditions, H. R. Rep. No. 93–1051, p. 4 (1974); 120 Cong. Rec. 12938 (1974) (remarks of Sen. Williams), there is nothing to suggest that Congress considered the status of university faculties.

12. The Act provides broadly that "employees" have organizational and other rights. 29 U.S.C. § 157. Section 2(3) defines "employee" in general terms, 29 U.S.C. § 152(3); § 2(12) defines "professional employee" in

some detail, 29 U.S.C. § 152(12); and § 9(b)(1) prohibits the Board from creating a bargaining unit that includes both professional and nonprofessional employees unless a majority of the professionals vote for inclusion, 29 U.S.C. § 159 (b)(1).

13. An employee may be excluded if he has authority over any one of 12 enumerated personnel actions, including hiring and firing. 29 U.S.C. §§ 152 (3), 152 (11), 164 (a). The Board has held repeatedly that professionals may be excluded as supervisors. *E.g.*, University of Vermont, 223 N.L.R.B. 423, 426 (1976); Presbyterian Medical Center, 218 N.L.R.B. 1266, 1267–1269 (1975).

or recommending discretionary actions that effectively control or implement employer policy.

The Board does not contend that the Yeshiva faculty's decisionmaking is too insignificant to be deemed managerial. Nor does it suggest that the role of the faculty is merely advisory and thus not managerial. Instead, it contends that the managerial exclusion cannot be applied in a straightforward fashion to professional employees because those employees often appear to be exercising managerial authority when they are merely performing routine job duties. The status of such employees, in the Board's view, must be determined by reference to the "alignment with management" criterion. The Board argues that the Yeshiva faculty are not aligned with management because they are expected to exercise "independent professional judgment" while participating in academic governance, and because they are neither "expected to conform to management policies [nor] judged according to their effectiveness in carrying out those policies." Because of this independence, the Board contends there is no danger of divided loyalty and no need for the managerial exclusion. In its view, union pressure cannot divert the faculty from adhering to the interests of the university, because the university itself expects its faculty to pursue professional values rather than institutional interests. The Board concludes that application of the managerial exclusion to such employees would frustrate the national labor policy in favor of collective bargaining.

This "independent professional judgment" test was not applied in the decision we are asked to uphold. The Board's opinion relies exclusively on its previous faculty decisions for both legal and factual analysis. But those decisions only dimly foreshadow the reasoning now proffered to the Court. Without explanation, the Board initially announced two different rationales for faculty cases, then quickly transformed them into a litany to be repeated in case after case: (i) faculty authority is collective, (ii) it is exercised in the faculty's own interest rather than in the interest of the university, and (iii) final authority rests with the board of trustees. *Northeastern University*, 218 N.L.R.B. 247, 250 (1975); *University of Miami*, 213 N.L.R.B. 634, 634 (1974); *see Tusculum College*, 199 N.L.R.B. 28, 30 (1972).[19] In their arguments in this case, the Board's lawyers have abandoned the first and third branches of this analysis, which in any event were flatly inconsistent with its precedents, and have transformed the second into a theory that does not appear clearly in any Board opinion.

The controlling consideration in this case is that the faculty of Yeshiva University exercise authority which in any other context unquestionably would be managerial. Their authority in academic matters is absolute. They decide what courses will be offered, when they will be scheduled, and to whom they will be taught. They debate and determine teaching methods, grading policies, and matriculation standards. They effectively decide which students will be admitted, retained, and graduated. On occasion their views have determined the size of the student body, the tuition to be charged, and the location of a school. When one considers the function of a university, it is

---

19. Citing these three factors, the Board concludes in each case that faculty are professional employees. It has never explained the reasoning connecting the premise with the conclusion, although an argument similar to that made by its lawyers in this case appears in one concurring opinion. Northeastern University, 218 N.L.R.B., at 257 (opinion of Member Kennedy).

difficult to imagine decisions more managerial than these. To the extent the industrial analogy applies, the faculty determines within each school the product to be produced, the terms upon which it will be offered, and the customers who will be served.[23]

The Board nevertheless insists that these decisions are not managerial because they require the exercise of independent professional judgment. We are not persuaded by this argument. There may be some tension between the Act's exclusion of managerial employees and its inclusion of professionals, since most professionals in managerial positions continue to draw on their special skills and training. But we have been directed to no authority suggesting that that tension can be resolved by reference to the "independent professional judgment" criterion proposed in this case. Outside the university context, the Board routinely has applied the managerial and supervisory exclusions to professionals in executive positions without inquiring whether their decisions were based on management policy rather than professional expertise. Indeed, the Board has twice implicitly rejected the contention that decisions based on professional judgment cannot be managerial. Since the Board does not suggest that the "independent professional judgment" test is to be limited to university faculty, its new approach would overrule *sub silentio* this body of Board precedent and could result in the indiscriminate recharacterization as covered employees of professionals working in supervisory and managerial capacities.

Moreover, the Board's approach would undermine the goal it purports to serve: To ensure that employees who exercise discretionary authority on behalf of the employer will not divide their loyalty between employer and union. In arguing that a faculty member exercising independent judgment acts primarily in his own interest and therefore does not represent the interest of his employer, the Board assumes that the professional interests of the faculty and the interests of the institution are distinct, separable entities with which a faculty member could not simultaneously be aligned. The Court of Appeals found no justification for this distinction, and we perceive none. In fact, the faculty's professional interests—as applied to governance at a university like Yeshiva—cannot be separated from those of the institution.

In such a university, the predominant policy normally is to operate a quality institution of higher learning that will accomplish broadly defined educational goals within the limits of its financial resources. The "business" of a university is education, and its vitality ultimately must depend on academic policies that largely are formulated and generally are implemented by faculty governance decisions. *See* K. Mortimer & T. McConnell, Sharing Authority Effectively 23–24 (1978). Faculty members enhance their own standing and fulfill their professional mission by ensuring that the university's objectives are met. But there can be no doubt that the quest for academic excellence and institutional distinction is a "policy" to which the administration expects the faculty to adhere, whether it be defined as a professional or

---

23. The record shows that faculty members at Yeshiva also play a predominant role in faculty hiring, tenure, sabbaticals, termination and promotion. *See supra*, at 859–860, and n. 5. These decisions clearly have both managerial and supervisory characteristics. Since we do not reach the question of supervisory status, we need not rely primarily on these features of faculty authority.

an institutional goal. It is fruitless to ask whether an employee is "expected to conform" to one goal or another when the two are essentially the same.[27]

The problem of divided loyalty is particularly acute for a university like Yeshiva, which depends on the professional judgment of its faculty to formulate and apply crucial policies constrained only by necessarily general institutional goals. The university requires faculty participation in governance because professional expertise is indispensable to the formulation and implementation of academic policy. It may appear, as the Board contends, that the professor performing governance functions is less "accountable" for departures from institutional policy than a middle-level industrial manager whose discretion is more confined. Moreover, traditional systems of collegiality and tenure insulate the professor from some of the sanctions applied to an industrial manager who fails to adhere to company policy. But the analogy of the university to industry need not, and indeed cannot, be complete. It is clear that Yeshiva and like universities must rely on their faculties to participate in the making and implementation of their policies. The large measure of independence enjoyed by faculty members can only increase the danger that divided loyalty will lead to those harms that the Board traditionally has sought to prevent.

We certainly are not suggesting an application of the managerial exclusion that would sweep all professionals outside the Act in derogation of Congress' expressed intent to protect them. The Board has recognized that employees whose decisionmaking is limited to the routine discharge of professional duties in projects to which they have been assigned cannot be excluded from coverage even if union membership arguably may involve some divided loyalty. Only if an employee's activities fall outside the scope of the duties routinely performed by similarly situated professionals will he be found aligned with management. We think these decisions accurately capture the intent of Congress, and that they provide an appropriate starting point for analysis in cases involving professionals alleged to be managerial.[31]

... The Court of Appeals ... determined that the faculty of Yeshiva University, "in effect, substantially and pervasively [operate] the enterprise." 582 F.2d, at 698. We find no reason to reject this conclusion....

27. At Yeshiva, administrative concerns with scarce resources and University-wide balance have led to occasional vetoes of faculty action. But such infrequent administrative reversals in no way detract from the institution's primary concern with the academic responsibilities entrusted to the faculty. The suggestion that faculty interests depart from those of the institution with respect to salary and benefits is even less meritorious. The same is true of every supervisory or managerial employee. Indeed, there is arguably a greater community of interest on this point in the university than in industry, because the nature and quality of a university depend so heavily on the faculty attracted to the institution. B. Richman & R. Farmer, Leadership, Goals, and Power in Higher Education 258 (1974); see D. Bornheimer, G. Burns, & G. Dumke, The Faculty in Higher Education 174–175 (1973).

31. We recognize that this is a starting point only, and that other factors not present here may enter into the analysis in other contexts. It is plain, for example, that professors may not be excluded merely because they determine the content of their own courses, evaluate their own students, and supervise their own research. There thus may be institutions of higher learning unlike Yeshiva where the faculty are entirely or predominantly non-managerial. There also may be faculty members at Yeshiva and like universities who properly could be included in a bargaining unit. It may be that a rational line could be drawn between tenured and untenured faculty members, depending upon how a faculty is structured and operates. But we express no opinion on these questions, for it is clear that the unit approved by the Board was far too broad.

■ MR. JUSTICE BRENNAN, with whom MR. JUSTICE WHITE, MR. JUSTICE MARSHALL and MR. JUSTICE BLACKMUN join, dissenting.

[T]he Court's vision is clouded by its failure fully to discern and comprehend the nature of the faculty's role in university governance.

Unlike the purely hierarchical decisionmaking structure that prevails in the typical industrial organization, the bureaucratic foundation of most "mature" universities is characterized by dual authority systems. The primary decisional network is hierarchical in nature: Authority is lodged in the administration, and a formal chain of command runs from a lay governing board down through university officers to individual faculty members and students. At the same time, there exists a parallel professional network, in which formal mechanisms have been created to bring the expertise of the faculty into the decisionmaking process. *See* J. Baldridge, Power and Conflict in the University 114 (1971); Finkin, The NLRB in Higher Education, 5 U. Toledo L. Rev. 608, 614–618 (1974).

What the Board realized—and what the Court fails to apprehend—is that whatever influence the faculty wields in university decisionmaking is attributable solely to its collective expertise as professional educators, and not to any managerial or supervisory prerogatives. Although the administration may look to the faculty for advice on matters of professional and academic concern, the faculty offers its recommendations in order to serve its own independent interest in creating the most effective environment for learning, teaching, and scholarship. And while the administration may attempt to defer to the faculty's competence whenever possible, it must and does apply its own distinct perspective to those recommendations, a perspective that is based on fiscal and other managerial policies which the faculty has no part in developing. The University always retains the ultimate decisionmaking authority, and the administration gives what weight and import to the faculty's collective judgment as it chooses and deems consistent with its own perception of the institution's needs and objectives.[8]

The premise of a finding of managerial status is a determination that the excluded employee is acting on behalf of management and is answerable to a higher authority in the exercise of his responsibilities. The Board has consistently implemented this requirement—both for professional and non-professional employees—by conferring managerial status only upon those

---

8. One must be careful not to overvalue the significance of the faculty's influence on academic affairs. As one commentator has noted, "it is not extraordinary for employees to seek to exert influence over matters embedded in an employment relationship for which they share a concern, or that management would be responsive to their strongly held desires." Finkin, The NLRB in Higher Education, 5 U. Toledo L. Rev. 608, 616 (1974). Who, after all, is better suited than the faculty to decide what courses should be offered, how they should be taught, and by what standards their students should be graded? Employers will often attempt to defer to their employees' suggestions, particularly where—as here—those recommendations relate to matters within the unique competence of the employees.

Moreover, insofar as faculty members are given some say in more traditional managerial decisions such as the hiring and promotion of other personnel, such discretion does not constitute an adequate basis for the conferral of managerial or supervisory status. Indeed, in the typical industrial context, it is not uncommon for the employees' union to be given the *exclusive* right to recommend personnel to the employer, and these hiring-hall agreements have been upheld even where the union requires a worker to pass a union-administered skills test as a condition of referral. *See, e.g.,* Local 42 (Catalytic Constr. Co.), 164 N.L.R.B. 916 (1967); *see generally* Teamsters v. NLRB, 365 U.S. 667 (1961).

employees "whose interests are closely aligned with management *as true representatives of management*." (Emphasis added.) Only if the employee is expected to conform to management policies and is judged by his effectiveness in executing those policies does the danger of divided loyalties exist.

Yeshiva's faculty, however, is not accountable to the administration in its governance function, nor is any individual faculty member subject to personal sanction or control based on the administration's assessment of the worth of his recommendations. When the faculty, through the schools' advisory committees, participates in university decisionmaking on subjects of academic policy, it does not serve as the "representative of management."[10] Unlike industrial supervisors and managers, university professors are not hired to "make operative" the policies and decisions of their employer. Nor are they retained on the condition that their interests will correspond to those of the university administration. Indeed, the notion that a faculty member's professional competence could depend on his undivided loyalty to management is antithetical to the whole concept of academic freedom. Faculty members are judged by their employer on the quality of their teaching and scholarship, not on the compatibility of their advice with administration policy. Board Member Kennedy aptly concluded in his concurring opinion in *Northeastern University*, 218 N.L.R.B. 247, 257 (1975):

> [The] influence which the faculty exercises in many areas of academic governance is insufficient to make them "managerial" employees. Such influence is not exercised "for management" or "in the interest of the employer," but rather is exercised in their own professional interest. The best evidence of this fact is that faculty members are generally not held accountable by or to the administration for their faculty governance functions. Faculty criticism of administration policies, for example, is viewed not as a breach of loyalty, but as an exercise in academic freedom. So, too, intervention by the university administration in faculty deliberations would most likely be considered an infringement upon academic freedoms. Conversely, university administrations rarely consider themselves bound by faculty recommendations.

> . . .

Moreover, the congruence of interests in this case ought not to be exaggerated. The university administration has certain economic and fiduciary responsibilities that are not shared by the faculty, whose primary concerns are academic and relate solely to its own professional reputation. The record evinces numerous instances in which the faculty's recommendations have been rejected by the administration on account of fiscal constraints

---

10. Where faculty members actually do serve as management's representatives, the Board has not hesitated to exclude them from the Act's coverage as managerial or supervisory personnel. *Compare* University of Vermont, 223 N.L.R.B. 423 (1976) (excluding department chairmen as supervisors), *and* University of Miami, 213 N.L.R.B. 634 (1974) (excluding deans as supervisors), *with* Northeastern University, 218 N.L.R.B. 247 (1975) (department chairmen included within bargaining unit because they act primarily as instruments of the faculty), *and* Fordham University, 193 N.L.R.B. 134 (1971) (including department chairmen because they are considered to be representatives of the faculty rather than of the administration). In fact, the bargaining unit approved by the Board in the present case excluded deans, acting deans, directors, and principal investigators of research and training grants, all of whom were deemed to exercise supervisory or managerial authority. *See ante*, at 678, n. 7.

or other managerial policies. Disputes have arisen between Yeshiva's faculty and administration on such fundamental issues as the hiring, tenure, promotion, retirement, and dismissal of faculty members, academic standards and credits, departmental budgets, and even the faculty's choice of its own departmental representative. The very fact that Yeshiva's faculty has voted for the Union to serve as its representative in future negotiations with the administration indicates that the faculty does not perceive its interests to be aligned with those of management. Indeed, on the precise topics which are specified as mandatory subjects of collective bargaining—wages, hours, and other terms and conditions of employment—the interests of teacher and administrator are often diametrically opposed.

Finally, the Court's perception of the Yeshiva faculty's status is distorted by the rose-colored lens through which it views the governance structure of the modern-day university. The Court's conclusion that the faculty's professional interests are indistinguishable from those of the administration is bottomed on an idealized model of collegial decisionmaking that is a vestige of the great medieval university. But the university of today bears little resemblance to the "community of scholars" of yesteryear.[14] Education has become "big business," and the task of operating the university enterprise has been transferred from the faculty to an autonomous administration, which faces the same pressures to cut costs and increase efficiencies that confront any large industrial organization. The past decade of budgetary cutbacks, declining enrollments, reductions in faculty appointments, curtailment of academic programs, and increasing calls for accountability to alumni and other special interest groups has only added to the erosion of the faculty's role in the institution's decisionmaking process.

These economic exigencies have also exacerbated the tensions in university labor relations, as the faculty and administration more and more frequently find themselves advocating conflicting positions not only on issues of compensation, job security, and working conditions, but even on subjects formerly thought to be the faculty's prerogative. In response to this friction, and in an attempt to avoid the strikes and work stoppages that have disrupted several major universities in recent years, many faculties have entered into collective-bargaining relationships with their administrations and governing boards.[17] An even greater number of schools—Yeshiva among

---

14. *See generally* J. Brubacher & W. Rudy, Higher Education in Transition: A History of American Colleges and Universities, 1636–1976 (3d ed. 1976). In one of its earliest decisions in this area, the Board recognized that the governance structure of the typical modern university does not fit the mold of true collegiality in which authority rests with a peer group of scholars. Adelphi University, 195 N.L.R.B. 639, 648 (1972). *Accord*, New York University, 205 N.L.R.B. 4, 5 (1973). Even the concept of "shared authority," in which university decisionmaking is seen as the joint responsibility of both faculty and administration, with each exerting a dominant influence in its respective sphere of expertise, has been found to be "an ideal rather than a widely adopted practice." K. Mortimer & T. McConnell, Sharing Authority Effectively 4

(1978). The authors conclude: "Higher education is in the throes of a shift from informal and consensual judgments to authority based on formal criteria.... There have been changes in societal and legislative expectations about higher education, an increase in external regulation of colleges and universities, an increase in emphasis on managerial skills and the technocratic features of modern management, and a greater codification of internal decision-making procedures. These changes raise the question whether existing statements of shared authority provide adequate guidelines for internal governance." *Id.*, at 269.

17. As of January 1979, 80 private and 302 public institutions of higher education had engaged in collective bargaining with their faculties, and over 130,000 academic

them—have endeavored to negotiate and compromise their differences informally, by establishing avenues for faculty input into university decisions on matters of professional concern.

Today's decision, however, threatens to eliminate much of the administration's incentive to resolve its disputes with the faculty through open discussion and mutual agreement. By its overbroad and unwarranted interpretation of the managerial exclusion, the Court denies the faculty the protections of the NLRA and, in so doing, removes whatever deterrent value the Act's availability may offer against unreasonable administrative conduct. Rather than promoting the Act's objective of funneling dissension between employers and employees into collective bargaining, the Court's decision undermines that goal and contributes to the possibility that "recurring disputes [will] fester outside the negotiation process until strikes or other forms of economic warfare occur." *Ford Motor Co. v. NLRB*, 441 U.S. 488, 499 (1979).

In sum, the Board analyzed both the essential purposes underlying the supervisory and managerial exclusions and the nature of the governance structure at Yeshiva University. Relying on three factors that attempt to encapsulate the fine distinction between those professional employees who are entitled to the NLRA's protections and those whose managerial responsibilities require their exclusion, the Board concluded that Yeshiva's full-time faculty qualify as the former rather than the latter. I believe the Board made the correct determination. But even were I to have reservations about the specific result reached by the Board on the facts of this case, I would certainly have to conclude that the Board applied a proper mode of analysis to arrive at a decision well within the zone of reasonableness. Accordingly, in light of the deference due the Board's determination in this complex area, I would reverse the judgment of the Court of Appeals.

Questions and Comments on *Yeshiva*

1. The majority and dissenters disagree about how Yeshiva University is run and whether it is the faculty or the administration that has the power to make decisions. Who is right? Is the majority correct when it says that "[f]aculty members enhance their own standing and fulfill their professional mission by ensuring that the university's objectives are met"?

2. The dissent points out differences between the hierarchical structure of a university and that of a typical industrial enterprise. How is the relationship between faculty and the administration different from the typical relationship between industrial

personnel had been unionized. National Center for the Study of Collective Bargaining in Higher Education, Directory of Faculty Contracts and Bargaining Agents in Institutions of Higher Education i-ii (1979). Although the NLRA is not applicable to any public employer, *see* 29 U.S.C. § 152 (2), as of 1976, 22 States had enacted legislation granting faculties at public institutions the right to unionize and requiring public employers to bargain with duly constituted bargaining agents. Mortimer & McConnell, *supra*, n. 14, at 53. *See also* Livingston & Christensen, State and Federal Regulation of Collective Negotiations in Higher Education, 1971 Wis. L. Rev. 91, 102. The upsurge in the incidence of collective bargaining has generally been attributed to the faculty's desire to use the process as a countervailing force against increased administrative power and to ensure that the ideals of the academic community are actually practiced. As the Carnegie Commission found, "[unionization] for [faculty] is more a protective than an aggressive act, more an effort to preserve the status quo than to achieve a new position of influence and affluence...." Carnegie Commission on Higher Education, Governance of Higher Education 40 (1973).

employees and management? Are university administrators more likely to defer to the suggestions of faculty than industrial managers are to their employees? Does your answer depend on whether the suggestions are about academic matters such as curriculum?

3. Should faculty be permitted to unionize? What are the benefits and costs of either approach? Are the same concerns that justify permitting other types of employees to unionize present in the case of college and university faculty?

LeMoyne–Owen College v. N.L.R.B.

United States Court of Appeals, District of Columbia Circuit, 2004.
357 F.3d 55.

■ ROBERTS, CIRCUIT JUDGE:

Petitioner LeMoyne–Owen College is a historically black college in Memphis, Tennessee that traces its roots to a school founded in 1862. The College's full-time faculty (numbering approximately sixty members) sought to unionize in the spring of 2002 to negotiate with management, but the College argued that the faculty members *were* management—that is, managerial employees not entitled to the protection of the National Labor Relations Act (NLRA). The National Labor Relations Board sided with the faculty, ordering the College to recognize and bargain with the faculty's representative. The College petitioned for review in this court, and the Board filed a cross-application to enforce its order.

1. The College relies primarily on *NLRB v. Yeshiva University*, 444 U.S. 672 (1980), the Supreme Court's leading (because only) case on determining the managerial status of an academic faculty. . . .

Recognizing that the governance structures of academic institutions differ from the standard industry model for which the NLRA was designed, the Court declined to adopt a *per se* rule on the managerial status of faculty members. Instead, the Court emphasized a number of factors that supported its conclusion that Yeshiva University's faculty were beyond the scope of the NLRA. . . .

2. As might be expected given such a long list of relevant factors and the exquisite variety of academic institutions across the country, the Board has developed a substantial body of cases that explicate and develop the *Yeshiva* standard. In *American International College*, 282 N.L.R.B. 189 (1986), for example, the Board held the approximately ninety faculty members to be managerial employees, noting the authority of faculty standing committees in such areas as admissions, curriculum issues, and graduation requirements. Although there were some instances in which the administration had vetoed faculty proposals, the NLRB said that "they are not substantial or predominant and do not show a pattern of unilateral action by the administration."

In *Livingstone College*, 286 N.L.R.B. 1308 (1987), the NLRB reached the same outcome, even though the faculty exercised their authority through standing committees of mixed membership—including administrators and students. The faculty's "substantial authority" in the development and implementation of policies in the academic sphere, outweighed the lack of faculty input into budget decisions or the tenure process.

The Board again found faculty members to be managerial employees in *Lewis and Clark College*, 300 N.L.R.B. 155 (1990). Faculty workload policies at the college were set by the administration, but committees (composed predominantly of faculty) made effective recommendations in areas such as admissions requirements and curriculum. The Board rejected a Regional Director's view that "umbrella committees" on which the faculty were a minority, addressing financial issues and long-term planning, negated the faculty's managerial status. As the Board found, "there is ... nothing inconsistent with the faculty members' having authority over one level of policy (e.g., academics), and the administration (including the board of trustees), having control over another (e.g., financial viability and long-term planning)." The Board further explained:

> The board of trustees and others in the administration are entrusted with the ultimate policy-making and fiduciary responsibility for the College, not the faculty. But, even as to those areas in which the administration has exercised its own managerial decision-making authority, high-level implementation of those decisions is performed by the faculty.

In *Elmira College*, 309 N.L.R.B. 842 (1992), the Board upheld, without comment, a Regional Director's conclusion that "without more, the nature of faculty involvement with respect to academic matters conclusively establishes their status as managerial employees." Under the college by-laws, the faculty had authority over admissions, courses, graduation requirements, the nature of available degrees, and related procedural matters. The Regional Director noted that some factors supported a lack of managerial status: "the college faculty does not participate in promotion decisions exclusive of tenure and, in a few instances, has been overruled in hiring decisions. Also, the faculty has only a limited voice in administrative decisions involving salary or benefits or the budget process." He did not find these factors controlling, because they "fall outside the crucial matters of academic governance considered dispositive by the Supreme Court in *Yeshiva*."

3. When the faculty of LeMoyne–Owen College petitioned the NLRB for recognition as a bargaining unit, the College responded by contending that "the instant case bears strong similarity to cases in which the Board, utilizing the principles set forth in *Yeshiva*, found that faculty members were managerial employees...." The College pointed to significant factual parallels between LeMoyne–Owen and the other institutions at which faculty members were deemed managerial employees—particularly when the comparison focuses primarily on academic matters and on "effective recommendation or control rather than final authority." For example, the LeMoyne–Owen faculty have, according to the *Faculty Handbook*, "policy and procedural authority" over a range of academic areas, including admissions standards, the curriculum, general education requirements, graduation requirements, standards for grading, candidates for graduation, and conditions of academic standing, suspension, and dismissal. *Faculty Handbook* § 3.00.

The faculty act largely through a Faculty Assembly, consisting of all full-time faculty members, and various standing committees. The standing committees include a Curriculum Committee, which approves curriculum changes and course additions or modifications, and an Academic Honors, Standards, and Selection Committee, which oversees the awarding of academic honors and handles cases of academic probation and dismissal. Faculty have discretion over their teaching methods and the content of their courses, within certain parameters described in the *Faculty Handbook*. For example, each full-time faculty member is obliged to teach twelve credit hours per semester, and for each course, the faculty member must prepare a detailed syllabus and file it with the appropriate division chair. College policy mandates that an evaluation of each student's English usage form at least ten percent of the student's grade.

Faculty recommendations on academic policies and other matters, such as tenure, often require the approval of the president and ultimately of the College's board of trustees. But the president testified that he had never, in six years as president, failed to approve a faculty recommendation on degree requirements or other matters related to the courses taught at the College. He also stated that he had forwarded all Faculty Assembly recommendations on curricular changes to the trustees, without exception, and that the trustees had never rejected any of those recommendations.

4. The Regional Director determined, however, that the faculty at LeMoyne–Owen were not managerial employees, and certified a bargaining unit consisting of all full-time faculty members. The Regional Director distinguished the College's faculty from the faculty at Yeshiva University, stating that "the faculty of LeMoyne–Owen College neither possess absolute control over any facet of the school's operations, nor 'effectively' recommend policies affecting its administration. They neither establish new policy nor effectively recommend changes to existing policy." In support of this conclusion, the Regional Director noted that committee recommendations at the College are "subject to multiple levels of review, and subject to change by higher levels of authority." *Id.* The existence of such multiple levels of authority, he stated, makes it less likely that faculty recommendations will be effective, because the recommendations can be altered on their way up the hierarchy. The Regional Director pointed to a number of other factors, including the presence of non-faculty on standing committees, an ad hoc core curriculum committee with significant non-faculty representation established by the president in apparent tension with the faculty Curriculum Committee, and the instructional policies in the *Faculty Handbook*, such as the English usage requirement and the rules governing course syllabi. He also stated that the faculty play "a limited role in the selection of applicants for hire, [and] no role in the decision to dismiss staff or faculty," and cited specific instances such as the firing of secretaries during a financial crunch at the College in 2000 and the hiring of a professor as a full-time faculty member despite a faculty recommendation that she be hired only as a visiting professor.

. . .

LeMoyne–Owen requested that the Board review the Regional Director's decision. . . . The Board denied the request by a 2–1 vote, declaring in a one-sentence order that the College had "raised no substantial issues warranting review." After the faculty voted to accept their bargaining representative, the Regional Director issued a formal certification of that representative and the College again sought the review of the Board. As it had before, the College argued that the LeMoyne–Owen faculty exercise authority comparable to that of the faculty members in *American International College* and the analogous post-*Yeshiva* cases. The Board again issued a terse order denying review, again with no discussion of the precedents. The College refused to bargain with the faculty, and the Board ultimately deemed the College guilty of unfair labor practices and ordered it to bargain. The matter is before this court on the College's petition for review of the order and the Board's cross-application for enforcement. The College's challenge brings the entire NLRB proceeding—including the Regional Director's underlying decision to certify the full-time faculty as a bargaining unit—before this court for review.

We accord deference to the Board's exercise of its authority under 29 U.S.C. § 159 to certify appropriate bargaining units. That deference is subject to certain limits, however, and one of those limits is that the Board "cannot ignore its own relevant precedent but must explain why it is not controlling." In this case, the Board has not provided any explanation—let alone an adequate one—of how its disposition is consistent with its contrary holdings in the post-*Yeshiva* cases that appear to have presented similar facts. The only opinion is that of the Regional Director, which did not discuss or even mention a single one of the precedents on which the College relied.

An agency is by no means required to distinguish every precedent cited to it by an aggrieved party. But where, as here, a party makes a significant showing that analogous cases have been decided differently, the agency must do more than simply ignore that argument. As this court noted in *Cleveland Construction*, 44 F.3d at 1016, "we cannot uphold silence." Emerson's advice to preachers—"emphasize your choice by utter ignoring of all that you reject," Ralph Waldo Emerson, *The Preacher, reprinted in* 10 LECTURES AND BIOGRAPHICAL SKETCHES 215, 235 (1904)—will not do for administrative agencies.

The need for an explanation is particularly acute when an agency is applying a multi-factor test through case-by-case adjudication. The "open-ended rough-and-tumble of factors" on which *Yeshiva* launched the Board and higher education, can lead to predictability and intelligibility only to the extent the Board explains, in applying the test to varied fact situations, which factors are significant and which less so, and why.

. . .

The NLRB may have an adequate explanation for the result it reached in this case. We cannot, however, assume that such an explanation exists until we see it. We therefore grant the petition for review, deny the cross-application for enforcement, and remand to the NLRB for further proceedings.

Note on *LeMoyne–Owen College*

On remand, the Board examined the record in light of *Yeshiva* and its progeny and held that the faculty of LeMoyne–Owen College are managerial employees:

> To summarize, we find that through individual faculty members, the curriculum committee, the academic standards committee, and the faculty assembly, the faculty make or effectively control decisions with regard to curriculum, courses of study and course content, degrees and degree requirements, majors and minors, academic programs, academic divisions, the addition and deletion of courses, course content, teaching methods, grading, academic retention, lists of graduates, selection of honors, admission standards, syllabi, and textbooks. The faculty also will have an effective voice in the outcome of the accreditation review, which was incomplete at the time of the hearing. The faculty also makes effective decisions in some nonacademic

areas, including tenure standards and selections, and faculty evaluation procedures.

We disagree with the Regional Director's analysis, which largely questions the independence and effectiveness of the faculty's recommendations. The Regional Director disputed the independence of the faculty standing committees and the faculty assembly because they included nonfaculty members. However, it is undisputed that the curriculum committee, academic standards committee, and the faculty assembly, which approve many academic decisions, are overwhelmingly comprised of faculty members...

... The Regional Director also disputed the effectiveness of faculty recommendations because of the "potential" for the decline in faculty influence as recommendations ascend through the "hierarchy of the review process." However, there is no factual basis for the Regional Director's supposition that faculty recommendations are compromised as they proceed through the administrative hierarchy. To the contrary, the evidence demonstrates that the faculty's recommendations have been routinely approved by the administration.

LeMoyne–Owen College, 345 N.L.R.B. 93 (2005), 2005 WL 2477119, at 12–13. Do you agree with the Board's characterization of the faculty at LeMoyne–Owen college?

To what extent are academic freedom and shared governance linked? Can one exist at a college or university without the other?

Minnesota State Board for Community Colleges v. Knight

Supreme Court of the United States, 1984.
465 U.S. 271, 104 S.Ct. 1058, 79 L.Ed.2d 299.

■ Justice O'Connor delivered the opinion of the Court.

In 1971, the Minnesota Legislature adopted the Public Employment Labor Relations Act (PELRA), Minn. Stat. § 179.61 *et seq.* (1982), to establish "orderly and constructive relationships between all public employers and their employees...." ... PELRA provides for the division of public employees into appropriate bargaining units and establishes a procedure, based on majority support within a unit, for the designation of an exclusive bargaining agent for that unit. The statute requires public employers to "meet and negotiate" with exclusive representatives concerning the "terms and conditions of employment," which the statute defines to mean "the hours of employment, the compensation therefore ... and the employer's personnel policies affecting the working conditions of the employees." The employer's and employees' representatives must seek an agreement in good faith.

PELRA also grants professional employees, such as college faculty, the right to "meet and confer" with their employers on matters related to employment that are outside the scope of mandatory negotiations. This provision rests on the recognition that "professional employees possess knowledge, expertise, and dedication which is helpful and necessary to the operation and quality of public services and which may assist public employers in developing their policies." The statute declares it to be the State's policy to "encourage close cooperation between public employers and professional employees" by providing for "meet and confer" sessions on all employment-related questions not subject to mandatory bargaining. There is no statutory provision concerning the "meet and confer" process, however, that requires good-faith efforts to reach agreement.

PELRA requires professional employees to select a representative to "meet and confer" with their public employer. If professional employees in an appropriate bargaining unit have an exclusive representative to "meet and negotiate" with their employer, that representative serves as the "meet and confer" representative as well. Indeed, the employer may neither "meet and negotiate" nor "meet and confer" with any members of that bargaining unit except through their exclusive representative. This restriction, however, does not prevent professional employees from submitting advice or recommendations to their employer as part of their work assignment. Moreover, nothing in PELRA restricts the right of any public employee to speak on any "matter related to the conditions or compensation of public employment or their betterment" as long as doing so "is not designed to and does not interfere with the full faithful and proper performance of the duties of employment or circumvent the rights of the exclusive representative if there be one."

Appellant Minnesota State Board for Community Colleges (State Board) operates the Minnesota community college system. At the time of trial, the system comprised 18 institutions located throughout the State. Each community college is administered by a president, who reports, through the chancellor of the system, to the State Board.

Prior to 1971, Minnesota's community colleges were governed in a variety of ways. On some campuses, faculty had a strong voice in administrative policymaking, expressed through organizations such as faculty senates. On other campuses, the administration consulted very little with the faculty. Irrespective of the level of faculty involvement in governance, however, the administrations of the colleges retained final authority to make policy.

Following enactment of PELRA, appellant Minnesota Community College Faculty Association (MCCFA) was designated the exclusive representative of the faculty of the State's community colleges, which had been deemed a single bargaining unit. MCCFA has "met and negotiated" and "met and conferred" with the State Board since 1971. The result has been the negotiation of successive collective-bargaining agreements in the intervening years and, in order to implement the "meet and confer" provision, a restructuring of governance practices in the community college system.

On the state level, MCCFA and the Board established "meet and confer" committees to discuss questions of policy applicable to the entire system. On the campus level, the MCCFA chapters and the college administrations created local "meet and confer" committees—also referred to as "exchange of views" committees—to discuss questions of policy applicable only to the campus. The committees on both levels have discussed such topics as the selection and evaluation of administrators, academic accreditation, student affairs, curriculum, and fiscal planning—all policy matters within the control of the college administrations and the State Board.

The State Board considers the views expressed by the statewide faculty "meet and confer" committees to be the faculty's official collective position. It recognizes, however, that not every instructor agrees with the official faculty view on every policy question. Not every instructor in the bargaining unit is a member of MCCFA, and MCCFA has selected only its own members to represent it on "meet and confer" committees. Accordingly, all faculty have been free to communicate to the State Board and to local administrations their views on questions within the coverage of the statutory "meet and confer" provision. They have frequently done so.[3] With the possible exception of a brief period of adjustment to the new governance structure, during which some administrators were reluctant to communicate informally with faculty, individual faculty members have not been impeded by either MCCFA or college administrators in the communication of their views on policy questions. Nor has PELRA ever been construed to impede such communication.[4]

Appellees are 20 Minnesota community college faculty instructors who are not members of MCCFA. In December 1974, they filed suit in the United States District Court for the District of Minnesota, challenging the constitutionality of MCCFA's exclusive representation of community college faculty in both the "meet and negotiate" and "meet and confer" processes. A three-judge District Court was convened to hear the case . . .

The court rejected appellees' attack on the constitutionality of exclusive representation in bargaining over terms and conditions of employment. . . . The court agreed with appellees, however, that PELRA, as applied in the community college system, infringes First and Fourteenth Amendment speech and associational rights of faculty who do not wish to join MCCFA. By granting MCCFA the right to select the faculty representatives for the "meet and confer" committees and by permitting MCCFA to select only its own members, the court held, PELRA unconstitutionally deprives non-MCCFA instructors of "a fair opportunity to participate in the selection of governance representatives." The court granted declaratory relief in accordance with its holdings and enjoined MCCFA from selecting "meet and confer" representatives without providing all faculty the fair opportunity that its selection practice had unconstitutionally denied.

Appellees, the State Board, and MCCFA all filed appeals with this Court. . . .

3. Indeed, both the Board and the local administrations have regularly made efforts to supplement the "official" advice with other, unofficial communications. Prior to each on-campus Board meeting, the Board has made itself available to persons who wish to express their views individually or in groups. In addition, many faculty members have met with or written to the Board or the system's chancellor to communicate their individual views. On the local level, college presidents have used a variety of means to solicit opinions from their instructors and students, including making themselves available at collegewide "town meetings" or at commons areas, hosting luncheons and breakfasts, appearing at faculty meetings, and inviting faculty advice through maintenance of an "open-door" policy. Thus, while the "meet and confer" process gives weight to an official collective faculty position as formulated by the faculty's exclusive representative, all instructors have ample opportunity to express their views to their employer on subjects within the purview of the "meet and confer" process.

4. The repeated suggestions in JUSTICE STEVENS' dissent that the state employer and state employees have been prohibited or deterred by the statute from talking with each other on policy questions misunderstand the statute and are flatly contradicted by the District Court's findings. All that the statute prohibits is the formal exchange of views called a "meet and confer" session. It in no way impairs the ability of individual employees or groups of employees to express their views to their employer outside that formal context, and there has been no suggestion in these cases that, after an initial period of adjustment to PELRA, any such communication of views has ever been restrained because it was challenged as constituting a formal "meet and confer" session. None of the testimony selectively quoted by JUSTICE STEVENS' dissent recites a single instance of such restraint, and the quoted passages make clear that the prohibition on the employer's holding "meet and confer" sessions with anyone but the exclusive representative has been understood to bar only a certain type of formal exchange, not other exchanges of views.

On March 28, 1983, the Court noted probable jurisdiction in the appeals by the Board and MCCFA. Several weeks later, following an election held pursuant to a newly established scheme for selecting "meet and confer" representatives, the three-judge District Court modified its injunction to require a specific voting system for the selection of faculty "meet and confer" representatives.[5] This Court permitted appellants to add to their appeal a challenge to this new relief.

Appellees do not and could not claim that they have been unconstitutionally denied access to a public forum. A "meet and confer" session is obviously not a public forum. It is a fundamental principle of First Amendment doctrine, articulated most recently in *Perry Education Assn. v. Perry Local Educators' Assn.*, 460 U.S. 37, 45–46 (1983), that for government property to be a public forum, it must by long tradition or by government designation be open to the public at large for assembly and speech. Minnesota college administration meetings convened to obtain faculty advice on policy questions have neither by long tradition nor by government designation been open for general public participation. The District Court did not so find, and appellees do not contend otherwise.

. . .

Indeed, the claim in these cases is not even a claim of access to a *nonpublic* forum, such as the school mail system at issue in *Perry Education Assn.* A private organization there claimed a right of access to government property for use in speaking to potentially willing listeners among a group of private individuals and public officials not acting in an official capacity. The organization claimed no right to have anyone, public or private, attend to its message. Appellees here make a claim quite different from those made in the nonpublic-forum cases. They do not contend that certain government property has been closed to them for use in communicating with private individuals or public officials not acting as such who might be willing to listen to them. Rather, they claim an entitlement to a government audience for their views.

"Meet and confer" sessions are occasions for public employers, acting solely as instrumentalities of the State, to receive policy advice from their professional employees. Minnesota has simply restricted the class of persons to whom it will listen in its making of policy. Thus, appellees' principal claim is that they have a right to force officers of the State acting in an official policymaking capacity to listen to them in a particular formal setting. . . .

The District Court agreed with appellees' claim to the extent that it was limited to faculty participation in governance of institutions of higher education. . . .

This conclusion is erroneous. Appellees have no constitutional right to force the government to listen to their views. They have no such right as

5. The Board and MCCFA established a new process for selecting "meet and confer" representatives and held the prescribed election before this Court noted probable jurisdiction. The new process allowed each faculty member to nominate candidates, to run for election, and to vote for each vacancy on both state and local committees. For a voter's ballot to be counted, though, the voter had to cast votes for as many candidates as there were slots to be filled. Only MCCFA members ran for the statewide committees. At the local level, several non-MCCFA instructors ran for office, and MCCFA ran slates of candidates at each institution. Only MCCFA members were elected.

members of the public, as government employees, or as instructors in an institution of higher education.

The Constitution does not grant to members of the public generally a right to be heard by public bodies making decisions of policy. In *Bi-Metallic Investment Co. v. State Board of Equalization*, 239 U.S. 441 (1915), this Court rejected a claim to such a right founded on the Due Process Clause of the Fourteenth Amendment. Speaking for the Court, Justice Holmes explained:

> Where a rule of conduct applies to more than a few people it is impracticable that every one should have a direct voice in its adoption. The Constitution does not require all public acts to be done in town meeting or an assembly of the whole. General statutes within the state power are passed that affect the person or property of individuals, sometimes to the point of ruin, without giving them a chance to be heard. Their rights are protected in the only way that they can be in a complex society, by their power, immediate or remote, over those who make the rule.

> . . .

> Policymaking organs in our system of government have never operated under a constitutional constraint requiring them to afford every interested member of the public an opportunity to present testimony before any policy is adopted. Legislatures throughout the Nation, including Congress, frequently enact bills on which no hearings have been held or on which testimony has been received from only a select group. Executive agencies likewise make policy decisions of widespread application without permitting unrestricted public testimony. Public officials at all levels of government daily make policy decisions based only on the advice they decide they need and choose to hear. To recognize a constitutional right to participate directly in government policymaking would work a revolution in existing government practices.

> . . .

> Appellees thus have no constitutional right as members of the public to a government audience for their policy views. As public employees, of course, they have a special interest in public policies relating to their employment. Minnesota's statutory scheme for public-employment labor relations recognizes as much. Appellees' status as public employees, however, gives them no special constitutional right to a voice in the making of policy by their government employer.

In *Smith v. Arkansas State Highway Employees*, [441 U.S. 463 (1979)] a public employees union argued that its First Amendment rights were abridged because the public employer required employees' grievances to be filed directly with the employer and refused to recognize the union's communications concerning its members' grievances. The Court rejected the argument.

> The public employee surely can associate, and speak freely and petition openly, and he is protected by the First Amendment from retaliation for doing so. But the First Amendment does not impose any affirmative obligation on the government to listen, to respond or, in this context, to recognize the association and bargain with it.

The Court acknowledged that "[the] First Amendment protects the right of an individual to speak freely, to advocate ideas, to associate with others, and to petition his government for redress of grievances." The government had not infringed any of those rights, the Court concluded. "[All] that the [government] has done in its challenged conduct is simply to ignore the union. That it is free to do."

The conduct challenged here is the converse of that challenged in *Smith*. There the government listened only to individual employees and not to the union. Here the government "meets and confers" with the union and not with individual employees. The applicable constitutional principles are identical to those that controlled in *Smith*. When government makes general policy, it is under no greater constitutional obligation to listen to any specially affected class than it is to listen to the public at large.

The academic setting of the policymaking at issue in these cases does not alter this conclusion. To be sure, there is a strong, if not universal or uniform, tradition of faculty participation in school governance, and there are numerous policy arguments to support such participation. But this Court has never recognized a constitutional right of faculty to participate in policymaking in academic institutions.

. . . Even assuming that speech rights guaranteed by the First Amendment take on a special meaning in an academic setting, they do not require government to allow teachers employed by it to participate in institutional policymaking. Faculty involvement in academic governance has much to recommend it as a matter of academic policy, but it finds no basis in the Constitution.

Although there is no constitutional right to participate in academic governance, the First Amendment guarantees the right both to speak and to associate. Appellees' speech and associational rights, however, have not been infringed by Minnesota's restriction of participation in "meet and confer" sessions to the faculty's exclusive representative. The State has in no way restrained appellees' freedom to speak on any education-related issue or their freedom to associate or not to associate with whom they please, including the exclusive representative. Nor has the State attempted to suppress any ideas.

. . .

Nor is appellees' right to speak infringed by the ability of MCCFA to "retaliate" for protected speech, as the District Court put it, by refusing to appoint them to the "meet and confer" committees. The State of Minnesota seeks to obtain MCCFA's views on policy questions, and MCCFA has simply chosen representatives who share its views on the issues to be discussed with the State. MCCFA's ability to "retaliate" by not selecting those who dissent from its views no more unconstitutionally inhibits appellees' speech than voters' power to reject a candidate for office inhibits the candidate's speech.

Similarly, appellees' associational freedom has not been impaired. Appellees are free to form whatever advocacy groups they like. They are not required to become members of MCCFA, and they do not challenge the monetary contribution they are required to make to support MCCFA's representation activities. Appellees may well feel some pressure to join the exclusive representative in order to give them the opportunity to serve on the "meet and confer" committees or to give them a voice in the representative's adoption of positions on particular issues. That pressure, however, is no different from the pressure they may feel to join MCCFA because of its unique status in the "meet and negotiate" process, a status the Court has summarily approved. Moreover, the pressure is no different from the pressure to join a majority party that persons in the minority always feel. Such pressure is inherent in our system of government; it does not create an unconstitutional inhibition on associational freedom.

Unable to demonstrate an infringement of any First Amendment right, appellees contend that their exclusion from "meet and confer" sessions denies them equal protection of the laws in violation of the Fourteenth Amendment. This final argument is meritless. The interest of appellees that is affected—the interest in a government audience for their policy views—finds no special protection in the Constitution. There being no other reason to invoke heightened scrutiny, the challenged state action "need only rationally further a legitimate state purpose" to be valid under the Equal Protection Clause. *Perry Education Assn. v. Perry Local Educators' Assn.*, 460 U.S., at 54. PELRA certainly meets that standard. The State has a legitimate interest in ensuring that its public employers hear one, and only one, voice presenting the majority view of its professional employees on employment-related policy questions, whatever other advice they may receive on those questions. Permitting selection of the "meet and confer" representatives to be made by the exclusive representative, which has its unique status by virtue of majority support within the bargaining unit, is a rational means of serving that interest.

If it is rational for the State to give the exclusive representative a unique role in the "meet and negotiate" process, as the summary affirmance in appellees' appeal in this litigation presupposes, it is rational for the State to do the same in the "meet and confer" process. The goal of reaching agreement makes it imperative for an employer to have before it only one collective view of its employees when "negotiating." *See Abood v. Detroit Board of Education*, 431 U.S., at 224. Similarly, the goal of basing policy decisions on consideration of the majority view of its employees makes it reasonable for an employer to give only the exclusive representative a particular formal setting in which to offer advice on policy. Appellees' equal protection challenge accordingly fails.

The District Court erred in holding that appellees had been unconstitutionally denied an opportunity to participate in their public employer's making of policy. Whatever the wisdom of Minnesota's statutory scheme for professional employee consultation on employment-related policy, in academic or other settings, the scheme violates no provision of the Constitution. The judgment of the District Court is therefore

Reversed.

■ Justice Marshall, concurring in the judgment.

I do not agree with the majority's sweeping assertion that no government official is ever constitutionally obliged, before making a decision on a matter of public policy, to afford interested citizens an opportunity to present their views.... The narrow question presented in these cases is the constitutional validity of a peculiar set of constraints on consultation between administrators and members of the faculties of state colleges; it can be sensibly resolved only by attending to the distinctive characteristics and needs of public institutions of higher education.

... In an appropriate case, I would be prepared to include within this collection of constitutionally protected avenues of communication a measure of freedom on the part of faculty members (as well as students) to present to college administrators their ideas on matters of importance to the mission of the academic community. Such freedom is essential if all members of the community are to participate meaningfully in the determination of the goals of the institution and the choice of means to achieve them. Such participation is, in turn, essential if our academic institutions are to fulfill their dual responsibility to advance the frontiers of knowledge through unfettered inquiry and debate, *see Sweezy v. New Hampshire*, 354 U.S. 234, 250 (1957), and to produce a citizenry willing and able to involve itself in the governance of the polity, *see id.* at 250–251; *see also Keyishian v. Board of Regents, supra*, at 603.

... As JUSTICE STEVENS suggests there are good reasons to be more suspicious when a state legislature instructs college administrators to listen to some faculty members but not others than when administrators decide on their own to listen to some faculty members but not others. Administrators are more accountable to slighted faculty members than are state legislators. Moreover, our solicitude for the rights of unpopular members of academic communities and our desire to keep open the channels of communication within those communities, should not blind us to the fact that, in general, colleges and universities are most likely to fulfill their crucial roles in our society if they are allowed to operate free of outside interference. That insight should prompt us to defer to the judgment of college administrators—persons we presume to be knowledgeable and to have the best interests of their institutions at heart—in circumstances in which we would not defer to the judgment of government officials who seek to regulate the affairs of the academy.

The difficult tasks of giving shape to these First Amendment rights and of assessing the state interests that might justify their abridgment can, however, be left to another day, because the proofs in these cases do not establish the kind of impairment of the ability of faculty members to communicate with administrators that would, in my view, give rise to constitutional difficulty. As the majority observes, there remains substantial opportunity, outside the formal "meet and confer" sessions, for administrators and faculty members in Minnesota community colleges to exchange ideas on a wide variety of topics. This is not to say that all faculty members have equal access to the most effective media for communicating with the administration; the findings of the District Court make plain that the representatives of the MCCFA enjoy greater freedom to express their views than appellees. But the Constitution does not require college administrators to give "equal time" to all persons competing for their attention. No more can legitimately be expected than that all members of the academic community be afforded a meaningful opportunity to make themselves heard. In my view, appellees have failed to show that the PELRA denies them that opportunity.

■ JUSTICE BRENNAN, dissenting.

Although I agree with much of JUSTICE STEVENS' dissent, I write separately to explain why, irrespective of other grounds, principles of academic freedom require affirmance of the District Court's holding that the "meet and confer" provisions deprive appellees of their constitutional rights.

It is crucial at the outset to recognize that two related First Amendment interests are at stake here. On the one hand, those faculty members who are barred from participation in "meet and confer" sessions by virtue of their refusal to join MCCFA have a First Amendment right to express their views on important matters of academic governance to college administrators. At the same time, they enjoy a First Amendment right to be free from compelled associations with positions or views that they do not espouse. In my view, the real vice of the Minnesota Public Employment Labor Relations Act (PELRA) is that it impermissibly forces nonunion faculty members to choose between these two rights.

The first right is rooted in our common understanding that the First Amendment safeguards the free exchange of ideas at institutions of higher learning. This First Amendment freedom to explore novel or controversial ideas in the classroom is closely linked to the freedom of faculty members to express their views to the administration concerning matters of academic governance. If the First Amendment is truly to protect the "free play of the spirit" within our institutions of higher learning, *Shelton v. Tucker, supra,* at 487, then the faculty at those institutions must be able to participate effectively in the discussion of such matters as, for example, curriculum reform, degree requirements, student affairs, new facilities, and budgetary planning. The freedom to teach without inhibition may be jeopardized just as gravely by a restriction on the faculty's ability to speak out on such matters as by the more direct restrictions struck down in *Keyishian* and in *Epperson*. In my view, therefore, a direct prohibition of some identified faculty group from submitting their views concerning academic policy questions for consideration by college administrators would plainly violate the principles of academic freedom enshrined in the First Amendment.

. . .

■ JUSTICE STEVENS, with whom JUSTICE BRENNAN joins in all but Part III, and with whom JUSTICE POWELL joins in all but Part II, dissenting.

. . .

We need not consider whether executives or legislators have any constitutional obligation to listen to unsolicited advice to decide this case. It is inherent in the republican form of government that high officials may choose—in their own wisdom and at their own peril—to listen to some of their constituents and not to others. But the First Amendment does guarantee an open marketplace for ideas—where divergent points of view can freely compete for the attention of those in power and of those to whom the powerful must account. The Minnesota statute places a significant restraint on that free competition, by regulating the communication that may take place between the government and those governed. As the District Court found, the statute gives only one speaker a realistic opportunity to present its views to state officials. All other communication is effectively prohibited, not by reference to the time, place, or manner of communication, or even by reference to the officials' willingness to listen, but rather by reference to the identity of the speaker. The statute is therefore invalid because the First Amendment does not permit any state legislature to grant a single favored speaker an effective monopoly on the opportunity to petition the government.

. . .

The breadth of the communication prohibited by this statute is remarkable. The "meet and confer" process in which only the majority union can participate is defined broadly to encompass "the exchange of views and concerns between employers and their respective employees." The statute itself imposes no limit on the subjects that might be covered by the "meet and confer" system; in its application to other agencies, that system could encompass the entire range of public policy questions. Thus, in terms the statute says that a public employee may not exchange any views on virtually any public policy question with his or her employer. Appellants suggest no narrowing construction of these statutory terms, nor would it be appropriate for this Court to attempt in the first instance to construe the statute to mean something other than what it plainly says. The District Court found that the statute has been applied to mean what it says. In the community college program, the District Court found that the "subjects covered by the meet and confer system include new course proposals and other curriculum matters, budgetary planning, development of facilities, student rights and student affairs generally, evaluation of administrators, selection of college presidents, academic accreditation of the community colleges, and other matters."

Not only are employees who are not selected to represent the majority union's views disabled from expressing their own opinions to their employers, but the union is guaranteed ample opportunities to do what no one else can. The statute places public employers under an obligation to meet and confer with the majority union's representative at least once every four months. Moreover, the statute acknowledges that the "meet and confer" process is critical to the process of formulating public policy.

As might be expected, the statutory prohibition has had an adverse impact on conversation and communication between teachers and administrators in the State's community college system. Although the "meet and confer" sessions with the majority union are open to all faculty members, no one can speak without the union's permission. In practice, observers have not been permitted to speak. The statute thus gives the majority union in the system an effective veto over the right of dissident faculty members to communicate their views to the administration. College administrators understand the PELRA to prohibit them from listening to the views except those of the majority union, and they have acted in accord with that understanding. As a result, much less communication between faculty members and college administrators occurs under the statute because both administrators and teachers fear that if they exchange views, especially when the exchange involves nonunion faculty members, they will be violating the PELRA. Those conversations that do still occur often are useless as a practical matter, since the administrator often responds only by saying that the subject must be discussed in a different forum. Thus the PELRA has substituted a union-controlled process for the formerly free exchange of views that took place between faculty and the administration. In practice, the union has a monopoly on the effective opportunity to present views to the administration on the wide range of subjects covered by the "meet and confer" process.

The District Court found that under the statute "the weight and significance of individual speech interests have been consciously derogated in favor of systematic, official expression." "[The] PELRA has made the formal meet and confer process the primary mechanism for *any significant faculty-administration communication* on such policy questions." It concluded that the "meet and confer" process "is the only significant forum for the faculty to resolve virtually every issue outside the scope of mandatory bargaining. *This structure effectively blocks any meaningful expression by faculty members who are excluded from the formal process.*" These findings may not be set aside unless clearly erroneous, and in any event are not challenged by appellants or the Court.

Both the plain language of the statute and the District Court's findings concerning its actual operation demonstrate that it is a law abridging the freedom of speech. This is true both because it grants unions especially favored positions in communicating with public policymaking bodies and because it curtails the ability of all other members of the public to communicate effectively with those public bodies.

. . .

The Court's analysis is rooted simply in the notion that "[appellees] have no constitutional right to force the government to listen to their views." No claim is made that college administrators do not want to hear what appellees have to say; to the contrary the administrators claim that they are willing to listen to the views of appellees. The problem is that the administrators are statutorily prohibited from listening. . . .

Moreover, the District Court found that prior to the passage of the challenged statute, appellees were able to participate in the "meet and confer" process.[20] Their former ability to communicate with the administration has been impaired not by the administration's unwillingness to listen, but by the challenged statute. Any realistic appraisal of the effects of such a restriction must lead to the conclusion that this statute has restricted the traditional freedom of speech appellees had once enjoyed. "[The] capacity of a group or individual 'to participate in the intellectual give and take of campus debate . . . [would be] limited by denial of access to the customary media for communicating with the administration, faculty members, and . . . students.' " *Widmar v. Vincent*, 454 U.S. 263, 267–268, n. 5 (1981) (quoting *Healy*, 408 U.S., at 181–182).

In short, by prohibiting the administration from listening to appellees, the PELRA ensures that appellees' speech can have no meaningful impact upon the administration. Appellees do not rely on the government's "obligation" to hear them; they rely only on their right to have a meaningful opportunity to speak. If a public employer does not wish to listen to appellees, that is its privilege, but the First Amendment at least requires that that decision be made in an open marketplace of ideas, rather than under a

---

20. "Traditionally, the subjects of meet and confer have been resolved through governance systems in which all faculty members have an opportunity to participate. In the present case, governance at community col-leges prior to passage of PELRA consisted of faculty senates and committees, selected through elections in which every faculty member was eligible to both vote and seek election." 571 F.Supp., at 8.

statutory scheme that does not permit appellees' speech to be considered, no matter how much merit it may contain.[21]

. . .

There is a simple, but fundamental, reason why the state interest in exclusivity cannot sustain this statute. That interest creates a preference for the views of majority unions which itself infringes the principles of the First Amendment. In *Police Department of Chicago v. Mosley*, 408 U.S. 92 (1972), the Court considered the constitutionality of a Chicago ordinance that granted labor unions access to a narrowly defined forum and denied such access to all other speakers. The forum in that case was the area "within 150 feet of any primary or secondary school building while the school is in session" and for one-half hour before and after school sessions; the method of communication was peaceful picketing. Unions, but no one else, were allowed access to that narrow forum. The Court unanimously held the ordinance unconstitutional. After pointing out that the ordinance allowed peaceful picketing on the subject of a school's labor-management dispute, but prohibited all other peaceful picketing, the Court continued:

> "Necessarily, then, under the Equal Protection Clause, not to mention the First Amendment itself, government may not grant the use of a forum to people whose views it finds acceptable, but deny use to those wishing to express less favored or more controversial views. And it may not select which issues are worth discussing or debating in public facilities. There is an 'equality of status in the field of ideas,' and government must afford all points of view an equal opportunity to be heard. Once a forum is opened up to assembly or speaking by some groups, government may not prohibit others from assembling or speaking on the basis of what they intend to say." *Id.*, at 96 (footnote omitted).

We have consistently adhered to the principle that government must "afford all points of view an equal opportunity to be heard." The majority claims that this principle does not apply to closed proceedings not open to any form of public access. In fact, however, the "meet and confer" sessions are open to the public and are held in public places. Moreover, the State permits participation by the union's representatives but no others. When a State permits some speakers but not others access to a forum for communica-

---

21. The Court finds this proposition "shocking," and concludes that it would destroy the ability of public officials from the President of the United States on down to select whomever it is that he or she wishes to consult. The Court is simply mistaken. Nothing I have said implies that public policymakers must listen to any given point of view, much less that they must give all persons individualized notice and opportunity for hearing, which is all that *Bi–Metallic Investment Co. v. State Board of Equalization*, 239 U.S. 441 (1915), relied upon by the majority, *ante*, at 283–285, involved. That case did not present, or consider, any First Amendment issue. An analogy much closer to the PELRA than *Bi–Metallic* would be a statute passed by a Democratic legislative majority prohibiting all legislators from consulting with their Republican constituents. Even this Court might balk at such a statute, but it would not offend the rationale of the majority's opinion. If the President, or a college administrator, does not think it worthwhile to consult with appellees, he of course is free to make that decision. The Minnesota statute, in contrast, does not permit that decision to be made. Minnesota has delegated public policymaking to various employers, but at the same time required that those policies be made in a closed environment where citizens are not even given any realistic opportunity to petition those policymakers for redress of grievances, and policymakers are not free to decide whether they wish to consider the views of disfavored speakers.

tion, it must justify its exclusions as viewpoint-neutral. Surely that principle cannot be avoided by the simple expedient of using the speaker's point of view as the criterion for defining the scope of access to a publicly sponsored forum. Indeed, the case on which the majority principally relies, *Perry Education Assn. v. Perry Local Educators' Assn.*, 460 U.S. 37 (1983), states that government may not restrict access to channels of communication as an attempt "to discourage one viewpoint and advance another."

Here, by giving the union exclusive rights with respect to the primary avenue for communication with college administration, the Minnesota statutory scheme plainly advances the union's viewpoint at the expense of all others. . . .

. . .

Because I am convinced that the statutorily mandated exclusive "meet and confer" process is constitutionally intolerable, I respectfully dissent.

Questions & Comments on *Knight*

Which opinion in *Knight* do you agree with? The majority holds there is no constitutional right for faculty to participate in academic decisionmaking. Should that holding be limited by the facts of this case to community colleges?

Do you agree with the majority when it equates faculty participation in governance with a public citizen informing a government decision-maker of his view on policy matters? Or, as Justice Marshall suggests, are there any First Amendment considerations that apply differently to faculty than to ordinary citizens? Can you identify these considerations?

University of New Hampshire Chapter of the AAUP v. Haselton

United States District Court for the District of New Hampshire, 1975.
397 F.Supp. 107.

■ BOWNES, DISTRICT JUDGE.

. . . Plaintiffs requested that a Three–Judge Court be convened to declare unconstitutional and permanently enjoin the operation of NH RSA 98:C as it applies to them. NH RSA 98:C is a public employment relations statute which confers upon state employees the right to engage in collective bargaining. The statute defines employees as:

> classified employees of the state, and non-academic employees (exclusive of department heads and executive officers) of the University of New Hampshire including Keene State College and Plymouth State College as defined by the board of trustees of the University. . . . NH RSA 98–C:1

The net effect of the statutory classification is to confer collective bargaining rights upon state employees in general, while specifically denying these rights to the academic employees of the State University System.

. . . On May 10, 1974, plaintiff Association, supported by the signatures of approximately one hundred sixty academic employees of the University of

New Hampshire at Durham, petitioned the defendants,[4] pursuant to the provisions of NH RSA 98:C, claiming the right and authority to act as the exclusive bargaining representative for the academic employees at the Durham campus.

On May 21, 1974, defendants refused to entertain plaintiffs' petition on the ground that Durham academic employees were excluded from the enabling provisions of NH RSA 98:C.

There are two issues before the court:

(1) Whether the State's refusal to confer collective bargaining rights upon academic employees is an abridgment of their First Amendment rights; and

(2) Whether the statutory classification created by NH RSA 98:C violates the equal protection clause of the Fourteenth Amendment.

The First Amendment rights of association, assembly, and freedom of speech guarantee to public employees the right to organize collectively and select representatives to engage in collective bargaining. The Supreme Court has characterized "the right to organize and select representatives for lawful purposes of collective bargaining ... as a 'fundamental right'...." *Auto Workers v. Wis. Board*, 336 U.S. 245, 259 (1948).

Plaintiffs do not allege nor has there been any showing that their First Amendment rights are impinged by the operation of NH RSA 98:C. As far as plaintiffs are concerned, the statute maintains the status quo; they are free to unionize in order to advance their ideas and interests. The State, however, does not have a constitutional obligation to respond to plaintiffs' demands or to enter into a contract with them. There is no constitutional right ... to make collective bargaining mandatory. As a matter of Constitutional law, this Court agrees with the other courts which have held that no such right exists. As was stated in [*Atkins v. City of Charlotte*], 296 F. Supp. at 1077:

"There is nothing in the United States Constitution which entitles one to have a contract with another who does not want it. It is but a step further to hold that the state may lawfully forbid such contracts with its instrumentalities. The solution, if there be one, from the viewpoint of the firemen, is that labor unions may someday persuade state government of the asserted value of collective bargaining agreements, but this is a political matter and does not yield to judicial solution." [The right to a collective bargaining agreement, so firmly entrenched in American labor-management relations, rests upon national legislation and not upon the federal Constitution.] *Confederation of Police v. City of Chicago*, 382 F. Supp. 624, 628–629 (N.D. Ill. 1974).

Traditionally, the right to be recognized in the collective bargaining process has been hammered out either through the legislative process or by the economic forge of the strike, and not by judicial decrees. The operation of NH RSA 98:C does not impede the plaintiffs' rights to collectively

4. Named as defendants are: Edward Haselton, Chairman of the State Personnel Commission, Robert Duvall, Commissioner of Labor, and Robert Stark, Secretary of State of the State of New Hampshire.

organize or participate in an economic strike. Plaintiffs' First Amendment rights remain untarnished and unaffected.

Whenever a state statute is alleged to be violative of the equal protection clause the court must inquire, as to the interests and rights affected by the statutory classification, in order to determine the appropriate standard of review. Since we find that the statutory classification, created by NH RSA 98:C, does not interfere with a "fundamental right," our standard of review is the rational basis test. . . .

Collective bargaining is a recent phenomenon in higher education.[6] The university community remained the last bastion against the spread of collective bargaining for two essential reasons: first, most universities have internal governance procedures; and, second, many academics believed that their professional status and independence would be tarnished by the collective bargaining process.

Ideally, the governance of a university is based upon the concept of "shared authority."[8] Central to the concept is the tenet that academics are given extensive authority to participate in university governance. The theory is that the university setting, unlike the industrial world, is a single community comprised of an amalgamation of components which, in a joint effort, create an atmosphere of mutuality and cooperation.

In order to effectuate the goals of shared authority, most higher institutions have established university senates. A properly balanced senate, which evenly disperses power and control, enabling the faculty to have an active participation in university governance, negates the need for collective bargaining. The need to collectively bargain arises only when academics believe that they are not effectively represented in the process of institutional decision-making.[10]

An examination of the governance system at the Durham campus indicates that academic authority is more elusive than shared. In 1969 the governing structure of the University was changed so that, for the first time in any university, undergraduates were given parity with the faculty in a single unicameral body. The traditional academic senate was abolished. At present, the University Senate serves as an advisory body to the Board of Trustees. The entire University community is represented in the Senate: students, hourly employees, and professional and technical employees. The faculty has only minority representation.

The major administrative officers of the University are appointed without either the advice or consent of the faculty. The faculty has no voice in matters of tenure, salary or faculty appointments. These decisions are made solely by the administration with only minimal faculty advisement.

---

6. "As of June 1, 1973, eighteen states have enacted public employment relation statutes applicable to academic employees in all state or local institutions of higher learning. Due to the rapidly expanding concept of bargaining in the public sector, there exist great difficulties at any point in time in determining exactly which states allow collective negotiations among their academic personnel." Gee, Organizing the Halls of Ivy: Developing a Framework for Viable Alternatives in Higher Education Employment, 1973 Utah L. Rev. 233, n.2. *See generally*, Wollett, The Status and Trends of Collective Negotiations for Faculty in Higher Education, 1971 Wis. L. Rev. 2.

8. For a working definition of shared authority see Gee, *supra* note 6, at n.57.

10. *Id.* at 278.

But the structure of the University's governance can change again, as it did in 1969. The New Hampshire University Senate was the subject of a recent study which suggested numerous changes in the Senate's structure so as to make it a more effective mechanism for faculty participation. (Azzi Commission on University Governance). At present, the proposal has not been initiated.

Despite the fact that the academic employees at the Durham campus do not effectively partake in the University's governance, as they do in many other universities, we find that a rational basis does exist for the legislature's refusal to extend collective bargaining to university academic employees.

Although collective bargaining in educational circles has gained increasing acceptance, its critics have pointed out that it injects into university decisionmaking an adversarial process resting on the influence of the bargaining unit.[11] The dynamics of this process, it is argued, is egalitarian and majoritarian, and, the process of making trade-offs to reach a settlement, may result in a failure to recognize the interests inherent in a wide diversity of disciplines,[12] with consequent adverse effect on some professors.[13]

Fearing the effect of these forces on an institution of higher learning, a Task Force of the American Association of Higher Education recommended, in 1966, that, in order to promote the spirit of cooperation, a university should use internal governance mechanisms rather than resorting to external bargaining techniques.[14] While controversy continues, the commentators seem to agree on one point—that the employment conditions in higher education are unique and deserve special statutory consideration. We cannot fail to observe also that where collective bargaining for academics has been introduced into public universities, it has been accomplished mainly by statute. *See* note 6, *supra*. And the Court of Appeals for this Circuit has implicitly recognized the propriety of legislative judgment in this area.

---

11. "Collective negotiations is itself a political system, and the leaders of a faculty collective negotiations structure—the negotiators, the executive boards, the departmental stewards—are themselves politicians. They are not enlisted in the service of reasonableness, rationality or the persuasive power of ideas. They are concerned with getting more, as management is with giving less. They understand that their ability to achieve this objective depends upon the effective mobilization and utilization of political power." Wollett, *supra* note 6, at 32.

12. "Collective negotiations in universities and colleges places all academic disciplines at the same bargaining table.... In some areas involving items such as curriculum, academic programs, admission requirements, and other similar variables, the diversity of disciplines could create significant problems of reconciliation for negotiators and their constituents.

"Collective bargaining involves tradeoffs in order to reach a mutual settlement. In the heat of negotiations, especially as a strike deadline looms over the proceedings, there is a strong temptation to trade items rather than settle on the true merits of each. This, of course, is characteristic of any bargaining situation, but 'horse-trading' of issues without careful consideration of the long-run impact could be exceedingly disastrous in such a highly-complex and diversified field as higher education." Allen, Organizing the Eggheads: Professors and Collective Bargaining, 23 Lab. L.J. 606, 614 (1972).

13. "Collective bargaining inherently subjects many policy determinations to the rule of the organizational majority, and majority rule often reflects deep suspicion of individual initiative or advantage. Thus, collective negotiations could have an adverse effect on teachers with special ability." Wollett, The Coming Revolution in Public School Management, 67 Mich. L. Rev. 1017, 1029 (1969). By the same token, we recognize that in the absence of collective bargaining many other junior faculty members of a faculty may feel equally adversely affected.

14. American Association of Higher Education Task Force Report, Faculty Participation in Academic Government cited in Brown, *supra* note 9, at 284.

We recite these observations not to take sides on an issue of great complexity, but to indicate that the New Hampshire legislature in excluding the Durham faculty from the collective bargaining statute was not lacking in a rational basis for its decision. Specifically, it could conclude that a faculty bargaining unit, particularly if it sought to bargain broadly on curriculum, admissions, degree requirements, and other educational policy matters, would undermine and disrupt its present effort at university-wide governance. No similar internal governance experiment is being undertaken at the vocational schools. The legislature could also conclude that the disparate interests of various academic departments in the University would not be as well served by collective treatment as the more unified interests of the vocational schools. We think there is sufficient dissimilarity between the vocational colleges and the University to support a legislative distinction. We note finally that the legislature may be given some latitude for experimentation in attempting to resolve the problems of internal relationships in the academic setting.

In balancing the benefits and detriments that collective bargaining in higher education could produce, we find that it is reasonable for the State to exclude University of New Hampshire academic employees from the benefits conferred by NH RSA 98:C.

Questions and Comments on *University of New Hampshire Chapter of the AAUP*

1. Having read the cases on shared governance, do you conclude that the First Amendment protects the faculty's right to speak out on governance issues at public colleges and universities? If so, what interests account for this protection? How should courts respond when college or university administrators suppress this kind of faculty speech? In what way is a member of the faculty discussing complaints about the governance of a university different from any other public employee commenting on their working conditions? Why should the speech of a faculty member be protected when the speech of other public employees is not?

2. Membership rates in unions have been declining in recent years across all industries in the United States. In 2007, 12.1 percent of employed wage and salary workers were unionized, compared to 20.1 percent in 1983. Workers in the public sector were five times more likely to be unionized than their private sector counterparts. News Release, Bureau of Labor Statistics, U.S. Dep't of Labor, Union Members in 2007 (Jan. 25, 2008), *available at* www.bls.gov/news.release/pdf/union2.pdf.

CHAPTER 8

DENYING AND TERMINATING TENURE

Every serious study of the tenure principle, including those that were commenced to find alternatives, have concluded there is no better one. Academic tenure remains the worst form of university employment save all of the others

-James J. Fishman[a]

Is tenure a necessary partner of academic freedom? The question continues to be debated by faculty, university administrators, governing boards, regulators, and the public. Although it is commonly assumed that tenure is synonymous with lifetime employment, even the AAUP 1915 Declaration makes clear that tenured faculty may be fired for cause. In the words of William W. Van Alstyne:

> Tenure, accurately and unequivocally defined, lays no claim whatever to a guarantee of lifetime employement. Rather, tenure provides only that no person continuously retained as a full-time faculty member beyond a specified lengthy period of probationary service may thereafter be dismissed without adequate cause.[b]

The notion that tenure is only about job protection also overlooks the important role played by the tenure process in maintaining both academic freedom and academic standards. An individual who seeks to become a faculty member must first undergo a rigorous academic training that includes completion of a Ph.D. or the equivalent before being hired to a position that may (or may not) lead to tenure. Once hired, faculty are in effect on probation for up to seven years. During this pretenure period they must demonstrate their skills as both teachers and scholars. Finally, they must be approved as deserving of tenure by a representative group of their academic peers—that is by faculty who have previously earned tenure. The 1915 AAUP Declaration, for example, states that a board or committee representative of the faculty should approve each candidate before tenure is awarded. Note that the Declaration does not say that if the faculty approves, tenure must be awarded. Faculty approval is thus necessary but not sufficient. Even if the faculty votes in favor of tenure, the governing board or the administration may turn down a candidate for appropriate reasons. For example, the standards applied by the faculty in the relevant department might not be sufficiently high.

---

a. James J. Fishman, *Tenure and Its Discontents: The Worst Form of Employment Relationship Save All of the Others*, 21 PACE L. REV. 159, 202 (2000).

b. William W. Van Alstyne, *Tenure: A Summary, Explanation, and "Defense,"* 57 AAUP BULL. 328 (1971).

It also has been argued that tenure promotes quality in the peer review process because "without it incumbents would never be willing to hire people who might turn out to be better than themselves."[c]

Given the importance of faculty peer review in the decision to award tenure, should courts be more deferential to decisions to deny tenure than they are to decisions to terminate a tenured faculty member?

Beitzell v. Jeffrey

United States Court of Appeals, First Circuit, 1981.
643 F.2d 870.

■ BREYER, CIRCUIT JUDGE.

Plaintiff, Robert E. Beitzell, an assistant professor at the University of Maine at Orono (UMO), a state university, was denied an appointment at the university with tenure. He brought this civil rights action under 42 U.S.C. § 1983 against UMO officials in the United States District Court for the District of Maine. He claimed that, in denying him tenure, the university deprived him of "liberty" and "property" without "due process of law." After a hearing the district court found there had been no such denial of Fourteenth Amendment rights and entered judgment for defendants....

... After teaching as an instructor at the University of Massachusetts, Beitzell accepted a one-year appointment as an assistant professor of history at UMO in 1967. He was reappointed as an assistant professor in 1968, and again in 1970. He was first considered for a permanent "tenured" appointment by the history department's "Policy Advisory Committee" (PAC) in November, 1971.

The PAC consisted of several tenured members of the history department, including its chairman, William Jeffrey. In the normal course of events, the PAC would recommend to the department chairman whether or not a faculty member should be granted tenure. In principle, the department chairman would decide whether or not to accept the recommendation. In practice, an unfavorable PAC recommendation was almost always followed by a denial of tenure. A favorable PAC recommendation, however, might still be reversed by the chairman, or someone higher in the university chain of command, such as the dean of the college, the vice-president for academic affairs or the university president. The procedures for awarding tenure at UMO, some of which are set out in the faculty handbook, generally follow those recommended by the American Association of University Professors, and are typical of procedures followed at numerous universities.[1] In October, 1971, the history department supplemented the handbook by publishing an explicit statement of its "Criteria for Promotion and Tenure." These criteria consist of classical tenure requirements: a mixture of scholarship, teaching and service. Scholarship was essentially defined as "significant publication," teaching as "satisfactory classroom performance," and "service" as "significant contributing membership" on university or professional committees.

c. H. Lorne Carmichael, *Incentives in Academics: Why Is There Tenure?*, 96 J. POL. ECON. 453, 454 (1988).

1. ... These recommendations and procedures are derived from AAUP, "1940 State-ment of Principles and Interpretive Comments," Policy Documents and Reports, the most widely accepted plan for tenure acquisition in the United States.

Beitzell's tenure case in 1971 was controversial. There is evidence that Jeffrey, the department chairman, felt that Beitzell was unstable and that Jeffrey repeated to various faculty members rumors that Beitzell drank too much. The district court found, however, that Jeffrey made a fair presentation to the PAC of Beitzell's professional qualifications for tenure. When the subject of Beitzell's drinking arose at the meeting, Jeffrey ruled it out of order and prevented further comment. At the end of a "free-wheeling" discussion, the PAC members voted unanimously against a tenure recommendation. Jeffrey, in his role as department head, accepted the negative recommendation and informed Beitzell of his decision. On an official personnel form (which was delayed in transmission to Beitzell for a year) Jeffrey wrote that Beitzell "had not lived up to his promise as a scholar," was "a less than adequate teacher," and "as advisor, he has been totally inadequate."

Beitzell was again considered for tenure in the Fall of 1972. By that time, Beitzell's book had been accepted for publication by a prestigious publisher. Galleys were made available to the PAC, as were summaries of interviews with students, largely favorable to Beitzell. Jeffrey invited Beitzell to a meeting of the PAC to make his own case, but Beitzell declined. Instead, Jeffrey made the presentation on his behalf a presentation described as "bland," but without offensive remarks. The district court found that all "relevant information supportive of plaintiff's application for tenure was accumulated in advance of the meeting and was available for inspection by members of the committee." The PAC again recommended that the chairman deny Beitzell tenure, this time by a vote of 7 to 6, with Jeffrey abstaining.

Beitzell then hired a lawyer. He sought review of the history department's decision by a Faculty Professional Relations Committee (FPRC) empowered to hear faculty grievances, to conciliate, and to make recommendations. The FPRC met with Beitzell, then with Jeffrey and others. After discussing the PAC decision in detail, Jeffrey made available to the FPRC a two and one-half page document he had prepared as a basis for his appearance before it. That document was very critical of Beitzell; it detailed behavior which it described as "irresponsible," it cast doubt on whether Beitzell's improved performance would continue, and it repeated allegations made by others that Beitzell drank too much. Beitzell met again with the FPRC to rebut some of the charges made against him, but the FPRC did not disclose all of the derogatory claims made by Jeffrey or others. The FPRC concurred in the decision of the PAC.

Beitzell next invoked a new, more formal, grievance procedure, which UMO had just created. Acting under this procedure, the UMO president created a special ad hoc board to hear Beitzell's grievance and make a recommendation. The Grievance Board held a hearing, with lawyers present, during which both Beitzell and representatives of the University were allowed to present testimony and documentary evidence and to cross-examine witnesses. Jeffrey testified and, after he made some references to the document he had used before the FPRC, Beitzell's counsel asked that it be placed in the record. Despite efforts to keep the proceedings confidential, word of Jeffrey's criticisms spread on the campus. The Grievance Committee eventually recommended that the PAC give Beitzell further consideration, particularly in respect to the quality of his book and his teaching. And, the Committee criticized Jeffrey, claiming that his FPRC testimony and the document he prepared were professionally speaking "unethical."

The UMO president then asked the PAC whether it felt it should reopen Beitzell's case. The PAC responded that its hearing had been fair and that it was up to the president to decide whether to reopen. Jeffrey evidently told the president the PAC opposed reopening, and the president wrote Beitzell, denied his request for reopening and affirmed that Beitzell's probationary appointment expired in the summer of 1973. Then, after learning that the PAC actually had not decided whether to reopen, the president gave Beitzell an extension of his appointment through the Fall and told the PAC to decide whether to reopen the case. The PAC voted 12 to 2 not to reopen; the decision was affirmed by a new UMO president; Beitzell exhausted all his internal appeals, and he then filed this lawsuit.

. . .

Beitzell, on appeal, contends that the University, in making public "false and stigmatizing" charges against him without a proper hearing, deprived him of "liberty" without "due process of law." He also claims that procedural protections UMO accorded him were constitutionally inadequate to protect his "property interest" in tenure.

We first take up the question of whether Beitzell had a constitutionally protected "property" interest in tenure. At least since 1970, the Fourteenth Amendment term "property" has referred not simply to "actual ownership of real estate, chattels, or money," but also to "interests that a person has already acquired in specific (governmental) benefits." *Board of Regents v. Roth*, 408 U.S. 564, 572 (1972); *Goldberg v. Kelly*, 397 U.S. 254, 262 (1970). As so interpreted, Fourteenth Amendment protections previously given land owners are provided as well to many others who depend heavily upon the continued availability of, for example, welfare, social security, or government employment.

The broadening of the term "property" to include this "new property"[7] has required the courts to determine when an interest in a government benefit rises to the level of protected "property." The Supreme Court has made clear that the answer depends in large part upon the extent to which a person has been made secure in the enjoyment of the benefit as a matter of substantive state or federal law. The greater the interest and protection accorded an interest by such substantive law, the more reasonable is the holder in expecting to continue to enjoy it and in making decisions in reliance upon that expectation, and the less reasonable it is for the state to interfere directly with that enjoyment without according a fair opportunity to the holder to contest that interference. Thus, in *Roth*, the Supreme Court stated that for an interest in a benefit to become a "property" interest, a person

"... must have more than a unilateral expectation of it. He must, instead, have a legitimate claim of entitlement to it. It is the purpose of the ancient institution of property to protect those claims upon which people rely in their daily lives, reliance that must not be arbitrarily undermined. It is a purpose of the constitutional right to

---

7. *See*, Reich, "The New Property", 73 Yale L.J. 733 (1964); Monaghan, "Of 'Liberty' and 'Property'", 62 Cornell L.Rev. 405 (1977); Van Alstyne, "Cracks In 'The New Property' Adjudicative Due Process in the Administrative State", 62 Cornell L.Rev. 445 (1977).

a hearing to provide an opportunity for a person to vindicate those claims." 408 U.S. at 577.

While these decisions provide no perfect touchstone for identifying "property," they suggest that the more circumscribed is the government's discretion (under substantive state or federal law) to withhold a benefit, the more likely that benefit constitutes "property." . . .

Thus, in the area of government employment, a person who holds a job from which he can be removed only "for cause," has a protected property interest, while one who can be removed "at will" does not. In the former case, the government's power to remove is seriously circumscribed; the person is likely to rely reasonably on remaining employed; and a hearing is likely to help determine whether cause exists. In the latter type of case, the opposite tends to be true. . . .

Neither is it surprising that every court that we have found to have considered the matter has held that, in the absence of unusual circumstances, a probationary university employee has no "property" interest in obtaining tenure. Tenure involves a long-term academic and financial commitment by a university to an individual, providing faculty with unusually secure positions tantamount to life contracts.[8] This security and the freedom of expression it allows, arguably help the university carry out a basic function, the vigorous exchange of ideas a function that itself enjoys constitutional protection. Given the university's overall mission, the creation and transmission of knowledge, the very need for strong procedural protections to prevent the wrongful dismissal of a tenured teacher concomitantly suggests a need for wide discretion in making an initial tenure award. Only at the initial tenure stage can the university look primarily to the interests of the students, of the discipline, and of its own administrative needs. As other courts have suggested, the initial decision to grant tenure, like various other academic matters, typically calls for the exercise of subjective judgment, confidential deliberation, and personal knowledge of both the candidate and the university community. *See, e. g., Sweeney v. Board of Trustees of Keene State College*, 569 F.2d 169, 176 (1st Cir.), *vacated and remanded on other grounds*, 439 U.S. 24 (1978); *Citron v. Jackson State University, supra*, 456 F. Supp. at 14; *Stebbins v. Weaver*, 537 F.2d 939, 943 n.2 (7th Cir. 1976), *cert. denied*, 429 U.S. 1041 (1977); *Faro v. New York University*, 502 F.2d 1229, 1231–32 (2d Cir. 1974); *Johnson v. University of Pittsburgh, supra*, 435 F. Supp. at 1346. The determination does not call for the use of adversarial procedures which are at the core of judicial notions of due process. These facts suggest why it would be objectively unreasonable for a probationary teacher to rely upon an award of tenure. And, they suggest the inappropriateness of courts determining what procedures universities ought to follow in making initial tenure awards.[9]

---

8. Courts have frequently found this to be the case. *See, e. g.,* Huang v. College of the Holy Cross, 436 F. Supp. 639, 653 (D.Mass. 1977); Labat v. Board of Higher Ed. of City of New York, 401 F. Supp. 753, 756 (S.D.N.Y. 1975). The Commission on Academic Tenure in Higher Education defines tenure as: "(A)n arrangement under which faculty appointments in an institution of higher education are continued until retirement for age or disability, subject to dismissal for adequate cause or unavoidable termination on account of financial exigency or change of institutional program." Commission on Academic Tenure in Higher Education, Faculty Tenure: A Report and Recommendations 256 (1973) (emphasis in original). (hereinafter Faculty Tenure).

9. Even if, as here, the trial court determines that the procedures required by the "due process" clause are minimal, the very fact of court supervision encourages a proliferation of procedural arguments on the campus

These cases and principles indicate that Beitzell had no protected "property" interest in obtaining tenure at UMO. The record makes clear that tenure at UMO does not differ significantly from tenure elsewhere. The UMO handbook points out that tenure is not granted as of right, but, rather, it is a permanent status provided after careful evaluation at both departmental and administrative levels. Beitzell was hired as a probationary employee. And, at UMO many probationary employees were not given tenure. The district court based its finding of a property "entitlement" upon the fact that the UMO history department promulgated criteria for a tenure award. But those criteria did not set objective standards conferring an automatic right to tenure, nor did they create a reasonable expectation of receiving it. Rather, they simply reiterated the traditional criteria for promotion at universities: teaching, scholarship, and service.[12] The government often promulgates criteria for selecting among applications for a particular job, but that fact alone does not create an automatic right in the applicant to the job, nor does it create an entitlement, or a property interest, in a job not yet possessed. Aside from the mere existence of these criteria, there is not a word in the record suggesting that UMO's "tenure" was meant to be granted routinely or to be withheld only for "cause," nor is there a word suggesting that the tenure procedure was meant to be less judgmental or subjective than elsewhere.

In addition to the history department criteria, Beitzell advanced two other grounds in his complaint to support his claim that UMO's tenure procedure created a property right. First, he contended that UMO automatically granted tenure after seven years of service; and, he stated that he had such service because his previous service at the University of Massachusetts should have been counted as part of the seven years under Section 3.3521[14] of UMO's regulations. The district court properly rejected this argument, pointing out that the regulation said that up to three years elsewhere "may" be counted, not that it must be. Second, Beitzell claimed that former Department Chairman Seager had written in letters of recommendation that "it is my intention to promote . . . (Beitzell) to a tenured position . . . when his book is published." The court reasonably found, however, that these letters were insufficient to create a reasonable expectation of tenure, and

---

as disappointed candidates seek to obtain appointments by transforming their substantive arguments into procedural ones.

12. . . . Depending on their needs, universities and colleges may give different weight to any of the criteria. Thus, for one school, publications and scholarship may be of prime importance; for another, teaching may be particularly essential.

14. Section 3.3521 provides:

"Probationary Status

No member of the faculty with instructor or professorial rank may be held in a probationary status at the University of Maine for more than seven years. If a new appointee has had full-time teaching experience at other institutions of higher education at the rank of instructor or

above, three of those years, depending on the nature of the experience, may be counted as part of the probationary period, in which case the probationary period at the University of Maine would not exceed four years. The duration of the probationary period shall be established in writing at the time of initial appointment. The possible seven-year probationary period shall in no way prevent the granting of tenure in a shorter period if the performance of an individual justifies such action." (Emphasis added.)

It should be noted that the object of the regulation is not necessarily to grant "automatic" tenure, but rather to make certain a tenure decision is made in time to allow the teacher, if necessary, to find employment elsewhere.

Beitzell's later actions in preparing for PAC consideration suggest that he had no such expectation.

In the absence of unusual circumstances, where a formal tenure system exists, that system confers no "property" interest on probationary employees. It would take highly unusual circumstances to show that plaintiff had been granted de facto tenure. No such circumstance is present here. Thus, Beitzell had no protected "property" interest. We need not then consider whether he received the process that was "due."

We believe that the district court was correct in holding that Beitzell failed to show he was deprived of any constitutionally protected "liberty." The definition of the term "liberty," provided procedural protection by the Fourteenth Amendment, has expanded well beyond its common law core, "the power of locomotion ... without imprisonment or restraint," W. Blackstone, Commentaries on the Law of England: Of the Rights of Persons *134, and includes other fundamental freedoms. In certain circumstances, the list of fundamental liberties accorded procedural protection includes an interest in reputation at least where the injury to reputation is likely to be sufficiently severe to interfere with the exercise of other fundamental freedoms such as those described in *Meyer v. Nebraska*, 262 U.S. 390, 399 (1923), as the right "to engage in any of the common occupations of life," or "to marry, to establish a home and bring up children." Thus, in *Roth*, the Court, after referring to *Meyer*, suggested that the Fourteenth Amendment offers protection against a severely defamatory charge, such as a claim of "dishonesty or immorality" that might "seriously damage" one's "standing and associations in his community" or impose a "stigma" that significantly interfered with his ability to "take advantage of other employment opportunities." And, the Court cited a series of cases, arising principally during the 1950's, where the charges made, of "subversive activities," were likely to have had just so serious an effect.

In *Paul v. Davis*, 424 U.S. 693, 701 (1976), the Supreme Court, making clear that the Fourteenth Amendment "liberty" does not include all interests protected by state tort law, held that it does not grant procedural protection to reputation alone, "apart from some more tangible interests such as employment". Rather, the injury to reputation must be accompanied by a change in the injured person's status or rights (under substantive state or federal law), perhaps as a touchstone (or concrete evidence) of the fact that the injury to reputation was inflicted as a result of a conscious government policy and is serious enough to interfere with other liberties of the sort suggested in *Meyer*. The Court has not interpreted the requirement of change in "rights" or "status" technically, for it has found the requisite change of status in the termination of government employment held at will. *Owen v. City of Independence*, 445 U.S. 622, 633 n.13 (1980). Thus, the cases suggest there is a core interest in reputation which is protected from interference by individualized government action; the Fourteenth Amendment procedurally protects reputation only where (1) government action threatens it, (2) with unusually serious harm, (3) as evidenced by the fact that employment (or some other right or status)[18] is affected.

---

18. Wisconsin v. Constantineau, 400 U.S. 433 (1971) (defamation plus denial of freedom to buy liquor within city limits). Other evidence of the seriousness of government threat of harm to reputation apart from effect on employment (or some other right or status) may be found in the nature of the government action itself. *Compare* Jenkins v.

Under these standards, Beitzell has not made out a claim of injury to a constitutionally protected interest. Beitzell cannot claim injury to a constitutionally protected interest in reputation prior to the time he invoked the University's grievance procedure. The fact that the PAC recommended that he not be retained does not injure his reputation sufficiently. In the words of *Roth*, "It stretches the concept too far to suggest that a person is deprived of 'liberty' when he simply is not rehired in one job but remains as free as before to seek another." 408 U.S. at 575. Nor does the discussion of Beitzell's tenure credentials whether he is an adequate teacher, scholar, member of the university community threaten his reputation insofar as it is constitutionally protected. Such discussions accompany many, if not all, decisions to hire, or to promote, as well as to discharge, an employee, and they threaten no special injury. Beitzell claims that, during this time, Jeffrey circulated rumors about his drinking habits. But in the district court's view, Beitzell failed to show that these rumors became public, that they were made available to other employers or that they interfered with his ability to obtain other employment. And, the record supports the finding of the district court.

Beitzell also claims that the charges contained in Jeffrey's memo, such as excessive drinking, were defamatory and that their circulation on campus after the meeting of the Grievance Committee infringed a protected "liberty" interest. Whether or not the Grievance Committee meeting is sufficiently related to employment termination to satisfy *Paul*, the University did not infringe any constitutionally protected interest in Beitzell's reputation. Such infringement has been found when the state has made seriously defamatory charges in public, for example, at public meetings or to the press. The fact that the statements are made in the form of charges by the government tends to lend them authority and credibility so that they stigmatize and the fact that they are made in public makes interference with future employment opportunities likely. E. Goffman, Stigma (1963); Note, "Reputation, Stigma and Section 1983: The Lessons of *Paul v. Davis*," 30 Stan.L.Rev. 191, 224 n.187, 226 n.195 (1977). In this instance, no such charge was made; rather, Jeffrey's views on Beitzell's drinking became known to the Grievance Committee as a result of Beitzell's attorney asking that the memo be placed in the record. The meeting was in private, and there is no evidence that University officials were responsible for spreading the information on campus. Any information spread on campus was the result apparently of unauthorized "leaks." In terms of likely stigmatizing effect, there is obviously a world of difference between official charges (say, of excessive drinking) made publicly and a campus rumor based upon hearsay extracted from one witness by Beitzell's attorney at a closed meeting. The district court reasonably found that any disclosure did not occur as a result of charges brought by University officials in connection with the nonrenewal of his contract. It also found that Beitzell failed to establish that Jeffrey's memorandum significantly interfered with his ability to find future employment a finding equally well supported in the record.

In any event, even were there a protected "liberty" interest at stake and we believe there is not we would also uphold the district court's decision that Beitzell received the process that was his due. The cases make clear that,

McKeithen, 395 U.S. 411 (1969) (defamation by state agency performing solely or predominantly accusatory function denies due process) *with* Hannah v. Larche, 363 U.S. 420 (1960) (defamation by purely investigatory agency not making affirmative determinations of criminal culpability held not to deny due process absent effect on other right or status).

when a constitutionally protected interest in reputation is at stake, the Fourteenth Amendment requires a proceeding at which plaintiff has an opportunity to clear his name. *Board of Regents v. Roth, supra*, 408 U.S. at 573 n.12.... Beitzell was given just such an opportunity by the Grievance Committee. He had his lawyer present and was offered the opportunity to present, and to cross-examine, witnesses. He thus could have rebutted Jeffrey's statements, correcting misstatements, had he wished to do so.

In sum, in failing to provide Beitzell with tenure, UMO did not deprive him of "property" within the meaning of the Fourteenth Amendment. And, it did not, during the tenure proceedings, interfere with any protected interests in "liberty." Therefore, the judgment of the district court is affirmed.

Questions and Comments on *Beitzell*

1. Consider the views of Clark Byse and Louis Joughin on the relationship between tenure and academic freedom:

> The principle justification for academic tenure is that it enables a faculty member to teach, study, and act free from a large number of restraints and pressures which otherwise would inhibit independent thought and action. This justification of freedom for teachers, customarily termed "academic freedom," is similar to that which accounts for the proscription in the Bill of Rights of governmental interference with the citizen's general freedoms of thought and expression. These general freedoms exist both because of the moral conviction that the political state should not limit the individual's inalienable rights of life and liberty and because of the pragmatic recognition that free trade in ideas is an indispensable condition to enlightened community decisions and action.

> But there is more to academic freedom. Teachers in colleges and universities in our society have the unique responsibility to help students to develop critical capacities. Teachers must also strive to make available the accumulated knowledge of the past, to expand the frontiers of knowledge, to appraise existing institutions, and to seek their correction or replacement in the light of reason and experience. If they are to perform these indispensable tasks, there must be free inquiry and discussion. This, as Professor Fritz Machlup has noted, demands more than mere "absence of governmental sanctions, more than a guarantee that ... [professors] will not be jailed for the expressions of their thoughts. If they are to be encouraged to pursue the truth wherever it may lead, to 'follow out any bold, vigorous, independent train of thought ...,' they need protection from all more material sanctions, especially from dismissal." Professor Machlup continues:

>> With regard to some occupations, it is eminently in the interest of society that men concerned speak their minds without fear of retribution.... The occupational work of the vast majority of people is largely independent of their thought and speech. The professor's work *consists* of his thought and speech. If he loses his position for what he writes or says, he will, as a rule, have to leave his profession, and may no longer be able effectively to question and challenge accepted doctrines. And if *some* professors lose their positions for what they write or say, the effect on many other professors will be such that their usefulness to their students and to society will be gravely reduced.

> ... Academic freedom and tenure do not exist because of a peculiar solicitude for the human beings who staff our academic institutions. They exist, instead, in order that society may have the benefit of honest judgment

and independent criticism which otherwise might be withheld because of fear of offending a dominant social group or transient social attitude.

CLARK BYSE & LOUIS JOUGHIN, TENURE IN AMERICAN HIGHER EDUCATION: PLANS, PRACTICES, AND THE LAW 2–4 (1959).

2. Courts are generally reluctant to second guess academic decisions to deny tenure provided proper procedures are followed and there is no evidence of discrimination. *See, e.g.*, University of Penn. v. E.E.O.C., 493 U.S. 182, 199 (1990) ("[J]udges ... asked to review the substance of a genuinely academic decision ... should show great respect for the faculty's professional judgment." (quoting Regents of Univ. of Mich. v. Ewing, 474 U.S. 214, 225 (1985))), *see supra* at 343; University of Baltimore v. Iz, 123 Md.App. 135, 716 A.2d 1107, 1117 (1998) ("[C]ourts should be wary of intruding into the world of university tenure decisions absent discrimination or other unlawful action by the university." (quoting Stern v. University of Okla. Bd. of Regents, 841 P.2d 1168, 1172 (Okla. Ct. App. 1992))); Halper v. University of the Incarnate Word, 90 S.W.3d 842, 846 (Tex. App. 2002) ("[J]udicial review must focus on the procedures followed, not the wisdom of the decision reached"). Is this deference appropriate?

Note on Faculty Handbooks

Most colleges and universities have faculty handbooks that include sections on tenure, faculty governance, and faculty benefits. Typically, the handbooks are incorporated by reference into faculty contracts, making them a relevant legal standard both for awarding and terminating tenure. *See, e.g.*, Sola v. Lafayette College, 804 F.2d 40 (3d Cir. 1986); Arenson v. Board of Trustees, 210 Ill.App.3d 844, 155 Ill.Dec. 252, 569 N.E.2d 252 (1991). They are also a window into the variety of institutional cultures. Consider:

1. Harvard University, Faculty of Arts and Sciences Handbook for Faculty available at Harvard University Website, *available at* http://www.fas.harvard.edu/home/academic _affairs/faculty_handbook.pdf.

RESOLUTION ON RIGHTS AND RESPONSIBILITIES

The central functions of an academic community are learning, teaching, research, and scholarship. By accepting membership in the University, an individual joins a community ideally characterized by free expression, free inquiry, intellectual honesty, respect for the dignity of others, and openness to constructive change. The rights and responsibilities exercised within the community must be compatible with these qualities.

The rights of members of the University are not fundamentally different from those of other members of society. The University, however, has a special autonomy and reasoned dissent plays a particularly vital part in its existence. All members of the University have the right to press for action on matters of concern by any appropriate means. The University must affirm, assure, and protect the rights of its members to organize and join political associations, convene and conduct public meetings, publicly demonstrate and picket in orderly fashion, advocate, and publicize opinion by print, sign, and voice.

The University places special emphasis, as well, upon certain values which are essential to its nature as an academic community. Among these are freedom of speech and academic freedom, freedom from personal force and violence, and freedom of movement. Interference with any of these freedoms must be regarded as a serious violation of the personal rights upon which the community is based. Furthermore, although the administrative processes and activities of the University cannot be ends in themselves, such functions are vital to the orderly pursuit of the work of all members of the University. Therefore, interference with members of the University in performance of their normal duties and activities must be regarded as unacceptable obstruction of the essential processes of the University. Theft or willful destruction of the property of the University or its members must also be considered an unacceptable violation of the rights of individuals or of the community as a whole.

Moreover, it is the responsibility of all members of the academic community to maintain an atmosphere in which violations of rights are unlikely to occur and to develop processes by which these rights are fully assured. In particular, it is the responsibility of officers of administration and instruction to be alert to the needs of the University community; to give full and fair hearing to reasoned expressions of grievances; and to respond promptly and in good faith to such expressions and to widely-expressed needs for change. In making decisions which concern the community as a whole or any part of the community, officers are expected to consult those affected by the decisions. Failures to meet these responsibilities may be profoundly damaging to the life of the University. Therefore, the University community has the right to establish orderly procedures consistent with imperatives of academic freedom to assess the policies and assure the responsibility of those whose decisions affect the life of the University.

No violation of the rights of members of the University, nor any failure to meet responsibilities, should be interpreted as justifying any violation of the rights of members of the University. All members of the community—students and officers alike—should uphold the rights and responsibilities expressed in this Resolution if the University is to be characterized by mutual respect and trust.

2. Yale University Faculty Handbook, *available at* http://www.yale.edu/provost/html/facultyhb.html (last visited Aug. 19, 2008):

Instructional and Institutional Responsibilities

The department chair, or, in a professional school, the dean, is charged with assigning faculty members classroom responsibilities that will provide students comprehensive and effective formal instruction. Varying instructional techniques and classroom demands mean that such assignments may differ among departments and schools. The obligations of a member of the teaching faculty go well beyond the classroom and other teaching duties. They include time spent on research, student advising, and various kinds of department and University service on committees and in administrative roles. While the proportion of these components vary from individual to individual and from time to time, faculty may not substitute time spent on sponsored research for their regular teaching duties without special permission from the Provost.

Members of the faculty are often called upon to write letters of recommendation for students or to offer their professional judgments on the qualifications of candidates for positions at Yale or elsewhere. It is understood that such judgments, expressed orally or in writing, will be consistent with the nondiscrimination policy of the University.

3. The University of Chicago Faculty Handbook (1999):

Teaching and University Service

The University expects excellence in teaching as well as excellence in research. Faculty should attend to teaching with the same care and concern they would commit to any other fundamental responsibility.

The active involvement of faculty in undergraduate teaching is a proud tradition at the University. Most divisional faculty, and some professional school faculty, hold joint appointments in the College. Members of the faculty bear primary responsibility for teaching the Core courses that are a central feature of the College's identity, as well as for instruction at the advanced, or concentration, level. Faculty are also responsible for teaching, advising, and evaluating the performance of graduate and professional students.

At all levels of teaching, faculty should give clear guidance to students about program and course requirements, should be reasonably available to students outside of class, and should provide forthright evaluations through grades and written assessments. A faculty member who observes special problems in a student's performance should promptly inform the relevant program committee, chair, or dean of students. There is as strong an obligation not to waste the time and resources of students who are not succeeding as to facilitate the success of those who do well. If second chances are accorded, the expectations must be clear. Faculty have a special obligation to assist students in placement and should provide prompt and fair recommendations.

Faculty bear a special responsibility to the students whose dissertations they oversee. A faculty member should not undertake to supervise dissertations if he or she does not have the time or the expertise to do so effectively. A faculty member should regularly and clearly communicate his or her expectations for a student's progress, define and enforce clear time limits for the completion of a student's work, and provide prompt and candid evaluations of the work a student submits. If there are early indications that a student has not performed sufficiently well to be admitted to candidacy, that message should be conveyed promptly.

Faculty members who want advice in these matters should speak with their department chair or dean.

4. University of California Academic Personnel Manual, *available at* University of California website: http://www.ucop.edu/acadadv/acadpers/apm/welcome.html (last visited Aug. 18, 2007).

Section 210–1 d. Criteria for Appointment, Promotion, and Appraisal

The review committee shall judge the candidate with respect to the proposed rank and duties, considering the record of the candidate's performance in (1) teaching, (2) research and other creative work, (3) professional activity, and (4) University and public service. In evaluating the candidate's qualifications within these areas, the review committee shall exercise reasonable flexibility, balancing when the case requires, heavier commitments and responsibilities in one area against lighter commitments and responsibilities in another. The review committee must judge whether the candidate is engaging in a program of work that is both sound and productive. As the University enters new fields of endeavor and refocuses its ongoing activities, cases will arise in which the proper work of faculty members departs markedly from established academic patterns. In such cases, the review committees must take exceptional care to apply the criteria with sufficient flexibility. However, flexibility does not entail a relaxation of high standards. *Superior intellectual attainment, as evidenced both in teaching and in research or other creative achievement, is an indispensable qualification for appointment or promotion to tenure positions.* Insistence upon this [sic] standards for holders of the professorship is necessary for maintenance of the quality of the University as an institution dedicated to the discovery and transmission of knowledge. Consideration should be given to changes in emphasis and interest that may occur in an academic career. The candidate may submit for the review file a presentation of his or her activity in all four areas. The University of California is committed to excellence and equity in every facet of its mission. Teaching, research, professional and public service contributions that promote diversity and equal opportunity are to be encouraged and given recognition in the evaluation of the candidate's qualifications. These contributions to diversity and equal opportunity can take a variety of forms including efforts to advance equitable access to education, public service that addresses the needs of California's diverse population, or research in a scholar's area of expertise that highlights inequalities. Mentoring and advising of students or new faculty members are to be encouraged and given recognition in the teaching or service categories of academic personnel actions. The criteria set forth below are intended to serve as guides for minimum standards in judging the candidate, not to set boundaries to exclude other elements of performance that may be considered.

(1) Teaching—Clearly demonstrated evidence of high quality in teaching is an essential criterion for appointment, advancement, or promotion. Under no circumstances will a tenure commitment be made unless there is clear documentation of ability and diligence in the teaching role. In judging the effectiveness of a candidate's

teaching, the committee should consider such points as the following: the candidate's command of the subject; continuous growth in the subject field; ability to organize material and to present it with force and logic; capacity to awaken in students an awareness of the relationship of the subject to other fields of knowledge; fostering of student independence and capability to reason; spirit and enthusiasm which vitalize the candidate's learning and teaching; ability to arouse curiosity in beginning students, to encourage high standards, and to stimulate advanced students to creative work; personal attributes as they affect teaching and students; extent and skill of the candidate's participation in the general guidance, mentoring, and advising of students; effectiveness in creating an academic environment that is open and encouraging to all students, including development of particularly effective strategies for the educational advancement of students in various underrepresented groups. The committee should pay due attention to the variety of demands placed on instructors by the types of teaching called for in various disciplines and at various levels, and should judge the total performance of the candidate with proper reference to assigned teaching responsibilities. The committee should clearly indicate the sources of evidence on which its appraisal of teaching competence has been based. In those exceptional cases when no such evidence is available, the candidate's potentialities as a teacher may be indicated in closely analogous activities. In preparing its recommendation, the review committee should keep in mind that a redacted copy of its report may be an important means of informing the candidate of the evaluation of his or her teaching and of the basis for that evaluation. It is the responsibility of the department chair to submit meaningful statements, accompanied by evidence, of the candidate's teaching effectiveness at lower-division, upper-division, and graduate levels of instruction. More than one kind of evidence shall accompany each review file. Among significant types of evidence of teaching effectiveness are the following: (a) opinions of other faculty members knowledgeable in the candidate's field, particularly if based on class visitations, on attendance at public lectures or lectures before professional societies given by the candidate, or on the performance of students in courses taught by the candidate that are prerequisite to those of the informant; (b) opinions of students; (c) opinions of graduates who have achieved notable professional success since leaving the University; (d) number and caliber of students guided in research by the candidate and of those attracted to the campus by the candidate's repute as a teacher; and (e) development of new and effective techniques of instruction, including techniques that meet the needs of students from groups that are underrepresented in the field of instruction. All cases for advancement and promotion normally will include:

(a) evaluations and comments solicited from students for most, if not all, courses taught since the candidate's last review;

(b) a quarter-by-quarter or semester-by-semester enumeration of the number and types of courses and tutorials taught since the candidate's last review;

(c) their level;

(d) their enrollments;

(e) the percentage of students represented by student course evaluations for each course;

(f) brief explanations for abnormal course loads;

(g) identification of any new courses taught or of old courses when there was substantial reorganization of approach or content;

(h) notice of any awards or formal mentions for distinguished teaching;

(i) when the faculty member under review wishes, a self evaluation of his or her teaching; and

(j) evaluation by other faculty members of teaching effectiveness.

When any of the information specified in this paragraph is not provided, the department chair will include an explanation for that omission in the candidate's dossier. If such information is not included with the letter of recommendation and its absence is not adequately accounted for, it is the review committee chair's responsibility to request it through the Chancellor.

(2) Research and Creative Work—Evidence of a productive and creative mind should be sought in the candidate's published research or recognized artistic production in original architectural or engineering designs, or the like. Publications of research and other creative accomplishment should be evaluated, not merely enumerated. There should be evidence that the candidate is continuously and effectively engaged in creative activity of high quality and significance. Work in progress should be assessed whenever possible. When published work in joint authorship (or other product of joint effort) is presented as evidence, it is the responsibility of the department chair to establish as clearly as possible the role of the candidate in the joint effort. It should be recognized that special cases of collaboration occur in the performing arts and that the contribution of a particular collaborator may not be readily discernible by those viewing the finished work. When the candidate is such a collaborator, it is the responsibility of the department chair to make a separate evaluation of the candidate's contribution and to provide outside opinions based on observation of the work while in progress. Account should be taken of the type and quality of creative activity normally expected in the candidate's field. Appraisals of publications or other works in the scholarly and critical literature provide important testimony. Due consideration should be given to variations among fields and specialties and to new genres and fields of inquiry. Textbooks, reports, circulars, and similar publications normally are considered evidence of teaching ability or public service. However, contributions by faculty members to the professional literature or to the advancement of professional practice or professional education, including contributions to the advancement of equitable access and diversity in education, should be judged creative work when they present new ideas or original scholarly research. In certain fields such as art, architecture, dance, music, literature, and drama, distinguished creation should receive consideration equivalent to that accorded to distinction attained in research. In evaluating artistic creativity, an attempt should be made to define the candidate's merit in the light of such criteria as originality, scope, richness, and depth of creative expression. It should be recognized that in music, drama, and dance, distinguished performance, including conducting and directing, is evidence of a candidate's creativity.

(3) Professional Competence and Activity—In certain positions in the administration, dentistry, engineering, law, medicine, etc., a demonstrated distinction in the special competencies appropriate to the field and its characteristic activities should be recognized as a criterion for appointment or promotion. The candidate's professional activities should be scrutinized for evidence of achievement and leadership in the field and of demonstrated progressiveness in the development or utilization of new approaches and techniques for the solution of professional problems, including those that specifically address the professional advancement of individuals in underrepresented groups in the the candidate's field. It is the responsibility of the department chair to provide evidence that the position in question is of the type described above and that the candidate is qualified to fill it.

(4) University and Public Service—The faculty plays an important role in the administration of the University and in the formulation of its policies. Recognition should therefore be given to scholars who prove themselves to be able administrators and who participate effectively and imaginatively in faculty government and the formulation of departmental, college, and University policies. Services by members of the faculty to the community, State, and nation, both in their special capacities as scholars and in areas beyond those special capacities when the work done is at a sufficiently high level and of sufficiently high quality, should likewise be recognized as evidence for promotion. Faculty service activities related to the improvement of elementary and secondary education represent one example of this kind of service.

Similarly, contributions to student welfare through service on student-faculty commit-tees and as advisers to student organizations should be recognized as evidence, as should contributions furthering diversity and equal opportunity within the University through participation in such activities as recruitment, retention, and mentoring of scholars and students. The Standing Orders of The Regents provide: "No political test shall ever be considered in the appointment and promotion of any faculty member or employee." This provision is pertinent to every stage in the process of considering appointments and promotions of the faculty.

A.   TERMINATING TENURE FOR CAUSE

Smith v. Kent State University

United States Court of Appeals for the Sixth Circuit, 1983.
696 F.2d 476.

■ PER CURIAM.

This case was brought . . . on constitutional grounds (primarily First and Fourteenth Amendment causes of action), against Kent State University ("KSU") its President, Board of Trustees, and other KSU officials involved in the termination of Dr. Joseph F. Smith ("Smith"), a former music professor at KSU. Smith seeks both damages and reinstatement in this proceeding. After a full hearing following a reference from the District Judge, the Magistrate entered a judgment for all defendants, concluding that Smith had breached his contractual obligations to KSU and that his discharge was "not in contravention of any constitutionally protected right." . . .

Smith first became a member of the faculty at KSU in 1967 in the Department of Philosophy. He could not "get along" within that department and was transferred to the School of Music in the fall of 1968. In that same year, he became active in the American Federation of Teachers ("AFT") and involved in solicitation of other Music Department faculty in AFT. A year later, Smith sought tenure, but the Music Department faculty committee recommended against granting this request. Upon the urging of the Director of the Music Department, appellee Merrill, the faculty committee reconsid-ered and recommended tenure. The next fall, however, 1970, Smith joined in a petition with other music teachers requesting that Merrill be removed because of alleged irregularities in his credentials; after discussion and debate, however, the music faculty voted for his retention. Subsequently Merrill initiated a suit in a state court based on libel against appellant and other signers of the petition.

Smith had received an unfavorable rating for his teaching a basic course in Music History, Music 280, one purportedly within his field of expertise. This unsatisfactory experience may well have been an appropriate basis for withholding his request for tenure for a year. Smith was appointed coordina-tor of the Music History and Literature Division within the Music Depart-ment to work on teaching assignments for 1971. The assistant director of the Department and Director Merrill both decided that Smith should teach a section of Music 280 in the fall of 1971. Smith did not agree to this assignment, and then advised the assistant director in writing that he would not teach the course. Merrill responded in writing that Smith was the logical person to be assigned this responsibility. Smith responded to the effect that to teach this course would somehow lower his standing among the academic community. Merrill again called upon Smith to teach the assigned course and again Smith forcefully declined. The KSU Department Dean, next in line of authority, then advised Smith that this assignment was reasonable and requested his written acceptance. The written response forthcoming, once more, was negative.

In view of these circumstances, Merrill then advised appellant that he would seek his dismissal for refusal to accept his academic assignment. KSU policies were followed in the ensuing steps resulting from the initiation of dismissal proceedings. The Faculty Hearing Committee, Smith's peers, approved assignment of the course but recommended against dismissal as too severe a sanction; it suggested that Smith be retained if he accepted the Music Director's further authority in respect to class assignments after consultation. Promptly thereafter such a department consultation procedure was adopted, since KSU President Olds accepted the faculty committee recommendation that Smith be retained provided he complied with Merrill's directions and teaching assignments.

After receipt of appellant's assurance that he would accede to the Director's authority, appellee Olds as KSU President sent Smith a contract for the 1972–1973 academic year subject to Board of Trustee approval. In September of 1972 the Board ratified Smith's contract on the following express condition:

> That, should Dr. Smith again refuse to teach what is in the opinion of the president, upon a hearing before him, a reasonable teaching assignment from the School of Music or his delegates, that he be automatically removed from the faculty.

Olds then forwarded a copy of this Board action to Smith. With respect to 1972–1973 assignments, Smith did not respond to Merrill's invitation to propose course offerings. In consultation initiated by Music Department administrators, however, when advised he would be asked to teach Music 280, Smith responded that he would take the matter up with his lawyers, and then, just before classes were to begin, advised the assistant Music Department director that it was "inappropriate for me to teach the Music History Survey [course 280] in question." Both Smith and his attorney refused to attend a meeting with the Music Department Executive Committee to discuss the situation regarding his fall assignments; instead, Smith attempted to appeal his assignment.

KSU's Music Department officials notified Smith that he was to teach the assigned Music 280 class pending decision on his asserted appeal. Smith did not meet the class for its first session as posted and assigned despite his clear knowledge of the position of KSU and its responsible officials. Thereafter, in response to the University invitation for a meeting, Smith's lawyer agreed that Smith would teach the class pending resolution of the dispute. Once again, however, when the class was again scheduled to convene, Smith failed to appear, and adamantly refused to discuss the matter with a designated faculty representative.

President Olds then advised Smith he would conduct a hearing in respect to his status in light of the aforementioned recent Board of Trustees resolution. Smith filed suit in the District Court below against KSU and its officials asserting first amendment and constitutional claims, demanding a full due process hearing which he contended was not what Olds had indicated was forthcoming. Judge Lambros ruled that a due process hearing could proceed before President Olds and that Smith might be suspended pending the hearing.

After further notice and hearing in accordance with Judge Lambros' decision in 1973, Olds notified Smith that he was terminated based on the record and the circumstances. This action ensued in 1974.

Under the facts related, Smith clearly received his full due process rights in the extended proceedings leading to his termination. The President of the University had authority to act on behalf of its Board of Trustees to effectuate the termination after a hearing and finding that contractual conditions set by the Board had been disregarded by appellant.

Under the facts set out, KSU had just cause to terminate Smith regardless of his tenured status, particularly in light of his persistent actions not only in flouting the authority of the Music Department director and assistant director but also in refusing to meet his scheduled classes. The latter conduct violated his own agreement, and it violated the right of KSU students to receive instruction. It was appellant himself whose actions initiated his suspension and ultimate termination.

Appellant asserts that his union activities and his petitioning for removal of Merrill constituted protected free speech, and that these were impermissible bases for his termination rather than his refusal to teach the class assigned. Appellant had the burden of proving that his activities did indeed constitute first amendment "speech" and that his termination was the consequence of his exercise of free speech. *Perry v. Sindermann*, 408 U.S. 593 (1972); *Nathanson v. United States*, 630 F.2d 1260 (8th Cir. 1980); *Rosaly v. Ignacio*, 593 F.2d 145 (1st Cir. 1979); and *Roseman v. Indiana University*, 520 F.2d 1364 (3d Cir. 1975).

Here Smith failed in his burden of establishing that his activities were of the nature which are protected under the First Amendment, and it was clear that such activities did interfere with the orderly administration of the Department of Music and KSU. *Pickering v. Board of Education*, 391 U.S. 563 (1968); *McLaughlin v. Tilendis*, 398 F.2d 287 (7th Cir. 1968). Finally, appellant failed in his burden of showing that his purported "speech" was in fact any motivating basis of his termination. *Mt. Healthy City School District Board v. Doyle*, 429 U.S. 274 (1977).

. . .

The decision of the district court is accordingly affirmed.

Korf v. Ball State University

United States Court of Appeals for the Seventh Circuit, 1984.
726 F.2d 1222.

■ COFFEY, CIRCUIT JUDGE.

Dr. William E. Korf appeals the district court's decision granting summary judgment to the defendants in an action brought by Dr. Korf following his termination as a tenured Associate Professor of Music History and Musicology at Ball State University, Muncie, Indiana. . . .

In February, 1981, Dr. Korf was informed by Lloyd Nelson, Dean of Ball State's College of Fine and Applied Arts, that certain of his current and former male students had accused him of sexual harassment. The students alleged that the harassment consisted of Dr. Korf's making unwelcomed sexual advances towards them and offering good grades contingent upon sexual involvement. Dean Nelson informed Dr. Korf that he intended to commence termination proceedings against him, and provided him the opportunity to resign. Dr. Korf denied the accusations and refused to resign. In accordance with established procedures, a committee was formed to investigate the charges. On April 2, 1981, the committee concluded that sufficient grounds existed to institute formal termination proceedings against Dr. Korf.

The president of Ball State, Dr. Robert P. Bell, reviewed the committee's recommendation and informed Dr. Korf of the committee's findings. Based on those findings, on April 24, 1981, Dr. Bell told Dr. Korf that formal termination proceedings were being commenced and that he had the right to a hearing before an *ad hoc* hearing committee, drawn from the University Senate Judicial Committee, to determine whether or not Dr. Korf should be removed from his position. Dr. Korf requested a hearing and the University complied with his request on May 20, 1981.

At that hearing, a student related the relationship he had had with Dr. Korf and testified that Dr. Korf gave him money and gifts in exchange for sexual acts.[1] In addition, the student alleged that he was promised good grades. While denying that grades were involved, Dr. Korf admitted his sexual involvement with this student. The committee also heard testimony from three individuals and had statements of four other individuals who recounted Dr. Korf's sexual advances towards them while or after they were his students.

On May 21, 1981, the committee made the following findings:

"Based on the evidence provided at the hearing on May 20, 1981, we find Dr. William E. Korf guilty of unethical conduct because he used his position and influence as a teacher to exploit students for his private advantage. The evidence indicates a pattern of behavior in which he frequently built a personal, friendly relationship, followed by sexual advances, often in his home.

"This pattern was evidenced by the testimony of six (6) witnesses who were either present or submitted signed statements ... and by two (2) individuals who made statements to the Affirmative Action Officer.... These eight (8) people are current or former students in one or more of Dr. Korf's classes.

"We find insufficient evidence to support the allegation that Dr. Korf encouraged dishonest academic conduct."

The committee based its finding that Dr. Korf engaged in unethical conduct on paragraph 2 of the American Association of University Professors ("AAUP") Statement on Professional Ethics which was adopted by Ball State University in 1967 and published in its *Faculty Handbook*.[2] Even though the

---

1. The relationship began while this student was a seventeen-year-old freshman at the University.

2. The statement reads in pertinent part that: "2. As a teacher, the professor encourages the free pursuit of learning in his students. He holds before them the best scholarly

committee found Dr. Korf guilty of unethical conduct, they recommended only that Dr. Korf be placed on a three-year period of probation, rather than discharged, because they did not feel that he had been provided "ample warning and opportunity for behavioral change."

Pursuant to established procedures, the Board of Trustees was presented with the hearing committee's report. After hearing arguments from University representatives and counsel for Dr. Korf on July 6, 1981, the Trustees agreed with the committee's finding of unethical conduct but refused to accept the committee's disciplinary recommendation of three years probation and directed that the committee's report and recommendations be returned to them for reconsideration. Upon reconsideration, the hearing committee, after a "close re-examination of the statement of ethics in the *Faculty Handbook*" and because of the realistic unenforceability of some of the proposed conditions of probation,[3] reversed its prior recommendation of probation and recommended that Dr. Korf be discharged from the University. Based upon this recommendation the Trustees terminated Dr. Korf's employment on July 24, 1981.

Dr. Korf initiated this action under 42 U.S.C. § 1983 on May 21, 1982, seeking both legal and equitable relief. . . .

On March 11, 1983, the district court granted defendants summary judgment on Dr. Korf's constitutional and state law claims. The court concluded that Ball State University was an instrumentality of the State of Indiana for the purposes of the Eleventh Amendment and therefore the University, its Board of Trustees and the individual defendants in their official capacities were immune from suit under § 1983. Because the affidavits presented on Dr. Korf's behalf failed to provide any evidence sufficient to create a genuine question whether the individual defendants acted in bad faith, the court also ruled that the defendants were immune from § 1983 liability under the doctrine of qualified or "good faith" immunity.

The main question we must decide is whether or not the district court committed error in granting the defendants' motion for summary judgment. Dr. Korf contends that since there were disputed issues of material fact concerning his substantive due process and equal protection claims, summary judgment was improper.

. . .

standards of his discipline. He demonstrates respect for the student as an individual and adheres to his proper role as intellectual guide and counselor. He makes every reasonable effort to foster honest academic conduct and to assure that his evaluation of his students reflects their true merits. He respects the confidential nature of the relationship between professor and student. *He avoids any exploitation of students for his private advantage* and acknowledges significant assistance from them. He protects their academic freedom." Ball State University *Faculty Handbook* at II–7 (Emphasis added).

3. The terms of the recommended probation were:

"1. He will not invite students to his home.

"2. He will not have students living in his home.

"3. He will hold no private meetings with any student without leaving his office, classroom or studio door open.

"4. He will be excluded from consideration for promotion.

"5. He will be ineligible for merit pay consideration.

"6. He will periodically be reviewed by appropriate administrators."

Dr. Korf argues that the record contains issues of material fact as to "whether he could have had adequate notice" of Ball State's "asserted prohibition of consensual sexual relations between faculty members and students." Dr. Korf does not contend he was unaware of the University's proscription of unethical faculty conduct; rather, he argues that the AAUP Statement on Professional Ethics could not be reasonably interpreted to include what he labels "consensual sexual relationships" with students but which the Hearing Committee expressly found to be "unethical behavior of exploiting students for his private advantage."

In support of his opposition to defendants' summary judgment motion, Dr. Korf failed to allege any specific facts which would tend to create a genuine issue challenging the reasonableness of the interpretation given to the AAUP Statement of Professional Ethics, paragraph 2, by his faculty peers on the Hearing Committee. While Dr. Korf argues that he was not "adequately put on notice" because he was the first Ball State University faculty member ever disciplined for conduct such as his or, for that matter, any unethical conduct, the only logical basis for this argument is that if another professor had previously been dismissed for conduct similar to his, Dr. Korf would have *definitely* known that his conduct would warrant discipline. The plaintiff-appellant has failed to cite any caselaw setting forth a constitutional requirement that such notice be provided to would-be offenders. Common sense, reason and good judgment should have made him cognizant of the fact that his conduct could and would be cause for termination. One cannot be heard to complain that it is somehow unfair to be the first one disciplined under a particular law, rule or regulation since if that were the case, no new law, rule or regulation could ever be enforced.

Dr. Korf also alleges that other "private and consensual" faculty/student sexual relationships had occurred and were presently occurring at Ball State University and that no steps had ever been taken against the faculty members allegedly involved. This argument also misses the mark. First, despite Dr. Korf's repeated characterization of his conduct as "private and consensual," the faculty Hearing Committee found that he engaged in unethical behavior by "exploiting students for his private advantage." Therefore, "consensual" sexual activity is not at issue as it does not concern a fact which is "outcome determinative under the governing law." In any event, while there is no evidence that the young student Dr. Korf admitted having a sexual relationship with did not consent to engage in sexual activity with him, Dr. Korf's conduct is not to be viewed in the same context as would conduct of an ordinary "person on the street." Rather, it must be judged in the context of the relationship existing between a professor and his students within an academic environment. University professors occupy an important place in our society and have concomitant ethical obligations. The AAUP Statement on Professional Ethics makes this clear:

1.) The professor, guided by a deep conviction of the worth and dignity of the advancement of knowledge, recognizes the special responsibilities placed upon him....

2.) ... He demonstrates respect for the student as an individual and adheres to his proper role as intellectual guide and counselor....

Ball State University *Faculty Handbook* at II–7. Furthermore, the Committee heard evidence of Dr. Korf's sexual advances towards seven students who refused his advances. One student recounted how he had to be "very assertive to get away from Dr. Korf's amorous advances." Such conduct certainly cannot be characterized as consensual sexual activity. Second, even if such alleged relationships between other faculty and students were relevant, all Dr. Korf has done is made bare assertions of faculty-student sexual relationships without any detailed information, much less supporting affidavits or proof. He must set forth *specific facts* in order to create a genuine issue of fact.

Dr. Korf further argues that it is significant that the AAUP Statement on Professional Ethics relied upon by the Board of Trustees as the basis for his termination does not make any reference to sexual conduct. While his observation that the statement does not specifically mention sexual conduct is correct, his conclusion regarding the omission's significance is misplaced and is contrary to reason and common sense. As is the case with other laws, codes and regulations governing conduct, it is unreasonable to assume that the drafters of the Statement on Professional Ethics could and must specifically delineate each and every type of conduct (including deviant conduct) constituting a violation. Nor have we been cited any case reciting that the language of the Constitution requires such precision.

> It is not feasible or necessary ... to spell out in detail all that conduct which will result in retaliation. The most conscientious of codes that define prohibited conduct of employees include "catch-all" clauses prohibiting employee "misconduct," "immorality," or "conduct unbecoming."

The lack of specific reference to sexual conduct in the Statement on Professional Ethics does not bar its application to Dr. Korf's conduct.

The Hearing Committee and the Board of Trustees relied upon that portion of the AAUP Statement warning against "any exploitation of students for ... private advantage" in reaching their decision to terminate Dr. Korf. Dr. Korf argues that this portion of the statement only prohibits the use of student research or assistance in an improper manner because this portion of the statement ends by stating "and acknowledges significant academic assistance from them." Construing "exploitation of students for ... private advantage" to include Dr. Korf's conduct was entirely reasonable. The narrow construction Dr. Korf asks us to accept is contrary to the express language of the provision as it proscribes "any exploitation of students" rather than merely "academic exploitation of students." We agree with his academic peers on the Hearing Committee and the Board of Trustees in their application of this provision of the AAUP Statement of Professional Ethics to Dr. Korf's conduct. They were well-qualified to interpret the AAUP Statement of Professional Ethics as well as to determine what is and is not acceptable faculty conduct within an academic setting. Furthermore, while the Hearing Committee based their initial recommendation on the particular portion of the AAUP Statement barring "exploitation of students ... for private advantage," they explained that they changed their recommendation after they undertook a "close re-examination of the Statement of Ethics in the *Faculty Handbook*." The pertinent paragraph of the AAUP Statement of Professional Ethics also states that a professor "demonstrates respect for the student as an individual and adheres to his proper role as intellectual guide and counselor." It is patently clear that Dr. Korf's conduct was also inconsistent with this provision of the AAUP Statement.

In sum, Dr. Korf's arguments merely consist of generalized allegations disparaging the reasonableness of the interpretation given to the AAUP Statement by the Hearing Committee and the Board of Trustees. Our examination of the record reveals no "genuine issue of material fact" precluding disposition of his substantive due process claim by summary judgment. When the record is viewed in the light most favorable to Dr. Korf, his bald allegations do not meet that standard of proof necessary to create a genuine issue of material fact as to whether he "had adequate notice of the standard of conduct to which he was being held." The facts and circumstances clearly demonstrate that he should have understood both the standards to which he was being held and the consequences of his conduct. Dr. Korf merely asserts that he was not afforded notice and thereby contends that an issue of fact exists. This assertion alone is "insufficient to raise a factual issue." Because of Dr. Korf's failure to allege any specific facts in support of his alleged lack of notice his substantive due process claim was ripe for summary judgment since "there [was] no genuine issue as to any material fact. . . ."

We also agree with the conclusions of law reached by the district court regarding the substantive due process issue and the court's express finding that "it cannot be seriously maintained that Dr. Korf's conduct was not clearly proscribed by University Regulations."

> The claim that a person is entitled to "substantive due process" means, as we understand the concept, that state action which deprives him of life, liberty, or property must have a rational basis— that is to say, the reason for the deprivation may not be so inadequate that the judiciary will characterize it as "arbitrary."

Jeffries v. Turkey Run Consolidated School District, 492 F.2d 1, 3–4 (7th Cir. 1974). We have no difficulty whatsoever concluding that Dr. Korf's termination was not "arbitrary" since the reasons for his termination were adequate. The University's interpretation of the AAUP Statement was entirely reasonable and rationally related to the duty of the University to provide a proper academic environment.

> [A] University has a right, and indeed a duty, to take all reasonable and lawful measures to prevent activities which adversely intrude into the teaching process, or which might adversely affect the University's image and reputation. It has a right to expect and demand the highest standards of personal behavior and teaching performance from its teachers and professors. It does not have to settle for less.

Naragon v. Wharton, 572 F. Supp. 1117, 1121 (M.D. La. 1983). (A university did not violate the constitutional rights of a graduate assistant when it changed her assignment from teaching to research after discovering that she had had a homosexual relationship with a student who was not in her classes.) We hold that the district court properly granted summary judgment to the defendants on Dr. Korf's substantive due process claim.

Dr. Korf's allegations contending that disputed issues of material fact exist which should have precluded summary judgment on his equal protection claim suffer the same infirmities as his allegations regarding his substantive due process claim. Simply put, his allegations when viewed in a light most favorable to him, do not create a genuine issue of material fact as to whether the University selectively enforced its regulations against him. Dr. Korf again incorrectly premises his arguments on involvement in "consensual sexual relations" and merely alleges selective enforcement without providing us with any specific facts to support that claim.

We do not agree with Dr. Korf's argument that he was terminated for his untraditional sexual preferences, since he was in fact terminated for his unethical conduct in violation of the AAUP Statement of Professional Ethics as a result of sexual advances toward his students. The record fails to even suggest that the University would hesitate to discharge a professor who acted in a manner similar to Dr. Korf but directed his or her advances towards students of the opposite sex rather than the same sex. . . .

. . . We hold that Dr. Korf's equal protection claim has no legal or factual basis and that the district court properly granted summary judgment to defendants on this claim.

Boise v. New York University

United States District Court for the Southern District of New York, 2005.
2005 WL 2899853.

■ SWEET, U.S.D.J.

The defendant New York University ("NYU" or the "University") has moved under Rule 56, Fed. R. Civ. P., to dismiss the complaint of plaintiff pro se William B. Boise ("Boise").

Boise filed his complaint in this action on August 6, 2003, alleging age discrimination arising out of his not having been assigned to teach courses during 2003 and 2004, the revocation of his tenure, and the refusal of NYU to renew his apartment lease for a three-year term, which acts are also alleged to constitute retaliation from his earlier age discrimination action against NYU.

Boise's first suit was dismissed by this Court on October 21, 2003, and the Second Circuit affirmed the dismissal on January 28, 2005. This first suit against NYU was an age discrimination suit based on an earlier time-frame not at issue in this case.

On April 21, 2003, Boise filed a charge with the U.S. Equal Employment Opportunity Commission ("EEOC"), alleging discrimination on the basis of age and retaliation. On July 31, 2003, the EEOC informed Boise that it was dismissing his claim, and it issued a Notice of Right to Sue. Boise's amended and supplemental complaint, prepared by his then counsel, alleging age discrimination and retaliation under the Age Discrimination in Employment Act (the "ADEA"), 29 U.S.C. § 621, *et seq.*, is dated January 26, 2004. This motion was marked submitted on July 6, 2005.

. . .

Boise was formerly a Professor of Public Administration in the Robert F. Wagner Graduate School of Public Service ("Wagner" or the "School") at NYU, a private university.

Ellen Schall assumed the position of Dean of Wagner in November 2002. In April 2003, due to Boise's history of aberrant grading practices, his harassment of faculty and staff members, and other instances of bizarre behavior, Dean Schall offered him an opportunity to retire, which would have enabled him to continue to live in NYU-owned housing. Boise did not accept Dean Schall's offer. Based on the recommendation of the Wagner Faculty Personnel Committee and with the required approval of the President of the University, Dean Schall instituted proceedings in December 2003 to revoke Boise's tenure at NYU. Boise was given notice of the proceedings in January 2004.

Boise retained counsel and was afforded a hearing over five days between March and June 2004, before a panel of five faculty members comprising the hearing panel of the Faculty Tenure Committee. In accordance with the University's Rules Regulating Proceedings to Terminate for Cause the Service of a Tenured Member of the Teaching Staff of the Faculty Handbook, the panel consisted of faculty representatives from different schools and colleges at the University, including one from Boise's own school. The panel was presented with evidence by both parties including the testimony of NYU students and professors, videotape clips of Boise's behavior, as well as other exhibits. Boise was represented by counsel until he discharged his attorney prior to the final day of the hearings. On June 21, 2004, the panel issued its decision revoking Boise's tenure based on his grading practices, his harassment of members of the NYU community, which the panel noted created "an inappropriate and sometimes threatening workplace environment," and his violations of the conditions put in place to allow him to continue to use his office while the proceedings were conducted. The panel concluded that Boise's behavior amounted to "conduct of a character seriously prejudicial to . . . the welfare of the University." Finally, the panel noted the extraordinary nature of the action that they were taking, adding that while some of Boise's behaviors alone might not have warranted termination, the sum total of the evidence convinced them that revocation was appropriate.

On September 22, 2004, the Tenure Appeal Committee unanimously affirmed the hearing panel's decision and found that the sanction of dismissal for cause was appropriate.

Boise testified at deposition held on January 31, 2005 that he has no evidence that indicates any age-based or retaliatory motivation on the part of NYU but instead has based each of his charges on personal speculation.

For a claim of discrimination, the plaintiff has the initial burden of proving a prima facie case. *McDonnell Douglas Corp. v. Green*, 411 U.S. 792, 802 (1973). . . .

. . .

In order to meet the fourth requirement of a prima facie case of age discrimination under *McDonnell Douglas*, Boise must proffer admissible evidence "showing circumstances that would be sufficient to permit a rational finder of fact to infer a discriminatory motive." *Chambers v. TRM Copy Centers Corp.*, 43 F.3d 29, 38 (2d Cir. 1994). . . . No such evidence has been submitted. Boise acknowledged at his deposition that no derogatory statements about his age were ever made by any agents of the University to him or in his presence. There is no evidence that any of the University's decisions were based on a discriminatory motive.

At his deposition, Boise stated that his claims were based solely on his own speculation. Personal speculation is insufficient to raise an inference of discrimination. Boise's speculation is particularly insufficient in light of the fact that courts in this Circuit have recognized that "because tenure decisions 'involve a myriad of considerations and are made by numerous individuals and committees over a lengthy period of time, a plaintiff faces an uphill battle in her efforts to prove discrimination.'" *Peterson v. City Coll.*, 32 F. Supp. 2d 675, 684–85 (S.D.N.Y. 1999).

As circumstantial evidence, Boise notes that he is 76 years old. Six individuals over 70 have taught on the Wagner faculty during Dean Schall's deanship, and no evidence has been submitted that any of these faculty members have ever been subject to discriminatory remarks or conduct on the part of NYU. None of these individuals have leveled allegations of age discrimination against Dean Schall in a grievance, EEOC charge, or lawsuit. Where the plaintiff's only evidence in support of his claim is the fact of his age, courts have granted summary judgment in favor of the employer defendant. . . .

In addition, the University has established a legitimate, non-discriminatory reason for its actions. The ADEA states that:

It shall not be unlawful for an employer . . . to take any action otherwise prohibited under subsections (a), (b), (c) or (e) of this section . . . where the differentiation is based on reasonable factors other than age. . . .

29 U.S.C. § 623(f)(1). The ADEA states further that employers are not subject to discrimination claims where their actions constitute the disciplining or discharging of an employee for good cause. *See* 29 U.S.C. § 623(f)(3) ("It shall not be unlawful for an employer . . . to discharge or otherwise discipline an individual for good cause.").

The University's Faculty Handbook, providing the University with the right to revoke the tenure of a faculty member for cause, is consistent with the ADEA. NYU established good cause because Boise engaged in grading practices in violation of school policy, improperly tampered with faculty mailboxes, and harassed members of the University community. The decision of the panel of faculty representatives from NYU, as well as the appeal panel, concluded the termination of tenure was appropriate.

Universities are entitled to a degree of deference in the exercise of academic judgment. *Boise I*, 2003 U.S. Dist. LEXIS 18639, 2003 WL 22390792, at *6 (citing *Univ. of Mich. v. Ewing*, 474 U.S. 214, 225 (1985)). . . .

By the time Dean Schall assumed the deanship, the Wagner School had received numerous complaints from the students enrolled in a course taught by Boise. Boise had failed to publish a scholarly work for many years and had not given a grade other than "A" for completed course-work at any time since the fall of 1992.

Boise had also been observed tampering with and removing the mail of other faculty members on several occasions. No reason has been put forth not to defer to the University's considered judgment based on good cause and reasonable factors other than age.

Boise has failed to adduce any evidence to rebut these legitimate non-discriminatory reasons for his termination. The termination of tenure was undertaken consistent with the elaborate procedures identified in the NYU Faculty Handbook, he was given notice of the proceedings, a hearing, and the opportunity to present his own witnesses and to cross-examine the University's witnesses. Boise conceded the appropriateness of this procedure at his deposition when he stated that "they followed this procedure," and that he was given "internal due process." Consequently, Boise has failed to present any evidence of an improper motivation by any of the numerous actors at NYU who played a role in the decision to terminate his tenure.

. . .

Based on the foregoing, there is no genuine issue of material fact regarding Boise's discrimination claim, and NYU is entitled to summary judgment. . . .

A viable claim for retaliation requires that plaintiff show:

that he engaged in protected activity, that the employer was aware of this activity, that the employer took adverse action against the plaintiff, and that a causal connection exists between the protected activity and the adverse action, i.e., that a retaliatory motive played a part in the adverse employment action.

In order to survive this motion, a plaintiff in Boise's situation must present some evidence of a causal connection between his first age discrimination suit and the adverse employment actions complained of herein. . . .

Boise has not presented direct evidence of any retaliatory motivation on the part of the University. He admitted at deposition that he does not have any evidence that the filing of the present suit caused NYU to take action against him, instead testifying that the retaliation against him was only due to his first age discrimination lawsuit. Regarding his first suit, Boise stated at his deposition that his retaliation claim was based exclusively on his own speculation. He has offered no evidence that fellow faculty members were treated differently for engaging in similar conduct.

At best, Boise has presented only a temporal proximity as an indirect basis for the causal connection to support his retaliation claim. . . .

Here, NYU's purportedly retaliatory actions were undertaken between the spring of 2003 and September 2004, while Boise's first lawsuit was commenced on or about October 16, 2000. The nearly three-year time difference fails to establish a link between Boise's first suit and the allegedly retaliatory actions that took place sufficient to prove retaliation. A claim of causal connection is further undermined by the evidence of his unprofessional conduct leading up to his termination.

Boise has not established that there was a causal connection to any purported retaliatory conduct.

Even if Boise had stated a prima facie case of retaliation, which he has not, the University had legitimate, non-discriminatory reasons for its actions. . . .

NYU was legitimately concerned that Boise could no longer provide the level of scholarly rigor or safety that students expect from the Wagner School and that he could no longer set a good example for those students. Boise has offered no evidence that these reasons were a pretext for retaliation.

As there is no genuine issue of material fact regarding Boise's retaliation claim, NYU is entitled to summary judgment.

Questions and Comments on Terminating Tenure for Cause

In each of these cases, the courts defer to the factual findings of the college and university committees for several important issues. Should courts be this deferential to university committee findings?

B.   TERMINATING TENURE FOR FINANCIAL EXIGENCY

American Association of University Professors v. Bloomfield College

Superior Court of New Jersey, Chancery Division, 1974.
129 N.J.Super. 249, 322 A.2d 846, *aff'd* 136 N.J.Super. 442, 346 A.2d 615 (1975).

■ ANTELL, J.S.C.

This is an action for declaratory relief and specific performance with respect to the academic tenure of faculty members at Bloomfield College, a private institution of higher education licensed under the laws of the State of New Jersey. Plaintiff American Association of University Professors, Bloomfield College Chapter (hereinafter AAUP) ... has been certified and recognized by the National Labor Relations Board as the exclusive representative for collective bargaining on behalf of the college faculty. The individual plaintiffs include faculty members who seek clarification of their claimed tenured status and those whose service has been terminated and seek reinstatement to their former positions. Their periods of accumulated service range from 8 to 22 years. In addition to Bloomfield College, also named as defendants are Merle F. Allshouse, president of the college, and the individual members of the college board of trustees.

The legal basis of plaintiffs' claim of tenure is to be found in the *Faculty Handbook* of the college under the heading of "Bloomfield College Policies on Employment and Tenure" (hereinafter "Policies"). This document forms an essential part of the contractual terms governing the relationship between the college and the faculty. Under paragraph C thereof

> Bloomfield College recognizes that tenure is a means to certain ends, specifically: (1) freedom of teaching and research and of extra-mural activities, and (2) a sufficient degree of economic security to make the profession attractive to men and women of ability. Freedom and security, hence tenure, are indispensable to the success of an institution in fulfilling its obligations to its students and to society.

Following a probationary period of seven years, which has been completed by all the individual plaintiffs, subparagraph C(3) provides:

> * * * a teacher will have tenure and his services may be terminated only for adequate cause, except in case of retirement for age, or under extraordinary circumstances because of financial exigency of the institution.

Pertinent also is subparagraph C(6) of the "Policies" which provides:

Termination of continuous appointment because of financial exigency of the institution must be demonstrably *bona fide*. A situation which makes drastic retrenchment of this sort necessary precludes expansion of the staff at other points at the same time, except in extraordinary circumstances.

On June 21, 1973 the board of trustees adopted Resolution R–58 which in material part resolved:

> * * * [U]pon the recommendation of the Executive Committee, the President, the Dean of the College, and with the advice of the special Evaluation Committee for the reduction of faculty size due to financial exigency, and in accordance with the action of the Board on March 1 and the recommendation of the Academic Affairs Committee that thirteen faculty members be terminated in the reduction of faculty size due to financial exigency, the following persons be informed that they will be terminated as of June 30, 1974, and their duties for the 1973–74 academic year be defined to include no teaching, participation in College governance, or voting privileges. * * *
>
> That every faculty member be informed on or before June 30, 1973 that all 1973–74 contracts are one-year terminal contracts. The Board of Trustees through its Academic Affairs Committee will call together from among the remaining 54 members of the faculty an evaluation committee to determine what faculty members will remain at the College beyond June 30, 1974. This Committee to Define and Evaluate Personnel Needs will define personnel needs for the new academic program priorities which are set and the curricular revisions which are made, and will evaluate existing faculty members to determine their qualifications for meeting these needs. Their recommendations are to be made no later than November 30, 1973. All faculty members will be notified by December 15, 1973, as to their contract status for the 1974–75 academic year.
>
> . . .

During the period between June 21, 1973 and the commencement of the school year in September 1973 the College engaged the services of 12 new and untenured teachers to serve on its faculty. Defendants assert that these were hired to replace others who were lost to the school over a period of time as the result of "normal attrition," not those who were terminated under Resolution R–58.

Among the roster of plaintiffs are included (1) those faculty members who received termination notices and seek reinstatement to their former positions, and (2) those whose employment was continued, but subject to one-year terminal contracts. The latter ask declaratory judgment that their tenured status is unaffected by the action of the board of trustees in adopting Resolution R–58. As is clearly implied by the excerpted documents, defendants justify the resolution on the basis of "financial exigency." The issue projected is whether the action accomplished by Resolution R–58 in abrogating tenure and terminating the employment of tenured faculty members at Bloomfield College was "demonstrably bona fide" as having been taken "under extraordinary circumstances because of the financial exigency of the institution." Complementary thereto is the question as to whether the circumstances were further "extraordinary" so as to allow at the same time for the hiring of 12 new teachers.

[Bloomfield College is a small institution founded in 1807 by the Presbyterian Church. Its student body is "ethnically mixed" and "presents a low academic profile." The college predominately enrolls students from poor families. Three-fourths of the school's financial support is derived from tuition. For the 1973–74 year, enrollment was 867, down from 1,069 in 1972. Enrollment projections for the 1974–75 year ranged between 450 and 638. In response to these declining numbers, the college decided to reduce the number of faculty from 76 to 54 in order to maintain a 17 to 1 student-faculty ratio. This reduction was achieved through the "normal attrition" of 21 teachers and the discharging of the 13 teachers. In addition, 12 new teachers were hired in 1973.

The college considered retaining the discharged faculty instead of hiring new ones, but this option was rejected under the belief that the old faculty would not fit with proposed changes to the university programs. The objective of these new programs was to increase enrollment by offering career oriented students a liberal arts foundation, enhancing the distinctiveness of Bloomfield, and responding "very seriously" to the personal needs of students. The practical changes to be accomplished by the new directions of the college were never clearly stated, and the revisions appeared to be "minor in nature." Additionally, the decisions about the direction of the institution were not made until the Fall of 1973, after the 13 teachers had been discharged. Enrollment projections continued to forecast reductions in the student body.]

... [T]he college's ... budget for the 1972–73 school year was $3,652,000. For the year 1973–74 it is $3,397,000. The planned cash deficit for 1972 was $123,000 and for 1973 $191,000, with estimates that it will probably rise to $231,000 for the year. Between June 30, 1973 and March 31, 1974 it reached $145,000. By cash deficit is meant the amount by which the accounts payable and direct loans exceed available cash. In June 1973 its operating deficit, *i.e.*, the amount by which current liabilities exceed current assets, was $368,000. In 1973 the college endowment fund was $945,000, reflecting a 21% decline from the previous year, of which 17.19% occurred between January 1 and March 31, 1973. Cash flow problems intensified around June 1973, with accounts payable accumulating to the point where some went back to February 1973, and were compounded by financing difficulties. Interest on loans rose from 8% to 11%, higher borrowing costs resulted from the college's loss of status as a prime lending risk some years ago, and the declining value of the endowment portfolio further restricted borrowing capacity. As the result of conferences—which were, coincidentally, carried on during the hearings and of which the court was kept aware—its bank will now determine its lending status on a week-to-week basis and will advance no funds other than those necessary to meet payrolls. Under these circumstances a freeze has been placed upon all expenses other than payroll.

It is recognized by the administration that existing mortgages could be recast in order to ease the cash situation, but this decision has been deferred for the reason that the ultimate costs would eventually increase the financial burden. The prospect of rising fixed costs, the built-in limitation on tuitions resulting from the economic character of the student body, and reductions of federal aid with no corresponding increases in state aid programs are additional negative factors. Lack of available scholarship aid is another deterrent to the college's financial reanimation. At present it can only put 4% of its budget into scholarships, a figure which should be as high as 15% to 17%. Help is needed from federal or other outside sources, and without such assistance the school is burdened by a "tuition-subsidy gap." It is believed that enrollment and tuition income will continue to decline for the following three reasons: (1) the pool from which the college has historically drawn in terms of age and economic background is itself being diminished, a widespread phenomenon; (2) inability to develop a sufficiently attractive academic program, and (3) costs. In addition, it is believed that the present location of the college in Essex County is not conducive to further growth for the reason that the area is already overburdened with educational facilities in terms of existing need.

The remaining significant asset of the college, in addition to its tuition income, the college property and its endowment fund, is the Knoll Golf Club. The Knoll is a property of 322 acres, having two golf courses, two club houses, a swimming pool and a few residences. It was purchased by the college around the end of 1966 or early 1967 with the intention of using it for the establishment of an educational plant. The purchase price was $3,325,000 and was paid for by $900,000 cash, a bank loan of $300,000 and a mortgage of $2,125,000. The $900,000 was provided as a gift to the college by the Presbyterian Church out of monies raised as part of its Fifty Million Dollar Fund, a fund-raising project conducted by the church. These monies are dedicated to purposes of educational capital development and cannot be used for any other purpose.

Conservative estimates as to the market value of The Knoll in its present condition lie between $5,000,000 and $7,000,000. The net yield to the college out of a $5,000,000 sale, after taxes and the liquidation of secured debts, would be around $1,536,000. At $7,000,000 the sale would yield $2,366,000. In addition, there would also be realized some $795,000 owing to the college's current operating fund as well as approximately $727,000, being the present value of the gift from the Fifty Million Dollar Fund, subject, of course, to the terms and restrictions of that benefaction.

Although the college does not carry The Knoll as a liability, the income received therefrom does not exceed what is necessary to meet carrying charges. It is required, however, to make substantial cash advances during the year to sustain the operation, and these, of course, are additional burdens upon its already strained cash position. At year's end 1972 and 1973 these advances totaled $263,000 and $269,000, respectively.

The salient economic features of this property in its present posture, therefore, are that it is altogether lacking in income-producing characteristics, that it compels some degree of cash diversion from the operating needs of the college, and that its sale would release sufficient cash to meet the college's immediate and reasonably foreseeable financial requirements.

Present plans for the future of the Knoll are uncertain. The one being most seriously entertained is the installation of a large development which would occupy 202.5 acres of land. Site plans and proposals show an 84–month building plan projecting 61 units of low-density housing, 240 units of luxury housing, 2 medium-rise buildings having 340 units, as well as medium-density townhouses and condominiums. Negotiations preliminary to necessary zoning applications are taking place, but even assuming zoning approval is obtained (a prospect which is by no means assured), a lead time of at least two years must precede actual construction. Needless to say, the successful completion of such a program would greatly enhance the value of The Knoll to the college as a sustaining asset, but it is obvious that retention of the property for long-term appreciation necessarily requires that the college forego the benefit of the improved cash position which would be realized from a near term sale.

Without question, the economic health of the college is poor. A more definitive diagnosis is that the problem is chiefly one of liquidity, a difficulty with which the college has been coping for many years. Although a recent audit shows $56,000 in cash as against accounts payable of $301,000, previous years' figures show that in 1968 there was only $808 against $985,000 in accounts payable, in 1971 $6,000 available against $1,247,000 in accounts payable, in 1972 $6,000 available as against $777,000, and as of June 30, 1973 $2,302 available as against $1,018,000. The college's dilemma is real, but not unique. Although financially beleaguered, as Mr. Ritterskamp, who testified on behalf of the college as an expert in the financing of higher education, said, "all private education is in financial trouble today."

Notwithstanding the problem of cash flow, Bloomfield College is a very substantial educational institution with a net worth of $6,600,000, reflecting assets of $12,600,000 and liabilities of $6,000,000, based upon book values which show The Knoll as an asset worth only $3,370,000. The college is by no means insolvent, even though it is difficult for it to meet obligations as they mature. Although its preference is to exploit The Knoll's long-term possibilities, its choices are by no means restricted to this course of action. The option of selling the property now is perhaps more realistic as a survival measure since it would supply immediate liquidity. Near-term infusion of needed cash could start an economic recovery leading the college at some future time to a firmer financial base from which to move into more speculative, more rewarding ventures of the kind now under consideration. While the program of development being investigated might eventually provide vast financial resources, they would not begin to benefit the college for many years during which it would presumably continue its penurious standards to the detriment of its standing as an educational institution.

Regardless, however, of what the future may offer, the sale of The Knoll as an available alternative to the abrogation of tenure is a viable one and fairly to be considered on the meritorious issues.

. . .

As recited in the Bloomfield College "Policies" and in the 1940 "Statement of Principles" "Tenure is a means to certain ends; specifically: (1) Freedom of teaching and research and of extra mural activities, and (2) A sufficient degree of economic security to make the profession attractive to men and women of ability." Practice undoubtedly varies from one institution to another, but under the "Statement of Principles" and the "Policies," tenure does not "automatically" arise. It is conferred after the faculty member has passed through a probationary period during which his qualifications are examined by his peers and the administration. Thus, it is only after a demonstration of professional competence that the faculty member arrives at a status where he will be free of outside pressures and influences that might interfere with the conduct of his research, his interpretations and his investigations, or lead him to compromise the search for truth in his discipline and in transmitting it to his students. Although academic tenure does not constitute a guarantee of life employment, *i.e.,* tenured teachers may be released for "cause" or for reasons of the kind here involved, it denotes clearly defined limitations upon the institution's power to terminate the teacher's services.

. . .

[The] adoption [of tenure] is not merely a reflection of solicitude for the staffs of academic institutions, but of concern for the general welfare by providing for the benefits of uninhibited scholarship and its free dissemination. The security provided therefor by the consensus of learned authority should not be indifferently regarded. It should be vigilantly protected by a court of equity except where, under agreed standards stringent to the point suggested by phrases such as "financial exigency," "drastic retrenchment," "extraordinary circumstances" and "demonstrably bona fide," the survival of the college is imperiled, and then only where the good faith of the administration in seeking the severance of tenured personnel has been clearly demonstrated as a measure reasonably calculated to preserve its existence as an academic institution. It is not a sufficient justification only that the college acted on the belief that the measure would in some degree advance the financial fortunes of the institution . . . .

A resolution of this controversy is not referable merely to the criterion of "financial exigency." . . . [T]he term is highly relative and must be applied within a given context. Its applicable register of meaning is to be found somewhere between the understanding offered by the chairman of the college's board of trustees as "an urgent financial situation about which something had to be done in order to stay in business," and that propounded by the Princeton professor of economics who advocated that financial exigency exists "when, taking into account all assets, potential assets, sources of funding, income and all alternative courses of action, the continued viability of the institution becomes impossible without abrogating tenure."

Conceding that the college is under financial stress, and that "something had to be done," it does not follow that the college's freedom of response extends to the unilateral revocation of a contractually protected employment status and the discharge of tenured teachers as a matter of unbridled discretion. Similarly, although it may be appropriate to inspect the available resources and alternatives open to the college, this does not imply authority on the part of the court to substitute its judgment for that of the trustees, to weigh the wisdom of their action, to modify wayward or imprudent judgments in their formulation of educational or financial policy, or to decide whether the survival of the institution remains "possible" by the choice of other courses of action. The trustees, after all, have the best insight into the college's problems and will have the continuing duty of determining and providing for its future priorities. Their considered judgment in matters of policy is not lightly to be displaced. Interests must be balanced, and while the court must refrain from interfering with the policy-making and administrative processes of the college, still, it is called upon to protect important contractual rights against excesses in the mobilization of administrative and policy-making powers.

. . .

In our search for the controlling standard we are struck by the great plasticity of the raw material presented. The very concept of "exigency" changes before our eyes. Its meaning varies with the light of surrounding circumstances. . . . In this sense, the only definition of exigency which suits our needs is that offered by Webster as "such need or necessity as belongs to the occasion." *Webster's Third New International Dictionary of the English Language* (1969).

That the parties intended that this evaluation not be left to the college free of restraint is shown by their choice of preconditions (1) that the Board's action be demonstrably bona fide, (2) extraordinary circumstances, (3) that staff expansions in other areas not be undertaken except in "extraordinary circumstances."

. . .

The test best suited to effectuate the intent of the parties on judicial review of the college's action, therefore, is whether the action taken followed from the board's demonstrably bona fide belief, under honestly formulated standards, in the existence of a financial exigency and extraordinary attendant circumstances, and in the necessity for terminating tenured faculty members as a means of relieving the exigent condition. Interrelated therewith is the question of whether sufficient credible evidence of "exigency" and "extraordinary circumstances" exists as to provide a basis for the conclusions reached in the exercise of a reasonable and prudent judgment.

Except for policy differences touching upon the presumption of correctness and burden of proof, the test proposed is materially comparable to that used on judicial review of actions by governmental administrative agencies and in cases involving the discharge of tenured teachers for cause. . . .

The court concludes that the actions of Bloomfield College with respect to the tenured status of its faculty members in terminating the services of some and placing others on one-year employment contracts under the circumstances presented overflowed the limits of its authority as defined by its own Policies, and therefore fail to constitute a legally valid interruption in the individual plaintiffs' continuity of service. Whatever other motivations defendants might have had, they have failed to demonstrate by a preponderance of the evidence that their purported action was in good faith related to a condition of financial exigency within the institution. These conclusions are compelled by the following enumerated considerations:

(1) Although some financial relief might have been realized by discontinuing the services of the 13 faculty members, it has not been suggested how the college could possibly have been similarly benefited by placing the entire remaining faculty, including tenured personnel, on one-year terminal contracts. This startling action could have produced no immediate financial benefit, could not have been inspired by financial exigency, and can only be interpreted as a calculated repudiation of a contractual duty without any semblance of legal justification. It was a gratuitous challenge to the principle of academic tenure. Its clear implication of ulterior design and lack of sensitivity to the question of moral correctness reflect adversely upon the

claimed bona fides of discharging the 13 faculty members for the same given reason.

(2) The hiring of 12 new faculty members between June 21 and September 30, 1973 (the period during which the action complained of took place) has not been justified by a showing of "extraordinary circumstances" as required by sub-paragraph C(6) of the Bloomfield College "Policies." The record is lacking, in fact, any evidence from which it can be determined what the financial consequences of these hirings were, whether they resulted in a savings to the college, and if so in what amount. The explanation that the newcomers were brought in to meet the demands of a modified curriculum is totally unacceptable. Although the testimony is richly festooned with references to "teaching-learning contracts," "interdisciplinary programs," "steady state," "new directions," and "career tracks," the phrases lack content of any value in understanding what the new program was all about. It was only topically delineated and no explanation was offered as to why the tenured faculty members could not meet its requirements. Further, the court is entirely unclear as to the dynamics by which the new directions program was expected to reverse the unfavorable enrollment prognosis. This is notable in view of the fact that the success which defendants claim was anticipated never, in fact, materialized. In any case, the new program was not inaugurated until the fall of 1973, some months after the adoption of Resolution R–58 and after the institution of this suit.

. . .

(3) The financial problem is one of liquidity, which, as the evidence demonstrates, has plagued the college for many years. The board chairman himself testified that he cannot "remember when financing was ever easy." Unless we are prepared to say that financial exigency is chronic at Bloomfield College, it is difficult to say how, by any reasonable definition, the circumstances can now be pronounced exigent.

Recognizing the right of the board of trustees to make its own business judgments as to how to improve cash flow, still, the yield from a sale of The Knoll has been conservatively estimated at between 1 1/2 and 4 million dollars. Apart from the discontinuation of cash advances to the golf club, the immediate benefits which the college would realize from such a cash infusion has been described. What effect this would have on the school's long-term future is, of course, uncertain. However, it clearly enhances the probability that it will be able to continue as a college for the foreseeable future. This much certainly cannot be said of the expansive development program now being explored. By so commenting, we do not suggest that one or the other of the courses is to be preferred, but that the college's claim of financial exigency can be validated only in its role as an educational institution, not as the aspiring proprietor of high-rise apartments, condominiums and luxury dwellings. Its desire to retain this investment for long-term appreciation is not a factor which the court may weigh in passing upon the existence of a financial exigency. Its immediate duty is to maintain its educational programs and refrain from acts of faithlessness toward the faculty members by whom it has been competently served. In this light the facts surrounding its economic existence cannot reasonably support its claim of demonstrably bona fide financial exigency.

(4) Internal memoranda transmitted within the college itself during the critical period of time are themselves revealing as to the real objectives to be achieved by the adoption of Resolution R–58. For example, in his memorandum to the faculty dated April 12, 1973 President Allshouse advised the faculty of his opposition to the "faculty substitute plan." Reason 3, upon which he places reliance, reads:

> The document explicitly placed adherence to the 1940 and 1958 AAUP Statements on academic freedom, tenure, and due process as the primary criterion for staff reductions rather than academic planning for the *long term viability of the College*. [Emphasis supplied]

It would appear that Dr. Allshouse's real concern is more fully addressed to balancing problems of long-term concern against basic contractual obligations, whereas the position relied on herein is a claim of financial exigency, an immediate, compelling crisis. His hostility to the basic concept of tenure is further elaborated in his report to the board of trustees dated June 21, 1973 wherein, under paragraph B, he analyzes at great length the faculty's "substitute plan" and in so doing engages almost entirely in partisan polemics having to do with the *pros* and *cons* of tenure unrelated to any question of financial crisis.

(5) Revealing also is the first paragraph in the report to the board of trustees from the college's Commission to Review Tenure and Retirement Policy dated June 21, 1973 in which it clearly focuses upon the issue of the "tenure system," not with a bona fide attempt to reconcile the fact of tenure with the reality of a true financial exigency:

> For the last six months, the Commission to Review Tenure and Retirement Policy has reviewed the present practices of the College regarding tenure, the debate over tenure throughout the country, and alternatives to a traditional tenure system. While it has studied the larger issues concerning tenure which are being faced by institutions across the country, it has attempted to focus on the needs of Bloomfield College as it faces the development of a new and distinctive mission to meet the challenge of the 1970's and 80's. As a result of our deliberations, we have concluded that the present tenure system be abolished and that a new term-contract system be established. At the October meeting of the Board, the Commission will present a series of proposals for a contract system, a plan for implementation (including timetables) and a series of revisions to the *Bloomfield College Policies on Employment and Tenure*.

(6) Further confirming the impression that the defendants' primary objective was the abolition of tenure at Bloomfield College, not the alleviation of financial stringency, is their careful eschewal of other obvious remedial measures such as across-the-board salary reductions for all faculty members and reduction of faculty size by nonrenewal of contracts with teachers on probationary status, rather than termination of those who had earned tenured status by years of competent service.

The conclusions herein reached are not in their nature unique. Courts have not hesitated to invalidate the dismissal of tenured personnel where the reasons of economy given for their dismissal were shown to have been used as a subterfuge.

Defendants' resistance to the remedy of specific performance rests upon that line of authority denying such relief in the case of contracts for personal services on the ground that equity will not compel the continuation of an obnoxious personal relationship. *See Sarokhan v. Fair Lawn Memorial Hospital*, 83 *N.J. Super.* 127, 133 (App. Div. 1964); 11 *Williston, Contracts* (3 ed. 1968), § 1450; 5A *Corbin, Contracts* § 1204 (1964); 42 *Am. Jur.* 2d, *Injunctions*, §§ 101, 102. The rationale of these authorities within the context of a teaching contract case is well expressed in *Greene v. Howard University*, 271 *F. Supp.* 609 (D.C.D.C. 1967), rem. on other grounds 134 *U.S. App. D.C.* 81, 412 *F.* 2d 1128 (1969). After stating that such a contract may not be enforced by specific performance, the court observed:

> It would be intolerable for the courts to interject themselves and to require an educational institution to hire or to maintain on its staff a professor or instructor whom it deemed undesirable and did not wish to employ. For the courts to impose such a requirement would be an interference with the operation of institutions of higher learning contrary to established principles of law and to the best tradition of education. [271 F. Supp. at 615]

But the conditions upon which this reasoning rests do not prevail in the case presented. The rule is not hard and fast, and, as Williston observes, "appealing factual situations may occasionally induce a court to enforce a personal service contract specifically, particularly in the absence of any personal relationship between the parties." 11 *Williston, Contracts*, § 1424 at 786–787. This is not a case in which termination was based on any dissatisfaction with the services rendered, but ostensibly only by reason of financial exigency. It was an action taken with deep regret and with recognition of the "invaluable contribution to the College" made by the terminated faculty members.

The dangers envisioned by *Greene v. Howard University, supra*, are conspicuously absent, and no reason appears as to why reinstatement cannot be ordered here as has been done so often in the numerous cases involving public educational institutions....

. . .

For the reasons given it is concluded that the individual plaintiffs who were terminated from their positions as faculty members of Bloomfield College are entitled to reinstatement under the terms and conditions of the "Bloomfield College Policies on Employment and Tenure." By way of declaratory relief it will further be adjudged that all plaintiffs serving as tenured faculty members of Bloomfield College prior to June 21, 1973 are now, and shall continue, on tenured status within the terms of the "Bloomfield College Policies on Employment and Tenure," and that the provisions of Resolution R–58 to the contrary, adopted on June 21, 1973 by the Bloomfield College Board of Trustees, as well as all administrative actions taken thereunder by defendants, are in all respects inefficacious.

Questions and Comments on *Bloomfield College*

The court notes that the terms "financial exigency" and "extraordinary circumstances" are not self-defining. What standard does the court apply? How would you define these terms?

The court also recognizes the problems with specific performance as a remedy for violations of the employment relationship. Is there any other adequate remedy when a professor has been terminated in violation of the principles of tenure? Given the problems colleges and universities have with long term planning, should they be allowed to terminate tenure based on a *projected* financial exigency?

Board of Trustees for Baltimore County–Essex Community College v. Adams

Maryland Court of Special Appeals, 1997.
117 Md.App. 662, 701 A.2d 1113.

■ Opinion by CATHELL, J.

. . . Appellees were tenured professors at Essex Community College. In 1991, the governing bodies, the State and County, that funded most of the operations of the college drastically reduced appropriations to the school. The college, believing that personnel and staff cutbacks were inevitable, began to study the programs and courses it offered to determine which, if any, programs were to be scaled back or terminated. A process was put in place by the "Division Chairs," presumably the heads of the various departments at the college, called the Four Flags for Andy[1] program. Under it, each department and program was evaluated in terms of enrollment, section size, and other considerations. A committee was then formed composed of the Dean of Instruction, a representative of the faculty senate, a representative of the Academic Council, and a representative "from the counseling area." The committee met over a period of several months considering all of the material on the budgetary crisis, enrollment, etc. This committee then made certain recommendations on how the financial difficulties should be addressed. It recommended termination of seven programs. The Board of Trustees, appellant, ultimately approved the program terminations in 1993. One of the programs terminated was the "Office Technology" program, in which appellees taught.

Appellees, in March of 1993, were apprised by a dean of the college that they would be terminated on July 1, 1994. Appellees submitted additional information to the dean, but the decision remained unchanged. Appellees then initiated the grievance process of the college. Ultimately, the grievance process ended with a hearing before the Board of Trustees—the final step in the grievance process. The Board denied the grievance. As a result of the termination of the program, appellees were ultimately terminated from their faculty positions in 1994. At no time were any allegations made that appellees were being terminated for behavioral or qualification problems.

. . .

The provisions of the contract executed in the early 1970s, that was apparently a standard form contract of that time, upon which appellant's complaint was based, provided in relevant part:

---

1.   Andy was the first name of the president of the college. The "flags" terminology was merely a way of trying to determine which programs were more appropriate for termination, if necessary. Each flag identified a negative attribute of a program. The higher the number of flags, the less justifiable, in terms of need, the program. Any program with four or more flags, in terms of need, enrollment, duplication, etc., was a candidate for termination.

After said faculty member has been placed on continuous tenure, his [her] appointment may not be terminated except as provided herein.

. . .

... The Board of Trustees may dismiss said faculty member ... for immorality, dishonesty, misconduct in office, incompetency, insubordination, or willful neglect of duty....

The contract contained no specific provisions relating to procedures that would apply if the college was forced to terminate programs for reasons not related to the personal performance or conduct of a professor. It contained no provisions for priorities between tenured professors, reassignments, relocations, retraining or the like. It is agreed by all parties that appellees' performance and conduct was not in question.

. . .

There is one primary underlying question for this Court to resolve:

May tenured faculty with no behavioral or qualification problems be terminated when the course or program she or he teaches is terminated due to financial difficulties?

The parties have not directed us to any Maryland cases directly on point. We have found only one, *County Bd. of Educ. v. Cearfoss*, 165 Md. 178, 166 A. 732 (1933), that suggests, in well reasoned dicta, that the answer is yes.... Our review of the authorities elsewhere indicates that the great weight of authority supports a holding that tenured professors may be terminated for reasons unrelated to them personally—such as discontinuance of courses, school consolidations, and, as in the case sub judice, financial shortfalls....

. . .

In the present case ... specific statutory authority was conferred ... permitting the Governor, under certain circumstances, to reduce the budget of the community college at issue here. In the case sub judice, no one challenges the validity of that statute or the reductions made under it. The challenge is directed only to the result of the reduction, the termination of tenured faculty....

. . .

... Dr. Joseph Testa, the Associate Dean of Instruction, was permitted to testify at trial:

Q. Did there come a time when the college began to experience financial difficulties in the budget area?

. . .

A. The college was experiencing financial difficulties at that time.

. . .

A. The State reduced the college's budget from the State by 25 percent. It amounted to several million dollars.... Much has been made about the fact that the college was not in a situation of financial exigency. That is correct. Technically, it was not. Financial exigency would have meant that there was simply not enough money to pay all of the college's bills. We were not in that situation. What we were in was a serious financial crisis in which there had been—there was no money for equipment. There was declining money for supplies. We were facing enrollment growths and yet a dramatic decrease in income.

. . .

Dr. Snope then testified:

. . .

[Appellant's attorney]: Dr. Snope, why wasn't the Board ever asked to declare a financial exigency?

A.   A financial exigency is a last resort. It is extreme action that involves laying off staff when there appears to be absolutely no other way to pay the bills. A state of financial exigency was not asked for because it was possible for us to make ends meet through all of the other steps that we implemented in response to very severe financial difficulties which exist to this day.

. . .

There was virtually no evidence contradicting the testimony of Dean Testa and Dr. Snope at trial, or the documents generated by the procedures before the college's governance entities that were later admitted in evidence. . . .

. . .

[A] relevant case . . . albeit a federal case, concerned a private Maryland college. In *Krotkoff v. Goucher College*, 585 F.2d 675 (4th Cir. 1978), a college professor brought suit against the college alleging that it had violated her tenure when it discharged her. The college contended that it terminated her employment as a "part of a general retrenchment prompted by severe financial problems." The college notified Krotkoff in June of 1975 that it would not renew her contract in June of 1976 "because of financial problems." The serious "financial situation [caused by substantial operating deficits,] convinced the trustees that action was needed to insure the institution's future."

As a part of its retrenchment, the college did not renew the contracts of [eleven] untenured and four tenured faculty members including Krotkoff. These professors were selected largely on the bases of the dean's study of enrollment projections and necessary changes in the curriculum. In addition, the faculty elected a committee to review curricular changes suggested by the administration. Among the administration's proposals were elimination of the classics department and the German section . . . which were staffed exclusively by tenured professors.

Following a study of enrollment projections, it was determined that only one position would remain in the German section of the modern language department. Krotkoff, a German faculty member, was terminated, while the other professor in the German section was retained because she had experience with elementary language courses and because she was also qualified to teach French. A faculty grievance committee recommended Krotkoff's retention but did not suggest that the other professor be terminated. The president did not accept the committee's recommendation, and the trustees sustained the president's decision.

The court framed the issue as "whether as a matter of law Krotkoff's contract permitted termination of her tenure by discontinuing her teaching position because of financial exigency." The tenure bylaws of the college provided for "continued service unless good cause be shown for termination." The court noted that "financial exigency is not mentioned in the bylaws, and the college concedes that it is not considered to be a ground of dismissal for cause." In its discussion, the court noted that the national academic community's understanding of tenure acknowledges that a tenured professor may be terminated because of financial necessity—so long as the necessity is "bona fide." The court discussed that termination of tenured professors was appropriate under two circumstances—the first being for cause and the second included "financial exigency." It also commented on a witness's reliance on a 1940 Statement of Principles on Academic Freedom and Tenure and noted that the statement recognized that termination for financial exigency was permitted so long as the financial exigency was demonstrably bona fide. The court, referring to this statement, said:

> All of the secondary authorities seem to agree that it is the "most widely-accepted academic definition of tenure."

> The reported cases support the conclusion that tenure is not generally understood to preclude demonstrably bona fide dismissal for financial reasons.... Where the contracts did not mention this term, the courts construed tenure as implicitly granting colleges the right to make bona fide dismissals for financial reasons. No case indicates that tenure creates a right to exemption from dismissal for financial reasons....

> A concept of tenure that permits dismissal based on financial exigency is consistent with the primary purpose of tenure. Tenure's "real concern is with arbitrary or retaliatory dismissals based on an administrator's or a trustee's distaste for the content of a professor's teaching or research.... Dismissals based on financial exigency, unlike those for cause or disability, are impersonal; they are unrelated to the views of the dismissed teachers."

Id. at 679–80 (citations omitted).

The court then noted that Goucher College's bylaws and the other relevant documents did not define the rights of tenured professors during financial exigency and that the tenured teachers believed that tenure precluded their dismissal for financial reasons. The court then stated that, in assessing whether the financial exigency was bona fide, it was improper for a fact finder, i.e., a trial court, to consider a college's land holdings or endowment, in that choices as to retention of land or usages of endowments were the proper business of the college and not the courts. It concluded: "The existence of financial exigency should be determined by the adequacy of a college's operating funds rather than its capital assets."

In respect to whether Krotkoff, or some other professor, should have been terminated, the court looked to Krotkoff's contract. It held that Krotkoff was entitled, under her contract, to insist that Goucher "use reasonable standards in selecting which faculty appointments to terminate, and ... that it take reasonable measures to afford her alternative employment." The court, nevertheless, ultimately held:

> The necessity for revising Goucher's curriculum was undisputed. A faculty committee accepted elimination of the classics department and reduction of the German section ... as reasonable responses to this need. The only substantial controversy was whether the college should have retained Krotkoff or Ehrlich, both tenured professors. . . .
>
> ... In the absence of an explicit contractual undertaking, the evidence discloses that tenure does not entitle a professor to training for appointment in another discipline.

Id. at 682 (emphasis added).

. . .

We hold that a tenured professor may be terminated when the reasons are not personal to the teacher, but are created by 1) the necessary or preferred discontinuance of courses or programs; 2) declining enrollment that alleviates the need for programs; or 3) when financial problems result in the necessity for termination of programs, positions, or courses. As long as the process of selecting the person(s) to be terminated complies with any institutional requirements and is otherwise fair and reasonable, such terminations are matters of policy and generally not the business of the judiciary. In the case sub judice, the evidence was uncontradicted that the college was in a condition of serious financial difficulty, as reflected by drastic reductions in its budget caused by State and county cutbacks. To the extent the trial judge found otherwise, his factual conclusions, as we have said, were clearly erroneous.

. . .

The trial judge apparently equated the formal declaration of a "financial exigency" with a necessary step in the existence of a financial crisis sufficient to justify the termination of any tenured faculty. As we perceive the law, that is incorrect. Terminations of tenured faculty were manifestly justified. Which professors or programs were to be terminated were policy decisions for the administrative body of the school.

We note, however, that the trial court was concerned, as are we, with the nature of the grievance process afforded appellees.

Because the trial court based its decision on what it perceived to be a complete lack of financial problems, i.e. no financial exigency, it found no reason for the terminations. That was wrong. The trial court, however, because of those findings, did not adequately consider or address whether, if the terminations were justified, the process of selection of tenured members for termination was done in compliance with the pertinent policies of the institution. That necessitates that these matters now be considered by the trial court.

. . .

We note, in closing, that if tenured teachers could force schools to maintain programs, courses, and positions, the teachers would, themselves, be the policymakers—rather than the administrative bodies of the colleges. This is especially pertinent when a college is a publicly supported institution, such as appellant. The institution cannot compel the legislative and executive branches of government to fund programs. In fact, all the legislative and executive branches would have to do would be to legislate the institution out of existence. Moreover, the courts are also ill situated, under the circumstances here present, to compel funding of institutions that are mandated into existence by legislative policy and where that branch of government has the power to abolish the entity it has created if it has the will.

Questions and Comments on *Adams*

Note the differences in approach between this case and *Bloomfield College*. The *Adams* court holds that the terminations were justified even though the college admitted there was no financial exigency. Does this finding comport with your conception of tenure? Additionally, the *Adams* court cites *Krotkoff v. Goucher* for the assertion that courts should not look at a college or university's capital holdings when determining whether a financial exigency exists, in contrast to the reasoning in *Bloomfield College*. Which approach makes better economic sense?

The *Adams* court also argues that teachers should not be the policymakers at the college. Is this correct? Does it depend on what kind of policy? Should faculty have a say in decisions to close programs? A veto?

C. PROCEDURAL PROTECTION

Perry v. Sindermann

Supreme Court of the United States, 1972.
408 U.S. 593, 92 S.Ct. 2694, 33 L.Ed.2d 570.

■ MR. JUSTICE STEWART delivered the opinion of the Court.

From 1959 to 1969 the respondent, Robert Sindermann, was a teacher in the state college system of the State of Texas. After teaching for two years at the University of Texas and for four years at San Antonio Junior College, he became a professor of Government and Social Science at Odessa Junior College in 1965. He was employed at the college for four successive years, under a series of one-year contracts. He was successful enough to be appointed, for a time, the cochairman of his department.

During the 1968–1969 academic year, however, controversy arose between the respondent and the college administration. The respondent was elected president of the Texas Junior College Teachers Association. In this capacity, he left his teaching duties on several occasions to testify before committees of the Texas Legislature, and he became involved in public disagreements with the policies of the college's Board of Regents. In particular, he aligned himself with a group advocating the elevation of the college to four-year status—a change opposed by the Regents. And, on one occasion, a newspaper advertisement appeared over his name that was highly critical of the Regents.

Finally, in May 1969, the respondent's one-year employment contract terminated and the Board of Regents voted not to offer him a new contract for the next academic year. The Regents issued a press release setting forth allegations of the respondent's insubordination.[a] But they provided him no official statement of the reasons for the nonrenewal of his contract. And they allowed him no opportunity for a hearing to challenge the basis of the nonrenewal.

The respondent then brought this action in Federal District Court. He alleged primarily that the Regents' decision not to rehire him was based on his public criticism of the policies of the college administration and thus infringed his right to freedom of speech. He also alleged that their failure to provide him an opportunity for a hearing violated the Fourteenth Amendment's guarantee of procedural due process. The petitioners—members of the Board of Regents and the president of the college—denied that their decision was made in retaliation for the respondent's public criticism and argued that they had no obligation to provide a hearing. On the basis of these bare pleadings and three brief affidavits filed by the respondent, the District Court granted summary judgment for the petitioners. . . .

The Court of Appeals reversed the judgment of the District Court. . . .

The first question presented is whether the respondent's lack of a contractual or tenure right to re-employment, taken alone, defeats his claim that the nonrenewal of his contract violated the First and Fourteenth Amendments. We hold that it does not.

For at least a quarter-century, this Court has made clear that even though a person has no "right" to a valuable governmental benefit and even though the government may deny him the benefit for any number of reasons, there are some reasons upon which the government may not rely. It may not deny a benefit to a person on a basis that infringes his constitutionally protected interests—especially, his interest in freedom of speech. For if the government could deny a benefit to a person because of his constitutionally protected speech or associations, his exercise of those freedoms would in effect be penalized and inhibited. This would allow the government to "produce a result which [it] could not command directly." *Speiser v. Randall*, 357 U.S. 513, 526. Such interference with constitutional rights is impermissible.

. . .

Thus, the respondent's lack of a contractual or tenure "right" to re-employment for the 1969–1970 academic year is immaterial to his free speech claim. Indeed, twice before, this Court has specifically held that the nonrenewal of a nontenured public school teacher's one-year contract may not be predicated on his exercise of First and Fourteenth Amendment rights. *Shelton v. Tucker*, [364 U.S. 479]; *Keyishian v. Board of Regents*, [385 U.S. 584]. We reaffirm those holdings here.

In this case, of course, the respondent has yet to show that the decision not to renew his contract was, in fact, made in retaliation for his exercise of the constitutional right of free speech. The District Court foreclosed any opportunity to make this showing when it granted summary judgment. Hence, we cannot now hold that the Board of Regents' action was invalid.

a. The press release stated, for example, that the respondent had defied his superiors by attending legislative committee meetings when college officials had specifically refused to permit him to leave his classes for that purpose.

But we agree with the Court of Appeals that there is a genuine dispute as to "whether the college refused to renew the teaching contract on an impermissible basis—as a reprisal for the exercise of constitutionally protected rights." The respondent has alleged that his nonretention was based on his testimony before legislative committees and his other public statements critical of the Regents' policies. And he has alleged that this public criticism was within the First and Fourteenth Amendments' protection of freedom of speech. Plainly, these allegations present a bona fide constitutional claim. For this Court has held that a teacher's public criticism of his superiors on matters of public concern may be constitutionally protected and may, therefore, be an impermissible basis for termination of his employment. *Pickering v. Board of Education*, [391 U.S. 563].

For this reason we hold that the grant of summary judgment against the respondent, without full exploration of this issue, was improper.

The respondent's lack of formal contractual or tenure security in continued employment at Odessa Junior College, though irrelevant to his free speech claim, is highly relevant to his procedural due process claim. But it may not be entirely dispositive.

We have held today in *Board of Regents v. Roth* that the Constitution does not require opportunity for a hearing before the nonrenewal of a nontenured teacher's contract, unless he can show that the decision not to rehire him somehow deprived him of an interest in "liberty" or that he had a "property" interest in continued employment, despite the lack of tenure or a formal contract. In *Roth* the teacher had not made a showing on either point to justify summary judgment in his favor.

Similarly, the respondent here has yet to show that he has been deprived of an interest that could invoke procedural due process protection. As in *Roth*, the mere showing that he was not rehired in one particular job, without more, did not amount to a showing of a loss of liberty. Nor did it amount to a showing of a loss of property.

But the respondent's allegations—which we must construe most favorably to the respondent at this stage of the litigation—do raise a genuine issue as to his interest in continued employment at Odessa Junior College. He alleged that this interest, though not secured by a formal contractual tenure provision, was secured by a no less binding understanding fostered by the college administration. In particular, the respondent alleged that the college had a *de facto* tenure program, and that he had tenure under that program. He claimed that he and others legitimately relied upon an unusual provision that had been in the college's official Faculty Guide for many years:

> *Teacher Tenure*: Odessa College has no tenure system. The Administration of the College wishes the faculty member to feel that he has permanent tenure as long as his teaching services are satisfactory and as long as he displays a cooperative attitude toward his co-workers and his superiors, and as long as he is happy in his work.

Moreover, the respondent claimed legitimate reliance upon guidelines promulgated by the Coordinating Board of the Texas College and University System that provided that a person, like himself, who had been employed as a teacher in the state college and university system for seven years or more has some form of job tenure. Thus, the respondent offered to prove that a teacher with his long period of service at this particular State College had no less a "property" interest in continued employment than a formally tenured teacher at other colleges, and had no less a procedural due process right to a statement of reasons and a hearing before college officials upon their decision not to retain him.

We have made clear in *Roth* that "property" interests subject to procedural due process protection are not limited by a few rigid, technical forms. Rather, "property" denotes a broad range of interests that are secured by "existing rules or understandings." A person's interest in a benefit is a "property" interest for due process purposes if there are such rules or mutually explicit understandings that support his claim of entitlement to the benefit and that he may invoke at a hearing.

A written contract with an explicit tenure provision clearly is evidence of a formal understanding that supports a teacher's claim of entitlement to continued employment unless sufficient "cause" is shown. Yet absence of such an explicit contractual provision may not always foreclose the possibility that a teacher has a "property" interest in re-employment. For example, the law of contracts in most, if not all, jurisdictions long has employed a process by which agreements, though not formalized in writing, may be "implied." 3 A. Corbin on Contracts §§ 561–572A (1960). Explicit contractual provisions may be supplemented by other agreements implied from "the promisor's words and conduct in the light of the surrounding circumstances." And, "the meaning of [the promisor's] words and acts is found by relating them to the usage of the past."

A teacher, like the respondent, who has held his position for a number of years, might be able to show from the circumstances of this service—and from other relevant facts—that he has a legitimate claim of entitlement to job tenure. Just as this Court has found there to be a "common law of a particular industry or of a particular plant" that may supplement a collective-bargaining agreement, *Steelworkers v. Warrior & Gulf Co.*, 363 U.S. 574, 579 (1960), so there may be an unwritten "common law" in a particular university that certain employees shall have the equivalent of tenure. This is particularly likely in a college or university, like Odessa Junior College, that has no explicit tenure system even for senior members of its faculty, but that nonetheless may have created such a system in practice. *See* C. Byse & L. Joughin, Tenure in American Higher Education 17–28 (1959).

In this case, the respondent has alleged the existence of rules and understandings, promulgated and fostered by state officials, that may justify his legitimate claim of entitlement to continued employment absent "sufficient cause." We disagree with the Court of Appeals insofar as it held that a mere subjective "expectancy" is protected by procedural due process, but we agree that the respondent must be given an opportunity to prove the legitimacy of his claim of such entitlement in light of "the policies and practices of the institution." Proof of such a property interest would not, of course, entitle him to reinstatement. But such proof would obligate college officials to grant a hearing at his request, where he could be informed of the grounds for his nonretention and challenge their sufficiency.

Therefore, while we do not wholly agree with the opinion of the Court of Appeals, its judgment remanding this case to the District Court is affirmed.

Note on *Perry v. Sindermann*

Several months after the decision by the Supreme Court, and three years after the beginning of dispute, Odessa Junior College decided to settle with Sindermann rather than continue to litigate. They paid him $48,000. Sindermann has said that in the years following the trial, he found it almost impossible to find academic employment, "appl[ying] for jobs at 225 colleges and universities and receiv[ing] only one bid." David Hudson, *Robert Sindermann Speaks Out About Famous Supreme Court Case Bearing His Name,* http://www.freedomforum.org/templates/document.astp?documentD=14370 (July 2001).

Trimble v. West Virginia Board of Directors

Supreme Court of Appeals of West Virginia, 2001.
209 W.Va. 420, 549 S.E.2d 294.

■ DAVIS, J.

George Trimble, appellant/petitioner below (hereinafter referred to as "Mr. Trimble"), appeals from a final order of the Circuit Court of Kanawha County affirming the decision of the Board of Directors of the West Virginia State College System (hereinafter referred to as "the Board")[1] to dismiss Mr. Trimble from his position as a tenured, full-time assistant professor of English at the Southern West Virginia Community and Technical College, appellee/respondent below (hereinafter referred to as "the College"). Mr. Trimble was terminated for alleged insubordination. Here, Mr. Trimble contends that his termination violated his First Amendment rights to freedom of speech and assembly. Mr. Trimble also contends that he had a property interest in his employment and that because of his property interest, the College was required to utilize progressive disciplinary measures prior to considering termination of his employment. . . .

Mr. Trimble began his employment with the College as an Instructor in the Fall of 1978. He was awarded tenure and promoted to the position of assistant professor in 1984. During his employment with the College, Mr. Trimble taught Literature and English in the College's Humanities Division. Prior to 1996, Mr. Trimble engaged in no conduct that required disciplinary action against him. In fact, Mr. Trimble consistently received favorable evaluations throughout his employment with the College.

Problems began to occur in 1996. In January of 1996, the College faculty unanimously voted a vote of no confidence for the College President, Travis Kirkland. The no confidence vote was prompted by numerous changes Mr. Travis attempted to institute at the College. Additionally, in August 1996, Mr. Trimble was instrumental in organizing WVEA/Southern (hereinafter referred to as "WVEA"), a teacher's labor organization. Mr. Trimble became President of the organization, which a majority of the College's faculty eventually joined. In fact, WVEA was extremely critical of many policy initiatives proposed by the College.

---

1. The Board ceased to exist on July 1, 2000, pursuant to W. Va. Code §§ 18B–2–1(e) & 18B–3–1(e) (2000) (Supp. 2000). The Legislature replaced the Board with the West Virginia Higher Education Policy Commission. *See* W. Va. Code § 18B–1B–1, *et seq*. Additionally, on July 1, 2001, an Institutional Board of Governors for each higher education institution will come into existence. *See* W. Va. Code § 18B–2A–1, *et seq.*

One of the changes sought by President Kirkland was the implementation of an assessment plan known as Instructional Performance Systems Incorporated (hereinafter referred to as "IPSI"). IPSI was a computer software program used for writing course syllabi. It was designed to allow for measuring competency-based goals which could be later used to evaluate student achievement. The College faculty was first advised of the assessment plan in a memorandum issued in August 1996. A few months later, President Kirkland mandated the use of the IPSI software. President Kirkland's decision was met with faculty opposition.

The Humanities Division objected to using IPSI. The position taken by the Humanities Division was that IPSI was impractical and unworkable for their courses, although it might have relevancy for technical or vocational programs offered by the College. Therefore, Mr. Trimble opposed the use of IPSI on the grounds that it interfered with the principles of academic freedom. The position taken by Mr. Trimble was printed in a newsletter published by WVEA.

Several informational meetings were conducted by the College concerning the use of the IPSI software on the Williamson campus. Mr. Trimble failed to attend several of the meetings. The College sent a memo to Mr. Trimble advising him of institutional policy mandating advanced written notice of non-emergency reasons for not attending required College meetings. Mr. Trimble was further advised that "continued non-attendance and disregard for these required meetings will result in a letter of reprimand being placed in your personnel file with additional action as needed."

As a result of opposition to the IPSI software by members of the Humanities Division, President Kirkland ordered every faculty member of the Humanities Division to prepare an IPSI-generated syllabus for a specific course by a certain deadline. Subsequently, Mr. Trimble and two other members of the Humanities Division filed a grievance challenging the mandatory use of the IPSI software.

The College advised Mr. Trimble in a memo dated March 17, 1997, that his resistance to the College's efforts to require the faculty to draft IPSI syllabi was being viewed as a "flagrant and willful disregard for directions and/or inquiries of your employer" which constitutes "insubordination." Mr. Trimble responded with a memo disputing the characterization of his actions as "insubordination."

During a Humanities Division meeting in April, 1997, Mr. Trimble and another faculty member indicated that they refused to complete a syllabus using the IPSI format pending resolution of their grievance. On April 14, 1997, Mr. Trimble received a letter directing him to appear in a vacant office on the College's Logan Campus at 9:00 a.m. on Wednesday, April 16, 1997, to complete a draft IPSI syllabus. Mr. Trimble failed to appear at the Logan campus on April 16, 1997.

By letter dated May 12, 1997, President Kirkland advised Mr. Trimble of the College's intention to terminate his employment, effective May 30, 1997, for insubordination. Mr. Trimble was offered the opportunity to meet with President Kirkland to rebut the charges. He never requested a meeting.

Accordingly, by letter dated May 30, 1997, Mr. Trimble's employment with the College was terminated.[5]

Mr. Trimble filed a grievance challenging his termination. An Institutional Hearing Committee (hereinafter referred to as "IHC") conducted evidentiary hearings on September 2 and 3, 1997. On September 22, 1997, IHC issued a letter decision in favor of Mr. Trimble, concluding that there was no proof that he was insubordinate. However, President Kirkland subsequently made his own findings and upheld Mr. Trimble's termination. Mr. Trimble appealed President Kirkland's decision to the Board. A hearing examiner was appointed to conduct evidentiary hearings.

The hearing examiner issued a decision on November 18, 1998, recommending that the termination decision be upheld. The Board adopted the recommendation on January 26, 1999. Mr. Trimble then filed an appeal with the Circuit Court of Kanawha County. The circuit court affirmed the Board's decision on August 2, 2000. It is from the circuit court's ruling that Mr. Trimble now appeals. . . .

Mr. Trimble makes two arguments regarding the claim that his termination violated his rights to free speech and assembly, as guaranteed under the First Amendment of the United States Constitution. First, Mr. Trimble asserts that he was fired because of his union activities in establishing a branch of WVEA at the College. Therefore, he argues, the First Amendment protected him from being fired for such activities. Second, he contends that his refusal to cooperate with implementing the IPSI program was a protest affecting the education of his students. Likewise, he contends the First Amendment protected him from being fired for such protest. The circuit court and hearing examiner concluded that Mr. Trimble failed to prove that his termination was due to the exercise of First Amendment freedoms.

[The court holds that Trimble had a constitutionally protected right to voice his concerns regarding the impact of the IPSI program on his students and peacefully organize a branch of WVEA at the College, but did not have a First Amendment right to refuse to attend training programs or to refuse to use the IPSI program. The court found, however, that Trimble did not prove that his protected conduct was a substantial or motivating factor for his discharge, and thus found no First Amendment violation on the part of the college.]

Next, Mr. Trimble contends that because he was a tenured assistant professor, he had a property interest in his employment. Further, he claims that because of the property interest, the College should not have fired him before resorting to other progressive disciplinary measures. . . .

[I]t is well-settled, and we so hold, that a tenured teacher has a protected property interest in his/her position, which raises constitutional due process considerations when a teacher is faced with termination of his/her employment. W. Va. Const. art. III, § 10. We recognize that the purpose of tenure is to protect competent and worthy teachers against arbitrary dismissal and to promote conditions which will encourage their professional growth. It does not, however, confer upon teachers special privileges or immunities to interfere in the efficient operation of an educational institution. In the instant proceeding there is no dispute, and the circuit court so found, that Mr. Trimble's status as a tenured assistant

---

5. In May of 1997, Mr. Trimble received his annual evaluation report. This evaluation rated Mr. Trimble's performance as "Good" for the 1996–1997 school year.

professor gave him a constitutionally protected property interest in continued employment with the College.

The cases decided by this Court that implicated a constitutionally protected property interest in employment dealt primarily with giving adequate notice or holding an adequate hearing prior to taking some disciplinary action against the employee. The issue of an adequate notice or hearing is not presented by the instant case. Instead, we are asked to determine whether Mr. Trimble's property interest in continued employment required the College to utilize progressive disciplinary measures before resorting to termination.

When an employee is determined to have a property interest in his or her employment, the extent of due process required is determined as follows:

> The extent of due process protection affordable for a property interest requires consideration of three distinct factors: first, the private interest that will be affected by the official action; second, the risk of an erroneous deprivation of a property interest through the procedures used, and the probable value, if any, of additional or substitute procedural safeguards; and finally, the government's interest, including the functions involved and the fiscal and administrative burdens that the additional or substitute procedural requirement would entail.

Constitutional due process protections are to be defined by the facts of a particular case. It is generally recognized that if it is determined that constitutional due process applies, "the question remains what process is due." *Cleveland Bd. of Educ. v. Loudermill*, 470 U.S. 532, 541 (1985) (internal quotation and citation omitted). Because of the "flexible" nature of due process, we believe, and accordingly hold, that constitutional due process principles may be used to determine whether disciplinary action taken by a public higher educational institution against a tenured teacher is too severe for the infraction occasioning such discipline. W. Va. Const. art. III, § 10.

. . .

The prior employment termination decisions of this Court and decisions in other jurisdictions, lead us to our conclusion and result and holding that constitutional due process is denied when a tenured public higher education teacher, who has a previously unblemished record, is immediately terminated for an incident of insubordination that is minor in its consequences. Under such circumstances, due process requires the educational institution to impose progressive disciplinary sanctions in an attempt to correct the teacher's insubordinate conduct before it may resort to termination. W. Va. Const. art. III, § 10.

Prior to Mr. Trimble's problems surrounding the IPSI program, he faithfully served the College without incident for 19 years. The circuit court specifically found that Mr. Trimble's "teaching ability, his quality as a teacher is not being called into question. . . . The parties stipulated that [Mr. Trimble's] work with students was not 'anything less than excellent.'" While we do not condone Mr. Trimble's failure to attend several IPSI meetings and his refusal to prepare an IPSI syllabus, we find that, in view of his 19 years of outstanding service and unblemished record, the College acted arbitrarily and capriciously in terminating him.

Because of Mr. Trimble's property interest in continued employment with the College and his previously unblemished record, due process required the College to utilize progressive disciplinary measures against Mr. Trimble. This conclusion is in keeping with a long held principle by this Court that " '[a] teacher may not be lightly shorn of the privileges for which he [or she] fairly contracted.' " *Fox v. Board of Ed. of Doddridge County*, 160 W. Va. at 672, 236 S.E.2d at 246, (quoting *White v. Board of Educ. of Lincoln County*, 117 W. Va. 114, 125, 184 S.E. 264, 268 (1936)). In other words, "the state may not convey a property interest, such as tenure, and then arbitrarily terminate employment in violation of that interest." *Wuest v. Winner Sch. Dist. 59-2*, 2000 SD 42, 607 N.W.2d 912, 918 (S.D. 2000). We therefore order that Mr. Trimble be reinstated with backpay and benefits from the effective date of his improper termination.

CHAPTER 9

THE UNIVERSITY AS EMPLOYER: ACADEMIC FREEDOM OR UNLAWFUL DISCRIMINATION?

University of Pennsylvania v. Equal Employment Opportunity Commission

Supreme Court of the United States, 1990.
493 U.S. 182, 110 S.Ct. 577, 107 L.Ed.2d 571.

[The opinion is set forth at pages 127–33, *supra*.]

Weinstock v. Columbia University

United States Court of Appeals for the Second Circuit, 2000.
224 F.3d 33.

■ MᴄLᴀᴜɢʜʟɪɴ, Cɪʀᴄᴜɪᴛ Jᴜᴅɢᴇ:

This case arises from Columbia University's denial of tenure to Shelley Weinstock. Weinstock contends that the decision to deny her tenure was the result of discrimination on the basis of her gender. Because this is an appeal from a grant of summary judgment to the defendant, we recite the facts in the light most favorable to the plaintiff. . . .

Weinstock was employed by Barnard College, an undergraduate college and affiliate of Columbia, as an Assistant Professor in its Chemistry Department from July 1985 to June 1994. Weinstock became eligible for tenure during the Spring semester of the 1992–1993 academic year. Pursuant to an affiliation agreement between Columbia and Barnard, the Byzantine tenure process for Barnard faculty proceeds through the following votes.

First, (1) the faculty member's academic department at Barnard; (2) the Barnard Committee on Appointments, Tenure and Promotions; and (3) the counterpart department at Columbia, all must vote in favor of tenure. Then, Barnard's President decides whether to recommend that the process move forward. If the President of Barnard votes favorably, she forwards the nomination to the Provost of Columbia. The Provost then convenes a five-person University ad hoc committee to review the nomination. Under the terms of the affiliation agreement, the ad hoc committee consists of two faculty members designated by the Provost, two Barnard faculty members, and one faculty member from an outside institution. The tenure appointment will be made if: (1) the review of the ad hoc committee is favorable; (2) the Provost accepts that review; (3) the President of Columbia follows the advice of the Provost; and, finally, (4) the Trustees of Barnard and Columbia grant tenure.

Weinstock received the support of: (1) the Barnard Chemistry Department; (2) the Barnard Committee on Appointments, Tenure and Promotions; and (3) the Columbia Chemistry Department. The President of Barnard, Ellen Futter, who initially had reservations about Weinstock's scholarship, then recommended that Weinstock's nomination be moved forward.

As required by the affiliation agreement between Barnard and Columbia, the Provost of Columbia, Jonathan Cole, convened an ad hoc committee. He appointed Professor Alan Tall, the Chair of Columbia's Department of Medicine, as the committee's Chair. He also appointed Professor Samuel Silverstein of Columbia's Department of Physiology and Cellular Biophysics, Professor Zanvil Cohn of Rockefeller University, Professor Lila Braine of Barnard's Department of Psychology and Professor Paul Hertz of Barnard's Department of Biological Sciences, as the committee's other members.

Protocol permits the Chair of an ad hoc committee to contact committee members before their meeting to determine whether they need more information to complete the candidate's file. Tall telephoned the committee members to discuss Weinstock's file, and to determine if any committee member wanted additional information. According to committee members Braine and Hertz, Tall also told each of them on the phone that he thought there were problems with Weinstock's candidacy. Both Braine and Hertz (from the Barnard faculty) reported these remarks, which they considered as going beyond a mere inquiry about lack of information, to Barnard's Dean, Robert McCaughey.

The ad hoc committee met on April 12, 1993. Present were all the committee members, Provost Cole and Dean McCaughey. At the outset of the meeting, Dean McCaughey questioned the extent of Tall's telephone calls to Professors Braine and Hertz. Provost Cole inquired whether any of the committee members' opinions of Weinstock had been tainted by their conversations with Tall. None of the members complained that they had been influenced. Provost Cole also reminded the ad hoc committee that the standards for tenure at Columbia were high, because Columbia is an internationally renowned research university. Professor Sally Chapman, the Chair of Barnard's Chemistry Department, then presented Weinstock's case for tenure.

During the meeting, committee members Tall and Silverstein referred to Weinstock, whom they had never met, by her first name, "Shelley," and allegedly commented that she seemed "nice." Weinstock also alleges that she heard from Chapman and Hertz that Tall and Silverstein observed that she (Weinstock) seemed "nurturing." However, neither Hertz, Silverstein nor Tall remembers hearing the word "nurturing."

Tall and Silverstein deemed Weinstock's publications and research papers insufficient to merit tenure. In their depositions, they testified that her research lacked originality and that the journals in which she published were not first-tier scientific journals. Tall and Silverstein were also unimpressed with Weinstock's letters of recommendation. Silverstein noted that the letters were lukewarm by comparison to letters he had examined in other tenure reviews.

The committee eventually voted 3–2 to grant Weinstock tenure. Braine, Hertz, and Cohn voted for tenure; Tall and Silverstein voted against it. A 3–2 favorable vote is considered "underwhelming [in terms of] support, according to Columbia's current President, George Rupp." . . .

The decision to accept or reject the committee's vote moved to Provost Cole's desk. Before Provost Cole made his decision though, he contacted Ronald Breslow, a member of the Columbia Chemistry Department, for his insights. Breslow stated bluntly that, measured by intellectual strength and scientific ability, Weinstock was not in the same league as other tenured members of the Barnard Chemistry Department.

Provost Cole also discussed Weinstock's candidacy with the Chair of the Columbia Chemistry Department, Richard Bersohn. From these inquiries, as well as from a previous inquiry of Bersohn by Associate Provost Stephen Rittenberg, Cole learned that: (1) the general sentiment of the Columbia Chemistry Department was that Weinstock's work was unimaginative and that her publication record was weak; (2) the Columbia Department did not deem her worthy of tenure; but (3) the Columbia Department had voted to recommend her for tenure as a courtesy to their counterpart department at Barnard.

Provost Cole eventually recommended against tenure for Weinstock because he felt that her scholarship was not up to snuff.

The President of Columbia, Michael Sovern, who followed provostal recommendations on tenure as a matter of course, accepted Cole's recommendation and denied Weinstock tenure.

Weinstock learned in May 1993 that she had been denied tenure. Dean McCaughey from Barnard immediately objected to alleged procedural flaws in the tenure process, and requested that Provost Cole either reverse his decision and follow the ad hoc committee's recommendation to grant tenure, or reconvene the ad hoc committee to consider the additional inputs that Provost Cole had gathered from Professors Breslow and Bersohn. Dean McCaughey apparently was disturbed that the committee did not have the benefit of the information—damning as it was—that Provost Cole had collected from Breslow and Bersohn. Provost Cole though, refused to change his recommendation or to reconvene the committee.

Under the rules of the tenure process for Barnard candidates, if the Provost does not accept the vote of the ad hoc committee, he must say why. Provost Cole did this only after Professor Braine wrote two letters requesting such a clarification. In his explanation, Provost Cole stated that: (1) a favorable vote of 3–2 was not a strong endorsement; (2) the two Columbia members of the committee, Tall and Silverstein, felt that Weinstock's research was limited and below the quality expected of a candidate for tenure; (3) candidates from Columbia and Barnard were to be judged for tenure by the same standards; (4) Cohn, the outside member of the ad hoc committee (Rockefeller University), had stated that Weinstock would not receive tenure at a research university such as Columbia even though he conceded that her research was adequate for an institution such as Barnard; and (5) he had collected evaluations from Breslow and Bersohn confirming his assessment that Weinstock did not merit tenure.

Citing procedural irregularities in Weinstock's tenure process, Barnard President Futter urged President Sovern to reject Provost Cole's recommendation and to accept the favorable recommendation of the ad hoc committee. In the alternative, President Futter requested that a new ad hoc committee be appointed to review Weinstock's application.

By this time, George Rupp had replaced Sovern as President of Columbia. In response to President Futter's protest, President Rupp wrote a letter informing President Futter that he had reviewed Weinstock's case and that he agreed with Provost Cole's determination that her research was not up to the standards expected of a tenured faculty member. President Rupp also indicated that he did not believe there were any procedural irregularities in Weinstock's tenure process. Accordingly, Rupp declined to interfere.

In February 1995, Weinstock filed a complaint in the United States District Court for the Southern District of New York (Keenan, J.), alleging that, by denying her tenure on the basis of her sex, Columbia violated: (1) Title VII of the Civil Rights Act of 1964, as amended, 42 U.S.C. § 2000e et seq.; (2) Title IX of the Education Amendments of 1972, as amended, 20 U.S.C. § 1681 et seq.; (3) the New York State Human Rights Law, New York Executive Law § 296 et seq.; and (4) the Administrative Code of the City of New York § 8–107 et seq.

Upon completion of discovery, Columbia filed a motion for summary judgment. The district court granted the motion, concluding that Weinstock had failed to produce any evidence to establish a triable issue of fact as to the pretextual nature of Columbia's legitimate, non-discriminatory reason for denying her tenure. Weinstock now appeals.

. . .

In a Title VII sex discrimination case such as this, where there is no direct or overt evidence of discriminatory conduct, we apply the three-part burden shifting framework of *McDonnell Douglas Corp. v. Green*, 411 U.S. 792, 802–04 (1973), to determine whether summary judgment is appropriate.

First, the plaintiff must establish a prima facie case of discrimination by showing that: (1) she is a member of a protected class; (2) she is qualified for her position; (3) she suffered an adverse employment action; and (4) the circumstances give rise to an inference of discrimination. Here, the district court, viewing the facts in the light most favorable to Weinstock, found that she satisfied her de minimis burden of proof at the prima facie stage.

That is not the end of the story, however. Even if the plaintiff succeeds in presenting a prima facie case, the defendant may rebut that showing by articulating a legitimate, non-discriminatory reason for the employment action. Upon the defendant's articulation of such a non-discriminatory reason for the employment action, the presumption of discrimination arising with the establishment of the prima facie case drops from the picture. For the case to continue, the plaintiff must then come forward with evidence that the defendant's proffered, non-discriminatory reason is a mere pretext for actual discrimination. The plaintiff must "produce not simply 'some' evidence, but 'sufficient evidence to support a rational finding that the legitimate, non-discriminatory reasons proffered by the [defendant] were false, and that more likely than not [discrimination] was the real reason for the [employment action].'" In short, the question becomes whether the evidence, taken as a whole, supports a sufficient rational inference of discrimination. To get to the jury, "it is not enough . . . to disbelieve the employer;

the factfinder must [also] believe the plaintiff's explanation of intentional discrimination."

Applying these standards here, the district court held that Columbia had articulated a legitimate reason for its tenure decision—namely, that Weinstock's scholarship was not up to its standards. The district court also found that Weinstock had failed to come up with any evidence that this reason was a pretext. We find no error in the district court's analysis.

Columbia's legitimate, non-discriminatory reason for denying Weinstock tenure was that she did not meet the standard for scholarship uniformly applicable within the University. There can be no doubt that this was a valid reason for her tenure decision.

When a college or university denies tenure for a valid, non-discriminatory reason, and there is no evidence of discriminatory intent, this Court will not second-guess that decision.

. . .

Here, ad hoc committee members Tall and Silverstein testified in their depositions that they believed that Weinstock's publications and research papers were insufficient to merit tenure. They also testified that her research lacked originality and that the journals in which she published were not first-tier scientific journals. Neither Tall nor Silverstein was impressed with Weinstock's letters of recommendation. Silverstein noted that the letters were lukewarm by comparison to other letters he had examined in other tenure reviews.

Even though the ad hoc committee voted 3–2 to grant Weinstock tenure, Provost Cole recommended against tenure because her scholarship was questionable. Rejecting a committee vote was nothing new, however, because, according to Columbia's current President George Rupp, a 3–2 favorable vote is considered "underwhelming in terms of support," and from 1989 to the present, as earlier noted, at least six tenure candidates (five male, one female) were denied tenure after an ad hoc committee voted 3–2 in favor of granting tenure.

Before Provost Cole made his recommendation to disagree with the 3–2 vote, he contacted Ronald Breslow, a member of the Columbia Chemistry Department for further comment. It should come as no surprise that Cole, who is not a biochemist, did not read Weinstock's publications during the decision-making process, but instead relied upon the input of other professors who had a better grasp of her work. Breslow stated that Weinstock was not in the same class as other tenured members of the Barnard Chemistry Department in terms of intellectual strength or scientific ability. Provost Cole also discussed Weinstock's candidacy with the Chair of the Columbia Chemistry Department, Richard Bersohn. From these inquiries, as well as from a previous inquiry of Bersohn by Associate Provost Rittenberg, Cole learned that: (1) the general sentiment of the Columbia Chemistry Department was that Weinstock's work was unimaginative and that her publication record was weak; (2) the Columbia Department did not deem her worthy of tenure; but (3) the Columbia Department had voted to recommend her for tenure as a courtesy to their counterpart department at Barnard.

We conclude that when Provost Cole recommended to the President of Columbia that Weinstock's tenure be denied, the legitimate, non-discriminatory reason that she was not academically qualified was established.

Weinstock contends, however, that this was all a mere cover for discrimination, because there exists evidence of: (1) gender stereotyping; (2) procedural irregularities in the ad hoc committee process; and (3) disparate treatment. . . .

Weinstock contends that during the ad hoc committee meeting, she was referred to in a patronizing tone and that statements were made that stereotyped her and demonstrated gender bias. Specifically, Weinstock claims that committee members Tall and Silverstein referred to her as "nice" and "nurturing," and that these statements are essentially code words for gender bias because they reflect feminine stereotypes. Weinstock argues that this is evidence of pretext. We disagree.

First, there appears to be no admissible evidence to support Weinstock's allegation that anyone on the committee referred to her as "nurturing." Weinstock claims that she heard from Chapman that the word "nurturing" was used. However, in Chapman's deposition, in which Weinstock's attorney took part, Chapman never stated that the word "nurturing" was used. Weinstock claims that Hertz, too, told her the word "nurturing" was used. However, when Hertz was deposed by Weinstock's attorney, Hertz stated, "I don't remember them using the word 'nurturing. . . .'" Silverstein, in his deposition, also stated that he did not remember the word "nurturing" being used. Tall, as well, stated that he did not remember the word "nurturing."

Weinstock has failed to offer any direct evidence, or any testimony, from any person present at the committee meeting, that the word "nurturing" was used during her tenure process. Hertz denies it; Silverstein does not remember it; and Chapman, when deposed, was never even queried on the matter. Therefore, because Rule 56 of the Federal Rules of Civil Procedure provides that an affidavit submitted in opposition to summary judgment "shall be made on personal knowledge, [and] shall set forth such facts as would be admissible in evidence," Weinstock has adduced no evidence sufficient to create a genuine issue of fact as to her contention that the word "nurturing" was used.

Second, even assuming that the words "nice" and "nurturing" were used, this fact alone provides no evidence of pretext or discriminatory intent on the part of Columbia. "Nice" and "nurturing" are simply not qualities that are stereotypically female.

Any reasonable person of either sex would like to be considered "nice." It is indefensible to conclude that an employer's use of the word "nice" evinces gender discrimination. Were it so, every time an employer said, "[Bob or Sue], you are a nice person and a hard worker, but I am going to have to let you go," such a statement would become a basis for a Title VII discrimination claim.

This is not a case like *Price Waterhouse v. Hopkins*, 490 U.S. 228 (1989), where the Supreme Court held that Title VII was violated when Ann Hopkins was denied a promotion because she was perceived negatively for lacking stereotypical feminine character traits. Specifically, her superior had advised her to "walk more femininely, talk more femininely, dress more femininely, wear make-up, have her hair styled, and wear jewelry." These statements were a clear indication that Hopkins' superiors had discriminated against her on the basis of sex, because she did not fit the sexual stereotype of what a woman should be. Weinstock, on the other hand, faced no such carping.

Nor can "nurturing" possibly be the basis for a Title VII action. The two primary definitions of the verb "nurture" are "to supply with food, nourishment, and protection" and "to train by or as if by instruction." Webster's Third International Dictionary (1961). These are definitions that are in no way stereotypically female.

Finally, there is no evidence that these words were ever used to describe Weinstock's quotidian research, which was the proffered non-discriminatory reason for Columbia's decision to deny her tenure. These words, if used at all, were spoken only in connection with Weinstock's teaching, i.e., her classroom performance. It is simply not objectively reasonable to label these innocuous words as semaphores for discrimination. To do so would preclude tenure committees from ever discussing a candidate's positive personal attributes as a teacher. Niceness and nurturing are not, after all, bad qualities to have in a teacher's mentoring capacity—particularly of undergraduates.

Weinstock contends that there was a series of procedural irregularities in her tenure process that evidences discriminatory intent on Columbia's part. Specifically, Weinstock takes issue with Tall's phone calls to the committee members before the committee convened, and Provost Cole's delay in explaining why he rejected the committee's vote and recommended denial of Weinstock's tenure. There is, however, no evidence that Weinstock's sex played a role in any alleged procedural irregularities, and there is, again, no evidence of pretext.

It is true that "departures from procedural regularity . . . can raise a question as to the good faith of the process where the departure may reasonably affect the decision." *Stern v. Trustees of Columbia Univ.*, 131 F.3d 305, 313 (2d Cir. 1997). In this case, however, whatever irregularities existed did not affect the final decision to deny Weinstock tenure. The phone calls that Tall made prior to the committee meeting had no effect on any committee member's assessment of Weinstock's candidacy for tenure. In deposition testimony, the committee members acknowledged as much. Moreover, the committee voted 3–2 in favor of granting her tenure. Provost Cole made his decision to reject the committee's recommendation; and his delay in explaining his recommendation did not affect that decision itself. Therefore, any possible procedural irregularities in the denial of Weinstock's tenure were not enough to suggest gender bias.

Furthermore, the dissent incorrectly concludes that "procedural defects in the tenure review process call into question Columbia's proffered nondiscriminatory reason for denying tenure." The phone calls that the dissent characterizes as a "procedural irregularity," in fact, only serve to support Columbia's proffered nondiscriminatory reason for denying Weinstock tenure. The deposition testimony of Professors Hertz, Silverstein, Braine, and Tall all support the conclusion that Professor Tall indicated from the very beginning that he had concerns about the quality of Weinstock's research and that he was concerned that the materials in her dossier were not of "tenurable" quality. The consistency of the viewpoint expressed by Tall—that Weinstock's research was subpar—only further supports Columbia's proffered nondiscriminatory reason for denying Weinstock tenure.

Weinstock also alleges that she was held to a stricter standard for tenure because she is a woman, and argues that this is evidence of discriminatory intent on Columbia's part. Specifically, she contends that Barnard professors are traditionally held to a lesser scholastic standard than Columbia professors, and complains that she was not cut this slack during her candidacy. The evidence, however, is to the contrary.

According to Columbia, the standard for quality of research that is expected of tenure candidates from Barnard and Columbia is identical, although a lower level of productivity in research and publication is accepted from Barnard candidates because they typically have a heavier teaching load. Any difference in productivity standards, however, is of no import, because Columbia's non-discriminatory reason for denying Weinstock tenure involved the quality, not the quantity, of her research. That the quality of research for both Columbia and Barnard professors must be uniform is undisputed by Presidents Rupp, Sovern and Futter.

Weinstock disagrees. She asserts that Columbia applied a stricter standard to her than to male Barnard candidates in the hard sciences; she believes she was measured by the "higher" standard for tenure required of a Columbia-based candidate. Weinstock's only support for this assertion is her contention that a year after she was denied tenure, Columbia granted tenure to a male Barnard faculty member in its Physics Department, Timothy Halpin–Healy, whose research was supposedly below the standard that would be expected by his counterpart department at Columbia.

Initially, Weinstock fails to support her claim that a different standard was used during the two tenure hearings in question. Provost Cole's notes unmistakably indicate that at both hearings the committee discussed whether the candidate would receive tenure at Columbia. Additionally, Weinstock's only evidence that Halpin–Healy's research was subpar in this regard was the fact that one unidentified member of his ad hoc committee may have expressed the opinion that his research was not up to Columbia University standards. However, there is no other evidence that any other member of his ad hoc committee shared this view, and in fact, the committee voted unanimously to grant Halpin–Healy tenure. It cannot be said therefore that Halpin–Healy was held to a laxer standard than Weinstock when he was granted tenure.

. . .

Columbia had a legitimate, non-discriminatory reason for denying Weinstock tenure—she lacked the requisite scholarship required. A claim that a single, supposedly less qualified male received tenure in the hard sciences at Barnard does not signify sex bias because "the record at best indicates a difference of opinion in evaluation of scholarly merit," and not gender discrimination aimed at Weinstock.

. . .

Notwithstanding the dissent's quixotic efforts to breathe life into this case, we cannot fault the district court for aborting it by granting a motion for summary judgment. The very purpose of summary judgment is to weed out those cases that are destined to be dismissed on a motion for a directed verdict, or as it is now termed, a motion for judgment as a matter of law. *See* Fed. R. Civ. P. 50(a). Plaintiff would have us follow the advice of David

Copperfield's mentor, the amicable Mr. Micawber, and let matters proceed in the hope that "something will turn up." This notion is inconsistent with the text and policy behind Rule 56 of the Federal Rules of Civil Procedure, which was intended to prevent such calendar profligacy.

. . .

Accordingly, we AFFIRM the grant of appellee's motion for summary judgment.

■ CARDAMONE, CIRCUIT JUDGE, dissenting:

. . .

The district court found that plaintiff failed to come forward with any proof of pretext. The majority could find no error in this conclusion. I think there was error. To avoid dismissal of her civil rights complaint plaintiff need not actually establish pretext. Her burden is only to raise a question of fact as to the validity of the reason proffered by defendant for its adverse employment decision. . . .

. . . From the start the provost had a negative view of Weinstock's candidacy. He took actions that violated both the letter and the spirit of Columbia's affiliation agreement with Barnard—an agreement executed to ensure fairness to Barnard in tenure matters. Despite the unanimous support for tenure of those most familiar with Weinstock's scholarship, namely her peers in the Chemistry Departments of Columbia and Barnard, the provost, who had no expertise in the field and had not read any of her publications, single-handedly denied her tenure, stating that, in his view, her scholarship was not up to Columbia's standards. From this it is fair to say that the provost evaluated plaintiff's candidacy for tenure through a gender-tainted lens, failing to recognize that his vast discretion did not permit him to violate the affiliation agreement, or to trample on the law forbidding discrimination on account of sex that Congress in 1964 enacted as Title VII of the Civil Rights Act. In particular, this record is marked by numerous contradictions and irregularities in the conduct of and rationales offered by Provost Jonathan Cole, the principal actor in this tenure decision. These inconsistencies are inexplicable in the absence of gender discrimination.

To fully explain the grounds on which I dissent, it is important to understand the relationship between Barnard, the college where Professor Weinstock sought tenure, and defendant Columbia University.

Barnard College and Columbia University are parties to a written affiliation agreement that requires Columbia's approval of tenure for Barnard faculty. The agreement requires that Barnard appoint faculty of comparable quality to Columbia and that there be a regular system for reviewing Barnard candidates for tenure. Yet, the University agrees that the procedures for Barnard candidates are not identical to those for Columbia candidates, and that this distinction is to ensure fairness to Barnard. Although the tenure review process embodies the same standards and provides for regular review, it recognizes the differences in the mission between Barnard College and Columbia University.

Barnard is a small, undergraduate, women's liberal arts college of several thousand students (this year's graduating class was about 570), while Columbia is a large, internationally known research university, teaching graduate as well as undergraduate students. Resources for research at the smaller College are more limited than at the University, which is a reason why "the procedures by which Barnard nominations [for tenure] are reviewed differ in some respects" under the agreement between the University and Barnard. Because there are no graduate students to assist in research and the research budget and facilities are more limited than at the larger University, the projects undertaken by Barnard professors in the Chemistry Department are necessarily narrower than those at the University. Thus, although the affiliation agreement states that faculty at Barnard and Columbia are to be of comparable quality, the more limited resources at Barnard require that the standards for tenure at the two institutions differ. This crucial difference is explored below.

Statistical evidence puts this matter in further perspective and makes plain how the University deviated from the standards it had agreed to abide by. Although not in the record before us, Columbia makes statistical information on its hiring patterns freely and widely available. *See* Office of Equal Opportunity and Affirmative Action (visited Aug. 8, 2000) <http://www.columbia.edu/cu/vpaa/eoaa/index.html>. Even though Columbia established a 33 percent hiring goal for women in the natural sciences in 1996–97, of the five new hires that year, none were women. Such disparity cannot be explained by a lack of women graduate students in scientific fields since women earned 45 percent of all doctorates awarded in life sciences (which includes biochemistry, Weinstock's field) in 1997; nor can it be explained by a restricted pipeline of candidates since even in 1987 women obtained 35 percent of all life science doctorates nationwide.

In fact, in the natural sciences (often known as "hard sciences"), where plaintiff teaches, only 15 percent of professors at Columbia were women. In over forty years, only two women have ever been tenured in Columbia's Chemistry Department, and the department has never had more than one woman tenured at a time. Columbia's record cannot be explained by supply and demand—the number of women obtaining doctorates and entering the academic job market in science has risen dramatically over the last decade. One Columbia professor characterized this abysmal record as a "scandal." The 15 percent women professors in natural sciences has held steady for the past 12 years, the same length of time the provost who made this tenure decision has held office. Statistical disparities like these are probative on the issue of discrimination because they are often the only way to demonstrate covert discrimination.

Next we look at plaintiff's background. Weinstock was an assistant professor in the Chemistry Department at Barnard for nine years from 1985 to 1994 when, after she was denied tenure, her employment was terminated. She is a biochemist whose research focused primarily on blood substitutes and artificial organs. Weinstock was educated at MIT and Harvard, published scholarly works in academic publications and received prestigious grants, including one from the National Institutes of Health, which funds less than 10 percent of all applications. Because the award of such a grant is highly selective it shows that she ranked near the top of her national peer group. In her tenure application, Weinstock received the unanimous support of the Barnard Chemistry Department. The Columbia Chemistry Department voted for plaintiff's tenure with not a single negative vote. The Barnard Committee for Tenure voted in her favor, and the president of Barnard favored granting plaintiff tenure. Weinstock's tenure dossier was extremely strong, containing excellent referee letters from leading scientists in her field. She was widely lauded as an excellent teacher and mentor.

Following the approval of the Chemistry Departments of Barnard and Columbia and the other approvals already recited, Professor Weinstock's application was turned over to Columbia Provost Cole, who, as provided for in the affiliation agreement, selected an ad hoc committee of five....

The two Columbia professors Cole appointed to the ad hoc, Alan Tall and Samuel Silverstein, were both from the medical school. Cole had known both professors for several years and with Silverstein shared a common interest in the "sociology of science," an area in which Cole has published several books.

As Chair of the ad hoc committee, Cole's other Columbia appointee, Professor Tall, called each of the ad hoc members before the committee convened and expressed criticism of Weinstock's candidacy. Tall admitted he called to express "his concerns." The majority dismisses these phone calls as "protocol," yet testimony from Lila Braine and Paul Hertz, the two Barnard professors on the committee, makes it very clear that Tall was not calling to schedule a convenient meeting time, inquiring about information perhaps missing from the dossier distributed to all members in advance, or attending to any other matters falling within the scope of such administrative "protocol."

Indeed, Braine testified that Tall was trying to "twist her arm" with his negative views of Weinstock. Both Braine and Hertz were so disturbed by the nature of Tall's phone calls that independently of each other they reported the phone calls to Robert McCaughey, the Dean of Barnard's Arts and Sciences faculty, who was to be present at the ad hoc. Columbia's then-President Michael Sovern, its current President George Rupp, Barnard's then-President Ellen Futter, and even Cole himself all agree that these phone calls would have been clearly "inappropriate" if Tall were expressing an opinion on Weinstock's candidacy, and would have constituted a procedural irregularity, because, according to Columbia's president, members of an ad hoc committee are to meet after reviewing the candidate's dossier "completely independently."

Yet when Dean McCaughey raised the issue at the ad hoc and requested that a new ad hoc be convened, Provost Cole dismissed his request, claiming that because neither Braine nor Hertz felt their opinions had changed as a result of Tall's phone calls, there was no procedural irregularity. Replicating Cole's argument, the majority finds that "whatever irregularities existed did not affect the final decision to deny Weinstock tenure." Whether Tall's arm-twisting was ultimately successful is irrelevant to the issue of gender discrimination. The very fact that the calls were made, that they were clearly inappropriate, and as such constituted procedural defects in the tenure review process, calls into question Columbia's proffered nondiscriminatory reason for denying Weinstock tenure. (issue #1) This evidence raises the first of 12 disputed questions of fact that I identify. Many of them relate to Cole's credibility. All of them are material to the issues of pretext and discrimination. At this stage of the case, all of these issues should have been resolved in plaintiff's favor.

Moreover, at the ad hoc deliberations, evidence of gender discrimination began to surface. Barnard Professors Braine and Hertz observed that Columbia Professors Silverstein and Tall, who had never met Weinstock, referred to her by her first name, "Shelley." Referring to a woman by her first name in this context may be probative on the issue of gender discrimination. Amici,[1] quoting an article from the Yale Journal of Law and Feminism, report that in 1,730 student evaluations of law school faculty, male professors were never referred to by their first names. Braine and Hertz also testified that Silverstein and Tall assumed a patronizing tone toward Weinstock, calling her "nice" and describing her as if she were nurturing. Although they do not specifically remember what words were used to describe Weinstock, they both believe that "nurturing" was consistent with the nature of Silverstein's and Tall's commentary.

The majority finds, as a matter of law, that these comments cannot possibly raise an inference of sex discrimination because "nice" and "nurturing" could: (1) conceivably be used to describe men, and (2) are positive qualities. Perhaps these are positive qualities in a motherhood contest, but during the tenure deliberations for a chemistry professor and scientist, they suggest gender discrimination. By describing her as "nice" and referring to her nurturing manner, Silverstein and Tall were not extolling her positive qualities—rather, they were using these qualities to highlight what they perceived to be her intellectual weakness.

At the ad hoc meeting the Barnard dean and Columbia provost are both present, supposedly as observers. But the provost took an active role and expressed a negative view of Weinstock and her chemistry research, a field in which he had no expertise. Cole admitted he had not read a single one of her many publications. Significantly, he denied in his deposition having expressed any opinion at the ad hoc meeting at all, yet three members of the committee who were present, including outside Professor Cohn, say Cole took an active role and was negative (Professor Cohn said the "sticking point" for Cole was Professor Weinstock's research). (issue #2)

The provost informed the members of the ad hoc committee that plaintiff should be judged as though she would receive tenure at Columbia, a standard that had not been applied to other Barnard candidates. According to the affiliation agreement between the two institutions, the procedures by which Barnard nominations for tenure are reviewed "differ in some respects" from Columbia nominations. The differences between the two institutions render the provost's purported standard a false and impossible one. (issue #3)

Provost Cole's predisposition against Professor Weinstock, evidenced by his active and deliberate role during the ad hoc, could explain why remarkably he sent Barnard College a letter stating that he agreed with the ad hoc's decision to deny Weinstock tenure and was thus denying her tenure. He generated this very important document despite the fact that the ad hoc committee had voted to grant plaintiff tenure. Alerted to his glaring error, Cole sent a follow-up letter to Barnard College, explaining that he had sought "additional information" after the ad hoc voted in her favor, which had convinced him to reject its recommendation. (issue #4)

---

1. A brief Amici Curiae was filed in this appeal jointly by Equal Rights Advocates, American Association of University Women, Association for Women in Science, and New York Chapter of the National Employment Lawyers Association.

The process by which Provost Cole collected his purported "additional information" is equally mendacious. He asked Associate Provost Stephen Rittenberg to compile a list of experts in Weinstock's field to consult about her candidacy. Although Rittenberg provided him with a list of expert faculty within Columbia University, Cole did not contact a single person on this list. Rather, he turned to Breslow and Bersohn, two professors in Columbia's Chemistry Department, neither of whom are experts in Weinstock's field. Professor Breslow had previously written a thoughtful letter supporting plaintiff's candidacy, but changed his tune in response to the provost, describing Weinstock as not aggressive, not tough, a "perfectly nice person" and a "pushover." Having obtained from Professor Breslow what he wanted, the provost then cited Breslow's advice in support of his decision to turn plaintiff's tenure application down. (issue #5)

When questioned during his deposition on why he did not contact any of the experts knowledgeable about Weinstock's area of research, Cole responded that he sought only to "confirm" his assessment of Weinstock and therefore did not need to consult an expert. His own notes of his conversation with Breslow are telling in that they touch only briefly on the supposedly central issue—the strength of Weinstock's research—but instead go on to describe personal characteristics, i.e., a "perfectly nice person," a "pushover." Cole found the confirmation he needed—confirmation of gender stereotypes that detracted from Weinstock's scholarly achievements. (issue #6)

In addition, from his conversation with Bersohn, Cole discredited the positive recommendation of Columbia's Chemistry Department, by describing it as a "courtesy" extended to Barnard. If the sincerity of the Columbia Chemistry Department's letter favoring Weinstock's tenure was ambiguous, the affiliation agreement sets forth formalized procedures for exploring its meaning, either through a written statement to the ad hoc, or by testimony before it. Neither option was followed. In light of the fact that Weinstock received 11 votes from Columbia's Chemistry Department in her favor, 4 abstentions from those unfamiliar with her research, and not a single negative vote, Cole's assertion that the recommendation was extended as a mere "courtesy" is to say the least, somewhat startling. The majority's assertion that this vote "was a mere 'courtesy' " at best raises a dispute about a material issue of fact. (issue #7)

Moreover, in assessing the credibility of Cole's reliance on two supposedly negative reports from members of the Columbia Chemistry Department, Weinstock is entitled to the inference from the departmental vote that either (a) Breslow and Bersohn thought well enough of her work to vote to tenure her; or (b) they were among those abstaining because they were unfamiliar with her work. Either inference casts doubt on the validity of Cole's reason. (issue #8)

Even when the ad hoc's vote is 3–2, it is rare for the provost to reject its recommendation. To justify, at least in part, taking the "rare" action of overruling a positive ad hoc committee vote, Cole in his report to the president of Columbia said that Rockefeller University's Professor Cohn—the only member of the ad hoc committee who was in plaintiff's field—thought Weinstock's research was "weak." Yet, according to two of the ad hoc members, Professor Cohn was positive about plaintiff's candidacy. In fact, in Professor Cohn's own letter to the Chair of Barnard's Chemistry Department following the denial of tenure, he expressed his unhappiness at Cole's decision to deny Weinstock tenure, stated that he had voted in her favor and had found her research "rather imaginative," and commented that she was an excellent teacher and mentor. Hardly the language used to describe a weak candidate. (issue #9)

Further, the affiliation agreement provided that the provost was to explain the reasons for his decision to the ad hoc whose recommendation he rejected. Cole offered none. After Barnard Professor Braine wrote two letters requesting an explanation, Cole finally answered, but qualified his response by stating that since Weinstock had filed a charge of discrimination with the EEOC, any explanation he offered must be made with the defense of Columbia University in mind. One might fairly ask what defense would be needed if the reason given was not pretextual. (issue #10)

For the reader to place Cole's conduct in proper context, some insight into his initial negative view of plaintiff as a woman candidate for tenure in the Chemistry Department can be gained by examining a book he wrote on this subject, Fair Science: Women in the Scientific Community (1979). In the book Provost Cole addresses the question of whether women scientists are subject to sex discrimination in matters of promotion. His answer, set forth in chapter 3, Woman's Place in the Scientific Community, is "no." Instead, he believes there is a high degree of fairness in the distribution of scientific rewards and that women's lack of success is based on what he terms "universalistic criteria," which, at page 5, he defines as merit. To put it bluntly, a rational juror could find that in the provost's view, women scientists are not subject to discrimination in denial of tenure cases; they simply lack merit.

Faced with such a strong tenure candidate, Cole explained his decision by insisting that Weinstock fell short of the standard needed to obtain tenure in Columbia's Chemistry Department, rather than Barnard's Chemistry Department. This rationale enabled him to mischaracterize all the positive reviews of her work, including Professor Cohn's, by insisting that these reviewers were only positive about Weinstock because they applied a lower standard. It is nonetheless clear from the affiliation agreement that the standards for tenure at Barnard, a small undergraduate institution with limited research facilities, differ from those at Columbia, a large research institution with advanced facilities and a substantial budget and graduate students to assist professors in their research. There is ample evidence to indicate that as a practical matter, two standards, one for tenure at Barnard and one for tenure at Columbia, had emerged. President Futter of Barnard appealed Cole's decision in writing—the first time she had ever appealed a tenure decision in her 12 years as Barnard's president. In his defense, Cole cited the affiliation agreement, arguing that it permitted him to apply identical standards to Barnard and Columbia professors, and that his broad discretion rendered his decision unreviewable.

Cole's nondiscriminatory rationale is from start to finish incredible. Even Professor Breslow, whose testimony he cites in support of his decision, agreed that Sally Chapman, the Chair of Barnard's Chemistry Department, would not have been granted tenure under the standard Cole claimed to impose on candidate Weinstock. Professor Weinstock was the first woman nominated for tenure in the natural sciences at Columbia or Barnard during Cole's term as provost, and it is apparent that Cole selectively applied a higher standard in her case. The tenure bar was raised for Weinstock because she is a woman. This point was made crystal clear the following year when a male professor in the Physics Department was granted tenure at Barnard despite the fact that at least one member of his ad hoc committee acknowledged that he would not have received tenure in the Physics Department at Columbia. That is, the tenure bar was lowered for a man. (issue #11) Standing alone this issue is significant enough to overcome a summary judgment motion.

Even Provost Cole's response to Professor Braine's letter inquiring as to his reasons for denying Weinstock tenure was suspect. Cole insisted that as provost he had to be concerned about the financial impact of tenure on University finances. That statement is inaccurate and disingenuous. The affiliation agreement with Columbia leaves the qualifications review up to the agreed-upon ad hoc process, but with respect to financial considerations, Barnard's decision is "final," as the president of Columbia conceded. (issue #12)

This record reflects gender discrimination incontrovertibly shown by gender stereotyping and by statistics. Further this discrimination occurred under the aegis of a provost granted vast discretion in tenure matters who, the record demonstrates, was guilty of procedural irregularities in violation of the affiliation agreement between Columbia and Barnard, as well as a very large number of credibility issues that cast doubt on the provost's veracity as a witness. In light of this evidence, a reasonable jury could find that the proffered reason for denial of tenure was pretextual, and that the real reason was sex discrimination in violation of Title VII.

In their zeal to "clear the calendar" of so-called "doomed lawsuits," my colleagues have overlooked the procedural posture of Weinstock's appeal. Summary judgment is appropriate only when the moving party has shown that there are no genuine issues of material fact and that it is entitled to judgment as a matter of law. See Fed. R. Civ. P. 56(c). In determining whether genuine issues of material fact exist, "a court must resolve all ambiguities and draw all reasonable inferences against the moving party. . . . Not only must there be no genuine issue as to the evidentiary facts, but there must also be no controversy regarding the inferences to be drawn from them."

In reviewing the facts of this case, the district court and the majority have done the precise opposite—resolved factual issues in Columbia's favor rather than Weinstock's, and disregarded the controversy surrounding 12 of its pivotal facts. These analytical errors are particularly egregious in a discrimination case, where an employer's intent is at issue. As we have repeatedly recognized, evidence of discriminatory intent is usually circumstantial and can only be gleaned from careful scrutiny of the entire record.

. . .

The discriminatory effect of gender stereotypes is precisely the problem the Supreme Court condemned in *Price Waterhouse v. Hopkins*, 490 U.S. 228 (1989). The majority believes *Price Waterhouse* is inapplicable to this case because unlike Ann Hopkins, who was advised to "walk more femininely, talk more femininely, dress more femininely, wear make-up, have her hair styled and wear jewelry," Weinstock did not face "carping." This logic misapprehends why stereotyping is discriminatory. The irony of *Price Water-*

house arose from the fact that Hopkins' so-called masculine qualities-what others perceived as her abrasiveness-would have been valued qualities in a man being considered for partnership. Price Waterhouse discriminated against Hopkins because although she performed the "masculine" role of competing successfully for business, the firm punished her for not *simultaneously* performing the "feminine" role of speaking softly and having a feminine appearance. The Supreme Court held that Hopkins' failure to fulfill this gendered role was an impermissible consideration in the partnership decision.

This case presents the mirror image of *Price Waterhouse*. Cole's decision to deny Weinstock tenure was based—ironically—on her perceived success at projecting a stereotypically "feminine" image at work. Weinstock was described as gentle and caring, "nice," a "pushover," and nurturing. Unfortunately for Weinstock, a stereotypically "feminine" person is not viewed in a male dominated field as a driven, scientifically-minded, competitive academic researcher. The inappropriate focus on Weinstock's "feminine" qualities in the tenure process led Cole and perhaps others to discount her "masculine" success as a researcher and professor. While Hopkins was punished for failing to perform a "feminine" role, Weinstock was punished for performing it too well.

The problem both Weinstock and Hopkins faced is that their employers demanded that they perform both "masculine" and "feminine" roles, yet perceived those roles as fundamentally incompatible. Unlike "masculine" men at Price Waterhouse, Hopkins was punished because her "masculinity" appeared inconsistent with gendered stereotypes of how women should look and behave; Weinstock was punished because her "femininity" appeared inconsistent with "masculine" success as a researcher. Yet if Weinstock had chosen to project a more "masculine" image, she could very well have suffered the same fate as Hopkins.

Questions and Comments on *Weinstock*

1. It is relatively rare for an academic plaintiff to win an employment suit against a university. One study of Title VII claims found that in cases that went to litigation, plaintiffs succeeded only 21 percent of the time. Martha S. West, *Gender Bias in Academic Robes: The Law's Failure to Protect Women Faculty*, 67 TEMP. L. REV. 67.

2. As the *Weinstock* majority observes, in Title VII litigation, proof of pretext does not mean the plaintiff wins the case. Rather, it means only that the issue of fact will go to the jury. As the Supreme Court has noted:

> Title VII does not award damages against employers who cannot prove a nondiscriminatory reason for adverse employment action, but only against employers who are proven to have taken adverse employment action by reason of (in the context of the present case) race. That the employer's proffered reason is unpersuasive, or even obviously contrived, does not necessarily establish that the plaintiff's proffered reason of race is correct. That remains a question for the factfinder to answer, subject, of course, to appellate review....

St. Mary's Honor Ctr. v. Hicks, 509 U.S. 502, 523–24 (1993).

3. Views on gender appear to have played a role in ending the presidency of Lawrence Summers at Harvard University. Summers publicly suggested that the reason women are not highly represented in math and science careers is because of innate differences between men and women. His statement provoked widespread reaction and media attention. Backlash from Harvard's faculty and governing board ultimately contributed to his resignation in 2006. Marcella Bombardieri & Maria Sacchetti, *Summers to Step Down, Ending Tumult at Harvard*, BOSTON GLOBE, Feb. 22, 2006, at A1.

4. During the 1979–80 academic year, Professor Julia Brown, an English professor at Boston University, sued the university after being denied tenure. At Boston University, candidates for tenure were reviewed during their sixth year for excellence in three areas: scholarship, teaching, and service to the university. Excellence was required in two of these three areas. Brown had authored a book on Jane Austen published by the Harvard University Press, and was working on another book on Oscar Wilde. Under the category of teaching, Brown listed the courses she taught at Boston University, including two classes she developed on her own. In addition, Brown had taken the time to advise students on course selection and graduate school programs.

A committee comprised of all the tenured professors in the English department was the first to review Brown's case. This committee unanimously recommended that brown be given tenure by a vote of 22–0. The chairman of this committee highly praised Brown's teaching and scholarship, and commented that the Jane Austen book had been widely recognized by noted critics. Next, the Appointments, Promotions and Tenure Committee (APT) of the College of Liberal Arts unanimously recommended tenure, again noting Brown's excellent teaching and first rate scholarly work. At this point the Dean of the College of Liberal Arts recommended Brown for tenure, but expressed concerns that she did not spend enough time advising students, and recommended a possible three year extension of Brown's probationary period so that her subsequent work on Oscar Wilde could be evaluated. At the next level of review, a university-wide APT recommended tenure by a vote of 9–2.

At this point in the process, the tenure decision moved to the Provost's office. The Provost concluded that Brown's scholarship was limited to a revised Ph.D. dissertation and three book reviews, and recommended that her probationary period be extended by three years in order to allow her to finish her major independent work. After Brown refused to agree to a three year extension, the Provost recommended that Brown not receive tenure.

Due to the dispute between the different levels of review, an ad hoc committee was formed to review Brown's candidacy. This committee voted 2–1 in favor of tenure. Based on the fact that Brown's report was not a "strong, unqualified endorsement of the candidate's work," John Silber, the president of Boston University recommended that the Trustees not grant tenure. Based on the president's recommendation, the Trustees denied Brown tenure. Brown sued the University under Title VII of the Civil Rights Act of 1964, claiming that it had discriminated against her on the basis of sex.

At trial, Brown brought tenure evidence that suggested that alleged "similarly situated" faculty members, particularly males, had been held to a lower tenure standard than she had been. The jury sided with Brown, and she was awarded damages and reinstatement to the position of associate professor with tenure. On appeal, the court upheld the upheld the verdict. On the issue of Brown's reinstatement, the court went on to note:

> Courts have quite rarely awarded tenure as a remedy for unlawful discrimination, and those that have, have done so under circumstances distinguishable from those here. The University argues that tenure is a significantly more intrusive remedy than remedies ordinarily awarded in Title VII cases, such as reinstatement or seniority, because a judicial tenure award mandates a lifetime relationship between the University and the professor. The University further contends that due to the intrusiveness of tenure awards and the First Amendment interest in academic freedom, a court should not award tenure unless there is no dispute as to a professor's

qualifications. Thus, the University concludes, the district court should not have awarded tenure to Brown, because there existed a dispute as to her qualifications.

We agree that courts should be "extremely wary of intruding into the world of university tenure decisions." However, once a university has been found to have impermissibly discriminated in making a tenure decision, as here, the University's prerogative to make tenure decisions must be subordinated to the goals embodied in Title VII. The Supreme Court has ruled that the remedial provision of Title VII requires courts to fashion the most complete relief possible for victims of discriminatory employment decisions. *Albemarle Paper Co. v. Moody*, 422 U.S. 405, 421, 95 S.Ct. 2362, 2373, 45 L.Ed.2d 280 (1975). Once Title VII liability has been imposed, a court should deny "make whole" relief "only for reasons which, if applied generally, would not frustrate the central statutory purposes of eradicating discrimination throughout the economy and making persons whole for injuries suffered through past discrimination."

We see no reason to deny Brown such "make whole" relief here. We disagree with the University's characterization of the tenure award as an infringement on its First Amendment right to determine for itself who may teach. In often-quoted language, Justice Frankfurter defined academic freedom as " 'an atmosphere in which there prevail the four essential freedoms of a university-to determine for itself on academic grounds who may teach, what may be taught, how it shall be taught, and who may be admitted to study.' " Academic freedom does not include the freedom to discriminate against tenure candidates on the basis of sex or other impermissible grounds. Our decisions in this area have formulated a university's prerogatives similarly. While we have been and remain hesitant to interfere with universities' independent judgment in choosing their faculty, we have said that we will respect universities' judgment only "so long as they do not discriminate."

The University also argues that the special needs of academic institutions counsel imposition of less restrictive alternative remedies. However, the University suggests none. Some amici suggest that Brown be reinstated for a three year probationary period, or be subjected to a non-discriminatory tenure decision. Aside from the impracticality of the latter, well over eight years after the original decision, these suggestions fall far short of remedies which will make Brown whole. According to the jury's verdict, she was offered the three year extension because of discrimination. The jury found that, "but for" sex discrimination, Brown would immediately have been granted tenure. Awarding her tenure is the only way to provide her the most complete relief possible.

. . . We add that Brown's near unanimous endorsement by colleagues within and without her department suggest strongly that there are no issues of collegiality or the like which might make the granting of tenure inappropriate.

Brown v. Trustees of Boston Univ., 891 F.2d 337 (1st Cir. 1989). Why do you think this case came out differently than *Weinstock*?

Shoucair v. Brown University

Supreme Court of Rhode Island, 2007.
917 A.2d 418.

■ JUSTICE SUTTELL, for the Court.

Professor Fred Shoucair was, by all accounts, a dedicated and qualified teacher in the division of engineering at Brown University, but in today's world of major research universities that is often not enough to merit tenure. After he was denied tenure in 1993, Shoucair filed a civil action against Brown, alleging unlawful employment practices in violation of the Fair Employment Practices Act. Brown maintained that, in effect, Shoucair fell short of tenure by virtue of a modern corollary to the venerable "publish or perish" adage—one that assesses professors/researchers on their ability to attract lucrative grants on a regular basis. It appears that the jury, however, found that Shoucair's demise at Brown resulted from his unfortunate encounter with another time-honored tradition of higher education: petty politics. Yet, contrary to the notoriously acerbic observation that "academic politics are so vicious precisely because the stakes are so small," the stakes for Fred Shoucair in this case loomed very large indeed.

Brown University now appeals from the trial justice's denial of its motion for judgment as a matter of law under Rule 50 of the Superior Court Rules of Civil Procedure. . . .

Fred Shoucair, Ph.D., joined the Brown faculty as an assistant professor in the electrical sciences group of the division of engineering in July 1987. His duties as assistant professor included teaching undergraduate-and grad-uate-level courses, supervising the research of doctoral candidates, conducting his own research and pursuing grants to finance that research. Shoucair's particular area of expertise focused on electronics for severe environment; his research in that vein aimed at enhancing the functional capacity of electronics at extremely high temperatures, among other things.

Shortly after Shoucair arrived at Brown, Professor Harvey Silverman invited him to join the Laboratory for Engineering Man/Machine Systems (LEMS group) and Shoucair accepted. The LEMS group consisted of a number of professors in the electrical sciences group, and they met regularly to discuss shared academic and research interests. But Shoucair left the group in May 1990 after he had a falling out with Silverman over a grading controversy that arose in one of Shoucair's undergraduate engineering classes. At that time, Silverman was the director of undergraduate programs in the division of engineering, and he summoned Shoucair to his office to discuss what Silverman deemed to be a disproportionately large number of noncredit grades Shoucair had turned in for his "Engineering 52" class. According to Shoucair, Silverman told him, "You graded like a son of a bitch, like a bastard," and demanded that he change the grades. When he refused, Shoucair testified, Silverman left the room, returned with two other professors, and proceeded to alter the grades on Shoucair's grade sheets. When then asked to sign the altered grade sheets, Shoucair said that he acquiesced only after the three professors agreed to write a note acknowledging that Shoucair was acting under protest. Subsequently, Shoucair wrote a letter of complaint to Professor Arto Nurmikko (head of the electrical science faculty) and to Dean of Engineering Alan Needleman. Dean Needleman then ordered that the original grades be restored. Still later, in June 1990, Dean Needleman requested that Shoucair meet with Nurmikko and another colleague, Professor Jan Tauc, to review the exams once more. Shoucair agreed to meet with Nurmikko and Tauc, and after that meeting he accepted their recommendation that he lower the passing score for the Engineering 52 exam by ten points and adjust his grades accordingly.

It is abundantly clear from a review of the voluminous trial transcripts that Harvey Silverman is the eminence grise of Shoucair's narrative, and that Shoucair's primary theory of recovery was ethnic discrimination. Most of his evidence tended to support his contention that Silverman carefully orchestrated the denial of his tenure. The jury, however, rejected this allegation and instead predicated Brown's liability on a second theory of recovery advanced by Shoucair, i.e., the retaliatory animus of Professor Maurice Glicksman, a close associate of Silverman's.

When Shoucair came up for tenure at Brown in 1992, Silverman, who then was the Dean of Engineering, appointed Glicksman to convene a tenure review committee to begin the evaluation process. Dean Silverman recused himself from the proceedings because in the wake of the 1990 grading dispute, he and Shoucair were not on speaking terms. Professor Glicksman enlisted Professor Nabil Lawandy and Professor Subra Suresh to round out the three-person tenure review committee (TRC). Professor Glicksman then contacted Shoucair to alert him to the composition of the committee and to request an updated curriculum vitae and a list of suggested references. Professor Shoucair complied, and the TRC mailed evaluation requests to ten references, some of whom had been suggested by Shoucair himself, and others whom the committee sought out independently.

As he was compiling Shoucair's tenure dossier over the course of the 1992–93 academic year, Glicksman was also co-chairing a search committee to hire a new faculty member in the electrical sciences division to replace Professor Jim Rosenberg, who was resigning. On February 19, 1993, Dean Silverman sent a memorandum to all tenured engineering faculty announcing that the search committee had recommended hiring Eli Kapon, Ph.D., and that a meeting to vote on this recommendation would convene on February 26, 1993. The tenured faculty approved the search committee's recommendation, but Brown's Affirmative Action Monitoring Committee (AAMC) was not prepared to accept the recommendation until, according to Glicksman's report to the Engineering Executive Committee (EEC), the department interviewed one more "viable under-represented minority candidate (Asian)." Between March 4 and March 16, 1993, Glicksman brought a qualified minority candidate to campus for interviews, and shortly thereafter he informed the EEC that the interview process was "concluded" and that an offer would be extended to Kapon, whom "the tenured faculty had already approved." At trial, there was some confusion about the timing of the minority candidate's interview and the official offer to Kapon. Bryan Shepp, dean of the faculty, testified that he made the official offer after clearing the EEC's recommendation with the AAMC, but he could not attach specific dates to those actions. Dean Silverman himself wrote to Kapon on March 19, 1993, to congratulate him on his appointment and to encourage him to accept it.

According to Shoucair, it was his belief Kapon had already been offered the position that led him to question Glicksman's secretary, Sandy Spinacci, when she contacted Shoucair in early March to ask that he interview the additional minority candidate. Professor Shoucair testified that he believed Silverman's February 19 memorandum meant that "the job had been offered to * * * [Mr.] Kapon" and that he was unaware of AAMC's subsequent objection and the resulting extension of the interview process. Professor Shoucair asked Ms. Spinacci to confirm which opening the candidate she was asking him to interview was applying to fill. Shoucair recalled that when Ms.

Spinacci called back to confirm that the interview was for the Rosenberg opening, she also informed him that the interview was being conducted for "some affirmative action considerations." Professor Shoucair testified that in declining to do the interview, he also noted to Ms. Spinacci his concern that it might be illegal to interview a candidate for a position that had already been offered to someone else. Ms. Spinacci testified that she was not aware at the time whether Brown had already offered another candidate the position that Rosenberg vacated.

Professor Shoucair also testified that a week or two after he told Ms. Spinacci that he did not wish to participate in the interview, Glicksman showed up at his office, unannounced, with the minority candidate whom Shoucair previously had declined to interview. Professor Glicksman asked Shoucair to spend roughly fifteen minutes with the candidate, and Shoucair, in spite of his earlier objections, reluctantly did so.

Shortly thereafter, on March 23, 1993, the TRC chaired by Glicksman voted to recommend Shoucair for tenure. The generally positive recommendation report that Glicksman authored came with a significant disclaimer, however; the committee members endorsed Shoucair for tenure, but professed that they were unable to do so "with enthusiasm." This caveat, according to the report, was based on the committee's opinion that Shoucair was "not contributing at the level we would like to see, to the visibility of our research program (in competitive, peer-reviewed on-site funding of research) and to the support of our graduate students and programs." Professor Glicksman distributed the tenure review committee's report to all tenured faculty in the electrical sciences group.

On March 24, 1993, seven of the electrical sciences group's nine members convened to review the TRC report and decide on their support for Shoucair's candidacy. Dean Silverman attended the meeting, but he and Glicksman both abstained from what turned out to be a five to zero vote in favor of a motion to allow Shoucair's contract to lapse at the end of the 1993–1994 academic year, and thus not to award him tenure. In the subsequent report that Glicksman disseminated to all tenured faculty in the engineering division, he explained that "although Fred Shoucair's record is a competent one, it is not one that promises some distinction, and the particular lack of contract/grant awards and the lack of support for graduate students do not show promise for future positive contributions." Professor Glicksman apprised Shoucair of this turn of events, and told Shoucair that he was entitled to attend the next engineering division meeting and make his case to the tenured faculty before they, too, assessed his candidacy. Professor Shoucair demurred, choosing rather to make himself available to answer any questions that might arise. There were no questions for Shoucair, and the tenured faculty of the engineering division followed the lead of the electrical sciences group, voting fifteen to five (with four abstentions) against tenure for Shoucair. Professor Glicksman conveyed this result to Shoucair and also informed Shoucair of his right to be heard when the Committee on Faculty Reappointment and Tenure (ConFRaT) met to consider his case before making its recommendation to the provost.

Professor Shoucair did appear at the ConFRaT meeting on May 17, 1993. After the committee had asked several questions of Silverman, Glicksman, and Lawandy, Dean Shepp introduced Shoucair and Professor Peter Richardson, a colleague of Shoucair's in the engineering division who was acting as his advisor. Professor Shoucair answered questions from those in attendance, including Provost Frank Rothman. At the meeting's conclusion, the ConFRaT members voted seven to one to deny Shoucair's tenure application and allow his contract to expire on June 30, 1994. In protest, Shoucair filed a grievance with the Faculty Executive Committee (FEC) on May 27, 1993, alleging violations of his academic freedom and a "failure of the University to follow prescribed procedures in matters relating to reappointment or promotion." Professor Shoucair named Silverman and Glicksman as respondents in his grievance, along with seven unknown "coconspirators" who participated in the electrical sciences group's vote against the initially positive, albeit unenthusiastic, endorsement of the tenure review committee. Most of Shoucair's complaints focused on Silverman's alleged bias because of the grading incident and failure to recuse himself completely from the tenure review proceedings. Professor Shoucair faulted Glicksman for his "reckless dissemination of the [electrical sciences] sub-group's tainted vote" and his failure to provide Shoucair with the engineering division's "Criteria for Evaluation and Promotion." Professor Shoucair also alleged that he had been "individually discriminated against because of ethnic origin."

Beginning in September 1993, an ad hoc committee convened by the FEC heard testimony pertaining to Shoucair's grievance. It was during these proceedings that Shoucair first alleged that Glicksman had undermined his tenure bid in retaliation for Shoucair's professed misgivings about interviewing the minority candidate for the Rosenberg opening. The ad hoc committee did not find this particular charge relevant to Shoucair's grievance and did not pursue it. Ultimately, this committee found "that the evidence presented * * * does not support the charges by Prof. Shoucair of violation of his academic freedom, failure of the University to follow prescribed procedures in matters relating to reappointment and promotion, or discrimination against him as an individual because of ethnic origin." Professor Shoucair made one last-ditch plea to Brown's then-President, Vartan Gregorian, but to no avail; after the ad hoc committee's decision, Shoucair effectively was finished at Brown. His contract expired on June 30, 1994.

Professor Shoucair remained in Providence for roughly another year and a half after he left Brown University. He worked as a consultant for a computer company owned by a former student of his, and he also continued to supervise the work of the last remaining doctoral candidate with whom he had been associated at Brown. Professor Shoucair testified at trial that he submitted "around the order of a hundred" employment applications to colleges and universities between 1994 and 1995, but had received no offers. In early 1996, Shoucair moved to California and accepted a part-time, adjunct teaching position at the University of California–Berkeley. He continued in that capacity at Berkeley until the end of 1999, but eventually left because he believed the position offered no opportunities for advancement. Since leaving UC–Berkeley, Shoucair has done some consulting and volunteer work, but has had "no steady income."

Professor Shoucair filed the lawsuit underlying the instant appeal in May 1996. He alleged that (1) Brown had "tolerated and even condoned" an ethnically hostile work environment created by Dean Silverman in the division of engineering; (2) Professor Glicksman, acting as an agent of Brown, had retaliated against Shoucair for opposing Glicksman's discriminatory interviewing practices; and (3) Shoucair was denied tenure because of his national/ancestral origin. Professor Shoucair sought a declaratory judgment that Brown's actions and practices in his case violated the Fair Employment Practices Act (FEPA), G.L. 1956 chapter 5 of title 28,[2] and in addition to back pay and benefits, compensatory damages, punitive damages and attorney's fees, he asked the court to direct Brown to place him "in the position he would have occupied but for defendant's discriminatory and retaliatory treatment of him." At the conclusion of the trial in May 2003, the jury found for Shoucair on the retaliation claim only and awarded him $400,000 in back pay, $175,000 in compensatory damages, and $100,000 in punitive damages. Brown then renewed the motion for judgment as a matter of law under Rule 50 that it had pressed at both the close of plaintiff's case and at the close of the evidence. In the alternative, Brown moved for a new trial based on Rule 59 of the Superior Court Rules of Civil Procedure. Brown also moved to strike the punitive and compensatory damage awards. Professor Shoucair moved for reinstatement or, alternatively, for an award of front pay; he also moved for attorney's fees.

After hearing arguments on the parties' respective motions, the trial justice denied Brown's Rule 50 and Rule 59 motions. . . . Brown timely filed a notice of appeal to this Court, and Shoucair followed with a timely cross-appeal.

. . .

The . . . theory on which Brown assails the trial court's decision posits that no reasonable jury could conclude that retaliatory intent fueled the decision to deny Shoucair tenure. Brown argues that legitimate academic and institutional needs were the only determinative factors, and that as a matter of law Shoucair failed to make the requisite showing of causation between his purportedly protected activity and Brown's decision to deny him tenure. Brown submits that, even if one allows that Shoucair made his prima facie case for retaliation, it countered with a permissible alternative explanation for his termination, and thus Shoucair had to go beyond his prima facie showing to prove Brown's explanation pretextual. Brown argued that Shoucair's highly specialized area of expertise placed him somewhat on the outskirts of the electrical sciences research landscape. Shoucair's limited field of study, according to Brown, had hindered his capacity to attract significant research grants in the six years leading up to his tenure review. Brown also pointed out that at every step of the tenure review process, Shoucair's own colleagues expressed doubts that his future research endeavors would be any more likely to bring in the desired level of funding or elevate the prestige of Brown's division of engineering. Brown contends that in the context of Title VII and FEPA cases alike, a defendant's articulation of a viable legal reason for termination imposes upon a plaintiff a burden to prove that reason "unworthy of credence" and that Shoucair has fallen short of that mark.

After our review of the evidence, however, we concur with the trial justice's thoughtful decision. In ruling on Brown's motion for judgment as a matter of law, she drew all reasonable inferences in favor of Shoucair and concluded that the evidence did not lead to only one legitimate conclusion

---

2. General Laws 1956 § 28–5–3 declares that it is

"the public policy of this state to foster the employment of all individuals in this state in accordance with their fullest capacities, regardless of their race or color, religion, sex, sexual orientation, gender identity or expression, disability, age, or country of ancestral origin, and to safeguard their right to obtain and hold employment without such discrimination."

about whether Brown's reason for denying him tenure was pretextual. Applying our appellate criteria, we, too, perceive no basis to disturb the verdict of the jury.

The jury and the trial justice were entitled to credit Shoucair's testimony over that of Glicksman and Spinacci, and Shoucair's version of the events, along with evidence he presented, refuted the alternative reasons Brown touted for denying him tenure sufficiently to support a finding of retaliation. As the trial justice pointed out, Shoucair presented testimony to support his qualifications for tenure from respected authorities in his field, and Brown's own tenure review committee recommended, albeit without enthusiasm, that the provost should grant Shoucair tenure. A reasonable person could surmise from this information that Shoucair merited tenure.

Professor Shoucair also testified that Glicksman had all but assured him of tenure just days before Shoucair had expressed reluctance to participate in what he deemed to be a "sham" interview and that almost immediately thereafter Glicksman sabotaged his tenure bid by authoring the TRC report with its ambiguous recommendation. Contrary to Brown's contention that mere temporal proximity is not enough to establish causation, an inference of causation is permissible when the adverse employment action comes so swiftly on the heels of the protected activity. A survey of persuasive authorities indicates that the week or so that elapsed between Shoucair's refusal of Glicksman's request to interview the minority candidate and the issuance of the tenure review committee's report was within an acceptable range to permit a reasonable inference of causation. *See, e.g., Richmond v. ONEOK, Inc.*, 120 F.3d 205, 209 (10th Cir. 1997) (three-month interval insufficient); *Reed v. A.W. Lawrence & Co.*, 95 F.3d 1170, 1178 (2d Cir. 1996) (twelve-day interval sufficient). That said, temporal proximity only suffices to establish prima facie causation, and once Brown articulated its legitimate, nonretaliatory reasons for denying Shoucair's tenure, the *McDonnell Douglas* [*Corp. v. Green*, 411 U.S. 792, 802–04 (1973)] paradigm required Shoucair to make more than a mere prima facie case. Indeed, the consensus of federal courts in the Title VII arena is that "[t]he proper standard of proof on the causation element of a . . . retaliation claim is that the adverse employment action taken against the plaintiff would not have occurred 'but for' [the employee's] protected conduct." *Septimus v. University of Houston*, 399 F.3d 601, 608 (5th Cir. 2005).

To meet his burden, Shoucair had to "do more than simply cast doubt upon the employer's justification." Shoucair had to build on his prima facie case to the extent that the sum of the evidence he presented was such that a reasonable jury could conclude that Brown's justifications for denying him tenure were "unworthy of credence." Professor Shoucair presented evidence suggesting that Glicksman was aware of Shoucair's refusal to interview the additional candidate and that shortly thereafter he authored a very qualified recommendation for Shoucair, submitted it to the electrical sciences group, and then abstained from that group's unanimous vote against Shoucair's tenure. As the trial justice noted, "multiple witnesses testified that this was the first instance they could recall in which the recommendation of the Tenure Review Committee was rejected by the tenured faculty." Professor Shoucair also presented evidence from which the jury could reasonably conclude that the group-level vote sealed his fate, and that the professed independent layers of review that followed were, in fact, nothing more than a formality. We are satisfied that a jury could survey the parties' conflicting testimony and reasonably choose to credit Shoucair's theory of recovery on his retaliation allegation.

Brown points out that the provost ultimately decided on Shoucair's tenure, and cites *Okruhlik v. University of Arkansas*, 395 F.3d 872, 879–80 (8th Cir. 2005), to support its contention that the qualified recommendation Shoucair alleged Glicksman introduced in the TRC report was merely an intermediate act in a many-layered process and therefore could not constitute an adverse employment action. Brown argues that only the final decision on tenure is actionable, and there is no evidence that the final decision-maker, the provost, knew anything about Shoucair's protected activity or harbored any ill will toward him as a result. But *Okruhlik* goes on to add that a jury reasonably may conclude that even a preliminary evaluation, if based on retaliation or discrimination, influenced the decision-making process and thereby infected the final decision.

In *Mato v. Baldauf*, 267 F.3d 444 (5th Cir. 2001), the United States Court of Appeals, Fifth Circuit provided a lucid explanation of the "rubber-stamp" theory Shoucair has invoked to link the provost's actions to Glicksman's alleged retaliatory animus:

> In establishing this causal connection, [plaintiff] must first identify who made the decision that resulted in her termination. For example, *Long v. Eastfield College*, 88 F.3d 300 (5th Cir. 1996), involved an executive officer, on the one hand, with the final authority to fire employees but who had no retaliatory animus toward the plaintiff; and, on the other hand, intermediate supervisors who appeared to have had an improper retaliatory intent and who recommended that an employee be fired. We explained that the causal link between the protected conduct and termination is broken where the official with final authority to fire employees conducts an "independent investigation" in the course of reaching his or her decision. The causal link is not broken, however, where the decision-maker "rubber-stamps" the firing recommendation of . . . subordinates' improper motive. *Id.*; *see also Russell v. McKinney Hospital Venture*, 235 F.3d 219, 226–27 (5th Cir. 2000) ('If the [plaintiff] can demonstrate that others had influence or leverage over the official decisionmaker, * * * it is proper to impute their discriminatory [or retaliatory] attitudes to the formal decisionmaker.'). Of course, the degree to which the executive's decision was based on his or her own independent evaluation is a question of fact.

Although it is true that Glicksman did not go so far as to recommend "firing" Shoucair, in the unique context of a tenure review process the jury nevertheless reasonably could have determined that his arguably subtler form of sabotage was just as damaging. The electrical sciences group, the division of engineering, ConFRaT, and the provost all cited the same concerns over Shoucair's research performance and prospects that Glicksman first red-flagged in his initial report. The fact that a subsequent report issued by the Accreditation Board of Engineering and Technology (ABET) during its independent and unrelated certification review of Brown's division of engineering gave Shoucair a "high" rating for his research belies Glicksman's alleged misgivings. And once the jury resolved that Glicksman's animus had contaminated the process, the key question became whether subsequent reviews were truly independent.

Professor Marc Richman, a faculty member in the division of engineering, testified that in his thirty-five years of experience at Brown, it was extremely rare for subsequent reviewers to disregard the recommendation of a professor's own group (in this case, Shoucair's electrical sciences group). Professor Shoucair also established that Silverman, Glicksman, Shepp, and the provost played bridge together and were friendly with one another. Glicksman and Silverman were particularly close, and given the power the two wielded within the electrical sciences group, it was hardly unreasonable for the jury to doubt the independence of that group's influential vote. *See Lam v. University of Hawaii*, 40 F.3d 1551, 1560–61 (9th Cir. 1994) (evidence of prejudice on the part of two voting faculty members, one of whom headed the appointments committee, sufficient as a matter of law to preclude summary judgment in favor of university); *Gutzwiller v. Fenik*, 860 F.2d 1317, 1327 (6th Cir. 1988) (two biased faculty votes sufficient to establish discriminatory employment decision in tenure process that required decisions at four separate levels). Shoucair presented a combination of factors that, taken as a whole, permitted the jury to conclude that the demise of Shoucair's tenure bid was a fait accompli once Glicksman's animus infected the process.

Brown contends that even if Glicksman did influence the process, Shoucair had the opportunity to make his case to subsequent reviewers and that in itself is enough to defeat his "rubber-stamp" argument. Shoucair admitted at trial that he had the chance to present written evidence to all reviewers and also to answer questions and speak on his own behalf at the division of engineering and ConFRaT meetings convened to consider his application for tenure.

Recently, the Supreme Judicial Court of Massachusetts cited several decisions from various courts in concluding that "[w]hen assessing the independence of the ultimate decision maker, courts place considerable emphasis on the decision maker's giving the employee the opportunity to address the allegations in question, and on the decision maker's awareness of the employee's view that the underlying recommendation is motivated by bias or a desire to retaliate." *Mole v. University of Massachusetts*, 442 Mass. 582, 814 N.E.2d 329, 344 (Mass. 2004).... Although we agree with the Supreme Judicial Court that an employee's opportunity to be heard by subsequent reviewers is a strong indicator that an independent investigation has taken place, we are not prepared to say that as a matter of law by granting Shoucair a limited opportunity to be heard during subsequent stages of review Brown completely purged all traces of Glicksman's alleged retaliation. Although Shoucair did have the opportunity to be heard before the division of engineering and ConFRaT, he did not have any such opportunity to address the electrical sciences group before their vote—the vote that arguably sealed his fate. The jurors heard testimony that the decisions made at the group level are rarely, if ever, reversed at the divisional level, and that ConFRaT and the provost invariably adopt the recommendation of the division.

In light of the remarkable deference all subsequent reviewers apparently accorded to the group-level decision, we are unwilling to disturb the jury's finding that the tenure decision was ultimately a product of Glicksman's retaliatory animus toward Shoucair. We recognize that this is an exceedingly close question, and that a rational jury easily could reach a contrary verdict. Nevertheless, we are satisfied that the evidence led to more than one permissible result. Accordingly, we affirm the judgment in favor of Shoucair on his allegation of retaliation.

Questions and Comments on *Shoucair*

In another denial of tenure case, Reginald Clark claimed he was denied tenure at Claremont Graduate School on the basis of his race. Clark, who was hired by Claremont for a position in multicultural and urban education, had published a 422–page dissertation study on 13 black students in Chicago from similar social backgrounds that performed differently in school. Clark's intent was for the dissertation to be the first part of a cross-cultural research project explaining differences in student success at school. The chairman of the Education Faculty at Claremont told Clark that he would probably receive tenure in three to four years if his book was finished by then. During the intervening years between when Clark began teaching at Claremont and his tenure review, several racially-related incidents occurred on campus. One of Clark's faculty colleagues referred to him by the name "Calhoun" after a stereotypical black character on the Amos and Andy television show. Another faculty member referred to Clark by the term "boy." On one occasion, Clark's office was broken into and racial insults were spray painted on his wall.

During Clark's tenure review, Clark happened to overhear the committee discussing his candidacy. Clark heard one committee member state "I mean, us [sic] white people have rights too." Another member stated "I don't know how I would feel working on a permanent base [sic] with a black man." After Clark was denied tenure, he sued Claremont claiming racial discrimination. On appeal, the court upheld a jury verdict for Clark. Clark v. Claremont Univ. Ctr. & Graduate Sch., 6 Cal.App.4th 639, 8 Cal.Rptr.2d 151 (1992).

Kimel v. Florida Board of Regents

Supreme Court of the United States, 2000.
528 U.S. 62, 120 S.Ct. 631, 145 L.Ed.2d 522.

■ JUSTICE O'CONNOR delivered the opinion of the Court.

The Age Discrimination in Employment Act of 1967 (ADEA or Act), 81 Stat. 602, as amended, 29 U.S.C. § 621 *et seq.* (1994 ed. and Supp. III), makes it unlawful for an employer, including a State, "to fail or refuse to hire or to discharge any individual or otherwise discriminate against any individual . . . because of such individual's age." 29 U.S.C. § 623(a)(1). In these cases, three sets of plaintiffs filed suit under the Act, seeking money damages for their state employers' alleged discrimination on the basis of age. . . .

. . .

The ADEA makes it unlawful for an employer "to fail or refuse to hire or to discharge any individual or otherwise discriminate against any individual with respect to his compensation, terms, conditions, or privileges of employment, because of such individual's age." 29 U.S.C. § 623(a)(1). The Act also provides several exceptions to this broad prohibition. For example, an employer may rely on age where it "is a bona fide occupational qualification reasonably necessary to the normal operation of the particular business." § 623(f)(1). The Act also permits an employer to engage in conduct otherwise prohibited by § 623(a)(1) if the employer's action "is based on reasonable factors other than age," § 623(f)(1), or if the employer "discharges or otherwise disciplines an individual for good cause," § 623(f)(3). Although the Act's prohibitions originally applied only to individuals "at least forty years of age but less than sixty-five years of age," Congress subsequently removed the upper age limit, and the Act now covers individuals age 40 and over. Any person aggrieved by an employer's violation of the Act "may bring a civil action in any court of competent jurisdiction" for legal or equitable relief. § 626(c)(1). . . .

Since its enactment, the ADEA's scope of coverage has been expanded by amendment. Of particular importance to these cases is the Act's treatment of state employers and employees. When first passed in 1967, the ADEA applied only to private employers. In 1974, in a statute consisting primarily of amendments to the FLSA, Congress extended application of the ADEA's substantive requirements to the States. Congress accomplished that expansion in scope by a simple amendment to the definition of "employer" contained in 29 U.S.C. § 630(b): "The term [employer] also means . . . a State or political subdivision of a State and any agency or instrumentality of a State or a political subdivision of a State. . . ." Congress also amended the ADEA's definition of "employee," still defining the term to mean "an individual employed by any employer," but excluding elected officials and appointed policymakers at the state and local levels. § 630(f). In the same 1974 Act, Congress amended 29 U.S.C. § 216(b), the [Fair Labor Standards Act] enforcement provision incorporated by reference into the ADEA. 88 Stat. 61. Section 216(b) now permits an individual to bring a civil action "against any employer (including a public agency) in any Federal or State court of competent jurisdiction." Section 203(x) defines "public agency" to include "the Government of a State or political subdivision thereof," and "any agency of . . . a State, or a political subdivision of a State." Finally, in the 1974 Act, Congress added a provision prohibiting age discrimination generally in employment at the Federal Government. 88 Stat. 74, 29 U.S.C. § 633a (1994 ed. and Supp. III). Under the current ADEA, mandatory age limits for law enforcement officers and firefighters—at federal, state, and local levels—are exempted from the statute's coverage.

In December 1994, Roderick MacPherson and Marvin Narz, ages 57 and 58 at the time, filed suit under the ADEA against their employer, the University of Montevallo, in the United States District Court for the Northern District of Alabama. In their complaint, they alleged that the university had discriminated against them on the basis of their age, that it had retaliated against them for filing discrimination charges with the Equal Employment Opportunity Commission (EEOC), and that its College of Business, at which they were associate professors, employed an evaluation system that had a disparate impact on older faculty members. MacPherson and Narz sought declaratory and injunctive relief, backpay, promotions to full professor, and compensatory and punitive damages. The University of Montevallo moved to dismiss the suit for lack of subject matter jurisdiction, contending it was barred by the Eleventh Amendment. No party disputes the District Court's holding that the University is an instrumentality of the State of Alabama. On September 9, 1996, the District Court granted the University's motion. The court determined that, although the ADEA contains a clear statement of Congress' intent to abrogate the States' Eleventh Amendment immunity, Congress did not enact or extend the ADEA under its Fourteenth

Amendment § 5 enforcement power. The District Court therefore held that the ADEA did not abrogate the States' Eleventh Amendment immunity.

In April 1995, a group of current and former faculty and librarians of Florida State University, including J. Daniel Kimel, Jr., the named petitioner in one of today's cases, filed suit against the Florida Board of Regents in the United States District Court for the Northern District of Florida. The complaint was subsequently amended to add as plaintiffs current and former faculty and librarians of Florida International University. The plaintiffs, all over age 40, alleged that the Florida Board of Regents refused to require the two state universities to allocate funds to provide previously agreed upon market adjustments to the salaries of eligible university employees. The plaintiffs contended that the failure to allocate the funds violated both the ADEA and the Florida Civil Rights Act of 1992, Fla. Stat. § 760.01 *et seq.* (1997 and Supp. 1998), because it had a disparate impact on the base pay of employees with a longer record of service, most of whom were older employees. The plaintiffs sought backpay, liquidated damages, and permanent salary adjustments as relief. The Florida Board of Regents moved to dismiss the suit on the grounds of Eleventh Amendment immunity. On May 17, 1996, the District Court denied the motion, holding that Congress expressed its intent to abrogate the States' Eleventh Amendment immunity in the ADEA, and that the ADEA is a proper exercise of congressional authority under the Fourteenth Amendment.

In May 1996, Wellington Dickson filed suit against his employer, the Florida Department of Corrections, in the United States District Court for the Northern District of Florida. Dickson alleged that the state employer failed to promote him because of his age and because he had filed grievances with respect to the alleged acts of age discrimination. Dickson sought injunctive relief, backpay, and compensatory and punitive damages. The Florida Department of Corrections moved to dismiss the suit on the grounds that it was barred by the Eleventh Amendment. The District Court denied that motion on November 5, 1996, holding that Congress unequivocally expressed its intent to abrogate the States' Eleventh Amendment immunity in the ADEA, and that Congress had authority to do so under § 5 of the Fourteenth Amendment.

The plaintiffs in the *MacPherson* case, and the state defendants in the *Kimel* and *Dickson* cases, appealed to the Court of Appeals for the Eleventh Circuit. The United States also intervened in all three cases to defend the ADEA's abrogation of the States' Eleventh Amendment immunity. The Court of Appeals consolidated the appeals and, in a divided panel opinion, held that the ADEA does not abrogate the States' Eleventh Amendment immunity. . . .

We granted certiorari to resolve a conflict among the Federal Courts of Appeals on the question whether the ADEA validly abrogates the States' Eleventh Amendment immunity.

The Eleventh Amendment states:

> "The Judicial power of the United States shall not be construed to extend to any suit in law or equity, commenced or prosecuted against one of the United States by Citizens of another State, or by Citizens or Subjects of any Foreign State."

Although today's cases concern suits brought by citizens against their own States, this Court has long " 'understood the Eleventh Amendment to stand not so much for what it says, but for the presupposition . . . which it confirms.' " *Seminole Tribe of Fla. v. Florida*, 517 U.S. 44, 54 (1996) (quoting *Blatchford v. Native Village of Noatak*, 501 U.S. 775, 779 (1991)). Accordingly, for over a century now, we have made clear that the Constitution does not provide for federal jurisdiction over suits against nonconsenting States. *College Savings Bank v. Florida Prepaid Postsecondary Ed. Expense Bd.*, 527 U.S. 666, 660–620. . . . Petitioners nevertheless contend that the States of Alabama and Florida must defend the present suits on the merits because Congress abrogated their Eleventh Amendment immunity in the ADEA. To determine whether petitioners are correct, we must resolve two predicate questions: first, whether Congress unequivocally expressed its intent to abrogate that immunity; and second, if it did, whether Congress acted pursuant to a valid grant of constitutional authority.

. . .

This is not the first time we have considered the constitutional validity of the 1974 extension of the ADEA to state and local governments. In *EEOC v. Wyoming*, 460 U.S. 226, 243 (1983), we held that the ADEA constitutes a valid exercise of Congress' power "to regulate Commerce . . . among the several States," and that the Act did not transgress any external restraints imposed on the commerce power by the Tenth Amendment. Because we found the ADEA valid under Congress' Commerce Clause power, we concluded that it was unnecessary to determine whether the Act also could be supported by Congress' power under § 5 of the Fourteenth Amendment. Resolution of today's cases requires us to decide that question.

In *Seminole Tribe*, we held that Congress lacks power under Article I to abrogate the States' sovereign immunity. "Even when the Constitution vests in Congress complete lawmaking authority over a particular area, the Eleventh Amendment prevents congressional authorization of suits by private parties against unconsenting States." . . . Under our firmly established precedent then, if the ADEA rests solely on Congress' Article I commerce power, the private petitioners in today's cases cannot maintain their suits against their state employers.

. . .

Section 5 of the Fourteenth Amendment, however, does grant Congress the authority to abrogate the States' sovereign immunity. In *Fitzpatrick v. Bitzer*, 427 U.S. 445 (1976), we recognized that "the Eleventh Amendment, and the principle of state sovereignty which it embodies, are necessarily limited by the enforcement provisions of § 5 of the Fourteenth Amendment." Since our decision in *Fitzpatrick*, we have reaffirmed the validity of that congressional power on numerous occasions. Accordingly, the private petitioners in these cases may maintain their ADEA suits against the States of Alabama and Florida if, and only if, the ADEA is appropriate legislation under § 5.

. . .

As we recognized most recently in *City of Boerne v. Flores*, 521 U.S. 507, 517 (1997), § 5 is an affirmative grant of power to Congress. "It is for Congress in the first instance to determine whether and what legislation is needed to secure the guarantes of the Fourteenth Amendment, and its conclusions are entitled to much deference." Congress' § 5 power is not confined to the enactment of legislation that merely parrots the precise wording of the Fourteenth Amendment. Rather, Congress' power "to enforce" the Amendment includes the authority both to remedy and to deter violation of rights guaranteed thereunder by prohibiting a somewhat broader swath of conduct, including that which is not itself forbidden by the Amendment's text.

Nevertheless, we have also recognized that the same language that serves as the basis for the affirmative grant of congressional power also serves to limit that power. For example, Congress cannot "decree the *substance* of the Fourteenth Amendment's restrictions on the States.... It has been given the power 'to enforce,' not the power to determine *what constitutes* a constitutional violation." 521 U.S. at 519 (emphases added). The ultimate interpretation and determination of the Fourteenth Amendment's substantive meaning remains the province of the Judicial Branch. In *City of Boerne*, we noted that the determination whether purportedly prophylactic legislation constitutes appropriate remedial legislation, or instead effects a substantive redefinition of the Fourteenth Amendment right at issue, is often difficult. The line between the two is a fine one. Accordingly, recognizing that "Congress must have wide latitude in determining where [that line] lies," we held that "there must be a congruence and proportionality between the injury to be prevented or remedied and the means adopted to that end."

In *City of Boerne*, we applied that "congruence and proportionality" test and held that the Religious Freedom Restoration Act of 1993 (RFRA) was not appropriate legislation under § 5. We first noted that the legislative record contained very little evidence of the unconstitutional conduct purportedly targeted by RFRA's substantive provisions. Rather, Congress had uncovered only "anecdotal evidence" that, standing alone, did not reveal a "widespread pattern of religious discrimination in this country." Second, we found that RFRA is "so out of proportion to a supposed remedial or preventive object that it cannot be understood as responsive to, or designed to prevent, unconstitutional behavior."

Last Term, we again had occasion to apply the "congruence and proportionality" test. In *Florida Prepaid*, we considered the validity of the Eleventh Amendment abrogation provision in the Patent and Plant Variety Protection Remedy Clarification Act (Patent Remedy Act). We held that the statute, which subjected States to patent infringement suits, was not appropriate legislation under § 5 of the Fourteenth Amendment. The Patent Remedy Act failed to meet our congruence and proportionality test first because "Congress identified no pattern of patent infringement *by the States*, let alone a pattern of constitutional violations." 527 U.S. at 640 (emphasis added). Moreover, because it was unlikely that many of the acts of patent infringement affected by the statute had any likelihood of being unconstitutional, we concluded that the scope of the Act was out of proportion to its supposed remedial or preventive objectives. Instead, "the statute's apparent and more basic aims were to provide a uniform remedy for patent infringement and to place States on the same footing as private parties under that regime." While we acknowledged that such aims may be proper congressional concerns under Article I, we found them insufficient to support an abrogation of the States' Eleventh Amendment immunity after *Seminole Tribe*.

Applying the same "congruence and proportionality" test in these cases, we conclude that the ADEA is not "appropriate legislation" under § 5 of the Fourteenth Amendment. Initially, the substantive requirements the ADEA imposes on state and local governments are disproportionate to any unconstitutional conduct that conceivably could be targeted by the Act. We have considered claims of unconstitutional age discrimination under the Equal Protection Clause three times. *See Gregory v. Ashcroft*, 501 U.S. 452 (1991); *Vance v. Bradley*, 440 U.S. 93 (1979); *Massachusetts Bd. of Retirement v. Murgia*, 427 U.S. 307 (1976) *(per curiam)*. In all three cases, we held that the age classifications at issue did not violate the Equal Protection Clause. Age classifications, unlike governmental conduct based on race or gender, cannot be characterized as "so seldom relevant to the achievement of any legitimate state interest that laws grounded in such considerations are deemed to reflect prejudice and antipathy." *Cleburne v. Cleburne Living Center, Inc.*, 473 U.S. 432, 440 (1985). Older persons, again, unlike those who suffer discrimination on the basis of race or gender, have not been subjected to a " 'history of purposeful unequal treatment.' " *Murgia, supra*, at 313 (quoting San Antonio Independent School Dist. v. Rodriguez, 411 U.S. 1, 28 (1973)). Old age also does not define a discrete and insular minority because all persons, if they live out their normal life spans, will experience it. Accordingly, as we recognized in *Murgia*, *Bradley*, and *Gregory*, age is not a suspect classification under the Equal Protection Clause.

States may discriminate on the basis of age without offending the Fourteenth Amendment if the age classification in question is rationally related to a legitimate state interest. The rationality commanded by the Equal Protection Clause does not require States to match age distinctions and the legitimate interests they serve with razorlike precision. As we have explained, when conducting rational basis review "we will not overturn such [government action] unless the varying treatment of different groups or persons is so unrelated to the achievement of any combination of legitimate purposes that we can only conclude that the [government's] actions were irrational." In contrast, when a State discriminates on the basis of race or gender, we require a tighter fit between the discriminatory means and the legitimate ends they serve. *See, e.g., Adarand Constructors, Inc. v. Pena*, 515 U.S. 200, 227 (1995) ("[Racial] classifications are constitutional only if they are narrowly tailored measures that further compelling governmental interests").... Under the Fourteenth Amendment, a State may rely on age as a proxy for other qualities, abilities, or characteristics that are relevant to the State's legitimate interests. The Constitution does not preclude reliance on such generalizations. That age proves to be an inaccurate proxy in any individual case is irrelevant. "Where rationality is the test, a State 'does not violate the Equal Protection Clause merely because the classifications made by its laws are imperfect.' " *Murgia, supra*, at 316. Finally, because an age classification is presumptively rational, the individual challenging its constitutionality bears the burden of proving that the "facts on which the classification is apparently based could not reasonably be conceived to be true by the governmental decisionmaker." *Bradley*, 440 U.S. at 111....

Our decisions in *Murgia*, *Bradley*, and *Gregory* illustrate these principles. In all three cases, we held that the States' reliance on broad generalizations with respect to age did not violate the Equal Protection Clause. In *Murgia*, we upheld against an equal protection challenge a Massachusetts statute requiring state police officers to retire at age 50. The State justified the provision on the ground that the age classification assured the State of the physical preparedness of its officers. Although we acknowledged that Officer Murgia himself was in excellent physical health and could still perform the duties of a state police officer, we found that the statute clearly met the requirements of the Equal Protection Clause. "That the State chooses not to determine fitness more precisely through individualized testing after age 50 [does not prove] that the objective of assuring physical fitness is not rationally furthered by a maximum-age limitation." In *Bradley*, we considered an equal protection challenge to a federal statute requiring Foreign Service officers to retire at age 60. We explained: "If increasing age brings with it increasing susceptibility to physical difficulties ... the fact that individual Foreign Service employees may be able to perform past age 60 does not invalidate [the statute] any more than did the similar truth undercut compulsory retirement at age 50 for uniformed state police in *Murgia*." Finally, in *Gregory*, we upheld a provision of the Missouri Constitution that required judges to retire at age 70. Noting that the Missouri provision was based on a generalization about the effect of old age on the ability of individuals to serve as judges, we acknowledged that "it is far from true that all judges suffer significant deterioration in performance at age 70," "it is probably not true that most do," and "it may not be true at all." Nevertheless, because Missouri's age classification was subject only to rational basis review, we held that the State's reliance on such imperfect generalizations was entirely proper under the Equal Protection Clause. These decisions thus demonstrate that the constitutionality of state classifications on the basis of age cannot be determined on a person-by-person basis. Our Constitution permits States to draw lines on the basis of age when they have a rational basis for doing so at a class-based level, even if it "is probably not true" that those reasons are valid in the majority of cases.

Judged against the backdrop of our equal protection jurisprudence, it is clear that the ADEA is "so out of proportion to a supposed remedial or preventive object that it cannot be understood as responsive to, or designed to prevent, unconstitutional behavior." *City of Boerne*, 521 U.S. at 532. The Act, through its broad restriction on the use of age as a discriminating factor, prohibits substantially more state employment decisions and practices than would likely be held unconstitutional under the applicable equal protection, rational basis standard. The ADEA makes unlawful, in the employment context, all "discrimination against any individual ... because of such individual's age." Petitioners, relying on the Act's exceptions, dispute the extent to which the ADEA erects protections beyond the Constitution's requirements. They contend that the Act's prohibition, considered together with its exceptions, applies only to arbitrary age discrimination, which in the majority of cases corresponds to conduct that violates the Equal Protection Clause. We disagree.

Petitioners stake their claim on § 623(f)(1). That section permits employers to rely on age when it "is a bona fide occupational qualification reasonably necessary to the normal operation of the particular business." Petitioners' reliance on the "bona fide occupational qualification" (BFOQ) defense is misplaced. Our interpretation of § 623(f)(1) in *Western Air Lines, Inc. v. Criswell*, 472 U.S. 400 (1985), conclusively demonstrates that the defense is a far cry from the rational basis standard we apply to age discrimination under the Equal Protection Clause. The petitioner in that case maintained that, pursuant to the BFOQ defense, employers must be permitted to rely on age when such reliance has a "rational basis in fact." We rejected that argument, explaining that "the BFOQ standard adopted in the statute is one of 'reasonable necessity,' not reasonableness," *id.*, at 419, and that the ADEA standard and the rational basis test are "significantly different," *id.*, at 421.

Under the ADEA, even with its BFOQ defense, the State's use of age is prima facie unlawful. *See* 29 U.S.C. § 623 (a)(1); *Western Air Lines*, 472 U.S. at 422 ("Under the Act, employers are to evaluate employees on their merits and not their age"). Application of the Act therefore starts with a presumption in favor of requiring the employer to make an individualized determination. In *Western Air Lines*, we concluded that the BFOQ defense, which shifts the focus from the merits of the individual employee to the necessity for the age classification as a whole, is " 'meant to be an extremely narrow exception to the general prohibition' of age discrimination contained in the ADEA." We based that conclusion on both the restrictive language of the statutory BFOQ provision itself and the EEOC's regulation interpreting that exception. To succeed under the BFOQ defense, we held that an employer must demonstrate either "a substantial basis for believing that *all or nearly all employees* above an age lack the qualifications required for the position," or that reliance on the age classification is necessary because "it is *highly impractical* for the employer to insure by individual testing that its employees will have the necessary qualifications for the job." Measured against the rational basis standard of our equal protection jurisprudence, the ADEA plainly imposes substantially higher burdens on state employers. Thus, although it is true that the existence of the BFOQ defense makes the ADEA's prohibition of age discrimination less than absolute, the Act's substantive requirements nevertheless remain at a level akin to our heightened scrutiny cases under the Equal Protection Clause.

. . .

That the ADEA prohibits very little conduct likely to be held unconstitutional, while significant, does not alone provide the answer to our § 5 inquiry. Difficult and intractable problems often require powerful remedies, and we have never held that § 5 precludes Congress from enacting reasonably prophylactic legislation. Our task is to determine whether the ADEA is in fact just such an appropriate remedy or, instead, merely an attempt to substantively redefine the States' legal obligations with respect to age discrimination. . . .

Our examination of the ADEA's legislative record confirms that Congress' 1974 extension of the Act to the States was an unwarranted response to a perhaps inconsequential problem. Congress never identified any pattern of age discrimination by the States, much less any discrimination whatsoever that rose to the level of constitutional violation. The evidence compiled by petitioners to demonstrate such attention by Congress to age discrimination by the States falls well short of the mark. That evidence consists almost entirely of isolated sentences clipped from floor debates and legislative reports. The statements of Senator Bentsen on the floor of the Senate are indicative of the strength of the evidence relied on by petitioners. See, *e.g.*, 118 Cong. Rec. 24397 (1972) (stating that "there is ample evidence that age discrimination is broadly practiced in government employment," but relying on newspaper articles about federal employees); *id.*, at 7745 ("Letters from my own State have revealed that State and local governments have also been guilty of discrimination toward older employees"); *ibid.* ("There are strong indications that the hiring and firing practices of governmental units discriminate against the elderly. . . .").

Petitioners place additional reliance on Congress' consideration of a 1966 report prepared by the State of California on age discrimination in its public agencies. *See* Hearings on H. R. 3651 et al. before the Subcommittee on Labor of the House of Representatives Committee on Education and Labor, 90th Cong., 1st Sess., pp. 161–201 (1967) (Hearings) (reprinting State of California, Citizens' Advisory Committee on Aging, Age Discrimination in Public Agencies (1966)). Like the assorted sentences petitioners cobble together from a decade's worth of congressional reports and floor debates, the California study does not indicate that the State had engaged in any *unconstitutional* age discrimination. In fact, the report stated that the majority of the age limits uncovered in the state survey applied in the law enforcement and firefighting occupations. Those age limits were not only permitted under California law at the time, but are also currently permitted under the ADEA. *See* 5 U.S.C. §§ 3307(d), (e); 29 U.S.C. § 623 (j) (1994 ed., Supp. III). Even if the California report had uncovered a pattern of unconstitutional age discrimination in the State's public agencies at the time, it nevertheless would have been insufficient to support Congress' 1974 extension of the ADEA to every State of the Union. The report simply does not constitute "evidence that [unconstitutional age discrimination] had become a problem of national import."

Finally, the United States' argument that Congress found substantial age discrimination in the private sector is beside the point. Congress made no such findings with respect to the States. Although we also have doubts whether the findings Congress did make with respect to the private sector could be extrapolated to support a finding of *unconstitutional* age discrimination in the public sector, it is sufficient for these cases to note that Congress failed to identify a widespread pattern of age discrimination by the States.

A review of the ADEA's legislative record as a whole, then, reveals that Congress had virtually no reason to believe that state and local governments were unconstitutionally discriminating against their employees on the basis of age. Although that lack of support is not determinative of the § 5 inquiry, Congress' failure to uncover any significant pattern of unconstitutional discrimination here confirms that Congress had no reason to believe that broad prophylactic legislation was necessary in this field. In light of the indiscriminate scope of the Act's substantive requirements, and the lack of evidence of widespread and unconstitutional age discrimination by the States, we hold that the ADEA is not a valid exercise of Congress' power under § 5 of the Fourteenth Amendment. The ADEA's purported abrogation of the States' sovereign immunity is accordingly invalid.

Our decision today does not signal the end of the line for employees who find themselves subject to age discrimination at the hands of their state employers. We hold only that, in the ADEA, Congress did not validly abrogate the States' sovereign immunity to suits by private individuals. State employees are protected by state age discrimination statutes, and may recover money damages from their state employers, in almost every State of the Union. Those avenues of relief remain available today, just as they were before this decision.

Because the ADEA does not validly abrogate the States' sovereign immunity, however, the present suits must be dismissed. Accordingly, the judgment of the Court of Appeals is affirmed.

Questions and Comments on *Kimel*

The decision in *Kimel* prohibits suits for money damages against public employers, including public universities, but does not prevent suits for injunctive relief. ADEA plaintiffs still may sue officers in their individual capacity at public universities, moreover. Claims for money damages as well as injunctive relief can be brought against private universities.

In a case similar to *Kimel*, but involving the Americans with Disabilities Act, the Supreme Court held that the Act did not abrogate the sovereign immunity of states. Board of Trs. of Univ. of Ala. v. Garrett, 531 U.S. 356 (2001). The Court in *Garrett* discussed the remedies still available to plaintiffs:

> Our holding here that Congress did not validly abrogate the States' sovereign immunity from suit by private individuals for money damages under Title I does not mean that persons with disabilities have no federal recourse against discrimination. Title I of the ADA still prescribes standards applicable to the States. Those standards can be enforced by the United States in actions for money damages, as well as by private individuals in actions for injunctive relief under *Ex parte Young*, 209 U.S. 123 (1908). In addition, state laws protecting the rights of persons with disabilities in employment and other aspects of life provide independent avenues of redress.

Board of Trs. of Univ. of Ala. v. Garrett, 531 U.S. 356, 374, n.9 (2001). For more discussion of the remedies available after the Court's holdings in *Kimel* and *Garrett*, see Ivan E. Bodensteiner & Rosalie B. Levinson, *Litigating Age and Disability Claims Against State and Local Government Employers in the New "Federalism" Era*, 22 BERKELEY J. EMP. & LAB. L. 99 (2001).

PART III

Student Access

CHAPTER 10

ADMISSIONS

JEROME KARABEL, THE CHOSEN: THE HIDDEN HISTORY OF ADMISSION
AND EXCLUSION AT HARVARD, YALE, AND PRINCETON
86–90, 92–93, 100–01, 108 (2005).

For anyone who doubted the existence of a "tipping point" of Jewish enrollment beyond which the WASP elite would abandon a college, Columbia served as a sobering example.... As early as 1908, the headmaster of Horace Mann, a leading private school in New York, reported to Columbia's president Nicholas Murray Butler that the prevailing view among parents with children in private school was the "the University undergraduate body contains a prepondering element of students who have had few social advantages and that as a consequence, there is little opportunity of making friendships of permanent value among them." As a result, most of the parents sent their children out of the city for college. One year later, a visitor to Princeton reported sentiment among the students that the Jews had already ruined Columbia....

.   .   .

The specter of Columbia was very much on the mind of President Lowell as he confronted Harvard's "Jewish problem." With Columbia and NYU taking active measures to limit Jewish enrollment, Lowell moved in February 1920 to inquire about the numbers of Jews at Harvard College. Although the dean's office did not provide a precise estimate, Lowell had ample reason to worry; a study of higher education enrollment patterns in 1918–1919 among the leading private colleges revealed that only Columbia and the University of Pennsylvania—the very institutions that many members of the eastern upper class believed had already been "ruined" by the Jews—had a higher percentage of Jewish students than Harvard.

Though the proportion of Jews in Harvard's freshman class had ranged from 13 to 20 percent between 1912 and 1919, Harvard retained its close connection to Boston's upper class throughout the 1910s. Indeed, the link between Harvard and Brahmin Boston was far tighter than the historical ties between the upper classes of New York and Philadelphia with Columbia and Penn respectively. By the 1910s, Harvard enrolled 85 percent of the sons of the Boston upper class, whereas just 52 and 6 percent of their counterparts in Philadelphia and New York matriculated at Penn and Columbia....

.   .   .

... In a letter to Julian Mack, a member of Harvard's Board of Overseers and a federal judge, Lowell made explicit some of the cultural assumptions behind his commitment to a Jewish quota: "It is the duty of Harvard to receive just as many boys who have come, or whose parents have come, to this country without our background as it can effectively educate: including in education the imparting, not only of book knowledge, but of the ideas and traditions of our people. Experience seems to place that proportion at about 15%."

By the spring of 1922, when Lowell moved decisively, the proportion of Jews had already reached 21.5 percent. Unless immediate measures were taken, Lowell wrote in a letter ... it would suffer the fate of Columbia....

   . . .

... At a [faculty] meeting on May 23, Lowell's brother-in-law and personal friend, James Hardy Ropes, the Hollis Professor of Divinity, introduced a three part motion: its most controversial elements instructed the Committee on Admissions "to take into account the proportionate size of racial and national groups in the membership of Harvard College" and declared that "it is not desirable that the number of students in any group which is not easily assimilated into the common life of the College should exceed fifteen percent of the whole college." Though the motion proposing a 15 percent quota ... was not approved, the meeting was a partial triumph for Lowell, for a slightly revised version of the other controversial element was passed.... It called upon the Committee on Admission, "pending further action by this Faculty ... to take into account the ... proportionate size of racial and national groups in the membership of Harvard College." This was a dramatic departure from Harvard's historic commitment to nondiscrimination....

   . . .

... By May 29, Lowell had received four separate petitions requesting that he call a special meeting to permit the faculty to reconsider the motions it had passed.... One petition, signed by 31 faculty members, described the "action of the Faculty relating to controlling the percentage of the Jews in Harvard College" as a radical departure from the spirit and practice of the college....

By now the eyes of the public were fixed on Harvard.... [A faculty motion to keep the proportion of Jews at its current level was] voted down ... 64–41—a major setback for Lowell....

Compounding Lowell's defeat was the faculty's decision to rescind by a vote of 69–25 the motions passed at the May 23 meeting. But the faculty stopped short of rejecting Lowell's initiatives altogether, leaving in place the earlier decision to appoint a special committee "to consider principles and methods for more effectively sifting candidates for admission."

... [I]n addition to the equivocal response of the faculty, there was the overwhelmingly negative reaction of the press. Within days of the announcement of Lowell's plan, the Boston Telegram ran an editorial: "Down Hill from Harvard to Lowell." In New York, the Times responded with an article, "Discrimination Against Jews Suspected in New Harvard Policy on Admission." And the Nation, despite its reference to "pushing young men with a foreign accent, accustomed to overcome discrimination by self-assertion," came out unequivocally against Jewish quotas. "A university which bars a persecution-scarred race ... cannot keep alive the tradition of intellectual integrity, of *noblesse oblige*, and of essential democracy which have made our elder universities play so great a role in American life—or it must open its doors frankly and fairly to all who can meet its requirements of scholarship."

Lowell's proposal also created a storm of political controversy. In addition to an attack from Boston's mayor James Michael Curley ("If the Jew is barred today, the Italian will be tomorrow, then the Spaniard, and the Pole, and at some future date the Irish.") and a formal resolution of opposition from Samuel Gompers, president of the American Federation of Labor, the proposal also generated a call for a legislative committee, to be appointed by Governor Channing Harris Cox, to investigate whether Harvard was acting in violation of a bill already on the books that mandated equality of opportunity....

. . .

A man of extraordinary hubris, Lowell had made a grave error in making public his plan to impose a Jewish quota. As his counterparts at Yale and Princeton grasped intuitively, the public declaration of an intent to discriminate violated core American principles and was likely to lead to a bitter public controversy. This is precisely what happened at Harvard.... Yet Lowell was utterly forthright about his intentions, making it impossible for Harvard to take measures in full public view that more prudent administrators elsewhere were already carrying out behind closed doors. It was a mistake that Lowell would not repeat.

. . .

... When the Report of the Special Committee Appointed to Consider the Limitation of Numbers was approved by the Board of Overseers on January 11, 1926, Lowell had every reason to be pleased.... [I]t recommended that "the application of the rule concerning candidates from the first seventh of their school be discretionary with the Committee on Admission"—a provision that would make it possible to eliminate schools that sent too many Jews to Harvard. Equally important, the committee decisively rejected an admissions policy based on scholarship alone, stating that "it is neither feasible nor desirable to raise the standards of the College so high that none but brilliant scholars can enter" while stipulating that "the standards ought never to be too high for serious and ambitious students of average intelligence."

When the faculty formally approved the report eight days later, Lowell was further elated, for they also approved measures making the admissions process even more subjective. In particular, the faculty called on [the director of admissions] to interview as many applicants as possible to gather additional information on "character and fitness and the promise of the greatest usefulness in the future as a result of a Harvard education." Henceforth, declared the faculty, a passport-sized photo would be "required as an essential part of the application for admissions."

Note on Admission Policies and Procedures

Karabel's book reveals that the admission forms and policies in widespread use today originated in the restrictive admission policies of the past. Do they need to be revised?

His book focuses almost entirely on three of the most selective universities in the United States: Harvard, Yale, and Princeton. They each have acceptance rates under 13 percent. But how representative are they?

David Hawkins of the National Association for College Admissions Counseling found that of 857 four-year, not-for-profit universities and colleges in the country that accepted more than 1,000 students in 2004, only 2.6 percent accepted fewer than 25 percent of their applicants, while 82.5 percent accepted more than half. *College Acceptance Rates: How Many Get In?*, USA TODAY, Nov. 8, 2006. In addition, most community colleges have open admissions policies and offer the possibility of transferring to a four year college after two years.

Despite the fact that only a small proportion of the colleges and universities have highly selective admissions policies, there is great interest in how those decisions are made. In recent years, many books have appeared that attempt to explain the process. *See, e.g.*, DANIEL GOLDEN, THE PRICE OF ADMISSION: HOW AMERICA'S RULING CLASS BUYS ITS WAY INTO ELITE COLLEGES—AND WHO GETS LEFT OUTSIDE THE GATES (2006); PETER SCHMIDT, COLOR AND MONEY: HOW RICH WHITE KIDS ARE WINNING THE WAR OVER COLLEGE AFFIRMATIVE ACTION (2007); JOSEPH A. SOARES, THE POWER OF PRIVILEGE: YALE AND AMERICA'S ELITE COLLEGES (2007); JACQUES STEINBERG, THE GATEKEEPERS: INSIDE THE ADMISSIONS PROCESS OF A PREMIER COLLEGE (2007); MITCHELL L. STEVENS, CREATING A CLASS, COLLEGE ADMISSIONS AND THE EDUCATION OF ELITES (2007).

Legacy preferences are perhaps the most controversial admissions practice used by colleges and universities aside from affirmative action. Under this practice, children of alumni are given an advantage in the admissions process over other applicants. Effectively, this preference benefits white applicants to a much greater degree than African American applicants, as African Americans were historically discriminated against in higher education. In 2002, Texas A & M University admitted 321 whites and only three African Americans who would not have been admitted without the legacy preference. Colleges and universities justify the use of legacy preferences as a way to generate contributions from alumni. Studies have shown that giving to colleges and university increased as children of alumni reached college age, and then dropped off dramatically thereafter. The decline is more dramatic when the child is not admitted. Federal courts have upheld the use of legacies for public colleges and universities on the ground that the preferences are a rational way to generate monetary support for the university. Because neither race nor any fundamental rights are involved, the policy must have a rational basis only. Adam Liptak, *A Hereditary Perk the Founding Fathers Failed to Anticipate*, N.Y. TIMES, Jan. 15, 2008, at A12. Adding to the controversy, a 2007 study by Princeton University showed that legacies are far more likely than minority students or athletes to have academic problems in college. Peter Schmidt, *Children of Alumni are Uniquely Harmed by Admissions Preferences, Study Finds*, CHRON HIGHER EDUC., Apr. 6, 2007, at 28. Are public colleges and universities justified in using legacy preferences?

Educational Attainment of the U.S. Population by Race and Gender, 2004

	8th grade or less	Some H.S.	H.S. diploma	Some college	Associate Degree	Bachelor's degree	Master's degree	Doctoral Degree	Professional Degree	Number Of adults (millions)
All	6.3%	8.6	32.0	17.0	8.4	18.1	6.7	1.3	1.6	186.9
Men	6.5%	8.7	31.1	16.8	7.5	18.6	6.9	1.8	2.1	89.6
Women	6.1%	8.5	32.8	17.3	9.3	17.6	6.6	0.8	1.1	97.3
Asian All	8.2%	5.0	19.8	10.3	7.3	29.9	12.2	3.6	3.8	8.0
A. Men	6.6%	4.7	17.5	10.8	6.7	29.1	15.0	5.4	4.3	3.8
A. Women	9.6%	5.4	21.8	9.9	7.8	30.6	9.6	2.0	3.3	4.2
Black All	5.8%	13.6	36.0	19.2	7.8	12.3	4.1	0.5	0.8	20.8
B. Men	6.4%	13.3	38.4	18.7	6.8	11.4	3.5	0.6	1.0	9.2
B. Women	5.3%	13.9	34.1	19.6	8.6	13.0	4.4	0.4	0.6	11.6
Hispanic All	25.1%	16.5	27.7	13.2	5.4	8.8	2.2	0.4	0.7	21.6
H. Men	25.1%	17.0	27.4	13.3	4.8	8.4	2.2	0.5	0.7	11.0
H. Women	24.6%	15.9	28.0	13.2	6.0	9.1	2.2	0.4	0.6	10.6
White All	3.3%	6.7	32.8	17.6	9.0	19.8	7.6	1.4	1.7	134.1
W. Men	3.3%	6.8	31.6	17.2	8.1	20.8	7.7	2.0	2.5	64.4
W. Women	3.3%	6.6	34.0	17.8	9.9	18.9	7.5	0.9	1.1	69.7

Source: Census Bureau Survey of 50,000 households conducted in March 2004.

Note on Degree Completion by Race and Income

The differences in educational attainment by race and income remain large as the table shows. In 2006, seventy-five percent of students from families in the top income quartile received bachelor's degrees by age twenty-four. Of students growing up in low-income families, by contrast, fewer than nine percent received a bachelor's degree by age twenty-four. African–Americans between twenty-five and twenty-nine attain bachelor's degrees at only one half, and Latinos at one-third the rate of Whites. Most of the gaps are growing larger. Kati Haycock, *Promise Abandoned: How Policy Choices and Institutional Practices Restrict College Opportunities,* Higher Education Trust (2006).

Minority students who enroll in college achieve lower graduation rates than their white colleagues. Less than half of all black students who start college at a four-year institution graduate in six years or less. This rate is more than twenty percentage points less than the rate for white students. In 2006, The median institutional graduation rate gap between white and black students was nearly ten percent. Kevin Carey, Graduation Rate Watch 1–2 (2008) *available at* http://www.educationsector.org /usr_doc/Graduation_Rate_Watch.pdf.

Degree completion is heavily affected by how prepared students are when they enter college. Only 29 percent of students who enroll in two-year colleges earn an associate's degree in three years or less. ACT, inc, ACT 2007 Retention/Completion Summary Tables (2007) *available at* http://www.act.org/research/policymakers/pdf/ retain_trends.pdf. Forty-two percent of the freshmen enrolled in community colleges are enrolled in at least one remedial course. JOHN WIRT ET AL., THE CONDITION OF EDUCATION 2004, at 84 (2004) *available at* http://nces.ed.gov/pubs2004/2004077.pdf. By contrast, more than half the students who enroll in four year colleges earn a bachelor's degree within six years. ACT 2007. About one third of them enroll in at least one remedial course. Overall, only thirty percent of students who have to take remedial reading in college ever earn a degree or certificate. THE CONDITION OF EDUCATION 2004, *supra*.

A. DISCRIMINATION ON THE BASIS OF RACE

Sweatt v. Painter

Supreme Court of the United States, 1950.
339 U.S. 629, 70 S.Ct. 848, 94 L.Ed. 1114.

[The opinion is set forth at pp. 92–95, *supra*.]

Brown v. Board of Education

Supreme Court of the United States, 1954.
347 U.S. 483, 74 S.Ct. 686, 98 L.Ed. 873.

■ MR. CHIEF JUSTICE WARREN delivered the opinion of the [unanimous] Court.

These cases come to us from the States of Kansas, South Carolina, Virginia, and Delaware....

In each of the cases, minors of the Negro race, through their legal representatives, seek the aid of the courts in obtaining admission to the public schools of their community on a nonsegregated basis. In each instance, they had been denied admission to schools attended by white children under laws requiring or permitting segregation according to race. This segregation was alleged to deprive the plaintiffs of the equal protection of the laws under the Fourteenth Amendment. In each of the cases other than the Delaware case, a three-judge federal district court denied relief to the plaintiffs on the so-called "separate but equal" doctrine announced by this Court in *Plessy v. Ferguson*, 163 U.S. 537 [(1896)]. Under that doctrine, equality of treatment is accorded when the races are provided substantially equal facilities, even though these facilities be separate. In the Delaware case, the Supreme Court of Delaware adhered to that doctrine, but ordered that the plaintiffs be admitted to the white schools because of their superiority to the Negro schools.

The plaintiffs contend that segregated public schools are not "equal" and cannot be made "equal," and that hence they are deprived of the equal protection of the laws....

 . . .

... In this Court, there have been six cases involving the "separate but equal" doctrine in the field of public education. In *Cumming v. County Board of Education*, 175 U.S. 528, and *Gong Lum v. Rice*, 275 U.S. 78, the validity of the doctrine itself was not challenged. In more recent cases, all on the graduate school level, inequality was found in that specific benefits enjoyed by white students were denied to Negro students of the same educational qualifications. *Missouri ex rel. Gaines v. Canada*, 305 U.S. 337; *Sipuel v. Oklahoma*, 332 U.S. 631; *Sweatt v. Painter*, 339 U.S. 629; *McLaurin v. Oklahoma State Regents*, 339 U.S. 637. In none of these cases was it necessary to re-examine the doctrine to grant relief to the Negro plaintiff. And in *Sweatt v. Painter, supra*, the Court expressly reserved decision on the question whether *Plessy v. Ferguson* should be held inapplicable to public education.

... Here, unlike *Sweatt v. Painter*, there are findings below that the Negro and white schools involved have been equalized, or are being equalized, with respect to buildings, curricula, qualifications and salaries of teachers, and other "tangible" factors. Our decision, therefore, cannot turn on merely a comparison of these tangible factors in the Negro and white schools involved in each of the cases. We must look instead to the effect of segregation itself on public education.

In approaching this problem, we cannot turn the clock back to 1868 when the Amendment was adopted, or even to 1896 when *Plessy v. Ferguson* was written. We must consider public education in the light of its full development and its present place in American life throughout the Nation. Only in this way can it be determined if segregation in public schools deprives these plaintiffs of the equal protection of the laws.

Today, education is perhaps the most important function of state and local governments. Compulsory school attendance laws and the great expenditures for education both demonstrate our recognition of the importance of education to our democratic society. It is required in the performance of our most basic public responsibilities, even service in the armed forces. It is the very foundation of good citizenship. Today it is a principal instrument in awakening the child to cultural values, in preparing him for later professional training, and in helping him to adjust normally to his environment. In these days, it is doubtful that any child may reasonably be expected to succeed in life if he is denied the opportunity of an education. Such an opportunity, where the state has undertaken to provide it, is a right which must be made available to all on equal terms.

We come then to the question presented: Does segregation of children in public schools solely on the basis of race, even though the physical facilities and other "tangible" factors may be equal, deprive the children of the minority group of equal educational opportunities? We believe that it does.

In *Sweatt v. Painter, supra*, in finding that a segregated law school for Negroes could not provide them equal educational opportunities, this Court relied in large part on "those qualities which are incapable of objective measurement but which make for greatness in a law school." In *McLaurin v. Oklahoma State Regents, supra*, the Court, in requiring that a Negro admitted to a white graduate school be treated like all other students, again resorted to intangible considerations: " ... his ability to study, to engage in discussions and exchange views with other students, and, in general, to learn his profession." Such considerations apply with added force to children in grade and high schools. To separate them from others of similar age and qualifications solely because of their race generates a feeling of inferiority as to their status in the community that may affect their hearts and minds in a way unlikely ever to be undone.... Whatever may have been the extent of psychological knowledge at the time of *Plessy v. Ferguson*, this finding is amply supported by modern authority. Any language in *Plessy v. Ferguson* contrary to this finding is rejected.

We conclude that in the field of public education the doctrine of "separate but equal" has no place. Separate educational facilities are inherently unequal. Therefore, we hold that the plaintiffs and others similarly situated for whom the actions have been brought are, by reason of the segregation complained of, deprived of the equal protection of the laws guaranteed by the Fourteenth Amendment. . . .

Questions and Comments on *Brown v. Board of Education*

Although *Brown* dealt with segregation in grades K to 12, it also sounded the death knell for de jure segregation in higher education as the next case shows. *Brown* also had the potential of increasing the number of minority students academically prepared for college.

Why did Thurgood Marshall and the NAACP Legal Defense Fund bring a case involving a law student to the Supreme Court before turning to elementary school segregation? *See generally* RICHARD KLUGER, SIMPLE JUSTICE: THE HISTORY OF *BROWN V. BOARD OF EDUCATION* AND BLACK AMERICA'S STRUGGLE FOR EQUALITY (1975); JAMES T. PATTERSON, *BROWN V. BOARD OF EDUCATION*: A CIVIL RIGHTS MILESTONE AND ITS TROUBLED LEGACY (2001).

In overturning *Plessy v. Ferguson*, *Brown* struck a decisive blow against Jim Crow. Nonetheless, a number of scholars have criticized the rationale of *Brown* and the slow enforcement of its holding. *See, e.g.*, CHARLES OGLETREE, ALL DELIBERATE SPEED: REFLECTIONS ON THE FIRST HALF-CENTURY OF *BROWN V. BOARD OF EDUCATION* (2004). *See also* DERRICK BELL, SILENT COVENANTS : *BROWN V. BOARD OF EDUCATION* AND THE UNFULFILLED HOPES FOR RACIAL REFORM (2004) (suggesting that African–American students would have been better off if the Supreme Court had ordered southern states to equalize black and white schools). *But see* Leland Ware, *The Story of* Brown v. Board of Education: *The Long Road to Racial Equality in* EDUCATION LAW STORIES 19, 45 (Michael A. Olivas & Ronna Greff Schneider eds., 2008):

> There have been many difficulties with school desegregation beginning with the era of massive resistance and continuing into the present with housing patterns that create segregated schools. But these problems cannot fairly be attributed to the opinions in *Brown*.

Who is right?

United States v. Fordice

Supreme Court of the United States, 1992.
505 U.S. 717, 112 S.Ct. 2727, 120 L.Ed.2d 575.

■ JUSTICE WHITE delivered the opinion of the Court.

In 1954, this Court held that the concept of " 'separate but equal' " has no place in the field of public education. *Brown v. Board of Education*, 347 U.S. 483, 495 *(Brown I)*. The following year, the Court ordered an end to segregated public education "with all deliberate speed." *Brown v. Board of Education*, 349 U.S. 294, 301 (1955) *(Brown II)*. Since these decisions, the Court has had many occasions to evaluate whether a public school district has met its affirmative obligation to dismantle its prior *de jure* segregated system in elementary and secondary schools. In these cases we decide what standards to apply in determining whether the State of Mississippi has met this obligation in the university context.

Mississippi launched its public university system in 1848 by establishing the University of Mississippi, an institution dedicated to the higher education exclusively of white persons. In succeeding decades, the State erected additional postsecondary, single-race educational facilities. Alcorn State University opened its doors in 1871 as "an agricultural college for the education of Mississippi's black youth." Creation of four more exclusively white institutions followed: Mississippi State University (1880), Mississippi University for Women (1885), University of Southern Mississippi (1912), and Delta State University (1925). The State added two more solely black institutions in 1940 and 1950: in the former year, Jackson State University, which was charged with training "black teachers for the black public schools," and in the latter year, Mississippi Valley State University, whose functions were to educate teachers primarily for rural and elementary schools and to provide vocational instruction to black students.

Despite this Court's decisions in *Brown I* and *Brown II*, Mississippi's policy of *de jure* segregation continued. The first black student was not admitted to the University of Mississippi until 1962, and then only by court order. *See Meredith v. Fair*, 306 F.2d 374 (CA5), *cert. denied*, 371 U. S. 828, *enf'd*, 313 F.2d 532 (1962) (en banc) *(per curiam)*. For the next 12 years the segregated public university system in the State remained largely intact. Mississippi State University, Mississippi University for Women, University of Southern Mississippi, and Delta State University each admitted at least one black student during these years, but the student composition of these institutions was still almost completely white. During this period, Jackson State and Mississippi Valley State were exclusively black; Alcorn State had admitted five white students by 1968.

Private petitioners initiated this lawsuit in 1975. They complained that Mississippi had maintained the racially segregative effects of its prior dual system of postsecondary education in violation of the Fifth, Ninth, Thirteenth, and Fourteenth Amendments, 42 U. S. C. §§ 1981 and 1983, and Title VI of the Civil Rights Act of 1964, 42 U. S. C. § 2000d. Shortly thereafter, the United States filed its complaint in intervention, charging that state officials had failed to satisfy their obligation under the Equal Protection Clause of the Fourteenth Amendment and Title VI to dismantle Mississippi's dual system of higher education.

After this lawsuit was filed, the parties attempted for 12 years to achieve a consensual resolution of their differences through voluntary dismantlement by the State of its prior separated system. [In 1981, the State assigned certain missions to Mississippi's public universities as they then existed. It classified University of Mississippi, Mississippi State, and Southern Mississippi, three exclusively white institutions under the prior system, as "comprehensive" universities having the most varied programs and offering graduate degrees. Two of the other historically white institutions, Delta State University and Mississippi University for Women, along with two of the historically black institutions, Alcorn State University and Mississippi Valley State University, were designated as "regional" universities with more limited programs and devoted primarily to undergraduate education. Jackson State University was classified as an "urban" university whose mission was defined by its urban location.]

By the mid–1980's, 30 years after *Brown*, more than 99 percent of Mississippi's white students were enrolled at University of Mississippi, Mississippi State, Southern Mississippi, Delta State, and Mississippi University for Women. The student bodies at these universities remained predominantly white, averaging between 80 and 91 percent white students. Seventy-one percent of the State's black students attended Jackson State, Alcorn State, and Mississippi Valley State, where the racial composition ranged from 92 to 99 percent black.

By 1987, the parties concluded that they could not agree on whether the State had taken the requisite affirmative steps to dismantle its prior *de jure* segregated system. They proceeded to trial. . . .

[The District Court] concluded that in the higher education context, "the affirmative duty to desegregate does not contemplate either restricting choice or the achievement of any degree of racial balance."

When it addressed the same aspects of the university system covered by the findings of fact in light of the foregoing standard, the court found no violation of federal law in any of them. "In summary, the court finds that current actions on the part of the defendants demonstrate conclusively that the defendants are fulfilling their affirmative duty to disestablish the former *de jure* segregated system of higher education."

The Court of Appeals reheard the action en banc and affirmed the decision of the District Court. . . .

We granted the respective writs of certiorari filed by the United States and the private petitioners.

. . .

Like the United States, we do not disagree with the Court of Appeals' observation that a state university system is quite different in very relevant respects from primary and secondary schools. Unlike attendance at the lower level schools, a student's decision to seek higher education has been a matter of choice. The State historically has not assigned university students to a particular institution. Moreover, like public universities throughout the country, Mississippi's institutions of higher learning are not fungible—they have been designated to perform certain missions. Students who qualify for admission enjoy a range of choices of which institution to attend. Thus, as the Court of Appeals stated, "it hardly needs mention that remedies common to public school desegregation, such as pupil assignments, busing, attendance quotas, and zoning, are unavailable when persons may freely choose whether to pursue an advanced education and, when the choice is made, which of several universities to attend."

We do not agree with the Court of Appeals or the District Court, however, that the adoption and implementation of race-neutral policies alone suffice to demonstrate that the State has completely abandoned its prior dual system. That college attendance is by choice and not by assignment does not mean that a race-neutral admissions policy cures the constitutional violation of a dual system. In a system based on choice, student attendance is determined not simply by admissions policies, but also by many other factors. Although some of these factors clearly cannot be attributed to state policies, many can be. Thus, even after a State dismantles its segregative *admissions* policy, there may still be state action that is traceable to the State's prior *de jure* segregation and that continues to foster segregation. . . . We also disagree with respondents that the Court of Appeals and District Court properly relied on our decision in *Bazemore v. Friday*, 478 U.S. 385 (1986). *Bazemore* neither requires nor justifies the conclusions reached by the two courts below.

Bazemore raised the issue whether the financing and operational assistance provided by a state university's extension service to voluntary 4–H and Homemaker Clubs was inconsistent with the Equal Protection Clause because of the existence of numerous all-white and all-black clubs. Though prior to 1965 the clubs were supported on a segregated basis, the District Court had found that the policy of segregation had been completely abandoned and that no evidence existed of any lingering discrimination in either services or membership; any racial imbalance resulted from the wholly voluntary and unfettered choice of private individuals. *Bazemore, supra,* at 407 (WHITE, J., concurring). In this context, we held inapplicable the . . . Court's judgment [in *Green v. School Bd. of New Kent County,* 391 U.S. 430 (1968)] that a voluntary choice program was insufficient to dismantle a *de jure* dual system in public primary and secondary schools, but only after satisfying ourselves that the State had not fostered segregation by playing a part in the decision of which club an individual chose to join.

Bazemore plainly does not excuse inquiry into whether Mississippi has left in place certain aspects of its prior dual system that perpetuate the racially segregated higher education system. If the State perpetuates policies and practices traceable to its prior system that continue to have segregative effects—whether by influencing student enrollment decisions or by fostering segregation in other facets of the university system—and such policies are without sound educational justification and can be practicably eliminated, the State has not satisfied its burden of proving that it has dismantled its prior system. . . .

Had the Court of Appeals applied the correct legal standard, it would have been apparent from the undisturbed factual findings of the District Court that there are several surviving aspects of Mississippi's prior dual system which are constitutionally suspect; for even though such policies may be race neutral on their face, they substantially restrict a person's choice of which institution to enter, and they contribute to the racial identifiability of the eight public universities. Mississippi must justify these policies or eliminate them.

. . .

We deal first with the current admissions policies of Mississippi's public universities. As the District Court found, the three flagship historically white universities in the system—University of Mississippi, Mississippi State University, and University of Southern Mississippi—enacted policies in 1963 requiring all entrants to achieve a minimum composite score of 15 on the test administered by the American College Testing Program (ACT). The court described the "discriminatory taint" of this policy, an obvious reference to the fact that, at the time, the average ACT score for white students was 18 and the average score for blacks was 7. The District Court concluded, and the en banc Court of Appeals agreed, that present admissions standards derived from policies enacted in the 1970's to redress the problem of student unpreparedness. Obviously, this midpassage justification for perpetuating a policy enacted originally to discriminate against black students does not make the present admissions standards any less constitutionally suspect.

The present admissions standards are not only traceable to the *de jure* system and were originally adopted for a discriminatory purpose, but they also have present discriminatory effects. Every Mississippi resident under 21 seeking admission to the university system must take the ACT test. Any applicant who scores at least 15 qualifies for automatic admission to any of the five historically white institutions except Mississippi University for Women, which requires a score of 18 for automatic admission unless the student has a 3.0 high school grade average. Those scoring less than 15 but at least 13 automatically qualify to enter Jackson State University, Alcorn State University, and Mississippi Valley State University. Without doubt, these requirements restrict the range of choices of entering students as to which institution they may attend in a way that perpetuates segregation. Those scoring 13 or 14, with some exceptions, are excluded from the five historically white universities and if they want a higher education must go to one of the historically black institutions or attend junior college with the hope of transferring to a historically white institution. Proportionately more blacks than whites face this choice: In 1985, 72 percent of Mississippi's white high school seniors achieved an ACT composite score of 15 or better, while less than 30 percent of black high school seniors earned that score. It is not surprising then that Mississippi's universities remain predominantly identifiable by race.

The segregative effect of this automatic entrance standard is especially striking in light of the differences in minimum automatic entrance scores among the regional universities in Mississippi's system. The minimum score for automatic admission to Mississippi University for Women is 18; it is 13 for the historically black universities. Yet Mississippi University for Women is assigned the same institutional mission as two other regional universities, Alcorn State and Mississippi Valley State—that of providing quality undergraduate education. The effects of the policy fall disproportionately on black students who might wish to attend Mississippi University for Women; and though the disparate impact is not as great, the same is true of the minimum standard ACT score of 15 at Delta State University—the other "regional" university—as compared to the historically black "regional" universities where a score of 13 suffices for automatic admission. The courts below made little, if any, effort to justify in educational terms those particular disparities in entrance requirements or to inquire whether it was practicable to eliminate them.

We also find inadequately justified by the courts below or by the record before us the differential admissions requirements between universities with dissimilar programmatic missions. We do not suggest that absent a discriminatory purpose different programmatic missions accompanied by different admissions standards would be constitutionally suspect simply because one or more schools are racially identifiable. But here the differential admissions standards are remnants of the dual system with a continuing discriminatory effect, and the mission assignments "to some degree follow the historical racial assignments." Moreover, the District Court did not justify the differing admissions standards based on the different mission assignments. It observed only that in the 1970's, the board of trustees justified a minimum ACT score of 15 because too many students with lower scores were not prepared for the historically white institutions and that imposing the 15 score requirement on admissions to the historically black institutions would decimate attendance at those universities. The District Court also stated that the mission of the regional universities had the more modest function of providing quality undergraduate education. Certainly the comprehensive universities are also, among other things, educating undergraduates. But we think the 15 ACT test score for automatic admission to the comprehensive universities, as compared with a score of 13 for the regionals, requires further justification in terms of sound educational policy.

Another constitutionally problematic aspect of the State's use of the ACT test scores is its policy of denying automatic admission if an applicant fails to earn the minimum ACT score specified for the particular institution, without also resorting to the applicant's high school grades as an additional factor in predicting college performance. The United States produced evidence that the American College Testing Program (ACTP), the administering organization of the ACT, discourages use of ACT scores as the sole admissions criterion on the ground that it gives an incomplete "picture" of the student applicant's ability to perform adequately in college. One ACTP report presented into evidence suggests that "it would be foolish" to substitute a 3– or 4–hour test in place of a student's high school grades as a means of predicting college performance. The record also indicated that the disparity between black and white students' high school grade averages was much narrower than the gap between their average ACT scores, thereby suggesting that an admissions formula which included grades would increase the number of black students eligible for automatic admission to all of Mississippi's public universities.[10]

The United States insists that the State's refusal to consider information which would better predict college performance than ACT scores alone is irrational in light of most States' use of high school grades and other indicators along with standardized test scores. The District Court observed that the board of trustees was concerned with grade inflation and the lack of comparability in grading practices and course offerings among the State's diverse high schools. Both the District Court and the Court of Appeals found this concern ample justification for the failure to consider high school grade performance along with ACT scores. In our view, such justification is inadequate because the ACT requirement was originally adopted for discriminatory purposes, the current requirement is traceable to that decision and seemingly continues to have segregative effects, and the State has so far failed to show that the "ACT-only" admissions standard is not susceptible to elimination without eroding sound educational policy.

. . .

We next address Mississippi's scheme of institutional mission classification, and whether it perpetuates the State's formerly *de jure* dual system. The District Court found that, throughout the period of *de jure* segregation, University of Mississippi, Mississippi State University, and University of Southern Mississippi were the flagship institutions in the state system. They received the most funds, initiated the most advanced and specialized programs, and developed the widest range of curricular functions. At their inception, each was restricted for the education solely of white persons. The

---

10. In 1985, 72 percent of white students in Mississippi scored 15 or better on the ACT test, whereas only 30 percent of black students achieved that mark, a difference of nearly 2½ times. By contrast, the disparity among grade averages was not nearly so wide. 43.8 percent of white high school students and 30.5 percent of black students averaged at least a 3.0, and 62.2 percent of whites and 49.2 percent of blacks earned at least a 2.5 grade point average. Though it failed to make specific factfindings on this point, this evidence, which the State does not dispute, is fairly encompassed within the District Court's statement that "black students on the average score somewhat lower [than white students]."

missions of Mississippi University for Women and Delta State University, by contrast, were more limited than their other all-white counterparts during the period of legalized segregation. Mississippi University for Women and Delta State University were each established to provide undergraduate education solely for white students in the liberal arts and such other fields as music, art, education, and home economics. When they were founded, the three exclusively black universities were more limited in their assigned academic missions than the five all-white institutions. Alcorn State, for example, was designated to serve as "an agricultural college for the education of Mississippi's black youth." Jackson State and Mississippi Valley State were established to train black teachers. Though the District Court's findings do not make this point explicit, it is reasonable to infer that state funding and curriculum decisions throughout the period of *de jure* segregation were based on the purposes for which these institutions were established.

. . .

The institutional mission designations adopted in 1981 have as their antecedents the policies enacted to perpetuate racial separation during the *de jure* segregated regime. . . . That different missions are assigned to the universities surely limits to some extent an entering student's choice as to which university to seek admittance. While the courts below both agreed that the classification and mission assignments were made without discriminatory purpose, the Court of Appeals found that the record "supports the plaintiffs' argument that the mission designations had the effect of maintaining the more limited program scope at the historically black universities." We do not suggest that absent discriminatory purpose the assignment of different missions to various institutions in a State's higher education system would raise an equal protection issue where one or more of the institutions become or remain predominantly black or white. But here the issue is whether the State has sufficiently dismantled its prior dual system; and when combined with the differential admission practices and unnecessary program duplication, it is likely that the mission designations interfere with student choice and tend to perpetuate the segregated system. On remand, the court should inquire whether it would be practicable and consistent with sound educational practices to eliminate any such discriminatory effects of the State's present policy of mission assignments.

. . .

Because the District Court and the Court of Appeals failed to consider the State's duties in their proper light, the cases must be remanded. To the extent that the State has not met its affirmative obligation to dismantle its prior dual system, it shall be adjudged in violation of the Constitution and Title VI and remedial proceedings shall be conducted. The decision of the Court of Appeals is vacated, and the cases are remanded for further proceedings consistent with this opinion.

■ JUSTICE THOMAS, concurring.

. . .

I agree with the Court that a State does not satisfy its obligation to dismantle a dual system of higher education merely by adopting race-neutral policies for the future administration of that system. . . .

. . .

[W]e do not foreclose the possibility that there exists "sound educational justification" for maintaining historically black colleges *as such*. Despite the shameful history of state-enforced segregation, these institutions have survived and flourished. Indeed, they have expanded as opportunities for blacks to enter historically white institutions have expanded. Between 1954 and 1980, for example, enrollment at historically black colleges increased from 70,000 to 200,000 students, while degrees awarded increased from 13,000 to 32,000. *See* S. Hill, National Center for Education Statistics, The Traditionally Black Institutions of Higher Education 1860 to 1982, pp. xiv-xv (1985). These accomplishments have not gone unnoticed:

> The colleges founded for Negroes are both a source of pride to blacks who have attended them and a source of hope to black families who want the benefits of higher learning for their children. They have exercised leadership in developing educational opportunities for young blacks at all levels of instruction, and, especially in the South, they are still regarded as key institutions for enhancing the general quality of the lives of black Americans. Carnegie Commission on Higher Education, From Isolation to Mainstream: Problems of the Colleges Founded for Negroes 11 (1971).

I think it undisputable that these institutions have succeeded in part because of their distinctive histories and traditions; for many, historically black colleges have become "a symbol of the highest attainments of black culture." J. Preer, Lawyers v. Educators: Black Colleges and Desegregation in Public Higher Education 2 (1982). Obviously, a State cannot maintain such traditions by closing particular institutions, historically white or historically black, to particular racial groups. Nonetheless, it hardly follows that a State cannot operate a diverse assortment of institutions—including historically black institutions—open to all on a race-neutral basis, but with established traditions and programs that might disproportionately appeal to one race or another. No one, I imagine, would argue that such institutional *diversity* is without "sound educational justification," or that it is even remotely akin to program *duplication*, which is designed to separate the races for the sake of separating the races. The Court at least hints at the importance of this value when it distinguishes *Green* in part on the ground that colleges and universities "are not fungible." Although I agree that a State is not constitutionally *required* to maintain its historically black institutions as such, I do not understand our opinion to hold that a State is *forbidden* to do so. It would be ironic, to say the least, if the institutions that sustained blacks during segregation were themselves destroyed in an effort to combat its vestiges.

Questions and Comments on *Fordice*

1. As Justice White's opinion for the Court notes, segregation in higher education is different from segregation in K–12 because college students are not assigned by the state to particular schools as younger students are. After the decision of the Supreme Court in *Fordice*, a private settlement was reached. Although some plaintiffs did not agree with the settlement, it was upheld in the courts. *See* 358 F.3d 356 (2004), *cert. denied*, 537 U.S. 861.

2. Remember Karabel's assertion that many of today's admissions practices can be traced to programs designed to restrict access for certain groups to particular institutions of higher learning. After *Fordice*, are these practices still justifiable for public colleges and universities? If such policies were initially established to discriminate based on race, how can a public college or university continue to justify their use?

3. Notice that the Court rejects state policies that have "segregative effects" on student enrollment decisions. How is a state to ensure that its policies do not disproportionately appeal to one or another race? Is it an equal protection problem if certain racial groups prefer certain educational environments over others?

4. Shortly after the *Fordice* decision, some commentators complained that the Court was insufficiently clear about what actions a state must take to dismantle the effects of former segregated public higher education systems:

> . . . While *Fordice* notes many of the issues relevant to college desegregation, it does not offer adequate analysis or guidance. Defendants will easily manipulate the *Fordice* standard because it is vague. *Fordice* fails to solve the voluntary/involuntary dilemma raised by *Bazemore*, and it provides no formula for allocating the burdens of desegregation.

Cory Todd Wilson, Note, *Mississippi Learning: Curriculum for the Post–*Brown *Era of Higher Education Desegregation*, 104 YALE L.J. 243, 253 (1994). Do you agree? What affirmative steps must states take to integrate public colleges and universities?

5. Justice Thomas's concurrence notes that historically black colleges with race-neutral admissions policies may present a sound educational justification for maintaining policies that disproportionately cater to non-white students. Leland Ware argues that these historically black institutions provide opportunities that are unavailable at predominately white universities. He finds that black institutions provide leadership opportunities, are freer of racial tensions, and focus on African–American culture and accomplishment in a way that white institutions do not. He concludes that historically black institutions are educationally justified because they provide a different type of educational environment than white colleges can offer. Leland Ware, *The Most Visible Vestige: Black Colleges After* Fordice, 35 B.C. L. REV. 633 (1994).

B.   DISCRIMINATION ON THE BASIS OF GENDER

United States v. Virginia

Supreme Court of the United States, 1996.
518 U.S. 515, 116 S.Ct. 2264, 135 L.Ed.2d 735.

■ JUSTICE GINSBURG delivered the opinion of the Court.

Virginia's public institutions of higher learning include an incomparable military college, Virginia Military Institute (VMI). The United States maintains that the Constitution's equal protection guarantee precludes Virginia from reserving exclusively to men the unique educational opportunities VMI affords. We agree.

[VMI was founded in 1839, and remains Virginia's sole single-sex school. It's distinctive mission is to produce "citizen-soldiers" prepared for leadership in civilian life and military service. To pursue this mission, VMI employs an "adversative method" of instruction. Through this process, cadets are subjected to physical rigor, mental stress, absence of privacy, minute regulation of behavior, and indoctrination in desirable values. The purpose of this method is to instill in the student a sense of their limits and capabilities.

The approximately 1,300 men currently enrolled at VMI live in barracks under constant surveillance. They wear uniforms, eat together in the mess hall, and regularly participate in drills. Entering students are incessantly exposed to the rat line, "an extreme form of the adversarial model," comparable in intensity to Marine Corps boot camp.]

VMI has notably succeeded in its mission to produce leaders; among its alumni are military generals, Members of Congress, and business executives. The school's alumni overwhelmingly perceive that their VMI training helped them to realize their personal goals. VMI's endowment reflects the loyalty of its graduates; VMI has the largest per-student endowment of all public undergraduate institutions in the Nation.

. . .

VMI attracts some applicants because of its reputation as an extraordinarily challenging military school, and "because its alumni are exceptionally close to the school." "[W]omen have no opportunity anywhere to gain the benefits of [the system of education at VMI]."

In 1990, prompted by a complaint filed with the Attorney General by a female high-school student seeking admission to VMI, the United States sued the Commonwealth of Virginia and VMI, alleging that VMI's exclusively male admission policy violated the Equal Protection Clause of the Fourteenth Amendment.

. . .

The District Court ruled in favor of VMI. . . .

The Court of Appeals for the Fourth Circuit disagreed and vacated the District Court's judgment. . . .

In response to the Fourth Circuit's ruling, Virginia proposed a parallel program for women: Virginia Women's Institute for Leadership (VWIL). The 4–year, state-sponsored undergraduate program would be located at Mary Baldwin College, a private liberal arts school for women, and would be open, initially, to about 25 to 30 students. Although VWIL would share VMI's mission—to produce "citizen-soldiers"—the VWIL program would differ, as does Mary Baldwin College, from VMI in academic offerings, methods of education, and financial resources.

. . .

Virginia returned to the District Court seeking approval of its proposed remedial plan, and the court decided the plan met the requirements of the Equal Protection Clause.

. . .

A divided Court of Appeals affirmed the District Court's judgment.

. . .

We note, the core instruction of this Court's pathmarking decisions in *J.E.B. v. Alabama ex rel. T.B.*, 511 U.S. 127, 136–137, and n. 6 (1994), and *Mississippi Univ. for Women* [*v. Hogan*], 458 U.S. 718, 724 (1982): Parties who seek to defend gender-based government action must demonstrate an "exceedingly persuasive justification" for that action.

Today's skeptical scrutiny of official action denying rights or opportunities based on sex responds to volumes of history. As a plurality of this Court acknowledged a generation ago, "our Nation has had a long and unfortunate history of sex discrimination." *Frontiero v. Richardson*, 411 U.S. 677, 684 (1973). Through a century plus three decades and more of that history, women did not count among voters composing "We the People";[5] not until 1920 did women gain a constitutional right to the franchise. And for a half century thereafter, it remained the prevailing doctrine that government, both federal and state, could withhold from women opportunities accorded men so long as any "basis in reason" could be conceived for the discrimination.

In 1971, for the first time in our Nation's history, this Court ruled in favor of a woman who complained that her State had denied her the equal protection of its laws. *Reed v. Reed*, 404 U.S. 71, 73 (holding unconstitutional Idaho Code prescription that, among " 'several persons claiming and equally entitled to administer [a decedent's estate], males must be preferred to females' "). Since *Reed*, the Court has repeatedly recognized that neither federal nor state government acts compatibly with the equal protection principle when a law or official policy denies to women, simply because they are women, full citizenship stature—equal opportunity to aspire, achieve, participate in and contribute to society based on their individual talents and capacities.

Without equating gender classifications, for all purposes, to classifications based on race or national origin, the Court, in post-*Reed* decisions, has carefully inspected official action that closes a door or denies opportunity to women (or to men). To summarize the Court's current directions for cases of official classification based on gender: Focusing on the differential treatment or denial of opportunity for which relief is sought, the reviewing court must determine whether the proffered justification is "exceedingly persuasive." . . .

The State must show "at least that the [challenged] classification serves 'important governmental objectives and that the discriminatory means employed' are 'substantially related to the achievement of those objectives.' " The justification must be genuine, not hypothesized or invented *post hoc* in response to litigation. And it must not rely on overbroad generalizations about the different talents, capacities, or preferences of males and females.

The heightened review standard our precedent establishes does not make sex a proscribed classification. Supposed "inherent differences" are no longer accepted as a ground for race or national origin classifications. *See Loving v. Virginia*, 388 U.S. 1 (1967). Physical differences between men and women, however, are enduring: "[T]he two sexes are not fungible; a community made up exclusively of one [sex] is different from a community composed of both." *Ballard v. United States*, 329 U.S. 187, 193 (1946).

"Inherent differences" between men and women, we have come to appreciate, remain cause for celebration, but not for denigration of the

---

5. As Thomas Jefferson stated the view prevailing when the Constitution was new: "Were our State a pure democracy . . . there would yet be excluded from their deliberations . . . women, who, to prevent depravation of morals and ambiguity of issue, should not mix promiscuously in the public meetings of men." Letter from Thomas Jefferson to Samuel Kercheval (Sept. 5, 1816), in 10 Writings of Thomas Jefferson 45–46, n. 1 (P. Ford ed. 1899).

members of either sex or for artificial constraints on an individual's opportunity. Sex classifications may be used to compensate women "for particular economic disabilities [they have] suffered," *Califano v. Webster*, 430 U.S. 313, 320 (1977) (*per curiam*), to "promot[e] equal employment opportunity," *see California Federal Sav. & Loan Assn. v. Guerra*, 479 U.S. 272, 289 (1987), to advance full development of the talent and capacities of our Nation's people.[7] But such classifications may not be used, as they once were, to create or perpetuate the legal, social, and economic inferiority of women.

Measuring the record in this case against the review standard just described, we conclude that Virginia has shown no "exceedingly persuasive justification" for excluding all women from the citizen-soldier training afforded by VMI. We therefore affirm the Fourth Circuit's initial judgment, which held that Virginia had violated the Fourteenth Amendment's Equal Protection Clause. Because the remedy proffered by Virginia—the Mary Baldwin VWIL program—does not cure the constitutional violation, i.e., it does not provide equal opportunity, we reverse the Fourth Circuit's final judgment in this case.

. . .

Virginia . . . asserts two justifications in defense of VMI's exclusion of women. First, the Commonwealth contends, "single-sex education provides important educational benefits," and the option of single-sex education contributes to "diversity in educational approaches." Second, the Commonwealth argues, "the unique VMI method of character development and leadership training," the school's adversative approach, would have to be modified were VMI to admit women. . . .

. . .

Neither recent nor distant history bears out Virginia's alleged pursuit of diversity through single-sex educational options. In 1839, when the State established VMI, a range of educational opportunities for men and women was scarcely contemplated. Higher education at the time was considered dangerous for women;[9] reflecting widely held views about women's proper

---

7. Several *amici* have urged that diversity in educational opportunities is an altogether appropriate governmental pursuit and that single-sex schools can contribute importantly to such diversity. Indeed, it is the mission of some single-sex schools "to dissipate, rather than perpetuate, traditional gender classifications." *See* Brief for Twenty–Six Private Women's Colleges as *Amici Curiae* 5. We do not question the State's prerogative evenhandedly to support diverse educational opportunities. We address specifically and only an educational opportunity recognized by the District Court and the Court of Appeals as "unique," an opportunity available only at Virginia's premier military institute, the State's sole single-sex public university or college. *Cf.* Mississippi Univ. for Women v. Hogan, 458 U.S. 718, 720, n. 1 (1982) ("Mississippi maintains no other single-sex public university or college. Thus, we are not faced with the question of whether States can provide 'separate but equal' undergraduate institutions for males and females.").

9. Dr. Edward H. Clarke of Harvard Medical School, whose influential book, Sex in Education, went through 17 editions, was perhaps the most well-known speaker from the medical community opposing higher education for women. He maintained that the physiological effects of hard study and academic competition with boys would interfere with the development of girls' reproductive organs. *See* E. Clarke, Sex in Education 38–39, 62–63 (1873); *id.* at 127 ("identical education of the two sexes is a crime before God and humanity, that physiology protests against, and that experience weeps over"); *see also* H. Maudsley, Sex in Mind and in Education 17 (1874) ("It is not that girls have not ambition, nor that they fail generally to run the intellectual race [in coeducational settings], but it is asserted that they do it at a cost to their

place, the Nation's first universities and colleges—for example, Harvard in Massachusetts, William and Mary in Virginia—admitted only men. VMI was not at all novel in this respect: In admitting no women, VMI followed the lead of the State's flagship school, the University of Virginia, founded in 1819.

"[N]o struggle for the admission of women to a state university," a historian has recounted, "was longer drawn out, or developed more bitterness, than that at the University of Virginia." 2 T. Woody, A History of Women's Education in the United States 254 (1929) (History of Women's Education). In 1879, the State Senate resolved to look into the possibility of higher education for women, recognizing that Virginia "has never, at any period of her history," provided for the higher education of her daughters, though she "has liberally provided for the higher education of her sons." Despite this recognition, no new opportunities were instantly open to women.

. . .

Ultimately, in 1970, "the most prestigious institution of higher education in Virginia," the University of Virginia, introduced coeducation and, in 1972, began to admit women on an equal basis with men. . . .

. . . Virginia describes the current absence of public single-sex higher education for women as "an historical anomaly." But the historical record indicates action more deliberate than anomalous: First, protection of women against higher education; next, schools for women far from equal in resources and stature to schools for men; finally, conversion of the separate schools to coeducation. The state legislature, prior to the advent of this controversy, had repealed "[a]ll Virginia statutes requiring individual institutions to admit only men or women." And in 1990, an official commission, "legislatively established to chart the future goals of higher education in Virginia," reaffirmed the policy "of affording broad access" while maintaining "autonomy and diversity." Significantly, the Commission reported:

> Because colleges and universities provide opportunities for students to develop values and learn from role models, it is extremely important that they deal with faculty, staff, and students without regard to sex, race, or ethnic origin.

This statement, the Court of Appeals observed, "is the only explicit one that we have found in the record in which the Commonwealth has expressed itself with respect to gender distinctions."

Our 1982 decision in *Mississippi Univ. for Women* prompted VMI to reexamine its male-only admission policy. Virginia relies on that reexamination as a legitimate basis for maintaining VMI's single-sex character. A Mission Study Committee, appointed by the VMI Board of Visitors, studied the problem from October 1983 until May 1986, and in that month counseled against "change of VMI status as a single-sex college." Whatever internal purpose the Mission Study Committee served—and however well-

---

strength and health which entails life-long suffering, and even incapacitates them for the adequate performance of the natural functions of their sex."); C. Meigs, Females and Their Diseases 350 (1848) (after five or six weeks of "mental and educational discipline," a healthy woman would "lose . . . the habit of menstruation" and suffer numerous ills as a result of depriving her body for the sake of her mind).

meaning the framers of the report—we can hardly extract from that effort any state policy evenhandedly to advance diverse educational options. As the District Court observed, the Committee's analysis "primarily focuse[d] on anticipated difficulties in attracting females to VMI," and the report, overall, supplied "very little indication of how th[e] conclusion was reached."

In sum, we find no persuasive evidence in this record that VMI's male-only admission policy "is in furtherance of a state policy of 'diversity.' " . . .

Virginia next argues that VMI's adversative method of training provides educational benefits that cannot be made available, unmodified, to women. . . .

. . .

It may be assumed, for purposes of this decision, that most women would not choose VMI's adversative method. As Fourth Circuit Judge Motz observed, however, in her dissent from the Court of Appeals' denial of rehearing en banc, it is also probable that "many men would not want to be educated in such an environment." (On that point, even our dissenting colleague might agree.) Education, to be sure, is not a "one size fits all" business. The issue, however, is not whether "women—or men—should be forced to attend VMI"; rather, the question is whether the State can constitutionally deny to women who have the will and capacity, the training and attendant opportunities that VMI uniquely affords.

The notion that admission of women would downgrade VMI's stature, destroy the adversative system and, with it, even the school, is a judgment hardly proved, a prediction hardly different from other "self-fulfilling prophec[ies]," once routinely used to deny rights or opportunities. When women first sought admission to the bar and access to legal education, concerns of the same order were expressed. . . .

A like fear, according to a 1925 report, accounted for Columbia Law School's resistance to women's admission, although

> [t]he faculty . . . never maintained that women could not master legal learning. . . . No, its argument has been . . . more practical. If women were admitted to the Columbia Law School, [the faculty] said, then the choicer, more manly and red-blooded graduates of our great universities would go to the Harvard Law School! The Nation, Feb. 18, 1925, p. 173.

. . .

Women's successful entry into the federal military academies, and their participation in the Nation's military forces, indicate that Virginia's fears for the future of VMI may not be solidly grounded.[15] The State's justification for excluding all women from "citizen-soldier" training for which some are qualified, in any event, cannot rank as "exceedingly persuasive," as we have explained and applied that standard.

---

15. Inclusion of women in settings where, traditionally, they were not wanted inevitably entails a period of adjustment. As one West Point cadet squad leader recounted: "[T]he classes of '78 and '79 see the women as women, but the classes of '80 and '81 see them as classmates." U.S. Military Academy, A. Vitters, Report of Admission of Women (Project Athena II) 84 (1978)

Virginia and VMI trained their argument on "means" rather than "end," and thus misperceived our precedent. Single-sex education at VMI serves an "important governmental objective," they maintained, and exclusion of women is not only "substantially related," it is essential to that objective. By this notably circular argument, the "straightforward" test *Mississippi Univ. for Women* described, was bent and bowed.

The State's misunderstanding and, in turn, the District Court's, is apparent from VMI's mission: to produce "citizen-soldiers," individuals

'imbued with love of learning, confident in the functions and attitudes of leadership, possessing a high sense of public service, advocates of the American democracy and free enterprise system, and ready . . . to defend their country in time of national peril.' 766 F. Supp., at 1425 (quoting Mission Study Committee of the VMI Board of Visitors, Report, May 16, 1986).

Surely that goal is great enough to accommodate women, who today count as citizens in our American democracy equal in stature to men. Just as surely, the State's great goal is not substantially advanced by women's categorical exclusion, in total disregard of their individual merit, from the State's premier "citizen-soldier" corps.[16] Virginia, in sum, "has fallen far short of establishing the 'exceedingly persuasive justification,'" *Mississippi Univ. for Women*, 458 U.S., at 731, that must be the solid base for any gender-defined classification.

. . .

Virginia chose not to eliminate, but to leave untouched, VMI's exclusionary policy. For women only, however, Virginia proposed a separate program, different in kind from VMI and unequal in tangible and intangible facilities. . . .

VWIL affords women no opportunity to experience the rigorous military training for which VMI is famed. . . .

VWIL students participate in ROTC and a "largely ceremonial" Virginia Corps of Cadets, but Virginia deliberately did not make VWIL a military institute. The VWIL House is not a military-style residence and VWIL students need not live together throughout the 4-year program, eat meals together, or wear uniforms during the school day. VWIL students thus do not experience the "barracks" life "crucial to the VMI experience," the spartan living arrangements designed to foster an "egalitarian ethic." "[T]he most important aspects of the VMI educational experience occur in the barracks," the District Court found, yet Virginia deemed that core experience nonessential, indeed inappropriate, for training its female citizen-soldiers.

VWIL students receive their "leadership training" in seminars, externships, and speaker series, episodes and encounters lacking the "[p]hysical

---

16. VMI has successfully managed another notable change. The school admitted its first African–American cadets in 1968. *See* The VMI Story 347–349 (students no longer sing "Dixie," salute the Confederate flag or the tomb of General Robert E. Lee at ceremonies and sports events). As the District Court noted, VMI established a Program on "retention of black cadets" designed to offer academic and social-cultural support to "minority members of a dominantly white and tradition-oriented student body." The school maintains a "special recruitment program for blacks" which the District Court found, "has had little, if any, effect on VMI's method of accomplishing its mission."

rigor, mental stress, . . . minute regulation of behavior, and indoctrination in desirable values" made hallmarks of VMI's citizen-soldier training. Kept away from the pressures, hazards, and psychological bonding characteristic of VMI's adversative training, VWIL students will not know the "feeling of tremendous accomplishment" commonly experienced by VMI's successful cadets.

Virginia maintains that these methodological differences are "justified pedagogically," based on "important differences between men and women in learning and developmental needs," "psychological and sociological differences" Virginia describes as "real" and "not stereotypes." The Task Force charged with developing the leadership program for women, drawn from the staff and faculty at Mary Baldwin College, "determined that a military model and, especially VMI's adversative method, would be wholly inappropriate for educating and training *most women*." The Commonwealth embraced the Task Force view, as did expert witnesses who testified for Virginia.

As earlier stated, generalizations about "the way women are," estimates of what is appropriate for *most women*, no longer justify denying opportunity to women whose talent and capacity place them outside the average description. Notably, Virginia never asserted that VMI's method of education suits *most men*. It is also revealing that Virginia accounted for its failure to make the VWIL experience "the entirely militaristic experience of VMI" on the ground that VWIL "is planned for women who do not necessarily expect to pursue military careers." By that reasoning, VMI's "entirely militaristic" program would be inappropriate for men in general or *as a group*, for "[o]nly about 15% of VMI cadets enter career military service."

In contrast to the generalizations about women on which Virginia rests, we note again [that some women can meet the physical standards imposed on men and would want to attend VMI if they had the opportunity.] It is on behalf of these women that the United States has instituted this suit, and it is for them that a remedy must be crafted,[19] a remedy that will end their exclusion from a state-supplied educational opportunity for which they are fit, a decree that will "bar like discrimination in the future." *Louisiana [v. United States]*, 380 U.S., at 154.

In myriad respects other than military training, VWIL does not qualify as VMI's equal. VWIL's student body, faculty, course offerings, and facilities hardly match VMI's. Nor can the VWIL graduate anticipate the benefits associated with VMI's 157–year history, the school's prestige, and its influential alumni network.

Mary Baldwin College, whose degree VWIL students will gain, enrolls first-year women with an average combined SAT score about 100 points lower than the average score for VMI freshmen. The Mary Baldwin faculty holds "significantly fewer Ph.D.'s," and receives substantially lower salaries.

---

19. Admitting women to VMI would undoubtedly require alterations necessary to afford members of each sex privacy from the other sex in living arrangements, and to adjust aspects of the physical training programs. *See* Brief for Petitioner 27–29. Experience shows such adjustments are manageable. *See* U.S. Military Academy, A. Vitters, N. Kinzer, & J. Adams, Report of Admission of Women (Project Athena I–IV) (1977–1980) (4–year longitudinal study of the admission of women to West Point); Defense Advisory Committee on Women in the Services, Report on the Integration and Performance of Women at West Point 17–§ 18 (1992).

Mary Baldwin does not offer a VWIL student the range of curricular choices available to a VMI cadet. VMI awards baccalaureate degrees in liberal arts, biology, chemistry, civil engineering, electrical and computer engineering, and mechanical engineering. VWIL students attend a school that "does not have a math and science focus," they cannot take at Mary Baldwin any courses in engineering or the advanced math and physics courses VMI offers.

For physical training, Mary Baldwin has "two multi-purpose fields" and "[o]ne gymnasium." VMI has "an NCAA competition level indoor track and field facility; a number of multi-purpose fields; baseball, soccer and lacrosse fields; an obstacle course; large boxing, wrestling and martial arts facilities; an 11–laps-to-the-mile indoor running course; an indoor pool; indoor and outdoor rifle ranges; and a football stadium that also contains a practice field and outdoor track."

Although Virginia has represented that it will provide equal financial support for in-state VWIL students and VMI cadets, and the VMI Foundation has agreed to endow VWIL with $5.4625 million, the difference between the two schools' financial reserves is pronounced. Mary Baldwin's endowment, currently about $19 million, will gain an additional $35 million based on future commitments; VMI's current endowment, $131 million—the largest per-student endowment in the Nation—will gain $220 million.

The VWIL student does not graduate with the advantage of a VMI degree. Her diploma does not unite her with the legions of VMI "graduates [who] have distinguished themselves" in military and civilian life. "[VMI] alumni are exceptionally close to the school," and that closeness accounts, in part, for VMI's success in attracting applicants. A VWIL graduate cannot assume that the "network of business owners, corporations, VMI graduates and non-graduate employers . . . interested in hiring VMI graduates," will be equally responsive to her search for employment.

Virginia, in sum, while maintaining VMI for men only, has failed to provide any "comparable single-gender women's institution." Instead, the Commonwealth has created a VWIL program fairly appraised as a "pale shadow" of VMI in terms of the range of curricular choices and faculty stature, funding, prestige, alumni support and influence.

Virginia's VWIL solution is reminiscent of the remedy Texas proposed 50 years ago, in response to a state trial court's 1946 ruling that, given the equal protection guarantee, African Americans could not be denied a legal education at a state facility. See *Sweatt v. Painter*, 339 U.S. 629 (1950). . . .

. . . In line with *Sweatt*, we rule here that Virginia has not shown substantial equality in the separate educational opportunities the State supports at VWIL and VMI.

. . . Valuable as VWIL may prove for students who seek the program offered, Virginia's remedy affords no cure at all for the opportunities and advantages withheld from women who want a VMI education and can make the grade. In sum, Virginia's remedy does not match the constitutional violation; the State has shown no "exceedingly persuasive justification" for withholding from women qualified for the experience premier training of the kind VMI affords.

. . .

For the reasons stated, the initial judgment of the Court of Appeals is affirmed, the final judgment of the Court of Appeals is reversed, and the case is remanded for further proceedings consistent with this opinion.

■ JUSTICE SCALIA, dissenting.

. . .

To reject the Court's disposition today . . . [i]t is only necessary to apply honestly the test the Court has been applying to sex-based classifications for the past two decades. . . . We have denominated this standard "intermediate scrutiny" and under it have inquired whether the statutory classification is "substantially related to an important governmental objective."

. . . Notwithstanding our above-described precedents and their " 'firmly established principles,' " the United States urged us to hold in this case "that strict scrutiny is the correct constitutional standard for evaluating classifications that deny opportunities to individuals based on their sex." (This was in flat contradiction of the Government's position below, which was, in its own words, to "stat[e] *unequivocally* that the appropriate standard in this case is 'intermediate scrutiny.' ") The Court, while making no reference to the Government's argument, effectively accepts it.

Although the Court in two places recites the test as stated in [*Mississippi Univ. for Women v. Hogan*, 458 U.S. 718 (1982)] which asks whether the State has demonstrated "that the classification serves important governmental objectives and that the discriminatory means employed are substantially related to the achievement of those objectives," the Court never answers the question presented in anything resembling that form. When it engages in analysis, the Court instead prefers the phrase "exceedingly persuasive justification" from *Hogan*. The Court's nine invocations of that phrase, and even its fanciful description of that imponderable as "the core instruction" of the Court's decisions in *J.E.B. v. Alabama ex rel. T.B.*, 511 U.S. 127 (1994), and *Hogan, supra,* would be unobjectionable if the Court acknowledged that *whether* a "justification" is "exceedingly persuasive" must be assessed by asking "[whether] the classification serves important governmental objectives and [whether] the discriminatory means employed are substantially related to the achievement of those objectives." Instead, however, the Court proceeds to interpret "exceedingly persuasive justification" in a fashion that contradicts the reasoning of *Hogan* and our other precedents.

That is essential to the Court's result, which can only be achieved by establishing that intermediate scrutiny is not survived if there are *some* women interested in attending VMI, capable of undertaking its activities, and able to meet its physical demands.

. . .

Intermediate scrutiny has never required a least-restrictive-means analysis, but only a "substantial relation" between the classification and the state interests that it serves. . . . There is simply no support in our cases for the notion that a sex-based classification is invalid unless it relates to characteristics that hold true in every instance.

Not content to execute a *de facto* abandonment of the intermediate scrutiny that has been our standard for sex-based classifications for some two decades, the Court purports to reserve the question whether, even in principle, a higher standard (*i.e.,* strict scrutiny) should apply. "The Court has," it says, "*thus far* reserved most stringent judicial scrutiny for classifications based on race or national origin," . . .; and it describes our earlier cases as having done no more than decline to "equat[e] gender classifications, *for all purposes*, to classifications based on race or national origin." The wonderful thing about these statements is that they are not actually false—just as it would not be actually false to say that "our cases have thus far reserved the 'beyond a reasonable doubt' standard of proof for criminal cases," or that "we have not equated tort actions, for all purposes, to criminal prosecutions." But the statements are misleading, insofar as they suggest that we have not already categorically *held* strict scrutiny to be inapplicable to sex-based classifications.

The Court's intimations are particularly out of place because it is perfectly clear that, if the question of the applicable standard of review for sex-based classifications were to be regarded as an appropriate subject for reconsideration, the stronger argument would be not for elevating the standard to strict scrutiny, but for reducing it to rational-basis review. The latter certainly has a firmer foundation in our past jurisprudence: Whereas no majority of the Court has ever applied strict scrutiny in a case involving sex-based classifications, we routinely applied rational-basis review until the 1970's, *see, e.g., Hoyt v. Florida*, 368 U.S. 57 (1961); *Goesaert v. Cleary*, 335 U.S. 464 (1948). And of course normal, rational-basis review of sex-based classifications would be much more in accord with the genesis of heightened standards of judicial review, the famous footnote in *United States v. Carolene Products Co.*, 304 U.S. 144 (1938), which said (intimatingly) that we did not have to inquire in the case at hand

> whether prejudice against discrete and insular minorities may be a special condition, which tends seriously to curtail the operation of those political processes ordinarily to be relied upon to protect minorities, and which may call for a correspondingly more searching judicial inquiry. *Id.*, at 152–153, n. 4.

It is hard to consider women a "discrete and insular minorit[y]" unable to employ the "political processes ordinarily to be relied upon," when they constitute a majority of the electorate. And the suggestion that they are incapable of exerting that political power smacks of the same paternalism that the Court so roundly condemns. Moreover, a long list of legislation proves the proposition false. . . .

Questions and Comments on *United States v. Virginia*

1.   In the aftermath of the decision in *United States. v. Virginia*, many influential VMI alumni called for the institute to privatize instead of admitting women. Ultimately, the Board of Visitors voted nine to eight to admit women. The process of preparing VMI for women cadets (a process the administration referred to as "assimilation") took over a year, and led to allegations by the United States Justice Department that VMI was intentionally delaying the admission of women. Unlike the federal military academies, VMI did not establish separate physical fitness benchmarks for women and men; women would have to meet the same sit-up, pull-up, and running requirements as men. In 2001, thirteen women graduated along with 220 men to form VMI's first coeducational class. PHILIPPA STRUM, WOMEN IN THE BARRACKS 297–328 (2002); *see also* LAURA FAIRCHILD BRODIE, BREAKING OUT (Vintage Books 2001) (2000).

2.   Many observers (including Justice Scalia in his dissent) argue that Justice Ginsburg's opinion in *United States v. Virginia* effectively blurs the line between intermediate and strict scrutiny. *See* Cornelia T.L. Pillard, United States v. Virginia: *The Virginia Military Institute, Where the Men are Men and So are the Women, in* CIVIL RIGHTS STORIES 265–92 (Myriam E. Gilles & Risa L. Goulboff eds., 2008); STRUM, *supra* at 287. Do you agree?

3. Observers also have criticized VMI for failing to adapt its educational procedures in response to the admission of women. Instead of using the outcome of the lawsuit as an opportunity to review established pedagogical techniques to see if they were appropriate for the education of students (both women and men), VMI was determined to change as little as possible in admitting women. This led Professor Pillard to write:

> VMI now belongs to its women as much as to its men. Any coeducational public college, VMI included, should be designed in a way that maximizes educational benefits while minimizing disproportionate adverse impact on any subgroup—in particular one that has been historically subjected to discrimination.... [I]t is the culture, not just the women, that should adapt.

Pillard, *supra*, at 289. Do you agree that VMI should have overhauled its pedagogical techniques in preparing for the admission of women, or is the formal equality of allowing both men and women to enroll in VMI and compete on the same terms enough? Compare Justice Thomas's concurrence in *Fordice*, where he argued that a public university could establish practices that might disproportionately appeal to a particular sub-category of society, as long as all groups had access to the institution?

Note on Gender and Admissions

1. Although Oberlin in the 1830s became the first college to admit women as well as men, a majority of the most selective universities remained closed to women until the 1970s. Consider JEROME KARABEL, THE CHOSEN 446 (2005):

> From today's vantage point, it is difficult to grasp just how thoroughly male the Big Three [Harvard, Yale, and Princeton,] were in 1960. Apart from the obvious fact that Yale and Princeton did not admit any female undergraduates and even Harvard relegated them to a separate and much smaller institution, there was the assumption that one could speak of the Yale man, the Princeton man, and the Harvard man, casually confidant that it was men—and men alone—who defined these institutions. Decisively reinforcing this feeling were the faculty itself, with no female full professors at Yale and Princeton in 1960 and just one woman out of a tenured faculty of 400 at Harvard.

> It was not until the mid–1960s that the idea of coeducation began to receive serious consideration at Yale and Princeton. Propelling it was less the conviction that women deserved equal opportunity than sheer institutional self-interest. As the data mounted on the reasons that admitted students chose not to enroll, the choice facing Yale and Princeton became clear: either admit women as undergraduates or risk falling behind Harvard and other institutions that included women.

> Yet this realization was not in and of itself enough to dislodge a tradition more than 200 years old. What gave the push for coeducation powerful (albeit indirect) momentum was the progressive opening of the Big Three to African Americans.... By 1968, with the influence of the black and student movements growing, the contradiction between the institutions' professed ideology of equal opportunity and the refusal to even accept applications from half the population had become too transparent to sustain....

> In 1968–1969, the barriers that had excluded women for so long at Yale and Princeton were finally cast aside.

At first the elite universities adopted quotas that limited the number of women admitted to the school, while simultaneously holding them to higher standards. By the early 1970s, however, after vocal criticism from feminists and a general change in public attitudes, Harvard, Princeton, and Yale finally adopted sex-blind admissions. *Id.* at 422, 438, 441.

2. There were once almost 250 all-male colleges in the nation. By 2006, however, only four remained: Hampden–Sydney, some sixty miles southwest of Richmond; Wabash College, forty-five miles northwest of Indianapolis; Moorehouse College in Atlanta; and Deep Springs, a two-year college limited to twenty-seven students in each class and located on a cattle ranch and alfalfa farm in eastern California. Peter Appleborne, *The Final Four*, N.Y. TIMES, EDUCATION LIFE, Apr. 23, 2006, at 20.

3. By contrast, in 2007 there were still some sixty women's colleges. Consider the explanation of Joanne Creighton, president of Mount Holyoke College:

> Key to understanding this is remembering how recently, and sometimes how begrudgingly, women have been invited into male institutions. It has been only for a generation or two, not long enough to wipe out the vestiges of sexism. Charles Eliot, a longtime president of Harvard, said in his 1869 inaugural address that he had doubts about the "natural mental capacities" of the female sex, a remark eerily echoed by a recent Harvard president.

> A woman's college, in contrast, is the equivalent of Virginia Woolf's "room of one's own," a college of women's own, free of many of the inhibiting presumptions of the male-dominated world. With its own powerful traditions, norms, and values, and a sense of wholeness sui generis, a woman's college helps to develop in students a sense of confidence, competence, and agency. Graduates are more able to see gender-repression when they encounter it and to distinguish between personal and systemic barriers to success.

> Women's colleges are not about separating women from the world but about encouraging them to be active agents within it. . . . Now more than ever the world needs them.

Joanne Creighton, *Why We Need Women's Colleges*, THE BOSTON GLOBE, May 21, 2007, at A9.

4. Recent studies have found that women who attend women's colleges may have a better educational experience then women who attend coeducational institutions. A study by the Indiana University Center for Postsecondary Research concluded: "In general, women at single-sex colleges are more engaged than women at coeducational institutions. . . . Specifically, women's college students indicated greater gains in understanding themselves and others, general education, ability to analyze quantitative problems, and desire to contribute to the welfare of their community." Jillian Kinzie et al., *Women Students at Coeducational and Women's Colleges: How Do Their Experiences Compare?*, 48 J.C. STUDENT DEV. 145, 154–55 (2007). Similarly, a study commissioned by the Women's College Coalition found that women's college alumnae were significantly more likely to earn a graduate degree than women graduating from coeducational institutions. Women who attended women's colleges generally rate their institutions more highly than those that attended coeducational colleges and universities. Scott Jaschik, *New Evidence Bolsters Women's Colleges*, INSIDE HIGHER ED, Mar. 4, 2008, *available at* http://www.insidehighered.com/news/2008/03/04/women.

Given the fact that female-only institutions seem to offer real benefits for women, why do so few male-only colleges remain? Do these studies support Justice Scalia's argument that single-gender instruction has benefits for both sexes, and thus Virginia should be allowed to provide single-sex instruction as a way of providing effective college education for its citizens? In light of this data, does it make sense to require that men and women be offered the same educational programs?

5. In the early 1980s, for the first time more women than men enrolled in colleges and universities. By 2007, women made up about 58 percent of undergraduates. Robin Wilson, *The New Gender Divide*, CHRON. HIGHER EDUC., Jan. 26, 2007, at A36.

> "Women are leading the charge here," says Jason Zelesky, associate dean of students at Clark University, in Massachusetts, where 60 percent of the students are female. "They are controlling our classrooms, they're dominating what have traditionally been male-oriented programs like business management and chemistry, and they tend to be getting our academic prizes and fellowships."

Id. In response, some schools are adding engineering programs and football teams, all in an effort to attract more men to enroll. Bill Pennington, *Small Colleges, Short of Men, Embrace Football*, N.Y. TIMES, July 10, 2006, at A2.

The gender gap is greatest among low-income students and disappears among students from the most affluent families according to the report, *Gender Equity in Higher Education: 2006*, published by the American Council of Education.

Women are also receiving more professional degrees. Between 1970 and 2000, their share of medical degrees rose from 8.4 percent to 42.7 percent; of law degrees from 5.4 percent to 45.9 percent, and of M.B.A.s from 3.6 percent to 39.8 percent. Andrew Hacker asserts that "the degree gap raises the possibility that as more women pursue new interests, there will be a shortfall of men to share those interests with." *How the B.A. Gap Widens the Chasm Between Men and Women*, CHRON. HIGHER EDUC., June 20, 2003, at B10. Do you agree?

C. DISCRIMINATION ON THE BASIS OF DISABILITIES

Southeastern Community College v. Davis

Supreme Court of the United States, 1979.
442 U.S. 397, 99 S.Ct. 2361, 60 L.Ed.2d 980.

■ MR. JUSTICE POWELL delivered the opinion of the Court.

This case presents a matter of first impression for this Court: Whether § 504 of the Rehabilitation Act of 1973, which prohibits discrimination against an "otherwise qualified handicapped individual" in federally funded programs "solely by reason of his handicap," forbids professional schools from imposing physical qualifications for admission to their clinical training programs.

Respondent, who suffers from a serious hearing disability, seeks to be trained as a registered nurse. During the 1973–1974 academic year she was enrolled in the College Parallel program of Southeastern Community College, a state institution that receives federal funds. Respondent hoped to progress to Southeastern's Associate Degree Nursing program, completion of which would make her eligible for state certification as a registered nurse. In the course of her application to the nursing program, she was interviewed by a member of the nursing faculty. It became apparent that respondent had difficulty understanding questions asked, and on inquiry she acknowledged a history of hearing problems and dependence on a hearing aid. She was advised to consult an audiologist.

On the basis of an examination at Duke University Medical Center, respondent was diagnosed as having a "bilateral, sensori-neural hearing loss." A change in her hearing aid was recommended, as a result of which it was expected that she would be able to detect sounds "almost as well as a person would who has normal hearing." But this improvement would not mean that she could discriminate among sounds sufficiently to understand normal spoken speech. Her lipreading skills would remain necessary for effective communication: "While wearing the hearing aid, she is well aware of gross sounds occurring in the listening environment. However, she can only be responsible for speech spoken to her, when the talker gets her attention and allows her to look directly at the talker."

Southeastern next consulted Mary McRee, Executive Director of the North Carolina Board of Nursing. On the basis of the audiologist's report, McRee recommended that respondent not be admitted to the nursing program. In McRee's view, respondent's hearing disability made it unsafe for her to practice as a nurse. In addition, it would be impossible for respondent to participate safely in the normal clinical training program, and those modifications that would be necessary to enable safe participation would prevent her from realizing the benefits of the program: "To adjust patient learning experiences in keeping with [respondent's] hearing limitations could, in fact, be the same as denying her full learning to meet the objectives of your nursing programs."

As previously noted, this is the first case in which this Court has been called upon to interpret § 504. . . . Section 504 by its terms does not compel educational institutions to disregard the disabilities of handicapped individuals or to make substantial modifications in their programs to allow disabled persons to participate. Instead, it requires only that an "otherwise qualified handicapped individual" not be excluded from participation in a federally funded program "solely by reason of his handicap," indicating only that mere possession of a handicap is not a permissible ground for assuming an inability to function in a particular context.

The court below, however, believed that the "otherwise qualified" persons protected by § 504 include those who would be able to meet the requirements of a particular program in every respect except as to limitations imposed by their handicap. Taken literally, this holding would prevent an institution from taking into account any limitation resulting from the handicap, however disabling. It assumes, in effect, that a person need not meet legitimate physical requirements in order to be "otherwise qualified." We think the understanding of the District Court is closer to the plain meaning of the statutory language. An otherwise qualified person is one who is able to meet all of a program's requirements in spite of his handicap.

. . .

The remaining question is whether the physical qualifications Southeastern demanded of respondent might not be necessary for participation in its nursing program. It is not open to dispute that, as Southeastern's Associate Degree Nursing program currently is constituted, the ability to understand speech without reliance on lipreading is necessary for patient safety during the clinical phase of the program. As the District Court found, this ability also is indispensable for many of the functions that a registered nurse performs.

Respondent contends nevertheless that § 504, properly interpreted, compels Southeastern to undertake affirmative action that would dispense with the need for effective oral communication. First, it is suggested that respondent can be given individual supervision by faculty members whenever she attends patients directly. Moreover, certain required courses might be dispensed with altogether for respondent. It is not necessary, she argues, that Southeastern train her to undertake all the tasks a registered nurse is licensed to perform. Rather, it is sufficient to make § 504 applicable if respondent might be able to perform satisfactorily some of the duties of a registered nurse or to hold some of the positions available to a registered nurse.

Respondent finds support for this argument in portions of [regulations promulgated by the Department of Health, Education and Welfare.] In particular, a provision applicable to postsecondary educational programs requires covered institutions to make "modifications" in their programs to accommodate handicapped persons, and to provide "auxiliary aids" such as sign-language interpreters. Respondent argues that this regulation imposes an obligation to ensure full participation in covered programs by handicapped individuals and, in particular, requires Southeastern to make the kind of adjustments that would be necessary to permit her safe participation in the nursing program.

We note first that on the present record it appears unlikely respondent could benefit from any affirmative action that the regulation reasonably could be interpreted as requiring. Section 84.44(d)(2), for example, explicitly excludes "devices or services of a personal nature" from the kinds of auxiliary aids a school must provide a handicapped individual. Yet the only evidence in the record indicates that nothing less than close, individual attention by a nursing instructor would be sufficient to ensure patient safety if respondent took part in the clinical phase of the nursing program. Furthermore, it also is reasonably clear that § 84.44(a) does not encompass the kind of curricular changes that would be necessary to accommodate respondent in the nursing program. In light of respondent's inability to function in clinical courses without close supervision, Southeastern, with prudence, could allow her to take only academic classes. Whatever benefits respondent might realize from such a course of study, she would not receive even a rough equivalent of the training a nursing program normally gives. Such a fundamental alteration in the nature of a program is far more than the "modification" the regulation requires.

Moreover, an interpretation of the regulations that required the extensive modifications necessary to include respondent in the nursing program would raise grave doubts about their validity. If these regulations were to require substantial adjustments in existing programs beyond those necessary to eliminate discrimination against otherwise qualified individuals, they would do more than clarify the meaning of § 504. Instead, they would constitute an unauthorized extension of the obligations imposed by that statute.

The language and structure of the Rehabilitation Act of 1973 reflect a recognition by Congress of the distinction between the evenhanded treatment of qualified handicapped persons and affirmative efforts to overcome the disabilities caused by handicaps. Section 501(b), governing the employment of handicapped individuals by the Federal Government, requires each federal agency to submit "an affirmative action program plan for the hiring, placement, and advancement of handicapped individuals. . . ." These plans "shall include a description of the extent to which and methods whereby the special needs of handicapped employees are being met." Similarly, § 503(a), governing hiring by federal contractors, requires employers to "take affirmative action to employ and advance in employment qualified handicapped individuals...." The President is required to promulgate regulations to enforce this section.

Under § 501(c) of the Act, by contrast, state agencies such as Southeastern are only "[encouraged] ... to adopt and implement such policies and procedures." Section 504 does not refer at all to affirmative action, and except as it applies to federal employers it does not provide for implementation by administrative action. A comparison of these provisions demonstrates that Congress understood accommodation of the needs of handicapped individuals may require affirmative action and knew how to provide for it in those instances where it wished to do so.

. . .

We do not suggest that the line between a lawful refusal to extend affirmative action and illegal discrimination against handicapped persons always will be clear. It is possible to envision situations where an insistence on continuing past requirements and practices might arbitrarily deprive genuinely qualified handicapped persons of the opportunity to participate in a covered program. Technological advances can be expected to enhance opportunities to rehabilitate the handicapped or otherwise to qualify them for some useful employment. Such advances also may enable attainment of these goals without imposing undue financial and administrative burdens upon a State. Thus, situations may arise where a refusal to modify an existing program might become unreasonable and discriminatory. Identification of those instances where a refusal to accommodate the needs of a disabled person amounts to discrimination against the handicapped continues to be an important responsibility of HEW.

In this case, however, it is clear that Southeastern's unwillingness to make major adjustments in its nursing program does not constitute such discrimination. The uncontroverted testimony of several members of Southeastern's staff and faculty established that the purpose of its program was to train persons who could serve the nursing profession in all customary ways. This type of purpose, far from reflecting any animus against handicapped individuals, is shared by many if not most of the institutions that train persons to render professional service. It is undisputed that respondent could not participate in Southeastern's nursing program unless the standards were substantially lowered. Section 504 imposes no requirement upon an educational institution to lower or to effect substantial modifications of standards to accommodate a handicapped person.

. . .

... Southeastern's program, structured to train persons who will be able to perform all normal roles of a registered nurse, represents a legitimate academic policy, and is accepted by the State. In effect, it seeks to ensure that no graduate will pose a danger to the public in any professional role in which he or she might be cast. Even if the licensing requirements of North Carolina or some other State are less demanding, nothing in the Act requires an educational institution to lower its standards.

One may admire respondent's desire and determination to overcome her handicap, and there well may be various other types of service for which she can qualify. In this case, however, we hold that there was no violation of § 504 when Southeastern concluded that respondent did not qualify for admission to its program. Nothing in the language or history of § 504 reflects an intention to limit the freedom of an educational institution to require reasonable physical qualifications for admission to a clinical training program. Nor has there been any showing in this case that any action short of a substantial change in Southeastern's program would render unreasonable the qualifications it imposed.

Accordingly, we reverse the judgment of the court below, and remand for proceedings consistent with this opinion.

Questions and Comments on Disability Discrimination

1. Davis conceded that her hearing disability meant that she would not be able to perform all of the duties that a nurse could be licensed to perform, but argued that there are other duties that her disability would not hinder her ability to perform. Does it make sense to bar disabled persons entirely from a professional program, even if they are still able to perform many of the tasks required of the profession?

2. The Supreme Court was much more deferential to the school in *Southeastern Community College* than it was in *University of Pennsylvania v. EEOC*. Can you reconcile the two opinions?

3. Applicants have been unsuccessful for the most part in asserting claims of disability discrimination in admissions. Because most standardized tests offer accommodations for students with disabilities, applicants challenging their denial of admission are usually unable to demonstrate that their lower credentials are the result of their disabilities. Universities often point to other students with disabilities currently enrolled at the school as proof that they do not discriminate. *See, e.g.*, Ohio Civil Rights Comm'n v. Case W. Reserve Univ., 76 Ohio St.3d 168, 666 N.E.2d 1376 (1996) (holding that denial of admission of a blind student to medical school did not violate the Rehabilitation Act of 1973). *See generally* LAURA ROTHSTEIN & JULIA ROTHSTEIN, DISABILITIES AND THE LAW §§ 3:4–3:7 (3d ed. 2006); Laura F. Rothstein, *Disability Law and Higher Education: A Road Map for Where We've Been and Where We May Be Heading*, 63 MD. L. REV. 122 (2004).

D.   CLASS BARRIERS

San Antonio Independent School District v. Rodriguez

Supreme Court of the United States, 1973.
411 U.S. 1, 93 S.Ct. 1278, 36 L.Ed.2d 16.

■ MR. JUSTICE POWELL delivered the opinion of the Court.

This suit attacking the Texas system of financing public education was initiated by Mexican–American parents whose children attend the elementary and secondary schools in the Edgewood Independent School District, an urban school district in San Antonio, Texas. They brought a class action on behalf of school children throughout the State who are members of minority groups or who are poor and reside in school districts having a low property tax base. . . . The complaint was filed in the summer of 1968 and a three-judge court was impaneled in January 1969. In December 1971 the panel rendered its judgment in a per curiam opinion holding the Texas school finance system unconstitutional under the Equal Protection Clause of the Fourteenth Amendment. The State appealed. . . .

. . .

Until recent times, Texas was a predominantly rural State and its population and property wealth were spread relatively evenly across the State. Sizable differences in the value of assessable property between local school districts became increasingly evident as the State became more industrialized and as rural-to-urban population shifts became more pronounced. The location of commercial and industrial property began to play a significant role in determining the amount of tax resources available to each school district. These growing disparities in population and taxable property between districts were responsible in part for increasingly notable differences in levels of local expenditure for education.

In due time it became apparent to those concerned with financing public education that contributions from the [State-financed] Available School Fund were not sufficient to ameliorate these disparities. . . .

. . .

The school district in which appellees reside, the Edgewood Independent School District, has been compared throughout this litigation with the Alamo Heights Independent School District. This comparison between the least and most affluent districts in the San Antonio area serves to illustrate the manner in which the dual system of finance operates and to indicate the extent to which substantial disparities exist despite the State's impressive progress in recent years. Edgewood is one of seven public school districts in the metropolitan area. Approximately 22,000 students are enrolled in its 25 elementary and secondary schools. The district is situated in the core-city sector of San Antonio in a residential neighborhood that has little commercial or industrial property. The residents are predominantly of Mexican–American descent: approximately 90% of the student population is Mexican–American and over 6% is Negro. The average assessed property value per pupil is $5,960—the lowest in the metropolitan area—and the median family income ($4,686) is also the lowest. At an equalized tax rate of $1.05 per $100 of assessed property—the highest in the metropolitan area—the district contributed $26 to the education of each child for the 1967–1968 school year above its Local Fund Assignment for the Minimum Foundation Program. The Foundation Program contributed $222 per pupil for a state-local total of $248. Federal funds added another $108 for a total of $356 per pupil.

Alamo Heights is the most affluent school district in San Antonio. Its six schools, housing approximately 5,000 students, are situated in a residential community quite unlike the Edgewood District. The school population is predominantly "Anglo," having only 18% Mexican–Americans and less than 1% Negroes. The assessed property value per pupil exceeds $49,000, and the median family income is $8,001. In 1967–1968 the local tax rate of $.85 per $100 of valuation yielded $333 per pupil. . . . Coupled with the $225 provided from [the Foundation] Program, the district was able to supply $558 per student. Supplemented by a $36 per-pupil grant from federal sources, Alamo Heights spent $594 per pupil.

. . .

This, then, establishes the framework for our analysis. We must decide, first, whether the Texas system of financing public education operates to the disadvantage of some suspect class or impinges upon a fundamental right explicitly or implicitly protected by the Constitution, thereby requiring strict judicial scrutiny. . . .

. . . In concluding that strict judicial scrutiny was required, [the District Court] relied on decisions dealing with the rights of indigents to equal treatment in the criminal trial and appellate processes, and on cases disapproving wealth restrictions on the right to vote. Those cases, the District Court concluded, established wealth as a suspect classification. . . . It then reasoned, based on decisions of this Court affirming the undeniable importance of education, that there is a fundamental right to education and that, absent some compelling state justification, the Texas system could not stand.

. . . [F]or the several reasons that follow, we find neither the suspect-classification nor the fundamental-interest analysis persuasive.

The wealth discrimination discovered by the District Court in this case, and by several other courts that have recently struck down school-financing laws in other States, is quite unlike any of the forms of wealth discrimination heretofore reviewed by this Court. Rather than focusing on the unique features of the alleged discrimination, the courts in these cases have virtually assumed their findings of a suspect classification through a simplistic process of analysis: since, under the traditional systems of financing public schools, some poorer people receive less expensive educations than other more affluent people, these systems discriminate on the basis of wealth. This approach largely ignores the hard threshold questions, including whether it makes a difference for purposes of consideration under the Constitution that the class of disadvantaged "poor" cannot be identified or defined in customary equal protection terms, and whether the relative—rather than absolute—nature of the asserted deprivation is of significant consequence. . . .

The precedents of this Court provide the proper starting point. The individuals, or groups of individuals, who constituted the class discriminated against in our prior cases shared two distinguishing characteristics: because of their impecunity they were completely unable to pay for some desired benefit, and as a consequence, they sustained an absolute deprivation of a meaningful opportunity to enjoy that benefit. [The Court reviews its precedents discussing discrimination based on wealth.]

Only appellees' first possible basis for describing the class disadvantaged by the Texas school-financing system—discrimination against a class of definably "poor" persons—might arguably meet the criteria established in these prior cases. Even a cursory examination, however, demonstrates that neither of the two distinguishing characteristics of wealth classifications can be found here. First, in support of their charge that the system discriminates against the "poor," appellees have made no effort to demonstrate that it operates to the peculiar disadvantage of any class fairly definable as indigent, or as composed of persons whose incomes are beneath any designated poverty level. Indeed, there is reason to believe that the poorest families are not necessarily clustered in the poorest property districts. A recent and exhaustive study of school districts in Connecticut concluded that "[i]t is clearly incorrect . . . to contend that the 'poor' live in 'poor' districts . . . Thus, the major factual assumption of *Serrano*[*v. Priest*, 487 P.2d 1241 (Cal. 1971)]—that the educational financing system discriminates against the 'poor'—is simply false in Connecticut."[53] Defining "poor" families as those below the Bureau of the Census "poverty level," the Connecticut study found, not surprisingly, that the poor were clustered around commercial and industrial areas—those same areas that provide the most attractive sources of property tax income for school districts. Whether a similar pattern would be discovered in Texas is not known, but there is no basis on the record in this case for assuming that the poorest people—defined by reference to any level of absolute impecunity—are concentrated in the poorest districts.

Second, neither appellees nor the District Court addressed the fact that, unlike each of the foregoing cases, lack of personal resources has not occasioned an absolute deprivation of the desired benefit. The argument here is not that the children in districts having relatively low assessable property values are receiving no public education; rather, it is that they are receiving a poorer quality education than that available to children in districts having more assessable wealth. Apart from the unsettled and disputed question whether the quality of education may be determined by the amount of money expended for it, a sufficient answer to appellees' argument is that, at least where wealth is involved, the Equal Protection Clause does not require absolute equality or precisely equal advantages. Nor, indeed, in view of the infinite variables affecting the educational process, can any system assure equal quality of education except in the most relative sense. Texas asserts that the Minimum Foundation Program provides an "adequate" education for all children in the State. By providing 12 years of free public-school education, and by assuring teachers, books, transportation, and operating funds, the Texas Legislature has endeavored to "guarantee, for the welfare of the state as a whole, that all people shall have at least an adequate program of education. This is what is meant by 'A Minimum Foundation Program of Education.'" The State repeatedly asserted in its briefs in this Court that it has fulfilled this desire and that it now assures "every child in every school district an adequate education." No proof was offered at trial persuasively discrediting or refuting the State's assertion.

For these two reasons—the absence of any evidence that the financing system discriminates against any definable category of "poor" people or that it results in the absolute deprivation of education—the disadvantaged class is not susceptible of identification in traditional terms.

. . .

However described, it is clear that appellees' suit asks this Court to extend its most exacting scrutiny to review a system that allegedly discriminates against a large, diverse, and amorphous class, unified only by the common factor of residence in districts that happen to have less taxable wealth than other districts. The system of alleged discrimination and the class it defines have none of the traditional indicia of suspectness: the class is not saddled with such disabilities, or subjected to such a history of purposeful unequal treatment, or relegated to such a position of political powerlessness as to command extraordinary protection from the majoritarian political process.

---

53. Note, *A Statistical Analysis of the School Finance Decisions: On Winning Battles and Losing*   *Wars*, 81 YALE L.J. 1303, 1328–1329 (1972).

We thus conclude that the Texas system does not operate to the peculiar disadvantage of any suspect class. [Appellees] also assert that the State's system impermissibly interferes with the exercise of a "fundamental" right and that accordingly the prior decisions of this Court require the application of the strict standard of judicial review....

. . .

... We are in complete agreement with the conclusion of the three-judge panel below that "the grave significance of education both to the individual and to our society" cannot be doubted. But the importance of a service performed by the State does not determine whether it must be regarded as fundamental for purposes of examination under the Equal Protection Clause. Mr. Justice Harlan, dissenting from the Court's application of strict scrutiny to a law impinging upon the right of interstate travel, admonished that "[v]irtually every state statute affects important rights." *Shapiro v. Thompson*, 394 U.S., at 655, 661. In his view, if the degree of judicial scrutiny of state legislation fluctuated depending on a majority's view of the importance of the interest affected, we would have gone "far toward making this Court a 'super-legislature.'" We would, indeed, then be assuming a legislative role and one for which the Court lacks both authority and competence. But Mr. Justice Stewart's response in *Shapiro* to Mr. Justice Harlan's concern correctly articulates the limits of the fundamental-rights rationale employed in the Court's equal protection decisions:

The Court today does not "pick out particular human activities, characterize them as 'fundamental,' and give them added protection...." To the contrary, the Court simply recognizes, as it must, an established constitutional right, and gives to that right no less protection than the Constitution itself demands.

Justice Stewart's statement serves to underline what the opinion of the Court in *Shapiro* makes clear. In subjecting to strict judicial scrutiny state welfare eligibility statutes that imposed a one-year durational residency requirement as a precondition to receiving AFDC benefits, the Court explained: "[I]n moving from State to State ... appellees were exercising a constitutional right, and any classification which serves to penalize the exercise of that right, unless shown to be necessary to promote a compelling governmental interest, is unconstitutional." The right to interstate travel had long been recognized as a right of constitutional significance, and the Court's decision, therefore, did not require an ad hoc determination as to the social or economic importance of that right.

. . .

The lesson of these cases in addressing the question now before the Court is plain. It is not the province of this Court to create substantive constitutional rights in the name of guaranteeing equal protection of the laws. Thus, the key to discovering whether education is "fundamental" is not to be found in comparisons of the relative societal significance of education as opposed to subsistence or housing. Nor is it to be found by weighing whether education is as important as the right to travel. Rather, the answer lies in assessing whether there is a right to education explicitly or implicitly guaranteed by the Constitution.

Education, of course, is not among the rights afforded explicit protection under our Federal Constitution. Nor do we find any basis for saying it is implicitly so protected. As we have said, the undisputed importance of education will not alone cause this Court to depart from the usual standard for reviewing a State's social and economic legislation. It is appellees' contention, however, that education is distinguishable from other services and benefits provided by the State because it bears a peculiarly close relationship to other rights and liberties accorded protection under the Constitution. Specifically, they insist that education is itself a fundamental personal right because it is essential to the effective exercise of First Amendment freedoms and to intelligent utilization of the right to vote. In asserting a nexus between speech and education, appellees urge that the right to speak is meaningless unless the speaker is capable of articulating his thoughts intelligently and persuasively. The "marketplace of ideas" is an empty forum for those lacking basic communicative tools. Likewise, they argue that the corollary right to receive information becomes little more than a hollow privilege when the recipient has not been taught to read, assimilate, and utilize available knowledge.

A similar line of reasoning is pursued with respect to the right to vote. Exercise of the franchise, it is contended, cannot be divorced from the educational foundation of the voter. The electoral process, if reality is to conform to the democratic ideal, depends on an informed electorate: a voter cannot cast his ballot intelligently unless his reading skills and thought processes have been adequately developed.

We need not dispute any of these propositions. The Court has long afforded zealous protection against unjustifiable governmental interference with the individual's rights to speak and to vote. Yet we have never presumed to possess either the ability or the authority to guarantee to the citizenry the most effective speech or the most informed electoral choice. That these may be desirable goals of a system of freedom of expression and of a representative form of government is not to be doubted. These are indeed goals to be pursued by a people whose thoughts and beliefs are freed from governmental interference. But they are not values to be implemented by judicial intrusion into otherwise legitimate state activities.

Even if it were conceded that some identifiable quantum of education is a constitutionally protected prerequisite to the meaningful exercise of either right, we have no indication that the present levels of educational expenditure in Texas provide an education that falls short. Whatever merit appellees' argument might have if a State's financing system occasioned an absolute denial of educational opportunities to any of its children, that argument provides no basis for finding an interference with fundamental rights where only relative differences in spending levels are involved and where—as is true in the present case—no charge fairly could be made that the system fails to provide each child with an opportunity to acquire the basic minimal skills necessary for the enjoyment of the rights of speech and of full participation in the political process.

Furthermore, the logical limitations on appellees' nexus theory are difficult to perceive. How, for instance, is education to be distinguished from the significant personal interests in the basics of decent food and shelter? Empirical examination might well buttress an assumption that the ill-fed, ill-clothed, and ill-housed are among the most ineffective participants in the political process, and that they derive the least enjoyment from the benefits of the First Amendment. . . .

. . .

. . . . Every step leading to the establishment of the system Texas utilizes today—including the decisions permitting localities to tax and expend locally, and creating and continuously expanding state aid—was implemented in an effort to extend public education and to improve its quality. Of course, every reform that benefits some more than others may be criticized for what it fails to accomplish. But we think it plain that, in substance, the thrust of the Texas system is affirmative and reformatory and, therefore, should be scrutinized under judicial principles sensitive to the nature of the State's efforts and to the rights reserved to the States under the Constitution.

It should be clear, for the reasons stated above and in accord with the prior decisions of this Court, that this is not a case in which the challenged state action must be subjected to the searching judicial scrutiny reserved for laws that create suspect classifications or impinge upon constitutionally protected rights.

. . .

In addition to matters of fiscal policy, this case also involves the most persistent and difficult questions of educational policy, another area in which this Court's lack of specialized knowledge and experience counsels against premature interference with the informed judgments made at the state and local levels. Education, perhaps even more than welfare assistance, presents a myriad of "intractable economic, social, and even philosophical problems." *Dandridge v. Williams*, 397 U.S., at 487. The very complexity of the problems of financing and managing a statewide public school system suggests that "there will be more than one constitutionally permissible method of solving them," and that, within the limits of rationality, "the legislature's efforts to tackle the problems" should be entitled to respect. *Jefferson v. Hackney*, 406 U.S., at 546–547. On even the most basic questions in this area the scholars and educational experts are divided. Indeed, one of the major sources of controversy concerns the extent to which there is a demonstrable correlation between educational expenditures and the quality of education—an assumed correlation underlying virtually every legal conclusion drawn by the District Court in this case. Related to the questioned relationship between cost and quality is the equally unsettled controversy as to the proper goals of a system of public education. And the question regarding the most effective relationship between state boards of education and local school boards, in terms of their respective responsibilities and degrees of control, is now undergoing searching re-examination. The ultimate wisdom as to these and related problems of education is not likely to be divined for all time even by the scholars who now so earnestly debate the issues. In such circumstances, the judiciary is well advised to refrain from imposing on the States inflexible constitutional restraints that could circumscribe or handicap the continued research and experimentation so vital to finding even partial solutions to educational problems and to keeping abreast of ever-changing conditions.

It must be remembered, also, that every claim arising under the Equal Protection Clause has implications for the relationship between national and state power under our federal system. Questions of federalism are always inherent in the process of determining whether a State's laws are to be accorded the traditional presumption of constitutionality, or are to be subjected instead to rigorous judicial scrutiny. While "[t]he maintenance of the principles of federalism is a foremost consideration in interpreting any of the pertinent constitutional provisions under which this Court examines state action," it would be difficult to imagine a case having a greater potential impact on our federal system than the one now before us, in which we are urged to abrogate systems of financing public education presently in existence in virtually every State.

[The Court next applies the rational basis test to the Texas system of school finance.]

[T]o the extent that the Texas system of school financing results in unequal expenditures between children who happen to reside in different districts, we cannot say that such disparities are the product of a system that is so irrational as to be invidiously discriminatory. Texas has acknowledged its shortcomings and has persistently endeavored—not without some success—to ameliorate the differences in levels of expenditures without sacrificing the benefits of local participation. The Texas plan is not the result of hurried, ill-conceived legislation. It certainly is not the product of purposeful discrimination against any group or class. On the contrary, it is rooted in decades of experience in Texas and elsewhere, and in major part is the product of responsible studies by qualified people. In giving substance to the presumption of validity to which the Texas system is entitled, it is important to remember that at every stage of its development it has constituted a "rough accommodation" of interests in an effort to arrive at practical and workable solutions. *Metropolis Theatre Co. v. City of Chicago*, 228 U.S. 61, 69–70 (1913). One also must remember that the system here challenged is not peculiar to Texas or to any other State. In its essential characteristics, the Texas plan for financing public education reflects what many educators for a half century have thought was an enlightened approach to a problem for which there is no perfect solution. We are unwilling to assume for ourselves a level of wisdom superior to that of legislators, scholars, and educational authorities in 50 States, especially where the alternatives proposed are only recently conceived and nowhere yet tested. The constitutional standard under the Equal Protection Clause is whether the challenged state action rationally furthers a legitimate state purpose or interest. *McGinnis v. Royster*, 410 U.S. 263, 270 (1973). We hold that the Texas plan abundantly satisfies this standard.

Questions and Comments on Rodriguez

1. The Court in *Rodriguez* quoted its statement in *Brown v. Board of Education* that education is one of the most important functions of local government, and must be provided on equal terms when a state has undertaken to provide it. In legitimizing differences in funding between school districts within a state, is the Court being faithful to the legacy of *Brown*?

2. Justice Powell acknowledges that there is a debate about what the goals of a system of public education should be. Nevertheless, he leaves this question unanswered, choosing to defer to local authorities. What do you think the purposes of public K–12 education should be? If preparing students for college is a goal, how can a state justify such differences in the quality of education provided?

3. Some authors have noted that the quality of a student's education and his or her chances of completing college are largely determined by the neighborhood where the student lives. As Professor Howard Gardner of Harvard's Graduate School of Education notes, "Tell me the zip code of a child and I will predict her chances of college completion and probable income; add the elements of family support (parental, grandparental, ethnic and religious values) and few degrees of freedom remain, at least in our country." Howard Gardner, *Paroxysms of Choice*, N.Y. REV. OF BOOKS, Oct. 19, 2000, at 44, 49. In the aftermath of *Rodriguez*, plaintiffs seeking to challenge the disparity of funding between school districts turned to state courts. Eventually, the Texas Supreme Court directed state lawmakers to fix the school financing system. This led to Texas Senate Bill 7, which had the effect of redistributing funds from wealthier school districts to their less wealthy counterparts. Despite these reforms, the correlations noted by Professor Gardner persist. Michael Heise, *The Story of San Antonio School District v. Rodriguez: School Finance, Local Control, and Constitutional Limits, in* EDUCATION LAW STORIES 51, 73 (Michael A. Olivas & Ronna Greff Schneider eds., 2008).

WILLIAM G. BOWEN, MARTIN P. KURZWEIL, AND EUGENE M. TOBIN, EQUITY AND EXCELLENCE IN AMERICAN HIGHER EDUCATION
95–105, 175–76 (2005).

We turn now to a detailed examination of new data showing how socio-economic status relates to admission, enrollment, and academic outcomes at 19 academically selective colleges and universities. . . .

[I]t would have been desirable to look at more schools, but focusing on this group of highly ranked organizations is worthwhile because of the depth of the analysis that it permits. . . . Furthermore, it is still often the case that the path to many positions of power and wealth in this country winds its way through these selective colleges and universities. It is important, from a societal vantage point, to know who is attending them.

The fundamental question is whether these highly regarded institutions should today be considered "engines of opportunity" or "bastions of privilege." The president of one of them posed a central question to us early on in this project: "In applying to my university, is an applicant better off, other things equal, being rich or poor?" Put another way: is there an admissions advantage associated with being poor, or with being the first member of your family to go to college, that is comparable to the advantage associated with being a minority student, a legacy; or a recruited athlete? Alternatively, does coming from a wealthy family, in and of itself, increase an applicant's chance of admission? . . .

. . . In the previous chapter we discussed the extent to which family circumstances affect decisions to take the SAT in the first place and then the extent to which they affect test-taking performance. We found that those in the top income quartile were about six times more likely to take the SAT *and* score above 1200 than were those in the bottom income quartile, and that young people with at least one parent who was educated beyond a high school diploma were nearly seven times more likely to achieve these high scores than those whose parents have no more than a high school diploma. Fewer than 2.5 percent of young people from low-income families, and fewer than 1 percent of the children of parents with low educational attainment, were in this category of high-scoring SAT-takers.

Of the candidates from low-[socioeconomic status (SES)] backgrounds who do end up with high SAT scores, more apply to selective and expensive schools such as those in our study than one might have expected. Data in a recent report by Richard Spies . . . indicate that, of all high-testing students from low-income families, about one-third apply to one or more of the selective colleges that he chose as a reference group—a set of institutions that is generally similar to ours. However, more than half of the high-testing students from high-income families applied to these schools.... Spies also finds evidence that the impact of family incomes is considerably smaller now than it was in earlier years.

... One reason is that highly selective institutions have stepped up the recruitment of disadvantaged students....

. . .

Applying to college is, of course, only the first step....

There are two major conclusions to be drawn from [our data]. First, the percentage of students from low-income families and the percentage who are first-generation college students are both small. Students whose families are in the bottom quartiles of the national incomes distribution [the cut-off in 1995 was under $25,000] represent roughly 10 to 11 percent of all students at these schools, and first-generation college students represent a little over 6 percent of these student populations. Nationally, the bottom quartile is, by definition, 25 percent of the population, while 38 percent of the national population of 16–year-olds have parents who never attended college.... When we combine the two measures ... and estimate the fraction of the enrollment at these schools that is made up of students who are *both* first-generation college-goers and from low-income families, we get a figure of about 3 percent. Nationally, the share of the same-age population who fell into this category was around 19 percent in 1992, making this doubly disadvantaged group even more underrepresented than students with just one of the two characteristics.

The second conclusion ... is that these percentages do not change very much as we move from the applicant pool to the group of students admitted, to those who enroll, and finally to those who graduate. *This consistent pattern suggests that socioeconomic status does not affect progression through these stages.* Thus, even in this basic figure (which does not take into account associated differences in SAT scores or other variables) we can begin to see the outline of what we regard as a striking finding: once disadvantaged students make it into the credible applicant pool of one of these highly selective schools (no easy accomplishment, to be sure), they have essentially the same experiences as their more advantaged peers....

. . .

The question of *admission preference* ... needs to be addressed directly....

[We compared] admission probabilities in relation to SAT scores for three other "special groups": underrepresented minority students, legacies, and recruited athletes. It is evident that applicants in each of these special groups have a *decidedly* better chance of being admitted, at any specified SAT level, than do other students, including those from low-SES categories.

Table 5.1

	Adjusted Admission Advantage
Income (relative to Middle Quartiles)	
Bottom quartile	−1.0
Top quartile	−3.1
Parental Education	
First-generation college student	4.1
Other Characteristics	
Recruited athlete	30.2
Underrepresented minority	27.7
Legacy	19.7
Early applicant	19.6

... The straightforward interpretation of these estimates is that an applicant with an admissions probability of, say, 40 percent based on SAT scores and other variables would have an admissions probability of 70 percent if he or she were also a recruited athlete, 68 percent if a member of an under-represented minority group, and 60 percent if a legacy or an early action/early decision applicant.

. . .

[W]e return to the central question . . . : how should students from poor families and from families with no previous history of college attendance be treated in the admissions process? If we were to poll presidents of leading colleges and universities, we are confident that a large majority would want their schools to be more than "neutral" in considering such candidates. The brief submitted to the Supreme Court in conjunction with the University of Michigan cases by Harvard, Brown, Chicago, Duke, Dartmouth, the University of Pennsylvania, Princeton, and Yale is unequivocal on this point. The relevant section reads as follows:

> Admission factors begin, of course, with the core academic criteria, including not just grades and test scores, but teacher recommendations and state, regional, national, and international awards. In some cases, those criteria will be all but decisive, either positively (very rarely) or negatively (more often). In the vast majority of cases, however, they are not themselves decisive, and the process continues. *Admissions officials give special attention to, among other, applicants from economically and/or culturally disadvantaged backgrounds,* those with unusual athletic ability, those with special artistic talents, *those who would be the first in their families to attend any college,* those whose parents are alumni or alumnae, *and those who have overcome various identifiable hardships.* (our emphasis)

What is striking is the juxtaposition of this clear statement of intent with the equally clear empirical finding that, at the schools in our study, there is absolutely no admissions advantage (about 4 percentile points) associated with being a first-generation college-goer; at least that was the case of the '95 entering cohort. We do not believe that this disjunction is due to any desire to be disingenuous or to "gild the lily." Rather, we believe it is due to a combination of lack of data at the institutional level on the background characteristics of all applicants (data that are hard to assemble), financial aid constraints, a commitment to being need-blind (and therefore purposefully ignoring SES) and the lack of vocal champions for students from low-income families when tough choices are being made among a large group of very well-qualified candidates.

. . . The president of one of the universities in our study told us that, on reflection, and on the basis of what he had seen in the admissions process at his own university, he was not at all surprised by the finding that admissions at these highly selective universities is truly need-blind, but not more than that. He said that when the admissions staff was considering an outstanding soccer player, it was as if "the lights went on" in the room; everyone paid close attention, and everyone knew that the coach and athletic director were, in effect, watching closely and would have to be dealt with. Similarly, when the staff considered a legacy candidate with strong ties to the university, it was clear that representatives of the alumni office, the development office, and perhaps even the president's officer, were "present" in spirit if not in person. Minority candidates also were considered carefully and sympathetically, in part because of the active involvement of recruiters and admissions staff members with a special commitment to racial diversity. But, the president continued, when an otherwise "normal" applicant from a family of modest circumstances was considered, the process just moved right ahead without anyone making a special plea. . . .

Note on the Relationship Between Financial Aid and Discrimination on the Basis of Class

Even if a college does not overtly discriminate against students from low-income families in the admissions process, the costs of attendance often constitute an insurmountable barrier. Most if not all of the schools in the Bowen study were wealthy enough to offer enough financial aid to admitted students to cover all of their costs. Until recently, much of the financial aid offered even by the weakest schools was in the form of loans, rather than grants, and that formed a significant barrier for students from low-income families. *See infra* pp. 815–17. Bowen et al. conclude that the presidents of colleges and universities should want their schools to be more than neutral when considering candidates from low-income families and who are the first generation in their family to attend college. Should colleges and universities prefer students from these types of backgrounds, or should admissions be entirely determined by academic credentials? If institutions should prefer these students, what policies should they adopt to ensure that low-income students are able to attend?

E.   INTERNATIONAL AND OUT-OF-STATE STUDENTS

Shim v. Rutgers
Supreme Court of New Jersey, 2007.
191 N.J. 374, 924 A.2d 465.

■ JUSTICE LONG announced the opinion of the Court.

Ezrina Shim was born in Montgomery County, Pennsylvania on November 5, 1984. Sometime later, Shim left the United States with her parents and settled in Korea. In August 1999, she moved back to the United States to live with her aunt and uncle, the Parks, in Mount Laurel, New Jersey. Her parents remained in Korea.

While living with Mr. and Mrs. Park, Shim attended four years of high school in Mount Laurel. She also obtained a New Jersey driver license; acquired and registered an automobile in New Jersey; opened a bank account in this State; worked several jobs here; filed New Jersey personal income tax returns; and registered to vote in Burlington County. In addition, Shim forged several meaningful social relationships in and around the State.

... She has represented to others that she considers New Jersey her home and has no intention of returning to live in Korea. She does not speak Korean fluently, and has no meaningful social life or close friends in Korea.

In September 2003, Shim, then eighteen years old, enrolled as an undergraduate student at Rutgers [University]. Prior to enrollment, the Admissions Office determined that Shim was not a resident of this State for tuition purposes because she was a dependent student whose parents were not domiciled here. Shim, however, claimed residency based on her living arrangement with her aunt and uncle.

. . .

... [Shim] noted that under [a New Jersey Statute,] N.J.S.A. 18A:62–4, all students who are domiciled in New Jersey are entitled to in-state tuition rates, and individuals who have lived in the state for twelve months prior to enrollment in a public university are presumed domiciliaries. As Shim had lived in the state for over four years before her enrollment at Rutgers, she argued that she should have been presumed eligible for, and received, in-state tuition rates.

[Rutgers argued that New Jersey Administrative regulations, N.J.A.C. 9A: 5–1.1(f) and N.J.A.C. 9A:9–2.6 mandate that an undergraduate student is presumed to have the residency status of her parents, unless the student is able to prove that she is independent of her parents. Since Shim had provided no evidence of independence, Rutgers presumed that she was not a resident of New Jersey for tuition purposes.

Shim appealed this decision to the New Jersey Superior Court, Appellate Division, arguing that the regulator presumption conflicted with the legislative presumption, and therefore was invalid. Alternatively, Shim argued that the regulation was void as an unauthorized exercise of agency power.

The Appellate Division held] that Rutgers' denial of Shim's application for in-state residency status was arbitrary and capricious because it was based upon an erroneous application of the relevant regulatory standard.

. . .

For over a century, New Jersey has afforded residents more favorable tuition rates at state institutions than their non-resident counterparts. Prior to 1979, the regulatory standard that governed in-state tuition eligibility was absolute—only twelve months residency in New Jersey prior to enrollment would suffice.

In 1979, the Legislature enacted N.J.S.A. 18A:62–4, the statute at issue here. It provides:

> Persons who have been resident within this State for a period of 12 months prior to enrollment in a public institution of higher education are presumed to be domiciled in this State for tuition purposes. Persons who have been resident within this State for less than 12 months prior to enrollment are presumed to be nondomiciliaries for tuition purposes. Persons presumed to be nondomiciled

or persons who are presumed to be domiciled, but whose domiciliary status is challenged by the institution, may demonstrate domicile according to rules and regulations established for that purpose by the Commission on Higher Education. Residence established solely for the purpose of attending a particular educational institution is not domicile for the purposes of this act.

The Senate Education Committee statement to the bill that became N.J.S.A. 18A:62–4 identified its core purpose:

> Present law requires that a student be a resident for 12 months prior to enrollment. The State Board of Higher Education cannot make an exception to this regulation. This penalizes individuals who have moved to New Jersey and established legal domicile less than a year prior to a student's enrollment in college. Under this bill, the State Board of Higher Education could make an exception for individuals who can demonstrate that they are legally domiciled in New Jersey.

That legislative history is critical to any analysis of the statute. It underscores that in enacting N.J.S.A. 18A:62–4, the Legislature had no intention of making it more difficult for a student who had actually resided here for a year prior to enrollment to establish in-state status for tuition purposes. Instead, that statute was enacted to broaden the class of students who might qualify for in-state tuition by softening the prior bright line rule of twelve-months residency. It is against that backdrop that we must interpret the statute.

A student seeking in-state tuition bears the burden of proving that she is domiciled here. Apropos of that obligation, in enacting N.J.S.A. 18A:62–4, the Legislature established, as the statute's point of departure, a set of presumptions regarding domicile.

. . .

Under N.J.S.A. 18A:62–4, twelve months residence in New Jersey is the basic fact that the Legislature has said establishes the presumed fact of domicile. Accordingly, length of residence is the preliminary inquiry. If the twelve-month standard has been satisfied, there is a mandatory inference that the student is a domiciliary. If not, there is a contrary mandatory inference that the student is a non-domiciliary.

At that point, the institution has two choices: it can either accept the student's presumed domicile, or it can challenge that status. The gravamen of such a challenge is found in the last sentence of N.J.S.A. 18A:62–4, which declares that "[r]esidence established solely for the purpose of attending a particular educational institution is not domicile for the purposes of this act." In other words, the Legislature itself has declared that residence in New Jersey solely for the purpose of obtaining admission and in-state tuition at a state college or university will not satisfy the statute. Accordingly the institution may challenge a student who has lived here for more than twelve months on that basis.

Upon such a challenge, N.J.S.A. 18A:62–4 declares that the student, like her presumptively non-domiciled counterparts, "may demonstrate domicile according to the rules and regulations established for that purpose by the Commission on Higher Education." Thus, the student, who is in the best position to do so, has the burden of producing the evidence enumerated in the applicable regulations. . . .

. . .

That brings us to the regulations and Rutgers' application of subsection (f) of N.J.A.C. 9A:5–1.1, which declares that "[d]ependent students as defined in the rules of the Higher Education Student Assistance Authority at N.J.A.C. 9A:9–2.6 are presumed to be domiciled in the state in which their parent(s) or legal guardian(s) is domiciled" and that "[d]ependent students whose parent(s) or legal guardian(s) is not domiciled in New Jersey are presumed to be in the State for the temporary purpose of obtaining an education and presumed not to be domiciled in New Jersey."

. . .

. . . Subsection (f) can reasonably be read as intending to declare that evidence of a student's financial dependence on her out-of-state parents is sufficient to raise a material issue of fact regarding the student's domicile, thus overcoming the presumption that flows from twelve months of residence here. Under that reading, which aligns with the law on presumptions, the playing field is evened and the student must prove her case, based on all the evidence, with no presumption either way.

That is the only interpretation of subsection (f) that renders the statute and regulations a coherent and seamless whole. Pursuant to it, a student who has lived in New Jersey for twelve months prior to enrollment is presumed to be a domiciliary for tuition purposes. If that student is, in fact, dependent on out-of-state parents, that dependence creates a genuine issue regarding domicile and the presumption in her favor is neutralized. Importantly, that does not give rise to the contrary presumption that she is a non-domiciliary. Rather, she is neither presumed a domiciliary nor presumed a non-domiciliary. Rutgers must then fully, fairly, and dispassionately consider all submitted evidence, including but not limited to evidence of the student's dependence on out-of-state parents. If a preponderance of the evidence indicates that the student's domicile is in New Jersey as defined in N.J.A.C. 9A:5–1.1(a), then it must classify her as a domiciliary for in-state tuition purposes.

In this case, Shim established that she lived in New Jersey for four years prior to her enrollment at Rutgers at age eighteen. Thus, under N.J.S.A. 18A:62–4, she was a presumed New Jersey domiciliary. Rutgers rejected that presumption under the terms of N.J.A.C. 9A:5–1.1(f), flatly stating that "[r]eflective of the applicable state regulations . . . an undergraduate student is presumed to have the residency status of her parents, unless she proves herself 'independent' as that term is defined[.]" Rutgers erred in applying that presumption of non-domicile and in refusing to consider the evidence Shim proffered that, notwithstanding her financial dependence on out-of-state parents, her domicile was, in fact, in New Jersey. To be sure, the financial details of Shim's support by her out-of-state parents were relevant to her domiciliary status and created a fact issue that overcame the presumption in her favor. However, financial support alone did not create a counter-presumption of non-domicile and thus could not be outcome determinative. Rather, Rutgers was required to fully and fairly weigh all the other evidence proffered by the student with no presumption either way. Only after doing so, could Rutgers have determined that Shim was a non-domiciliary, and then only if the weight of the evidence on the record supported its conclusion.

By standing on what it incorrectly understood to be a presumption of non-domicile and limiting consideration of Shim's evidence to that which bore on her parents' financial support, Rutgers interpreted the regulations in a way that violated N.J.S.A. 18A:62–4 and denied Shim a fair opportunity to prove her domicile. We therefore affirm the judgment of the Appellate Division and remand the case to Rutgers for reconsideration in light of the principles to which we have adverted.

Questions and Comments on International and Out of State Students

1. Does *Shim* make college more or less accessible for students? If Shim is unable to establish residency in New Jersey for tuition purposes, a state where she lives, pays taxes, and votes, will she be able to obtain in-state tuition at any public university?

2. An estimated 2.7 million students in the world attended an institute of higher education outside of their home country in 2007. Of those, twenty-two percent left their home country to attend a post-secondary institution in the United States. The country with the next highest percentage was the United Kingdom, where thirteen percent of internationally mobile students went for their education. Global Destinations for International Students, Atlas of Student Mobility Website of the Institute of International Education, http://www.atlas.iienetwork.org/?p=48027 (last visited June 20, 2008). What sorts of challenges do American colleges and universities face when educating this many foreign students?

F.   AFFIRMATIVE ACTION

Affirmative action became an official policy of the federal government on September 24, 1965, when President Lyndon Johnson issued Executive Order 11246. It provided in pertinent part:

[A]ll Government contracting agencies shall include in every Government contract hereafter entered into the following provisions:

During the performance of this contract, the contractor agrees as follows:

(1) The contractor will not discriminate against any employee or applicant for employment because of race, color, religion, sex, or national origin. The contractor will take affirmative action to ensure that applicants are employed, and that employees are treated during employment, without regard to their race, color, religion, sex[a] or national origin. Such action shall include, but not be limited to the following: employment, upgrading, demotion, or transfer; recruitment or recruitment advertising; layoff or termination; rates of pay or other forms of compensation; and selection for training, including apprenticeship. The contractor agrees to post in conspicuous places, available to employees and applicants for employment, notices to be

---

a. Women were not added to the Executive Order until 1967.

provided by the contracting officer setting forth the provisions of this nondiscrimination clause.

(2) The contractor will, in all solicitations or advancements for employees placed by or on behalf of the contractor, state that all qualified applicants will receive consideration for employment without regard to race, color, religion, sex or national origin.

The term "affirmative action" has been traced back to the days immediately after the inauguration of John F. Kennedy as President in 1961. Three lawyers gathered in the Willard Hotel to write the first draft of what became Executive Order 10925, which established the President's Committee on Equal Employment Opportunity: Abe Fortas, Arthur Goldberg, (both future supreme court justices) and Hobart Taylor, Jr, whose father was a businessman in Houston and an ally of Lyndon Johnson. Taylor later recalled that he added the phrase "affirmative action" as an afterthought to "give a sense of positiveness to performance under that Executive Order."[b]

From the beginning, affirmative action has been fiercely debated both inside and outside the judiciary. The debate over affirmative action in college admissions has been particularly fierce.

As you read the materials in this section, consider what are the strongest arguments for and against affirmative action. If you were a justice on the Supreme Court would you vote to uphold affirmative action in college admissions? Why or why not?

Regents of the University of California v. Bakke

Supreme Court of the United States, 1978.
438 U.S. 265, 98 S.Ct. 2733, 57 L.Ed.2d 750.

■ MR. JUSTICE POWELL announced the judgment of the Court.

This case presents a challenge to the special admissions program of the petitioner, the Medical School of the University of California at Davis, which is designed to assure the admission of a specified number of students from certain minority groups. The Superior Court of California sustained respondent's challenge, holding that petitioner's program violated the California Constitution, Title VI of the Civil Rights Act of 1964, 42 U.S.C. § 2000d *et seq.*, and the Equal Protection Clause of the Fourteenth Amendment. . . . The Supreme Court of California affirmed those portions of the trial court's judgment declaring the special admissions program unlawful and enjoining petitioner from considering the race of any applicant. It modified that portion of the judgment denying respondent's requested injunction and directed the trial court to order his admission.

For the reasons stated in the following opinion, I believe that so much of the judgment of the California court as holds petitioner's special admissions program unlawful and directs that respondent be admitted to the Medical School must be affirmed. For the reasons expressed in a separate opinion,

b. NICHOLAS LEMANN, THE BIG TEST: THE SECRET HISTORY OF THE AMERICAN MERITOCRACY 162 (1999).

my Brothers The Chief Justice, Mr. Justice Stewart, Mr. Justice Rehnquist, and Mr. Justice Stevens concur in this judgment.

I also conclude for the reasons stated in the following opinion that the portion of the court's judgment enjoining petitioner from according any consideration to race in its admissions process must be reversed. For reasons expressed in separate opinions, my Brothers Mr. Justice Brennan, Mr. Justice White, Mr. Justice Marshall, and Mr. Justice Blackmun concur in this judgment.

The Medical School of the University of California at Davis opened in 1968 with an entering class of 50 students. In 1971, the size of the entering class was increased to 100 students, a level at which it remains. No admissions program for disadvantaged or minority students existed when the school opened, and the first class contained three Asians but no blacks, no Mexican–Americans, and no American Indians. Over the next two years, the faculty devised a special admissions program to increase the representation of "disadvantaged" students in each Medical School class. The special program consisted of a separate admissions system operating in coordination with the regular admissions process.

[Under the regular admissions procedure, candidates whose overall undergraduate grade point average fell below 2.5 on a scale of 4.0 were summarily rejected. The remaining candidates were given a numerical benchmark score based on an interview, the candidate's overall grade point average, grade point average in science courses, scores on the Medical College Admissions Test (MCAT), letters of recommendation, extracurricular activities, and other biographical data. The admissions committee then reviewed the score and file of each applicant and made offers of admissions on a rolling basis.

The special admissions program was operated separately from the regular admissions procedure. In 1973, candidates were asked to indicate whether they wished to be considered as "economically and/or educationally disadvantaged" applicants. In 1973, students were asked if they wished to be considered as members of a "minority group" including "Blacks," "Chicanos," "Asians," and "American Indians." If an applicant answered affirmatively to either of these questions, their application was forwarded to a special committee. The committee screened each of these applications to see whether it reflected economic or educational deprivation. These applicants were not automatically rejected if their overall grade point average fell below 2.5. After a benchmark score was calculated in the same manner as in the regular procedure, the special committee recommended its top choices until a prescribed number of special admissions had been met. Although disadvantaged whites applied to the special program in large numbers, none received an offer of admission through that process.

Allan Bakke is a white male who applied to the Davis Medical School under the general admissions program in 1973 and 1974. Despite strong benchmark scores, Bakke was rejected both times. In both years, applicants were admitted under the special program with grade point averages, MCAT scores, and benchmark scores significantly lower than Bakke's.]

After the second rejection, Bakke filed the instant suit in the Superior Court of California....

. . .

In this Court the parties neither briefed nor argued the applicability of Title VI of the Civil Rights Act of 1964. Rather, as had the California court, they focused exclusively upon the validity of the special admissions program under the Equal Protection Clause. Because it was possible, however, that a decision on Title VI might obviate resort to constitutional interpretation, *see Ashwander v. TVA*, 297 U.S. 288, 346–348 (1936) (concurring opinion), we requested supplementary briefing on the statutory issue.

The language of § 601 [of Title VI] like that of the Equal Protection Clause, is majestic in its sweep:

> No person in the United States shall, on the ground of race, color, or national origin, be excluded from participation in, be denied the benefits of, or be subjected to discrimination under any program or activity receiving Federal financial assistance.

The concept of "discrimination," like the phrase "equal protection of the laws," is susceptible of varying interpretations. . . . We must, therefore, seek whatever aid is available in determining the precise meaning of the statute before us. Examination of the voluminous legislative history of Title VI reveals a congressional intent to halt federal funding of entities that violate a prohibition of racial discrimination similar to that of the Constitution. Although isolated statements of various legislators, taken out of context, can be marshaled in support of the proposition that § 601 enacted a purely colorblind scheme, without regard to the reach of the Equal Protection Clause, these comments must be read against the background of both the problem that Congress was addressing and the broader view of the statute that emerges from a full examination of the legislative debates.

. . .

In view of the clear legislative intent, Title VI must be held to proscribe only those racial classifications that would violate the Equal Protection Clause or the Fifth Amendment.

Petitioner does not deny that decisions based on race or ethnic origin by faculties and administrations of state universities are reviewable under the Fourteenth Amendment. The parties do disagree as to the level of judicial scrutiny to be applied to the special admissions program. Petitioner argues that the court below erred in applying strict scrutiny, as this inexact term has been applied in our cases. That level of review, petitioner asserts, should be reserved for classifications that disadvantage "discrete and insular minorities." *See United States v. Carolene Products Co.*, 304 U.S. 144, 152 n. 4 (1938). Respondent, on the other hand, contends that the California court correctly rejected the notion that the degree of judicial scrutiny accorded a particular racial or ethnic classification hinges upon membership in a discrete and insular minority and duly recognized that the "rights established [by the Fourteenth Amendment] are personal rights." *Shelley v. Kraemer*, 334 U.S. 1, 22 (1948).

En route to this crucial battle over the scope of judicial review, the parties fight a sharp preliminary action over the proper characterization of the special admissions program. Petitioner prefers to view it as establishing a "goal" of minority representation in the Medical School. Respondent, echoing the courts below, labels it a racial quota.

This semantic distinction is beside the point: The special admissions program is undeniably a classification based on race and ethnic background. To the extent that there existed a pool of at least minimally qualified minority applicants to fill the 16 special admissions seats, white applicants could compete only for 84 seats in the entering class, rather than the 100 open to minority applicants. Whether this limitation is described as a quota or a goal, it is a line drawn on the basis of race and ethnic status.

. . .

Petitioner urges us to adopt for the first time a more restrictive view of the Equal Protection Clause and hold that discrimination against members of the white "majority" cannot be suspect if its purpose can be characterized as "benign." The clock of our liberties, however, cannot be turned back to 1868. It is far too late to argue that the guarantee of equal protection to *all* persons permits the recognition of special wards entitled to a degree of protection greater than that accorded others. "The Fourteenth Amendment is not directed solely against discrimination due to a 'two-class theory'—that is, based upon differences between 'white' and Negro."

Once the artificial line of a "two-class theory" of the Fourteenth Amendment is put aside, the difficulties entailed in varying the level of judicial review according to a perceived "preferred" status of a particular racial or ethnic minority are intractable. The concepts of "majority" and "minority" necessarily reflect temporary arrangements and political judgments. As observed above, the white "majority" itself is composed of various minority groups, most of which can lay claim to a history of prior discrimination at the hands of the State and private individuals. Not all of these groups can receive preferential treatment and corresponding judicial tolerance of distinctions drawn in terms of race and nationality, for then the only "majority" left would be a new minority of white Anglo–Saxon Protestants. There is no principled basis for deciding which groups would merit "heightened judicial solicitude" and which would not.[36] Courts would be asked to evaluate the

---

36. As I am in agreement with the view that race may be taken into account as a factor in an admissions program, I agree with my Brothers Brennan, White, Marshall, and Blackmun that the portion of the judgment that would proscribe all consideration of race must be reversed. But I disagree with much that is said in their opinion. They would require as a justification for a program such as petitioner's, only two findings: (i) that there has been some form of discrimination against the preferred minority groups by "society at large" and (ii) that "there is reason to believe" that the disparate impact sought to be rectified by the program is the "product" of such discrimination: "If it was reasonable to conclude—as we hold that it was—that the failure of minorities to qualify for admission at Davis under regular procedures was due principally to the effects of past discrimination, then there is a reasonable likelihood that, but for pervasive racial discrimination, respondent would have failed to qualify for admission even in the absence of Davis' special admissions pro-

gram." The breadth of this hypothesis is unprecedented in our constitutional system. The first step is easily taken. No one denies the regrettable fact that there has been societal discrimination in this country against various racial and ethnic groups. The second step, however, involves a speculative leap: but for this discrimination by society at large, Bakke "would have failed to qualify for admission" because Negro applicants—nothing is said about Asians—would have made better scores. Not one word in the record supports this conclusion, and the authors of the opinion offer no standard for courts to use in applying such a presumption of causation to other racial or ethnic classifications. This failure is a grave one, since if it may be concluded *on this record* that each of the minority groups preferred by the petitioner's special program is entitled to the benefit of the presumption, it would seem difficult to determine that any of the dozens of minority groups that have suffered "societal discrimination" cannot also claim it, in any area of social intercourse.

extent of the prejudice and consequent harm suffered by various minority groups. Those whose societal injury is thought to exceed some arbitrary level of tolerability then would be entitled to preferential classifications at the expense of individuals belonging to other groups. Those classifications would be free from exacting judicial scrutiny. As these preferences began to have their desired effect, and the consequences of past discrimination were undone, new judicial rankings would be necessary. The kind of variable sociological and political analysis necessary to produce such rankings simply does not lie within the judicial competence—even if they otherwise were politically feasible and socially desirable.

Moreover, there are serious problems of justice connected with the idea of preference itself. First, it may not always be clear that a so-called preference is in fact benign. Courts may be asked to validate burdens imposed upon individual members of a particular group in order to advance the group's general interest. Nothing in the Constitution supports the notion that individuals may be asked to suffer otherwise impermissible burdens in order to enhance the societal standing of their ethnic groups. Second, preferential programs may only reinforce common stereotypes holding that certain groups are unable to achieve success without special protection based on a factor having no relationship to individual worth. Third, there is a measure of inequity in forcing innocent persons in respondent's position to bear the burdens of redressing grievances not of their making.

By hitching the meaning of the Equal Protection Clause to these transitory considerations, we would be holding, as a constitutional principle, that judicial scrutiny of classifications touching on racial and ethnic background may vary with the ebb and flow of political forces. Disparate constitutional tolerance of such classifications well may serve to exacerbate racial and ethnic antagonisms rather than alleviate them. Also, the mutability of a constitutional principle, based upon shifting political and social judgments, undermines the chances for consistent application of the Constitution from one generation to the next, a critical feature of its coherent interpretation. . . .

If it is the individual who is entitled to judicial protection against classifications based upon his racial or ethnic background because such distinctions impinge upon personal rights, rather than the individual only because of his membership in a particular group, then constitutional standards may be applied consistently. Political judgments regarding the necessity for the particular classification may be weighed in the constitutional balance, *Korematsu v. United States*, 323 U.S. 214 (1944), but the standard of justification will remain constant. This is as it should be, since those political judgments are the product of rough compromise struck by contending groups within the democratic process. When they touch upon an individual's race or ethnic background, he is entitled to a judicial determination that the burden he is asked to bear on that basis is precisely tailored to serve a compelling governmental interest. The Constitution guarantees that right to every person regardless of his background.

. . .

If petitioner's purpose is to assure within its student body some specified percentage of a particular group merely because of its race or ethnic origin, such a preferential purpose must be rejected not as insubstantial but as facially invalid. Preferring members of any one group for no reason other than race or ethnic origin is discrimination for its own sake. This the Constitution forbids.

The State certainly has a legitimate and substantial interest in ameliorating, or eliminating where feasible, the disabling effects of identified discrimination. The line of school desegregation cases, commencing with *Brown*, attests to the importance of this state goal and the commitment of the judiciary to affirm all lawful means toward its attainment. In the school cases, the States were required by court order to redress the wrongs worked by specific instances of racial discrimination. That goal was far more focused than the remedying of the effects of "societal discrimination," an amorphous concept of injury that may be ageless in its reach into the past.

We have never approved a classification that aids persons perceived as members of relatively victimized groups at the expense of other innocent individuals in the absence of judicial, legislative, or administrative findings of constitutional or statutory violations. . . .

Petitioner does not purport to have made, and is in no position to make, such findings. Its broad mission is education, not the formulation of any legislative policy or the adjudication of particular claims of illegality. . . . [I]solated segments of our vast governmental structures are not competent to make those decisions, at least in the absence of legislative mandates and legislatively determined criteria. Before relying upon these sorts of findings in establishing a racial classification, a governmental body must have the authority and capability to establish, in the record, that the classification is responsive to identified discrimination. Lacking this capability, petitioner has not carried its burden of justification on this issue.

Hence, the purpose of helping certain groups whom the faculty of the Davis Medical School perceived as victims of "societal discrimination" does not justify a classification that imposes disadvantages upon persons like respondent, who bear no responsibility for whatever harm the beneficiaries of the special admissions program are thought to have suffered. To hold otherwise would be to convert a remedy heretofore reserved for violations of legal rights into a privilege that all institutions throughout the Nation could grant at their pleasure to whatever groups are perceived as victims of societal discrimination. That is a step we have never approved.

. . .

[Another] goal asserted by petitioner is the attainment of a diverse student body. This clearly is a constitutionally permissible goal for an institution of higher education. Academic freedom, though not a specifically enumerated constitutional right, long has been viewed as a special concern of the First Amendment. The freedom of a university to make its own judgments as to education includes the selection of its student body. Mr. Justice Frankfurter summarized the "four essential freedoms" that constitute academic freedom:

> It is the business of a university to provide that atmosphere which is most conducive to speculation, experiment and creation. It is an atmosphere in which there prevail "the four essential freedoms" of a university—to determine for itself on academic grounds who may teach, what may be taught, how it shall be taught, and who may be

admitted to study. *Sweezy v. New Hampshire*, 354 U.S. 234, 263 (1957) (concurring in result).

. . .

The atmosphere of "speculation, experiment and creation"—so essential to the quality of higher education—is widely believed to be promoted by a diverse student body.[48] As the Court noted in *Keyishian* [*v. Board of Regents*, 385 U.S. 589 (1967)], it is not too much to say that the "nation's future depends upon leaders trained through wide exposure" to the ideas and mores of students as diverse as this Nation of many peoples.

Thus, in arguing that its universities must be accorded the right to select those students who will contribute the most to the "robust exchange of ideas," petitioner invokes a countervailing constitutional interest, that of the First Amendment. In this light, petitioner must be viewed as seeking to achieve a goal that is of paramount importance in the fulfillment of its mission.

It may be argued that there is greater force to these views at the undergraduate level than in a medical school where the training is centered primarily on professional competency. But even at the graduate level, our tradition and experience lend support to the view that the contribution of diversity is substantial. . . .

Physicians serve a heterogeneous population. An otherwise qualified medical student with a particular background—whether it be ethnic, geographic, culturally advantaged or disadvantaged—may bring to a professional school of medicine experiences, outlooks, and ideas that enrich the training of its student body and better equip its graduates to render with understanding their vital service to humanity.

Ethnic diversity, however, is only one element in a range of factors a university properly may consider in attaining the goal of a heterogeneous student body. Although a university must have wide discretion in making the sensitive judgments as to who should be admitted, constitutional limitations protecting individual rights may not be disregarded. Respondent urges—and the courts below have held—that petitioner's dual admissions program is a racial classification that impermissibly infringes his rights under the Fourteenth Amendment. As the interest of diversity is compelling in the context of a university's admissions program, the question remains whether the program's racial classification is necessary to promote this interest.

---

48. The president of Princeton University has described some of the benefits derived from a diverse student body: "[A] great deal of learning occurs informally. It occurs through interactions among students of both sexes; of different races, religions, and backgrounds; who come from cities and rural areas, from various states and countries; who have a wide variety of interests, talents, and perspectives; and who are able, directly or indirectly, to learn from their differences and to stimulate one another to reexamine even their most deeply held assumptions about themselves and their world. As a wise graduate of ours observed in commenting on this aspect of the educational process, 'People do not learn very much when they are surrounded only by the likes of themselves. . . .' In the nature of things, it is hard to know how, and when, and even if, this informal 'learning through diversity' actually occurs. It does not occur for everyone. For many, however, the unplanned, casual encounters with roommates, fellow sufferers in an organic chemistry class, student workers in the library, teammates on a basketball squad, or other participants in class affairs or student government can be subtle and yet powerful sources of improved understanding and personal growth." Bowen, Admissions and the Relevance of Race, Princeton Alumni Weekly 7, 9 (Sept. 26, 1977).

It may be assumed that the reservation of a specified number of seats in each class for individuals from the preferred ethnic groups would contribute to the attainment of considerable ethnic diversity in the student body. But petitioner's argument that this is the only effective means of serving the interest of diversity is seriously flawed. In a most fundamental sense the argument misconceives the nature of the state interest that would justify consideration of race or ethnic background. It is not an interest in simple ethnic diversity, in which a specified percentage of the student body is in effect guaranteed to be members of selected ethnic groups, with the remaining percentage an undifferentiated aggregation of students. The diversity that furthers a compelling state interest encompasses a far broader array of qualifications and characteristics of which racial or ethnic origin is but a single though important element. Petitioner's special admissions program, focused *solely* on ethnic diversity, would hinder rather than further attainment of genuine diversity.

. . .

The experience of other university admissions programs, which take race into account in achieving the educational diversity valued by the First Amendment, demonstrates that the assignment of a fixed number of places to a minority group is not a necessary means toward that end. An illuminating example is found in the Harvard College program:

> In recent years Harvard College has expanded the concept of diversity to include students from disadvantaged economic, racial and ethnic groups. Harvard College now recruits not only Californians or Louisianans but also blacks and Chicanos and other minority students. . . .
>
> In practice, this new definition of diversity has meant that race has been a factor in some admission decisions. When the Committee on Admissions reviews the large middle group of applicants who are 'admissible' and deemed capable of doing good work in their courses, the race of an applicant may tip the balance in his favor just as geographic origin or a life spent on a farm may tip the balance in other candidates' cases. A farm boy from Idaho can bring something to Harvard College that a Bostonian cannot offer. Similarly, a black student can usually bring something that a white person cannot offer. . . .
>
> In Harvard College admissions the Committee has not set target-quotas for the number of blacks, or of musicians, football players, physicists or Californians to be admitted in a given year. . . . But that awareness [of the necessity of including more than a token number of black students] does not mean that the Committee sets a minimum number of blacks or of people from west of the Mississippi who are to be admitted. It means only that in choosing among thousands of applicants who are not only "admissible" academically but have other strong qualities, the Committee, with a number of criteria in mind, pays some attention to distribution among many types and categories of students. App. to Brief for Columbia University, Harvard University, Stanford University, and the University of Pennsylvania, as *Amici Curiae* 2–3.

In such an admissions program, race or ethnic background may be deemed a "plus" in a particular applicant's file, yet it does not insulate the individual from comparison with all other candidates for the available seats. The file of a particular black applicant may be examined for his potential contribution to diversity without the factor of race being decisive when compared, for example, with that of an applicant identified as an Italian–American if the latter is thought to exhibit qualities more likely to promote beneficial educational pluralism. Such qualities could include exceptional personal talents, unique work or service experience, leadership potential, maturity, demonstrated compassion, a history of overcoming disadvantage, ability to communicate with the poor, or other qualifications deemed important. In short, an admissions program operated in this way is flexible enough to consider all pertinent elements of diversity in light of the particular qualifications of each applicant, and to place them on the same footing for consideration, although not necessarily according them the same weight. Indeed, the weight attributed to a particular quality may vary from year to year depending upon the "mix" both of the student body and the applicants for the incoming class.

This kind of program treats each applicant as an individual in the admissions process. The applicant who loses out on the last available seat to another candidate receiving a "plus" on the basis of ethnic background will not have been foreclosed from all consideration for that seat simply because he was not the right color or had the wrong surname. It would mean only that his combined qualifications, which may have included similar nonobjective factors, did not outweigh those of the other applicant. His qualifications would have been weighed fairly and competitively, and he would have no basis to complain of unequal treatment under the Fourteenth Amendment.[52]

It has been suggested that an admissions program which considers race only as one factor is simply a subtle and more sophisticated—but no less effective—means of according racial preference than the Davis program. A facial intent to discriminate, however, is evident in petitioner's preference program and not denied in this case. No such facial infirmity exists in an admissions program where race or ethnic background is simply one element—to be weighed fairly against other elements—in the selection process. "A boundary line," as Mr. Justice Frankfurter remarked in another connection, "is none the worse for being narrow." *McLeod v. Dilworth*, 322 U.S. 327, 329 (1944). And a court would not assume that a university, professing to employ a facially nondiscriminatory admissions policy, would operate it as a cover for the functional equivalent of a quota system. In short, good faith would be presumed in the absence of a showing to the contrary in the manner permitted by our cases. *See, e.g., Arlington Heights v. Metropolitan Housing Dev. Corp.*, 429 U.S. 252 (1977); *Washington v. Davis*, 426 U.S. 229 (1976); *Swain v. Alabama*, 380 U.S. 202 (1965).

. . .

The fatal flaw in petitioner's preferential program is its disregard of individual rights as guaranteed by the Fourteenth Amendment. Such rights

---

52. The denial to respondent of this right to individualized consideration without regard to his race is the principal evil of petitioner's special admissions program. No- where in the opinion of Mr. Justice Brennan, Mr. Justice White, Mr. Justice Marshall, and Mr. Justice Blackmun is this denial even addressed.

are not absolute. But when a State's distribution of benefits or imposition of burdens hinges on ancestry or the color of a person's skin, that individual is entitled to a demonstration that the challenged classification is necessary to promote a substantial state interest. Petitioner has failed to carry this burden. For this reason, that portion of the California court's judgment holding petitioner's special admissions program invalid under the Fourteenth Amendment must be affirmed.

In enjoining petitioner from ever considering the race of any applicant, however, the courts below failed to recognize that the State has a substantial interest that legitimately may be served by a properly devised admissions program involving the competitive consideration of race and ethnic origin. For this reason, so much of the California court's judgment as enjoins petitioner from any consideration of the race of any applicant must be reversed.

With respect to respondent's entitlement to an injunction directing his admission to the Medical School, petitioner has conceded that it could not carry its burden of proving that, but for the existence of its unlawful special admissions program, respondent still would not have been admitted. Hence, respondent is entitled to the injunction, and that portion of the judgment must be affirmed.

■ MR. JUSTICE MARSHALL.

While I applaud the judgment of the Court that a university may consider race in its admissions process, it is more than a little ironic that, after several hundred years of class-based discrimination against Negroes, the Court is unwilling to hold that a class-based remedy for that discrimination is permissible. In declining to so hold, today's judgment ignores the fact that for several hundred years Negroes have been discriminated against, not as individuals, but rather solely because of the color of their skins. It is unnecessary in 20th-century America to have individual Negroes demonstrate that they have been victims of racial discrimination; the racism of our society has been so pervasive that none, regardless of wealth or position, has managed to escape its impact. The experience of Negroes in America has been different in kind, not just in degree, from that of other ethnic groups. It is not merely the history of slavery alone but also that a whole people were marked as inferior by the law. And that mark has endured. The dream of America as the great melting pot has not been realized for the Negro; because of his skin color he never even made it into the pot.

These differences in the experience of the Negro make it difficult for me to accept that Negroes cannot be afforded greater protection under the Fourteenth Amendment where it is necessary to remedy the effects of past discrimination. In the *Civil Rights Cases*, the Court wrote that the Negro emerging from slavery must cease "to be the special favorite of the laws." 109 U.S., at 25. We cannot in light of the history of the last century yield to that view. Had the Court in that decision and others been willing to "do for human liberty and the fundamental rights of American citizenship, what it did ... for the protection of slavery and the rights of the masters of fugitive slaves," 109 U.S., at 53 (Harlan, J., dissenting), we would not need now to permit the recognition of any "special wards."

Most importantly, had the Court been willing in 1896, in *Plessy v. Ferguson*, to hold that the Equal Protection Clause forbids differences in treatment based on race, we would not be faced with this dilemma in 1978. We must remember, however, that the principle that the "Constitution is colorblind" appeared only in the opinion of the lone dissenter. 163 U.S., at 559. The majority of the Court rejected the principle of color blindness, and for the next 60 years, from *Plessy* to *Brown v. Board of Education*, ours was a Nation where, *by law*, an individual could be given "special" treatment based on the color of his skin.

It is because of a legacy of unequal treatment that we now must permit the institutions of this society to give consideration to race in making decisions about who will hold the positions of influence, affluence, and prestige in America. For far too long, the doors to those positions have been shut to Negroes. If we are ever to become a fully integrated society, one in which the color of a person's skin will not determine the opportunities available to him or her, we must be willing to take steps to open those doors. I do not believe that anyone can truly look into America's past and still find that a remedy for the effects of that past is impermissible.

Questions and Comments on *Bakke*

1. After the Court's decision, Allan Bakke released a statement through his lawyers, "I am pleased and, after five years of waiting, I look forward to entering medical school in the fall." HOWARD BALL, THE *BAKKE* CASE 143 (2000). He entered the University of California, Davis School of Medicine in September 1978. On the first day of classes, hundreds of protesters came to the campus to demonstrate their opposition to the *Bakke* decision. Bakke himself passed by the protestors completely unnoticed. *Id.* at 173. Bakke graduated in 1982, and worked as an anesthesiologist in Rochester, Minnesota. He invented a device that warms refrigerated blood for transfusions. He is now retired. Peter Schmidt, *'Bakke' Set a new Path to Diversity for Colleges*, CHRON. HIGHER EDUC., June 20, 2008, at 1.

2. One of the main points of disagreement between Justice Powell and Justice Marshall was whether a class-based advantage is an appropriate remedy for the history of discrimination against African Americans. Are class-based affirmative action programs necessary to remedy such past discrimination? If so, how can you justify imposing burdens on an individual who may have no history of engaging in discrimination?

3. What do you think of Justice Powell's reliance on the Court's academic freedom decisions to find that attaining educational diversity is a compelling government interest? Should a public college be able to make decisions based, at least partially, on race when other state institutions may not?

Grutter v. Bollinger

Supreme Court of the United States, 2003.
539 U.S. 306, 123 S.Ct. 2325, 156 L.Ed.2d 304.

[The text is set forth on pages 345–60, *supra*.]

Gratz v. Bollinger

United States Supreme Court, 2003.
539 U.S. 244, 123 S.Ct. 2411, 156 L.Ed.2d 257.

■ CHIEF JUSTICE REHNQUIST delivered the opinion of the Court.

We granted certiorari in this case to decide whether "the University of Michigan's use of racial preferences in undergraduate admissions violates the Equal Protection Clause of the Fourteenth Amendment, Title VI of the Civil Rights Act of 1964 (42 USC § 2000d [42 USCS § 2000d]), or 42 USC § 1981." ...

Petitioners Jennifer Gratz and Patrick Hamacher both applied for admission to the University of Michigan's (University) College of Literature, Science, and the Arts (LSA) as residents of the State of Michigan. Both petitioners are Caucasian. [In both cases LSA deferred making a final determination after an initial review of their application materials. Neither petitioner was offered admission. Gratz ultimately enrolled in and graduated from the University of Michigan at Dearborn, while Hamacher enrolled at Michigan State University.]

In October 1997, Gratz and Hamacher filed a lawsuit in the United States District Court for the Eastern District of Michigan against the University of Michigan.... Petitioners sought, *inter alia*, compensatory and punitive damages for past violations, declaratory relief finding that respondents violated petitioners' "rights to nondiscriminatory treatment," an injunction prohibiting respondents from "continuing to discriminate on the basis of race in violation of the Fourteenth Amendment," and an order requiring the LSA to offer Hamacher admission as a transfer student.

. . .

The University has changed its admissions guidelines a number of times during the period relevant to this litigation, and we summarize the most significant of these changes briefly. The University's Office of Undergraduate Admissions (OUA) oversees the LSA admissions process. In order to promote consistency in the review of the large number of applications received, the OUA uses written guidelines for each academic year. Admissions counselors make admissions decisions in accordance with these guidelines.

OUA considers a number of factors in making admissions decisions, including high school grades, standardized test scores, high school quality, curriculum strength, geography, alumni relationships, and leadership. OUA also considers race. During all periods relevant to this litigation, the University has considered African–Americans, Hispanics, and Native Americans to be "underrepresented minorities," and it is undisputed that the University admits "virtually every qualified ... applicant" from these groups.

During 1995 and 1996, OUA counselors evaluated applications according to grade point average combined with what were referred to as the "SCUGA" factors. These factors included the quality of an applicant's high school (S), the strength of an applicant's high school curriculum (C), an applicant's unusual circumstances (U), an applicant's geographical residence (G), and an applicant's alumni relationships (A). After these scores were combined to produce an applicant's "GPA 2" score, the reviewing admissions counselors referenced a set of "Guidelines" tables, which listed GPA 2 ranges on the vertical axis, and American College Test/Scholastic Aptitude Test (ACT/SAT) scores on the horizontal axis. Each table was divided into cells that included one or more courses of action to be taken, including admit, reject, delay for additional information, or postpone for reconsideration.

In both years, applicants with the same GPA 2 score and ACT/SAT score were subject to different admissions outcomes based upon their racial or ethnic status. For example, as a Caucasian in-state applicant, Gratz's GPA 2 score and ACT score placed her within a cell calling for a postponed decision on her application. An in-state or out-of-state minority applicant with Gratz's scores would have fallen within a cell calling for admission.

In 1997, the University modified its admissions procedure. Specifically, the formula for calculating an applicant's GPA 2 score was restructured to include additional point values under the "U" category in the SCUGA factors. Under this new system, applicants could receive points for underrepresented minority status, socioeconomic disadvantage, or attendance at a high school with a predominantly underrepresented minority population, or underrepresentation in the unit to which the student was applying (for example, men who sought to pursue a career in nursing). Under the 1997 procedures, Hamacher's GPA 2 score and ACT score placed him in a cell on the in-state applicant table calling for postponement of a final admissions decision. An underrepresented minority applicant placed in the same cell would generally have been admitted.

Beginning with the 1998 academic year, the OUA dispensed with the Guidelines tables and the SCUGA point system in favor of a "selection index," on which an applicant could score a maximum of 150 points. This index was divided linearly into ranges generally calling for admissions dispositions as follows: 100–150 (admit); 95–99 (admit or postpone); 90–94 (postpone or admit); 75–89 (delay or postpone); 74 and below (delay or reject).

Each application received points based on high school grade point average, standardized test scores, academic quality of an applicant's high school, strength or weakness of high school curriculum, in-state residency, alumni relationship, personal essay, and personal achievement or leadership. Of particular significance here, under a "miscellaneous" category, an applicant was entitled to 20 points based upon his or her membership in an underrepresented racial or ethnic minority group. The University explained that the " 'development of the selection index for admissions in 1998 changed only the mechanics, not the substance of how race and ethnicity were considered in admissions.' "

In all application years from 1995 to 1998, the guidelines provided that qualified applicants from underrepresented minority groups be admitted as soon as possible in light of the University's belief that such applicants were more likely to enroll if promptly notified of their admission. Also from 1995 through 1998, the University carefully managed its rolling admissions system to permit consideration of certain applications submitted later in the academic year through the use of "protected seats." Specific groups—including athletes, foreign students, ROTC candidates, and underrepresented minorities—were "protected categories" eligible for these seats. A committee called the Enrollment Working Group (EWG) projected how many applicants from each of these protected categories the University was likely to receive after a given date and then paced admissions decisions to permit full consideration of expected applications from these groups. If this space was not filled by qualified candidates from the designated groups toward the end of the admissions season, it was then used to admit qualified candidates remaining in the applicant pool, including those on the waiting list.

During 1999 and 2000, the OUA used the selection index, under which every applicant from an underrepresented racial or ethnic minority group was awarded 20 points. Starting in 1999, however, the University established an Admissions Review Committee (ARC), to provide an additional level of consideration for some applications. Under the new system, counselors may, in their discretion, "flag" an application for the ARC to review after determining that the applicant (1) is academically prepared to succeed at the University,[8] (2) has achieved a minimum selection index score, and (3) possesses a quality or characteristic important to the University's composition of its freshman class, such as high class rank, unique life experiences, challenges, circumstances, interests or talents, socioeconomic disadvantage, and underrepresented race, ethnicity, or geography. After reviewing "flagged" applications, the ARC determines whether to admit, defer, or deny each applicant.

The parties filed cross-motions for summary judgment with respect to liability. . . .

The District Court . . . granted petitioners' motion for summary judgment with respect to the LSA's admissions programs in existence from 1995 through 1998, and respondents' motion with respect to the LSA's admissions programs for 1999 and 2000. [The Court granted certiorari despite the lack of a decision by the Court of Appeals so as to consider the case at the same time as *Grutter v. Bollinger*.]

. . .

To withstand our strict scrutiny analysis, respondents must demonstrate that the University's use of race in its current admission program employs "narrowly tailored measures that further compelling governmental interests." Because "racial classifications are simply too pernicious to permit any but the most exact connection between justification and classification," our review of whether such requirements have been met must entail " 'a most searching examination.' " We find that the University's policy, which automatically distributes 20 points, or one-fifth of the points needed to guarantee admission, to every single "underrepresented minority" applicant solely because of race, is not narrowly tailored to achieve the interest in educational diversity that respondents claim justifies their program.

. . .

Justice Powell's opinion in *Bakke* emphasized the importance of considering each particular applicant as an individual, assessing all of the qualities that individual possesses, and in turn, evaluating that individual's ability to contribute to the unique setting of higher education. The admissions program Justice Powell described, however, did not contemplate that any single characteristic automatically ensured a specific and identifiable contribution to a university's diversity. . . .

The current LSA policy does not provide such individualized consideration. The LSA's policy automatically distributes 20 points to every single applicant from an "underrepresented minority" group, as defined by the University. The only consideration that accompanies this distribution of points is a factual review of an application to determine whether an individual is a member of one of these minority groups. Moreover, unlike Justice

8. LSA applicants who are Michigan residents must accumulate 80 points from the selection index criteria to be flagged, while out-of-state applicants need to accumulate 75 points to be eligible for such consideration.

Powell's example, where the race of a "particular black applicant" could be considered without being decisive, the LSA's automatic distribution of 20 points has the effect of making "the factor of race . . . decisive" for virtually every minimally qualified underrepresented minority applicant.

Also instructive in our consideration of the LSA's system is the example provided in the description of the Harvard College Admissions Program, which Justice Powell both discussed in, and attached to, his opinion in *Bakke*. The example was included to "illustrate the kind of significance attached to race" under the Harvard College program. It provided as follows:

> The Admissions Committee, with only a few places left to fill, might find itself forced to choose between A, the child of a successful black physician in an academic community with promise of superior academic performance, and B, a black who grew up in an inner-city ghetto of semi-literate parents whose academic achievement was lower but who had demonstrated energy and leadership as well as an apparently abiding interest in black power. If a good number of black students much like A but few like B had already been admitted, the Committee might prefer B; and vice versa. If C, a white student with extraordinary artistic talent, were also seeking one of the remaining places, his unique quality might give him an edge over both A and B. Thus, the critical criteria are often individual qualities or experience *not dependent upon race but sometimes associated with it. Ibid.* (emphasis added).

This example further demonstrates the problematic nature of the LSA's admissions system. Even if student C's "extraordinary artistic talent" rivaled that of Monet or Picasso, the applicant would receive, at most, five points under the LSA's system. At the same time, every single underrepresented minority applicant, including students A and B, would automatically receive 20 points for submitting an application. Clearly, the LSA's system does not offer applicants the individualized selection process described in Harvard's example. Instead of considering how the differing backgrounds, experiences, and characteristics of students A, B, and C might benefit the University, admissions counselors reviewing LSA applications would simply award both A and B 20 points because their applications indicate that they are African–American, and student C would receive up to 5 points for his "extraordinary talent."

Respondents emphasize the fact that the LSA has created the possibility of an applicant's file being flagged for individualized consideration by the ARC. We think that the flagging program only emphasizes the flaws of the University's system as a whole when compared to that described by Justice Powell. Again, students A, B, and C illustrate the point. First, student A would never be flagged. This is because, as the University has conceded, the effect of automatically awarding 20 points is that virtually every qualified underrepresented minority applicant is admitted. Student A, an applicant "with promise of superior academic performance," would certainly fit this description. Thus, the result of the automatic distribution of 20 points is that the University would never consider student A's individual background, experiences, and characteristics to assess his individual "potential contribution to diversity." Instead, every applicant like student A would simply be admitted.

It is possible that students B and C would be flagged and considered as individuals. This assumes that student B was not already admitted because of the automatic 20–point distribution, and that student C could muster at least 70 additional points. But the fact that the "review committee can look at the applications individually and ignore the points," once an application is flagged, is of little comfort under our strict scrutiny analysis. The record does not reveal precisely how many applications are flagged for this individualized consideration, but it is undisputed that such consideration is the exception and not the rule in the operation of the LSA's admissions program. Additionally, this individualized review is only provided *after* admissions counselors automatically distribute the University's version of a "plus" that makes race a decisive factor for virtually every minimally qualified underrepresented minority applicant.

Respondents contend that "the volume of applications and the presentation of applicant information make it impractical for [LSA] to use the ... admissions system" upheld by the Court today in *Grutter*. But the fact that the implementation of a program capable of providing individualized consideration might present administrative challenges does not render constitutional an otherwise problematic system. Nothing in Justice Powell's opinion in *Bakke* signaled that a university may employ whatever means it desires to achieve the stated goal of diversity without regard to the limits imposed by our strict scrutiny analysis.

We conclude, therefore, that because the University's use of race in its current freshman admissions policy is not narrowly tailored to achieve respondents' asserted compelling interest in diversity, the admissions policy violates the Equal Protection Clause of the Fourteenth Amendment.[22] We further find that the admissions policy also violates Title VI and 42 USC § 1981 [42 USCS § 1981]. Accordingly, we reverse that portion of the District Court's decision granting respondents summary judgment, with respect to liability and remand the case for proceedings consistent with this opinion.

It is so ordered.

■ JUSTICE O'CONNOR, concurring.

[T]he record before us does not support the conclusion that the University of Michigan's admissions program for its College of Literature, Science, and the Arts—to the extent that it considers race—provides the necessary individualized consideration. The University, of course, remains free to modify its system so that it does so. But the current system, as I understand it, is a nonindividualized, mechanical one. As a result, I join the Court's opinion reversing the decision of the District Court.

---

22. Justice Ginsburg in her dissent observes that "one can reasonably anticipate ... that colleges and universities will seek to maintain their minority enrollment ... whether or not they can do so in full candor through adoption of affirmative action plans of the kind here at issue." She goes on to say that "if honesty is the best policy, surely Michigan's accurately described, fully disclosed College affirmative action program is preferable to achieving similar numbers through winks, nods, and disguises." These observations are remarkable for two reasons. First, they suggest that universities—to whose academic judgment we are told in *Grutter v. Bollinger* we should defer—will pursue their affirmative-action programs whether or not they violate the United States Constitution. Second, they recommend that these violations should be dealt with, not by requiring the universities to obey the Constitution, but by changing the Constitution so that it conforms to the conduct of the universities.

■ JUSTICE BREYER, concurring in the judgment.

I concur in the judgment of the Court though I do not join its opinion. I join Justice O'Connor's opinion except insofar as it joins that of the Court. I join Part I of Justice Ginsburg's dissenting opinion, but I do not dissent from the Court's reversal of the District Court's decision. I agree with Justice Ginsburg that, in implementing the Constitution's equality instruction, government decisionmakers may properly distinguish between policies of inclusion and exclusion, for the former are more likely to prove consistent with the basic constitutional obligation that the law respect each individual equally, *see* U. S. Const., Amdt. 14.

■ JUSTICE STEVENS, with whom JUSTICE SOUTER joins, dissenting.

Petitioners seek forward-looking relief enjoining the University of Michigan from continuing to use its current race-conscious freshman admissions policy. Yet unlike the plaintiff in *Grutter v. Bollinger,* the petitioners in this case had already enrolled at other schools before they filed their class-action complaint in this case. Neither petitioner was in the process of reapplying to Michigan through the freshman admissions process at the time this suit was filed, and neither has done so since. There is a total absence of evidence that either petitioner would receive any benefit from the prospective relief sought by their lawyer. While some unidentified members of the class may very well have standing to seek prospective relief, it is clear that neither petitioner does. Our precedents therefore require dismissal of the action.

■ JUSTICE GINSBURG, with whom JUSTICE SOUTER joins, dissenting.*

Educational institutions, the Court acknowledges, are not barred from any and all consideration of race when making admissions decisions. But the Court once again maintains that the same standard of review controls judicial inspection of all official race classifications. This insistence on "consistency," would be fitting were our Nation free of the vestiges of rank discrimination long reinforced by law. But we are not far distant from an overtly discriminatory past, and the effects of centuries of law-sanctioned inequality remain painfully evident in our communities and schools.

In the wake "of a system of racial caste only recently ended," large disparities endure. Unemployment, poverty, and access to health care vary disproportionately by race. Neighborhoods and schools remain racially divided. African–American and Hispanic children are all too often educated in poverty-stricken and underperforming institutions. Adult African–Americans and Hispanics generally earn less than whites with equivalent levels of education. Equally credentialed job applicants receive different receptions depending on their race. Irrational prejudice is still encountered in real estate markets and consumer transactions. "Bias both conscious and unconscious, reflecting traditional and unexamined habits of thought, keeps up barriers that must come down if equal opportunity and nondiscrimination are ever genuinely to become this country's law and practice." [*Adarand Constructors, Inc. v. Pena*, 515 U.S. 200, 274 (1995)] (Ginsburg, J., dissenting); *see generally* Krieger, Civil Rights Perestroika: Intergroup Relations After Affirmative Action, 86 Calif. L. Rev. 1251, 1276–1291 (1998).

The Constitution instructs all who act for the government that they may not "deny to any person . . . the equal protection of the laws." Amdt. 14,

---

* Justice Breyer joins Part I of this opinion.

§ 1. In implementing this equality instruction, as I see it, government decisionmakers may properly distinguish between policies of exclusion and inclusion. Actions designed to burden groups long denied full citizenship stature are not sensibly ranked with measures taken to hasten the day when entrenched discrimination and its after effects have been extirpated. *See* Carter, When Victims Happen To Be Black, 97 Yale L. J. 420, 433–434 (1988) ("To say that two centuries of struggle for the most basic of civil rights have been mostly about freedom from racial categorization rather than freedom from racial oppression is to trivialize the lives and deaths of those who have suffered under racism. To pretend . . . that the issue presented in [*Bakke*] was the same as the issue in [*Brown*] is to pretend that history never happened and that the present doesn't exist.").

Our jurisprudence ranks race a "suspect" category, "not because [race] is inevitably an impermissible classification, but because it is one which usually, to our national shame, has been drawn for the purpose of maintaining racial inequality." But where race is considered "for the purpose of achieving equality," no automatic proscription is in order. For, as insightfully explained, "the Constitution is both color blind and color conscious. To avoid conflict with the equal protection clause, a classification that denies a benefit, causes harm, or imposes a burden must not be based on race. In that sense, the Constitution is color blind. But the Constitution is color conscious to prevent discrimination being perpetuated and to undo the effects of past discrimination." *United States v. Jefferson County Bd. of Ed.*, 372 F.2d 836, 876 (CA5 1966) (Wisdom, J.); *see* Wechsler, The Nationalization Of Civil Liberties And Civil Rights, Supp to 12 Tex. Q. 10, 23 (1968) (*Brown* may be seen as disallowing racial classifications that "impl[y] an invidious assessment" while allowing such classifications when "not invidious in implication" but advanced to "correct inequalities"). Contemporary human rights documents draw just this line; they distinguish between policies of oppression and measures designed to accelerate *de facto* equality.

The mere assertion of a laudable governmental purpose, of course, should not immunize a race-conscious measure from careful judicial inspection. Close review is needed "to ferret out classifications in reality malign, but masquerading as benign," *Adarand*, 515 U.S., at 275 (Ginsburg, J., dissenting), and to "ensure that preferences are not so large as to trammel unduly upon the opportunities of others or interfere too harshly with legitimate expectations of persons in once-preferred groups," *id.*, at 276.

Examining in this light the admissions policy employed by the University of Michigan's College of Literature, Science, and the Arts (College), . . . I see no constitutional infirmity. . . .

The stain of generations of racial oppression is still visible in our society, and the determination to hasten its removal remains vital. One can reasonably anticipate, therefore, that colleges and universities will seek to maintain their minority enrollment—and the networks and opportunities thereby opened to minority graduates—whether or not they can do so in full candor through adoption of affirmative action plans of the kind here at issue. Without recourse to such plans, institutions of higher education may resort to camouflage. For example, schools may encourage applicants to write of their cultural traditions in the essays they submit, or to indicate whether English is their second language. Seeking to improve their chances for admission, applicants may highlight the minority group associations to which they belong, or the Hispanic surnames of their mothers or grandparents. In turn, teachers' recommendations may emphasize who a student is as much as what he or she has accomplished. If honesty is the best policy, surely Michigan's accurately described, fully disclosed College affirmative action program is preferable to achieving similar numbers through winks, nods, and disguises.[11]

Questions and Comments on *Grutter* and *Gratz*

1. Do you think the affirmative action in admissions approved in *Grutter* will continue to be upheld by the Supreme Court now that Justice O'Connor has resigned from the Court?

A heavily fractured Court may have given a partial answer to this question in 2007 when it struck down programs in Seattle and Kentucky that took into account racial composition when assigning students to K–12 public schools. The Court noted that it had recognized two interests that qualify as compelling for purposes of evaluating the use of racial classifications in the school context. The first is the compelling interest of remedying the effects of past intentional discrimination. The Court continued:

> The second government interest we have recognized as compelling for purposes of strict scrutiny is the interest in diversity in higher education upheld in *Grutter*, 539 U.S., at 328. The specific interest found compelling in *Grutter* was student body diversity "in the context of higher education." The diversity interest was not focused on race alone but encompassed "all factors that may contribute to student body diversity." . . .

> . . . [W]hat was upheld in *Grutter* was consideration of "a far broader array of qualifications and characteristics of which racial or ethnic origin is but a single though important element." . . .

> The entire gist of the analysis in *Grutter* was that the admissions program at issue there focused on each applicant as an individual, and not simply as a member of a particular racial group. The classification of applicants by race upheld in *Grutter* was only as part of a "highly individualized, holistic review," 539 U.S. at 337. As the Court explained, "[t]he importance of this individualized consideration in the context of a race-conscious admissions program is paramount." The point of the narrow tailoring analysis in which the *Grutter* Court engaged was to ensure that the use of racial classifications was indeed part of a broader assessment of diversity, and not simply an effort to achieve racial balance, which the Court explained would be "patently unconstitutional."

> . . .

> In upholding the admissions plan in *Grutter* . . . this Court relied upon considerations unique to institutions of higher education, noting that in light of "the expansive freedoms of speech and thought associated with the university environment, universities occupy a special niche in our constitutional tradition." 539 U.S., at 329. *See also Bakke* [438 U.S. at] 312, 313 (opinion of Powell, J.). The Court explained that "[c]ontext matters" in applying strict scrutiny, and repeatedly noted that it was addressing the use of race "in the context of higher education." *Grutter*, [539 U.S.] at 327, 328,

---

11. Contrary to the Court's contention, I do not suggest "changing the Constitution so that it conforms to the conduct of the universities." In my view, the Constitution, properly interpreted, *permits* government officials to respond openly to the continuing importance of race. Among constitutionally permissible options, those that candidly disclose their consideration of race seem to me preferable to those that conceal it.

334. The Court in *Grutter* expressly articulated key limitations on its holding-defining a specific type of broad-based diversity and noting the unique context of higher education ...

Parents Involved in Cmty. Sch. v. Seattle Sch. Dist. No. 1, ___ U.S. ___, ___ – ___, 127 S.Ct. 2738, 2753–55 (2007). The Court held that the school assignment plans were unconstitutional because the school districts failed to show that relying upon racial classifications in making school assignments was narrowly tailored to achieve a compelling government interest. *Id.* In his concurrence, Justice Kennedy rejected the plurality's view that race cannot be a factor in many situations where it could be considered. In his view, the government has an interest in ensuring that all people have equal opportunity regardless of their race. Thus, school authorities may use race-conscious measures to ensure equal educational opportunity for all students so long as they do not treat students differently solely on the basis of race. *Id.* at 2791 (Kennedy, J., concurring).

Some have suggested that *Parents Involved* will have the effect of shrinking the pool of minority students that are well prepared for admission to the most selective higher education institutions. *See* Robert O'Neil, *The Supreme Court, Affirmative Action, and Higher Education*, ACADEME, Jan.-Feb. 2008, at 17, 19. Do you agree?

2. On November 7, 2006, the citizens of Michigan voted in favor of Proposal 2 which amended their state constitution to ban affirmative-action programs in all state agencies, including public colleges and universities, thus overturning the decision in *Grutter* in the state of Michigan. The proposal passed with 58 percent of the vote, and made Michigan the third state in the nation to approve such a ballot initiative following California in 1996 and Washington State in 1998. The Michigan Civil Rights Initiative committee, the group that got the measure on the ballot, was headed by Jennifer Gratz, the lead plaintiff in *Gratz v. Bollinger*. Peter Schmidt, *Michigan Overwhelmingly Adopts Ban on Affirmative–Action Preferences*, CHRON. HIGHER EDUC., Nov. 17, 2006, at A23.

In January, 2005, a federal judge ordered the University of Michigan to pay $672,000 in fees to the lawyers for Gratz and her co-lead-plaintiff, Patrick Hamacher. In January 2007, Gratz and Hamacher were each awarded $10,000 to cover their miscellaneous costs under a settlement agreement with the University of Michigan. Terry Pell, the president of the Center for Individual Rights, which represented the plaintiffs in their class action law suit, announced that the settlement opens the door for others damaged by the University's admissions policy to seek relief. Maria Schultz, *Lawsuit Challenging U–M Undergraduate Admissions Policy Dismissed After 10 Years*, DETROIT NEWS, Jan. 31, 2007.

3. The percentage of African American, Hispanic and Native American students admitted to the University of Michigan Law School for 2007 fell from 39.6 percent before the adoption of Proposal 2, to 5.5 percent. Elizabeth Redden, *Now and Then: Minorities and Michigan*, INSIDE HIGHER ED, June 25, 2007, *available at* http://inside highered.com/news/2007/06/19/michigan.

4. The adoption of Proposition 209 by voters in California in 1996 led to a significant decrease in the number of black students at UCLA. In the fall of 2006, only 96 black students, or 2 percent of the freshman class of 48,852 enrolled at UCLA, the lowest figure since 1973. The figure was only one-third of what it had been in 1995, the year before Proposition 209 was adopted. In 2007, UCLA adopted a new, "holistic" approach to making admission decisions. Under this approach, every application is read in its entirety and the evaluators give consideration to the opportunities that were or were not available to the applicant. The new process has increased the number of black students accepted. Peter Schmidt, *UCLA Reverses Decline in Black Admissions but Rejects More Asians*, CHRON HIGHER EDUC., Apr. 20, 2007, at 42.

5. White applicants are not the only students claiming to be harmed by affirmative action admission policies. In 2008, the Department of Education Office for Civil

Rights initiated a compliance review of Princeton University's admissions system after Jian Li, an Asian American student, filed a complaint that racial bias had blocked his admission to the university. Likening the treatment of Asian American students to the treatment of Jewish students in the 1920s, Li's complaint alleged that Asian Americans are held to tougher standards than other applicants. A study of elite colleges by two Princeton scholars indicated that without affirmative action programs, the admission rates of Asian students would rise 5.8 percent, while white admission rates would hold steady, and African American and Hispanic rates would drop dramatically. College officials responded that Princeton rejects thousands of well qualified applicants every year from every racial and ethnic group. Scott Jaschick, *Inquiry Into Alleged Anti-Asian Bias Expands*, INSIDE HIGHER EDUC., June 11, 2008, *available at* https://www.insidehighered.com/news/2008/06/11/asians.

6. Consider the critique of the *Bakke* rationale put forth by Professor Charles Lawrence:

> When Bowen, Bok, [authors of THE SHAPE OF THE RIVER: LONG TERM CONSEQUENCES OF CONSIDERING RACE IN COLLEGE AND UNIVERSITY ADMISSIONS (1998)] and other liberals argue that affirmative action is required for racial diversity, when they say diversity works, and when they cite evidence of friendship between black and white students and professional colleagues as proof thereof, they make a moral argument, an argument that is not just a matter of policy or practical consequence but of principle. Their argument supports affirmative action because it is just and because we are ethically bound to live out the ideals of our democracy and participate in the ongoing struggle to make democracy live. If the contradiction between the unifying American dream of inclusion and the reality of America's racism is, as Swedish sociologist Gunnar Myrdal observed, our American dilemma, then America's leading institutions of learning and research must make the resolution of that contradiction central to their mission.
>
> The liberal argument for race-sensitive admissions is, in part, a utilitarian one. It is premised on a widely shared belief that the primary mission of colleges and universities is to educate those students who are likely to become the leaders of society in an increasingly diverse world. In Bowen and Bok's words, "The advantages of being able to understand how others think and function, to cope across racial divides, and to lead groups composed of diverse individuals are certain to increase." Education for leadership, however, is more than skills training for business executives, doctors, and lawyers. Our best colleges and universities have always played a central role in shaping our society's moral vision. We socialize our students. We teach them values by engaging them in moral discourse, but even more importantly, we teach by the example of our own leadership in the construction of our nation's conscience.
>
> The argument for racial diversity cannot in the end rest only upon a university's choice to expose its students to a more colorful, more culturally diverse universe, or on a cost-benefit analysis of the need for an integrated elite in a soon-to-be majority non-white nation, or, as the *Bakke* Court argued, on the faculty's First Amendment right to academic freedom. We must integrate our universities because we cannot fulfill our democratic ideal until we have conquered the scourge of American apartheid. And we cannot teach and learn about racism in classrooms where only white folks are present.

Charles R. Lawrence, III, *Two Views of the River: A Critique of the Liberal Defense of Affirmative Action*, 101 COLUM. L. REV. 928, 963–64 (2001).

Note on the History of the SAT

Carl Brigham, a Princeton psychology professor, became an expert in intelligence testing when he worked during World War I with Robert Yerkes administering

Army IQ tests. After the War, Brigham administered the army test to all Princeton freshman and found it could identify those who excelled academically. By 1926, after some refinements, the Army test had been transformed into the SAT.

In 1933, James Bryant Conant, the new president of Harvard wanted a way to assess Midwestern public-school boys for a new scholarship program. There were exams offered by the College Entrance Examination Board, an association founded in 1900 by a small group of private schools and colleges, but they were not designed to assess public school graduates. In 1934, Conant directed his staff to use the SAT in addition to transcripts and recommendations to select ten outstanding young men from the Midwest who were named Harvard National Scholars.

Harvard then reached out to Princeton, Columbia, and Yale to use a similar process for their scholarship students. By 1937, the Scholarship Examinations were administered at 150 sites around the nation to more than 2,000 high school seniors.

On December 7, 1941, a group of College Board officials were meeting and discussed the possibility of abolishing the old College Board's essay examination in favor of using the SAT for all applicants. The meeting was interrupted with news of the bombing of Pearl Harbor. Within two weeks, the essay exams were suspended on the ground that they were too administratively complicated to use during a national emergency—and never used again.

On January 1, 1948, the Educational Testing Service (ETS) was founded to develop and administer the tests for the College Board, a partnership that endures. Nicholas Lemann, The Big Test: The Secret History of the American Meritocracy 27–31, 38–39, 51, 65 (1999).

The ETS is a 501 (c)(3) non-profit entity headquartered just outside Princeton, New Jersey. With a budget that exceeds $900 million and more than 2700 employees, critics assert that its nonprofit status give it both competitive advantages, and little public disclosure. More than 3 million students take the SAT annually.

CHAPTER 11

FINANCIAL AID

Financial aid has a more direct impact on the accessibility of higher education than almost any other factor. A 2007 study by the Educational Policy Institute found that in the countries where a college degree is most affordable, it is not always the most accessible. The United States ranked thirteenth for affordability in the world because of its generally high tuition and cost of living. It ranked fourth for accessibility (behind the Netherlands, Finland and Britain), however, because of the amount of financial aid provided.[a] The same pattern holds true when a student compares the costs of two schools. One may charge higher tuition than the other, but if enough financial aid is offered, the price to the student may be lower.

There is intense debate about how to account for financial aid. Some argue it is analogous to the way airlines price seats. They contend financial aid should be viewed as a discounting mechanism designed to fill seats. Some of the most selective private schools, on the other hand, which could easily fill their seats with full-tuition paying students, nonetheless offer significant financial aid to students who are not from wealthy families in order to achieve a diverse student body. The debate is at the heart of the first case in this section, a case that was triggered by a report in the *Wall Street Journal* that described how some of the most selective colleges met annually to compare financial aid offers before they were provided to applicants. The *Journal* called it "price-fixing."[b]

United States v. Brown University

United States Court of Appeals for the Third Circuit, 1993.
5 F.3d 658.

CIRCUIT JUDGE.

The Antitrust Division of the United States Department of Justice ("Division") brought this civil antitrust action against appellant Massachusetts Institute of Technology ("MIT") and eight Ivy League colleges and universities. The Division alleged that MIT violated section one of the Sherman Antitrust Act, 15 U.S.C. § 1, by agreeing with the Ivy League schools to distribute financial aid exclusively on the basis of need and to collectively

---

a. Sara Lipka, *15–Nation Study Finds Cheap Tuition Does Not Always Increase Access,* CHRON. HIGHER EDUC., Apr. 22, 2005, at A46.

b. Gary Putka, *Do Colleges Collude on Financial Aid?—Elite Schools Compare Notes on Applicants,* Wall St. J., May 2, 1989. Two years after the *Wall Street Journal* story, on May 22,

1991, the Antitrust Division of the Justice Department filed a civil suit seeking relief against MIT and the other eight schools of Ivy overlap. Michael Petronio, Comment, *Eliminating the Social Cost of Higher Education: The Third Circuit Allows Social Welfare Benefits to Justify Horizontal Restraints of Trade,* 83 GEO. L. J. 189 (1994).

determine the amount of financial assistance commonly admitted students would be awarded.

   . . .

MIT, founded in 1861, is a private nonprofit institution of higher education offering undergraduate and graduate programs. . . .

MIT has vast resources. It has an operating budget of $1.1 billion and an endowment of $1.5 billion, among the ten largest in the nation. It receives in excess of $200 million annually in tuition and room and board payments. Although the annual student budget (tuition, room and board, books and incidental expenses) is approximately $25,000, MIT still operates its undergraduate educational program at a significant loss. Alumni contributions and investment income from the endowment heavily subsidize the cost of MIT's educational services.

Each year, MIT receives between six and seven thousand applications for admission to its undergraduate program. MIT then evaluates applicants' grades, class rank, standardized test scores and personal accomplishments, and admits approximately 2,000 students. Approximately 1,100 of the accepted students ultimately matriculate at MIT. MIT accepts only exceptionally talented students. In the 1991–92 academic year, eighty-three percent of the first-year class were in the top five percent of their high school class and eighty percent had math SAT scores over 700. MIT's principal competitors for these high quality undergraduate students are Harvard, Princeton, Yale and Stanford. In 1988, eighty-two percent of all students admitted to MIT chose to attend either MIT, an Ivy League school or Stanford.

Although MIT could fill its entire entering class with students able to pay the full tuition, it utilizes a need-blind admissions system under which all admission decisions are based entirely on merit without consideration of an applicant's ability to pay tuition. Because financial status is irrelevant, very intelligent but needy students are preferred over less accomplished but more affluent ones. To provide admitted needy students with a realistic opportunity to enroll, MIT also is committed to satisfying the full financial aid needs of its student body. This commitment is expensive. In the 1991–92 academic year, fifty-seven percent of the entering class received some financial aid. The combination of need-blind admissions and full need-based aid allows many students to attend MIT who otherwise could not afford to attend. For the 1991–92 academic year, minorities comprised forty-four percent of the entering class, while thirty years earlier minorities represented only three to four percent of the undergraduate class.

. . . Under the federal financial aid program, students and their families must use their combined assets to pay for the students' college education. When family assets are insufficient to meet expenses, the student is eligible for federal loans and loan guarantees. To qualify for federal financial aid, students and their parents must disclose financial information to the College Scholarship Service ("CSS"). CSS processes this information and distributes the results to the United States Department of Education, which calculates each aid applicant's expected family contribution using the "Congressional Methodology" formula. The family contribution is the amount the student and his or her family may reasonably be expected to contribute annually toward educational expenses. CSS then forwards these results to participating institutions.

Under the Congressional Methodology, schools may increase or decrease the family contribution determination using their professional judgment. Professional judgment may be used only on a case-by-case basis when special circumstances exist. Through the exercise of professional judgment, schools may have differing family contribution determinations for the same applicant. If a student receives any federal aid, however, he or she may not receive supplemental aid from an institution that would exceed his or her need as computed under the Congressional Methodology.

In 1958, MIT and the eight Ivy League schools[1] formed the "Ivy Overlap Group" to collectively determine the amount of financial assistance to award to commonly admitted students.... The Ivy Overlap Group expressly agreed that they would award financial aid only on the basis of demonstrated need. Thus, merit-based aid was prohibited. To ensure that aid packages would be comparable, the participants agreed to share financial information concerning admitted candidates and to jointly develop and apply a uniform needs analysis for assessing family contributions.

. . .

The Ivy Overlap Group conducted their needs analysis pursuant to the "Ivy Methodology," which differed from the Congressional Methodology in several significant respects. For example, when a family has two or more children simultaneously attending college, the Congressional Methodology evenly apportions the parental contribution while the Ivy Methodology apportions the contribution based on the relative cost of the colleges. When a student's parents are divorced, the Congressional Methodology expects a parental contribution only from the custodial parent while the Ivy Methodology expects a contribution from both the custodial and noncustodial parents. Each deviation resulted in less generous aid packages than under the Congressional Methodology.

Although each Ivy Overlap institution employed the same analysis to compute family contributions, discrepancies in the contribution figures still arose. To eliminate these discrepancies, the Overlap members agreed to meet in early April each year to jointly determine the amount of the family contribution for each commonly admitted student. Prior to this conference, the Overlap schools independently determined the family contribution of each student they admitted, and transmitted this data to Student Aid Services. Student Aid Services then compiled rosters. A bilateral roster listed aid applicants who were admitted to two Ivy Overlap Group schools, and a multilateral roster compiled applicants admitted to more than two participating schools. For each student, the rosters showed each school's student budget, proposed student and parent contributions, self-help levels, and grant awards.

At the two-day spring Overlap conference, the schools compared their family contribution figures for each commonly admitted student. Family contribution differences of less than $500 were ignored. When there was a disparity in excess of $500, the schools would either agree to use one school's

---

1. The eight Ivy League schools include Brown University, Columbia University, Cornell University, Dartmouth College, Harvard University, Princeton University, the University of Pennsylvania, and Yale University. These schools were also named as defendants in this case, but each signed a consent decree with the United States immediately after the complaint was filed.

figure or meet somewhere in the middle. Due to time constraints, the schools spent only a few minutes discussing an individual and the agreed upon figures were more a result of compromise than of a genuine effort to accurately assess the student's financial circumstances.

All Ivy Overlap Group institutions understood that failing to comply with the Overlap Agreement would result in retaliatory sanctions. Consequently, noncompliance was rare and quickly remedied. For example, in 1986, Princeton began awarding $1,000 research grants to undergraduates based on academic merit. After a series of complaints from other Overlap institutions who viewed these grants as a form of scholarship, Princeton terminated this program.

Stanford represented the Overlap schools' only meaningful competition for students. The Ivy Overlap Group, fearful that Stanford would lure a disproportionate number of the highest caliber students with merit scholarships, attempted to recruit Stanford into the group. Stanford declined this invitation.

In 1991, the Antitrust Division of the Justice Department brought this civil suit alleging that the Ivy Overlap Group unlawfully conspired to restrain trade in violation of section one of the Sherman Act, 15 U.S.C. § 1, by (1) agreeing to award financial aid exclusively on the basis of need; (2) agreeing to utilize a common formula to calculate need; and (3) collectively setting, with only insignificant discrepancies, each commonly admitted students' family contribution toward the price of tuition. The Division sought only injunctive relief. All of the Ivy League institutions signed a consent decree with the United States, and only MIT proceeded to trial. After a ten-day bench trial, the district court held that the Ivy Overlap Group's conduct constituted "trade or commerce" under section one of the Sherman Act. Rejecting MIT's argument that financial aid is pure charity and thus exempt from the dictates of the Sherman Act, the district court characterized the Overlap Agreement as setting a selective discount off the price of educational services.

. . .

Faced with what it believed was a plainly anticompetitive agreement, the district court applied an abbreviated version of the rule of reason and took only a "quick look" to determine if MIT presented any plausible procompetitive affirmative defenses that justified the Overlap Agreement. MIT argued that Overlap widened the pool of applicants to Overlap institutions by providing needy students with the ability to enroll if accepted. This, MIT asserted, increased consumer choice and enhanced the quality of the education provided to all students by opening the doors of the most elite colleges in the nation to diversely gifted students of varied socio-economic backgrounds. The district court deemed these explanations to be social welfare justifications and flatly rejected the contention that the elimination of competition may be justified by non-economic considerations. The court based its reasoning on the unambiguous pronouncements of the Supreme Court in landmark Sherman Act cases, which preclude substituting Congress' view of the social benefits of competition for that of a defendant. In two cases which the district court deemed closely analogous to the present case, the Supreme Court had rejected social welfare justifications for the anti-competitive designs of certain professional associations. *National Society of Professional*

Engineers v. United States, 435 U.S. 679 (1978); *FTC v. Indiana Federation of Dentists*, 476 U.S. 447, 463 (1986)....

[MIT appealed the order of the district court.]

As a threshold matter, we must decide whether section one of the Sherman Act applies to the challenged conduct—MIT's agreement with the other Overlap institutions to award financial aid only to needy students and to set the amount of family contribution from commonly admitted students. Section one, by its terms, does not apply to all conspiracies, but only to those which restrain "trade or commerce." MIT characterizes its conduct as disbursing charitable funds to achieve the twin objectives of advancing equality of access to higher education and promoting socio-economic and racial diversity within the nation's most elite universities. This alleged pure charity, MIT argues, does not implicate trade or commerce, and is thus exempt from antitrust scrutiny.

.   .   .

We thus come to the crux of the issue—is providing financial assistance solely to needy students a selective reduction or "discount" from the full tuition amount, or a charitable gift? If this financial aid is a component of the process of setting tuition prices, it is commerce. If it is pure charity, it is not.

When MIT admits an affluent student, that student must pay approximately $25,000 annually (tuition plus room, board and incidental expenses) if he or she wishes to enroll at MIT. If MIT accepts a needy student and calculates that it will extend $10,000 in financial aid to that student, the student must pay approximately $15,000 to attend MIT. The student certainly is not free to take the $10,000 and apply it toward attendance at a different college. The assistance package is only available in conjunction with a complementary payment of approximately $15,000 to MIT. The amount of financial aid not only impacts, but directly determines the amount that a needy student must pay to receive an education at MIT. The financial aid therefore is part of the commercial process of setting tuition.[6]

MIT suggests that providing aid exclusively to needy students and setting the amount of that aid is not commercial because the price needy students are charged is substantially below the marginal cost of supplying a year of education to an undergraduate student. Because profit maximizing companies would not engage in such economically abnormal behavior, MIT concludes that such activity must be noncommercial. MIT's concession, however, that setting the full tuition amount is a commercial decision subject to antitrust scrutiny undermines this argument. The full tuition figure, like the varying amounts charged to needy students, is significantly below MIT's marginal cost. Therefore, whether the price charged for educational services is below marginal cost is not probative of the commercial or noncommercial nature of the methodology utilized to determine financial aid packages.

The fact that MIT is not obligated to provide any financial aid does not transform that aid into charity. Similarly, discounting the price of educational services for needy students is not charity when a university receives tangible benefits in exchange. Regardless of whether MIT's motive is al-

---

6. At least one Overlap member apparently agrees with this conclusion. In a paper entitled "Tuition Income," Yale explains that "tuition, modified by student aid expenditures, is in essence the price that the University charges for its educational programs."

truism, self-enhancement or a combination of the two,[7] MIT benefits from providing financial aid. MIT admits that it competes with other Overlap members for outstanding students. By distributing aid, MIT enables exceptional students to attend its school who otherwise could not afford to attend. The resulting expansion in MIT's pool of exceptional applicants increases the quality of MIT's student body. MIT then enjoys enhanced prestige by virtue of its ability to attract a greater portion of the "cream of the crop." The Supreme Court has recognized that nonprofit organizations derive significant benefit from increased prestige and influence. *See American Society of Mechanical Engineers, Inc. v. Hydrolevel Corp.*, 456 U.S. 556, 576 (1982). Although MIT could fill its class with students able to pay the full tuition, the caliber of its student body, and consequently the institution's reputation, obviously would suffer. Overlap affords MIT the benefit of an overrepresentation of high caliber students, with the concomitant institutional prestige, without forcing MIT to be responsive to market forces in terms of its tuition costs. By immunizing itself through the Overlap from competition for students based on a price/quality ratio, MIT achieves certain institutional benefits at a bargain.

. . .

We hold that financial assistance to students is part and parcel of the process of setting tuition and thus a commercial transaction. Although MIT's status as a nonprofit educational organization and its advancement of congressionally-recognized and important social welfare goals does not remove its conduct from the realm of trade or commerce, these factors will influence whether this conduct violates the Sherman Act.

Section one of the Sherman Act provides that "every contract, combination in the form of trust or otherwise, or conspiracy, in restraint of trade or commerce among the several states . . . is declared to be illegal." 15 U.S.C. § 1. . . Because even beneficial business contracts or combinations restrain trade to some degree, section one has been interpreted to prohibit only those contracts or combinations that are "unreasonably restrictive of competitive conditions." *Standard Oil Co. v. United States*, 221 U.S. 1, 58 (1911).

. . . Most restraints are analyzed under the traditional "rule of reason." . . . The plaintiff bears an initial burden under the rule of reason of showing that the alleged combination or agreement produced adverse, anti-competitive effects within the relevant product and geographic markets. The plaintiff may satisfy this burden by proving the existence of actual anticompetitive effects, such as reduction of output, increase in price, or deterioration in quality of goods or services. Such proof is often impossible to make, however, due to the difficulty of isolating the market effects of challenged conduct.

---

7. The district court did not make a factual finding with respect to MIT's motivation for joining the Overlap Agreement. There is ample evidence that MIT's indirect objective was to promote equal access to higher education and diversity within the student body. We cannot overlook, however, that MIT also desired to attract the most talented students at the least expense to itself, a result which would also flow directly from the elimination of price competition among the Ivy Overlap member institutions. In fact, we could conjecture a number of self-serving reasons why MIT might have entered the Overlap Agreement, not the least of which might have been the market power which typically accompanies combinations. The higher than competitive tuition prices which MIT and the other Overlap members were able to charge, absent tuition competition, enhances "revenues", if not "profits", which can be allocated to any conceivable internal institutional purpose. . . .

Accordingly, courts typically allow proof of the defendant's "market power" instead. Market power, the ability to raise prices above those that would prevail in a competitive market, *Jefferson Parish Hosp. Dist. No. 2 v. Hyde*, 466 U.S. 2, 27 n.46 (1984), is essentially a "surrogate for detrimental effects."
. . .

While the rule of reason typically mandates "an elaborate inquiry into the reasonableness of a challenged business practice," *Arizona v. Maricopa County Medical Society*, 457 U.S. 332, 343 (1982), "there are certain agreements or practices which because of their pernicious effect on competition and lack of any redeeming virtue are conclusively presumed to be unreasonable," *Northern Pacific Ry. Co. v. United States*, 356 U.S. 1, 5 (1958). Such "plainly anticompetitive" agreements or practices are deemed to be "illegal per se." *National Society of Professional Engineers v. United States*, 435 U.S. 679, 692 (1978). . . .

In addition to the traditional rule of reason and the per se rule, courts sometimes apply what amounts to an abbreviated or "quick look" rule of reason analysis. The abbreviated rule of reason is an intermediate standard. It applies in cases where per se condemnation is inappropriate, but where "no elaborate industry analysis is required to demonstrate the anticompetitive character" of an inherently suspect restraint. . . .

In the present case, the district court applied the abbreviated rule of reason analysis . . . in deference to Supreme Court precedents counseling special scrutiny of restraints involving professional associations. Accordingly, rather than immediately condemning the Overlap because of its apparent quintessentially anti-competitive nature, the court afforded MIT an opportunity to proffer a procompetitive affirmative defense—an acknowledged "heavy burden."

. . .

The district court found that the "Ivy Overlap Group members, which are horizontal competitors, agreed upon the price which aid applicants and their families would have to pay to attend a member institution to which that student had been accepted." Based on this finding, the Division argues that MIT's conduct was per se unlawful price fixing. We disagree.

. . .

Antitrust analysis is based largely on price theory, which "assures us that economic behavior . . . is primarily directed toward the maximization of profits." R. Bork, The Antitrust Paradox 116 (1978) (emphasis in original). The rationale for treating professional organizations differently is that they tend to vary somewhat from this economic model. *See Professional Engineers*, 435 U.S. at 696 ("by their nature, professional services may differ significantly from other business services, and, accordingly, the nature of the competition in such services may vary"). Specifically, while professional organizations aim to enhance the profits of their members, they and the professionals they represent may have greater incentives to pursue ethical, charitable, or other non-economic objectives that conflict with the goal of pure profit maximization. While it is well settled that good motives themselves "will not validate an otherwise anticompetitive practice," courts often look at a party's intent to help it judge the likely effects of challenged conduct. Thus, when bona fide, non-profit professional associations adopt a restraint which they claim is motivated by "public service or ethical norms," economic harm to consumers may be viewed as less predictable and certain. In such circumstances, it is proper to entertain and weigh procompetitive justifications proffered in defense of an alleged restraint before declaring it to be unreasonable.

The same rationale counsels against declaring Overlap per se unreasonable. As a qualified charitable organization under 26 U.S.C. § 501(c)(3), MIT deviates even further from the profit-maximizing prototype than do professional associations. While non-profit professional associations advance the commercial interests of their for-profit constituents, MIT is, as its 501(c)(3) status suggests, an organization "operated exclusively for . . . educational purposes . . . no part of the net earnings of which inures to the benefit of any private shareholder or individual." 26 U.S.C. § 501(c)(3). This does not mean, of course, that MIT and other bona fide charitable organizations lack incentives to increase revenues. Nor does it necessarily mean that commercially motivated conduct of such organizations should be immune from per se treatment. Like the defendant associations in *Indiana Dentists* and *Professional Engineers*, however, MIT vigorously maintains that Overlap was the product of a concern for the public interest, here the undisputed public interest in equality of educational access and opportunity, and alleges the absence of any revenue maximizing purpose.

This alleged pure altruistic motive and alleged absence of a revenue maximizing purpose contribute to our uncertainty with regard to Overlap's anti-competitiveness, and thus prompts us to give careful scrutiny to the nature of Overlap, and to refrain from declaring Overlap per se unreasonable. . . .

. . .

MIT does not dispute that the stated purpose of Overlap is to eliminate price competition for talented students among member institutions. Indeed, the intent to eliminate price competition among the Overlap schools for commonly admitted students appears on the face of the Agreement itself. In addition to agreeing to offer financial aid solely on the basis of need and to develop a common system of needs analysis, the Overlap members agreed to meet each spring to compare data and to conform one another's aid packages to the greatest possible extent. Because the Overlap Agreement aims to restrain "competitive bidding" and deprive prospective students of "the ability to utilize and compare prices" in selecting among schools, it is anticompetitive "on its face." Price is "the central nervous system of the economy," *Socony–Vacuum Oil*, 310 U.S. at 224 n.59, and "the heart of our national economic policy long has been faith in the value of competition," *Standard Oil Co. v. FTC*, 340 U.S. 231, 248 (1951). We therefore agree that Overlap initially "requires some competitive justification even in the absence of a detailed market analysis."

MIT's principal counterargument is that an abbreviated rule of reason analysis is appropriate only where economic harm to consumers may fairly be presumed; and such harm may be presumed only when evidence establishes that "the challenged practice, unlike Overlap, manifestly has an adverse effect on price, output, or quality." As the Division aptly points out, however, if an abbreviated rule of reason analysis always required a clear evidentiary showing of a detrimental effect on price, output, or quality, it would no longer be abbreviated. This is because proof of actual adverse effects generally will require the elaborate, threshold industry analysis that an abbreviated inquiry is designed to obviate.

. . .

Since the Overlap Agreement is a price fixing mechanism impeding the ordinary functioning of the free market, MIT is obliged to provide justification for the arrangement. . . .

The district court did not make any conclusive findings with regard to [the] consequences of price fixing in the present case. First, the district court did not find, and we do not understand the Division to suggest, that Overlap has caused or is even likely to cause any reduction of output. Second, while the parties sharply dispute the effect of Overlap on the price of education at the member colleges, the district court expressed doubt as to whether price effects could be determined to a reasonable degree of economic certainty. The court therefore assumed without deciding that the cooperation among the schools had no aggregate effect on the price of an MIT education. Thus, while MIT bears the burden of establishing an affirmative justification for Overlap, the absence of any finding of adverse effects such as higher price or lower output is relevant, albeit not dispositive, when the district court considers whether MIT has met this burden. . . .

. . .

On appeal, MIT first contends that by promoting socio-economic diversity at member institutions, Overlap improved the quality of the education offered by the schools and therefore enhanced the consumer appeal of an Overlap education. The Supreme Court has recognized improvement in the quality of a product or service that enhances the public's desire for that product or service as one possible procompetitive virtue. The district court itself noted that it cannot be denied "that cultural and economic diversity contributes to the quality of education and enhances the vitality of student life." Albeit in a different context, the Supreme Court also has recognized that "the atmosphere of 'speculation, experiment and creation'—so essential to the quality of higher education—is widely believed to be promoted by a diverse student body." *Regents of the Univ. of California v. Bakke*, 438 U.S. 265, 312 (1978) (opinion of Powell, J.).

MIT also contends that by increasing the financial aid available to needy students, Overlap provided some students who otherwise would not have been able to afford an Overlap education the opportunity to have one. In this respect, MIT argues, Overlap enhanced consumer choice. The policy of allocating financial aid solely on the basis of demonstrated need has two obvious consequences. First, available resources are spread among more needy students than would be the case if some students received aid in excess of their need. Second, as a consequence of the fact that more students receive the aid they require, the number of students able to afford an Overlap education is maximized. In short, removing financial obstacles for the greatest number of talented but needy students increases educational access, thereby widening consumer choice. Enhancement of consumer choice is a traditional objective of the antitrust laws and has also been acknowledged as a procompetitive benefit.

Finally, MIT argues that by eliminating price competition among participating schools, Overlap channeled competition into areas such as curriculum, campus activities, and student-faculty interaction. As the Division correctly notes, however, any competition that survives a horizontal price restraint naturally will focus on attributes other than price. This is not the kind of procompetitive virtue contemplated under the Act, but rather one mere consequence of limiting price competition.

MIT next claims that beyond ignoring the procompetitive effects of Overlap, the district court erroneously refused to consider compelling social welfare justifications. MIT argues that by enabling member schools to maintain a steadfast policy of need-blind admissions and full need-based aid, Overlap promoted the social ideal of equality of educational access and opportunity.

Congress has sought to promote the same ideal of equality of educational access and opportunity for more than twenty-five years. Testimony at trial established that a primary objective of federal financial aid policy is to promote "horizontal equity" and "vertical equity." In other words,

> federal financial aid policy aims to ensure that similarly situated students are treated the same regardless of which institution, or aid officer within that institution, reviews their applications, and that students with less financial need do not receive more aid than those students with more financial need.

Brown University, 805 F. Supp. At 291. The federal government seeks to effectuate these goals through programs that distribute financial aid exclusively on the basis of need.

As the evidence attested, MIT has sought to promote similar social and educational policy objectives by limiting financial aid to those with demonstrated need, although the district court found that the Ivy Needs Analysis Methodology differed significantly from the Congressional Methodology. The Overlap Agreement states:

> Member institutions agree that the primary purpose of a college financial aid program for all students is to provide financial assistance to students who without such aid would be unable to attend that institution. Financial aid should only be awarded after it is determined that family resources are inadequate to meet the student's educational expenses, and such aid should not exceed the difference between educational expenses and family resources....

Brown University, 805 F. Supp. at 292–93. Although the percentage of American minorities comprising MIT's student body has dramatically risen over the last three decades,[11] which MIT attributes to the Overlap policy, the Ivy Methodology for performing a student needs analysis was ironically less generous to needy students in certain key ways than the Congressional Methodology. The district court noted three main areas in which the Ivy Methodology departed from the Congressional Methodology, including the way in which the Overlap apportions family income when multiple siblings attend college simultaneously,[12] the requirements of separate payment from

---

11. In the 1991–1992 academic year, American minorities comprised 44% of MIT's undergraduate enrollment, up from 3% to 4% just three decades earlier.

12. The district court found that:

When more than one child in a family is attending college, the Congressional Methodology evenly apportions the parental contribution; for example, if two children in one family are attending col-non-custodial parents where there is a divorce or separation,[13] and the way Overlap treats capital losses, depreciation losses, and losses from secondary business which are reported on the parents' tax returns. Despite these discrepancies, the facts certainly attest that MIT has widened the access of certain minorities to its educational institution, whether or not the Overlap was mainly responsible for or necessary to that result. . . .

The district court was not persuaded by the alleged social welfare values proffered for Overlap because it believed the Supreme Court's decisions in *Professional Engineers* and *Indiana Dentists* required a persuasive procompetitive justification, or a showing of necessity, neither of which it believed that MIT demonstrated. In *Professional Engineers*, the engineers maintained that an ethics rule banning competitive bidding was reasonable because price competition for projects would induce engineers to offer their services at unsustainably low prices and compensate by cutting corners on the quality of their work, because consumers in most instances award contracts to the lowest bidder, regardless of quality, competitive bidding "would be dangerous to the public health, safety and welfare." The Court flatly rejected the engineers' "public safety" argument, viewing it as nothing more than an attempt to impose "[their own] views of the costs and benefits of competition on the entire marketplace." The Court explained that "the Rule of Reason does not support a defense based on the assumption that competition itself is unreasonable."

In *Indiana Dentists*, where a group of dentists agreed to withhold x-rays from patients' insurers, the dentists association argued that certain noncompetitive "quality of care" effects of the agreement were relevant to the Court's analysis under the rule of reason. According to the Court,

> [t]he gist of the claim is that x rays, standing alone, are not adequate bases for diagnosis of dental problems or for the formulation of an acceptable course of treatment. Accordingly ... there is a danger that [insurers] will erroneously decline to pay for treatment that is in fact in the interest of the patient, and that the patient will as a result be deprived of fully adequate care.

Id. at 462–63. Unconvinced, the Court explained that "precisely such a justification for withholding information from customers was rejected as illegitimate in the [*Professional Engineers*] case." The Court continued:

> The argument is, in essence, that an unrestrained market in which consumers are given access to the information they believe to be relevant to their choices will lead them to make unwise and even dangerous choices. Such an argument amounts to "nothing less than a frontal assault on the basic policy of the Sherman Act."

Id. (quoting *Professional Engineers*, 435 U.S. at 695).

---

lege, half the parental contribution would be attributed to each child. By contrast, the Ivy methodology apportioned the family contribution for multiple siblings based on the cost of the colleges the children were attending. The more a college costs, the greater part of the family contribution would be attributed to the student attending that college.

13. The district court found that "in the event a student's parents were divorced or separated, the Congressional Methodology expects a contribution from the custodial parent only. The Ivy Overlap Group schools considered the income of the non-custodial parent."

Both the public safety justification rejected by the Supreme Court in *Professional Engineers* and the public health justification rejected by the Court in *Indiana Dentists* were based on the defendants' faulty premise that consumer choices made under competitive market conditions are "unwise" or "dangerous." Here MIT argues that participation in the Overlap arrangement provided some consumers, the needy, with additional choices which an entirely free market would deny them. The facts and arguments before us may suggest some significant areas of distinction from those in *Professional Engineers* and *Indiana Dentists* in that MIT is asserting that Overlap not only serves a social benefit, but actually enhances consumer choice. Overlap is not an attempt to withhold a particular desirable service from customers, as was the professional combination in *Indiana Dentists*, but rather it purports only to seek to extend a service to qualified students who are financially "needy" and would not otherwise be able to afford the high cost of education at MIT. Further, while Overlap resembles the ban on competitive bidding at issue in *Professional Engineers*, MIT alleges that Overlap enhances competition by broadening the socio-economic sphere of its potential student body. Thus, rather than suppress competition, Overlap may in fact merely regulate competition in order to enhance it, while also deriving certain social benefits. If the rule of reason analysis leads to this conclusion, then indeed Overlap will be beyond the scope of the prohibitions of the Sherman Act.

We note the unfortunate fact that financial aid resources are limited even at the Ivy League schools. A trade-off may need to be made between providing some financial aid to a large number of the most needy students or allowing the free market to bestow the limited financial aid on the very few most talented who may not need financial aid to attain their academic goals. Under such circumstances, if this trade-off is proven to be worthy in terms of obtaining a more diverse student body (or other legitimate institutional goals), the limitation on the choices of the most talented students might not be so egregious as to trigger the obvious concerns which led the Court to reject the "public interest" justifications in *Professional Engineers* and *Indiana Dentists*. However, we leave it for the district court to decide whether full funding of need may be continued on an individual institutional basis, absent Overlap, whether tuition could be lowered as a way to compete for qualified "needy" students, or whether there are other imaginable creative alternatives to implement MIT's professed social welfare goal.

. . .

On remand if the district court, under a full scale rule of reason analysis, finds that MIT has proffered a persuasive justification for the Overlap Agreement, then the Antitrust Division of the Justice Department, the plaintiff in this case, must prove that a reasonable less restrictive alternative exists. The district court should consider, if and when the issue arises, whether the Antitrust Division has shown, by a preponderance of the evidence, that another viable option, perhaps the free market, can achieve the same benefits as Overlap.

For the foregoing reasons, we will reverse the judgment of the district court and remand for further proceedings consistent with this opinion.

Questions and Comments on *U.S. v. Brown*

Following the Third Circuit decision, MIT and the Department of Justice reached a settlement. Under the terms of the settlement, eligible colleges will not be able to share information about the amount of financial aid offered to a particular student, but they may discuss general guidelines for granting aid. Independent auditors will review the scholarship information and report gross disparities in awards by different universities in the network that might indicate that a member was using high awards for recruiting purposes. The schools also will be able to compare need claims presented by applicants to discourage fraud. To be eligible, a college must have a "need-blind and full-need" admissions policy. William H. Honan, *M.I.T. Wins Right to Share Financial Aid Data in Antitrust Accord*, N.Y. TIMES, Dec. 23, 1993. MIT President Charles Vest said of the settlement that it provided "maybe 98 percent" of what MIT had sought, and that it authorized "a more modern system to replace the overlap process." Steve Stecklow & William M. Bulkeley, *Antitrust Case Against MIT is Dropped, Allowing Limited Exchange of Aid Data*, WALL ST. J., Dec. 23, 1993.

Vest later called this application of the Sherman Anti–Trust Act "bizarre," and noted that U.S. attorney general Richard Thornburgh who brought the formal complaint left the administration the next week to run for the U.S. Senate. CHARLES M. VEST, THE AMERICAN RESEARCH UNIVERSITY FROM WORLD WAR II TO WORLD WIDE WEB 64 (2007). Leon Higgenbotham, who had served as chief justice of the Third Circuit before the hearing, offered to submit an amicus brief in support of MIT. In 1995, Higgenbotham said that the two pro bono legal endeavors he was most proud of were representing Nelson Mandela and testifying on behalf of MIT because he believed in merit-based admissions. *Id.* at 66.

On October 20, 1994, Congress enacted Section 568 of the Improving America's Schools Act of 1994, which proscribes the application of antitrust laws to the award of need-based financial aid to students. *See* Pub. L. No. 103–382, 108 Stat. 3518 (1994) (codified in Sherman Anti–Trust Act, 15 U.S.C. § 1 (2000)). Section 568 also modifies the settlement reached between MIT and the government. Colleges that practice need-blind admissions, but cannot meet the full financial need of admitted students, may now participate in the kind of financial aid discussion permitted by the MIT settlement. *See* Antitrust Compliance Policy, *available at* http://ogc.yale.edu/legal_reference/antitrust.html.

Section 568 authorizes colleges and universities "to agree or attempt to agree:

(1) to award . . . financial aid only on the basis of demonstrated financial need . . . ;

(2) to use common principles of analysis for determining the need of such students for financial aid . . . ;

(3) to use a common aid application form for need-based financial aid . . . ; or

(4) to exchange through an independent third party, *before* awarding need-based financial aid to any . . . student who is commonly admitted to the institutions . . . ."

Id. Section 568 will expire in 2008 unless it is extended by Congress.

In 2000, in order to encourage more merit aid, twenty-eight selective universities and colleges including MIT publicly committed to merit-based admission and a common methodology for measuring need. 568 Presidents' Group, *The 568 Presidents' Group Consensus Methodology Policy Guidelines* (2000), http://568group.org/docs/cmmanual-non.pdf.

In 2001, Congress amended Section 568 to require the United States Government Accountability Office (GAO) to "conduct a study of the effect of the antitrust exemption on institutional student aid under section 568. . . ." Need–Based Education Act of 2001, § 3(a)(1). The GAO report, issued in 2006, after reviewing twenty-five out of twenty-eight private four-year institutions using the antitrust exemption, concluded that the exemption created "virtually no difference in the amount students and their families were expected to pay between schools using the exemption and similar schools not using the exemption." It also found that the participating colleges and universities did not enroll significantly more or fewer low-income or minority students since implementing the cooperative financial aid practices. U.S. Gov't Accountability Office, GAO–06–963, Schools' Use of the Antitrust Exemption Has Not Significantly Affected College Affordability or Likelihood of Student Enrollment to Date, Sept. 2006, *available at* http://www.gao.gov/new.items/d06963. pdf.

The Institute for College Access and Success released a proposal in 2008 urging Congress to create temporary additional exemptions from antitrust laws in order to allow colleges and universities with need-blind admissions policies to coordinate aid packages. Under the proposed exemptions, institutions would be able to collaborate subject to continued monitoring to ensure that any agreements result in increased affordability and access. Scott Jaschik, *Could Collaboration Shift Colleges' Aid Policies?*, Inside Higher Ed, June 13, 2008, *available at* http://insidehighered.com/news/2008/06/13/antitrust. Do you think that allowing institutions of higher education to collaborate on student aid packages would increase access or would such an antitrust exemption merely enable colleges and universities to lower the costs of competing for highly qualified students?

Fabrizio v. U.S. Department of Education (*In re* Fabrizio)

United States Bankruptcy Court for the Western District of Pennsylvania, 2007.
369 B.R. 238.

■ Agresti, J.

On October 2, 2005 . . . Anthony Robert Fabrizio ("Debtor"), filed a voluntary petition for relief under Chapter 7 of the Bankruptcy Code. On February 14, 2006, the Debtor filed a "Motion" pursuant to *11 U.S.C. § 523(a)(8)* seeking discharge of approximately $43,000 in consolidated, student loan obligations owed the Defendant. . . .

The Debtor is 51 years of age residing in an apartment located in Erie, Pa. He owns no real property. From 1984 through 1991, the Debtor obtained a number of subsidized Stafford loans as a means to fund his educational pursuits. On January 16, 2004, the Debtor consolidated his outstanding loans into the William D. Ford Direct Loan Program creating a single, total obligation amounting to $40,583.00. After consolidation, the monthly educational loan payments were fixed at $279.02. The Debtor never made any payments on the consolidated loan. As of March 12, 2006, the outstanding balance on the consolidated loan had grown to $42,898.78.

In 1973, the Debtor obtained his high school degree from the Cathedral Preparatory School. In 1989, he received a B.S. in Management and Finance from Gannon University. The Debtor later took classes towards his MBA, but only completed approximately half of the requirements for that degree. In the last ten years, the Debtor has received professional certificates for education in communication, social studies and mathematics from the Commonwealth of Pennsylvania, as well as local certificates in sales consulting and for proficiency in various computer skills.

As of November 1, 2006, the Debtor obtained employment as a car salesman. As stipulated by the Debtor, his net earnings for the month of December, 2006 totaled $2,333.63. Prior to that, from March, 2006, through the end of October, 2006, the Debtor was unemployed and during that period received monthly Pennsylvania unemployment compensation benefits in the amount of $1180. Before this recent period of unemployment, for all practical purposes, the Debtor was continuously employed for the prior eighteen (18) year period. The Debtor estimates his average annual income over the last ten (10) years approximated $30,000.

The Debtor currently lives alone. Even though he has twice been married and divorced in 1994 and 2000, he has no current alimony or spousal obligations and there is no indication he has ever been required to make such payments. The Debtor is responsible for monthly child support payments totaling $364 for the care of his 13 year-old son and will be obligated to make those payments for the next five years until his son reaches the age of majority.

As of January 4, 2007, the Debtor incurred monthly living expenses of $1,188. The Debtor managed to significantly reduce his expenses from those experienced during his previous six month period of unemployment. At the time of argument on the Motion, Debtor's Counsel contended that . . . Debtor's expenses were expected to increase now that the Debtor had obtained what appears to be regular employment. . . .

Finally, the Debtor admits he has no physical or mental disabilities or other personal limitations that would in any way impair his ability to maintain future, gainful employment.

. . .

As a general rule, discharge of a student loan indebtedness is not available to a debtor seeking relief under the Bankruptcy Code. However, an exception to this general rule is found in § 523(a)(8) of the Code which provides in relevant part:

> (a) A discharge under section 727, 1141, 1228(a), 1228(b), or 1328(b) of this title does not discharge an individual debtor from any debt—
>
> > . . .
>
> > (8) unless excepting such debt from discharge under this paragraph would impose an *undue hardship* on the debtor and the debtor's dependents, for—
>
> > (A)(i) an educational benefit overpayment or loan made, insured or guaranteed by a governmental unit, or made under any program funded in whole or in part by a governmental unit or nonprofit institution. . . .

11 U.S.C. § 523(a)(8) (emphasis added).

While Congress did not specifically define the phrase "undue hardship" in the Bankruptcy Code, the meaning of the "term" is "settled law" in the Third Circuit since the decision rendered in *Pennsylvania Higher Education Assistance Agency v. Faish (In re Faish)*, 72 F.3d 298 (3d Cir. 1995). In *Faish*, for purposes of § 523(a)(8), the Court of Appeals for the Third Circuit adopted the "undue hardship" test as originally set forth in *Brunner v. New York State Higher Education Corp.*, 831 F.2d 395 (2d Cir. 1987).

Under this test, "undue hardship" requires a showing that: (1) the debtor cannot maintain, based on current income and expenses, a minimal standard of living for himself and his dependents if forced to repay the loans; (2) additional circumstances exist indicating that this state of affairs is likely to persist for a significant portion of the student loan repayment period; and (3) the debtor has made good faith efforts to repay the loans. Student loan debtors bear the burden of proof in advancing a student loan discharge complaint. The standard of proof by which a debtor must establish each of the elements is by a preponderance of the evidence. Because the test is written in the conjunctive, if one of the three elements of the test is not proven, the inquiry ends there and the student loan cannot be discharged. Finally, the test must be strictly construed. Equitable concerns or other extraneous factors not contemplated by the test may not be imported into the "undue hardship" analysis.

. . . [T]he Court will begin its analysis by examining the third prong of the *Brunner* test. Under this prong, the Debtor must prove that he has made a "good faith" effort to repay the loan over the entire time period from the date on which the first loan payment became due to the date on which the debtor filed his bankruptcy petition. The "good faith" inquiry is guided by the understanding that undue hardship encompasses a notion that the Debtor may not negligently or willfully cause his own default. Instead, his financial plight must be due to factors beyond his reasonable control. This prong also fulfills the purpose behind the adoption of the *§ 523(a)(8)* student loan discharge provision of the Bankruptcy Code which was enacted in response to a "rising incidence of consumer bankruptcies of former students motivated primarily to avoid payment of education loan debts."

In order for the Debtor to avail himself of the student loan discharge rights contained in *§ 523(a)(8)*, the Court is required to focus on the specific loan or loans sought to be discharged. Here we are dealing with a consolidation loan governed by the *Higher Education Act, 20 U.S.C. § 1074(a)*, which statutory language makes clear that "federal consolidation loans are new agreements which discharge the liabilities of the old loans and create their own obligations." Acknowledging the foregoing at the time of argument, the Debtor stipulated that the relevant time period for consideration of whether a "good faith repayment" attempt occurred began with the January 16, 2004 loan consolidation date and ended with the October 2, 2005 petition filing date. During this time period the Debtor admittedly never made any payments toward his loan obligation. As such, the record is clear that the Debtor failed to make any attempt at paying his loan during the appropriate time period even though for all but six months of that time he was earning $37,000 in his position as a senior account executive/director of marketing. As such, without more, the Court is unable to find that the Debtor made any "good faith repayment" effort during the relevant time period.

. . .

Finally, when evaluating "good faith," some courts have analyzed the ratio of a debtor's student loan debt to total debt to be discharged. Here, upon review of the Debtor's Schedules, the Debtor's student loan debt constitutes approximately 80% of the original debt to be discharged. *Compare In re Kelly*, 351 B.R. 45 (Bankr. E.D.N.Y. 2006) (where the debtor's student loan debt constituted more than 70% of the debt sought to be discharged, the court found that the debtor failed to establish that she made good faith efforts to repay her student loans). Such a high ratio of student loan debt in the instant matter in light of the undisputed facts before the Court further supports the conclusion that, under any scenario, the Debtor is unable to sustain his burden in establishing good faith pursuant to the third prong of the undue hardship test. Therefore, since the Debtor is unable to meet the third prong of the *§ 523(a)(8)* "undue hardship" test, the entry of summary judgment in favor of the Defendant is appropriate.

Since the *Brunner § 523(a)(8)* undue hardship test requires all three prongs to be independently proven in order for its application to result in the discharge of a student loan obligation, because of the above finding, it is unnecessary to review the applicability of the remaining elements of the test. Nonetheless, since alternate reasons exist in this case for the grant of summary judgment, further discussion is warranted.

The second prong of the *Brunner* test, sometimes referred to as the "additional circumstances test," requires the Debtor to show that his current state of affairs will not improve for a significant portion of the student loan repayment period. Courts considering this prong of the test have found it to be a "demanding requirement" since it is not enough for the Debtor to prove financial straits or a "present inability to fulfill financial commitment." Rather, he must prove a total incapacity to repay the loan in the future for reasons beyond the Debtor's control. *In re Cehula,* 327 B.R. 241 (Bankr. W.D. Pa. 2005); *In re Brightful,* 267 F.3d at 328....

The Debtor is well-educated. In addition to obtaining his Bachelor of Science degree in Management and Finance, he has completed a significant portion of the required classes towards his Masters of Business Administration. In the last ten years, the Debtor has received professional certificates from the Commonwealth of Pennsylvania for education in communication, social studies and mathematics, in addition to local certificates in sales consulting and for proficiency in various computer skills. The Debtor clearly possesses an educational background that increases his marketability for obtaining future employment and would appeal to a wide array of prospective employers. He also possesses extensive experience in sales and, specifically, automotive sales. As of the date of the summary judgment argument he was employed as a car salesman with an annualized, gross income of $28,000 based upon his experience for the month of December, 2006.

. . .

For all the above reasons and resolving all reasonable inferences of fact in favor of the Debtor, the Court finds that, as to the second prong of the undue hardship test, the Debtor has failed to demonstrate any ability to satisfy his burden of proof at trial. No relevant additional circumstances have been demonstrated that the Debtor's state of financial affairs is likely to persist for a significant portion of the student loan repayment period. As such, summary judgment is appropriate in this regard as well.... Now that it has been determined that the Debtor failed to sustain his independent burden of proof as to two separate prongs of the "undue hardship" test, there is no need for the Court to go any further prior to entering summary judgment in favor of the Defendant....

Questions and Comments on *Fabrizio*

As *Fabrizio* demonstrates, it is very difficult to discharge student loan debts in bankruptcy. Indeed, the Bankruptcy Abuse Prevention and Consumer Protection Act of 2005, Pub. L. No. 109–8, 119 Stat. 23 (2005), extended the prohibition on discharging in bankruptcy that already applied to most student loans funded and guaranteed by the federal government or nonprofit institutions to student loans that are privately funded. There are, however, other options available to some borrowers. For example, they may be able to work out a plan to repay the loan over a longer period of time. In some circumstances, partial or total forgiveness may be available as the next case demonstrates.

Consider the three-part "undue hardship" test. Should a debtor be required to show anything more than an inability to pay back the loans and maintain a minimum standard of living? Why should an individual need to show good faith in attempting to pay off his debts?

What if a student attends college by taking out educational loans, but does not acquire any marketable skills? Some courts have held that educational loans are dischargeable when the student does not financially benefit from the education that the loans helped to finance. *See, e.g.,* Clay v. Westmar Coll. (*In re* Clay), 12 B.R. 251, 255 (Bankr. N.D. Iowa 1981) (discharging a student loan for a former student who became a water meter reader); Littell v. Oregon Bd. of Higher Ed. (*In re* Little), 6 B.R. 85, 88 (Bankr. D. Or. 1980) ("There is thus great pressure and temptation on the part of college authorities to encourage students to apply for loans and grant them when in effect it is not a sound economic thing to do. This should be a substantial factor in determining whether a student loan should be dischargeable."). Do you agree that student loans should be forgiven if the student does not financially benefit from the education he or she receives?

De La Mota v. United States Department of Education

United States Court of Appeals, Second Circuit, 2005.
412 F.3d 71.

■ B.D. PARKER, CIRCUIT JUDGE:

Marisol De La Mota, Froebel Chungata, and Oren Doron are public service attorneys employed by New York City's Administration for Children's Services ("ACS"). ACS defines its mission as "to ensure the safety and well-being of all the children of New York" and to employ "all available means to be certain that children do not live in danger of abuse and neglect." De La Mota and Chungata work in the Child Support Litigation Unit to secure financial support for children in low-income families primarily by litigating paternity and child support actions. Doron works in the Division of Legal Services where he prosecutes child abuse and neglect cases on behalf of low income children. Appellants believed that they had been improperly denied cancellation of their student Perkins Loans under a provision of the Higher Education Act ("HEA" or "the Act") of 1965, authorizing cancellation to borrowers "providing, or supervising the provision of, services to high-risk children who are from low-income communities and the families of such children." 20 U.S.C. § 1087ee(a)(2)(I). They sued under the Administrative Procedure Act, challenging the Department of Education's ("DOE") interpretation of eligibility requirements for cancellation of Perkins Loans. They now appeal from a judgment of the United States District Court for the Southern District of New York dismissing their claims. . . .

Title IV of the HEA directs the Secretary of the Department of Education to implement various federal student financial aid programs. The Perkins Loan Program is one such program, designed to assist institutions of higher education in financing low-interest loans to financially needy students. *See* 20 U.S.C. §§ 1070 et seq. Congress delegated to the Secretary the authority to implement Perkins Loans, including the authority to promulgate regulations governing the program. The Secretary has promulgated regulations under this section. *See* 34 C.F.R. § 674.

Under the program, the DOE provides federal monies to participating institutions. The institution makes matching capital contributions and the funds are the source of loans to eligible students. Once the student graduates or leaves the school, the loan is to be repaid. The institution's fund is revolving and repaid loans are deposited into the fund and then supplemented by new federal and institutional funds. In other words, Perkins Loans are "campus-based": The schools independently determine eligibility, advance funds, collect payments and make decisions concerning loan forgiveness.

Low-interest Perkins Loans are intended to assist undergraduate and graduate students with exceptional financial need. Customarily, a student obtains Perkins Loans in concert with other financial aid devices such as Stafford Loans, Pell Grants, private loans, work study and scholarships. Perkins Loans are often a crucial element in financial aid packages. Under the program, undergraduates may borrow up to $4000 and graduate students may borrow up to $6000 per year. 20 U.S.C. § 1087dd(a)(2)(A).

In 1985, Congress reauthorized and amended the 1965 HEA, renaming one of the loan programs in honor of Carl D. Perkins, long-time Chairman of the House Education and Labor Committee. At the same time, Congress amended the statute to encourage graduates to work in various areas of public service, such as teaching and the Peace Corps. This encouragement took the form of partial or total Perkins Loan cancellation. See 20 U.S.C. § 1087ee. Subsequent amendments to the HEA further expanded the categories of public service that qualify for loan cancellation to include law enforcement, nursing and additional types of childcare.

The section of the statute pivotal to this appeal was added by a 1992 Amendment. *See* Pub. L. 102–325, § 465(a)(5), 106 Stat. 448 (July 23, 1992). It provides that "loans shall be canceled . . . for service": "(I) as a full-time employee of a public or private nonprofit child or family service agency who is providing, or supervising the provision of, services to high-risk children who are from low-income communities and the families of such children." 20 U.S.C. § 1087ee(a)(2). The HEA defines "low-income communities" as "communities in which there is a high concentration of children eligible to be counted under Title I of the Elementary and Secondary Education Act of 1965." 20 U.S.C. § 1087ii(a). The HEA defines "high-risk children" as "individuals under the age of 21 who are low-income or at risk of abuse or neglect, have been abused or neglected, have serious emotional, mental, or behavioral disturbances, reside in placements outside their homes, or are involved in the juvenile justice system." Id. at § 1087ii(b). The HEA does not define the term "providing . . . services." As noted, in order to cancel Perkins Loans, a borrower applies to the lending school, which, rather than the DOE, bears the responsibility for determining the applicant's eligibility for loan cancellation.

Since the 1992 amendments, the DOE, through handbooks and advice via telephone and e-mail, has wrestled with determining and giving participating institutions guidance about eligibility for loan cancellation for child or family service. The extent to which we are required to defer to these efforts is the critical issue on this appeal.

In 1995, the DOE enacted a regulation purportedly implementing the child or family service cancellation provision. In doing so, the DOE did not add institutional gloss or agency wisdom but rather incorporated verbatim the statute, 20 U.S.C. § 1087ee(a)(2)(I), into its own regulation–34 C.F.R § 674.56(b)(1). It provides:

> An institution must cancel up to 100 percent of the outstanding balance on a borrower's Federal Perkins or NDSL made on or after July 23, 1992, for service as a full-time employee in a public or private nonprofit child or family service agency who is providing, or supervising the provision of, services to high-risk children who are from low-income communities and the families of these children.

34 C.F.R § 674.56(b)(1). In addition to the rule, each year the Federal Student Aid Office of the DOE issues a Student Financial Aid Handbook to participating institutions to assist them in responding to loan cancellation requests. The Handbooks introduced a new qualification for loan cancellation based on child or family service not found in the statute, requiring that the services be extended "only" to high-risk children:

> To receive loan cancellation for being employed at a child or family services agency, a borrower must be providing services only to high-risk children who are from low-income communities. The borrower may also be providing services to adults, but these adults must be members of the families of the children for whom services are provided. The services provided to adults must be secondary to the services provided to the high-risk children. [DOE] has determined that an elementary or secondary school or a hospital is not an eligible employing agency.

DOE Student Financial Aid Handbook (2001–2002).

. . .

De La Mota applied for loan cancellation in 2000 through three academic institutions: City University of New York ("CUNY") and Manhattanville College where she did her undergraduate work, and New York Law School ("NYLS"). In the ACS Child Support Litigation Unit, she litigates paternity actions and prosecutes child support cases. For two years her loans were forgiven, but in the third year, one school, NYLS, rejected her application and demanded back payment for the previous two years. CUNY and Manhattanville continued to forgive her loans.

The DOE advised NYLS not to cancel her loans, because the services she provided to children were neither "direct" nor "only to high-risk children." The word "only" originated in the Handbooks, not the HEA statute or the DOE regulation. The requirement of "direct" services is not contained in the HEA statute, the DOE regulation, or the Handbooks. Rather it first appeared in an April 12, 2001 informal e-mail from a DOE Program Specialist to NYLS: "The borrower must be providing services directly to the high-risk children. In this case, the borrower is providing services to the City of New York as an attorney, she is not providing services directly to high-risk children." Subsequently, a letter from a DOE Ombudsman to De La Mota defended and relied on the "directly" and "only" requirements of the Handbooks and e-mail. Upon advice from the Program Specialist that De La Mota's services and supervision of the provision of services were not "directly" nor "only" targeted to low-income, high-risk children, NYLS rejected her application, informing her that the DOE had determined that her position at ACS did not qualify for loan cancellation, reversed her previous cancellations, and directed her to make back payments. . . .

Chungata, also a NYLS graduate, applied for loan forgiveness in 2001 based on his ACS employment where he also litigates paternity actions and prosecutes child support cases. NYLS informed Chungata that the DOE deemed him ineligible for loan cancellation. This decision was based solely on the e-mail from the Program Specialist concerning De La Mota's application for loan cancellation.

Doron prosecutes neglect and child abuse cases for ACS in Brooklyn Family Court. He also petitions the court to determine permanent placement for abused and neglected children. He applied for cancellation through Tulane and Rutgers, the two schools from which he had received Perkins Loans. His application for loan cancellation drew conflicting responses: Tulane approved his application and canceled his debt, but Rutgers rejected his application and referred him to the DOE. When Doron contacted the DOE, the same Program Specialist e-mailed him that he was ineligible for cancellation because "[he] represent[s] the City of New York. . . . [He does] not provide services directly and exclusively to high-risk children." The Program Specialist also explained, "The Department of Education does not make the determination of eligibility for Federal Perkins Loan Program cancellation benefits. This is the responsibility of the college or university. . . ." Despite the DOE's expressed lack of authority, it nonetheless issued an after-the-fact endorsement of Rutgers' rejection of Doron, stating: "We concur with the decision of Rutgers University to deny [Doron's] request for a cancellation of [his] Federal Perkins Loan."

The Appellants then sought judicial review under the Administrative Procedure Act of the DOE's interpretation of § 1087ee(a)(2)(I) and the denial of loan cancellation benefits. *See* 5 U.S.C. § 701. They also named their respective law schools as defendants. The DOE moved for summary judgment, which the District Court granted.

⋅   ⋅   ⋅

As an initial matter, we note that the Appellants appear comfortably to meet the statute's textual qualifications for loan forgiveness. They are "full-time employee[s] of a public . . . nonprofit child or family service agency" who are "providing . . . services to high-risk children who are from low-income communities and the families of such children." 20 U.S.C. § 1087ee(a)(2)(I). The legislative history makes clear that the statute was intended "to encourage qualified individuals to seek [such] employment." Congress thought cancellation subsidies were necessary because, traditionally, child and family service work tended to be low-paying, and the subsidies would encourage qualified graduates to enter the field.

Notwithstanding the text of the statute and its intended purposes, the DOE recommended rejection of the applications for loan forgiveness by applying its interpretation of the statute as articulated through the two agency Handbooks in the record and a few *ad hoc* e-mails. . . .

⋅   ⋅   ⋅

The DOE representative who explained the rejection to De La Mota justified his understanding of the "exclusively" requirement as follows: "If even a small percentage of the children a borrower was providing services to did not meet that criteria, the borrower would not qualify for a child or family services cancellation." The requirement of utter exclusivity generates a result impossible to administer and at odds with Congress' goals in establishing the loan cancellation program.

Perhaps most importantly, the DOE interpreted the statute in an advisory capacity. The DOE argued in its brief: "Plaintiffs, however, cannot impute to DOE the positions taken by CUNY Law School or Tulane University.... As DOE has maintained throughout this litigation, it is the individual educational institutions that render decisions upon loan cancellation, not DOE." In proceedings below, the DOE conceded that it "does not make the determination of whether a borrower qualifies for a cancellation but *upon request provides guidance* to institutions that make the decisions." (emphasis added). We are especially disinclined to defer to an agency when it does not purport to speak authoritatively. In the past we have declined to show an agency deference when "there is no indication in the record of the process through which [the agency] arrived at its interpretation" and the agency itself "labels its interpretation as 'tentative'" because "we cannot say with confidence that [the agency's] interpretation came about as the result of a reasoned process." *Rabin v. Wilson–Coker*, 362 F.3d 190, 198 (2d Cir. 2004).

In sum, the DOE's interpretation—the addition of "only" in the Handbooks, coupled with the use of "directly" and "exclusively" in an advisory role—lacks the power to persuade, and the DOE fails to show thoroughness in its consideration or validity in its reasoning. Thus, even assuming arguendo that the agency offered consistent guidance, we are not bound to defer to its construction of the statute.

20 U.S.C. § 1087ee(a)(2)(I) provides loan cancellation to anyone who, as "as a full-time employee of a public or private nonprofit child or family service agency ... is providing, or supervising the provision of, services to high-risk children who are from low-income communities and the families of such children." Congress expected that the indeterminate elements of this formulation would be clarified by regulation, but the Secretary has not provided such guidance. The resulting uncertainty impairs incentives for students to undertake careers aiding high-risk children and for educational institutions to train these students-schools must choose between financial risk and cheating their graduates.

Because we find no basis for deference to the several *ad hoc* or unreasoned manuals and e-mails issued by DOE employees who lack authority to make policy, we are left for now with nothing but the statutory text and the apparent congressional intent to encourage qualified individuals to borrow the costs of preparing to serve children in poor communities. While we agree with the DOE that this evident purpose would be defeated unless the provided services target and reach at risk children predominately, a more restrictive reading of the statute is not compelled. Therefore, unless and until the DOE adopts such a reading in some form that commands deference or persuades, we will adhere to the only available analysis.

De La Mota, Chungata, and Doron are full-time employees of a public nonprofit child service agency. Through litigation, they provide services to neglected, abused, or unsupported children, who predominately are by definition the high-risk children targeted by the statute. De La Mota, Chungata, and Doron qualify for cancellation of their Perkins Loan obligations.

We reverse the judgment of the District Court and remand for further proceedings consistent with this opinion.

Note on Student Loan Debt

Financial Aid continues to be an important determinant of whether a high school graduate will be able to attend college. It also means that many students graduate from universities and colleges with large amounts of debt. Although the average price per year at public universities has been rising about 6 percent annually, the federal government has *reduced* the amount of money it provides to low-income students in the form of Pell grants over the same period. In 1975, the maximum Pell Grant given by the federal government to low-income students covered approximately eighty-four percent of the cost of attending a public college or university. Today it covers only 36 percent. Of the current institutional expenditures on student aid, moreover, 52 percent, or more than $45 billion, are not based on need. Kati Haycock, *Promise Abandoned: How Policy Choices and Institutional Practices Restrict College Opportunities,* Higher Education Trust (2006). Education officials report that the reduction in need-based aid was caused by heightened competition among colleges for students who will raise the school's grade and score averages that are used by rankings such as the one by *U.S. News & World Report.* Merit-based aid tends to go to students who come from wealthier families. In addition, the bulk of the federal government's education tax benefits go to middle and upper income families. The result is that the cost of attending four years colleges paid by families who earn less than $35,000 has risen by several hundred dollars in the past few years, while the amount paid by students from families earning between $63,000 and $95,000 has remained flat at public universities and has fallen by almost $900 at private colleges. Kim Clark, *Reports: Needy Students Got Less Scholarship Money,* U.S. NEWS & WORLD REP., Oct. 24, 2006, *available at* http://www.usnews.com/usnews/biztech/articles/061024/24finaid.htm.

Mirroring the move from grants to loans by colleges and universities, the federal government now provides more aid in the form of loans instead of grants. For the 1991–1992 school year, 63 percent of federal aid to undergraduate students took the form of grants, while only 35 percent were loans. By the 2006–2007 academic year, this ratio had flipped to 46 percent grants and 49 percent loans. COLLEGE BOARD, TRENDS IN STUDENT AID 15 (2007) *available at* http://www.collegeboard.com/prod_down loads/about/news_info/trends/trends_aid_07.pdf.

State governments have increased the amount of money they provide to students on the basis of need, but they continue to provide much larger amounts in merit-based scholarship programs. Sandy Baum and Lucie Lapovsky, in their report for the College Board, *Tuition Discounting: Not Just a Private College Practice,* found that "only about 40 percent of the institutional grant aid in the public four-year sector fills documented financial need, while more than 60 percent of the institutional aid in the private sector and the public two-year sector is merit-based." In part the difference reflects the fact that most athletic scholarships do not go to financially needy students. Doug Lederman, *Documenting the Shift to Merit,* INSIDE HIGHER ED., Sept. 12, 2006, *available at* http://www.insidehighered.com/news/2006/09/12/discounting.

Individual institutions have attempted to increase the enrollment of students from low-income families by increasing the amount of grant aid. Princeton in 1998 announced that it would replace loans with grants for all students from families with annual incomes less than $46,500. In 2003, it extended the policy to all undergraduates. In 2004 Harvard announced that it would not ask parents who earned less than $40,000 a year to contribute any money for their children's education. In 2006 that qualifying income was raised to $60,000. Stanford followed suit in 2006, and the

University of Pennsylvania said it would replace loans with grants for students from families with incomes of $50,000 or less. Karen Arenson, *Harvard Extends Breaks for Low–Income Parents*, N.Y. TIMES, Mar. 31, 2006, at A10. In 2007, Swarthmore College announced a similar plan to replace loans with grants for all students who qualify for financial aid. Dan Hardy et al., *No-Loan Plan at Swarthmore*, PHILA. INQUIRER, Dec. 13, 2007, at A1. Several public universities also offer special assistance to students from low-income families. The University of North Carolina at Chapel Hill, for example, has established the Carolina Covenant, which provides enough grant money for low-income students that they do not need to borrow to pay for their education. *Grappling with the Access Problem*, INSIDE HIGHER ED., Sept. 12, 2006, *available at* http://inside highered.com/news/2006/09/12/unc.

In 2007 and 2008, colleges and universities announced new financial aid initiatives designed to increase access to students based on need. Harvard capped tuition for families with incomes of up to $180,000 at ten percent of their earnings. Kim Clark, *The Markdown at Harvard*, U.S. NEWS & WORLD REP., Dec. 24, 2007, at 66. Under a new Yale system, families earning $60,000 to $120,000 will contribute between 1 to 10 percent of their income per year, while families earning between $120,000 to $200,000 will pay an average of 10 percent of their income. Families earning less than $60,000 will not have to contribute. Eric Hoover, *Yale Follows Harvard in Announcing Big Student–Aid Jump*, CHRON. HIGHER EDUC., Jan. 15, 2008, *available at* http://chronicle. com/daily/2008/01/1235n.htm.

Looking at all public and private four-year institutions, the proportion of Pell Grant recipients decreased 7 percent between 2004–2005 and 2006–2007. Robert Shireman of the Institute for College Access and Success blames this decrease on the decreased purchasing power of the Pell Grant, which caused many needy students to turn to two-year colleges. Karin Fischer, *Wealthy Colleges Show Drop in Enrollments of Needy Students*, CHRON. HIGHER EDUC. Apr. 24, 2008, *available at* http://chronicle.com/ free/2008/04/2604n.htm

In response to these concerns, Congress passed the College Cost Reduction and Access Act of 2007 (CCRAA). The House Education and Labor Committee indicated that one of the goals of the legislation was to "ensure that all qualified students, regardless of their background, . . . [have] access to higher education[,] . . . and graduate to achieve their goals." H.R. REP. NO. 110–210, at 41 (2007). The Act reduced federal subsidies to private loan companies, increased federal grants, reduced interest rates on federally subsidized loans for low-income students, capped repayments at a percentage of a college graduate's income, and offered loan forgiveness for students who hold public service jobs for ten years. Ian Shapira, *Bush Signs Sweeping Student Loan Bill Into Law, Adding an Asterisk*, WASH. POST, Sept. 28, 2007, at A6.

In 2008, many lenders stopped offering college loans to students. The lenders claimed that the cut in subsidies made it impossible for them to offer student loans at a profitable rate, and that the global credit crisis had elevated their capital costs. The Democratic senators responsible for passing CCRA responded that the lenders were overstating the impact of the cut in subsidies, and that the cuts were helping students. David Cho & Maria Glod, *Credit Crisis May Make College Loans More Costly; Some Firms Stop Lending to Students*, WASH. POST, Mar. 3, 2008, at A1. In 2008, the Department of Education announced a plan to purchase college loans from lenders to stabilize the student loan market. Sam Dillon & Jonathan Glater, *Education Agency's Plan Shores Up Market for Loans to College Students*, N.Y. TIMES, May 22, 2008, at A22.

The CCRAA included a new system of student loan repayment to assist graduates who take low-income positions after graduating with high debt. Under the new law, graduates may elect to repay government guaranteed loans under an income contingent repayment plan. Repayments under this plan are limited to 15 percent of the borrower's discretionary income, defined as adjusted gross income minus 150 percent of the poverty level. After twenty-five years, any remaining debt is forgiven. If the graduate works in a full-time public service job for ten years, their loans may be forgiven after only ten years. One of the main purposes of the law was to assist law school graduates who, like the plaintiffs in *De La Mota*, wish to pursue public interest careers after law school to be able to afford the high cost of legal education. As Professor Schrag has noted, the new law will not only help lawyers and law students who desire public interest careers, but will also help "all high-debt/lower-income borrowers to be able to pursue long-term public service careers in many different fields of work." Philip G. Schrag, *Federal Student Loan Repayment Assistance for Public Interest Lawyers and Other Employees of Governments and Nonprofit Organizations*, 36 HOFSTRA L. REV. 27, 35 (2007).

STUDENTS AND THE LAW

From the founding of the first colonial colleges through most of the nineteenth century, faculty were responsible for overseeing student conduct as well as teaching:

> Nineteenth-century . . . [c]olleges tended to be small, financially shaky, and extremely authoritarian. The life of the mind was not unknown, but neither was it usually central. The curriculum was largely prescribed, and the pedagogy consisted mainly of daily assignments and recitations. Extracurricular life was also closely regulated, and an enormous amount of energy seems to have gone into keeping unruly students from misbehaving. Corporal punishment was common, and the students often responded with violent rioting.[a]

Toward the end of the nineteenth century, as more faculty were scholars and colleges and universities became less religious, the relationship between faculty and students changed. President Timothy Dwight of Yale replaced the extreme code of 1745 with what Frederick Rudolph termed the "treat-them-like-gentlemen" approach, or more simply "treat them like men instead of like minions of the devil."[b] In the twentieth century, most faculty withdrew from the disciplinary process, turning it over to administrators and/or students,[c] and colleges and universities abandoned most of their *in loco parentis* role.

In recent years, however, tort and contract law have been used to impose obligations to students on schools. Beginning in the 1960s, courts increasingly have intervened to protect the constitutional rights of students including due process, free speech, and the free exercise of religion. Courts have also imposed duties on colleges and universities to protect students from foreseeable harms. As you read the materials in this part, consider whether these judicial decisions have strengthened or weakened the academic experience of students.

---

a. CHRISTOPHER JENCKS & DAVID RIESMAN, THE ACADEMIC REVOLUTION 29–30 (1968).

b. FREDERICK RUDOLPH, THE AMERICAN COLLEGE & UNIVERSITY: A HISTORY 107 (John R. Thelin ed., 1990) (1962).

c. LAWRENCE R. VEYSEY, THE EMERGENCE OF THE AMERICAN UNIVERSITY 312 (1965).

CHAPTER 12

STUDENT RIGHTS AND RESPONSIBILITIES

A. ACADEMIC STANDARDS

Examinations and grading are central to the judgments faculty make about student academic achievement. This section examines what rights, if any, students have to challenge those judgments. May an "unfair" grade or exam be successfully challenged in court? Does the answer depend on whether the student is enrolled in a public or private institution of higher education? Should it?

Board of Curators of the University of Missouri v. Horowitz

Supreme Court of the United States, 1978.
435 U.S. 78, 98 S.Ct. 948, 55 L.Ed.2d 124.

■ MR. JUSTICE REHNQUIST delivered the opinion of the Court.

Respondent, a student at the University of Missouri–Kansas City Medical School, was dismissed by petitioner officials of the school during her final year of study for failure to meet academic standards. Respondent sued petitioners under 42 U.S.C. § 1983 ... alleging ... that petitioners had not accorded her procedural due process prior to her dismissal. The District Court, after conducting a full trial, concluded that respondent had been afforded all of the rights guaranteed her by the Fourteenth Amendment to the United States Constitution and dismissed her complaint. The Court of Appeals for the Eighth Circuit reversed.... We granted certiorari to consider what procedures must be accorded to a student at a state educational institution whose dismissal may constitute a deprivation of "liberty" or "property" within the meaning of the Fourteenth Amendment....

Respondent was admitted with advanced standing to the Medical School in the fall of 1971. During the final years of a student's education at the school, the student is required to pursue in "rotational units" academic and clinical studies pertaining to various medical disciplines such as obstetrics-gynecology, pediatrics, and surgery. Each student's academic performance at the School is evaluated on a periodic basis by the Council on Evaluation, a body composed of both faculty and students, which can recommend various actions including probation and dismissal. The recommendations of the Council are reviewed by the Coordinating Committee, a body composed solely of faculty members, and must ultimately be approved by the Dean. Students are not typically allowed to appear before either the Council or the Coordinating Committee on the occasion of their review of the student's academic performance.

685

In the spring of respondent's first year of study, several faculty members . . . noted that respondent's "performance was below that of her peers in all clinical patient-oriented settings," that she was erratic in her attendance at clinical sessions, and that she lacked a critical concern for personal hygiene. Upon the recommendation of the Council on Evaluation, respondent was advanced to her second and final year on a probationary basis.

[During her second year, respondent's clinical skills were rated "unsatisfactory." The Council concluded that she should not be considered for graduation in June and that, absent "radical improvement," she should be dropped from the school.

As an "appeal" to the decision not to permit her to graduate, it was arranged for respondent to spend time with seven practicing physicians. Two of them recommended that she be graduated on schedule, two that she be dropped from the school, and three that she not be permitted to graduate but be retained at the school on probation.] Upon receipt of these recommendations, the Council on Evaluation reaffirmed its prior position.

[After respondent received a "low-satisfactory" rank on her surgery rotation and a negative evaluation on her emergency rotation, the Council unanimously recommended dismissing her. The Dean and the Coordinating Committee approved the dismissal, and the Provost sustained the dismissal after the respondent appealed.]

To be entitled to the procedural protections of the Fourteenth Amendment, respondent must in a case such as this demonstrate that her dismissal from the school deprived her of either a "liberty" or a "property" interest. Respondent has never alleged that she was deprived of a property interest. Because property interests are creatures of state law, *Perry v. Sindermann,* 408 U.S. 593, 599–603 (1972), respondent would have been required to show at trial that her seat at the Medical School was a "property" interest recognized by Missouri state law. Instead, respondent argued that her dismissal deprived her of "liberty" by substantially impairing her opportunities to continue her medical education or to return to employment in a medically related field.

. . .

We need not decide, however, whether respondent's dismissal deprived her of a liberty interest in pursuing a medical career. Nor need we decide whether respondent's dismissal infringed any other interest constitutionally protected against deprivation without procedural due process. Assuming the existence of a liberty or property interest, respondent has been awarded at least as much due process as the Fourteenth Amendment requires. The school fully informed respondent of the faculty's dissatisfaction with her clinical progress and the danger that this posed to timely graduation and continued enrollment. The ultimate decision to dismiss respondent was careful and deliberate. These procedures were sufficient under the Due Process Clause of the Fourteenth Amendment. We agree with the District Court that respondent "was afforded full procedural due process by the [school]. In fact, the Court is of the opinion, and so finds, that the school went beyond [constitutionally required] procedural due process by affording [respondent] the opportunity to be examined by seven independent physicians in order to be absolutely certain that their grading of the [respondent] in her medical skills was correct."

In *Goss v. Lopez*, 419 U.S. 565 (1975), we held that due process requires, in connection with the suspension of a student from public school for disciplinary reasons, "that the student be given oral or written notice of the charges against him and, if he denies them, an explanation of the evidence the authorities have and an opportunity to present his side of the story." The Court of Appeals apparently read *Goss* as requiring some type of formal hearing at which respondent could defend her academic ability and performance. All that *Goss* required was an "informal give-and-take" between the student and the administrative body dismissing him that would, at least, give the student "the opportunity to characterize his conduct and put it in what he deems the proper context." But we have frequently emphasized that "[t]he very nature of due process negates any concept of inflexible procedures universally applicable to every imaginable situation." *Cafeteria Workers v. McElroy*, 367 U.S. 886, 895 (1961). The need for flexibility is well illustrated by the significant difference between the failure of a student to meet academic standards and the violation by a student of valid rules of conduct. This difference calls for far less stringent procedural requirements in the case of an academic dismissal.[3]

Since the issue first arose 50 years ago, state and lower federal courts have recognized that there are distinct differences between decisions to suspend or dismiss a student for disciplinary purposes and similar actions taken for academic reasons which may call for hearings in connection with the former but not the latter. Thus, in *Barnard v. Inhabitants of Shelburne*, 216 Mass. 19, 102 N.E. 1095 (1913), the Supreme Judicial Court of Massachusetts rejected an argument . . . that school officials must also grant a hearing before excluding a student on academic grounds. According to the court, disciplinary cases have "no application. . . . Misconduct is a very different matter from failure to attain a standard of excellence in studies. A determination as to the facts involves investigation of a quite different kind. A public hearing may be regarded as helpful to the ascertainment of misconduct and useless or harmful in finding out the truth as to scholarship."

A similar conclusion has been reached by the other state courts to consider the issue. . . . Indeed, until the instant decision by the Court of Appeals for the Eighth Circuit, the Courts of Appeals were also unanimous in concluding that dismissals for academic (as opposed to disciplinary) cause do not necessitate a hearing before the school's decisionmaking body. These prior decisions of state and federal courts, over a period of 60 years, unanimously holding that formal hearings before decisionmaking bodies need not be held in the case of academic dismissals, cannot be rejected lightly.

Reason, furthermore, clearly supports the perception of these decisions. A school is an academic institution, not a courtroom or administrative

---

3. We fully recognize that the deprivation to which respondent was subjected—dismissal from a graduate medical school—was more severe than the 10–day suspension to which the high school students were subjected in *Goss*. And a relevant factor in determining the nature of the requisite due process is "the private interest that [was] affected by the official action." *Mathews v. Eldridge*, 424 U.S. 319, 335 (1976). But the severity of the deprivation is only one of several factors that must be weighed in deciding the exact due process owed. We conclude that considering all relevant factors, including the evaluative nature of the inquiry and the significant and historically supported interest of the school in preserving its present framework for academic evaluations, a hearing is not required by the Due Process Clause of the Fourteenth Amendment.

hearing room. In *Goss,* this Court felt that suspensions of students for disciplinary reasons have a sufficient resemblance to traditional judicial and administrative factfinding to call for a "hearing" before the relevant school authority. . . .

. . .

Even in the context of a school disciplinary proceeding, however, the Court stopped short of requiring a *formal* hearing since "further formalizing the suspension process and escalating its formality and adversary nature may not only make it too costly as a regular disciplinary tool but also destroy its effectiveness as a part of the teaching process."

Academic evaluations of a student, in contrast to disciplinary determinations, bear little resemblance to the judicial and administrative factfinding proceedings to which we have traditionally attached a full-hearing requirement. In *Goss,* the school's decision to suspend the students rested on factual conclusions that the individual students had participated in demonstrations that had disrupted classes, attacked a police officer, or caused physical damage to school property. The requirement of a hearing, where the student could present his side of the factual issue, could under such circumstances "provide a meaningful hedge against erroneous action." The decision to dismiss respondent, by comparison, rested on the academic judgment of school officials that she did not have the necessary clinical ability to perform adequately as a medical doctor and was making insufficient progress toward that goal. Such a judgment is by its nature more subjective and evaluative than the typical factual questions presented in the average disciplinary decision. Like the decision of an individual professor as to the proper grade for a student in his course, the determination whether to dismiss a student for academic reasons requires an expert evaluation of cumulative information and is not readily adapted to the procedural tools of judicial or administrative decisionmaking.

Under such circumstances, we decline to ignore the historic judgment of educators and thereby formalize the academic dismissal process by requiring a hearing. The educational process is not by nature adversary; instead it centers around a continuing relationship between faculty and students, "one in which the teacher must occupy many roles—educator, adviser, friend, and, at times, parent-substitute." *Goss v. Lopez,* 419 U.S., at 594 (Powell, J., dissenting). This is especially true as one advances through the varying regimes of the educational system, and the instruction becomes both more individualized and more specialized. In *Goss,* this Court concluded that the value of some form of hearing in a disciplinary context outweighs any resulting harm to the academic environment. Influencing this conclusion was clearly the belief that disciplinary proceedings, in which the teacher must decide whether to punish a student for disruptive or insubordinate behavior, may automatically bring an adversary flavor to the normal student-teacher relationship. The same conclusion does not follow in the academic context. We decline to further enlarge the judicial presence in the academic community and thereby risk deterioration of many beneficial aspects of the faculty-student relationship. We recognize, as did the Massachusetts Supreme Judicial Court over 60 years ago, that a hearing may be "useless or harmful in finding out the truth as to scholarship." *Barnard v. Inhabitants of Shelburne,* 216 Mass., at 23, 102 N.E., at 1097.

"Judicial interposition in the operation of the public school system of the Nation raises problems requiring care and restraint.... By and large, public education in our Nation is committed to the control of state and local authorities." *Epperson v. Arkansas*, 393 U.S. 97, 104 (1968). We see no reason to intrude on that historic control in this case.[6]

. . .

The judgment of the Court of Appeals is therefore reversed.

Questions and Comments on *Horowitz*

1. In *Waugh v. Board of Trustees*, 237 U.S. 589 (1915), the Supreme Court upheld a state ban on membership in a fraternity at the University of Mississippi against a substantive due process challenge brought by college students. In *Hamilton v. Board of Regents of California*, 293 U.S. 245 (1934), the Court similarly upheld a Regent's rule that students must take a course in military science and tactics. In justifying its ruling in *Hamilton*, the Court emphasized that attending college is a privilege not a right, a distinction that has fallen out of favor in recent years. *See, e.g.*, Roy Lucas, *The Right to Higher Education*, 41 J. HIGHER EDUC. 55 (1970); William W. Van Alstyne, *The Demise of the Right–Privilege Distinction in Constitutional Law*, 81 HARV. L. REV. 1439 (1968).

2. In *Horowitz*, the Court specifically declined to decide whether an academic dismissal from a college or university violates a liberty or property interest. Instead, it simply assumed such an interest was at stake for purposes of the analysis. Should lower courts find that students have a property or liberty interest under the Due Process Clause in completing a college education? If so, is that interest violated by a university's failure to follow its own grade review procedures?

3. On what basis does the Court distinguish *Goss*? Is this distinction convincing? Should an academic dismissal process be as adversarial as a disciplinary procedure? Does the majority give clear guidance about what procedure, if any, is required in academic dismissals?

4. In *Horowitz*, the Court described the university's decision to dismiss a student for academic reasons as "subjective and evaluative," but also noted that such a judgment "requires an expert evaluation of cumulative information." Do the different descriptions of academic decisions (subjective versus expert) provide different reasons for the Court to defer to the university on academic matters? Does the deference afforded to academic decisions by *Horowitz* permit a university to change its standards of evaluation after a student has been admitted to an academic program? In *Ezekwo v. New York City Health & Hospitals Corp.*, 940 F.2d 775, 785 (2d Cir. 1991), the court held that a medical student was denied due process when the school changed the selection criteria for the position of "Chief Resident" from a rotational to a merit

---

6. Respondent contends in passing that she was not dismissed because of "clinical incompetence," an academic inquiry, but for disciplinary reasons similar to those involved in *Goss*.... In this regard, respondent notes that the school warned her that significant improvement was needed not only in the area of clinical performance but also in her personal hygiene and in keeping to her clinical schedules. The record, however, leaves no doubt that respondent was dismissed for purely academic reasons, a fact assumed without discussion by the lower courts. Personal hygiene and timeliness may be as important factors in a school's determination of whether a student will make a good medical doctor as the student's ability to take a case history or diagnose an illness. Questions of personal hygiene and timeliness, of course, may seem more analogous to traditional factfinding than other inquires that a school may make in academically evaluating a student. But in so evaluating the student, the school considers and weighs a variety of factors, not all of which, as noted earlier, are adaptable to the factfinding hearing. And the critical faculty-student relationship may still be injured if a hearing is required.

based system midway during the student's residency without informing the student of the change.

Regents of the University of Michigan v. Ewing

Supreme Court of the United States, 1985.
474 U.S. 214, 106 S.Ct. 507, 88 L.Ed.2d 523.

[The opinion is set forth at pages 341–45, *supra*.]

Questions and Comments on *Ewing*

1. In the wake of *Ewing*, lower courts have disagreed whether continuing a college or university education is a constitutionally protected liberty or property interest. *See* Fernand N. Dutile, *Students and Due Process in Higher Education: Of Interests and Procedures*, 2 FLA. COASTAL L. J. 243 (2001). *See generally* Robert Firester, *Does 42 U.S.C. 1983 Redress Arbitrary, Capricious, or Unfair Student Dismissals from State Colleges*, 22 DAYTON L. REV. 209 (1997); Thomas A. Schweitzer, *Academic Challenge Cases: Should Judicial Review Extend to Academic Evaluations of Students*, 41 AM. U. L. REV. 267 (1992).

2. In *Ewing*, the Court left open a "narrow avenue" for judicial review of academic dismissals if the dismissal constitutes "such a substantial departure from accepted academic norms as to demonstrate that the faculty did not exercise professional judgment." What would constitute a substantial departure from academic norms?

3. *Horowitz* and *Ewing* both involved public universities. On what basis, if any, may a student in a private college or university challenge a dismissal?

4. In *Green v. Lehman*, 544 F.Supp. 260 (D.Md.1982), a student at the United States Naval Academy challenged his academic dismissal. The student was dismissed after he failed to achieve the minimum required GPA for two semesters in a row. The student complained that he should not have been dismissed because his cumulative GPA for the four-year period exceeded the minimum standard. *Id.* at 262. The court noted that narrowly prescribed judicial review of military discharge procedures may be appropriate in some circumstances. The court held that in this circumstance, however, where the student failed to meet clearly established academic requirements, judicial review was not appropriate. *Id.* at 263.

In re Susan M. v. New York Law School

Court of Appeals of New York, 1990.
76 N.Y.2d 241, 556 N.E.2d 1104, 557 N.Y.S.2d 297.

■ ALEXANDER, J.

In this article 78 proceeding, petitioner challenges her dismissal for academic deficiency from respondent law school. . . . Petitioner enrolled at respondent law school in the fall of 1985. In accordance with respondent's published rules, petitioner was automatically placed on academic probation at the end of her first year for having failed to achieve a 2.0, or "C" cumulative average. The law school rules further provided that a student on probation who thereafter fails to achieve both a semester and a cumulative average of 2.0 is subject to academic dismissal at the discretion of the law school's Academic Status Committee (Committee). Such a student, however, has the right to present written and oral statements to the Committee explaining his or her failure to meet the school's academic standards.

Although petitioner earned a cumulative average of 2.001 at the end of her third semester, in her fourth semester her average dropped to 1.546, lowering her cumulative average to 1.89. Consequently she was notified that the Academic Status Committee would be considering whether she would be permitted to continue her studies. She submitted a written statement to the Committee, describing factors that she claimed affected her performance. In this written statement, petitioner blamed her less than "C" average on the grades she received in two of her fourth semester courses, namely, Constitutional Law II, in which she received a "C–," and Corporations, in which she received a "D." She argued that these grades did not fairly and accurately reflect the knowledge she had demonstrated on the exams in those courses. Petitioner also appeared before the Committee to state her case orally. She contends that when she attempted to raise the subject of the two grades, she was immediately interrupted by the Committee chairperson who told her that the Committee would not consider them. Petitioner then gave other reasons for her below average performance. They were unavailing and the Committee voted unanimously to dismiss her for failure to meet the law school's academic standards. Petitioner requested reconsideration of her case, and submitted an additional statement offering still further reasons for her substandard academic performance. The Committee accepted the new submission, but declined to reconsider its decision.

Con Law 2 (C–)

Corporations (D)

... [P]etitioner alleges that the Committee's decision to dismiss her was arbitrary and capricious....

Petitioner also alleges that when she met with the Corporations professor to discuss her grade, the professor told her that she was given zero credit on an essay question worth 30% of the exam because she analyzed the problem under both Delaware law and New York law when only Delaware law was called for, that her answer did correctly analyze the problem under Delaware law and that she would have received full credit on this question had she only refrained from mentioning New York law. Notwithstanding petitioner's claim that she only mentioned New York law to get extra credit, the professor allegedly insisted that petitioner gave two answers to the question, thereby indicating that she did not know which one was correct, and was therefore not entitled to any credit. Petitioner also alleges that the professor advised her that points were deducted from the Corporations exam because she had misused the term "oppressive conduct" and because the exam was written in the style of a first-year student.

Corps Prof,

The responding affidavits of respondent's Dean of Academic Affairs and the Corporations professor asserted that the grading of the exam was purely a matter of academic discretion and that the exam grade was based upon the over-all quality of petitioner's answer and not on any narrow, formalistic concerns.

Supreme Court dismissed the petition, concluding that petitioner had not demonstrated that her dismissal was arbitrary, capricious or ordered in bad faith. The Appellate Division rejected most of petitioner's claims, but reversed Supreme Court and granted the petition to the extent of remanding the matter to respondent for further consideration of the Corporations grade to determine whether the grade given on the exam, including the disputed essay, was a rational exercise of discretion. Respondent appeals and petitioner cross-appeals....

– Rational exercise of discretion

. . .

Strong policy considerations militate against the intervention of courts in controversies relating to an educational institution's judgment of a student's academic performance (*Matter of Olsson v. Board of Higher Educ.*, 49 N.Y.2d 408, 413; . . . *see also, Board of Curators, Univ. of Mo. v. Horowitz*, 435 U.S. 78, 89–90). Unlike disciplinary actions taken against a student, institutional assessments of a student's academic performance, whether in the form of particular grades received or actions taken because a student has been judged to be scholastically deficient, necessarily involve academic determinations requiring the special expertise of educators. These determinations play a legitimate and important role in the academic setting since it is by determining that a student's academic performance satisfies the standards set by the institution, and ultimately, by conferring a diploma upon a student who satisfies the institution's course of study, that the institution, in effect, certifies to society that the student possesses the knowledge and skills required by the chosen discipline. Thus, to preserve the integrity of the credentials conferred by educational institutions, the courts have long been reluctant to intervene in controversies involving purely academic determinations.

Accordingly, although we have emphasized that the determinations of educational institutions as to the academic performance of their students are not completely beyond the scope of judicial review that review is limited to the question of whether the challenged determination was arbitrary and capricious, irrational, made in bad faith or contrary to Constitution or statute. This standard has rarely been satisfied in the context of challenges to academic determinations because the courts have repeatedly refused to become involved in the pedagogical evaluation of academic performance. Thus, we have declined, in the absence of bad faith, to compel a university to award a diploma where a student alleged that he had failed a final comprehensive exam because of his reliance on the professor's misstatement as to how the exam would be graded (*Matter of Olsson v. Board of Higher Educ.*, *supra*), or to compel a medical school to permit a student who had failed a number of courses to repeat a year (*Matter of Patti Ann H. v. New York Med. Coll.*, 88 A.D.2d 296, *aff'd* 58 NY2d 734, *supra*), and we have concluded that a college did not act arbitrarily in refusing to "round off" a senior's grade so that she might graduate (*Matter of McIntosh v. Borough of Manhattan Community Coll.*, 55 N.Y.2d 913, *aff'g* 78 A.2d 839).

As a general rule, judicial review of grading disputes would inappropriately involve the courts in the very core of academic and educational decision making. Moreover, to so involve the courts in assessing the propriety of particular grades would promote litigation by countless unsuccessful students and thus undermine the credibility of the academic determinations of educational institutions. We conclude, therefore, that, in the absence of demonstrated bad faith, arbitrariness, capriciousness, irrationality or a constitutional or statutory violation, a student's challenge to a particular grade or other academic determination relating to a genuine substantive evaluation of the student's academic capabilities, is beyond the scope of judicial review.

Petitioner's allegations do not meet this standard; rather, they go to the heart of the professor's substantive evaluation of the petitioner's academic performance and as such, are beyond judicial review. The claim that this Corporations grade resulted in petitioner's arbitrary dismissal from the law school was properly dismissed by Supreme Court.

Questions and Comments on *Susan M.*

Like Susan M., most students have failed to meet the challenge of presenting "a judicially cognizable claim" in academic dismissal cases. This "formidable roadblock" of judicial deference has meant that even when plaintiffs prevail at trial, the decisions are often reversed on appeal. *See* Thomas A. Schweitzer, *Academic Challenge Cases: Should Judicial Review Extend to Academic Evaluations of Students*, 41 AM. U. L. REV. 267, 272 (1992). There have been a few exceptions to this pattern, however, as the next case illustrates.

Sylvester v. Texas Southern University

United States District Court for the Southern District of Texas, 1997.
957 F.Supp. 944.

■ HUGHES, UNITED STATES DISTRICT JUDGE.

A law student complained about the process the law school used in her appeal of a grade. The school has consistently disregarded every aspect of fair procedure, including its own rules and court orders. In an effort to minimize court intervention, the school was not enjoined at the beginning, and it was given two additional opportunities to correct its mistreatment of the student. Rather than comply with it responsibilities, the school manipulated the process, proving itself unable to obey the law it teaches....

Karen Sylvester, a student at Texas Southern University's Thurgood Marshall School of Law, enrolled in James Bullock's course in wills and trusts in the spring of 1994. Bullock gave the final examination in May 1994 and posted grades in July. Sylvester got a D. The result of this grade is that Sylvester's class rank dropped from first to third. With a grade of C or pass, Sylvester would have remained first.

Sylvester immediately protested orally to Associate Dean Carrington. She protested in writing on August 20, 1994. The school did not respond. She continued to protest orally between August 1994 and March 1995. Sylvester protested in writing a second time on March 26, 1995; this time she wrote the law school's Academic Standards Committee, requesting a review of her wills-and-trusts grade. Sylvester never received a formal response. When she was about to graduate, Bullock informed Sylvester that her examination was lost. When Bullock was ordered to see that the examination was found, it was.

On May 10, 1995, Sylvester sought to enjoin her law school's graduation ceremony. Claiming that she had been denied review of her examination, Sylvester sued to preserve her right to appeal the grade because school policy says that a student may not appeal after graduation. The court did not restrain graduation on the school's representation that it would later adjust the grade if needed.

TSU's regulations include procedures for disputing grades. The regulations allow students to seek grade changes on the basis of clerical errors that a faculty member refuses to correct or on the basis of discrimination against a specific student through the use of a grossly inconsistent standard for that student. The student is required to protest in writing.

The regulations say that the academic standing committee will review the protested grade and that the dean's office will notify the student in writing of the disposition. TSU did neither.

Bullock was defiant. The school agreed to a court-ordered session between Sylvester and Bullock to review the grade. When Sylvester flew to Houston to meet with Bullock at a time set by the dean, Bullock had no key to the answers and no comparable answers for Sylvester to use in judging the deficiencies in her answers. At the next hearing after the truncated review, the court ordered Bullock to pay her expenses of $200 for coming from Dallas and to attend all further conferences and hearings. He did neither.

At the next session in court, Bullock refused to appear. He had to be brought to court by the marshal, although he admitted under oath that he had known for three months that he had been ordered to pay Sylvester's expenses and to attend all proceedings. Counsel for TSU and Bullock stressed that they had notified Bullock of the order and setting. Bullock was ordered to pay Sylvester her lawyer's fees and the marshal its costs. Parenthetically, throughout this bureaucratic shuffle, counsel for the school have been candid and responsible; they are not to blame for the clients' behavior.

The school agreed to have its committee review Sylvester's examination. At its first meeting, the committee ruled that it lacked jurisdiction to review Sylvester's grade because of defects in her federal-court complaint. At that session, the committee had no comparable answers, although Bullock swore that he had given the committee a key to the answers.

The court sent the protest back to the committee to do the review, leaving the complaint to the parties and court.

The committee chairman unilaterally decided to expel the student members of the committee. Her ground for this *coup* was that it was inappropriate for the students to participate because they would be obliged in the review to become aware of the contents of other students' papers. This is true—and irrelevant—of every action before the standards committee. It contradicts the school's policy, which is manifest in its having put students on the committee in the first place. One member of a committee cannot reconstitute the committee whatever her motives.

The committee review resulted in a report that simply said the review was done and no inconsistencies were found.

One member of the committee abstained from voting and wrote a specific dissent. From this detailed report, the court learned that Bullock still had not furnished a complete set of answers. Despite swearing in court that he had long ago provided a complete key to the examination, Bullock gave "yes" as the full answer to part of question V, and he gave no answer for another section. No student could have received a perfect score for answering "yes" to an essay question on a law school final, yet that was the correct answer on Bullock's key.

The committee was illegally composed and had no means of making an informed judgment about Sylvester's answers; it especially did not have the evidence of comparable examinations required by the school's rules.

TSU claims that Sylvester was not entitled to process besides notification of her grade. . . .

The state may require its institutions to meet standards for regular process that are in excess of the national constitutional standard; therefore, violating a higher state-imposed standard would not necessarily violate the federal law. On the other hand, the Constitution does not define the benefits that a state must furnish nor the process it may use other than to require that similarly situated people be treated similarly. Because in the exercise of its state authority TSU has afforded a meaningful review to other students who protested their grades, TSU must provide that benefit to Sylvester. Governmental actions cannot be arbitrary. Having no basis for comparison is arbitrary. Changing the committee on the chairman's malicious whim is arbitrary. Once the committee had been changed from the official, university-constituted form it was nothing but a mob.

arbitrary

While it is true that the assignment of a test grade is a purely academic evaluation, Sylvester is entitled to due process in that evaluation. TSU is a state institution, funded by tax dollars and operating in the public interest. TSU must adhere to procedural requirements like other state institutions.

This court has no opinion on the quality of Sylvester's answers to Bullock's questions. Because the school institutionally and through several of its high-paid, life-tenured professors breached its duty under the Constitution to discharge its responsibilities through a process that is regular and can be seen to be regular, Sylvester will be given a new grade. Bullock had three opportunities to evaluate Sylvester's work—first when he graded it; second when she asked for a review; and third when the court ordered and the dean set a review conference.

breached Constitutional Duty

The school's committee had two opportunities to review—first it attempted to circumvent its duty by refusing to review the paper, and second it conducted a flawed one because the committee was illegal under the regulations governing committee composition and the material reviewed was not consistent with school requirements.

Based on the well-documented acts of the school, Sylvester will receive an equitable adjustment in her grade, a form of relief from which none of the actors, institutional or individual, is immune.

Sylvester will be assigned a "pass" in Bullock's wills and trusts class at TSU. The original grade may have been exactly correct, but we will never know. No review by anyone at TSU at this point could be reasonably accepted. Between active manipulation and sullen intransigence, the faculty, embodying arbitrary government, have mistreated a student confided to their charge. This violates their duty to conduct the public's business in a rationally purposeful manner.

Sylvester was entitled to a review of her final that complied with school rules about grade disputes. She did not receive that review. TSU has persisted in its inability to obey the Constitution, to follow its rules, to speak candidly, or to act responsibly.

Although a "pass" will change her class rank from third to first, she will share that position with the current valedictorian.

— share the position

Questions and Comments on *Sylvester*

1. If the university had not permitted students to serve on the Academic Standards Committee, would the result in *Sylvester* have been the same? Can you reconcile *Sylvester* with *In re Susan M.*?

2. Although the District Court changed Sylvester's grade from "D" to pass, it stated that the grade of "D" might have been correct. Does the action of the District Court suggest that the primary focus of its review was not the fairness of the grade per se, but rather the fairness of the process for assigning and appealing the grade? Why might judicial review be more appropriate for the latter case than the former?

Fairness of Process

Atria v. Vanderbilt University

United States Court of Appeals, Sixth Circuit, 2005.
142 Fed.Appx. 246.

■ ALICE M. BATCHELDER, CIRCUIT JUDGE.

Plaintiff–Appellant Nicklaus Atria appeals the district court's order granting summary judgment in favor of the Defendant–Appellee Vanderbilt University on his claims of negligence, negligence per se, breach of contract, and promissory estoppel. . . .

Nicklaus Atria was a pre-med student at Vanderbilt University when the events giving rise to this litigation occurred. During the spring semester of 2002, Atria was enrolled in an Organic Chemistry class taught by Professor B.A. Hess. On January 29, 2002, Professor Hess gave an examination that required students to record their answers on an answer sheet. Professor Hess's system for returning the graded tests is—at least in our experience—unusual. After grading the tests, Professor Hess would place the answer sheets in a stack on a table outside of the class room. Before the next class, students would thumb through the stack and locate their answer sheets, which were conspicuously marked with their names and social security numbers. Professor Hess testified that he did not know the names of most students and had no way of knowing whether students were picking up their own tests. After class, Professor Hess would gather those tests that had not been retrieved from the table and distribute them directly to the students during the next class period. Atria was absent from class on Friday, February 1, 2002, the day that the graded answer sheets were put out for general retrieval. He therefore, received his graded test on the following Monday.

Professor Hess allows any student who believes that an answer on his test was incorrectly marked as wrong to resubmit the answer sheet for a "re-grade." To prevent students from seeking a re-grade after altering incorrect answers, Professor Hess retained photocopies of all of the answer sheets. Atria, who had taken another chemistry class from Professor Hess in the fall of 2001, testified that he was aware of Professor Hess's practice of photocopying the original answer sheets. According to Atria, when he picked up his answer sheet on Monday, the answer recorded for question number six was "b>c>a," which is the correct answer. Because question six was marked as incorrect on his answer sheet, Atria returned his test to Professor Hess for a re-grade. According to the photocopy retained by Professor Hess, however, Atria's original answer to question number six was "b>a>a." It appeared to Professor Hess that an "a" in question number six had been changed to a "c." Professor Hess reported this irregularity to Vanderbilt's Honor Council and accused Atria of fraudulently modifying his answer sheet to get credit for question number six. . . .

Vanderbilt's Student Handbook contains a detailed description of the University's honor system, including its Honor Code, the applicability of the Code, procedures for the adjudication of asserted violations, and appeals from a finding of guilt. When a violation of the Honor Code is reported, the Honor Council appoints two investigators who meet with the accused and present him with a written statement of the charges. The Student Handbook provides that "an accused may obtain professional legal representation, advice, and counsel. However, an attorney may not participate in or be present during an Honor Council hearing. The Honor Council is a student tribunal untrained in the law." An Honor Council hearing is conducted by a twelve-member panel consisting of the President of the Honor Council and eleven members of the Council appointed by the President. Proof of a student's guilt must be "clear and convincing" and ten of the twelve members must vote "guilty" to convict.

A student found guilty by the Honor Council may appeal the decision to the Appellate Review Board ("ARB") by filing a petition with the Honor Council's faculty advisor....

On March 19, 2002, Vanderbilt's Honor Council conducted a hearing in Atria's case.... During the hearing, Atria testified that he was not guilty of the charges and that his answer sheet could have been smudged while in his book bag. At the conclusion of the hearing, the Council advised Atria that he had been found guilty as charged and imposed a sentence of failure in Organic Chemistry and a suspension from the University during the summer session. Several days later, Atria paid for and took a polygraph test conducted by a local polygraph examiner. According to the examiner's analysis of the results, Atria's statements that he did not alter the answer to question six were "truthful."

[Atria appealed the decision of the Honor Council, but the appeal was denied by the Chairman of the Appellate Review Board, Francis Wells, who testified that he had the power to reject petitions that presented insufficient grounds for appeal without allowing the full panel to hear it.]

Atria filed suit against Vanderbilt in United States District Court.... [T]he district court granted Vanderbilt's motion for summary judgment on all claims. Atria timely appealed.

. . .

Atria alleges that Professor Hess was negligent in the manner in which he redistributed the graded answer sheets from his Organic Chemistry exam....

To make out the prima facie case for negligence, Atria must prove each of the following five elements: 1) a duty of care owed by the defendant to the plaintiff; 2) a breach of that duty; 3) an injury or loss; 4) cause in fact; and 5) proximate legal causation ... Vanderbilt and its agents owe everyone, including Atria, a duty to refrain from conduct that poses an unreasonable and foreseeable risk of harm....

The facts in this case are in dispute as to whether the manner in which Professor Hess distributed graded answer sheets posed an unreasonable risk of harm. A jury could certainly conclude that the burden on Professor Hess to engage in alternative conduct that would have prevented the harm is at most *de minimis*: instead of handing back the students' original answer sheets he could have retained the originals and handed back the photocopies,

Negligence Claim which could not be altered.[3] A jury could find that the harm caused by Professor Hess's conduct was foreseeable. [Mark] Bandas, [the advisor to the Honor Counsel] testified that he met with Professor Hess in the Fall of 2002 because "[Professor Hess] had been submitting a number of cases to the honor council based on students altering, you know, score sheets for a re-grade. He was actually submitting a sufficient number of them, and that it was putting a heavy load on the honor council's docket." In a prior Honor Council proceeding, a student accused by Professor Hess asserted, as a defense, that another student tampered with her test before it was returned to Hess for a re-grade. Though this student subsequently admitted to altering her own answer sheet, a jury could easily find that this incident should have alerted Professor Hess to the possibility that one student might tamper with another's answer sheet. Indeed, the record supports the inference that Professor Hess was actually well aware of the risk posed by his redistribution system, inasmuch as he made photocopies of the answer sheets in an effort to combat dishonesty on the part of students seeking a re-grade.

The gravity of the harm posed by Hess's distribution system is severe: a wrongful conviction by a disciplinary committee could ruin a student's chances of admittance to graduate school. In sum, a jury reasonably could conclude that Professor Hess's distribution system created an unreasonable risk of harm because the foreseeable probability of, and the gravity of the harm resulting from, a wrongful Honor Council conviction outweigh the burden on Professor Hess to redistribute the photocopy of the answer sheet rather than the original.

Prox. Cause Atria must ... show that Vanderbilt's actions were the proximate cause of his injury.... Tennessee has adopted a three-pronged test for proximate causation: 1) the tortfeasor's conduct must have been a "substantial factor" in bringing about the harm being complained of; 2) there is no rule or policy that should relieve the wrongdoer from liability because of the manner in which the negligence has resulted in the harm; and 3) the harm giving rise to the action could reasonably have been foreseen or anticipated by a person of ordinary intelligence and prudence. There are two possible causes of Atria's Honor Council conviction: either he cheated and caused his own injury or, he did not cheat, someone else made the alteration on his answer sheet before Atria retrieved it, and Professor Hess's method of returning the tests was the proximate cause of his Honor Council conviction. Because the record contains evidence that could lead reasonable people to disagree about the cause of Atria's Honor Council conviction, the question of proximate cause is one for the jury.

Jury question Vanderbilt ... argues that Atria's injury was not foreseeable because a professor could not have imagined that a student, in an effort to improve his position in the curve, would sabotage another student's test. We suspect that a jury would not think that conjuring up this scenario would take much imagination, particularly in today's competitive academic institutions. In any event, it is for the jury to determine....

3. In fact, Professor Hess admitted that Bandas met with him in the Fall of 2002, after Atria's Honor Council hearing, and suggested that he redistribute the photocopies instead. When asked how he responded to Bandas's suggestion, Professor Hess testified "I tell you, I don't recall much about the meeting to be frank because I was kind of put off by the meeting, that I felt that they were encroaching on my academic freedom, and I'm pretty strong on academic freedom. So I basically dismissed what they were talking about."

For the foregoing reasons, we reverse the district court's order granting summary judgment on Atria's negligence claim.

. . .

Atria's breach of contract claims are based on Vanderbilt's alleged failure to follow the Honor Council's procedural rules, as embodied in the Student Handbook, in the handling of his case and his appeal. . . . Specifically, Atria alleges that the University breached its own procedures by dismissing his appeal without submitting the petition to the entire ARB; holding an Honor Council meeting without requiring the presence of Professor Hess, the accuser; refusing to consider the results of the polygraph examination; failing to provide an unbiased appellate body; and refusing to accept a petition that was signed by Atria's attorney. . . .

Though Vanderbilt's Student Handbook, which states that its policies "are not intended to be all-inclusive and do not constitute a contract," its provisions may be enforced in Tennessee if it creates an implied contract. *See Givens v. Mullikin ex rel. Estate of McElwaney*, 75 S.W.3d 383, 405 (Tenn. 2002). This court, applying Tennessee's law, has stated that "the student-university relationship is contractual in nature although courts have rejected a rigid application of contract law in this area." *Doherty v. Southern College of Optometry*, 862 F.2d 570, 577 (6th Cir. 1988). Catalogs, manuals, handbooks, bulletins, circulars and regulations of a university may help define this contractual relationship. The district court held that dismissal of Atria's breach of contract claim was necessary because a federal court is an inappropriate forum in which to challenge academic matters. We disagree with the district court's characterization of this claim as one challenging academic matters. "Courts have adopted different standards of review when educators' decisions are based upon disciplinary versus academic criteria—applying a more intrusive analysis of the former and a far more deferential examination of the latter." The case at bar involves a disciplinary action by the university, and does not arise in the context of any academic finding, and may appropriately be brought in this court.

An issue of material fact exists as to whether Vanderbilt breached this implied contract when Wells personally dismissed Atria's petition as presenting insufficient grounds for review rather than submitting it to the entire ARB. Vanderbilt has conflicting rules about whether the ARB chairman or the entire ARB performs the gatekeeping function of determining whether the petition states sufficient grounds for appeal. The Student Handbook says "if the chair determines that the petition, when considered in the light most favorable to the petitioner, does not set forth a basis sufficient to provide the relief sought by the petitioner, the ARB Chair will dismiss the petition. The ARB Chair's decision is final." However, the Procedures of the Appellate Review Board provides,

> the panel will review the petition and, by majority vote, will determine whether the petition presents sufficient grounds for an appeal. . . . If the panel determines that the petition does set forth sufficient grounds for the appeal, the panel will proceed to a full consideration of the appeal.

Vanderbilt asserts that the provisions of the Student Handbook, which were adopted in 1999, supercede the "Procedures of the Appellate Review Board," which were adopted in 1995. While Vanderbilt has the right to amend its procedures, there is nothing in the record to suggest that the University did, in fact, amend the Procedures of the Appellate Review Board. Vanderbilt's argument that the Student Handbook preempts the Procedures of the Appellate Review Board is inconsistent with the Handbook itself, which incorporates the Procedures by reference: "[a] copy of the Appellate Review Board's procedures is available at the offices of the Vice Chancellor for Student Life and Chair of the Conduct Councils." Because Vanderbilt admitted in its responses to Atria's requests for admission that that the Procedures of the Appellate Review Board were in force at the time of Atria's Honor Council conviction, the conflict between these procedures and the Student Handbook raises a factual issue as to whether Vanderbilt substantially complied with its own rules.

. . .

For the foregoing reasons, we REVERSE the district court's order granting summary judgment on Atria's negligence claim, REVERSE in part the order granting summary judgment on the breach of contract claims, AFFIRM the district court's order on all other respects, and REMAND this case for further proceedings consistent with this opinion.

Questions and Comments on *Atria*

1. After the Sixth Circuit reversed the district court's summary judgment, Atria and Vanderbilt reached a settlement, the terms of which were not disclosed. Telephone Interview by Matthew Edgar with John C. Callison, Senior Deputy General Counsel, Vanderbilt University (July 21, 2008). According to Mr. Callison, while the lawsuit was pending, Professor Hess changed his method for distributing exams and the university refined its rules for challenging grades. The revised rules ban polygraph evidence and expert witness testimony. *Id.*

2. *Atria* demonstrates that students at private universities may successfully challenge arbitrary actions as violations of tort or contract law. *See also* Russell v. Salve Regina College, 890 F.2d 484 (1st Cir. 1989), *rev'd on other grounds*, 499 U.S. 225 (1991), *reinstating damages on remand*, 938 F.2d 315 (1st Cir. 1991). In *Russell*, a nursing student sued her college for dismissing her solely because she was obese. The college argued that Russell was dismissed for failing a required course, but the court found that the failure was mostly due to her weight. After finding that a contract with Russell was created by "the various catalogs, manuals, handbooks, etc." and that the contract had been breached by the college's failure to educate her, the court awarded her more than $30,000. 890 F.2d at 488. Compare the facts of *Russell* to those of *Horowitz*. Would the plaintiff in *Horowitz* have faired better if she had brought her claim in contract law?

3. Is a university better or worse off if it has detailed procedures for handling academic wrongdoing and dismissals? How can it avoid having inconsistent policies?

4. What do you think of Professor Hess's belief that the honor council was "encroaching on [his] academic freedom" by suggesting that he hand out photocopies of the exams? At what point, if any, do procedures for academic wrongdoing and dismissals encroach on the academic freedom of faculty?

Constantine v. The Rectors and Visitors of George Mason University

United States Court of Appeals, Fourth Circuit, 2005.
411 F.3d 474.

■ Shedd, Circuit Judge:

Carin Constantine sued The Rectors and Visitors of George Mason University ("GMU") and several members of GMU's law school faculty (the "individual defendants"), asserting a First Amendment retaliation claim under 42 U.S.C. § 1983 and disability discrimination claims under Title II of the Americans with Disabilities Act ("ADA") and § 504 of the Rehabilitation Act. The defendants moved to dismiss the complaint on the grounds that (1) the Eleventh Amendment barred all claims against GMU and the individual defendants in their official capacities, and (2) the complaint failed to state a claim upon which relief could be granted. The district court declined to rule on the Eleventh Amendment issues but dismissed the complaint for failure to state a claim. . . .

Constantine was a student in Professor Nelson Lund's constitutional law course at GMU, a state university that receives federal funds.[1] Constantine suffered from "intractable migraine syndrome," for which she took prescription medication. While taking Professor Lund's final exam, Constantine suffered a migraine headache. She alerted exam administrators to her condition and requested additional time to complete the exam, but they refused. Constantine failed the exam. She then requested a grade appeal and reexamination, but those requests were denied as well.

Constantine complained to Professor Lund, the dean of the law school, and other law school officials about the construction of Professor Lund's exam and GMU's grade appeals process. She publicized her complaints in an article she wrote for the law school newspaper.

About three months after Constantine made her initial request for re-examination, and after she voiced criticism of the grade appeals process, the dean agreed to give Constantine a second chance to take Professor Lund's final exam. Because Constantine was carrying a full load of law school courses during the spring semester, the parties agreed that the re-examination would take place "sometime in June" 2003. On May 17, 2003, however, Constantine received an e-mail notifying her that she must present herself for the re-examination on May 21, 2003.

Constantine notified the dean, the law school registrar, and two other administrators that she would not be able to take Professor Lund's exam at that time because she had a conflict related to another law school course and, in any event, the dean had told her that she would be re-examined in June. These law school officials told Constantine that she should appear for re-examination at the time specified or forfeit her right to take the exam. Constantine requested an opportunity to take the exam in June, but that request was denied.

Constantine then filed this lawsuit and moved the district court for a temporary restraining order. After a hearing, the district court denied the motion. Constantine declined to take Professor Lund's exam on May 21, 2003. GMU later offered to give Constantine another chance to take Professor Lund's exam, but Constantine believes that in retaliation for her criticism of GMU's handling of her case, GMU decided in advance to give her an "F" on the exam. Constantine eventually took Professor Lund's exam, and she received an "F."

---

1. Because we are reviewing the dismissal of Constantine's complaint, we accept as true all well-pleaded allegations and view the complaint in the light most favorable to her.

As a result of this failing grade in constitutional law, Constantine was not able to graduate on time. Delayed graduation compromised her ability to begin on time the judicial clerkship that she had previously accepted, so Constantine had to inform her judge of the failing grade and obtain special permission to start work a year later. According to Constantine, the "F" on her transcript continues to hamper her employment prospects.

Constantine sued GMU and the individual defendants in their official and individual capacities. She alleges that the defendants' failure to accommodate her physical disability violated her rights under the ADA and the Rehabilitation Act. She further alleges that the individual defendants retaliated against her for criticizing GMU's grade appeals policies and thus violated her First Amendment right to free speech. Constantine seeks monetary damages as well as declaratory and injunctive relief.

The defendants moved to dismiss Constantine's suit, arguing that the Eleventh Amendment bars her claims against GMU and against the individual defendants in their official capacities. Further, the defendants argued that Constantine had failed to state a claim upon which relief can be granted. The district court granted the motion to dismiss under Rule 12(b)(6), ruling only that Constantine had failed to state a claim upon which relief can be granted. This appeal followed.

. . .

[The court holds that the Eleventh Amendment does not bar Constantine's claims under the ADA and the Rehabilitation Act].

Title II of the ADA provides that "no qualified individual with a disability shall, by reason of such disability, be excluded from participation in or be denied the benefits of the services, programs, or activities of a public entity, or be subjected to discrimination by any such entity." 42 U.S.C. § 12132. Similarly, § 504 of the Rehabilitation Act provides that "no otherwise qualified individual with a disability . . . shall, solely by reason of her or his disability, be excluded from the participation in, or be denied the benefits of, or be subjected to discrimination under any program or activity receiving Federal financial assistance." 29 U.S.C. § 794(a). In general, a plaintiff seeking recovery for violation of either statute must allege that (1) she has a disability, (2) she is otherwise qualified to receive the benefits of a public service, program, or activity, and (3) she was excluded from participation in or denied the benefits of such service, program, or activity, or otherwise discriminated against, on the basis of her disability.[17] The district court ruled that Constantine's complaint failed to allege facts showing that (1) Constantine was "otherwise qualified" as a law student or (2) she was actually denied the benefits of an educational program or service.

A plaintiff is "qualified" if she is "an individual with a disability who, with or without reasonable modifications to rules, policies, or practices . . . meets the essential eligibility requirements for the receipt of services or the

---

17. Although "the ADA and Rehabilitation Act generally are construed to impose the same requirements," we have recognized that the causation standards under Title II of the ADA and § 504 of the Rehabilitation Act are "significantly dissimilar." *Baird*, 192 F.3d at 469. A plaintiff seeking relief under Title II of the ADA must prove that disability "played a motivating role" in the adverse action, while a plaintiff seeking relief under § 504 of the Rehabilitation Act must prove that the defendants' discriminatory conduct was "solely by reason" of the plaintiff's disability. *Id*. at 469–70.

participation in programs or activities provided by a public entity." 42 U.S.C. § 12131(2). According to the complaint, Constantine "is qualified to be a student at GMU and is able to perform all the essential functions of being a student with reasonable accommodations. If she received additional time as a reasonable accommodation for her disability, she would not have any problem complying [with] GMU's examination policy." The complaint further alleges that Constantine carried a full load of law school courses in the spring of 2003 and completed her other final exams "without incident." Taken together, these allegations are sufficient to make a *prima facie* case that Constantine, with reasonable modifications to exam administration policies or practices, met the essential eligibility requirements for participation in GMU's law school programs.

... Constantine's complaint alleges that she was unable to complete Professor Lund's exam because of her disability; that the defendants initially refused to accommodate her disability by giving her additional time to complete the exam, resulting in her failing the exam; that when the defendants agreed months later to allow a re-examination, they gave her only three days to prepare; that when she alerted the defendants to a conflict with other law school responsibilities, they refused to alter the date for re-examination; and that when she sought a temporary restraining order to prevent the re-examination on the date set by the defendants, they determined that she would fail any subsequent re-examination. If these allegations are true, then Constantine can demonstrate that the defendants excluded her from meaningful participation in Professor Lund's course or denied her the benefits of that course, or at least discriminated against her with respect to that course. Whatever may happen at summary judgment or trial, these allegations are sufficient to satisfy Rule 12(b)(6).

Constantine also asserts a claim against the individual defendants for First Amendment retaliation in violation of 42 U.S.C. § 1983. Specifically, Constantine alleges that the defendants violated her First Amendment right to free speech by retaliating against her after she complained about Professor Lund's constitutional law exam and GMU's grade appeals policies.

Constantine alleges that she complained to GMU officials about the construction of Professor Lund's exam and the procedures available to challenge her grade. She then repeated her complaints about the grade appeals process in an article printed in the law school newspaper. It is undisputed that Constantine engaged in protected First Amendment activity.

Constantine further alleges that GMU, in response to these complaints, (1) denied her initial request to re-take the exam, (2) denied her request to have a different professor determine whether the original exam was defective or graded unfairly, and (3) refused to grant her a hearing before the Academic Standing Committee to challenge her grade....

First Amendment retaliation is actionable because "retaliatory actions may tend to chill individuals' exercise of constitutional rights." *American Civil Liberties Union, Inc. v. Wicomico County*, 999 F.2d 780, 785 (4th Cir. 1993). Not all retaliatory conduct tends to chill First Amendment activity, however, and a plaintiff seeking to recover for retaliation must show that the defendant's conduct resulted in something more than a "*de minimis* inconvenience" to her exercise of First Amendment rights, *American Civil Liberties Union, Inc.*, 999 F.2d at 786 n. 6. Of course, conduct that tends to chill the exercise of constitutional rights might not itself deprive such rights, and a plaintiff need not actually be deprived of her First Amendment rights in order to establish First Amendment retaliation.

We reject the defendants' suggestion that this inquiry depends upon the actual effect of the retaliatory conduct on a particular plaintiff. We have never held that a plaintiff must prove that the allegedly retaliatory conduct caused her to cease First Amendment activity altogether. The cause of action targets conduct that tends to *chill* such activity, not just conduct that *freezes* it completely. Moreover, such a subjective standard would expose public officials to liability in some cases, but not in others, for the very same conduct, depending upon the plaintiff's will to fight. We believe that an objective standard better instructs public officials as to their obligations under the First Amendment. . . .

Constantine alleges that in response to her public criticism of Professor Lund's exam and GMU's grade appeals policies, the defendants denied her requests to sit for a re-examination, to have another professor review her original exam, and even to have a hearing before an administrative committee. When the defendants finally allowed a re-examination, they gave Constantine only three days' notice and, according to the complaint, determined in advance that she would receive a failing grade. Because such conduct would tend to chill a reasonable person's exercise of First Amendment rights, we conclude that Constantine has adequately alleged adverse action.

. . .

We conclude that . . . Constantine's complaint adequately alleges claims for disability discrimination in violation of Title II of the ADA and § 504 of the Rehabilitation Act, as well as a First Amendment retaliation claim under § 1983. Accordingly, we reverse the judgment of the district court and remand this case for further proceedings.

Questions and Comments on *Constantine*

1. According to Thomas Beck, the attorney for George Mason:

> After the case was remanded to the district court, the plaintiff voluntarily dismissed her Section 1983 claim for First Amendment retaliation and, shortly thereafter, the court dismissed her remaining claim for disability discrimination due to her failure to cooperate in discovery and otherwise to prosecute her claim. The failing grade that the plaintiff received in her initial Constitutional Law class was not dropped or changed in any way.

E-mail from Thomas Beck, Attorney, Jones Day, July 3, 2007, 1:07 p.m. (on file with author).

2. Should migraines qualify as a disability under the Americans with Disabilities Act? *Compare* Price v. National Bd. of Med. Examiners, 966 F.Supp. 419 (S.D.W.Va. 1997) (holding that, although they had some learning difficulties, medical students with ADHD were not disabled because there was no evidence demonstrating that their disorder impaired their scholastic abilities). For a discussion of the issues universities face under the ADA, see Oren R. Griffin, *Accommodating the Learning Disabled Student on Campus*, 78 U. DET. MERCY L. REV. 547 (2001). *See also* Scott Weiss, *Contemplating Greatness: Learning Disabilities and the Practice of Law*, 6 SCHOLAR 219 (2004).

3. In *Constantine*, the Fourth Circuit insisted on an objective standard for determining when First Amendment retaliation has occurred. What does the court tell us about this standard? What if Constantine deserved an "F" on the exam she eventually took? Can the court determine whether the final grade was retaliatory without deciding whether the grade was justified on the merits?

Ross v. Creighton University

United States Court of Appeals, Seventh Circuit, 1992.
957 F.2d 410.

■ RIPPLE, CIRCUIT JUDGE.

Kevin Ross filed suit against Creighton University (Creighton or the University) for negligence and breach of contract arising from Creighton's alleged failure to educate him. The district court dismissed Mr. Ross' complaint for failure to state a claim. . . .

. . .

In the spring of 1978, Mr. Ross was a promising senior basketball player at Wyandotte High School in Kansas City, Kansas. Sometime during his senior year in high school, he accepted an athletic scholarship to attend Creighton and to play on its varsity basketball team.

Creighton is an academically superior university. Mr. Ross comes from an academically disadvantaged background. At the time of his enrollment at Creighton, Mr. Ross was at an academic level far below that of the average Creighton student. For example, he scored in the bottom fifth percentile of college-bound seniors taking the American College Test, while the average freshman admitted to Creighton with him scored in the upper twenty-seven percent. According to the complaint, Creighton realized Mr. Ross' academic limitations when it admitted him, and, to induce him to attend and play basketball, Creighton assured Mr. Ross that he would receive sufficient tutoring so that he "would receive a meaningful education while at Creighton."

Mr. Ross attended Creighton from 1978 until 1982. During that time he maintained a D average and acquired 96 of the 128 credits needed to graduate. However, many of these credits were in courses such as Marksmanship and Theory of Basketball, and did not count towards a university degree. Mr. Ross alleges that he took these courses on the advice of Creighton's Athletic Department, and that the department also employed a secretary to read his assignments and prepare and type his papers. Mr. Ross also asserts that Creighton failed to provide him with sufficient and competent tutoring that it had promised.

When he left Creighton, Mr. Ross had the overall language skills of a fourth grader and the reading skills of a seventh grader. Consequently, Mr. Ross enrolled, at Creighton's expense, for a year of remedial education at the Westside Preparatory School in Chicago. At Westside, Mr. Ross attended classes with grade school children. He later entered Roosevelt University in Chicago, but was forced to withdraw because of a lack of funds. In July 1987, Mr. Ross suffered what he terms a "major depressive episode," during which he barricaded himself in a Chicago motel room and threw furniture out the window. To Mr. Ross, this furniture "symbolized" Creighton employees who had wronged him.

Mr. Ross filed suit against Creighton in Cook County (Illinois) Circuit Court for negligence and breach of contract. Creighton, which is located in

Omaha, Nebraska, removed the case to federal court on diversity grounds. . . .

Mr. Ross' complaint advances three separate theories of how Creighton was negligent towards him. First, he contends that Creighton committed "educational malpractice" by not providing him with a meaningful education and preparing him for employment after college. Second, Mr. Ross claims that Creighton negligently inflicted emotional distress upon him by enrolling him in a stressful university environment for which he was not prepared, and then by failing to provide remedial programs that would have helped him survive there. Third, Mr. Ross urges the court to adopt a new cause of action for the tort of "negligent admission," which would allow recovery when an institution admits, and then does not adequately assist, a woefully unprepared student. The complaint also sets forth a contract claim, alleging that Creighton contracted to provide Mr. Ross "an opportunity . . . to obtain a meaningful college education and degree, and to do what was reasonably necessary . . . to enable [Mr. Ross] to obtain a meaningful college education and degree." It goes on to assert that Creighton breached this contract by failing to provide Mr. Ross adequate tutoring; by not requiring Mr. Ross to attend tutoring sessions; by not allowing him to "red-shirt," that is, to forego a year of basketball, in order to work on academics; and by failing to afford Mr. Ross a reasonable opportunity to take advantage of tutoring services. Mr. Ross also alleges that Creighton breached a promise it had made to him to pay for a college education.

Creighton moved to dismiss the complaint under Federal Rule of Civil Procedure 12(b)(6), and the district court granted this motion. . . .

. . .

As an appellate court, we review de novo a Rule 12(b)(6) dismissal for failure to state a claim. . . .

. . .

1.   Educational malpractice

Illinois courts have never ruled on whether a tort cause of action exists against an institution for educational malpractice. However, the overwhelming majority of states that have considered this type of claim have rejected it. Only Montana allows these claims to go forward, and its decision was based on state statutes that place a duty of care on educators, a circumstance not present here. *B.M. v. State,* 200 Mont. 58, 649 P.2d 425, 427–28 (Mont. 1982).

Courts have identified several policy concerns that counsel against allowing claims for educational malpractice. First, there is the lack of a satisfactory standard of care by which to evaluate an educator. Theories of education are not uniform, and "different but acceptable scientific methods of academic training [make] it unfeasible to formulate a standard by which to judge the conduct of those delivering the services." *Swidryk v. St. Michael's Medical Center,* 201 N.J. Super. 601, 493 A.2d 641, 643 (N.J. Super. Ct. Law Div. 1985) (citing *Peter W. v. San Francisco Unified School Dist.,* 60 Cal. App. 3d 814, 131 Cal. Rptr. 854, 859 (Ct. App. 1976)). Second, inherent uncertainties exist in this type of case about the cause and nature of damages. "Factors such as the student's attitude, motivation, temperament, past experience and home environment may all play an essential and immeasurable role in learning." *Donohue v. Copiague Union Free School Dist.*, 47 N.Y.2d 440, 391 N.E.2d 1352, 1355, 418 N.Y.S.2d 375 (N.Y. 1979) (Wachtler, J., concurring). Consequently, it may be a "practical impossibility [to] prove that the alleged malpractice of the teacher proximately caused the learning deficiency of the plaintiff student." A third reason for denying this cause of action is the potential it presents for a flood of litigation against schools. As the district court noted, "education is a service rendered on an immensely greater scale than other professional services." *Ross v. Creighton Univ.*, 740 F. Supp. 1319, 1329 (N.D. Ill. 1990). The sheer number of claims that could arise if this cause of action were allowed might overburden schools. *Id.* This consideration also suggests that a common-law tort remedy may not be the best way to deal with the problem of inadequate education. A final reason courts have cited for denying this cause of action is that it threatens to embroil the courts into overseeing the day-to-day operations of schools. *Donohue*, 391 N.E.2d at 1354; *Hoffman v. Board of Educ.*, 49 N.Y.2d 121, 424 N.Y.S.2d 376, 400 N.E.2d 317, 320 (N.Y. 1979). This oversight might be particularly troubling in the university setting where it necessarily implicates considerations of academic freedom and autonomy.

We believe that the Illinois Supreme Court would find the experience of other jurisdictions persuasive and, consequently, that these policy considerations are compelling. Consequently, the Illinois Supreme Court would refuse to recognize the tort of educational malpractice. We therefore affirm the district court's dismissal of Mr. Ross' claim based on that theory.

2. "Negligent admission"

In his complaint, Mr. Ross alleges that Creighton owed him a duty "to recruit and enroll only those students reasonably qualified and able to academically perform at CREIGHTON." He then contends that Creighton breached this duty by admitting him, not informing him of how unprepared he was for studies there, and then not providing tutoring services or otherwise enabling him to receive a meaningful education. As a result, Mr. Ross underwent undue stress, which brought about, among other things, the incident at the motel.

We believe that Illinois would reject this claim for "negligent admission" for many of the same policy reasons that counsel against recognizing a claim for educational malpractice. First, this cause of action would present difficult, if not insuperable, problems to a court attempting to define a workable duty of care. Mr. Ross suggests that the University has a duty to admit only students who are "reasonably qualified" and able to perform academically. However, determining who is a "reasonably qualified student" necessarily requires subjective assessments of such things as the nature and quality of the defendant institution and the intelligence and educability of the plaintiff. Such decisions are not open to ready determination in the judicial process. Second, such a cause of action might unduly interfere with a university's admissions decisions, to the detriment of students and society as a whole. As the district court noted, if universities and colleges faced tort liability for admitting an unprepared student, schools would be encouraged to admit only those students who were certain to succeed in the institution. The opportunities of marginal students to receive an education therefore would likely be lessened. Also, the academic practice of promoting diversity by admitting students from disadvantaged backgrounds might also be jeopardized.

3.   Negligent infliction of emotional distress

[The court held that the same policy reasons that led Illinois to deny Mr. Ross' claim for educational malpractice and negligent admission would also lead it to deny his claim for negligent infliction of emotional distress.]

The Contract Claims

In counts two and three of his complaint, Mr. Ross alleges that Creighton breached an oral or a written contract that it had with him. When read as a totality, these allegations fairly allege that Creighton agreed, in exchange for Mr. Ross' promise to play on its basketball team, to allow him an opportunity to participate, in a meaningful way, in the academic program of the University despite his deficient academic background. The complaint further alleges, when read as a totality, that Creighton breached this contract and denied Mr. Ross any real opportunity to participate in and benefit from the University's academic program when it failed to perform five commitments made to Ross: (1) "to provide adequate and competent tutoring services," (2) "to require [Mr. Ross] to attend tutoring sessions," (3) to afford Mr. Ross "a reasonable opportunity to take full advantage of tutoring services," (4) to allow Mr. Ross to red-shirt, and (5) to provide funds to allow Mr. Ross to complete his college education.

It is held generally in the United States that the "basic legal relation between a student and a private university or college is contractual in nature. The catalogues, bulletins, circulars, and regulations of the institution made available to the matriculant become a part of the contract." *Zumbrun v. University of Southern California,* 25 Cal. App. 3d 1, 101 Cal. Rptr. 499, 504 (Ct. App. 1972) (collecting cases from numerous states).... It is quite clear, however, that Illinois would not recognize all aspects of a university-student relationship as subject to remedy through a contract action. [*De Marco v. University of Health Sciences,* 352 N.E.2d 356 (Ill. App. Ct. 1976),] makes the point quite clearly. "A contract between a private institution and a student confers duties upon both parties which cannot be arbitrarily disregarded and may be judicially enforced." However, "a decision of the school authorities relating to the academic qualification of the students will not be reviewed.... Courts are not qualified to pass an opinion as to the attainments of a student ... and ... courts will not review a decision of the school authorities relating to academic qualifications of the students." *Id.*

There is no question, we believe, that Illinois would adhere to the great weight of authority and bar any attempt to repackage an educational malpractice claim as a contract claim. As several courts have noted, the policy concerns that preclude a cause of action for educational malpractice apply with equal force to bar a breach of contract claim attacking the general quality of an education. "Where the essence of the complaint is that the school breached its agreement by failing to provide an effective education, the court is again asked to evaluate the course of instruction ... [and] is similarly called upon to review the soundness of the method of teaching that has been adopted by an educational institution." *Paladino v. Adelphi Univ.,* 89 A.D.2d 85, 454 N.Y.S.2d 868, 872 (App. Div. 1982).

To state a claim for breach of contract, the plaintiff must do more than simply allege that the education was not good enough. Instead, he must point to an identifiable contractual promise that the defendant failed to honor. Thus, as was suggested in *Paladino,* if the defendant took tuition money and then provided no education, or alternately, promised a set number of hours of instruction and then failed to deliver, a breach of contract action may be available. *Paladino*, 454 N.Y.S.2d at 873; *see also Zumbrun*, 25 Cal. App. 3d 1, 101 Cal. Rptr. 499 (breach of contract action allowed against university when professor declined to give lectures and final exam, and all students received a grade of "B"). Similarly, a breach of contract action might exist if a student enrolled in a course explicitly promising instruction that would qualify him as a journeyman, but in which the fundamentals necessary to attain that skill were not even presented. *See Wickstrom*, 725 P.2d at 156–58. In these cases, the essence of the plaintiff's complaint would not be that the institution failed to perform adequately a promised educational service, but rather that it failed to perform that service at all. Ruling on this issue would not require an inquiry into the nuances of educational processes and theories, but rather an objective assessment of whether the institution made a good faith effort to perform on its promise.

We read Mr. Ross' complaint to allege more than a failure of the University to provide him with an education of a certain quality. Rather, he alleges that the University knew that he was not qualified academically to participate in its curriculum. Nevertheless, it made a specific promise that he would be able to participate in a meaningful way in that program because it would provide certain specific services to him. Finally, he alleges that the University breached its promise by reneging on its commitment to provide those services and, consequently, effectively cutting him off from any participation in and benefit from the University's academic program. To adjudicate such a claim, the court would not be required to determine whether Creighton had breached its contract with Mr. Ross by providing deficient academic services. Rather, its inquiry would be limited to whether the University had provided any real access to its academic curriculum at all.

Accordingly, we must disagree respectfully with our colleague in the district court as to whether the contract counts of the complaint can be dismissed at the pleadings stage. In our view, the allegations of the complaint are sufficient to warrant further proceedings. We emphasize, however, the narrow ground of our disagreement. We agree—indeed we emphasize—that courts should not "take on the job of supervising the relationship between colleges and student-athletes or creating in effect a new relationship between them." We also recognize a formal university-student contract is rarely employed and, consequently, "the general nature and terms of the agreement are usually implied, with specific terms to be found in the university bulletin and other publications; custom and usages can also become specific terms by implication." Nevertheless, we believe that the district court can adjudicate Mr. Ross' specific and narrow claim that he was barred from *any* participation in and benefit from the University's academic program without second-guessing the professional judgment of the University faculty on academic matters.

Accordingly, the judgment of the district court is affirmed in part and reversed and remanded in part for proceedings consistent with this opinion.

Questions and Comments on *Ross*

1. In *Ross*, the court rejected the negligent admission cause of action because the determination of who is a " 'reasonably qualified student' necessarily requires subjective assessments of such things as . . . the intelligence and educability of the plaintiff." Does the wide divergence between Mr. Ross's score on the American College Test and the average score of admitted Creighton students provide an objective basis for determining that Ross was negligently admitted? Was Mr. Ross's poor performance at Creighton reasonably foreseeable, given his low test score?

2. When news broke that Ross was functionally illiterate, despite having attended Creighton for four years, the dispute garnered national attention. Jack Curry, *Suing for 2d Chance to Start Over*, N.Y. TIMES, Jan. 30, 1990. Ross testified before Congress, met President Reagan, and used funds from speaking engagements to help pay for his education at Roosevelt University. *Outside the Lines: Unable to Read* (ESPN television broadcast Mar. 17, 2002), *transcript available at* http://sports.espn.go.com/page2/tv listings/show103transcript.html. Ross became depressed after money from speaking was no longer available, leading to the incident in the hotel that sparked his lawsuit against Creighton. *Id.* He settled the lawsuit with Creighton for $30,000 and is now a janitor and substitute teacher at his former junior high. *Id.*

Note on Educational Malpractice

1. Educational malpractice claims have continued to fare badly in the courts. Since *Ross*, seven more states have rejected such claims including Montana, the one state *Ross* claimed recognized the tort. *See* Ogbaegbe v. Hampton Univ., 141 Fed. Appx. 100 (4th Cir. 2005) (holding that educational malpractice claims are not cognizable in Virginia); Brantley v. District of Columbia, 640 A.2d 181 (D.C. 1994); Key v. Coryell, 86 Ark.App. 334, 185 S.W.3d 98 (2004); Tolman v. CenCor Career Colls., Inc., 851 P.2d 203 (Colo.App. 1992); Jamieson v. Vatterott Educ. Ctr., Inc., 473 F. Supp. 2d 1153 (D. Kan. 2007); Furlong v. Carroll Coll., 2001 ML 1594 (Mont. Dist. 2001); Lawrence v. Lorain County Cmty. Coll., 127 Ohio App.3d 546, 713 N.E.2d 478 (1998). For an overview of the challenges facing educational malpractice claims see Todd A. DeMitchell & Terri A. DeMitchell, *Statutes and Standards: Has the Door to Educational Malpractice Been Opened?*, 2003 BYU EDUC. & L. J. 485 (2003). For a discussion of why contract law may be a better basis for student suits against universities than tort law *see* Hazel Glenn Beh, *Student Versus University: The University's Implied Obligations of Good Faith and Fair Dealing*, 59 MD. L. REV. 183 (2000).

2. Students in community colleges and proprietary schools have had some success with claims based in contract law. *See generally* Patrick F. Linehan, Note, *Dreams Protected: A New Approach to Policing Proprietary Schools' Misrepresentations*, 89 GEO. L.J. 753 (2001). In *Cencor, Inc. v. Tolman*, 868 P.2d 396 (Colo. 1994), a group of students sued a vocational school for failure to provide a variety of the services it originally advertised. The students primarily alleged claims of negligence, breach of contract, and misrepresentation. Noting that educational malpractice claims were not recognized in the jurisdiction, the Colorado Supreme Court dismissed the negligence claims, but upheld the contract and misrepresentation claims. *Id.* at 398, 400. The court noted that when "educational institutions have failed to provide specifically promised educational services, such as a failure to offer any classes or a failure to deliver a promised number of hours of instruction, such claims have been upheld on the basis of the law of contracts." *Id.* at 399.

Compare Cencor with Andre v. Pace Univ., 170 Misc.2d 893, 655 N.Y.S.2d 777 (1996). In *Andre*, students enrolled in a computer programming class that a school administrator had promised would require only basic math and computer skills. After attending the class for five weeks and finding the instruction and textbook to require more math and computer skills than they were promised, the students sued. The trial court found for the students based on breach of contract, breach of fiduciary duty, misrepresentation, and educational malpractice law. *Id.* at 896. The appellate court reversed the judgment, including the breach of contract claims, explaining:

> the public policy considerations underlying judicial noninterference in tort-based educational malpractice claims is equally applicable when the action is brought against a private educational institution and is formulated in con-

tract... In determining that the defendant had breached its contract, on the ground, *inter alia*, that the "textbook [was] plainly unsuited for the plaintiffs and the rest of the class," the court below improperly engaged in judicial evaluation of a course of instruction that the courts of this State have consistently held is the proper domain of educators and educational institutions entrusted to the task.

Id. at 897–98.

B. STUDENT MISCONDUCT

Dixon v. Alabama State Board of Education

United States Court of Appeals Fifth Circuit, 1961.
294 F.2d 150.

■ Opinion by RIVES, J.

The question presented by the pleadings and evidence, and decisive of this appeal, is whether due process requires notice and some opportunity for hearing before students at a tax-supported college are expelled for misconduct....

The misconduct for which the students were expelled has never been definitely specified. Defendant Trenholm, the President of the College, testified that he did not know why the plaintiffs and three additional students were expelled and twenty other students were placed on probation. The notice of expulsion which Dr. Trenholm mailed to each of the plaintiffs assigned no specific ground for expulsion, but referred in general terms to "this problem of Alabama State College."

The acts of the students considered by the State Board of Education before it ordered their expulsion are described in the opinion of the district court:

> On the 25th day of February, 1960, the six plaintiffs in this case were students in good standing at the Alabama State College for Negroes in Montgomery, Alabama.... On this date, approximately twenty-nine Negro students, including these six plaintiffs, according to a prearranged plan, entered as a group a publicly owned lunch grill located in the basement of the county courthouse in Montgomery, Alabama, and asked to be served. Service was refused; the lunchroom was closed; the Negroes refused to leave; police authorities were summoned; and the Negroes were ordered outside where they remained in the corridor of the courthouse for approximately one hour. On the same date, John Patterson, as Governor of the State of Alabama and as chairman of the State Board of Education, conferred with Dr. Trenholm, a Negro educator and president of the Alabama State College, concerning this activity on the part of some of the students. Dr. Trenholm was advised by the Governor that the incident should be investigated, and that if he were in the president's position he would consider expulsion and/or other appropriate disciplinary action. On February 26, 1960, several hundred Negro students from the Alabama State College, including several if not all of these plaintiffs, staged a mass attendance at a

trial being held in the Montgomery County Courthouse, involving the perjury prosecution of a fellow student. After the trial these students filed two by two from the courthouse and marched through the city approximately two miles back to the college. On February 27, 1960, several hundred Negro students from this school, including several if not all of the plaintiffs in this case, staged mass demonstrations in Montgomery and Tuskegee, Alabama. On this same date, Dr. Trenholm advised all of the student body that these demonstrations and meetings were disrupting the orderly conduct of the business at the college and were affecting the work of other students, as well as work of the participating students. Dr. Trenholm personally warned plaintiffs Bernard Lee, Joseph Peterson and Elroy Embry, to cease these disruptive [demonstrations] immediately, and advised the members of the student body at the Alabama State College to behave themselves and return to their classes. . . .

On or about March 1, 1960, approximately six hundred students of the Alabama State College engaged in hymn singing and speech making on the steps of the State Capitol. Plaintiff Bernard Lee addressed students at this demonstration, and the demonstration was attended by several if not all of the plaintiffs. Plaintiff Bernard Lee at this time called on the students to strike and boycott the college if any students were expelled because of these demonstrations.

As shown by the findings of the district court . . . the only demonstration which the evidence showed that all of the expelled students took part in was that in the lunch grill located in the basement of the Montgomery County Courthouse. . . .

[The plaintiffs' complaint alleged that Members of the State Board of Education expelled the plaintiffs as retaliation for the demonstration, without regard to any valid rule or regulation concerning student conduct. The court noted that members of the Board gave different grounds for their decision to expel the plaintiffs. Mr. Harry Ayers alone cited the demonstration at the lunch counter attended by all the plaintiffs as the reason for expulsion. He claimed that the demonstration violated the law of Alabama "separating the races in public places of that kind." Governor Patterson claimed that, if no action were taken against the plaintiffs, violence and disorder might result. Superintendent of Education Stewart claimed the plaintiffs violated a rule against demonstrations without the consent of the University president. Other members gave different reasons.]

The district court found . . . :

On or about March 2, 1960, the State Board of Education met and received reports from the Governor of the State of Alabama, which reports embodied the investigations that had been made and which reports identified these six plaintiffs, together with several others, as the "ring leaders" for the group of students that had been participating in the above-recited activities. During this meeting, Dr. Trenholm, in his capacity as president of the college reported to the assembled members of the State Board of Education that the action of these students in demonstrating on the college campus and in certain downtown areas was having a disruptive influence on the work of the other students at the college and upon the orderly operation of the college in general. Dr. Trenholm further reported to the Board that, in his opinion, he as president of the college could not control future disruptions and demonstrations. There were twenty-nine of the Negro students identified as the core of the organization that was responsible for these demonstrations. This group of twenty-nine included these six plaintiffs. After hearing these reports and recommendations and upon the recommendation of the Governor as chairman of the Board, the Board voted unanimously, expelling nine students, including these six plaintiffs, and placing twenty students on probation. This action was taken by Dr. Trenholm as president of the college, acting pursuant to the instructions of the State Board of Education. Each of these plaintiffs, together with the other students expelled, was officially notified of his expulsion on March 4th or 5th, 1960. No formal charges were placed against these students and no hearing was granted any of them prior to their expulsion.

The evidence clearly shows that the question for decision does not concern the sufficiency of the notice or the adequacy of the hearing, but is whether the students had a right to any notice or hearing whatever before being expelled.... After careful study and consideration, we find ourselves unable to agree with the conclusion of the district court that no notice or opportunity for any kind of hearing was required before these students were expelled.

. . .

It is not enough to say, as did the district court in the present case, "The right to attend a public college or university is not in and of itself a constitutional right." That argument was emphatically answered by the Supreme Court in [*Cafeteria and Restaurant Workers Union v. McElroy*, 81 S.Ct. 1743 (1961)] when it said that the question of whether ... summarily denying Rachel Brawner access to the site of her former employment violated the requirements of the Due Process Clause of the Fifth Amendment ... cannot be answered by easy assertion that, because she had no constitutional right to be there in the first place, she was not deprived of liberty or property by the Superintendent's action. "One may not have a constitutional right to go to Bagdad, but the Government may not prohibit one from going there unless by means consonant with due process of law." [S]o here, it is necessary to consider "the nature both of the private interest which has been impaired and the governmental power which has been exercised."

. . .

The precise nature of the private interest involved in this case is the right to remain at a public institution of higher learning in which the plaintiffs were students in good standing. It requires no argument to demonstrate that education is vital and, indeed, basic to civilized society. Without sufficient education the plaintiffs would not be able to earn an adequate livelihood, to enjoy life to the fullest, or to fulfill as completely as possible the duties and responsibilities of good citizens.

There was no offer to prove that other colleges are open to the plaintiffs. If so, the plaintiffs would nonetheless be injured by the interruption of their course of studies in mid-term. It is most unlikely that a public college would accept a student expelled from another public college of the same state. Indeed, expulsion may well prejudice the student in completing his education at any other institution. Surely no one can question that the right to remain at the college in which the plaintiffs were students in good standing is an interest of extremely great value.

Turning then to the nature of the governmental power to expel the plaintiffs, it must be conceded, as was held by the district court, that that power is not unlimited and cannot be arbitrarily exercised. Admittedly, there must be some reasonable and constitutional ground for expulsion or the courts would have a duty to require reinstatement. The possibility of arbitrary action is not excluded by the existence of reasonable regulations. There may be arbitrary application of the rule to the facts of a particular case. Indeed, that result is well nigh inevitable when the Board hears only one side of the issue. In the disciplining of college students there are no considerations of immediate danger to the public, or of peril to the national security, which should prevent the Board from exercising at least the fundamental principles of fairness by giving the accused students notice of the charges and an opportunity to be heard in their own defense. Indeed, the example set by the Board in failing so to do, if not corrected by the courts, can well break the spirits of the expelled students and of others familiar with the injustice, and do inestimable harm to their education.

. . .

We are confident that precedent as well as a most fundamental constitutional principle support our holding that due process requires notice and some opportunity for hearing before a student at a tax-supported college is expelled for misconduct.

For the guidance of the parties in the event of further proceedings, we state our views on the nature of the notice and hearing required by due process prior to expulsion from a state college or university. They should, we think, comply with the following standards. The notice should contain a statement of the specific charges and grounds which, if proven, would justify expulsion under the regulations of the Board of Education. The nature of the hearing should vary depending upon the circumstances of the particular case. The case before us requires something more than an informal interview with an administrative authority of the college. By its nature, a charge of misconduct, as opposed to a failure to meet the scholastic standards of the college, depends upon a collection of the facts concerning the charged misconduct, easily colored by the point of view of the witnesses. In such circumstances, a hearing which gives the Board or the administrative authorities of the college an opportunity to hear both sides in considerable detail is best suited to protect the rights of all involved. This is not to imply that a full-dress judicial hearing, with the right to cross-examine witnesses, is required. Such a hearing, with the attending publicity and disturbance of college activities, might be detrimental to the college's educational atmosphere and impractical to carry out. Nevertheless, the rudiments of an adversary proceeding may be preserved without encroaching upon the interests of the college. In the instant case, the student should be given the names of the witnesses against him and an oral or written report on the facts to which each witness testifies. He should also be given the opportunity to present to the Board, or at least to an administrative official of the college, his own defense against the charges and to produce either oral testimony or written affidavits of witnesses in his behalf. If the hearing is not before the Board directly, the results and findings of the hearing should be presented in a report open to the student's inspection. If these rudimentary elements of fair play are followed in a case of misconduct of this particular type, we feel that the requirements of due process of law will have been fulfilled.

The judgment of the district court is reversed and the cause is remanded for further proceedings consistent with this opinion.

Question and Comments on *Dixon*

1. In *Nash v. Auburn,* 812 F.2d 655 (11th Cir.1987), the court held that *Dixon* does not require a university to give students facing disciplinary hearings "the names of the witnesses against them and a summary of their expected testimony, when the opposing witnesses will testify in the presence of the accused." 812 F.2d at 662–63. Is that a fair reading of *Dixon?*

2. Why does the court hold that cross-examination of witnesses is not necessary for a hearing to be fair, even though it concedes that witnesses may be biased? The court balances the students' right to a fair hearing with the interest of the university or college. What legitimate interests does the university have in limiting the procedural requirements of a disciplinary hearing?

3. How should colleges and universities respond to disruptive student protests? Students at the University of Southern California chained themselves together and occupied the office of the president of the university to protest the use of sweatshop labor in the manufacture of the institution's branded apparel. Andy Guess, *A Standout Sit–In*, Inside Higher Ed., May 1, 2006, *available at* http://insidehighered.com/news/2007/05/01/ protests. The university gave the students an ultimatum: either leave the office by the end of the day or face "interim suspension," meaning that they could not attend classes, remain on campus, or stay in university housing until after a judicial process began. *Id.* University officials also contacted the students' parents. *Id.* In light of the holding in *Dixon,* should the students have been provided with some judicial process or disciplinary hearing before being given an interim suspension?

Gomes v. University of Maine System

United States District Court, District of Maine, 2005.
365 F. Supp. 2d 6.

■ JOHN A. WOODCOCK, JR., UNITED STATES DISTRICT JUDGE.

On September 25, 2002, following a disciplinary hearing, the Student Conduct Code Committee (Hearing Committee) of the University of Maine found that the Plaintiffs, Stefan Gomes and Paris Minor, undergraduates at the University, had sexually assaulted a female student and, thereby, violated the Student Conduct Code. The University suspended them for one year. After the Plaintiffs' administrative appeals failed, they turned to this Court for relief, asserting the disciplinary process was substantially flawed....

Following an incident on June 10, 2002, a female University student (Complainant) accused two male University students of sexually assaulting her. The two male students, former members of the University football team, are the Plaintiffs in this case.

The University has adopted a Student Conduct Code (Code), which sets forth the procedures it follows upon notice of a potential violation. Under the Code, the University designates a campus official, denominated the

"Officer," to investigate alleged violations of the Code, to notify the respondent of his conclusions, and, if appropriate, to impose sanctions. If the Officer concludes there is doubt whether a violation occurred or what sanction should be imposed, he may refer the matter directly to the Hearing Committee.

... The Hearing Committee is charged with holding a hearing to receive evidence, determining whether the respondent violated the Code, and, if so, imposing a sanction. If the Hearing Committee suspends or dismisses the respondent, the Code provides for two appeals. The first appeal is to a new person or group (the Appeal Committee); the second appeal is to the President or designee. The appeals are limited to a review of the procedures followed and the appropriateness of the sanction.

[On July 16, 2002, David Fiacco, the designated Officer, received information from the Old Town Police Department that Complainant had filed a charge of sexual assault against Plaintiffs. On August 17, 2002, the Complainant signed a University incident report, prompting Mr. Fiacco to investigate the incident and refer the case to the Hearing Committee.]

The Hearing Committee, chaired by Dr. Elizabeth Allan, consisted of five members. The Hearing Committee held a hearing on September 24, 2002, and by letter dated September 25, 2002, the Chair informed the Plaintiffs that it had concluded they had violated the Code by committing a sexual assault. The Hearing Committee suspended the Plaintiffs from the University through May 31, 2003 and made the suspensions effective immediately. The Hearing Committee ruled the suspensions would not be stayed pending any appeal "for the protection of other persons." ...

The Plaintiffs appealed the Hearing Committee's decision to the Appeal Committee.... On October 16, 2002, the Appeal Committee concluded the Hearing Committee did not commit procedural error and found the sanctions appropriate. The Plaintiffs exercised their right to a second appeal before the President's designee.... On November 18, 2002, [President Hoff's designee] concluded that the procedures "were in substantial conformity to the requirements of the code and afforded the Respondents fundamental fairness." He also determined that "the sanctions imposed on the Respondents were appropriate given the findings of the committee."

Summary judgment is appropriate only if the record shows "that there is no genuine issue as to any material fact and that the moving party is entitled to a judgment as a matter of law." ... In determining whether this burden is met, the court must view the record in the light most favorable to the nonmoving party and give that party the benefit of all reasonable inferences in its favor....

... This Court's review is substantially circumscribed; the law does not allow this Court to retry the University's disciplinary proceeding.

... This Court draws no opinion, therefore, about whether a sexual assault occurred, whether the acts were consensual, who among the Plaintiffs and the Complainant is credible, and who is not. This decision, which grants summary judgment in favor of the Defendants, is not a judicial finding either in favor or against the Plaintiffs or in favor or against the Complainant on the merits of her claims and their defenses.

. . .

The First Circuit has held that a student's interest "in pursuing an education is included within the fourteenth amendment's protection of liberty and property." *Gorman v. Univ. of Rhode Island*, 837 F.2d 7, 12 (1st Cir. 1988). A student "facing expulsion or suspension from a public educational institution is entitled to the protections of due process." Here, the Plaintiffs were students at a public university and potentially subject to expulsion or suspension. They are, therefore, entitled to the protections of due process. *See generally* Curtis J. Berger & Vivian Berger, *Academic Discipline: A Guide to Fair Process for the University Student*, 99 Colum. L. Rev. 289 (1999).

Determining an interest is protected by the due process clause of the Constitution is "only the beginning of the inquiry"; the question remains "what process is due." Due process is "not a fixed or rigid concept, but, rather, is a flexible standard which varies depending upon the nature of the interest affected, and the circumstances of the deprivation." At a minimum, students facing disciplinary action, such as a suspension, must be given "some kind of notice and afforded some kind of hearing." *Goss v. Lopez*, 419 U.S. 565, 579 (1975). Judge Gignoux of this Court adopted Professor Wright's description of the minimum requirements of due process in an academic setting:

> (1) The student must be advised of the charges against him; (2) he must be informed of the nature of the evidence against him; (3) he must be given an opportunity to be heard in his own defense; and (4) he must not be punished except on the basis of substantial evidence.

Keene v. Rodgers, 316 F. Supp. 217, 221 (D. Me. 1970) (quoting Charles Alan Wright, *The Constitution on the Campus*, 22 Vand. L. Rev. 1027, 1071–72 (1969)). To these factors, *Keene* added: 1) the student must be permitted the assistance of a lawyer, at least in major disciplinary proceedings; 2) he must be permitted to confront and to cross-examine the witnesses against him; and, 3) he must be afforded the right to an impartial tribunal, which must make written findings.

The law seeks to counterbalance the tension between two principles. A university is not a court of law, and it is neither practical nor desirable it be one. Yet, a public university student who is facing serious charges of misconduct that expose him to substantial sanctions should receive a fundamentally fair hearing. In weighing this tension, the law seeks the middle ground.

One factor is the seriousness of the charge and the potential consequences—what the Supreme Court described as the "private interest" affected by the official action. *Mathews v. Eldridge*, 424 U.S. 319, 334 (1976). Here, the private interest is compelling. The Plaintiffs faced charges of sexual assault against a fellow student, charges that could have led to their expulsions and did lead to their suspensions. The potential consequences reach beyond their immediate standing at the University. The Supreme Court has noted that " 'where a person's good name, reputation, honor, or integrity is at stake because of what the government is doing to him,' the minimal requirements of the [Due Process] Clause must be satisfied." *Goss*, 419 U.S. at 574. The University's decision could "interfere with later opportunities for higher education and employment." *Id.* at 575. The Plaintiffs argue, and this Court accepts, that these charges could "have a major immediate and life-long impact on [their] personal life, education, employment, and public engagement." The Plaintiffs also have an interest in avoiding "an erroneous deprivation" of their private interest through the University's procedures.

At the same time, a major purpose of the administrative process and hearing is to avoid formalistic and adversarial procedures. Justice White wrote in *Goss*, "further formalizing the suspension process and escalating its formality and adversary nature may not only make it too costly as a regular disciplinary tool but also destroy its effectiveness as part of the teaching process." In *Gorman*, the First Circuit advised courts reviewing an educational institution's administrative process of the following:

> In fostering and insuring the requirements of due process, however, the courts have not and should not require that a fair hearing is one that necessarily must follow the traditional common law adversarial method. Rather, on judicial review the question presented is whether, in the particular case, the individual has had an opportunity to answer, explain, and defend, and not whether the hearing mirrored a common law criminal trial.
>
> . . .
>
> . . . The question presented is not whether the hearing was ideal, or whether its procedure could have been better. In all cases the inquiry is whether, under the particular circumstances presented, the hearing was fair, and accorded the individual the essential elements of due process. In the words of Justice White, "the Due Process Clause requires, not an 'elaborate hearing' before a neutral party, but simply 'an informal give-and-take between student and disciplinarian' which gives 'the student an opportunity to explain his version of the facts.'"

The Plaintiffs claim the Defendants violated their due process rights by failing to inform them before the hearing of certain evidence: 1) they were not provided with a summary of a statement the Complainant gave to the Old Town Police Department; 2) they were not provided with a witness list before the day of the hearing; and, 3) they were not provided with the Complainant's medical records until the day of the hearing.

Following the June 10, 2002 incident, the Complainant notified the Old Town Police Department, which initiated an investigation. The police officers conducted four interviews of the Complainant. . . . The Plaintiffs assert the records of these interviews . . . call the Complainant's "credibility into serious doubt." . . .

. . . The University has admitted that, even though it provided a statement from the Old Town Police Department records to the Complainant's attorney, it provided nothing in the police report to the Plaintiffs. . . .

The Defendants contend there is no due process requirement in a university disciplinary hearing to provide the responding student with exculpatory or impeachment evidence. The Defendants further state the Plaintiffs themselves failed to act prudently to obtain the records from the District Attorney or request a continuance of the disciplinary hearing. Finally, the Defendants say the Plaintiffs still received a fundamentally fair hearing.

The Defendants are correct about discovery in university student disciplinary proceedings. Other than the limited notice provisions set forth in *Keene*—requiring that the student be advised of the charges and the nature of the evidence—there is no formal right to discovery. It is likely the University could have given neither the Complainant nor the Plaintiffs any police documents at all and survived a due process challenge.

The Plaintiffs' point remains, nevertheless, a potentially significant one. . . . In view of the nature of the charge and its circumstances, the Hearing Committee was required to determine who to believe. There were only three people in the Complainant's room the night of the incident. The Complainant stated she had consensual sex with Mr. Minor, non-consensual sex with Mr. Gomes, and then non-consensual sex with Mr. Minor; the Plaintiffs agreed they had sexual relations with the Complainant, but said their sexual relations with her were entirely consensual. The credibility of these three individuals ran to the heart of the disciplinary hearing.

[According to the Plaintiffs, the report shows that: Complainant did not mention non-consensual sex with Mr. Minor until the third police interview; she consumed alcohol before the incident; she took prescription medication that might have interacted with the alcohol. The Plaintiffs also note that the Complainant complained of "numerous errors and gross inaccuracies" in the report.] These issues, as well as certain other matters, would have at least been appropriate for the Hearing Committee's consideration; however, none of the information in the police reports was presented to the Hearing Committee. In fact, at the hearing, the Complainant was asked no questions at all: none by members of the Hearing Committee and none by the Plaintiffs.

The Plaintiffs argue the hearing generated the misimpression that the Complainant had been entirely consistent from the date of the incident onward. . . .

Mr. Fiacco's refusal to give the Plaintiffs what he had given the Complainant becomes more potentially significant in light of their respective roles in this proceeding. Under the Code, the Complainant and Mr. Fiacco, as the Officer, assume the roles of presenting the case against the Plaintiffs.[16] Mr. Fiacco and the Complainant had a complete copy of the police report, but the Plaintiffs did not, and Mr. Fiacco had failed to turn documents over to the Plaintiffs when requested to do so. The question is whether a university may, consistent with the requirements of due process, make potentially significant documents available to one side and not the other. . . . On its face, the University's actions raise a question as to whether this procedure was fundamentally fair and complied with the basic protections of due process.

The analysis cannot, however, end there. *Gorman* has reminded us not to "impose on educational institutions all the procedural requirements of a common law criminal trial." There are a number of factors to consider: 1) what precisely was given to one side that was not given to the other; 2) timing; 3) the reason the University provided unequal access; 4) the University's role in not supplying the full record; and, 5) the significance of the withheld information.

---

16. On September 17, 2002, the Complainant, through her attorney, informed Mr. Fiacco that she did not wish him to present the results of the investigation to the Hearing Committee. SMF ¶ 178. She presented the case herself with the advice of her lawyer.

What was given remains unclear. Mr. Fiacco [testified that he] "shared a component of the [police] report with the woman," . . . that "summarized her statement of the events." There is no clarification as to what "component" was given to the Complainant. This Court cannot assess the impact of an uneven distribution of material unless the Plaintiffs establish what material was distributed.

The timing is constrained. [Mr. Fiacco received the police records on July 16, 2002. The Complainant signed an incident report on August 17, 2002. Mr. Fiacco began a formal investigation and referred the matter to the Hearing Committee on September 9, 2002. The hearing was set for September 16, 2002, and postponed until September 24, 2002, at Plaintiffs' request.]

Between the referral and the hearing, there was a flurry of activity. [The Plaintiffs' attorney, Mr. Costlow, requested the component of the police report from the University's in-house counsel, Ms. Lavoie, and from Mr. Fiacco. Ms. Lavoie did not comply with the request, because she was concerned that doing so would violate Maine law. Mr. Fiacco did not give Mr. Costlow a copy of the report.

Lawyers for the Complainant and Plaintiffs sought complete copies of the police report from the District Attorney's Office. Assistant District Attorney Clifford provided the Complainant's lawyer a full copy of the report on September 20, 2002, along with a note stating that the full report would also be made available to the Plaintiff's lawyer. Nevertheless, the Plaintiff's attorney did not receive a full copy from the District Attorney until after the September 24, 2002 hearing.]

This chronology reflects the tight deadlines attendant to student disciplinary hearings from complaint to resolution. In *Nash*, for example, . . . the Eleventh Circuit concluded [a period of six days between the charge and the hearing] was "reasonable," because it allowed the students to retain counsel, to successfully argue for more certain notice and a short delay, and to appear at the hearing with supporting witnesses and documents. This tight timeframe, a timeframe not uncommon in university disciplinary hearings, makes it less appropriate to impose strict legal document production requirements on the parties. . . .

Why did the University not turn over the entire police report? The University was confronted with a provision of Maine statutory law that restricts the disclosure of the police reports. The police reports constituted "record information" under § 613, and University counsel was concerned that this statute may have prohibited dissemination to any third party, including the Plaintiffs and the Complainant.[19] The University, through Attorney Lavoie, made an effort to clarify whether the law prohibited it from releasing material.

What was the University's role? Upon review, the University's actions were not as significant as the Plaintiffs would have them be. It was on September 9, 2002 that Mr. Fiacco gave the Complainant one unidentified statement from the police report, but it was on September 20, 2002, the

---

19. The record reflects that in-house counsel Nina Lavoie was concerned not only about the release of the police reports to the Plaintiffs, but also about whether Mr. Fiacco's release of the statement in the report to the Complainant constituted a violation of law. It should be noted as well that Mr. Fiacco released the statement to the Complainant before questions about the legality of its release were raised.

Complainant received by fax from ADA Clifford a complete copy of the entire police file. The District Attorney's Office is not the University of Maine, and its actions are not attributable to the University. ADA Clifford's uneven distribution of the entire report eclipses the University's uneven distribution of one statement in the report. The Complainant had the entire report one full week ahead of the hearing and her possession of one statement from the report eleven days earlier has not been shown to have had any impact on the hearing. Because the Complainant later obtained the same statement through other sources, the Plaintiffs' claim cannot be based on the Complainant's possession of the statement, but rather must be based solely on their non-possession of this one statement.

What was the impact of the University's actions? This leaves the Plaintiffs' contention that their non-possession of one unidentified statement constituted a denial of due process. Having failed to identify which statement they did not receive, it would be speculative to intuit what effect its non-production had on the proceeding. On the state of the record before it, this Court can draw no conclusions.

Upon analysis, the Plaintiffs' claim of a violation of due process based on the University's failure to distribute a statement in the police report to them before the hearing must fail. Tight time constraints, a general rule against imposing discovery requirements on university disciplinary proceedings, the Complainant's access to the same material from a non-university source, and the Plaintiffs' failure to identify the statement itself require this Court to conclude there is no genuine issue of material fact on the issue of whether the uneven distribution of a statement from the police records constituted a denial of due process.

Several days before the hearing, the Defendants provided a witness list to the Plaintiffs. . . . [At the hearing, the Complainant called two additional "rebuttal witnesses." Mr. Costlow objected, but he acknowledged that the decision to include the testimony was "at the discretion of the chair." The Plaintiffs were present for the rebuttal witnesses' testimony and had an opportunity to cross-examine the witnesses.]

Mr. Costlow was correct in acknowledging the Chair's discretion. If this hearing had been before a court, the judge would have had the discretion to allow or exclude the testimony of unlisted witnesses. A trial judge's decision to allow the Government to call a rebuttal witness in a criminal trial is reviewed for abuse of discretion. The decision to allow the testimony of unlisted witnesses would have been upheld in a judicial proceeding and was well within the Chair's discretion as presiding officer at the disciplinary hearing.

Moreover, due process in the context of academic discipline does not necessarily require students be given a list of witnesses and exhibits prior to the hearing, provided the students are allowed to attend the hearing itself. *Nash v. Auburn Univ.*, 812 F.2d 655, 662–63 (11th Cir. 1987) ("We did not require in *Dixon* that students facing a hearing on charges of misconduct be given the names of witnesses against them and a summary of their expected testimony, when the opposing witnesses will testify in the presence of the accused."). Because [the rebuttal witnesses] testified in the presence of the Plaintiffs, it was not a due process requirement to give the Plaintiffs their names and a summary of their expected testimony before the hearing.

[The Plaintiffs argued that they were due greater procedural protections than the students in *Nash*, because the charge of sexual assault is more serious than the charge of academic dishonesty (*Nash*). The District Court rejected the distinction because it would "require nuanced judgments about gradations of seriousness among differing charges and a perilous attempt to translate tonal levels of gravity to sets of due process rights." The District Court argued that the severity of the sanction should determine the level of due process. Noting the similarity of the sanctions in this case, *Nash*, and *Dixon*, the District Court refused to conclude that "due process clause requires [Plaintiffs] be supplied in advance with a witness list, when those students are present at the hearing and have the right to listen to the statements and ask questions."]

. . .

Finally, the University's decision not to allow voir dire is consistent with the Code, which does not permit voir dire, but does permit challenges for cause. The parties were advised at the outset of the hearing of their right to challenge for cause, but the Plaintiffs made no challenge. Allowing challenges for cause, but not voir dire, reduces the risk the committee hearing will be transformed into a full blown trial. On the other hand, if the parties are aware of reasons that would disqualify a committee member, they are allowed to bring them forward. Striking this balance, the University has not violated the due process clause.

. . .

In light of the disposition of this case, the claim for punitive damages is dismissed.

This Court grants the Defendants' Motion for Summary Judgment; judgment is to be entered in favor of the Defendants and against the Plaintiffs on all remaining counts.

Questions and Comments on *Gomes*

1. *Gomes* dealt with student misconduct at a public university where, according to most courts, a student is guaranteed procedural due process before being suspended or expelled. What guarantees do students at private universities have? Because private universities do not qualify as state actors, students generally must rely on contract law and argue that the university should follow its written procedures in discipline cases.

2. Many colleges and universities include provisions in their disciplinary codes about behavior off-campus. Should universities be able to suspend students for their actions off-campus? Stanford and Cornell have recently proposed revisions to their codes of conduct that would allow the administration to investigate and respond to off-campus activity. Elia Powers, *Extending the Arm of Campus Law*, INSIDE HIGHER ED., Nov. 20, 2007, *available at* http://insidehighered.com/news/2007/11/20/offcampus. The University's off-campus enforcement is directed at major code infractions, such as sexual assault and hazing, not minor infractions such as underage drinking. *Id.* Complaints from neighbors living near the University of Washington about disruptive student behavior have led a state senator to propose legislation compelling state universities to extend their disciplinary code to off-campus neighborhoods. Christine Frey, *UW May Expand Student Conduct Code to Cover Off–Campus Behavior*, SEATTLE POST-INTELLI-GENCER, Jan. 22. 2007, *available at* http://seattlepi.nwsource.com/local/300601_conduct code22html. Both university officials and students oppose the measure. *Id. See also,*

Krasnow v. Virginia Polytechnic Inst., 414 F.Supp. 55 (W.D.Va. 1976) (holding universities may regulate activity off-campus), *aff'd* 551 F.2d 591 (4th Cir. 1977); Kusnir v. Leach, 64 Pa.Cmwlth. 65, 70, 439 A.2d 223 (1982) ("a college has a vital interest in the character of its students, and may regard off-campus behavior as a reflection of a student's character and his fitness to be a member of the student body").

3. The 2006 Duke lacrosse scandal demonstrates the dangers a university faces if it rushes to discipline students when they are accused, but not yet convicted, of crimes. When three lacrosse players at Duke University were accused of raping a stripper hired to perform at their party, the university suspended the students. Some members of the faculty, dubbed the group of 88, published an ad in the university newspaper which raised questions about the racist culture at Duke entitled "What Does Social Disaster Sound Like?" As the case against the lacrosse players fell apart, the group of 88 and the university faced mounting criticism from the community for rushing to judgment against the students. *See* Rob Copeland, *"Group of 88" Faculty Hears Criticism in Wake of Sex Scandal*, THE CHRONICLE, Nov. 7, 2006, available at www. dukechronicle.com; Stuart Taylor Jr. & K.C. Johnson, *Guilty in the Duke Case*, WASHINGTON POST, Sept. 7, 2007, at A21. By the time all charges were dropped a year later, the three accused students had filed lawsuits against the university, which were eventually settled for an undisclosed amount. Wenjia Zhang, *"A Great Day For North Carolina:" Families, Duke Agree To Terms Of Settlement*, THE CHRONICLE, June 21, 2007, at 1, available at www.dukechronicle.com. Other members of the team have also filed suit, alleging that Duke violated a special duty of care by failing to protect the players from harassment, harm to their reputation, and a rogue criminal investigation. Sara Lipka, *More than 3 Dozen Lacrosse Players Sue Duke, Alleging Privacy Violations and Neglect of Duty*, CHRON. HIGHER EDUC., Feb. 22, 2008, *available at* http://chronicle.com/daily/2008/02/1797n.htm. The president of the university has since apologized for failing to offer more support to the accused students. Lawrence Biemiller, *Duke U. President Apologizes for Handling of Rape Accusations*, CHRON. HIGHER EDUC., Sept. 29, 2007, *available at* http://chronicle.com/news/index.php?id=3144. What should a university do when a student is faced with charges but has not yet been convicted? Could a university face liability for failing to discipline students charged with crimes? *See* Williams v. Bd. of Regents *infra* at p. 828.

4. In *Gomes*, the plaintiffs argued that Dr. Allan was biased against them because she was an advocate for rape victims. They also alleged that other members of the Hearing Committee might be biased against football players. Was the court right to dismiss the charges as unfounded? Arguably, the group of 88's rush to judge the Duke lacrosse players stemmed from the group's ideological and political commitments. *See* STEWART TAYLOR JR. & KC JOHNSON, UNTIL PROVEN INNOCENT, 103–117 (2007) (arguing that political correctness and radical left-wing ideology led many prominent academics at Duke to presuppose that the privileged white male students on the lacrosse team had raped the underprivileged black woman.) Should the political or associational affiliations of a faculty member be a relevant factor in determining whether the faculty member should be allowed to serve on a disciplinary committee?

5. May a university deny a student who has completed all academic requirements a degree for disciplinary reasons? In *Harwood v. Johns Hopkins University*, 130 Md.App. 476, 747 A.2d 205 (2000), *appeal denied*, 360 Md. 486, 759 A.2d 231 (2000), the court held that a student who murdered another student could be expelled without receiving a degree, despite the fact that he had completed all relevant coursework. The court noted that the relationship between the student and Johns Hopkins, a private university, was contractual, and that the Student Handbook formed part of the contract. The Handbook explicitly stated that students will not receive a degree based solely on the completion of coursework and that students must comply with the university's policies, including its rule prohibiting violence against other students, in order to receive a degree. Given these provisions of the handbook and the administrative hearing provided to the student before his dismissal, the expulsion of the student was upheld.

C. ACADEMIC MISCONDUCT

Napolitano v. Trustees of Princeton University

Superior Court of New Jersey, Appellate Division, 1982.
186 N.J.Super. 548, 453 A.2d 263.

■ MATTHEWS, P.J.A.D.

When this action was instituted plaintiff was a student in her senior year at Princeton University, a member of the Class of 1982. Were it not for the disciplinary action which precipitated this litigation, she would have been eligible to graduate on June 8, 1982. She is presently eligible to graduate in June 1983, at which time she will receive a Bachelor of Arts degree, with a major in English.

Defendant, The Trustees of Princeton University, is an educational corporation in the State of New Jersey. It operates a private institution of higher education known as Princeton University....

Defendant William G. Bowen is the President of Princeton University. He has held that position since July of 1972....

Among the many functions exercised by President Bowen is the power to review and, when appropriate, to modify the penalties imposed by various disciplinary bodies at Princeton, including the Faculty–Student Committee on Discipline (COD).

Defendant Peter Onek is an Assistant Dean of Student Affairs at Princeton, having held that position since August of 1977. As Assistant Dean of Student Affairs, Dean Onek is Secretary of the COD, but not a voting member. Dean Onek's duties as Secretary include (1) receiving disciplinary charges from faculty members, proctors or others, (2) notifying students of such charges, (3) counseling students on their rights and the procedures of the COD, (4) coordinating the presentation of documentary and other evidence to the COD and (5) taking and, when appropriate, preparing the minutes of the COD meetings. Dean Onek performed each of those duties in connection with the first disciplinary hearing but was voluntarily replaced for the second hearing, although replacement was not required by the trial judge.

Defendant Sylvia Molloy is a Professor of Spanish in the Department of Romance Languages and Literatures.... In 1973 Professor Molloy was promoted to Associate Professor, a tenured position. In 1981 she became a full Professor.

During the Fall Term of the 1981–1982 academic year Professor Molloy taught Spanish 341, a course entitled "The Spanish American Novel." Plaintiff elected to become a student in that course. It was her submission of a term paper for that course which gave rise to the disciplinary proceedings here under review.

. . .

All disciplinary matters concerning undergraduates which do not involve in-class examinations are subject to the jurisdiction of the COD. This includes academic violations, such as plagiarism on essays, term papers or laboratory reports, and nonacademic violations, such as disorderly conduct or drug-related offenses. The COD is a Standing Committee of the Faculty of Princeton University. Rules and Procedures of the Faculty of Princeton University (July 1978 with Addenda).

A general description of some of the rules and procedures of the COD is found in a booklet entitled Rights, Rules, Responsibilities—1980 Edition (RRR–1980). The penalty section lists the following penalties:

Range of Penalties. For violation of University-wide rules of conduct, members of the community are subject to several kinds of penalties. The applicability and exact nature of each penalty varies for faculty, students, professional staff, and employees; but in general the penalties, in ascending order of severity, are:

1. *Warning....*

2. *Disciplinary Probation.* A more serious admonition assigned for a definite amount of time, up to two years. It implies that any future violation, of whatever kind, during that time, may be grounds for suspension, required withdrawal, or in especially serious cases, for expulsion, from the University.

3. *Suspension.* Removal from membership in, or employment by, the University for a specified period of time.

4. *Required Withdrawal....*

5. *Expulsion....*

6. *Censure....*

A withheld degree, the penalty imposed upon plaintiff, is a less severe variation of suspension. It is imposed only upon second semester seniors. It permits them to finish their academic requirements and wait the prescribed period to receive their degree, rather than requiring them to lose their tuition and repeat their last semester in the following academic year. Excluding plaintiff's case, Princeton has withheld 20 degrees for disciplinary reasons since the 1972–1973 academic year.

There are two avenues of appeal from the decision and penalty of the COD: to the Judicial Committee of the Council of the Princeton University Community (Judicial Committee) and to the President of the University. Only the Judicial Committee avenue of appeal appears in the written material. A direct appeal to President Bowen from the COD is not mentioned in RRR–1980 or any other University publication, but, we are advised, is the avenue chosen in the overwhelming number of cases in which there is an appeal.

The appellate jurisdiction exercised by the President of the University is generally confined to a review of the penalty. It is accurately described in the RRR section concerning appeals from the Judicial Committee.

RRR contains a lengthy section concerning the "general requirements" or "fundamental principles" for the acknowledgment of sources in academic work:

The academic departments of the University have varying requirements for the acknowledgment of sources, but certain fundamental principles apply to all levels of work. In order to prevent any misunderstanding, students are expected to study and comply with the following basic requirements.

Quotations. Any quotations, however small, must be placed in quotation marks or clearly indented beyond the regular margin. Any quotation must be accompanied (either within the text or in a footnote) by a precise indication of the source—identifying the author, title, place and date of publication (where relevant), and page numbers. Any sentence or phrase which is not the original work of the student must be acknowledged.

Paraphrasing. Any material which is paraphrased or summarized must also be specifically acknowledged in a footnote or in the text. A thorough rewording or rearrangement of an author's text does not relieve one of this responsibility. Occasionally, students maintain that they have read a source long before they wrote their papers and have unwittingly duplicated some of its phrases or ideas. This is not a valid excuse. The student is responsible for taking adequate notes so that debts of phrasing may be acknowledged where they are due.

Ideas and Facts. Any ideas or facts which are borrowed should be specifically acknowledged in a footnote or in the text, even if the idea or fact has been further elaborated by the student. . . .

. . .

Footnotes and Bibliography. All the sources which have been consulted in the preparation of an essay or report should be listed in a bibliography, unless specific guidelines (from the academic department or instructor) request that only works cited be so included. However, the mere listing of a source in a bibliography shall not be considered a "proper acknowledgement" for specific use of that source within the essay or report.

. . .

This description of "fundamental principles" is followed by a series of definitions of "academic fraud" within the jurisdiction of the COD:

With regard to essays, laboratory reports, or any other written work submitted to fulfill an official academic requirement, the following are considered academic fraud:

Plagiarism. The deliberate use of any outside source without proper acknowledgment. "Outside source" means any work, published or unpublished, by any person other than the student.

. . .

Because of the importance of original work in the Princeton academic community, each student is required to attest to the originality of the submitted work and its compliance with University regulations:

At the end of an essay, laboratory report, or any other requirement, the student is to write the following sentence and sign his or her name: *"This paper represents my own work in accordance with University regulations."* [Emphasis in original]

- Sign honor code

. . .

At the first class meeting of Spanish 341 Professor Molloy announced that the course requirements would be a term paper and midterm and final examinations. The term paper was to be a critical analysis of one of the works read for the course, on a topic which was to be chosen by the student but approved by Professor Molloy. The paper could be handed in at any time during the Fall Term, but no later than January 13, 1982, the last day of Princeton's reading period.

Plaintiff did not meet with Professor Molloy to seek approval of her topic until December 16, 1981, the last day of classes before the Christmas recess. She was one of the last, if not the last, to seek such approval from Professor Molloy.

Plaintiff told Professor Molloy that she wanted to write her paper on the family ties in a novel entitled *Cien anos de soledad (100 Years of Solitude)* by Gabriel Garcia Marquez. Professor Molloy approved the topic and told plaintiff that she ought to read *Cien anos de soledad: una interpretacion* by Josefina Ludmer (Ludmer), a book which Professor Molloy had put on library reserve at the beginning of the Fall Semester. . . .

Plaintiff has testified that *Ludmer* was the only book to which she referred in writing her paper. Although she also testified that she did not have *Ludmer* in front of her when she wrote her paper, she admitted that she did refer to her notes, all of which had been prepared while she was reading *Ludmer*.

Plaintiff's paper was entitled *"Un analisis de la estructura de Cien anos de soledad."* . . . The paper was written in Spanish.

A simple comparison of plaintiff's paper and *Ludmer* reveals numerous sections of the paper which are taken verbatim, or in other portions virtually verbatim, from *Ludmer*, but which are not put into quotation marks or indented and which are not footnoted. At the end of her paper plaintiff wrote and signed the acknowledgment of originality required by RRR, in Spanish: "This paper represents my own work in accordance with University regulations."

On or about January 21, 1982 Professor Molloy began to correct plaintiff's paper. As soon as she began reading the first page she "sensed there was something wrong" and wrote, "Is this yours?", in Spanish, on the margin. She did not go beyond the first page, which contains no footnote or reference to *Ludmer*, before she "realized that Gabrielle Napolitano had not written what [she] was reading."

On January 22, 1982, after completing her review of plaintiff's paper and *Ludmer*, Professor Molloy consulted RRR–1980 and the Faculty Rules. Pursuant to the instruction at page 80 of the Faculty Rules, Professor Molloy telephoned Dean Onek and told him about plaintiff's paper. Dean Onek told her to send him a letter, with the paper and *Ludmer*, to present the copied material as clearly as possible and to turn in an "Incomplete" as plaintiff's grade in the course.

On January 26, 1982 Professor Molloy sent the letter Dean Onek had requested, setting forth her charge of plagiarism against plaintiff.

Between his receipt of Professor Molloy's letter and the date of the first COD hearing, Dean Onek met with plaintiff on four separate occasions. In the course of those meetings Dean Onek explained the various written and unwritten rules and procedures of the COD. He gave plaintiff copies of her paper, *Ludmer* and Professor Molloy's letter. He also sent plaintiff a formal letter notifying her of the hearing. At plaintiff's request Dean Onek spoke by telephone to her parents' attorney during one of their meetings.

The first COD hearing took place on Thursday, February 11. Plaintiff arrived at about 8 a.m. While she and her advisor waited in Dean Onek's office, the Dean distributed copies of Professor Molloy's letter, plaintiff's paper and the photocopy of *Ludmer* to members of the COD for their review. . . .

. . .

After the COD unanimously voted to find plaintiff guilty of plagiarism and withhold her degree for one year, Dean Onek informed her of the decision and subsequently met with her to explain the right of appeal.

Plaintiff met with President Bowen's assistant to discuss the appeal sometime before February 18, 1982, the date on which she wrote a letter to President Bowen, appealing to him for "clemency."

Plaintiff met with President Bowen and his assistant on Friday, February 26, 1982. President Bowen and plaintiff discussed her appeal. Although plaintiff claims that President Bowen stated that her conduct was an "unconscious act," there is no independent support of that found in the record.

President Bowen reviewed the file materials regarding proceedings before the COD and also received a letter on plaintiff's behalf from Professor Aarsleff. On March 1, 1982 President Bowen wrote to plaintiff to inform her that he had decided to uphold the determination of the COD.

A verified complaint was filed on April 22, 1982, at which time the trial judge entered an order to show cause scheduling a hearing on plaintiff's request for injunctive relief. Plaintiff's 14–count, verified complaint stated a wide variety of legal theories, all of which were directed to an attack upon the finding of plagiarism at Princeton University and the resulting penalty. . . .

. . .

After several procedural motions, including a motion by defendants to disqualify the trial judge (which he denied), and various conferences among counsel and the judge, the parties were directed to bring cross-motions for summary judgment on [a number of issues, including whether the COD applied the appropriate standard in finding plaintiff guilty of plagiarism, whether plaintiff had a right to call witnesses to speak on her behalf, and whether the plaintiff had a right to counsel at the disciplinary hearing.]

The first summary hearing was held on May 24, 1982. . . .

After hearing oral argument the trial judge decided to remand the matter for a rehearing at Princeton. He found that a conviction for the academic fraud offense of plagiarism must be based upon a finding of "intent to pass off the submitted work as the student's own." He also required that plaintiff be permitted to call "any witnesses she wished on her own behalf, subject only to reasonable regulation by the presiding officer."

He rejected plaintiff's argument that she was entitled to be represented by counsel at the rehearing. He retained jurisdiction and scheduled a further hearing....

The trial judge also directed counsel to prepare a set of instructions to the Faculty–Student Committee on Discipline, setting forth its responsibilities at the hearing. That document was prepared with the agreement of both counsel and presented to COD. [The instructions provided, among other things: (1) the Committee was to proceed in its usual manner, except as specifically set forth in the "charge"; (2) the Committee was free to reach the same or a different result; (3) plaintiff could call any witness, subject to "reasonable limitation in terms of numbers, length of presentation, and the like"; (4) the Committee was "not limited in any way to information presented at the earlier hearing"; (5) the decision was to "be based solely on the information presented at the rehearing"; (6) the entire proceedings, including deliberations, were to be tape-recorded and (7) the minutes or "summary" of the proceedings were to be prepared by the acting secretary and approved by each member of the Committee.

With respect to the COD's responsibilities in rehearing the accusation against plaintiff, the instructions provided, in full:

> The Committee should first focus upon whether the offense of plagiarism has occurred. In so doing, it should determine whether there has been deliberate use of an outside source without proper acknowledgment. In this regard, "deliberate" means "intention to pass off the work as one's own." If the question of a penalty is reached, the Committee should then focus upon: (a) the seriousness of the offense that has been found to have been committed, (b) the character and accomplishments of the person who has committed the offense, (c) the penalties assigned in other cases, and (d) the purposes—including educative—of the penalty to be assigned in this matter....

The rehearing took place on May 27, 1982, commencing at 8 a.m. Plaintiff was accompanied into the hearing room by her chosen advisor, Professor Jameson W. Doig, who spoke on her behalf....

After hearing the opening and closing remark of Professor Doig, plaintiff's statement and the questioning of Professor Molloy, plaintiff and other witnesses, ... [t]he Committee unanimously found plaintiff guilty of plagiarism (8–0) and, with one abstention, imposed the penalty of withholding her degree for one year (7–1).

On May 30, 1982 plaintiff and Professor Doig met with President Bowen to discuss her appeal. Plaintiff's parents also met with President Bowen on that date. On June 1, 1982 President Bowen affirmed the decision reached by the COD at the rehearing.

The trial judge held a final summary hearing on June 2, 1982.... [H]e found that the decision on the remand was supported by the evidence. He stated that the "Committee's findings concerning intent are explicit and substantiated in the record as set forth in some detail on pages two and three of the summary of the hearing dated May 28, 1982"; that "there is no question from plaintiff's extensive use of unattributed material, that the committee was justified in concluding that she committed the offense with the intention to pass off the quoted material as her own." While he emphasized his personal disagreement with the severity of the penalty, he held that he could not find "that Princeton could not in good faith have assessed the penalties it did against plaintiff."

. . .

The principal issue, as we see it, is whether the trial judge properly viewed his role as limited to a determination of whether Princeton substantially complied with its own regulations in disciplining plaintiff and, if so, whether Princeton's decision was supported by the evidence adduced at the hearing, and whether the penalty imposed was within Princeton's authority to impose.

. . .

Plaintiff complains that the trial judge gave total deference to the results of the second hearing at the University and thereby abdicated his role as a Chancery Division judge. Contrary to plaintiff's contentions, the trial judge did not determine his role in reviewing the proceedings before the University and the penalty without recourse to authority. In the opinion he filed after the proceedings there may be found citation to several cases dealing with academic discipline and the role that courts should play in dealing with the rights of students *vis-à-vis* the university in which they are enrolled. Because of the lack of precedent in this jurisdiction, he referred to our law of private associations, as set forth in *Higgins v. American Society of Clinical Pathologists*, 51 N.J. 191 (1968). He also noted the comprehensive opinion filed by Judge Ackerman in the United States District Court in *Clayton v. Princeton University*, 519 F.Supp. 802 (D.N.J.1981).

In *Higgins v. American Society of Clinical Pathologists* Justice Proctor, speaking for the court, described the relationship between a private organization and one of its members, and the rights of each, in the following terms:

> While the general rule is that courts will not compel admission of an individual into a voluntary association, they have been willing to intervene and compel the reinstatement of a member who has been wrongfully expelled: "The law accords important rights and status to members of voluntary organizations not extended to mere aspirants to membership therein...."
>
> The rights accorded to members of an association traditionally have been analyzed either in terms of property interests—that is, some interest in the assets of the organization, . . . or in terms of contract rights—that is, reciprocal rights and duties laid down in the constitution and bylaws.... These theories, however, are incomplete since they often prevent the courts from considering the genuine reasons for and against relief . . . and have been extensively criticized. *See, e.g.,* Note, *Judicial Control of Actions of Private Associations*, 76 HARV. L. REV. 983, 998–1002 (1963); Note, 15 RUTGERS L. REV. 327, 330–33 (1960). Leading commentators have pointed out that the real reason for judicial relief against wrongful expulsion is the protection of the member's valuable personal relationship to the association and the status conferred by that relationship.... As Professor Chafee has noted, "the wrong is a tort, not a breach of contract, and the tort consists in the destruction of the relation rather than in a deprivation of the remote and conjectural right to

receive property." ... The loss of *status* resulting from the destruction of one's relationship to a professional organization ofttimes may be more harmful than a loss of property or contractual rights and properly may be the subject of judicial protection....

. . .

... In determining whether the deprivation of plaintiff's status was justified, our examination of the reason for her expulsion must be limited. Courts ordinarily ought not to intrude upon areas of associational decision involving specialized knowledge.... Private associations must have considerable latitude in rule-making in order to accomplish their objectives and their private law generally is binding on those who wish to remain members. However, courts will relieve against any expulsion based on rules which are in conflict with public policy.... [51 N.J. at 199–202; citations omitted]

We do not believe, however, that the law of private associations delineates completely the relationship between a student and a university. The relationship is unique. The status of a private university such as Princeton was referred to by Justice Handler in his opinion for the court in *State v. Schmid*, 84 N.J. 535 (1980), in these terms:

A private educational institution such as Princeton University involves essentially voluntary relationships between and among the institution and its students, faculty, employees, and other affiliated personnel, and the life and activities of the individual members of this community are directed and shaped by their shared educational goals and the institution's educational policies.

The student comes to the academic community (the university) seeking to be educated in a given discipline. The student pays a tuition which might, in some instances, represent a contractual consideration. The university undertakes to educate that student through its faculty and through the association of other students with that student and the faculty. Transcending that bare relationship is the understanding that the student will abide by the reasonable regulations, both academic and disciplinary, that the student will meet the academic standards established by the faculty and that the university, on the successful completion of studies, will award the degree sought to the student. Such a relationship, we submit, cannot be described either in pure contractual or associational terms. In those instances where courts have dealt with the relationship of a private university to its students in contractual terms, they have warned against a rigid application of the law of contracts to students' disciplinary proceedings. Thus, in *Slaughter v. Brigham Young Univ.*, 514 F.2d 622 (10th Cir.1975), it was held:

It is apparent that *some* elements of the law of contracts are used and should be used in the analysis of the relationship between plaintiff and the University to provide some framework into which to put the problem of expulsion for disciplinary reasons. This does not mean that "contract law" must be rigidly applied in all its aspects, nor is it so applied even when the contract analogy is extensively adopted. There are other areas of the law which are also used by courts and writers to provide elements of such a framework. These included in times past *parens patriae*, and now include private associations such as church membership, union membership, professional societies; elements drawn from "status" theory, and others. Many sources have been used in this process, and combinations thereof, and in none is it assumed or required that all the elements of a particular doctrine be applied. The student-university relationship is unique, and it should not be and cannot be stuffed into one doctrinal category. It may also be different at different schools.

. . .

Courts have also recognized the necessity for independence of a university in dealing with the academic failures, transgressions or problems of a student. We ... regard the problem before the court as one involving academic standards and not a case of violation of rules of conduct. Plaintiff, apparently ignoring the distinction, seeks a full panoply of procedural safeguards under a claim of due process.

Courts have been virtually unanimous in rejecting students' claims for due process in the constitutional sense where academic suspensions or dismissal are involved.

. . .

Considering Princeton's status as a private university under our law, *State v. Schmid*, we believe that the principles set forth in the cases cited above, culminating with *Board of Curators, Univ. of Mo. v. Horowitz*, accurately state our law with respect to the proceedings here under review. We agree with the trial judge that he should not have become a super-trier under due process considerations.

In support of our conclusion we note that deference has always been afforded to the internal decision-making process under our law of associations. . . .

Plaintiff persists, however, in her contention that the charge of plagiarism against her was not proved by the University before the COD and that the trial judge should have conducted a full hearing on the substantive offense. No authority is cited to us to support this view, and we know of none. . . .

Our independent examination of the record satisfies us that the COD properly concluded that plaintiff had plagiarized. Her paper constitutes a mosaic of the *Ludmer* work in an attempt to pass off Ludmer's ideas as plaintiff's own. While plaintiff persists in her argument that she did not intend to plagiarize and that there is nothing in the proofs to show that she did so intend, the mosaic itself is the loudest argument against her. The creation of that mosaic can only lead to one conclusion: that plaintiff intended to deceive her preceptor that the paper was original. An excerpt from the summary prepared by the COD with respect to the basis of its finding of intent is illuminating:

> A series of questions and comments concerning the contents of the paper followed Ms. Napolitano's presentation. It was pointed out that the entire paper consisted almost exclusively of a literal or slightly paraphrased rendering of various portions of the one secondary source used, without proper attribution, except in occasional instances. In addition, Professor Molloy and some members of the

Committee mentioned a number of points in the paper which at the very least suggested that Ms. Napolitano did indeed intend to give the impression that the borrowings from her source were in fact her own. Among these were:

dated to plagiarize

> 1) A few statements from the source had been put in quotation marks but not the rest. This could indicate, on the other hand, that Ms. Napolitano had made an effort to use outside sources and, on the other, that the portions of the paper that were not in direct quotations were her own work.

> 2) The use, in the paper, of phrases such as "it is evident that," "it is important to note that," "one can assume that," etc. suggests that what follows is Ms. Napolitano's own thoughts and words, when in fact, in virtually all instances, what follows is words borrowed from the one source without attributions.

> 3) In several instances, there are quotes from the novel which is the subject of the paper. These quotes were used by the secondary source [the *Ludmer* text] to illustrate various points. In making these same points (usually using the words of the secondary source), Ms. Napolitano used the same quotes but changed the page numbers of the quotes to correspond to the edition of the novel used in the course. This gives the appearance that Ms. Napolitano had found the quotes herself in the novel, which, in fact, she did not.

> 4) The verb tenses in the material borrowed from the source were all changed to the present tense for the sake of consistency in the paper.

> 5) Small words and phrases from the borrowed source were deleted in cases where these words may have seemed too technical or awkward.

The COD did not accept plaintiff's explanations, finding them unsatisfactory, especially in light of the signed statement at the conclusion of the paper that it was her work in accordance with University regulations.

. . .

Plaintiff's final argument relates to the penalty which was imposed upon her, the postponement of her degree for a period of one year until June 1983. The question of the penalty was troublesome to the trial judge. From the very institution of this action until the time he rendered his final decision, the judge expressed personal disagreement with the decision of the COD and President Bowen to defer the granting of plaintiff's degree from June 1982 until June 1983. Despite that disagreement the judge correctly held that he could not substitute his own views for those of a duly constituted administrative body within a private institution. He reached this conclusion and the holding as to the correctness of the penalty on the basis of the law of contracts. Plaintiff persists in arguing, however, that the penalty imposed demonstrates bias on the part of defendants because (a) the penalty imposed is inconsistent with penalties imposed in similar cases over the years and (b)

argued penalty is too harsh

it is actually "out of line" with the offense with which she was charged. We reject these arguments with the following observations.

Defendants in their brief describe plaintiff as maintaining a "strong" academic record at the University. [T]he first count of her complaint [highlighted: (a) Ms. Napolitano's academic achievements at Princeton (she maintained a G.P.A. of 3.7 on a 4.0 scale, she missed only three classes during her four years at Princeton, she had been considered as a nominee for a Rhodes Scholarship, and she was described by her faculty thesis advisor as one the finest students he had taught in thirty years), (b) her personal integrity (she was described by educators, coaches, and fellow students as incapable of deceit), and (c) her contribution to the University's Athletic Department (she was scheduled to play basketball at Princeton, but suffered a debilitating injury her freshman year; thereafter, she devoted herself to team management, paper work, and other support services for the basketball team).]

It must be apparent that everyone involved in this action regarded plaintiff as a somewhat gifted if not unusual student of high achievement. She had obviously earned her place in the University community by her achievements. Under those circumstances should not the community of Princeton University have been entitled to expect more of plaintiff? Should not the reaction of a University community such as that at Princeton been one of dismay? We merely pose these questions. We do not answer them. We pose them principally because of plaintiff's persistent complaints that the University did not "prove" that she was a plagiarist, especially in the face of her continued denials of plagiarism or the intent to deceive Professor Molloy. It is apparent to us that plaintiff has neglected to view her position in the university community and the effect that the charges against her have had on the entire community.

Viewed in this light, we find little purpose in reviewing plaintiff's argument which attempts to demonstrate that in 20 or more disciplinary cases arising out of the same or similar incidents the individuals there involved were not penalized as severely as she was. To us this is totally irrelevant. Each penalty obviously must be tailored to the offense committed, and the offense committed must be viewed with regard to the offender and the community. We believe it is readily ascertainable that the University softened the penalty because of the status that plaintiff had attained in the University community and the fact that she had never transgressed any of the University regulations before. Recall that this incident occurred at the beginning of the second semester. Precedent would permit the COD and the President to have imposed a penalty of suspension for the entire second semester, with the result that plaintiff would have had to repeat that semester during the winter and spring of 1983 at the additional expense of another tuition. Under the penalty imposed, plaintiff was permitted to continue her work and complete her requirements for her degree. Her penalty was that the degree was not awarded to her and will not be until June 1983. We find nothing unreasonable in this determination.

One last observation. Plaintiff claims that the penalty is supposed to provide something educative in its imposition. She argues that the penalty here is improper because there is no educational value to be found in it. Perhaps plaintiff's self-concern blinds her to the fact that the penalty imposed on her, as a leader of the University community, has to have some educative effect on other student members of the community. In addition, to paraphrase the poet, "the child is mother to the woman," we believe that the lesson to be learned here should be learned by Gabrielle Napolitano and borne by her for the rest of her life. We are sure it will strengthen her in her resolve to become a success in whatever endeavor she chooses.

The judgment of the Chancery Division is affirmed with no costs to any party.

Questions and Comments on *Napolitano*

1. In *Clayton v. Trustees of Princeton University*, 608 F.Supp. 413 (D.N.J. 1985), Clayton was suspended for a year after he was convicted of cheating on a biology exam by a student-run disciplinary committee. During his hearing, the committee deviated from the procedures outlined in the student code in several ways, including telling the student defense counselor that his job was to provide a balanced portrayal of the event, not just to advocate for his client. In the first round of the trial, the court ruled in favor of the student, emphasizing that the court expected "substantial compliance" with university procedures. *Id.* at 804. Four years later, the same judge, abandoning the "substantial compliance" standard and, emphasizing fundamental fairness, ruled in favor of the university. 608 F.Supp. at 439. Would the result have been the same if the case involved nonacademic misconduct?

2. Why did the court in *Napolitano* decide that the student was entitled only to an academic rather than a disciplinary hearing? Should plagiarism be treated the same way as other forms of cheating? *See* Roger Billings, *Plagiarism in Academia and Beyond: What is the Role of the Courts?*, 38 U.S.F. L. REV. 391 (2004).

3. Was the penalty for plagiarism given to Napolitano unduly harsh? Under what circumstances should a court review the adequacy of the penalty? What is a fair penalty for plagiarism?

4. How common is plagiarism and cheating on college campuses? In a survey of MIT students, 83 percent admitted to some form of cheating, while a study of over 15,000 students revealed that 87 percent of business majors and 67 percent of humanities majors cheated at least once during college. *83 Percent at MIT Admit They Cheated*, WASH. POST, Dec. 15, 1993, at A17. Cheating is also a problem in graduate and professional schools. *See, e.g.*, Paula Wasley, *46 Students Are Disciplined for Cheating at Indiana University's Dental School*, CHRON. HIGHER EDUC., May 9, 2007, *available at* http://chronicle.com/daily/2007/05/2007050907n.htm (over half of second-year class disciplined for viewing files prior to an exam); Jeffrey Young, *Cheating Incident Involving 34 Students at Duke Is Business School's Biggest Ever*, CHRON. HIGHER EDUC., Apr. 30, 2007, *available at* http://chronicle.com/daily/2007/04/2007043002n.htm (thirty-three students found to have collaborated on an exam in Duke's Fuqua School of Business). What penalties are appropriate for cheating or plagiarism? In the Duke business school case, students received penalties ranging from one-year suspension to an "F" in the course. *Id.* The University of Ohio revoked the master's degree of one mechanical-engineering student for plagiarism of his thesis and allowed twenty others to rewrite and resubmit plagiarized portions of their master's theses. Paula Wasley, *Ohio U. Revokes a Degree for First Time in Investigation of Plagiarism in Engineering Theses*, CHRON. HIGHER EDUC., Mar. 29, 2007, *available at* http://chronicle.com/daily/2007/03/2007032904n.htm. Fifteen cadets at the Air Force Academy were expelled and three resigned after being caught sharing answers to a weekly quiz. Dan Frosch, *18 Air Force Cadets Exit Over Cheating*, N.Y. TIMES, May 2, 2007, *available at* http://www.nytimes.com/2007/05/02/education/02cheat.html. What steps may a university take to detect and prevent plagiarism? In *A.V. v. iParadigms*, 544 F.Supp.2d 473 (E.D. Va. 2008), the court held that turnitin.doc, a plagiarism detection service that stores copies of students' papers in a database, does not violate students' copyrights. Although some academics saw the ruling as a relief, others criticized the service for creating an atmosphere of mistrust between students and professors. Jeffrey Young, *Academic Reaction to Court Decision About Plagiarism Detection is Mixed*, CHRON. HIGHER EDUC., Mar. 26, 2008, *available at* http://chroncile.com/wiredcampus/article/2844.

CHAPTER 13

STUDENT FIRST AMENDMENT RIGHTS

A. SPEECH AND RELIGION

Free speech ... represents the very dignity of what a human being is .... That's what marks us off from the stones and the stars. You can speak freely.... It is the thing that marks us as just below the angels.   Mario Savio, 1994

Widmar v. Vincent

Supreme Court of the United States, 1981.
454 U.S. 263 (1981).

[The opinion is set forth at pp. 192–98, *supra*].

Rosenberger v. Rector and Visitors of the University of Virginia

Supreme Court of the United States, 1995.
515 U.S. 819, 115 S.Ct. 2510, 132 L.Ed.2d 700.

■ KENNEDY, J. delivered the opinion of the Court.

The University of Virginia, an instrumentality of the Commonwealth for which it is named and thus bound by the First and Fourteenth Amendments, authorizes the payment of outside contractors for the printing costs of a variety of student publications. It withheld any authorization for payments on behalf of petitioners for the sole reason that their student paper "primarily promotes or manifests a particular belief in or about a deity or an ultimate reality." That the paper did promote or manifest views within the defined exclusion seems plain enough. The challenge is to the University's regulation and its denial of authorization, the case raising issues under the Speech and Establishment Clauses of the First Amendment.

The public corporation we refer to as the "University" is denominated by state law as "the Rector and Visitors of the University of Virginia," Va. Code Ann. § 23–69 (1993), and it is responsible for governing the school. Founded by Thomas Jefferson in 1819, and ranked by him, together with the authorship of the Declaration of Independence and of the Virginia Act for Religious Freedom, Va. Code Ann. § 57–1 (1950), as one of his proudest achievements, the University is among the Nation's oldest and most respected seats of higher learning. It has more than 11,000 undergraduate students, and 6,000 graduate and professional students....

Before a student group is eligible to submit bills from its outside contractors for payment by the fund described below, it must become a "Contracted Independent Organization" (CIO).... A standard agreement signed between each CIO and the University provides that the benefits and opportunities afforded to CIO's "should not be misinterpreted as meaning that those organizations are part of or controlled by the University, that the University is responsible for the organizations' contracts or other acts or omissions, or that the University approves of the organizations' goals or activities."

All CIO's may exist and operate at the University, but some are also entitled to apply for funds from the Student Activities Fund (SAF). Established and governed by University Guidelines, the purpose of the SAF is to support a broad range of extracurricular student activities that "are related to the educational purpose of the University." ... The SAF receives its money from a mandatory fee of $14 per semester assessed to each full-time student....

Some, but not all, CIO's may submit disbursement requests to the SAF. The Guidelines recognize 11 categories of student groups that may seek payment to third-party contractors because they "are related to the educational purpose of the University of Virginia." One of these is "student news, information, opinion, entertainment, or academic communications media groups." The Guidelines also specify, however, that the costs of certain activities of CIO's that are otherwise eligible for funding will not be reimbursed by the SAF. The student activities that are excluded from SAF support [include] religious activities ... and ... political activities. The prohibition on "political activities" is defined so that it is limited to electioneering and lobbying. The Guidelines provide that "these restrictions on funding political activities are not intended to preclude funding of any otherwise eligible student organization which ... espouses particular positions or ideological viewpoints, including those that may be unpopular or are not generally accepted." A "religious activity," by contrast, is defined as any activity that "primarily promotes or manifests a particular belief in or about a deity or an ultimate reality."

... If an organization seeks SAF support, it must submit its bills to the Student Council, which pays the organization's creditors upon determining that the expenses are appropriate. No direct payments are made to the student groups. During the 1990–1991 academic year, 343 student groups qualified as CIO's. One hundred thirty-five of them applied for support from the SAF, and 118 received funding. Fifteen of the groups were funded as "student news, information, opinion, entertainment, or academic communications media groups."

Petitioners' organization, Wide Awake Productions (WAP), qualified as a CIO. Formed by petitioner Ronald Rosenberger and other undergraduates in 1990, WAP was established "to publish a magazine of philosophical and religious expression," "to facilitate discussion which fosters an atmosphere of sensitivity to and tolerance of Christian viewpoints," and "to provide a unifying focus for Christians of multicultural backgrounds." WAP publishes Wide Awake: A Christian Perspective at the University of Virginia. The paper's Christian viewpoint was evident from the first issue, in which its editors wrote that the journal "offers a Christian perspective on both personal and community issues, especially those relevant to college students at the University of Virginia." The editors committed the paper to a two-fold mission: "to challenge Christians to live, in word and deed, according to the faith they proclaim and to encourage students to consider what a personal relationship with Jesus Christ means." The first issue had articles about racism, crisis pregnancy, stress, prayer, C. S. Lewis' ideas about evil and free will, and reviews of religious music. In the next two issues, Wide Awake featured stories about homosexuality, Christian missionary work, and eating disorders, as well as music reviews and interviews with University professors. Each page of Wide Awake, and the end of each article or review, is marked by a cross. The advertisements carried in Wide Awake also reveal the Christian perspective of the journal. For the most part, the advertisers are churches, centers for Christian study, or Christian bookstores. By June 1992, WAP had distributed about 5,000 copies of Wide Awake to University students, free of charge.

WAP had acquired CIO status soon after it was organized. This is an important consideration in this case, for had it been a "religious organization," WAP would not have been accorded CIO status. As defined by the Guidelines, a "religious organization" is "an organization whose purpose is to practice a devotion to an acknowledged ultimate reality or deity." At no stage in this controversy has the University contended that WAP is such an organization.

[The Appropriations Committee of the Student Council denied WAP's request for SAF funding on the grounds that Wide Awake was a "religious activity," i.e., that it "promoted or manifested a particular belief in or about a deity or an ultimate reality." WAP lost on appeal to the full Student Council and the Student Activities Committee.]

Having no further recourse within the University structure, WAP, Wide Awake, and three of its editors and members filed suit in the United States District Court for the Western District of Virginia, challenging the SAF's action as violative of Rev. Stat. § 1979, 42 U.S.C. § 1983. They alleged that refusal to authorize payment of the printing costs of the publication, solely on the basis of its religious editorial viewpoint, violated their rights to freedom of speech and press, to the free exercise of religion, and to equal protection of the law. . . . The suit sought damages for the costs of printing the paper, injunctive and declaratory relief, and attorney's fees.

On cross-motions for summary judgment, the District Court ruled for the University, holding that denial of SAF support was not an impermissible content or viewpoint discrimination against petitioners' speech, and that the University's Establishment Clause concern over its "religious activities" was a sufficient justification for denying payment to third-party contractors. . . .

The United States Court of Appeals for the Fourth Circuit, in disagreement with the District Court, held that the Guidelines did discriminate on the basis of content. . . .

It is axiomatic that the government may not regulate speech based on its substantive content or the message it conveys. *Police Dept. of Chicago v. Mosley*, 408 U.S. 92, 96 (1972). Other principles follow from this precept. In the realm of private speech or expression, government regulation may not favor one speaker over another. Discrimination against speech because of its message is presumed to be unconstitutional. These rules informed our determination that the government offends the First Amendment when it imposes financial burdens on certain speakers based on the content of their expression. When the government targets not subject matter, but particular views taken by speakers on a subject, the violation of the First Amendment is all the more blatant. Viewpoint discrimination is thus an egregious form of content discrimination. The government must abstain from regulating speech when the specific motivating ideology or the opinion or perspective of the speaker is the rationale for the restriction.

These principles provide the framework forbidding the State from exercising viewpoint discrimination, even when the limited public forum is one of its own creation. In a case involving a school district's provision of school facilities for private uses, we declared that "there is no question that the District, like the private owner of property, may legally preserve the property under its control for the use to which it is dedicated." *Lamb's Chapel v. Center Moriches Union Free School Dist.*, 508 U.S. 384, 390 (1993). The necessities of confining a forum to the limited and legitimate purposes for which it was created may justify the State in reserving it for certain groups or for the discussion of certain topics. Once it has opened a limited forum, however, the State must respect the lawful boundaries it has itself set. The State may not exclude speech where its distinction is not "reasonable in light of the purpose served by the forum," nor may it discriminate against speech on the basis of its viewpoint. Thus, in determining whether the State is acting to preserve the limits of the forum it has created so that the exclusion of a class of speech is legitimate, we have observed a distinction between, on the one hand, content discrimination, which may be permissible if it preserves the purposes of that limited forum, and, on the other hand, viewpoint discrimination, which is presumed impermissible when directed against speech otherwise within the forum's limitations.

The SAF is a forum more in a metaphysical than in a spatial or geographic sense, but the same principles are applicable. The most recent and most apposite case is our decision in *Lamb's Chapel, supra*. There, a school district had opened school facilities for use after school hours by community groups for a wide variety of social, civic, and recreational purposes. The district, however, had enacted a formal policy against opening facilities to groups for religious purposes. Invoking its policy, the district rejected a request from a group desiring to show a film series addressing various child-rearing questions from a "Christian perspective." There was no indication in the record in *Lamb's Chapel* that the request to use the school facilities was "denied, for any reason other than the fact that the presentation would have been from a religious perspective." 508 U.S. at 393–394. Our conclusion was unanimous: "It discriminates on the basis of viewpoint to permit school property to be used for the presentation of all views about family issues and child rearing except those dealing with the subject matter from a religious standpoint."

The University does acknowledge (as it must in light of our precedents) that "ideologically driven attempts to suppress a particular point of view are presumptively unconstitutional in funding, as in other contexts," but insists that this case does not present that issue because the Guidelines draw lines based on content, not viewpoint. As we have noted, discrimination against one set of views or ideas is but a subset or particular instance of the more general phenomenon of content discrimination. And, it must be acknowledged, the distinction is not a precise one. It is, in a sense, something of an understatement to speak of religious thought and discussion as just a viewpoint, as distinct from a comprehensive body of thought. The nature of our origins and destiny and their dependence upon the existence of a divine being have been subjects of philosophic inquiry throughout human history. We conclude, nonetheless, that here, as in *Lamb's Chapel*, viewpoint discrimination is the proper way to interpret the University's objections to Wide Awake. By the very terms of the SAF prohibition, the University does not exclude religion as a subject matter but selects for disfavored treatment those student journalistic efforts with religious editorial viewpoints. Religion may be a vast area of inquiry, but it also provides, as it did here, a specific premise, a perspective, a standpoint from which a variety of subjects may be discussed and considered. The prohibited perspective, not the general subject matter, resulted in the refusal to make third-party payments, for the subjects discussed were otherwise within the approved category of publications.

The dissent's assertion that no viewpoint discrimination occurs because the Guidelines discriminate against an entire class of viewpoints reflects an insupportable assumption that all debate is bipolar and that antireligious speech is the only response to religious speech. Our understanding of the complex and multifaceted nature of public discourse has not embraced such a contrived description of the marketplace of ideas. If the topic of debate is, for example, racism, then exclusion of several views on that problem is just as offensive to the First Amendment as exclusion of only one. It is as objectionable to exclude both a theistic and an atheistic perspective on the debate as it is to exclude one, the other, or yet another political, economic, or social viewpoint. The dissent's declaration that debate is not skewed so long as multiple voices are silenced is simply wrong; the debate is skewed in multiple ways.

The University's denial of WAP's request for third-party payments in the present case is based upon viewpoint discrimination not unlike the discrimination the school district relied upon in *Lamb's Chapel* and that we found invalid. The church group in *Lamb's Chapel* would have been qualified as a social or civic organization, save for its religious purposes. Furthermore, just as the school district in *Lamb's Chapel* pointed to nothing but the religious views of the group as the rationale for excluding its message, so in this case the University justifies its denial of SAF participation to WAP on the ground that the contents of Wide Awake reveal an avowed religious perspective....

The University tries to escape the consequences of our holding in *Lamb's Chapel* by urging that this case involves the provision of funds rather than access to facilities. The University begins with the unremarkable proposition that the State must have substantial discretion in determining how to allocate scarce resources to accomplish its educational mission. Citing our decisions in *Rust v. Sullivan*, 500 U.S. 173 (1991), *Regan v. Taxation with Representation of Wash.*, 461 U.S. 540 (1983), and *Widmar v. Vincent*, 454 U.S. 263 (1981), the University argues that content-based funding decisions are both inevitable and lawful. Were the reasoning of *Lamb's Chapel* to apply to funding decisions as well as to those involving access to facilities, it is urged, its holding "would become a judicial juggernaut, constitutionalizing the ubiquitous content-based decisions that schools, colleges, and other government entities routinely make in the allocation of public funds."

To this end the University relies on our assurance in *Widmar v. Vincent, supra*. There, in the course of striking down a public university's exclusion of religious groups from use of school facilities made available to all other student groups, we stated: "Nor do we question the right of the University to make academic judgments as to how best to allocate scarce resources." The quoted language in *Widmar* was but a proper recognition of the principle that when the State is the speaker, it may make content-based choices. When the University determines the content of the education it provides, it is the University speaking, and we have permitted the government to regulate the content of what is or is not expressed when it is the speaker or when it enlists private entities to convey its own message. In the same vein, in *Rust v. Sullivan, supra,* we upheld the government's prohibition on abortion-related advice applicable to recipients of federal funds for family planning counseling. There, the government did not create a program to encourage private speech but instead used private speakers to transmit specific information pertaining to its own program. We recognized that when the government appropriates public funds to promote a particular policy of its own it is entitled to say what it wishes. When the government disburses public funds to private entities to convey a governmental message, it may take legitimate and appropriate steps to ensure that its message is neither garbled nor distorted by the grantee.

It does not follow, however, and we did not suggest in *Widmar,* that viewpoint-based restrictions are proper when the University does not itself speak or subsidize transmittal of a message it favors but instead expends funds to encourage a diversity of views from private speakers. A holding that the University may not discriminate based on the viewpoint of private persons whose speech it facilitates does not restrict the University's own speech, which is controlled by different principles. . . .

[handwritten margin note: not proper of viewpoint Discrimination]

The distinction between the University's own favored message and the private speech of students is evident in the case before us. The University itself has taken steps to ensure the distinction in the agreement each CIO must sign. The University declares that the student groups eligible for SAF support are not the University's agents, are not subject to its control, and are not its responsibility. Having offered to pay the third-party contractors on behalf of private speakers who convey their own messages, the University may not silence the expression of selected viewpoints.

The University urges that, from a constitutional standpoint, funding of speech differs from provision of access to facilities because money is scarce and physical facilities are not. Beyond the fact that in any given case this proposition might not be true as an empirical matter, the underlying premise that the University could discriminate based on viewpoint if demand for space exceeded its availability is wrong as well. The government cannot justify viewpoint discrimination among private speakers on the economic fact of scarcity. Had the meeting rooms in *Lamb's Chapel* been scarce, had the demand been greater than the supply, our decision would have been no different. It would have been incumbent on the State, of course, to ration or allocate the scarce resources on some acceptable neutral principle; but nothing in our decision indicated that scarcity would give the State the right to exercise viewpoint discrimination that is otherwise impermissible.

Vital First Amendment speech principles are at stake here. The first danger to liberty lies in granting the State the power to examine publications to determine whether or not they are based on some ultimate idea and, if so, for the State to classify them. The second, and corollary, danger is to speech from the chilling of individual thought and expression. That danger is especially real in the University setting, where the State acts against a background and tradition of thought and experiment that is at the center of our intellectual and philosophic tradition. In ancient Athens, and, as Europe entered into a new period of intellectual awakening, in places like Bologna, Oxford, and Paris, universities began as voluntary and spontaneous assemblages or concourses for students to speak and to write and to learn. *See generally* R. PALMER & J. COLTON, A HISTORY OF THE MODERN WORLD 39 (7th ed. 1992). The quality and creative power of student intellectual life to this day remains a vital measure of a school's influence and attainment. For the University, by regulation, to cast disapproval on particular viewpoints of its students risks the suppression of free speech and creative inquiry in one of the vital centers for the Nation's intellectual life, its college and university campuses.

The Guideline invoked by the University to deny third-party contractor payments on behalf of WAP effects a sweeping restriction on student thought and student inquiry in the context of University sponsored publications. The prohibition on funding on behalf of publications that "primarily promote or manifest a particular belief in or about a deity or an ultimate reality," in its ordinary and common-sense meaning, has a vast potential reach. The term "promotes" as used here would comprehend any writing advocating a philosophic position that rests upon a belief in a deity or ultimate reality. *See* WEBSTER'S THIRD NEW INTERNATIONAL DICTIONARY 1815 (1961) (defining "promote" as "to contribute to the growth, enlargement, or prosperity of: further, encourage"). And the term "manifests" would bring within the scope of the prohibition any writing that is explicable as resting upon a premise that presupposes the existence of a deity or ultimate reality. *See id.* at 1375 (defining "manifest" as "to show plainly: make palpably evident or certain by showing or displaying"). Were the prohibition applied with much vigor at all, it would bar funding of essays by hypothetical student contributors named Plato, Spinoza, and Descartes. And if the regulation covers, as the University says it does, those student journalistic efforts that primarily manifest or promote a belief that there is no deity and no ultimate reality, then undergraduates named Karl Marx, Bertrand Russell, and Jean–Paul Sartre would likewise have some of their major essays excluded from student publications. If any manifestation of beliefs in first principles disqualifies the writing, as seems to be the case, it is indeed difficult to name renowned thinkers whose writings would be accepted, save perhaps for articles disclaiming all connection to their ultimate philosophy. Plato could contrive perhaps to submit an acceptable essay on making pasta or peanut butter cookies, provided he did not point out their (necessary) imperfections.

Based on the principles we have discussed, we hold that the regulation invoked to deny SAF support, both in its terms and in its application to these petitioners, is a denial of their right of free speech guaranteed by the First Amendment. It remains to be considered whether the violation following from the University's action is excused by the necessity of complying with the Constitution's prohibition against state establishment of religion. . . .

. . .

The governmental program here is neutral toward religion. There is no suggestion that the University created it to advance religion or adopted some ingenious device with the purpose of aiding a religious cause. The object of the SAF is to open a forum for speech and to support various student enterprises, including the publication of newspapers, in recognition of the diversity and creativity of student life. The University's SAF Guidelines have a separate classification for, and do not make third-party payments on behalf of, "religious organizations," which are those "whose purpose is to practice a devotion to an acknowledged ultimate reality or deity." The category of support here is for "student news, information, opinion, entertainment, or academic communications media groups," of which Wide Awake was 1 of 15 in the 1990 school year. WAP did not seek a subsidy because of its Christian editorial viewpoint; it sought funding as a student journal, which it was.

The neutrality of the program distinguishes the student fees from a tax levied for the direct support of a church or group of churches. A tax of that sort, of course, would run contrary to Establishment Clause concerns dating from the earliest days of the Republic. The apprehensions of our predecessors involved the levying of taxes upon the public for the sole and exclusive purpose of establishing and supporting specific sects. The exaction here, by contrast, is a student activity fee designed to reflect the reality that student life in its many dimensions includes the necessity of wide-ranging speech and inquiry and that student expression is an integral part of the University's educational mission. The fee is mandatory, and we do not have before us the question whether an objecting student has the First Amendment right to demand a pro rata return to the extent the fee is expended for speech to which he or she does not subscribe. We must treat it, then, as an exaction upon the students. But the $14 paid each semester by the students is not a general tax designed to raise revenue for the University. The SAF cannot be used for unlimited purposes, much less the illegitimate purpose of supporting one religion....

Government neutrality is apparent in the State's overall scheme in a further meaningful respect. The program respects the critical difference "between *government* speech endorsing religion, which the Establishment Clause forbids, and *private* speech endorsing religion, which the Free Speech and Free Exercise Clauses protect." In this case, "the government has not fostered or encouraged" any mistaken impression that the student newspapers speak for the University. *Capitol Square Review and Advisory Bd. v. Pinette.* The University has taken pains to disassociate itself from the private speech involved in this case. The Court of Appeals' apparent concern that Wide Awake's religious orientation would be attributed to the University is not a plausible fear, and there is no real likelihood that the speech in question is being either endorsed or coerced by the State.

The Court of Appeals (and the dissent) are correct to extract from our decisions the principle that we have recognized special Establishment Clause dangers where the government makes direct money payments to sectarian institutions, citing *Roemer v. Board of Public Works of Md.*, 426 U.S. 736, 747 (1976); *Bowen v. Kendrick*, 487 U.S. 589, 614–615 (1988); *Hunt v. McNair*, 413 U.S. at 742; *Tilton v. Richardson*, 403 U.S. 672, 679–680; *Board of Ed. of Central School Dist. No. 1 v. Allen*, 392 U.S. 236 (1968). The error is not in identifying the principle, but in believing that it controls this case. Even assuming that WAP is no different from a church and that its speech is the same as the religious exercises conducted in *Widmar* (two points much in doubt), the Court of Appeals decided a case that was, in essence, not before it, and the dissent would have us do the same. We do not confront a case where, even under a neutral program that includes nonsectarian recipients, the government is making direct money payments to an institution or group that is engaged in religious activity. Neither the Court of Appeals nor the dissent, we believe, takes sufficient cognizance of the undisputed fact that no public funds flow directly to WAP's coffers.

It does not violate the Establishment Clause for a public university to grant access to its facilities on a religion-neutral basis to a wide spectrum of student groups, including groups that use meeting rooms for sectarian activities, accompanied by some devotional exercises. This is so even where the upkeep, maintenance, and repair of the facilities attributed to those uses is paid from a student activities fund to which students are required to contribute. The government usually acts by spending money. Even the provision of a meeting room, as in *Mergens* and *Widmar*, involved governmental expenditure, if only in the form of electricity and heating or cooling costs. The error made by the Court of Appeals, as well as by the dissent, lies in focusing on the money that is undoubtedly expended by the government, rather than on the nature of the benefit received by the recipient. If the expenditure of governmental funds is prohibited whenever those funds pay for a service that is, pursuant to a religion-neutral program, used by a group for sectarian purposes, then *Widmar*, *Mergens*, and *Lamb's Chapel* would have to be overruled. Given our holdings in these cases, it follows that a public university may maintain its own computer facility and give student groups access to that facility, including the use of the printers, on a religion neutral, say first-come-first-served, basis. If a religious student organization obtained access on that religion-neutral basis and used a computer to compose or a printer or copy machine to print speech with a religious content or viewpoint, the State's action in providing the group with access would no more violate the Establishment Clause than would giving those groups access to an assembly hall. There is no difference in logic or principle, and no difference of constitutional significance, between a school using its funds to operate a facility to which students have access, and a school paying a third-party contractor to operate the facility on its behalf. . . .

Were the dissent's view to become law, it would require the University, in order to avoid a constitutional violation, to scrutinize the content of student speech, lest the expression in question—speech otherwise protected by the Constitution—contain too great a religious content. The dissent, in fact, anticipates such censorship as "crucial" in distinguishing between "works characterized by the evangelism of Wide Awake and writing that merely happens to express views that a given religion might approve." That eventuality raises the specter of governmental censorship, to ensure that all student writings and publications meet some baseline standard of secular orthodoxy. To impose that standard on student speech at a university is to imperil the very sources of free speech and expression. As we recognized in *Widmar*, official censorship would be far more inconsistent with the Establishment Clause's dictates than would governmental provision of secular printing services on a religion-blind basis.

. . .

To obey the Establishment Clause, it was not necessary for the University to deny eligibility to student publications because of their viewpoint. The neutrality commanded of the State by the separate Clauses of the First Amendment was compromised by the University's course of action. The viewpoint discrimination inherent in the University's regulation required public officials to scan and interpret student publications to discern their underlying philosophic assumptions respecting religious theory and belief. That course of action was a denial of the right of free speech and would risk fostering a pervasive bias or hostility to religion, which could undermine the very neutrality the Establishment Clause requires. There is no Establishment Clause violation in the University's honoring its duties under the Free Speech Clause.

The judgment of the Court of Appeals must be, and is, reversed.

Questions and Comments on *Rosenberger*

1. Can you reconcile *Rosenberger* with *Locke v. Davey*, 540 U.S. 712 (2004)? In *Locke*, the Court held that Washington's denial of scholarship funds to theology students was constitutional because of the state's compelling interest in not violating the Establishment Clause. Would the result in *Rosenberger* be different if the university had argued that it was trying to avoid violating an Establishment Clause in the state constitution? *See* Alan Trammell, Note, *The Cabining of* Rosenberger: Locke v. Davey *and the Broad Nondiscrimination Principle that Never Was*, 92 VA. L. REV. 1957 (2007).

2. Does *Rosenberger* provide sufficient guidance to university administrators? *See* Kristine Kuenzli, *Opportunity Wasted: The Supreme Court's Failure to Clarify Religious Liberty Issues in* Rosenberger v. Rector and Visitors of the University of Virginia, 32 GONZ. L. REV. 85 (1996).

3. Does the Court adequately distinguish a tax from a student fee? Could an avowed evangelical group ask for a subsidy in printing its pamphlets? Could a student bible study group be funded by a public university? Consider *Christian Legal Society v. Walker, infra* p. 782.

4. Students at the United States Naval Academy, assisted by the American Civil Liberties Union, have complained to the Navy about the practice of commencing mandatory daily lunch meetings with a prayer. Neela Banerjee, *Religion and its Role are in Dispute at the Service Academies*, N.Y. TIMES, June 25, 2008, at A14. A recent graduate of the Naval Academy stated that the practice of daily prayers "make[s] it very clear that this is the standard, and the standard is Judaism or Christianity." *Id.* at A19. Students at West Point have made similar complaints about the prevalence of religion, specifically evangelical Christianity, at the academy. *Id.* Army and Navy officials have declined to review or modify their current practices. *Id.* The Air Force Academy, in contrast, issued guidelines in 2005 instructing officials to ensure that their "words and actions cannot reasonably be construed as either official endorsement or disapproval ..." of religion. The reforms at the Air Force Academy came after an official investigation revealed that the academy sponsored a showing of "The Passion of the Christ" and placed a banner in a locker room stating that student athletes played for "Team Jesus." *Id.*

Board of Regents of the University of Wisconsin v. Southworth

Supreme Court of the United States, 2000.
529 U.S. 217, 120 S.Ct. 1346, 146 L.Ed.2d 193.

■ JUSTICE KENNEDY delivered the opinion of the Court.

For the second time in recent years we consider constitutional questions arising from a program designed to facilitate extracurricular student speech at a public university. Respondents are a group of students at the University of Wisconsin. They brought a First Amendment challenge to a mandatory student activity fee imposed by petitioner Board of Regents of the University of Wisconsin and used in part by the University to support student organizations engaging in political or ideological speech. Respondents object to the speech and expression of some of the student organizations. Relying upon our precedents which protect members of unions and bar associations from being required to pay fees used for speech the members find objectionable, both the District Court and the Court of Appeals invalidated the University's student fee program. The University contends that its mandatory student activity fee and the speech which it supports are appropriate to further its educational mission.

. . .

The University of Wisconsin is a public corporation of the State of Wisconsin. *See* Wis. Stat. § 36.07(1) (1993–1994). . . . Some 30,000 undergraduate students and 10,000 graduate and professional students attend the University's Madison campus, ranking it among the Nation's largest institutions of higher learning. Students come to the renowned University from all 50 States and from 72 foreign countries. . . .

The responsibility for governing the University of Wisconsin System is vested by law with the board of regents. The same law empowers the students to share in aspects of the University's governance. One of those functions is to administer the student activities fee program. By statute the "students in consultation with the chancellor and subject to the final confirmation of the board [of regents] shall have the responsibility for the disposition of those student fees which constitute substantial support for campus student activities." § 36.09(5). The students do so, in large measure, through their student government, called the Associated Students of Madison (ASM), and various ASM subcommittees. The program the University maintains to support the extracurricular activities undertaken by many of its student organizations is the subject of the present controversy.

It seems that since its founding the University has required full-time students enrolled at its Madison campus to pay a nonrefundable activity fee. For the 1995–1996 academic year, when this suit was commenced, the activity fee amounted to $331.50 per year. The fee is segregated from the University's tuition charge. Once collected, the activity fees are deposited by the University into the accounts of the State of Wisconsin. The fees are drawn upon by the University to support various campus services and extracurricular student activities. In the University's view, the activity fees "enhance the educational experience" of its students by "promoting extracurricular activities," "stimulating advocacy and debate on diverse points of view," enabling "participation in political activity," "promoting student participation in campus administrative activity," and providing "opportunities to develop social skills," all consistent with the University's mission.

The board of regents classifies the segregated fee into allocable and nonallocable portions. The nonallocable portion approximates 80% of the total fee and covers expenses such as student health services, intramural sports, debt service, and the upkeep and operations of the student union facilities. Respondents did not challenge the purposes to which the University commits the nonallocable portion of the segregated fee.

The allocable portion of the fee supports extracurricular endeavors pursued by the University's registered student organizations or RSO's. To qualify for RSO status students must organize as a not-for-profit group, limit membership primarily to students, and agree to undertake activities related to student life on campus. During the 1995–1996 school year, 623 groups had RSO status on the Madison campus. To name but a few, RSO's included the Future Financial Gurus of America; the International Socialist Organization; the College Democrats; the College Republicans; and the American Civil Liberties Union Campus Chapter. As one would expect, the expressive activities undertaken by RSO's are diverse in range and content, from displaying posters and circulating newsletters throughout the campus, to hosting campus debates and guest speakers, and to what can best be described as political lobbying.

RSO's may obtain a portion of the allocable fees in one of three ways. Most do so by seeking funding from the Student Government Activity Fund (SGAF), administered by the ASM. SGAF moneys may be issued to support an RSO's operations and events, as well as travel expenses "central to the purpose of the organization." As an alternative, an RSO can apply for funding from the General Student Services Fund (GSSF), administered through the ASM's finance committee. During the 1995–1996 academic year, 15 RSO's received GSSF funding. These RSO's included a campus tutoring center, the student radio station, a student environmental group, a gay and bisexual student center, a community legal office, an AIDS support network, a campus women's center, and the Wisconsin Student Public Interest Research Group (WISPIRG). The University acknowledges that, in addition to providing campus services (e.g., tutoring and counseling), the GSSF-funded RSO's engage in political and ideological expression.

The GSSF, as well as the SGAF, consists of moneys originating in the allocable portion of the mandatory fee. The parties have stipulated that, with respect to SGAF and GSSF funding, "the process for reviewing and approving allocations for funding is administered in a viewpoint-neutral fashion," and that the University does not use the fee program for "advocating a particular point of view."

A student referendum provides a third means for an RSO to obtain funding. While the record is sparse on this feature of the University's program, the parties inform us that the student body can vote either to approve or to disapprove an assessment for a particular RSO. One referendum resulted in an allocation of $45,000 to WISPIRG during the 1995–1996 academic year. At oral argument, counsel for the University acknowledged that a referendum could also operate to defund an RSO or to veto a funding decision of the ASM. In October 1996, for example, the student body voted to terminate funding to a national student organization to which the University belonged. Both parties confirmed at oral argument that their stipulation regarding the program's viewpoint neutrality does not extend to the referendum process.

With respect to GSSF and SGAF funding, the ASM or its finance committee makes initial funding decisions. The ASM does so in an open session, and interested students may attend meetings when RSO funding is discussed. It also appears that the ASM must approve the results of a student referendum. Approval appears *pro forma*, however, as counsel for the University advised us that the student government "voluntarily views the referendum as binding." Once the ASM approves an RSO's funding application, it forwards its decision to the chancellor and to the board of regents for their review and approval. Approximately 30% of the University's RSO's received funding during the 1995–1996 academic year.

RSO's, as a general rule, do not receive lump-sum cash distributions. Rather, RSO's obtain funding support on a reimbursement basis by submitting receipts or invoices to the University. Guidelines identify expenses appropriate for reimbursement. Permitted expenditures include, in the main, costs for printing, postage, office supplies, and use of University facilities and equipment. Materials printed with student fees must contain a disclaimer that the views expressed are not those of the ASM. The University also reimburses RSO's for fees arising from membership in "other related and non-profit organizations."

The University's policy establishes purposes for which fees may not be expended. RSO's may not receive reimbursement for "gifts, donations, and contributions," the costs of legal services, or for "activities which are politically partisan or religious in nature." (The policy does not give examples of the prohibited expenditures.) A separate policy statement on GSSF funding states that an RSO can receive funding if it "does not have a *primarily* political orientation (i.e. is not a registered political group)." The same policy adds that an RSO "shall not use [student fees] for any lobbying purposes." . . .

. . .

In March 1996, respondents, each of whom attended or still attend the University's Madison campus, filed suit in the United States District Court for the Western District of Wisconsin against members of the board of regents. Respondents alleged, *inter alia*, that imposition of the segregated fee violated their rights of free speech, free association, and free exercise under the First Amendment.... The District Court decided the fee program compelled students "to support political and ideological activity with which they disagree" in violation of respondents' First Amendment rights to freedom of speech and association. The court did not reach respondents' free exercise claim. The District Court's order enjoined the board of regents from using segregated fees to fund any RSO engaging in political or ideological speech.

The United States Court of Appeals for the Seventh Circuit affirmed in part, reversed in part, and vacated in part....

. . .

It is inevitable that government will adopt and pursue programs and policies within its constitutional powers but which nevertheless are contrary to the profound beliefs and sincere convictions of some of its citizens. The government, as a general rule, may support valid programs and policies by taxes or other exactions binding on protesting parties. Within this broader principle it seems inevitable that funds raised by the government will be spent for speech and other expression to advocate and defend its own policies. *See, e.g., Rust v. Sullivan*, 500 U.S. 173 (1991); *Regan v. Taxation With Representation of Wash.*, 461 U.S. 540, 548–549 (1983). The case we decide here, however, does not raise the issue of the government's right, or, to be more specific, the state-controlled University's right, to use its own funds to advance a particular message. The University's whole justification for fostering the challenged expression is that it springs from the initiative of the students, who alone give it purpose and content in the course of their extracurricular endeavors. . . .

The University of Wisconsin exacts the fee at issue for the sole purpose of facilitating the free and open exchange of ideas by, and among, its students. We conclude the objecting students may insist upon certain safeguards with respect to the expressive activities which they are required to support. Our public forum cases are instructive here by close analogy. This is true even though the student activities fund is not a public forum in the traditional sense of the term and despite the circumstance that those cases most often involve a demand for access, not a claim to be exempt from supporting speech. *See, e.g., Lamb's Chapel v. Center Moriches Union Free School Dist.*, 508 U.S. 384 (1993); *Widmar v. Vincent*, 454 U.S. 263 (1981). The standard of viewpoint neutrality found in the public forum cases provides the standard we find controlling. We decide that the viewpoint neutrality requirement of the University program is in general sufficient to protect the rights of the objecting students. The student referendum aspect of the program for funding speech and expressive activities, however, appears to be inconsistent with the viewpoint neutrality requirement.

We must begin by recognizing that the complaining students are being required to pay fees which are subsidies for speech they find objectionable, even offensive. The *Abood* and *Keller* cases, then, provide the beginning point for our analysis. *Abood v. Detroit Bd. of Ed.*, 431 U.S. 209 (1977); *Keller v. State Bar of Cal.*, 496 U.S. 1 (1990).

. . .

In *Abood*, some nonunion public school teachers challenged an agreement requiring them, as a condition of their employment, to pay a service fee equal in amount to union dues. The objecting teachers alleged that the union's use of their fees to engage in political speech violated their freedom of association guaranteed by the First and Fourteenth Amendments. The Court agreed and held that any objecting teacher could "prevent the Union's spending a part of their required service fees to contribute to political candidates and to express political views unrelated to its duties as exclusive bargaining representative." The principles outlined in *Abood* provided the foundation for our later decision in *Keller*. There we held that lawyers admitted to practice in California could be required to join a state bar association and to fund activities "germane" to the association's mission of "regulating the legal profession and improving the quality of legal services." The lawyers could not, however, be required to fund the bar association's own political expression.

The proposition that students who attend the University cannot be required to pay subsidies for the speech of other students without some First Amendment protection follows from the *Abood* and *Keller* cases. Students enroll in public universities to seek fulfillment of their personal aspirations and of their own potential. If the University conditions the opportunity to receive a college education, an opportunity comparable in importance to joining a labor union or bar association, on an agreement to support objectionable, extracurricular expression by other students, the rights acknowledged in *Abood* and *Keller* become implicated. It infringes on the speech and beliefs of the individual to be required, by this mandatory student activity fee program, to pay subsidies for the objectionable speech of others without any recognition of the State's corresponding duty to him or her. Yet recognition must be given as well to the important and substantial purposes of the University, which seeks to facilitate a wide range of speech.

In *Abood* and *Keller* the constitutional rule took the form of limiting the required subsidy to speech germane to the purposes of the union or bar association. The standard of germane speech as applied to student speech at a university is unworkable, however, and gives insufficient protection both to the objecting students and to the University program itself. Even in the context of a labor union, whose functions are, or so we might have thought, well known and understood by the law and the courts after a long history of government regulation and judicial involvement, we have encountered difficulties in deciding what is germane and what is not. . . .

. . .

Just as the vast extent of permitted expression makes the test of germane speech inappropriate for intervention, so too does it underscore the high potential for intrusion on the First Amendment rights of the objecting students. It is all but inevitable that the fees will result in subsidies to speech which some students find objectionable and offensive to their personal beliefs. If the standard of germane speech is inapplicable, then, it might be argued the remedy is to allow each student to list those causes which he or she will or will not support. If a university decided that its students' First Amendment interests were better protected by some type of optional or refund system it would be free to do so. We decline to impose a system of that sort as a constitutional requirement, however. The restriction could be so disruptive and expensive that the program to support extracurricular speech would be ineffective. The First Amendment does not require the University to put the program at risk.

The University may determine that its mission is well served if students have the means to engage in dynamic discussions of philosophical, religious, scientific, social, and political subjects in their extracurricular campus life outside the lecture hall. If the University reaches this conclusion, it is entitled to impose a mandatory fee to sustain an open dialogue to these ends.

The University must provide some protection to its students' First Amendment interests, however. The proper measure, and the principal standard of protection for objecting students, we conclude, is the requirement of viewpoint neutrality in the allocation of funding support. Viewpoint neutrality was the obligation to which we gave substance in *Rosenberger v. Rector and Visitors of Univ. of Va.*, 515 U.S. 819 (1995). . . . While *Rosenberger* was concerned with the rights a student has to use an extracurricular speech program already in place, today's case considers the antecedent question, acknowledged but unresolved in *Rosenberger*: whether a public university may require its students to pay a fee which creates the mechanism for the extracurricular speech in the first instance. When a university requires its students to pay fees to support the extracurricular speech of other students, all in the interest of open discussion, it may not prefer some viewpoints to others. There is symmetry then in our holding here and in *Rosenberger*: Viewpoint neutrality is the justification for requiring the student to pay the fee in the first instance and for ensuring the integrity of the program's operation once the funds have been collected. We conclude that the University of Wisconsin may sustain the extracurricular dimensions of its programs by using mandatory student fees with viewpoint neutrality as the operational principle.

The parties have stipulated that the program the University has developed to stimulate extracurricular student expression respects the principle of viewpoint neutrality. If the stipulation is to continue to control the case, the University's program in its basic structure must be found consistent with the First Amendment.

We make no distinction between campus activities and the off-campus expressive activities of objectionable RSO's. Those activities, respondents tell us, often bear no relationship to the University's reason for imposing the segregated fee in the first instance, to foster vibrant campus debate among students. If the University shares those concerns, it is free to enact viewpoint neutral rules restricting off-campus travel or other expenditures by RSO's, for it may create what is tantamount to a limited public forum if the principles of viewpoint neutrality are respected. We find no principled way, however, to impose upon the University, as a constitutional matter, a requirement to adopt geographic or spatial restrictions as a condition for RSO's entitlement to reimbursement. Universities possess significant interests in encouraging students to take advantage of the social, civic, cultural, and religious opportunities available in surrounding communities and throughout the country....

Our decision ought not to be taken to imply that in other instances the University, its agents or employees, or—of particular importance—its faculty, are subject to the First Amendment analysis which controls in this case. Where the University speaks, either in its own name through its regents or officers, or in myriad other ways through its diverse faculties, the analysis likely would be altogether different. *See Rust v. Sullivan*, 500 U.S. 173 (1991); *Regan v. Taxation With Representation of Wash.*, 461 U.S. 540 (1983). The Court has not held, or suggested, that when the government speaks the rules we have discussed come into play.

When the government speaks, for instance to promote its own policies or to advance a particular idea, it is, in the end, accountable to the electorate and the political process for its advocacy. If the citizenry objects, newly elected officials later could espouse some different or contrary position. In the instant case, the speech is not that of the University or its agents. It is not, furthermore, speech by an instructor or a professor in the academic context, where principles applicable to government speech would have to be considered.

It remains to discuss the referendum aspect of the University's program. While the record is not well developed on the point, it appears that by majority vote of the student body a given RSO may be funded or defunded. It is unclear to us what protection, if any, there is for viewpoint neutrality in this part of the process. To the extent the referendum substitutes majority determinations for viewpoint neutrality it would undermine the constitutional protection the program requires. The whole theory of viewpoint neutrality is that minority views are treated with the same respect as are majority views. Access to a public forum, for instance, does not depend upon majoritarian consent. That principle is controlling here. A remand is necessary and appropriate to resolve this point; and the case in all events must be reexamined in light of the principles we have discussed.

The judgment of the Court of Appeals is reversed, and the case is remanded for further proceedings consistent with this opinion. In this Court the parties shall bear their own costs.

■ JUSTICE SOUTER, with whom JUSTICE STEVENS and JUSTICE BREYER join, concurring in the judgment.

[The concurring opinion is set forth at pp. 328, *supra*.]

Questions and Comments on *Southworth*

1. Do you agree with Justices Souter, Stevens, and Breyer that content neutrality is not an appropriate standard to apply to decisions made by colleges and universities? If you do not, how would your answer their question about instructing in plutocracy?

2. For a thoughtful discussion of *Southworth*'s role in compelled subsidization cases, see Gregory Klass, *The Very Idea of a First Amendment Right Against Compelled Subsidization*, 38 U.C. DAVIS L. REV. 1087 (2005).

3. The Respondents objected to funding for several organizations, including: Amnesty International; International Socialist Organization; Lesbian, Gay, and Bisexual Campus Center; Progressive Student Network; and UW Greens. Brief of Respondent at 1–2, University of Wisconsin v. Southworth, 529 U.S. 217 (2000). Would a system allowing students to opt out of funding organizations they found objectionable better protect the First Amendment rights of students, or would it tend to chill free speech, especially by marginalized groups? Why might a university find it important to subsidize unpopular and potentially offensive speech?

Hosty v. Carter

United States Court of Appeals for the Seventh Circuit, 2005.
412 F.3d 731, *cert. denied*, 546 U.S. 1169 (2006).

■ CIRCUIT JUDGE EASTERBROOK delivered the opinion of the Court.

Controversy began to swirl when Jeni Porche became editor in chief of the *Innovator*, the student newspaper at Governors State University. None of the articles concerned the apostrophe missing from the University's name. Instead the students tackled meatier fare, such as its decision not to renew the teaching contract of Geoffrey de Laforcade, the paper's faculty adviser.

[Hosty attacked the integrity of Roger Oden, Dean of the College of Arts and Sciences, in the *Innovator*. When the university administration objected, the *Innovator* declined to retract the statements or to print the administration's response. Patricia Carter, Dean of Student Affairs and Services, then told *Innovator*'s printer not to print issues that she had not reviewed in advance. Publication of the *Innovator* ceased in November 2000.] Porche, Hosty, and Steven Barba, another of the paper's reporters, have continued the debate in court, suing the University, all of its trustees, most of its administrators, and several of its staff members for damages under 42 U.S.C. § 1983.

Defendants moved for summary judgment, and the district court granted the motion with respect to all except Dean Carter. Some defendants prevailed because, in the district judge's view, they had not done anything wrong (or, indeed, anything at all, and § 1983 does not create vicarious liability); others received qualified immunity....

When entertaining an interlocutory appeal by a public official who seeks the shelter of qualified immunity, the threshold question is: "Taken in the light most favorable to the party asserting the injury, do the facts alleged show the [public official's] conduct violated a constitutional right?" *Saucier v. Katz*, 533 U.S. 194, 201 (2001). Only if the answer is affirmative does the court inquire whether the official enjoys qualified immunity. "If a violation could be made out on a favorable view of the parties' submissions, the next, sequential step is to ask whether the right was clearly established." *Saucier*, 533 U.S. at 201. . . .

Hazelwood School District v. Kuhlmeier, 484 U.S. 260 (1988), provides our starting point. A high school's principal blocked the student newspaper (which was financed by public funds as part of a journalism class) from publishing articles that the principal thought inappropriate for some of the school's younger students and a potential invasion of others' privacy. When evaluating the students' argument that the principal had violated their right to freedom of speech, the Court first asked whether the paper was a public forum. After giving a negative answer based on the school's established policy of supervising the writing and reviewing the content of each issue, the Court observed that the school's subvention of the paper's costs distinguished the situation from one in which students were speaking independently, as in *Tinker v. Des Moines Independent Community School District*, 393 U.S. 503 (1969). When a school regulates speech for which it also pays, the Court held, the appropriate question is whether the "actions are reasonably related to legitimate pedagogical concerns." "Legitimate" concerns, the Court stated, include setting "high standards for the student speech that is disseminated under its auspices—standards that may be higher than those demanded by some newspaper publishers or theatrical producers in the 'real' world—and [the school] may refuse to disseminate student speech that does not meet those standards. In addition, a school must be able to take into account the emotional maturity of the intended audience in determining whether to disseminate student speech on potentially sensitive topics, which might range from the existence of Santa Claus in an elementary school setting to the particulars of teenage sexual activity in a high school setting." Shortly after this passage the Court dropped a footnote: "A number of lower federal courts have similarly recognized that educators' decisions with regard to the content of school-sponsored newspapers, dramatic productions, and other expressive activities are entitled to substantial deference. We need not now decide whether the same degree of deference is appropriate with respect to school-sponsored expressive activities at the college and university level."

Picking up on this footnote, plaintiffs argue, and the district court held, that *Hazelwood* is inapplicable to university newspapers and that post-secondary educators therefore cannot ever insist that student newspapers be submitted for review and approval. Yet this footnote does not even hint at the possibility of an on/off switch: high school papers reviewable, college papers not reviewable. It addresses degrees of deference. Whether *some* review is possible depends on the answer to the public-forum question, which does not (automatically) vary with the speakers' age. Only when courts need assess the reasonableness of the asserted pedagogical justification in non-public-forum situations does age come into play, and in a way suggested by the passage we have quoted from *Hazelwood*'s text. To the extent that the justification for editorial control depends on the audience's maturity, the difference between high school and university students may be important. (Not that any line could be bright; many high school seniors are older than some college freshmen, and junior colleges are similar to many high schools.) To the extent that the justification depends on other matters—not only the desire to ensure "high standards for the student speech that is disseminated under [the school's] auspices" (the Court particularly mentioned "speech that is . . . ungrammatical, poorly written, inadequately researched, biased or prejudiced, vulgar or profane, or unsuitable for immature audiences", 484 U.S. at 271) but also the goal of dissociating the school from "any position other than neutrality on matters of political controversy"—there is no sharp difference between high school and college papers.

The Supreme Court itself has established that age does not control the public-forum question. So much is clear not only from decisions such as *Tinker*, which held that public school students have a right of non-disruptive personal expression on school premises, but also from the decisions concerning the use of school funds and premises for religious expression. *See, e.g., Lamb's Chapel v. Center Moriches Union Free School District*, 508 U.S. 384 (1993); *Rosenberger v. Rector and Visitors of the University of Virginia*, 515 U.S. 819 (1995). These decisions hold that no public school, of any level—primary, secondary, or post-secondary—may discriminate against religious speech in a public forum (including classrooms made available to extracurricular activities), or withhold funding that would be available to student groups espousing sectarian views. *Good News Club [v. Milford Central School*, 533 U.S. 98 (2001)], which dealt with student clubs in an elementary school, deemed dispositive a decision about the first amendment rights of college students. Having opened its premises to student clubs, and thus created a limited-purpose public forum, even an elementary school could not supervise or censor the views expressed at a meeting of the Good News Club.

If private speech in a public forum is off-limits to regulation even when that forum is a classroom of an elementary school, *see Good News Club*, then speech at a non-public forum, and underwritten at public expense, may be open to reasonable regulation even at the college level—or later, as *Rust v. Sullivan*, 500 U.S. 173 (1991), shows by holding that the federal government may insist that physicians use grant funds only for the kind of speech required by the granting authority. We hold, therefore, that *Hazelwood*'s framework applies to subsidized student newspapers at colleges as well as elementary and secondary schools. . . .

Hazelwood's first question therefore remains our principal question as well: was the reporter a speaker in a public forum (no censorship allowed?) or did the University either create a non-public forum or publish the paper itself (a closed forum where content may be supervised)? . . .

[The district court held and plaintiffs argued that *Hazelwood* applies only to curricular speech, e.g., a newspaper prepared as part of a course on journalism, not to the *Inovator*, which was an extracurricular activity. Judge Easterbrook rejected this distinction. He noted that, if a University recruited students to write for its alumni magazine as an extracurricular activity, the University would clearly be allowed to censor the speech.]

What, then, was the status of the *Innovator*? Did the University establish a public forum? Or did it hedge the funding with controls that left the University itself as the newspaper's publisher? . . . We do not think it possible on this record to determine what kind of forum the University established or evaluate Dean Carter's justifications. But the question posed by *Saucier* is not who wins in the end, but whether the evidence makes out a constitutional claim when taken in the light most favorable to the plaintiff. These facts would permit a reasonable trier of fact to conclude that the *Innovator* operated in a public forum and thus was beyond the control of the University's administration.

The *Innovator* did not participate in a traditional public forum. Freedom of speech does not imply that someone else must pay. The University does not hand out money to everyone who asks. But by establishing a subsidized student newspaper the University may have created a venue that goes by the name "designated public forum" or "limited-purpose public forum." Participants in such a forum, declared open to speech *ex ante*, may not be censored *ex post* when the sponsor decides that particular speech is unwelcome. The classrooms used for meetings in *Good News Club* were designated public forums, and because the school allowed any student group to use the space the Court held that it could not forbid religious speech. In the same way, a school may declare the pages of the student newspaper open for expression and thus disable itself from engaging in viewpoint or content discrimination while the terms on which the forum operates remain unaltered. Dean Carter did not purport to alter the terms on which the *Innovator* operated; that authority belonged to the Student Communications Media Board. And the rules laid down by the Board, though ambiguous, could be thought (when considered as favorably to plaintiffs as the record allows) to create a designated public forum.

Defendants concede that the Board is the publisher of the *Innovator* and other subsidized print and broadcast media. The Board has seven members, all chosen by the Student Senate: four students, two faculty members, and one "civil service or support unit employee of the university." The Board determines how many publications it will underwrite (subject to the availability of funds, which as in *Southworth* and *Rosenberger* come from student activities fees), and the general character of each. It appoints "for the period of one year, the head of each student media staff." The Board's policy is that each funded publication "will determine content and format . . . without censorship or advance approval." If this is all there is to it, then the *Innovator* is in the same position as the student speakers in *Southworth* and *Rosenberger*: a designated public forum has been established, and the faculty cannot censor speech within it. When viewing matters in the light most favorable to the students, we stop here, because other matters are cloudy.

. . .

Qualified immunity nonetheless protects Dean Carter from personal liability unless it should have been "clear to a reasonable [public official] that his conduct was unlawful in the situation he confronted." "This inquiry, it is vital to note, must be undertaken in light of the specific context of the case, not as a broad general proposition." One might well say as a "broad general proposition" something like "public officials may not censor speech in a designated public forum," but whether Dean Carter was bound to know that the *Innovator* operated in such a forum is a different question altogether.

The district court held that any reasonable college administrator should have known that (a) the approach of *Hazelwood* does not apply to colleges; and (b) only speech that is part of the curriculum is subject to supervision.

We have held that neither of these propositions is correct—that *Hazelwood*'s framework is generally applicable and depends in large measure on the operation of public-forum analysis rather than the distinction between curricular and extra-curricular activities.

But even if student newspapers at high schools and colleges operate under different constitutional frameworks, as both the district judge and our panel thought, it greatly overstates the certainty of the law to say that any reasonable college administrator had to know that rule. The question had been reserved in *Hazelwood*, and the Supreme Court does not identify for future decision questions that already have "clearly established" answers. Post-*Hazelwood* decisions likewise had not "clearly established" that college administrators must keep hands off all student newspapers.... [T]he tenth and eleventh circuits have used *Hazelwood* as the framework for evaluating the acts of colleges as well as high schools. One circuit has said otherwise. *See Student Government Ass'n v. University of Massachusetts*, 868 F.2d 473, 480 n.6 (1st Cir. 1989) (asserting, in sole reliance on *Hazelwood*'s footnote 7, that the Supreme Court itself "holds" that *Hazelwood*'s approach does not apply to post-secondary education). The approach of others is hard to classify. *See Kincaid v. Gibson*, 236 F.3d 342, 346 n.5 (6th Cir. 2001) (en banc) (stating, in reliance on the parties' agreement, that *Hazelwood* has "little application" to collegiate publications but not explaining what this means, or how a constitutional framework can apply "just a little.") ...

. . .

... For reasons that should by now be evident, the implementation of *Hazelwood* means that both legal and factual uncertainties dog the litigation— and it is the function of qualified immunity to ensure that such uncertainties are resolved by prospective relief rather than by financial exactions from public employees. "Qualified immunity shields an official from suit when she makes a decision that, even if constitutionally deficient, reasonably misapprehends the law governing the circumstances she confronted." ...

Public officials need not predict, at their financial peril, how constitutional uncertainties will be resolved. Disputes about both law and fact make it inappropriate to say that any reasonable person in Dean Carter's position in November 2000 had to know that the demand for review before the University would pay the *Innovator*'s printing bills violated the first amendment. She therefore is entitled to qualified immunity from liability in damages.

■ Evans, Circuit Judge, joined by Rovner, Wood, and Williams, Circuit Judges, dissenting.

In concluding that *Hazelwood* extends to a university setting, the majority applies limitations on speech that the Supreme Court created for use in the *narrow* circumstances of elementary and secondary education. Because these restrictions on free speech rights have no place in the world of college and graduate school, I respectfully dissent.

The majority's conclusion flows from an incorrect premise—that there is no legal distinction between college and high school students. In reality, however, "the Court long has recognized that the status of minors under the law is unique in many respects." Age, for which grade level is a very good indicator,[1] has always defined legal rights. As the Court has noted:

> Constitutional rights do not mature and come into being magically only when one attains the state-defined age of majority. Minors, as well as adults, are protected by the Constitution and possess constitutional rights. The Court indeed, however, long has recognized that the State has somewhat broader authority to regulate the activities of children than of adults. *Planned Parenthood of Missouri. v. Danforth*, 428 U.S. 52 (1976).

. . .

There are two reasons why the law treats high school students differently than it treats college students, who "are, of course, young adults," *Widmar v. Vincent*, 454 U.S. 263, 274 n.14 (1981): high school students are less mature and the missions of the respective institutions are different. These differences make it clear that *Hazelwood* does not apply beyond high school contact.

It is self-evident that, as a general matter, juveniles are less mature than adults. Indeed, "during the formative years of childhood and adolescence, minors often lack the experience, perspective, and judgment to recognize and avoid choices that could be detrimental to them." *Bellotti*, 443 U.S. at 635. . . . In *Hazelwood*, the Court emphasized that a different First Amendment standard is appropriate in a high school setting because those students are young, emotionally immature, and more likely to be inappropriately influenced by school-sponsored speech on controversial topics. . . . It was, therefore, reasonable to restrict publication of an article about teenage pregnancy. *Bethel School District No. 403 v. Fraser*, 478 U.S. 675 (1986), where the Court permitted a high school to sanction a student for making a lewd student council election speech, makes a similar point. The Court emphasized that "the speech could well be seriously damaging to its *less mature* audience." . . .[2] The same concerns simply do not apply to college students, who are certainly (as a general matter) more mature, independent thinkers. *Tilton v. Richardson*, 403 U.S. 672, 686 (1971), establishes this point. The Court upheld a federal law that provided funding to church-related colleges and universities for construction of facilities for secular educational purposes. The Court noted that pre-college students may not have the maturity to make their own decisions on religion; however, "college students are less impressionable and less susceptible to religious indoctrination."

Not only is there a distinction between college and high school students themselves, the missions of the two institutions are quite different. Elementary and secondary schools have "custodial and tutelary responsibility for

---

1. According to the U.S. Census Bureau, only about one percent of those enrolled in American colleges and universities in 2002 were under the age of 18. *See* 2002 U.S. Census Bureau Current Population Survey (CPS) Rep., Table A–6, "Age Distribution of College Students 14 Years Old and Over, by Sex: October 1947 to 2002."

2. Other decisions of the Court outside the free speech arena likewise emphasize that greater restrictions are permitted on the rights of juveniles because they are less mature. For example, in *Lee v. Weisman*, 505 U.S. 577 (1992), the Court noted that "there are heightened concerns with protecting freedom of conscience from subtle coercive pressure in the elementary and secondary public schools." *Id.* at 592.

children," *Bd. of Educ. of Indep. Sch. Dist. No. 92 v. Earls*, 536 U.S. 822, 829–30 (2002) (holding that "Fourth Amendment rights ... are different in public schools than elsewhere"), and are largely concerned with the "inculcation" of "values." *Fraser*, 478 U.S. at 683; *see also Ambach v. Norwick*, 441 U.S. 68, 76 (1979) ("The importance of public schools in the preparation of individuals for participation as citizens, and in the preservation of the values on which our society rests, long has been recognized by our decisions[.]") A university has a different purpose—to expose students to a "marketplace of ideas." *Keyishian v. Bd. of Regents of the Univ. of N.Y.*, 385 U.S. 589 (1967) (emphasizing that the "Nation's future depends upon leaders trained through wide exposure to that robust exchange of ideas....")

As the Supreme Court perhaps best articulated in *Healy v. James*:

The precedents of this Court leave no room for the view that, because of the acknowledged need for order, *First Amendment* protections should apply with less force on college campuses than in the community at large. Quite to the contrary, "the vigilant protection of constitutional freedoms is nowhere more vital than in the community of American schools." The college classroom with its surrounding environs is peculiarly the " 'market-place of ideas,' " and we break no new constitutional ground in affirming this Nation's dedication to safeguarding academic freedom.

408 U.S. 169, 180–81 (1972) (quoting *Shelton v. Tucker*, 364 U.S. 479, 487 (1960), and *Keyishian*, 385 U.S. at 603). Based on this important notion, I do not believe it is appropriate for this court to extend *Hazelwood* to the college and university setting.

Questions and Comments on *Hosty*

1. Should the court have given greater weight to the maturity of college students? What rights do student newspapers have at private universities?

2. *Compare Hosty with* Kincaid v. Gibson, 236 F.3d 342 (6th Cir. 2001) (en banc) (holding that a university was a limited public forum and confiscation of the student yearbook by the university president was arbitrary and unreasonable) *and* Student Gov't Ass'n. v. Board of Trustees, 868 F.2d 473, 480 (1st Cir. 1989) ("*Hazelwood* ... is not applicable to college newspapers").

3. *Hosty* prompted much criticism for dampening free speech on college campuses. *See, e.g.*, Virginia J. Nimick, Note, *Schoolhouse Rocked:* Hosty v. Carter *and the Case Against* Hazelwood, 14 J.L. & Pol'y 941 (2006); Chris Sanders, Commentary, *Censorship 101: Anti–Hazelwood Laws and the Preservation of Free Speech at Colleges and Universities*, 58 Ala. L. Rev. 159 (2006). *But see* Jeff Sklar, Note, *The Presses Won't Stop Just Yet: Shaping Student Speech Rights in the Wake of* Hazelwood's *Application to Colleges*, 80 S. Cal. L. Rev. 641 (2007) (arguing that criticism of *Hosty* is exaggerated because most college papers are public forums and few interests rise to the level of legitimate pedagogical concerns worthy of censorship).

4. In response to *Hosty*, the Illinois Legislature passed the "College Campus Press Act," a bill making all publications at Illinois public colleges and universities public forums. The Act makes student editors and reporters responsible for all content and advertising decisions. Michael Beder, Student Press Law Center, Sept. 4, 2007, *available at* http://www.splc.org/newsflash.asp?id=1597.

B. ASSOCIATION

Healy v. James

Supreme Court of the United States, 1972.
408 U.S. 169, 92 S.Ct. 2338, 33 L.Ed.2d 266.

[The opinion is set forth at pp. 119–25, *supra.*]

Frank v. Ivy Club

Supreme Court of New Jersey, 1990.
120 N.J. 73, 576 A.2d 241, *cert. denied*, 498 U.S. 1073 (1991).

■ GARIBALDI, JUDGE.

This appeal concerns whether the New Jersey Division on Civil Rights (Division) followed the proper administrative procedure in concluding that it had jurisdiction under the New Jersey Law Against Discrimination, N.J. Stat. Ann. § 10:5–1 to–42 (LAD), over the Tiger Inn and Ivy Club (Clubs), all-male eating Clubs at Princeton University. Central to the resolution of the jurisdictional issue is whether the Clubs are "places of accommodation" within the meaning of LAD, or are exempt from LAD because they are "distinctly private." The Division found that the Clubs have an integral relationship of mutual benefit with Princeton which deprives them of private status and makes them subject to the Division's jurisdiction....

. . .

This case has a protracted history. Plaintiff, Sally Frank was a student in Princeton in 1979 when she commenced the action. She since has graduated from Princeton, finished Law School, and is now counsel of record in this case. The record consists of 31 volumes, comprising nearly 6,000 pages.

[In February, 1979 the Division refused to process a complaint filed by Frank against Princeton and three male-only eating clubs.]

In November of 1979 Frank filed another complaint, again alleging gender discrimination by the same parties. This complaint asserted that the Clubs were "public accommodations" because the Clubs functioned as "arms of Princeton ..." and because they were public accommodations in their own right. The Club filed answers denying that they were places of public accommodation and denying that they functioned as arms of Princeton. They claimed they were "bona fide private clubs" and therefore exempt from jurisdiction under N.J. Stat. Ann. § 10:5–5l. Princeton filed an answer denying that it was a place of public accommodation "with respect to the eating and social activities of its students." Princeton also claimed that as a factual matter, the Clubs were not part of the University.

The Civil Rights Division dismissed Frank's complaints. The Appellate Division, emphasizing that it was taking no position of the merits, vacated the Division's order because of the Division's failure to make findings of fact and to grant a hearing, and remanded the matter to the Division for further proceedings consistent with its opinion.

. . .

The Division issued a "Finding of Probable Cause" on May 14, 1985 (the "Finding"). The Finding established that the Division had jurisdiction over the Clubs and that probable cause existed to believe that the Clubs had discriminated against women. . . .

Princeton University is a private, non-sectarian institution of higher education, founded in 1746. The University is located in Princeton, New Jersey. From 1746 to 1968, Princeton University admitted only male students as undergraduates. In 1969, the University for the first time admitted women as undergraduate degree candidates.

From approximately 1803 to 1843, Princeton University required all undergraduate students to take their meals in commons operated by the college steward. In 1843, Princeton permitted its undergraduate students to board off-campus. The Princeton college refectory burned down in 1856 and was closed for fifty years. During that time, all students took their meals in boarding houses that were not affiliated with the college. In the mid–1800's several groups of Princeton students formed "select associations" to reduce the cost of their off campus living and dining expenses. By 1876 twenty-five "select associations" or eating clubs were in existence.

The club system associated with Princeton University, which began with these "select associations," presently [sic.] consists of thirteen clubs, eight of which are non-selective clubs and five of which are selective clubs. Campus, Charter, Cloister Inn, Colonial, Dial Lodge, Elm, Quadrangle and Terrace are the eight non-selective clubs. These clubs, formerly all male and selective, are now co-ed. The non-selective clubs offer social, recreational and dining activities.

Admission to the non-selective or open clubs is by a lottery system. . . .

The five selective clubs are Ivy, Cottage, Tiger Inn, Cap & Gown and Tower. The selective clubs also offer social, recreation and dining activities. Tower, Cap & Gown and Cottage accept male and female members. From their inception until the present, Ivy and Tiger have only accepted male members.

. . .

Ivy . . . owns the land and clubhouse at 143 Prospect Street in Princeton and pays all of its local and state taxes, maintenance, utility and insurance costs. Ivy is incorporated in New Jersey, tax-exempt under the Internal Revenue Code. . . .

. . .

Membership in the selective clubs is presently by invitation only. The general public is not invited to join Tiger or Ivy. Bicker is the term the five selective Clubs use for the process of interviewing and selecting new members. The sophomore class at one time administered Bicker, but ceased doing so in 1978. Since 1978, the sophomore class has not provided direct funding for the Bicker process. The process is now totally funded by the individual Clubs.

. . .

Undergraduate members of Ivy are elected by consensus at a meeting of a majority of its current membership. . . .

The Clubs require their undergraduate members to pay an initiation fee together with a yearly fee for board and social activities. All fees are paid by the student directly to the clubs. These fees are not part of Princeton University's undergraduate tuition. Membership dues and contributions to Ivy and Tiger are not tax deductible as contributions to educational institutions. Respondent Clubs provide food for consumption on their premises by contract with club members, the club agreeing to provide specific meals to their members for specific sums. All the Clubs charge members who bring a guest to dinner for the guest's meal unless the guest holds a University dining contract, and both the club member and the guest uses the Meal Exchange Program.

Respondent Clubs [occasionally place announcements in The Daily Princetonian and they rent the Club for events attended by non-members.] Employees of the Clubs are not employees of Princeton University. Employees of the Clubs are not covered by University-provided benefits such as health insurance, pension plans or Social Security contributions.

The Clubs use zip code 08540. Zip code 08544 is only used by Princeton University. Respondent clubs do not have campus mail delivery, nor can they use Princeton University's non-profit mailing permit.

Princeton University requires all freshman and sophomore students to have University dining contracts. Princeton University juniors and seniors generally dine in one of the following ways (figures are for 1983–84): DS (dining service) contracts (191); club membership (1570); living off-campus (98); living in Spelman Hall, apartment-style with kitchens (156); living at 2 Dickinson Street and participating in the co-op there (20); and living in other upperclass residential halls and eating in an undetermined manner (194).

. . .

The Club system has consistently been the most popular eating option available to upperclass students. In school year 1983–84, 1570 out of 2230 of Princeton's juniors and seniors took meals at one of the eating clubs. . . .

. . .

From at least 1977, Tiger and Ivy have not been listed as officially recognized student organizations by the Dean of Students of Princeton University. Princeton University does not presently provide any assistance to Tiger or Ivy in their fundraising efforts. However, the Princeton University Alumni Records and Mailing Services ("ARMS") makes certain services available to University alumni, including supplying updated mailing lists and processing mailings. There is a single rate-sheet for all such services, applicable to the eating clubs and to other outside organizations. Tiger and Ivy have used some of these services.

. . .

Sally Frank was a student at Princeton University from September 1976 through June 1980, when she graduated. During that time, Sally Frank did not join any of the non-selective eating clubs. During spring 1979 Bicker, Sally Frank was permitted to Bicker at the Ivy Club. However, Ivy's president told her that she could speak to Ivy members only when there were no sophomore men waiting to speak to Ivy members. Sally Frank spoke to at least one Club member at each of the Bicker sessions. She did not receive a bid from Ivy. During spring 1979 Bicker, Sally Frank Bickered at Tower Club and Cap & Gown. She did not receive a bid. During Bicker of 1980, Tiger Inn, Cottage and Ivy refused to permit Sally Frank to Bicker.

From these facts, the Division issued eleven factual conclusions. . . .

1. A Club system provides dining facilities for a majority of upper-class students attending Princeton University.

2. Respondent Clubs are part of this Club system associated with Princeton University.

3. Princeton University relies on these Clubs to feed a majority of their upperclass students.

4. Without the Clubs, Princeton University would incur substantial costs and would have to make major changes in the provision of dining services for upperclass students.

5. Princeton University has an interest in the continued viability of the Club system and has taken actions based on that interest.

6. The Clubs are characterized by the Clubs and Princeton University as servicing Princeton students and recruit members almost exclusively from Princeton University.

7. The Clubs work with one another and with Princeton University through organizations like the C.B.A. and the Interclub Council.

8. The link that ties the individual Clubs together is their association with Princeton University.

9. The Clubs would not continue in their present form with Princeton University.

10. Princeton University and the Clubs are integrally connected in a mutually beneficially relationship.

11. Non-members of respondent Clubs, particularly but not exclusively, Princeton University students, can participate in many of the respondent Clubs' activities and use the respondent Clubs' facilities.

The Division concluded based on these facts that the relationship between the Clubs and Princeton University is one of integral connection and mutual benefit that negates the Clubs claims that they are "distinctly private" entities. The Division rejected the argument that the Club members' constitutional free-association rights would be violated if the Clubs were subject to LAD. The Division then discussed briefly the issue of discrimination. On the basis of undisputed facts, the Division determined that probable cause existed to believe that the Clubs discriminated on the basis of gender.

. . .

[After the Finding of Probable Cause was issued, Frank succeeded in transferring the case to the Office of Administrative Law (OAL). On the basis of undisputed facts, the Administrative Law Judge (ALJ) granted Frank's motion for partial summary judgment on the issue of liability. The ALJ proposed the following remedies: (a) that Ms. Frank be awarded $2,500 in compensatory damages by the two Clubs; (b) that Ms. Frank *not* be awarded membership in either club; (c) that the two Clubs should sever certain ties to Princeton in order to attain "distinctly private" status; (d) that Princeton should avoid reference to the two Clubs as being affiliated or connected with the University in all future publications. Frank and Princeton agreed to a separate settlement.

The Director issued a final decision and order. Frank's damages were increased to $5,000. The Director ordered the Clubs to accept women, noting that the ALJ's decision "ordering the clubs to sever ties instead of ceasing their discriminatory practices was counter to the purpose of the LAD." [2]]

Ivy and Tiger appealed to the Appellate Division. The Appellate Division partially reversed the Division and remanded the case to the Division for new proceedings....

The court based its reversal ... on the fact that the Chief had exceeded his authority by resolving disputed facts and that the Division, by relying on the facts as resolved by the Chief, had abused its discretion....

Sally Frank then petitioned this Court for certification, arguing that the Appellate Division failed to defer to the Division's substantively correct and procedurally fair decision....

. . .

In analyzing the materiality of the facts, it is critical to understand that the Division rejected the theory that the Clubs themselves were places of accommodation. Instead, the Division premised its conclusion that the Clubs were not distinctly private on its finding that "the relationship between the Clubs and Princeton University is one of integral connection and mutual benefit." Jurisdiction over the Clubs is, essentially, based on jurisdiction over Princeton and supported by undisputed facts of the present day interdependence of the Clubs and Princeton. There no longer is any question that Princeton is a place of public accommodation under LAD. *Peper v. Trustees of Princeton University*, 77 N.J. 55, 67–68, 389 A.2d 465 (1978).

. . .

The finding of an integral and symbiotic relationship is based on the undisputed factual conclusions that the Clubs need the University and the University needs the Clubs, rather than on any particular act of control or integration. Where a place of public accommodation and an organization that deems itself private share a symbiotic relationship, particularly where the allegedly "private" entity supplies an essential service which is not provided by the public accommodation, the servicing entity loses its private character and becomes subject to laws against discrimination. *Hebard v. Basking Ridge Volunteer Fire Company*, 164 N.J.Super. 77, 395 A.2d 870 (App.Div.1978), *cert. den.* 81 N.J. 294, 405 A.2d 838 (1979) (volunteer fire

---

2. Both clubs recently voted to end their policy of not admitting women. In order for the policy change to become final, however, each club will need to confirm its vote within one year of the initial vote and then each club's graduate board consisting of alumni must approve the policy change.

department that refused to admit women had sufficient ties to municipality to make it subject to LAD*); Franklin v. Order of United Commercial Travelers*, 590 F.Supp. 255 (D.Mass.1984) (fraternal benefit society is not exempt from State anti-discrimination law because its relationship to city's police department deprives it of private status); *Adams v. Miami Police Benevolent Ass'n*, 454 F.2d 1315 (5th Cir.1972) *cert. den.*, 409 U.S. 843 (1972) (an association held subject to anti-discrimination law based on connection to city's police department, a non-exempt body). It would be disingenuous for the Clubs to assert that they could ever exist apart from Princeton University. The Clubs gather their membership from Princeton and, in turn, provide the service of feeding Princeton students. Because of this, the Clubs lack the distinctly private nature that would exempt them from LAD.

The Division's conclusion that the Clubs are not distinctly private is based on undisputed evidence. . . .

. . .

. . . There are no disputed facts material to the jurisdictional issue. Therefore, no plenary hearing was necessary before the Division properly asserted jurisdiction over the Clubs.

We also find that the undisputed facts establish that the Clubs and Princeton have an interdependent relationship that deprives the Clubs of private status and makes them subject to the Division's jurisdiction.

Gender discrimination is contrary to the legislative policy of the State of New Jersey. "The eradication of 'the cancer of discrimination' has long been one of our State's highest priorities." *Dixon v. Rutgers, The State University of N.J.*, 110 N.J. 432, 451, 541 A.2d 1046 (1988), quoting from *Fuchilla v. Layman*, 109 N.J. 319, 334, 537 A.2d 652 (1988). The Legislature enacted LAD to reflect the belief that "discrimination threatens not only the rights and proper privileges of the inhabitants of the State but menaces the institutions of a free democratic state." N.J. Stat. Ann. § 10:5–3. The elimination of discrimination in educational institutions is particularly critical. *Dixon v. Rutgers, The State University of N.J.*, *supra*, 110 N.J. at 452–53, 541 A.2d 1046. The intent of the legislature to eliminate discrimination in educational institutions is evidenced by the designation in N.J. Stat. Ann. 10:5–5(*l*), as a "place of accommodation," of any "college and university, or any educational institution under the supervision of the State Board of Education, or the Commissioner of Education of the State of New Jersey."

The Clubs have fiercely contested the threshold issue of jurisdiction because, once jurisdiction is established, there is no question that the Clubs discriminated against women. It is undisputed that the Clubs had a general policy that excluded females from consideration as members. It is also undisputed that the Clubs applied this policy to Frank when she attempted to Bicker at the clubs. That policy constituted discrimination in violation of LAD. On the basis of the facts in this record, we agree with the Division that the Clubs cannot sever their ties to the University or remove themselves from the jurisdiction of the Division. Instead, the Clubs must obey this State's substantive legal proscriptions against discrimination and discontinue their practice of excluding women purely on the basis of gender.

We reverse the Appellate Division. . . .

Questions and Comments on *Frank*

1. Ivy became coed in 1990 when the New Jersey Supreme Court ruled in Frank's favor. Tiger Inn, however, asked the U.S. Supreme Court to hear the case, but their petition for certiorari was denied. Tiger Inn v. Frank, 498 U.S. 1073 (1991). Tiger Inn then opened to women. Lee Williams, *Sally Frank '80, Who Ten Years Ago Forced the Last Three All–Male Eating Clubs to Go Co-ed, Will Speak Today*, DAILY PRINCETONIAN, Feb. 28, 2000, *available at* http://dailyprincetonian.com.

2. What rights against discrimination by other quasi-private clubs do students have? *See generally* Sally Frank, *The Key to Unlocking the Clubhouse Door: The Application of Antidiscrimination Laws to Quasi–Private Clubs*, 2 MICH. J. GENDER & L. 27 (1994) (written by the plaintiff in *Frank* who is now a law professor at Drake Law School).

Chi Iota Colony of Alpha Epsilon Pi Fraternity v. City University of New York

United States Court of Appeals, Second Circuit, 2007.
502 F.3d 136.

■ LEVAL, J.

This is an appeal by the defendant City University of New York, a public university, from a preliminary injunction imposed by the United States District Court for the Eastern District of New York (Irizarry, J.) barring the university's constituent, the College of Staten Island ("CSI"), from enforcing against the plaintiff fraternity, Chi Iota Colony ("the Fraternity"), a non-discrimination policy, which restricts official recognition of a student group to those that do not discriminate on the basis of gender.

. . .

The College of Staten Island is a public college within the City University of New York system. As of 2004, CSI had about 11,000 undergraduates, 40% of whom were male. CSI is committed to pluralism and diversity. The school's mission statement says that it hopes to instill in its students "a sensitivity to pluralism and diversity," and that it views "[e]fforts to promote diversity and to combat bigotry [as] an inextricable part of [its] educational mission." The school requires all students to fulfill a "Pluralism and Diversity" requirement by taking at least one course on that topic. CSI also has a policy of "provid[ing] services for students without regard to . . . sex."

CSI encourages students to form clubs in order to "support, enrich, extend, and amplify the goals of CSI's educational mission." In order to be officially recognized and to qualify for various benefits, "the purpose and goals of the student organization must exhibit a clear relationship with the educational mission of [CSI] by demonstrating a commitment to one or more" enumerated objectives. The list of enumerated objectives includes general values such as "promotion of service," "spiritual growth and development," and "promotion and development of cultural diversity and awareness."

In order for a student group to gain recognition, it must comply with CSI's non-discrimination policy:

[M]embership and participation in it must be available to all eligible students of the College. In addition, in order to be recognized, each organization must agree not to discriminate on the basis of ... gender....

. . .

A group that is recognized is entitled to [use CSI facilities and services, including a mailbox and workspace in the Campus Center; use the CSI name in conjunction with the group; solicit contributions outside the college and apply for special funding through the CSI Student Government; include group events in the CSI monthly calendars and have the group's public interest events covered in the student newspaper. Recognition also makes an association eligible to receive insurance through the CSI Association.] A group which fails to gain recognition is not banned or forbidden to meet or function; it is, however, not accorded the privileges listed above.

Chi Iota Colony is a male, social fraternity, which draws its members primarily from the CSI student body. As of September 2005, the Fraternity had eighteen members who were CSI students and one member who was not. The Fraternity has placed no limit on its size but has never before exceeded twenty members.

The Fraternity identifies itself as a Jewish organization.... Though most Fraternity members are non-practicing Jews, the group welcomes non-Jewish members, and several current members are not Jewish.

The Fraternity does not admit women. According to its president, "The selective, single-sex, all-male nature of the Fraternity is essential to achieving and maintaining the congeniality, cohesion and stability that enable it to function as a surrogate family and to meet [the] social, emotional and cultural needs of its members." He explained that admitting women might lead to romantic relationships between members, causing "inevitable jealousies and other conflicts." Even admitting lesbians might disrupt the special bonds between Fraternity members, because "[h]aving a female in the fraternity is an issue itself."

The Fraternity selects its members through a process called "rush." [The Fraternity meets most of the men that it invites to rush through its participation in Jewish groups such as Hillel and the Jewish Awareness Movement ("JAM").] ... The rush process ... is intended to ensure that offers of membership are extended "only [to] those who themselves and [the Fraternity] feel are compatible with the current members."

... Every prospective member goes through an interview regarding "the reason for and nature of his interest in the Fraternity, his family and other personal aspects of his life, his academic and career plans, [and] his religion and his attitudes about religion." Decisions about whom to invite to join the Fraternity are made by a five-member executive board in consultation with the group's members. No offer is ever made if more than one member is seriously opposed. Of those who repeatedly attend rush events, the majority are asked to "pledge" the Fraternity. Not everyone accepts the offer; somewhere between six and ten students pledge each semester. The Fraternity's president says that it hopes one day to have about fifty pledges, but he doubts that membership will ever exceed fifty, "because CSI is a heavily commuter campus."

. . .

Not all pledges become Fraternity members.... Of the six to ten pledges each semester, "most but not all, perhaps five to six" are initiated as members of the Fraternity. Initiation takes place in a private ceremony, usually at the house of one of the current members. The ceremony is secret and ritualized, and the Fraternity's president described it as "very special."....

Fraternity members participate in a variety of activities, some of which are open to the public and some of which are not. [Meetings concerning Fraternity business and membership are private.

The Fraternity also participates in JAM activities with non-members and holds for-profit parties to which non-members, including women, are invited.]

The Fraternity is seeking to become a chapter of Alpha Epsilon Fraternity, Inc. ("AEPi"), an international umbrella organization for Jewish fraternities.... AEPi's constitution limits membership to men, and the Fraternity's president specified that "[i]f the Fraternity is to maintain its affiliation with, and eventually meet its goal of becoming a chapter of, AEPi, it may have as members only male students."

On or about March 3, 2004, the Fraternity applied to become a chartered and officially recognized CSI student group. On March 29, Carol Brower, CSI's Director of the Office of Student Life, denied the Fraternity's application. One reason given was the group's failure to comply with CSI's non-discrimination policy....

While the Fraternity has continued to exist despite its inability to obtain official recognition, it claims that its "existence has been and continues to be made much more difficult." The Fraternity has been forbidden to set up recruitment tables at student orientations, to receive funding from CSI, to hand out fliers or advertise on campus, or to appear in a published list of student organizations. Some students who have been approached about joining the Fraternity have declined to explore membership because of the Fraternity's need to hold its events off-campus. Even some existing members have ceased participating in Fraternity activities because of transportation difficulties. Only when the Fraternity is participating in an event sponsored by a recognized student group can it meet on campus.

On June 17, 2005, the Fraternity and its eighteen CSI-student members (collectively, "the Fraternity") filed suit in the United States District Court for the Eastern District of New York, alleging that CSI was violating their rights under the First and Fourteenth Amendments, under federal anti-discrimination law, and under New York state law.... The Fraternity sought damages, as well as an injunction forcing CSI to recognize the Fraternity as an official student group.

. . .

The right to intimate association protects the close ties between individuals from inappropriate interference by the power of the state. *See Roberts v. U.S. Jaycees*, 468 U.S. 609, 619 (1984). To determine whether a governmental rule unconstitutionally infringes on an associational freedom, courts balance the strength of the associational interest in resisting governmental interference with the state's justification for the interference. This will require an assessment of: (1) the strength of the associational interests asserted and their importance to the plaintiff; (2) the degree to which the rule interferes with those interests; (3) the public interests or policies served by the rule imposed; and (4) the tailoring of the rule to effectuate those interests or policies. The more important the associational interest asserted, and the more the challenged governmental rule burdens the associational freedom, the more persuasive must be the state's reasons for the intrusion, and the more precisely tailored the state's policy must be.

. . .

Rather than balancing CSI's interests in its non-discrimination policy against the Fraternity's interests in opposing the policy, the district court adopted a categorical approach: Either the policy affected a constitutionally protected liberty or it did not. . . .

This categorical approach is inappropriate for dealing with association-rights cases. It fails to account for the "broad range of human relationships that may make greater or lesser claims to constitutional protection from particular incursions by the State." *Roberts*, 468 U.S. at 620.

Associational claims populate all ground from the heart of the First Amendment to its periphery, resisting facile attempts to divide them neatly into two piles. Moreover, governmental regulations may burden associational freedoms substantially, or minimally, or somewhere in between. Thus, the appropriate question in evaluating an associational-interest claim is not—as the district court asked—whether the associational interest claimed receives constitutional protection. Rather, the question is: Upon a balancing of all pertinent factors, do the state's interests, and its means of achieving them, justify the state's intrusion on the particular associational freedom?

The right to intimate association "reflects the realization that individuals draw much of their emotional enrichment from close ties with others," ties that allow for the cultivation and transmittal of shared beliefs. *Id.* at 619. [To determine the level of protection afforded to a relationship or association,] the Court has instructed that relationships must be "locate[d] . . . on a spectrum from the most intimate to the most attenuated of personal attachments." *Bd. of Dirs. of Rotary Int'l v. Rotary Club of Duarte*, 481 U.S. 537, 546 (1987). Criteria used to measure the strength of an association's interest in intimacy include "size, purpose, selectivity, and whether others are excluded from critical aspects of the relationship." *Id.* We examine these particulars in the context of the Fraternity's claim.

Size: The Fraternity currently has nineteen members. . . . But the Fraternity places no limit on membership size. The fact that the membership roll is not larger is due to the fact that CSI is primarily a commuter campus. Thus, the size limitation is the product of circumstances, not a desire to maintain intimacy. These characteristics render the Fraternity similar to other groups whose intimate-association interests were held to be weak. *See, e.g., id.* ("The size of local Rotary Clubs ranges from *fewer than 20* to more than 900." (emphasis added)); *id.* ("There is no upper limit on the membership of any local Rotary Club.").

Selectivity: The Fraternity employs some care in selecting recruits in order to ensure that all its members are compatible. Every prospective member goes through a screening interview that involves personal questions, and decisions about whom to invite are made in consultation with all current members.

However, upon each year's graduation, the Fraternity presumably ceases to associate regularly with a quarter of its members and seeks to replace them with new members. Like the Rotary Clubs in *Duarte*, the Fraternity must "keep a flow of prospects coming to make up for . . . attrition and gradually to enlarge the membership." *Id.* at 546 (quotation marks omitted). The Fraternity thus aggressively recruits new members from the CSI student body. *See Pi Lambda Phi Fraternity, Inc. v. Univ. of Pittsburgh*, 229 F.3d 435, 442 (3d Cir. 2000) (finding associational interest to be weak where chapter annually recruited new members). . . . [A] relatively high percentage of Jewish men at CSI who express an interest in the Fraternity are invited to join. The degree of selectivity displayed by the Fraternity in choosing new members thus compares unfavorably with that employed in creating the strongest of associational interests, as in the cases of marriage or adoption.

Purpose: The Fraternity's purposes are generally inclusive. The Fraternity aims to "foster and promote brotherly love, to inaugurate a spirit of cooperation and helpfulness, . . . [and] to encourage vigorous participation in university, college and general activities in [the] community. . . ." The Fraternity hopes to promote in its members a respect for "the traditional values of men's college social fraternities . . . , community service, and the expression of Jewish culture." These are broad, public-minded goals that do not depend for their promotion on close-knit bonds. *See Duarte*, 481 U.S. at 546–47 (Rotary Club's goal, "an inclusive fellowship for service based on diversity of interest, . . . does not suggest the kind of private or personal relationship to which we have accorded protection under the First Amendment.").

To be sure, the Fraternity also seeks to foster personal, intimate relationships between its members. According to its president, Fraternity brothers form "deep attachments and commitments" and share "a community of thoughts, experiences, beliefs and distinctly personal aspects of their lives." But the same can be said of nearly any student group in which members become close friends. As the Supreme Court explained in rejecting a facial challenge to an anti-discrimination law that affected clubs with more than 400 members:

> It may well be that a considerable amount of private or intimate association occurs in such a setting, as is also true in many restaurants and other places of public accommodation, but that fact alone does not afford the entity as a whole any constitutional immunity to practice discrimination when the government has barred it from doing so.

N.Y. State Club Ass'n, Inc. v. City of N.Y., 487 U.S. 1, 12 (1988).

Exclusion of Non–Members: It is true that some Fraternity activities take place only among its members. . . .

Nonetheless, the Fraternity involves non-members in several crucial aspects of its existence. Many rush events are held in public places such as local cafes or pool halls. During its February 2003 rush, the Fraternity planned several events requiring the interaction of current and prospective members with non-members—a party, as well as outings to a strip club, a karaoke bar, and a laser tag establishment. *See Roberts*, 468 U.S. at 621 ("[M]uch of the activity central to the formation and maintenance of the association involves the participation of strangers to that relationship.").

Once they join, many Fraternity members attend public weekly meetings with the JAM and a rabbi. The Fraternity also participates with the JAM in other Jewish-themed events. *See Pi Lambda Phi*, 229 F.3d at 442 (finding associational interest to be weakened by chapter's participation in many public university events). The Fraternity gives parties, sometimes at a profit, at which non-members—including women—are encouraged to attend. *See N.Y. State Club Ass'n*, 487 U.S. at 12 (regular receipt of payments from non-members is "at least as significant in defining the nonprivate nature of these associations, because of the kind of role that strangers play in their ordinary existence, as is the regular participation of strangers at meetings"). Social events involving non-members occur "perhaps once or twice a month."

Furthermore, the Fraternity seeks affiliation with AEPi, a national organization. Association with AEPi would involve the members to some extent in activities of the national group and would thus dilute the intimacy of the Fraternity. The Fraternity opposes admitting women at least in part because admitting them would make the Fraternity ineligible for this affiliation. The Fraternity's desire to associate itself with this national organization is in some tension with the purpose of the right to intimate association.

. . .

Also important is the fact that CSI's non-discrimination policy interferes only to a limited extent with the Fraternity's associational rights. CSI's policy does not prevent the Fraternity from continuing to exist, to hold intimate meetings, to exclude women, or to exercise selectivity in choosing new members. Denial of recognition has consequences primarily for the Fraternity's non-intimate aspects. CSI's denial of use of school facilities interferes more with the Fraternity's ability to solicit strangers from future classes to become new members than it interferes with the ability of its existing members to gather and share intimate associations. The Fraternity has not shown that the unavailability of school facilities makes it impossible, or even difficult, to find suitable places for meetings. CSI's refusal to subsidize the Fraternity's activities does not constitute a substantial imposition on the group's associational freedom. *See Lyng v. Int'l Union, United Auto., Aerospace and Agr. Implement Workers of Am., UAW*, 485 U.S. 360, 368 (1988) (upholding the government's refusal to extend food stamp benefits to workers who strike, because "the strikers' right of association does not require the Government to furnish funds to maximize the exercise of that right"); *Lyng v. Castillo*, 477 U.S. 635, 638 (1986) (upholding law lowering food stamp allotments for certain family members living together below levels they would have received if they had lived separately or been unrelated, because the law does not " 'directly and substantially' interfere with family living arrangements and thereby burden a fundamental right"); *Regan v. Taxation with Representation of Washington*, 461 U.S. 540, 546 (1983) ("We again reject the notion that First Amendment rights are somehow not fully realized unless they are subsidized by the State").

CSI's interests in applying its non-discrimination policy are substantial. As the district court acknowledged, "[t]here is undoubtedly a compelling interest in eradicating discrimination based on gender." *See Bd. of Dirs. of Rotary Int'l v. Rotary Club of Duarte*, 481 U.S. 537, 549 (1987) ("[P]ublic accommodations laws 'plainly serv[e] compelling state interests of the highest order.' ") (quoting *Roberts*, 468 U.S. at 624). The school's mission statement declares that "[e]fforts to promote diversity and to combat bigotry . . . are an inextricable part of the educational mission of the University." CSI encourages students to form clubs in order to support the school's goals. To gain recognition, a club must "exhibit a clear relationship with the educational mission" of CSI. By denying recognition to student groups that reject members based on gender, CSI's anti-discrimination policy directly promotes the significant, consistent commitment the school has made to oppose discrimination.

Though recognizing the importance of eradicating discrimination, the district court minimized the state interest in doing so in the present context. The court noted that fraternities and sororities have long existed as single-sex institutions, and that federal anti-discrimination laws specifically exempt fraternities and sororities from their reach. It attached considerable importance to the fact that there "is no law deeming single-sex organizations per se unconstitutional or against national policy." The district court concluded that while eliminating sex discrimination *in general* is a compelling state interest, preventing fraternities from discriminating is not.

The fact that a practice is lawful does not mean that a state may not have a substantial interest in opposing it. An interest need not be protected by federal statutes before it can be considered compelling. In *Roberts*, for instance, the Supreme Court found that Minnesota's public accommodations law served a compelling interest—eradicating discrimination in private clubs—even though the law went further than federal anti-discrimination laws. 468 U.S. at 623; *see also Grutter v. Bollinger*, 539 U.S. 306, 327–33 (2003) (recognizing that states have a compelling interest in promoting a diverse student body at public universities, even though no federal law requires affirmative action in education). The state's interest in prohibiting sex discrimination is no less compelling because federal anti-discrimination statutes exempt fraternities.

Moreover, CSI has a substantial interest in making sure that its resources are available to all its students. When a student group is officially recognized by CSI, it becomes entitled to a range of benefits, including use of CSI facilities and services, eligibility for insurance through the school, the right to use the CSI name in conjunction with the group, and the opportunity to apply for funding from the student government. These benefits are funded in part by tuition paid by CSI's students; CSI's non-discrimination policy ensures that all its students have access to the organizations that enjoy these benefits. *See Roberts*, 468 U.S. at 624 (state has a compelling interest in "assuring its citizens equal access to publicly available goods and services").

. . .

In sum, the Fraternity's interests in intimate association are relatively weak; CSI's non-discrimination policy imposes no great burden on the plaintiffs' enjoyment of those interests; the policy serves several important state interests; and the policy is well tailored to effectuate those interests. Given this balance of the pertinent factors, we believe the district court erred in granting a preliminary injunction barring CSI from enforcing its policy of denial of recognition to a group that categorically excludes members on the basis of gender.

The preliminary injunction is vacated and the case is remanded for further proceedings.

Questions and Comments on *Chi Iota Colony*

In balancing CSI's interest in its non-discrimination policy with the students' interest in freedom of association, the court held that the protection afforded to students depends upon the intimacy of the association. Examining the size, purpose, selectivity, and exclusivity of the fraternity, the court found that the association was not so intimate that it merited the court's protection. The president of the fraternity, in contrast, described it as a "surrogate family." Did the court misjudge the intimacy of the relationship? For example, was the court right to hold that friendship is no more a central goal of the fraternity than it is of any public interest student group? If the fraternal association were more intimate than the court acknowledged, would the state's interest in ending gender discrimination still outweigh the students' freedom of association?

IOTA XI Chapter of Sigma Chi Fraternity v. George Mason University

United States Court of Appeals for the Fourth Circuit, 1993.
993 F.2d 386.

■ SPROUSE, SENIOR CIRCUIT JUDGE.

George Mason University appeals from a summary judgment granted by the district court to the Iota Chi Chapter of Sigma Chi Fraternity in its action for declaratory judgment and an injunction seeking to nullify sanctions imposed on it by the University because it conducted an "ugly woman contest" with racist and sexist overtones....

Sigma Chi has for two years held an annual "Derby Days" event, planned and conducted both as entertainment and as a source of funds for donations to charity. The "ugly woman contest," held on April 4, 1991, was one of the "Derby Days" events. The Fraternity staged the contest in the cafeteria of the student union. As part of the contest, eighteen Fraternity members were assigned to one of six sorority teams cooperating in the events. The involved Fraternity members appeared in the contest dressed as caricatures of different types of women, including one member dressed as an offensive caricature of a black woman. He was painted black and wore stringy, black hair decorated with curlers, and his outfit was stuffed with pillows to exaggerate a woman's breasts and buttocks. He spoke in slang to parody African–Americans.

There is no direct evidence in the record concerning the subjective intent of the Fraternity members who conducted the contest. The Fraternity, which later apologized to the University officials for the presentation, conceded during the litigation that the contest was sophomoric and offensive.

[After the contest, two hundred fifty-seven students, including many minorities, filed a petition condemning the act. The Dean for Student Services, Kenneth Bumgarner, met with the offended students, members of Sigma Chi, and the student government. The student government agreed that the behavior created a hostile learning environment for women and minorities. Sigma Chi was subject to sanctions, including a ban on all activities for the remainder of the academic year and a two-year ban on social activities except for pledging and events with an educational purpose related to gender discrimination and cultural diversity.]

On June 5, 1991, Sigma Chi brought this action under 42 U.S.C. § 1983 against the University and Dean Bumgarner. It requested declaratory judgment and injunctive relief to nullify the sanctions as violative of the First and Fourteenth Amendments. Sigma Chi moved for summary judgment on its First Amendment claims on June 28, 1991. . . .

. . . [T]he University submitted the affidavits of [Dean Bumgarner and] other officials, including that of University President George W. Johnson and Vice–President Earl G. Ingram. President Johnson, by his affidavit, [affirmed that the mission of the university is to promote a culturally and racially diverse student body, and that, in keeping with this goal, the university has implemented "a plan incorporating affirmative steps designed to attract and retain minorities to this campus." Vice President Ingram added that the "University's affirmative action plan is a part of an overall state plan designed, in part, to desegregate the predominately 'white' and 'black' public institutions of higher education in Virginia," and that the behavior of Sigma Chi impeded this goal.]

The district court granted summary judgment to Sigma Chi on its First Amendment claim.

. . .

We initially face the task of deciding whether Sigma Chi's "ugly woman contest" is sufficiently expressive to entitle it to First Amendment protection. . . . The answer to the question of whether the First Amendment protects the Fraternity's crude attempt at entertainment . . . is all the more difficult because of its obvious sophomoric nature.

First Amendment principles governing live entertainment are relatively clear: short of obscenity, it is generally protected. As the Supreme Court announced in *Schad v. Borough of Mount Ephraim*, 452 U.S. 61 (1981), "entertainment, as well as political and ideological speech, is protected; motion pictures, programs broadcast by radio and television, and live entertainment . . . fall within the First Amendment guarantee." Expression devoid of "ideas" but with entertainment value may also be protected because "the line between the informing and the entertaining is too elusive."

Thus, we must determine if the skit performed by Sigma Chi comes within the constitutionally protected rubric of entertainment. Unquestionably, some forms of entertainment are so inherently expressive as to fall within the First Amendment's ambit regardless of their quality. For example, in *Ward v. Rock Against Racism*, 491 U.S. 781 (1989), the Supreme Court flatly ruled that "music, as a form of expression and communication, is protected under the First Amendment." Justice Kennedy explained:

> Music is one of the oldest forms of human expression. From Plato's discourse in the Republic to the totalitarian state in our own times, rulers have known its capacity to appeal to the intellect and to the emotions, and have censored musical compositions to serve the needs of the state. The Constitution prohibits any like attempts in our own legal order.

Even crude street skits come within the First Amendment's reach. In overturning the conviction of an amateur actor for wearing a military uniform in violation of a federal statute, the Supreme Court discussed the statute's "theatrical production" exception.[3] *Schacht v. United States*, 398 U.S. 58, 61–62 (1970). Responding to the Government's argument that the amateur skit was not a "theatrical production," Justice Black, writing for the majority, stated:

> It may be that the performances were crude and amateurish and perhaps unappealing, but the same thing can be said about many theatrical performances. We cannot believe that when Congress wrote out a special exception for theatrical productions it intended to protect only a narrow and limited category of professionally produced plays.
>
> . . .

Bearing on this dichotomy between low and high-grade entertainment are the Supreme Court's holdings relating to nude dancing. *See Barnes v. Glen Theatre, Inc.*, 115 L. Ed. 2d 504 (1991); *Schad v. Borough of Mount Ephraim*, 452 U.S. 61, 65–66 (1981); *Doran v. Salem Inn, Inc.*, 422 U.S. 922, 932–33 (1975); *California v. LaRue*, 409 U.S. 109, 116–18 (1972). Most recently, in *Barnes*, the Supreme Court conceded that nude dancing is expressive conduct entitled to First Amendment protection. In *Barnes*, [115 L.Ed.2d 504 (1991)], the Court reviewed ... a Seventh Circuit opinion authored by Judge Flaum, *Miller v. Civil City of South Bend*, 904 F.2d 1081 (7th Cir. 1990) (en banc), *rev'd sub nom.*, ... which thoroughly analyzed the questions of whether and how nude dancing is expression entitled to First Amendment protection. The Miller opinion noted that dance is inherently expressive entertainment, as it conveys emotions and ideas. Judge Flaum refused to distinguish "high" art from "low" entertainment on the asserted basis that low entertainment "fails to communicate a defined intellectual thought." Applying the test enunciated in *Texas v. Johnson*, 491 U.S. 397, 404 (1989),[4] he concluded that nude dancing communicated a message of eroticism and sensuality, understood by its viewers as such. *Miller*, 904 F.2d at 1087. Thus, notwithstanding its artistic quality, nude dancing was sufficiently expressive to entitle it to First Amendment protection. Justice White's dissent in *Barnes* echoed Judge Flaum's opinion:

> While the entertainment afforded by a nude ballet at Lincoln Center to those who can pay the price may differ vastly in content (as viewed by judges) or in quality (as viewed by critics), it may not differ in substance from the dance viewed by the person who ... wants some "entertainment" with his beer or shot of rye.

In sum, although the *Barnes* plurality did not explore these views, it appears that the low quality of entertainment does not necessarily weigh in the First Amendment inquiry. It would seem, therefore, that the Fraternity's

3. 10 U.S.C. § 772(f) provides:

While portraying a member of the Army, Navy, Air Force, or Marine Corps, an actor in a theatrical or motion-picture production may wear the uniform of that armed force if the portrayal does not tend to discredit that armed force.

4. In *Texas v. Johnson*, discussed *infra*, the Supreme Court stated: "In deciding whether particular conduct possesses sufficient communicative elements to bring the First Amendment into play, we have asked whether 'an intent to convey a particularized message was present, and [whether] the likelihood was great that the message would be understood by those who viewed it.'" *Johnson*, 491 U.S. at 404 (quoting *Spence v. Washington*, 418 U.S. 405, 410–11 (1974)).

skit, even as low-grade entertainment, was inherently expressive and thus entitled to First Amendment protection.

The University nevertheless contends that discovery will demonstrate that the contest does not merit characterization as a skit but only as mindless fraternity fun, devoid of any artistic expression. It argues further that entitlement to First Amendment protection exists only if the production was intended to convey a message likely to be understood by a particular audience. From the summary judgment record, the University insists, it is impossible to discern the communicative intent necessary to imbue the Fraternity's conduct with a free speech component.

As indicated, we feel that the First Amendment protects the Fraternity's skit because it is inherently expressive entertainment. Even if this were not true, however, the skit, in our view, qualifies as expressive conduct under the test articulated in *Texas v. Johnson*. It is true that the *Johnson* test for determining the expressiveness of conduct requires " 'an intent to convey a particularized message' " and a great likelihood " 'that the message would be understood by those who viewed it.' " . . . [H]owever, the intent to convey a message can be inferred from the conduct and the circumstances surrounding it. Thus viewed, the University's argument is self-defeating. The affidavit from the University's Vice–President, Earl Ingram, stated that the message conveyed by the Fraternity's conduct—that racial and sexual themes should be treated lightly—was completely antithetical to the University's mission of promoting diversity and providing an educational environment free from racism and sexism. . . .

Importantly, the affidavits establish that the punishment was meted out to the Fraternity because its boorish message had interfered with the described University mission. It is manifest from these circumstances that the University officials thought the Fraternity intended to convey a message. The Fraternity members' apology and post-conduct contriteness suggest that they held the same view. To be sure, no evidence suggests that the Fraternity advocated segregation or inferior social status for women. What is evident is that the Fraternity's purposefully nonsensical treatment of sexual and racial themes was intended to impart a message that the University's concerns, in the Fraternity's view, should be treated humorously. From the Fraternity's conduct and the circumstances surrounding it, we have no difficulty in concluding that it intended to convey a message.

As to the second prong of the Johnson test, there was a great likelihood that at least some of the audience viewing the skit would understand the Fraternity's message of satire and humor. Some students paid to attend the performance and were entertained. What the Fraternity did not anticipate was the reaction to their crude humor by other students on campus and University officials who opposed the racist and sexist implications of the Fraternity's skit.

Even considering, therefore, the sparsity of the evidentiary record, we are persuaded that the Fraternity's "ugly woman contest" satisfies the *Johnson* test for expressive conduct.

If this were not a sufficient response to the University's argument, the principles relating to content and viewpoint discrimination recently emphasized in *R.A.V. v. City of St. Paul*, 120 L.Ed.2d 305 (1992), provide a definitive answer. Although the Court in *St. Paul* reviewed the constitutional effect of a city "hate speech" ordinance, and we review the constitutionality of sanctions imposed for violating University policy, St. Paul's rationale applies here with equal force. Noting that St. Paul's city ordinance prohibited displays of symbols that "arouse anger, alarm or resentment in others on the basis of race, color, creed, religion or gender," but did not prohibit displays of symbols which would advance ideas of racial or religious equality, Justice Scalia stated: "The First Amendment does not permit St. Paul to impose special prohibitions on those speakers who express views on disfavored subjects."

As evidenced by their affidavits, University officials sanctioned Sigma Chi for the message conveyed by the "ugly woman contest" because it ran counter to the views the University sought to communicate to its students and the community. The mischief was the University's punishment of those who scoffed at its goals of racial integration and gender neutrality, while permitting, even encouraging, conduct that would further the viewpoint expressed in the University's goals and probably embraced by a majority of society as well. "The First Amendment generally prevents government from proscribing ... expressive conduct because of disapproval of the ideas expressed."

The University, however, urges us to weigh Sigma Chi's conduct against the substantial interests inherent in educational endeavors. *See Tinker v. Des Moines Indep. Community Sch. Dist.*, 393 U.S. 503 (1969). The University certainly has a substantial interest in maintaining an educational environment free of discrimination and racism, and in providing gender-neutral education. Yet it seems equally apparent that it has available numerous alternatives to imposing punishment on students based on the viewpoints they express.[8] We agree wholeheartedly that it is the University officials' responsibility, even their obligation, to achieve the goals they have set. On the other hand, a public university has many constitutionally permissible means to protect female and minority students. We must emphasize, as have other courts, that "the manner of [its action] cannot consist of selective limitations upon speech." *St. Paul*, 112 S.Ct. at 2548; *see also Carey v. Brown*, 447 U.S. 455, 471 (invalidating a ban on residential picketing that exempted labor picketing); *Schacht v. United States*, 398 U.S. 58, 62–63 (1970) (invalidating a law that allowed wearing military uniforms only in dramatic portrayals that did not "tend to discredit the military"). The First Amendment forbids the government from "restricting expression because of its message or its ideas." *Police Dept. v. Mosley*, 408 U.S. 92, 95 (1972). The University should have accomplished its goals in some fashion other than silencing speech on the basis of its viewpoint.

The decision of the district court is affirmed.

Note on Fraternity Hazing

1. Hazing is common at many universities, both in Greek organizations and in sports. One survey found that eighty percent of college athletes had been subjected to

---

8. In *St. Paul*, the Court rejected the Minnesota Supreme Court's pronouncement that St. Paul's "hate speech" ordinance was narrowly tailored to serve St. Paul's compelling interest in "ensuring the basic human rights of members of groups that had historically been subjected to discrimination." *St.* *Paul*, 112 S.Ct. at 2549. Although the Court acknowledged that this interest was compelling, it concluded that the content discrimination contained in the ordinance was not "reasonably necessary to achieve St. Paul's compelling interests." *Id.*

some form of hazing. Joshua A. Sussberg, Note, *Shattered Dreams: Hazing in College Athletics*, 24 CARDOZO L. REV. 1421, 1427 (2003). Anti-hazing laws have been passed in almost every state and some students have been formally charged in hazing incidents. Massachusetts, for example, has made hazing punishable by a fine of up to three thousand dollars and/or one year in prison. Mass. Gen. Laws ch. 269, § 17 (2002). The statute defines hazing as "any conduct or method of initiation into any student organization . . . which willfully or recklessly endangers the physical or mental health of any student or other person" and removes consent as a defense to prosecution. *Id.* Massachusetts also has made failure to report hazing punishable. Mass. Gen. Laws ch. 269, § 18 (2002). *See also* Cal. Penal Code § 245.6 (West 2007); N.Y. Penal Law § 120.16 (McKinney 2004).

Florida has enacted one of the toughest anti-hazing laws, making hazing resulting in serious physical injury a felony punishable by up to five years in prison. Fla. Stat § 1006.63(2) (2004). In a recent case, two members of Kappa Alpha Psi at Florida A & M University were sentenced to two years in prison for felony hazing. Elia Powers, *Testing an Anti–Hazing Law*, INSIDE HIGHER ED., Jan. 31, 2007, *available at* http://insidehighered.com/layout/set/print/news/2007/01/31/hazing. The fraternity members beat a pledge with a wooden paddle and boxing gloves, causing the pledge to suffer a ruptured eardrum and injury to his buttocks. *Id.* While not speaking on behalf of the university, some university officials, including the former president, a former Board of Trustees chairman, and the current assistant director for recreation, pleaded for leniency in the sentencing. Susan Lipkins, a psychologist specializing in campus conflict, criticized the university officials for sending "mixed messages." *Id.* *See also* Lisa W. Foderaro, *3 Plead Guilty in Inquiry into Fatal College Hazing*, N.Y. TIMES, Oct. 11, 2003, at B5; Joseph A. Slobodzian, *Penn Students Guilty in '05 Hazing Incident*, Philly.com, Nov. 21, 2006, *available at* http://www.insidehazing.com/headline. php?id=344.

2. What steps should a university take to stop hazing? Consider *Furek v. University of Delaware*, 594 A.2d 506 (Del.1991), in which a college student sued the University of Delaware after suffering injuries during a fraternity hazing incident:

> In the fall of 1980, Furek began his pledge period at Sig Ep. The pledge period is an eight-week initiation process during which pledges, those seeking to become members of the fraternity, are instructed concerning the history of the fraternity and undergo a process known as "brotherhood development." The pledges are also subjected to various forms of harassment known as "hazing". The culmination of the initiation process is a secret ritual known as "Hell Night" . . . After assembling across the street from the Sig Ep house, wearing only T-shirts and jeans, the pledges were ordered to crawl on their hands and knees to the fraternity house while being sprayed by a fire extinguisher. Once inside the house, the pledges were ushered to various rooms where they were humiliated and degraded. Among other things, they were paddled, forced to do calisthenics and ordered to eat food out of a toilet.

> Donchez, a member of the fraternity, was stationed in the kitchen and assigned the task of pouring food on the pledges. The pledges were escorted into the kitchen blindfolded, and pancake batter, ketchup and other foodstuffs was poured on their heads. During this process, Donchez poured a container containing a lye-based liquid oven cleaner over the back and neck of Furek. . . . He was then taken to the hospital and treated for first- and second-degree chemical burns. As a result of the events of Hell Night, Sig Ep had its charter revoked by the National Fraternity and the University withdrew the registration of the fraternity. Furek, permanently scarred, subsequently withdrew from the University and forfeited his football scholarship.

> Although official policy directives from the University and the National Fraternity forbade hazing, Sig Ep and other fraternities on the Newark

campus had engaged in various forms of hazing for at least five years previous to the incident in question.

The court upheld the jury award of $30,000 in damages against the university, stating that although there is "no duty on the part of a college or university to control its students based *merely* on the university-student relationship, where there is direct university involvement in, and knowledge of, certain dangerous practices of its students, the university cannot abandon its residual duty of control."

Id. at 519–20 (emphasis in original).

The university's previous knowledge of hazing incidents was a key factor in *Furek*. In contrast, Cornell was not held liable after a similar incident because it lacked knowledge of prior hazing incidents. Lloyd v. Alpha Phi Alpha Fraternity, 1999 WL 47153 (N.D.N.Y. 1999). By regulating fraternities and punishing them for past incidents of hazing, did the University of Delaware inadvertently expose themselves to more liability?

3. What liability should individual fraternity members have for injuries resulting from hazing? In a recent case involving a non-university-recognized fraternity at the State University of New York College at Plattsburgh, the family of a student who died from hazing was awarded 1.5 million dollars in compensatory and punitive damages from an individual fraternity member. *Parents are Awarded 1.5–Million in Hazing Death of SUNY–Plattsburgh Student,* CHRON. HIGHER EDUC., Dec. 4, 2007, *available at* http://chronicle.com/news/article/3554/parents-are-awarded-15-million. The student died from swelling of the brain after being forced to drink several gallons of water. *Id.*

Romeo v. Seton Hall University

Superior Court of New Jersey, Appellate Division, 2005.
378 N.J.Super. 384, 875 A.2d 1043.

■ PETRELLA, P.J.A.D.

Anthony Romeo is an openly gay student at Seton Hall University. He claims he elected to attend Seton Hall in part because of its published antidiscrimination policy, which he argues created a "unilateral contract" binding upon it. On November 13, 2003, he applied to the Seton Hall University Department of Student Affairs for provisional recognition of a gay and lesbian student organization to be named "TRUTH," an acronym for the phrase "Trust, Respect and Unity at The Hall." Dr. Laura A. Wankel, Vice President of Student Affairs at Seton Hall, responded to Romeo's application in a December 18, 2003 letter, stating in pertinent part:

> The most compelling guidance from the Church directs us to care for the human person whose fundamental identity is as a "child of God"—not as a "heterosexual" or a "homosexual." The Church teaches that an exclusive focus on a person's sexual orientation denies the fullness of human dignity and diminishes persons in a way that is both reductionist and marginalizing. As a result, although SOAC [Student Organization Activities Committee] recommended to me that "TRUTH" be approved, I am informing you that your application for provisional recognition has been denied. No organization based solely upon sexual orientation may receive formal University recognition.

. . .

... [T]he Division of Student Affairs remains prepared to work with gay and lesbian students to meet their needs. I am committed to working collaboratively with you and other students in fostering a positive, safe and caring community. To that end, I am providing the following plan that outlines how we may move forward.

The plan referenced in her letter was entitled "Memorandum of Understanding," and provided guidelines for gay and lesbian students wishing to operate as a group within the Seton Hall University community. The guidelines in the memorandum offered privileges, including the ability to: (1) sponsor educational events, meetings and programs; (2) sponsor volunteer and community service initiatives; (3) provide a forum for the exchange of views; (4) support gay students through campus educational programs aimed against discrimination; (5) elect officers and have ad hoc committees; and (6) request funds for particular activities and the use of other resources.

This proposal was not satisfactory to the students, and thus, Romeo filed his complaint on March 10, 2004, alleging violations of the [New Jersey Law Against Discrimination] LAD and breach of contract. The complaint was dismissed, but on a reconsideration motion the dismissal was vacated and Romeo was granted leave to amend. The appeal is from that order.

. . .

Under N.J. Stat. Ann. § 10:5–12(f) the owner of a place of public accommodation may not discriminate against any person on various grounds stated, including "sexual orientation." This term is broad and not defined in the statute.

However, Seton Hall argues that it is exempt from the provisions of the LAD by virtue of N.J. Stat. Ann. § 10:5–5(l), which states: "nor shall anything herein contained apply to any educational facility operated or maintained by a bona fide religious or sectarian institution."

... It is not disputed that Seton Hall qualifies as an educational facility operated by a bona fide religious institution. Thus, by its very terms the provisions of LAD, including the prohibition of discrimination based on sexual orientation, *see* N.J. Stat. Ann. § 10:5–3, do not apply to such religiously affiliated institutions.

Romeo argues that Seton Hall waived its exemption through the written statement found in its "Non Discrimination Policy":

No person may be denied employment or related benefits or admission to the University or to any of its programs or activities, either academic or nonacademic, curricular or extracurricular, because of race, color, religion, age, national origin, gender, sexual orientation, handicap and disability, or veteran's status.

It was conceded by Romeo's attorney at oral argument that Romeo was not denied "admission to the University or to any of its programs or activities" based on his "sexual orientation."

In response to Romeo's contention that Seton Hall, through its internal "Non Discrimination Policy" which is listed on its website and in its handbooks, waived the statutory exemption, Seton Hall argues that it could not waive its exemption and did not do so by adopting its antidiscrimination policy. It asserts that First Amendment protections and considerations under the United States Constitution also apply. It thus argues that Romeo's complaint must be dismissed as a matter of law.

Our Supreme Court has utilized Title VII case law "for guidance in developing standards to govern the resolution of LAD claims."

In *Little v. Wuerl*, 929 F.2d 944 (3d Cir.1991), the Third Circuit discussed the issue of waiver of a religious exemption in the Title VII context. The court held: "Once Congress stated that '[t]his title shall not apply' to religiously-motivated employment decisions by religious organizations, no act by Little [the plaintiff] or the Parish [the defendant] could expand the statute's scope."

.   .   .

In *Egan v. Hamline United Methodist Church*, 679 N.W.2d 350 (Minn. Ct. App. 2004), the Minnesota Court of Appeals addressed a similar issue. The plaintiff in *Egan* argued that the church had waived its exemption to a statute prohibiting discrimination on the basis of sexual orientation due to the church's commitment to nondiscrimination on the basis of sexual orientation, as provided in the church's *Personnel Handbook* and the United Methodist Church's The Book of Discipline. *Id.* at 352–356. After discussing the waiver issue in the Title VII context, in particular *Little* and *Hall,* the court held:

> we would not take the rule from the Title VII cases to its logical extreme. We do not hold that it is impossible for churches to waive their exemption from the MHRA. If the waiver is specific and unequivocal, and if the scope of that waiver is evident, then there is not a risk of entanglement. It ought to be recognized. It would be illogical and unjust to ignore such a waiver; however, a pronouncement by the religious organization that it will conform to the principle of nondiscrimination only indicates an intent to voluntarily embrace that principle. Without greater clarity, we would be compelled to conduct an examination and interpret statements of Hamline Methodist and the United Methodist Church on doctrinal policy as it relates to the alleged reason for an employee's discharge. This invites an unconstitutional entanglement of the church with the judicial and administrative branches of government.

The court proceeded to hold that the policy at issue did not constitute an effective waiver. . . .

Cases such as *Little* persuade us to conclude that the exemption in N.J. Stat. Ann. § 10:5–5(*l*) of the LAD cannot be waived. But, even if Seton Hall could waive the exemption, its antidiscrimination policy is general and akin to that in *Egan* which the Minnesota Court of Appeals deemed inadequate to constitute a waiver. Thus, Romeo's claim under the LAD fails as a matter of law.

Seton Hall also argues that its antidiscrimination policy did not create a unilateral contract, and therefore, could not be breached as alleged by Romeo. It contends that as a matter of law, Romeo's breach of contract claim cannot stand.

.   .   .

In determining whether Seton Hall's antidiscrimination policy constitutes a unilateral contract, the parties dispute the appropriateness of applying the standard in *Woolley v. Hoffmann–La Roche, Inc.*, 99 N.J. 284, 307, 491 A.2d 1257 (1985), *modified*, 101 N.J. 10, 499 A.2d 515 (1985). *Woolley* held that an employment manual's provisions on job security constituted a binding contract between the employer and the employee "unless the manual elsewhere prominently and unmistakably indicates that those provisions shall not be binding or unless there is some other similar proof of the employer's intent not to be bound."

Seton Hall asserts that *Woolley* does not apply here because the university-student relationship markedly differs from an employer-employee relationship. We agree. The situation here is more appropriately analyzed under *Mittra v. University of Medicine & Dentistry of New Jersey*, 316 N.J. Super. 83, 719 A.2d 693 (App. Div.1998), where we said:

> the relationship between the university and its students should not be analyzed in purely contractual terms. As long as the student is afforded reasonable notice and a fair hearing in general conformity with the institution's rules and regulations, we defer to the university's broad discretion in its evaluation of academic performance.

In *Mittra* we ruled that a contractual relationship was not created by the UMDNJ's dissemination of a student handbook containing a student evaluation process. . . .

. . .

The standard in *Woolley* cannot be applied here in light of the inherent differences between the employer-employee relationship and the university-student relationship. . . .

. . .

Even if *Woolley* applied, Seton Hall's policy "prominently and unmistakably indicates" that student clubs, organizations and associations can only be formed that "respect the values and mission of the University." The values and mission of Seton Hall as a private religious university were fully analyzed in Dr. Wankel's December 18, 2003 letter denying "TRUTH" provisional recognition under church policy.

The position of the Catholic Church on its values and mission regarding homosexuality is described in various documents in the record. These documents were attached as exhibits to a certification in support of defendant's motion to dismiss. Included was an October 1, 1986 "Letter to the Bishops of the Catholic Church on the Pastoral Care of Homosexual Persons," which was approved by Pope John Paul II and adopted by the Congregation for the Doctrine of the Faith, on the subject. That document states in pertinent part that "Homosexual activity is not a complementary union, able to transmit life; and so it thwarts the call to a life of that form of self-giving which the Gospel says is the essence of Christian living. . . ." The document further states that the human person cannot adequately be "described by a reductionist reference to his or her sexual orientation." The Church, it is said, does not consider an individual as a "heterosexual" or a "homosexual," but rather "insists that every person has a fundamental Identity: the creature of God, and by grace, his child and heir to eternal life." In addition, a March 20, 1992 opinion letter from the New Jersey

Office of Legislative Services to a State Assemblyman regarding amendments to the LAD and other statutes, states that the New Jersey Catholic Conference was of the view that Catholic teaching "finds homosexual activity to be morally wrong."

In reaching her conclusion, Dr. Wankel analyzed the proposed recognition of "TRUTH" in light of the values and mission of the Catholic Church, as contemplated by the student handbook. Therefore, even under *Woolley* the student application for provisional recognition of an entity neither created a contract nor provided a basis for a breach of contract claim. Rather, the case is more akin to *Mittra*. A contractual relationship cannot be based on isolated provisions in a student manual. Just as in *Mittra,* where the evaluation of a student's academic performance is left to the judgment of the university, a private religious university's values and mission must be left to the discretion of the university. The case for such discretion is even greater, where as here, the very values and mission in question address fundamental religious ideals. Courts should avoid entanglement in religious disputes involving ecclesiastical "polity or doctrine," as well as policy. *Elmora Hebrew Center, Inc. v. Fishman*, 125 N.J. 404, 415–416, 593 A.2d 725 (1991).

Romeo's breach of contract claim cannot stand as a matter of law.

Questions and Comments on *Romeo*

After *Boy Scouts of America v. Dale*, 530 U.S. 640 (2000) (holding that freedom of association enabled the Boy Scouts to bar homosexual members), may a public university refuse to recognize student groups that discriminate against homosexual members? *See* David E. Bernstein, *Trends in First Amendment Jurisprudence: Antidiscrimination Laws and the First Amendment*, 66 MO. L. REV. 83 (2001); Mark Andrew Snider, Note, *Viewpoint Discrimination by Public Universities: Student Religious Organizations and Violations of University Nondiscrimination Policies*, 61 WASH. & LEE L. REV. 841 (2004).

Christian Legal Society v. Walker

United States Court of Appeals, Seventh Circuit, 2006.
453 F.3d 853.

■ SYKES, C.J.

The dean of Southern Illinois University's School of Law ("SIU") revoked the official student organization status of the Christian Legal Society ("CLS") chapter at SIU because he concluded that CLS's membership policies, which preclude membership to those who engage in or affirm homosexual conduct, violate SIU's nondiscrimination policies. CLS sued SIU for violating its First Amendment rights to free speech, expressive association, and free exercise of religion, and its Fourteenth Amendment rights of equal protection and due process. CLS moved for a preliminary injunction, asking that its official student organization status be restored, but the district court denied the motion. We reverse.

Southern Illinois University at Carbondale and its School of Law, a public university and law school, encourage and support a wide variety of student organizations and invite them to apply for official recognition. The benefits of recognition are several. If an organization is officially recognized by the law school, benefits include access to the law school List–Serve (the law school's database of e-mail addresses), permission to post information on law school bulletin boards, an appearance on lists of official student organizations in law school publications and on its website, the ability to reserve conference rooms and meeting and storage space, a faculty advisor, and law school money. During the 2004–2005 school year, SIU School of Law recognized seventeen student organizations—among them, the Black Law Student Association, the Federalist Society, the Hispanic Law Student Association, Law School Democrats, Lesbian and Gay Law Students and Supporters, SIU Law School Republicans, the Student Animal Legal Defense Fund, Women's Law Forum, and CLS. . . .

CLS is a nationwide association of legal professionals and law students who share (broadly speaking) a common faith—Christianity. Members are expected to subscribe to a statement of faith and agree to live by certain moral principles. One of those principles, the one that has caused the dispute in this case, is that sexual activity outside of a traditional (one man, one woman) marriage is forbidden. That means, in addition to fornication and adultery, CLS disapproves active homosexuality. CLS welcomes anyone to its meetings, but voting members and officers of the organization must subscribe to the statement of faith, meaning, among other things, that they must not engage in or approve of fornication, adultery, or homosexual conduct; or, having done so, must repent of that conduct.

In February 2005 someone complained to SIU about CLS's membership and leadership requirements that preclude active homosexuals from becoming voting members or officers. . . . [CLS explained to SIU that a person] "who may have engaged in homosexual conduct in the past but has repented of that conduct, or who has homosexual inclinations but does not engage in or affirm homosexual conduct, would not be prevented from serving as an officer or member."

In response, the law school dean revoked CLS's registered student organization status, telling CLS that the "tenets of the national CLS" violated two university policies. The first is SIU's Affirmative Action/Equal Employment Opportunity Policy. In pertinent part, the policy states that SIU will "provide equal employment and education opportunities for all qualified persons without regard to race, color, religion, sex, national origin, age, disability, status as a disabled veteran of the Vietnam era, sexual orientation, or marital status." The second is a policy of the SIU Board of Trustees which provides that "[n]o student constituency body or recognized student organization shall be authorized unless it adheres to all appropriate federal or state laws concerning nondiscrimination and equal opportunity." As a result of [SIU's action, CLS lost the benefits of university recognition.]

CLS brought suit against the dean and several other SIU officials—we will use the shorthand "SIU" to refer to all the defendants—and quickly moved for a preliminary injunction. CLS claimed that SIU violated CLS's First Amendment rights of expressive association, free speech, and free exercise of religion. CLS also alleged that it was denied equal protection and due process. On the basis of the record information we have recounted here, the district court denied the motion, holding that CLS's likelihood of success on the merits was "at best . . . a close question." The district court also held that CLS had not suffered irreparable harm because CLS still existed as an organization, just without the official student organization recognition and benefits conferred by the university. At most, said the district judge, the harm from derecognition was "speculative." As the judge saw it, CLS would merely have to "use other meeting areas and other ways to communicate" with students.

CLS appealed and moved for an injunction pending appeal, focusing primarily on its expressive association claim and its right of access to a speaking forum. . . .

. . .

In a First Amendment case, we are required to make an independent review of the record because "the reaches of the First Amendment are ultimately defined by the facts it is held to embrace," and the reviewing court must decide independently whether "a given course of conduct falls on the near or far side of the line of constitutional protection." *Hurley v. Irish–American Gay, Lesbian & Bisexual Group of Boston*, 515 U.S. 557, 567 (1995); *see also BSA v. Dale*, 530 U.S. 640, 648–49 (2000). . . . Our task is simplified here because only the first two injunction factors are disputed. The loss of First Amendment freedoms is presumed to constitute an irreparable injury for which money damages are not adequate, and injunctions protecting First Amendment freedoms are always in the public interest.

The district court concluded that because derecognition did not preclude CLS from meeting and expressing itself (it just had to do so without the benefits that official student organization status brings), CLS had not shown a likelihood of success on the merits. We disagree. . . .

1.   Whether CLS Violated a University Policy

As an initial matter, it is doubtful that CLS violated either of the policies SIU cited as grounds for derecognition. One is a Board of Trustees policy providing that "[n]o student constituency body or recognized student organization shall be authorized unless it adheres to all appropriate federal or state laws concerning nondiscrimination and equal opportunity." Through two rounds of briefing in this Court—one for the injunction pending appeal and one on the merits—SIU failed to identify which federal or state law it believes CLS violated. . . . This raises the specter of pretext; at the least, this asserted ground for derecognition simply drops out of the case.

SIU also claims CLS violated the university's Affirmative Action/EEO policy, which states that SIU will "provide equal employment and education opportunities for all qualified persons without regard to [,among other things,] sexual orientation." We are skeptical that CLS violated this policy. CLS requires its members and officers to adhere to and conduct themselves in accordance with a belief system regarding standards of sexual *conduct,* but its membership requirements do not exclude members on the basis of sexual *orientation.* CLS's statement of faith specifies, among other things, a belief in the sinfulness of "all acts of sexual conduct outside of God's design for marriage between one man and one woman, which acts include fornication, adultery, and homosexual conduct." Those who engage in sexual conduct outside of a traditional marriage are not invited to become CLS members unless they repent the conduct and affirm the statement of faith.

In response to the law school's inquiry about its membership policies, CLS explained that it interprets its statement of faith to allow persons "who may have homosexual inclinations" to become members of CLS as long as they do not engage in or affirm homosexual conduct. The same is true of unmarried heterosexual persons: heterosexual persons who do not participate in or condone heterosexual conduct outside of marriage may become CLS members; those who engage in unmarried heterosexual conduct and do not repent that conduct and affirm the statement of faith may not. CLS's membership policies are thus based on belief and behavior rather than status, and no language in SIU's policy prohibits this.

There are other reasons we are skeptical that CLS violated SIU's Affirmative Action/EEO policy. First, CLS does not employ anyone. Second, it is not readily apparent (though certainly an argument could be made) that CLS should be considered an SIU "education opportunity" for purposes of applying the policy. On this latter point, the Affirmative Action/EEO policy by its terms applies to SIU, and there is no support in the record for the proposition that CLS is an extension of SIU. CLS is a private speaker, albeit one receiving (until it was derecognized) the public benefits associated with recognized student organization status. But subsidized student organizations at public universities are engaged in private speech, not spreading state-endorsed messages. *See Rosenberger v. Rector & Visitors of Univ. of Va.*, 515 U.S. 819, 833–34 (1995) (explaining the difference between government funding of private groups to spread a government-controlled message and government funding of private groups simply to encourage a diversity of views from private speakers); *see also Bd. of Regents of Univ. of Wis. Sys. v. Southworth*, 529 U.S. 217, 229, 233 (2000). It would be a leap, and one SIU does not take, to suggest that student organizations are mouthpieces for the university.

Accordingly, CLS has demonstrated a likelihood of success on the threshold question of whether either of SIU's stated grounds for derecognition actually applies. . . .

2.   Expressive Association

Implicit in the First Amendment freedoms of speech, assembly, and petition is the freedom to gather together to express ideas—the freedom to associate. *Rumsfeld v. Forum for Academic & Institutional Rights, Inc.*, 547 U.S. 47, 66–68 (2006) ("FAIR"); *Dale*, 530 U.S. at 647–48; *Roberts v. United States Jaycees*, 468 U.S. 609, 622 (1984); *Healy v. James*, 408 U.S. 169, 181 (1972). The freedom to associate assures that the majority (or a powerful or vocal minority) cannot force its views on groups that choose to express unpopular ideas. Government action may impermissibly burden the freedom to associate in a variety of ways; two of them are "impos[ing] penalties or withold[ing] benefits from individuals because of their membership in a disfavored group" and "interfer[ing] with the internal organization or affairs of the group."

The Supreme Court has held that "[t]here can be no clearer example of an intrusion into the internal structure or affairs of an association than a regulation that forces the group to accept members it does not desire." Freedom to associate "plainly presupposes a freedom not to associate." *Dale*, 530 U.S. at 648 (quoting *Roberts*, 468 U.S. at 623). When the government forces a group to accept for membership someone the group does not welcome and the presence of the unwelcome person "affects in a significant way the group's ability to advocate" its viewpoint, the government has infringed on the group's freedom of expressive association. However, "the freedom of expressive association, like many freedoms, is not absolute." Infringements on expressive association are subject to strict scrutiny; the right of expressive association "may be overridden 'by regulations adopted to serve compelling state interests, unrelated to the suppression of ideas, that cannot be achieved through means significantly less restrictive of associational freedoms.' "

Dale and *Hurley* were "forced inclusion" expressive association cases. The Supreme Court held in *Dale* that a New Jersey law prohibiting discrimination in public accommodations could not be constitutionally applied to the Boy Scouts to force the Scouts to accept an openly gay scoutmaster. The Court held that the presence of an openly gay scoutmaster "would significantly burden the organization's right to oppose or disfavor homosexual conduct" and "[t]he state interests embodied in New Jersey's public accommodations law do not justify such a severe intrusion on the Boy Scouts' rights to freedom of expressive association." Similarly, in *Hurley*, the Court held that Massachusetts' public accommodations law could not be constitutionally applied to force a Boston St. Patrick's Day parade organization to accept a parade unit marching under the banner of an Irish gay and lesbian group. The Court held that "[w]hen the law is applied to expressive activity in the way it was done here, its apparent object is simply to require speakers to modify the content of their expression to whatever extent beneficiaries of the law choose to alter it with a message of their own." This, the Court said, "is a decidedly fatal objective."

CLS alleges that SIU's application of its antidiscrimination policy as a justification for revocation of CLS's student organization status unconstitutionally intrudes upon its right of expressive association. The likelihood of success on this claim turns on three questions: (1) Is CLS an expressive association? (2) Would the forced inclusion of active homosexuals significantly affect CLS's ability to express its disapproval of homosexual activity? and (3) Does CLS's interest in expressive association outweigh the university's interest in eradicating discrimination against homosexuals?

. . . CLS is a group of people bound together by their shared Christian faith and a commitment to "[s]howing the love of Christ to the campus community and the community at large by proclaiming the gospel in word and deed" and "[a]ddressing the question, 'What does it mean to be a Christian in law?' " . . . It would be hard to argue—and no one does—that CLS is not an expressive association.

Our next question is whether application of SIU's antidiscrimination policy to force inclusion of those who engage in or affirm homosexual conduct would significantly affect CLS's ability to express its disapproval of homosexual activity. To ask this question is very nearly to answer it. . . . There can be little doubt that requiring CLS to [accept active homosexuals as members] would impair its ability to express disapproval of active homosexuality.

CLS is a faith-based organization. One of its beliefs is that sexual conduct outside of a traditional marriage is immoral. It would be difficult for CLS to sincerely and effectively convey a message of disapproval of certain types of conduct if, at the same time, it must accept members who engage in that conduct. CLS's beliefs about sexual morality are among its defining values; forcing it to accept as members those who engage in or approve of homosexual conduct would cause the group as it currently identifies itself to cease to exist. We have no difficulty concluding that SIU's application of its nondiscrimination policies in this way burdens CLS's ability to express its ideas.

Our final question is this: Does SIU's interest in preventing discrimination against homosexuals outweigh CLS's interest in expressing its disapproval of homosexual activity? In order to justify interfering with CLS's freedom of expressive association, SIU's policy must serve a compelling state interest that is not related to the suppression of ideas and that cannot be achieved through a less restrictive means. Certainly the state has an interest in eliminating discriminatory conduct and providing for equal access to opportunities. But the Supreme Court has made it clear that antidiscrimination regulations may not be applied to expressive conduct with the purpose of either suppressing or promoting a particular viewpoint.

"While the law is free to promote all sorts of conduct in place of harmful behavior, it is not free to interfere with speech for no better reason than promoting an approved message or discouraging a disfavored one, however enlightened either purpose may strike the government." What interest does SIU have in forcing CLS to accept members whose activities violate its creed other than eradicating or neutralizing particular beliefs contained in that creed? SIU has identified none. The only apparent point of applying the policy to an organization like CLS is to induce CLS to modify the content of its expression or suffer the penalty of derecognition.

On the other side of the scale, CLS's interest in exercising its First Amendment freedoms is unquestionably substantial. "The First Amendment protects expression, be it of the popular variety or not," and "public or judicial disapproval of a tenet of an organization's expression does not justify the State's effort to compel the organization to accept members where such acceptance would derogate from the organization's expressive message." CLS has carried its burden of proving a likelihood of success on its claim for violation of its right of expressive association.

SIU objects that this is not a "forced inclusion" case like *Dale* or *Hurley* because it is not forcing CLS to do anything at all, but is only withdrawing its student organization status. SIU argues, and the district court held, that the consequences of derecognition are too insignificant to constitute a constitutional violation. The Supreme Court rejected this argument in *Healy*, a case that parallels this one in all material respects.

. . .

3. Free Speech

The government violates the Free Speech Clause of the First Amendment when it excludes a speaker from a speech forum the speaker is entitled to enter. SIU has created a speech forum for student organizations and has bestowed certain benefits on those who are qualified to enter the forum. CLS alleges that SIU violated its free speech rights by ejecting it from that speech forum without a compelling reason.

[The level of scrutiny applied to the government's action depends on the nature of the forum from which the speaker has been excluded. In both a traditional public forum and a designated public forum, state restrictions are subject to strict scrutiny. *See Rosenberger*, 515 U.S. at 829 (once a university designates a forum to be open, it may not renege). Speech restriction in a non-public forum is subject to less scrutiny.]

. . .

Whether SIU's student organization forum is a public, designated public, or nonpublic forum is an inquiry that will require further factual development, and that is a task properly left for the district court. But even assuming at this stage of the litigation that SIU's student organization forum is a nonpublic forum—making the lowest level of scrutiny applicable—we believe CLS has the better of the argument. . . .

. . .

B. Balancing of Harms

The district court also held that CLS was not suffering irreparable harm as a result of derecognition, focusing on the fact that CLS could still hold meetings on campus and could communicate with students by means other than university bulletin boards and listservs. The district court believed that CLS was not being forced to include anyone, but was simply being told that if it desires the benefits of recognized student organization status, it must abide by SIU's antidiscrimination policy. We have already explained the flaws in this analysis; violations of First Amendment rights are presumed to constitute irreparable injuries, and *Healy* holds that denying official recognition to a student organization is a significant infringement of the right of expressive association. CLS has shown a reasonable likelihood of success on its expressive association claim under *Healy*, *Dale*, and *Hurley*. CLS has also demonstrated a likelihood of success on its claim that SIU has unconstitutionally excluded it from a speech forum in which it is entitled to remain. One way or the other, CLS has shown it likely that SIU has violated its First Amendment freedoms.

The district court simply misread the legal standards, and that is necessarily an abuse of discretion. The district court did not address the question whether SIU would be harmed by the issuance of a preliminary injunction. On appeal, the only harm SIU claims is the hardship associated with being required to recognize a student organization it believes is violating the university's antidiscrimination policy. But if SIU is applying that policy in a manner that violates CLS's First Amendment rights—as CLS has demonstrated is likely—then SIU's claimed harm is no harm at all.

For the foregoing reasons, we Reverse the district court's decision and Remand this case with directions to enter a preliminary injunction against SIU.

Questions and Comments on *Christian Legal Society*

1. After the decision by the Seventh Circuit, Southern Illinois settled with CLS. As part of the settlement, the university agreed to grant full recognition to the group, to pay their attorney fees, and to establish a $10,000 annual scholarship to be administered by CLS. Alliance Defense Fund, *Southern Illinois University Settles Lawsuit with Christian Legal Society*, May 22, 2007, *available at* http://www.alliancedefensefund.org/news/pressrelease.aspx?cid=4126.

2. For a critique of the *Christian Legal Society* decision, see *Recent Case*, 120 HARV. L. REV. 1112 (2007). *See generally* Eugene Volokh, *Freedom of Expressive Association and Government Subsidies*, 58 STAN. L. REV. 1919 (2006).

3. CLS maintained that its exclusion of "active homosexuals" was based on belief and behavior, not their status as homosexuals. Why is this distinction important? To what extent does the Seventh Circuit's holding rest on this distinction? Would the holding of *Christian Legal Society* have been different if the university's antidiscrimination policy explicitly stated that student groups could not discriminate against active homosexuals?

C. PRIVACY

Prostrollo v. University of South Dakota

United States Court of Appeals, Eighth Circuit, 1974.
507 F.2d 775, *cert. denied*, 421 U.S. 952 (1975).

■ LAY, CIRCUIT JUDGE.

The University of South Dakota, Dr. Richard Bowen, its President, A. L. Schnell, Director of Resident Services, and the Board of Regents of the State of South Dakota appeal from a decision of the district court declaring certain University housing regulations unconstitutional. The named plaintiffs, Gail Prostrollo and Lynn Severson, are students at the University of South Dakota. They brought this suit on behalf of themselves and other students similarly situated to challenge a regulation which requires all single freshman and sophomore students to live in University residence halls. They contend that enforcement of this rule encroaches upon their right of privacy and denies them equal protection of the laws. The district court found that the *primary* purpose of the regulation was to ensure housing income sufficient to pay off the revenue bonds which had been issued to finance the construction of the dormitories. It concluded that the regulation was unconstitutional, since it established an arbitrary and unreasonable classification which had no rational relationship to this purpose and therefore denied petitioners equal protection of the laws.

The challenged regulation provides:

> All single freshman and sophomore students are required to live in university residence halls. Exceptions to this policy must be approved by the Director of Resident Services prior to the beginning of the semester.

School officials offered several justifications for this parietal rule.[2] Dr. Richard L. Bowen, the University president, said that the rule had at least two purposes. First, he stated, it was intended to provide a standard level of occupancy to ensure repayment of the government bonds which provided capital for the dormitory construction. Second, he said, it was meant to ensure that younger students who must of necessity live away from home while attending the University would avail themselves of the learning experience in self-government, group discipline, and community living that dorm life provides, as well as the increased opportunity for enriching relationships with the staff and other students. Aaron Schnell, Director of Resident

2. Both parties and the court below consistently use the term "parietal" rule in describing the housing regulation. The New Webster's Dictionary of the English Language defines that term as an adjective meaning "of or relating to life within college walls or its order or regulation." Its derivation is discussed in *Pratz v. Louisiana Polytechnic Institute*, 316 F. Supp. 872, 876 n.2 (W.D. La. 1970), *aff'd*, 401 U.S. 1004 (1971).

Services, emphasized the educational benefits of living on campus, such as the availability of films and discussion forums. Dr. Richard Gibb, the Commissioner of Higher Education for the South Dakota Board of Regents, freely admitted the financial reasons for the rule, but throughout his testimony, he also emphasized the various educational advantages of dormitory living. Michael Easton, the Director of Student Services, observed:

> The facilities for studying are more accessible to those people who live on campus. It's easier for them to get to the library, for example; the atmosphere on campus is more conducive to study. It's encouraged.... There are control factors which eliminate the amount of confusion and noise. The emphasis on campus is academic ... where off campus it's frequently not.

The overall evidence demonstrates that these University officials believe that dormitory living provides an educational atmosphere which assists *younger* students, as underclassmen, in adjusting to college life.[4] The testimo-

---

4. The defendants have adopted answers to interrogatories from another pending case in the federal district court in the Southern District of Iowa. Iowa university officials were asked to list the advantages and disadvantages of dormitory living. They listed them as follows:

ADVANTAGES	DISADVANTAGES
1) meals prepared	1) too restrictive
2) maid service	2) isolation from the opposite sex
3) meet more people	3) student not responsible for self
4) group activities, movies	4) can't study
5) ideal location	5) too noisy
6) laundry service	6) too expensive
7) activities	7) no liquor
8) communication	8) rooms too crowded
9) more a part of campus life	9) parking
10) experiencing different life styles	10) standing in line
11) supervision for young and immature	11) poor quality of food
12) equipment available	12) lack of privacy
13) develop feeling of belonging	13) no choice of roommates
14) educational environment	14) having roommates
15) counselors available	15) not sufficient study lounges
16) advisors spot problems early	16) prolongs adolescence
17) feel a part of group	17) too social
18) Reserve Library	18) maybe escape

ny reflects a belief that students who become "established" and well-oriented in their early years are more prone to develop those good study habits which will assist them in their years as upperclassmen. Despite this testimony, the district court ... emphasized its factual conclusion that the *primary* purpose of the parietal rule was to defray the costs of the revenue bonds. It found the reasons relating to educational values expressed by school officials to be "unconvincing and unsupported by the evidence." It was on the basis of the finding of this primary purpose that the court concluded that the classification had no rational connection to the purpose of the regulation and therefore denied plaintiffs equal protection of the law.

We need not decide whether the court's finding regarding the primary purpose of the rule is clearly erroneous. The district court's error, we believe, was in deciding the reasonableness of the classification on the basis of a single "primary" purpose in the face of evidence revealing multiple purposes. This is a misapplication of the standards governing the equal protection clause. In discussing equal protection principles, the Supreme Court recently observed:

> Our decisions do not authorize courts to pick and choose among legitimate legislative aims to determine which is primary and which subordinate. Rather, legislative solutions must be respected if the "distinctions drawn have some basis in practical experience," *South Carolina v. Katzenbach*, 383 U.S. 301 (1966), or if some legitimate state interest is advanced, *Dandridge v. Williams*, 397 U.S., at 486. So long as the state purpose upholding a statutory class is legitimate and nonillusory, its lack of primacy is not disqualifying.
>
> ... The search for legislative purpose is often elusive enough, without a requirement that primacy be ascertained. Legislation is frequently multi-purposed: the removal of even a "subordinate" purpose may shift altogether the consensus of legislative judgment supporting the statute. Permitting nullification of statutory classifications based rationally on a nonprimary legislative purpose would allow courts to peruse legislative proceedings for subtle emphases supporting subjective impressions and preferences. The Equal Pro-

19) forced to meet people and get along

_____

20) more recreational opportunities

_____

21) vending machines

_____

22) stores in dorms

_____

23) refrigerators

_____

24) freedom from household duties

_____

25) learn to be more tolerant of others

_____

26) easier to keep up with current activities

_____

27) help one another with homework

_____

28) easier to meet people

tection Clause does not countenance such speculative probing into the purposes of a coordinate branch. We have supplied no imaginary basis or purpose for this statutory scheme, but we likewise refuse to discard a clear and legitimate purpose because the court below perceived another to be primary.

The district court concluded that the challenged classification (freshmen and sophomores) had no rational connection to the purpose of paying off the bonds. We would agree. However, there is no evidence on the record that the classification in question was ever intended to have any connection with that purpose.... To the contrary in the present case, the only evidence of why the classification was created was the testimony of University officials that they felt that freshman and sophomore students benefited more directly from the educational values of dormitory living.

When no suspect classification is involved or fundamental right infringed, any "rational basis" may justify classifications which have been made. We find there exists a rational connection between one of the permissible purposes for the regulation and the classification made.

Although the district court did not pass on the plaintiffs' other contention, i.e., that the regulation violates their right of privacy, this claim is argued on appeal and we must decide it. Aside from equal protection arguments, any law may, of course, be invalid if it clearly violates a fundamental constitutional right. Plaintiffs urge, however, that it is now recognized that when a legislative classification appears to have been made on a suspect basis or encroaches upon a fundamental right, the state has the burden of demonstrating a "compelling interest" which required it. We agree that when those circumstances exist closer judicial scrutiny is required under an equal protection challenge. That is not the case here, however.

First, we think it obvious that the classification involved was not made on a "suspect" basis. The class within the regulation is created on the basis of educational attainment. This classification has never been recognized as an inherently irrational basis for differentiating between persons otherwise equal.

. . .

The basic challenge asserted by plaintiffs is that the parietal rule affects (a) their right of privacy and (b) their freedom of association. Plaintiffs rely on *Shapiro v. Thompson*, 394 U.S. 618 (1969), which requires the demonstration of a "compelling state interest" before a fundamental right may be encroached upon. However, before applying the compelling interest rule it is basic that both the nature and importance of the rights affected and the extent or nature of the encroachment must first be weighed to determine if the challenged rule constitutes a serious abridgement of a basic interest.

Plaintiffs urge that inherent within the right of privacy is the right to choose one's home and to live with whomever one chooses. As much as we may strive to protect these goals, we cannot agree that the right to choose one's place of residence is necessarily a fundamental right. Cases too numerous to mention have upheld restrictions on this interest. *See, e.g., Village of Belle Terre v. Boraas*, 416 U.S. 1 (1974) (zoning ordinance). This "right" is akin to the interest in education, which the Supreme Court recently held not to be the kind of interest which will invoke the compelling interest test. *See San Antonio School District v. Rodriguez*, 411 U.S. 1 (1973). This is not, it must be noted, a case in which the right to live in a given geographic area is affected or in which freedom to travel and relocate is abridged.... The interest in living precisely where one chooses is not fundamental within our constitutional scheme.

Freedom of association has been recognized as a fundamental right, *NAACP v. Alabama*, 357 U.S. 449 (1958), but even fundamental rights are not so absolute as to be protected from all incidental effects of otherwise legitimate legislation. For example, in *Village of Belle Terre v. Boraas, supra,* a case challenging zoning laws, one of the rights supposedly infringed was the right of association and, admittedly, the ordinance prevented more than two unmarried adults from living in a single dwelling. The Court found these incidental effects to be too insignificant to invoke strict scrutiny of the statute. The analogy to the instant case is apparent.

. . .

Fundamental to our reasoning is the fact that we are dealing with education, an area in which "school authorities are traditionally charged with broad power to formulate and implement educational policy...." *Swann v. Board of Education*, 402 U.S. 1, 16 (1971). We are also cognizant of the wisdom of Mr. Justice Holmes' statement in *Missouri, Kansas & Texas Ry. Co. v. May*, 194 U.S. 267 (1904), where he observed:

> When a state legislature has declared that in its opinion policy requires a certain measure, its action should not be disturbed by the courts under the Fourteenth Amendment, unless they can see clearly that there is no fair reason for the law that would not require with equal force its extension to others whom it leaves untouched.

Id. at 269.

This parietal rule and its challenged classification are directed toward a permissible objective. The classification is not based on any patently invidious basis. We conclude that the rule is reasonable and not arbitrary and that it "bears a rational relationship to a permissible state objective." We find this test to be met here.

The judgment of the district court is reversed and the cause is remanded to the district court to enter judgment in favor of the defendants....

Questions and Comments on *Prostrollo*

1. Compare the deference shown by courts to the university in *Prostrollo* with that shown in *Healy* or *Kegan*. Is there any justification for the difference?

2. *Compare Prostrollo with* Hack v. President and Fellows of Yale College, 237 F.3d 81 (7th Cir. 2001), *cert. denied*, 534 U.S. 888 (2001), *supra* p. 149 (upholding Yale's mandatory dormitory residence for unmarried students under the age of twenty-one, despite objections made by Orthodox Jews who claimed that such living arrangements violated their religion.)

People v. Superior Court

California Court of Appeals, Sixth District, 2006.
143 Cal.App.4th 1183, 49 Cal.Rptr.3d 831.

■ DUFFY, J.

A 19–year-old college student, defendant/real party in interest Christopher Eugene Walker (defendant), was charged with possession of marijuana for sale. Critical evidence supporting that charge was obtained from defendant's dormitory room at Santa Clara University (University) as a result of a warrantless search and seizure by police officers of the City of Santa Clara.

[The superior court granted the defendant's motion to suppress evidence against him—i.e., marijuana, a digital scale, and $1,800 cash (collectively, the contraband)—on the grounds that it was illegally seized by the police. The superior court rejected the argument that the search was reasonable because a University security officer, who was legally in the room, authorized the search. The People filed a petition for writ of mandate challenging the suppression order.]

. . .

At the hearing on defendant's motion to suppress on May 24, 2005, the parties stipulated that Kim Payne (Payne), a University safety officer, would have testified . . . as follows:

> [Payne observed the defendant smoking marijuana outside of Sobrato Hall. When asked, the defendant told Payne that the marijuana was for medicinal purposes. The defendant spontaneously said that Payne could come to his room. The defendant unlocked the door of his room for Payne and escorted him into the room. The defendant showed Payne a small bag of marijuana and a medical release form that purported to authorize use of marijuana for therapeutic purposes. Noting that the defendant acted suspiciously near his closet drawers, Payne checked the drawers. He uncovered two sandwich-sized bags full of marijuana, $1800 cash, and several small plastic bags with marijuana remnants. A subsequent search of the closet yielded two more sandwich-sized bags full of marijuana and additional plastic bags.]

The parties agreed further at the hearing on the motion to suppress that Officer Tyson Green of the Santa Clara Police Department would have testified as follows:

> [The University Campus Safety Office contacted the Santa Clara Police Department and informed them that a large amount of marijuana had been discovered in a dorm room. When police officers approached the defendant's room, Payne swung open the door and said "you have got to see this." While standing in the hallway, the officers were able to observe the marijuana in the room, which was in plain view. The police officers asked Payne if he had received consent search the room. Payne replied that he had received consent and added that consent was not necessary because of the waiver the defendant had signed in his Residence Housing Contract. The police then entered the room.]

In addition to the stipulated testimony of Payne and Officer Green, the housing agreement between the University and the defendant (Housing Contract) was before the court. The "Terms and Conditions of Occupancy" appended to the contract provided in relevant part: "Room entry and inspection may occur periodically. The University balances the right to privacy of the resident students with the responsibility to maintain a safe environment for all students and staff in the residence halls. The University will take all reasonable steps to ensure the residents of a room receive reasonable notice prior to entry by University personnel for the purposes of repair, inventory, construction, and/or inspection. The University also reserves the right to enter a residence room without notice for responding to real or reasonably perceived emergencies, ... and/or for response to situations where there is a reasonable suspicion that a violation of the law or University policies is occurring or has occurred inside a particular room. Under such circumstances, it is not necessary that the room's resident(s) be present; nor will a resident's refusal, either verbal or physical, prevent an entry or inspection. By entering into the University Residence Hall Contract ... the student consents to the room entry and inspection under those circumstances indicated." The appendix to the agreement provided further that "[r]esidents agree to abide by all applicable laws and University regulations.... Students who fail to abide by this agreement will be subject to University disciplinary procedures as well as possible termination of their University Residence Hall Contract." Included among specified acts subjecting the resident student to disciplinary action is the "[v]iolation of state laws regarding possession and/or consumption of controlled substances."

The People contend that the court erred in suppressing the contraband for [the following reasons:]

1. The police officers' entry into defendant's dormitory room was lawful because they had valid third-party consent (from Payne); under the circumstances, the officers' conduct was justified because Payne had either actual or apparent authority to consent to the entry.

. . .

[2.] Even if the police officers' entry into the dorm room was unlawful, the seized contraband that would have otherwise been subject to the exclusionary rule was admissible under the inevitable discovery rule.

. . .

The Fourth Amendment to the Constitution of the United States provides: "The right of the people to be secure in their persons, houses, papers, and effects, against unreasonable searches and seizures, shall not be violated, and no Warrants shall issue, but upon probable cause, supported by Oath or affirmation, and particularly describing the place to be searched, and the persons or things to be seized." ... As the Supreme Court has explained: "The touchstone of the Fourth Amendment is reasonableness. [Citation.] The Fourth Amendment does not proscribe all state-initiated searches and seizures; it merely proscribes those which are unreasonable." *Florida v. Jimeno* 500 U.S. 248, 250 (1991); *see also Brigham City, Utah v. Stuart* 547 U.S. 398 (2006).

"[T]he Fourth Amendment protects people, not places." *Katz v. United States*, 389 U.S. 347, 351 (1967).... "[I]n order to claim the protection of the Fourth Amendment, a defendant must demonstrate that he personally has an expectation of privacy in the place searched, and that his expectation is reasonable." *Minnesota v. Carter* (525 U.S. 83, 88 (1998)); *see, e.g., Minnesota v. Olson* 495 U.S. 91, 99 (1990) (houseguest has legitimate expectation of privacy in host's home.) ...

" '[P]rivate residences are places in which the individual normally expects privacy free of governmental intrusion not authorized by a warrant, and that expectation is plainly one that society is prepared to recognize as justifiable.' [Citations.]" *People v. Robles, supra,* 23 Cal. 4th at 795, 97 Cal. Rptr. 2d 914, 3 P.3d 311, quoting *United States v. Karo,* 468 U.S. 705, 714 (1984). Therefore, searches and seizures conducted without a warrant "are per se unreasonable under the Fourth Amendment [of the United States Constitution]—subject only to a few specifically established and well-delineated exceptions." *Katz v. United States,* 389 U.S. at 357. . . .

. . .

The reason for this presumption that warrantless searches are unreasonable (and hence illegal) is plain: "An intrusion by the state into the privacy of the home for any purpose is one of the most awesome incursions of police power into the life of the individual. . . . It is essential that the dispassionate judgment of a magistrate, an official dissociated from the 'competitive enterprise of ferreting out crime' [citation], be interposed between the state and the citizen at this critical juncture." *People v. Ramey,* 16 Cal. 3d 263, 275, 127 Cal. Rptr. 629, 545 P.2d 1333 (1976).

. . .

Thus, "the Fourth Amendment has drawn a firm line at the entrance to the house. Absent exigent circumstances, that threshold may not reasonably be crossed without a warrant." *Payton v. New York, supra,* 445 U.S. at 590; *see also Johnson v. United States, supra,* 333 U.S. at 14–15 (warrant required save in cases involving "exceptional circumstances"); *People v. Ramey, supra,* 16 Cal. 3d at 270, 127 Cal. Rptr. 629, 545 P.2d 1333 (warrantless searches "unreasonable per se in the absence of one of a small number of carefully circumscribed exceptions.")

The People contend that the police officers had valid third-party consent to enter defendant's dormitory room because University employee Payne had actual authority to consent to the police officers' entry into the room. In the alternative, the search and seizure of the contraband were reasonable because the police officers reasonably believed that Payne had authority to consent to their entry. . . .

A recognized exception to the Fourth Amendment's proscription against warrantless searches is a search that is based upon consent. *Schneckloth v. Bustamonte,* 412 U.S. 218, 219 (1973). That consent may be given by the party later challenging the search's constitutional validity. Alternatively, "a third party who possesses common authority over the premises" may consent to the search. *Illinois v. Rodriguez,* 497 U.S. 177, 181 (1990); *see also People v. Boyer,* 38 Cal. 4th 412, 445, 42 Cal. Rptr. 3d 677, 133 P.3d 581 (2006) (search without warrant may "be based on the consent of a person, other than the accused, who has joint dominion or control over the area or thing to be searched.")

The validity of a third party's consent to search is founded upon the nature and extent of that party's access to and control over the property. As the United States Supreme Court has explained: "The [common] authority which justifies the third-party consent does not rest upon the law of property, with its attendant historical and legal refinements [citations] but rests rather on mutual use of the property by persons generally having joint access or control for most purposes, so that it is reasonable to recognize that any of the co-inhabitants has the right to permit the inspection in his own right and that the others have assumed the risk that one of their number might permit the common area to be searched." *United States v. Matlock*, 415 U.S. 164, 171 (1974). Third-party consent is valid where it is given by one "who possess[es] common authority over or other sufficient relationship to the premises or effects sought to be inspected." *Id*. at 171. . . .

The law also permits a search based upon consent by a person with apparent authority where the officers conducting the search reasonably believe that the person is empowered to give that consent. In *Rodriguez, supra*, 497 U.S. at 186, the Supreme Court held that where the police conduct a warrantless search based upon the consent of a third party whom they reasonably believe at the time to have the authority to give it, no Fourth Amendment violation occurs. The high court reasoned: "It is apparent that in order to satisfy the 'reasonableness' requirement of the Fourth Amendment, what is generally demanded of the many factual determinations that must regularly be made by agents of the government—whether the magistrate issuing a warrant, the police officer executing a warrant, or the police officer conducting a search or seizure under one of the exceptions to the warrant requirement—is not that they always be correct, but that they always be reasonable." *Id*. at 185. . . .

Thus, the owners of property may consent to a police search thereof as long as no other persons are legitimately occupying that property. *People v. Carr*, 8 Cal.3d 287, 298, 104 Cal.Rptr. 705, 502 P.2d 513 (1972). Likewise, a co-occupant—i.e., "one who possesses common authority over premises," *Matlock, supra*, 415 U.S. at 170—may give valid consent to a search of the premises "as against the absent, nonconsenting person with whom that authority is shared." *Id*.; *see also Frazier v. Cupp*, 394 U.S. 731, 740 (1969) (cousin had authority to consent to search of the defendant's duffel bag which both men used and which had been left with cousin.) For example, the co-occupant may be the defendant's spouse, *Coolidge, supra*, 403 U.S. at 488–489, the defendant's lover posing as his wife, *Matlock, supra*, at 176, or the defendant's mistress, *People v. Smith*, 63 Cal. 2d 779, 799, 48 Cal. Rptr. 382, 409 P.2d 222 (1966). . . .

But a landlord may not give valid third-party consent to a police search of a house rented to another. *Chapman v. United States*, 365 U.S. 610, 616–618 (1961); *People v. Escudero*, 23 Cal.3d 800, 807, 153 Cal. Rptr. 825, 592 P.2d 312 (1979). The same principle applies to prevent a finding of third-party consent where the leased property is an apartment unit, *People v. Roberts*, 47 Cal. 2d 374, 377, 303 P.2d 721 (1956), a room in a boarding house, *McDonald v. United States*, 335 U.S. 451 (1948), a garage, *People v. Roman*, 227 Cal. App. 3d 674, 680, 278 Cal. Rptr. 44 (1991), or a locker, *People v. Baker*, 12 Cal. App. 3d 826, 836, 96 Cal. Rptr. 760 (1970). Likewise, a hotel clerk may not consent to the search of an occupant's room. *Stoner v. California*, 376 U.S. 483, 488–489 (1964); *People v. Burke*, 208 Cal. App. 2d 149, 160, 24 Cal. Rptr. 912 (1962); *see also People v. Bennett*, 17 Cal. 4th 373, 384, 70 Cal. Rptr. 2d 850, 949 P.2d 947 (1998) (motel).

There are surprisingly few cases addressing the constitutional validity of searches of college dormitory rooms. *See generally* Annotation, *Search Conducted by School Official or Teacher as Violation of Fourth Amendment or Equivalent State Constitutional Provision*, 31 A.L.R. 5th 229, 296–300 (1995), § 8 and cases cited. Only one case was decided in California. *See People v. Kelly*, 195 Cal. App. 2d 669, 16 Cal. Rptr. 177 (1961). Many of the cases have involved the legality of searches by college officials only, and have not addressed whether police searches abridged the Fourth Amendment rights of dormitory room occupants....[12]

In *Kelly, supra*, the defendant (a college student attending California Institute of Technology) contended that his conviction of two counts of burglary was based upon evidence illegally seized from his dormitory room. After the police obtained information concerning several burglaries that led them to suspect the defendant, they contacted the college dean, who in turn contacted the house master, who had general responsibility over all resident students at the college. The house master advised the police that he had "free inspection rights to all rooms" and was specifically authorized under the housing rules to use his master key to enter any of the rooms in case of emergency. The police then accompanied the house master to the defendant's room. As they approached the room, the door was open at an angle of approximately 35 degrees. The house master opened the door further as he went into the room; an officer then entered the room, found no one present, and searched for the defendant under the bed and in the closet. The police officer located one stolen article in the closet and observed a toolbox in the room. He found a gun in the toolbox and removed it and two other articles believed to have been stolen.

The appellate court characterized the defendant's right to occupy the dorm room as being "quite different from the usual relationship of landlord and tenant," apparently placing considerable reliance upon the housing rules: "[The defendant's] occupancy of the room was conditional upon his accepting the responsibility of practicing the school's traditional principle of personal honor and upon his agreeing to abide by the house rules." It found further that the defendant, through the rules, had implicitly agreed that the house master might enter the room for the purpose of "upholding the high disciplinary standards and integrity of the school." The *Kelly* court upheld the denial of the motion to suppress, based upon (1) the police having reasonable cause to believe that the defendant had participated in a series of burglaries; (2) the general authority that the house master possessed over the occupancy and use of the dorm rooms; (3) the house master telling the police that he had the authority to enter rooms and that the housing rules specifically permitted such entry in an emergency; and (4) the police officer's assertion that a felony investigation constituted an emergency. It concluded: "The evidence was sufficient to support a finding that the officers believed in good faith that the master had authority to permit them to enter the room."

As one authority has observed: "[I]n the case of the [college dormitory] room, ... the educational institution's position is more akin to that of any other landlord. This being the case, courts are understandably reluctant to put the student who has the college as a landlord in a significantly different position than 'a student who lives off campus in a boarding house.' The

---

12. We note that in 1981, the Supreme Court decided a case in which it assumed (without expressly stating) that the Fourth Amendment applies to the search of a state university dormitory room. *See Washington v. Chrisman*, 455 U.S. 1 (1982). In that case, the Supreme Court, applying the plain-view doctrine, found constitutional the warrantless search of the defendant's dorm room and the ensuing seizure of marijuana, LSD, and a pipe used for smoking marijuana found in the room. *Id*. at 6–7.

latter student is quite obviously protected by the Supreme Court's ruling in *Chapman*, 365 U.S. 610, that a landlord may not consent to a police search of his tenant's quarters merely because he has some right of entry of his own in connection with his position as landlord.... [T]he same may be said of the college landlord." 4 LaFave, Search and Seizure § 8.6(e), 260–261 (4th ed. 2004) § 8.6(e) (footnotes omitted). Consistent with this viewpoint, there are cases at odds with *Kelly*, in which courts in other jurisdictions have held unreasonable the warrantless police searches of college dormitory rooms, even where school officials themselves had the lawful right of entry and gave the police consent.

For instance, an Ohio appellate court held recently that "[a] college student's dormitory room is entitled to the same protection against unreasonable search and seizure that is afforded to a private home for purposes of the Fourth Amendment." *State v. Ellis* (Ohio Ct. App., Mar. 31, 2006, No. 05CA78) 2006 WL 827376 at *2, ¶ 13. In *Ellis*, Central State University resident assistants discovered marijuana in the defendant's dorm room while they were conducting an authorized, unannounced safety inspection. Campus police officers were then notified and went to the room. While the campus police did not participate in the search, they were present in the room at the resident assistants' invitation. The *Ellis* court concluded that the seizure of the marijuana was unconstitutional. It found that while the resident assistants' search was authorized under the university's policies and procedures, the later police entry into the room was unlawful because it was made without a warrant, consent, or exigent circumstances. The court explained: "The problem arises in this case because, after the resident advisors initially discovered marijuana in [the] Defendant's room and notified campus police, the campus police then came to the scene and entered [the] Defendant's room.... By entering [the] Defendant's dormitory room, campus police infringed upon the reasonable expectation of privacy that [the] Defendant had in that place which ... is entitled to the same level of protection against unreasonable search and seizure as a private home. In order to lawfully enter [the] Defendant's room, police needed either a warrant, which they did not have, or an established exception to the warrant requirement."

Similarly, in *Piazzola v. Watkins*, 442 F.2d 284 (5th Cir.1971), the court invalidated a warrantless search of several Troy State University dormitory rooms conducted by the police in conjunction with school officials. There, a regulation provided that " '[t]he college reserves the right to enter rooms for inspection purposes.' " In holding that the search was unreasonable, the Fifth Circuit stated: "[A] student who occupies a college dormitory room enjoys the protection of the Fourth Amendment. True the University retains broad supervisory powers which permit it to adopt the regulation heretofore quoted, provided that regulation is reasonably construed and is limited in its application to further the University's function as an educational institution. The regulation cannot be construed or applied so as to give consent to a search for evidence for the primary purpose of a criminal prosecution. Otherwise, the regulation itself would constitute an unconstitutional attempt to require a student to waive his protection from unreasonable searches and seizures as a condition to his occupancy of a college dormitory room. [Citation.] Clearly the University had no authority to consent to or join in a police search for evidence of crime." *Id.* at 289–290 (footnotes omitted).

. . .

Finally, in *People v. Cohen*, 57 Misc. 2d 366, 292 N.Y.S.2d 706, 709 (1968), the court rejected the argument that the defendant (a Hofstra University student) gave his implied consent to a police search of his dormitory room under the theory that "a student impliedly consents to entry into his room by University officials at any time, except at late hours." After noting that the search conducted by police and university officials was "a fishing expedition calculated to discover narcotics," the court concluded that "even if the doctrine of implied consent were imported into this case, the consent is given, not to police officials, but to the University and the latter cannot fragmentize, share or delegate it." *Id.*; *see also* Smith & Strope, *The Fourth Amendment: Dormitory Room Searches in Public Universities*, 97 Ed. Law Rep. 985, 987 (1995) (where student signs waiver giving university officials permission to search dorm room for health, safety or maintenance reasons, "officials cannot delegate their authority to other individuals to conduct a search for other reasons.")

As we have noted, valid third-party consent to a warrantless search occurs where the party giving that consent "possesses common authority over the premises." *Rodriguez, supra*, 497 U.S. 177, 181; *see also People v. Boyer, supra*, 38 Cal.4th at p. 445, 42 Cal.Rptr.3d 677, 133 P.3d 581. That common authority is founded "on mutual use of the property by persons generally having joint access or control for most purposes." *Matlock, supra*, 415 U.S. 164, 171, n. 7. And the burden rests with the People to establish the existence of common authority supporting the contention that the search was based on third-party consent. Also, where the facts available to the officer at the time of the search would lead a reasonable person to believe "that the consenting party had authority over the premises," the search is valid even if it ultimately turns out that no actual authority to consent existed. *Id.* at 188–189.

. . .

. . . We start by reiterating the Supreme Court's caution that common authority is not determined merely by virtue of the third party's interest in the property. *Matlock, supra*, 415 U.S. at 171, n. 7. Here, the University's property interest notwithstanding, its relationship to the dormitories (specifically, to defendant's dorm room) is atypical of instances in which courts have found third-party consent based upon common authority. This is not a case in which the third party allegedly giving consent—the University employee— had common authority over the dorm room. It differs greatly from the case of consent given by a spouse of a home's occupant, *Coolidge, supra*, 403 U.S. at 488–489, or by the host/homeowner who offered lodging to a guest, *People v. Welch, supra*, 20 Cal. 4th at 747–748, 85 Cal. Rptr. 2d 203, 976 P.2d 754. Rather, the relationship between the University, defendant, and defendant's dormitory room is more closely akin to relationships in which the Supreme Court has rejected third-party-consent arguments, such as landlord-tenant, *Chapman, supra*, 365 U.S. 610, or hotel-occupant relationships, *Stoner, supra*, 376 U.S. 483. *See also People v. O'Keefe*, 222 Cal. App. 3d 517, 521, 271 Cal. Rptr. 769 (1990) (college dormitory "analogous to a hotel or apartment complex," and "each student lives and enjoys separate privacy in each of their individual dormitory rooms.") In this respect, borrowing the Supreme Court's language in *Stoner, supra*, at 489, "[i]t is important to bear in mind that it was [defendant-student's] constitutional right which was at stake here, and not the [security officer's] nor the [University's]."

Within the plain language of *Matlock*, the University had neither "mutual use" of defendant's dorm room, nor "joint access or control for most purposes" over it. Likewise, it could hardly be said that defendant "assumed the risk that [the University] might permit" inspection of his dorm room by others, such as the police. On the surface, therefore, the University did not have common authority over the dorm room.[16]

We perceive of no legitimate reason to distinguish between privacy expectations reasonably enjoyed by college students in occupying dormitory rooms with those experienced by tenants occupying houses or apartments. Nor do we believe that college students should have less protection from unreasonable searches and seizures in their dorm rooms than occupants have in their hotel rooms. . . .

Our conclusion is not altered by the fact that defendant signed a Housing Contract that authorized the University (1) to conduct routine room inspections on reasonable notice to the resident student, and (2) to enter rooms without notice "where there is a reasonable suspicion that a violation of the law or University policies is occurring or has occurred inside a particular room." These terms of occupancy, while constituting consent to the University's entry into defendant's dorm room under certain circumstances, cannot be reasonably construed as defendant having given such consent to others. *See Piazzola v. Watkins, supra*, 442 F.2d at 289–290; *Com. v. Neilson, supra*, 666 N.E.2d at 987. In particular, these contract terms do not constitute defendant's agreement to nonconsensual warrantless searches and seizures of his private residence by the police. Nor could the Housing Contract be so construed, since such purported advance consent to warrantless police searches would be an illegal waiver of defendant's constitutional rights under the Fourth Amendment. *See Piazzola v. Watkins, supra*, at 289 (regulation authorizing college to inspect dorm rooms could not be interpreted as student's "consent to a search for evidence for the primary purpose of a criminal prosecution" (fn. omitted)); *Devers v. Southern University, supra*, 712 So.2d at 204–207 (lease provision reserving college's right to inspect dorm room with police unconstitutionally abridged student's Fourth Amendment rights); *cf.* § 626.11, subd. (b) (purported waiver of student-occupant's protection from unreasonable search and seizure in college housing agreement void.)

We therefore conclude that the University had no actual authority to give valid third-party consent to a police search of defendant's dorm room.

We have concluded that the University did not have actual common authority over defendant's dormitory room to consent to a police search or seizure. But if the police officers' entry into defendant's dorm room was based upon their reasonable (but mistaken) belief that University employee Payne had the authority to consent to that entry, the police search and

16. As Justice Souter recently explained, the third-party-consent exception to the proscription against warrantless searches and seizures is founded in significant part on the "commonly held understanding about the authority that co-inhabitants may exercise in ways that affect each other's interests." *Georgia v. Randolph, supra*, 547 U.S. at 111. "A person on the scene who identifies himself, say, as a landlord or a hotel manager calls up no cus- tomary understanding of authority to admit guests without the consent of the current occupant. [Citations]." *Id.* at 112. Like a landlord or a hotel manager, here the University's exertion of administrative control over a dormitory suggests no customary understanding that it has the authority to admit third persons into an individual dorm room absent the student-occupant's consent.

seizure would be deemed to have been reasonable. *Rodriguez, supra,* 497 U.S. 177.

As the Supreme Court has explained, the question of apparent authority is determined objectively by asking whether "the facts available to the officer at the moment . . . warrant a man of reasonable caution in the belief that the consenting party had authority over the premises." *Rodriguez, supra,* 497 U.S. at 188, quoting *Terry v. Ohio,* 392 U.S. 1, 21–22 (1968). If the answer is "yes," the warrantless search is valid. And as the Supreme Court has made plain, "in order to satisfy the 'reasonableness' requirement of the Fourth Amendment, what is generally demanded of the many factual determinations that must regularly be made by agents of the government— . . . the police officer conducting a search or seizure under one of the exceptions to the warrant requirement—is not that they always be correct, but that they always be reasonable." *Id.* at 185.

The People, citing *Rodriguez, supra,* 497 U.S. 177, and *Kelly, supra,* 195 Cal.App.2d 669, 16 Cal. Rptr. 177, argue that the police had a reasonable basis for believing that Payne could consent to their entry. Defendant, citing *Chapman, supra,* 365 U.S. 610, and *People v. Escudero, supra,* 23 Cal.3d 800, 807, 153 Cal. Rptr. 825, 592 P.2d 312, responds that a landlord may not consent to a police search of a tenant's property—and thus argues (inferentially) that apparent authority is inapplicable in this instance because the University was essentially acting as defendant's landlord.

The police officers asked whether Payne had received consent to search the room. Payne responded in part that he had defendant's consent. By itself, this was insufficient to support a finding of reasonableness. This inquiry and Payne's response concerned only whether the University officials had the right to be in defendant's dorm room; it did not address whether the University could consent on defendant's behalf to a police search or seizure of the room. In the ordinary case, the police may not reasonably rely on a landlord's claimed authority over a rented room as being a sufficient basis for consent to a search. *See Chapman, supra,* 365 U.S. at 616–618; *People v. Escudero, supra,* 23 Cal. 3d at 807, 153 Cal. Rptr. 825, 592 P.2d 312 (ranch owner could not give consent to search of foreman's house under principle that landlord may not ordinarily consent to police entry of premises occupied by tenant). Likewise, here, the relationship between the University and the student-resident, defendant, was akin to a landlord-tenant relationship, and the mere fact that Payne stated that he had defendant's consent to search the room did not give rise to a reasonable conclusion that that University official could agree to a police search of the room on defendant's behalf. *See Piazzola v. Watkins, supra,* 442 F.2d at 289–290.

Payne's additional response to the police that defendant's consent was unnecessary "because of the waiver the defendant had signed in" the Housing Contract was also insufficient to support the reasonableness of the search. This was not a direct statement that Payne could consent to the officers' entry or that defendant had expressly given him that right of consent. Absent clarification as to what Payne meant by the defendant's "waiver" in the Housing Contract, the police could not have reasonably concluded that Payne had the authority to consent to a search of the dorm room.

But *Kelly, supra,* might support a contrary conclusion, i.e., that the officers' conduct was reasonable solely on the basis of Payne's two statements concerning defendant's consent and Housing Contract "waiver." . . .

We believe that *Kelly* has limited precedential value. *Kelly* was decided nearly 45 years ago, prior to the development of Fourth Amendment law that today controls suppression motions. College life and societal norms as a whole have changed significantly since 1961. Also since *Kelly* was decided, the Legislature, by its enactment of section 626.11 in 1975, gave express recognition to the constitutional rights of college students, including the right of privacy and the right to be free from unreasonable searches and seizures. That statute made inadmissible in any administrative proceeding any evidence seized by officials of any University of California, California state university, or public community college, in violation of another's constitutional rights (§ 626.11, subd. (a)); declared that any provision in such an institution's housing agreement purporting to waive the student-occupant's protection from unreasonable searches and seizures was against public policy and void (§ 626.11, subd. (b)); and made inadmissible in any administrative proceeding any evidence seized by officials of any such institution through a nonconsensual search of a dormitory room, where the evidence was "not directly related to the purpose for which the entry was initially made" (§ 626.11, subd. (c)).

Moreover, it is questionable whether *Kelly*'s reasoning—including its seemingly antiquated view that the college student had impliedly agreed that the house master could search the dorm room to uphold the disciplinary standards and integrity of the institution—would pass constitutional muster today. As the district court reasoned in *Morale v. Grigel, supra,* 422 F.Supp. at 997: "While the school also has a 'legitimate interest in preventing disruption on the campus,' its interests are limited by its function as an educational institution. A college cannot, in this day and age, protect students under the aegis of *in loco parentis* authority from the rigors of society's rules and laws, just as it cannot, under the same aegis, deprive students of their constitutional rights." We therefore conclude—*Kelly* and its reasoning notwithstanding— that Payne's statements, by themselves, were insufficient to justify police entry into the dorm room under apparent authority.

. . .

In our evaluation of the reasonableness of the officers' conduct, "we are mindful of the rule applicable to unprecedented factual situations involving the reasonableness of police conduct as restricted by the Fourth Amendment. 'There is no exact formula for the determination of reasonableness.' " *People v. Superior Court (York),* 3 Cal. App. 3d 648, 659, 83 Cal. Rptr. 732 (1970). Here, however, we need not decide the issue of whether the police reasonably believed that Payne had authority to consent to their entry, because as we discuss below, the contraband would have been inevitably discovered.

The People argue as an additional reason that the suppression motion should have been denied: "Although the police conduct in this case was not improper, it was inevitable that after completing its private search, the University would have turned the marijuana and marijuana paraphernalia over to the Santa Clara Police." Therefore (the People argue) the inevitable discovery doctrine should have been applied by the court below to prevent operation of the exclusionary rule. The court below found that the inevitable discovery doctrine did not apply because it was not supported by the evidence. Assuming that the warrantless search was unreasonable, we find that the contraband would have been inevitably discovered.

. . . Here, the record supports a finding that the contraband would have been inevitably discovered. The University contacted the Santa Clara Police Department to report that "a considerable amount of drugs had been found in a Residence Hall room." The police arrived at the dormitory, met Campus Safety Officer Brady, who then accompanied them to defendant's dorm room, announcing (as he opened the door), "You've got to see this." After Brady opened the door, the large quantity of marijuana and cash were easily visible to the police. It defies logic (and common sense) to conclude that the University safety officers—having contacted the police, gathered the contraband (apparently for inspection by the police), and displayed the contraband to the police—thereafter would have withheld the contraband from the police to pursue their own internal investigation. The probability that the University would have involved the police further is heightened by the fact that the safety officers' investigation had disclosed a potentially significant marijuana sales enterprise on the University campus (evidenced by a "large quantity" of marijuana, several boxes of packaging materials, an electronic scale, and $1,800 cash)—a possible crime that is a far cry from possession of a small quantity of the drug for personal use. While it would not be unreasonable to conclude that the University might have handled a student's possession of a small quantity of marijuana privately, the converse is likewise true where (as here) the student was in possession of a significant quantity of the drug along with evidence of sales activity. In resolving this question, this "court does not leave its common sense at the door." *Government Employees Ins. Co. v. Superior Court*, 79 Cal. App. 4th 95, 102, 93 Cal. Rptr. 2d 820 (2000). Under these circumstances, it is plain that the contraband " 'would have been eventually secured through legal means regardless of the [allegedly] improper official conduct.' " *People v. Superior Court (Tunch)*, 80 Cal. App.3d 665, 673, 145 Cal. Rptr. 795 (1978).

. . .

The prosecution bears the burden of proving by a preponderance of the evidence that evidence otherwise unlawfully obtained would have been inevitably discovered. *People v. Coffman and Marlow, supra*, 34 Cal. 4th at p. 62, 17 Cal. Rptr. 3d 710, 96 P.3d 30; *People v. Carpenter*, 21 Cal. 4th 1016, 1040, 90 Cal. Rptr. 2d 607, 988 P.2d 531 (1999). On the record before us, we conclude that the prosecution met that burden.

Questions and Comments on *People v. Superior Court*

1. In *People v. Superior Court*, the California Court of Appeals argued that there is "no legitimate reason to distinguish between privacy expectations reasonably enjoyed by college students in occupying dormitory rooms with those experienced by tenants occupying houses or apartments." Is the relationship between a student occupying a dorm room and the university truly analogous to the relationship between a landlord and a tenant, or does the educational mission of the university make the student-university relationship special? In *State v. Hunter*, 831 P.2d 1033, 1036 (Utah App.1992), for instance, the court ruled that "[t]he right of privacy protected by the fourth amendment does not include freedom from reasonable inspection of a school-operated dormitory room by school officials" if the search is "designed to protect campus order and discipline and to promote an environment consistent with the educational process." Should the level of protection afforded to students depend on whether the search is performed for educational or disciplinary purposes, on the one hand, or law enforcement purposes on the other? In *Devers v. Southern Univ.*, 712 So.2d 199 (La.App.1998), the court suppressed evidence of drug possession arising from a warrantless search of a student's dorm room. The student had signed a standard university housing contract that included a provision stating that "[t]he University reserves all rights in connection with assignments of rooms, inspection of rooms with police, and the termination of room occupancy." Although acknowledging the constitutionality of waivers permitting university officials to search dorm rooms for purposes related to the university's educational mission, the court ruled that the contract provision was unconstitutional on its face because it purported to authorize warrantless searches by police that were unconnected to the educational mission of the university. *Id.* at 205. The court then ruled that the search was unconstitutional because it was coordinated with a police investigation. For an insightful discussion of the Fourth Amendment rights of students in dorms, see Kristal Otto Stanley, *The 4th Amendment and Dormitory Searches—a New Truce*, 65 U. CHI. L. REV. 1403 (1998).

2. What privacy rights do students have when they connect to student networks? In *Warner Bros. v. Does 1–6*, 527 F.Supp.2d 1 (D.D.C. 2007), the court compelled Georgetown University to turn over the names of six students whom Warner Bros. Recording, Inc. believed were illegally distributing copyrighted material using peer-to-peer networks. The court noted that Georgetown's disclosure of the information would not violate the Family Educational Rights and Privacy Act because the disclosure would be made pursuant to a court order.

In *U.S. v. Heckenkamp*, 482 F.3d 1142 (9th Cir. 2007), the Ninth Circuit upheld a search of a computer performed by a university security official. After receiving a complaint that a university student was hacking into a network in California, Jeffrey Savoy, a computer network investigator at the University of Wisconsin, discovered that the same student user had gained unauthorized access to the university's "Mail 2" server, which processed over 250,000 emails a day. Savoy traced the intrusions to a dorm room and computer account belonging to Heckenkamp, a computer science graduate student. Savoy decided that Heckenkamp's computer needed to be taken offline immediately to avoid disruption of email service. Without obtaining a warrant, Savoy entered Heckenkamp's dorm room with police officers while Heckenkamp was not present. Savoy wanted to access Heckenkamp's computer directly to confirm that it was the computer used in the hacking, but he did not have the password. When Heckenkamp returned to his room with the police, he gave Savoy his password and authorized Savoy to make a copy of his hard drive. The following day, federal agents obtained a warrant and seized Heckenkamp's computer. *Id.* at 1145.

The Ninth Circuit held that the defendant had an objectively reasonable expectation of privacy in his computer that was not destroyed when he attached the computer to a university network. *Id.* at *1146*. The court noted that the student's computer was "protected by a screen-saver password, located in his dormitory room, and subject to no policy allowing the university actively to monitor or audit his computer usage." *Id.* at 1147. Nevertheless, the court held that Savoy's search of the computer was justified under the "special needs" exemption to the warrant requirement. *Id.* The court emphasized the fact that Savoy was motivated by the need to protect the university's email system, not by a need to collect evidence for law enforcement purposes. Moreover, the court found that Savoy's actions were consistent with university policy, which authorized him to " 'rectif[y] emergency situations that threaten the integrity of campus computer or communication systems[,] provided that the use of accessed files is limited solely to maintaining or safeguarding the system.' " *Id.*

Tracy Mitrano, director of the Computer Policy and Law Program at Cornell University, said the decision was a "good thing for privacy advocates. . . . On the basis of this case one could say, 'just because something is technologically possible, i.e., remote inspection of a hard drive, does not necessarily make it legal.' " Scott Jaschik, *Defining Privacy—and Its Limits*, INSIDE HIGHER ED., Apr. 10, 2007, *available at* http://insidehighered.com/news/2007/04/09/heckenkamp. Do you agree? She also said that the case highlighted the importance of good computer usage policy at colleges and universities: "not only should a policy allow for free expression ('no monitoring of the network or devices attached to it for content as a practice') but also for circumstances under which exceptions will be made ('security, network maintenance, regulatory compliance, contractual obligations and investigations of violations of law or policy')." *Id.*

CHAPTER 14

OBLIGATIONS OF COLLEGES AND UNIVERSITIES TO STUDENTS

A. DOCTRINE OF IN LOCO PARENTIS

Gott v. Berea College

Court of Appeals of Kentucky, 1913.
156 Ky. 376, 161 S.W. 204.

■ NUNN, J.

The appellant, J.S. Gott, about the first of September, 1911, purchased and was conducting a restaurant in Berea, Kentucky, across the street from the premises of Berea College. A restaurant had been conducted in this same place for quite a long while by the party from whom Gott purchased. For many years it has been the practice of the governing authorities of Berea College to distribute among the students at the beginning of each scholastic year a pamphlet entitled "Students' Manual," containing the rules and regulations of the college for the government of the student body. Subsection three of this manual under the heading "Forbidden Places," enjoined the students from entering any "place of ill repute, liquor saloons, gambling houses, etc."

During the 1911 summer vacation the faculty, pursuant to their usual practice of revising the rules, added another clause to this rule as to forbidden places, and the rule was announced to the student body at chapel exercises on the first day of the fall term which began September 11th. The new rule is as follows:

> (b) Eating houses and places of amusement in Berea, not controlled by the College, must not be entered by students on pain of immediate dismission. The institution provides for the recreation of its students, and ample accommodation for meals and refreshment, and cannot permit outside parties to solicit student patronage for gain.

Appellant's restaurant was located and conducted mainly for the profits arising from student patronage. During the first few days after the publication of this rule two or three students were expelled for its violation, so that the making of the rule, and its enforcement, had the effect of very materially injuring, if not absolutely ruining appellant's business because the students were afraid to further patronize it.

On the 20th day of September appellant instituted this action in equity, and procured a temporary restraining order and injunction against the enforcement of the rule above quoted, and charging that the college and its officers unlawfully and maliciously conspired to injure his business by adopting a rule forbidding students entering eating houses. For this he claimed damages in the sum of $500. By amended petitions, he alleged that in pursuance of such conspiracy the college officers had uttered slanderous remarks concerning him, and his business, and increased his prayer for damages to $2,000. The slanderous remarks were alleged to have been spoken at chapel, and other public exercises to the student body as a reason for the rule, and were to the effect that appellant was a boot-legger, and upon more than one occasion had been charged and convicted of illegally selling whiskey. Berea College answered, and denied that any slanderous remarks had been made as to appellant, or that they had conspired maliciously, or otherwise, or that the rule adopted was either unlawful, or unreasonable. In the second paragraph the college affirmatively set forth that it is a private (incorporated) institution of learning, supported wholly by private donations, and its endowment, and such fees as it collects from students or parents of students who desire to become affiliated with said institution, and abide by, and conform to the rules and regulations provided by the governing authorities of the college for the conduct of the students; that every student upon entering said institution agrees upon pain of dismissal to conform to such rules and regulations as may be from time to time promulgated; that the institution aims to furnish an education to inexperienced country, mountain boys and girls of very little means at the lowest possible cost; that practically all of the students are from rural districts, and unused to the ways of even a village the size of Berea, and that they are of very limited means. It is further alleged that they have been compelled from time to time to pass rules tending to prevent students from wasting their time and money, and to keep them wholly occupied in study; that some of the rules prohibited the doing of things not in themselves wrong, or unlawful, but which the governing authorities have found, and believe detrimental to the best interest of the college, and the student body. For these reasons the rule in question was adopted, but they say at the time that they had no knowledge that the plaintiff owned, or was about to acquire a restaurant, and that the rule was in no way directed at the plaintiff. Upon motion the restraining order was dissolved, but on account of allegations charging slanderous remarks the lower court overruled demurrer to the petition. After filing of the answer, proof was heard, the case submitted, and tried by the court with the result that the petition was dismissed, and Gott appeals to this court.

. . .

The [question] we are called here to pass upon, is whether the rule forbidding students entering eating houses was a reasonable one, and within the power of the college authorities to enact, and the further question whether, in that event, appellant Gott, will be heard to complain. That the enforcement of the rule worked a great injury to Gott's restaurant business cannot well be denied, but unless he can show that the college authorities have been guilty of a breach of some legal duty which they owe to him, he has no cause of action against them for the injury. One has no right of action against a merchant for refusal to sell goods, nor will an action lie, unless such means are used as of themselves constitute a breach of legal duty, for inducing or causing persons not to trade, deal, or contract with another, and it is a well established principle that when a lawful act is performed in the proper manner, the party performing it is not liable for mere incidental consequences injuriously resulting from it to another.

College authorities stand *in loco parentis* concerning the physical and moral welfare, and mental training of the pupils, and we are unable to see why to that end they may not make any rule or regulation for the government, or betterment of their pupils that a parent could for the same purpose. Whether the rules or regulations are wise, or their aims worthy, is a matter left solely to the discretion of the authorities, or parents as the case may be, and in the exercise of that discretion, the courts are not disposed to interfere, unless the rules and aims are unlawful, or against public policy. Section 881, of the Kentucky Statutes, applicable to corporations of this character, provides that they may "adopt such rules for their government and operation, not inconsistent with law, as the directors, trustees, or managers may deem proper." The corporate charter of Berea College empowers the board of trustees to "make such by-laws as it may deem necessary to promote the interest of the institution, not in violation of any laws of the State or the United States." This reference to the college powers shows that its authorities have a large discretion, and they are similar to the charter and corporate rights under which colleges and such institutions are generally conducted. Having in mind such powers, the courts have without exception held to the rule which is well settled in 7 Cyc., 288.

"A college or university may prescribe requirements for admission and rules for the conduct of its students, and one who enters as a student impliedly agrees to conform to such rules of government."

The only limit upon this rule is as to institutions supported in whole, or in part, by appropriations from the public treasury. In such cases their rules are viewed somewhat more critically, but since this is a private institution it is unnecessary to notice further the distinction.

. . .

There is nothing in the case to show that the college had any contract, business, or other direct relations with the appellant. They owed him no special duty, and while he may have suffered an injury, yet he does not show that the college is a wrong-doer in a legal or any sense. Nor does he show that in enacting the rules they did it unlawfully, or that they exceeded their power, or that there was any conspiracy to do anything unlawful. Their right to enact the rule comes within their charter provision, and that it was a reasonable rule cannot be very well disputed. Assuming that there were no other outside eating houses in Berea, and that there never had been a disorderly one, or one in which intoxicating liquors had been sold, still it would not be an unreasonable rule forbidding students entering or patronizing appellant's establishment. In the first place the college offers an education to the poorest, and undertakes to offer them the means of a livelihood within the institution while they are pursuing their studies, and at the same time provides board and lodging for a nominal charge. Whatever profit was derived, served to still further reduce expenses charged against the pupil. It stands to reason that when the plans of the institution are so prepared, and the support and maintenance of the students are so ordered, that there must be the fullest co-operation on the part of all the students, otherwise there will be disappointment if not failure in the project. It is also a matter of common knowledge that one of the chief dreads of college authorities is the outbreak of an epidemic, and against which they should take the utmost precaution. These precautions, however, may wholly fail if students carelessly, or indiscriminately visit or patronize public or unsanitary eating houses. Too often those operating such places are ignorant of, or indifferent to even the simplest sanitary requirements. As a safeguard against disease infection from this source there is sufficient reason for the promulgation of the rule complained of. But even if it might be conceded that the rule was an unreasonable one, still appellant Gott is in no position to complain. He was not a student, nor is it shown that he had any children as students in the college. The rule was directed to and intended to control only the student body. For the purposes of this case the school, its officers and students are a legal entity, as much so as any family, and like a father may direct his children, those in charge of boarding schools are well within their rights and powers when they direct their students what to eat and where they may get it; where they may go and what forms of amusement are forbidden. A case very similar, and often quoted is that of *People v. Wheaton College*, 40 Ill. 186. It illustrates the principles here announced so well that we quote with approval the following from it:

> Wheaton College is an incorporated institution, resting upon private endowments, deriving no aid whatever from the State or from taxation. Its charter gives the trustees and faculty power to adopt and enforce such rules as may be deemed expedient in the government of the institution, a power which they would have possession without such express grant, because incident to the very object of their incorporation, and indispensable to the successful management of the college. Among the rules they have deemed it expedient to adopt is one forbidding students to become a member of secret societies. We perceive nothing unreasonable in the rule itself since all persons familiar with college life know that the tendency of secret societies is to withdraw students to some extent from the control of the faculty and to impair the discipline of the institution. Such may not always be the effect, but such is their general tendency. But whether the rule be judicious or not, it violates neither good morals nor the laws of the land, and is, therefore, clearly within the power of the college authorities to make and enforce.... It is urged that the Good Templars are a society established for the promotion of temperance and incorporated by the Legislature and that any citizen has a right to join it. We do not doubt the beneficent object of the society and we admit that any citizen has the right to join it if the society consent. But this right is not of so high and solemn a character that it cannot be surrendered and the son of the relator did voluntarily surrender it when he became a student of Wheaton College, for he knew, or must be taken to have known, that by the rules of the institution which he was voluntarily entering, he would be precluded from joining any secret society....

There is no similarity between this and the case of the *Standard Oil Co. v. Doyle*, 118 Ky. 662, and many others of like import relied upon by appellant. These all relate to unlawful combinations and conspiracies between trading corporations or between individuals in trade, together with the use of unlawful, and fraudulent measures in restraint of trade, and to throttle competition. Of course trading corporations have no such wide latitude or discretion in the scope and character of rules and by-laws they may adopt or enforce in conducting their business. They are limited and controlled both by statute and common law. But the mere fact that one's trade has been restrained, as Gott's admittedly has, gives him no ground to invoke the law, unless the means used to restrain it have been malicious and wrongful. And as above indicated the proof shows neither malice nor wrong on the part of appellee.

Considering the whole case the judgment of the lower court is affirmed.

Questions and Comments on *In Loco Parentis*

1.   Berea College was founded in 1859 as the first co-educational, interracial college in the south. The founders were abolitionists dedicated to creating an affordable institution of higher education that would be open to all classes and races. In 1904, the school was forced to stop enrolling black students when Kentucky passed the Day Law, which prohibited education of black and white students together even at private schools. The college fought the law all the way to the Supreme Court, but was forced to set up a separate school for blacks when it lost the case. Berea College v. Kentucky, 211 U.S. 45 (1908). After the Day Law was amended in 1950 to permit post-secondary schools to teach blacks and whites, Berea again opened its doors to black students. The school continues to serve a diverse student body. Admission is limited to students with demonstrated financial need, and each admitted student is awarded a full tuition scholarship. Additional costs, such as room, board, and fees are covered by the college depending on financial need of the student. Students are also required to work at least ten hours a week at a job on campus. *See* Berea College's website, www.berea.edu (last visited July 7, 2008).

2.   The doctrine of *in loco parentis* provided colleges and universities with the ability to make rules and regulations governing student behavior, but it also insulated their disciplinary proceedings from judicial intervention. *See, e.g.*, John B. Stetson Univ. v. Hunt, 88 Fla. 510, 102 So. 637 (1924) (upholding student's dismissal for violating vague rule against "offensive behavior"; her actions included hazing, ringing cow bells and parading in the hallways at forbidden hours); Woods v. Simpson, 146 Md. 547, 126 A. 882 (1924) (upholding dismissal of student for refusing to admit to anonymously making charges of sexual harassment in the student newspaper); Anthony v. Syracuse Univ., 224 A.D. 487, 231 N.Y.S. 435 (1928) ("While no adequate reason was assigned by the university for the [student's] dismissal, [the court] find[s] nothing in the record on which to base a finding that no such record exists.").

Did *in loco parentis* impose any duties on the university in addition to providing it with the power to regulate student behavior? If a university failed to act like a parent, for example by failing to protect its students from injuries on campus, could the student sue? Consider ROBERT D. BICKEL & PETER F. LAKE, THE RIGHTS AND RESPONSIBIL-ITIES OF THE MODERN UNIVERSITY 29 (1999) ("*in loco parentis* was not-ever-a liability/responsibility/duty creating norm. It was only a legal tool of immunity for universities when they deliberately chose to discipline students."). *See also* Theodore C. Stamatakos, Note, *The Doctrine of In Loco Parentis, Tort Liability and the Student–College Relationship*, 65 IND. L.J. 471 (1990).

3.   *In loco parentis* fell out of favor with the courts beginning with *Dixon v. Alabama State Bd. of Educ.*, 294 F.2d 150 (5th Cir.1961). Along with increased recognition of students' rights to due process came a decrease in deference towards a university's authority to regulate student life. *See, e.g.*, Lansdale v. Tyler Junior College, 470 F.2d 659 (5th Cir. 1972) (granting an injunction against the school's rule prohibiting long hair on male students). Many courts and scholars declared that by the 1970s, "the era of *in loco parentis* was dead." BICKEL & LAKE at 48.

B.   COLLEGE AS BYSTANDER

Bradshaw v. Rawlings

United States Court of Appeals, Third Circuit, 1979.
612 F.2d 135, *cert. denied*, 446 U.S. 909 (1980).

■ ALDISERT, CIRCUIT JUDGE:

The major question for decision in this diversity case tried under Pennsylvania law is whether a college may be subject to tort liability for injuries sustained by one of its students involved in an automobile accident when the driver of the car was a fellow student who had become intoxicated at a class picnic.... The district court permitted the question of negligence to go to the jury against the college, the beer distributor and the municipality. From an adverse verdict of $1,108,067 each of the defendants has appealed, advancing separate arguments for reversal. The plaintiff has filed a conditional cross-appeal.[1]

Donald Bradshaw, an eighteen-year old student at Delaware Valley College, was severely injured on April 13, 1975 in Doylestown, Pennsylvania, while a backseat passenger in a Saab automobile driven by a fellow student, Bruce Rawlings. Both were sophomores and had attended their class picnic at a grove owned by the Maennerchor Society on the outskirts of the borough. Returning to the college from the picnic, Rawlings drove through Doylestown on Union Street. Union Street is colloquially known as "Dip Street" because it was constructed with drainage dips, instead of sewers, to carry surface water runoff. While proceeding through one of the dips, Rawlings lost control of the automobile which then struck a parked vehicle. As a result of the collision Bradshaw suffered a cervical fracture which caused quadriplegia.

The picnic, although not held on college grounds, was an annual activity of the sophomore class. A faculty member who served as sophomore class advisor participated with the class officers in planning the picnic and co-signed a check for class funds that was later used to purchase beer. The advisor did not attend the picnic, nor did he get another faculty member to attend in his place. Flyers announcing the picnic were prominently displayed across the campus. They were mimeographed by the college duplicating facility and featured drawings of beer mugs. Approximately seventy-five students attended the picnic and consumed six or seven half-kegs of beer. The beer was ordered from Marjorie Moyer, trading as Sunny Beverages, by the sophomore class president who was underage.

The legal drinking age in Pennsylvania was, and is, twenty-one years, but the great majority of the students drinking at the picnic were sophomores of either nineteen or twenty years of age. Rawlings had been at the picnic for a number of hours. He testified that he had no recollection of what occurred from the time he left the picnic until after the accident. Bradshaw testified that Rawlings had been drinking and another witness, Warren Wylde, expressed his opinion that Rawlings was under the influence of alcohol when he left the picnic grove. That there was sufficient evidence on the question of Rawlings' intoxication to submit to the jury cannot be seriously questioned.

On appeal, the college argues that Bradshaw failed to present sufficient evidence to establish that it owed him a duty for the breach of which it could be held liable in tort. The district court, apparently assuming that such a duty existed, submitted the question of the college's liability to the jury, stating:

1. For convenience we refer to the plaintiff in the singular although joining the injured plaintiff, Donald Bradshaw, were his mother and stepfather who recovered $5,000 each.

In any event, the college owes a duty to use due care under the circumstances to prevent an unreasonable risk of harm to sophomores who attend a class function. Restatement (Second) of Torts §§ 282 and 283 (1965) provide:

§ 282. Negligence Defined

In the Restatement of this Subject, negligence is conduct which falls below the standard established by law for the protection of others against unreasonable risk of harm. It does not include conduct recklessly disregardful of an interest in others.

§ 283. Conduct of a Reasonable Man:

The Standard

Unless the actor is a child, the standard of conduct to which he must conform to avoid being negligent is that of a reasonable man under like circumstances.

Bradshaw v. Rawlings, 464 F.Supp. 175, 181 (E.D.Pa.1979)....

The college's argument strikes at the heart of tort law because a negligence claim must fail if based on circumstances for which the law imposes no duty of care on the defendant. "Negligence in the air, so to speak, will not do."[4] As Professor Prosser has emphasized, the statement that there is or is not a duty begs the essential question, which is whether the plaintiff's interests are entitled to legal protection against the defendant's conduct. "Duty" is not sacrosanct in itself, but only an expression of the sum total of those considerations of policy which lead the law to say that a particular plaintiff is entitled to protection.[5] Thus, we may perceive duty simply as an obligation to which the law will give recognition in order to require one person to conform to a particular standard of conduct with respect to another person.

These abstract descriptions of duty cannot be helpful, however, unless they are directly related to the competing individual, public, and social interests implicated in any case. An interest is a social fact, factor, or phenomenon existing independently of the law which is reflected by a claim, demand, or desire that people seek to satisfy and that has been recognized as socially valid by authoritative decision makers in society. Certainly, the plaintiff in this case possessed an important interest in remaining free from bodily injury, and thus the law protects his right to recover compensation from those who negligently cause him injury. The college, on the other hand, has an interest in the nature of its relationship with its adult students, as well as an interest in avoiding responsibilities that it is incapable of performing.

Our beginning point is a recognition that the modern American college is not an insurer of the safety of its students. Whatever may have been its responsibility in an earlier era, the authoritarian role of today's college administrations has been notably diluted in recent decades. Trustees, administrators, and faculties have been required to yield to the expanding rights

---

4. F. POLLOCK, LAW OF TORTS 468 (13th ed. 1929).

5. W. PROSSER, LAW OF TORTS 333 (3d ed. 1964).

and privileges of their students. By constitutional amendment,[7] written[8] and unwritten law, and through the evolution of new customs, rights formerly possessed by college administrations have been transferred to students. College students today are no longer minors; they are now regarded as adults in almost every phase of community life. For example, except for purposes of purchasing alcoholic beverages, eighteen-year old persons are considered adults by the Commonwealth of Pennsylvania. They may vote, marry, make a will, qualify as a personal representative, serve as a guardian of the estate of a minor, wager at racetracks, register as a public accountant, practice veterinary medicine, qualify as a practical nurse, drive trucks, ambulances and other official fire vehicles, perform general fire-fighting duties, and qualify as a private detective. Pennsylvania has set eighteen as the age at which criminal acts are no longer treated as those of a juvenile, and eighteen-year old students may waive their testimonial privilege protecting confidential statements to school personnel. Moreover, a person may join the Pennsylvania militia at an even younger age than eighteen[23] and may hunt without adult supervision at age sixteen. As a result of these and other similar developments in our society, eighteen-year old students are now identified with an expansive bundle of individual and social interests and possess discrete rights not held by college students from decades past. There was a time when college administrators and faculties assumed a role *in loco parentis*. Students were committed to their charge because the students were considered minors. A special relationship was created between college and student that imposed a duty on the college to exercise control over student conduct and, reciprocally, gave the students certain rights of protection by the college. The campus revolutions of the late sixties and early seventies were a direct attack by the students on rigid controls by the colleges and were an all-pervasive affirmative demand for more student rights.[25] In general, the students succeeded, peaceably and otherwise, in acquiring a new status at colleges throughout the country. These movements, taking place almost simultaneously with legislation and case law lowering the age of majority, produced fundamental changes in our society. A dramatic reapportionment of responsibilities and social interests of general security took place. Regulation by the college of student life on and off campus has become limited. Adult students now demand and receive expanded rights of privacy in their college life including, for example, liberal, if not unlimited, partial visiting hours. College administrators no longer control the broad arena of general morals. At one time, exercising their rights and duties *in loco parentis*, colleges were able to impose strict regulations. But today students vigorously claim the right to define and regulate their own lives. Especially have they demanded and received satisfaction of their interest in self-assertion in both physical and mental activities, and have vindicated what may be called the

---

7. Section one of the twenty-sixth amendment to the United States Constitution provides: "The right of citizens of the United States, who are eighteen years of age or older, to vote shall not be denied or abridged by the United States or by any State on account of age."

8. *See, e.g., Goss v. Lopez,* 419 U.S. 565 (1975); *Papish v. Board of Curators,* 410 U.S. 667 (1973) (per curiam); *Healy v. James,* 408 U.S. 169 (1972); *Grayned v. City of Rockford,* 408 U.S. 104 (1972); *Tinker v. Des Moines School District,* 393 U.S. 503 (1969).

23. 51 Pa. Cons. Stat. § 301 (seventeen years, six months).

25. *See generally Scheuer v. Rhodes,* 416 U.S. 232 (1974); *Healy v. James,* 408 U.S. 169, 171 (1972); *See also* REPORT OF THE PRESIDENT'S COMMISSION ON CAMPUS UNREST (1970); REPORT OF THE AMERICAN BAR ASSOCIATION COMMISSION ON CAMPUS GOVERNMENT AND STUDENT DISSENT (1970); STEVEN KELMAN, PUSH COMES TO SHOVE: THE ESCALATION OF STUDENT PROTEST (1970); ALAN ADELSON, SDS (4th ed. 1970).

interest in freedom of the individual will. In 1972 Justice Douglas summarized the change:

> Students who, by reason of the Twenty-sixth Amendment, become eligible to vote when 18 years of age are adults who are members of the college or university community. Their interests and concerns are often quite different from those of the faculty. They often have values, views, and ideologies that are at war with the ones which the college has traditionally espoused or indoctrinated.

Healy v. James, 408 U.S. 169, 197 (1972) (Douglas, J., concurring).

Thus, for purposes of examining fundamental relationships that underlie tort liability, the competing interests of the student and of the institution of higher learning are much different today than they were in the past. At the risk of oversimplification, the change has occurred because society considers the modern college student an adult, not a child of tender years. It could be argued, although we need not decide here, that an educational institution possesses a different pattern of rights and responsibilities and retains more of the traditional custodial responsibilities when its students are all minors, as in an elementary school, or mostly minors, as in a high school. Under such circumstances, after weighing relevant competing interests, Pennsylvania might possibly impose on the institution certain duties of protection, for the breach of which a legal remedy would be available. But here, because the circumstances show that the students have reached the age of majority and are capable of protecting their own self interests, we believe that the rule would be different. We conclude, therefore, that in order to ascertain whether a specific duty of care extended from Delaware Valley College to its injured student, we must first identify and assess the competing individual and social interests associated with the parties.

In the process of identifying the competing interests implicated in the student-college relationship, we note that the record in this case is not overly generous in identifying the interests possessed by the student, although it was Bradshaw's burden to prove the existence of a duty owed him by the college in order to establish a breach thereof. Bradshaw has concentrated on the school regulation imposing sanctions on the use of alcohol by students. The regulation states: "Possession or consumption of alcohol or malt beverages on the property of the College or at any College sponsored or related affair off campus will result in disciplinary action. The same rule will apply to every student regardless of age." We are not impressed that this regulation, in and of itself, is sufficient to place the college in a custodial relationship with its students for purposes of imposing a duty of protection in this case. We assume that the average student arrives on campus at the age of seventeen or eighteen, and that most students are under twenty-one during the better part of their college careers. A college regulation that essentially tracks a state law and prohibits conduct that to students under twenty-one is already prohibited by state law does not, in our view, indicate that the college voluntarily assumed a custodial relationship with its students so as to make operative the provisions of § 320 of the Restatement (Second) of Torts.

Thus, we predict that the Pennsylvania courts would not hold that by promulgating this regulation the college had voluntarily taken custody of Bradshaw so as to deprive him of his normal power of self-protection or to subject him to association with persons likely to cause him harm. Absent proof of such a relationship, we do not believe that a prima facie case of custodial duty was established in order to submit the case to the jury on this theory.

We next examine the facts adduced at trial to determine whether a special relationship existed as a matter of law, which would impose upon the college either a duty to control the conduct of a student operating a motor vehicle off campus or a duty to extend to a student a right of protection in transportation to and from off campus activities. We conclude that Bradshaw also failed to meet his burden of proving either of these duties. Bradshaw's primary argument is that the college had knowledge that its students would drink beer at the picnic, that this conduct violated a school regulation and state law, that it created a known probability of harm to third persons, and that knowledge by the college of this probable harm imposed a duty on the college either to control Rawling's conduct or to protect Bradshaw from possible harm.

Although we are aware of no Pennsylvania decision that has addressed this precise issue, the supreme court of that state has held that a private host who supplies intoxicants to a visibly intoxicated guest may not be held civilly liable for injuries to third parties caused by the intoxicated guest's negligence. *Manning v. Andy*, 454 Pa. 237, 310 A.2d 75 (1973). Only licensed persons engaged in the sale of intoxicants have been held civilly liable to injured parties, *id.* at 239, 310 A.2d at 76 (citing *Jardine v. Upper Darby Lodge*, 413 Pa. 626, 198 A.2d 550 (1964)), and the source of this liability derives from the common law, *Corcoran v. McNeal*, 400 Pa. 14, 161 A.2d 367 (1960), as well as from a violation of Pennsylvania's Dram Shop statute, 47 P.S. § 4–493(1), *Majors v. Brodhead Hotel*, 416 Pa. 265, 205 A.2d 873 (1965). Because the Pennsylvania Supreme Court has been unwilling to find a special relationship on which to predicate a duty between a private host and his visibly intoxicated guest, we predict that it would be even less willing to find such a relationship between a college and its student under the circumstances of this case.

The centerpiece of Bradshaw's argument is that beer-drinking by underage college students, in itself, creates the special relationship on which to predicate liability and, furthermore, that the college has both the opportunity and the means of exercising control over beer drinking by students at an off campus gathering. These contentions miss the mark, however, because they blur the distinction between establishing the existence of a duty and proving the breach thereof. Bradshaw does not argue that beer drinking is generally regarded as a harm-producing act, for it cannot be seriously controverted that a goodly number of citizens indulge in this activity. Our national public policy, insofar as it is reflected by industry standards or by government regulation of certain types of radio-television advertising, permits advertising of beer at all times of the day and night even though Congress has banned advertisement of cigarettes and the broadcasting industry has agreed to ban the advertisement of liquor. What we know as men and women we must not forget as judges, and this panel of judges is able to bear witness to the fact that beer drinking by college students is a common experience. That this is true is not to suggest that reality always comports with state law and college rules. It does not. But the Pennsylvania law that prohibits sales to, and purchases by, persons under twenty-one years of age, is certainly not a universal practice in other countries, nor even the general rule in North America. Moreover in New Jersey, the bordering state from which the majority of Delaware Valley College students come, the legal drinking age is eighteen. Under these circumstances, we think it would be placing an impossible burden on the college to impose a duty in this case.

. . .

Therefore, we conclude that Bradshaw failed to establish a prima facie case against the college that it should be charged with a duty of custodial care as a matter of law and that the district court erred by submitting the case to the jury.

Questions and Comments on *Bradshaw*

1. Although many courts in recent years have been willing to hold colleges and universities liable for some student injuries, *Bradhaw* illustrates the dominate judicial view that they are not liable for most alcohol related injuries and deaths. *See, e.g.,* Albano v. Colby Coll., 822 F.Supp. 840 (D. Me. 1993) (college not liable for drinking related student injury on a school sponsored tennis trip); Booker v. Lehigh Univ., 800 F.Supp. 234, 239 (E.D.Pa.1992) (refusing to hold university's alcohol policy constituted an assumption of duty); Baldwin v. Zoradi, 123 Cal.App.3d 275, 176 Cal.Rptr. 809 (1981) (university not liable for student injury resulting from car race accident after drinking in a campus dormitory); University of Denver v. Whitlock, 744 P.2d 54 (Colo.1987) (overturning an imposition of liability on university for students alcohol-related injury on a trampoline); Allen v. Rutgers, 216 N.J.Super. 189, 523 A.2d 262 (App.Div.1987) (college not liable for drinking-related fall over stadium wall at school football game); Beach v. University of Utah, 726 P.2d 413 (Utah 1986) (university not liable for a student's-drinking related injury on a field trip, even though the university was aware that student had a history of similar behavior and the teacher sponsoring the trip was also drinking); Houck v. University of Wash., 60 Wash.App. 189, 803 P.2d 47 (1991) (university has no duty to prevent underage students from drinking on campus and is not liable for student's drinking related injury). Courts have also resisted holding colleges or universities liable for drug-related student injuries and deaths. *See, e.g.,* Bash v. Clark Univ., 22 Mass. L. Rep. 84 (Mass.Super.Ct. 2006) (university not liable for student's on-campus heroin overdose).

2. A college or university that voluntarily implements measures to control underage drinking or to curb drunk driving on campus may expose itself to liability. In *Coghlan v. Beta Theta Pi Fraternity*, 133 Idaho 388, 987 P.2d 300 (1999), for example, the court held that the university assumed a duty to protect its students from those serving alcohol to minors when it voluntarily assigned university employees to supervise all on-campus parties. Similarly in *McClure v. Fairfield University*, 2003 WL 21524786 (Conn.Super.Ct. 2003), the court ruled in favor of a student who was hit by a drunk driver late at night while walking to campus. The court held that the university assumed liability for the safe transportation of its students by offering a free shuttle service at night. *Id* at 8. Does this mean schools should not take any safety precautions?

3. If a university decides to confront the problem of alcohol, what steps should it take? A growing number of universities are contacting parents when students are caught using alcohol or drugs. Elizabeth Bernstein, *Colleges Move Boldly on Student Drinking*, Wall St. J., Dec. 6, 2007, at D1. Although the Family Education Rights and Privacy Act (FERPA) generally protects the privacy of students' disciplinary record, an exception created in 1998 allows universities to contact parents if a student under twenty-one commits an alcohol or drug violation. Although proponents of the measure point to the important role that parents can play in addressing the problem of alcohol abuse at universities, opponents feel that the measure violates the privacy and independence of students. What do you think?

A former president of Middlebury College, John M. McCardell, Jr., has argued that the best way to combat the problems associated with underage drinking is to allow eighteen to twenty year olds to drink after they have completed an alcohol education program. Paula Wasley, CHRON. HIGHER EDUC., April 6, 2007 at A35–36. Mr. McCardell believes that the current law encourages irresponsible drinking habits among underage students. The measure has drawn support from other university officials who complain that the age–21 law forces them to punish students as opposed to educating them about the proper use of alcohol. *Id.* The age–21 law is supported by Mother's Against Drunk Driving, which claims that, since the age–21 law was adopted, there have been roughly one thousand fewer deaths from drunk driving per year. Mr. McCardell contends that MADD's statistics are flawed, and that other safety measures, including increased use in seatbelts, account for the reduction in alcohol-related automobile fatalities in the past twenty years. *Id.* Do you agree with the McCardell proposal?

4. Bickel and Lake characterize decisions like *Bradshaw* as "cast[ing] the university in the legal and cultural role of helpless 'bystander' to student life and danger." BICKEL & LAKE, THE RIGHTS AND RESPONSIBILITIES OF THE MODERN UNIVERSITY 49 (1999). Do you think this is an accurate characterization? How important in *Bradshaw* was the fact that college students are now considered adults? Should a university be liable for a student's drinking related injury if the student is not yet eighteen? *See, e.g.,* Hartman v. Bethany College, 778 F.Supp. 286, 295 (N.D.W.Va.1991) ("Because no *in loco parentis* relationship exists, the college owes its seventeen year old students no heightened duty" to protect them from drinking related injuries off-campus.).

5. What responsibility does a student who provides alcohol to another student bear if the student becomes ill or dies? In a recent case at Clemson University, three fraternity members were charged with transferring alcohol to a minor after a student died from alcohol poisoning. Meg Kinnard, *3 Charged After Freshman's Alcohol Death*, USA TODAY, Jan. 30, 2008, *available at* http://www.usatoday.com/news/nation/2008–01–30–1921182376_x.htm. Should the students also be civilly liable?

C.   MODERN LIABILITY CASES

Nova Southeastern University v. Gross

Supreme Court of Florida, 2000.
758 So.2d 86.

■ QUINCE, J.

We have for review a decision on the following question certified by the Fourth District Court of Appeal ... to be of great public importance:

> Whether a university may be found liable in tort where it assigns a student to an internship site which it knows to be unreasonably dangerous but gives no warning, or inadequate warning, to the student, and the student is subsequently injured while participating in the internship?

. . .

Bethany Jill Gross, a twenty-three year old graduate student attending Nova Southeastern University, was criminally assaulted while leaving an off-campus internship site. Gross filed a negligence action against Nova based on Nova's alleged negligence in assigning her to perform an internship at a facility which Nova knew was unreasonably dangerous and presented an unreasonable risk of harm. The trial court granted summary judgment for Nova, finding that there was no duty. . . .

The facts, as alleged in the sworn affidavits and other record evidence, and presented in the light most favorable to [Gross], the non-moving party, are briefly summarized as follows. . . . [Gross] moved to Fort Lauderdale from North Carolina to study at Nova Southeastern University in the doctorate psychology program. As part of the curriculum, she was required to complete an eleven-month internship, called a "practicum." Nova provides each student with a listing of the approved practicum sites, complete with a description of the type of experience offered at each site. Each student selects six internships from the list and is placed, by Nova, at one of the selected sites. [Gross] submitted her six selections and was assigned, by Nova, to Family Services Agency, Inc. ("FSA").

. . . One evening, when leaving FSA, [Gross] was accosted by a man in the parking lot. [He pointed a gun at her head just after she started her car. He subsequently abducted, robbed, and sexually assaulted her.] There was evidence that prior to [Gross's] attack, Nova had been made aware of a number of other criminal incidents which had occurred at or near the FSA parking lot. *Gross*, 716 So.2d at 338.[1]

The Fourth District reversed the trial court's summary judgment in favor of Nova. . . . Analysis is necessary in this case only because the injury was caused by the allegedly "foreseeable" acts of a third party.

. . .

Nova argues it did not owe Gross a duty because she was an adult student, and therefore not within the ambit of a special relationship between a school and a minor student. The special relationship doctrine creates a duty between parties, which would not exist but for their relationship. Nova points out that in *Rupp v. Bryant*, 417 So. 2d 658 (Fla. 1982), the Court stated:

> The genesis of this supervisory duty is based on the school employee standing partially in place of the student's parents. Mandatory schooling has forced parents into relying on teachers to protect children during school activity. But our problem is complicated by the fact that the injury did not occur during the school day or on school premises. As such, we must define the scope of the school's and employee's duty to supervise.

Thus, Nova argues it is inappropriate for the Fourth District to find there is a special relationship between a university, where attendance is not mandatory, and an adult student because the university is not standing *in loco parentis* to an adult student. While the Fourth District discussed the special relationship doctrine, the court did not base Nova's duty to Gross on the type of relationship that exists between a minor child and public school officials.

Although Nova is correct that the school-minor student special relationship evolved from the *in loco parentis* doctrine, the district court recognized that any duty owed by Nova to Gross was not the same duty a school and its employees owe to a minor student. The district court further recognized a

---

1. Gross settled her claim against Family Services Agency, Inc. for $900,000.

different relationship existed between the university and its adult students, a relationship which does not necessarily preclude the university from owing a duty to students assigned to mandatory and approved internship programs. In *Rupp*, we said the extent of the duty a school owes to its students should be limited by the amount of control the school has over the student's conduct. Here, the practicums were a mandatory part of the curriculum that the students were required to complete in order to graduate. Nova also had the final say in assigning students to the locations where they were to do their practicums.

As Nova had control over the students' conduct by requiring them to do the practicum and by assigning them to a specific location, it also assumed the Hohfeldian correlative duty[3] of acting reasonably in making those assignments. In a case such as this one, where the university had knowledge that the internship location was unreasonably dangerous, it should be up to the jury to determine whether the university acted reasonably in assigning students to do internships at that location.

Moreover, the Fourth District's analysis is supported by fundamental principles of tort law. In *Union Park Memorial Chapel v. Hutt*, 670 So.2d 64, 66–67 (Fla. 1996), we stated:

> It is clearly established that one who undertakes to act, even when under no obligation to do so, thereby becomes obligated to act with reasonable care. *See Slemp v. City of North Miami*, 545 So.2d 256 (Fla. 1989) (holding that even if city had no general duty to protect property owners from flooding due to natural causes, once city has undertaken to provide such protection, it assumes the responsibility to do so with reasonable care); *Banfield v. Addington*, 104 Fla. 661, 667, 140 So. 893, 896 (1932) (holding that one who undertakes to act is under an implied legal duty to act with reasonable care to ensure that the person or property of others will not be injured as a result of the undertaking); *Kowkabany v. Home Depot, Inc.*, 606 So.2d 716, 721 (Fla. 1st DCA 1992) (holding that by undertaking to safely load landscaping timbers into vehicle, defendant owed duty of reasonable care to bicyclist who was struck by timbers protruding from vehicle window); *Garrison Retirement Home v. Hancock*, 484 So.2d 1257, 1262 (Fla. 4th DCA 1985) (holding that retirement home that assumed and undertook care and supervision of retirement home resident owed duty to third party to exercise reasonable care in supervision of resident's activities). As this Court recognized over sixty years ago in *Banfield v. Addington*, "in every situation where a man undertakes to act, ... he is under an implied legal obligation or duty to act with reasonable care, to the end that the person or property of others may not be injured." *Id.*; *see also Pate v. Threlkel*, 661 So.2d 278, 280 (Fla. 1995) ("A duty is thus established when the acts of a defendant in a particular case create a foreseeable zone of risk."). We find this fundamental principle of tort law is equally applicable in this case. There is no reason why a university may act without regard to the consequences of its actions while

---

3. *See* Wesley Newcomb Hohfeld, *Some Fundamental Legal Conceptions as Applied in Judi-* *cial Reasoning*, 23 YALE L. J. 16 (1913).

every other legal entity is charged with acting as a reasonably prudent person would in like or similar circumstances.

Nova also argues it did not owe Gross a duty because she knew FSA was in a dangerous location, and Nova's knowledge of the dangerous location was not superior to Gross's knowledge. While this is a correct statement of the law with regard to negligence actions based upon premises liability, this is not a premises liability case. Gross is suing Nova under a common law negligence theory based upon Nova assigning her to do her mandatory practicum at an unreasonably dangerous location. Issues of Gross's knowledge should be considered when determining the issues of breach of duty and proximate cause of her injury and in attributing proportional fault. However, it does not eliminate the university's duty to use reasonable care in assigning students to practicum locations.

Lastly, Nova argues even if it had a duty to warn Gross, the failure to warn her did not cause her injury. This argument is one that this Court need not reach but is better left to the trier of fact. In this case, the motion for summary judgment was based solely upon Nova's lack of duty. Therefore, this Court will not consider whether Nova's failure to warn Gross caused her injuries.

Gross cross-petitions for review claiming the Fourth District's emphasis on Nova's failure to warn implies Nova only had a duty to warn. We do not read the Fourth District's opinion so narrowly. The court stated, "We need not go so far as to impose a general duty of supervision, as is common in the school-minor student context, to find that Nova had a duty, in this limited context, to use ordinary care in providing educational services and programs to one of its adult students." We read this statement broadly as an indication that the duty, one of ordinary care under the circumstances, could include but is not necessarily limited to warning of the known dangers at this particular practicum site.

We do not make any specific findings as to what duty Nova owed Gross, other than to hold a jury should determine whether Nova acted reasonably in light of all of the circumstances surrounding the case. As the court said in *Silvers v. Associated Technical Institute, Inc.*, 1994 Mass. Super. LEXIS 506, *8, No. 93–4253 (Mass. Super. Ct. Oct. 12, 1994), "students . . . could reasonably expect that the school's placement office would make some effort to avoid placing [students] with an employer likely to harm them." This is the type of duty owed under the circumstances of this case.

Accordingly, we answer the certified question in the affirmative and approve the decision of the Fourth District.

Questions and Comments on *Nova*

1. For a discussion of *Nova Southeastern* and its implications see Kathleen Connolly Butler, *Shared Responsibility: The Duty to Legal Externs*, 106 W. VA L. REV. 51 (2003). For more information on liability for crime on and off campus, see Oren R. Griffin, *Confronting the Evolving Safety and Security Challenge at Colleges and Universities*, 5 PIERCE L. REV. 413 (2007).

2. The Supreme Court of Florida rejected the argument that Nova Southeastern University owed no duty to Gross because of the demise of the *in loco parentis* doctrine. Does the court's holding mean that colleges will no longer be treated differently from businesses on the subject of liability?

Kleisch v. Cleveland State University

Ohio Court of Appeals, Tenth Appellate District, 2006.
2006 Ohio 1300, 2006 WL 701047.

■ Petree, J.

Plaintiff-appellant, Marie G. Kleisch, appeals from a judgment of the Court of Claims of Ohio in favor of defendant-appellee, Cleveland State University ("university" or "CSU"). . . .

At approximately 9 a.m. in the morning on August 3, 2001, a stranger attacked and raped plaintiff, who at that time was a CSU student and was studying in a university lecture hall for a final examination that was to be held there approximately one hour later that same day. Thereafter, in July 2003, alleging four causes of action and seeking declaratory relief and monetary damages, plaintiff sued the university, university police, and the university's chief of police in both his official and individual capacity. In her complaint, plaintiff claimed, among other things, that: (1) the university's chief of police acted with malice, in bad faith, or in a wanton or reckless manner and, consequently he was not entitled to civil immunity under R.C. 9.86 and 2743.02(F); (2) the university and university police were negligent under the common law and under the doctrine of *res ipsa loquitur*; and (3) the university and university police violated R.C. 4101.11, thereby breaching a duty of care toward plaintiff.

After a bench trial wherein the issues of liability and damages were bifurcated, the trial court found that the university's chief of police was entitled to civil immunity and the trial court also rendered judgment in favor of the university. From the trial court's judgment, plaintiff now appeals. In this appeal, plaintiff does not challenge the trial court's determination that the university's chief of police was entitled to civil immunity under R.C. 9.86 and former 2743.02(F).

Plaintiff assigns a single error for our consideration:

The trial court erred as a matter of law by finding that a rape of a state college student in a classroom during business hours was not foreseeable and by finding that appellant failed to prove any duty owed to her that proximately caused her injury.

. . .

Under Ohio common law of premises liability, the status of the person who enters upon the land of another, specifically, trespasser, licensee, or invitee, defines the scope of the legal duty that a landowner owes the entrant.

"A trespasser is one who, without express or implied authorization, invitation or inducement, enters private premises purely for his own purposes or convenience." By comparison, "invitees are persons who rightfully come upon the premises of another by invitation, express or implied, for some purpose which is beneficial to the owner." . . .

Here, plaintiff was a CSU student at the time of the rape and was studying in a classroom on the CSU campus in preparation for a final examination that was to be held there later in the morning. We therefore conclude that plaintiff's presence on university property afforded her the status of an invitee, and, as a consequence, the university owed plaintiff a duty " 'to exercise ordinary care and to protect [her] by maintaining the premises in a safe condition.' "

By her sole assignment of error, plaintiff suggests, among other things, that the trial court found that the university did not owe any duty toward plaintiff. Rather than finding an absence of duty, the trial court in fact found that plaintiff failed to prove that defendant breached any duty owed to plaintiff. In its decision, the trial court stated: "The court finds that plaintiff failed to prove that defendant breached any duty owed to her that proximately caused her injury." Thus, to the extent that plaintiff contends that the trial court found that the university owed no duty of care toward plaintiff, such a contention is not supported by the plain language of the trial court's judgment.

.   .   .

In *Simpson v. Big Bear Stores Co.* (Dec. 30, 1993), Franklin App. No. 93AP–852, 1993 Ohio App. LEXIS 6250, *aff'd* (1995), 73 Ohio St.3d 130, 1995 Ohio 203, 652 N.E.2d 702, this court explained:

> ... Under Ohio law, ordinarily no duty exists to prevent a third person from harming another unless a "special relationship" exists between the actor and the other. *Gelbman v. Second Natl. Bank of Warren* (1984), 9 Ohio St. 3d 77, 9 Ohio B. 280, 458 N.E.2d 1262 (adopting 2 Restatement of the Law 2d, Torts (1965) 122, Section 315(b)). Such a "special relationship" exists between a business and its business invitees. *Reitz v. May Co. Dept. Stores* (1990), 66 Ohio App. 3d 188, 583 N.E.2d 1071; *see also,* Restatement, *supra,* at 118, Section 314(A); Restatement, *supra,* at 123, Section 315, Comment c. Thus, a business may be subject to liability for harm caused to a business invitee by the criminal conduct of third persons. *Rogers, supra; Taylor v. Dixon* (1982), 8 Ohio App.3d 161, 8 Ohio B. 219, 456 N.E.2d 558; *see* Restatement, *supra,* at 223–226, Section 344. Nonetheless, a business is not an insurer of the safety of its business invitees while they are on its premises. *Rogers, supra,* at paragraph two of the syllabus. Consequently, a business has a duty to warn or protect its business invitees from criminal acts of third persons only where the business knows or should know in the exercise of ordinary care that such acts present a danger to its business invitees. *Rogers, supra,* at paragraph three of the syllabus; *Reitz, supra,* at 191.

Applying *Simpson,* the inquiry here is whether plaintiff's rape was reasonably foreseeable and whether the university breached a duty of ordinary care by failing to take measures to protect plaintiff from being attacked and raped by a stranger.

Ordinarily, whether a defendant properly discharged a duty of care and whether a breach of a duty of care proximately caused plaintiff's injuries are questions for the trier of fact.

In this appeal, although not expressly claiming that the trial court's judgment is against the manifest weight of the evidence, we find that plaintiff's argument advances such a claim. As to civil judgments, "judgments supported by some competent, credible evidence going to all the essential elements of the case will not be reversed by a reviewing court as being against the manifest weight of the evidence." When considering whether a judgment is against the manifest weight of the evidence, an appellate court is guided by a presumption that the findings of the trier of fact were correct. "An appellate court should not substitute its judgment for that of the trial court when there exists ... competent and credible evidence supporting the findings of fact and conclusions of law...."

Here, the trial court concluded that "after careful consideration of all the testimony and other evidence presented, the court finds that it was not foreseeable that plaintiff would be raped in a classroom on a weekday morning when final examinations were going to be held."

Relying heavily upon plaintiff's expert's opinion, plaintiff contends that her rape was foreseeable for the following reasons: (1) the university police department is undermanned as there are only approximately three to five officers on duty during each shift, and these officers must patrol a campus that is located in a high-risk crime area and that spans approximately 85 acres and approximately 38 buildings; (2) under such circumstances, a deployment of approximately three to five officers per shift cannot adequately secure campus buildings; (3) because a deployment of approximately three to five officers per shift cannot adequately secure the campus, university classrooms should be locked when classes are not in session; (4) classrooms at the university had existing hardware that allowed classrooms to be locked when they were not in use; (5) although classrooms were able to be locked, the university failed to lock classrooms when they were not in use and failed to have a policy requiring classrooms to be locked when they were not in use; (6) due to the classroom's design and construction, the unlocked classroom where the rape occurred was isolated and nearly soundproof and, therefore, more susceptible to criminal activity; (7) although university police locked exterior doors at night after classes ended, interior rooms were not searched and, therefore, potential intruders could remain in university buildings undetected after classes ended; and (8) the amount of violent crime at the university purportedly was underreported, was not consistent with the requirements of the Clery Act,[9] and this purported underreporting conveyed a false sense of security to students and prospective students.

Relying upon its own expert witness, the university disputes plaintiff's contention that plaintiff's rape was foreseeable. According to the university, prior to plaintiff's rape, the last rape at the campus occurred approximately 16 months earlier at a separate but connected building from where plaintiff was raped. Moreover, the university contends that the circumstances of the earlier rape differed from the rape at issue. For example, in the previous rape, a rapist attacked a woman in a women's restroom; here, plaintiff's attacker assaulted plaintiff in a classroom, which is a more open environment than a restroom. The university also asserts that the manner in which its police personnel are allocated and the university police's procedures are discretionary and, therefore, decisions concerning the allocation of university police personnel and procedures of the university police are protected by discretionary immunity. *See, e.g., Reynolds v. State, Div. of Parole & Community Services* (1984), 14 Ohio St.3d 68, 70, 14 Ohio B. 506, 471 N.E.2d 776 (construing a former version of R.C. 2743.02 to mean "that the state cannot

---

9. *See, generally,* Section 1092, Title 20, U.S.Code. *See also, Allocco v. Coral Gables* (S.D. Fla. 2002), 221 F.Supp.2d 1317, fn. 12, affirmed (2003), 88 Fed. Appx. 380 (stating that "the Clery Act, 20 U.S.C. § 1092, requires United States colleges and universities to collect and publish data on student safety, campus security policies, and campus crime statistics").

be sued for its legislative or judicial functions or the exercise of an executive or planning function involving the making of a basic policy decision which is characterized by the exercise of a high degree of official judgment or discretion").

"Ohio courts are split on the appropriate test for foreseeability." *Whisman v. Gator Invest. Properties, Inc.*, 149 Ohio App.3d 225, 2002 Ohio 1850, at P24, 776 N.E.2d 1126, citing *Heys v. Blevins* (June 13, 1997), Montgomery App. No. 16291, 1997 Ohio App. LEXIS 2536. As the *Whisman* court explained: "The totality-of-the-circumstances test takes into consideration not only past experiences but also 'such factors as the location of the business and the character of the business to determine whether the danger was foreseeable.' " "Under this test, the totality of the circumstances must be 'somewhat overwhelming' to result in a duty to protect third parties against criminal acts of others." However, "under the other test, 'the occurrence of prior similar acts suggests that the danger was foreseeable.' "

. . .

Here, the evidence suggests that in the four or five years prior to plaintiff's rape, only one rape occurred on the university campus, and this rape occurred in a restroom in a building adjacent to the building where plaintiff was raped approximately one year and four months prior to plaintiff's rape.

Recognizing that the university was not an absolute insurer of plaintiff's safety and that criminal behavior by third persons is not predictable to any particular degree of certainty, we cannot conclude that a rape at CSU nearly one and one-half years before plaintiff's rape is sufficient as a matter of law to give the university reason to know that plaintiff likely would be raped in a classroom while she studied at 9 a.m. in the morning for a final examination. We therefore cannot conclude in this case that the totality of the circumstances is somewhat overwhelming such that the requisite foreseeability was established to hold the university liable for breaching a duty of care toward plaintiff.

Furthermore, we cannot conclude that the trial court's judgment was against the manifest weight of the evidence. When questioned whether, from a security standpoint, the occurrence of a rape approximately one and one-half years before plaintiff's rape mandated a change in university security policy, defendant's expert witness testified:

I think it could, but not necessarily.

. . .

... I think it depends on the circumstances of the event. As I recall, the previous rape had occurred in a restroom in an adjacent building. This occurred in a classroom facility, which was typically an open environment.

The university's expert witness also testified, as follows:

Q.   [By Assistant Attorney General Tracy M. Greuel] Okay. Is there anything unique about the crime of rape in general that mandates special security concerns, or is there anything special that can be done to prevent it?

A. Well, that's kind of an open question. But the answer is there are—there certainly are things that can be done to prevent rape, but not always. Not every crime is preventable. In the case of rape, part of the solution is to be aware of these situations when they come up and to have—when the opportunity exists, to have police involved and extra patrols and so forth, if there's something to look for, a suspect to be had. But more importantly, to disseminate the information to students and staff so that people are aware that this has occurred, and these are the things that one should watch out for, and these are the steps that one might take to prevent that—or to avoid from being put in that situation.

Defendant's expert further testified that the university's crime prevention program was viable. Defendant's expert testified:

> ... I thought they presented the information that the police department needs to present to its students, faculty, staff, and visitors. I thought it was easy to get the information. I liked the fact that they had a program for new students and that they require new students to attend that program. So I thought they did a good job in disseminating that information to their population.

Ultimately, defendant's expert witness opined to a reasonable degree of professional certainty that the university complied with requirements under the Clery Act and that it had acceptable standards and best practices in place at the time of plaintiff's rape.

We find defendant's expert's testimony, if believed by the trial court, as the trier of fact, constitutes some competent, credible evidence to support the trial court's judgment that defendant did not breach any duty of care toward plaintiff, notwithstanding the trial court's view that plaintiff was a victim and a very believable witness.

Accordingly ... we overrule plaintiff's sole assignment of error and affirm the judgment of the Court of Claims of Ohio.

Questions and Comments on *Kleisch*

1. *Compare Kleisch with* Nero v. Kansas State Univ., 253 Kan. 567, 861 P.2d 768 (1993). In *Nero*, a student was raped in the laundry room of her co-ed dormitory by a male student who previously had been accused of raping another student on campus. The university was aware of the previous allegation of rape and had taken steps to separate the male student from female student dorms. The court held that the university had a legal duty to protect students living on campus from foreseeable criminal conduct and remanded the case for trial. *See also* Mullins v. Pine Manor College, 389 Mass. 47, 449 N.E.2d 331, 335–36 (1983) (despite the decline of *in loco parentis*, "[p]arents, students, and the general community still have a reasonable expectation, fostered in part by colleges themselves, that reasonable care will be exercised to protect resident students from foreseeable harm."). When does a crime become reasonably foreseeable?

2. Does a specific pattern of rape or sexual assault have to occur before the university needs to take steps to protect its students? Should a university be required to take affirmative steps to educate female students about the dangers they may face? In *Stanton v. University of Maine System*, 773 A.2d 1045 (Me. 2001), the Maine Supreme Court noted that "the concentration of young people, especially young women, on a college campus, creates a favorable opportunity for criminal behavior" and "that many of the students tend to be away from home for the first time and may not be fully conscious of the dangers that are present ... thus that the threat of criminal behavior is self-evident." *Id.* at 1050. The court found that the university had a "duty to reasonably warn and advise students of steps they could take to improve their personal safety." *Id.*

3. In contrast, in *Tanja H. v. Regents of University of California*, 228 Cal.App.3d 434, 278 Cal.Rptr. 918 (1991), when the appellant, a female college student who was the victim of a gang rape at a party on campus, pointed to statistics demonstrating the widespread nature of sexual assault at universities, the court dismissed the statistics as being irrelevant to whether the university could be held liable. The court explained:

> College students are generally young adults who do not always have a mature understanding of their own limitations or the dangers posed by alcohol and violence. However, the courts have not been willing to require college administrators to reinstitute curfews, bed checks, dormitory searches, hall monitors, chaperons, and the other concomitant measures which would be necessary in order to suppress the use of intoxicants and protect students from each other.... In this respect, a university in its residual role as the operator of a dormitory used as living quarters by students is more akin to an innkeeper, who does not have a duty to search guests for contraband, separate them from each other, or monitor their private social activities.

Id. at 921.

Which court is correct? Should universities be required to take affirmative steps to protect or warn students? Or are they just educational innkeepers? Is it possible to strike a balance between the position taken in *Tanja H.* and a full blown return to *in loco parentis*?

4. After a highly publicized sex scandal at the Air Force Academy in 2004, Congress launched an investigation into sexual harassment at the military academies. Paul Fain, *Military Academies Have Made Progress in Dealing with Sexual Assault, Pentagon Report Finds*, CHRON. HIGHER EDUC., Dec. 10, 2007, *available at* http://chronicle.com/daily/2007/12/930n.htm. The Congressional investigation revealed that, prior to the scandal, over two-thirds of cases of sexual assault and harassment in the military academies went unreported. *Id.* In response, the academies launched an educational campaign and instituted a new system that allows cadets to report incidents of sexual assault confidentially, without triggering official investigations or criminal prosecutions. A recent report from the Pentagon suggests that the changes have led to fewer sexual assaults and a heightened sense of safety in the academies, though some cadets still worry about the possibility of reprisal if they report an incident. *Id.*

5. How will the mass shootings at Virginia Tech transform the nature and scope of universities' liability for crimes against students? Peter Lake, the director of the Center for Excellence in Higher Education Law and Policy at Stetson University College of Law, argues that the incident will accelerate a trend toward the "application of general principles of business-liability law to colleges." Peter Lake, *Higher Education Called to Account*, CHRON. HIGHER EDUC., June 29, 2007, at B6. Institutions of higher education no longer can assume that their special status will shield them from liability. Lake cites six specific consequences of this trend for colleges and universities: (1) "[c]ourts will require colleges to provide reasonably safe campus environments for their students and other people by attending to foreseeable dangers"; (2) security officials will need to work together with resident staff members and other university officials to recognize dangers in advance; (3) colleges will have to comply with the law of agency, i.e., it will be assumed that what the employee knows is known to the college; (4) colleges can no longer hide behind the "no duty" argument of *Bradshaw*, but rather must always assume and act as if a duty of care is owed to its students and other persons; (5) college mental-health officials will need to recognize circumstances in which safety concerns trump confidentiality and privacy; (6) colleges will continue to face the indeterminacy of the law surrounding their liability for student suicide. *Id.* at B7. Do you agree?

Note on Obligations to Visitors to Campus

When a non-student visitor sues for injuries that occurred on campus, the outcome often turns on whether the visitor is classified as a trespasser, a licensee, or an invitee. Traditionally, the common law drew a distinction between these categories to determine the level of care that a landowner was required to provide an entrant onto his land. Thus, with respect to a trespasser or licensee, the landowner was not liable for ordinary negligence, but only for injuries caused by willful, wanton, or intentional conduct. Landowners owe a further duty to a licensee to use reasonable care if the landowner expects the licensee will "not discover or realize the danger." Generally, an invitee enters the land on the understanding that reasonable care has been used to ensure his safety. In order to qualify as an invitee, the plaintiff must have been invited to enter the land for a purpose connected with business dealings with the possessor of the land. In some states, a person entering land for a purpose for which the land is held open to the public is considered a "public invitee." A licensee, on the other hand, is a person that the landowner has merely permitted to access the land. Although many states have moved away from the common law system, some continue to follow the common law rules. *See* Robert S. Driscoll, Note, *The Law of Premises Liability in America: Its Past, Present, and Some Considerations for its Future*, 82 NOTRE DAME L. REV. 881 (2006) (reviewing the policies behind the common law distinctions and the reasons some states have abandoned them); David M. Dumas, Note, *Defective Buildings and Grounds—A Dangerous Condition for Colleges and Universities*, 17 J.C. & U.L. 351, 357–66 (1991) (applying the concept of premises liability to the relationship of a college or university to its students).

In the states that still use the common law distinctions, liability for college and university campuses largely depends on how the court defines the legal status of the visitor. *See, e.g.,* Osadchy v. Southern Methodist Univ., 232 S.W.3d 844 (Tex. App. 2007) (holding that university owed no duty to a member of the Dallas Chamber Orchestra because he was merely a licensee); Blust v. Berea Coll., 431 F.Supp.2d 703 (E.D. Ky. 2006) (college owed no duty to warn licensee of the danger of falling from a cliff on campus because the cliff was "open and obvious").

Williams v. Board of Regents of the University System of Georgia

United States Court of Appeals, Eleventh Circuit, 2007.
477 F.3d 1282.

■ KRAVITCH, CIRCUIT JUDGE:

The primary question in this appeal is whether petitioner, a student at the University of Georgia, alleged facts sufficient to withstand defendants' motion to dismiss her Title IX claim based on student-on-student sexual harassment.

Here, as alleged in her complaint, at approximately 9:00 p.m. on January 14, 2002, Tiffany Williams ("Williams"), then a student at the University of Georgia ("UGA"), received a telephone call from UGA basketball player Tony Cole. Cole invited Williams to his room in McWhorter Hall, the main dormitory for student-athletes on the university campus. Shortly after Williams arrived at Cole's room, the two engaged in consensual sex. Unbeknownst to Williams, Brandon Williams, a UGA football player, whom Williams did not know, was hiding in Cole's closet. Cole and Brandon had previously agreed that Brandon would hide in the closet while Cole had sex with Williams. When Cole went to the bathroom and slammed the door behind him, Brandon emerged from the closet naked, sexually assaulted Williams, and attempted to rape her.

As Brandon was sexually assaulting Williams, Cole was on the telephone with Steven Thomas, Cole's teammate, and Charles Grant, Brandon Williams's teammate. Cole told Thomas and Grant that they were "running a train" on Williams.[3] Thomas came to Cole's room, and Cole allowed Thomas to enter the room. With Cole's encouragement, Thomas sexually assaulted and raped Williams.

[Williams returned to her dormitory at 11:00 p.m. and called a friend, Jennifer Shaughnessy. Shaughnessy came to William's room and found her visibly upset and crying. After Williams described the earlier incident, Shaughnessy encouraged Williams to call the police and report a rape, but Williams did not because she was afraid. While Shaughnessy was in William's room, Thomas called twice and attempted to speak with Williams.]

Williams then called her mother, who notified UGA Police of the incident that occurred in Cole's room. UGA Police arrived at Williams's room shortly after 1:00 a.m. on January 15 and arranged for Williams to have a sexual assault exam performed. Later that same day, Williams requested that UGA Police process the charges against Cole, Brandon Williams, and Thomas. After filing her complaint with UGA Police, Williams permanently withdrew from UGA.

UGA Police conducted an investigation, as part of which, the police obtained Cole's telephone records. The records show that Cole called Williams's dorm room several times in the days immediately following the incident and Williams's withdrawal. Within forty-eight hours of the incident, UGA's Chief of Police notified UGA's Director of Judicial Programs of the incident and provided her with a written explanation. On April 17, 2002, a lieutenant from UGA Police provided the Director of Judicial Programs with additional information about the investigation. Several of the individuals who spoke with UGA Police supported Williams's allegations.

The actions of Cole, Brandon Williams, and Thomas constitute sexual harassment under the Sexual Harassment Policy of the University of Georgia. The policy applicable in January 2002, however, provided that "[s]exual harassment between students, neither of whom is employed by the University should be treated as a disciplinary matter and should be reported to the Office of Student Affairs" and not dealt with under the Sexual Harassment Policy. Cole, Brandon Williams, and Thomas were charged with disorderly conduct under UGA's Code of Conduct. Additionally, their coaches suspended them from their sports teams after an Athens–Clarke County grand jury indicted them in early April 2002.[4] A UGA judiciary panel, consisting of one staff member and two university students, held hearings almost a year after the January 2002 incident and decided not to sanction Cole, Brandon Williams, or Thomas. By the time of the hearing, Cole and Brandon Williams no longer attended UGA. Thomas left UGA in September 2003. The three also faced criminal charges, but a jury acquitted Brandon

---

3. "Running a train" is a slang expression for a gang rape.

4. Williams alleges that Cole and Thomas did not suffer any negative consequences as a result of the suspension because the basket-ball season had already ended when they were indicted and that Brandon Williams suffered little or no adversity as the spring football season ended a few days after the indictment.

Williams, and the prosecutor dismissed the charges against Cole and Thomas.

Williams's complaint also alleges that defendants James Harrick, former head coach of UGA's men's basketball team, Vincent Dooley, Athletic Director of the University of Georgia Athletic Association ("UGAA"), and Michael Adams, President of UGA and UGAA, were personally involved in recruiting and admitting Cole even though they knew he previously had disciplinary and criminal problems, particularly those involving harassment of women, at other colleges.

While coaching the men's basketball team at the University of Rhode Island ("URI"), Harrick recruited Cole to attend URI. When Cole could not gain admission to URI, Harrick helped Cole gain admission to the Community College of Rhode Island ("CCRI"). Cole was eventually dismissed from CCRI after allegations that in December 1999 and February 2000 he sexually assaulted two part-time employees of the college's athletic department by groping the women, putting his hands down their pants, and threatening them when they rejected his advances. Cole pleaded no contest to criminal charges of misdemeanor trespass in connection with the two sexual assaults.[5]

Furthermore, while attending Wabash Valley College ("WVC") in Mount Carmel, Illinois, Cole was dismissed from the basketball team because of disciplinary problems, including an incident in which he whistled at and made lewd suggestions to a female store clerk. Adams, Harrick, and Dooley knew of the incident when they recruited and admitted Cole. By the time Cole was dismissed from WVC, Harrick was at UGA and again recruited Cole. Because Cole did not meet UGA's standards for admission, Harrick requested that Adams admit Cole through UGA's special admissions policy. Adams is the sole decision maker when admitting an applicant under the special admissions policy. Cole was admitted to attend UGA on a full scholarship.

Finally, Williams alleges that UGA officials received suggestions from student-athletes that coaches needed to inform the student-athletes about UGA's sexual harassment policy. Despite Adams's and Dooley's duties to ensure student-athletes' compliance with UGA's policy, UGA and UGAA failed to ensure that the student-athletes received adequate information concerning UGA's sexual harassment policy applicable to student-athletes and failed to enforce the policy against football and basketball players.

Williams brought suit against: (1) UGA, the Board of Regents of the University System of Georgia ("Board of Regents"), and UGAA for violation of Title IX; (2) Adams, Harrick, and Dooley as individuals and in their official capacities as UGA and UGAA President, former head basketball coach, and Athletic Director of UGAA for violation of 42 U.S.C. § 1983; (3) UGA and the Board of Regents for violation of 42 U.S.C. § 1983; and (4) Cole, Brandon Williams, and Thomas for state law torts. She also sought "injunctive relief ordering the defendants to implement policies, and procedures to protect students like Plaintiff from student-on-student sexual harassment prohibited by Title IX."

---

5. Additionally, Adams, Harrick, and Dooley knew about several other violent incidents involving Cole, such as Cole's May 2001 arrest for violating a protective order that his foster mother requested after he assaulted one of her friends and an incident in prep school when Cole punched another player in the face during a game.

UGA, UGAA, the Board of Regents, Adams, Harrick, and Dooley all filed motions to dismiss Williams's claims. Williams then moved to amend her complaint, adding additional factual allegations to support her claims, providing a more specific request for injunctive relief, and requesting declaratory relief against UGA, UGAA, and the Board of Regents. . . . [T]he district court dismissed all the claims.

Williams now appeals. After a thorough review of the record and the benefit of oral argument, we reverse the district court's decisions to dismiss Williams's Title IX claims against UGA and UGAA and to deny Williams's motion to amend her complaint. In all other respects, we affirm the district court.

. . .

This case presents a factually distinct scenario from our and the Supreme Court's precedents. In each of those cases, the defendant did not learn about the alleged harasser's proclivities until the alleged harasser became a teacher or a student at the defendant's school. *Davis v. Monroe County Bd. of Educ.*, 526 U.S. 629 (1999) (student); *Gebser v. Lago Vista Indep. Sch. Dist.*, 524 U.S. 274 (1998) (teacher); *Hawkins v. Sarasota County Sch. Bd.*, 322 F.3d 1279 (11th Cir. 2003) (student). Here, however, Williams has alleged that Adams, Dooley, and Harrick knew about Cole's past sexual misconduct when they recruited him and gained his admission to UGA. Furthermore, UGA and UGAA knew about student-athletes' suggestions that the athletic coaches should inform student-athletes about the applicable sexual harassment policy. Although, a Title IX recipient cannot be held liable for misconduct that occurred before the alleged harasser was affiliated with the recipient, as we explain later, Adams, Dooley, and Harrick's preexisting knowledge of Cole's past sexual misconduct and the student-athletes' suggestions are relevant when determining whether Williams alleged facts sufficient to survive the defendants' motion to dismiss her Title IX complaint.

Title IX states, in pertinent part: "No person . . . shall, on the basis of sex, be excluded from participation in, be denied the benefits of, or be subjected to discrimination under any education program or activity receiving Federal financial assistance." 20 U.S.C. § 1681(a). Although Title IX does not expressly permit private enforcement suits, the Supreme Court has found an implied private right of action for individuals to enforce the mandates of Title IX. *Cannon v. Univ. of Chi.*, 441 U.S. 677 (1979). The Court also has held that private individuals can obtain monetary damages. *Franklin v. Gwinnett County Pub. Sch.*, 503 U.S. 60, 76 (1992).

" '[S]exual harassment' is 'discrimination' in the school context under Title IX" and in certain narrow circumstances, a plaintiff may be able to recover for student-on-student harassment. *Davis v. Monroe County Bd. of Educ.*, 526 U.S. 629, 650 (1999). A plaintiff seeking recovery for a violation of Title IX based on student-on-student harassment must prove four elements. First, the defendant must be a Title IX funding recipient. Second, an "appropriate person" must have actual knowledge of the discrimination or harassment the plaintiff alleges occurred. *Gebser v. Lago Vista Indep. Sch. Dist.*, 524 U.S. 274, 290 (1998). "[A]n 'appropriate person' . . . is, at a minimum, an official of the recipient entity with authority to take corrective action to end the discrimination." Third, a funding recipient is liable for student-on-student harassment only if "the funding recipient acts with deliberate indifference to known acts of harassment in its programs or activities." *Davis*, 526 U.S. at 633. In considering this element, we analyze the conduct of the funding recipient, not the alleged harasser; we do this to ensure that we hold the funding recipient liable only if the funding recipient's deliberate indifference "subjected" the plaintiff to discrimination. Therefore, we will not hold a funding recipient liable solely because a person affiliated with the funding recipient discriminated against or harassed the plaintiff. Fourth, the discrimination must be "so severe, pervasive, and objectively offensive that it effectively bars the victim's access to an educational opportunity or benefit." *Davis*, 526 U.S. at 633.

As an initial matter, we hold that the district court properly dismissed Williams's Title IX claim against the Board of Regents. Even if we construe Williams's initial complaint and first amended complaint broadly and construe all the allegations in her favor, we cannot find any allegations that an "appropriate person" with the Board of Regents had "actual knowledge of discrimination in the recipient's programs and fail[ed] adequately to respond." ...

Turning to the Title IX claims against UGA and UGAA, for the reasons that follow, we hold that the district court erred in dismissing those claims.

As to the first element, the parties agree that UGA is a funding recipient properly subject to Title IX liability. [UGAA disputes that it is a funding recipient because it receives federal funds only indirectly, through the UGA.] We are persuaded, however, ... that if we allowed funding recipients to cede control over their programs to indirect funding recipients but did not hold indirect funding recipients liable for Title IX violations, we would allow funding recipients to receive federal funds but avoid Title IX liability. *Cmtys. for Equity v. Mich. High Sch. Athletic Ass'n*, 80 F. Supp. 2d 729, 733–34 (W.D. Mich. 2000). We hold that Williams's complaint sufficiently alleges this element, and we leave for the discovery process and the district court to determine whether to treat UGAA like a funding recipient.

As to the second element, we agree with Williams that an "appropriate person" at both UGA and UGAA had actual knowledge of the harassment. According to Williams, Adams, the President of UGA and UGAA, and Dooley, the Athletic Director of UGAA, had actual knowledge of the three forms of discrimination or harassment that Williams allegedly faced: (1) Cole's recruitment and admission despite his past misconduct at several other schools; (2) the January 14, 2002 incident involving Cole, Brandon Williams, and Thomas; and (3) the discrimination that Williams faced as a result of UGA's failure to respond adequately to her allegations against Cole, Brandon Williams, and Thomas. Additionally, Williams has sufficiently alleged—and Adams and Dooley do not dispute—that Adams and Dooley had authority to take corrective measures for UGA and UGAA to end the alleged discrimination. Thus, we must turn to the final two elements of a Title IX cause of action.

The *Davis* Court held that funding recipients are deliberately indifferent "only where the recipient's response to the harassment or lack thereof is clearly unreasonable in light of the known circumstances." ... Williams has alleged sufficient facts in her complaint to demonstrate that UGA and UGAA were deliberately indifferent to the alleged discrimination and that the district court erred in concluding that [UGA and UGAA's] response was "not 'clearly unreasonable' as a matter of law."

The factual distinctiveness of this case is most relevant when determining whether UGA and UGAA were deliberately indifferent to the alleged discrimination. In *Gebser*, the Supreme Court adopted the deliberate indifference standard for determining when a Title IX recipient would be liable for teacher-on-student harassment, and in *Davis*, adopted the same standard for determining liability for student-on-student harassment. Prior to *Gebser*, the Court adopted the deliberate indifference standard when determining a municipality's liability "for claims under § 1983 alleging that a municipality's actions in failing to prevent a deprivation of federal rights was the cause of the violation." In adopting the deliberate indifference standard in Title IX cases that do not involve allegations of discrimination resulting from the Title IX recipient's official policy, the *Gebser* Court noted that "comparable considerations"—namely, to impose liability only for official decisions by the defendant not to remedy the violation and not for the independent actions of employees—supported the use of the deliberate indifference standard in both Title IX and § 1983 municipality liability cases.

In the municipality liability context, this circuit has held that a plaintiff can show deliberate indifference by proving that "the municipality knew of a need to ... supervise in a particular area and the municipality made a deliberate choice not to take any action." *Gold v. City of Miami*, 151 F.3d 1346, 1350–51 (11th Cir. 1998). This precedent guides our decision here to the extent that we deal with a scenario that is factually distinct from *Gebser*, *Davis*, and *Hawkins*, but we stress that Title IX has important requirements for establishing deliberate indifference that cannot be scuttled simply because the plaintiff can meet the standard applicable to municipality liability cases.

First, Title IX requires that the plaintiff prove that the deliberate indifference occurred in response to discrimination she faced. *Davis*, 526 U.S. at 633. Second, as *Davis* requires, a Title IX recipient may not be liable for damages unless its deliberate indifference "subject[s]" its students to harassment. That is, the deliberate indifference must, at a minimum, "cause [students] to undergo" harassment or "make them liable or vulnerable" to it. *Id.* at 644–45. Based on the *Davis* Court's language, we hold that a Title IX plaintiff at the motion to dismiss stage must allege that the Title IX recipient's deliberate indifference to the initial discrimination subjected the plaintiff to further discrimination.

As stated earlier, Adams, Dooley, and Harrick's decision to recruit Cole and admit him through UGA's special admission process was a form of discrimination that Williams suffered. According to Williams, Adams, Dooley, and Harrick knew at that point of the need to supervise Cole for two reasons. First, UGA and UGAA officials had received suggestions from student-athletes that UGA and UGAA ensure that athletic coaches inform their athletes about the sexual harassment policy applicable to student-athletes. Second, and more importantly, Williams alleges that Adams, Harrick, and Dooley knew about Cole's past sexual misconduct. Nevertheless ... UGA and UGAA failed to adequately supervise Cole. Williams's allegations of UGA and UGAA's failures are sufficient at this stage to establish deliberate indifference under our municipality liability precedent. But to satisfy our Title IX precedent, Williams must go further and sufficiently allege that the deliberate indifference subjected her to further discrimination.

Williams meets the Title IX standard through her allegations regarding the January 14 incident.... By placing Cole in a student dormitory and failing to supervise him in any way or to inform him of their expectations of him under the applicable sexual harassment policy, UGA and UGAA substantially increased the risk faced by female students at UGA.

Furthermore, viewing the evidence in the light most favorable to Williams, UGA acted with deliberate indifference again when it responded to the January 14 incident. Although UGA Police seem to have performed a thorough investigation, UGA failed to provide an adequate response. Within forty-eight hours of the incident, UGA had a preliminary report providing details about the incident, and by April 2002, had a full report, including information about interviews with suspects and witnesses, from UGA Police. Nevertheless, UGA waited another eight months before conducting a disciplinary hearing to determine whether to sanction the alleged assailants. By that point, two of the alleged assailants no longer attended UGA....

Once again, UGA's deliberate indifference was followed by further discrimination, this time in the form of effectively denying Williams an opportunity to continue to attend UGA. Although Williams withdrew from UGA the day after the January 14 incident, we do not believe that at this stage her withdrawal should foreclose her argument that UGA continued to subject her to discrimination.... Viewing the evidence in the light most favorable to Williams, UGA failed to take any precautions that would prevent future attacks from Cole, Thomas, Brandon Williams, or like-minded hooligans should Williams have decided to return to UGA, either by, for example, removing from student housing or suspending the alleged assailants, or implementing a more protective sexual harassment policy to deal with future incidents. Considering what had already occurred, UGA's failure was inexplicable and discriminatory.

... Placed together, Williams's allegations that she faced several forms of harassment and that UGA and UGAA repeatedly responded with deliberate indifference are sufficient to meet Williams's burden on a motion to dismiss.

As for the first part of the final element, we conclude that the discrimination was "severe, pervasive, and objectively offensive." "Whether gender-oriented conduct rises to the level of actionable 'harassment' thus 'depends on a constellation of surrounding circumstances, expectation, and relationships,' including, but not limited to, the ages of the harasser and the victim and the number of individuals involved." "[T]o have a 'systemic effect' of denying the victim equal access to an educational program or activity ... gender discrimination must be more widespread than a single instance of one-on-one peer harassment...." *Hawkins*, 322 F.3d at 1289 (citing *Davis*, 526 U.S. at 652–53).

According to Williams's allegations, a conspiracy between at least two of the alleged perpetrators began before she entered Cole's room because Brandon Williams was already in Cole's closet, with Cole's permission and without her knowledge, when she entered the room. Viewing the allegations in the light most favorable to Williams, Cole and Brandon agreed before Williams arrived that Brandon would emerge from the closet and attempt to have sex with Williams once she and Cole finished having sex. Then, during Brandon's sexual assault of Williams, Cole called Thomas and Charles Grant and invited them to continue "running a train" on Williams. Even though Williams successfully fended off Brandon's attempted rape, the situation worsened further when Thomas arrived and raped her. Moreover, Thomas later telephoned her twice.

The January 14 events differ markedly from the rarely actionable, theoretical single incident mentioned in *Davis* and *Hawkins*. The incident involved a ringleader who lured the victim to his territory and then conspired with two friends to commit two separate acts of sexual assault and so constitutes a continuous series of events. Although occurring in one room over two hours, the acts are sufficient to meet the requirements of severity and objective offensiveness. Based upon these facts, together with the discrimination that occurred before and after the incident, we conclude that Williams has alleged sufficient facts at this stage to show that the discrimination was pervasive.

This leaves us to resolve whether the discrimination "effectively bar[red] the victim's access to an educational opportunity or benefit." *Davis*, 526 U.S. at 633. As we noted, this case involves a cycle of discrimination and deliberate indifference that lasted for more than one year, ultimately resulting in Williams's withdrawal from and decision not to return to UGA. Williams alleges that she may return to the university if UGA implements more effective procedures to deal with student-on-student harassment. Although UGA and UGAA neither formally forced Williams to leave nor banned her from returning, the discrimination in which they engaged or they allowed to occur on campus caused Williams to withdraw and not return. When Williams was faced with decisions to leave or to return to UGA, she knew the following: (1) UGA and UGAA recruited and admitted a student-athlete despite knowledge of his past sexual misconduct; (2) UGA and UGAA failed to supervise dangerous students or properly instruct student-athletes on the applicable sexual harassment policy; (3) she was sexually assaulted and raped by three student-athletes, including one whose past sexual misconduct was known to UGA and UGAA officials; and (4) the response to her complaints did nothing to assuage her concerns of a future attack should she return to UGA. Considering these circumstances, we conclude that Williams has alleged sufficient facts at this stage to show that the alleged discrimination "effectively bar[red] [her] access to an educational opportunity or benefit," namely pursuing an education at UGA.

. . .

Next we consider Williams's § 1983 claims against Adams, Harrick, and Dooley, as individuals and in their official capacities, and against the Board of Regents and UGA. The district court dismissed the claims against Adams, Harrick, and Dooley as individuals based on Williams's failure to state a claim and the defendants' qualified immunity. The district court dismissed all other claims based on Eleventh Amendment immunity.

Title 42 U.S.C. § 1983 provides every person with the right to sue those acting under color of state law for violations of federal constitutional and statutory provisions. 42 U.S.C. § 1983. Section 1983 is merely a vehicle by which to bring these suits; it does not create any substantive federal rights. Therefore, the plaintiff must point to a specific federal right that the defendant violated.

Here, Williams asserts that Adams, Harrick, and Dooley, while acting under color of state law—a finding that the defendants do not dispute— deprived her of her federal rights: (1) under Title IX by failing to implement policies and procedures to ensure compliance with the statute and (2) under the Equal Protection Clause for discrimination based on sex. Williams also asserts a § 1983 claim against the three defendants because they exhibited deliberate indifference by recruiting and admitting Cole despite his troubled past. Williams fails to explain what statutory or constitutional right the defendants violated through their deliberate indifference, so we consider those allegations as relevant to both the Title IX and equal protection claims. Additionally, Williams asserts that UGA and the Board of Regents violated the Equal Protection Clause by implementing a sexual harassment policy that treats student-on-student harassment differently from harassment involving other members of the university community.

The district court dismissed Williams's first § 1983 claim against Adams, Harrick, and Dooley as individuals because a plaintiff cannot assert a § 1983 action based on a violation of Title IX. We agree. Title IX does not allow claims against individual school officials; only funding recipients can be held liable for Title IX violations. *Hartley v. Parnell*, 193 F.3d 1263, 1270 (11th Cir. 1999). Although this court has never considered whether a plaintiff can use § 1983 to assert a Title IX claim against an individual school official, we conclude that to allow plaintiffs to use § 1983 in this manner would permit an end run around Title IX's explicit language limiting liability to funding recipients.

The district court dismissed Williams's second § 1983 claim against Adams, Harrick, and Dooley as individuals, holding that the defendants have qualified immunity and that Williams failed to state a claim. We need not address whether Williams failed to state a claim because we affirm the district court's holding on qualified immunity grounds.

"Qualified immunity shields governmental officials executing discretionary responsibilities from civil damages 'insofar as their conduct does not violate clearly established statutory or constitutional rights of which a reasonable person would have known.' " *Courson v. McMillian*, 939 F.2d 1479, 1486 (11th Cir. 1991) (citing *Harlow v. Fitzgerald*, 457 U.S. 800, 818 (1982)). If a defendant asserts a qualified immunity defense in a Rule 12(b)(6) motion to dismiss, the court should grant qualified immunity if the plaintiff's complaint fails to allege a violation of a clearly established constitutional or statutory right. *Williams v. Ala. State Univ.*, 102 F.3d 1179, 1182 (11th Cir. 1997) (per curiam).

. . .

[If, as the parties agree here, the defendant acted within the scope of discretionary authority when performing the challenged conduct] the plaintiff must [then] establish that the state of the law when the challenged events occurred was such that the defendant had fair warning that his alleged treatment of the plaintiff was unconstitutional. *Willingham v. Loughnan*, 321 F.3d 1299, 1301 (11th Cir. 2003). The plaintiff does not have to show that the precise conduct in question has been held unlawful. Nevertheless, for a federal right to be clearly established, its parameters "must be sufficiently clear that a reasonable official would understand that what he is doing violates that right."

The Equal Protection Clause confers a federal constitutional right to be free from sex discrimination. *Pers. Adm'r of Mass. v. Feeney*, 442 U.S. 256, 273 (1979). Here, Williams has alleged a harrowing incident, similar to other allegations that unfortunately have become increasingly common on today's university campuses.[10] . . . Nevertheless, Williams has failed to present any cases that show the three defendants violated her clearly established equal protection rights by recruiting and admitting an individual like Cole. Therefore, Williams cannot meet her burden under the second step of the qualified immunity analysis, and we hold that Adams, Harrick, and Dooley are entitled to qualified immunity.

Williams also brings § 1983 claims against Adams, Harrick, and Dooley, in their official capacities. The district court dismissed these claims based on Eleventh Amendment immunity. Without addressing the district court's reasoning, we hold instead that the claims were properly dismissed for the same reasons we dismissed the claims against those defendants in their individual capacities.

As for the § 1983 claims against UGA and the Board of Regents, we hold that the Eleventh Amendment bars suit against those defendants. Under most circumstances, the Eleventh Amendment bars suits against states and state entities by their citizens. *Hans v. Louisiana*, 134 U.S. 1, 20–21 (1890). Williams does not dispute that UGA and the Board of Regents are state entities for Eleventh Amendment purposes. But even in those situations in which the Eleventh Amendment bars suits, a party may sue the state if the state has waived its immunity or if Congress has validly abrogated the state's immunity.

Williams correctly notes that Congress validly abrogated the states' immunity from Title IX suits. *Gebser*, 524 U.S. at 284. This is why the Eleventh Amendment did not bar the direct Title IX action against UGA, UGAA, and the Board of Regents. Here, however, Williams is trying to use § 1983 to bring a Title IX claim. Congress has not abrogated states' immunity from § 1983 suits. *Miller v. King*, 384 F.3d 1248, 1259–60 (11th Cir. 2004). Nor has UGA or the Board of Regents waived its Eleventh Amendment immunity. Therefore, the Eleventh Amendment bars Williams's § 1983 claims against UGA and the Board of Regents.

Finally, Williams asserts that the district court erred in dismissing her claim for injunctive relief. . . . In her initial complaint, Williams sought an injunction "ordering the defendants to implement policies and procedures to protect students like Plaintiff from student-on-student sexual harassment prohibited by Title IX." . . .

The district court rejected Williams's claims because she lacked standing.

. . .

We agree with the district court's reasoning and hold that Williams lacked standing to pursue injunctive relief because the threat of future harm to Williams and other students is merely conjectural. First, the alleged assailants no longer attend UGA. Therefore, as for harm that may come from them, granting injunctive relief would not prevent future harm to Williams or other students or remedy the past harm Williams suffered.

---

10. *See, e.g.*, Diane Carman, *Finally, A Debacle CU's Barnett Can't Survive*, DENVER POST, Dec. 8, 2005, at B05; *Six UTC Players Charged with Rape*, MOBILE REGISTER, Nov. 9, 2005, at C7; Simone Weichselbaum, *Athletes: Campus Life Raunchy, Raucous Partygoers, Others at La Salle Talk of Alleged Sexual Assaults*, PHILA. DAILY NEWS, July 1, 2004, at 10.

Second, Williams no longer attends UGA. Williams alleges that if UGA adopts an equal and more protective sexual harassment policy—presumably the one she asks this court to order—she may pursue undergraduate or graduate studies at UGA. Furthermore, she alleges that in the absence of such a policy, the current students at UGA who are the victims of student-on-student harassment suffer from prohibited inequality. Williams's claim that an equal and more protective sexual harassment policy would prevent future harm is too conjectural to warrant injunctive relief. Consequently, we affirm the district court's decision that Williams lacks standing to obtain the injunctive relief she seeks.

. . .

In conclusion, we remand to the district court for further proceedings on Williams's Title IX claims against UGA and UGAA. . . .

Questions and Comments on *Williams*

1. Without admitting liability, the University of Georgia settled the lawsuit with Ms. Williams. Charles Huckabee, *U. of Georgia Settles Harassment Suit in Case Involving Former Basketball Player*, Chron. Higher Educ., Apr. 29, 2007, *available at* http://chronicle.com/news/index.php?id=2194. The settlement amount was not disclosed, but Ed Tolley, an attorney for the university's athletic association, reported that it was in the six figures. *Id.*

2. In *Simpson v. University of Colorado*, 500 F.3d 1170 (10th Cir. 2007), two female students sued the university under Title IX after they were raped at a party by a group of football players and recruits. The Tenth Circuit overturned a district court's grant of summary judgment to the University of Colorado, holding that the evidence that was before the district court would support findings that (1) the Coach had general knowledge of the serious risk of sexual harassment and assault; (2) that he nonetheless maintained an unsupervised player-host program to show high-school recruits "a good time"; and (3) that he knew there had been no change in atmosphere since 1997 when a prior assault occurred. Thus a jury could have concluded that the coach was "deliberately indifferent" to the risk. To settle the lawsuit, the University of Colorado agreed to pay the women $2.85 million and to create a Title IX-advisor position to help the university prevent sexual harassment. Libby Sander, *U. of Colorado Settles Lawsuit over Alleged Gang Rapes*, Chron. Higher Educ., Dec. 14, 2007, at A20. As a result of controversy surrounding the incident, the Athletic Director, Richard Thurp, and the University's President, Elizabeth Hoffman, resigned. The Football Coach, Gary Barnett, also resigned after reaching a $3–million settlement with the university. *Id.* When asked what the university learned from the incident, the current university president, Hank Brown said that "it's one thing to have policies, but . . . we have to be very diligent about making sure that people understand them and are tested on them." *University of Colorado President Speaks Out*, Rocky Mountain News, Dec. 6, 2007, http://www.rockymountainnews.com/news/2007/dec/06/university-of-colorado-speaks-out. *See also* Jenni E. Spies, Comment, *Winning at All Costs: An Analysis of a University's Potential Liability for Sexual Assaults Committed by Its Student Athletes*, 16 Marq. Sports L. Rev. 429 (2006).

3. Should statutory rape be considered sexual harassment under Title IX? *See* Benefield v. Board of Trs. of the Univ. of Ala. at Birmingham, 214 F.Supp.2d 1212 (N.D.Ala. 2002) (holding that consensual sex by a fifteen year old college student with multiple members of the college football team was not sexual harassment).

4. Why have so many athletes been the subject of sexual harassment suits? Some "contend that a potent mix of alcohol, arrogance, and ignorance, as well as an inherent propensity towards violence, makes the male athlete a particularly dangerous creature." Christopher M. Parent, *Personal Fouls: How Sexual Assault by Football Players is Exposing Universities to Title IX Liability*, 13 FORDHAM INTELL. PROP. MEDIA & ENT. L.J. 617, 636 (2003). Whatever the reasons, it is clear that university athletic departments need to be aware of the requirements of Title IX. For more on how a university can comply with Title IX requirements and best support rape and sexual harassment victims *see generally* Holly Hogan, *What Athletic Departments Must Know About Title IX And Sexual Harassment*, 16 MARQ. SPORTS L. REV. 317 (2006); Kathryn M. Reardon, *Beyond Prosecution: Sexual Assault Victim's Rights in Theory and Practice Symposium: Acquaintance Rape at Private Colleges and Universities: Providing for Victims' Educational and Civil Rights*, 38 SUFFOLK U. L. REV. 395 (2005).

Jain v. Iowa

Supreme Court of Iowa, 2000.
617 N.W.2d 293.

■ NEUFMAN, JUSTICE.

This appeal concerns the tragic death of Sanjay Jain, a freshman at the University of Iowa. Sanjay committed suicide in his dormitory room. His father and administrator of his estate, Uttam Jain, sued the university for wrongful death, claiming it negligently failed to exercise reasonable care and caution for Sanjay's safety. In particular he claimed that if the university had followed its policy of notifying parents of a student's self-destructive behavior, the suicide could have been prevented.

On the university's motion for summary judgment, the district court dismissed Uttam's suit. It concluded the university owed no legal duty to Sanjay Jain to prevent him from harming himself, nor did it breach any legally recognized duty of care by failing to notify his parents of an earlier suicide attempt. For the reasons that follow, we affirm.

Sanjay Jain had just celebrated his eighteenth birthday when he enrolled as a freshman at the University of Iowa and moved into an off-campus university dormitory, the Mayflower. Sanjay came to Iowa from Addison, Illinois, the second of three children born to Uttam and Anita Jain. By all accounts they were a close-knit family.

Sanjay had enjoyed a successful academic career in high school and planned to major in biomedical engineering at the university. That course of study proved difficult. By the middle of the first semester his personal life as well as academic performance were showing the strain. He became moody and skipped many classes.... [H]e was placed on one-year disciplinary probation for smoking marijuana in his room. Beth Merritt, the hall coordinator for the Mayflower dorm, imposed this discipline and ordered him to attend a series of alcohol and drug education classes.

Sanjay's parents and family were unaware of these difficulties. University policy calls for privacy with respect to the university's relationships with its adult students. Although Sanjay confided to his mother that he wished to switch his major from engineering to computer science, he told his father and brother that he liked biomedical engineering and his classes were going well. His frequent phone conversations with his parents were reportedly upbeat. Sanjay, in his father's words, described everything about college as "awesome."

In the early morning hours of November 20, 1994, resident assistants on duty at the Mayflower were called to a "domestic" dispute outside Sanjay's apartment. When they arrived they observed Sanjay and his girlfriend, Roopa, fighting over a set of keys to Sanjay's moped. Sanjay had moved the motorized cycle into his room. Roopa asserted that Sanjay was preparing to commit suicide by inhaling exhaust fumes and she was merely trying to stop him. Sanjay was interviewed independently. He, too, reported that he was trying to commit suicide. The RAs concluded from their conversation that Sanjay "had a lot of frustrations about family life and academics." After discussing the situation for about an hour, the group disbanded. Sanjay assured the RAs that he would seek counseling after getting a good night's rest.

Beth Merritt met with Sanjay the next day. He was reportedly evasive and refused to admit or deny that he had tried to commit suicide. he encouraged him to seek help at the university counseling service. She also demanded that he remove the moped from his room because storing it there violated university policy. He agreed to do so. Merritt also gave Sanjay her home phone number, urging him to call her "if he thought he was going to hurt himself." Sanjay assured her he would do so. He reportedly claimed that he just really needed to talk to his family and looked forward to doing so during the Thanksgiving break that would start the next day.

In keeping with university protocol, Merritt discussed the Sanjay incident with her supervisor, David Coleman, the assistant director for residence life.... She ... advised Coleman that she requested permission to contact Sanjay's parents about the incident, but he refused to consent. Coleman concurred in Merritt's decision to encourage Sanjay to seek counseling. He took no further action on the matter.

Evidently Sanjay's visit with his family at Thanksgiving did not include discussion of the turmoil in his life. His parents and siblings perceived nothing amiss in his attitude or behavior. Sanjay returned to the university when classes resumed on November 28. Merritt encountered him briefly and inquired about how things were going. Sanjay responded "good." Unbeknownst to Merritt, however, the moped was back in Sanjay's room. In a statement given after Sanjay's death, his roommate, Scott, reported that the vehicle had been stored in Sanjay's room for roughly three weeks. Sanjay reportedly told Scott that "he would kill himself by running the cycle in the room . . . when Scott was not there."

This threat, apparently taken in jest by Scott, played out on December 4. Scott planned to spend the weekend in Cedar Rapids. Sanjay called his brother to make arrangements for a ride home over the upcoming winter break, then joined friends for a night of drinking downtown. They stayed until the bars closed at 2 a.m. Sanjay was described as "visibly intoxicated but coherent." His friends fed him sandwiches when they returned to the dorm. One friend was reportedly reluctant to leave him alone in his room, telling him she would post herself outside his door until Scott returned. Sanjay convinced her this was not necessary, and she retired to her room around 4 a.m.

At approximately 10:30 a.m., one of Sanjay's suite-mates awoke to the smell of something "unusual." He ignored it but, thirty minutes later, he felt dizzy when he tried to get up. He suspected the pilot light might have gone out on the apartment's stove. When he opened the door to the kitchen a cloud of exhaust smoke appeared there and in the bathroom. Fearing another suicide attempt by Sanjay, he knocked on his door but received no answer. All he heard was loud music coming from the room. He contacted the RA on duty, who unlocked the door and found Sanjay unconscious, the moped still running. Emergency medical personnel were summoned and the dormitory was evacuated. Sanjay was pronounced dead of self-inflicted carbon monoxide poisoning.

The record reveals that an unwritten university policy dealing with self-destructive behavior dictates that, with evidence of a suicide attempt, university officials will contact a student's parents. The decision to do so rests solely with Phillip Jones, the dean of students. The dean bases his decision on information gathered from a variety of sources. In this case, no information concerning Sanjay Jain was transmitted to the dean's office until after his death.

Plaintiff Uttam Jain commenced this wrongful death action against the university in accordance with the "state agency" provisions of the State Tort Claims Act. *See* Iowa Code § 669.2 (1995). The suit claimed that Sanjay's death proximately resulted from university employees' negligent failure to exercise care and caution for his safety. The state generally denied the claims and asserted, by way of affirmative defenses, the doctrine of superseding-intervening cause and the discretionary function exemption to the State's waiver of sovereign immunity. Extensive discovery ensued. By the close of discovery, the only specification of negligence seriously advanced by plaintiff was his claim that Sanjay's death resulted from the university's failure to notify his parents of his earlier suicide attempt.

The State moved for summary judgment. Following hearing, the district court ruled that (1) no special relationship existed between the university and Sanjay that would give rise to an affirmative duty to prevent his suicide, (2) by adopting a policy of notifying parents of a student's suicide attempt, the university did not thereby assume a voluntary duty to prevent Sanjay's self-inflicted death, and (3) the facts, viewed in the light most favorable to the plaintiff, do not establish an exception to the general rule that suicide is an intentional intervening act which supersedes any alleged negligence by the defendant. The court therefore concluded the State was entitled to judgment as a matter of law. This appeal by plaintiff followed.

. . .

At the outset plaintiff concedes that the law generally imposes no duty upon an individual to protect another person from self-inflicted harm in the absence of a "special relationship," usually custodial in nature. Restatement (Second) of Torts § 314, at 116 (1965). . . . Plaintiff claims no reliance on the "custody or control" exception here, conceding the university's relationship with its students is not custodial in nature. What plaintiff *does* claim is that the university's knowledge of Sanjay's "mental condition or emotional state requiring medical care" created a special relationship giving rise to an affirmative duty of care toward him.

Plaintiff's focus is on the Restatement (Second) of Torts section 323. It states:

> One who undertakes, gratuitously or for consideration, to render services to another which he should recognize as necessary for the protection of the other's person or things, is subject to

liability to the other for physical harm resulting from his failure to exercise reasonable care to perform his undertaking, if

(a) his failure to exercise such care increases the risk of such harm, or

(b) the harm is suffered because of the other's reliance upon the undertaking.

Restatement (Second) of Torts § 323, at 135. He posits two possible circumstances that could establish the university's special duty to Sanjay under this record: (1) its adherence to an exception in federal legislation known as the "Buckley Amendment" that otherwise protects the confidentiality of student records, or (2) the university's adoption of a policy to notify parents of a student's self-destructive behavior. Alternatively, Plaintiff asserts that Sanjay's "intervening" act of suicide constituted a significant part of the risk inherent in the university's negligent failure to notify, thereby rendering inapplicable the intervening-superseding cause doctrine relied upon by the district court.

The state counters that plaintiff has not preserved his argument concerning the Buckley Amendment. It then argues that the university's voluntary conduct created no actionable duty under section 323 of the Restatement and, because there existed no legally-recognized special relationship between Sanjay and the university, the superseding-intervening act doctrine absolves the university of liability as a matter of law. We shall consider the arguments in turn.

Congress enacted the Family Educational Rights and Privacy Act (FERPA) to ensure access to educational records for students and parents while protecting the privacy of such records from the public. *See generally* 20 U.S.C. § 1232g (1990). The Act, commonly known as the "Buckley Amendment," strives to achieve its purpose by conditioning federal educational funding on compliance with its privacy requirements. *Student Press Law Ctr. v. Alexander,* 778 F. Supp. 1227, 1228 (D.D.C. 1991). At issue here is an exception that permits institutions to disclose otherwise confidential information to "appropriate parties" when an "emergency" makes it necessary "to protect the health or safety of the student or other persons." 20 U.S.C. § 1232g(b)(1)(I). According to the terms of the implementing administrative regulations, the exception is discretionary in nature. *See* 34 C.F.R. § 99.36(a) (1994) (educational institution "may" disclose pertinent information "if" knowledge necessary to protect student). A companion regulation directs that the exception be "strictly construed." *Id.* at § 99.36(b).

Jain contends an emergency existed with respect to his son, Sanjay, and it was vitally important for Sanjay's parents to have information concerning the situation so they could intervene on his behalf. He then seems to argue that because the exception to the Buckley Amendment would have authorized revelation of the pertinent facts, the university was duty bound to reveal them. In other words, Jain claims the university misapplied the Buckley Amendment to his son's detriment, thereby giving rise to a cause of action "for any reasonably foreseeable injuries resulting therefrom."

We entertain serious doubts about the merits of plaintiff's argument. His claim rests, after all, not on a violation of the Act but on an alleged failure to take advantage of a discretionary exception to its requirements. We need not resolve the question, however, because [the claim was not raised before the district court or ruled upon in its decision.]

That brings us to the crux of Plaintiff's claim—that the university has voluntarily adopted a policy (consistent with the Buckley Amendment) of notifying parents when a student engages in self-destructive behavior but it negligently failed to act on that policy in the case of Sanjay Jain. By not following its own policy, plaintiff argues, the "university deprived Sanjay of the medical intervention he so desperately needed."

The argument implicates section 323 of the Restatement (Second) of Torts. Although this court has applied section 323 in a variety of settings, we have not before had occasion to consider the rule's application in the context of an allegedly preventable death by suicide. *See, e.g., American State Bank v. Enabnit*, 471 N.W.2d 829, 832 (Iowa 1991) (rejecting cause of action by bank against lawyer for alleged gratuitous undertaking with respect to escrow funds); *DeBurkarte v. Louvar*, 393 N.W.2d 131, 135 (Iowa 1986) (recognizing section 323 encompasses cause of action for "lost chance of survival"); *Van Iperen v. Van Bramer*, 392 N.W.2d 480, 485 (Iowa 1986) (traditional proof of causation in medical malpractice case not affected by section 323).

In *Power v. Boles*, the Ohio Court of Appeals neatly summarized what a plaintiff must prove to show assumption of a duty under section 323:

> Cases interpreting section 323(a) have made it clear that the increase in the risk of harm required is not simply that which occurs when a person fails to do something that he or she reasonably should have. Obviously, the risk of harm to the beneficiary of a service is always greater when the service is performed without due care. Rather, as the court stated in *Turbe v. Government of Virgin Islands, Virgin Island Water & Power Auth.*, 938 F.2d 427, 432 (3d Cir. 1991):
>
>> [Section] 323(a) applies only when the defendant's actions increased the risk of harm to plaintiff relative to the risk that would have existed had the defendant never provided the services initially. Put another way, the defendant's negligent performance must somehow put the plaintiff in a worse situation than if the defendant had never begun performance. . . . To prevail under a theory of increased harm a plaintiff must "identify the sins of commission rather than sins of omission."

Power, 110 Ohio App. 3d 29, 673 N.E.2d 617, 620 (Ohio Ct. App. 1996) (citations omitted). Likewise with respect to the "reliance" prong of section 323(b), the *Power* court noted the general requirement that the plaintiff show "actual or affirmative reliance, i.e., reliance 'based on specific actions or representations which cause a person to forego other alternatives of protecting themselves.'" 673 N.E.2d at 621; *accord* Restatement (Second) of Torts § 323 cmt. C, at 137.

Plaintiff argues, in essence, that once university employees discovered Sanjay and Roopa fighting over the moped keys, elicited comments suggestive of a suicide threat and referred Sanjay to counseling, they were bound under section 323 to follow through with their undertaking. In this case, plaintiff argues, that meant bringing the matter to the attention of the dean of students for the purpose of notifying Sanjay's parents.

Although, in hindsight, plaintiff's contention carries considerable appeal, the duty he seeks to impose upon the university cannot be squared with section 323(a) or (b). The record, read in the light most favorable to the plaintiff, reveals that Sanjay may have been at risk of harming himself. No affirmative action by the defendant's employees, however, increased that risk of self-harm. To the contrary, it is undisputed that the RAs appropriately intervened in an emotionally-charged situation, offered Sanjay support and encouragement, and referred him to counseling. Beth Merritt likewise counseled Sanjay to talk things over with his parents, seek professional help, and call her at any time, even when she was not at work. She sought Sanjay's permission to contact his parents but he refused. In short, no action by university personnel prevented Sanjay from taking advantage of the help and encouragement being offered, nor did they do anything to prevent him from seeking help on his own accord.

The record is similarly devoid of any proof that Sanjay relied, to his detriment, on the services gratuitously offered by these same personnel. To the contrary, it appears by all accounts that he failed to follow up on recommended counseling or seek the guidance of his parents, as he assured the staff he would do. *See Power*, 673 N.E.2d at 622 (summary judgment proper in absence of proof that decedent abandoned other available opportunities to protect himself in reliance on defendant-city's gratuitous undertaking).

This case is distinctly different from the only case relied upon by plaintiff in support of his section 323 argument, *United States v. Gavagan*, 280 F.2d 319 (5th Cir. 1960). *Gavagan* involved the question of governmental liability for the unsuccessful rescue of a ship in distress at sea. Although plaintiff understandably looks to the case as a metaphor for the failed rescue perceived in the case before us, the court's affirmance of a verdict for the estates of the deceased crew members in *Gavagan* turned on proof of the essential elements of Restatement section 323. The case reveals that but for negligent mistakes in the conveyance of vital information concerning the vessel's location, lives lost would have been saved. Crucial to the court's decision was proof that the mistakes greatly increased the likelihood that the ship would not be found before dark, and reliance on the misleading information led others to abandon their search.

By contrast to *Gavagan*, the record before us reveals that the university's limited intervention in this case neither increased the risk that Sanjay would commit suicide nor led him to abandon other avenues of relief from his distress. Thus no legal duty on the part of the university arose under Restatement section 323 as a matter of law. The district court was correct in so ruling.

In Iowa and elsewhere, it is the general rule that unless the possibility of accident or innocence can be reasonably determined, the act of suicide is considered a deliberate, intentional and intervening act that precludes another's responsibility for the harm. As already noted earlier in this opinion, an exception to this general rule arises from the existence of a special relationship that imposes upon the defendant the duty to prevent foreseeable harm to the plaintiff. In such a case, the doctrine of intervening-superseding act will not relieve a defendant of liability. That is because the intervening act (in this case, suicide) is the very risk the special duty is meant to prevent.

Here, the district court logically concluded that because no legally-recognized special relationship existed between the university and Sanjay, plaintiff could not rely on the exception to the intervening-superseding cause doctrine to counter the university's affirmative defense. We agree. Accordingly we affirm the district court's summary judgment for the State of Iowa.

Shin v. Massachusetts Institute of Technology

Superior Court of Massachusetts, at Middlesex, 2005.
19 Mass. L. Rep. 570.

■ McEvoy, J.

Following the suicide of their daughter, Elizabeth H. Shin, a sophomore at the Massachusetts Institute of Technology, the Plaintiffs filed a twenty-five (25)-count complaint against the Defendants Massachusetts Institute of Technology, MIT Medical Professionals, MIT Administrators, and MIT Campus Police Officers. . . .

Elizabeth Shin ("Elizabeth") was born on September 26, 1980, and enrolled at Massachusetts Institute of Technology ("MIT") in September 1998. Elizabeth lived in Random Hall, a coeducational dormitory that houses both first-year students and upperclassmen.

Elizabeth's annual tuition and room and board at MIT totaled approximately $35,000.00 for the 1998–1999 academic year. MIT, as a modest sized city, provides a multitude of services to its students, faculty and staff. MIT provides housing, food service, educational and medical services to the members of its community. MIT Medical Services Department offers comprehensive health services funded, in part, by tuition payments and administered by Blue Cross/Blue Shield. Prior to beginning freshman classes, MIT sent Elizabeth information about its Medical Services Department and the health services available to her upon arrival at MIT.

Elizabeth first experienced psychiatric problems at MIT in February 1999, during the spring semester of her freshman year. She was hospitalized following an overdose of Tylenol with codeine. Elizabeth was initially taken to Massachusetts General Hospital by MIT ambulance. From there she was admitted to McLean Hospital ("McLean") for a one-week psychiatric hospitalization. During her treatment at McLean, Elizabeth revealed that she suffered from mental health problems and engaged in cutting behavior while she was in high school.

After obtaining Elizabeth's consent, Nina Davis–Mills ("Davis–Mills"), Elizabeth's housemaster at Random Hall, called Elizabeth's parents to inform them of their daughter's hospitalization at McLean. The Shins came to visit their daughter at McLean, where they met with treating clinicians and a social worker. The clinicians at McLean recommended that Elizabeth seek psychotherapy following her discharge from McLean. Prior from her discharge from McLean, Elizabeth's father, Mr. Shin, brought Elizabeth to MIT's Mental Health Services Department to meet with Dr. Kristine Girard ("Girard"), one of the full-time psychiatrists at MIT. Girard discussed treatment options with Mr. Shin and Elizabeth, which included treatment at MIT, referral to a mental health facility outside MIT, or taking a leave from MIT to focus on her treatment elsewhere. Girard recommended that Elizabeth accept a referral for weekly treatment outside MIT, but Elizabeth refused. They agreed that Elizabeth would begin treatment with Girard with appointments every two or three weeks.

On February 23, 1999, Girard treated Elizabeth during a fifty-minute therapy session and diagnosed her with "adjustment disorder." Girard also noted that Elizabeth was speaking with Counseling and Support Services ("CSS") Dean Ayida Mtembu ("Mtembu") to assist her with her academic extensions. On March 11, 1999, Mtembu attempted to contact Girard to discuss Elizabeth's mental condition because Mtembu learned that Elizabeth made a suicidal comment to her boyfriend who she broke up with two days prior.

On April 7, 1999, Girard treated Elizabeth during a forty-five minute therapy session where Girard noted that Elizabeth was considering transferring from MIT due to her marginal performance in some of her classes. Girard noted that Elizabeth was suffering from "situational issues" and as a plan of treatment, recommended she read "Feeling Good" by David Burns, Ph.D. On May 3, 1999, Girard again met with Elizabeth who described her own medical condition as "not so good." Elizabeth explained that she was having conflicts with her boyfriend and poorly performing in some of her classes. Elizabeth told Girard she was going to home to live with her parents in New Jersey for the summer break. Girard again diagnosed Elizabeth as suffering from "situational issues" and instructed Elizabeth to return for therapy at the beginning of her sophomore year.

On October 6, 1999, Mtembu sent Elizabeth to MIT Mental Health for an immediate assessment because she was concerned for Elizabeth's safety after she told Mtembu she was thinking of killing herself. MIT psychiatrist, Dr. Lesley Egler ("Egler") treated Elizabeth in a fifty-minute therapy session. Egler noted that Elizabeth was cutting herself without suicidal intent, had a history of mood disorder, was having passive suicidal ideation without any plan or intent, suicidal thoughts had dissipated and were more "abstract" than "concrete," reduced sleep, erratic eating habits, and that she did not feel she was in any immediate danger of harming herself. Egler advised Elizabeth to return within the next day or two for a walk-in appointment as needed and gave her MIT's telephone number for reaching an after-hours mental health clinician.

On October 12, 1999, Girard treated Elizabeth noting Elizabeth was "feeling significantly better this week," but Girard was cautiously optimistic because Elizabeth's affect was dramatic with "underlying sadness."

On November 9, 1999, Elizabeth met with CSS Dean Arnold Henderson ("Henderson") and told him that she had been cutting herself intentionally. Observing the self-inflicted scratches, Henderson arranged for Elizabeth to meet with a MIT psychiatrist immediately because he believed it was an "urgent" situation.

On December 6, 1999, Henderson received an email from Elizabeth's biology instructor stating that Elizabeth had told a teaching assistant she bought a bottle of sleeping pills with the intention to take them, but had decided not to. Henderson contacted Elizabeth to see how she was doing, and she appeared to be doing well. Nonetheless, Henderson reported the incident to Davis–Millis and Girard.

Elizabeth's mental health problems resurfaced in March of 2000, her second semester of her sophomore year. In the early morning hours of

March 18, 2000, a student notified Davis–Millis that Elizabeth was cutting herself and extremely upset. Believing the situation to be an emergency, Davis–Millis persuaded Elizabeth to go to MIT Mental Health early in the morning of March 18, 2000. Elizabeth met with MIT physician, K. Vassen ("Vassen") who documented that Elizabeth was "very upset." Elizabeth also told the physician that she did not feel safe alone. Vassen contacted the on-call psychiatrist, Dr. Reisen ("Reisen"), who instructed Vassen to keep Elizabeth there until he arrived. After meeting with Elizabeth, Reisen decided that she could not return to Random Hall and should be admitted for observation at MIT's infirmary. Reisen also prescribed a tranquilizer. Reisen then examined Elizabeth on March 19, 2000 and permitted her to return to Random Hall. A student spoke with Elizabeth and reported to Davis–Millis that Elizabeth sounded distraught. Davis–Millis did not relay this information to Reisen or any other person within MIT Mental Health Department.

The next day, with Elizabeth's consent, Davis–Millis contacted Mr. and Mrs. Shin to inform them that Elizabeth was in the infirmary. Mr. Shin drove to MIT the following day and took Elizabeth home to New Jersey.

Upon returning from spring break, Elizabeth resumed treatment at MIT with a new psychiatrist, Dr. Linda Cunningham ("Cunningham"). Prior to meeting with Elizabeth for the first time on March 23, 2000, Cunningham did not review Elizabeth's medical record or speak with any other clinician about her mental health history. Cunningham prescribed an anti-depressant, Celexa, and a tranquilizer. Ultimately, Cunningham diagnosed Elizabeth to be suffering from borderline personality disorder and depression.

Between the end of March 2000 through April 10, 2000, Davis–Millis began receiving frequent reports from Random Hall students and Graduate Resident Tutors ("GRTs") indicating that Elizabeth's mental health was deteriorating.

On March 26, 2000, Davis–Millis, at the request of Cunningham through Henderson, discouraged Elizabeth from pursuing her earlier mentioned desire to move out of Random Hall. On March 29, 2000, Henderson counseled Elizabeth after Davis–Millis communicated her and other Random Hall persons' concern that Elizabeth might harm herself. On that day and the following day, Henderson began to speak with Elizabeth's professors about postponing her examinations scheduled for the following week.

At 11:00 a.m. on March 30, 2000, Elizabeth met with Cunningham where Cunningham diagnosed Shin as suffering from a major depressive episode—"severe." At Cunningham's request, Elizabeth returned that day at 3:00 p.m. and Cunningham increased Shin's daily dosage of Celexa, continued the prescription for the tranquilizer, and informed Elizabeth that she would try and locate an outside therapist for her. Cunningham noted that Elizabeth was having "recurrent suicidal gestures" and her condition was "deteriorating" regarding her ability to cope with stress associated with academic pressures. Cunningham further documented that Elizabeth might be required to be hospitalized.

On April 3, 2000, Elizabeth contacted Henderson requesting that he speak with a professor about postponing an exam Elizabeth originally told the professor she would be able to take as scheduled. Henderson obliged Shin's request and continued to stay in contact with Davis–Millis regarding Elizabeth's condition.

On April 4, 2000 Elizabeth visited the MIT Mental Health Department as a walk-in and spoke with Dr. Lili Gottfried ("Gottfried"). Elizabeth was unable to tell Gottfried why she had come in that day. On the same day, at the recommendation of Cunningham, Elizabeth met with Eleanor Temelini ("Temelini"), a licensed social worker who specializes in the treatment of patients suffering from BPD.

In late March and early April, Cunningham and Temelini discussed treatment options for Elizabeth outside of MIT. Specifically, they discussed an out-patient treatment program in dialectic behavioral therapy (BPT) at the Two Brattle Center treatment facility in Cambridge, Massachusetts. Elizabeth was scheduled to have an intake appointment on April 11, 2000.

On April 6, 2000, Elizabeth met with Cunningham for a therapy session. Elizabeth commented that she continued to feel "overwhelmed by symptoms" and that she was "feeling isolated." Cunningham noted that Elizabeth "fluctuates between severe overwhelming anxiety and emptiness, both of which are unbearable and cause disturbing sudden onset of suicidal thoughts." During this therapy session Cunningham raised the possibility that Elizabeth might need to be hospitalized at Beth Israel Hospital. Cunningham directed Elizabeth to return later in the afternoon for another treatment session.

At 12:30 p.m., Elizabeth returned for a second treatment session with Cunningham. Cunningham discussed the BPT program and Elizabeth seemed "interested." Cunningham noted that she was considering adding another drug, Resperdal, to Elizabeth's medicine regime.

On April 5, Margarita Ribas Groeger ("Groeger"), Elizabeth's Spanish I professor from the prior semester, contacted Davis–Millis to express her concerns about Elizabeth after Maria Skufca ("Skufca"), Elizabeth's Spanish II professor, indicated she was worried about Elizabeth's health. Davis–Millis notified Henderson about Groeger's concerns.

On April 6, Skufca contacted Groeger about cuts on Elizabeth's arms. Groeger placed four phone calls to Henderson before she spoke with him. The following day Henderson informed Groeger that there was no reason to be concerned because actions were being taken to take care of Elizabeth.

On the evening of April 8, Elizabeth informed another student residing in Random Hall that she was going to kill herself with a knife. The student called MIT Campus Police and officers transported Elizabeth and the other student to MIT's Mental Health Center. Upon arriving at the center, Dr. Heller ("Heller"), a MIT staff physician, evaluated Elizabeth. Heller called the on-call psychiatrist, Dr. Van Niel ("Van Niel") at his home. Van Niel spoke with Elizabeth on the phone for less than five minutes. Determining that Elizabeth was not acutely suicidal, Van Niel instructed Elizabeth to return to Random Hall without any restrictions or planned follow-up.

At approximately 12:30 a.m. on Monday, April 10, 2000, two Random Hall students notified Davis–Millis that Elizabeth had told them that she planned to kill herself that day and requested one of the students to erase her computer files. Davis–Millis testified that she believed Elizabeth intended to carry out her suicide plan. Davis–Millis called MIT Mental Health to contact the on-call psychiatrist. Van Niel called Davis–Millis back and she relayed the students' revelations to him. Van Niel instructed Davis–Millis to check on Elizabeth, but it would not be necessary to bring her in to the MIT

Medical considering (1) Elizabeth had assured him that she was fine and (2) her friends had overreacted on the April 8 episode. He then told Davis–Millis he would contact her at 6:30 a.m.

At 6:30 a.m., Davis–Millis told Van Niel that she had gone to check on Elizabeth, had found all was quiet, and had decided not to wake her. Van Niel asked Davis–Millis to convey her assessment to Henderson, who would be going to the "deans and psychs" meeting later that morning. Davis–Millis contacted Henderson and conveyed the events of the preceding night.

Next, Davis–Millis sent Elizabeth an email asking her to contact Davis–Millis when she woke up. Elizabeth called her at about 9:45 a.m. A disturbing conversation ensued where Elizabeth accused Davis–Millis of wanting to send her home and told her, "You won't have to worry about me any more," or words to that effect. Concerned more than ever, Davis–Millis contacted Henderson following the phone conversation with Elizabeth. He assured her he would convey her concerns to everyone attending the "deans and psychs" meeting.

The aforementioned "deans and psychs" meeting convened at 11:00 a.m. on Monday, April 10th. Henderson, other CCS deans, Reich, Girard, and Gottfried were among those in attendance. The attendees discussed Elizabeth's case, including her statement to the two students that she intended to kill herself that day.[2] It is contested what, if any, treatment options were discussed at the meeting, including hospitalization, the DBT program, and a medical withdrawal from MIT. At the conclusion of the meeting, Reich made an appointment at Two Brattle Center for Elizabeth for the next day. He left a voice message on Elizabeth's answering machine and notified her of the appointment and that he would be available for the rest of the day.

That night, shortly before 9:00 p.m., students in Random Hall heard the smoke alarm sounding in Elizabeth's room. The MIT Campus Police were called and both Campus Police and Cambridge Fire Department personnel responded within minutes. The Campus Police broke open Elizabeth's door and found her with her clothing engulfed in flames. Officer Munnelly ("Munnelly") pulled Elizabeth into the lobby area. The MIT police officers put out the flames and immediately began CPR. Elizabeth was transported to the emergency room at Massachusetts General Hospital. In the ambulance, she showed a non-verbal level of consciousness. As a result of the fire, Elizabeth suffered third-degree burns over 65% of her body.

On April 14, 2000, Mr. and Mrs. Shin were notified that Elizabeth suffered irreversible neurological brain damage and recommended termination of life support. At 1:50 a.m. on April 14, 2000, Elizabeth Shin was pronounced dead as a result of injuries suffered in the fire.

On April 18, 2000, the medical examiner determined that the cause of death was "self-inflicted thermal burns." Reich and MIT Chief of Police concurred that Elizabeth's death was a suicide.

. . .

2. Reich testified that he was not aware of Elizabeth's suicide plan to kill herself at the time of the meeting.

In their complaint, the Plaintiffs allege that they had an express and/or implied contract with MIT supported by adequate consideration, or in the alternative through promissory estoppel, to provide necessary and reasonable medical services for the benefit of Elizabeth. Elizabeth was an intended beneficiary under the agreement between MIT and the Plaintiffs.

"To state a claim for breach of contract under Massachusetts law, a plaintiff must allege, at a minimum, that there was a valid contract, that the defendant breached its duties under its contractual agreement, and that the breach caused the plaintiff damage." *Guckenberger v. Boston Univ.*, 974 F. Supp. 106, 150 (D.Mass. 1997). "Even in the absence of consideration to support a binding contractual agreement between the parties, a party reasonably relying on a promise may prevail under a theory of promissory estoppel. A claim in promissory estoppel is essentially a claim in breach of contract; however, the plaintiff must prove *reasonable reliance* on a promise, offer, or commitment by the defendant rather than the existence of consideration."

While it is well-established that "the relationship between a university and a student is contractual in nature," courts should be "slow to intrude into the sensitive area of the student-college relationship" and contract law need not be "rigidly applied." Under Massachusetts law, statements in handbooks, policy manuals, brochures, catalogs, advertisements, and other promotional materials can form the basis of a valid contract. *See Russell v. Salve Regina College*, 890 F.2d 484, 488 (1st Cir. 1989), *rev'd on other grounds*, 499 U.S. 225 (1991), and reinstated on remand, 938 F.2d 315 (1st Cir. 1991). However, the promise must be "definite and certain so that the promisor should reasonably foresee that it will induce reliance. . . ." *Guckenberger*, 974 F. Supp. at 150.

In *Guckenberger*, students brought suit against Boston University ("BU") after BU declined to extend certain accommodations for the students' learning disabilities. A federal court interpreting Massachusetts law declined to decide whether there was an enforceable contract based on BU brochures.[3] Instead, it found an enforceable contract between BU and three students based on "specific promises" BU faculty made to the students and their parents concerning the accommodation of their learning disabilities.

In *Morris v. Brandeis Univ.*, a student challenged the university's finding that he plagiarized his term paper. The Appeals Court found the basis for a valid contract in the detailed procedural standards of the student judicial process contained in Brandeis' student handbook. However, the court noted that the "generalized representations" to treat students with "fairness and beneficence" in Brandeis' promotional materials were "too vague and indefinite to form an enforceable contract." 60 Mass. App. Ct. 1119, n.6, 804 N.E.2d 961 (2004) (unpublished opinion).

In the instant case, the Plaintiffs first argue that the representations made in MIT's Medical Department brochure to incoming students and its Medical Department By–Laws formed the basis of an enforceable contract. While the Plaintiffs do not point to specific language in the MIT Medical Department brochure, the Court looks to the following language:

---

3. The BU brochures touted BU's "highly trained staff" and the option of "reasonable accommodations in testing and coursework" which would "be available throughout the student's academic career." *Id.* at 151.

This gives you access to a full range of physicians and other health care professionals who can care for your physical and psychological needs. These care givers also will help you maintain good health.

It is not unusual for new students, especially those from other countries and cultures, to have some adjustment issues after arriving at MIT. If you have any such difficulties, we offer you—at no charge—a wide range of mental health professionals to assist with this transition.

We want to help you maintain your physical, psychological and emotional well-being, and hope that you will take advantage of our wide range of services.

In the MIT Medical Department By–Laws, the Court looks to the following language:

The Medical Department, under the governance of the Medical Management Board, has the responsibility to provide high quality, low barrier comprehensive health services to the MIT Community. . . .

The Plaintiffs also argue that "MIT representatives did induce reliance as shown by Elizabeth's multiple visits to the MIT mental health services and meetings with Arnold Henderson, Dean of Counseling and Support Services." Additionally, the Plaintiffs point to a meeting with Davis–Millis in February 1999 where all agreed that Mr. and Mrs. Shin would be kept informed of any subsequent problems with Elizabeth.

The representations made in the MIT Medical Department brochure and By–Laws are merely "generalized representations" of the purpose and medical services available to the MIT community. Unlike the well-defined policies and procedures found to be the basis of an enforceable contract in *Sullivan* and *Morris*, such statements are not "definite and certain" and "too vague and indefinite to form an enforceable contract."

Likewise, Davis–Millis' statement that she would keep the Plaintiffs informed of any subsequent developments to Elizabeth's health does not rise to the level of a "specific promise" that the Plaintiffs relied upon. The other statements, which the Plaintiffs refer to generally and fail to allege with any specificity, allegedly made by MIT medical personnel and administrators were to Elizabeth, and not to the Plaintiffs. Therefore, the Plaintiffs could not have relied on these representations. Moreover, there is nothing in the summary judgment record relating to any "specific promises" MIT medical personnel and administrators made to Elizabeth. Accordingly, there was no contract between MIT and the Plaintiffs and MIT's motion for summary judgment on Counts I, II, and III is Allowed.

. . .

II.   Claims Against MIT Medical Professionals

Defendants Reich, Cunningham, Girard, and Van Niel have moved for partial summary judgment on the Plaintiff's claims of gross negligence (Count XIII), negligent infliction of emotional distress (Count XV), and violation of G.L.c. 93A (Count XVI). Girard also independently moved for summary judgment on all the rest of the claims brought against her.

A.   Gross Negligence (Count XIII)

In *Altman v. Aronson*, the Supreme Judicial Court defined gross negligence as follows:

> Gross negligence is substantially and appreciably higher in magnitude than ordinary negligence. It is materially more want of care than constitutes simple inadvertence. It is an act or omission respecting legal duty of an aggravated character as distinguished from mere failure to exercise ordinary care. It is very great negligence, or the absence of slight diligence, or the want of even scant care. It amounts to indifference to present legal duty and to utter forgetfulness of legal obligations so far as other persons may be affected. It is a heedless and palpable violation of legal duty respecting the rights of others.

The Plaintiffs argue that the MIT medical professionals individually and collectively failed to coordinate Elizabeth's care. As a "treatment team," the professionals failed to secure Elizabeth's short-term safety in response to Elizabeth's suicide plan in the morning hours of April 10. During the "deans and psychs" meeting on the morning of April 10, plans to assist Elizabeth were discussed, however, an immediate response to Elizabeth's escalating threats to commit suicide was not formulated. By not formulating and enacting an immediate plan to respond to Elizabeth's escalating threats to commit suicide, the Plaintiffs have put forth sufficient evidence of a genuine issue of material fact as to whether the MIT Medical Professionals were grossly negligent in their treatment of Elizabeth. Accordingly, the MIT Medical Professionals' partial motion for summary judgment as to Count XIII for gross negligence is Denied.

. . .

D.   Girard's Motion for Summary Judgment

Girard moves independently for summary judgment on all claims against her arguing that she had no duty to Elizabeth and was not a "substantial, contributing cause" to Elizabeth's death. Girard argues that as of April 2000, there was no physician-patient relationship between herself and Elizabeth because Girard did not personally treat Elizabeth after October 12, 1999. hus, the Plaintiffs cannot recover under their medical malpractice causes of action. According to testimony, Girard, among others, attended the April 10, 2000 "deans and psychs" meeting. Van Neil relayed the information reported to him by Davis–Millis regarding Elizabeth's suicide plan she conveyed to students in the early morning hours on April 10. Reich testified that he considered Girard familiar with Elizabeth and relied on Girard's opinion to form his opinion that Elizabeth was a "very help-resistant person." Accordingly, the Plaintiffs provided sufficient evidence to raise a genuine issue of material fact as to whether Girard was a part of the "treatment team" treating Elizabeth at the time of the suicide; thereby establishing a physician-patient relationship at the time of Elizabeth's suicide. Therefore, Girard's motion for summary judgment as to all claims against her is Denied.

III.   Claims Against MIT Administrators

A.   MIT Administrators' Duty to Elizabeth

Defendants Henderson and Davis–Millis have moved for summary judgment on all the counts against them (Counts V–X). Their primary argument rests on the proposition that they, as MIT Administrators, had no duty to prevent Elizabeth's suicide. Such a view is consistent with the basic tort principle that ordinarily "we do not owe others a duty to take action to rescue or protect them from conditions we have not created." *Cremins v. Clancy*, 415 Mass. 289, 296, 612 N.E.2d 1183 (1993). More specifically Henderson and Davis–Millis point to Massachusetts law which states that persons who are not treating clinicians have a duty to prevent suicide only if (1) they caused the decedent's uncontrollable suicidal condition, or (2) they had the decedent in their physical custody, such as a mental hospital or prison, and had knowledge of the decedent's risk of suicide. Henderson and Davis–Millis correctly assert that neither of these two situations occurred in this case and therefore, they owed no duty to prevent Elizabeth's suicide.

However, Section 314A of the Restatement (2nd) of Torts expressly recognizes that there exist "special relationships" which give rise to a duty to act or protect a person where otherwise no duty would exist:

> This Section states exceptions to the general rule, stated in § 314 that the fact that the actor realizes or should realize that this action is necessary for the aid and protection of another does not in itself impose upon him any duty to act. The duties stated in this Section arise out of special relationships between the parties, which create a special responsibility, and take the case out of the general rule. The relations [common carrier, innkeeper, land owner, one who is required by law or voluntarily takes custody of another] are not intended to be exclusive, and are not necessarily the only ones in which a duty of affirmative action for the aid and protection of another may be found.... The law appears, however, to be working slowly toward a recognition of the duty to aid or protect in any relation of dependence....

In *Mullins v. Pine Manor College*, the plaintiff was abducted from her dormitory and raped by an unidentified assailant. 389 Mass. 47, 449 N.E.2d 331 (1983). The SJC held that the college and an administrator owed a duty to exercise care to protect the well-being of their resident students, including seeking to protect them against the criminal acts of third parties. The Court noted that it found the source for imposing such a duty in "existing social values and customs."

One year later, in *Irwin v. Town of Ware*, the SJC further explained the basis for imposing a duty where a "special relationship" exists:

> A duty to act with reasonable care to prevent harm to a plaintiff which, if violated, may give rise to tort liability is based on a "special relationship" between the plaintiff and the defendant. *See* W. Prosser, TORTS § 56 (4th ed. 1971). While several different categories of such special relationships are recognized in the common law, they are based to a large extent on a uniform set of considerations. Foremost among these is whether a defendant reasonably could foresee that he would be expected to take affirmative action to protect the plaintiff and could anticipate harm to the plaintiff from the failure to do so. It has been said that such foreseeability can be based on reasonable reliance by the plaintiff, impeding other persons who might seek to render aid, statutory duties, property ownership or some other basis. As the harm which safely may be considered foreseeable to the defendant changes with the evolving

expectations of a maturing society, so change the "special relationships" upon which the common law will base tort liability for the failure to take affirmative action with reasonable care. 392 Mass. 745, 756–57, 467 N.E.2d 1292 (1984).

In *Irwin*, the SJC held that there was a "special relationship between a police officer who negligently failed to remove an intoxicated motorist from the highway, and a member of the public who suffers injury as a result of that failure." More recently, in *Schieszler v. Ferrum College*, a similar case to the instant case, a U.S. District Court in Virginia denied a motion to dismiss on the issue of whether a duty was owed to a student who committed suicide. 236 F. Supp. 2d 602 (W.D. Va. 2002). The campus police and resident assistant responded to a domestic disturbance between the decedent and his girlfriend. Shortly thereafter, the decedent sent a note to his girlfriend indicating that he intended to hang himself with his belt. The resident assistant and campus police were shown the note and went to the decedent's room. They found the decedent with bruises on his head that he admitted were self-inflicted. The campus police notified the dean of student affairs. Days later, the decedent wrote to a friend stating "tell Crystal [his girlfriend] that I love her." The decedent's girlfriend told the defendants but they took no action. Soon thereafter, the decedent wrote another note stating "only God can help me now," which his girlfriend again passed on to the defendants. When the defendants visited the decedent's room, they found that he had hung himself with his belt. The estate of the student filed a wrongful death suit against the college and administrators (dormitory resident assistant and dean of student affairs) alleging (1) that the defendants knew or should have know that the decedent was likely to attempt to hurt himself if not properly supervised and (2) that the defendants were negligent by failing to take adequate precautions to insure that the decedent did not hurt himself.

Following an analysis similar to the SJC in *Mullins* and *Irwin*, the federal court concluded that the defendants owed a duty to the decedent because of a special relationship between them. The court found that a trier of fact could conclude that there was "an imminent probability" that the decedent would try to hurt himself, and the defendants had notice of this specific harm.

In the instant case, Henderson and Davis–Millis were well aware of Elizabeth's mental problems at MIT from at least February 1999. Davis–Millis received numerous reports from students at Random Hall about Elizabeth's self-destructive behavior from February 1999 to April 10, 2000, including the report that Elizabeth was planning to commit suicide on April 10, 2000. Davis–Millis reported these incidents to Henderson and had several conversations with him discussing Elizabeth's fragile state. Henderson received reports from Elizabeth's professors, GRTs, and Davis–Millis who were concerned for her safety. Henderson met with Elizabeth on numerous occasions to discuss her mental health. On one occasion, on November 9, 1999, Henderson referred Elizabeth to MIT Mental Health for an immediate assessment after observing self-inflicted wounds. Henderson was also in regular communication with MIT psychiatrists regarding Elizabeth's treatment. Additionally, Henderson attended weekly "deans and psychs" meetings, including the meeting on April 10 where Elizabeth's mental problems were discussed with other MIT medical professionals. The Plaintiffs have provided sufficient evidence that Henderson and Davis–Millis could reasonably foresee that Elizabeth would hurt herself without proper supervision. Accordingly, there was a "special relationship" between the MIT Administrators, Henderson and Davis–Millis, and Elizabeth imposing a duty on Henderson and Davis–Millis to exercise reasonable care to protect Elizabeth from harm.

B. Gross Negligence (Count VIII)

The Plaintiffs have provided sufficient evidence that Henderson and Davis–Millis were actively a part of Elizabeth's "treatment team." As discussed in the analysis of the MIT Medical Professionals' motion for summary judgment, as a "treatment team," the professionals and administrators failed to secure Elizabeth's short-term safety in response to Elizabeth's suicide plan in the morning hours of April 10. By not formulating and enacting an immediate plan to respond to Elizabeth's escalating threats to commit suicide, the Plaintiffs have put forth sufficient evidence of a genuine issue of material fact as to whether the MIT Administrators were grossly negligent in their treatment of Elizabeth. Accordingly, the MIT Administrators' motion for summary judgment as to Count VIII for gross negligence is Denied.

C. Negligence/Wrongful Death (Counts VI and VII)

For the same reasons discussed in the gross negligence analysis, the Plaintiffs have provided sufficient evidence to raise a genuine issue of material fact as to whether the MIT Administrators breached their duty and proximately caused Elizabeth's death. *See Mullins*, 389 Mass. at 56, 58 (questions of negligence and causation are generally questions of fact for the jury). Accordingly, the MIT Administrators' motion for summary judgment as to Count VI for negligence and Count VII for wrongful death is Denied.

Note on Student Suicide

1. The *Shin* parties eventually settled out of court. Surprisingly, the case which may change the legal landscape on student suicide may not have been a suicide. *See* Marcella Bombardieri, *Parents Strike Settlement with MIT in Death of Daughter*, BOSTON GLOBE, Apr. 4, 2006, at B1 (noting that Shin's parents now believe her death was an accident).

2. Three converging trends make *Shin* and similar cases particularly important for college administrators: an increase in student suicides, an increase in suits against universities, and an increase in the number of students with mental health problems going on to higher education. *See* Heather E. Moore, Note, *University Liability When Students Commit Suicide: Expanding the Scope of the Special Relationship*, 40 IND. L. REV. 423, 424–27 (2007). After alcohol, suicide has now become a leading concern for many university administrators. How should universities handle potentially suicidal students? Should they notify parents of a student's suicidal behavior? Might notification conflict with the student's right to privacy? Would a policy of parental notification deter students from seeking help?

In a recent case, a jury decided that a university mental health counselor and Allegheny College should not be held liable for failing to contact parents prior to a student's suicide. Elizabeth Bernstein, *After a Suicide, Privacy on Trial*, WALL ST. J., March 24–25, 2007, at A1. The counselor testified that she did not contact the parents, despite clear signs of suicidal behavior, because the student requested that his parents not be contacted and she worried that doing so might worsen his depression. *Id.* at A7. Allegheny had a policy of sending letters to all parents asking them to discuss with their children the option of signing a privacy waiver that would allow the college to contact parents on a range of issues, including student safety. The parents of the deceased acknowledged that they did not discuss the waiver with their son. Members of the jury cited the parents' failure to discuss the waiver as a key factor in their decision. *Id.*

Cornell, in contrast, has successfully cut its suicide rate in half over the past six years by implementing a plan that places safety above privacy. Elizabeth Bernstein, *Bucking Privacy Concerns, Cornell Acts as Watchdog*, WALL ST. J., Dec. 28, 2007, at A1. Cornell has trained all of its employees, from janitors to professors, to recognize and report the signs of depression to an "alert team" of campus administrators, police, and counselors. The team meets weekly to compare notes on students suffering emotional problems. *Id.* Exploiting an exception in FERPA for students who are listed as dependents on their parents' tax returns, Cornell also plans to contact parents whom it thinks are suffering emotionally without the permission of students. *Id.*

By taking steps to prevent a suicide, does a university expose itself to increased liability? If a university avoids taking any responsibility for the mental health of its students, might it also be held liable? May universities force students to move off campus after making suicide threats? May schools require counseling sessions in exchange for allowing the student to remain on campus?

Virginia has become the first state to pass legislation barring public colleges for expelling or punishing students "solely for attempting to commit suicide." Robert B. Smith & Dana L. Fleming, *Student Suicide and Colleges' Liability*, CHRON. HIGHER EDUC., Apr. 20, 2007, at B24. Critics charge that the law, taken together with the holding in *Shin*, places colleges in a double bind: either they avoid dealing with students' emotional problems, thereby putting students at risk, or they attempt to help at-risk students, thereby creating a "special relationship" and exposing themselves to liability. Smith and Fleming suggests a number of possible ways that colleges may address the problem, including screening programs for early identification of emotional problems and requiring students to report mental illnesses. *Id.* Would such programs be lawful? Would they be successful? *See* Marlynn H. Wei, *College and University Policy and Procedural Responses to Students at Risk of Suicide*, 34 J.C. & U.L. 285 (2008); Peter Lake, *Still Waiting: The Slow Evolution of the Law in Light of the Ongoing Student Suicide Crisis*, J.C. & U.L. 253 (2008); Susanna Dyer, Note, *Is There a Duty? Limiting College and University Liability for Student Suicide*, 106 MICH. L. REV. 1379 (2008).

D.   LITIGATION DEFENSES

1.   PUBLIC COLLEGES AND UNIVERSITIES

Prairie View A & M University of Texas v. Mitchell

Texas Court of Appeals, First District, 2000.
27 S.W.3d 323.

■ J. MIRABAL.

Prairie View A & M University brings this interlocutory appeal from the trial court's order denying its plea to the jurisdiction based on sovereign immunity.

Michael Mitchell and his wife, Yvette Mitchell, sued Prairie View A & M University, asserting negligence claims arising from the university's alleged misrepresentations that Michael had not graduated from the university.[2]

---

2. The Mitchells also sued Robert F. Ford, as registrar and individually; Ford is not involved in this appeal.

... [T]he Mitchells alleged that Michael graduated from the university on May 3, 1981 with a Bachelor of Science Degree in Civil Engineering, having completed a total of 167 credit hours. The Mitchells unequivocally state that Michael attended the university, completed the curriculum, and earned the degree. After graduating, Michael was employed as a civil engineer by Chevron from 1981 to 1990 and by Stubbs and Overtech from 1991 to 1993. Michael accepted an employment offer from Bechtel Corporation in June 1993 as a Senior Engineer working in California.

In August, 1993, Bechtel Corporation contacted the university to confirm Michael's qualifications. The university told Bechtel Corporation that Michael did not complete his course work and did not obtain a degree. The petition alleges that Bechtel Corporation required Michael to take a leave of absence without pay, "on grounds that Bechtel Corporation could not (after numerous efforts) obtain confirmation from A & M that Mr. Mitchell did in fact graduate with a Bachelor of Science in Civil Engineering Degree in May of 1981." When the Mitchells, after numerous efforts, were unable to resolve the matter, they filed suit against the university.

. . .

The university filed a plea to the jurisdiction asserting sovereign immunity as a bar to the suit. The university argued that the Mitchells' claims, which were based on alleged negligence in the operation of computers, typewriters, and other tangible record-keeping devices, did not constitute claims coming within the waiver of immunity provisions of the Texas Tort Claims Act. After a hearing, the trial court denied the plea to the jurisdiction.

In a single issue, the university asserts the trial court erred because the Mitchells have not stated a claim under the Texas Tort Claims Act for an injury caused by the use or condition of tangible personal property.

It is uncontroverted that the university is a governmental unit that is immune from tort liability except when that immunity has been waived by the legislature. The issue in this case is whether the Mitchells have alleged a cause of action that falls within the immunity waiver provisions of section 101.021(2) of the Texas Tort Claims Act, which reads:

A governmental unit in the state is liable for:

. . .

(2) personal injury and death so caused by a condition or use of tangible personal or real property if the governmental unit would, were it a private person, be liable to the claimant according to Texas law. TEX. CIV. PRAC. & REM. CODE ANN. § 101.021(2) (Vernon 1997).

Our task is to examine the pleadings, to take as true the facts pleaded, and to determine whether those facts support jurisdiction in the trial court....

. . .

This Court has specifically addressed the issue of "whether use of a computer or information contained in a computer printout constitutes use of tangible personal property under the Texas Tort Claims Act." *See Sawyer v. Texas Dep't of Criminal Justice*, 983 S.W.2d 310, 311 (Tex. App.—Houston [1st Dist.] 1998, pet. denied). In *Sawyer*, a prison inmate received a computer printout showing December 2024 as his parole review date. That printout contradicted earlier printouts indicating the inmate's parole reviews date would be 26 years earlier, in September 1998. In fact, the Texas Department of Criminal Justice (TDCJ) had made a mistake, and it later corrected the error with a letter indicating September 1998 was the correct parole review date. The inmate sued, claiming the miscommunication caused him emotional distress.

The inmate in *Sawyer*, as the Mitchells in the present case, alleged the governmental unit used tangible personal property under the Texas Tort Claims Act because it used a computer to create the erroneous printout. Alternatively, the inmate argued the computer printout was itself tangible personal property. Similarly, the Mitchells maintain the printed transcript and diploma constitute tangible personal property. We rejected the inmate's positions in *Sawyer*, reasoning as follows:

> Here . . . equipment used to communicate information was not the source of the alleged injuries. Rather, the alleged injury arose from the information conveyed.
>
> . . . Tangible personal property refers to something that is corporeal, concrete, and has a palpable existence. [*University of Tex. Med. Branch v. York*, 871 S.W.2d 175, 178 (Tex. 1994)]. As *York* clarified, use, misuse, or nonuse of medical information does not constitute use, misuse, or nonuse of tangible personal property under section 101.021(2). Information is not tangible because it lacks corporeal, concrete, and palpable qualities. Although the paper on which the information is printed is tangible, in that it can be seen and touched, the information itself has no such properties. Therefore, a governmental unit does not waive its sovereign immunity by using or misusing information.
>
> . . . Information or misinformation remains *information*, whether it is transmitted by electronic equipment or by word of mouth. The medium used to communicate information does not alter its intangible nature. . . .
>
> We hold that the TDCJ did not waive the sovereign immunity afforded by the Texas Tort Claims Act through the erroneous use of information contained in the computer or the computer printout.

Sawyer, 983 S.W.2d at 312 (emphasis in original).

Sawyer controls the disposition of the present case. Here, the Mitchells alleged injury arose from the information conveyed (that Michael did not have a Bachelor of Science Degree in Civil Engineering). This misinformation (not the computers) was the source of the Mitchells' injury. Although the misinformation was printed on paper (the transcript), and correct information was misused or nonused because it was not printed on paper (a diploma), the information itself is not "tangible personal property." *See University of Tex. Med. Branch v. York*, 871 S.W.2d 175, 178–79 (Tex. 1994); *Sawyer*, 983 S.W.2d at 312. Use, misuse, or nonuse of information does not constitute use, misuse, or nonuse of tangible personal property under section 101.021(2). Therefore, a governmental unit does not waive its sovereign immunity by using or misusing information.

Because the Mitchells' pleadings do not assert facts supporting a claim for injury caused by a condition or use of tangible personal property under section 101.021(2), the trial court erred when it denied the university's plea to the jurisdiction. Accordingly, we sustain the university's sole issue.

We reverse the trial court's order denying the plea to the jurisdiction, and we render judgment dismissing the claims against appellant Prairie

View A & M University of Texas without prejudice for lack of subject-matter jurisdiction.

Questions and Comments on Sovereign Immunity

The doctrine of sovereign immunity can be traced to our colonial period. *See* THE FEDERALIST No. 81 (Alexander Hamilton) ("It is inherent in the nature of sovereignty not to be amenable to the suit of an individual *without its consent.*"); Guy I. Seidman, *The Origins of Accountability: Everything I Know About the Sovereign's Immunity, I Learned from King Henry III*, 49 ST. LOUIS L.J. 393 (2005). Sovereign immunity is both grounded in the common law and included in the constitutions of most states. *See, e.g.*, KY. CONST. § 231; WASH. CONST. art. II, § 26; State v. Baltimore & O.R. Co., 34 Md. 344, 374 (1871). Like Texas, most states have passed tort claims acts, which allow some suits against the state. *See, e.g.*, ALASKA STAT. § 09.50.250; CAL. GOV. CODE § 811.2 (2007); MD. CODE ANN., State Gov't §§ 12–101 to 12–110 (2007). Most state tort claims acts mirror the Federal Torts Claims Act, which was originally adopted in 1946. 28 U.S.C. § 2671 (2007). Sovereign immunity is also commonly waived in contract cases either by statute or common law. *See, e.g.*, MD. CODE ANN., State Gov't § 12–201 (2007); *Ex parte* McLeod, 718 So.2d 682 (Ala. 1997) (holding that sovereign immunity did not bar professor's suit over contract dispute). Many state courts have abrogated the common law doctrine of sovereign immunity. *See, e.g.*, Stone v. Arizona Highway Comm'n, 93 Ariz. 384, 381 P.2d 107, 109 (1963).

As *Prairie View A & M University of Texas* demonstrates, sovereign immunity can be a powerful defense for public colleges and universities. The success of suits against such universities will often depend upon a court's interpretation of the state's tort claims act. *Compare Prairie View A & M University of Texas with* Lowe v. Texas Tech University, 540 S.W.2d 297 (Tex. 1976).

For further discussion of state sovereign immunity, see James A. Burt, *The Tortured Trail of Sovereign Immunity in Missouri*, 54 J. MO. B. 189 (1998); Steven G. Carlino, *The History of Governmental Immunity in Ohio*, 32 OHIO N.U.L. REV. 59 (2006); Angela S. Fetcher, *Outdated, Confusing, and Unfair: A Glimpse at Sovereign Immunity in Kentucky*, 41 BRANDEIS L.J. 959 (2003); Shawn A. Grinolds, *Judicial Abrogation of North Dakota's Sovereign Immunity Results in its Possible Legislative Reassertion and Legislation to Provide Injured Parties a Remedy for the Torts Committed by the State or Its Agents*, 71 N. DAK. L. REV. 761 (1995); Karen J. Kruger, *Governmental Immunity in Maryland: A Practitioner's Guide to Making and Defending Tort Claims*, 36 U. BALT. L. REV. 37 (2006); Michael Shaunessy, *Sovereign Immunity and the Extent of the Waiver of Immunity Created by the Texas Tort Claims Act*, 53 BAYLOR L. REV. 87 (2001); Debra L. Stephens & Bryan P. Harnetiaux, *The Value of Government Tort Liability: Washington State's Journey from Immunity to Accountability*, 30 SEATTLE UNIV. L. R. 35 (2006).

Kimel v. Florida Board of Regents

Supreme Court of the United States, 2000.
528 U.S. 62, 120 S.Ct. 631, 145 L.Ed.2d 522.

[The opinion is set forth at pages 577–86, *supra*].

Joseph v. Board of Regents of the University of Wisconsin System

United States Court of Appeals for the Seventh Circuit, 2005.
432 F.3d 746.

■ FLAUM, CHIEF JUDGE.

Plaintiff Michael Joseph attended college at the University of Wisconsin ("University"). He has completed his studies, but still owes the University over $18,000 in tuition. He alleges that the University violated his constitutional rights by charging him out-of-state tuition while he was a student.... The defendant, the Board of Regents of the University of Wisconsin System, claims that the suit is barred by the Eleventh Amendment, or, in the alternative, that it is without merit. The defendant has also moved to sanction the plaintiff's attorney for filing a frivolous appeal.

. . .

Michael Joseph, a resident of Colorado, attended high school in Maryland. He attended the University of Wisconsin for five semesters. He was charged the nonresident tuition rate of $9,000 per semester. Joseph has paid $27,000 to the University, but still owes approximately $18,500 in back tuition.

During the period when Joseph attended the University, the tuition for Wisconsin residents was approximately $2,500 per semester. Tuition for Minnesota residents, because of a reciprocity agreement between the two states' university systems, was only slightly higher.

Tuition rates for the University are set by the Board of Regents of the University of Wisconsin System ("the Board"). The Board is composed of seventeen members. Fifteen of those members are appointed by the governor of Wisconsin with the advice and consent of the state senate. The Board has the primary responsibility of governing the state university system, consistent with the mandates of Wisconsin statutes. The Wisconsin State Treasurer is the Board's treasurer, and the Board must submit its biennial budget to the State of Wisconsin Department of Administration to be incorporated into the state's budget. This budget is subject to legislative control during the state budget process, and the Department of Administration oversees the University's financial affairs throughout the year.

Joseph sued the Board under 42 U.S.C. § 1983 ("§ 1983"), claiming that the University's tuition policy is unconstitutional. Specifically, Joseph claims that the tuition policy violates the Equal Protection Clause and Article I, Section 10 of the Constitution. The Board moved to dismiss the complaint, under Federal Rule of Civil Procedure 12(b)(6), for failure to state a claim upon which relief can be granted. The district court granted the motion, ruling that the Eleventh Amendment barred the suit. Joseph now appeals.

. . .

We find that the district court properly dismissed Joseph's complaint because it is barred by the Eleventh Amendment of the United States Constitution. The Eleventh Amendment bars private litigants' suits against non-consenting states in federal courts, with the exception of causes of action where Congress has abrogated the states' traditional immunity through its powers under the Fourteenth Amendment. The Supreme Court has held that state agencies, as "arms of the state," *Kroll v. Bd. of Trustees of Univ. of Ill.*, 934 F.2d 904, 907 (7th Cir. 1991), and state officials in their official capacities are also immune from suit under the Eleventh Amendment. *Will v. Mich. Dep't of State Police*, 491 U.S. 58, 70–71 (1989). Additionally, the Court has ruled that states and their departments are not "persons" within the meaning of § 1983. *Id.* at 66, 71.

The Board is an "arm of the state" for Eleventh Amendment purposes. *Romco Ltd. v. Outdoor Aluminum, Inc.*, 725 F. Supp. 1033 (W.D. Wis. 1989) (applying the factors in *Kashani v. Purdue*, 813 F.2d 843 (7th Cir. 1987), to determine if the Board is an "arm of the state" for Eleventh Amendment purposes, and holding that it is); *see also EEOC v. Bd. of Regents of the Univ. of Wis. Sys.*, 288 F.3d 296, 299 (7th Cir. 2002) ("If this case was to be prosecuted in federal court, the EEOC had to do it. The individual charging parties were barred by the Eleventh Amendment from suing the state (and therefore the Board of Regents of the state university system).").

Joseph argues that Congress abrogated the Board's immunity when passing § 1983. He cites three cases in support of his argument, none of which are convincing. The first, *Vlandis v. Kline*, 412 U.S. 441 (1973), was a § 1983 suit involving a public university. That case does not, however, "definitively rule[] that students have the right under § 1983 to sue a state university," as Joseph claims. The plaintiffs in that case sued the director of admissions as an individual, and therefore the Eleventh Amendment was not implicated. Joseph misplaces his reliance on *Gratz v. Bollinger*, 539 U.S. 244 (2003), as well. The plaintiffs in that case sued under a law in which Congress has specifically abrogated the states' Eleventh Amendment rights. The Supreme Court has expressly held that Congress has not abrogated the state' immunity in § 1983 suits. *Quern v. Jordan*, 440 U.S. 332, 341–45 (1979). Finally, Joseph relies on *Monell v. Dep't of Social Services*, 436 U.S. 658 (1978), to support his position. The Court has been clear, however, that *Monell's* holding applies only to municipalities and not states or states' departments.

Because the Board is an "arm of the state" and Congress has not abrogated its immunity in § 1983 actions, this suit is barred by the Eleventh Amendment.

Questions and Comments on the Eleventh Amendment

Eleventh Amendment immunity can be particularly important in suits based on federal legislation such as Title VII, Title IX, and the Americans with Disabilities Act. The Supreme Court has held that Congress may validly abrogate state sovereign immunity only if (1) its desire to do so is unequivocally expressed in the statute, Seminole Tribe of Fla. v. Florida, 517 U.S. 44, 55 (1996), (2) the statute is enacted pursuant to Congress's enforcement power granted through the Fourteenth Amendment, *id.*, and (3) "[t]here must be a congruence and proportionality between the injury to be prevented or remedied and the means adopted to that end," City of Boerne v. Flores, 521 U.S. 507 (1997). The Court's holdings have resulted in a series of decisions about when a state can claim Eleventh Amendment immunity. *See, e.g.*, Nevada Dep't of Human Res. v. Hibbs, 538 U.S. 721 (2003) (finding a valid abrogation of states' immunity in family-leave provision of Family Medical Leave Act), Toeller v. Wisconsin Dep't of Corr., 461 F.3d 871 (7th Cir. 2006) (holding no valid abrogation of states' immunity in self-care provision of Family Medical Leave Act); Hurst v. Texas Dep't of Assistive & Rehab. Serv., 392 F. Supp. 2d 794, 798–802 (W.D. Tex. 2005) (deciding that immunity is waived under Section 504 of the Rehabilitation Act but not under Section 102 of the Act).

To qualify for Eleventh Amendment immunity, a college or university must be an arm of the state and not of a political subdivision. Most public colleges and universities have been recognized as arms of the state. *See, e.g.*, Hall v. Medical College of Ohio, 742 F.2d 299, 301 (6th Cir. 1984) (citing cases that have found public colleges to be arms of the state for Eleventh Amendment purposes). *See generally* Frank H. Julian, *The Promise and Perils of Eleventh Amendment Immunity in Suits Against Public Colleges and Universities*, 36 S. Tex. L. Rev. 85 (1995); Note, *Public Universities and the Eleventh Amendment*, 78 Geo. L.J. 1723 (1990). Courts have been more divided over whether community colleges are entitled to Eleventh Amendment immunity. *Compare* Central Virginia Cmty. College v. Katz, 546 U.S. 356 (2006) (holding that they are) *with* Hander v. San Jacinto Junior College, 519 F.2d 273 (5th Cir. 1975) (holding community college is like a municipal corporation so state is not a real party of interest).

2.   Private Colleges and Universities

Southern Methodist University v. Clayton

Supreme Court of Texas, 1943.
142 Tex. 179, 176 S.W.2d 749.

■ Judge Brewster, of the Commission of Appeals, delivered the opinion for the Court.

During a football game between the teams of petitioner, Southern Methodist University, and Texas A. & M. College, at Dallas, on November 9, 1940, a temporary bleacher collapsed. This is a suit by respondent, J. B. Clayton, to recover damages for injuries sustained by his wife, who was seated in the bleacher when it fell. After Clayton rested his case the trial court sustained the university's motion for an instructed verdict. That action was reversed by the Court of Civil Appeals and the cause was remanded for a new trial.

There is no dispute as to the material facts. Southern Methodist University is incorporated under the laws of Texas as an institution of higher education. It is owned and maintained by the Methodist Church and is governed by a board of trustees elected by subordinate bodies of the church. It has no capital stock and nobody can receive any pecuniary profit from its operation. In addition to a college of arts and sciences, it conducts schools of theology, law, engineering, music, business and the like. It also has a department of athletics, supervised by a professor of physical education, and every student is required to take some form of physical training. Football is one of them, but it is not self-sustaining. Over a period of fifteen years this department showed a net loss of $55,000 to the university's general fund. Besides moneys received from athletic contests, this general fund is constituted by tuition and fees collected from students and by income realized from gifts and endowments. From it all expenses of the university's operation are paid.

One L. B. Morgan had been employed by the university for about fifteen years with the duty, among others, of supervising the football field. That included the erection of temporary bleachers when it was expected that the permanent stands would not seat the spectators. The stand that fell and injured Mrs. Clayton was finished about five days before the game in question. Morgan directed the work.

Clayton alleged that the university was negligent (1) in permitting this stand to be crowded beyond its normal capacity; (2) in failing sufficiently to brace it; and (3) in constructing it of old and defective material. . . .

Because it is devoted to public education without private gain, the university is a charitable institution, despite the fact that it is under the control of a religious denomination and charges tuition. There is a divergence of opinion in our several American jurisdictions as to the tort liability of such an institution to its beneficiaries or to strangers. Some extend absolute immunity, others recognize a limited liability, while a few hold to the doctrine of respondeat superior. Since the limitation generally is based on the theory that it is better that the injured individual go without his damages than that the assets of the charity be dissipated to pay them, it is sometimes held that liability exists but that it cannot be enforced by levy of execution on property exclusively devoted to charity purposes. Obviously this holding is to permit the injured party to get the benefit of indemnity insurance carried by the charity. *O'Connor v. Boulder Colorado Sanitation Association*, 105 Col. 259, 96 Pac. (2d) 835, 133 A.L.R. 819. See 10 Am. Jur., Charities, secs. 140 to 143, inc.; Annotation in 14 A.L.R., beginning at page 572; and *President and Directors of Georgetown College v. Hughes*, 130 Fed. (2d) 810, for excellent reviews of the various holdings.

It seems definitely established in this state that a charity corporation is liable to an employee for injuries proximately caused by the negligence of its officers, vice principals or agents. *Armendarez v. Hotel Dieu* (Civ. App.) 145 S.W. 1030; same case, 167 S.W. 181, 210 S.W. 518. On the other hand, it is equally well settled that it is not liable for such injuries to beneficiaries of the charity, provided it is not negligent in hiring or keeping the agent whose negligence proximately causes the injuries. The principle has been applied in several cases where injuries were received by patients in charity hospitals because of the alleged negligence of nurses.

Whether this rule is to be extended to strangers to the charity is the question we have to decide. It is contended that since the Claytons were on the university's campus as guests paying to watch a football game, they were strangers to the university's charitable purpose of promoting education and are entitled to damages for the injuries sustained by Mrs. Clayton. Or, as respondent puts it in his brief, "If J. B. Clayton had been a student at the University at the time of the injury, the University would have been liable in damages only if it had been negligent in the hiring of L. B. Morgan. But since it is patently clear that Clayton was not a student and was a stranger to the charities of the institution, its negligence in hiring Morgan becomes of no consequence, if the institution is otherwise found to have been negligent." We do not believe there is any solid ground for such a distinction. No Texas case is cited which supports it, nor have we found any. However, *Vermillion v. Woman's College of Due West*, 104 S.C. 197, 88 S.E. 649, a decision by the Supreme Court of South Carolina, is on all fours with this case. There the college gave a musical entertainment in its new auditorium, to which the public was invited for an admission fee of fifty cents each. Plaintiff's intestate was present as a paying guest. While the entertainment was in progress a balcony fell on him, inflicting the injuries from which he died. In an effort to avoid the effect of an earlier decision by that court in *Lindler v. Hospital*, 98 S.C. 25, 81 S.E. 512, that a charity is not liable for injuries suffered by a beneficiary, Vermillion sought to make the identical distinction that Clayton seeks to make here, that is, that his intestate was not a beneficiary of the charity but was "a stranger, sustaining no relation to the charity, except that of an invited guest upon its premises, who had paid for his right to be there." In overruling it, that court said:

> These differences in the facts of the two cases make no difference in the applicable law, because the exemption of public charities

from liability in actions for damages for tort rests not upon the relation of the injured person to the charity, but upon grounds of public policy, which forbids the crippling or destruction of charities which are established for the benefit of the whole public to compensate one or more individual members of the public for injuries inflicted by the negligence of the corporation itself, or of its superior officers or agents, or of its servants or employes. The principle is that, in organized society, the rights of the individual must, in some instances, be subordinated to the public good. It is better for the individual to suffer injury without compensation than for the public to be deprived of the benefit of the charity. The law has always favored and fostered public charities in ways too numerous to mention, because they are most valuable adjuncts of the state in the promotion of many of the purposes for which the state itself exists.

To hold the university liable in damages to Clayton would unquestionably take from it, to the extent of the judgment, funds which would otherwise be devoted to its charity purpose. It would, to that extent, deprive the public of the benefit of the charity. The principle of respondeat superior, if applied to situations like that presented in this case, could result in impairing or destroying the university, in the face of a clear public policy demand that it be preserved. We must agree, therefore, with the holding of the Supreme Court of South Carolina in the *Vermillion* case ... that no liability exists. As said in that case:

> This rule does not put such charities above the law, for their conduct is subject to the supervision of the court of equity; nor does it deny an injured person a remedy for his wrong. It is merely an exception to the rule of respondeat superior, which is itself based on reasons of public policy. The injured person has his remedy against the actual wrongdoer. It is said, however, that he may be and often is financially irresponsible. But the answer is that the law does not undertake to provide a solvent defendant for every wrong done. There are many cases of wrongful injury not compensated, because the wrongdoer is insolvent. Questions of public policy must be determined upon consideration of what on the whole will best promote the general welfare.

> ... [W]e think sound public policy demands that charity corporations be held immune from liability for the torts of their agents, in the absence of negligence in employing or keeping the latter, whether the injured party be a beneficiary of the trust or a stranger to it, since the result to the charity would be the same in either case.

>   . . .

The judgment of the Court of Civil Appeals is reversed and that of the district court is affirmed.

Questions and Comments on the Doctrine of Charitable Immunity

By the 1940s, most states had adopted the doctrine of charitable immunity. *See* Bradley C. Canon & Dean Jaros, *The Impact of Changes in Judicial Doctrine: The Abrogation of Charitable Immunity*, 13 L. & SOC'Y REV. 969, 971 (1979). Charitable immunity ensured that few tort suits against private colleges or universities prevailed.

One year before *Southern Methodist University*, the tide began to change. In *Georgetown College v. Hughes*, 76 U.S.App.D.C. 123 (D.C.Cir.1942), future Justice Rutledge thoroughly analyzed the arguments for and against charitable immunity:

> For it are various commonly advanced arguments: Liability would violate the donor's intention; misappropriate the funds to unauthorized purposes and to persons not within the intended class of beneficiaries; and in effect indemnify the trustees, if the charity is organized as a trust, against the consequences of their own or their subordinate's misconduct. More persuasive apparently, but hardly more substantial, are the frequently expressed fears that imposing liability would dissipate the fund in damages and deprive the favored class or the public of the charity's benefit. A variant is the assumed danger that donors would be deterred from creating the charity and from adding to its funds by subsequent donations. Other considerations are mentioned, but these are the principal ones.
>
> . . .
>
> As against the factors favoring it, may be mentioned the tendency of immunity to foster neglect and of liability to induce care and caution; the departure from the general rule of liability; the anomaly of exempting charitable corporations and trust funds, when charity is not a defense to others; the injustice of giving benefit to some at the cost of injury to others and of the injured individual's having to bear the loss wrongfully inflicted upon him, at a time when the direction of the law is toward social distribution of losses through liability for fault, liability without fault, and legislation which gives the person disabled to work what is commonly but inaccurately called "social" security. There are others we do not stop to mention.

Id. at 824. After noting that the reasons advanced in favor of the doctrine no longer had as much force as they once did, the court abolished charitable immunity as a defense. "The incorporated charity should respond as do private individuals, business corporations and others, when it does good in the wrong way." *Id.* at 828.

Following *Georgetown College*, most states have rejected the doctrine of charitable immunity. *See, e.g.*, Albritton v. Neighborhood Centers Ass'n for Child Dev., 12 Ohio St.3d 210, 466 N.E.2d 867 (1984); Flagiello v. Pennsylvania Hosp., 417 Pa. 486, 208 A.2d 193 (1965). A few states retain the defense and either bar negligence suits entirely, permit suits only against an institution's insurance company, or limit recovery to the extent of the institution's insurance coverage. *See, e.g.*, George v. Jefferson Hosp. Ass'n, Inc., 337 Ark. 206, 987 S.W.2d 710 (1999); Wells v. Rogers, 281 Ga.App. 473, 636 S.E.2d 171 (2006); Coulombe v. Salvation Army, 790 A.2d 593 (Me. 2002); Abramson v. Reiss, 334 Md. 193, 638 A.2d 743 (1994); O'Connell v. State, 171 N.J. 484, 795 A.2d 857 (2002); Ola v. YMCA of S. Hampton Rds, Inc., 270 Va. 550, 621 S.E.2d 70 (2005). Other states cap the amount of damages that can be awarded. *See* Tex. Civ. Prac. & Rem. Code § 84.006; Goldberg v. Northeastern Univ., 805 N.E.2d 517 (Mass.App.Ct. 2004); James v. Lister, 331 S.C. 277, 500 S.E.2d 198 (App. 1998).

*

P A R T V

UNIVERSITY GOVERNANCE

CHAPTER 15

GOVERNING BOARDS AND PRESIDENTS

Chapter 7 examined shared governance of academic matters. This chapter, by contrast, focuses on the overall roles and responsibilities of presidents and governing boards. Today, most private colleges and universities, following the examples set by Harvard and William & Mary in the seventeenth century, are nonprofit corporations subject to the authority of a governing board and the president they appoint. Most public colleges and universities have similar structures, although some campus governing boards are subject to the authority of a state-wide board. By tradition, a majority of the members of academic governing boards are business leaders and alumni rather than academics, although a majority of the board members of some religious colleges and universities are clerics.

A. GOVERNING BOARDS

A. Lawrence Lowell,[a] *The Relation Between Faculties and Governing Boards, in* AT WAR WITH ACADEMIC TRADITIONS IN AMERICA
281–82, 285–91 (1934, reprinted 1970).

The question of the organization of universities and colleges, of the relation between the faculties and the governing boards, has of late years provoked much discussion.... The form of corporate organization with which we are most familiar is the industrial. Concerns of this kind are created by capitalists who take all the risks of the business, conduct it through a board of directors whom they select, and employ the various grades of persons who serve it. The rights and duties of all persons employed are fixed by a contract with the corporation, that is with the owners of the property, and extend only so far as they are contractual. The main reason for the present form of industrial organization is that capital originates the enterprise and takes the risk. For that reason, the board is elected by the capital.... [W]hatever other forms of corporate organization might exist, it is natural that we should take our ideas from the one to which we are most accustomed, and apply them to institutions of all kinds. Yet to do so in the case of universities and colleges, where the conditions are very different, creates confusion and does harm. In this case, there are no owners

---

a. Lowell earned both an A.B. and a law degree from Harvard. For seventeen years he practiced law in a Boston law firm before returning to Harvard. He was a professor of government from 1900 to 1909 and then served as president for a quarter of a century. II AMERICAN HIGHER EDUCATION: A DOCUMENTARY HISTORY 832 (Richard Hofstadter & Wilson Smith eds., 1961).

who take the risk of the business. The institutions are not founded for profit, but for the purpose of preserving, transmitting, and increasing knowledge. The trustees, or whatever the members of the governing boards may be called, although vested with the legal title to the property, are not the representatives of private owners, for there are none. They are custodians, holding the property in trust to promote the objects of the institution.

In the Middle Ages, when the universities first appeared, their property was held and the enterprise conducted practically by the academic body. This is the condition today of the colleges in Oxford and Cambridge, where the property of a college is vested in, and all its affairs are conducted by, the Fellows. In most places this state of things has not continued. In continental Europe the property has become vested, as a rule, in the State, which has also the ultimate power of control. In the American endowed universities it has become vested in a board or boards, distinct, for the most part, from the teaching staff.

        . . .

The transition which has taken place at Harvard [set forth at pp. 15 of this casebook, *supra*] is an example of the differentiation of functions that comes with the growth in size and complexity of institutions. More recent universities and colleges in America have not gone through this evolution, but have started with a body quite distinct from the instructing staff, and containing none of its members except the President; yet a body in which the title to the property and the complete ultimate control are legally vested. This legal situation has no doubt led to the present unfortunate tendency to regard the boards of trustees of institutions of learning as analogous to the boards of directors of business corporations, their legal position being the same. In spite, however, of the difference in legal organization, the best and most fruitful conception of a university or college is the ancient one of a society or guild of scholars associated together for preserving, imparting, increasing, and enjoying knowledge.

If a university or college is a society or guild of scholars why does it need any separated body of trustees at all? Why more than learned societies, which are obviously groups of scholars, and have no such boards recruited outside their own membership? One reason is to be found in the large endowments of our institutions of learning that require for investment a wide knowledge and experience of business affairs. In fact, as already pointed out, the vast complexity of a modern university has compelled specialization of functions, and one aspect thereof is the separation of the scholarly and business organs. Another reason is that higher education has assumed more and more of a public character; its importance has been more fully recognized by the community at large; it must therefore keep in touch with public needs, make the public appreciate its aims and the means essential to attain them; and for this purpose it must possess the influence and obtain the guidance of men conversant with the currents of the outer world.

There is a further reason more fundamental if less generally understood. Teaching in all its grades is a public service, and the administration of every public service must comprise both expert and lay elements. Without the former it will be ineffectual; without the latter it will become in time narrow, rigid, or out of harmony with its public object. Each has its own distinctive function, and only confusion and friction result if one of them strives to perform the function of the other. From this flows the cardinal principle, popularly little known but of well-nigh universal application, that experts should not be members of a non-professional body that supervises experts. One often hears that men with a practical knowledge of teaching should be elected to school boards, but unless they are persons of singular discretion they are likely to assume that their judgment on technical matters is better than that of the teachers, with effects that are sometimes disastrous. Laymen should not attempt to direct experts about the method of attaining results, but only indicate the results to be attained. Many years ago the Board of Overseers, after a careful examination, came to the conclusion that the writing of English by Harvard undergraduates was sadly defective. In this they were acting wholly within their proper province, and the result was a notable improvement in the teaching of English composition. They would not have known, as the instructing staff did, how it should be done, and they would have exasperated and disheartened the teachers.

But another question may well be asked. Granted that there should be both expert and non-professional elements in the management of a university or college, why in a society or guild of scholars should the non-professional organ be the final authority? For this there are three reasons. In the first place, so far as the object is public—and where teaching is conducted on a large scale the object cannot fail to concern the public deeply—that object must in the final analysis be determined by public, that is by non-professional, judgment. In an endowed university the governing board does not, indeed, represent the public in the sense that it is elected by popular vote, but it is not on that account any less truly a trustee for the public.

In the second place, the non-professional board is responsible for the financial administration, and the body that holds the purse must inevitably have the final control.

Thirdly, the non-professional board is the only body, or the most satisfactory body, to act as arbiter between the different groups of experts. Everyone knows that in an American university or college there is a ceaseless struggle for the means of development between different departments, and someone must decide upon the relative merits of their claims. In a university with good traditions the professors would be more ready to rely on the fairness and wisdom of a well constituted board of trustees than on one composed of some of their own number each affected almost unavoidably by a bias in favor of his particular subject.

Let it be observed, however, that although the governing board is the ultimate authority it is not in the position of an industrial employer. It is a trustee not to earn dividends for stockholders, but for the purposes of the guild. Its sole object is to help the society of scholars to accomplish the object for which they are brought together. They are the essential part of the society; and making their work effective for the intellectual and moral training of youth and for investigation is the sole reason for the existence of trustees, of buildings, of endowments, and of all the elaborate machinery of a modern university. If this conception be fully borne in mind most of the sources of dissension between professors and governing boards will disappear....

The differences between the ordinary industrial employment and the conduct of a society or guild of scholars in a university are wide. In the industrial system of employment the employee is paid according to the value of his services; he can be discharged when no longer wanted; and his duties are prescribed as minutely as may be desired by the employer. In a university there is permanence of tenure; substantial equality of pay within each academic grade; and although the duties in general are well understood, there is great freedom in the method of performing them. It is not difficult to see why each of these conditions prevails, and is in fact dependent upon the others. Permanence of tenure lies at the base of the difference between a society of scholars in a university and the employees in an industrial concern. In the latter … men are employed in order to promote its earning power. In a university the concern exists to promote the work of the scholars and of the students whom they teach. Therefore in the industrial concern an unprofitable employee is discharged, but in the university the usefulness of the scholar depends largely upon his sense of security, upon the fact that he can work for an object that may be remote and whose value may not be easily demonstrated. In a university, barring positive misconduct, permanence of tenure is essential for members who have passed the probationary period. The equality of pay goes with the permanence of tenure. In an industrial establishment the higher class of officials, those who correspond most nearly to the grade of professors, can be paid what they may be worth to the concern, and discharged if they are not worth their salaries. How valuable they are can be fairly estimated, and their compensation can be varied accordingly. But professors, whose tenure is permanent, cannot be discharged if they do not prove so valuable as they were expected to be. Moreover, it is impossible to determine the value of scholars in the same way as commercial officials. An attempt to do so would create injustice and endless discontent; and it could offer a temptation to secure high pay, from their own or another institution, by a display wholly inconsistent with the scholarly attitude of mind. The only satisfactory system is that of paying salaries on something very close to a fixed scale…. In an industrial concern the prospect of a high salary may be needed to induce the greatest effort; but indolence among professors is seldom found…. [A] man may desire to do research who is better fitted for teaching, or he may prefer to teach advanced students when there is a greater need of the strongest men in more elementary instruction; but failure to work hard is rare.

The governing boards of universities having, then, the ultimate legal control in their hands, and not yet being in the position of industrial employers, it is pertinent to inquire what their relation to the professors should be. If we bear in mind the conception of a society or guild of scholars, that relation usually becomes in practice clear. The scholars, both individually and gathered into faculties, are to provide the expert knowledge; the governing board the financial management, the general coordination, the arbitral determinations, and the preservation of the general direction of public policy. In the words of a former member of the Harvard Corporation, their business is to "serve tables." The relation is not one of employer and employed, of superior and inferior, of master and servant, but one of mutual cooperation for the promotion of the scholars' work. Unless the professors have confidence in the singleness of purpose and in the wisdom of the governing boards, and unless these in their turn recognize that they exist to promote the work of the society of scholars the relations will not have the harmony that they should. The relation is one that involves constant seeking of opinion, and in the main the university must be conducted, not by authority, but by persuasion. There is no natural antagonism of interest between trustees and professors. To suggest it is to suggest failure in their proper relation to one another; to suppose it, is to provoke failure; to assume it is to ensure failure.

. . .

Attempts have been made to define, and express in written rules the relation between the faculties and the governing boards; but the best element in that relation is an intangible, an undefinable, influence. If a husband and wife should attempt to define by regulations their respective rights and duties in the household, that marriage could safely be pronounced a failure. The essence of the relation is mutual confidence and mutual regard; and the respective functions of the faculties and governing boards—those things that each had better undertake, those it had better leave to the other, and those which require mutual concession—are best learned from experience and best embodied in tradition. Tradition has great advantages over regulations. It is a more delicate instrument; it accommodates itself to things that are not susceptible of sharp definition; it is more flexible in its application, making exceptions and allowances which it would be difficult to foresee or prescribe. It is also more stable. Regulations can be amended; tradition cannot, for it is not made, but grows, and can be altered only by a gradual change in general opinion, not by a majority vote. In short, it cannot be amended, but only outgrown.

Questions and Comments on the Lowell Essay

1. Do you agree with Lowell's description of the ideal relationship between faculty and board? Are there any alternatives that would work as well or better? Why does Lowell assume that professors are seldom "indolent"? Do you agree?

2. Do Lowell's principles give adequate guidance to faculties and boards as to the scope of their respective responsibilities? How should a board resolve disputes over which body has the ultimate authority?

3. One of Lowell's justifications for preferring a lay-governing board to an expert board is that the board should serve as an intermediary between the institution and the public. How responsive to the public should a college or university be? Does it matter whether the institution is public or private?

4. Consider the governing structure of The University of California. Under the California constitution:

> The University of California shall constitute a public trust, to be administered by the existing corporation known as "The Regents of the University of California," will full powers of organization and government. . . . [The Regents] shall be in form a board composed of seven ex officio members, which shall be: the Governor, the Lieutenant Governor, the Speaker of the Assembly, the Superintendent of Public Instruction, the president and the vice president of the alumni association of the university and the acting president of the university, and 18 appointive members appointed by the Governor and approved by the Senate, a majority of the membership concurring . . .
>
> . . .
>
> The members of the board may . . . appoint to the board . . . a person enrolled as a student at a campus of the university for each regular academic term during his service as a member of the board.

. . .

... The Regents ... shall be vested with the legal title and the management and disposition of the property of the university and ... shall also have all the powers necessary or convenient for the effective administration of its trust.

CAL. CONST. art. IX, § 9.

Under the standing orders of the Regents, the President of the University is appointed by a vote of the Board. Among the responsibilities of the president of the university are:

(a) The President shall be the executive head of the University and shall have full authority and responsibility over the administration of all affairs and operations of the University ...

(b) The President is authorized in the name of The Regents to award degrees to candidates recommended by the Academic Senate for degrees in course and certified by the respective registrars, and to confer honorary degrees, the award of which has been approved by the Board....

(c) The President of the University, in accordance with such regulations as the President may establish, is authorized to appoint, determine compensation, promote, demote, and dismiss University employees, except as otherwise provided in the Bylaws and Standing Orders....

. . .

(f) The President annually, through the appropriate Standing Committee, shall present to the Board recommendations as to the budget of the University, recommendations as to the Capital Improvement Program of the University, and recommendations as to requests for appropriations of funds for the University.

. . .

(j) The President shall consult with the Chancellors and the Academic Senate regarding the educational and research policies of the University....

(k) The President shall develop, initiate, implement, and approve fundraising campaigns for the benefit of the University in accordance with the policies of the Board.

The Regents of the University of California, Standing Order 100.4: Duties of the President of the University, http://www.universityofcalifornia.edu/regents/bylaws/so 1004.html. The president is responsible directly to the Board, whereas all other officers of the university are responsible to the president. *Id.* at 1001.

Furthermore, the Regents authorized the creation of an Academic Senate in order to establish a system of shared governance between the Board and the faculty:

(a) The Academic Senate, subject to the approval of the Board, shall determine the conditions for admission, for certificates, and for degrees other than honorary degrees. It shall recommend to the President all candidates for degrees in course and shall be consulted through committees appointed in such manner as the President may determine in connection with the award of all honorary degrees.

(b) The Academic Senate shall authorize and supervise all courses and curricula offered under the sole or joint jurisdiction of the departments, colleges, schools, graduate divisions, or other University academic agencies approved by the Board....

. . .

(d) The Academic Senate is authorized to select a committee or committees to advise a Chancellor concerning a campus budget and to select a committee or committees to advise the President concerning the University budget.

(e) The Academic Senate shall have the right to lay before the Board, but only through the President, its views on any matter pertaining to the conduct and welfare of the University.

The Regents of the University of California, Standing Order 105.2: Duties, Powers, and Privileges of the Academic Senate, http://www.universityofcalifornia.edu/regents/bylaws/so1052.html. Does the University of California system achieve the ideals set forth by Lowell?

5. In October 2006, the Board of Governors of the American Red Cross issued a report analyzing its governance procedures. Although the report terms the Red Cross "unique in the size and complexity of its operations and responsibilities," including responsibility for a more than $2 billion-a-year blood-related business, the report provides information of use to all nonprofits including colleges and universities.

The Red Cross began as a small, Washington, D.C.-based nonprofit association in 1881 under the leadership of Clara Barton. In recognition of the importance of its work, the Red Cross was chartered by Congress in 1900 primarily to fulfill the obligation of the United States under the Geneva Conventions to care for sick and wounded soldiers on the battlefield. The Red Cross is today the only nonprofit organization with a Congressional mandate to provide disaster relief domestically and internationally.

A governance audit was performed to guide the report; it found that over time the distinction between the governance and management functions of the organization had been blurred. The Report recommended a number of steps that should be taken to clarify the Board's role:

1. The Bylaws should be amended to include a statement clarifying the Board's role as a governance and strategic oversight board and to outline areas of Board Responsibility, including, but not limited to:

    - reviewing and approving the mission statement. . . .
    - approving and overseeing the . . . strategic plan and maintaining strategic oversight of operational matters;
    - selecting, evaluating and determining the level of compensation of the . . . CEO;
    - evaluating the performance and establishing the compensation of the senior leadership team, and providing for management succession;
    - overseeing the financial reporting and audit processes, internal controls and legal compliance;
    - holding management accountable for performance;
    - providing oversight of the financial stability of the organization;
    - ensuring the inclusiveness and diversity [of the organization];
    - providing oversight of the protection of the . . . brand and
    - assisting with fundraising.

2. The Bylaws should be amended to:

    - clarify that the management responsibility of the Board under both the Charter and the Bylaws consist of overseeing management; and
    - explicitly delegate management responsibility for operations and day-to-day management. . . .

3. In addition to amending the Bylaws, the Board should adopt a detailed statement of its core governance responsibilities. This statement should be incorporated into a set of governance principles that would be approved by the Board.

4. The Board should focus its meetings on in-depth discussion and may include outside experts at Board meetings.

AMERICAN RED CROSS, AMERICAN RED CROSS FOR THE 21ST CENTURY: A REPORT OF THE BOARD OF GOVERNORS 37–38 (2006), *available at* http://www.redcross.org/report/bogoct 2006.

Assume you are counsel to a university committed to shared governance. What changes would you make in the Red Cross recommendations to provide faculty with primary responsibility for academic matters? Does the experience of the Red Cross refute Lowell's contention that the relationship between the faculty and the governing board should be governed by tradition, rather than regulation?

Benner v. Oswald

United States Court of Appeals, Third Circuit, 1979.
592 F.2d 174, *cert. denied*, 444 U.S. 832.

■ ALDISERT, CIRCUIT JUDGE.

The question is whether the equal protection clause of the fourteenth amendment requires undergraduate student participation in the election of certain members of the Pennsylvania State University (Penn State) board of trustees. The district court ruled that the students had no such right. They have appealed. . . .

. . . The board of trustees is composed of 32 members. Five serve as ex officio members including the president of the University, the state governor and three members of his cabinet. Six other trustees are appointed by the governor with the consent of the senate. The student appellants do not challenge the method by which these eleven trustees are selected, but they do challenge the selection of the remaining 21 trustees. Of this latter group, 9 trustees are elected by the alumni association and 12 are elected by the members of county agricultural and industrial societies of Pennsylvania. Students qua students, therefore, do not participate in the election process. They complain that the refusal to allow them to participate in the selection process of these 21 trustees denies them rights guaranteed by the equal protection clause.

They argue preliminarily that the selection process involves state action, thus affording them a procedural vehicle under 42 U.S.C. § 1983 to obtain relief in a federal forum. Substantively, they mount alternative arguments: first, they contend that *Kramer v. Union Free School District*, 395 U.S. 621 (1969), is controlling judicial precedent requiring appellees to demonstrate that a compelling state interest justifies the trustee selection process. Alternatively, they argue that the selection process cannot pass scrutiny under the less rigorous rational relationship test. . . .

Alumni trustees are chosen for staggered three-year terms and are elected in a process that begins early in each year when nomination ballots are mailed by the University to alumni who have been active members of the alumni association or who have contributed to the University within the past two years or who specifically request a nomination ballot. Approximately 50,000 nomination ballots are mailed. All nominees receiving 50 or more votes are eligible for the election if they consent. Normally between 8 and 12 nominees vie for the three positions. Election ballots are then mailed to the alumni and approximately 14,000 alumni cast their ballots each year.

Agricultural and industrial trustees, also chosen for staggered three-year terms, are elected by specially chosen delegates during the annual commencement week. The agricultural trustee selection process begins around January when the University sends to all county agricultural extension directors the list of agricultural societies which were eligible to send delegates during the previous year. Each county agricultural extension director determines whether the agricultural societies for his county remain eligible and whether there are new societies to be added to the eligibility list. At the time of the district court hearing there were 397 agricultural societies eligible to send delegates. The industrial trustee selection process is similar. The University determines which industrial societies and associations were eligible to send delegates the previous year. The list is sent to five officials who are responsible for updating the list. At the time of the district court hearing, 160 mining, manufacturing and engineering societies were eligible to send delegates. Approximately 450 delegates participate annually. In 1977, there were 207 delegates representing agricultural societies, and 198 delegates representing industrial societies.

Our inquiry into state action must begin with a description of the University.

Penn State was created by statute in 1855 ... and was originally known as the Farmers' High School of Pennsylvania. The enabling act provided great detail about the purposes of the school and the subjects to be taught: "the English language, grammar, geography, history, mathematics, chemistry and such other branches of the natural and exact sciences as will conduce to the proper education of a farmer." The statute also established the time and place of the first meeting of the trustees, and directed them to obtain a tract of land and to make improvements thereon for "an institution properly adapted to the instruction of youth in the art of farming...." The statute also set the number of original trustees, specified that the governor, the secretary of the commonwealth, the "principal of the institution," and the president of the state agricultural society shall be ex officio members of the board, and designated the nine other trustees by name. Successors to the original designated trustees were to be elected annually by delegates of each county agricultural society in the commonwealth.

The institution broadened somewhat in 1862 when Congress passed the Morrill Act, which established land grant colleges. The commonwealth agreed to [the conditions established by Congress]. Annually, trustees adopt the operating budget and determine the level of tuition to be paid by students in the next academic year.... The commonwealth provides an annual appropriation to the University, representing over 30% of the total revenues received. In addition it makes grants for special projects; students have received substantial scholarship aid from Pennsylvania ranging from $6 million to $9 million annually from 1971 through 1976.

In addition, the Pennsylvania General State Authority (GSA) has provided physical facilities to the University for many years. Since 1968 the GSA has constructed on the campuses of the University educational buildings valued at approximately 95 million dollars.... The GSA holds legal title to these buildings and to the land upon which they are constructed. In every instance, the University has conveyed title to the land by general warranty deed, and utilizes the GSA buildings in its educational functions and for no other purpose.

University employees may be members of the State Employees' Retirement System; the University pays its employer's contribution into the retirement system fund from its general operating revenues. Roads on University campuses may be constructed by the Pennsylvania Department of Transportation.

Appellees ... contend that although Pennsylvania supplies funds for the operation of the University, no members of either the executive or the legislative branches of the commonwealth participate officially in the selection process of the board. They argue that other than the ex officio trustees and the trustees appointed by the governor, no state officers participate in formulating essential University policy. Accordingly, they urge us to conclude that the requisite connection between the commonwealth and the University is not present....

.   .   .

We ... conclude that the district court properly analyzed and applied the teachings of this court by determining that state action could be found, either (1) when the state and the entity whose activities were challenged are joint participants in a symbiotic relationship or (2) where the entity is pervasively regulated by the state and a sufficient nexus exists between the state and the challenged activity....

.   .   .

The student appellants advance two arguments in their constitutional attack on the trustee selection process. Primarily, they contend they are being denied a fundamental right to vote and the selection process must therefore be scrutinized under the compelling state interest test.... [T]he students assert that the teaching of *Kramer v. Union School District*, 395 U.S. 621 (1969), and similar cases should control the disposition of this case. Alternatively they urge that even if we examine the selection process under the less stringent rational basis test we should find it constitutionally defective.

.   .   .

In *Kramer, supra*, at issue was a New York statute that limited the right to vote in local school board elections to persons, otherwise eligible to vote in general elections, who owned or leased taxable real property in the school district or who had children enrolled in public school in the particular district. The Court held that in an election of general interest, voting restrictions other than those pertaining to residence, age and citizenship must promote a compelling state interest in order to be constitutional. Because the New York statute in question did not accomplish the articulated state goal with sufficient precision, it was struck down as a denial of equal protection.

Likewise, in *Hadley v. Junior College District of Kansas City*, 397 U.S. 50 (1970), certain residents and taxpayers of the Kansas City school district, one of eight school districts which made up the junior college district of metropolitan Kansas City, mounted a constitutional assault on the Missouri statute that apportioned their right to vote for the trustees who conducted and managed the affairs of the junior college district. The statute provided for the election of six trustees and for the apportionment to be made on the basis of the number of school age children who reside in each district. The

Kansas City school district contained approximately 60% of the total number of school age children in the junior college district but was apportioned only 50% of the total number of trustees. In holding that the right to vote for trustees had been unconstitutionally diluted, the Court determined that "as a general rule, whenever a state or local government decides to select persons by popular election to perform governmental functions, the Equal Protection Clause of the Fourteenth Amendment requires that each qualified voter must be given an equal opportunity to participate in that election...." *Id.* at 56.

Examining these teachings we note that the cases involve general government elections. Such elections are seen as directly relating to the Constitution: "statutes distributing the franchise constitute the foundation of our representative society." *Kramer, supra*, 395 U.S. at 626....

But we refuse to accept the formulation of the student appellants that the right to vote for a university trustee is equivalent to a right to vote in a participatory democracy. We will not conclude that the University trustee selection process is a general public election, or that the trustees perform general governmental functions. The University's board of trustees controls no viable political sub-division and has less power than a local school district. It cannot acquire property by condemnation, levy or collect taxes, or pass on petitions to annex school districts. It simply does not possess the minimum governmental powers associated with municipal, school district, county, state, or federal offices. At most, the board has the authority to approve a budget and set a level of tuition. And even in the setting of tuition, they do not have a free hand. The parties have stipulated that "(t)he level of tuition is based upon estimates of expense and of income from other sources, including the estimated amount of the state appropriation, endowment income, recovery of indirect costs on government contracts and other miscellaneous sources."

. . .

We therefore conclude that the duties of the trustees are not commensurate with the duties of elected public officials; that these duties do not involve the responsibilities going to "the essence of a democratic society," and do not implicate decisions that are "preservative of all rights." Because the trustees' duties do not approach the quantum of responsibilities of officials selected in a political democracy, we conclude that any individual interests affected by the selection process classifications are not fundamental rights so as to require recourse to the strict judicial scrutiny standard.

Our remaining task is to decide whether any rational basis exists to support the distinction which limits participation in the trustee selection process to members of local agricultural and industrial societies and alumni.

... We agree with Judge Muir's determination:

> Penn State argues that because of its historic commitment to both agriculture and industrial goals, it is entitled to give members of agricultural and industrial societies a voice in the operation of the university to the exclusion of other interested groups. The Court cannot say as a matter of law that the distinction made between agricultural and industrial societies and other interested groups, including undergraduate students, is wholly unrelated to the achievement of Penn State's underlying objective which is the governance of the affairs of the University. Therefore the charter provisions which give local agricultural and industrial societies a

voice in selecting members of Penn State's board of trustees but which deny it to undergraduate students do not violate the equal protection clause.

444 F. Supp. at 561–62.

Allowing alumni to participate in the selection process is justified by the premise that those alumni who cast ballots are graduates of the University who have a continuing interest in its affairs. Alumni support of their Alma mater is a universal phenomenon in the United States and alumni provide an important source of political, social, and financial sustenance. The record here reveals that for the period 1953 through 1977 alumni have contributed the sum of $11,247,076 through lifetime gifts or testamentary bequests. An alumni association has been active at Penn State for over 100 years, and the record demonstrates significant participation in University activities.

Applying the rational basis test, we cannot conclude that the trustee selection process which limits participation to alumni and agricultural and industrial groups is irrational. "A statutory discrimination will not be set aside if any state of facts reasonably may be conceived to justify it." *McGowan v. Maryland*, 366 U.S. 420, 426 (1961).

. . .

The judgment of the district court will be affirmed.

Questions and Comments on *Benner v. Oswald*

Do you agree that a university board of trustees has "less power than a local school district"? Why is it reasonable to give voting power to alumni, but deny it to current students?

In contrast to Penn State, many universities have student members on their governing boards, including the University of Illinois, University of Illinois Board of Trustees Home Page, http://uillinois.edu/trustees, and California State University, CSU Board of Trustees Home Page, http://www.calstate.edu/PA/info/BOT/shtml.

McKinney v. Board of Trustees of Mayland Community College

United States Court of Appeals, Fourth Circuit, 1992.
955 F.2d 924.

■ ERVIN, CHIEF JUDGE.

The plaintiffs,[1] former employees of Mayland Community College, which is a part of the North Carolina community college system, sued the defendants in state court alleging that they had been unlawfully discharged because of their political affiliations, or, in the case of Barbara McKinney, for writing a letter critical of how the college selected its president. The defendants removed the case to federal district court and sought summary judgment. After the plaintiffs moved to remand the case to state court, the

---

1. Because there are McKinneys on both sides of the v., to avoid confusion we will refer to the plaintiffs-appellants as "the plaintiffs" rather than by name. For consistency, we will refer to the defendants-appellees as "the defendants."

district court denied the plaintiffs' motion to remand and granted the defendants' motion for summary judgment. The plaintiffs appeal[led]. . . .

. . . The plaintiffs have alleged that their contracts were not renewed because of either their political affiliation or their statements criticizing Mayland. In such a case, plaintiffs have the burden of showing that their conduct was constitutionally protected and that their conduct was a substantial factor in their employer's decision not to rehire them. If the plaintiffs carry their burden, the employer may defend its action by showing by a preponderance of the evidence that it would have reached the same decision in the absence of the protected conduct. *Mt. Healthy City Bd. of Educ. v. Doyle*, 429 U.S. 274, 287 (1977).

We . . . set out the facts relevant to the plaintiffs' claim in the light most favorable to the plaintiffs. Virginia Foxx became President of Mayland Community College in January 1987. Foxx was a Republican whose previous position was an appointive office in Raleigh to which Governor Martin, also a Republican, appointed her. Three of the defendant trustees, all Republicans, had successfully lobbied for her selection at Mayland. Before their efforts, Foxx was not high on the list of candidates. At the time of her selection, nine of the twelve trustees at Mayland were Republicans. Defendant trustee Bill Slagle, a Republican county commissioner in Mitchell County, looked up the political affiliation of Mayland's employees and repeatedly said that too many of them were Democrats. Another Republican trustee, defendant Ted McKinney, said several times that the Republicans planned to fire all the Democrats at Mayland.

At a board of trustees meeting in April 1987, Foxx recommended that the board not renew the contracts of nine administrators and faculty members. All nine were Democrats. Foxx then recommended the nonrenewal of a tenth employee, Barbara McKinney. Barbara McKinney had written a letter criticizing the process that led to the selection of Foxx. The trustees had been visibly angered when they read McKinney's letter at an earlier board meeting.[5] The board then voted not to renew the contracts of all ten employees. Afterwards, defendant Slagle said that the Democrats had gotten what they deserved.

The trustees did not follow Mayland's usual procedures for dismissing the ten employees, and their dismissal caused a considerable controversy in the community. On May 18, 1987, the board voted to rescind its earlier decision. Foxx then began to meet individually with the employees, as Mayland's policy on nonrenewal called for. However, she did not meet with three of them. When she met with plaintiff Ronald McKinney, Foxx broke down and cried, telling McKinney that she was having to make decisions that were not of her choosing and that her decision did not reflect on McKinney personally.

At the next board meeting, Foxx recommended that the same employees not be renewed. The board followed her recommendation. Later, after Republicans in the community expressed strong support for one of the fired employees, Sandra Lusk, she was rehired. In addition to the above evidence of the trustees' political motivation, the plaintiffs also presented evidence that the performance of at least some of the employees had never been criticized, Mayland's budget increased during the period when the defendants claim

---

5. It appears from the plaintiffs' reply brief that Barbara McKinney was also a registered Democrat at the time her contract was not renewed, although until that brief was filed the parties believed that she was a registered Republican at the time of her nonrenewal.

that there was a budget crisis, Foxx's reorganization plan that supposedly necessitated the firings was a sham, and Foxx and the trustees repeatedly did not follow Mayland's employment procedures.

After reviewing the record *de novo*, we believe that the plaintiffs have carried their burden of showing that their protected conduct may have been a substantial factor in the trustees' employment decision. In finding that the trustees would have made the same decision in the absence of the plaintiffs' protected conduct, the district court seems to have drawn several inferences in the *defendants'* favor. For example, the district court explained away defendant Slagle's apparent political motivation by noting that he was not present at the April board meeting. However, the plaintiffs argue that the trustees at that meeting may have just rubberstamped an already formed plan, and Slagle was present at the later board meeting at which the nonrenewals were actually implemented. The district court also found that Mayland was in the midst of a budget crisis at the time of the nonrenewals, although there is conflicting evidence on that point. In addition, the district court completely ignored two pieces of potentially incriminating evidence: (1) defendant Ted McKinney's statement that the Republicans were planning to fire Mayland's Democratic employees, and (2) Foxx's breakdown before plaintiff Ronald McKinney and statement to him that she was having to make decisions not of her choosing. Viewing the evidence in its entirety, we agree with the plaintiffs that it is possible that Foxx's reorganization plan was pretextual. Finally, it is not dispositive that Mayland has improved since the dismissal of the plaintiffs, with attendance and other measures of success up. That improvement alone does not show that these firings were properly motivated. In making these several inferences in the defendants' favor, the district court failed to adhere strictly to the legal standard appropriate to motions for summary judgment.

Of course, the defendants may win at trial. There may have been perfectly acceptable reasons for not renewing the plaintiffs' contracts. The plaintiffs' positions were mostly eliminated or filled by other Democrats. George Fouts, who was the interim president before Foxx took over and apparently non-partisan, recommended that most of the plaintiffs not be renewed. However, despite these facts, there were far too many suspicious aspects about the nonrenewals to rule in the defendants' favor as a matter of law. We therefore reverse the granting of the defendants' motion for summary judgment and remand the case to the district court for proceedings not inconsistent with this opinion.

Note on Holding Governing Boards Accountable

If the Board of Directors of a public corporation fails to discharge its duties, there are a number of mechanisms to hold it to account including shareholder derivative suits. What can be done in the case of a nonprofit corporation such as a university? This question is the focus of the next case.

Summers v. Cherokee Children & Family Services

Tennessee Court of Appeals, 2002.
112 S.W.3d 486.

■ PATRICIA J. COTTRELL, J., delivered the opinion of the court.

In this appeal, the Attorney General filed suit to dissolve two nonprofit public benefit corporations.... The trial court granted summary judgment for the Attorney General finding that the nonprofit corporations had abandoned their charitable purposes. . . .

This is a case of first impression in this State wherein the Attorney General sought to involuntarily dissolve Cherokee Children and Family Services, Inc. ("CCFS") and Cherokee Children Nutrition, Inc. ("CCN") via the authority granted in Tenn. Code Ann. § 48–64–301(a)(1). CCFS and CCN are two related nonprofit public benefit corporations that are tax-exempt under state and federal law. The Attorney General sought appointment of a receiver to marshal the remaining nonprofit assets, dissolve the corporations, and distribute the assets to other "legitimate" nonprofit organizations. . . .

[WillieAnn Madison incorporated CCFS and CCN as nonprofit public benefit corporations. Both were granted tax exempt status under 501(c) (3) of the Internal Revenue Code. Neither corporation had any members. According to its charter, CCFS was founded to "provide transitional child care services for children of low-income families referred by the Department of Human Services [DHS]." CCN was organized to handle certain portions of the food program for which CCFS was responsible in accordance with contracts between CCFS and DHS.]

Under the 1990 contract with DHS, the State compensated CCFS and CCN by reimbursing the company for expenses incurred. The contracts in effect from 1992 to 1999 significantly changed the payment program by providing that CCFS and CCN would be paid a percentage (between 3% and 3.5%) of the funds DHS paid to daycare centers for Cherokee-placed children. CCFS was not required to report its costs to DHS under this type of contract. From January 1, 2000, to August 21, 2000, the parties operated under a third contract that reverted to the cost reimbursement plan.

Our Supreme Court has recently described the relationship between CCFS and the State:

> Between 1990 and 2000, Cherokee contracted with TDHS to perform certain functions related to government-subsidized child care services in Shelby County. It is important to note here that Cherokee did not 'care for' or 'keep' children in the strictest sense. Rather, it served as a 'brokering agency' that screened applicants and assisted eligible applicants in locating approved child care providers. TDHS paid the child care subsidies directly to the care centers; Cherokee, therefore, was not involved in the payment of subsidies for the child care services. Virtually all of Cherokee's operating revenue, however, came from government sources.

Memphis Publ'g Co. v. Cherokee Children & Family Services, 87 S.W.3d 67 (Tenn.2002).

As the Supreme Court found, the vast majority of the income of both CCFS and CCN has come from contracts with DHS or other government programs. The total revenue received from DHS by CCFS and CCN, including earned commissions, was $3,055,004 in 1998, $6,869,465 in 1999, and $4,910,477.08 in 2000. . . .

Mrs. Madison has been the Executive Director of CCFS and CCN since their inception. Her compensation included a salary and, from time to time, she has received additional compensation or bonuses. According to CCFS, this additional compensation was based on the success of the program.

The State canceled its contract with CCFS by letter dated August 21, 2000....

After the Attorney General began the investigation that led to the institution of this action, the current Board of Directors, which consists of two longtime members and two new members, undertook to review past corporate actions or transactions, including related party transactions, as well as the allegations of the complaint regarding misapplication or wasting of assets. The Board ratified many of the prior transactions, instituted new controls, reduced its operating expenses significantly because of the loss of the State contracts, and settled an issue of rent overpayments....

. . .

The Attorney General's action is based on Tenn. Code Ann. § 48–64–301(a)(1) which authorizes a court to dissolve a nonprofit corporation in an action brought by the Attorney General if it is established that the corporation:

(A) Obtained its charter through fraud;

(B) Has exceeded or abused the authority conferred upon it by law;

(C) Has violated any provision of law resulting in the forfeiture of its charter;

(D) Has carried on, conducted, or transacted its business or affairs in a persistently fraudulent or illegal manner;

(E) Is a public benefit corporation and the corporate assets are being misapplied or wasted; or

(F) Is a public benefit corporation and is no longer able to carry out its purposes; provided, that the enumeration of these grounds for dissolution shall not exclude actions or special proceedings by the attorney general and reporter or other state officials for the dissolution of a corporation for other causes as provided in this chapter or in any other statute of this state....

. . .

The two corporations were both formed pursuant to the Tennessee Nonprofit Corporation Act, TENN. CODE ANN. §§ 48–51–101 *et. seq.* Nonprofit corporations in Tennessee can be religious corporations, public benefit corporations, or mutual benefit corporations. Both corporations herein are public benefit corporations.

. . .

... A basic distinction between for profit and nonprofit entities is the possibility of private enrichment. Thus, "in general terms, a nonprofit enterprise is an organization in which no part of the income is distributable to its members, directors or officers...." RONALD LEE GILMAN, TENNESSEE CORPORATIONS § 11B–1 (2001).... To be more precise,

one crucial feature distinguishes nonprofit corporate governance from that of for-profit corporations: nonprofit corporations are subject to the non-distribution constraint. The non-distribution constraint prevents the organization from distributing its net earnings to those in control of the corporation. . . .

Developments in the Law—Nonprofit Corporations, 105 HARV. L. REV. 1578, 1582 (May 1992) (footnotes omitted).

· · ·

. . . Under TENN. CODE ANN. § 48–63–101 a nonprofit corporation may make no distributions that are not authorized by TENN. CODE ANN. § 48–63–102. That section provides that a public benefit corporation may make distributions to its members: (1) who are public benefit corporations; and (2) if in conformity with its charitable purposes. TENN. CODE ANN. § 48–64–102(b). "Distribution" is defined as "the direct or indirect transfer of assets or any part of the income or profit of a corporation, to its members, directors, or officers." TENN. CODE ANN. § 48–51–201(11). Thus, in combination, these statutes clearly prohibit the transfer of assets, income, or accumulated revenue to any individual who is a member, director, or officer of the corporation. The statutory exception to that prohibition is found in the definition "distribution."

"Distribution" does not include:

(A) The payment of compensation in a reasonable amount to its members, directors, or officers for services rendered;

(B) Conferring benefits on its members in conformity with its purposes;

(C) Repayment of debt obligations in the normal and ordinary course of conducting business activities; or

(D) The incurrence of indebtedness, whether directly or indirectly (including through a guaranty), for or on behalf of a member, director or officer.

In addition to these limitations on distributions, nonprofit corporations are specifically prohibited from lending money to, or guaranteeing the obligation of, a director or officer of the corporation. TENN. CODE ANN. § 48–58–303.

Nonprofit corporations are eligible for beneficial treatment in a number of areas, particularly taxation. Such treatment is in recognition of the benefit to the public good resulting from the work of most nonprofit organizations. Exemption from federal taxation and tax-deductibility of donations are benefits of classification as a § 501(C)(3) entity, but that classification is based upon essentially charitable purposes where the public good is served, not the private interest of any corporate insider.

· · ·

Similarly, the Tennessee Constitution authorizes the legislature to exempt from taxation property held and used for purposes purely religious, charitable, scientific, literary, or educational. Tenn. Const. art. II, § 28. The legislature has enacted statutes providing for such exemption, but has specifically stated the property of institutions shall not be exempt if:

The organization thereof for any such avowed purpose be a guise or pretense for directly or indirectly making any other pecuniary profit for such institution, or for any of its members or employees, or if it not be in good faith organized or conducted exclusively for one (1) or more of these [religious, charitable, scientific, or educational] purposes.

TENN. CODE ANN. § 67–5–212(a)(3)(B).

This exemption and the liberal interpretation applied to tax exempt statutes are based upon the "benefit conferred on the public by such institutions, and a consequent relief, to some extent, of the burden upon the state to care for and advance the interests of its own citizens."

Thus, it is clear that the bargain made with the government, the taxpayers, and the public in return for benefits such as tax exemption is that the organization will be operated for the public good and not to enrich those involved in running it.

. . .

Adherence to the fundamental character of a nonprofit corporation is intended to be insured, in part, by the fiduciary duties imposed on officers and directors of such corporations. It is well established that officers and directors of a for profit corporation owe a fiduciary duty to the corporation and its members or shareholders. Directors and officers of corporations are bound to the exercise of the utmost good faith, loyalty, and honesty toward the corporation. "The directors of a corporation have to see to it that the corporation had the benefit of their best judgment and act solely and always with reasonable care in good faith to promote its welfare."

Directors and officers of nonprofit corporations also owe a fiduciary duty to the corporation. There are two basic fiduciary duties: the duty of care and the duty of loyalty. They are embodied in the Revised Model Nonprofit Corporation Act and have been enacted in Tennessee:

(a) A director shall discharge all duties as a director, including duties as a member of a committee:

(1) In good faith;

(2) With the care an ordinarily prudent person in a like position would exercise under similar circumstances; and

(3) In a manner the director reasonably believes to be in the best interests of the corporation.

TENN. CODE ANN. § 48–58–301. A corporate officer with discretionary authority is subject to the same standards. TENN. CODE ANN. § 48–58–403.

These statutory standards of conduct for directors and officers of nonprofit corporations are similar to those for their counterparts in for profit corporations. However, because the missions of the two types of corporations are different, the duty of loyalty is defined somewhat differently. The officers and directors of a for profit corporation are to be guided by their duty to maximize long term profit for the benefit of the corporation and the shareholders. A nonprofit public benefit corporation's reason for existence, however, is not to generate a profit. Thus, a director's duty of loyalty lies in pursuing or ensuring pursuit of the charitable purpose or public benefit which is the mission of the corporation.

. . .

In addition to the duties of care and loyalty, or as part of them, certain transactions, called conflict of interest transactions, between the corporation and a director or officer are subject to close scrutiny. "Close investigation is accorded a corporation's transactions with an officer or director, and the burden of proof is placed upon the officer or director because of his fiduciary capacity." [*Johns v. Caldwell*, 601 S.W.2d 37, 411 (Tenn. Ct. App. 1980)]. At common law, an absolute prohibition existed against contracts between corporations with common directors, but that prohibition has been modified by statute.

A conflict of interest transaction is statutorily defined as "a transaction with the corporation in which a director or officer of the corporation has a direct or indirect interest." TENN. CODE ANN. § 48–58–302(a). A director or officer has such an interest if, but not only if, "another entity in which the director or officer has a material interest. . . . is a party to the transaction" or "another entity of which the director or officer is a director, officer, or trustee is a party to the transaction." TENN. CODE ANN. § 48–58–302(c).

Under the Revised Model Nonprofit Corporation Act, any conflict of interest transaction is voidable by the corporation, and may be the basis for liability of a director or officer, unless the transaction was fair at the time it was entered into or is approved in accordance with statutory provisions. TENN. CODE ANN. § 48–58–302(a). A conflict of interest transaction may be approved if:

(1) The material facts of the transaction and the director's or officer's interest were disclosed or known to the board of directors or a committee consisting entirely of members of the board of directors and the board of directors or such committee authorized, approved, or ratified the transaction;

(2) The material facts of the transaction and the director's or officer's interest were disclosed or known to the members and they authorized, approved, or ratified the transaction; or

(3) Approval is obtained from:

(A) The attorney general and reporter; or

(B) A court of record having equity jurisdiction in an action in which the attorney general and reporter is joined as a party.

TENN. CODE ANN. § 48–58–302(b). Any approval by the board requires the affirmative vote of a majority of the directors who have no direct or indirect interest in the transaction, but no such transaction may be approved by a single member of the board.

Approval meeting the statutory requirements, however, simply removes the voidability of the transaction by the corporation, or personal liability for directors and officers. In addition, directors considering such approval must comply with their fiduciary duties in deciding whether to approve. Such approval does not obviate the requirements of nondistribution to corporate insiders and use of assets for public benefit purposes.

Where corporate officers and directors do not, contrary to their fiduciary duties, advance the corporation's charitable goals, protect its assets, and ensure that its resources are used to achieve the corporation's purposes and not to enrich those who control the corporation, other remedies exist. TENN.

CODE ANN. § 48–64–301(a)(2) authorizes dissolution of a nonprofit corporation in a proceeding brought by a specified number or percentage of voting members upon proof of one of several grounds, including where "the corporate assets are being misapplied or wasted" or where "the directors or those in control of the corporation have acted, are acting, or will act in a manner that is illegal, oppressive, or fraudulent." TENN. CODE ANN. § § 48–64–301(a)(2)(B) & (D).

Even before the adoption of the Revised Model Nonprofit Corporation Act, Tennessee recognized the right of members of a nonprofit corporation to bring the equivalent of a shareholder derivative action against the directors and officers for wasting corporate assets and using corporate assets for personal gain. *Bourne v. Williams*, 633 S.W.2d 469 (Tenn. Ct. App. 1981)....

This right, however, is not effective where, as here, a nonprofit corporation has no members. Consequently, statutory authority has been given to the Attorney General to act in the public good in enforcing the requirements applicable to nonprofit corporations, particularly public benefit corporations. *State ex rel. Adventist Health Care Sys. v. Nashville Mem'l Hosp., Inc.*, 914 S.W.2d 903, 907 (Tenn. Ct. App. 1995). The Tennessee statutes mirror the provisions of the Revised Model Nonprofit Corporation Act, and the authority given therein to the Attorney General was designed to protect the public interest in the operation of nonprofit public benefit corporations.

> Since the enactment of the Statute of Charitable Uses in the sixteenth century, a major device for regulating charities has been the power of the attorney general to regulate or investigate charitable trusts. Over time, this power has been recognized and applied to nonprofit corporations organized for charitable purposes. The Revised [Model Nonprofit Corporation] Act has extended this concept to reach all nonprofit corporations in varying degrees. The state under the Revised Act has limited power to regulate mutual benefit and religious corporations, but it has broad power of supervision over the public benefit corporation. This is one of the features of the Revised Act that is both most criticized and most complimented. The Drafting Committee, however, accepted such provisions on the rationale that public benefit corporations, which usually have no participants with a sufficient economic interest to assure oversight, can only be made accountable for their use of assets if there are broad powers of regulation in a state officer. To that end, the Revised Act provides standing to the attorney general to protect the public interest.

[Lizabeth A. Moody, *The Who, What and How of the Revised Model Nonprofit Corporation* Act, 16 KY. LAW REV. 251, 262–63.][25] The drafters of the Revised

---

25. In addition to the provision authorizing the action brought herein, pursuant to TENN. CODE ANN. § 48–58–110(a)(1), the Attorney General may bring an action to remove a director of a public benefit corporation who is "engaged in fraudulent or dishonest conduct, or gross abuse of authority or discretion, with respect to the corporation." Further, a dissolving public benefit corporation must notify the Attorney General of its intent to dissolve and the distribution of its assets, and no assets may be transferred until the passage of twenty (20) days, consent by the Attorney General, or notice that the Attorney General will take no action regarding the transfer. TENN. CODE ANN. § 48–64–103. Under this section, the Attorney General has "authority to bring any action he deemed necessary to protect the public inter-

Model Act intended that the Attorney General of the incorporating state have wide discretion and broad powers in regulating public benefit corporations to ensure that they operate as nonprofits.

An official comment to the Revised Act provides:

> The failure to set forth an explicit limitation on a nonprofit organization's activities [in terms of limiting corporate purposes] does not mean that an enterprising entrepreneur can improperly and with impunity operate in the nonprofit form. In general, public benefit and religious corporations cannot make distributions to members or controlling persons. Unreasonable compensation cannot be paid to members or controlling persons. In addition, the attorney general has broad powers to ensure that a public benefit corporation is not operating for the private benefit of any individual.

The statute itself, TENN. CODE ANN. § 48–64–301, establishes grounds for dissolution of nonprofit corporations in general. . . . There can be no question that the legislature intended to provide oversight of public benefit corporation assets to ensure their proper use and prevent their misapplication. Thus, the Attorney General, acting in the public interest, has authority to seek dissolution of a nonprofit public benefit corporation which fails to devote its assets to a public, rather than a private, interest. Where such a corporation is operated for the private benefit of an individual in contravention of the principles governing nonprofit status and its accompanying benefits, or where, as the trial court phrased it, the corporation has abandoned its public benefit, charitable purpose, action by the Attorney General and the courts is warranted.

. . .

. . . Mrs. Madison was the incorporator of both corporations. She served as the executive director throughout the corporate existence. Her husband, John Madison, Sr. was the corporations' accountant. Her father, William Davis, was on the Board of Directors of CCFS for a number of years. The Board also included Rev. C.E. Ware, Mrs. Madison's pastor, who testified that Mr. Madison, as presiding elder over the church district, was Rev. Ware's immediate supervisor. Two of Mrs. Madison's children were employees of the corporation(s), as were her nephew, her stepson, and her husband's nephew.

Most of the various members of the Board had some association with a childcare provider: as owner, manager, director, or employee. Mr. and Mrs. Madison operated a day care center, referred to as Little People. Mr. Davis served on the board of two day care providers. Rev. Joyner, also a member of the CCFS Board of Directors for some years, was pastor of a church which operated a day care center. Rev. Ware was the chairman of the board of directors for his church's day care center. Ida Porter, a longtime Board member, was the director of a daycare program. Phyllis Herring, Mrs. Madison's sister, owned a child care center. As a broker for child care services, CCFS provided parents with lists of available child care centers in their area. All the Board members who gave depositions testified that CCFS

est. . . ." *State ex rel. Adventist Health Care Sys.,* 914 S.W.2d at 906. Additionally, the Attorney General is authorized to bring an action to enjoin a corporate act on the ground the corporation lacked power to act. TENN. CODE ANN. § 48–53–104(b).

did not directly refer any parents to their child care centers; the choice of centers was made by the parents.

CCFS regularly did business with its officers and directors, as more specifically detailed below. The record is replete with references by the auditors to related party transactions. They included purchasing travel arrangements through a charter travel company owned and operated by the church of which Rev. Joyner is the pastor. In addition, CCFS purchased insurance through one Board member and has done a significant amount of business with an equipment rental business owned or managed by a recently appointed Board member. As one Board member expressed it:

If a person was giving his time to the Board most—I think it is unkind if you didn't make purchases from them. If they were giving their time serving on the volunteer Board I think it would be unkind if they had a business and you needed something they had, I think it would be unkind not to purchase from them.

Perhaps the most telling description of how the corporations operated came from longtime Board member, Mr. Davis, as he expressed his view of CCFS while testifying about his approval of a particular transaction:

A. Let me say this. As a Board member I did not know whether we were operating directly for Cherokee [CCFS] or directly for her [Mrs. Madison], I didn't understand that.

Q. Okay. So during Board meetings it was not necessarily clear whether you were operating on behalf of the corporation or operating on behalf of your daughter?

A. That's right.

Q. Why did you fail to understand that distinction?

A. Because I thought it was all one.

Q. Okay. As a Board member you thought that the financial affairs of the corporation and the financial affairs of your daughter were the same?

A. Yes.

. . .

According to CCFS's 990 filings, CCFS paid as compensation to officers and directors the following: In FY 95, $100,000 (all to Mrs. Madison); in FY 96, $150,000 (of which $100,000 was paid to Mrs. Madison); in FY 97, $165,508 (all to Mrs. Madison); in FY 98, $239,402 (of which $177,000 was paid to Mrs. Madison); in FY 99, $200,000 (of which $125,000 was paid to Mrs. Madison). Each of these forms listed by name other corporate officers and stated that those officers received no compensation. The implication is that the difference was paid to directors, but the difference is unexplained in the record before us.

CCFS made interest-free loans to several employees. Most significant among those was a loan of $10,396.15 to John Madison, Jr., the son of John Madison, Sr. and the stepson of Mrs. Madison. He was an employee of CCFS at the time of the loan. According to the independent auditor, CCFS's books reflected this as a "no interest" loan made May 18, 1999. The auditors listed this loan, describing it as a related party loan, on its FY 99 report as a "reportable condition" because IRS regulations require that interest be charged on a loan exceeding $10,000. The Madisons testified that the loan was made to John Madison, Jr. to pay off a student loan and to foreclose garnishment proceedings. CCFS does not dispute the facts surrounding this loan, but states that interest including retroactive interest "was eventually charged" to John Madison, Jr. and that he repaid the loan in full including all interest.

The Attorney General has pointed out a number of expenditures made by the corporations which he alleges involve substantial benefit to the Madisons, their family, and other persons employed by or controlling the corporations, including primarily personal expenses. These include travel expenses, particularly trips to London and Hawaii. In specific, the Attorney General's statement was, "Madison paid her personal credit card with corporate money. These bills amounted to and included foreign trips." . . .

. . .

The testimony of several Board members demonstrates that they were less than vigilant or probing in examining corporate activities and in remaining knowledgeable about the corporation. They relied upon Mrs. Madison for information and recommendations and generally did not question her recommendations. For example, Rev. Ware testified he did not know if Mrs. Madison was being compensated by both corporations, or by one on behalf of both, and he did not inquire into it. He also testified that he was not aware of the financial condition or resources of CCFS; he did not look at financial statements; he had not ever looked into the financial condition of the corporation. The testimony of several Board members indicates their lack of knowledge of the duties imposed by law upon corporate directors.

. . .

It is not necessary for this court to address the corporations' arguments regarding the sufficiency of the proof of fraudulent or illegal operations; neither must we address the arguments as to whether specific transactions constituted a waste or misapplication of assets. We are of the opinion that the trial court correctly recognized the central issue in this case: whether the corporations complied with the requirements of nonprofit public benefit corporations in fulfilling their charitable or nonprofit purposes, or whether they were operated for private financial gain. To the extent the corporations were operated for private gain, their assets were misapplied. Thus, the question is whether the undisputed facts demonstrate that CCFS and CCN were operated for the private benefit of Mrs. Madison, her family, or other corporate insiders.

A review of the record . . . leads to the inevitable conclusion that the corporations were operated for the private gain of Mrs. Madison, her family, and/or other individuals in control of the corporations. The facts demonstrate a consistent pattern of disregard of the corporations as separate entities from Mrs. Madison. They also demonstrate a disregard of the fundamental nature of a nonprofit public benefit corporation.

Even based on the figures provided by the corporations, although they are not entirely reconcilable, Mrs. Madison was paid a substantial salary, but was regularly awarded bonuses of 50% or more of her stated salary. Corporate records and corporate memory are ambiguous about the exact amounts so paid, although several $50,000 bonuses were awarded her. The corporations' inexact records on this issue simply demonstrate the inattention paid to distributions to Mrs. Madison by anyone other than Mrs. Madison. Although the corporations attempt to justify the raises in salary and the large bonuses as merited by the success of the program, including the financial success, that argument misses the point. The goal of a nonprofit public benefit corporation is not to generate profit; neither is it to reduce its "profit" or excess revenues by increasing operating expenses which enrich corporate insiders. Excess revenues are intended to be used to further the charitable or public benefit mission of the corporation. We do not imply that a public benefit corporation cannot reward its officers with salary increases or other compensation if that compensation is reasonable. Although the corporations argue vehemently that they proved that Mrs. Madison's salary was reasonable, that proof was related to her 2000 salary disclosed as $125,000, an amount the corporations describe as the highest salary level she reached. We find no proof to support an argument that regular yearly grants of additional compensation of 50% or more of her salary is reasonable. In any event, it is not a question of whether any particular amount was proven to be reasonable or unreasonable. Rather, the apparently cavalier way in which the corporation regularly gave its creator and executive director significant "additional compensation" plus her also increasing salary demonstrates to us that the corporations' assets were treated as a ready source of economic benefit to an individual.

Another example of the manner in which the corporate resources were used involves payment for personal expenses. Mrs. Madison freely used corporate funds for personal expenses for herself and her family, such as the travel described earlier. In those instances, no one in the corporation apparently questioned the original payment of the expenses by the corporation, and the corporation was never repaid, even though there is no dispute that the trips had no business purpose.

. . .

These circumstances as well as others demonstrate a failure of those in control of the corporations to ensure adherence to the basic requirement of a nonprofit public benefit entity: that it be operated exclusively for a charitable purpose, that it serve a public rather than a private interest, and that its income or assets not be distributed to individuals in control of the entity. . . .

While we need not specifically address some of the issues raised by the corporations because they relate to grounds other than the one we find determinative, there remains one argument which we interpret as a general defense to dissolution. In essence, the corporations argue that they established a defense to many of the Attorney General's allegations because the directors' judgment with respect to the challenged financial transactions was insulated from "second-guessing" by the business judgment rule. Essentially, the corporations argue that decisions by the Board regarding compensation, payment of expenses, investment, leasing, etc. are committed to the sound discretion of the Board and should not be second-guessed by the courts.

. . .

We conclude that the business judgment rule has no application to the case before us. While the business judgment rule reflects a judicial policy of declining to substitute a court's judgment for that of a corporation's directors when they have acted in good faith and in the exercise of honest judgment in furtherance of corporate purposes, that policy has no application to allegations that a public benefit corporation has abandoned any charitable purpose and has pursued private, rather than public, interests. Similarly, while Tennessee courts have adopted a non-interventionist policy with regard to internal corporate matters, *McRedmond v. Estate of Marianelli*, 46 S.W.3d 730, 736 (Tenn. Ct. App. 2000), that policy is inapplicable here because the legislature has specifically given the Attorney General and the courts authority and responsibility to ensure that nonprofit public benefit corporations operate in the public interest and not for private gain. The public policy of this state, as expressed by the legislature, is that the Attorney General and the courts intervene in such situations because the public interest is involved and the activities involved are not merely "internal corporate matters."

. . .

After a careful consideration of the record, we have determined that the trial court was correct in granting summary judgment for the Attorney General, appointing a receiver, and ordering the dissolution of CCFS and CCN. Therefore, we affirm the decision of the trial court and remand the case for any further proceedings consistent with this opinion which may be necessary.

Questions and Comments on *Summers*

For further discussion of oversight of nonprofits, see generally PANEL ON THE NONPROFIT SECTOR, PRINCIPLES FOR GOOD GOVERNANCE AND ETHICAL PRACTICE: A GUIDE FOR CHARITIES AND FOUNDATIONS (2007) *available at* http://www.nonprofitpanel.org/Report/principles/Principles_Guide.pdf; Marion R. FREMONT-SMITH, GOVERNING NONPROFIT ORGANIZATIONS (2004); Ronald Chester, *Improving Enforcement Mechanisms in the Charitable Sector: Can Increased Disclosure of Information Be Utilized Effectively?*, 40 NEW ENG. L. REV. 447 (2006); Denise Ping Lee, Note, *The Business Judgment Rule: Should It Protect Nonprofit Directors?*, 103 COLUM. L. REV. 925 (2003); Dana Brakman Reiser & Evelyn Brody, *Chicago-Kent Symposium: Who Guards the Guardians?: Monitoring and Enforcement of Charity Governance*, 80 CHI.-KENT. L. REV. 543 (2005).

In the Matter of Adelphi University v. Board of Regents of the State of New York

Supreme Court of New York, Appellate Division, 1997.
229 A.D.2d 36, 652 N.Y.S.2d 837.

■ CARPINELLO, J.

Petitioners to this proceeding are Adelphi University, a private, not-for-profit university in Nassau County, and its 20 duly appointed trustees and officers. They seek a judgment against respondents staying and prohibiting respondent Board of Regents from conducting a hearing against the trustees pursuant to Education Law § 226(4).... They also seek a declaration that such hearing, in any event, must be conducted pursuant to the State Administrative Procedure Act.... Supreme Court dismissed the petition finding, *inter alia,* that the remedy of prohibition does not lie in this proceeding. Petitioners appeal....

. . .

The important legal question before this Court is whether the present removal proceeding pending against the trustees is in violation of the Education Law because the Board of Regents exceeded its authorized quasi-judicial powers by impermissibly delegating its authority to initiate and prosecute such proceedings to private citizens. Because the Board of Regents neither drafted the trustee removal petition nor verified the accuracy of the factual allegations contained therein before scheduling the removal hearing and is not itself prosecuting the allegations against the trustees, petitioners would have us answer this question in the affirmative....

The Board of Regents, as head of the State Department of Education (*see,* NY Const, art V, § 4), has been given full authority to regulate and manage educational institutions in this State, including Adelphi and the trustees thereof (*see* Education Law §§ 201, 202). Of critical importance to the implementation of the Board of Regents' powers is the broad legislative function with which it has been endowed, i.e., to "establish rules for carrying into effect the laws and policies of the [S]tate, relating to education" (Education Law § 207). There can be no dispute that a trustee removal procedure pursuant to Education Law § 226 (4) rightly belongs within the jurisdiction of the Board of Regents.

Education Law § 226(4) provides, as is relevant here, that "[t]he [Board of Regents] may remove any trustee ... for misconduct, incapacity, neglect of duty, or where it appears to the satisfaction of the [Board of Regents] that the corporation has failed or refuses to carry into effect its educational purposes." The only express requirement enunciated under the statute is a hearing before the Board of Regents or its committee on notice to the trustees. Education Law § 206 further mandates that "any decision or determination ... shall be made by the [Board of Regents]." Notably, no mechanism has been set up under the Education Law for either the investigatory or prosecutorial phases of trustee removal proceedings. In the absence of such mechanism, this Court will not impose one.

Given the paucity of a detailed procedure under Education Law § 226(4), the Board of Regents was necessarily left to determine the procedure most suitable to accomplish the legislative goal of permitting and conducting trustee removal proceedings. To this end, we note that the Board of Regents was granted the authority to remove university trustees over 75 years ago. Since then, the record reveals, there have been only four trustee removal proceedings, which includes the proceeding at issue in this case. And, although not dispositive, it is noteworthy that each of the preceding petitions for removal was filed by a third party....

In this case, in response to allegations of neglect and misconduct on the part of the trustees and a request that an "Education Law § 226 ... action be initiated," respondent Gayle D. Insler was advised by a representative of the Department of Education that "a formal petition under Education Law § 226 is needed before the Board of Regents can review this matter." Insler was further advised, *inter alia,* that "[t]he petition must be verified, must set forth the ground or grounds upon which each named trustee is subject to removal, and should provide statements sufficiently particular to give the Board of Regents and the other parties notice of the transactions, occurrences, or series of transactions or occurrences, intended to be proved." Our review of the amended petition seeking removal of the trustees convinces us that these procedures were in fact complied with by respondents. The amended trustee removal petition is verified and sufficiently detailed. More importantly, *prior* to convening the three-member panel to hear the charges, the Board of Regents reviewed the removal petition for legal sufficiency.

In view of the broad policy-making powers granted to the Board of Regents by the Legislature under Education Law § 207 and the lack of any detailed procedures within Education Law § 226 (4) as to how and by whom said proceedings *must* be initiated and conducted, we find that it was permissible for the Board of Regents to establish procedures for same. In so doing, the Board of Regents was merely filling the interstices of the legislative policy to remove recalcitrant, incapacitated or neglectful trustees.

More importantly, we find that the Board of Regents is acting within its authority in opting to permit third parties to draft and prosecute trustee removal petitions rather than do so itself. We are unpersuaded that this constitutes an impermissible delegation of the Board of Regents' powers....

Moreover, to the extent that permitting private parties to draft and prosecute trustee removal petitions can be construed as a delegation of the Board of Regents' authority, we find it to be a reasonable and necessary act on its part to further the legislative schemes of promoting educational policies in this State and removing trustees whose acts fall within the conduct proscribed under the statute. As a practical matter, only individuals and organizations closely associated with a particular university would possess sufficient information regarding a trustee's alleged misconduct, incapacity or neglect of duty to be able to fairly and adequately detail same in a removal petition. It is not unreasonable, therefore, that these individuals or organizations be permitted to initiate a removal proceeding by way of a detailed, verified petition and also have the burden of proving the allegations at a hearing before the Board of Regents or a committee thereof. Moreover, ... the removal of trustees in this State cannot be *determined* by the whim of private citizens who may be motivated by selfish reasons because the Board of Regents alone possesses adjudicatory authority.

Since petitioners failed to demonstrate that the removal proceeding against them is being conducted in excess of the Board of Regents' jurisdiction, they have not demonstrated a clear legal right to the relief requested. Accordingly, prohibition does not lie. As a final matter, the issue of whether the State Administrative Procedure Act applies to the instant proceeding does not encroach on the Board of Regents' fundamental jurisdiction and therefore petitioners are not entitled to the requested relief of prohibition on this basis. We further note that this issue can be raised in a CPLR article 78 proceeding in the event of an adverse determination by the Board of Regents.

Questions and Comments on *In the Matter of Adelphi University*

Shortly after the court decision, the Board of Regents removed all but one of the trustees. A newly appointed Board of Trustees quickly fired Peter Diamandopoulos, the Adelphi University president whose large compensation package, which included a 1.3 million dollar apartment in Manhattan, was at the center of the controversy. Dr. Diamandopolus, citing tenure rights, continued to be paid over $98,000 as a professor and live in his $1.3 million apartment until the university reached a settlement with him and the former trustees in 1998. As part of the settlement, the former trustees paid over a million dollars in legal fees that the university had accumulated in the process. Dr. Diamandopolus also agreed to give up his tenured position and the million dollar apartment, while receiving over $600,000 in deferred compensation from Adelphi. *See* Courtney Leatherman, *Adelphi's Former Trustees Reach Multimillion–Dollar Settlement With University*, CHRON. HIGHER EDUC., Nov. 27, 1998, at A34. How could board oversight of compensation and spending packages be improved?

Note on Sarbanes–Oxley

In the wake of Enron and other corporate scandals, Congress passed the Sarbanes–Oxley Act of 2002, Pub. L. No. 107–204, 116 Stat. 745 (2002). With the exception of sections relating to obstruction of government proceedings and retaliation against whistle-blowers, the Act does not apply to nonprofit corporations and, therefore, does not apply to most colleges and universities. Dana Brakman Reiser, *Enron.org: Why Sarbanes–Oxley Will Not Ensure Comprehensive Nonprofit Accountability*, 38 U.C. DAVIS L. REV. 205 (2004); Wendy K. Szymanski, *An Allegory of Good (and Bad) Governance: Applying the Sarbanes–Oxley Act to Nonprofit Organizations*, 2003 UTAH L. REV. 1303 (2003). Nonetheless, many nonprofit boards are voluntarily adopting some of the Sarbanes–Oxley provisions that are now considered best practices. In addition, some states, including California, have adopted state regulations for nonprofits that are modeled on Sarbanes Oxley. *See* Nicole Gilkeson, Note, *For-Profit Scandal in the Nonprofit World: Should States Force Sarbanes–Oxley Provisions onto Nonprofit Corporations?*, 95 GEO. L.J. 831 (2007); Lumen N. Mulligan, *What's Good For The Goose Is Not Good For The Gander: Sarbanes–Oxley–Style Nonprofit Reforms*, 105 MICH. L. REV. 1981 (2007).

Sarbanes–Oxley:

- mandates adoption of a company-wide code of ethics even at companies that already have extensive policies on corporate behavior;
- mandates adoption of mechanisms for the board to receive, out of channels, confidential complaints from employees on virtually any topic;
- calls for written assurance by the chief executive officer and chief financial officer that the company's financial statements contain no material misstatements or omissions;
- imposes a regime for adoption of strict internal financial controls, and requires the board to oversee administration of the controls;
- provides that the board must have a separate audit committee, excludes management personnel from membership on the committee, requires that the committee have a comprehensive written charter, and necessitates inclusion of financial experts on audit committees;
- obliges the audit committee to receive the company's audit engagement letter and be responsible for appointing and compensating the auditor and overseeing the audit; and
- forbids the auditor from performing various non-audit services for the company and requires periodic rotation of auditors.

Martin Michaelson, *The Significance of Sarbanes–Oxley for College and University Boards*, TRUSTEESHIP, May/June 2005, at 15.

Which of these provisions do you think are most important for a nonprofit college or university to adopt? Which standard(s) might have prevented the Adelphi scandal?

Compare CAL. GOV. CODE § 12586(e) (Deering 2007):

Every charitable corporation, unincorporated association, and trustee required to file reports with the Attorney General pursuant to this section that receives or accrues in any fiscal year gross revenue of two million dollars ($2,000,000) or more, exclusive of grants from, and contracts for services with, governmental entities for which the governmental entity requires an accounting of the funds received, shall do the following:

(1) Prepare annual financial statements using generally accepted accounting principles that are audited by an independent certified public accountant in conformity with generally accepted auditing standards. For any nonaudit services performed by the firm conducting the audit, the firm and its individual auditors shall adhere to the standards for auditor independence set forth in the latest revision of the Government Auditing Standards, issued by the Comptroller General of the United States (the Yellow Book). The Attorney General may, by regulation, prescribe standards for auditor independence in the performance of nonaudit services, including standards different from those set forth in the Yellow Book. If a charitable corporation or unincorporated association that is required to prepare an annual financial statement pursuant to this subdivision is under the control of another organization, the controlling organization may prepare a consolidated financial statement. The audited financial statements shall be available for inspection by the Attorney General and by members of the public no later than nine months after the close of the fiscal year to which the statements relate. A charity shall make its annual audited financial statements available to the public in the same manner that is prescribed for IRS Form 990 by the latest revision of Section 6104(d) of the Internal Revenue Code and associated regulations.

(2) If it is a corporation, have an audit committee appointed by the board of directors. The audit committee may include persons who are not members of the board of directors, but the member or members of the audit committee shall not include any members of the staff, including the president or chief executive officer and the treasurer or chief financial officer. If the corporation has a finance committee, it must be separate from the audit committee. Members of the finance committee may serve on the audit committee; however, the chairperson of the audit committee may not be a member of the finance committee and members of the finance committee shall constitute less than one-half of the membership of the audit committee. Members of the audit committee shall not receive any compensation from the corporation in excess of the compensation, if any, received by members of the board of directors for service on the board and shall not have a material financial interest in any entity doing business with the corporation. Subject to the supervision of the board of directors, the audit committee shall be responsible for recommending to the board of directors the retention and termination of the independent auditor and may negotiate the independent auditor's compensation, on behalf of the board of directors. The audit committee shall confer with the auditor to satisfy its members that the financial affairs of the corporation are in order, shall review and determine whether to accept the audit, shall assure that any nonaudit services performed by the auditing firm conform with standards for auditor independence referred to in paragraph (1), and shall approve performance of nonaudit services by the auditing firm. If the charitable corporation that is required to have an audit committee pursuant to this subdivision is under the control of another corporation, the audit committee may be part of the board of directors of the controlling corporation.

Sarbanes–Oxley was designed to ensure that boards of public companies are more involved in effective oversight of management. Is a similar change needed in higher education? If governing boards become more involved in the business aspects of a college or university, will they still be able to defer to faculty expertise on academic matters as suggested by President Lowell? Could increased regulation and the possibility of trustee personal liability deter capable individuals from serving on university governing boards?

B. PRESIDENTS

A. Bartlett Giamatti, A Free and Ordered Space: The Real World of the University

17, 24–25, 29–30 (Norton ed., 1990) (1988).

Being president of a university is no way for an adult to make a living. Which is why so few adults actually attempt to do it. It is to hold a mid-nineteenth century ecclesiastical position on top of a late-twentieth-century corporation. But there are those lucid moments, those crystalline experiences, those Joycean epiphanies, that reveal the numinous beyond and lay bare the essence of it all. . . .

. . .

. . . The university today is very different from the one twenty-five years ago, or fifty, or one hundred or two hundred and fifty years ago, and yet it is not different. It is still a constant conversation between young and old, between students, among faculty; between faculty and students; a conversation between past and present, a conversation the culture has with itself, on behalf of the country. . . .

Perhaps it is the sound of all those voices, over centuries overlapping, giving and taking, that is finally the music of civilization, the sound of human beings shaping and sharing, mooring ideals to reality, making the world, for all its pain, work. The university is the place where the seeds of speech first grow and where most of us first began to find a voice. It is neither a paradise nor the worst spot we have ever been in; it is a good place that continues to want to make her children better.

Its essence is that give-and-take, the civil conversation in its innumerable forms. . . . Of all the threats to the institution, the most dangerous come from within. Not the least among them is the smugness that believes the institution's value is so self-evident that it no longer needs explication, its mission so manifest that it no longer requires definition and articulation.

Without constant attempts to redefine and reassert publicly their nature and purposes, universities become frozen in internal mythology, in a complacent self-perpetuation. Universities are profoundly conservative institutions, meant to transmit the past, built to remember. . . . When they are not challenged within themselves to justify themselves, to themselves as well as to the society they serve; when they are not held accountable by themselves and are not constantly urged to examine their presuppositions, their processes and acts, they stiffen up and lose their evolving complementarity to other American institutions.

. . .

. . . [S]ince World War II . . . institutions of higher education . . . have tended to lurch into new structures and programs with no thought of consequences, and then spastically to reinstitute what had been jettisoned in a new, watered-down form. . . .

When the university lurches spasmodically rather than changes in a patient, inefficient, but purposeful way, a larger society that hears nothing about the principles and purposes of higher education from clear voices within higher education also sees the whole class of institutions as floundering, as growing more expensive when costs supposedly are going down; as abdicating the role of *in loco parentis* just when the family is under increasing stress; as asking more and more of government (while wishing to be independent) just when government, at the federal level in particular, is arguing for a New Federalism and a less intrusive (and supportive) federal role; as seemingly indifferent to drugs or drinking just when the public grows in awareness of the evils of substance abuse.

A clear instance: the central cry, heard on all sides, is, Why don't our colleges teach "moral values"? The cry is cried out constantly, and not only from outside the Academy. And here we come full circle. Without anyone clearly and forthrightly telling students and their parents (and everyone else) that a college or university teaches "moral values" by its *acts as an institution*, by its institutional behavior, and not by causing some dogma or doctrine to be propounded exclusively in its classrooms, there is no education of the public, or the academic world, regarding the nature of the modern, nonsectarian American college or university. Silence does not make the point that families are where moral values (or immoral values) are first and longest implanted; that churches or synagogues or other houses of worship are where moral values are supposed to be taught; and that the classroom, or the academic part of the university, is where values of all kinds are meant to collide, to contest, to be tested, debated, disagreed about—freely, openly, civilly (as opposed to coercively). Silence does not assert that institutional behavior—how the university or college treats the people within it, invests its money, admits students, promotes faculty, comports itself vis-à-vis other social institutions—is every day, in a thousand different forms, how the college or university teaches. The place teaches by example. In this fashion, it is a model for ethical or moral behavior or it is not, but however it acts, people—within and without—draw lessons.

Other Views on the Presidency

1. Derek Bok, Beyond the Ivory Tower: Social Responsibilities of the Modern University 84–86 (1982):

> Unlike armies, corporations, and other hierarchical organizations, universities are communities in which authority is widely shared instead of being concentrated in the hands of a few leaders. Individual professors are largely immune from administrative control over their teaching and research by virtue of the doctrine of academic freedom. Acting collectively, faculties typically have the power to fix the content of the curriculum, set academic requirements, search for new professors, and shape the standards for admission. Students do not have much power to initiate policy directly. Nevertheless, they do exert considerable influence on policy—not so much by collective action, but by their ability not to attend institutions they do not like and to force changes in curriculum and teaching methods by the slow, silent pressure of apathy and disapproval. Alumni likewise have considerable power to block developments they oppose by withholding contributions or voicing their discontent through boards of trustees or in other embarrassing ways. . . .

In this environment of shared authority, president and deans have limited, though significant powers. To begin with, they generally have the means to block particular programs or initiatives that they consider unwise or improper—either by refusing to allow the institution to sponsor the activities or award the necessary degrees or, indirectly, by declining to assist in obtaining funds or providing other forms of essential support to the enterprise. There are various reasons for exercising such power. A president or dean may block a program because he believes that it does not meet accepted standards of quality, because it invades the jurisdictional prerogatives of other units in the university, because it permits outside influence over matters of academic policy, or because its administrations and financing seem inadequate.

In addition, academic leaders have a responsibility to curb activities and programs that promise to violate generally accepted norms of society or to inflict unwarranted harm on others. . . .

. . . In exercising . . . authority, of course, presidents and deans must avoid interfering arbitrarily or indiscriminately. In particular, they must refrain from using their authority to impose their private political views on the university. Any attempt to do so would threaten to violate the academic freedom of individuals holding contrary opinions. Such action would also constitute an abuse of office, since academic leaders are appointed to serve the interests of a wide variety of groups who support the university and benefit from its activities. Finally, efforts to use the university for particular ideological goals would jeopardize the independence of the institution by inviting the intervention of outside groups who will respect the university's autonomy only so long as it does not seek to become a mechanism to achieve specific political reforms. It is in this sense that the university administration must be neutral. Any president or dean who ignores that principle not only will violate his trust but will almost certainly be stymied by the opposition of faculty, alumni, and trustees.

. . . [P]residents and deans can also exert a positive influence to encourage new ventures, since their position gives them special opportunities to present proposals, have them considered carefully by the faculty, and find the funds and facilities to carry them out. . . . Yet the extent of a president's influence is limited by the fact that his proposals will succeed only if they command the genuine interest and support of the professor who must put them into practice and the funding agencies that must provide continuing financial support.

2. NANNERL O. KEOHANE, HIGHER GROUND: ETHICS AND LEADERSHIP IN THE MODERN UNIVERSITY 112–18 (2006):

The American college presidency is a distinctive institution, invented in the early days of our republic to compensate for the lack of a guild of respected scholars accustomed to self-governance. . . . At a time when captains of industry are once again dominating our world with daunting feats of economic power . . . the comparison with anemic college presidents is especially compelling. . . .

Thus, it is to be expected that many of those who trace [the problems of higher education] to defects in our governance system have hit upon an obvious solution: strengthen the presidency. If only the head of Stanford or Michigan would act more like the head of IBM or General Electric, striking off the fetter of entitlements and veto powers, we would be well on the way to reforming higher education.

In certain moods, all university presidents must thrill at such suggestions. I know I have. Why, indeed, are we such wimps? Would it not be refreshing to single-handedly shut down a program or department to cut costs and reallocate resources? Or to have the deans function more like line managers and less like feudal barons?

But life is not that simple.... [C]onsider the modern campus as a political system.

Like the government supported by the U.S. Constitution, our higher education system is characterized by extensive checks and balances, rather than by a clear hierarchy or single locus of power. One of the major elements of our federal political system is the belief that different interest groups will effectively compete with one another to prevent the dominance of any single one. As developed in James Madison's classic essay in the *Federalist Papers* (especially ... no. 10), such a system is designed primarily to avoid the abuse of power.

... [O]ur version is even more blocked by check and counterchecks than the federal government's including not only all the campus forces described above but others who have a significant stake in our work: employees, legislators, alumni, parents, neighbors. In combination with the cautious "political culture" of academia, this makes it very difficult to provide inspiration or incentives for acting boldly or expeditiously.

The view that our problems of governance should be solved by strengthening the presidency can be called Hamiltonian. Alexander Hamilton was prominent among those who argued against the Madisonian position and for a stronger, quasi-monarchical presidency....

. . .

... How might this Hamiltonian approach work in practice?

According to the bylaws of most higher education institutions, the board of trustees already delegates to the president a great deal of formal authority for the general management and governing of the institution. To expand the scope of this power, the most significant step would be to weaken or remove the powers granted to other constituencies, especially the faculty.... [A] board could rewrite the bylaws to stipulate that the president has the prerogative to create or dissolve academic programs, and to hire and terminate faculty members, without the approval of faculty councils....

Such a bold move would immediately raise serious issues of prior contractual obligations to faculty members and to donors of endowments for existing academic program.... More fundamentally, some positive defining elements about an institution of higher education would be lost.

Our present system has evolved because each of the major players brings something important to the table. The trustees as stewards, presidents as institutional leaders and managers, and faculty members, including deans and department chairs, as those most knowledgeable about what education and research offer and require—each of these elements in our governance structure is crucial to the successful functioning of the institution. Only a system that gives appropriate voice and authority to each of the major constituencies offers us a chance to maintain what James A. Perkins of Cornell called "the internal coherence" of higher education.

. . .

To make our campus governance system work effectively, we need both Madison and Hamilton. Presidents must be willing and able to lead, to inspire, to make tough choices, to bring others onto common ground, to envision....

Faculty members must be willing to learn enough about complex challenges to provide informed perspectives and help make hard choices. . . .

. . .

Boards and presidents need to recognize the fundamental contributions that faculty members make to the essential work of the university, rather than lament faculty power as a regrettable drag on the system. Yet all of us need to acknowledge that the tendency towards lengthy consultations . . . can easily be overdone in the governance of the institution. As one of our trustees says, if he learns that the end of the world is at hand, he will immediately come to Duke, because everything takes a year longer here. . . .

3. FRANK H.T. RHODES, THE CREATION OF THE FUTURE: THE ROLE OF THE AMERICAN UNIVERSITY 223–25 (2001):

. . . The task of the college president, reduced to its essentials, is to define and articulate the mission of the institution, develop meaningful goals, and then recruit the talent, build the consensus, create the climate, and provide the resources to achieve them. All else is peripheral.

. . .

The president should devote his or her best skills to dream the institution into something new, to challenge it to greatness, to elevate its hopes and extend its reach, to energize it to new levels of success and galvanize it to higher levels of achievement in every area of institutional life.

And it is here that most presidents fail. "Make no little plans," Daniel Burnham once urged. "They have no magic to stir men's blood." But it is not setting small goals, it is setting no goals that leads to presidential failure. Aimless day-to-day management, busy inertia, preoccupied drift, and high-minded indecision mark too many presidencies because incumbents set no goals. . . .

Creating this visionary purpose is not the work of a day or a week. Nor can it be a solo effort. It requires imagination, perception, cultivation, creativity, and boldness. It also requires help, criticism, and time. By building on the traditions of the institution, harnessing its strengths, recognizing emerging needs, seizing new opportunities, developing new niches, building new constituencies, the president shapes the vision and the mission, which are then tested, refined, and sharpened in active debate with all the stakeholders, both on and off the campus.

. . .

Creating the campus climate is among the most challenging and most subtle of all presidential roles. . . .

The president creates the atmosphere. He or she is everywhere, walking the campus, meeting with students at breakfast, faculty at brown bag lunches, alumni at reunions, everyone at campus events, entertaining at home. The president understands the hopes and concerns of the campus, energizes its efforts, challenges its complacency, raises its aspirations. No encounter is too brief, no event too small, no action too limited to have an influence—positive or negative—on the atmosphere of the campus.

4. Derek Bok, who served as president of Harvard from 1971 to 1991, returned to serve as interim president from 2006–07. Consider his most recent statement on university governance:

. . . Are universities, as currently organized and governed, truly capable of responding quickly and effectively enough to the challenges that confront them? Skeptics are not difficult to find. As I was once told by a wise older colleague, the late Milton Katz: "Leading a large university is like trying to steer a dog by its tail." Recent reports on higher education make much the same point, albeit in less colorful language. A group of past and current presidents from major research universities has announced that "many observers of university life (including the authors) believe that the environment is now changing too rapidly and some external constraints, like the financial constraints, have become too strong to maintain the present decision process." In a similar vein, a report from the National Commission on the Academic Presidency has concluded: "At a time when higher education should be alert and nimble, it is slow and cautious instead, hindered by traditions and mechanisms of governance that do not allow the responsiveness and decisiveness that the times require."

. . .

... Such questions have been much on my mind this year as I have worked my way through my brief, unanticipated return to academic administration.

Listening to discussions about reorganizing universities, I have discovered that much of the talk comes down to a desire to expand the power of university leaders at the expense of the faculty. Proposals of this kind are by no means unique to Harvard.... The most common justification is that the world is changing so fast ... that there is simply no time to engage in widespread faculty consultation without missing out on important opportunities. As the former president of the University of Michigan, James Duderstadt, puts it: "The academic tradition of extensive consultation, debate, and consensus building ... will be one of our greatest challenges, since this process is simply incapable of keeping pace with the profound changes swirling about higher education."

Such pronouncements sound plausible; they play upon a pervasive unease that changes are sweeping over America that existing institutions are unable to address adequately. Nevertheless, the diagnosis does not ring true to my experience. In four decades of observing the world of higher education, I have yet to encounter a significant problem that developed at anything approaching "warp speed," let alone a speed too rapid to allow for thoughtful deliberation....

Looking further at proposals to strengthen the hand of those in charge, I suspect that they proceed from an unspoken premise that unilateral decisions by the leadership will somehow be bolder, sounder, and more creative than decisions arrived at through faculty debate.... Countless tales have been told through the years about the inherent conservatism and political infighting of university faculties. When asked why he gave up the Princeton presidency to enter public life, Woodrow Wilson famously replied that he "left the hard politics of Princeton for the easier politics of Washington." ...

It is certainly true that professors can resist change and that, like most human beings, they are often loath to give up their prerogatives. For all that, however, American universities have fared quite well over the past 50 years, the very period when faculty power reached its zenith. As the international rankings attest, they have done better than most of our more hierarchical institutions in holding their own against foreign competition. Moreover, when I try to recall serious errors of judgment on the part of universities, I find it easier to think of examples beyond the customary purview of faculties, such as the excesses of intercollegiate athletics or the money lost through expensive forays into for-profit distance education, than to list comparable mistakes at the hands of professors.

It is also well to remember that there are severe limits to what one can accomplish by adding power to the administration. In universities like

Harvard, where professors do not belong to unions, the most important activities under faculty control have to do with teaching and research. Such functions are not likely to be improved by removing them from the faculty and placing them under executive control. No one ever raised the level of scholarship by ordering professors to write better books, nor has the quality of teaching ever improved by telling instructors to give more interesting classes. In these domains, good work depends on the talent and enthusiasm of professors. Much of the time taken up by faculty deliberation, however frustrating it may seem, is not wasted. Rather, it is a necessary process for generating the sense of ownership and shared commitment that is needed to elicit the best teaching and research.

Derek Bok, President Bok's Annual Report, June 6, 2007, *available at* http://www.harvardmagazine.com/go/Bok_report07 (last visited Aug. 18, 2007).

5. Stephen J. Trachtenberg, *Lessons from the Top*, Chron. Higher Educ., Nov. 2, 2007, at 5:

When I came to George Washington, my point of view was to transform the university from being a commuter institution—or so it was perceived, though not quite accurately—with a negligible reputation and small endowment into a residential research university with an international reputation and some money in the bank. I tried to make incremental changes through alliances, not fiat—to make trustees, faculty members, and administrators my collaborators. Instead of laying out a vision and commanding it, I described one goal and why I thought it was good, and then I asked others to help me achieve it. Then I did it over and over, goal by goal.

Some people have called me a true visionary. But I just had a point of view on one matter and then another and so on and was able to persuade colleagues to turn those ideas into specific goals that we would capture together.

Beyond learning such lessons, I have adopted a handful of techniques over the years. I write a personal reply to every letter and message that I receive. While time-consuming, it enables me to engage with strangers and reconnect with those familiar to me. . . .

I also recognize that a big idea—like curricular overhaul—is just something written down on paper. To make it work requires the appropriate tactics. In my presidencies, I've always tried to present my ideas privately, but consistently, to various groups with a stake in the outcome. I ask for their thoughts and probe any reluctance that they may have. I make my case and ask them to make theirs. The idea is to align our points of view as closely as possible without the inevitable drama that comes from a many-sided public discussion. It is amazing and gratifying how smoothly such tactics can achieve agreement.

I have also always appreciated the importance of casual perception, of how I appear to others as I walk down the street. If we want collegiality and civility, then we must be collegial and civil. If we want energy and enthusiasm, then we must project energy and enthusiasm. That is part of the job, always. It won't do to be welcoming and cheerful at ceremonial occasions if we are habitually gruff and glum.

. . . Academic administration is not an easy trade to follow . . . [but it] is rewarding and important. The faculty is not going to run admissions or see that meals are available to students or that the computers are secure. No one else is going to volunteer to provide students with transcripts, raise money, or handle the legal affairs of the university.

We administrators do all these things and more. Perhaps we can be seen as the logistical battalion. Without us, the more prominent missions of learning and service are impossible.

Do you agree with any of these former presidents as to how a president of a university should approach the position? To what extent do their views overlap or conflict? Would you envision a role different from those presented?

Note on American University Governance Dispute

1. In recent years there have been several, highly-publicized, conflicts between presidents at major universities and faculty or governing boards. Consider the events at American University:

In January 2004, American University President Benjamin Ladner and AU board chair George Collins took their wives to St. John in the Virgin Islands.

... Ladner and Collins had become friends. They dined together after board meetings, sailed together, vacationed together.

. . .

But by 2004 the mix of business and fun wasn't always pleasant. Ladner was lobbying the board for a raise, and he couldn't leave it in the board-room. During the trip to St. John, Ladner kept talking about money. At the time Ladner was making $880,750 year.... This put him among the nation's best paid presidents, but he wanted more.

In a confidential memo to Collins, Ladner had made the case for a package of bonuses and investments that would have added $5 million on top of his base salary over the next five years. He would be making more than any college president in the nation.

. . .

In many ways, the previous 11 years were exceptional for American University. The campus at DC's Ward Circle ... had undergone major renovations. Applications had risen during Ladner's tenure from 4,829 to 13,565, and freshman entered with higher test scores. The endowment had bloomed from $29 million to $281 million....

. . .

The responsibility for overseeing President Ladner belonged to the American University Board of Trustees.... With 24 members, it met just three times a year. A board member who joined in 1999 called it "a cocktail board."

. . .

An anonymous letter came to George Collins and other executive committee members the first week of March 2005. It accused the Ladners of "severe expense account violations." It said the Ladners had charged the university for their son's engagement party, lavish presents for their children, a personal French chef, long weekends in Europe for pleasure, maintenance of their personal residence in Maryland including ... daily wine for lunch and dinner at $50 to $100 per bottle, etc....

Collins set in motion an investigation.... The job of running the investigation fell to Leonard Jaskol, the recently appointed chair of the board's audit committee.

. . .

On August 19, the [outside] auditors ... delivered a 31–page report, in which they examined the purpose and cost of every foreign trip, every party, every chauffeured ride to the hairdresser.

"The whistleblower was accurate," Jaskol says. "It was basically all true."

The *Washington Post* had been covering the controversy since late July, when it received a copy of the whistleblower's letter.

. . .

The reaction at American University was immediate. Students rallied outside an informal board meeting on September 28. HAIL TO THE THIEF read one of the signs. . . .

. . .

The October 10 meeting [of the Board] took place with the campus in revolt, the scandal unfolding daily in the media, and federal investigators seeking documents.

Len Jaskol presented the final audit report, which said Ladner should reimburse the university $125,000 for personal expenses and pay taxes on $398,000 in imputed income during the three years the audit covered.

Ladner's allies wanted to alter the audit in his favor by switching funds from the amount he must give back to AU to the amount he owed taxes on so he would pay less out of pocket.

"I will not accept those changes," Jaskol said. "I will not sign the audit letter. I will not be party to a lie."

Without Jaskol's signature as chair of the audit committee, the university would not receive the blessing of its outside accountants. Its loans could then be called in. . . .

The board voted to accept the audit.

. . . [Then the] board voted [to dismiss Ladner].

Harry Jaffe, *Let Them Eat Truffles*, WASHINGTONIAN, April 2006, at 76.

2. On May 12, 2006, the American University Board of Trustees Special Committee on Governance, which had been formed in October of 2005, released a Report and Recommendations that provided in part:

The Committee recommends that the Board adopt as part of the Board Policies and apply the following statement on expectations for each American University Trustee:

To serve on a university governing board is a rare privilege in our society. With this honor come considerable responsibilities, obligations, and expectations. . . .

. . . Trustees of American University will:

1. Contribute to the Board efforts to sustain and advance the University's mission, integrity, traditions, values, reputation as an institution extraordinarily committed to service to others, civility in human relationships, and devotion to the pursuit of knowledge and truth. . . .

2. Energetically and consistently participate in Board and Board committee meetings. . . .

3. Provide donations in line with our financial capacity and each year as is expected for all trustees.

4. Call to the attention of the President or chief advancement officer the names of individuals, corporations or foundations that may be willing to invest in the University.

5. Conscientiously participate when feasible in campus activities and events....

6. Conduct ourselves in word and action ... from the perspective that we serve, individually and collectively, the whole institution rather than any one part of it or any group within it or outside it, or any partisan or political cause....

7. Be thoughtful in how we represent the University through our actions and words....

8. Avoid bringing even the appearance of a conflict of interest to our trusteeship activity....

9. Refrain from asking the President or other University executive and academic officers or staff for special favors on behalf of ourselves, family or friends.

10. Strictly maintain the confidentiality of the Board's executive sessions....

11. Assist the Board and the President to set the strategic direction of the University....

12. Participate ... in a self-assessment survey designed to help the Committee review our trusteeship service.

The report recommended that the President in the future should be a non-voting ex officio member of the Board. It then took up the question of whether the President should attend Executive Committee Meetings and concluded yes but added "there should ordinarily be a session of each such meeting attended only by the voting trustee members and the University Secretary." One aim of so proceeding is to allay concerns that the President is being unnecessarily excluded from Executive Committee deliberations; the practice of conducting some part of each meeting without the President is intended to foster realistic and proper expectations concerning the relationship between the Executive Committee and the President.

The recommendations of the Special Committee were adopted by the full American University Board in May 2006. Paul Fain, *American U.'s Chastened Trustees Approve Wide–Ranging Reforms*, CHRON. HIGHER EDUC., JUNE 2, 2006, at A25.

Do you agree with some or all of these recommendations? Do you think the governance problems experienced by American would have been avoided if the Committee's recommendations had been adopted before the problems started? Consider—Paul Fain, *Dos and Don'ts of Writing Presidential Contracts*, CHRON. HIGHER EDUC., Nov. 24, 2006, at B8.

CHAPTER 16

MANAGING THE ACADEMIC CORPORATION

Hutchins once described the modern university as a series of separate schools and departments held together by a central heating system. In an area where heating is less important and the automobile more, I have sometimes thought of it as a series of individual faculty entrepreneurs held together by a common grievance over parking.

—CLARK KERR, THE USES OF THE UNIVERSITY 15 (5th ed. 2001).

Governing boards and the presidents they appoint have formal authority over universities, although governance on academic matters is often shared with the faculty. In recent decades, students also have been given a voice, if not a vote. Increasingly, however, key functions at many institutions of higher education are performed by full time administrators, most of whom are not members of the faculty. This change had led to increased tension between faculty and administrators and between students and administrators. It also creates leadership challenges for presidents who must both oversee faculty, who are notoriously difficult to "manage" and hard to fire, and manage administrators and staff, who are organized in a more traditional corporate structure.

HENRY ROSOVSKY, THE UNIVERSITY: AN OWNERS MANUAL

261–88 (1990).

Governance concerns power: who is in charge; who makes decisions; who has a voice; and how loud is that voice? These are always complicated and contentious questions, especially in higher education. The reasons are clear. To begin with, universities and colleges are schools for adults, and the requirements of schooling and adulthood can be difficult to reconcile. Secondly, universities in America are often seen as agents of social change, as producers of research that could affect policy and also as places where entry or membership confers life-long advantages on selected individuals. It is understandable that many people are anxious to influence some of these outcomes. Thirdly, in our country colleges and universities can also be wealthy foundations as well as large enterprises that use their resources for a wide range of purposes more or less related to education. Universities are large employers; they manage sizeable investment portfolios, own residential real estate, operated restaurants, gift shops, campuses abroad, and much else. How wealthy foundations and enterprises dispose of resources is of legitimate concern to all sorts of people, inside and outside of their walls, and they demand a hearing. Finally, nearly all of higher education—public and private—receives funds or subsidies from taxpayers. (Somewhat over 20 percent of Harvard's budget come from government funds.) Taking money from the public means that representatives of the people, including the press, have a legitimate interest in how authority is exercised by the recipients.

In considering issues frequently associated with university governance . . . I have found the principles outlined below to be useful. . . .

The First Principle: Not everything is improved by making it more democratic.

I shudder as I write this sentence. No doubt future generations of students and colleagues will have additional proof of my deeply reactionary leanings. Even so, this principle is not placed first for nothing.

The United States and a few other countries attempt to practice political democracy. Although practice may fall short of the philosophical ideal, "one man [person], one vote" describes the legitimate goal of our political life. Formally, every vote is of equal weight and most of us believe that in our relations with government more is better than less democracy. . . .

A strong belief in the value of political democracy is not inconsistent with the practice of less democratic ways in other areas of life. Families are not usually run on democratic principles; neither are armies, hospitals, or most workplaces. Formal or informal hierarchies are in place: some voices are more powerful than others, and we know from experience that the functioning of these institutions is not necessarily improved by distributing power more equally.

Most social institutions have both democratic and hierarchical characteristics, and that applies to American universities. As a generalization, I would suggest that the relations *between* major university constituencies, faculty, students, staff—are hierarchical; *within* constituencies, relations tend to be more democratic. Even this proposition leaves me slightly uncomfortable, because of the many distinctions that prevail within groups. Some faculty members are tenured; others are not. Non-academic positions include senior vice presidents earning six-figure salaries and groundskeepers mowing the lawn for quite a bit less. These voices do not carry the same weight. . . .

The most basic force creating hierarchy in all education is the interaction between students and teachers—the constituencies for whom the university primarily exists. . . . I am obviously describing an unequal or undemocratic teacher-student relationship, but it should not imply student oppression or the arbitrary exercise of authority by teachers. . . .

Democratizing universities can have many meanings. One might be concerned about how the faculty governs itself or the prerogatives of faculty vis-à-vis administration, and much else. In recent years, especially since the 1960s, the issue of democracy has acquired another by now well-recognized meaning: more power for students, probationary members of the faculty, and non-academic employees in the setting of university policy. . . .

The limiting case exists in some European universities where the practice of "parity" was born in the 1960s. Power over virtually all decisions came to be equally shared between students, faculty, and employees (*drittelparitat*)—and not infrequently the government. The educational results have been disastrous. Academic standards declined and a sense of mission was lost. . . . The Dutch government amended university governance and instituted a version of parity in 1972. Within a few years, many of the better research institutes had lost their professors. This was especially true in the sciences, where escape to industry was possible and inviting.

Excessive democracy—and by that I mean parity, unclear lines of authority, and similar forms of administrative paralysis—may not be an accidental outcome. It can be the understandable reaction to arrogance and abuse of power by those in charge—administrators, professors, or ministry bureaucrats. . . .

The Second Principle: There are basic differences between the rights of citizenship in a nation and the rights that are attained by joining a voluntary organization.

As American citizens, we are equal in terms of political rights after reaching the age of eighteen, provided that we have not been convicted of a crime. . . .

Membership in a university community or university citizenship is quite different. It is always acquired by application and/or invitation and that should legitimize constraints. Just as corporations can sell restricted shares that no one has to buy, and clubs can enforce certain rules since no one is forced to join, so can schools offer positions or admission with limited rights. . . . Accordingly, students are invited to study and not to govern the university. Faculty members are invited to teach and do research and to set educational policy in their sphere of knowledge.

Indeed, faculty rights are also limited. Some areas of governance and policy are properly deemed beyond faculty jurisdiction, usually for reasons of lack of specialized competence or conflict of interest. These matters are generally considered the responsibility of trustees. I do not wish to suggest that restricted rights mean no rights. Everyone should be able to express opinions freely, and mechanisms for "voice" or "input" for all groups are more than merely desirable—they are mandatory if we wish to create a just university. . . .

The Third Principle: Rights and responsibilities in universities should reflect the length of commitment to the institution.

During my years as a dean, I made a statement to a group of undergraduates that became notorious and provoked much student hostility. I . . . said: "Remember, you—the [undergraduate] students are here for four years; the [tenured] faculty is here for life; and the institution is here forever." . . .

Why should a longer time horizon increase one's voice? That is certainly what I was saying to students, *not* because of their youth, but rather because they are transients. Almost all forms of organization recognize that long association (past and prospective) gives special competence and deserves recognition—up to a point. . . . We do so because length of service is an indicator of experience and loyalty, and a certain sign that short-term exploitation is not a goal of the individual.

Universities encounter a special problem: the mixture of constituencies assures that those with the shortest time horizons will outnumber everyone else; those with the least knowledge and experience are a majority. . . . Former students become alumni . . . and this large group certainly has a long-term though less direct stake in the university in which they studied: the value of their degree is closely related to an institution's overall standing. Furthermore, many alumni show a lifetime commitment by providing their institutions with financial and other types of support. Most of them, however, are very removed from the daily life of their universities. . . . Non-tenured faculty, unless promoted, may stay eight to ten years, whereas a typical tenured career will last twenty-five years or more. We must also mention those serving on the governing boards, the lawful owners of the university-assigned fiduciary responsibilities. . . .

What would be the net effect of majority rule? One man one vote would give those with the shortest time horizon the greatest influence. Influence would not be sufficiently weighted by the degree to which one has to live with the consequences of decisions and actions, and that is a bad idea. . . .

The Fourth Principle: In a university, those with knowledge are entitled to a greater say.

I do not mean general knowledge. Student opinions concerning the desirability of a Democratic or Republican administration in Washington are as valid as those of their professors. An employee who works in the facilities and maintenance division should know more than professors about the upkeep of buildings. . . . And of course, the large number of alumni embody a vast amount of knowledge about most everything. . . . What these constituencies lack—with the exception of some individual alumni—is expert knowledge about the primary mission of universities: teaching and research. . . . The individuals with expert knowledge are to be found almost entirely among the academic staff.

These are not . . . unqualified absolutes. Students are consumers of teaching and usually have worthy notions about the quality of instruction; their opinions deserve consideration. Former students (alumni) especially of the professional schools, tend to be shrewd judges of their education and of the effectiveness of programs. These voices need to be taken into account. All of us also recognize that professional university administrators, and secretaries and technical personnel, store much wisdom in their heads. But reasonable opinions are not the same things as deep understanding and ultimate responsibility.

Final judgments on educational questions are best left in the hands of those with professional qualifications: academics who have experienced a lengthy period of apprenticeship and have given evidence of performing high-quality work, in teaching and research, as judged by their peers on the basis of broad evidence. This applies particularly to faculty control of curriculum. The chances of having courses taught well—with verve and imagination—are greatly diminished when content and structure are imposed by "outsiders" without debate and discussion. . . .

. . .

The Fifth Principle: In universities, the quality of decisions is improved by consciously preventing conflict of interest.

When private advantage and public obligations clash, we are faced with a conflict of interest. Universities are complex structures: many of their citizens have communitywide (i.e. quasi-public) responsibilities, and we may reasonably assume that few of us are immune to the temptations of pursuing private interests.

. . .

. . . Some authority is properly delegated to higher levels, thereby not placing individuals or groups in a position where the temptation to pursue private—or for that matter short-term—interests could prove irresistible. That is why we do not allow professors to determine their own salaries and benefits. . . .

. . .

The logic of minimizing conflict of interest implies that students, faculty members, and employees should only rarely serve as trustees of their own university. They would be the equivalent of "inside directors," and good business practice dictates, I believe, that this category should be a distinct minority on well-constituted boards, since the fundamental purpose of the boards or trustees is to evaluate management, not to join its ranks.

The Sixth Principle: University governance should improve the capacity for teaching and research.

Teaching and research are the main missions of universities and a suitable system of governance should, therefore, make these activities as efficient as possible. . . . Given the university's main mission, the entire enterprise has to be organized so as to allow members of the instructional staff maximum opportunity to do their work, and to minimize, insofar as possible, even officially encouraged diversions, primarily excessive administrative responsibilities. These priorities apply with equal validity to students. . . .

I insist on the consideration of this principle because it is so often understood in theory and ignored in practice. The desire to participate is great, but self-governance comes only at a high price: it requires much time, knowledge, [and] commitment. . . . In some university activities—examples might be promotions, chairing departments, curricular requirements—faculty participation is essential and well worth the cost. No other group can be an adequate substitute.

All too often, however, the benefits of such faculty participation are illusory. . . . [Faculty] sit on innumerable committees without complaint, spending hours in fruitless and inconsequential debates. . . .

The Seventh Principle: To function well, a hierarchical system of governance requires explicit mechanisms of consultation and accountability.

I list this principle last, not because it is least important. It is just as important as all the others, and may actually be *the* most central because the efficiency and sincerity with which consultation and accountability are handled determine the overall quality of governance. . . .

Consultation encourages input into policy issues from the many constituencies of a modern American university: students, white-and blue-collar employees, faculty, alumni, the community, and perhaps some others. This process generally moves from the bottom up—for example, from students to faculty or from secretaries to senior administrators. . . .

Accountability, operating from the top down, is the other side of this coin. It applies primarily to those with authority and describes how they should carry out their responsibilities. . . .

. . . Universities in this country are not administered as participatory democracies, and there are few occasions to cast votes. . . . [F]or the system to work requires the belief that it operates reasonably and justly, that it is not arbitrary....

Communication is a major form of accountability. Those in charge should regularly make information available concerning their views and policies. As a dean, I started the practice of sending an annual budget letter to all faculty members—also available to anyone else in the community—which presented the current fiscal year in great detail. Accountability is the willingness to explain decisions, backed by evidence, when questioned by students, a colleague, or anyone else. In the form of consultation, it is also a means of making sure that the many voices of a community are heard....

Accountability also means that those entrusted with authority should report to some individual or group. Thus professors should be responsible to chairmen, most particularly when it comes to teaching responsibilities. Chairmen report to deans, who are appointed and, if necessary, discharged by provosts or presidents. And presidents report to boards of trustees....

... In performing their jobs, non-academic employees all have bosses, just as if they were working in any ordinary business. The same holds true for all administrators, academic and non-academic. Deans, chairmen, vice-presidents, all serve at the pleasure of a higher-up, and that is well accepted. But the concept of accountability becomes more subtle when it is applied to the professoriate.... [O]ne way of defining a professorship is to say that it is a job without a boss. Faculty members are the beneficiaries of enormous freedom: their formal obligations are limited to a few hours in the classroom and are far less significant than the unspecified parts of the job—research, discussion and guidance of students and colleagues, university and professional service, and the like.... Do they serve entirely at their own pleasure?

Not at all, although accountability is more difficult to enforce. In nearly all universities, salaries will reflect the individual's research and teaching performance. Those who set salaries—primarily chairmen and deans—usually pay close attention to peer review and evaluation of teaching by students.... In the university environment it is also understood—perhaps too vaguely—that "grave misconduct" and "neglect of duty" are failings for which professors can be held accountable by higher administrative authorities. If the transgressions that belong in these categories are widely known and clearly defined, accountability can be enforced.

During my years on the Harvard faculty I have known of a number of professors who resigned because they feared—and probably would have faced—charges of grave misconduct. If these had been formalized, alleged offenses would have ranged from financial improprieties to sexual harassment.

... Nevertheless, I am ready to admit that in all our universities the rights of professors are far better understood and advertised than their responsibilities. That this situation is allowed to persist is a major administrative—dare I say managerial—failure ...

Questions and Comments on Rosovsky

Do you agree with all of Rosovsky's principles? If not, why not? Are you persuaded that professors are held accountable for their work? Why do so many students think that the teaching ability of professors is not valued as much as their research? Why would a university value research more than teaching? Consider Giamatti's assertion that the form of an academic institution should be justified by its goals and functions. In what ways does the unique environment of an academic institution dictate the ways administrators should manage the institution? What is the best way to balance the interests of the competing constituencies of a college or university?

A. ADMINISTRATORS

Ollman v. Toll

United States District Court, District of Maryland, 1981.
518 F.Supp. 1196, *aff'd*,704 F.2d 139 (4th Cir. 1983).

■ HARVEY, II, J.

Bertell Ollman, the plaintiff in this civil action, is a Marxist. He has here sued various representatives of the University of Maryland under 42 U.S.C. § 1983, claiming that in 1978 he was rejected for the position of Professor and Chairman of the Department of Government and Politics at the College Park campus of the University because of his political beliefs and associations. Named as defendants are John S. Toll, President of the University of Maryland, Wilson H. Elkins, the past President of the University, and the University's Board of Regents. As relief, plaintiff seeks an injunction which would require the University to appoint him as Professor and Chairman of the Department in question, back pay, compensatory and punitive damages, attorneys' fees and other relief.

. . .

The University of Maryland is a large, public institution, with branches in various parts of the State and even overseas. At any one time, there are approximately 50,000 students at the College Park campus of the University. The total faculty numbers some 4,000 persons, with some 2500 faculty members located at College Park.

The Department of Government and Politics at the College Park campus is one of the larger departments of the University.[2] In September 1977, Professor Davis P. Bobrow, who had come to Maryland in 1974, resigned as Chairman of the Department. In accordance with University procedures, a Search Committee was appointed to locate a successor for this important position.

After considering a list of approximately 100 persons during the final three months of 1977, the Search Committee by early January of 1978 had not come up with a likely candidate to recommend for the position. Dr. Bertell Ollman, the plaintiff, was at the time an Associate Professor of the Department of Politics at New York University (hereinafter "N.Y.U.").[3] His name was not on the original lengthy list which the Search Committee had considered. However, in early January, three members of the Committee

---

2. At the time of the matters in suit, there were some forty-one faculty members within the Department of Government and Politics.

3. Dr. Ollman did not become a full Professor at New York University until May of 1980.

suggested plaintiff's name for the position, and the Committee ultimately recommended him and one other candidate for the position. The other candidate was Dr. Robert T. Holt, who is a Professor of the Department of Political Science at the University of Minnesota and presently Chairman of that Department. Both Dr. Holt and Dr. Ollman came to the College Park campus on several occasions and were interviewed.

Under University procedures, a Search Committee is required to report its recommendations for filling a position of this sort to the Provost of the particular Division of the faculty. The Department of Government and Politics was within the Division of Behavioral and Social Sciences, and the Provost was Dr. Murray Lee Polakoff, who, in February 1978, had been with the University for some seven months. Following receipt of the Search Committee's recommendation, the Provost was in turn required to make his recommendation to the Chancellor for Academic Affairs, in this instance, Dr. Robert L. Gluckstern. Dr. Gluckstern in turn would forward his recommendation for the position to the President of the University. Under the By-laws of the Board of Regents, it was the President who had the final authority to appoint a person Chairman of a Department. However, it was the practice that all recommendations for faculty appointments to be made by the President would first come to the Vice President of Academic Affairs for review. In the spring of 1978, Dr. R. Lee Hornbake had occupied this post for some eighteen years. He regularly reviewed recommendations of this sort from the Chancellor, and in turn, made recommendations to the President before final action was taken.

In the spring of 1978, Dr. Wilson H. Elkins had been President of the University of Maryland for some twenty-four years. He had previously announced his retirement effective June 30, 1978, and Dr. John S. Toll had been selected to replace him as President, commencing on July 1, 1978. Dr. Toll had been President of the State University of New York at Stony Brook, New York, for some thirteen years. . . .

Acting with some urgency between early January and late February, 1978, the Search Committee for the Department of Government and Politics recommended both Dr. Holt and Dr. Ollman for appointment as Chairman of the Department. In a meeting with Provost Polakoff, the same members of the Committee who had initially suggested plaintiff's name urged that he be selected for the position. The Provost agreed and, after reviewing the matter with the Chancellor and receiving his concurrence, telephoned plaintiff on March 3, 1978 and offered the post to him, provided that the President approved the appointment. When he had originally reviewed the qualifications of the candidates, Chancellor Gluckstern had rated Dr. Holt over Dr. Ollman, but he was later persuaded by the Provost that the position should be offered to Dr. Ollman.

More than six weeks then elapsed before Chancellor Gluckstern forwarded his recommendation to Dr. Hornbake and Dr. Elkins. Various steps were taken during that period to have the files on the recommended appointment put in proper form for submission to the President. Meanwhile, on April 18, 1978, an article appeared in The Diamondback, the campus newspaper, reporting that plaintiff, a Marxist, was being recommended for appointment as Chairman of the Department of Government and Politics. This first press report led in the following weeks to a veritable storm of publicity relating to the appointment. . . .

When the formal papers eventually reached Dr. Hornbake and were reviewed by him, he was disturbed by certain irregularities which he concluded had occurred in the search procedures.... After further study of the file and discussions with various faculty members, Dr. Hornbake eventually recommended to President Elkins that plaintiff not be appointed. Meanwhile, the publicity and controversy over the appointment continued. Since late April, President Elkins had been aware that if the appointment was rejected by him, a suit in federal court would be filed against him by Dr. Ollman.

By this time it was late May of 1978, a very busy time of the year for a University President.... Fearing that if he went along with the recommendation of Dr. Hornbake he would be involved in lengthy litigation which would come to trial after his retirement, President Elkins decided to seek the help of the Board of Regents.... At a meeting of the Board held on June 21, the Board formally requested President Elkins to give the Board a written report on the matter before he left office .....

President Elkins left office without having acted on the appointment. On June 30, as requested, he submitted to the Board his written report, together with pertinent materials from Chancellor Gluckstern, Provost Polakoff and the Search Committee. On July 1, 1978, defendant Toll assumed his new duties as President of the university and was confronted immediately with the Ollman matter. After considering the posture of the appointment at that time, he decided that he alone should make the final decision....

After discussing the matter with Dr. Hornbake and reviewing all documents in University files, President Toll decided that he would not rely merely on information in the files but would himself make an independent investigation of the qualifications of the plaintiff to be Chairman of the Department of Government and Politics. He held an open meeting with members of the Department on July 11, 1978, soliciting their views. Various Professors and other faculty members presented their comments both pro and con concerning the appointment of plaintiff to this position. Most favored the appointment but one-third of those present opposed it, including two former Chairmen of the Department and the Acting Chairman. On his own, President Toll had prepared a list of political science experts and others for consultation, and in early July, President Toll personally communicated with these individuals. Most of the persons on this so-called "referee list" were political scientists, and many were persons known and respected by President Toll. Some of the comments were favorable to Dr. Ollman but most were unfavorable.

Finally, on July 20, 1978, President Toll announced his decision. In a prepared statement, he said that after appropriate consultation and review, he had decided not to approve the appointment of plaintiff for the position of Professor and Chairman of the Department of Government and Politics at the University of Maryland at College Park. President Toll stated that his decision had been based on his own evaluation of whether or not the proposed candidate was the best qualified person for the position. His decision was announced at a special meeting of the Board of Regents held on the morning of July 20, 1978.

On August 1, 1978, this civil action was filed. Plaintiff contends that defendant Toll's stated reason for disapproving the appointment was a mere pretext and that defendant Toll was actually motivated to reject plaintiff because of his Marxist beliefs . . .

It is well established that a state university may not refuse to employ a prospective member of its faculty if the decision is made by reason of the exercise by the applicant of constitutionally protected First Amendment rights. Marxist or Communist beliefs, like other political beliefs, are protected under the First and Fourteenth Amendments, and such beliefs or one's association with others holding them is protected activity for which a state may not impose civil disabilities such as exclusion from employment by a state university. *Cooper v. Ross*, 472 F. Supp. 802 (E.D. Ark.1979).

It is equally well established that, in a case of this sort, the fact finder must bear in mind that it is not the function of a federal court to second guess the decision of an official of a state university on matters within his discretion which do not rise to the level of a constitutional deprivation. . . . A federal court should not set aside the decision of a school administrator which the court may view as lacking in wisdom or compassion or because of mistake. As the Supreme Court emphasized in *Mt. Healthy* [*City Board of Education v. Doyle*, 429 U.S. 274 (1977)], an applicant for a position at a public institution does not have the right to prevent his prospective employer from assessing his record and reaching a decision not to employ on the basis of that record merely because he has beliefs or associations which are constitutionally protected.

> . . .

Quite clearly, plaintiff has satisfied the first part of the burden placed upon him in a case of this sort. Dr. Ollman was a Marxist and was known for professing those political beliefs. Whether or not plaintiff's Marxist beliefs are popular ones and whether or not they have the approval of other citizens of this country, they are entitled to the full protection of the First Amendment. No more direct assault on academic freedom can be imagined than for school authorities to refuse to hire a teacher because of his or her political, philosophical or ideological beliefs. *See Board of Regents v. Roth*, 408 U.S. 564, 581 (1972) (Mr. Justice Douglas dissenting). Thus, an official of a state university may not restrict speech or association, even by the subtle or indirect coercion of refusal to hire, simply because that official finds the views expressed by any group or individual to be abhorrent.

The second portion of plaintiff's burden is a much more difficult one. Plaintiff must go beyond proving that his Marxism was a factor in his rejection. To be entitled to the relief he seeks, plaintiff in this case has the burden of showing that his beliefs or associations were a substantial or motivating factor in the decision of one or more of the defendants that he would not be hired at the University of Maryland. . . .

Although plaintiff has contended that President Elkins and the Board of Regents played a part in rejecting him for employment at the University, it is abundantly clear that President Toll and only President Toll made the final decision which is being challenged. . . . Therefore, it is the reasons given by President Toll for acting as he did which must be examined critically and in detail. . . .

Most of the voluminous evidence in the case related to events that occurred before President Toll assumed his duties at the University on July 1, 1978. These facts are of course relevant, because many of the events occurring in the first six months of 1978 were later brought to the attention of President Toll when he assumed office on July 1, 1978 and reviewed extensive University files relating to the matter. But, much more significant are the critical events that occurred between July 1, when President Toll took office, and July 20, when he announced that he would not appoint plaintiff to the position in question. . . .

. . .

Although Dr. Toll's term of office did not commence until July 1, 1978, he arrived at the University on June 30 and met with the Vice Presidents that Friday afternoon so that he might have a "running start." That meeting was mainly concerned with various other matters, but procedural aspects of the Ollman appointment were also discussed. By that time, President Toll had learned that the decision in the Ollman appointment had not been made by retiring President Elkins but that the matter was under discussion by the Board of Regents. . . .

. . .

After assuming office on Saturday, July 1, . . . President Toll flew back to his summer home on Long Island that night. He took with him the thick packet of materials prepared by President Elkins for the Board relating to the Ollman matter. In the report . . . President Elkins described in detail the steps he had taken in connection with the Ollman matter since he had first been officially advised by Chancellor Gluckstern that the recommendation would be forthcoming. Following his review of materials received from the Chancellor, President Elkins had concluded that the procedures followed in arriving at a decision to offer plaintiff the position lacked credibility. It was his opinion that Dr. Ollman's academic accomplishments would not bring academic stature to the Department of Government and Politics, that Dr. Ollman lacked administrative experience necessary for directing a large department such as this one, and that Dr. Ollman's lack of diversification in the field of political science was not conducive to effective leadership in a department which was marked with dissension and the absence of intellectual harmony. For these reasons, President Elkins had concluded that plaintiff's qualifications to be Chairman of the Department were not sufficiently strong to justify his appointment. He so stated in his report to the Board of Regents, which was included in the papers turned over to President Toll.

Over the long Fourth of July weekend following assumption of his new duties, President Toll for the first time reviewed in detail all documents in the file pertaining to the recommended appointment. At the outset, he was struck by apparent irregularities in the search procedures. An offer to plaintiff had been made before the search process had been completed. One of the promising candidates, Dr. Charles F. Cnudde, who was Chairman of the Department of Politics at Michigan State University, was actually visiting the Maryland campus after a decision had been made to offer the position to plaintiff.

In particular, President Toll noted a misleading statement contained in Dr. Polakoff's letter of April 7, 1978 to Chancellor Gluckstern, recommending Dr. Ollman for the position. That letter indicated that by January 1978, the list of candidates for the position had been reduced from over one hundred names to five, that these five candidates were then invited to the University for interviews, that the two highest candidates (who were Ollman and Holt) were then invited to return for further discussions and that from this "thorough" search process, Dr. Ollman evolved as the leading candidate. Since Dr. Cnudde came to the campus in early March after a decision had been reached to make an offer to plaintiff, Dr. Polakoff's statement concerning the thoroughness of the search process raised questions in President Toll's mind.

In the course of President Toll's further review of these materials, other concerns arose. The Search Committee had been given a specific charge which outlined the qualifications for individuals to be recommended for the position in question. In its entirety, the charge was as follows:

CHARGE TO GOVERNMENT AND POLITICS SEARCH COMMITTEE

A nationwide search for the Chair of Government and Politics at the University of Maryland. Suggested qualifications: Outstanding scholarly reputation, highly energetic, capable administrator, interested in interdisciplinary and applied programs and research. Experienced in obtaining research grants.

Professor Toll concluded that this was a reasonable statement of the necessary qualifications of candidates for the position, and used the charge itself in judging the qualifications of plaintiff. Included in the file before him were letters to Chancellor Gluckstern from Dr. Martin C. McGuire, Chairman of the Search Committee, recommending both Professor Robert T. Holt and plaintiff for the position. Dr. McGuire's letter of February 21, 1978, which attached a copy of Professor Holt's Curriculum Vitae (hereinafter "C.V."), stated that Professor Holt had been "enthusiastically" endorsed by the Search Committee as a candidate for Chairman of the Department of Government and Politics. Dr. McGuire stated that Professor Holt had "a superb record as a scholar," "a proven track record as an administrator" and that he would "be most adept" at bringing research grant money into the Department. Dr. McGuire's shorter letter of February 24, 1978, which attached a copy of plaintiff's C.V., stated that plaintiff had been "warmly" endorsed by the Committee as a candidate for the position. Although stating that plaintiff was "a world renowned student of Marx" who had "captured the imagination" of the Search Committee, Dr. McGuire made no mention of any administrative experience of plaintiff nor of any experience he had in obtaining research grants.

When he read these letters and the attached C.V.'s, President Toll concluded that Holt appeared to be a much stronger candidate than Ollman.[10] He wondered why an offer had not been made to Holt. Dr. Holt had been promoted in 1964 to a full professorship in the Department of Political Science at the University of Minnesota, which, according to Dr. McGuire's letter, was one of the top six political science departments in the nation. Unlike plaintiff, Holt had been on the original list of 100 names that had been compiled by the Search Committee. Holt's C.V. indicated that he was a top flight scholar, that he had published extensively in recognized journals and that he had considerable administrative experience.[12] Furthermore, Holt

---

10. Defendant Toll also read Dr. Cnudde's C.V. and concluded that Cnudde was likewise a stronger candidate than Ollman. Cnudde was Chairman of the Political Science Department at Michigan State University, a major state institution.

12. Chancellor Gluckstern had also rated Holt over Ollman, but had been persuaded

had experience in research development. President Toll felt that it was important for the University of Maryland to have as Chairman of the Department of Government and Politics an individual who would know how to obtain research grants and develop graduate research programs. Since the Department at Maryland was a large one and since the University occupied a unique location so close to the seat of the national government in Washington, D.C., President Toll believed that one of the important missions of the Department was to develop strong graduate research programs.

. . .

During his long weekend review of these files, President Toll also studied plaintiff's C.V. and other materials submitted in support of the Chancellor's recommendation of plaintiff for the appointment. Unlike the other leading candidates, plaintiff was not at the time a full Professor but merely an Associate Professor at N.Y.U. President Toll noted that plaintiff's principal contribution as a scholar was his book entitled Alienation: Marx's Conception of Man in Capitalist Society, published in 1971. This was recognized as plaintiff's major work, but it was apparently based in substantial part on his 1967 doctoral dissertation. Information contained in the files before him did not indicate to President Toll that plaintiff possessed the administrative experience to be Chairman of a large Department such as this one. Many of the letters of recommendation contained statements to the effect that the author of the letter had little knowledge of plaintiff's experience in this regard.

. . .

On Thursday, July 6, 1978, President Toll went to St. Louis to attend a meeting called by the Association of American Universities. While there, he continued his investigation of plaintiff's qualifications. President Toll telephoned or spoke in person to five different individuals about plaintiff before he left St. Louis on Saturday, July 8. Most of the comments he received were unfavorable. . . .

. . .

On July 10, President Toll returned to the Maryland campus. On the evening of July 11, a previously scheduled meeting was held with the full time faculty members of the Department of Government and Politics so that President Toll might personally hear their views concerning the controversial Ollman appointment. Also present at the meeting were Chancellor Gluckstern, Provost Polakoff, Dr. Hornbake and other administrative officials of the University. The meeting lasted for some one to two hours, and some seventeen members of the Department's faculty attended and freely presented their views concerning the qualifications of plaintiff for the position in question and the procedures employed for recommending him.

What became abundantly clear during this meeting was that the faculty of the Department had sharply differing views both as to the procedural aspects of the selection of plaintiff and as to the substantive qualifications of plaintiff to be the Department's Chairman. That there was serious dissension

by Provost Polakoff to recommend Ollman for the position. When he interviewed Holt on February 23, Dr. Gluckstern in his notes described Holt as "astute, personable, will have very high expectations, first class." Moreover, it was Dr. Gluckstern's judgment that Holt's scholarship was somewhat stronger than that of Ollman.

and a sharp split in the Department was nothing new and was well known in University circles. When Dr. Bobrow, the previous Chairman, had assumed the position in 1974, the Department of Government was badly divided. When he left in 1977, the internecine conflicts had, if anything, been intensified. In an attempt to upgrade the Department, Dr. Bobrow had brought in promising young professors but had downgraded and disparaged senior members of the faculty.

Although he testified that it would have been improper for him to have a formal role in the search procedures, the evidence indicates that Dr. Bobrow had a good deal to do with the selection of the Search Committee's Chairman and its members. . . . Quite clearly, the "old guard" was not represented on the Search Committee, and Dr. Bobrow's "new guard" had been placed in control. Senior members of the Department were unhappy about the composition and methods of the Search Committee, and this intra-department bitterness and divisiveness continued during the entire period when plaintiff's proposed appointment was pending before the President of the University.

Plaintiff's name had not been included on the original list of some 100 possible candidates for the position. However, in early January, Drs. Young, Hardin and Elkin had met together at a delicatessen and had agreed that plaintiff's name should be proposed to the Committee. At Committee meetings, these three backed plaintiff over all other candidates, and they continued vigorous efforts in his behalf during the course of the entire controversy. At a meeting with Provost Polakoff, they had persuaded the Provost to recommend plaintiff for the appointment.

Most of the members of the faculty who attended the July 11 meeting favored the appointment but approximately one-third of those attending expressed their opposition. Members of the Search Committee spoke in support of the process which had resulted in the recommendation of plaintiff for the position, claiming that it was an open and fair procedure. Members of the faculty who had not been on the Search Committee pointed out irregularities in the process, particularly during the later period of the search. The composition of the Committee was attacked by some of those who spoke. It was noted that letters of recommendation supporting plaintiff were solicited and received after the offer had been made and accepted. The observation was also made that a serious candidate was visiting the campus at the time the offer was made to plaintiff. It was further pointed out that no vote among the faculty had been taken concerning the offer of a professorship to plaintiff until after the offer had been made.[26] When this omission had been called to his attention, Professor Polakoff had eventually arranged for such a vote on April 12. Although the vote was in favor of plaintiff, the procedures employed were criticized. Signed ballots were required and later retained by the Provost. Some members of the faculty feared reprisals from the Provost, who had already recommended plaintiff at the time the vote was taken. Others saw the voting process as, in effect, a vote of confidence for Provost Polakoff by those faculty members who were enthusiastic about the new Provost and who were thus eager to support him. . . .

---

26. To be Chairman of the Department, plaintiff would have to be appointed a full Professor. It had generally been the practice at Maryland for members of the faculty of a Department to vote on professorships before any such offers were made.

. . . Members of the Department who had not been able to attend the July 11 meeting were asked by President Toll to submit letters giving their views on the Ollman matter. A number of letters were received and reviewed by President Toll during the week following the faculty meeting, some in support of and some in opposition to the appointment. President Toll also communicated with several other political scientists during that time period and considered their comments concerning the appointment. He also spoke briefly with Dr. McGuire, Chairman of the Search Committee, and learned that Dr. McGuire had not made his own evaluation of the qualifications of plaintiff but had relied primarily on the members of the political science faculty on the Committee.

. . .

On July 19, President Toll met with Dr. Hornbake and discussed the Ollman appointment. For many years, Dr. Hornbake, as one of his most important responsibilities as Academic Vice President of the University of Maryland, had been reviewing papers relating to faculty appointments which had been forwarded to the President and had been making recommendations to the President concerning the action to be taken. When the Ollman recommendation had been forwarded to President Elkins in late April, Dr. Hornbake, in the course of his review, had noted various irregularities in the search procedures. Questions had also arisen in his mind concerning plaintiff's qualifications for the position. Dr. Hornbake had read, among other works of plaintiff, his article entitled "On Teaching Marxism." *See* The Insurgent Sociologist, Vol. VI, No. 4, Summer 1976, pp. 37–50. . . . Among the other statements made by plaintiff in this article were the following (pp. 48–49):

> What are the practical results of my course on Marxism? How can one judge them? Most students who answer the question, "Why are you or aren't you a Marxist?", indicate at the end of the course that they now accept Marx's analysis (although the majority are still wary of the label "Marxist"). Where this happens, these students know better than most comrades with whom I have talked when and how they adopted a Marxist outlook.

> If non-Marxists see my concern with such questions as an admission that the purpose of my course is to convert students to socialism, I can only answer that in my view a view which denies the fact/value distinction a correct understanding of Marxism (as indeed of any body of scientific truths) leads automatically to its acceptance.

. . .

From his readings, Dr. Hornbake had concluded that plaintiff was doctrinaire in his approach to the teaching of Marxism and that plaintiff intended to indoctrinate his students concerning the truth of his beliefs. Dr. Hornbake passed along to Dr. Elkins the conclusions he had reached from his review of plaintiff's works.

Dr. Hornbake had eventually prepared for President Elkins a memorandum dated June 15, questioning plaintiff's administrative experience for heading a department as large as this one and further questioning Dr. Ollman's national reputation as a scholar. Thereafter, Dr. Hornbake had recommended to President Elkins that plaintiff not be appointed to the position.

After July 1, Dr. Hornbake continued his review of the matter and considered the new information which had come to light during the first two weeks of July. When he met with President Toll on July 19, his overall assessment was that the appointment should not be approved. From his knowledge of the complexity of the Department of Government and Politics and its size and state of being, it was Dr. Hornbake's opinion that more administrative talent and ability were required for the Chairman than that possessed by the plaintiff. Dr. Hornbake furthermore had reservations concerning plaintiff's scholarship, noting that plaintiff was an Associate Professor at N.Y.U. with no indication of further development which would suggest promotion to a full Professorship either at N.Y.U. or at Maryland. He also pointed out to President Toll that Dr. Ollman had no experience in obtaining research grants and that this was a specific requirement included in the charge to the Search Committee. Dr. Hornbake was disturbed that Dr. Ollman had stated his intention of making the Maryland Department of Government and Politics the leading one in the country for the study and use of Marxist approaches in the political science field. According to Dr. Hornbake, this was a change in the direction which the Department had taken in the past and would involve the commitment of new resources.

It is apparent from the record that President Toll considered and gave weight to Dr. Hornbake's opinion concerning the Ollman appointment. President Toll had known and worked with Dr. Hornbake when Toll was at Maryland between 1953 and 1965 as Professor and Chairman of the Department of Physics. President Toll had tremendous respect for Dr. Hornbake's ability as an academic officer, and in his testimony, characterized Dr. Hornbake as "truly one of the finest academic officers, chief academic officers, that any university ever had."

President Toll reached his final decision to reject the proposed appointment during the evening of July 19. The next day, he announced his decision at a meeting of the Board of Regents. In his written statement presented at that meeting, President Toll, among other things said the following:

> . . .
>
> In each decision on appointments, I make a determination on the basis of my judgment of the qualifications for a particular appointment of the candidate who has been proposed. I wish to stress that, in my opinion, it would be improper and illegal to base any decision on a candidate's personal opinions, political beliefs, or religious convictions. My responsibility is to judge the qualifications of a candidate to perform the duties of teaching, research, and service and, in addition for a candidate for chairman, to perform the important administrative responsibilities of that position. We aim in our search procedures to determine the best possible candidate for each appointment.
>
> . . .
>
> There has been wide public discussion of this proposed appointment, much of it focusing on issues that are not appropriate. For example, some persons have said that they felt I should

approve the recommendation, even though it was not merited, because others might believe that the appointment had been refused on account of the candidate's political beliefs. I must stress as clearly as I can that appointment decisions at the University of Maryland are not and shall not be based on political beliefs, but shall be based on the qualifications of the candidate for the duties of the position involved.

Some people who have agreed that this candidate is not the best who could be made Chairman of the Department of Government and Politics at College Park have nevertheless urged that the appointment be made because of the editorials that have been written in major newspapers or the indications that national organizations might criticize the University if the appointment is not made. I believe that a university must be willing to stand up firmly to such outside pressures.

One person has said that, although in his judgment the candidate did not have the qualifications in teaching, scholarship, and administrative ability that one should seek for this post, he was tempted to recommend the appointment in order to avoid the threat of a legal suit. I believe that academic administrators must have the courage to defend proper academic standards against all forms of outside pressure. In my opinion, it would be just as wrong to give in to the threat of a legal suit as to any other outside pressure.

In summary, although there has been considerable pressure for this proposed appointment from outside the University, mostly from people who have not carefully examined the qualifications of the candidate, I have viewed such pressure as irrelevant in reaching my decision. To the best of my ability, the decision has been based upon my evaluation of whether or not the proposed candidate is the best qualified person we can reasonably hope to get as Professor and Chairman of the Department of Government and Politics at UMCP.

On the record here, this Court finds and concludes that plaintiff has not met his burden of proving that his Marxist beliefs were a substantial or motivating factor in President Toll's decision not to appoint him as Professor and Chairman of the Department of Government and Politics at the University of Maryland....

The evidence indicates that the reasons assigned by President Toll for his decision were sincere ones, that there was an adequate factual basis for the conclusions reached and that he had fairly and conscientiously reviewed the entire matter before reaching his decision. Whether or not this Court might agree with President Toll concerning the direction which the Department should take and the qualifications of a Chairman to lead the Department in that direction, it is not for this Court to substitute its judgment for that of the University's Chief Executive Officer, so long as a legally impermissible reason was not the substantial or motivating factor.

Even if this Court were to conclude (as it has not) that plaintiff had carried his initial burden and had proved that his political beliefs were a motivating factor in President Toll's decision, the result in this case would still be the same. For the reasons stated at length herein, this Court finds and concludes that defendants have shown by a preponderance of the evidence that President Toll would have reached the same decision as to plaintiff's employment even in the absence of the protected beliefs. *See Mt. Healthy City Board of Education v. Doyle, supra* 429 U.S. at 287. As the Supreme Court there explained, the rule of causation in a case such as this one should not focus solely on whether the plaintiff's protected activity played a part in the decision not to hire him. In *Mt. Healthy*, the Supreme Court pointed out that if such an approach were adopted, a person like plaintiff would be placed "in a better position as a result of the exercise of constitutionally protected conduct than he would have (otherwise) occupied.... The constitutional principle at stake is sufficiently vindicated if such an employee is placed in no worse a position than if he had not engaged in the conduct." Whether or not plaintiff was a Marxist and whether or not that fact had significance to President Toll, plaintiff did not in President Toll's judgment possess the qualifications for the position. Defendants have thus here met their burden of showing that plaintiff would not have been hired in any event.

. . .

For the reasons stated, judgment will be entered in favor of the defendants, with costs.

Questions and Comments on *Ollman*

1. Consider the AAUP 1915 Declaration on Academic Freedom and Academic Tenure, set forth at pp. 68–79, *supra*. Under the Declaration, does the information Toll looked at in reaching his decision support the conclusion that Ollman intended to indoctrinate his students?

2. Many of the selections in Chapter 15 indicated that the president of a college or university should be a leader and provide direction for the goals of a university. If a president is limited in the reasons why he or she may choose to reject the appointment of a department chair, does this affect that president's ability to set the direction of the institution? Should the administration of colleges and universities be allowed to consider the views of a candidate for an administrative position?

3. What difficulties arise when an administrator declines to hire or promote a prospective faculty member with unpopular views? How can a reviewing court differentiate a pretextual reason from a valid one?

Jennings v. University of North Carolina

United States Court of Appeals for the Fourth Circuit, en banc, 2007.
482 F.3d 686.

■ MICHAEL, CIRCUIT JUDGE:

Melissa Jennings, a former student and soccer player at the University of North Carolina at Chapel Hill (UNC or the University), claims that her coach, Anson Dorrance, persistently and openly pried into and discussed the sex lives of his players and made sexually charged comments, thereby creating a hostile environment in the women's soccer program. Jennings sued UNC, Dorrance, Susan Ehringhaus (Assistant to the Chancellor and legal counsel to UNC), and several other individuals associated with the University, alleging violations of Title IX of the Educational Amendments of

1972 (20 U.S.C. § 1681 *et seq.*), 42 U.S.C. § 1983, and the common law. The district court awarded summary judgment to the defendants. . . .

Because Jennings was the non-movant in the summary judgment proceedings, we recite the facts, with reasonable inferences drawn, in her favor. UNC has the country's most successful women's soccer program at the college level. The UNC team, with Dorrance as head coach, has won the most national championships in the history of the sport. . . . Dorrance personally recruited Jennings while she was in high school, and she joined the UNC team at the start of her freshman year in August 1996. Jennings was one of four goalkeepers until Dorrance cut her from the team in May 1998, at the end of her sophomore year. Jennings was seventeen when she started playing for Dorrance, and he was forty-five.

Once Jennings became a member of the UNC team, she was distressed to learn that Dorrance engaged in sexually charged talk in team settings. Dorrance bombarded players with crude questions and comments about their sexual activities and made comments about players' bodies that portrayed them as sexual objects. In addition, Dorrance expressed (once within earshot of Jennings) his sexual fantasies about certain players, and he made, in plain view, inappropriate advances to another. This behavior on Dorrance's part occurred on a regular basis, particularly during team warm-up time at the beginning of practice. The sex-focused talk that Dorrance initiated or encouraged occurred at other times as well, or, as one player put it, "anytime the team was together," whether "on a plane, in a car, or on a bus, in a hotel, at practice, out of town, at events." . . .

In front of the entire team, Dorrance asked one player nearly every day "who [her] fuck of the minute is, fuck of the hour is, fuck of the week [is]," whether there was a "guy [she] ha[dn't] fucked yet," or whether she "got the guys' names as they came to the door or . . . just took a number." He asked a second player if she was "going to have sex with the entire lacrosse team," and advised a third, "[Y]ou just have to keep your knees together . . . you can't make it so easy for them." Dorrance frequently focused on a fourth player's sex life with questions such as whether she was going to have a "shag fest" when her boyfriend visited and whether she was "going to fuck him and leave him." The coach "direct[ed] inquir[ies]" to a fifth player about the size of her boyfriend's genitalia.

. . .

Dorrance did not limit himself to inappropriate speech. He showed overt affection—affection of the sort that was not welcomed—for one player, Keller, in front of the entire team. He paid inordinate attention to Keller, frequently brushing her forehead, hugging her, rubbing her back, whispering in her ear, dangling a hand in front of her chest, or touching her stomach. . . . Also, one evening Dorrance telephoned for Keller at home, and one of her roommates (not a soccer player) told him that Keller was out with her boyfriend. Dorrance retorted, "What is she doing, out having sex all over Franklin Street?" Dorrance told Keller that he "couldn't hide his affection for [her]" and said that "in a lifetime you should be as intimate with as many people as you can."

Jennings listened as Dorrance focused on the sex life of one player after another. Jennings sought desperately to avoid Dorrance's questions and ridicule about her personal life. She therefore tried to "stay out of [his] radar" by not participating in the discussions. She was targeted nevertheless. During a fall tournament in California at the end of Jennings's freshman season, Dorrance held one-on-one meetings with players in his hotel room to assess their performance for the season. Dorrance told Jennings that she was in danger of losing her eligibility to play soccer if her grades did not improve. In the midst of this discussion, Dorrance asked Jennings, "Who are you fucking?" She replied that it was "[n]one of his God damn business" what she did off field. As Jennings described the scene, "I was 17 when he asked me that in a dark hotel room, knee-to-knee, bed not made, sitting at one of those tiny tables." She felt acutely uncomfortable.

Jennings herself heard most of the comments recounted above that Dorrance made in front of the team. . . .

Jennings again found herself the target of Dorrance's sexual inquiries in a warm-up session during her sophomore year. . . . One player asked, using Jennings's nickname, "[W]ell, what about Trim'n?," and Dorrance immediately "chimed in," saying "[Y]es, what about Trim'n?" The coach wanted to know whether Jennings had "the same good weekend" as the player whose weekend he had just described as a shag fest. Dorrance thus encouraged the interrogation about personal sexual activity to "slide over" to Jennings for several minutes. She felt humiliated and refused to respond.

. . .

During the fall of her freshman year Jennings notified UNC about the hostile sexual environment that Dorrance had created within the women's soccer program. She lodged a complaint in a meeting with Susan Ehringhaus, legal counsel to the University and Assistant to the Chancellor. Jennings "gave [Ehringhaus] a [complete] run-down" about Dorrance's persistence in talking about players' sex lives when the team was assembled for practice or other activities. She reported her feelings of humiliation and discomfort. Ehringhaus dismissed these concerns and suggested that Jennings simply "work it out" with Dorrance. Jennings's complaint thus remained unaddressed by the UNC administration.

Jennings stayed on the team until she was cut by Dorrance during exams at the end of her sophomore year. He cited inadequate fitness as the reason. Over the next several days, Jennings's parents submitted several complaints to the Chancellor's office about Dorrance's regular involvement in discussions about the sexual activities of his players. Thereafter, the Director of Athletics, Richard Baddour, conducted an administrative review pursuant to UNC's sexual harassment policy. Dorrance admitted that he participated in group discussions with players about their sex lives, but claimed that his comments were only "of a jesting or teasing nature." The review ended with Athletic Director Baddour sending a letter of apology to Jennings's father and a brief, mild letter of reprimand to Dorrance. Baddour wrote to Mr. Jennings on June 9, 1998, apologizing for Dorrance's "inappropriate . . . involvement in [sexual] discussions" with his team members. Dorrance indicated his own apology by counter-signing the letter. One day later, Baddour wrote to Dorrance declaring it "inappropriate for [Dorrance] to have conversations with members of [the] team (individually or in any size group) regarding their sexual activity."

August 1998, at the start of Jennings's junior year, she and Keller brought this action against UNC and several individuals associated with the

University, including Dorrance and Ehringhaus.... After the lawsuit was filed, Jennings was threatened and harassed to the extent that UNC officials warned her that they could not guarantee her safety on campus. At UNC's urging, she spent her senior year at another school and was then awarded a UNC degree. Keller settled her claims and took a dismissal with prejudice. Jennings's case proceeded to the entry of summary judgment in favor of the defendants. She appealed and a divided panel of this court affirmed the judgment. We vacated the panel decision and reheard the case en banc....

Jennings claims that UNC discriminated against her in violation of Title IX by allowing Dorrance, the women's soccer coach, to subject her to severe and pervasive sexual harassment in the women's soccer program. Title IX provides that "[n]o person ... shall, on the basis of sex, be excluded from participation in, be denied the benefits of, or be subjected to discrimination under any education program or activity receiving Federal financial assistance." 20 U.S.C. § 1681(a). Discrimination under Title IX includes coach-on-student sexual harassment that creates a hostile environment in a school sports program....

To establish a Title IX claim on the basis of sexual harassment, a plaintiff must show that (1) she was a student at an educational institution receiving federal funds, (2) she was subjected to harassment based on her sex, (3) the harassment was sufficiently severe or pervasive to create a hostile (or abusive) environment in an educational program or activity, and (4) there is a basis for imputing liability to the institution....

Jennings can establish the first element of her Title IX claim without dispute: she was a student at UNC, an institution receiving federal funds. On the second element of her claim, Jennings must proffer facts showing that Dorrance subjected her to harassment (verbal in this case) based on her sex. Sexual harassment occurs when the victim is subjected to sex-specific language that is aimed to humiliate, ridicule, or intimidate. A coach's sexually charged comments in a team setting, even if not directed specifically to the plaintiff, are relevant to determining whether the plaintiff was subjected to sex-based harassment.

UNC argues that Dorrance's sex-focused comments were "of a joking and teasing nature" that did not amount to sexual harassment. The facts, when viewed in the light most favorable to Jennings, show that Dorrance's persistent, sex-oriented discussions, both in team settings and in private, were degrading and humiliating to his players because they were women. His conduct went far beyond simple teasing and qualified as sexual harassment.

Dorrance, in front of the entire team, frequently singled out individual players to find out whether, with whom, and how often they were having sex. These sorts of questions and comments, which frequently carried the strong suggestion of promiscuity, provoked in several players acute feelings of humiliation and degradation that were directly linked to their gender.... Finally, Dorrance's reckless comments about his sexual fantasies—to a trainer that he would like to have group sex with his Asian players and to Debbie Keller that he would like to be a fly on the wall the first time one player had sex—assist in demonstrating that his pronounced interest in discussing his players' sex lives transcended simple teasing or joking. In short, Jennings proffers sufficient facts for a jury to find that Dorrance subjected her to sexual harassment.

We next consider whether Jennings proffers facts to permit a finding that Dorrance's sex-based harassment was sufficiently severe or pervasive to create a hostile or abusive environment in the women's soccer program. Harassment reaches the sufficiently severe or pervasive level when it creates "an environment that a reasonable person would find hostile or abusive" and that the victim herself "subjectively perceive[s] . . . to be abusive." *Harris,* 510 U.S. at 21. Whether gender-oriented harassment amounts to actionable (severe or pervasive) discrimination "depends on a constellation of surrounding circumstances, expectations, and relationships." . . . These standards for judging hostility ensure that Title IX does not become a "general civility code." *See Oncale,* 523 U.S. at 80. "[S]imple teasing, offhand comments, and isolated incidents (unless extremely serious) will not amount to discrimi-nat[ion]." . . . Here, a jury could reasonably find that Dorrance's persistent sexual harassment was sufficiently degrading to young women to create a hostile or abusive environment.

Dorrance was not just any college coach. He was and still is the most successful women's soccer coach in U.S. college history, and he has coached the national team. Dorrance thus had tremendous power and influence over a player's opportunity for achievement in the soccer world, both at UNC and beyond. As Jennings put it, "[g]irls would cut off their right arm to be [at UNC]" and play for Dorrance. Dorrance encouraged his players to confide in him about all aspects of their personal lives, including the details of their sexual activities. He professed to them that he wanted to be a father figure. In reality, Dorrance abused his power as coach to ask his players questions a father would not ask; he pried into and talked openly about his players' sex lives in a way that was disrespectful and degrading. The disparity in power between Dorrance and his players trapped players into responding to his questions and enduring the environment. As the coach, Dorrance controlled everything: team membership, position, playing time, and scholarship eligi-bility. Even Debbie Keller, the team captain and a star player, was acutely mindful of Dorrance's enormous power and influence, and she took care not to provoke him. Keller was troubled by Dorrance's persistent focus on sex. "[A]ll [of his] comments about his affection" for her, together with the inappropriate touching, "made [her] skin crawl" and made her "fe[el] dirty." Dorrance's conduct put constant pressure on Keller because she "didn't want to tick him off to a point . . . where he would take it out on [her] by not playing [her]." . . .

Any age disparity between the harasser and his victim is also relevant to gauging whether there was a hostile or abusive sexual environment. Here, Dorrance was a forty-five-year-old man probing into and commenting about the sexual activities of young women, some of whom, like Jennings, were as young as seventeen. . . .

Jennings had good reason to fear that she too would be targeted by Dorrance, for he had subjected her to a general environment of sexual harassment. She had witnessed his degrading and persistent focus on the sex lives of other players. She observed Dorrance's sex-based humiliation of several of her teammates, and she heard his demeaning comments. . . .

. . .

In sum, Jennings has proffered sufficient facts for a jury to find that Dorrance's degrading and humiliating conduct was sufficiently severe or pervasive to create a sexually hostile environment. This conclusion takes into account the informal, sometimes jocular, college sports team atmosphere that fosters familiarity and close relationships between coaches and players. A male coach might use sexual slang in front of his women players, and the players might do the same in front of the coach. Title IX is not a civility code for the male coach who coaches women, and it is not meant to punish such a coach for off-color language that is not aimed to degrade or intimidate. What happened in this case, if Jennings's version of the facts is believed, is that Dorrance took advantage of the informal team setting to cross the line and engage in real sexual harassment that created a hostile or abusive environment.

A Title IX plaintiff completes her hostile environment showing at the summary judgment stage if, based on her proffered evidence, the sexual harassment *"can be said* to deprive [her] of access to . . . educational opportunities or benefits." [*Davis v. Monroe County Bd. of Educ.*, 526 U.S. 629, 650 (1999)] (emphasis added). *Davis* explains that a sexual harassment victim "can be said" to have been deprived of access to educational opportunities or benefits in several circumstances, including when the harassment (1) results in the physical exclusion of the victim from an educational program or activity; (2) "so undermines and detracts from the victim['s] educational experience" as to "effectively den[y her] equal access to an institution's resources and opportunities"; or (3) has "a concrete, negative effect on [the victim's] ability" to participate in an educational program or activity. . . .

Jennings has met the burden here with evidence showing that Dorrance's severe and pervasive sexual harassment concretely and negatively affected her ability to participate in the soccer program. . . .

. . .

Finally, Jennings must provide a basis for imputing liability to UNC for Dorrance's conduct. . . .

Jennings's facts show that in the fall of 1996 Jennings met with Susan Ehringhaus, Assistant to the Chancellor and counsel to the University. Ehringhaus was UNC's highest ranking lawyer and an official responsible for fielding sexual harassment complaints. Jennings informed Ehringhaus that Dorrance had created an abusive environment in the women's soccer program. Ehringhaus was given vivid details of Dorrance's sexual comments about his players when the team was together. Jennings also reported that the situation was causing her intense feelings of discomfort and humiliation. Ehringhaus dismissed this complaint by telling Jennings that Dorrance was a "great guy" and that she should work out her problems directly with him. Ehringhaus took no action on the complaint, and Dorrance's harassment continued. These facts are sufficient to establish that Jennings gave Ehringhaus, and by extension UNC, actual notice of the hostile environment created by Dorrance. This notice and the University's failure to take any action to remedy the situation would allow a rational jury to find deliberate indifference to ongoing discrimination.

For the foregoing reasons, Jennings has presented sufficient evidence to raise triable questions of fact on all disputed elements of her Title IX claim against UNC, and the district court erred in granting the University's motion for summary judgment.

Jennings asserts § 1983 claims for sexual harassment against Dorrance, Ehringhaus, and several other individuals who were employed by UNC. These defendants, according to Jennings, acted "under color of" state law to deprive her of "rights, privileges or immunities secured by the Constitution and laws" of the United States, 42 U.S.C. § 1983, specifically her Fourteenth Amendment equal protection right to be free from sexual harassment in an educational setting. . . .

To survive Dorrance's motion for summary judgment on her § 1983 sexual harassment claim against him, Jennings must show that he was a state actor, he harassed her because of sex, and the harassment was sufficiently severe or pervasive to interfere unreasonably with her educational activities. . . . As we spell out [above] Jennings has proffered evidence (1) that Dorrance was a state actor, functioning in his capacity as a coach, when he engaged in sexual harassment and (2) that the harassment was sufficiently severe or pervasive to interfere with her educational activities. The district court therefore erred in granting summary judgment to Dorrance on the § 1983 claim for sexual harassment.

.   .   .

Jennings's § 1983 claim against Ehringhaus is based on the theory of supervisory liability. *See Baynard v. Malone,* 268 F.3d 228, 235 (4th Cir. 2001) ("It is well settled that 'supervisory officials may be held liable in certain circumstances for the constitutional injuries inflicted by their subordinates.'" (quoting *Shaw v. Stroud,* 13 F.3d 791, 798 (4th Cir. 1994))). . . . Jennings's evidence would allow a jury to find that Ehringhaus had actual knowledge of Dorrance's misconduct; that her response was "so inadequate as to show deliberate indifference to or tacit authorization of the alleged offensive practices"; and that there exists "an affirmative causal link" between Ehringhaus's inaction and Jennings's constitutional injury. Ehringhaus is therefore not entitled to summary judgment on Jennings's § 1983 claim against her for supervisory liability.

.   .   .

For the reasons stated above, we vacate the district court's grant of summary judgment on Jennings's Title IX claim against UNC, her § 1983 claim against Dorrance for sexual harassment, and her § 1983 claim against Ehringhaus for sexual harassment based on supervisory liability. We affirm the grant of summary judgment on Jennings's remaining claims against the individual defendants, and we affirm the procedural rulings. The case is remanded for further proceedings on the open Title IX and § 1983 claims.

Questions and Comments on *Jennings*

On January 14, 2008, the University of North Carolina announced it would pay $385,000 to settle Jennings' law suit. As part of the settlement, the coach, Anson Dorrance, must apologize to players on the teams he coached between 1996 and 1998 for making inappropriate sexual comments to women. In settling the case, the university admitted no wrongdoing. Brad Wolverton, *U. of North Carolina Settles Sex–Harassment Suit Against Coach,* CHRON. HIGHER EDUC., Jan. 15, 2008, *available at* http://chronicle.com/daily/2008/01/1231n.htm.

Consider how UNC responded to the allegations of sexual harassment. If you had been in Ehringhaus's position, how would you have responded? What steps should colleges and universities take to avoid these kinds of law suits?

B. ALUMNI

Ad Hoc Committee of the Baruch Black and Hispanic Alumni Association v. Bernard M. Baruch College

United States District Court, Southern District New York, 1989.
726 F.Supp. 522.

■ RICHARD OWEN, UNITED STATES DISTRICT JUDGE.

Implicit in this case is the question of what responsibility, if any, a college has to its alumni, collectively or individually. Obviously, a college has a contractual duty to educate its undergraduates who pay to come to it and a duty to treat each student fairly and non-discriminatorily. But upon the departure of a student from its halls of learning, does any legally cognizable duty continue?

Clearly, since many graduates of colleges have formed enduring friendships with classmates and take away fond memories of shared experiences, most colleges generally disseminate an alumni magazine with collected news of alumni "doings," and provide opportunities and facilities for periodic reunions, and colleges are grateful if such old-school ties foster a desire in their graduates to make much-needed gifts to the alma mater. The way the alumni-college relationship is structured or fostered is, however, much varied from college to college. One may have an alumni association with a charter and a dues requirement. Another does not, all matriculants belonging to the association whose operations are funded by the college. Still another may have no association, but a national organization which is a federation of local, city and state clubs.

Thus, in the absence of any other factors, it is apparent that, upon graduation, one may no longer look to one's alma mater for other than such things as a transcript of grades as needed. This view of the relationship between a college and its alumni leads me to conclude that, unlike at the undergraduate level, *see Healy v. James*, 408 U.S. 169 (1972), the First Amendment does not require colleges to fund or recognize alumni groups. Moreover, a college does not unlawfully impede the associational rights of its alumni when it declines to recognize an alumni group. However, if a college does involve itself in establishing an alumni relationship structure, it must act non-discriminatorily.

Turning to the parties in this case, defendant Bernard B. Baruch College ("the College"), a branch of the City University of New York, has and recognizes a single alumni association for all graduates of its undergraduate program. It gave permission to that organization to use its name—as to which it has a proprietary interest—and to incorporate under New York State law as the Bernard M. Baruch Alumni Association (BCAA) with a charter and 7000 dues-paying alumni, among whom are many black and Hispanic members, a number of whom have served as its officers, including president.

Plaintiffs Ad Hoc Committee of the Baruch Black and Hispanic Alumni Association ("the Committee") and its Chairman Joseph Sellman have sought and by this action are seeking from defendants Bernard B. Baruch College and Baruch College President Joel Segall official recognition, including the right to use the Baruch name for a corporation it wishes to form under New York State law and thereafter to function as an independent alumni association. This is opposed, the College suggesting that the plaintiffs organize and work within the existing alumni association. Plaintiffs decline this suggestion, observing that without separate recognition, plaintiffs may not command and utilize the College's facilities or resources. Plaintiffs allege under 42 U.S.C. § 1983 that defendants' refusal to grant such recognition amounts to a violation of both the First Amendment to the United States Constitution (freedom of speech) and the Fourteenth Amendment (equal protection of the law). Both parties move for summary judgment.

As can be seen, the form of organization for conducting Baruch College's alumni affairs is one of the several forms colleges and/or their alumni have adopted to handle the relationship. While, as observed, these differ in structural approach, one factor is generally common, which is that there is a single umbrella organization, special interest groups existing, if at all, as affiliates within the larger structure. The BCAA is no exception, for its bylaws contemplate the existence of "Constituent Societies, Chapters, and Affiliates," and the record reveals that although black alumni at several other colleges have initiated separate programs, they have done so within the framework of alumni relations established at their respective colleges.

So here, consistent with this perspective on the conduct of alumni affairs as perceived by the Baruch College administrators, they responded encouragingly when they first learned about the existence of the Committee, anticipating that plaintiffs would work within the established framework of the BCAA and, indeed, plaintiffs initially suggested that was how they would proceed. As time passed, however, it became apparent that the Committee's organizers sought to establish a separate alumni entity.

The parties now have reached an impasse. In a nutshell, plaintiffs decline to pursue their interests under the aegis of the BCAA and claim a First Amendment right to the College's name and the use of its resources. In addition, they allege that the College's position is discriminatorily motivated in violation of the Equal Protection Clause. The College, on the other hand, asserts a right to restrict its recognition to the single organization open to all and, denying any unlawful motives, proffers several legitimate justifications for their position.

Although I conclude that colleges and universities have no First Amendment obligation to fund or recognize alumni groups, if they do assist any such group the Equal Protection clause precludes them from acting discriminatorily. While asserting that the administration has so acted, plaintiffs have not introduced any evidence of political or racial bias to support an Equal Protection claim.[4] On the contrary, the record indicates that legitimate

---

4. Plaintiffs allege that defendants denied the Committee recognition for the following reasons: 1) defendants' desire to have a single, unified alumni association with a call on its resources and facilities; 2) defendants' view that minority interests would better be served by cooperation within the existing alumni association; 3) defendants' requirement that an alumni group to which it furnishes resources is to restrict itself to alumni relationships and not involve itself in matters relating to College administrative

administrative concerns underlie the College's position and defendants have a constitutionally permissible reason for preferring that plaintiffs conduct their activities through the BCAA. Since the BCAA is a relatively small organization, the College justifiably fears that solicitation efforts by a separate alumni group would unduly burden and possibly alienate alumni. That type of administrative reasoning falls well within the discretion of the College. Moreover, the College has encouraged the Committee's efforts and President Segall's gestures of support make it apparent that the College in no way opposes the communicating and airing of minority views at the alumni level by any group even if critical of the administration.

In sum, the forum for the Committee's agenda already exists: the BCAA. As an affiliate of the BCAA, the Committee would have its appropriate share of access to the goal it seeks: the College's resources. However, plaintiffs have not demonstrated a constitutional basis to require that the College give the Committee the same, but separate, status it gives the BCAA, particularly when, through the BCAA, the Committee can share in the benefits of all. And in any event, the College in no way is restricting the Committee's freedom of speech or right of association regardless of whether it is with or without the assistance of the College.

Accordingly, plaintiffs' motion for summary judgment is denied, and defendants' motion for summary judgment is granted dismissing the complaint.

Questions and Comments on *Ad Hoc Committee*

In 1999, a group of alumni from Dartmouth College sued to prevent the college from eliminating single-sex fraternities. Between 1991 and 1996, Dartmouth had undertaken a campaign to raise money from alumni to fund certain aspects of the college, including the building of a new library, improving the curriculum, and keeping tuition costs down. After hearing of the trustees' plan to change the fraternity and sorority system at Dartmouth, the alumni sued the board of trustees, alleging a breach of a fiduciary duty owed by the trustees to the alumni. The alumni argued that the trustees had misrepresented the purposes of the fundraising campaign, and that the alumni donations created a fiduciary duty to the alumni with respect to the use of those funds to implement a major policy change to the residential and social system of the college. The alumni also argued that the inclusion of alumni-elected seats on the board of trustees created an inference of a fiduciary relationship between alumni and the board. Defining a fiduciary relationship as a "comprehensive term [that] exists wherever influence has been acquired and abused or confidence has been reposed and betrayed," the Supreme Court of New Hampshire held that there was no basis to support the existence of a fiduciary relationship between the group of alumni and the trustees. Even the fact that some of the alumni

---

policies or practices; 4) defendants' belief that recognition of the Committee would itself violate equal access and non-discrimination principles; 5) defendants' desire to respect opposition voiced by members of the BCAA; 6) defendants' belief that the Committee has reasonable alternatives to official recognition. I note in particular with respect to the third ground above that alumni groups have no standing to challenge college policies in a court of law because they lack a concrete interest in those administrative practices. *See, e.g., McCormack v. Nat'l Collegiate Athletic Ass'n*, 845 F.2d 1338 (5th Cir. 1988). Moreover, after an appropriate inquiry, I am not convinced that any of the foregoing reasons, even accepting truth as alleged, would constitute a showing of political or racial bias requiring the Committee's separate recognition and I conclude that there is no support for any claim that the College was motivated by an "invidious discriminatory purpose." *Arlington Heights v. Metropolitan Housing Corp.*, 429 U.S. 252, 266 (1976).

had donated money to Dartmouth did not create a fiduciary relationship, because the donation was a voluntary gift by the alumni to the college for the benefit of the college. The court held:

> [T]he presence of an alumni trustee on the board does not create a fiduciary relationship in and of itself. A college does not acquire influence over its alumni by soliciting donations in a capital campaign, or by the receipt of donations from alumni. The nature of the transaction is a voluntary gift by the alumni to the college for the benefit of the college.... [No] fiduciary relationship has been created by the transaction.

Brzica v. Trustees of Dartmouth Coll., 147 N.H. 443, 791 A.2d 990, 994–95 (2002). Taken together, these cases suggest that a college or university does not normally owe any duty to alumni. Do you agree, or should institutions of higher education be required to consider the views of alumni?

C.   GENERAL COUNSEL

Stephen Dunham, Who is the Client?

2007

The first question a lawyer must ask herself in almost any legal representation of a college or university is "Who is the client?" Does the lawyer represent the president, the dean of a school, individual faculty, a department or committee, trustees or all of the above? What duties does a university lawyer owe to students, parents, government funding agencies, donors, alumni, creditors and the public?

This question affects fundamental issues of professional responsibility and ethics. It determines confidentiality, loyalty, conflicts of interest, disclosure of wrongdoing, privilege and other ethical obligations. It is also a highly practical question, helping the lawyer understand how the university is organized, what its governance and management structure is, what its policies are and how they work, to whom authority is delegated, who to talk to, who calls the shots—in short, how decisions are made and who makes them.

The black letter answer to the ethics question is easy to state. Rule 1.13 of the Model Rules of Professional Conduct states the entity theory of representation this way: "A lawyer employed or retained by an organization represents the organization acting through its duly authorized constituents." But universities are unusually complex organizations, with multiple and shifting constituents and purposefully ambiguous lines of authority, so in practice, particularly in hard cases where the "who is the client question" may be paramount, the question is very difficult to answer and apply.

The analysis requires multiple steps. The university "organization" is typically a corporation, which of course is a legal fiction, or a governmental entity with a corporate form. While for some purposes it may be true that "corporations are people too," the university lawyer cannot talk to a legal fiction.

For most purposes, state corporation or non-profit laws tell us that the highest group of real people who can speak for the corporate entity is the board of directors (usually "trustees" in university parlance). But a college or university board may only meet three or four times a year, and trustees are seldom involved in day-to-day operational issues that are the bread and butter of university legal matters. A university lawyer trying to figure out who the client is must frequently drill down another level.

Following the language of Rule 1.13, the next step is to find a "duly authorized constituent." The "constituent" may be an individual, and "authorization" may be by a formal Board by-law, resolution or written policy. In such a case it is fairly easy for the lawyer to decide who the client is for the particular purpose. For example, the by-laws or Board approved policy may state which institutional official has authority to sign certain contracts or settle a lawsuit or sell property or invest the endowment or engage in financing transactions. The named official would usually be the "client" for legal issues related to the specific subject.

In many other situations the lawyer will find a policy describing a decision making process rather than an individual decision maker, and the "policy" may be based on practice or custom rather than a formalized procedure. The process may have multiple stages with different decision makers at each stage, and the decision makers may be departments or programs or "faculties" rather than individuals. The process may even be ad hoc, created for a particular purpose in response to particular events. The lawyer's "client," and therefore the constituency to which she owes her duties, is ambiguous and it changes over time as the process moves forward.

Tenure disputes are a good example. Among the most important decisions a university makes, one with substantial legal obligations and significant risks, is the decision to grant or deny tenure to a faculty member. A favorable decision is a significant commitment of the institution's resources over a period of decades. An unfavorable decision may prompt a lawsuit alleging, among other things, discrimination, retaliation, breach of contract and other theories. The university's tenure policy, approved by the Board, constitutes a delegation of authority, but to whom? In effect, the policy, as modified by historical practice, creates multiple client "constituents" for each stage in the process. To generalize, the tenure decision may begin with a request by a department chair to a faculty committee to review an individual for tenure; the committee may make a recommendation up or down back to the chair, who then adds his own position and forwards a recommendation to the dean of the particular school. There may be a school level committee that reviews the recommendation, or it may go to an all-campus or all-university committee. That committee may then make a recommendation to the Dean, or the Provost, or the President, or all three, one after the other. In the case of a favorable decision, the final administrator in the chain typically makes a recommendation to the Board, which has the ultimate authority. The authority for a negative decision more typically lies with the President or chief academic officer.

So who is the client? The answer depends in part on the stage of the process. As the process winds along the lawyer acquires new and different clients. Or, to be more accurate, the client stays the same—it is the entity— but the "authorized constituent," through which or whom the client speaks, changes. So, in the tenure case, when the dean asks for advice, the lawyer represents the dean in his capacity as dean. When a faculty committee asks for advice, the committee and its members are, in both practical and professional responsibility terms, the client. The same is true for the individual or group decision maker at every stage in the process. Usually this representation is of the individual in her official role, not in her individual capacity, though the representation may be individual as well. *See* Model Rule 1.13(g). Among other issues, these multiple and overlapping "clients" create significant potential for conflicts of interest. *See* Model Rule 1.7.

Additional complications arise when, as is frequently true, parallel with the tenure decision making process there is a simultaneous dispute of some kind. At the same time that the "university" is making its tenure decision, "it"—the university entity—may also be ruling on an internal grievance. The professor may have a pending dispute with the dean arising out of last year's salary decision, or he may be the respondent in a sexual harassment claim by a student, or he may be involved in a research misconduct investigation. For each of these proceedings there is likely a university policy that sets forth its own procedures—a charging party, a faculty committee, appeal to another committee, appeal to a higher official. Each of these separate policies thus has its own set of "authorized constituents" who are the lawyer's client for the particular role they are assigned under the particular policy.

This scenario—which is not uncommon—is made more complicated when the university's policies that define the "authorized constituents" for a particular decision are not written down in clear form, but instead are based on custom or tradition (which of course frequently varies across the institution), or reason, logic and common sense (as determined by whatever official is asking for advice) or just the proverbial "that is how things are done around here" standard, which the would-be client asserts to be the equivalent of a rule of law.

Most decisions in a legal representation are made by the client. The lawyer must defer to these decisions. *See* Model Rule 1.2. But for issues of professional responsibility, including deciding who the client is who can tell the lawyer what to do, the lawyer is on her own. For ethics issues, the lawyer is her own client. Faced with the maze of conflicting constituents that may arise in the not atypical tenure case described above, the lawyer must decide who the client is before ever getting to the substantive issue.

And of course the substantive legal question posed by the "client" will vary depending on who the client is. The ultimate issue for the entity may be whether a particular professor should get tenure; the lawyer's job is at the same time more discrete but also broader. For any particular constituent along the road to the final tenure decision, the legal issue may be quite different—was the professor guilty of harassment, did he engage in research misconduct, did the dean retaliate against the professor for a previous claim, did the committee rely on appropriate evidence, did the committee apply the right standard, were proper procedures followed, is certain information public or available to the professor, can one of the "clients" talk to another while the process is pending, etc. etc.

The challenge of multiple constituents and ambiguous "authorization" exists in all entity representations, but the "who is the client" question is particularly complex for colleges and universities. There are many reasons for this, but four stand out.

First, based on history and custom, frequently embodied in university policies, the faculty play a uniquely important role in university governance. Because of this role, individual faculty and groups of faculty (including committees and academic departments) are "authorized constituents" and exercise "client" functions much more than equivalent managers or administrators or professionals in a corporate or governmental entity. There are many caveats, and the faculty are frequently not the final decision makers, but as a general matter the faculty play a significant role in setting curriculum, approving academic standards for admission and graduation, deciding what and how to teach, controlling the research functions of the university, deciding what is misconduct, exploring new academic initiatives, and in general carrying out the academic mission of the university. In carrying out all of these functions, the faculty, individually and collectively, are clients who determine a lawyer's ethical responsibilities, make decisions for the entity, and control, or at least affect, the course of the legal representation.

Second, many universities are more decentralized and have less rigid decision making structures than corporations. The university lawyer therefore has less guidance in deciding who the client is in a particular matter. This difference has narrowed substantially in the past 30 years. As a result of federal compliance obligations, an increase in litigation and an increased willingness of regulators and some courts to second guess academic decisions, universities have been forced to be more defensive in their operations, which means they are more corporate, more structured and more formal. Nevertheless, the culture of many colleges and universities remains one of autonomy, independence, individuality, and distrust of rules and formal chains of command. Faculty (and students) often are not required to, and they do not, do as they are told. For a lawyer, these attributes make for an interesting and exciting client, but figuring out who that client is, precisely, is frequently a challenge.

Third, universities have students, and other entities don't. For the university lawyer, under the rules of professional responsibility, most students, most of the time, are third party bystanders, witnesses, even adverse plaintiffs, but not "clients." *See* Model Rules 4.1–4.4. But there are exceptions. Students serving on boards of trustees, or on committees, or running extracurricular activities or clubs may, depending on the issue, be at least a member of an "authorized constituent." Further, even in the normal case when students are not "authorized" clients, they are still constituents who have a very substantial effect on the legal issues facing a college or university. Universities have legal duties to students and students create liabilities for universities. The role of students in a university thus makes the university "entity" very different from a corporation.

Finally, most colleges and universities are not-for-profit entities with a mission to provide education and serve the public. Although a lawyer represents clients, not ideas, nevertheless the mission of colleges and universities helps define the lawyer's role. For example, in following Rule 1.13, the lawyer may need to decide if the "authorized constituent" she is dealing with has violated the law or acted in a way that does substantial harm to the organization. If so, the Rule has certain mandatory "up the ladder" reporting obligations and permissive "reporting out" rights. In working through this analysis, which is among the more difficult challenges faced by a university lawyer, the mission of the institution plays a critical role in helping the lawyer decide what is right and what is wrong and what to do and who decides.

The "who is the client" question is hard enough for the lawyer to answer herself when faced with a discrete legal question. But in practice the question is harder still because the answer often depends both on who asks the question and on the context in which it is asked. In other words, who wants to know, and why?

Let us take a concrete example. Suppose, hypothetically, that a graduate student teaching assistant is accused by an undergraduate in his class of sexual assault/ harassment at an off-campus party organized by the department to improve student/faculty relations. The professor was also at the party and was a witness to the alleged harassment. The victim files a grievance as part of the student disciplinary process. The student affairs dean appoints a committee to investigate. The victim also lodges a complaint with the equal opportunity office, which opens its own investigation. The campus police, employed by the university, opens an investigation. While the grievance is pending the victim sues the university board of trustees, as a group and individually, and the dean of students under Title IX for damages caused by the sexual assault.

The university lawyer knows that she represents the university Board in defense of the litigation. That much is easy, but who her other "clients" are will be determined in part by who wants to know and the purpose for which the question is asked.

For example, if the lawyer talks to the professor who was at the party, is the conversation subject to the attorney client privilege? The answer would be determined by state privilege law and the privilege might apply for some purposes and not others. The professor might be part of the university client for discussions related to how the professor employed, trained and paid the graduate assistant, and this part of the conversation would be privileged, but the conversation about what he witnessed at the party might be as a third party non-client that is not privileged.

As another example, if the victim's lawyer called the professor to interview him, is he a represented party under Rule 4.2 of the Model Rules whom the lawyer cannot talk to without permission of the university counsel? This would depend on the particular interpretation of Rule 4.2 in the state, which might or might not follow the privilege analysis.

If the graduate assistant and the Dean of Students ask the lawyer to represent them individually in the lawsuit, the lawyer will have to review the university's defense and indemnification policy to decide if it covers the claim. This likely requires analysis of the underlying facts—are the acts for which the individuals are sued within the scope of their employment, is there sufficient basis to believe that the TA committed sexual assault/harassment which would take the claim outside of the policy, even if attendance at the party were an official job function, and who decides this? If the lawyer agrees to represent one or both individuals in the case, she needs to analyze possible conflicts of interest (Model Rules 1.7 and 1.13 (g)) that exist now or might exist in the future (what happens if the school fires the Dean for unrelated conduct during the course of the litigation?).

Assume that during the course of the proceedings the student disciplinary process concludes that the graduate teaching assistant is in fact guilty of sexual assault and has a prior record of sexual assault. However, the TA's father is a major donor and the Vice President for Student Affairs decides to take no disciplinary action against the TA. The TA remains on campus and the lawyer is concerned that he is a threat to other students and that the university is violating the law by being deliberately indifferent to this threat. The lawyer needs to decide if she must go "up the ladder" under Rule 1.13 to tell a higher "constituent" in the university, such as the President or even the board. If she does so, and is unsuccessful in turning around the decision, she may, depending on the language of Model Rules 1.6 and 1.13 in her state, be permitted to "go public" with her concern. In this latter event, the client is, in effect, the public, because the lawyer has decided to act in contravention of a direction from the highest authorized constituent of the university.

The scenario raises many other issues of professional responsibility that the lawyer can only resolve by working through the "who is the client" analysis. At different times and for different purposes the lawyer may owe duties to the campus police, to individuals (including students) who serve on the student disciplinary board, to staff and administrators involved in the various decisions, to the Dean, the professor, the graduate student, the victim and the public. These individuals may be clients under Rule 1.13 or third parties under Rules 4.1–4.4 or adverse parties that create conflict of interest problems under Rules 1.7. The university may also owe duties to these individuals (such as the university's duty not to discriminate against employees or students and contractual duties to follow policies) and it may be the lawyer's duty to the university to ensure that the university follows it policies and does not harm others. And the lawyer has duties to the public, both because of the not-for-profit status of the university and the lawyer's own professional responsibilities. These are hard issues, but they are what make the university client so complex and interesting and the job of the university lawyer so challenging and, ultimately, rewarding.

Questions and Comments on Dunham

Is the approach that Dunham describes the best way for colleges and universities to operate with respect to their general counsel? What reforms, if any, are necessary to streamline the process and make the lines of authority clearer? What are the benefits of leaving these complex relationships between attorney and client as they are?

*

PART VI

THE PROMISE AND PERIL OF REGULATION

CHAPTER 17

Licensure and Accreditation

Shelton College v. State Board of Education

Supreme Court of New Jersey, 1967.
48 N.J. 501, 226 A.2d 612.

[The opinion is set forth at pages 214–18, *supra*.]

Moore v. Board of Regents of the University of the State of New York

Court of Appeals of New York, 1978.
44 N.Y.2d 593, 407 N.Y.S.2d 452, 378 N.E.2d 1022.

■ Jasen, J.

Presented for our review on this appeal is the issue whether the Board of Regents, through the Commissioner of Education, has the power to deny registration of doctoral degree programs offered by the State University of New York on the ground that they do not satisfy academic standards prescribed by the commissioner.

Appellants, the Chancellor and Trustees of the State University of New York and certain professors and doctoral students in the History and English Departments of the State University of New York at Albany, commenced this action seeking a declaration that the Trustees of the State University constitute the body charged with the operation of university programs, courses and curricula, thus invalidating the directive of the commissioner denying registration of doctoral programs in history and English, as made in excess of his powers. Special Term granted summary judgment to respondents, the Board of Regents and the Commissioner of Education, holding that respondents do possess the power to review academic programs offered by the State University to determine whether such programs should be registered ... On appeal, the Appellate Division unanimously affirmed. Before this court, appellants ... limit their challenge to the power of respondents to require registration of programs offered by the State University.

. . .

... When first created by the Legislature, the Regents of the University of the State of New York succeeded to the powers of the governors of Kings College, which was then renamed Columbia College. This grant of power endowed the Regents with full authority to govern and manage any college established in New York, all such institutions to be deemed part of the University of New York. Subsequently, however, the Legislature altered the role of the Regents by granting to a board of trustees of Columbia College autonomous control over the operation of the college. Concomitantly, this act endowed all colleges established in New York with the same rights and privileges vested in the trustees of Columbia College. As a result, the Regents underwent a metamorphosis, the effect of which was to clothe it with a broad policy-making function over higher education in New York, leaving the day-to-day operation of the colleges to their own governing bodies. With the advent of the State University of New York, however, the Regents became enmeshed in the day-to-day operation of this semi-independent educational corporation. To alter this governing structure, the Legislature subsequently vested in the Board of Trustees of the State University the same power to administer the day-to-day operations of the State University as trustees of private institutions of higher education had been granted. Viewed in this historical perspective, the issue in the instant case can be framed as whether the Regents, as a policy-making body, possesses the power to require registration of doctoral degree programs or whether control over the offer-ing of such programs lies within the ambit of the Trustees of the State University.

At the outset, we note that a critical function of the Regents is its preparation, once every four years, of a master plan "for the development and expansion of higher education" in New York. This plan includes public as well as private institutions. The 1972 master plan, prepared by the Regents, and approved by the Governor, recognized the need for strength-ening graduate programs and recommended that "institutions should with-draw those programs which, upon evaluation, prove to be (a) inactive or underenrolled, (b) of marginal quality and which cannot be strengthened by sharing resources with other institutions, and (c) below the minimum stan-dards set by Commissioner's Regulations." Separate and apart from the policy recommendations concerning graduate programs contained in the 1972 master plan, section 210 of the Education Law specifically gives the Regents the power to "register domestic and foreign institutions in terms of New York standards."

It is true that read literally section 210 speaks only of the registration of domestic and foreign institutions and is silent as to the registration of particular programs offered by such institutions. However, we do not believe the power of registration granted to the Regents need be construed so narrowly. . . . [S]ection 215 of the Education Law . . . authorizes the Regents or the Commissioner of Education to "visit, examine into and inspect, any institution in the university" and to "require, as often as desired, duly verified reports therefrom giving such information and in such form as the regents or the commissioner of education shall prescribe." In the event that an institution violates "any law or any rule of the university," the Regents is empowered to "suspend the charter or any of the rights and privileges of such institution."

We see no reason why sections 210 and 215 should not be read together as the statutory authority for the power of the Regents to require registration of doctoral degree programs offered by institutions of higher education in New York. If the Regents, in the first instance, has the power to register institutions "in terms of New York standards" and the power to suspend the rights and privileges of an institution violating "any rule or law of the university," it would not appear unreasonable to conclude that the Regents also possesses the power to deny the registration of doctoral degree pro-grams which it believes do not conform with standards set for institutions of higher education. Of course, the standards for registration set by the Regents must not be arbitrary or capricious, either in the abstract or in application to specific programs. To hold that the Regents is empowered to require registration of doctoral degree programs is not to insulate such administrative action from judicial scrutiny.

Of critical importance to the effectuation of the Regents' powers is the legislative function with which it has been endowed: that is, to determine the educational policies of the State and to "establish rules for carrying into effect the laws and policies of the state, relating to education, and the functions, powers, duties and trusts conferred or charged upon the university and the education department." Implementing this power, the Regents, based upon the policy recommendations made in the 1972 master plan, established a rule providing the Commissioner of Education with authority to promulgate regulations governing the registration of courses of study in colleges, as well as in professional, technical and other schools. Acting upon this mandate, the commissioner promulgated a regulation requiring the registration of "[every] curriculum creditable toward a degree offered by institutions of higher education."[1]

To effectuate this registration requirement, the commissioner also promulgated a regulation setting forth standards to be employed in the determination whether to grant or deny the registration of degree programs offered by all institutions of higher education, both private and public. This regulation provided, *inter alia*, that "[e]ach member of the academic staff shall have demonstrated by his training, earned degrees, scholarship, experience, and by classroom performance or other evidence of teaching potential, his competence to offer the courses and discharge the other academic responsibilities which are assigned to him."

In reviewing the qualifications of the faculty of the English and History Departments at the State University of New York at Albany to offer doctoral programs, the commissioner, based upon reports submitted by the site visitation team and program evaluation committee, as well as upon the recommendation of the doctoral council,[2] determined that the faculty in these departments were not sufficiently productive or prominent to support a doctoral program and, therefore, declined to register the programs.

Indicia of faculty productivity or prominence relied upon by the commissioner focused upon the extent of research and publications credited to members of the faculty of the doctoral programs evaluated. Concerning the history program, the report of the visitation team concluded that the department was not widely known and that "[with] one outstanding exception ... the members of the department, individually and collectively [did] not represent the kind of prominent scholars to whom one refers undergraduates in all parts of the country for graduate training." Similarly, the report of the visitation team evaluating the English program concluded "that in general the members of the department are not recognized nationally by

---

1. Pursuant to this regulation, approximately 13,000 degree and certificate programs, over 2,000 of which were offered by the State University, have been registered by the Department of Education.

2. In addition to reviewing the report of the evaluation committee, the doctoral council, a body composed of 14 leaders of graduate education in New York, two each from the State University and the City University of New York and 10 from private institutions, conducted a meeting attended by representatives of the State University and of the State University at Albany at which representatives of the latter submitted statements in support of the history and English doctoral programs being reviewed.

appointment to national honorary bodies, MLA committees, or editorial boards."

In concluding that the Commissioner of Education did not act in excess of his powers in denying registration of these programs based upon this criteria, we reject, at the outset, appellant's contention that the power of the Regents is limited pursuant to chapter 388 of the Laws of 1961 to supervision and approval of the State University Trustees' master plan. . . .

. . .

As a word of caution we add that the power of the Regents is not unbridled. Its function is one of an overseer: a body possessed of broad policy-making attributes. In its broadest sense, the purpose of the Regents is "to encourage and promote education," a purpose which must be realized only through the powers granted to the Regents by the Legislature. In the absence of a specific grant of power by the Legislature, the Regents cannot transform section 207 of the Education Law, the fountainhead of the Regents' rule-making power, into an all-encompassing power permitting the Regents' intervention in the day-to-day operations of the institutions of higher education in New York. Were this provision interpreted otherwise, it would run afoul of the constitutional prohibition against the Legislature's delegation of lawmaking power to other bodies. In view, however, of the specific powers granted by the Legislature to the Regents previously discussed, we believe that, in the present case, section 207 operates as a means for the effectuation of independent powers, rather than as their source.

Accordingly, the order of the Appellate Division should be affirmed, without costs.

Questions and Comments on *Shelton* and *Moore*

The New York State Education Department continues to monitor colleges and universities in the state by such actions as notifying the public about falsified transcripts and closing institutions that fail to meet its standards. *See* New York State Education Department website, Office of College and University Evaluation, http://www.highered.nysed.gov/ocue (last visited Aug. 18, 2007). At what point, if any, do state accreditation and licensing procedures hinder academic freedom?

Nova University v. Educational Institution Licensure Commission

District of Columbia Court of Appeals, 1984.
483 A.2d 1172, *cert. denied*, 470 U.S. 1054 (1985).

■ Newman, Associate Judge.

Nova University (Nova) seeks review of an Order of the Educational Institution Licensure Commission (Commission) denying Nova's application for a license to offer Doctorate of Public Administration degree courses in the District of Columbia. The Commission denied the license, without prejudice, on the grounds that Nova had not complied with the District's licensing statutes and regulations with respect to adequate full-time faculty and adequate library resources.

Nova challenges the denial of its application for a license on the grounds that: (1) D.C. CODE § 29–815 (1981), the District's licensing statute, is not applicable to schools, such as Nova, whose degrees are conferred outside the District of Columbia; (2) D.C. CODE § 29–815 is unconstitutional on its face and as applied to Nova because it violates the First Amendment; (3) D.C. CODE § 29–815 and the regulations guiding the issuance of licenses are unconstitutionally vague; and (4) the Commission's denial of a license was arbitrary, capricious, and unsupported by substantial evidence in the record.

. . .

A preliminary review of the legislation relevant to this case and its history is helpful to place in context the issues raised by Nova. In 1929, the District of Columbia was not only the capital of the United States, but the "capital" for practically all diploma mills operating not only in the District, but throughout the United States and the world. This dubious distinction resulted from the District's lax laws relating to the incorporation of educational institutions, the power these institutions had to confer degrees under their general charters, and the opportunity to advertise themselves as operating under the authority of the United States Government or Congress. Hundreds of fraudulent institutions of "learning" incorporated in the District and sold degrees from baccalaureate to doctoral in every conceivable field of study with little or no academic work; in addition, the charters themselves were sold to individuals who carried on the "educational" programs in other states and countries. At the urging of the United States Attorney's Office, local citizens and schools, sister jurisdictions and foreign countries, Congress enacted a statute "to Regulate Degree–Conferring Institutions in the District of Columbia." Pub. L. No. 70–949, § 586a, 45 Stat. 1504 (1929) (codified at D.C. CODE §§ 29–815 to 818 (1981)). The statute requires licensing of all degree-conferring institutions incorporated in the District or incorporated in another state but operating in the District. . . .

The statute provides for criminal penalties against anyone "who shall, directly or indirectly, participate in, aid, or assist in the conferring of any degree by any unlicensed . . . institution. . . ." D.C. CODE § 29–819 (1981).

In 1977, the Council of the District of Columbia established the Educational Institution Licensure Commission to perform licensing functions under D.C. CODE § 29–815. . . .

In 1980, the Council amended the 1977 statute, giving legislative sanction to regulations previously promulgated by the Commission's predecessor, the Board of Higher Education. D.C. CODE § 31–1606(a) (1981). These regulations set forth the procedures and criteria by which licenses are issued and revoked.

Section III of the Regulations contains eleven criteria the Commission is to consider in issuing licenses, involving inquiry into: institutional control; administrative staff and procedures; financial resources; number and quality of faculty; curricula, correspondence, extension, and summer session programs; admission requirements; library; physical plant and equipment; student personnel, health, and recreational services; and institutional publications. Applicants for a license are required to submit a statement as to how they plan to meet the criteria or give reasons why they consider themselves justified in not meeting a particular requirement. The regulations provide for flexibility, recognizing that "the . . . criteria will not be equally applicable to each institution wishing to award degrees." Applicants are entitled to a de novo hearing prior to the denial of a license, and to judicial review if a license is denied.

. . . Nova University is a non-profit corporation organized and existing under the laws of Florida. In addition to undergraduate, graduate, and professional curricula taught at its home campus in Fort Lauderdale, Nova has instituted a variety of field-based, or external degree programs, designed to lead to the conferral by Nova in Florida of various degrees for professional persons. The field-based program of concern here is the Doctorate of Public Administration (DPA). Candidates for this degree are not required to fulfill traditional residence requirements at the Nova campus in Fort Lauderdale. Instead, they form "clusters" of 20 to 25 students who meet at a site in the areas where they live. At the time of the hearing, Nova was operating 11 clusters at various locations throughout the United States, with plans to increase to 15 in the near future.

Nova's DPA program requires a minimum of three years to complete and consists of nine sequences (analogous to semesters or quarters), with each sequence consisting of three to four "units" (analogous to courses). Six of the nine sequences are taught at the cluster sites, and each of the units meets once a month for approximately eighteen to twenty hours from Friday night through Saturday. The remaining three sequences are taught in residence in Ft. Lauderdale. Each of these last about one week and occur annually.

The faculty of the DPA program consists of approximately nine professors from Nova's Florida campus and thirty-three national members, called preceptors. Generally, preceptors travel to the clusters to teach local course units and the Florida-based faculty teaches Florida units. Preceptors are academicians and practitioners in the public administration field, most of whom also teach at universities with traditional residence requirements. In addition, each cluster is coordinated by a cluster director, a contract employee living in the cluster area whose role consists of administrative and recruitment duties as well as counseling students.

In addition to preparing papers in anticipation of the unit sessions, students must complete a series of research papers, pass comprehensive written and oral examinations, and complete a final paper, an "analytical research project," which Nova deems to be the equivalent of a doctoral dissertation. The research papers are supervised by Nova's faculty in Ft. Lauderdale, during the annual week long conferences, as well as by telephone and written communication. The two-day comprehensive written examination is prepared and graded by the faculty in Florida, but administered locally. The oral examination is taken in Florida and administered by faculty members. If a student successfully completes the course work, comprehensive oral and written tests, and analytical research project, Nova awards a Doctor of Public Administration, under powers derived from its incorporation in Florida.

Since 1971, Nova has been accredited by the Southern Association of Colleges and Schools (SACS), the officially recognized regional accrediting association of the southeastern United States. Nova's accreditation was most recently affirmed for a ten-year period after a review in 1974–75 of its educational programs, including its external degree programs, such as the one here at issue. In 1980, SACS separately reviewed Nova's field-based programs, including the DPA program, and this review had no effect on Nova's accreditation.

In October 1980, Nova applied to the Commission for a license to offer DPA degree courses in the District of Columbia. In response to Nova's application, the Commission appointed a three-person evaluation team, composed of non-members of the Commission and approved by Nova, to visit Nova in Florida to determine whether Nova's DPA program met the District's statutory and regulatory criteria for licensing.

The team issued a report recommending denial of a license. Nova responded to the team report, pointing out what it believed were factual errors, and providing the Commission with additional information and proposals. The Commission then appointed a Task Force, made up of two Commission members, to evaluate the team's report and Nova's response. On March 4, 1981, the Task Force submitted its findings and concluded that the Commission should deny licensure. The Commission approved the recommendations of the site evaluation team and notified Nova of its intention to deny a license, the reasons for this intent, and Nova's right to request a hearing.

A de novo hearing was held before the Commission on August 19, 23, and 24, 1982. On January 19, the Commission rendered its decision denying Nova's license application, concluding that Nova failed to demonstrate that it would have adequate full-time faculty or adequate library resources in the District of Columbia as required by D.C. CODE § 29–815(4) and the Regulations § IV(e). Although the Commission denied the license, it did so without prejudice to Nova renewing its application, and offered to explain to Nova how it could meet the faculty and library requirements

. . . .

... The language of the statute, as well as its legislative history, plainly indicate Congress' intention to comprehensively regulate degree conferring institutions operating in the District of Columbia, whether the institutions were incorporated in the District or were foreign corporations seeking to operate in the District.

We turn now to Nova's argument that § 29–815 violates the First Amendment "on its face" and as applied to Nova.... D.C. CODE § 29–815 requires private educational institutions incorporated in the District to obtain a license as a condition to conferring a degree. Nova does not challenge this aspect of the statute, stating that the District may arguably regulate the "conduct" of degree conferral. However, Nova contends that the additional statutory requirement that private schools incorporated elsewhere and which undertake to confer degrees obtain a license as a condition to "operating" in the District, is unconstitutional because it licenses and regulates "pure speech" on the basis of quality. Nova points out that it has the authority to confer degrees from the state of Florida and seeks only to teach its degree program in the District. Because the District has no extrajurisdictional power to regulate Nova's degree conferral, Nova contends that the District is necessarily licensing teaching.

We reject this argument at the outset as well as the artificial conduct/speech distinction Nova draws because it has no practical or First Amendment substance. First, § 29–815 does not regulate or license teaching or "pure speech." The "operating" clause of § 29–815 merely subjects out-of-District schools to the same regulations as schools incorporated in the District, e.g. both have unfettered freedom to teach so long as no degree credits or degrees are promised or given. According to the Senate Report, "institutions which do not undertake to confer degrees do not come within the purview of this bill." S. REP. No. 611, 70th Cong., 1st Sess., at 4 (1928).... In short, Nova would not have needed to apply to the Commission for a license (an application requesting "a License to Offer Doctorate of Public Administration Degree Courses in the District of Columbia") nor would Nova be before this court if it did nothing in the District of Columbia but teach.

. . .

Our holding that D.C. CODE § 29–815 regulates the business conduct of degree conferral and leaves schools free to teach does not end our First Amendment inquiry, for although degree conferral and the operation of degree programs are "privileges" granted by the District, the District can not place conditions on the receipt of these privileges that themselves violate the Constitution or require the [recipient] to forego the exercise of fundamental rights.

Educational institutions, as well as individuals, have a First Amendment right to teach and to academic freedom. . . .

. . .

In determining whether § 29–815 violates the First Amendment, we look first to whether the statute is content-neutral, for however valid the government's interest in regulating, it generally cannot be pursued by discriminating between particular viewpoints and information. The Supreme Court has consistently recognized that if the constitutional guarantee means anything, it means that, ordinarily at least, "government has no power to restrict expression because of its message, its ideas, its subject matter, or its content." *Police Department of Chicago v. Mosley*, 408 U.S. 92, 95 (1972). We think it evident that the general rule that forbids the government to regulate speech on the basis of content has no application to this case, for there is not even a hint of bias or censorship in Congress' enactment or the Commission's enforcement of D.C. CODE § 29–815.... [C]ontrary to Nova's suggestion, we do not believe that Commission inquiry into faculty qualifications, library resources, and curriculum content necessarily makes the statute content-related or amounts to a constraint on academic freedom. This inquiry is limited to neutral, sound, academic criteria, not intended or likely to intrude upon the legitimate intellectual life of a university, but to ensure that when a university confers a degree, it does indeed have an intellectual life and the minimal resources essential to support that life. Nor is there any suggestion that the Commission denied Nova a license because of the particular subjects it teaches, content of books it provides, or views of its teachers. Nova was denied a license because the Commission found that Nova's plans to use Howard University's library facilities rather than providing their own, and Nova's use of field-based teachers with no resident faculty in the District, did not meet the District's requirements for adequate faculty and library resources. Although application of the statute to Nova may be burdensome in a financial and administrative sense, and limits Nova's institutional prerogatives, we do not believe these constraints intrude upon Nova's right to academic freedom or free speech. It cannot be said that requiring a library and teachers is incompatible with the academic endeavor or with intellectual freedom within a university.[10]

When governmental regulation, as in this case, is not aimed at the content of speech but nevertheless has an incidental impact on the exercise of communicative activity, the regulation will not violate the First Amendment so long as it does not unduly restrict the communication of ideas. *Cox v. New Hampshire*, 312 U.S. 569, 574 (1941).

In *United States v. O'Brien*, 391 U.S. 367 (1968), the Supreme Court set forth the framework for reviewing a viewpoint neutral regulation of this kind:

> [A] government regulation is sufficiently justified if it is within the constitutional power of the Government; if it furthers an important or substantial governmental interest; if the governmental interest is unrelated to the suppression of free expression; and if the incidental restriction on alleged First Amendment freedoms is no greater than is essential to the furtherance of that interest.

We have already addressed the power of the District to regulate the business activities of its own educational institutions and we have held that the District's interest in this case is not aimed at suppressing speech, but rather in preventing the harms that arise when educational institutions abuse their degree-conferring authority. Thus, the critical inquiries in this case are whether D.C. CODE § 29–815 furthers a substantial interest and whether the effect of the statute on speech and academic freedom is no greater than necessary to protect the District's interest.

The interest that the District asserts is that of ensuring minimal educational standards among degree-conferring institutions within its borders. The substantial interest and broad discretion that the state has in regulating its schools and the quality of education provided to its citizens is also well established.

The interest the District has in regulating degree conferral was well set out by the New Jersey Supreme Court in *Shelton College v. State Board of Education*, 48 N.J. 501, 226 A.2d 612 (1967) (*Shelton* I), in which the court upheld a licensing scheme similar to our own in the face of a First Amendment freedom of speech challenge. . . .

. . . .

Like the New Jersey Supreme Court, we find that the District's interest in this case is substantial. Indeed, as already discussed, such regulation is essential if the purposes of the statute are to be met.

Nova contends that however substantial the District's interests are, they are not being furthered by the licensing statute. First, Nova points out that education in our society occurs in a national marketplace and that the District cannot prevent persons, including its own citizens, from receiving degrees from other jurisdictions with less stringent incorporation and degree

---

10. *See Kunda v. Muhlenberg College*, 621 F.2d 532 (3d Cir. 1980), a Title VII case in which the court held that a court order reinstating and granting tenure to a professor did not interfere with the academic freedom of a university where the employment decision was not made on academic grounds, noting that "it does not follow that because academic freedom is inextricably related to the educational process it is implicated in every employment decision of an educational institution."

conferral laws, and then returning to the District to use the degree. Second, Nova argues that the licensing criteria are not rationally related to determining whether an educational institution is substandard.

We do not agree that the licensing statute is ineffective in or unrelated to accomplishing the District's purposes. We reject at the outset any suggestion that because the District cannot impose its educational standards nationwide, the statute is ineffective and the District must forego all attempts to ensure that educational standards are met by those schools operating in the District. Moreover, Nova's assertion that the licensing criteria are unrelated to determining whether an educational institution is substandard is not only incorrect but flows from the erroneous premise that nothing less than actual proved fraud or lack of quality would justify denying Nova a license. Section 29–815 is a prophylactic regulation—intended to prevent harm before it occurs. The Commission in denying a license is not deciding that an educational institution is in fact "substandard, transient, unethical, deceptive, or fraudulent," D.C. CODE § 31–1601(1) (1981), but rather that the applicant's failure to meet District criteria creates the probability that the harms with which the District is concerned will occur. We do not believe it can be accurately said that the licensing criteria in general and as specifically applied to Nova are not generally recognized indicia of legitimate and minimally qualified institutions of higher learning. Moreover, the regulations expressly recognize that the criteria will not apply equally in all situations, thereby providing the flexibility essential to ensure quality and legitimacy without discouraging diversity and innovation in higher education or injuring nascent education institutions....

The next question we must ask is whether the effect of § 29–815 on the free speech and academic freedom of educational institutions is no greater than necessary to further the District's interests. Nova contends that the principle that statutes touching First Amendment freedoms must be narrowly drawn dictates that the District must aim specifically at the fraudulent educational institutions and the out-and-out diploma mill and leave "quality" determinations to private accrediting associations and the educational consumer. This argument not only ignores the practical difficulties of detecting illegal activities by educational institutions and successfully prosecuting them under criminal fraud laws but overlooks the fact that the District has a substantial interest in preventing degree conferral by non-fraudulent but nevertheless substandard educational institutions. And although private accrediting institutions serve a valuable role in providing information to the public regarding the academic standards at various schools, these organizations are voluntary and can do nothing to prevent the substandard or fraudulent school from conferring a degree. Requiring full disclosure from schools and letting the educational consumer choose is inadequate. That individuals may choose with full knowledge to spend their money for a degree that has no academic substance does not mean that the District may not act to foreclose that choice where it is inherently harmful to the integrity of legitimate educational institutions, employers, and the public in general.

Finally, Nova asserts that § 29–815 creates such substantial burdens on the exercise of First Amendment freedoms that it cannot be justified despite the District's substantial interest. Specifically, Nova points to the lengthy and expensive administrative process it went through only to be denied a license in the final analysis "merely" because Nova would provide no library of its own and would utilize national faculty rather than placing any faculty in the

District. Although we recognize the burdens this statute places on Nova, we do not believe they amount to a First Amendment violation. There is simply no evidence that the length and complexity of the administrative process in this case arose from a lack of diligence on the Commission's part or of covert hostility toward Nova's educational program, or any particular subject taught or opinion held by Nova's teachers. Nova's application was denied without prejudice and the record reflects that the Commission is prepared to exercise the flexibility provided for in the Regulations to accommodate Nova's external degree program. Requiring Nova to provide some resident faculty and a library for District students does not prevent Nova from implementing its unique field-based program—it merely requires Nova to devote more resources to the program in the District.

[The Court next rejects Nova's claim that the statutory standards for licensure violate the First Amendment because they are impermissibly vague.]

The final question we address is whether the Commission's decision to deny Nova a license was error under D.C. law. . . .

The facts upon which the Commission rested its conclusion that Nova did not meet the District's library and faculty standards are essentially undisputed. As to library facilities, the Commission found that Nova had no library in the District of Columbia and no plans to establish one. Rather, Nova arranged with George Mason and Howard Universities to have their libraries available for Nova's students, and intended to rely on existing public and governmental institutions in the District.

As to faculty resources, the Commission found that Nova's faculty for the DPA program consisted of nine full-time Florida members and 33 part-time national faculty members (preceptors) for a projected 15 clusters, or approximately 380 students. The Florida faculty provides 50% of the DPA instruction as well as teaching in other departments and performing administrative duties. The turnover rate among the Florida faculty was 50% between August 1981 and August 1982. As we have previously stated, the preceptors, who contract with Nova to teach specific courses at the various clusters, are scholars prominent in the public administration field. Each cluster, consisting of 20–25 students, is coordinated by a cluster director, who is a part-time contractor, paid monthly by Nova under a three-year contract, and generally employed in a full-time position elsewhere. Cluster directors administer comprehensive examinations, arrange and assist in cluster sessions, counsel students, and assist the faculty in research and reading of student papers. Other than the contact students have with preceptors and cluster directors during weekend teaching sessions, contact is by special appointment, telephone and written communication.

Based upon these findings, the Commission concluded that Nova did not meet the District's requirements for adequate full-time faculty and library resources . . .

. . . .

. . . The record reflects that the Commission's concern was that none of Nova's faculty, full-time or otherwise, was consistently present in the District of Columbia. Considerable evidence was presented during the hearing regarding the importance in doctoral programs of face-to-face interaction between faculty and students, particularly for supervision and counseling during research projects. Not only was student-faculty interaction significantly reduced by the lack of any Nova faculty in the District, but evidence suggested that Nova's nine DPA faculty members in Florida could not provide adequate supervision and continuity in that they were non-tenured, subject to high turnover rates, and had significant responsibilities outside the DPA program. And despite the recognized excellence of Nova's preceptorial faculty, these teachers had only limited contact with students. Under these circumstances, the Commission's conclusion that Nova must satisfy faculty requirements in the District independently of its faculty in Florida was not unreasonable, and its conclusion that Nova's plans did not provide for sufficient full-time faculty to assure adequate interaction between faculty and student and continuity and stability in the overall program was supported by substantial evidence.

Nor do we believe that the Commission's conclusion that Nova did not meet the District's requirements for adequate library resources was unsupported by substantial evidence or erroneous as a matter of law. D.C. CODE § 29–815(4) requires degree-conferring institutions to be "possessed of suitable ... library equipment." The Regulations require, *inter alia*, an adequate "collection of books" and "continuous acquisition of current library materials." The Commission reasonably interpreted this language as requiring educational institutions to establish their own libraries, rather than rely on the public or private libraries otherwise available in the District or suburbs of the District. This interpretation is consistent not only with the language but with the purpose of the statute in that it ensures that an educational institution has materials appropriate to the degree program as well as library hours that meet student needs and assures some degree of stability and continuity due to the substantial investment it requires from an institution. Of course, the Commission has the discretion to waive this as well as other requirements when it believes the requirement is inapplicable or unnecessary in particular cases. However, we cannot say that the Commission's failure to do so in this case was irrational or not based on substantial evidence. Not only were Nova's arrangements with Howard and George Mason Universities contrary to the express mandate of the statute and regulations, Nova's arrangements did not ensure that the purposes of this requirement would be met. As the Commission points out, George Mason and Howard University do not have doctoral programs in public administration and Nova would have no control over their acquisitions; the arrangements have no guaranty of permanence because any of the schools could revoke the agreements; and Nova is not committed to an investment that would encourage stability and permanence of their program in the District.

Finally, we cannot say that the Commission erred in its conclusion that the library and faculty deficiencies in Nova's program justified denying Nova a license.... Given the complete lack of faculty and library resources in the District, we hold that the Commission's decision was justified by the evidence and in accord with the law.

Marjorie Webster Junior College v. Middle States Association of Colleges and Secondary Schools

United States Court of Appeals, District of Columbia Circuit, 1970.
432 F.2d 650, *cert. denied*, 400 U.S. 965 (1970).

■ BAZELON, CHIEF JUDGE.

Middle States Association of Colleges and Secondary Schools, Inc., is a voluntary nonprofit educational corporation, the successor to an unincorporated association of the same name established in 1887. Its general purposes are to aid and encourage the development of quality in secondary schools and institutions of higher education located within its geographical domain (New York, New Jersey, Pennsylvania, Delaware, Maryland, and the District of Columbia) or outside of the continental United States. Chief among its activities is that of accrediting member institutions and applicants for membership. Marjorie Webster Junior College, Inc., is a proprietary junior college for women located in the District of Columbia. In 1966, it applied to Middle States for accreditation. Relying upon a policy statement of the Federation of Regional Accrediting Commissions of Higher Education,[2] and upon its own past practice,[3] Middle States refused to consider Marjorie Webster for accreditation because the latter was not "a nonprofit organization with a governing board representing the public interest." Following this refusal, Marjorie Webster brought suit to compel its consideration for accreditation without regard to its proprietary character. The District Court found Middle States' refusal to consider proprietary institutions of higher education for accreditation a violation of § 3 of the Sherman Act and of the developing common law regarding exclusion from membership in private associations.

Appellee strongly urges, and the court below concluded, that once it be determined that appellee is engaging in "trade," restraint of that "trade" by appellant's conduct is subject to the limitations of the Sherman Act. If this were the ordinary case of a trade association alleged to have transgressed the bounds of reasonable regulation designed to mitigate the evils afflicting a particular industry, this reasoning might be conclusive. But in our view, the character of the defendant association, and the nature of the activities that it regulates, require a finer analysis.

Despite the broad wording of the Sherman Act, it has long been settled that not every form of combination or conspiracy that restrains trade falls within its ambit. For the language of the Act, although broad, is also vague; and in consequence of that vagueness, "perhaps not uncalculated, the courts have been left to give content to the statute, and in the performance of that function it is appropriate that courts should interpret its word in light of its legislative history and of the particular evils at which the legislation was aimed." The Act was a product of

> the era of "trusts" and of "combinations" of businesses and of capital organized and directed to control of the market by suppression of competition in the marketing of goods and services, the monopolistic tendency of which had become a matter of public concern.

Apex Hosiery Co. v. Leader, 310 U.S. 469, 492–93 (1940).

---

2. The Federation, which is made up of Middle States and the five other regional liberal arts accrediting associations, was established in 1964 to coordinate the policies of the six associations, to speak for them in matters of common interest, and to exchange information, experience, and personnel.

3. Middle States has never accredited or evaluated a proprietary institution of higher education. This restriction has been explicit since at least 1928. Middle States has, however, accredited three proprietary secondary schools and continues to do so.

The Court in *Apex* recognized that the Act is aimed primarily at combinations having commercial objectives and is applied only to a very limited extent to organizations, like labor unions, which normally have other objectives.

That appellant's objectives, both in its formation and in the development and application of the restriction here at issue, are not commercial is not in dispute. Of course, when a given activity falls within the scope of the Sherman Act, a lack of predatory intent is not conclusive on the question of its legality. But the proscriptions of the Sherman Act were "tailored . . . for the business world," not for the noncommercial aspects of the liberal arts and the learned professions. In these contexts, an incidental restraint of trade, absent an intent or purpose to affect the commercial aspects of the profession, is not sufficient to warrant application of the antitrust laws.

We are fortified in this conclusion by the historic reluctance of Congress to exercise control in educational matters.[19] We need not suggest that this reluctance is of such depth as to immunize any conceivable activity of appellant from regulation under the antitrust laws. It is possible to conceive of restrictions on eligibility for accreditation that could have little other than a commercial motive; and as such, antitrust policy would presumably be applicable.[21] Absent such motives, however, the process of accreditation is an activity distinct from the sphere of commerce; it goes rather to the heart of the concept of education itself. We do not believe that Congress intended this concept to be molded by the policies underlying the Sherman Act.

The increasing importance of private associations in the affairs of individuals and organizations has led to substantial expansion of judicial control over "The Internal Affairs of Associations not for Profit." [Chafee, *The Internal Affairs of Associations not for Profit*, 43 HARV. L. REV. 992, 1023 (1930).] Where membership in, or certification by, such an association is a virtual prerequisite to the practice of a given profession, courts have scrutinized the standards and procedures employed by the association notwithstanding their recognition of the fact that professional societies possess a specialized competence in evaluating the qualifications of an individual to engage in professional activities. The standards set must be reasonable, applied with an even hand, and not in conflict with the public policy of the jurisdiction.[25] Even where less than complete exclusion from practice is

---

19. *E.g.*, 20 U.S.C. § 401 (1964): "The Congress reaffirms the principle and declares that the States and local communities have and must retain control over and primary responsibility for public education." *Id.* § 402: "Nothing contained in this Act shall be construed to authorize any department, agency, officer, or employee of the United States to exercise any direction, supervision, or control over the curriculum, program of instruction, administration, or personnel of any educational institution or school system."

21. For example, if accreditation were denied any institution purchasing textbooks from a supplier who did not provide special discounts for association members, it would be hard to imagine other than a commercial motive for the action.

25. Higgins v. American Soc'y of Clinical Pathologists, 51 N. J. 191, 238 A.2d 665 (1968). The classic statement of the rationale for judicial intervention is that of the New Jersey Supreme Court in *Falcone* [*v. Middlesex County Medical Soc'y*], 170 A.2d [791], 799 [(1961)]: When courts originally declined to scrutinize admission practices of membership associations they were dealing with social clubs, religious organizations, and fraternal associations. Here the policies against judicial intervention were strong and there were no significant countervailing policies. When the courts were later called upon to deal with trade and professional associations exercising virtually monopolistic control, different factors were involved. The intimate personal relationships which pervaded the social, religious and fraternal organizations were hardly in evi-

involved, deprivation of substantial economic or professional advantages will often be sufficient to warrant judicial action.

The extent of judicial power to regulate the standards set by private professional associations, however, must be related to the necessity for intervention. Particularly when, as here, judicial action is predicated not upon a legislative text but upon the developing doctrines of the common law, general propositions must not be allowed to obscure the specific relevant facts of each individual case. In particular, the extent to which deference is due to the professional judgment of the association will vary both with the subject matter at issue and with the degree of harm resulting from the association's action.

With these factors in mind, we turn to consider the harm appellee will suffer by virtue of the challenged exclusion. We note in this regard that denial of accreditation by Middle States is not tantamount to exclusion of appellee from operating successfully as a junior college. t has been, and without regard to accreditation by appellant will remain, accredited by the District of Columbia Board of Education, and licensed to award the Associate in Arts degree. The record indicates that appellee's listing in the major publications available for use by high school guidance counselors (and often, by students and their families) does not depend upon its accreditation by appellant.[31] Appellee's lack of accreditation does not appear to render it, or its students, ineligible to receive federal aid.[32] Appellee's students seeking to transfer to four-year colleges at the completion of their programs are not necessarily barred from obtaining credit for their studies because of the unaccredited status of the institution. We recognize, as the trial court found, that lack of accreditation may be a not insignificant handicap to appellee both in the effect that such lack may have on students considering application for admission, and in the loss of the substantial benefits that the accreditation process itself has upon the institution under study. But appellee has operated successfully as a junior college since 1947. Although it suffered a decline in applications for admission in the years immediately preceding the instant suit, this decline was shared by the other women's institutions in the District of Columbia. In the last year for which figures were introduced, it received over 100 more applications than Mount Vernon Junior College, the institution receiving the second highest number. We do

dence and the individual's opportunity of earning a livelihood and serving society in his chosen trade or profession appeared as the controlling policy consideration.

31. Appellee is not listed in either the Junior College Directory, which lists both accredited and unaccredited institutions but not proprietary ones; or in Cass & Birnbaum's Guide to American Colleges, which lists only four-year colleges. It is fully listed in Lovejoy's College Guide; Barron's Guide to the Two–Year Institution; Chronicle Guidance Publications and View Deck; and the Association of College Admissions Officers' Admissions Search Kit. 302 F. Supp. at 475–76.

32. Eligibility for a number of federal funding programs that provide grants to institutions or their students does turn upon the institution's being accredited by a "nationally recognized accrediting agency" listed by the Commissioner of Education. *See, e.g.,* 20 U.S.C. § 403(b) (5) (National Defense Education Act of 1958), 751(f)(5) (grants and loans for construction of academic facilities) (1964 & Supp. IV, 1969). However, as an alternative to such accreditation, an institution or its students will become eligible upon showing that its credits "are accepted on transfer by not less than three institutions which are so accredited, for credit on the same basis as if transferred from an institution so accredited." This is known as "three-letter certification," and appellee has such certification at the Office of Education. It appears that appellee is ineligible for federal funds, if at all, because the applicable statutes preclude grants and loans to proprietary liberal arts institutions or their students.

not believe, therefore, that the record supports the conclusion that appellee will be unable to operate successfully as a junior college unless it is considered for accreditation by appellant.

Accordingly, we believe that judicial review of appellant's standards should accord substantial deference to appellant's judgment regarding the ends that it serves and the means most appropriate to those ends. Accreditation, as carried out by appellant, is as involved with educational philosophy as with yardsticks to measure the "quality" of education provided. As found by the trial court,

> [Appellant] seeks to determine in broad qualitative terms whether an institution has clearly defined appropriate objectives, whether it has established conditions under which it can reasonably be expected to obtain them, and whether it appears to be obtaining them. Under this criteria [sic], Middle States, in its publication, THE NATURE OF A MIDDLE STATES EVALUATION, notes that "Organization, administration, facilities, and resources are not important in themselves." Accreditation means that the institution has achieved quality within the context of its own aims and program—not that such institution is more qualified than any other accredited or unaccredited institution.

Appellee does not challenge this view of the accreditation process as improper. And given this view, we cannot say that appellant's refusal to consider proprietary institutions is an unreasonable means of seeking to reach the ends sought. Of course no institution, no matter how well endowed, can afford to entirely ignore the balance sheet. But when the institution itself is responsible in large part for setting the measure by which it is to be judged, we do not think it has been shown to be unreasonable for appellant to conclude that the desire for personal profit might influence educational goals in subtle ways difficult to detect but destructive, in the long run, of that atmosphere of academic inquiry which, perhaps even more than any quantitative measure of educational quality, appellant's standards for accreditation seek to foster.[37] Likewise, we may recognize that, even in nonprofit institutions, the battle for academic freedom and control of educational policy is still sporadically waged; but this factor would seem to strengthen, rather than weaken, the reasonableness of appellant's judgment that motives of personal profit should not be allowed to influence the outcome. Finally, we need not say that appellant's views of the proper measure for accreditation of an educational institution are the only, the best, or even particularly well chosen ones. The core of appellant's argument is not that proprietary institutions are unworthy of accreditation, but rather that they, like many trade and professional schools, should properly be measured by standards different from those used by appellant, and which appellant is possessed of no special competence or experience in using. In this regard appellee is unlike the individual denied membership in or

---

37. Needless to say, a failing institution may be forced to sacrifice its own view of educational quality for economic reasons, and doubtless even the best-endowed university would be grateful for additional funds to spend on education. But where funds may not be siphoned off from educational purposes, even the most stringent budget-cutting must find its limit. We need not here decide how or whether our conclusion would differ if appellee could show that its profits could never exceed a certain amount or percentage of income, in which case the profit-taking aspect of its operations would, as in the case of nonprofit institutions, have a definite limit.

certification by a professional society. Rarely, if ever, could it be said that such an individual could realistically be expected to combine with others excluded on the same grounds to form his own association. Appellee, however, is free to join with other proprietary institutions in setting up an association for the accreditation of institutions of such character; and such an association, if recognized, could obtain for its members all the benefits of accreditation by appellant save, perhaps, prestige. Appellee has made no attempt to show that any such course has ever been attempted. In these circumstances, we do not think that appellant's refusal to consider appellee for accreditation as a proprietary institution lacks sufficient basis in reason to warrant judicial intervention.

. . .

What has been said above should also dispose of so much of appellee's argument as is based upon the Due Process Clause. We may assume, without deciding, that either the nature of appellant's activities or the federal recognition which they are awarded renders them state action subject to the limitations of the Fifth Amendment. If so, however, the burden remains with appellee to show the unreasonableness of the restriction, not simply in the abstract but as applied specifically to it. We need not decide here the precise limits of those circumstances under which governmental action may restrict or injure the activities of proprietary educational institutions. For the reasons already discussed, we conclude that appellee has failed to show that the present restriction was without reasonable basis. Accordingly, it must be upheld.

Note on Federal Control of Accreditation

A 1992 amendment to the Higher Education Act gave the federal government a larger role in accreditation. For a university or college to receive funds from federal financial aid to students, the school must be accredited by a nationally recognized accreditation organization. 20 U.S.C.S § 100 (2007). The Act grants the Secretary of Education broad powers to recognize accreditation organizations, including the power to suspend or terminate recognition. 20 U.S.C.S. § 1099b (2007).

The American Bar Association (ABA) has long been recognized as the accreditor of law schools. That recognition was called into question, however, by the Department of Education which challenged the ABA's diversity standard, a standard that requires law schools to take concrete steps towards increasing minority enrollment. The Secretary of Education in the end granted recognition of the ABA for only eighteen months as opposed to the customary five years. Molly McDonough, *See You in 18 Months: Education Department Puts ABA Accreditation Role on a Short Leash*, ABA J., Feb. 2007, *available at* http://www.abajournal.com/magazine/see_you_in_18_months.

When Massachusetts School of Law (MSL) was denied accreditation by the ABA, the school sued the ABA, the Association of American Law Schools, and the Law School Admissions Council, Inc. *Massachusetts School of Law at Andover, Inc. v. American Bar Association*, 107 F.3d 1026 (3d Cir. 1997). The Massachusetts Board of Regents authorized MSL to grant J.D. degrees, but the ABA denied accreditation for the following reasons: the high student/faculty ratio, over reliance on part-time faculty, the heavy teaching load of full-time faculty, the lack of adequate sabbaticals for faculty, the use of a for-credit bar review class, the failure to limit the hours students may be employed, and the failure to use the LSAT or give evidence validating its own admission test. *Id.* at 1029–31. MSL alleged that "the ABA, AALS, [and] the LSAC . . . combined and conspired to organize and enforce a group boycott in violation of section 1 of the Sherman Act and conspired to monopolize legal education, law school accreditation, and the licensing of lawyers, in violation of section 2 of the Sherman

Act. 15 U.S.C. §§ 1–2." *Id.* at 1031. MSL claimed that the ABA's allegedly anti-competitive accreditation standards: (1) placed MSL at a competitive disadvantage because students from unaccredited schools cannot take the bar in most states; (2) stigmatized MSL; (3) forced MSL to raise faculty salaries; (4) created a boycott of unaccredited schools.

The Third Circuit upheld a motion for summary judgment against MSL. The court noted that individual states have final responsibility for determining who may take the bar examination, though states often take into account accreditation decisions made by the ABA. Consequently, the first injury alleged by MLS, namely the inability of its students to take the bar, was a result of government action, not the accreditation determination made by the ABA. Citing *Eastern R.R. Presidents Conference v. Noerr Motor Freight, Inc.,* 365 U.S. 127, 136 (1961), the court held that the ABA did not violate the Sherman Act because "where a restraint upon trade or monopolization is the result of valid governmental action, no violation of the Act can be made out." *Id.* at 1035. The Third Circuit held the stigma injury was incidental to the ABA's petitioning activity, that is, the ABA's justification of its accreditation decisions to state government officials, and that such non-commercial petitioning activity is immune from the Sherman Act. *Id.* at 1037–38. The court also found that MSL raised its faculty salaries for reasons independent of the ABA accreditation process. *Id.* at 1039. Finally, the court held that, though the ABA does prohibit accredited schools from accepting transfers from non-accredited schools, MSL failed to produce any evidence that it was harmed by a boycott of unaccredited schools. In fact, it was the policy of MSL to convince students not to transfer out of the school. *Id.* at 1040.

A. Lee Fritschler, *Government Should Stay Out of Accreditation*

CHRON. HIGHER EDUC., May 18, 2007, at B20.

. . . Last September a report by the Spellings Commission on the Future of Higher Education expressed grave concern about the quality and purpose of colleges and universities. The report cited statistics that implied that higher-education institutions are slipping behind their counterparts in many other industrialized nations, particularly in the rate at which students complete their degrees. It also noted that the cost of educating students in the United States exceeds, by a substantial amount, that in almost every other country. Although some of the data were used in questionable ways—the United States, for example, continues to have among the highest rates of bachelor's-degree attainment—those are nonetheless serious concerns that should not go unanswered.

One remedy that the Education Department has proposed would give accrediting agencies responsibility not only to evaluate institutions for access to federal student-aid money but also to set and enforce minimum standards for "student achievement." Under draft rules, if the department decides that the learning standards that an accreditor applies to institutions are not sufficiently high, it can withdraw the accrediting agency's power to accredit. What seems to be arising out of the mists are various proposals for a higher-education version of No Child Left Behind, with the federal government taking a more active role in reviewing what institutions teach and what students learn.

Those fixes won't work. While on their face they might seem reasonable, in reality they represent a misdirected effort that will move us further away from improving the quality and containing the cost of a college education.

Accrediting agencies, many of which predate federal student-aid programs by many years, have been the primary gateway between colleges and the federal government and, of course, federal funds. An institution that lost its accreditation could be out of business; it might not survive if its students were deemed ineligible for federal grants and loans. Becoming, and remaining, accredited is a high-stakes business. One problem with accrediting agencies, however, is that their decisions are so starkly up or down that, as a consequence, they hardly ever deny accreditation. As a regulatory tool, they are about as effective as a sledgehammer.

The traditional role of accreditors has been to work with institutions to help them correct deficiencies uncovered in the review process. Accreditation in America is based on principles of peer review and self-regulation that have their roots in the distant past, and have served us well in many respects. They have contributed to the development of a strong system of higher education largely free from government intrusion in curriculum, teaching, evaluation, and research. In fact, they provide a much-needed buffer between the political process and the core business of higher education.

Another important role of accreditation, at least in theory, is to persuade institutions to improve their performance. But accreditors cannot be expected to carry the quality-improvement agenda on their own. They do contribute to quality improvement, but by slow, rather indirect routes—most accrediting agencies visit campuses only once in 10 years. And accreditors cannot fill that role as forcefully as they might, in part because so much weight is placed on their gatekeeping function for student-aid eligibility.

Proposals to evaluate the performance and progress of higher education through the glasses of elementary and secondary education, with some version of a No Child Left Behind policy, are also inappropriate. Higher education touches students at a different stage in their development. Its mission is to motivate students to work on their own and develop mature habits of mind. It offers a wide variety of courses of study, for which there are no common norms or sets of learning skills. It would be impossible and counterproductive to organize skills testing on a national or statewide basis.

... [T]hroughout history political involvement in the classroom has yielded negative consequences, including, most visibly, outright purges of faculty members and courses in Eastern Europe and prohibitions on teaching evolution in the United States. Less extreme but more prevalent are the bureaucratic excesses that result from political intrusion in the classroom; they are one of the things that account for the static higher-education systems.

Involving accrediting agencies or the federal government in evaluating and regulating teaching and learning is an unhealthy departure from traditional arrangements. Outside involvement in those activities runs the risk of curbing the innovation and high levels of creativity that have been the hallmarks of American higher education for decades.

. . .

If we are serious about improving the quality of teaching and learning, we should support research to determine what works best in the classroom, and create incentives for institutions to reward good teaching rather than just good research. Maybe we need a new nongovernmental organization charged with improving college teaching and learning, with adequate resources to do the job. That approach could be more effective and less costly than the enforcement of the intrusive and bureaucratic national standards being proposed by the Department of Education. In exchange, we should hold institutional officials accountable for explaining what they are doing to improve the quality of their enterprise.

CHAPTER 18

FEDERAL REGULATION

There has been a dramatic increase in the amount of federal regulation of colleges and universities since World War II, prompted in part, no doubt, by the significant increase in federal funding during the same period. This chapter examines federal statutes and court decisions that are directed primarily at higher education or that raise problems of applicability because of the distinctive mission and structure of institutions of higher education.

Federal restrictions on discrimination in faculty hiring and admission of students are covered in Chapters 9 and 10 respectively.

A. TITLE IX (1972)

Cohen v. Brown University

United States Court of Appeals, First Circuit, 1996.
101 F.3d 155, *cert. denied*, 520 U.S. 1186 (1997).

■ BOWNES, SENIOR CIRCUIT JUDGE.

This is a class action lawsuit charging Brown University, its president, and its athletics director (collectively "Brown") with discrimination against women in the operation of its intercollegiate athletics program, in violation of Title IX of the Education Amendments of 1972, 20 U.S.C. §§ 1681–1688 ("Title IX"), and its implementing regulations, 34 C.F.R. §§ 106.1–106.71. The plaintiff class comprises all present, future, and potential Brown University women students who participate, seek to participate, and/or are deterred from participating in intercollegiate athletics funded by Brown.

This suit was initiated in response to the demotion in May 1991 of Brown's women's gymnastics and volleyball teams from university-funded varsity status to donor-funded varsity status. Contemporaneously, Brown demoted two men's teams, water polo and golf, from university-funded to donor-funded varsity status. As a consequence of these demotions, all four teams lost not only their university funding, but most of the support and privileges that accompany university-funded varsity status at Brown.

Prior to the trial on the merits that gave rise to this appeal, the district court granted plaintiffs' motion for class certification.... [A]fter hearing fourteen days of testimony, the district court granted plaintiffs' motion for a preliminary injunction, ordering, *inter alia*, that the women's gymnastics and volleyball teams be reinstated to university-funded varsity status, and prohibiting Brown from eliminating or reducing the status or funding of any existing women's intercollegiate varsity team until the case was resolved on the merits. *Cohen v. Brown Univ.*, 809 F. Supp. 978, 1001 (D.R.I. 1992) ("*Cohen I*"). A panel of this court affirmed the district court's decision granting a preliminary injunction to the plaintiffs. *Cohen v. Brown Univ.*, 991 F.2d 888, 907 (1st Cir. 1993) ("*Cohen II*"). In so doing, we upheld the district court's analysis and ruled that an institution violates Title IX if it ineffectively accommodates its students' interests and abilities in athletics under 34 C.F.R. § 106.41(c)(1) (1995), regardless of its performance with respect to other Title IX areas.

On remand, the district court determined after a lengthy bench trial that Brown's intercollegiate athletics program violates Title IX and its supporting regulations. *Cohen v. Brown Univ.*, 879 F. Supp. 185, 214 (D.R.I. 1995) ("*Cohen III*")....This appeal followed.

. . .

As a Division I institution within the National Collegiate Athletic Association ("NCAA") with respect to all sports but football, Brown participates at the highest level of NCAA competition. Brown operates a two-tiered intercollegiate athletics program with respect to funding: although Brown provides the financial resources required to maintain its university-funded varsity teams, donor-funded varsity athletes must themselves raise the funds necessary to support their teams through private donations. The district court noted that the four demoted teams were eligible for NCAA competition, provided that they were able to raise the funds necessary to maintain a sufficient level of competitiveness, and provided that they continued to comply with NCAA requirements. The court found, however, that it is difficult for donor-funded varsity athletes to maintain a level of competitiveness commensurate with their abilities and that these athletes operate at a competitive disadvantage in comparison to university-funded varsity athletes. For example, the district court found that some schools are reluctant to include donor-funded teams in their varsity schedules and that donor-funded teams are unable to obtain varsity-level coaching, recruits, and funds for travel, equipment, and post-season competition.

Brown's decision to demote the women's volleyball and gymnastics teams and the men's water polo and golf teams from university-funded varsity status was apparently made in response to a university-wide cost-cutting directive. The district court found that Brown saved $62,028 by demoting the women's teams and $15,795 by demoting the men's teams, but that the demotions "did not appreciably affect the athletic participation gender ratio."

Plaintiffs alleged that, at the time of the demotions, the men students at Brown already enjoyed the benefits of a disproportionately large share of both the university resources allocated to athletics and the intercollegiate participation opportunities afforded to student athletes. Thus, plaintiffs contended, what appeared to be the even-handed demotions of two men's and two women's teams, in fact, perpetuated Brown's discriminatory treatment of women in the administration of its intercollegiate athletics program....

In the course of the trial on the merits, the district court found that, in 1993–94, there were 897 students participating in intercollegiate varsity athletics, of which 61.87% (555) were men and 38.13% (342) were women. During the same period, Brown's undergraduate enrollment comprised 5,722 students, of which 48.86% (2,796) were men and 51.14% (2,926) were women. The district court found that, in 1993–94, Brown's intercollegiate athletics program consisted of 32 teams, 16 men's teams and 16 women's teams. Of the university-funded teams, 12 were men's teams and 13 were women's teams; of the donor-funded teams, three were women's teams and four were men's teams. At the time of trial, Brown offered 479 university-funded varsity positions for men, as compared to 312 for women; and 76 donor-funded varsity positions for men, as compared to 30 for women. In 1993–94, then, Brown's varsity program—including both university-and donor-funded sports—afforded over 200 more positions for men than for women. Accordingly, the district court found that Brown maintained a 13.01% disparity between female participation in intercollegiate athletics and female student enrollment, and that "although the number of varsity sports offered to men and women are equal, the selection of sports offered to each gender generates far more individual positions for male athletes than for female athletes."

. . .

Title IX provides that "no person in the United States shall, on the basis of sex, be excluded from participation in, be denied the benefits of, or be subjected to discrimination under any education program or activity receiving Federal financial assistance." 20 U.S.C.A. § 1681(a) (West 1990). As a private institution that receives federal financial assistance, Brown is required to comply with Title IX.

Title IX also specifies that its prohibition against gender discrimination shall not "be interpreted to require any educational institution to grant preferential or disparate treatment to the members of one sex on account of an imbalance which may exist" between the total number or percentage of persons of that sex participating in any federally supported program or activity, and "the total number or percentage of persons of that sex in any community, State, section, or other area." Subsection (b) also provides, however, that it "shall not be construed to prevent the consideration in any . . . proceeding under this chapter of statistical evidence tending to show that such an imbalance exists with respect to the participation in, or receipt of the benefits of, any such program or activity by the members of one sex."

Applying § 1681(b), the prior panel held that Title IX "does not mandate strict numerical equality between the gender balance of a college's athletic program and the gender balance of its student body." *Cohen II*, 991 F.2d at 894. The panel explained that, while evidence of a gender-based disparity in an institution's athletics program is relevant to a determination of noncompliance, "a court assessing Title IX compliance may not find a violation solely because there is a disparity between the gender composition of an educational institution's student constituency, on the one hand, and its athletic programs, on the other hand."

Congress enacted Title IX in response to its finding—after extensive hearings held in 1970 by the House Special Subcommittee on Education—of pervasive discrimination against women with respect to educational opportunities.

Title IX was passed with two objectives in mind: "to avoid the use of federal resources to support discriminatory practices," and "to provide individual citizens effective protection against those practices." *Cannon v. University of Chicago*, 441 U.S. 677, 704 (1979). To accomplish these objectives, Congress directed all agencies extending financial assistance to educational institutions to develop procedures for terminating financial assistance to institutions that violate Title IX.

The agency responsible for administering Title IX is the United States Department of Education ("DED"), through its Office for Civil Rights ("OCR"). Congress expressly delegated to DED the authority to promulgate regulations for determining whether an athletics program complies with Title IX. Pub. L. No. 93–380, 88 Stat. 612 (1974)....

. . .

In 1978, several years after the promulgation of the regulations, OCR published a proposed "Policy Interpretation," the purpose of which was to clarify the obligations of federal aid recipients under Title IX to provide equal opportunities in athletics programs. "In particular, this Policy Interpretation provides a means to assess an institution's compliance with the equal opportunity requirements of the regulation which are set forth at [34 C.F.R. §§ 106.37(c) and 106.41(c)]." 44 Fed. Reg. at 71,415. After considering a large number of public comments, OCR published the final Policy Interpretation. While the Policy Interpretation covers other areas, this litigation focuses on the "Effective Accommodation" section, which interprets 34 C.F.R. § 106.41(c)(1), the first of the non-exhaustive list of ten factors to be considered in determining whether equal athletics opportunities are available to both genders. The Policy Interpretation establishes a three-part test, a two-part test, and factors to be considered in determining compliance under 34 C.F.R. § 106.41(c)(1). At issue in this appeal is the proper interpretation of the first of these, the so-called three-part test, which inquires as follows:

> (1) Whether intercollegiate level participation opportunities for male and female students are provided in numbers substantially proportionate to their respective enrollments; or

> (2) Where the members of one sex have been and are underrepresented among intercollegiate athletes, whether the institution can show a history and continuing practice of program expansion which is demonstrably responsive to the developing interest and abilities of the members of that sex; or

> (3) Where the members of one sex are underrepresented among intercollegiate athletes, and the institution cannot show a continuing practice of program expansion such as that cited above, whether it can be demonstrated that the interests and abilities of the members of that sex have been fully and effectively accommodated by the present program.

The district court held that, "because Brown maintains a 13.01% disparity between female participation in intercollegiate athletics and female student enrollment, it cannot gain the protection of prong one." Nor did Brown satisfy prong two. While acknowledging that Brown "has an impressive history of program expansion," the district court found that Brown failed to demonstrate that it has "maintained a continuing practice of intercollegiate program expansion for women, the underrepresented sex." The court noted further that, because merely reducing program offerings to the overrepresented gender does not constitute program expansion for the underrepresented gender, the fact that Brown has eliminated or demoted several men's teams does not amount to a continuing practice of program expansion for women. As to prong three, the district court found that Brown had not "fully and effectively accommodated the interest and ability of the underrepresented sex 'to the extent necessary to provide equal opportunity in the selection of sports and levels of competition available to members of both sexes.'"

. . .

Title IX is an anti-discrimination statute, modeled after Title VI of the Civil Rights Act of 1964, 42 U.S.C. § 2000d ("Title VI"). *See Cannon*, 441 U.S. at 696 ("The drafters of Title IX explicitly assumed that it would be interpreted and applied as Title VI had been during the preceding eight years."). Thus, Title IX and Title VI share the same constitutional underpinnings. . . .

Although the statute itself provides for no remedies beyond the termination of federal funding, the Supreme Court has determined that Title IX is enforceable through an implied private right of action, *Cannon*, 441 U.S. at 703, and that damages are available for an action brought under Title IX, *Franklin v. Gwinnett County Pub. Sch.*, 503 U.S. 60, 76 (1992). The right to injunctive relief under Title IX appears to have been impliedly accepted by the Supreme Court in *Franklin*. In addition, a majority of the Court in *Guardians Ass'n v. Civil Serv. Comm'n*, 463 U.S. 582 (1983), agreed that injunctive relief and other equitable remedies are appropriate for violations of Title VI.

. . .

In *Cohen II*, a panel of this court squarely rejected Brown's constitutional and statutory challenges to the Policy Interpretation's three-part test, upholding the district court's interpretation of the Title IX framework applicable to intercollegiate athletics, as well as its grant of a preliminary injunction in favor of the plaintiffs. . . .

. . .

Brown contends that the district court misconstrued and misapplied the three-part test. Specifically, Brown argues that the district court's interpretation and application of the test is irreconcilable with the statute, the regulation, and the agency's interpretation of the law, and effectively renders Title IX an "affirmative action statute" that mandates preferential treatment for women by imposing quotas in excess of women's relative interests and abilities in athletics. Brown asserts, in the alternative, that if the district court properly construed the test, then the test itself violates Title IX and the United States Constitution.

We emphasize two points at the outset. First, notwithstanding Brown's persistent invocation of the inflammatory terms "affirmative action," "preference," and "quota," this is not an affirmative action case. Second, Brown's efforts to evade the controlling authority of *Cohen II* by recasting its core legal arguments as challenges to the "district court's interpretation" of the law are unavailing; the primary arguments raised here have already been litigated and decided adversely to Brown in the prior appeal.

. . .

Like other anti-discrimination statutory schemes, the Title IX regime permits affirmative action.[11] In addition, Title IX, like other anti-discrimina-

---

11. As previously noted, Title IX itself specifies only that the statute shall not be interpreted to require gender-based preferential or disparate treatment. 20 U.S.C.

tion schemes, permits an inference that a significant gender-based statistical disparity may indicate the existence of discrimination. Consistent with the school desegregation cases, the question of substantial proportionality under the Policy Interpretation's three-part test is merely the starting point for analysis, rather than the conclusion; a rebuttable presumption, rather than an inflexible requirement. In short, the substantial proportionality test is but one aspect of the inquiry into whether an institution's athletics program complies with Title IX.

Also consistent with the school desegregation cases, the substantial proportionality test of prong one is applied under the Title IX framework, not mechanically, but case-by-case, in a fact-specific manner. As with other anti-discrimination regimes, Title IX neither mandates a finding of discrimination based solely upon a gender-based statistical disparity, nor prohibits gender-conscious remedial measures.

Another important distinction between this case and affirmative action cases is that the district court's remedy requiring Brown to accommodate fully and effectively the athletics interests and abilities of its women students does not raise the concerns underlying the Supreme Court's requirement of a particularized factual predicate to justify voluntary affirmative action plans. In reviewing equal protection challenges to such plans, the Court is concerned that government bodies are reaching out to implement race-or gender-conscious remedial measures that are "ageless in their reach into the past, and timeless in their ability to affect the future," [*Wyant v. Jackson Bd. of Educ.*, 476 U.S. 267 (1986)] on the basis of facts insufficient to support a prima facie case of a constitutional or statutory violation, [*City of Richmond v. J.A. Croson Co.*, 488 U.S. 469, 500 (1989)], to the benefit of unidentified victims of past discrimination.... Accordingly, the Court has taken the position that voluntary affirmative action plans cannot be constitutionally justified absent a particularized factual predicate demonstrating the existence of "identified discrimination," because "societal discrimination, without more, is too amorphous a basis for imposing a racially classified remedy."

From a constitutional standpoint, the case before us is altogether different. Here, gender-conscious relief was ordered by an Article III court, constitutionally compelled to have before it litigants with standing to raise the cause of action alleged; for the purpose of providing relief upon a duly adjudicated determination that specific defendants had discriminated against a certified class of women in violation of a federal anti-discrimination statute; based upon findings of fact that were subject to the Federal Rules of Evidence. The factual problem presented in affirmative action cases is, "Does the evidence support a finding of discrimination such that race-or gender-conscious remedial measures are appropriate?" We find these multiple indicia of reliability and specificity to be sufficient to answer that question in the affirmative.

. . .

Brown has contended throughout this litigation that the significant disparity in athletics opportunities for men and women at Brown is the result of a gender-based differential in the level of interest in sports and that the

---

§ 1681(b). However, although Congress could easily have done so, it did not ban affirmative action or gender-conscious remedies under Title IX....

district court's application of the three-part test requires universities to provide athletics opportunities for women to an extent that exceeds their relative interests and abilities in sports. Thus, at the heart of this litigation is the question whether Title IX permits Brown to deny its female students equal opportunity to participate in sports, based upon its unproven assertion that the district court's finding of a significant disparity in athletics opportunities for male and female students reflects, not discrimination in Brown's intercollegiate athletics program, but a lack of interest on the part of its female students that is unrelated to a lack of opportunities.

We view Brown's argument that women are less interested than men in participating in intercollegiate athletics, as well as its conclusion that institutions should be required to accommodate the interests and abilities of its female students only to the extent that it accommodates the interests and abilities of its male students, with great suspicion. To assert that Title IX permits institutions to provide fewer athletics participation opportunities for women than for men, based upon the premise that women are less interested in sports than are men, is (among other things) to ignore the fact that Title IX was enacted in order to remedy discrimination that results from stereotyped notions of women's interests and abilities.

Interest and ability rarely develop in a vacuum; they evolve as a function of opportunity and experience. The Policy Interpretation recognizes that women's lower rate of participation in athletics reflects women's historical lack of opportunities to participate in sports. *See* 44 Fed. Reg. at 71,419 ("Participation in intercollegiate sports has historically been emphasized for men but not women. Partially as a consequence of this, participation rates of women are far below those of men.").

Moreover, the Supreme Court has repeatedly condemned gender-based discrimination based upon "archaic and overbroad generalizations" about women. The Court has been especially critical of the use of statistical evidence offered to prove generalized, stereotypical notions about men and women.

Thus, there exists the danger that, rather than providing a true measure of women's interest in sports, statistical evidence purporting to reflect women's interest instead provides only a measure of the very discrimination that is and has been the basis for women's lack of opportunity to participate in sports. Prong three requires some kind of evidence of interest in athletics, and the Title IX framework permits the use of statistical evidence in assessing the level of interest in sports. Nevertheless, to allow a numbers-based lack-of-interest defense to become the instrument of further discrimination against the underrepresented gender would pervert the remedial purpose of Title IX. We conclude that, even if it can be empirically demonstrated that, at a particular time, women have less interest in sports than do men, such evidence, standing alone, cannot justify providing fewer athletics opportunities for women than for men. Furthermore, such evidence is completely irrelevant where, as here, viable and successful women's varsity teams have been demoted or eliminated. We emphasize that, on the facts of this case, Brown's lack-of-interest arguments are of no consequence. As the prior panel recognized, while the question of full and effective accommodation of athletics interests and abilities is potentially a complicated issue where plaintiffs seek to create a new team or to elevate to varsity status a team that has never competed in varsity competition, no such difficulty is presented here, where plaintiffs seek to reinstate what were successful university-funded teams right up until the moment the teams were demoted.[16]

On these facts, Brown's failure to accommodate fully and effectively the interests and abilities of the underrepresented gender is clearly established. Under these circumstances, the district court's finding that there are interested women able to compete at the university-funded varsity level is clearly correct. Finally, the tremendous growth in women's participation in sports since Title IX was enacted disproves Brown's argument that women are less interested in sports for reasons unrelated to lack of opportunity. *See, e.g.,* Mike Tharp et al., *Sports crazy! Ready, set, go. Why we love our games,* U.S. NEWS & WORLD REPORT, July 15, 1996, at 33–34 (attributing to Title IX the explosive growth of women's participation in sports and the debunking of "the traditional myth that women aren't interested in sports").

Brown's relative interests approach is not a reasonable interpretation of the three-part test. This approach contravenes the purpose of the statute and the regulation because it does not permit an institution or a district court to remedy a gender-based disparity in athletics participation opportunities. Instead, this approach freezes that disparity by law, thereby disadvantaging further the underrepresented gender. Had Congress intended to entrench, rather than change, the status quo—with its historical emphasis on men's participation opportunities to the detriment of women's opportunities—it need not have gone to all the trouble of enacting Title IX.

. . .

It does not follow from our statutory and constitutional analyses that we endorse the district court's remedial order. Although we decline Brown's invitation to find that the district court's remedy was an abuse of discretion, we do find that the district court erred in substituting its own specific relief in place of Brown's statutorily permissible proposal to comply with Title IX by cutting men's teams until substantial proportionality was achieved.

In *Cohen II* we stated that it is "established beyond peradventure that, where no contrary legislative directive appears, the federal judiciary possesses the power to grant any appropriate relief on a cause of action appropriately brought pursuant to a federal statute." 991 F.2d at 901 (citing *Franklin,* 503 U.S. at 70–71). We also observed, however, that "we are a society that cherishes academic freedom and recognizes that universities deserve great leeway in their operations." 991 F.2d at 906 (citing *Wynne v. Tufts Univ. Sch. of Med.,* 976 F.2d 791, 795 (1st Cir. 1992), *cert. denied,* 507 U.S. 1030 (1993); *Lamphere v. Brown Univ.,* 875 F.2d 916, 922 (1st Cir. 1989)). Nevertheless, we have recognized that academic freedom does not embrace the freedom to discriminate. *Villanueva v. Wellesley College,* 930 F.2d 124, 129 (1st Cir. 1991) (citations omitted).

The district court itself pointed out that Brown may achieve compliance with Title IX in a number of ways:

16. The district court found that the women's gymnastics team had won the Ivy League championship in 1989–90 and was a "thriving university-funded varsity team prior to the 1991 demotion;" that the donor-funded women's fencing team had been successful for many years and that its request to be upgraded to varsity status had been supported by the athletics director at the time; that the donor-funded women's ski team had been consistently competitive despite a meager budget; and that the club-status women's water polo team had demonstrated the interest and ability to compete at full varsity status.

It may eliminate its athletic program altogether, it may elevate or create the requisite number of women's positions, it may demote or eliminate the requisite number of men's positions, or it may implement a combination of these remedies. I leave it entirely to Brown's discretion to decide how it will balance its program to provide equal opportunities for its men and women athletes. I recognize the financial constraints Brown faces; however, its own priorities will necessarily determine the path to compliance it elects to take.

Cohen III, 879 F.Supp. at 214; *see also Cohen II*, 991 F.2d at 898 n.15 (noting that a school may achieve compliance with Title IX by "reducing opportunities for the overrepresented gender").

. . .

Brown's proposed compliance plan stated its goal as follows:

The plan has one goal: to make the gender ratio among University-funded teams at Brown substantially proportionate to the gender ratio of the undergraduate student body. To do so, the University must disregard the expressed athletic interests of one gender while providing advantages for others. The plan focuses only on University-funded sports, ignoring the long history of successful donor-funded student teams.

In its introduction, Brown makes clear that it "would prefer to maintain its current program" and that the plan submitted

is inconsistent with Brown's philosophy to the extent that it grants advantages and enforces disadvantages upon student athletes solely because of their gender and curbs the historic role of coaches in determining the number of athletes which can be provided an opportunity to participate. Nevertheless, the University wishes to act in good faith with the order of the Court, notwithstanding issues of fact and law which are currently in dispute.

Brown states that it "seeks to address the issue of proportionality while minimizing additional undue stress on already strained physical and fiscal resources."

The general provisions of the plan may be summarized as follows: (i) Maximum squad sizes for men's teams will be set and enforced. (ii) Head coaches of all teams must field squads that meet minimum size requirements. (iii) No additional discretionary funds will be used for athletics. (iv) Four new women's junior varsity teams—basketball, lacrosse, soccer, and tennis—will be university-funded. (v) Brown will make explicit a de facto junior varsity team for women's field hockey.

The plan sets forth nine steps for its implementation, and concludes that "if the Court determines that this plan is not sufficient to reach proportionality, phase two will be the elimination of one or more men's teams."

The district court found Brown's plan to be "fatally flawed" for two reasons. First, despite the fact that 76 men and 30 women participated on donor-funded varsity teams, Brown's proposed plan disregarded donor-funded varsity teams. Second, Brown's plan "artificially boosts women's varsity numbers by adding junior varsity positions on four women's teams." As to the propriety of Brown's proposal to come into compliance by the addition of junior varsity positions, the district court held:

Positions on distinct junior varsity squads do not qualify as "intercollegiate competition" opportunities under the Policy Interpretation and should not be included in defendants' plan. As noted in *Cohen*, 879 F. Supp. at 200, "intercollegiate" teams are those that "regularly participate in varsity competition." Junior varsity squads, by definition, do not meet this criterion. Counting new women's junior varsity positions as equivalent to men's full varsity positions flagrantly violates the spirit and letter of Title IX; in no sense is an institution providing equal opportunity if it affords varsity positions to men but junior varsity positions to women.

The district court found that these two flaws in the proposed plan were sufficient to show that Brown had "not made a good faith effort to comply with this Court's mandate."

In criticizing another facet of Brown's plan, the district court pointed out that

> an institution does not provide equal opportunity if it caps its men's teams after they are well-stocked with high-caliber recruits while requiring women's teams to boost numbers by accepting walk-ons. A university does not treat its men's and women's teams equally if it allows the coaches of men's teams to set their own maximum capacity limits but overrides the judgment of coaches of women's teams on the same matter.

After rejecting Brown's proposed plan, but bearing in mind Brown's stated objectives, the district court fashioned its own remedy:

> I have concluded that Brown's stated objectives will be best served if I design a remedy to meet the requirements of prong three rather than prong one. In order to bring Brown into compliance with prong one under defendants' Phase II, I would have to order Brown to cut enough men's teams to eradicate approximately 213 men's varsity positions. This extreme action is entirely unnecessary. The easy answer lies in ordering Brown to comply with prong three by upgrading the women's gymnastics, fencing, skiing, and water polo teams to university-funded varsity status. In this way, Brown could easily achieve prong three's standard of "full and effective accommodation of the underrepresented sex." This remedy would entail upgrading the positions of approximately 40 women. In order to finance the 40 additional women's positions, Brown certainly will not have to eliminate as many as the 213 men's positions that would be cut under Brown's Phase II proposal. Thus, Brown will fully comply with Title IX by meeting the standards of prong three, without approaching satisfaction of the standards of prong one.

> It is clearly in the best interest of both the male and the female athletes to have an increase in women's opportunities and a small decrease in men's opportunities, if necessary, rather than, as under Brown's plan, no increase in women's opportunities and a large decrease in men's opportunities. Expanding women's athletic opportunities in areas where there is proven ability and interest is the very purpose of Title IX and the simplest, least disruptive, route to Title IX compliance at Brown.

The district court ordered Brown to "elevate and maintain women's gymnastics, women's water polo, women's skiing, and women's fencing to university-funded varsity status." The court stayed this part of the order pending appeal and further ordered that, in the interim, the preliminary injunction prohibiting Brown from eliminating or demoting any existing women's varsity team would remain in effect.

We agree with the district court that Brown's proposed plan fell short of a good faith effort to meet the requirements of Title IX as explicated by this court in *Cohen II* and as applied by the district court on remand. Indeed, the plan is replete with argumentative statements more appropriate for an appellate brief. It is obvious that Brown's plan was addressed to this court, rather than to offering a workable solution to a difficult problem.

It is clear, nevertheless, that Brown's proposal to cut men's teams is a permissible means of effectuating compliance with the statute. Thus, although we understand the district court's reasons for substituting its own specific relief under the circumstances at the time, and although the district court's remedy is within the statutory margins and constitutional, we think that the district court was wrong to reject out-of-hand Brown's alternative plan to reduce the number of men's varsity teams. After all, the district court itself stated that one of the compliance options available to Brown under Title IX is to "demote or eliminate the requisite number of men's positions." *Cohen III*, 879 F. Supp. at 214. Our respect for academic freedom and reluctance to interject ourselves into the conduct of university affairs counsels that we give universities as much freedom as possible in conducting their operations consonant with constitutional and statutory limits. *Cohen II*, 991 F.2d at 906; *Villanueva*, 930 F.2d at 129.

Brown therefore should be afforded the opportunity to submit another plan for compliance with Title IX. The context of the case has changed in two significant respects since Brown presented its original plan. First, the substantive issues have been decided adversely to Brown. Brown is no longer an appellant seeking a favorable result in the Court of Appeals. Second, the district court is not under time constraints to consider a new plan and fashion a remedy so as to expedite appeal. Accordingly, we remand the case to the district court so that Brown can submit a further plan for its consideration. In all other respects the judgment of the district court is affirmed. The preliminary injunction issued by the district court in *Cohen I*, 809 F. Supp. at 1001, will remain in effect pending a final remedial order.

There can be no doubt that Title IX has changed the face of women's sports as well as our society's interest in and attitude toward women athletes and women's sports. *See, e.g.*, Frank DeFord, *The Women of Atlanta*, NEWSWEEK, June 10, 1996, at 62–71; Tharp, *supra*, at 33; Robert Kuttner, *Vicious Circle of Exclusion*, WASHINGTON POST, September 4, 1996, at A15. In addition, there is ample evidence that increased athletics participation opportunities for women and young girls, available as a result of Title IX enforcement, have had salutary effects in other areas of societal concern. *See* DeFord, *supra*, at 66.

One need look no further than the impressive performances of our country's women athletes in the 1996 Olympic Summer Games to see that Title IX has had a dramatic and positive impact on the capabilities of our women athletes, particularly in team sports. These Olympians represent the first full generation of women to grow up under the aegis of Title IX. The unprecedented success of these athletes is due, in no small measure, to Title IX's beneficent effects on women's sports, as the athletes themselves have acknowledged time and again. What stimulated this remarkable change in the quality of women's athletic competition was not a sudden, anomalous upsurge in women's interest in sports, but the enforcement of Title IX's mandate of gender equity in sports. Kuttner, *supra*, at A15.

Affirmed in part, reversed in part, and remanded for further proceedings. No costs on appeal to either party.

Questions and Comments on *Cohen*

1.   Brown ultimately settled the lawsuit. Brown agreed to guarantee funding for women's gymnastics, skiing, fencing, and water polo and to ensure that women's participation rate in intercollegiate sports remains within 3.5 percent of women's undergraduate enrollment rate. Press Release, Trial Lawyers for Public Justice, *Brown University Agrees to Guarantee Participation Rates for Women Athletes and Funding for Contested Women's Teams*, June 23, 1998, *available at* http://www.tlpj.org/pr/brow2pr. htm. Brown also agreed that, if it eliminates a women's varsity team without eliminating a men's team, or adds a men's varsity team without adding a women's team, it will bring women's athletic participation rates within 2.25 percent of women's enrollment rates. *Id.*

2.   For the most part, Title IX has been applied to intercollegiate sports, but there is growing pressure in Congress to apply it to science education as well. John Tierney, *A New Frontier for Title IX: Science*, N.Y. TIMES, July 15, 2008, *available at* http://www.ny times.com/2008/07/15/science/15tier.html. Although women earn the majority of doctorates in life science and social sciences, they are in the minority in physical sciences, engineering, and computer science. *Id.* Is this discrepancy a result of discrimination against women? In a study of over 5,000 mathematically-gifted students, psychologists at Vanderbilt University found that adolescents' interests and abilities, not their sex, were the best predictors of their career path. *Id.* A similar study found that men and women in the computer industry prefer manipulating machines and objects to interacting with other people; once one controls for this personality variable, there is no significant gender gap in the computer industry. *Id.* How would the *Brown* court respond to the "interests and abilities" argument? Would the response be convincing?

Williams v. Board of Regents of the University System of Georgia

United States Court of Appeals for the Eleventh Circuit, 2007.
477 F.3d 1282.

[The opinion is set forth at pages 828–39, *supra*.]

Jennings v. University of North Carolina

United States Court of Appeals for the Fourth Circuit, 2007.
482 F.3d 686.

[The opinion is set forth at pages 924–30, *supra*.]

Questions and Comments on Title IX

What constitutes sexual harassment under Title IX? Is staring enough? *See* Bougher v. University of Pittsburgh, 882 F.2d 74 (3d Cir. 1989). Do repeated comparisons of a student to Monica Lewinsky in front of the class qualify as sexual harassment? *See* Oden v. Northern Marianas College, 440 F.3d 1085 (9th Cir. 2006). Do sexual advances by a professor qualify as sexual harassment if the students are no longer in his class? *See* Waters v. Metropolitan State Univ., 91 F. Supp. 2d 1287 (D. Minn. 2000). Does harassment during a required off-campus internship qualify as harassment? *See* Crandell v. New York Coll. of Osteopathic Med., 87 F. Supp. 2d 304 (S.D.N.Y. 2000). How often must a professor be accused of sexually harassing students before a university is charged with knowledge that the faculty member poses a threat? Is one accusation of sexual harassment and two past consensual relationships with students enough to provide notice? *See* Escue v. Northern Okla. Coll., 450 F.3d 1146 (10th Cir. 2006). How quickly must a university respond to an alleged incident of sexual harassment? *See* Oden v. Northern Marianas Coll., 440 F.3d 1085 (9th Cir. 2006). *See generally* Diane Heckman, *The Glass Sneaker: Thirty Years of Victories and Defeats Involving Title IX and Sex Discrimination in Athletics*, 13 FORDHAM INTELL. PROP. MEDIA & ENT. L.J. 551 (2003).

B.   FERPA (1974)

Gonzaga University v. Doe

Supreme Court of the United States, 2002.
536 U.S. 273, 122 S.Ct. 2268, 153 L.Ed.2d 309.

■ CHIEF JUSTICE REHNQUIST delivered the opinion of the Court.

The question presented is whether a student may sue a private university for damages under Rev. Stat. § 1979, 42 U.S.C. § 1983 (1994 ed., Supp. V), to enforce provisions of the Family Educational Rights and Privacy Act of 1974 (FERPA or Act), 88 Stat. 571, 20 U.S.C. § 1232g, which prohibit the federal funding of educational institutions that have a policy or practice of releasing education records to unauthorized persons. . . .

Respondent John Doe is a former undergraduate in the School of Education at Gonzaga University, a private university in Spokane, Washington. He planned to graduate and teach at a Washington public elementary school. Washington at the time required all of its new teachers to obtain an affidavit of good moral character from a dean of their graduating college or university. In October 1993, Roberta League, Gonzaga's "teacher certification specialist," overheard one student tell another that respondent engaged in acts of sexual misconduct against Jane Doe, a female undergraduate. League launched an investigation and contacted the state agency responsible for teacher certification, identifying respondent by name and discussing the allegations against him. Respondent did not learn of the investigation, or that information about him had been disclosed, until March 1994, when he was told by League and others that he would not receive the affidavit required for certification as a Washington schoolteacher.

Respondent then sued Gonzaga and League (petitioners) in state court. He alleged violations of Washington tort and contract law, as well as a pendent violation of § 1983 for the release of personal information to an "unauthorized person" in violation of FERPA. A jury found for respondent on all counts, awarding him $1,155,000, including $150,000 in compensatory damages and $300,000 in punitive damages on the FERPA claim.

The Washington Court of Appeals reversed in relevant part, concluding that FERPA does not create individual rights and thus cannot be enforced under § 1983. The Washington Supreme Court reversed that decision, and ordered the FERPA damages reinstated. The court acknowledged that "FERPA itself does not give rise to a private cause of action," but reasoned that FERPA's nondisclosure provision "gives rise to a federal right enforceable under section 1983."

... We ... granted certiorari to resolve the conflict among the lower courts and in the process resolve any ambiguity in our own opinions.

Congress enacted FERPA under its spending power to condition the receipt of federal funds on certain requirements relating to the access and disclosure of student educational records. The Act directs the Secretary of Education to withhold federal funds from any public or private "educational agency or institution" that fails to comply with these conditions. As relevant here, the Act provides:

> No funds shall be made available under any applicable program to any educational agency or institution which has a policy or practice of permitting the release of education records (or personally identifiable information contained therein....) of students without the written consent of their parents to any individual, agency, or organization. 20 U.S.C. § 1232g(b)(1).

The Act directs the Secretary of Education to enforce this and other of the Act's spending conditions. The Secretary is required to establish an office and review board within the Department of Education for "investigating, processing, reviewing, and adjudicating violations of [the Act]." § 1232g(g). Funds may be terminated only if the Secretary determines that a recipient institution "is failing to comply substantially with any requirement of [the Act]" and that such compliance "cannot be secured by voluntary means."

Respondent contends that this statutory regime confers upon any student enrolled at a covered school or institution a federal right, enforceable in suits for damages under § 1983, not to have "education records" disclosed to unauthorized persons without the student's express written consent. But we have never before held, and decline to do so here, that spending legislation drafted in terms resembling those of FERPA can confer enforceable rights.

In *Maine v. Thiboutot*, 448 U.S. 1 (1980), six years after Congress enacted FERPA, we recognized for the first time that § 1983 actions may be brought against state actors to enforce rights created by federal statutes as well as by the Constitution. There we held that plaintiffs could recover payments wrongfully withheld by a state agency in violation of the Social Security Act. A year later, in *Pennhurst State School and Hospital v. Halderman*, 451 U.S. 1 (1981), we rejected a claim that the Developmentally Disabled Assistance and Bill of Rights Act of 1975 conferred enforceable rights, saying:

> In legislation enacted pursuant to the spending power, the typical remedy for state noncompliance with federally imposed conditions is not a private cause of action for noncompliance but rather action by the Federal Government to terminate funds to the State.

We made clear that unless Congress "speaks with a clear voice," and manifests an "unambiguous" intent to confer individual rights, federal funding provisions provide no basis for private enforcement by § 1983.

Since *Pennhurst*, only twice have we found spending legislation to give rise to enforceable rights. In *Wright v. Roanoke Redevelopment and Housing Authority*, 479 U.S. 418 (1987), we allowed a § 1983 suit by tenants to recover past overcharges under a rent-ceiling provision of the Public Housing Act, on the ground that the provision unambiguously conferred "a mandatory [benefit] focusing on the individual family and its income." The key to our inquiry was that Congress spoke in terms that "could not be clearer," and conferred entitlements "sufficiently specific and definite to qualify as enforceable rights under *Pennhurst*." Also significant was that the federal agency charged with administering the Public Housing Act "had never provided a procedure by which tenants could complain to it about the alleged failures [of state welfare agencies] to abide by [the Act's rent-ceiling provision]."

Three years later, in *Wilder v. Virginia Hosp. Ass'n*, 496 U.S. 498 (1990), we allowed a § 1983 suit brought by health care providers to enforce a reimbursement provision of the Medicaid Act, on the ground that the provision, much like the rent-ceiling provision in *Wright*, explicitly conferred specific monetary entitlements upon the plaintiffs. Congress left no doubt of its intent for private enforcement, we said, because the provision required States to pay an "objective" monetary entitlement to individual health care providers, with no sufficient administrative means of enforcing the requirement against States that failed to comply.

Our more recent decisions, however, have rejected attempts to infer enforceable rights from Spending Clause statutes. In *Suter v. Artist M.*, 503 U.S. 347 (1992), the Adoption Assistance and Child Welfare Act of 1980 required States receiving funds for adoption assistance to have a "plan" to make "reasonable efforts" to keep children out of foster homes. A class of parents and children sought to enforce this requirement against state officials under § 1983, claiming that no such efforts had been made. We read the Act "in the light shed by *Pennhurst*," and found no basis for the suit....

Similarly, in *Blessing v. Freestone*, 520 U.S. 329 (1997), Title IV–D of the Social Security Act required States receiving federal child-welfare funds to "substantially comply" with requirements designed to ensure timely payment of child support. Five Arizona mothers invoked § 1983 against state officials on grounds that state child-welfare agencies consistently failed to meet these requirements. We found no basis for the suit, saying,

> Far from creating an *individual* entitlement to services, the standard is simply a yardstick for the Secretary to measure the *systemwide* performance of a State's Title IV–D program. Thus, the Secretary must look to the aggregate services provided by the State, not to whether the needs of any particular person have been satisfied.

. . .

Respondent reads this line of cases to establish a relatively loose standard for finding rights enforceable by § 1983. He claims that a federal statute confers such rights so long as Congress intended that the statute "benefit" putative plaintiffs. He further contends that a more "rigorous" inquiry would conflate the standard for inferring a private right of action under § 1983 with the standard for inferring a private right of action directly from the statute itself, which he admits would not exist under FERPA. As authority, respondent points to *Blessing* and *Wilder*, which, he says, used the term "benefit" to define the sort of statutory interest enforceable by § 1983.

. . .

We ... reject the notion that our cases permit anything short of an unambiguously conferred right to support a cause of action brought under § 1983. Section 1983 provides a remedy only for the deprivation of "rights, privileges, or immunities secured by the Constitution and laws" of the United States. Accordingly, it is *rights*, not the broader or vaguer "benefits" or "interests," that may be enforced under the authority of that section. This being so, we further reject the notion that our implied right of action cases are separate and distinct from our § 1983 cases. To the contrary, our implied right of action cases should guide the determination of whether a statute confers rights enforceable under § 1983.

We have recognized that whether a statutory violation may be enforced through § 1983 "is a different inquiry than that involved in determining whether a private right of action can be implied from a particular statute." But the inquiries overlap in one meaningful respect—in either case we must first determine whether Congress *intended to create a federal right* . . . .

Plaintiffs suing under § 1983 do not have the burden of showing an intent to create a private remedy because § 1983 generally supplies a remedy for the vindication of rights secured by federal statutes. Once a plaintiff demonstrates that a statute confers an individual right, the right is presumptively enforceable by § 1983. But the initial inquiry—determining whether a statute confers any right at all—is no different from the initial inquiry in an implied right of action case, the express purpose of which is to determine whether or not a statute "confers rights on a particular class of persons." This makes obvious sense, since § 1983 merely provides a mechanism for enforcing individual rights "secured" elsewhere, i.e., rights independently "secured by the Constitution and laws" of the United States. "One cannot go into court and claim a 'violation of § 1983'—for § 1983 by itself does not protect anyone against anything." *Chapman v. Houston Welfare Rights Organization*, 441 U.S. 600, 617 (1979).

A court's role in discerning whether personal rights exist in the § 1983 context should therefore not differ from its role in discerning whether personal rights exist in the implied right of action context. Both inquiries simply require a determination as to whether or not Congress intended to confer individual rights upon a class of beneficiaries. Accordingly, where the text and structure of a statute provide no indication that Congress intends to create new individual rights, there is no basis for a private suit, whether under § 1983 or under an implied right of action.

. . .

With this principle in mind, there is no question that FERPA's nondisclosure provisions fail to confer enforceable rights. To begin with, the provisions entirely lack the sort of "rights-creating" language critical to showing the requisite congressional intent to create new rights. Unlike the individually focused terminology of Titles VI and IX ("no person shall be subjected to discrimination"), FERPA's provisions speak only to the Secretary of Education, directing that "no funds shall be made available" to any "educational agency or institution" which has a prohibited "policy or practice." 20 U.S.C. § 1232g(b)(1). This focus is two steps removed from the interests of individual students and parents and clearly does not confer the sort of "*individual* entitlement" that is enforceable under § 1983. As we said in [*Cannon v. U. of Chicago*, 441 U.S. 677 (1979)]:

> There would be far less reason to infer a private remedy in favor of individual persons if Congress, instead of drafting Title IX with an unmistakable focus on the benefited class, had written it simply as a ban on discriminatory conduct by recipients of federal funds or as a prohibition against the disbursement of public funds to educational institutions engaged in discriminatory practices.

FERPA's nondisclosure provisions further speak only in terms of institutional policy and practice, not individual instances of disclosure. See 1232g(b)(1)-(2) (prohibiting the funding of "any educational agency or institution which has a *policy or practice* of permitting the release of education records" (emphasis added)). Therefore, as in *Blessing*, they have an "aggregate" focus, they are not concerned with "whether the needs of any particular person have been satisfied," and they cannot "give rise to individual rights." Recipient institutions can further avoid termination of funding so long as they "comply substantially" with the Act's requirements. § 1234c(a). This, too, is not unlike *Blessing*, which found that Title IV–D failed to support a § 1983 suit in part because it only required "substantial compliance" with federal regulations. . . .

Our conclusion that FERPA's nondisclosure provisions fail to confer enforceable rights is buttressed by the mechanism that Congress chose to provide for enforcing those provisions. Congress expressly authorized the Secretary of Education to "*deal with violations*" of the Act, § 1232g(f) (emphasis added), and required the Secretary to "establish or designate [a] review board" for investigating and adjudicating such violations, § 1232g(g). Pursuant to these provisions, the Secretary created the Family Policy Compliance Office (FPCO) "to act as the Review Board required under the Act and to enforce the Act with respect to all applicable programs." 34 CFR §§ 99.60(a) and (b) (2001). The FPCO permits students and parents who suspect a violation of the Act to file individual written complaints. If a complaint is timely and contains required information, the FPCO will initiate an investigation, notify the educational institution of the charge, and request a written response. If a violation is found, the FPCO distributes a notice of factual findings and a "statement of the specific steps that the agency or institution must take to comply" with FERPA. These administrative procedures squarely distinguish this case from *Wright* and *Wilder*, where an aggrieved individual lacked any federal review mechanism, and further counsel against our finding a congressional intent to create individually enforceable private rights.

.   .   .

In sum, if Congress wishes to create new rights enforceable under § 1983, it must do so in clear and unambiguous terms—no less and no more than what is required for Congress to create new rights enforceable under an implied private right of action. FERPA's nondisclosure provisions contain no rights-creating language, they have an aggregate, not individual, focus, and they serve primarily to direct the Secretary of Education's distribution of public funds to educational institutions. They therefore create no rights enforceable under § 1983. Accordingly, the judgment of Supreme Court of Washington is reversed, and the case is remanded for further proceedings not inconsistent with this opinion.

Questions and Comments on FERPA

1.   May colleges and universities use FERPA to deny student newspapers access to campus law enforcement records? *See* Bauer v. Kincaid, 759 F.Supp. 575 (W.D.Mo. 1991); Student Press Law Center v. Alexander, 778 F.Supp. 1227 (D.D.C.1991). What qualifies as an "educational record" under FERPA? Do negative letters of recommendation qualify? *See* Olsson v. Indiana Univ. Bd. of Tr., 571 N.E.2d 585 (Ind.App. 1991).

2.   FERPA contains an exception that permits a university to disclose records to parents or other "appropriate parties" in the case of an emergency. The implementing regulations provide:

> an educational agency or institution may disclose personally identifiable information from an educational record to appropriate parties in connection with an emergency if knowledge of the information is necessary to protect the health or safety of the student or other individuals. 34 C.F.R. § 99.36 (2006).

Should FERPA *require* notification of parents in cases of suicide threats or attempts? Consider John S. Gearan, *When Is it Ok to Tattle? The Need to Amend the Family Educational Rights and Privacy Act*, 39 SUFFOLK U. L. REV. 1023 (2006).

3.   After *Gonzaga,* how concerned should colleges and universities be about improper disclosures of student records? Although a § 1983 suit is now out of the question, students and their families may still pursue relief under state law breach of contract or tort claims. In fact, John Doe was ultimately able to prevail on that basis. *See* Doe v. Gonzaga Univ., 143 Wash.2d 687, 24 P.3d 390 (2001). *See also* Benjamin F. Sidbury, Gonzaga University v. Doe *and Its Implications: No Right to Enforce Student Privacy Rights Under FERPA*, 29 J.C. & U.L. 655 (2003).

C.   CLERY ACT (1990)

Havlik v. Johnson & Wales University

United States Court of Appeals for the First Circuit, 2007.
509 F.3d 25.

■ SELYA, SENIOR CIRCUIT JUDGE.

The Clery Act, 20 U.S.C. § 1092(f) (the Act), requires colleges and universities that participate in federal financial aid programs to notify their constituent communities of certain reported crimes. This case requires us to construe, for the first time at the federal appellate level, the Act's notification requirements. After analyzing the language and purpose of the Act, charting the dimensions of the plaintiff's claims, and sifting through the factual record, we affirm the district court's entry of summary judgment in favor of the defendant university.

The plaintiff, Christopher Havlik, is a citizen and resident of New York. In 2002, he enrolled as an undergraduate at Johnson & Wales University (the University) in Providence, Rhode Island. The events that led to this litigation occurred early in his junior year.

In the late night or wee morning hours of September 16–17, 2004, the plaintiff engaged in a heated exchange with another student, Donald Ratcliffe, on a sidewalk near the intersection of Richmond and Pine Streets in Providence. In the course of this encounter, the plaintiff punched Ratcliffe, knocking him to the ground. As a result, Ratcliffe hit his head on the sidewalk.

The Providence police responded and investigated the incident. Acquaintances of each protagonist had witnessed the fracas and gave somewhat differing accounts of what had transpired. One witness told the police that the plaintiff was holding a knife at the time of the confrontation.

The police arranged for Ratcliffe to be taken by ambulance to a local hospital, where he was found to have sustained a concussion and a fractured skull. Then, after concluding their probe, the police lodged a criminal charge against the plaintiff.

The incident was duly reported to the University's campus safety and security office. That office commenced its own inquiry. This inquiry culminated in an incident report, which indicated that the episode probably had been triggered by fraternity-related animosities; that the plaintiff was the likely aggressor; and that he reputedly flashed a knife at the time. At least one witness stated that he and a friend (also a witness) feared that the plaintiff or his fraternity brothers would retaliate against them for cooperating in the investigation.

On September 20, the University's student conduct office notified the plaintiff of his temporary suspension for violating rules contained in the student code of conduct (the Code). The notice cited three violations: assaulting another student, possessing a knife, and engaging in criminal behavior. The notice advised the plaintiff that he had a right to a hearing and scheduled one for the following day.

The hearing went forward the next morning before the student conduct board (the Board). The plaintiff explained his actions and presented witnesses who testified on his behalf. Other evidence also was adduced. After mulling all the proof, the Board found the plaintiff "responsible" for assaulting another student and for engaging in lawless behavior (the first and third charges). It found him "not responsible" for possessing a knife (the second charge). The Board then recommended that the plaintiff be dismissed from the University for having transgressed the Code and notified him of his right to appeal its decision.

During the course of these proceedings, other (related) events were occurring on a parallel track. On the same day that the plaintiff received notice of his suspension, the University's chief in-house counsel, Barbara Bennett, reviewed and revised a draft of a "crime alert" that she had received that day from the campus safety and security office. The crime alert was, in effect, a notice designed to inform the University community of a reported crime.

While both versions of the crime alert included statements that a blow had been struck and a knife had been brandished, Bennett's version contained two facts not included in the original draft. First, it noted that members of a particular fraternity (ZBT), whose enrollment included the plaintiff, were involved in the incident. Second, it named the plaintiff as the party reportedly responsible for the crime.

When her work was finished, Bennett sent the final version of the crime alert back to the campus safety and security office. Personnel from that office posted it in various locations some time after 4:00 pm on September 21. The record indicates that, at the relevant times, neither Bennett nor the campus safety and security office had any knowledge of the outcome of the disciplinary hearing before the Board.

The plaintiff decided to appeal the Board's decision, as was his right. Prior to going forward with his appeal, he and his mother conferred with Ronald Martel, the University's vice-president for student affairs. At the meeting, Martel accused the plaintiff of dissembling about the incident and called his fraternity brothers "thugs." The plaintiff nonetheless persisted in his appeal and Martel (to whom the letter of appeal was sent) turned the matter over to the designated appeal officer, Veera Sarawgi (also a vice-president of the University).

Although Sarawgi was not deposed, she would in the normal course of events have received, along with the letter of appeal, the hearing notification, a statement of applicable hearing procedures, the Board's decision, and the University's incident report. Sarawgi also asked Martel whether he knew of any reason that the Board's proposed sanction should be tempered or overturned. Martel replied in the negative. Nothing in the record indicates that he shared his views about either ZBT or the plaintiff's veracity with Sarawgi. On September 29, Sarawgi affirmed the plaintiff's dismissal.

During and after this time frame, a criminal prosecution was being mounted. The Providence police had charged the plaintiff with criminal assault. *See* R.I. GEN. LAWS § 11–5–3. The case originally was heard in the state district court and the plaintiff was found guilty after a bench trial. He appealed to the superior court and claimed his right to a de novo jury trial. *See id.* § 12–17–1. In May of 2005, a jury acquitted him.

Disgruntled by the disruption of his scholarly pursuits, the plaintiff filed a civil action against the University in Rhode Island's federal district court. He premised jurisdiction on diversity of citizenship and the existence of a controversy in the requisite amount. His complaint alleged defamatory publication of false information by means of the crime alert and breach of contract for the University's failure to provide a fair appeal process. The University denied the material allegations of the complaint and, after the close of discovery, moved for summary judgment. The district court granted the motion. This timely appeal followed.

We review a district court's entry of summary judgment de novo. . . .

A.   *The Clery Act.*

To put the relevance of the Clery Act into perspective, we deem it useful to begin by delineating the anatomy of the plaintiff's defamation claim. Defamation is a common law cause of action that arises under state law (here, the law of Rhode Island—the place of publication).

In Rhode Island, defamation requires proof that (i) the defendant made a false and defamatory statement regarding another, (ii) published it to a third party without an attendant privilege and (iii) was at least negligent in making the publication, with the result that (iv) the defamed party incurred harm. *Kevorkian* v. *Glass*, 913 A.2d 1043, 1047 (R.I. 2007). Consistent with this formulation, the defendant may avoid liability by showing that the publication enjoys a qualified privilege. *See Mills* v. *C.H.I.L.D., Inc.*, 837 A.2d 714, 720 (R.I. 2003).

In this instance, the district court assumed for argument's sake that the crime alert was defamatory. *Havlik*, 490 F. Supp. 2d at 255. It determined, however, that the University enjoyed a qualified privilege, stemming from its duty under the Act, to publish the crime alert. The court further determined that, in issuing the crime alert, the University acted without ill will or malice, so that the qualified privilege protected it from liability.

The plaintiff advances three primary claims of error with respect to this multi-part determination. In addressing them sequentially, we assume *arguendo*, as did the district court, that the crime alert contained defamatory statements.

1. *The Qualified Privilege.* Under Rhode Island law, a qualified privilege attaches if "the publisher acting in good faith correctly or reasonably believes that he has a legal, moral or social duty to speak out, or that to speak out is necessary to protect either his own interests, or those of third persons, or certain interests of the public." *Ponticelli* v. *Mine Safety Appl. Co.*, 104 R.I. 549, 247 A.2d 303, 305–06 (R.I. 1968). Thus, the privilege may apply when the speaker's perception of his duty to speak, though incorrect, is nonetheless reasonable. *See id.*

With this legal landscape in mind, the plaintiff argues that the University had no duty under the Act to report his involvement in the putative crime to the campus community and that, therefore, it had no qualified privilege to publish the crime alert. The University demurs, insisting that it had a legal duty to report the putative crime and set out the known particulars. On that basis, it defends the district court's holding that a qualified privilege obtained.

To determine whether the University enjoyed a qualified privilege, we must first determine whether its professed belief in its legal duty was reasonable. This brings us to the Clery Act,[2] so a brief exposition of the Act's provisions and legislative purpose is in order.

The Clery Act mandates that all colleges and universities that accept federal funding must notify the constituent campus communities—students, faculty, employees, and the like—when certain crimes are brought to their attention. Specifically, the Act requires every covered entity to make "timely reports to the campus community on [certain] crimes considered to be a threat to other students and employees ... that are reported to campus security or local law police agencies." 20 U.S.C. § 1092(f)(3).

The Act has both qualitative and situational limitations. As to the former, the Act does not reach all types of crimes but only encompasses murder, manslaughter, aggravated assault, sex offenses, robbery, burglary, motor vehicle theft, arson, liquor, drug, and weapons offenses, and hate crimes. *Id.* § 1092 (f)(1)(F)(i)-(ii). An aggravated assault is a covered crime, and in this venue the plaintiff does not contest that his confrontation with Ratcliffe qualifies under that rubric.

---

2. In its original incarnation, the Act was given the short title "Crime Awareness and Campus Security Act of 1990." Congress amended the Act in 1998 and renamed it the "Jeanne Clery Disclosure of Campus Security Policy and Campus Crime Statistics Act." Most commentators now use the shorthand "the Clery Act," and so do we.

Paragraph (1)(F) of the Act contains the relevant situational limitations. It describes the loci of crimes that must be reported. *See* 20 U.S.C. § 1092(f)(1)(F). That paragraph speaks of crimes that occur "on campus, in or on noncampus buildings or property, and on public property...." *Id.* The Act then proceeds to define each of these terms. "[N]oncampus building[s] or property" are those owned or controlled by the institution that are outside the "reasonably contiguous geographic area of the institution," *id.* § 1092(f)(6)(A)(ii); "public property" is non-owned property within the area reasonably contiguous to the institution and adjacent to a facility owned or controlled by the institution, *id.* § 1092(f)(6)(A)(iii).

The goal of the notification requirement is to protect members of the constituent campus communities by "aid[ing] in the prevention of similar occurrences." *Id.* § 1092(f)(3). The Act's history illuminates the centrality of this goal. Congress passed the original version of the Act in 1990 amid concerns that the proliferation of campus crime created a growing threat to students, faculty, and school employees. *See* H.R. Rep. No. 101–518, at 7 (1990), *reprinted in* 1990 U.S.C.C.A.N. 3363, 3369. Congress recognized that contemporary campus communities had become increasingly dangerous places. Furthermore, it noted that, in roughly eighty percent of crimes on campus, both the perpetrator and the victim were students. *See* Crime Awareness and Campus Security Act of 1990, Pub. L. No. 101–542, § 202, 104 Stat. 2381, 2384 (codified as amended at 20 U.S.C. § 1092(f)).

Notwithstanding these concerns, the first iteration of the Act restricted the reporting requirement to crimes committed on campus. *See* 20 U.S.C. §§ 1092(f)(1)(F) & (f)(3) (1990); *see also* H.R. Rep. No. 101–518, at 8, *reprinted in* 1990 U.S.C.C.A.N. at 3371 (disclaiming any intention "that institutions report ... offenses which occur outside of the campus"). Over time, however, Congress became dissatisfied with this restriction. In 1996, the House of Representatives expressed its displeasure with current enforcement efforts and passed a resolution calling for the Department of Education to make "[s]afety of students ... the number one priority." H.R. Rep. No. 104–875 (1997), *reprinted in* 1997 WL 10633, at *61 (citing H.R. Res. 470, 104th Cong. (1996)).

Two years later, Congress amended the Act to provide broader protections. Through the Higher Education Amendments of 1998, Congress expanded the Act's coverage to reach not only crimes committed on campus but also crimes committed on "noncampus" and "public" property, so long as (i) the property on which a crime occurs is owned or controlled by, or adjacent to a facility owned or controlled by, the institution, and (ii) that property or facility is used by the institution in direct support of, or in a way related to, its educational mission. Higher Education Amendments of 1998, Pub. L. No. 105–244, 112 Stat. 1581, 1744 (codified as amended at 20 U.S.C. § 1092(f)(6)(A)).

From the start, Congress made manifest a desire that educational institutions retain the ability to tailor security procedures to particularized needs. *See, e.g.*, H.R. Rep. No. 101–518, at 9, *reprinted in* 1990 U.S.C.C.A.N. at 3371 (stating that the legislation was designed "to encourage campuses to develop campus security policies and procedures which are appropriate to the unique conditions of [each particular] campus"). The 1998 amendments did not retreat from this aspiration. *See, e.g.*, 20 U.S.C. § 1092(f)(2) (declining "to authorize the Secretary [of Education] to require particular policies, procedures, or practices by institutions of higher education with respect to campus crimes or campus security"). As we read the Act, it vests substantial discretion in each campus security office to phrase and disseminate reports in those ways that the particular institution deems best suited to apprise its constituent campus communities of incipient criminal activity.

In this case, the district court determined that the locus of the incident fell under the Act's definition of "public property." *Havlik*, 490 F. Supp. 2d at 257; *see* 20 U.S.C. § 1092(f)(6)(A)(iii) (defining "public property" as "all property that is within the same reasonably contiguous geographic area of the institution, such as a sidewalk . . . and is adjacent to a facility owned or controlled by the institution" so long as "the facility is used by the institution in direct support of, or in a manner related to the institution's educational purposes"). On appeal, the plaintiff remonstrates that the University was not careful enough in gauging the location of the incident. Building on this foundation, he engages in an exegetic discourse about the meaning of terms such as "campus," "noncampus," and "public property," culminating in an assertion that the locus of the incident falls outside the compass of those definitions (and, thus, outside the compass of the Act).

We do not doubt the importance of the meaning that Congress assigned to each of these terms. Nevertheless, we reject the notion that the coverage of the Act turns exclusively on the use of a surveyor's theodolite. Reasonableness is the beacon by which institutions must steer, and reasonableness is not totally constrained by mathematically precise metes and bounds. So, too, common sense must inform a court's assessment of the reasonableness of a university's belief that the reporting of a crime is compulsory under the Act. And in making that assessment, the need to assure safety and security for campus communities counsels that doubts should be resolved in favor of notification.

In the case at hand, Bennett—the official who authored the final version of this crime alert—testified without contradiction that when advising school hierarchs whether a duty to publish a timely notification exists, she first determines whether the crime is of a type covered by the Act; she then determines whether it has been reported to campus security or local law enforcement; and she then determines whether the underlying conduct signals a threat to the University community (a determination that takes into account where the incident happened). She believed that all of these factors supported notification in this instance.

Nothing in the record undermines the reasonableness of Bennett's professed belief that the University had a responsibility under the Act to issue a timely notification about the incident. There is absolutely no evidence that the University thought that the incident had occurred outside the geographic purview of the Act. Moreover, while Bennett stated that she was not concerned with the specific street address at which the brouhaha erupted, she did consider the location of the crime to the extent of satisfying herself that it had taken place "in the vicinity of [the] campus and [in] an area that [the University's] students were known to frequent."

No more was exigible: school officials must act expeditiously to satisfy their responsibilities under the Clery Act, and a reasonable belief—even if later shown to be incorrect in some particular—is all that is required for the qualified privilege to attach.

That ends this phase of our inquiry. Because Bennett's belief that the University had a duty to report the crime was reasonable,[3] that belief sufficed to place publication of the crime within the ambit of the qualified privilege conferred by the Act.

2. *The University's Primary Motive.* The plaintiff next argues that even if the Act applies, the district court erred in upholding the qualified privilege because he adduced sufficient evidence to make out a genuine issue of material fact as to whether that privilege was vitiated. . . .

A qualified privilege is not a jujube that, like some magical charm, wards off liability for defamation, come what may. In Rhode Island, as elsewhere, such a privilege may be abrogated if the plaintiff proves that the privilege-holder published the offending statement out of spite, ill will, or malice. *See Kevorkian*, 913 A.2d at 1048; *Mills*, 837 A.2d at 720. To carry this burden, the plaintiff must show that malice—we use that word as a generic shorthand that includes ill will and spite—comprised the defendant's primary motive in publishing the statement. *Mills*, 837 A.2d at 720. To accomplish this goal, the plaintiff cannot rest on naked assertions or bare conclusions but, rather, must proffer facts sufficient to support a finding of malice as a primary motive.

Here, the plaintiff argues that summary judgment was improvident because the University's use of his name and fraternity affiliation in the crime alert and Martel's negative statements about him and his fraternity were sufficient to support an inference of malice. He adds that the statement in the crime alert about his possession of a knife buttresses this inference, given the Board's finding, hours before the crime alert issued, that he was "not responsible" on the knife-wielding charge. We do not agree.

At the outset, it is important to note that every university is different, and each one has its own culture. Mindful of this diversity, the Act stipulates no hard-and-fast rules but, instead, gives institutions of higher learning substantial leeway to decide how notices should be phrased and disseminated so as most effectively to prevent future incidents. *See, e.g.*, 20 U.S.C. § 1092(f)(3) (directing colleges and universities to make timely reports "in *a manner* . . . that will aid in the prevention of similar occurrences" (emphasis supplied)); *see also* H.R. Rep. No. 101–518, at 8, *reprinted in* 1990 U.S.C.C.A.N. at 3371 (explaining that reports should be constructed to permit students "to better protect themselves"). Given this mise-en-scene, the plaintiff has proffered nothing that might suffice to show malice in the composition of the crime alert.

The record shows that Bennett, who made the decision to include the plaintiff's name and fraternity affiliation in the text of the crime alert, believed that the information would be useful to the campus community and

---

3. In all events, Bennett's belief was quite probably correct. The plaintiff argues that the sidewalk where the fracas occurred did not constitute "public property" within the purview of the Act because it is adjacent to a parking lot owned by a third party. This argument overlooks, however, that the University presented uncontradicted evidence showing that this parking lot was owned by one of its subsidiary corporations, that it (the University) maintained the parking lot, and that the lot was used, at least in part, for employee and student parking and similar activities related to the University's educational mission. Because the only plausible conclusion that can be drawn from this undisputed evidence is that the University controlled the parking lot, the sidewalk adjacent to it was public property within the purview of the Act.

would assist in preventing future incidents. Bennett testified that she thought the plaintiff represented a threat to others on campus both because his fraternity had been involved in past misbehavior—she knew of at least one previously reported incident—and because the campus safety and security office had been told that witnesses feared retaliation at the hands of ZBT. On this record, Bennett's belief, whether or not unarguably correct, was clearly reasonable and, thus, inspires no inference of malice.

In pursuing this line of attack, the plaintiff makes much of Martel's deposition testimony that, during his two-year tenure, there were approximately five other crime alerts that involved students allegedly responsible for crimes that did not name the alleged perpetrator. In her deposition, however, Bennett explained that in all but one of those cases the student's identity was not known until after publication of the crime alert. On at least one other occasion, a student perpetrator's name was mentioned in a crime alert. She further explained that, in this instance, she chose to use the plaintiff's name because "we knew his identity."

That explanation seems sufficient, especially in view of three related facts. First, the crime alert as a whole appears consistent with the general tenor of the incident report and the police report. Second, there is no hint that Bennett even knew the plaintiff, let alone that she harbored any animus toward him. Last—but surely not least—the crime alert appears reasonably calculated to help prevent similar incidents. A finding of malice would, therefore, be totally at odds with the record.

To be sure, Martel—who accused the plaintiff of prevarication and called his fraternity brothers "thugs"—arguably may have harbored some hostility toward the plaintiff. The plaintiff insists that this ill will should be imputed to the University. But Martel's statements were made *after* the publication of the crime alert, and there is simply no evidence that Martel played any part in the preparation of that document. The motives of an employee who has no connection to a publication decision cannot be imputed to the institution for which he works and, thus, cannot defenestrate the institution's qualified privilege.

This leaves the fact that the Board found the plaintiff not responsible for possessing a knife a few hours before the University posted the crime alert. As to this item, there is a gap in the plaintiff's proof: the absence of any evidence that the University officials responsible for the publication were aware of the Board's finding at the time of publication. Bennett testified that she had no such knowledge until after publication had occurred, and there is no indication in the record that the campus safety and security office was any better informed. Finally, there is nothing to show that the University willfully blinded itself to the Board's finding. We conclude, therefore, that the inclusion of the "knife" language in the crime alert cannot support an inference of malice.

3. *Punitive Damages.* The plaintiff's third assignment of error—that the district court blundered in squelching his quest for punitive damages—need not detain us. In this case, punitive damages are not a separate cause of action but, rather, an element of damages in, and thus wholly derivative of, the plaintiff's defamation claim. Because the district court appropriately terminated that claim at the summary judgment stage, *see supra*, the plaintiff has no conceivable basis for an award of punitive damages.

B.   *The Contract.*

A student's relationship to his university is based in contract. *Mangla* v. *Brown Univ.*, 135 F.3d 80, 83 (1st Cir. 1998). The plaintiff's final claim of error in this case is that the lower court erred in granting summary judgment in favor of the University on his breach of contract claim.

The relevant terms of the contractual relationship between a student and a university typically include language found in the university's student handbook. We interpret such contractual terms in accordance with the parties' reasonable expectations, giving those terms the meaning that the university reasonably should expect the student to take from them. *See id.* Thus, if the university explicitly promises an appeal process in disciplinary matters, that process must be carried out in line with the student's reasonable expectations. *See Cloud v. Trustees of Boston Univ.*, 720 F.2d 721, 724–25 (1st Cir. 1983).

In this instance, the contract between the plaintiff and the University is governed by Rhode Island law. That body of jurisprudence requires, among other things, that parties to a contract act pursuant to an implied duty of good faith and fair dealing. Good faith and fair dealing cannot be separated from context, however—and in evaluating those covenants in the educational milieu, courts must accord a school some measure of deference in matters of discipline. *See Schaer v. Brandeis Univ.*, 432 Mass. 474, 735 N.E.2d 373, 381 (2000) (stating that universities must be given broad discretion in disciplining students). . . .

The University prepares and distributes to those who enroll a student handbook. With respect to matters of student conduct, the handbook designates the rudimentary contractual terms between the parties vis-à-vis the appeal process. In pertinent part, it gives a student a right of appeal from the Board's decision against charges of violating the Code. It specifies the bases on which a student may appeal, including the imposition of an inappropriate sanction.

Once the student submits a letter stating the basis for his appeal, the appeal officer must engage in a "further review of the [Board's] decision." The handbook does not limn the procedures to be followed by the appeal officer, nor does it pair particular types of code violations with particular sanctions. It is likewise silent as to the kinds of materials that an appeal officer may review.

To the extent the handbook's terms are explicit, it is plain that the University complied with them. The plaintiff asserts, however, that the University breached its implied duty of good faith and fair dealing because the appeal officer (Sarawgi) was improperly influenced by the phraseology of the crime alert and her conversation with Martel.

Given the sketchy nature of the appeal provision in the handbook and the straightforward nature of the materials that were made available to Sarawgi, *see supra*, it seems entirely reasonable for her to have considered that information. *Cf. Schaer*, 735 N.E.2d at 380 (holding that plaintiff had no reasonable expectation for judicial proceedings where "nothing in the contract suggests that disciplinary proceedings will be conducted as though they were judicial proceedings"). Her consultation with Martel also seems within the realm of reasonableness. Martel, after all, was the University's vice-president for student affairs.

In any event, the plaintiff's assertions of improper influence fail in light of the uncontested facts. The plaintiff presented no evidence that Martel repeated his negative sentiments to Sarawgi. *See Bennett*, 507 F.3d at 31 [2007 WL 3227393, at *7] ("[C]onjecture cannot take the place of proof in the summary judgment calculus.").

To say more on this point would be to paint the lily. In the absence of any probative evidence that the appeal officer ignored promised protections, improperly consulted certain proof, acted arbitrarily in carrying out the procedures outlined in the handbook, or made her decision in bad faith, there has been no showing that the plaintiff's reasonable expectations were thwarted. It follows that the University was entitled to summary judgment on the breach of contract claim.

Questions and Comments on the Clery Act

On April 5, 1986, Jeanne Clery "was tortured, raped, sodomized and murdered in her dormitory room at Lehigh University." Howard Clery & Connie Clery, What Jeanne Didn't Know, Security on Campus, Inc., http://www.securityoncampus.org/aboutsoc/didntknow.html (last visited Aug. 11, 2008). After discovering that there had been numerous other unreported crimes on the campus, Jeanne Clery's parents took action. After more than three years of lobbying, the "Jeanne Clery Disclosure of Campus Security Policy and Campus Crime Statistics Act" was signed into law in 1990. Originally named "Crime Awareness and Campus Security Act of 1990," the act requires that colleges report violent crimes that occur on or near campus. The information is also made available to prospective students and families through the Department of Education website.

How effective is the Act? Were you aware of your college's crime statistics when you chose which school to attend? Should colleges be required to report crimes that occur off-campus in locations frequented by students, such as in popular off-campus apartments? Is there an inherent conflict in the Act between the privacy rights of accused students and the reporting requirement? Should schools be required to report the names of accused students? Should they be required to report when a student is found innocent? *See, e.g.*, Bonnie S. Fisher, Jennifer L. Hartman, Francis T. Cullen & Michael G. Turner, *Making Campuses Safer For Students: The Clery Act As A Symbolic Legal Reform*, 32 STETSON L. REV. 61 (2002); Dennis E. Gregory & Steven M. Janosik, *The Clery Act: How Effective Is It? Perceptions from the Field—The Current State of the Research and Recommendations for Improvement*, 32 STETSON L. REV. 7 (2002); Tamu K. Walton, Note, *Protecting Student Privacy: Reporting Campus Crimes as an Alternative to Disclosing Student Disciplinary Records*, 77 IND. L.J. 143 (2002).

D. SOLOMON AMENDMENT (2003)

Rumsfeld v. Forum for Academic and Institutional Rights

Supreme Court of the United States, 2006.
547 U.S. 47, 126 S.Ct. 1297, 164 L.Ed.2d 156.

■ CHIEF JUSTICE ROBERTS delivered the opinion of the Court.

When law schools began restricting the access of military recruiters to their students because of disagreement with the Government's policy on homosexuals in the military, Congress responded by enacting the Solomon Amendment. *See* 10 U.S.C.A. § 983 (Supp. 2005). That provision specifies that if any part of an institution of higher education denies military recruiters access equal to that provided other recruiters, the entire institution would lose certain federal funds. The law schools responded by suing, alleging that the Solomon Amendment infringed their First Amendment freedoms of speech and association. The District Court disagreed but was reversed by a divided panel of the Court of Appeals for the Third Circuit, which ordered the District Court to enter a preliminary injunction against enforcement of the Solomon Amendment. We granted certiorari.

Respondent Forum for Academic and Institutional Rights, Inc. (FAIR), is an association of law schools and law faculties. Its declared mission is "to promote academic freedom, support educational institutions in opposing discrimination and vindicate the rights of institutions of higher education." FAIR members have adopted policies expressing their opposition to discrimination based on, among other factors, sexual orientation. They would like to restrict military recruiting on their campuses because they object to the policy Congress has adopted with respect to homosexuals in the military. *See* 10 U.S.C. § 654.[1] The Solomon Amendment, however, forces institutions to choose between enforcing their nondiscrimination policy against military recruiters in this way and continuing to receive specified federal funding.

In 2003, FAIR sought a preliminary injunction against enforcement of the Solomon Amendment, which at that time—it has since been amended—prevented the Department of Defense (DOD) from providing specified federal funds to any institution of higher education "that either prohibits, or in effect prevents" military recruiters "from gaining entry to campuses." § 983(b).[2] FAIR considered the DOD's interpretation of this provision particularly objectionable. Although the statute required only "entry to campuses," the Government—after the terrorist attacks on September 11, 2001—adopted an informal policy of " 'requir[ing] universities to provide military recruiters access to students equal in quality and scope to that provided to other recruiters.' " Prior to the adoption of this policy, some law schools sought to promote their nondiscrimination policies while still complying with the Solomon Amendment by having military recruiters interview on the undergraduate campus. But under the equal access policy, military recruiters had to be permitted to interview at the law schools, if other recruiters did so.

FAIR argued that this forced inclusion and equal treatment of military recruiters violated the law schools' First Amendment freedoms of speech and association. According to FAIR, the Solomon Amendment was unconstitutional because it forced law schools to choose between exercising their First Amendment right to decide whether to disseminate or accommodate a

---

1. Under this policy, a person generally may not serve in the Armed Forces if he has engaged in homosexual acts, stated that he is a homosexual, or married a person of the same sex. Respondents do not challenge that policy in this litigation.

2. The complaint named numerous other plaintiffs as well. The District Court concluded that each plaintiff had standing to bring this suit. 291 F. Supp. 2d 269, 284–296 (D.N.J. 2003). The Court of Appeals for the Third Circuit agreed with the District Court

that FAIR had associational standing to bring this suit on behalf of its members. 390 F.3d 219, 228, n. 7 (2004). The Court of Appeals did not determine whether the other plaintiffs have standing because the presence of one party with standing is sufficient to satisfy Article III's case-or-controversy requirement. *Ibid.* (citing Bowsher v. Synar, 478 U.S. 714, 721 (1986)). Because we also agree that FAIR has standing, we similarly limit our discussion to FAIR.

military recruiter's message, and ensuring the availability of federal funding for their universities.

[The District Court denied the preliminary injunction, holding that including "an unwanted periodic visitor" did not significantly affect that law's schools ability to express its viewpoint, and that recruiting is conduct, not speech.] The District Court held that Congress could regulate [the] expressive aspect of the conduct under the test set forth in *United States v. O'Brien*, 391 U.S. 367 (1968).

[After the District Court rejected the DOD's proposed interpretation of the statute requiring "access to students that is at least equal in quality in scope," . . .] Congress codified the DOD's informal policy. *See* H. R. Rep. No. 108–443, pt. 1, p 6 (2004). . . . The Solomon Amendment now prevents an institution from receiving certain federal funding if it prohibits military recruiters "from gaining access to campuses, or access to students . . . on campuses, for purposes of military recruiting in a manner that is at least equal in quality and scope to the access to campuses and to students that is provided to any other employer." 10 U.S.C.A. § 983(b) (Supp. 2005).[3]

FAIR appealed the District Court's judgment, arguing that the recently amended Solomon Amendment was unconstitutional for the same reasons as the earlier version. A divided panel of the Court of Appeals for the Third Circuit agreed. According to the Third Circuit, the Solomon Amendment violated the unconstitutional conditions doctrine because it forced a law school to choose between surrendering First Amendment rights and losing federal funding for its university. Unlike the District Court, the Court of Appeals did not think that the *O'Brien* analysis applied because the Solomon Amendment, in its view, regulated speech and not simply expressive conduct. The Third Circuit nonetheless determined that if the regulated activities were properly treated as expressive conduct rather than speech, the Solomon Amendment was also unconstitutional under *O'Brien*. . . .

We granted certiorari.

The Solomon Amendment denies federal funding to an institution of higher education that "has a policy or practice . . . that either prohibits, or in effect prevents" the military "from gaining access to campuses, or access to students . . . on campuses, for purposes of military recruiting in a manner that is at least equal in quality and scope to the access to campuses and to students that is provided to any other employer." 10 U.S.C.A. § 983(b) (Supp. 2005). The statute provides an exception for an institution with "a longstanding policy of pacifism based on historical religious affiliation." § 983(c)(2). The Government and FAIR agree on what this statute requires: In order for a law school and its university to receive federal funding, the law school must offer military recruiters the same access to its campus and students that it provides to the nonmilitary recruiter receiving the most favorable access.

---

3. The federal funds covered by the Solomon Amendment are specified at 10 U.S.C.A. § 983(d)(1) (Supp. 2005) and include funding from the Departments of Defense, Homeland Security, Transportation, Labor, Health and Human Services, and Education, and the Central Intelligence Agency and the National Nuclear Security Administration of the Department of Energy. Funds provided for student financial assistance are not covered. § 983(d)(2). The loss of funding applies not only to the particular school denying access but university-wide. § 983(b).

Certain law professors participating as *amici,* however, argue that the Government and FAIR misinterpret the statute. *See* Brief for William Alford et al. as *Amici Curiae* 10–18; Brief for 56 Columbia Law School Faculty Members as *Amici Curiae* 6–15. According to these *amici,* the Solomon Amendment's equal-access requirement is satisfied when an institution applies to military recruiters the same policy it applies to all other recruiters. On this reading, a school excluding military recruiters would comply with the Solomon Amendment so long as it also excluded any other employer that violates its nondiscrimination policy.

. . .

We conclude that . . . the Government and FAIR correctly interpret the Solomon Amendment. The statute requires the Secretary of Defense to compare the military's "access to campuses" and "access to students" to "the access to campuses and to students that is provided to *any other employer*." (Emphasis added.). . . .

The Solomon Amendment does not focus on the *content* of a school's recruiting policy, as the *amici* would have it. Instead, it looks to the *result* achieved by the policy and compares the "access . . . provided" military recruiters to that provided other recruiters. Applying the same policy to all recruiters is therefore insufficient to comply with the statute if it results in a greater level of access for other recruiters than for the military. Law schools must ensure that their recruiting policy operates in such a way that military recruiters are given access to students at least equal to that "*provided* to any other employer." (Emphasis added.)

. . . . Under *amici*'s interpretation, [the recent revision of the Solomon amendment would have] no effect—law schools could still restrict military access, so long as they do so under a generally applicable nondiscrimination policy. Worse yet, the legislative change made it *easier* for schools to keep military recruiters out altogether: under the prior version, simple access could not be denied, but under the amended version, access could be denied altogether, so long as a nonmilitary recruiter would also be denied access. That is rather clearly *not* what Congress had in mind in codifying the DOD policy. We refuse to interpret the Solomon Amendment in a way that negates its recent revision, and indeed would render it a largely meaningless exercise.

We therefore read the Solomon Amendment the way both the Government and FAIR interpret it. It is insufficient for a law school to treat the military as it treats all other employers who violate its nondiscrimination policy. Under the statute, military recruiters must be given the same access as recruiters who comply with the policy.

The Constitution grants Congress the power to "provide for the common Defence," "[t]o raise and support Armies," and "[t]o provide and maintain a Navy." Art. I, § 8, cls. 1, 12–13. Congress' power in this area "is broad and sweeping," and there is no dispute in this case that it includes the authority to require campus access for military recruiters. That is, of course, unless Congress exceeds constitutional limitations on its power in enacting such legislation. *See Rostker v. Goldberg,* 453 U.S. 57, 67 (1981). But the fact that legislation that raises armies is subject to First Amendment constraints does not mean that we ignore the purpose of this legislation when determining its constitutionality; as we recognized in *Rostker,* "judicial deference . . . is at its apogee" when Congress legislates under its authority to raise and support armies.

. . .

Congress' power to regulate military recruiting under the Solomon Amendment is arguably greater because universities are free to decline the federal funds. In *Grove City College v. Bell*, 465 U.S. 555, 575–576 (1984), we rejected a private college's claim that conditioning federal funds on its compliance with Title IX of the Education Amendments of 1972 violated the First Amendment. We thought this argument "warrant[ed] only brief consideration" because "Congress is free to attach reasonable and unambiguous conditions to federal financial assistance that educational institutions are not obligated to accept." We concluded that no First Amendment violation had occurred—without reviewing the substance of the First Amendment claims—because Grove City could decline the Government's funds.

Other decisions, however, recognize a limit on Congress' ability to place conditions on the receipt of funds. We recently held that " 'the government may not deny a benefit to a person on a basis that infringes his constitutionally protected . . . freedom of speech even if he has no entitlement to that benefit.' " *United States v. Am. Library Ass'n*, 539 U.S. 194, 210 (2003) (quoting *Board of Comm'rs, Wabaunsee Cty. v. Umbehr*, 518 U.S. 668, 674 (1996)). Under this principle, known as the unconstitutional conditions doctrine, the Solomon Amendment would be unconstitutional if Congress could not directly require universities to provide military recruiters equal access to their students.

This case does not require us to determine when a condition placed on university funding goes beyond the "reasonable" choice offered in *Grove City* and becomes an unconstitutional condition. It is clear that a funding condition cannot be unconstitutional if it could be constitutionally imposed directly. *See Speiser v. Randall*, 357 U.S. 513, 526 (1958). Because the First Amendment would not prevent Congress from directly imposing the Solomon Amendment's access requirement, the statute does not place an unconstitutional condition on the receipt of federal funds.

The Solomon Amendment neither limits what law schools may say nor requires them to say anything. Law schools remain free under the statute to express whatever views they may have on the military's congressionally mandated employment policy, all the while retaining eligibility for federal funds. *See* Tr. of Oral Arg. 25 (Solicitor General acknowledging that law schools "could put signs on the bulletin board next to the door, they could engage in speech, they could help organize student protests"). As a general matter, the Solomon Amendment regulates conduct, not speech. It affects what law schools must *do*—afford equal access to military recruiters—not what they may or may not *say*.

Nevertheless, the Third Circuit concluded that the Solomon Amendment violates law schools' freedom of speech in a number of ways. First, in assisting military recruiters, law schools provide some services, such as sending e-mails and distributing flyers, that clearly involve speech. The Court of Appeals held that in supplying these services law schools are unconstitutionally compelled to speak the Government's message. Second, military recruiters are, to some extent, speaking while they are on campus. The Court of Appeals held that, by forcing law schools to permit the military

on campus to express its message, the Solomon Amendment unconstitutionally requires law schools to host or accommodate the military's speech.
Third, although the Court of Appeals thought that the Solomon Amendment
regulated speech, it held in the alternative that, if the statute regulates
conduct, this conduct is expressive and regulating it unconstitutionally
infringes law schools' right to engage in expressive conduct. We consider
each issue in turn.[4]

Some of this Court's leading First Amendment precedents have established the principle that freedom of speech prohibits the government from
telling people what they must say. In *West Virginia Bd. of Ed. v. Barnette*, 319
U.S. 624, 642 (1943), we held unconstitutional a state law requiring schoolchildren to recite the Pledge of Allegiance and to salute the flag. And in
Wooley v. Maynard, 430 U.S. 705, 717 (1977), we held unconstitutional
another that required New Hampshire motorists to display the state motto—
"Live Free or Die"—on their license plates.

The Solomon Amendment does not require any similar expression by
law schools. Nonetheless, recruiting assistance provided by the schools often
includes elements of speech. For example, schools may send e-mails or post
notices on bulletin boards on an employer's behalf. Law schools offering such
services to other recruiters must also send e-mails and post notices on behalf
of the military to comply with the Solomon Amendment. As FAIR points out,
these compelled statements of fact ("The U. S. Army recruiter will meet
interested students in Room 123 at 11 a.m."), like compelled statements of
opinion, are subject to First Amendment scrutiny.

This sort of recruiting assistance, however, is a far cry from the compelled speech in *Barnette* and *Wooley*. The Solomon Amendment, unlike the
laws at issue in those cases, does not dictate the content of the speech at all,
which is only "compelled" if, and to the extent, the school provides such
speech for other recruiters. There is nothing in this case approaching a
Government-mandated pledge or motto that the school must endorse.

The compelled speech to which the law schools point is plainly incidental to the Solomon Amendment's regulation of conduct, and "it has never
been deemed an abridgment of freedom of speech or press to make a course
of conduct illegal merely because the conduct was in part initiated, evidenced, or carried out by means of language, either spoken, written, or
printed." *Giboney v. Empire Storage & Ice Co.*, 336 U.S. 490, 502 (1949).
Congress, for example, can prohibit employers from discriminating in hiring
on the basis of race. The fact that this will require an employer to take down
a sign reading "White Applicants Only" hardly means that the law should be
analyzed as one regulating the employer's speech rather than conduct. *See*

---

4. The Court of Appeals also held that
the Solomon Amendment violated the First
Amendment because it compelled law schools
to subsidize the Government's speech "by putting demands on the law schools' employees
and resources." We do not consider the law
schools' assistance to raise the issue of subsidizing Government speech as that concept has
been used in our cases. *See* Johanns v. Live-
stock Mktg. Ass'n, 544 U.S. 550, 559 (2005).
The accommodations the law schools must
provide to military recruiters are minimal, are

not of a monetary nature, and are extended to
all employers recruiting on campus, not just
the Government. And in *Johanns*, which was
decided after the Third Circuit's decision in
this case, we noted that our previous com-
pelled-subsidy cases involved subsidizing private speech, and we held that "[c]itizens may
challenge compelled support of private
speech, but have no First Amendment right
not to fund government speech." The military
recruiters' speech is clearly Government
speech.

R.A.V. v. St. Paul, 505 U.S. 377, 389 (1992) ("[W]ords can in some circumstances violate laws directed not against speech but against conduct"). Compelling a law school that sends scheduling e-mails for other recruiters to send one for a military recruiter is simply not the same as forcing a student to pledge allegiance, or forcing a Jehovah's Witness to display the motto "Live Free or Die," and it trivializes the freedom protected in *Barnette* and *Wooley* to suggest that it is.

Our compelled-speech cases are not limited to the situation in which an individual must personally speak the government's message. We have also in a number of instances limited the government's ability to force one speaker to host or accommodate another speaker's message. *See Hurley v. Irish–American Gay, Lesbian and Bisexual Group of Boston, Inc.*, 515 U.S. 557, 566 (1995) (state law cannot require a parade to include a group whose message the parade's organizer does not wish to send); *Pacific Gas & Elec. Co. v. Public Util. Comm'n of Cal.*, 475 U.S. 1, 20–21 (1986)(plurality opinion); *accord, id.*, at 25 (Marshall, J., concurring in judgment) (state agency cannot require a utility company to include a third-party newsletter in its billing envelope); *Miami Herald Publishing Co. v. Tornillo*, 418 U.S. 241, 258 (1974) (right-of-reply statute violates editors' right to determine the content of their newspapers). Relying on these precedents, the Third Circuit concluded that the Solomon Amendment unconstitutionally compels law schools to accommodate the military's message "[b]y requiring schools to include military recruiters in the interviews and recruiting receptions the schools arrange."

The compelled-speech violation in each of our prior cases, however, resulted from the fact that the complaining speaker's own message was affected by the speech it was forced to accommodate. The expressive nature of a parade was central to our holding in *Hurley*. 515 U.S. at 568 ("Parades are . . . a form of expression, not just motion, and the inherent expressiveness of marching to make a point explains our cases involving protest marches"). We concluded that because "every participating unit affects the message conveyed by the [parade's] private organizers," a law dictating that a particular group must be included in the parade "alter[s] the expressive content of th[e] parade." As a result, we held that the State's public accommodation law, as applied to a private parade, "violates the fundamental rule of protection under the First Amendment, that a speaker has the autonomy to choose the content of his own message."

The compelled-speech violations in *Tornillo* and *Pacific Gas* also resulted from interference with a speaker's desired message. In *Tornillo*, we recognized that "the compelled printing of a reply . . . tak[es] up space that could be devoted to other material the newspaper may have preferred to print," and therefore concluded that this right-of-reply statute infringed the newspaper editors' freedom of speech by altering the message the paper wished to express. The same is true in *Pacific Gas*. There, the utility company regularly included its newsletter, which we concluded was protected speech, in its billing envelope. Thus, when the state agency ordered the utility to send a third-party newsletter four times a year, it interfered with the utility's ability to communicate its own message in its newsletter. A plurality of the Court likened this to the situation in *Tornillo* and held that the forced inclusion of the other newsletter interfered with the utility's own message.

In this case, accommodating the military's message does not affect the law schools' speech, because the schools are not speaking when they host interviews and recruiting receptions. Unlike a parade organizer's choice of parade contingents, a law school's decision to allow recruiters on campus is not inherently expressive. Law schools facilitate recruiting to assist their students in obtaining jobs. A law school's recruiting services lack the expressive quality of a parade, a newsletter, or the editorial page of a newspaper; its accommodation of a military recruiter's message is not compelled speech because the accommodation does not sufficiently interfere with any message of the school.

The schools respond that if they treat military and nonmilitary recruiters alike in order to comply with the Solomon Amendment, they could be viewed as sending the message that they see nothing wrong with the military's policies, when they do. We rejected a similar argument in *Prune-Yard Shopping Center v. Robins*, 447 U.S. 74 (1980). In that case, we upheld a state law requiring a shopping center owner to allow certain expressive activities by others on its property. We explained that there was little likelihood that the views of those engaging in the expressive activities would be identified with the owner, who remained free to disassociate himself from those views and who was "not . . . being compelled to affirm [a] belief in any governmentally prescribed position or view."

The same is true here. Nothing about recruiting suggests that law schools agree with any speech by recruiters, and nothing in the Solomon Amendment restricts what the law schools may say about the military's policies. We have held that high school students can appreciate the difference between speech a school sponsors and speech the school permits because legally required to do so, pursuant to an equal access policy. *Board of Educ. of Westside Community Schools v. Mergens*, 496 U.S. 226, 250 (1990) (plurality opinion); *accord, id.*, at 268 (Marshall, J., concurring in judgment). . . .

Having rejected the view that the Solomon Amendment impermissibly regulates *speech*, we must still consider whether the expressive nature of the *conduct* regulated by the statute brings that conduct within the First Amendment's protection. In *O'Brien*, we recognized that some forms of " 'symbolic speech' " were deserving of First Amendment protection. But we rejected the view that "conduct can be labeled 'speech' whenever the person engaging in the conduct intends thereby to express an idea." Instead, we have extended First Amendment protection only to conduct that is inherently expressive. In *Texas v. Johnson*, 491 U.S. 397, 406 (1989), for example, we applied *O'Brien* and held that burning the American flag was sufficiently expressive to warrant First Amendment protection.

Unlike flag burning, the conduct regulated by the Solomon Amendment is not inherently expressive. Prior to the adoption of the Solomon Amendment's equal-access requirement, law schools "expressed" their disagreement with the military by treating military recruiters differently from other recruiters. But these actions were expressive only because the law schools accompanied their conduct with speech explaining it. For example, the point of requiring military interviews to be conducted on the undergraduate campus is not "overwhelmingly apparent." An observer who sees military recruiters interviewing away from the law school has no way of knowing whether the law school is expressing its disapproval of the military, all the law school's interview rooms are full, or the military recruiters decided for reasons of their own that they would rather interview someplace else.

The expressive component of a law school's actions is not created by the conduct itself but by the speech that accompanies it. The fact that such explanatory speech is necessary is strong evidence that the conduct at issue here is not so inherently expressive that it warrants protection under *O'Brien*. If combining speech and conduct were enough to create expressive conduct, a regulated party could always transform conduct into "speech" simply by talking about it. For instance, if an individual announces that he intends to express his disapproval of the Internal Revenue Service by refusing to pay his income taxes, we would have to apply *O'Brien* to determine whether the Tax Code violates the First Amendment. Neither *O'Brien* nor its progeny supports such a result.

Although the Third Circuit also concluded that *O'Brien* does not apply, it held in the alternative that the Solomon Amendment does not pass muster under *O'Brien* because the Government failed to produce evidence establishing that the Solomon Amendment was necessary and effective. The Court of Appeals surmised that "the military has ample resources to recruit through alternative means," suggesting "loan repayment programs" and "television and radio advertisements." As a result, the Government—according to the Third Circuit—failed to establish that the statute's burden on speech is no greater than essential to furthering its interest in military recruiting.

We disagree with the Court of Appeals' reasoning and result. We have held that "an incidental burden on speech is no greater than is essential, and therefore is permissible under *O'Brien*, so long as the neutral regulation promotes a substantial government interest that would be achieved less effectively absent the regulation." *United States v. Albertini*, 472 U.S. 675, 689 (1985). The Solomon Amendment clearly satisfies this requirement. Military recruiting promotes the substantial Government interest in raising and supporting the Armed Forces—an objective that would be achieved less effectively if the military were forced to recruit on less favorable terms than other employers. The Court of Appeals' proposed alternative methods of recruiting are beside the point. The issue is not whether other means of raising an army and providing for a navy might be adequate. *See id.*, at 689 (regulations are not "invalid simply because there is some imaginable alternative that might be less burdensome on speech"). That is a judgment for Congress, not the courts. *See* U.S. Const., Art. I, § 8, cls. 12–13; *Rostker*, 453 U.S. at 64–65. It suffices that the means chosen by Congress add to the effectiveness of military recruitment. Accordingly, even if the Solomon Amendment were regarded as regulating expressive conduct, it would not violate the First Amendment under *O'Brien*.

The Solomon Amendment does not violate law schools' freedom of speech, but the First Amendment's protection extends beyond the right to speak. We have recognized a First Amendment right to associate for the purpose of speaking, which we have termed a "right of expressive association." *See, e.g., BSA v. Dale*, 530 U.S. 640, 644 (2000). The reason we have extended First Amendment protection in this way is clear: The right to speak is often exercised most effectively by combining one's voice with the voices of others. *See Roberts v. United States Jaycees*, 468 U.S. 609, 622 (1984). If the government were free to restrict individuals' ability to join together and speak, it could essentially silence views that the First Amendment is intended to protect.

FAIR argues that the Solomon Amendment violates law schools' freedom of expressive association. According to FAIR, law schools' ability to express their message that discrimination on the basis of sexual orientation is wrong is significantly affected by the presence of military recruiters on campus and the schools' obligation to assist them. Relying heavily on our decision in *Dale*, the Court of Appeals agreed.

In *Dale*, we held that the Boy Scouts' freedom of expressive association was violated by New Jersey's public accommodations law, which required the organization to accept a homosexual as a scoutmaster. After determining that the Boy Scouts was an expressive association, that "the forced inclusion of Dale would significantly affect its expression," and that the State's interests did not justify this intrusion, we concluded that the Boy Scout's First Amendment rights were violated.

The Solomon Amendment, however, does not similarly affect a law school's associational rights. To comply with the statute, law schools must allow military recruiters on campus and assist them in whatever way the school chooses to assist other employers. Law schools therefore "associate" with military recruiters in the sense that they interact with them. But recruiters are not part of the law school. Recruiters are, by definition, outsiders who come onto campus for the limited purpose of trying to hire students—not to become members of the school's expressive association. This distinction is critical. Unlike the public accommodations law in *Dale*, the Solomon Amendment does not force a law school "to accept members it does not desire." The law schools *say* that allowing military recruiters equal access impairs their own expression by requiring them to associate with the recruiters, but just as saying conduct is undertaken for expressive purposes cannot make it symbolic speech, so too a speaker cannot "erect a shield" against laws requiring access "simply by asserting" that mere association "would impair its message."

FAIR correctly notes that the freedom of expressive association protects more than just a group's membership decisions. For example, we have held laws unconstitutional that require disclosure of membership lists for groups seeking anonymity, *Brown v. Socialist Workers '74 Campaign Comm.*, 459 U.S. 87, 101–102 (1982), or impose penalties or withhold benefits based on membership in a disfavored group, *Healy v. James*, 408 U.S. 169, 180–184 (1972). Although these laws did not directly interfere with an organization's composition, they made group membership less attractive, raising the same First Amendment concerns about affecting the group's ability to express its message.

The Solomon Amendment has no similar effect on a law school's associational rights. Students and faculty are free to associate to voice their disapproval of the military's message; nothing about the statute affects the composition of the group by making group membership less desirable. The Solomon Amendment therefore does not violate a law school's First Amendment rights. A military recruiter's mere presence on campus does not violate a law school's right to associate, regardless of how repugnant the law school considers the recruiter's message.

. . .

In this case, FAIR has attempted to stretch a number of First Amendment doctrines well beyond the sort of activities these doctrines protect. The law schools object to having to treat military recruiters like other recruiters, but that regulation of conduct does not violate the First Amendment. To the extent that the Solomon Amendment incidentally affects expression, the law schools' effort to cast themselves as just like the schoolchildren in *Barnette*, the parade organizers in *Hurley*, and the Boy Scouts in *Dale* plainly overstates the expressive nature of their activity and the impact of the Solomon Amendment on it, while exaggerating the reach of our First Amendment precedents.

Because Congress could require law schools to provide equal access to military recruiters without violating the schools' freedoms of speech or association, the Court of Appeals erred in holding that the Solomon Amendment likely violates the First Amendment. We therefore reverse the judgment of the Third Circuit and remand the case for further proceedings consistent with this opinion.

Questions and Comments on *Rumsfeld v. FAIR*

1. The implementation regulations for the Solomon Amendment require:

> access to students on their campuses in a manner that is at least equal in quality and scope to the access to campuses and to students provided to any other employer, or access to student-recruiting information. The term "equal in quality and scope" means the same access to campus and students provided by the school to the nonmilitary recruiters or employers receiving the most favorable access.

Military Recruiting and Reserve Officer Training Corps Program Access to Institutions of Higher Education, 73 Fed. Reg. 16525 (Mar. 28, 2008) (to be codified at 32 C.F.R. pt. 216). Does the statute authorize this standard?

2. After *FAIR*, at least three law schools decided to forgo federal funding and to refuse to allow military recruiters on campus. Major Anita J. Fitch, *The Solomon Amendment: A War on Campus*, ARMY LAW., May 2006, at 12. All were freestanding law schools, that is, not attached to universities. Unlike the three schools that chose to forgo federal funding, many law schools are associated with universities that receive significant amounts of money for federal research. Harvard, for instance, receives more than $400 million in federal grants per year. Considering that most schools cannot risk losing federal funding, how can they voice their opposition to the military's policies? The majority opinion mentioned that protests, signs, and other forms of opposition could be voiced, but would doing so violate the law's mandate to treat military recruiters as well as recruiters receiving "the most favorable access"?

*

Appendix A

American Association of University Professors and Association of American Colleges 1940 Statement of Principles on Academic Freedom and Tenure With 1940 and 1970 Interpretive Comments

In 1940, following a series of joint conferences begun in 1934, representatives of the American Association of University Professors and of the Association of American Colleges agreed upon a restatement of principles set forth in the 1925 Conference Statement on Academic Freedom and Tenure. *This restatement is known to the profession as the* 1940 Statement of Principles on Academic Freedom and Tenure.

The 1940 Statement *is printed below, followed by Interpretive Comments as developed by representatives of the American Association of University Professors and the Association of American Colleges during 1969. The governing bodies of the associations, meeting respectively in November 1989 and January 1990, adopted several changes in language in order to remove gender-specific references from the original text.*

The purpose of this statement is to promote public understanding and support of academic freedom and tenure and agreement upon procedures to assure them in colleges and universities. Institutions of higher education are conducted for the common good and not to further the interest of either the individual teacher (The word "teacher" as used in this document is understood to include the investigator who is attached to an academic institution without teaching duties) or the institution as a whole. The common good depends upon the free search for truth and its free exposition.

Academic freedom is essential to these purposes and applies to both teaching and research. Freedom in research is fundamental to the advancement of truth. Academic freedom in its teaching aspect is fundamental for the protection of the rights of the teacher in teaching and of the student to freedom in learning. It carries with it duties correlative with rights.[1] (Bold-faced numbers in brackets refer to Interpretive Comments which follow.)

Tenure is a means to certain ends; specifically: (1) freedom of teaching and research and of extramural activities, and (2) a sufficient degree of economic security to make the profession attractive to men and women of ability. Freedom and economic security, hence, tenure, are indispensable to the success of an institution in fulfilling its obligations to its students and to society.

Academic Freedom

1. Teachers are entitled to full freedom in research and in the publication of the results, subject to the adequate performance of their other academic duties; but research for pecuniary return should be based upon an understanding with the authorities of the institution.

2. Teachers are entitled to freedom in the classroom in discussing their subject, but they should be careful not to introduce into their teaching controversial matter which has no relation to their subject.[2] Limitations of academic freedom because of religious or other aims of the institution should be clearly stated in writing at the time of the appointment.[3]

3.   College and university teachers are citizens, members of a learned profession, and officers of an educational institution. When they speak or write as citizens, they should be free from institutional censorship or discipline, but their special position in the community imposes special obligations. As scholars and educational officers, they should remember that the public may judge their profession and their institution by their utterances. Hence they should at all times be accurate, should exercise appropriate restraint, should show respect for the opinions of others, and should make every effort to indicate that they are not speaking for the institution.[4]

Academic Tenure

After the expiration of a probationary period, teachers or investigators should have permanent or continuous tenure, and their service should be terminated only for adequate cause, except in the case of retirement for age, or under extraordinary circumstances because of financial exigencies.

In the interpretation of this principle it is understood that the following represents acceptable academic practice:

1.   The precise terms and conditions of every appointment should be stated in writing and be in the possession of both institution and teacher before the appointment is consummated.

2.   Beginning with appointment to the rank of full-time instructor or a higher rank, [5] the probationary period should not exceed seven years, including within this period full-time service in all institutions of higher education; but subject to the proviso that when, after a term of probationary service of more than three years in one or more institutions, a teacher is called to another institution it may be agreed in writing that the new appointment is for a probationary period of not more than four years, even though thereby the person's total probationary period in the academic profession is extended beyond the normal maximum of seven years. [6] Notice should be given at least one year prior to the expiration of the probationary period if the teacher is not to be continued in service after the expiration of that period.[7]

3.   During the probationary period a teacher should have the academic freedom that all other members of the faculty have.[8]

4.   Termination for cause of a continuous appointment, or the dismissal for cause of a teacher previous to the expiration of a term appointment, should, if possible, be considered by both a faculty committee and the governing board of the institution. In all cases where the facts are in dispute, the accused teacher should be informed before the hearing in writing of the charges and should have the opportunity to be heard in his or her own defense by all bodies that pass judgment upon the case. The teacher should be permitted to be accompanied by an advisor of his or her own choosing who may act as counsel. There should be a full stenographic record of the hearing available to the parties concerned. In the hearing of charges of incompetence the testimony should include that of teachers and other scholars, either from the teacher's own or from other institutions. Teachers on continuous appointment who are dismissed for reasons not involving moral turpitude should receive their salaries for at least a year from the date of notification of dismissal whether or not they are continued in their duties at the institution.[9]

5.   Termination of a continuous appointment because of financial exigency should be demonstrably bona fide.

1940 Interpretations

At the conference of representatives of the American Association of University Professors and of the Association of American Colleges on November 7–8, 1940, the following interpretations of the 1940 *Statement of Principles on Academic Freedom and Tenure* were agreed upon:

1.   That its operation should not be retroactive.

2.   That all tenure claims of teachers appointed prior to the endorsement should be determined in accordance with the principles set forth in the 1925 *Conference Statement on Academic Freedom and Tenure*.

3.   If the administration of a college or university feels that a teacher has not observed the admonitions of paragraph (c) of the section on Academic Freedom and believes that the extramural utterances of the teacher have been such as to raise grave doubts concerning the teacher's fitness for his or her position, it may proceed to file charges under paragraph (a)(4) of the section on Academic Tenure. In pressing such charges the administration should remember that teachers are citizens and should be accorded the freedom of citizens. In such cases the administration must assume full responsibility, and the American Association of University Professors and the Association of American Colleges are free to make an investigation.

1970 Interpretive Comments

Following extensive discussions on the 1940 Statement of Principles on Academic Freedom and Tenure with leading educational associations and with individual faculty members and administrators, a joint committee of the AAUP and the Association of American Colleges met during 1969 to reevaluate this key policy statement. On the basis of the comments received, and the discussions that ensued, the joint committee felt the preferable approach was to formulate interpretations of the Statement in terms of the experience gained in implementing and applying the Statement for over thirty years and of adapting it to current needs.

The committee submitted to the two associations for their consideration the following "Interpretive Comments." These interpretations were adopted by the Council of the American Association of University Professors in April 1970 and endorsed by the Fifty-sixth Annual Meeting as Association policy.

In the thirty years since their promulgation, the principles of the 1940 Statement *of Principles on Academic Freedom and Tenure* have undergone a substantial amount of refinement. This has evolved through a variety of processes, including customary acceptance, understandings mutually arrived at between institutions and professors or their representatives, investigations and reports by the American Association of University Professors, and formulations of statements by that association either alone or in conjunction with the Association of American Colleges. These comments represent the attempt of the two associations, as the original sponsors of the 1940 *Statement*, to formulate the most important of these refinements. Their incorporation here as Interpretive Comments is based upon the premise that the 1940 *Statement* is not a static code but a fundamental document designed to set a framework of norms to guide adaptations to changing times and circumstances.

Also, there have been relevant developments in the law itself reflecting a growing insistence by the courts on due process within the academic community which parallels the essential concepts of the 1940 *Statement*; particularly relevant is the identification by the Supreme Court of academic freedom as a right protected by the First Amendment. As the Supreme Court said in *Keyishian v. Board of Regents* 385 U.S. 589 (1967), "Our Nation is deeply committed to safeguarding academic freedom, which is of transcendent value to all of us and not merely to the teachers concerned. That freedom is therefore a special concern of the First Amendment, which does not tolerate laws that cast a pall of orthodoxy over the classroom."

The numbers refer to the designated portion of the 1940 *Statement* on which interpretive comment is made.

1. The Association of American Colleges and the American Association of University Professors have long recognized that membership in the academic profession carries with it special responsibilities. Both associations either separately or jointly have consistently affirmed these responsibilities in major policy statements, providing guidance to professors in their utterances as citizens, in the exercise of their responsibilities to the institution and to students, and in their conduct when resigning from their institution or when undertaking government-sponsored research. Of particular relevance is the Statement on Professional Ethics, adopted in 1966 as Association policy. (A revision, adopted in 1987, was published in Academe: Bulletin of the AAUP 73 [July–August 1987]: 49.)

2. The intent of this statement is not to discourage what is "controversial." Controversy is at the heart of the free academic inquiry which the entire statement is designed to foster. The passage serves to underscore the need for teachers to avoid persistently intruding material which has no relation to their subject.

3. Most church-related institutions no longer need or desire the departure from the principle of academic freedom implied in the 1940 Statement, and we do not now endorse such a departure.

4. This paragraph is the subject of an interpretation adopted by the sponsors of the 1940 Statement immediately following its endorsement which reads as follows:

If the administration of a college or university feels that a teacher has not observed the admonitions of paragraph (c) of the section on Academic Freedom and believes that the extramural utterances of the teacher have been such as to raise grave doubts concerning the teacher's fitness for his or her position, it may proceed to file charges under paragraph (a)(4) of the section on Academic Tenure. In pressing such charges the administration should remember that teachers are citizens and should be accorded the freedom of citizens. In such cases the administration must assume full responsibility, and the American Association of University Professors and the Association of American Colleges are free to make an investigation.

Paragraph (c) of the 1940 Statement should also be interpreted in keeping with the 1964 "Committee A Statement on Extramural Utterances" (AAUP Bulletin 51 [1965]: 29), which states inter alia: "The controlling principle is that a faculty member's expression of opinion as a citizen cannot constitute grounds for dismissal unless it clearly demonstrates the faculty member's unfitness for his or her position. Extramural utterances rarely bear upon the faculty member's fitness for the position. Moreover, a final decision should take into account the faculty member's entire record as a teacher and scholar."

*-*Paragraph V of the Statement on Professional Ethics also deals with the nature of the "special obligations" of the teacher. The paragraph reads as follows:

As members of their community, professors have the rights and obligations of other citizens. Professors measure the urgency of other obligations in the light of their responsibilities to their subject, to their students, to their profession, and to their institution. When they speak or act as private persons they avoid creating the impression of speaking or acting for their college or university. As citizens engaged in a profession that depends upon freedom for its health and integrity, professors have a particular obligation to promote conditions of free inquiry and to further public understanding of academic freedom.

Both the protection of academic freedom and the requirements of academic responsibility apply not only to the full-time probationary as well as to the tenured teacher, but also to all others, such as part-time faculty and teaching assistants, who exercise teaching responsibilities.

5. The concept of "rank of full-time instructor or a higher rank" is intended to include any person who teaches a full-time load regardless of the teacher's specific title. (For a discussion of this question, see the "Report of the Special Committee on Academic Personnel Ineligible for Tenure," AAUP Bulletin 52 [1966]: 280–82.)

6. In calling for an agreement "in writing" on the amount of credit for a faculty member's prior service at other institutions, the Statement furthers the general policy of full understanding by the professor of the terms and conditions of the appointment. It does not necessarily follow that a professor's tenure rights have been violated because of the absence of a written agreement on this matter. Nonetheless, especially because of the variation in permissible institutional practices, a written understanding concerning these matters at the time of appointment is particularly appropriate and advantageous to both the individual and the institution. (For a more detailed statement on this question, see "On Crediting Prior Service Elsewhere as Part of the Probationary Period," AAUP Bulletin64 [1978]: 274–75.)

7. The effect of this subparagraph is that a decision on tenure, favorable or unfavorable, must be made at least twelve months prior to the completion of the probationary period. If the decision is negative, the appointment for the following year becomes a terminal one. If the decision is affirmative, the provisions in the 1940 Statement with respect to the termination of services of teachers or investigators after the expiration of a probationary period should apply from the date when the favorable decision is made.

The general principle of notice contained in this paragraph is developed with greater specificity in the *Standards for Notice of Nonreappointment*, endorsed by the Fiftieth Annual Meeting of the American Association of University Professors (1964). These standards are:

Notice of nonreappointment, or of intention not to recommend reappointment to the governing board, should be given in writing in accordance with the following standards:

1. *Not later than March 1 of the first academic year of service*, if the appointment expires at the end of that year; or, if a one-year appointment terminates during an academic year, at least three months in advance of its termination.

2. *Not later than December 15 of the second academic year of service,* if the appointment expires at the end of that year; or, if an initial two-year appointment terminates during an academic year, at least six months in advance of its termination.

3. At least twelve months before the expiration of an appointment after two or more years in the institution.

Other obligations, both of institutions and of individuals, are described in the *Statement on Recruitment and Resignation of Faculty Members,* as endorsed by the Association of American Colleges and the American Association of University Professors in 1961.

8. The freedom of probationary teachers is enhanced by the establishment of a regular procedure for the periodic evaluation and assessment of the teacher's academic performance during probationary status. Provision should be made for regularized procedures for the consideration of complaints by probationary teachers that their academic freedom has been violated. One suggested procedure to serve these purposes is contained in the *Recommended Institutional Regulations on Academic Freedom and Tenure,* prepared by the American Association of University Professors.

9. A further specification of the academic due process to which the teacher is entitled under this paragraph is contained in the *Statement on Procedural Standards in Faculty Dismissal Proceedings,* jointly approved by the American Association of University Professors and the Association of American Colleges in 1958. This interpretive document deals with the issue of suspension, about which the 1940 Statement is silent.

The 1958 *Statement* provides: "Suspension of the faculty member during he proceedings is justified only if immediate harm to the faculty member or others is threatened by the faculty member's continuance. Unless legal considerations forbid, any such suspension should be with pay." A suspension which is not followed by either reinstatement or the opportunity for a hearing is in effect a summary dismissal in violation of academic due process.

The concept of "moral turpitude" identifies the exceptional case in which the professor may be denied a year's teaching or pay in whole or in part. The statement applies to that kind of behavior which goes beyond simply warranting discharge and is so utterly blameworthy as to make it inappropriate to require the offering of a year's teaching or pay. The standard is not that the moral sensibilities of persons in the particular community have been affronted. The standard is behavior that would evoke condemnation by the academic community generally.

Endorsers

Association of American Colleges and Universities—1941

American Association of University Professors—1941

American Library Association (adapted for librarians)—1946

Association of American Law Schools—1946

American Political Science Association—1947

American Association for Higher Education—1950

American Association of Colleges for Teacher Education—1950

Eastern Psychological Association—1950

Southern Society for Philosophy and Psychology—1953

American Psychological Association—1961

American Historical Association—1961

Modern Language Association of America–1962

American Economic Association—1962

American Agricultural Economics Association—1962

Midwest Sociological Society—1963

Organization of American Historians—1963

American Philological Association—1963

American Council of Learned Societies—1963

Speech Communication Association—1963

American Sociological Association—1963

Southern Historical Association—1963

American Studies Association—1963

Association of American Geographers—1963

Southern Economic Association—1963

Classical Association of the Middle West and South—1964

Southwestern Social Science Association—1964

Archaeological Institute of America—1964

Southern Management Association—1964

American Theatre Association—1964

South Central Modern Language Association—1964

Southwestern Philosophical Society—1964

Council of Independent Colleges—1965

Mathematical Association of America—1965

Arizona–Nevada Academy of Science—1965

American Risk and Insurance Association—1965

Academy of Management—1965

American Catholic Historical Association—1966

American Catholic Philosophical Association—1966

Association for Education in Journalism and Mass Communication—1966

Western History Association—1966

Mountain–Plains Philosophical Conference—1966

Society of American Archivists—1966

Southeastern Psychological Association—1966

Southern Speech Communication Association—1966

American Association for the Advancement of Slavic Studies—1967

American Mathematical Society—1967

College Theology Society—1967

Council on Social Work Education—1967

American Association of Colleges of Pharmacy—1967

American Academy of Religion—1967

Association for the Sociology of Religion—1967

American Society of Journalism School Administrators—1967

John Dewey Society—1967

South Atlantic Modern Language Association—1967

American Finance Association—1967

Association for Social Economics—1967

Phi Beta Kappa Society—1968

American Society of Christian Ethics—1968

American Association of Teachers of French—1968

Eastern Finance Association—1968

American Association for Chinese Studies—1968

American Society of Plant Physiologists—1968

University Film and Video Association—1968

American Dialect Society—1968

American Speech–Language–Hearing Association—1968

Association of Social and Behavioral Scientists—1968

College English Association—1968

National College Physical Education Association for Men—1969

American Real Estate and Urban Economics Association—1969

History of Education Society—1969

Council for Philosophical Studies—1969

American Musicological Society—1969

American Association of Teachers of Spanish and Portuguese—1969

Texas Community College Teachers Association—1970

College Art Association of America—1970

Society of Professors of Education—1970

American Anthropological Association—1970

Association of Theological Schools—1970

Association of Schools of Journalism and Mass Communication-1971

American Business Law Association—1971

American Council for the Arts—1972

New York State Mathematics Association of Two–Year Colleges—1972

College Language Association—1973

Pennsylvania Historical Association—1973

Massachusetts Regional Community College Faculty Association—1973

American Philosophical Association—1974 (Endorsed by the Association's Western Division in—1952, Eastern Division in—1953, and Pacific Division in—1962.)

American Classical League—1974

American Comparative Literature Association—1974

Rocky Mountain Modern Language Association—1974

Society of Architectural Historians—1975

American Statistical Association—1975

American Folklore Society—1975

Association for Asian Studies—1975

Linguistic Society of America—1975

African Studies Association—1975

American Institute of Biological Sciences—1975

North American Conference on British Studies—1975

Sixteenth–Century Studies Conference—1975

Texas Association of College Teachers—1976

Society for Spanish and Portuguese Historical Studies—1976

Association for Jewish Studies—1976

Western Speech Communication Association—1976

Texas Association of Colleges for Teacher Education—1977

Metaphysical Society of America—1977

American Chemical Society—1977

Texas Library Association—1977

American Society for Legal History—1977

Iowa Higher Education Association—1977

American Physical Therapy Association—1979

North Central Sociological Association—1980

Dante Society of America—1980

Association for Communication Administration—1981

American Association of Physics Teachers—1982

Middle East Studies Association—1982

National Education Association—1985

American Institute of Chemists—1985

American Association of Teachers of German—1985

American Association of Teachers of Italian—1985

American Association for Applied Linguistics—1986

American Association of Teachers of Slavic and East European Languages—1986

American Association for Cancer Education—1986

American Society of Church History—1986

Oral History Association—1987

Society for French Historical Studies—1987

History of Science Society—1987

American Association of Pharmaceutical Scientists—1988

American Association for Clinical Chemistry—1988

Council for Chemical Research—1988

Association for the Study of Higher Education—1988

Association for Psychological Science—1989

University and College Labor Education Association—1989

Society for Neuroscience—1989

Renaissance Society of America—1989

Society of Biblical Literature—1989

National Science Teachers Association—1989

Medieval Academy of America—1990

American Society of Agronomy—1990

Crop Science Society of America—1990

Soil Science Society of America—1990

International Society of Protistologists-1990

Society for Ethnomusicology—1990

American Association of Physicists in Medicine—1990

Animal Behavior Society—1990

Illinois Community College Faculty Association—1990

American Society for Theatre Research—1990

National Council of Teachers of English—1991

Latin American Studies Association—1992

Society for Cinema and Media Studies—1992

American Society for Eighteenth–Century Studies—1992

Council of Colleges of Arts and Sciences—1992

American Society for Aesthetics—1992

Association for the Advancement of Baltic Studies—1994

American Council of Teachers of Russian—1994

Council of Teachers of Southeast Asian Languages—1994

American Association of Teachers of Arabic—1994

Association of Teachers of Japanese—1994

Academic Senate for California Community Colleges—1996

National Council for the Social Studies—1996

Council of Academic Programs in Communication Sciences and Disorders—1996

Association for Women in Mathematics—1997

Philosophy of Time Society—1998

World Communication Association—1999

The Historical Society—1999

Association for Theatre in Higher Education—1999

National Association for Ethnic Studies—1999

Association of Ancient Historians—1999

American Culture Association—1999

American Conference for Irish Studies—1999

Society for Philosophy in the Contemporary World—1999

Eastern Communication Association—1999

Association for Canadian Studies in the United States—1999

American Association for the History of Medicine—2000

Missouri Association of Faculty Senates—2000

Association for Symbolic Logic—2000

Chinese Historians in the United States—2001

The Group for the Use of Psychology in History—2001

Society for the Scientific Study of Religion—2001

Eastern Sociological Society—2001

American Jewish Historical Society's Academic Council—2001

Society for German–American Studies—2001

American Society of Criminology—2001

New England Historical Association—2001

Society for Historians of the Gilded Age & Progressive Era—2002

Eastern Sociological Society—2001

Chinese Historian in the United States—2001

Community College Humanities Association—2002

Immigration and Ethnic History Society—2002

Agriculture History Society—2004

National Council for Accreditation of Teacher Education—2005

American Council for the Teaching of Foreign Languages—2005

Society for the study of Social Biology—2005

Association of Black Sociologists—2005

Society for the Study of Social Problems—2005

Dictionary Society of North America—2005

Society for Buddhist–Christian Studies—2005

National Women's Studies Association—2006

National Coalition for History—2006

Society for Armenian Studies—2006

Society for the Advancement of Scandinavian Study—2006

American Physiological Society—2006

College Forum of the National Council of Teachers of English—2006

Society for Military History—2006

Society for Industrial and Applied Mathematics—2006

Association for Research on Ethnicity and Nationalism in the Americas—2006

Society of Dance History Scholars—2006

Association of Literary Scholars and Critics—2006

Society for Applied Anthropology—2006

Society for Music Theory—2006

Society for Historians of American Foreign Relations—2006

American Society of Plant Taxonomists—2006

Law and Society Association—2006

Appendix B

Statement on Government of Colleges and Universities

The statement that follows is directed to governing board members, administrators, faculty members, students, and other persons in the belief that the colleges and universities of the United States have reached a stage calling for appropriately shared responsibility and cooperative action among the components of the academic institution. The statement is intended to foster constructive joint thought and action, both within the institutional structure and in protection of its integrity against improper intrusions.

It is not intended that the statement serve as a blueprint for governance on a specific campus or as a manual for the regulation of controversy among the components of an academic institution, although it is to be hoped that the principles asserted will lead to the correction of existing weaknesses and assist in the establishment of sound structures and procedures. The statement does not attempt to cover relations with those outside agencies that increasingly are controlling the resources and influencing the patterns of education in our institutions of higher learning: for example, the United States government, state legislatures, state commissions, interstate associations or compacts, and other interinstitutional arrangements. However, it is hoped that the statement will be helpful to these agencies in their consideration of educational matters.

Students are referred to in this statement as an institutional component coordinate in importance with trustees, administrators, and faculty. There is, however, no main section on students. The omission has two causes: (1) the changes now occurring in the status of American students have plainly outdistanced the analysis by the educational community, and an attempt to define the situation without thorough study might prove unfair to student interests, and (2) students do not in fact at present have a significant voice in the government of colleges and universities; it would be unseemly to obscure, by superficial equality of length of statement, what may be a serious lag entitled to separate and full confrontation. The concern for student status felt by the organizations issuing this statement is embodied in a note, "On Student Status," intended to stimulate the educational community to turn its attention to an important need.

This statement was jointly formulated by the American Association of University Professors, the American Council on Education (ACE), and the Association of Governing Boards of Universities and Colleges (AGB). In October 1966, the board of directors of the ACE took action by which its council "recognizes the statement as a significant step forward in the clarification of the respective roles of governing boards, faculties, and administrations," and "commends it to the institutions which are members of the Council." The Council of the AAUP adopted the statement in October 1966, and the Fifty-third Annual Meeting endorsed it in April 1967. In November 1966, the executive committee of the AGB took action by which that organization also "recognizes the statement as a significant step forward in the clarification of the respective roles of governing boards, faculties, and administrations," and "commends it to the governing boards which are members of the Association." (In April 1990, the Council of the AAUP adopted several changes in language in order to remove gender-specific references from the original text.)

1. Introduction

This statement is a call to mutual understanding regarding the government of colleges and universities. Understanding, based on community of interest and producing joint effort, is essential for at least three reasons. First, the academic institution, public or private, often has become less autonomous; buildings, research, and student tuition are supported by funds over which the college or university exercises a diminishing control. Legislative and executive governmental authorities, at all levels, play a part in the making of important decisions in academic policy. If these voices and forces are to be successfully heard and integrated, the academic institution must be in a position to meet them with its own generally unified view. Second, regard for the welfare of the institution remains important despite the mobility and interchange of scholars. Third, a college or university in which all the components are aware of their interdependence, of the usefulness of communication among themselves, and of the force of joint action will enjoy increased capacity to solve educational problems.

2. The Academic Institution: Joint Effort

a. *Preliminary Considerations.* The variety and complexity of the tasks performed by institutions of higher education produce an inescapable interdependence among governing board, administration, faculty, students, and others. The relationship calls for adequate communication among these components, and full opportunity for appropriate joint planning and effort.

Joint effort in an academic institution will take a variety of forms appropriate to the kinds of situations encountered. In some instances, an initial exploration or recommendation will be made by the president with consideration by the faculty at a later stage; in other instances, a first and essentially definitive recommendation will be made by the faculty, subject to the endorsement of the president and the governing board. In still others, a substantive contribution can be made when student leaders are responsibly involved in the process. Although the variety of such approaches may be wide, at least two general conclusions regarding joint effort seem clearly warranted: (1) important areas of action involve at one time or another the initiating capacity and decision-making participation of all the institutional components, and (2) differences in the weight of each voice, from one point to the next, should be determined by reference to the responsibility of each component for the particular matter at hand, as developed hereinafter.

b. *Determination of General Educational Policy.* The general educational policy, i.e., the objectives of an institution and the nature, range, and pace of its efforts, is shaped by the institutional charter or by law, by tradition and historical development, by the present needs of the community of the institution, and by the professional aspirations and standards of those directly involved in its work. Every board will wish to go beyond its formal trustee obligation to conserve the accomplishment of the past and to engage seriously with the future; every faculty will seek to conduct an operation worthy of scholarly standards of learning; every administrative officer will strive to meet his or her charge and to attain the goals of the institution. The interests of all are coordinate and related, and unilateral effort can lead to confusion or conflict. Essential to a solution is a reasonably explicit statement on general educational policy. Operating responsibility and authority, and procedures for continuing review, should be clearly defined in official regulations.

When an educational goal has been established, it becomes the responsibility primarily of the faculty to determine the appropriate curriculum and procedures of student instruction.

Special considerations may require particular accommodations: (1) a publicly supported institution may be regulated by statutory provisions, and (2) a church-controlled institution may be limited by its charter or bylaws. When such external requirements influence course content and the manner of instruction or research, they impair the educational effectiveness of the institution.

Such matters as major changes in the size or composition of the student body and the relative emphasis to be given to the various elements of the educational and research program should involve participation of governing board, administration, and faculty prior to final decision.

c. *Internal Operations of the Institution.* The framing and execution of long-range plans, one of the most important aspects of institutional responsibility, should be a central and continuing concern in the academic community.

Effective planning demands that the broadest possible exchange of information and opinion should be the rule for communication among the components of a college or university. The channels of communication should be established and maintained by joint endeavor. Distinction should be observed between the institutional system of communication and the system of responsibility for the making of decisions.

A second area calling for joint effort in internal operation is that of decisions regarding existing or prospective physical resources. The board, president, and faculty should all seek agreement on basic decisions regarding buildings and other facilities to be used in the educational work of the institution.

A third area is budgeting. The allocation of resources among competing demands is central in the formal responsibility of the governing board, in the administrative authority of the president, and in the educational function of the faculty. Each component should therefore have a voice in the determination of short-and long-range priorities, and each should receive appropriate analyses of past budgetary experience, reports on current budgets and expenditures, and short-and long-range budgetary projections. The function of each component in budgetary matters should be understood by all; the allocation of authority will determine the flow of information and the scope of participation in decisions.

Joint effort of a most critical kind must be taken when an institution chooses a new president. The selection of a chief administrative officer should follow upon a cooperative search by the governing board and the faculty, taking into consideration the opinions of others who are appropriately interested. The president should be equally qualified to serve both as the executive officer of the governing board and as the chief academic officer of the institution and the faculty. The president's dual role requires an ability to interpret to board and faculty the educational views and concepts of institutional government of the other. The president should have the confidence of the board and the faculty.

The selection of academic deans and other chief academic officers should be the responsibility of the president with the advice of, and in consultation with, the appropriate faculty.

Determinations of faculty status, normally based on the recommendations of the faculty groups involved, are discussed in Part 5 of this statement; but it should here be noted that the building of a strong faculty requires careful joint effort in such actions as staff selection and promotion and the granting of tenure. Joint action should also govern dismissals; the applicable principles and procedures in these matters are well established.[1]

d. *External Relations of the Institution.* Anyone—a member of the governing board, the president or other member of the administration, a member of the faculty, or a member of the student body or the alumni—affects the institution when speaking of it in public. An individual who speaks unofficially should so indicate. An individual who speaks officially for the institution, the board, the administration, the faculty, or the student body should be guided by established policy.

It should be noted that only the board speaks legally for the whole institution, although it may delegate responsibility to an agent.

The right of a board member, an administrative officer, a faculty member, or a student to speak on general educational questions or about the administration and operations of the individual's own institution is a part of that person's right as a citizen and should not be abridged by the institution.[2] There exist, of course, legal bounds relating to defamation of character, and there are questions of propriety.

3. The Academic Institution: The Governing Board

The governing board has a special obligation to ensure that the history of the college or university shall serve as a prelude and inspiration to the future. The board helps relate the institution to its chief community: for example, the community college to serve the educational needs of a defined population area or group, the church-controlled college to be cognizant of the announced position of its denomination, and the comprehensive university to discharge the many duties and to accept the appropriate new challenges which are its concern at the several levels of higher education.

The governing board of an institution of higher education in the United States operates, with few exceptions, as the final institutional authority. Private institutions are established by charters; public institutions are established by constitutional or statutory provisions. In private institutions the board is frequently self-perpetuating; in public colleges and universities the present membership of a board may be asked to suggest candidates for appointment. As a whole and individually, when the governing board confronts the problem of succession, serious attention should be given to

---

1. See the 1940 "Statement of Principles on Academic Freedom and Tenure," AAUP, *Policy Documents and Reports,* 10th ed. (Washington, D.C., 2006), 3–11, and the 1958 "Statement on Procedural Standards in Faculty Dismissal Proceedings," *ibid.,* 12–15. These statements were jointly adopted by the Association of American Colleges (now the Association of American Colleges and Universities) and the American Association of University Professors; the 1940 "Statement" has been endorsed by numerous learned and scientific societies and educational associations.

2. With respect to faculty members, the 1940 "Statement of Principles on Academic Freedom and Tenure" reads: "College and university teachers are citizens, members of a learned profession, and officers of an educational institution. When they speak or write as citizens, they should be free from institutional censorship or discipline, but their special position in the community imposes special obligations. As scholars and educational officers, they should remember that the public may judge their profession and their institution by their utterances. Hence they should at all times be accurate, should exercise appropriate restraint, should show respect for the opinions of others, and should make every effort to indicate that they are not speaking for the institution" (*Policy Documents and Reports,* 3–4).

obtaining properly qualified persons. Where public law calls for election of governing board members, means should be found to ensure the nomination of fully suited persons, and the electorate should be informed of the relevant criteria for board membership.

Since the membership of the board may embrace both individual and collective competence of recognized weight, its advice or help may be sought through established channels by other components of the academic community. The governing board of an institution of higher education, while maintaining a general overview, entrusts the conduct of administration to the administrative officers—the president and the deans—and the conduct of teaching and research to the faculty. The board should undertake appropriate self-limitation.

One of the governing board's important tasks is to ensure the publication of codified statements that define the overall policies and procedures of the institution under its jurisdiction.

The board plays a central role in relating the likely needs of the future to predictable resources; it has the responsibility for husbanding the endowment; it is responsible for obtaining needed capital and operating funds; and in the broadest sense of the term it should pay attention to personnel policy. In order to fulfill these duties, the board should be aided by, and may insist upon, the development of long-range planning by the administration and faculty. When ignorance or ill will threatens the institution or any part of it, the governing board must be available for support. In grave crises it will be expected to serve as a champion. Although the action to be taken by it will usually be on behalf of the president, the faculty, or the student body, the board should make clear that the protection it offers to an individual or a group is, in fact, a fundamental defense of the vested interests of society in the educational institution.[3]

4. The Academic Institution: The President

The president, as the chief executive officer of an institution of higher education, is measured largely by his or her capacity for institutional leadership. The president shares responsibility for the definition and attainment of goals, for administrative action, and for operating the communications system that links the components of the academic community. The president represents the institution to its many publics. The president's leadership role is supported by delegated authority from the board and faculty.

As the chief planning officer of an institution, the president has a special obligation to innovate and initiate. The degree to which a president can envision new horizons for the institution, and can persuade others to see

3. Traditionally, governing boards developed within the context of single-campus institutions. In more recent times, governing and coordinating boards have increasingly tended to develop at the multi-campus regional, systemwide, or statewide levels. As influential components of the academic community, these supra-campus bodies bear particular responsibility for protecting the autonomy of individual campuses or institutions under their jurisdiction and for implementing policies of shared responsibility. The American Association of University Professors regards the objectives and practices recommended in the "Statement on Government" as constituting equally appropriate guidelines for such supra-campus bodies, and looks toward continued development of practices that will facilitate application of such guidelines in this new context. [Preceding note adopted by the AAUP's Council in June 1978.]

them and to work toward them, will often constitute the chief measure of the president's administration.

The president must at times, with or without support, infuse new life into a department; relatedly, the president may at times be required, working within the concept of tenure, to solve problems of obsolescence. The president will necessarily utilize the judgments of the faculty but may also, in the interest of academic standards, seek outside evaluations by scholars of acknowledged competence.

It is the duty of the president to see to it that the standards and procedures in operational use within the college or university conform to the policy established by the governing board and to the standards of sound academic practice. It is also incumbent on the president to ensure that faculty views, including dissenting views, are presented to the board in those areas and on those issues where responsibilities are shared. Similarly, the faculty should be informed of the views of the board and the administration on like issues.

The president is largely responsible for the maintenance of existing institutional resources and the creation of new resources; has ultimate managerial responsibility for a large area of nonacademic activities; is responsible for public understanding; and by the nature of the office is the chief person who speaks for the institution. In these and other areas the president's work is to plan, to organize, to direct, and to represent. The presidential function should receive the general support of board and faculty.

5. The Academic Institution: The Faculty

The faculty has primary responsibility for such fundamental areas as curriculum, subject matter and methods of instruction, research, faculty status, and those aspects of student life which relate to the educational process.[4] On these matters the power of review or final decision lodged in the governing board or delegated by it to the president should be exercised adversely only in exceptional circumstances, and for reasons communicated to the faculty. It is desirable that the faculty should, following such communication, have opportunity for further consideration and further transmittal of its views to the president or board. Budgets, personnel limitations, the time element, and the policies of other groups, bodies, and agencies having jurisdiction over the institution may set limits to realization of faculty advice.

The faculty sets the requirements for the degrees offered in course, determines when the requirements have been met, and authorizes the president and board to grant the degrees thus achieved.

Faculty status and related matters are primarily a faculty responsibility; this area includes appointments, reappointments, decisions not to reappoint, promotions, the granting of tenure, and dismissal. The primary responsibility of the faculty for such matters is based upon the fact that its judgment is central to general educational policy. Furthermore, scholars in a particular field or activity have the chief competence for judging the work of their

---

4. With regard to student admissions, the faculty should have a meaningful role in establishing institutional policies, including the setting of standards for admission, and should be afforded opportunity for oversight of the entire admissions process. [Preceding note adopted by the Council in June 2002.]

colleagues; in such competence it is implicit that responsibility exists for both adverse and favorable judgments. Likewise, there is the more general competence of experienced faculty personnel committees having a broader charge. Determinations in these matters should first be by faculty action through established procedures, reviewed by the chief academic officers with the concurrence of the board. The governing board and president should, on questions of faculty status, as in other matters where the faculty has primary responsibility, concur with the faculty judgment except in rare instances and for compelling reasons which should be stated in detail.

The faculty should actively participate in the determination of policies and procedures governing salary increases.

The chair or head of a department, who serves as the chief representative of the department within an institution, should be selected either by departmental election or by appointment following consultation with members of the department and of related departments; appointments should normally be in conformity with department members' judgment. The chair or department head should not have tenure in office; tenure as a faculty member is a matter of separate right. The chair or head should serve for a stated term but without prejudice to reelection or to reappointment by procedures that involve appropriate faculty consultation. Board, administration, and faculty should all bear in mind that the department chair or head has a special obligation to build a department strong in scholarship and teaching capacity. Agencies for faculty participation in the government of the college or university should be established at each level where faculty responsibility is present. An agency should exist for the presentation of the views of the whole faculty. The structure and procedures for faculty participation should be designed, approved, and established by joint action of the components of the institution. Faculty representatives should be selected by the faculty according to procedures determined by the faculty.[5]

The agencies may consist of meetings of all faculty members of a department, school, college, division, or university system, or may take the form of faculty-elected executive committees in departments and schools and a faculty-elected senate or council for larger divisions or the institution as a whole.

The means of communication among the faculty, administration, and governing board now in use include: (1) circulation of memoranda and reports by board committees, the administration, and faculty committees; (2) joint ad hoc committees; (3) standing liaison committees; (4) membership of faculty members on administrative bodies; and (5) membership of faculty members on governing boards. Whatever the channels of communication, they should be clearly understood and observed.

On Student Status

When students in American colleges and universities desire to participate responsibly in the government of the institution they attend, their wish

---

5. The American Association of University Professors regards collective bargaining, properly used, as another means of achieving sound academic government. Where there is faculty collective bargaining, the parties should seek to ensure appropriate institutional governance structures which will protect the right of all faculty to participate in institutional governance in accordance with the "Statement on Government." [Preceding note adopted by the Council in June 1978.]

should be recognized as a claim to opportunity both for educational experience and for involvement in the affairs of their college or university. Ways should be found to permit significant student participation within the limits of attainable effectiveness. The obstacles to such participation are large and should not be minimized: inexperience, untested capacity, a transitory status which means that present action does not carry with it subsequent responsibility, and the inescapable fact that the other components of the institution are in a position of judgment over the students. It is important to recognize that student needs are strongly related to educational experience, both formal and informal.

Students expect, and have a right to expect, that the educational process will be structured, that they will be stimulated by it to become independent adults, and that they will have effectively transmitted to them the cultural heritage of the larger society. If institutional support is to have its fullest possible meaning, it should incorporate the strength, freshness of view, and idealism of the student body.

The respect of students for their college or university can be enhanced if they are given at least these opportunities: (1) to be listened to in the classroom without fear of institutional reprisal for the substance of their views, (2) freedom to discuss questions of institutional policy and operation, (3) the right to academic due process when charged with serious violations of institutional regulations, and (4) the same right to hear speakers of their own choice as is enjoyed by other components of the institution.

INDEX

References are to pages.